Lecture Notes in Computer Science 15364

Founding Editors

Gerhard Goos
Juris Hartmanis

The series Lecture Notes in Computer Science (LNCS), including its subseries Lecture Notes in Artificial Intelligence (LNAI) and Lecture Notes in Bioinformatics (LNBI), has established itself as a medium for the publication of new developments in computer science and information technology research, teaching, and education.

LNCS enjoys close cooperation with the computer science R & D community, the series counts many renowned academics among its volume editors and paper authors, and collaborates with prestigious societies. Its mission is to serve this international community by providing an invaluable service, mainly focused on the publication of conference and workshop proceedings and postproceedings. LNCS commenced publication in 1973.

Elette Boyle · Mohammad Mahmoody
Editors

Theory
of Cryptography

22nd International Conference, TCC 2024
Milan, Italy, December 2–6, 2024
Proceedings, Part I

 Springer

Editors
Elette Boyle
NTT Research
Sunnyvale, CA, USA

Reichman University
Herzliya, Israel

Mohammad Mahmoody
University of Virginia
Charlottesville, VA, USA

ISSN 0302-9743   ISSN 1611-3349 (electronic)
Lecture Notes in Computer Science
ISBN 978-3-031-78010-3   ISBN 978-3-031-78011-0 (eBook)
https://doi.org/10.1007/978-3-031-78011-0

This Springer imprint is published by the registered company Springer Nature Switzerland AG
The registered company address is: Gewerbestrasse 11, 6330 Cham, Switzerland

If disposing of this product, please recycle the paper.

Preface

The 22nd Theory of Cryptography Conference (TCC 2024) was held during December 2–6, 2024, at Bocconi University in Milano, Italy. It was sponsored by the International Association for Cryptologic Research (IACR). The general chair of the conference was Emmanuela Orsini.

The conference received 172 submissions, of which the Program Committee (PC) selected 68 for presentation, giving an acceptance rate of 39.5%. Each submission was reviewed by at least three PC members in a single-blind process. The 50 PC members (including PC chairs), all top researchers in our field, were helped by 185 external reviewers, who were consulted when appropriate. These proceedings consist of the revised versions of the 68 accepted papers. The revisions were not reviewed, and the authors bear full responsibility for the content of their papers.

We are extremely grateful to Kevin McCurley for providing fast and reliable technical support for the HotCRP review software. We also thank Kay McKelly for her help with the conference website.

This was the tenth year that TCC presented the Test of Time Award to an outstanding paper that was published at TCC at least eight years ago, making a significant contribution to the theory of cryptography, preferably with influence also in other areas of cryptography, theory, and beyond. This year, the Test of Time Award Committee selected the following paper, published at TCC 2004: "Notions of Reducibility between Cryptographic Primitives," by Omer Reingold, Luca Trevisan, and Salil P. Vadhan. The award committee recognized this paper "for providing a rigorous and systematic taxonomy of reductions in cryptography, and in particular coining fully black-box reductions and motivating their use in barrier results."

We are greatly indebted to the many people who were involved in making TCC 2024 a success. Thank you to all the authors who submitted papers to the conference and to the PC members for their hard work, dedication, and diligence in reviewing and selecting the papers. We are also thankful to the external reviewers for their volunteered hard work and investment in reviewing papers and answering questions. Finally, thank you to the general chair Emmanuela Orsini and her team at Bocconi University, as well as to the TCC Steering Committee.

October 2024   Elette Boyle
                                                                       Mohammad Mahmoody

Organization

General Chair

Emmanuela Orsini   Bocconi University, Italy

Program Committee Chairs

Elette Boyle   Reichman University, Israel & NTT Research, USA

Mohammad Mahmoody   University of Virginia, USA

Steering Committee

Yuval Ishai   Technion, Israel

Huijia (Rachel) Lin   University of Washington, USA

Tal Malkin   Columbia University, USA

Jesper Buus Nielsen   Aarhus University, Denmark

Krzysztof Pietrzak   Institute of Science and Technology Austria, Austria

Manoj M. Prabhakaran   IIT Bombay, India

Salil Vadhan   Harvard University, USA

Program Committee

Prabhanjan Ananth   UC Santa Barbara, USA

Benny Applebaum   Tel Aviv University, Israel

Amos Beimel   Ben-Gurion University of the Negev, Israel

Chris Brzuska   Aalto University, Finland

Yilei Chen   Tsinghua University, China

Ran Cohen   Reichman University, Israel

Geoffroy Couteau   CNRS, IRIF, Université Paris Cité, France

Itai Dinur   Ben-Gurion University of the Negev, Israel

Yevgeniy Dodis   New York University, USA

Stefan Dziembowski   University of Warsaw & IDEAS NCBR, Poland

Nils Fleischhacker   Ruhr University Bochum, Germany

Additional Reviewers

Behzad Abdolmaleki
Anasuya Acharya
Amit Agarwal
Divesh Aggarwal
Andris Ambainis
Gilad Asharov
Thomas Attema
David Balbás
Laasya Bangalore
James Bartusek
Tyler Besselman
Rishabh Bhadauria
Kaartik Bhushan
Alexander Bienstock
Aniruddha Biswas
Alexander Block
Jeremiah Blocki
Katharina Boudgoust
Nicholas Brandt
Rares Buhai
Alper Cakan
Matteo Campanelli
Ran Canetti
Rutchathon Chairattana-Apirom
Benjamin Chan
Anirudh Chandramouli
Rohit Chatterjee
Megan Chen
Jessica Chen
Binyi Chen
Arka Rai Choudhuri
Sandro Coretti-Drayton
Quand Dao
Pratish Datta
Giovanni Deligios
Marian Dietz
Fangqi Dong
Nico Döttling
Ehsan Ebrahimi
Christoph Egger
Saroja Erabelli
Grzegorz Fabiański
Pooya Farshim

Giacomo Fenzi
Ben Fisch
Pouyan Forghani
Cody Freitag
Phillip Gajland
Karthik Gajulapalli
Rachit Garg
Sanjam Garg
Riddhi Ghosal
Satrajit Ghosh
Suparno Ghoshal
Niv Gilboa
Eli Goldin
Tian Gong
Junqing Gong
Jiaxin Guan
Aditya Gulati
Taiga Hiroka
Iftach Haitner
David Heath
Aditya Hegde
Hans Heum
Minki Hhan
Yao-ching Hsieh
Zihan Hu
Jihun Hwang
Yuval Ishai
Abhishek Jain
Daniel Jost
Eliran Kachlon
Fatih Kaleoglu
Chethan Kamath
Simon Kamp
Julia Kastner
Shuichi Katsumata
Hannah Keller
Hamidreza Amini Khorasgani
Taechan Kim
Elena Kirshanova
Ohad Klein
Karen Klein
Dimitris Kolonelos
Chelsea Komlo

Manu Kondapaneni

Venkata Koppula

Alexis Korb

Nishat Koti

Roman Langrehr

Seunghoon Lee

Keewoo Lee

Zeyong Li

Yunqi Li

Hanjun Li

Xiao Liang

Fuchun Lin

Chuanwei Lin

Haoxing Lin

Yao-Ting Lin

Tianren Liu

Jiahui Liu

Chen-Da Liu-Zhang

Zhenjian Lu

Donghang Lu

Vadim Lyubashevsky

Ulysse Léchine

Nir Magrafta

Bernardo Magri

Nathan Manohar

Xinyu Mao

Marcin Mielniczuk

Ethan Mook

Tomoyuki Morimae

Changrui Mu

Saachi Mutreja

Anne Müller

Varun Narayanan

Barak Nehoran

Ky Nguyen

Hai Hoang Nguyen

Guilhem Niot

Oded Nir

Aysan Nishaburi

Mahak Pancholi

Aditi Partap

Anat Paskin-Cherniavsky

Rutvik Patel

Shravani Patil

Sikhar Patranabis

Alice Pellet-Mary

Paola de Perthuis

Naty Peter

Spencer Peters

Bertram Poettering

Guru Vamsi Policharla

Alexander Poremba

Luowen Qian

Rajeev Raghunath

Debasish Ray Chawdhuri

Hanlin Ren

Doreen Riepel

Ron D. Rothblum

Adeline Roux-Langlois

Lawrence Roy

Elahe Sadeghi

Pratik Sarkar

Rahul Satish

Benjamin Schlosser

Akash Shah

Jad Silbak

Mark Simkin

Fabrizio Sisinni

Tomer Solomon

Fang Song

Katerina Sotiraki

Noah Stephens-Davidowitz

Gilad Stern

Björn Tackmann

Kel Zin Tan

Er-cheng Tang

Athina Terzoglou

Jean-Pierre Tillich

Pratyush Ranjan Tiwari

Daniel Tschudi

Prashant Vasudevan

Ivan Visconti

Benedikt Wagner

William Wang

Benjamin Wesolowski

Jiawei Wu

David Wu

Yu Xia

Zhiye Xie

Jeff Xu

Anshu Yadav
Sophia Yakoubov
Chao Yan
Yibin Yang
Xiuyu Ye

Eylon Yogev
Albert Yu
Ilias Zadik
Runzhi Zeng

Contents – Part I

Proofs I

Instance-Hiding Interactive Proofs: (Extended Abstract) 3
    Changrui Mu and Prashant Nalini Vasudevan

The Power of NAPs:: Compressing OR-Proofs via Collision-Resistant
Hashing 35
    Katharina Boudgoust and Mark Simkin

zkSNARKs in the ROM with Unconditional UC-Security 67
    Alessandro Chiesa and Giacomo Fenzi

The Brave New World of Global Generic Groups and UC-Secure
Zero-Overhead SNARKs 90
    Jan Bobolz, Pooya Farshim, Markulf Kohlweiss, and Akira Takahashi

Hamming Weight Proofs of Proximity with One-Sided Error 125
    Gal Arnon, Shany Ben-David, and Eylon Yogev

Untangling the Security of Kilian's Protocol: Upper and Lower Bounds 158
    *Alessandro Chiesa, Marcel Dall'Agnol, Ziyi Guan, Nicholas Spooner,
    and Eylon Yogev*

Kolmogorov and One-Way Functions

Lower Bounds for Levin–Kolmogorov Complexity 191
    Nicholas Brandt

On One-Way Functions, the Worst-Case Hardness of Time-Bounded
Kolmogorov Complexity, and Computational Depth 222
    Yanyi Liu and Rafael Pass

One-Way Functions and pKt Complexity 253
    Shuichi Hirahara, Zhenjian Lu, and Igor C. Oliveira

On Bounded Storage Key Agreement and One-Way Functions 287
    Chris Brzuska, Geoffroy Couteau, Christoph Egger, and Willy Quach

Rate-1 Zero-Knowledge Proofs from One-Way Functions 319
    Noor Athamnah, Eden Florentz – Konopnicki, and Ron D. Rothblum

Consensus and Messaging

Consensus in the Presence of Overlapping Faults and Total Omission 353
  Julian Loss, Kecheng Shi, and Gilad Stern

On the (Im)possibility of Game-Theoretically Fair Leader Election
Protocols 383
  Ohad Klein, Ilan Komargodski, and Chenzhi Zhu

The Cost of Maintaining Keys in Dynamic Groups with Applications
to Multicast Encryption and Group Messaging 413
  Michael Anastos, Benedikt Auerbach, Mirza Ahad Baig,
  Miguel Cueto Noval, Matthew Kwan, Guillermo Pascual-Perez,
  and Krzysztof Pietrzak

Compact Key Storage in the Standard Model 444
  Yevgeniy Dodis and Daniel Jost

Bruisable Onions: Anonymous Communication in the Asynchronous
Model 476
  Megumi Ando, Anna Lysyanskaya, and Eli Upfal

Author Index 509

Proofs I

Instance-Hiding Interactive Proofs
(Extended Abstract)

Changrui Mu$^{(\boxtimes)}$ (iD) and Prashant Nalini Vasudevan (iD)

National University of Singapore, Singapore, Singapore
changrui.mu@u.nus.edu, prashant@comp.nus.edu.sg

Abstract. In an Instance-Hiding Interactive Proof (IHIP) [BFS90], an efficient verifier with a *private* input x interacts with an unbounded prover to determine whether x is contained in a language $\mathcal{L}$. In addition to completeness and soundness, the *instance-hiding* property requires that the prover should not learn anything about x in the course of the interaction. Such proof systems capture natural privacy properties, and may be seen as a generalization of the influential concept of Randomized Encodings [IK00, AIK04, AIKPC15], and as a counterpart to Zero-Knowledge proofs [GMR89].

We investigate the properties and power of such instance-hiding proofs, and show the following:
1. Any language with an IHIP is contained in $\mathsf{NP}/\mathsf{poly} \cap \mathsf{coNP}/\mathsf{poly}$.
2. If an average-case hard language has an IHIP, then infinitely-often One-Way Functions exist.
3. There is an oracle with respect to which there is a language that has an IHIP but not an SZK proof.
4. IHIP's are closed under composition with any efficiently computable function.
   We further study a stronger version of IHIP (that we call Simulatable IHIP) where the view of the honest prover can be efficiently simulated. For these, we obtain stronger versions of some of the above:
5. Any language with a Simulatable IHIP is contained in $\mathsf{AM} \cap \mathsf{coAM}$.
6. If a *worst-case* hard language has a Simulatable IHIP, then One-Way Functions exist.

1 Introduction

An Interactive Proof system (IP) [BM88, GMR89] for a language $\mathcal{L}$ is an interactive protocol between a polynomial-time verifier A and a computationally unbounded prover P where both are given as input a string x, and the prover tries to prove to the verifier that $x \in \mathcal{L}$. Such proofs are required to be complete – if $x \in \mathcal{L}$, the verifier will accept at the end of the interaction – and sound – if $x \notin \mathcal{L}$, no prover strategy P^* can make the verifier accept with large probability. Such proofs are very powerful and have been shown to exist for all languages computable with polynomial space (PSPACE) [LFKN92, Sha92].

Often in applications of interactive proof systems, one or both of the parties may hold some secret that they do not want the other to learn in the course

© International Association for Cryptologic Research 2025
E. Boyle and M. Mahmoody (Eds.): TCC 2024, LNCS 15364, pp. 3–34, 2025.
https://doi.org/10.1007/978-3-031-78011-0_1

of the interaction. For instance, the prover P may hold a secret key and wish to prove to the verifier something about a ciphertext encrypted using that key, without revealing the key itself. A powerful general formalization of a property that enables this is *Zero-Knowledge (ZK)* [GMR89]. This requires that there be a computationally efficient simulator that, for any $x \in \mathcal{L}$, can simulate the entire view of the verifier A interacting with P on input x. This ensures that the verifier learns nothing from the interaction other than the membership of x in $\mathcal{L}$.

This simulation may be perfect (PZK), statistically close to (SZK), or computationally indistinguishable from (CZK) the actual view. In contrast to general interactive proofs, it is known that languages that have PZK or SZK proofs are contained in AM ∩ coAM [For87, AH91]. Using computational assumptions, however, one can again construct CZK proofs for all languages in PSPACE [GMW91, BGG+88]. ZK proofs have been and continue to be the subject of extensive research, have found numerous applications in practice, and we understand them quite well (see, e.g., references in [Vad99, Tha22]).

Instance-Hiding Interactive Proofs. Whereas Zero-Knowledge provides security for the prover, *Instance-Hiding Interactive Proofs (IHIP)* [BFS90] provide a similar security guarantee for the verifier. In an IHIP, the input x is given only to the verifier A. Apart from completeness and soundness as in an IP, it is required that the protocol be instance-hiding – for any *prover* strategy P*, there should exist a simulator (computationally unbounded) that, given just the length of the input, can simulate the view of P* when interacting with A on any input x. This ensures that the prover cannot learn anything about the input except at most its length.

In other words, the prover proves to the verifier that $x \in \mathcal{L}$ without knowing anything at all about x. Seemingly paradoxical, such proof systems can, in fact, be constructed for several strutured languages, such as those that have certain random self-reduction properties [AFK89, FO91]. Nevertheless, a theorem of Abadi et al. [AFK89] implies that any language that has an IHIP in which the simulation of the prover's view is *perfect* is contained in NP/poly ∩ coNP/poly. In particular, this implies that NP-hard languages do not have perfect IHIP protocols unless the polynomial hierarchy collapses [Yap83].

Despite the fact that they capture this fundamental cryptographic property of protocols, not much else is known about the complexity of IHIP's today, decades after they were first defined. Further, even the aforementioned results do not hold if even a negligible amount of statistical error is allowed in the hiding property – that is, when the prover's view corresponding to any instance can have non-zero but negligibly small statistical distance from the simulator's output. In this paper, we undertake a systematic study of the complexity of such general imperfect IHIP's, with the objective of understanding what properties they have, how powerful they are, what kinds of structure they create, and how they compare to other cryptographic protocols like ZK proofs.

1.1   Our Results

In the rest of the paper, we simply use IHIP to denote instance-hiding IP's that have a negligible statistical hiding error as described above. We also study a strengthening of these proofs where the simulator that simulates the honest prover's view is required to be efficient; we refer to these as *Simulatable* IHIP *'s*. A number of natural constructions of IHIP's do, in fact, have this stronger property (see, e.g., full version [MV24, Appendix A]). We show a collection of results about various aspects of these proof systems, some of which follow from techniques common in the study of Secure Multi-Party Computation (MPC) and SZK proofs, while others require the development of new methods. We define these proof systems in Sect. 2, and in full version [MV24, Appendix A] we present examples of non-trivial languages that have such proof systems, including one that seems to require multiple rounds of interaction.

Power of Instance-Hiding Proofs. We start by asking which languages can possibly have IHIP's. The results of Abadi et al. [AFK89] imply that languages that have *perfect* IHIP's are contained in NP/poly ∩ coNP/poly. However, their techniques stop working if there is even a small amount of error in the hiding property. Using some carefully designed interactive proofs, we show that any language that has an IHIP with small enough hiding error is still contained in NP/poly ∩ coNP/poly. Further, if the IHIP has an efficient simulator for the honest prover and the simulator and verifier are uniform, we can get rid of the non-uniformity and show that the language lies in AM ∩ coAM.

Theorem 1.1 (Theorems 2 and 3). If a language $\mathcal{L}$ has an IHIP, then both $\mathcal{L}$ and its complement $\bar{\mathcal{L}}$ have constant-round public-coin interactive proofs with non-uniform verifiers. Further, if $\mathcal{L}$ has a simulatable IHIP, this conclusion holds with uniform verifiers.

This too implies that NP-hard problems do not have such proofs unless the polynomial hierarchy collapses [Yap83,FF91]. This upper bound on the power of such proofs is complemented by the existence a number of interesting non-trivial languages do have instance-hiding interactive proofs – see the examples in [MV24, Appendix A] and the connections to Randomized Encodings in [MV24, Appendix C].

Implications for One-Way Functions. Investigating further the implications of non-trivial languages having instance-hiding proofs, we show that the existence of hard languages with such proofs implies the existence of One-Way Functions (OWF's).

Theorem 1.2 (Theorems 4 and 5). One-Way Functions are implied by the existence of either of the following:

– An average-case hard language that has an IHIP
– A worst-case hard language that has a simulatable IHIP

The proof of the first statement in the theorem above is non-constructive – we prove that an OWF exists, but given an explicit average-case hard language with an IHIP, our proof does not construct an explicit function that is one-way.

Relationship with SZK. Both the above properties – membership in $\mathsf{AM} \cap \mathsf{coAM}$ [For87, AH91] and the implication of OWFs from average-case hardness [Ost91] – are shared by the class SZK of languages that have Statistical Zero Knowledge proofs. Intuitively, SZK proofs and IHIP's seem to rely on different properties of the underlying language, and it seems unlikely that one is contained in the other. We provide some evidence for this in the form of an oracle separation between SZK and $\mathsf{Simulatable\text{-}IHIP}$, the class of languages that have simulatable IHIP's.

Theorem 1.3 (Theorem 6). There exists an oracle $\mathcal{O}$ with respect to which $\mathsf{Simulatable\text{-}IHIP}^{\mathcal{O}} \not\subseteq \mathsf{SZK}^{\mathcal{O}}$.

We essentially prove this statement in the Generic Group Model [Sho97] – we show a group problem that cannot be decided by SZK protocols that treat the group in a certain "generic" manner, but can be decided by a similarly generic IHIP protocol. Showing an oracle separation in the other direction is an interesting open problem here.

Closure Properties. Finally, we show that IHIP's have rather strong closure properties – that they are closed under composition with any efficiently computable function. For any language $\mathcal{L}$, and functions $f : \{0,1\}^* \to \{0,1\}$ and $k : \mathbb{N} \to \mathbb{N}$, consider the "composed" language $f \circ \mathcal{L}^{\otimes k}$, in which an instance consists of $k = k(n)$ strings x_i of length n, which is in the language if and only if $f(\mathcal{L}(x_1), \ldots, \mathcal{L}(x_k)) = 1$. That is, given these k strings x_i, first check whether each of these is in $\mathcal{L}$, and then compute the function f on the result of these checks.

Theorem 1.4 (Theorem 1). Consider any language $\mathcal{L}$ that has an IHIP protocol, and any efficiently computable function $f : \{0,1\}^* \to \{0,1\}$. For any polynomial $k : \mathbb{N} \to \mathbb{N}$, the composed language $f \circ \mathcal{L}^{\otimes k}$ also has an IHIP protocol.

Similar properties for SZK are only known to hold for composition with polynomial-sized *formulas* (or NC^1) [SV97], whereas the above corresponds to polynomial-sized *circuits* (or P). This is another indication that this class is likely to be different from SZK.

The above theorem implies, in particular, that IHIP is closed under complement. While not directly implied by the theorem, our proof also shows that the OR or AND of two languages that have IHIP's also has an IHIP. This extends to the statement that for any constant k and languages $\mathcal{L}_1, \ldots, \mathcal{L}_k$ that all have IHIP's, any language expressible as a function of membership in these languages also has an IHIP.

Our proof of this theorem goes through Instance-Hiding Delegation [FO91], which are an alternative formulation of instance-hiding protocols that are interesting in their own right. See Sect. 3.5 for details.

Useful Tools. In the course of our constructions and proofs, we also show two lemmas that are meaningful outside this context – a protocol for proving lower bounds on a weighted sum of the sizes of sets (see full version [MV24, Section 3]), and an equivalence between randomized and deterministic advice for interactive proofs ([MV24, Section 3]).

1.2   Technical Overview

We now present an overview of the proofs of Theorems 1.1 to 1.3. The proof of Theorem 1.4 follows from a straightforward extension of existing work together with some standard transformations, so we leave its details to the relevant section.

Instance-Hiding to AM Proofs

Suppose a language $\mathcal{L}$ has an instance-hiding IP with prover P and verifier A – denoted $\langle \mathsf{P}, \mathsf{A} \rangle$. We will use this to construct a constant-round interactive proof $\langle \mathsf{M}, \mathsf{A} \rangle$ with non-uniform verifier A for $\mathcal{L}$. We will then show how to remove the non-uniformity if there is an efficient simulator for the honest prover.

Denote by $r \in \mathcal{R}_\mathsf{A}$ the random string used by the verifier. For any input x, denote by S_x the distribution over the transcript $s = (u_1, y_1, \ldots, u_q, y_q)$ generated by the execution of the protocol $\langle \mathsf{P}, \mathsf{A}(x; r) \rangle$, where u_i and y_i denote the verifier's and prover's message in i^{th} round respectively. For simplicity, assume that P is deterministic[1]. Given input x, our approach is to have M prove to A that the probability that $\langle \mathsf{P}, \mathsf{A}(x; r) \rangle$ accepts is large. Towards discussing this, we define the following two sets for any x and transcript s:

$$\beta_s^x = \{r \mid s \text{ is the transcript of } \langle \mathsf{P}, \mathsf{A}(x; r) \rangle\}$$
$$\alpha_s^x = \{r \mid r \in \beta_s^x \text{ and } \langle \mathsf{P}, \mathsf{A}(x; r) \rangle \text{ accepts}\}$$

We start with the observation that the probability of acceptance may be expressed as follows:

$$\Pr_r\left[\langle \mathsf{P}, \mathsf{A}(x; r) \rangle \text{ accepts}\right] = \frac{\sum_s |\alpha_s^x|}{|\mathcal{R}_\mathsf{A}|} = \sum_s \frac{|\beta_s^x|}{|\mathcal{R}_\mathsf{A}|} \cdot \frac{|\alpha_s^x|}{|\beta_s^x|} = \mathbb{E}_{s \leftarrow S_x}\left[\frac{|\alpha_s^x|}{|\beta_s^x|}\right] \quad (1)$$

So it is sufficient to construct a sound protocol where, for the given input x, M proves to A that the above expectation is large. Notice that for any s, the membership of a string r in the set α_s^x can be efficiently verified. This means that we can use the Goldwasser-Sipser set lower bound protocol [GS86] to prove lower bounds on the size of α_s^x. Now suppose the following three conditions were satisfied:

1. A has the ability to sample transcripts s from the distribution S_x
2. For s sampled as above, A can find out the value of $|\beta_s^x|$, and,
3. With high probability over s sampled from S_x, the value of $\frac{|\alpha_s^x|}{|\beta_s^x|}$ is close to its expectation

---

[1] In general interactive proofs, this assumption is without loss of generality. It is not clear that this is the case with instance-hiding interactive proofs without some worsening of parameters. In our actual proof, we do not need this assumption and the randomness of the prover is easy to deal with.

Then, we can construct the required protocol as follows:

- A samples an $s \leftarrow S_x$, and computes $|\beta_s^x|$
- M and A run the GS protocol where M proves that $|\alpha_s^x| \gg |\beta_s^x|/2$

If $x \in \mathcal{L}$, then with high probability over s, the condition involved in the GS protocol above is true, and A will accept with high probability. Similarly, if $x \notin \mathcal{L}$, this condition is false and A will reject with high probability.

   If the protocol $\langle \mathsf{P}, \mathsf{A} \rangle$ were *perfectly* instance-hiding, then the distribution S_x is the same for any x of a given length, as is the size of the set β_s^x for any s – call this common distribution S and the common set size b_s. Then, we can handle the first two conditions above by providing to A a sample s from S and the corresponding value b_s as non-uniform advice[2] (these are now independent of x). One catch here is that the completeness and soundness would then only hold for such randomly sampled advice. We show that an AM protocol with this property can be derandomized to a standard AM protocol with deterministic non-uniform advice ([GS86]).

   However, our protocol is only *statistically* instance-hiding, and so there may be no such common distribution. So we instead pick some canonical instance x_0, and use a sample s from the distribution S_{x_0} and the quantity $|\beta_s^{x_0}|$ as advice instead. Then we show that the instance-hiding property implies that the quantities $\mathbb{E}_{s \leftarrow S_x} \left[\frac{|\alpha_s^x|}{|\beta_s^x|} \right]$ and $\mathbb{E}_{s \leftarrow S_{x_0}} \left[\frac{|\alpha_s^x|}{|\beta_s^{x_0}|} \right]$ are close for any x. We use this to then show that using x_0 instead of x in the sampling of the advice will not affect the protocol by much.

   All that is left is to ensure that the third condition above holds – that with high probablity $|\alpha_s^x|/|\beta_s^x|$ is close to its expectation. But it very well might not be. We deal with this by using instead the sum of many independent copies of this random variable: $\sum_{i \in [g]} (|\alpha_{s_i}^x| / |\beta_{s_i}^x|)$, where each s_i is sampled independently. By the Hoeffding bound, this sum is indeed close to its expectation with high probability. Now, instead of proving a lower bound on the size of a single set, M needs to prove that the weighted sum of the sizes of a number of sets is large. We design an AM protocol for this by extending the Goldwasser-Sipser protocol ([GS86]).

Overall, the final constant-round protocol with randomized advice is as follows on input x:

- A receives as advice several samples $s_1, \ldots, s_g \leftarrow S_{x_0}$, and the quantities $|\beta_{s_1}^{x_0}|, \ldots, |\beta_{s_g}^{x_0}|$
- M and A run our weighted set-lower-bound protocol where M proves that:
$$\sum_i \frac{|\alpha_{s_i}^x|}{|\beta_{s_i}^{x_0}|} \gg \frac{g}{2}$$

An AM protocol can be obtained from this constant-round IP following standard transformations [GS86].

---

[2] In fact, [FF91] show that AM/poly is equivalent to NP/poly.

Uniform Verifier from Simulatable-IHIP. Midway through the argument above, we observed that it is sufficient for the verifier to be able to obtain a number of samples s from S_x, together with the values $|\beta_s^x|$. Above, we resolved this by providing approximations of these as non-uniform advice. If we have an efficient simulator Sim (that only takes the size of the instance as input) for the view of the honest prover, however, we can compute these in the protocol itself, without needing such advice. The first part is clear – if we sample s from $\mathsf{Sim}(n)$, its distribution is guaranteed to be close to S_x for any x, by the instance-hiding property.

What remains is to arrange for the verifier to learn the (approximate) value of $|\beta_s^x|$ for such s. We do this by taking advantage of the fact that for any x and s, by the instance-hiding property, the probability that $\mathsf{Sim}(n)$ outputs s is a reasonably good approximation of the probability that the protocol with verifier input x results in the transcript s. To be more specific, define the following quantity for any s:

$$\zeta_s = \{r_{\mathsf{Sim}} \mid s \text{ is the transcript of } \mathsf{Sim}(n; r_{\mathsf{Sim}})\}$$

Let the randomness space of the simulator be $\mathcal{R}_{\mathsf{Sim}}$. Then, we show that the simulator's output being negligibly close to the actual transcript implies the following for any x, with high probability over s sampled from either S_x or $\mathsf{Sim}(n)$:

$$\frac{1}{2} \cdot \frac{|\zeta_s|}{|\mathcal{R}_{\mathsf{Sim}}|} \leq \frac{|\beta_s^x|}{|\mathcal{R}_{\mathsf{A}}|} \leq 2 \cdot \frac{|\zeta_s|}{|\mathcal{R}_{\mathsf{Sim}}|}$$

Thus, if M can prove good bounds on the size of ζ_s to A, these would also imply good bounds on the size of β_s^x, and we can the proceed with the protocol as before. Notice that membership in ζ_s is again efficiently testable. So a lower-bound on $|\zeta_s|$ can again be proven using the GS protocol.

To prove an upper bound, we use the set upper-bound protocol of Fortnow [For87]. This protocol requires, in addition to membership in the set being testable, that the verifier privately obtain a uniformly random element from the set. This is easy for us to arrange – the verifier A simply samples a random $r \in \mathcal{R}_{\mathsf{Sim}}$, runs $\mathsf{Sim}(n; r)$ to obtain s, sends s to the prover M and keeps r private. Here, according to M, r is indeed a uniformly random element in ζ_s.

The entire protocol is now roughly as follows on input x:

- A samples $\{s_i \leftarrow \mathsf{Sim}_\mathsf{P}(n; r_i)\}_{i \in [g]}$, and sends the s_i's to M
- M and A run upper and lower bound protocols for A to obtain an approximation of each $|\zeta_{s_i}|$
- A assumes that $|\beta_{s_i}^x| = |\zeta_{s_i}| \cdot (|\mathcal{R}_\mathsf{A}| / |\mathcal{R}_{\mathsf{Sim}}|)$, using the values obtained above for the right-hand side
- M and A run our weighted set-lower-bound protocol where M proves that:
$$\sum_i \frac{|\alpha_{s_i}^x|}{|\beta_{s_i}^x|} \gg \frac{g}{2}$$

The actual protocol is slightly different because the set upper-bound protocol's guarantees are a bit weaker than ideal, but in essence it is as above. We refer the reader to full version [MV24, Section 4] for details.

One-Way Functions from IHIP for Hard Problems

Recall that Theorem 1.2 shows that if a *worst-case hard* (resp. *average-case hard*) problem has a Simulatable-IHIP (resp. IHIP), then there is explicit constructions of one-way functions (resp. non-explicit construction). The proofs assume, for the sake of contradiction, the non-existence of one-way function, and then use the efficient inverter algorithm for efficient functions guaranteed by the assumption to decide the problem.

Specifically, we assume the non-existence of distributional one-way function, which is implied by the non-existence of one-way functions [IL89]. If an efficient function f is not distributionally one-way, then there exists an efficient inverter A, which takes a random image of f as input, and samples preimages almost-uniformly. For the overview, we assume that the inverters work perfectly and sample uniformly random preimages[3], and also will focus on perfect-hiding protocols, and later describe how to make everything work with errors.

Non-explicit OWFs from Average-Case Hard IHIP

Consider any language $\mathcal{L}$ that has a q-round IHIP with prover P and verifier A, with a computationally unbounded simulator Sim for the honest prover's view. Further, there is an efficiently sampleable distribution X over which it is hard. We will work with $q = 2$ for this overview, which is sufficient to demonstrate the ideas behind the proof. Denote the algorithm of the verifier that computes the next message at any point in the protocol using random string r by $A(x, u_1, \ldots, y_i; r)$. As before, for any (possibly partial) transcript s, denote by β_s^x the set of random strings r consisted with s, and by α_s^x the set of r that lead to A accepting with transcript s.

We observe that if $\langle P, A \rangle$ is a one-round (two-message $s = (u_1, y_1)$) protocol, then it is easy to show that $F_1(x, r_1) = (x, A(x; r_1))$ must be an distributional one-way function[4]. Suppose not, there must exist an efficient inverter A_1, that on a random image (x, u_1) as input, samples r_1^* uniformly over $\beta_{u_1}^x$. Now consider a non-uniform adversary B^s that has as advice a random transcript $s = (u_1, y_1)$ sampled according to the simulation $Sim(n)$, and works as follows on input x:

- $B^s(x)$ runs $A_1(x, u_1)$ to obtain a random $r_1^* \in \beta_{u_1}^x$ and accepts if and only if $A(x, u_1, y_1; r_1^*)$ accepts.

This last event above happens with probability $|\alpha_s^x| / |\beta_s^x|$. So in expectation over s, by (1), the probability that B^s accepts will be large if x is in $\mathcal{L}$ and small otherwise. The fact that the advice s is random in this algorithm is not

---

[3] This assumption clearly loses generality. If it were true, then one would obtain OWF's from worst-case hard problems in SZK and IHIP rather than needing average-case hardness.

[4] In case X is not uniform distribution, F should instead take the randomness used by the sampler of X rather than x as input.

a concern – by taking multiple s and repeating B^s several times, one can then show that there is a single set of transcripts s that works well as advice for all possible instances of size n. This gives us a non-uniform algorithm for $\mathcal{L}$, which is a contradiction, so F_1 must be a distributional OWF.

In general, if we can set up an efficiently computable function such that inverting it lets us sample a random element of β_s^x given x and s, we can repeat the above argument. When the protocol $\langle \mathsf{P}, \mathsf{A} \rangle$ is more than one round (even just two rounds), however, this approach is not straightforward. This is because the messages of the verifier starting from the second round are dependent on prover's messages and are in general not guaranteed to be efficiently sampleable in the way the first message is. For instance, a natural candidate for such a function might be defined as $F_2^{(u_1, y_1)}(x, r) = \mathsf{A}(x, u_1, y_1; r)$. However, we are only interested in inverses of this function where the r is consistent with the first message u_1, and this might not be efficiently sampleable.

Instead, we use an recursive argument that either finds a distributional one-way function or obtain a "useful" efficient sampler for define F_2. The argument proceeds as follows:

First, if F_1 is already a distributional OWF, we are done with our proof. If not, consider a (perfect) inverter A_1 for F_1. Let $\mathsf{C}_1(x, u_1)$ be the algorithm that computes $(x, r_1) \leftarrow \mathsf{A}(x, u_1)$, and just outputs r_1. We define the function $F_2^{(u_1, y_1)}$ for any (u_1, y_1) as follows:

$$F_2^{(u_1, y_1)}(x, r_2) = (x, \mathsf{A}(x, u_1, y_1; \mathsf{C}_1(x, u_1; r_2)))$$

That is, $F_2^{(u_1, y_1)}(x, r_2)$ first runs C_1 with randomness r_2 to sample an r_1 that is contained in $\beta_{u_1}^x$, and then runs A on the partial transcript (u_1, y_1) with that r_1 to produce the next verifier message u_2 in the protocol. If C_1 is perfect, this achieves what the earlier attempt at defining F_2 did not – any output of $\mathsf{C}_1(x, u_1)$ is a random element of $\beta_{u_1}^x$, so we are never in a situation where we have in hand a verifier random string r that is not consistent with the partial transcript so far.

Let us look at the property of random inverses of F_2 more closely. First, given a random r_2, $\mathsf{C}_1(x, u_1; r_2)$ is a random element of $\beta_{u_1}^x$, and so also of $\beta_{(u_1, y_1)}^x$. So a random inverse of $F_2^{(u_1, y_1)}$ on output (x, u_2) is a random (x, r_2) such that $\mathsf{C}_1(x, u_1; r_2)$ is also further contained in $\beta_{(u_1, y_1, u_2)}^x$. So given a random inverse (x, r_2) of $F_2^{(u_1, y_1)}$ on output (x, u_2), the output of $\mathsf{C}_1(x, u_1; r_2)$ is distributed uniformly over $\beta_{(u_1, y_1, u_2)}^x$, and thus also β_s^x for $s = (u_1, y_1, u_2, y_2)$ for any y_2. So given a random such $s = (u_1, y_1, u_2, y_2)$ from the simulator $\mathsf{Sim}(n)$ along with a perfect distributional inverter for $F_2^{(u_1, y_1)}$, we can efficiently sample from β_s^x, which is exactly what we needed! So unless $F_2^{(u_1, y_1)}$ is distributionally one-way for such an s, we can decide $\mathcal{L}$ on infinitely often n.

There are two remaining issues here – one is that we do not actually have a perfect distributional inverter, only a very good one; the other is the question of where the distributional inverters come from for the eventual algorithm we construct for $\mathcal{L}$. The solution to the latter is non-uniform advice. As before, we can argue that there is a set of transcripts s that work for all instances, and then if the F_2's defined with those transcripts are not distributionally one-way, their inverters can be provided as non-uniform advice. The former issue can again be dealt with using standard techniques to carefully account for the inversion (and also hiding) errors and show that it remains small enough to not matter.

This process can then be inductively carried out for every round of the protocol if there are more rounds. Finally note that the reason this does not extend to being able to use the *worst-case* hardness of $\mathcal{L}$ is that the functions F_1, etc., that we construct take x as an input. So inverting them on random outputs cannot give guarantees for every possible x.

Explicit OWFs from Worst-Case Hard Simulatable-IHIP

Consider any language $\mathcal{L}$ that has a q-round Simulatable-IHIP with prover P, verifier A and efficient honest-prover simulator Sim. Our approach is to use the possibility of inverting any efficiently computable function to efficiently implement the "simulation-based prover" [AH91] for this interactive proof for any instance. This proof is almost the same as the proof that average-case hardness of SZK implies OWF's [Ost91], though see below for further discussion.

The simulation-based prover $\mathsf{P}_{\mathsf{Sim}}$ is defined to behave as follows on interaction with verifier A: at any point in the protocol, if the current transcript is $(u_1^*, \ldots, y_{i-1}^*, u_i^*)$, it samples an $s = (u_1, \ldots, u_i, y_i)$ from $\mathsf{Sim}(n)$ conditioned on $u_j = u_j^*$ for $j \leq i$ and $y_j = y_j^*$ for $j < i$, and then responds to A with the message y_i. By the instance-hiding property, the view of the verifier generated by A interacting with $\mathsf{P}_{\mathsf{Sim}}$ is statistically close to that when interacting with the honest verifier P. Thus, due to the completeness and soundness of the protocol, if $\mathsf{P}_{\mathsf{Sim}}$ can be implemented efficiently, the language can also be decided efficiently.

For each $i \in [q]$, define the efficiently computable function $\mathsf{Sim}_i(n, r)$ that runs $\mathsf{Sim}(n; r)$ (with randomness r), and outputs the first $(2i - 1)$ messages $(u_1, y_1, \ldots, u_i)$. If each Sim_i had a perfect distributional inverter, then given $(u_1^*, \ldots, u_i^*)$, the inverter can be used to sample a uniformly random r that when used by $\mathsf{Sim}(n; r)$ as randomness produces this partial transcript. Then computing $\mathsf{Sim}(n; r)$ can be used to sample the y_i that is exactly as required by the simulation-based prover. So if every efficiently computable function can be perfectly distributionally inverted, then the simulation-based prover can be implemented efficiently, giving us the contradiction we want. If the distributional inverter available is not perfect, there are some errors that come up throughout this process, but they can be handled using standard techniques.

This proof is very similar to the proof that average-case hardness of SZK implies OWF's [Ost91]. In the SZK case, the simulator also takes as input the instance x, and therefore being able to invert the simulator does not necessarily imply that the language can be decided for all instances x, which is why average-case hardness is needed. In this case, however, the simulator works for all instances x, and so inverting it gives an algorithm for all instances x, and worst-case hardness is sufficient.

Oracle Separation from SZK

To demonstrate an oracle separation between IHIP and SZK, we construct an oracle language for which these two protocols have different query complexities. This separation in query complexity can then be translated into an oracle separation using standard diagonalization techniques.

Our language is defined using the Discrete Log problem with a generic group oracle [Sho97]. For any $n \in \mathbb{N}$, and a prime number $N \approx 2^n$, given any bijection $\sigma : \mathbb{Z}_N \rightarrow [N]$, the generic group oracle $\mathcal{G}_\sigma$ encodes the group $\mathbb{Z}_N$ using otherwise meaningless labels from $[N]$. Given inputs $g, h \in [N]$, $\mathcal{G}_\sigma(g, h)$ is equal to $\sigma(\sigma^{-1}(g) + \sigma^{-1}(h))$. Consider in addition to this another oracle $\mathcal{I} : \mathbb{Z}_N \rightarrow \{0, 1\}$. We define our language (technically, promise problem) as:

$$\mathcal{L}^{\mathcal{I},\sigma} = \{(\sigma(1), \sigma(x)) \mid \mathcal{I}(x) = 1\}$$

This language has an IHIP for any σ and $\mathcal{I}$ when the parties are given access to $\mathcal{I}$ and $\mathcal{G}_\sigma$ as oracles. This is as follows: given input $(\sigma(1), \sigma(x))$, compute $y = \sigma(x+r)$ for a random $r \in \mathbb{Z}_N$, send y to the prover, who is supposed to return $r' \leftarrow \sigma^{-1}(y)$. Check that $\sigma(r') = y$, and if so output $\mathcal{I}(r' - r)$. The efficiency of the verifier here relies on the fact that $\sigma(r)$ for any r can be computed using $\text{poly}(n)$ calls to $\mathcal{G}_\sigma$ using repeated doubling. Completeness and soundness follow from the fact that (r, r') is an NP witness for the instance, and simulatable instance-hiding follows from the fact that the prover only sees a uniformly random element of $[N]$.

On the other hand, it is known from generic lower-bounds for the Discrete Log problem [Sho97, CGK18] that no algorithm can compute x given $(\sigma(1), \sigma(x))$ and oracle access to $\mathcal{G}_\sigma$ for a random σ with substantially fewer than $\sqrt{N}$ queries. This implies that any candidate efficient SZK simulator would, with very high probability, not query oracle $\mathcal{I}$ on x given input $(\sigma(1), \sigma(x))$ and oracle access to $\mathcal{G}_\sigma$. The simulation property then implies that if $\mathcal{I}(x) = 1$, then the verifier for the corresponding protocol, with high probability, would not query $\mathcal{I}$ on x either. If this happens, then the outcome of the protocol would have been the same irrespective of whether $\mathcal{I}(x)$ was 0 or 1. This shows that at least one of zero-knowledge, completeness, or soundness breaks at such an input x. This shows the required query complexity lower bound.

1.3 Related Work

The concept of instance-hiding proof systems was first introduced, albeit in the multi-prover setting, by Beaver et al. [BFS90]. Their definition was based on that of instance-hiding *schemes* as defined by Abadi et al. [AFK89], which may be seen as honest-prover instance-hiding proofs without the soundness property. The latter also showed that any language that has a perfect instance-hiding scheme (which is implied by a proof) is contained in NP/poly ∩ coNP/poly. The former showed that a language has a multi-prover instance-hiding proof iff it is contained in NEXP ∩ coNEXP, and further that such a proof could be made zero-knowledge.

Feigenbaum and Ostrovsky [FO91] and Beaver et al. [BFOS93] showed further connections between (single-prover) instance-hiding schemes and proofs assuming the existence of one-way permutations. To be more accurate, most of these papers consider instance-hiding proofs for certifying the evaluations of functions and discuss the feasibility of such proofs based on the complexity of these functions. Multi-prover instance-hiding schemes were also studied by Beaver and Feigenbaum [BF90], who showed that they exist for all functions.

Randomized Encodings. Randomized Encodings are closely related to instance-hiding proofs. The properties we show for simulatable IHIP – membership in AM ∩ coAM and the implication of OWFs from *worst-case* hardness [AR16] – are also shared by the class of languages that have Statistical Randomized Encodings (SRE) [IK00, AIK04, AIKPC15]. An SRE for a language $\mathcal{L}$ is a randomized function whose output on an input x reveals whether $x \in \mathcal{L}$ and nothing else about x, in a statistical sense. Randomized encodings with very low complexity have been used extensively in constructing MPC protocols [Yao86, Kil88, IK00, FKN03, AIK04, . . .]. Agrawal et al. [AIKPC15] showed examples of languages that have SREs that, under reasonable computational assumptions, are not efficiently computable.

It is known that languages that have an SRE also have SZK proofs [App14] (and the above oracle separation also carries over). Techniques from the literature also show that any language that has an SRE also has an IHIP (see e.g. [AIK10], and references in Sect. 1.1 therein). For completeness, we include a self-contained proof of this statement in full version [MV24, Appendix C]. These techniques can further be extended to show that an interactive version of Randomized Encodings (as defined by Applebaum et al. [AIK10]) is equivalent to IHIP.

1.4 Discussion and Open Problems

There are number of fundamental questions about the properties and power of instance-hiding proofs that are yet to be answered. We list a few of these below.

1. Are there natural complete problems for the class of languages that have instance-hiding proofs?
2. What is the relationship between this class and SZK? Both of them are contained in NP/poly ∩ coNP/poly, but is one contained in the other? In this work, we provide an oracle separation $\mathsf{IHIP}^O \not\subseteq \mathsf{SZK}^O$; can we show one in the other direction?
3. Is Simulatable-IHIP closed under complement?
4. Are there other cryptographic consequences of the existence of hard problems in this class, beyond one-way functions?
5. Can worst-case hard IHIP imply one-way function? This question is also open for SZK.
6. Can the instance-hiding error be amplified? Note that this question is also open for SRE.
7. Is there a separation between perfect and imperfect instance-hiding proofs?
8. What is the power of *computational* instance-hiding proofs? What assumptions are needed for these to be constructed for all of NP?

9. Similarly, what is the power of instance-hiding *argument systems*, which have efficient provers (given, say, an NP witness) and only computational soundness? How do we even define these, given that the witness might already reveal information about the witness?

There is also a looming non-technical question here that it would be useful to know the answer to. Instance-hiding proofs and zero-knowledge proofs were defined at around the same time. The initial results regarding these – multi-prover constructions for large classes of languages, limitations of perfect single-prover constructions, etc. – seem to have been similar. In strong contrast to zero-knowledge proofs, however, research on instance-hiding proofs (at least explicitly) has been very sparse after a brief period following their definition. Why is this the case? Could it be because we succeeded in constructing computational ZK proofs for all of NP shortly thereafter, whereas similar results for instance-hiding proofs were lacking? Given the more advanced cryptographic toolkit available to us today, can we construct computational instance-hiding proofs for large classes of languages? Would they be as useful as ZK proofs?

2   Instance-Hiding Interactive Proofs

In this section, we define Instance-Hiding Interactive Proofs.

Definition 1 (Instance-Hiding Interactive Proof (IHIP) [BFS90]). *Consider a promise problem $\Pi = (\text{YES}, \text{NO})$, and functions $\delta, \epsilon : \mathbb{N} \to [0,1]$. A (δ, ϵ)-Instance-Hiding Interactive Proof (IHIP) for Π is a protocol $\langle \mathsf{P}, \mathsf{A} \rangle$ in which a probabilistic polynomial-time verifier A interacts with a computationally unbounded prover P. For some $n \in \mathbb{N}$, the verifier gets a private input $x \in \text{YES}_n \cup \text{NO}_n$, while the prover only gets the input length n. At the end of the interaction, A outputs either 1 (Accept) or 0 (Reject). The protocol is required to satisfy the following properties for all large enough $n \in \mathbb{N}$:*

– **Completeness:** *For any input $x \in \text{YES}_n$:*

$$\Pr\left[\langle \mathsf{P}(n), \mathsf{A}(x) \rangle = 1\right] \geq 1 - \delta(n).$$

– **Soundness:** *For any input $x \in \text{NO}_n$, and any prover P^*:*

$$\Pr\left[\langle \mathsf{P}^*(n), \mathsf{A}(x) \rangle = 1\right] \leq \delta(n).$$

– **Hiding:** *For any prover P^*, there exists a computationally unbounded randomized algorithm $\mathsf{Sim}_{\mathsf{P}^*}$, called a simulator, such that for any input $x \in \{0,1\}^n$,*

$$\Delta\big(\mathsf{Sim}_{\mathsf{P}^*}(n), \text{VIEW}_{\mathsf{P}^*}(\mathsf{P}^*(n), \mathsf{A}(x))\big) \leq \epsilon(n).$$

If the simulator corresponding to the honest prover runs in polynomial time in n, we say the protocol is Simulatable-Instance-Hiding (Simulatable-IHIP). The protocol is perfectly-hiding IHIP if $\epsilon(n) = 0$ for all n. If a simulator is only guaranteed to exist only for the honest prover P, the protocol is honest-prover IHIP.

Definition 2 (Class IHIP, IHIP/poly**).** *The class* IHIP *consists of all promise problems that have a* (δ, ϵ)*-IHIP with uniform verifier protocol for some negligible* $\delta(n)$ *and* $\epsilon(n)$*. For concrete functions* (δ, ϵ)*, we denote by* (δ, ϵ)*-*IHIP *the class of problems possessing* (δ, ϵ)*-IHIP. Similarly,* IHIP/poly *denotes the class of promise problem that have a* (δ, ϵ)*-IHIP with non-uniform verifier protocol for some negligible* $\delta(n)$ *and* $\epsilon(n)$

Remark 1. Prior work in this area, such as Beaver et al. [BFS90], defined instance-hiding proof systems for function delegation rather than promise problem decision. For a function f, at the end of the protocol, completeness required that the verifier learn $f(x)$ when interacting with the honest prover; and soundness required that no prover could convince the verifier of an incorrect value of $f(x)$. Definition 1 is weaker than just the restriction of this to Boolean functions, in that we only require completeness guarantees to hold for YES instances $(\Pi(x) = 1)$, and soundness guarantees for NO instances $(\Pi(x) = 0)$. This relaxed definition is still meaningful, and lets us compare IHIPs directly to IPs, ZK proofs, etc., that are also similarly defined. The relaxation also makes it harder to prove our containment results and closure properties. Some of our results also extend to the definition involving function delegation – see Sect. 3.5 for this definition and further details.

Remark 2. Earlier definitions of instance-hiding proof systems only considered *perfect* instance-hiding. In this case, every transcript with non-zero probability mass is a valid transcript for all instances. This made showing containment of problems with such proofs in NP and coNP considerably simpler than our proofs showing containment of problems with imperfect instance-hiding proofs in AM and coAM.

Remark 3. As we show in full version [MV24, Appendix C], instance-hiding IPs are closely related to the notion of Randomized Encodings (RE) of promise problems [AIK04] (see also [AIK05]). In fact, using the techniques in that section, instance-hiding IPs (for non-negligible values of the hiding error) can be shown to be equivalent to an interactive version of RE as defined by Applebaum et al. [AIK10].

3   Properties

In this section, we present properties of instance-hiding interactive proofs. Due to page constraints, we include only the formal statement of theorem. The full proofs are deferred to the full version [MV24].

3.1   Closure Properties and Amplification

Since their inception, the composition properties of zero-knowledge proofs have been extensively studied. It is established that Statistical Zero-Knowledge (SZK) is preserved under sequential repetition, and that the existence of an SZK proof is preserved under composition with arbitrary polynomial-sized formulas [GK96, Oka00, DSDCPY08, CD96, SV97]. However, similar properties for instance-hiding have not received as much attention yet. In this subsection, we present positive results regarding these properties of IHIP. We show that the existence of such proofs is preserved under composition with any efficiently computable function, and not just polynomial-sized formulas.

For any promise problem $\Pi = (\text{YES}, \text{NO})$, we also denote by $\Pi : \{0,1\}^* \to \{0,1,\perp\}$ its characteristic function, which outputs 1 on any input $x \in \text{YES}$, 0 on any $x \in \text{NO}$, and $\perp$ on all other inputs. Similarly, given any function $f : \{0,1\}^* \to \{0,1,\perp\}$, we define the corresponding promise problem Π_f whose characteristic function it is. Consider any function $f : \{0,1,\perp\}^* \to \{0,1,\perp\}$ satisfying the property that its output is $\perp$ whenever any of its inputs is $\perp$. For any function $k : \mathbb{N} \to \mathbb{N}$, we define the composed promise problem $f \circ \Pi^{\otimes k}$ as follows:

$$\text{YES}_n(f \circ \Pi^{\otimes k}) = \left\{ (x_1, \ldots, x_{k(n)}) \mid \forall i : |x_i| = n \wedge f(\Pi(x_1), \ldots, \Pi(x_{k(n)})) = 1 \right\}.$$

$$\text{NO}_n(f \circ \Pi^{\otimes k}) = \left\{ (x_1, \ldots, x_{k(n)}) \mid \forall i : |x_i| = n \wedge f(\Pi(x_1), \ldots, \Pi(x_{k(n)})) = 0 \right\}.$$

Theorem 1 (Closure under Composition with Efficient Functions). *Consider any promise problems Π that has an IHIP protocol, and any efficiently computable function $f : \{0,1,\perp\}^* \to \{0,1,\perp\}$ whose output is $\perp$ whenever any of its inputs is $\perp$. For any polynomial $k : \mathbb{N} \to \mathbb{N}$, the composed promise problem $f \circ \Pi^{\otimes k}$ also has an IHIP protocol.*

An important special case of this theorem, which we use in its proof, is the closure of IHIP under complementation. This is stated in the following lemma:

Lemma 1 (Closure under Complementation). *Suppose, for some negligible functions δ, ϵ, that a problem Π has a (δ, ϵ)-IHIP (possibly with a non-uniform verifier). Then the complement of Π has a (δ', ϵ')-IHIP (resp. with a non-uniform verifier if starting with a non-uniform verifier), where δ', ϵ' are also negligible.*

Corollary 1. IHIP/poly = coIHIP/poly *and* IHIP = coIHIP.

Another component of the proof of Theorem 1 is the following lemma regarding the behavior of instance-hiding proofs under repetition in parallel that is significant on its own. In contrast to zero-knowledge proofs, instance-hiding proofs show robustness under parallel repetition.

Lemma 2 (Preservation of Instance-Hiding Under Parallel Repetition). *For any functions $k : \mathbb{N} \to \mathbb{N}$ and $\epsilon : \mathbb{N} \to [0,1]$, consider the protocol $\langle \mathbf{P}, \mathbf{A} \rangle$ where $\mathbf{A}$ takes as input $k(n)$ instances/inputs $x_1, \ldots, x_{k(n)}$, each of size n, and executes $\langle \mathsf{P}_1(n), \mathsf{A}_1(x_1) \rangle, \ldots, \langle \mathsf{P}_k(n), \mathsf{A}_k(x_k) \rangle$ independently in parallel, where each $\langle \mathsf{P}_i, \mathsf{A}_i \rangle$ is ϵ-instance-hiding. Then $\langle \mathbf{P}, \mathbf{A} \rangle$ is $(k \cdot \epsilon)$-instance-hiding.*

This gives us a round-efficient way to strongly amplify the completeness and soundness in an instance-hiding proof at a small cost in the instance-hiding error.

3.2   Upper Bounds

While the existence of IHIP is noteworthy, it is also important to explore the limitations of such constructions. Abadi et al. [AFK89] established an upper-bound for *perfect* instance-hiding proofs, showing that problems that have such proofs are contained in NP/Poly ∩ coNP/Poly.

Our work in this section extends these results by showing that every promise problem that has a (δ, ϵ)-IHIP, even with δ, ϵ as large as some small constant, is still contained in NP/poly ∩ coNP/poly.

Theorem 2. *Consider functions* $\delta, \epsilon : \mathbb{N} \to [0, 1]$ *such that for all sufficient large* n, *we have* $\delta(n), \epsilon(n) < \frac{1}{32}$. *If a promise problem* Π *possesses an honest-prover* (δ, ϵ)-IHIP, *where the verifier can be non-uniform, then* $\Pi \in$ NP/poly ∩ coNP/poly.

Setup. The *AM* protocol is presented in Fig. 1 with the advice oracle is presented in Fig. 2. We set up some notation for IHIP and Simulatable-IHIP proofs. Suppose $\langle P, A \rangle$ is a *q-round* (δ, ϵ)-IHIP (or (δ, ϵ)-Simulatable-IHIP) for a promise problem Π, and for any prover P^* denote by Sim_{P^*} the corresponding simulator of the prover's view. The only difference between IHIP and simulatable IHIP is the efficiency of Sim_P on simulating the view of honest prover. The $\langle P, A \rangle$ can be viewed as two deterministic algorithms on the input, random seed, and public view (transcript) of the protocol:

- A : $\mathcal{X} \times \mathcal{R}_A \times \Sigma^* \to \mathcal{U} \cup \{0, 1\}$,
- P : $\mathcal{R}_P \times \Sigma^* \to \mathcal{Y}$,

where $\mathcal{X}$, $\mathcal{R}_A$ (resp., $\mathcal{R}_P$) are the space of possible input instances and verifier's (resp., prover's) random seed respectively, and Σ^* is the space of the public view of the protocol. $\mathcal{U}$ and $\mathcal{Y}$ are verifier's and prover's message space respectively. The outputs $\{0, 1\}$ represent the verifier accepting or rejecting at the end of the interaction. Let $u_i \in \mathcal{U}, y_i \in \mathcal{Y}$ be the messages of verifier and prover at round i respectively, and denote by $s_i = (u_1, y_1, \ldots, u_i, y_i)$ the public view up to the end of ith round ($s_0 = \phi$). We denote $A\big(x, r_A, (u_1, y_1, \ldots, u_i, y_i)\big) = u_{i+1}$ that A on input instance x, with random seed r_A, and current public view s_i produces the next message $u_{i+1} \in \mathcal{U}$. Let $r_A \in \mathcal{R}_A, r_P \in \mathcal{R}_P$ be the randomness of A/P respectively. For $i \in [q]$, we have:

- $A(x, r_A, s_i) = u_{i+1}$.
- $P(r_P, (s_i, u_{i+1})) = y_{i+1}$.

For conciseness, we denote by $\boldsymbol{S}_x(r_A, r_P)$ the public view in the protocol $\langle P, A \rangle$ when the instance is x and random seeds are r_A, r_P respectively. Abusing notation, $\boldsymbol{S}_x$ also represents the output distribution of $\boldsymbol{S}_x(U_{\mathcal{R}_A}, U_{\mathcal{R}_P})$. Let $\mathcal{S}$ be the union of supports of $\boldsymbol{S}_x$ for all x, and for any x and $s \in \mathcal{S}$, define:

- $\beta_s^x = \{r_A \in \mathcal{R}_A \mid \forall i \in [q] : A(x, r_A, s_{i-1}) = u_i\}$.
- $\alpha_s^x = \{r_A \in \beta_s^x \mid A(x, r_A, s) = 1\}$.

- $\gamma_s = \{r_\mathsf{P} \in \mathcal{R}_\mathsf{P} \mid \forall i \in [q] : \mathsf{P}\left(r_\mathsf{P}, (s_{i-1}, u_i)\right) = y_i\}$.

Intuitively, β_s^x (resp. γ_s) is the set of A's (resp. P's) randomnesses that, when instance is x, makes A (resp. P) behave as in view s. α_s^x is a subset of β_s^x with which A accepts in the end seeing the instance x, randomness r_A and public view s. We denote by $\mathcal{R}_\mathsf{Simp}$ the simulator's random space and let

- $\zeta_{r_\mathsf{P}, s} = \{r_\mathsf{Sim} \mid \mathsf{Simp}(n; r_\mathsf{Sim}) = (r_\mathsf{P}, s)\}$

This is the set of Simp's randomness consistent with transcript s. On a random drawn $r_\mathsf{Sim} \leftarrow \mathcal{R}_\mathsf{Sim}$, let $(r_\mathsf{P}, s) \leftarrow \mathsf{Simp}(n; r_\mathsf{Sim})$ be the simulated view. The following claims apply to any instance-hiding protocol $\langle \mathsf{P}, \mathsf{A} \rangle$.

Claim. For any $s \in \mathcal{S}$ and any x,

$$\Pr_{(r_\mathsf{A}, r_\mathsf{P}) \leftarrow \mathcal{R}_\mathsf{A} \times \mathcal{R}_\mathsf{P}} [\boldsymbol{S}_x(r_\mathsf{A}, r_\mathsf{P}) = s] = \frac{|\beta_s^x|}{|\mathcal{R}_\mathsf{A}|} \cdot \frac{|\gamma_s|}{|\mathcal{R}_\mathsf{P}|}.$$

Corollary 2. $\mathsf{IHIP}/\mathsf{poly} \subseteq \mathsf{NP}/\mathsf{poly} \cap \mathsf{coNP}/\mathsf{poly}$.

Lemma 3 ([BT03, **Lemma 4**]). *If* $\mathsf{coNP} \subseteq \mathsf{AM}/\mathsf{poly}$*, then the polynomial hierarchy collapses to the third level.*

Combining with Lemma 3, the corollary follows:

Corollary 3. *If* $\mathsf{NP} \subseteq \mathsf{IHIP}/\mathsf{poly}$*, the polynomial hierarchy collapses to the third level.*

Further, we show that if the proof is simulatablely instance-hiding (that is, with an efficient simulator for the honest prover), then the problem is contained in $\mathsf{AM} \cap \mathsf{coAM}$. Here we need the errors to be negligible, though.

Theorem 3. *For any negligible functions* δ, ϵ*, if a promise problem* Π *has a simulatable honest-prover* (δ, ϵ)*-IHIP, then both* Π *and its complement* $\bar{\Pi}$ *have constant-round public-coin interactive proofs with uniform verifiers (that is, an* AM *proof system).*

The transformation protocol for Theorem 3 is presented in Fig. 3, with the proof deferred in [MV24, Section 4].

Corollary 4. $\mathsf{Simulatable}\text{-}\mathsf{IHIP} \subseteq \mathsf{AM} \cap \mathsf{coAM}$.

Remark 4. Theorem 2 and 3 can in fact be extended to similar but stronger statements with the hypothesis only requiring protocols that have ϵ-hiding, completeness, and soundness against the honest prover, because our proofs don't depend on the protocols' behavior with malicious provers.

AM protocol for Π: $\langle \mathsf{M}, \mathsf{A} \rangle^{\mathsf{Q}}(x)$

Parameters: input length n, g

Inputs:
  – An instance $x \in \mathrm{YES}(\Pi_n) \cup \mathrm{NO}(\Pi_n)$

Outputs: $d \in \{0, 1\}$

Ingredients:
  – $\langle \mathsf{P}, \mathsf{V} \rangle$ is an (δ, ϵ)-Instance-Hiding Interactive Proof
  – Advice: Takes advice $s^{(1)}, \ldots, s^{(g)}, b_1, \ldots, b_g$ from advide oracle Q
  – $\mathsf{WSLBP}^{\mathsf{O}_S}(c, K)$: Weighted Sets Lowerbound Protocol from [MV24, Section 3.2] for the sets $S_1, \ldots, S_g$, with input c, and errors negligible in n.
  – For $i \in [g]$ and transcript $s^{(i)}$, we define the efficient membership oracle for set $\alpha_{s^{(i)}}^x$ as follows:

Algorithm $\mathsf{O}_{\alpha_{s^{(i)}}^x}(r)$:
  1. $s^{(i)} = (u_1, y_1, \ldots, u_q, y_q)$
  2. $s_0 \leftarrow \phi$ *(the empty string)*
  3. **For** $j \leftarrow 1$ to q
     Check $\mathsf{V}\big(x, r, (u_1, y_1, \ldots, u_{j-1}, y_{j-1})\big) = u_j$, if not output 0.
  4. **If** $\mathsf{V}(x, r, s) = 1$ output 1; **Else** output 0.

Protocol:

1. M and A run the protocol $\mathsf{WSLBP}^{\mathsf{O}_{\alpha_{s^{(1)}}^x}, \ldots, \mathsf{O}_{\alpha_{s^{(g)}}^x}}$ with membership oracles access to $\mathsf{O}_{\alpha_{s^{(1)}}^x}, \ldots, \mathsf{O}_{\alpha_{s^{(g)}}^x}$ and inputs $(\frac{1}{b_1}, \ldots, \frac{1}{b_g})$, $(\frac{1}{2} \cdot g)$:

$$d \leftarrow \mathsf{WSLBP}^{\mathsf{O}_{\alpha_{s^{(1)}}^x}, \ldots, \mathsf{O}_{\alpha_{s^{(g)}}^x}} \left(\left(\frac{1}{b_1}, \ldots, \frac{1}{b_g} \right), \frac{1}{2} \cdot g \right).$$

2. A outputs d.

Fig. 1. AM Protocol from (δ, ϵ)-IHIP

3.3   Implications for One-Way Functions

As suggested in [Imp95], it is unclear whether hardness of problems in NP implies the existence of one-way function. This is important in the sense that if our world is in "Pessiland" or "Heuristica", where NP problems are hard either on average or on worst case but one-way functions do not exist, a huge set of cryptography primitives including pseudorandom generator [Yao82,BM82] and digital signatures [GMR88] would be impossible in a strong sense.

In this section, we provide positive implications by assuming the hard problem also possessing an instance-hiding interactive proof. We show two separate proofs – one for problems that only have an IHIP with *average-case hardness*, and another for those that have a simulatable IHIP with only *worst-case hard-*

Advice oracle $Q_w(P, V, n)$

Inputs:
- Input length n (Omitted when clear from context).
- $\langle P, V \rangle$ is an (δ, ϵ)-IHIP protocol for Π.

Ingredients:
- w is some arbitrary instance of Π.

Procedure:
1. **For** $i \leftarrow 1$ to g

    Samples random seed for verifier: $r_v^i \leftarrow \mathcal{R}_V$

    Samples random seed for prover: $r_p^i \leftarrow \mathcal{R}_P$

    Simulate the view with the prover's and verifier's algorithm and randomness:
    $$s^{(i)} \leftarrow \langle P(r_p^i), V(w, r_v^i) \rangle.$$

    Computes number of verifier's randomness consistent to the view $s^{(i)}$:
    $$b_i \leftarrow |\beta_{s^{(i)}}^w|.$$

2. Output $s^{(1)}, \ldots, s^{(g)}, b_1, \ldots, b_g$.

Fig. 2. Advice Oracle $Q_w(P, A, n)$ for AM Protocol From IHIP

ness. The former proof is non-constructive – we can only prove that a one-way function exists given an average-hard problem has IHIP. Moreover, this construction of one-way functions uses potential adversaries in a non-blackbox manner. Similar techniques have found use in the context of collision-resistant hash functions [KY18, RV22].

The latter proof is constructive – we show a construction of one-way function from any worst-case hard problem that has a Simulatable-IHIP, where the simulator is efficient. Implications similar to this are known for other classes such as SRE [AR16] (and SZK [Ost91], though that needs average-case hardness), which similarly rely on the efficiency of the simulator (or the encoding function in case of SRE).

OWFs from Average-Case Hard IHIP

Definition 3 (Average-Case Hard Problems). *Consider a promise problem $\Pi = (\text{YES}, \text{NO})$, and an ensemble of efficiently sampleable distributions $X = \{X_n\}_{n \in \mathbb{N}}$, where X_n is supported on $(\text{YES}_n \cup \text{NO}_n)$. Π is said to be* hard on average *over X if for any (non-uniform, if specified) polynomial-time algorithm A, there is a negligible function negl such that for all large enough n,*

$$\Pr_{x \leftarrow X_n} [A(x) = \Pi(x)] \leq \frac{1}{2} + \text{negl}(n).$$

Remark 5. In the above definition, we require that X_n be supported fully on $(\text{YES}_n \cup \text{NO}_n)$, and also be efficiently sampleable. Often in natural hard problems, these may not be simultaneously perfectly satisfied – a natural efficiently

---

Constant-round IP for Π: $\langle \mathsf{M}, \mathsf{A} \rangle(x)$

Parameters: Input length n, amplification parameter g.

Inputs: A promise instance x of Π_n.

Outputs: Verifier's decision $d \in \{0, 1\}$

Ingredients:

- $\langle \mathsf{P}, \mathsf{V} \rangle$: An (δ, ϵ)-simulatable instance-hiding interactive proof for Π.
- For any transcript $s \in \mathcal{S}$, we define the efficient membership oracle for set α_s^x as follows:

Algorithm $\mathsf{O}_{\alpha_s^x}(r)$:
1. Interpret s as $(u_1, y_1, \ldots, u_q, y_q)$
2. Denote by s_i the prefix $(u_1, y_1, \ldots, u_i, y_i)$, with s_0 being the empty string
3. **For** $j \leftarrow 1$ to q
   Check $\mathsf{V}(x, r, s_{j-1}) = u_j$, if not output 0.
4. **If** $\mathsf{V}(x, r, s) = 1$ output 1; **Else** output 0.

- For any $s \in \mathcal{S}$ and $r_\mathsf{P} \in \mathcal{R}_\mathsf{P}$, define the efficient membership oracles for sets $\zeta_{r_\mathsf{P}, s}$ and ζ_{r_P} as:

Algorithm $\mathsf{O}_{\zeta_{r_\mathsf{P}, s}}(r)$:
1. **If** $\mathsf{Sim}_\mathsf{P}(n; r) = (r_\mathsf{P}, s)$ output 1; **Else** output 0.

Algorithm $\mathsf{O}_{\zeta_{r_\mathsf{P}}}(r)$:
1. $(r'_\mathsf{P}, s) \leftarrow \mathsf{Sim}_\mathsf{P}(n; r)$.
2. **If** $r'_\mathsf{P} = r_\mathsf{P}$ output 1; **Else** output 0.

- $\mathsf{LBP}^{\mathsf{O}_S}(K)$: Set Lower-Bound protocol from [GS86] for the set S, with input K, and errors negligible in n.
- $\mathsf{UBP}^{\mathsf{O}_S}(K, r)$: Set Upper-Bound protocol from [For87] for the set S, with public input K, and verifier's private input r.

Protocol:

For $i \leftarrow 1$ to g, in parallel:
1. A samples $r_i \leftarrow \mathcal{R}_\mathsf{Sim}$, computes $(r_\mathsf{P}^{(i)}, s^{(i)}) \leftarrow \mathsf{Sim}_\mathsf{P}(n; r_i)$ and sends $(r_\mathsf{P}^{(i)}, s^{(i)})$ to prover M.
2. Honest M sets proposed lower bound $k_{\alpha_i} = |\alpha_{s^{(i)}}^x|$ (for size of $\alpha_{s^{(i)}}^x$), and $k_{r_\mathsf{P}^{(i)}} = |\zeta_{r_\mathsf{P}^{(i)}}|$, and upper bound $k_{r_\mathsf{P}^{(i)}, s^{(i)}} = 4 \cdot g \cdot |\zeta_{r_\mathsf{P}, s}|$ (for size of $\zeta_{r_\mathsf{P}^{(i)}, s^{(i)}}$), and sends $k_{\alpha_i}, k_{r_\mathsf{P}^{(i)}}, k_{r_\mathsf{P}^{(i)}, s^{(i)}}$ to verifier A.
3. A and M run lowerbound protocol on $\alpha_{s^{(i)}}^x$: $d_{\alpha_i} \leftarrow \mathsf{LBP}^{\mathsf{O}_{\alpha_{s^{(i)}}^x}}(k_{\alpha_i})$.
4. A and M run lowerbound protocol on ζ_{r_P}: $d_{r_\mathsf{P}, i} \leftarrow \mathsf{LBP}^{\mathsf{O}_{\zeta_{r_\mathsf{P}^{(i)}}}}(k_{r_\mathsf{P}^{(i)}})$.
5. A and M run upperbound protocol on $\zeta_{r_\mathsf{P}^{(i)}, s^{(i)}}$ with private input r_i:
$$d_{\zeta_i} \leftarrow \mathsf{UBP}^{\mathsf{O}_{\zeta_{r_\mathsf{P}^{(i)}, s^{(i)}}}}(k_{r_\mathsf{P}^{(i)}, s^{(i)}}, r_i).$$
6. If $d_{\alpha_i} = 0$, or $d_{\zeta_i} = 0$, or $d_{r_\mathsf{P}, i} = 0$: A outputs 0 (Reject).
Let $t_\mathsf{V} = |\mathcal{R}_\mathsf{V}|$ be the size of verifier's random space. A computes $\bar{k} \leftarrow \frac{1}{g} \cdot \sum_{i \in [g]} \frac{k_{r_\mathsf{P}^{(i)}} \cdot k_{\alpha_i}}{t_\mathsf{V} \cdot k_{r_\mathsf{P}^{(i)}, s^{(i)}}}$.
If $\bar{k} \geq \frac{1}{10 \cdot g}$, A outputs 1 (Accept); Otherwise Reject.

Fig. 3. Constant-Round IP from simulatable (δ, ϵ)-IHIP

sampleable hard distribution might have a small probability of not satisfying the promise. While we do not explicitly state this in our theorems, our proofs are robust to this and continue to hold as long as the probability of not satisfying the promise is small enough, e.g. negligible.

Theorem 4. *If any problem that is hard on average against non-uniform probabilistic polynomial-time algorithms possesses a (δ, ϵ)-instance-hiding interactive proof for some negligible functions δ and ϵ, then non-uniform infinitely-often one-way functions exist.*

One of the building blocks for our proof is the notion of distributional one-way function defined in [IL89], which also proved that the existence of distribitionally one-way functions imply existence of one-way functions.

Definition 4 ([IL89]). *Consider a family of efficiently computable functions $F = \{f_n : \{0,1\}^n \to \{0,1\}^{m(n)}\}_{n \in \mathbb{N}}$. For any $n \in \mathbb{N}$ and algorithm A, define the following two distributions: $D_{0,n}\left(x \leftarrow \{0,1\}^n,\ \text{outputs}\ (x, f(x))\right)$ and $D_{1,n}^A\left(x \leftarrow \{0,1\}^n,\ \text{outputs}\ \left(A(f(x)), f(x)\right)\right)$. $F = \{f_n\}$ is said to be distributionally one-way if, there is a constant $c > 0$ such that, for any efficient algorithm A, for all large enough n,*

$$\Delta(D_{0,n}, D_{1,n}^A) > n^{-c}.$$

Remark 6. While the above definition refers to the distribution of the input x being uniform over some $\{0,1\}^n$, we will treat it as coming from some sampleable distribution. That is, we will construct functions f_n where the above lower bound on statistical distance holds when x is sampled from some efficiently sampleable distribution X_n rather than $\{0,1\}^n$. This is sufficient because this function f_n composed with the efficient sampling algorithm for X_n then satisfies Definition 4.

Lemma 4 ([IL89]). *If there is a distributional one-way function then there is a one-way function. Further, there is an explicit transformation from any distributional one-way function to a one-way function. This transformation also works for non-uniform (distributional) one-way functions, and preserves uniformity.*

The proof sketch using a distributional one-way function is outlined in the technical overview, with the complete proof deferred to the full version [MV24, Section 5].

Explicit OWFs from Worst-Case Hard Simulatable IHIP

In addition to the positive result regarding OWF, this section also providing insights for comparing IHIP/Simulatable-IHIP with classes SZK and SRE by examining the consequences of the existence of hard problems within these classes. For instance, Ostrovsky [Ost91] proves an implication of *average-case hard* SZK of OWFs, while Applebaum and Raykov [AR16] demonstrate a similar implication of *worst-case hard* SRE. In this subsection, we present an implication of *worst-case* hard Simulatable-IHIP on OWF.

Definition 5 (Worst-Case Hard Problems). *A promise problem $\Pi = (\text{Yes}, \text{No})$ is said to be* worst-case hard *if for any (non-uniform, if specified) polynomial-time algorithm* A, *there is a negligible function* negl, *such that for all large enough n, there exists an instance $x \in \text{Yes}_n \cup \text{No}_n$,*

$$\Pr_{A} [A(x) = \Pi(x)] \leq \frac{1}{2} + \text{negl}(n).$$

Theorem 5. *If any worst-case hard problem has a honest-prover simulatable (δ, ϵ)-instance-hiding interactive proof for some negligible functions δ and ϵ, then there is an explicit construction of one-way functions. This one-way function is uniform if the simulator of the IHIP is uniform, and it is secure against non-uniform adversaries if the problem is worst-case hard against non-uniform algorithms.*

Remark 7. Unlike the OWF in Theorem 4, which incorporates the verifier algorithm A as part of the construction, the explicit construction of OWF from Simulatable-IHIP uses solely the efficient simulator Sim_P, which does not take the instance x as input. This is what allows the worst-case hardness of the problem to be useful in proving one-wayness of the latter function. Notably, the construction of OWF in [Ost91], based on SZK simulator, also takes the instance as part of the input, thus requiring hardness also over some distribution of instances. It is of interest to find whether a *worst-case hard* with just IHIP, which is not guaranteed an efficient similator for honest prover, implies OWF.

3.4   Oracle Separation from SZK

Given that SZK and IHIP are both contained in $\text{NP}/\text{poly} \cap \text{coNP}/\text{poly}$, it is natural to ask whether one is contained in the other. While we don't know how to construct IHIP protocols for SZK problems such as Statistical Difference and Graph Non-Isomorphism, it is also unclear whether IHIP is contained in SZK. Towards understanding their relationship, we exhibit an oracle relative to which IHIP $\not\subset$ SZK. Before advancing, it is essential to define the associated complexity classes.

Definition 6 (Class SZK). *A promise problem $\Pi = (\text{Yes}, \text{No})$ is in SZK if there exists a protocol $\langle P, A \rangle$, where the verifier runs in polynomial time, satisfying the following:*

- *$\langle P, A \rangle$ is an interactive proof for Π (where both P and A get the input instance) with negligible completeness and soundness errors.*
- *There exists an efficient algorithm Sim such that for any efficient A^* and any $x \in \text{Yes}_n$,*

$$\Delta\Big(\text{Sim}_{A^*}(x), \text{View}_{A^*}\big(P(x), A^*(x)\big)\Big) \leq \text{negl}(n).$$

Definition 7. *An oracle protocol is a protocol $\langle P, A \rangle$ in which both P and A are allowed to make calls to an oracle. For any oracle $\mathcal{O} : \{0,1\}^* \rightarrow \{0,1\}^*$, such a protocol with oracle $\mathcal{O}$ is denoted by $\langle P, A \rangle^{\mathcal{O}}$. The view of each party in such a protocol also includes the set of oracle queries it makes and the corresponding responses. The conditions for $\langle P, A \rangle^{\mathcal{O}}$ being a (Simulatable) instance-hiding proof (resp. SZK) system for a promise problem are the same as those in Definition 1 (resp. Definition 6), except that the simulator is also allowed access to the same oracle.*

Definition 8. *For any oracle $\mathcal{O} : \{0,1\}^* \rightarrow \{0,1\}^*$, Simulatable-IHIP$^{\mathcal{O}}$ (resp. SZK$^{\mathcal{O}}$) is the class of promise problems that have a simulatable instance-hiding proof (resp. SZK proof) system with oracle $\mathcal{O}$. This includes promise problems whose definitions involve properties of the oracle.*

Theorem 6. *There exists an oracle $\mathcal{O}$ such that Simulatable-IHIP$^{\mathcal{O}} \not\subseteq$ SZK$^{\mathcal{O}}$.*

Looking ahead, our oracle separation will use oracles based on the generic group model [Sho97]. Rather than Shoup's original formulation of this model, we will use the following formulation as in Corrigan-Gibbs and Kogan [CGK18], which will be more convenient to use.

Definition 9 (Generic Group Oracles). *For any $N \in \mathbb{N}$, and bijective function $\sigma : \mathbb{Z}_N \rightarrow [N]$, the oracle $\mathcal{G}_{\sigma} : [N] \times [N] \rightarrow [N]$ is defined as: $\mathcal{G}_{\sigma}(g, h) = \sigma(\sigma^{-1}(g) + \sigma^{-1}(h))$. We refer to elements of $[N]$ in this context as the group elements, and the corresponding inverses of σ as their discrete logarithms.*

Let $\mathcal{N} : \mathbb{N} \rightarrow \mathbb{N}$ be the function that, on input any $n \in \mathbb{N}$, outputs the smallest prime number larger than 2^{n-1}. For any family of bijective functions $\sigma = \left\{ \sigma_n : \mathbb{Z}_{\mathcal{N}(n)} \rightarrow [\mathcal{N}(n)] \right\}_{n \in \mathbb{N}}$ and family of oracles $\mathcal{I} = \left\{ \mathcal{I}_n : \mathbb{Z}_{\mathcal{N}(n)} \rightarrow \{0,1\} \right\}_{n \in \mathbb{N}}$, we define the promise problem $\Pi^{\mathcal{I}, \sigma} = (\text{YES}, \text{NO})$ as follows:

$$\text{YES}_n = \{(n, \mathcal{N}(n), \sigma_n(1), \sigma_n(x)) \mid \mathcal{I}_n(x) = 1\}.$$
$$\text{NO}_n = \{(n, \mathcal{N}(n), \sigma_n(1), \sigma_n(x)) \mid \mathcal{I}_n(x) = 0\}.$$

We extend the notation $\mathcal{G}_{\sigma}$ in the natural manner to denote the family of oracles $\mathcal{G}_{\sigma_n}$ for all $n \in \mathbb{N}$. Similarly, note that to define $\text{YES}_n(\Pi^{\mathcal{I}, \sigma})$ and $\text{NO}_n(\Pi^{\mathcal{I}, \sigma})$, only $\mathcal{I}_n$ and σ_n need to be specified; we denote the corresponding promise problem restricted to instances of size n by $\Pi^{\mathcal{I}_n, \sigma_n}$.

We show that there is an instance-hiding oracle protocol that, given oracle access to $\mathcal{I}$ and $\mathcal{G}_{\sigma}$, is a valid instance-hiding proof for $\Pi^{\mathcal{I}, \sigma}$, whereas every oracle protocol fails to be an SZK proof for this language for most such oracles. This already gives a separation between "generic" instance-hiding and SZK protocols that only use group elements in a generic manner. To show the oracle separation, a careful diagonalization argument is needed. We first state the following two lemmas alongside two additional imported lemmas that show the above statements, and then set up and perform the required diagonalization, which proves Theorem 6. The proof is deferred to the full version [MV24].

Lemma 5. *There is an oracle protocol $\langle P, A \rangle$ such that, for any $\mathcal{I}$ and σ as above, $\langle P, A \rangle^{\mathcal{I}, \mathcal{G}_\sigma}$ is a simulatable instance-hiding proof system for $\Pi^{\mathcal{I}, \sigma}$.*

Lemma 6. *For any oracle protocol $\langle P, A \rangle$ and polynomial-time oracle algorithm Sim, there is an $n_0 \in \mathbb{N}$ such that for all $n \geq n_0$, there exists some $\mathcal{I}_n$ and σ_n as above such there is either an input in $\mathrm{NO}_n(\Pi^{\mathcal{I}_n, \sigma_n})$ on which $\langle P, A \rangle^{\mathcal{I}_n, \mathcal{G}_{\sigma_n}}$ has soundness error $\Omega(1/n)$, or an input in $\mathrm{YES}_n(\Pi^{\mathcal{I}_n, \sigma_n})$ on which it has either completeness error $\Omega(1/n)$, or honest-verifier statistical zero-knowledge error $\Omega(1/n)$ with $\mathrm{Sim}^{\mathcal{I}_n, \mathcal{G}_{\sigma_n}}$ as the simulator.*

Our proof of Lemma 6 relies on the hardness of the discrete logarithm problem for generic algorithms, which require at least $N^{1/2}$ time on groups of order N, as shown by Shoup [Sho97]. Our modelling of such algorithms is more general than Shoup's, so we instead use the following corollary of a theorem of Corrigan-Gibbs and Kogan [CGK18, Theorem 2].

Lemma 7. *For any prime $N \in \mathbb{N}$ and oracle algorithm A that receives at most $\sqrt{N}$-bit non-uniform advice and runs in time T,*

$$\Pr_{\sigma, x}[A^{\mathcal{G}_\sigma}(\sigma(1), \sigma(x)) = x] \leq \frac{T^{2.01}}{\sqrt{N}}.$$

where σ is a uniformly random bijective function from $\mathbb{Z}_N$ to $[N]$, and x is uniformly random over $\mathbb{Z}_N$.

Then, we use Lemma 6 to construct functions $\mathcal{I}$ and σ such that with respect the oracles $(\mathcal{I}, \mathcal{G}_\sigma)$, the problem $\Pi^{\mathcal{I}, \sigma}$ does not have an SZK protocol. The standard approach to doing so is diagonalization: to enumerate all possible oracle protocols and simulators, and for each pick an input size n and corresponding $\mathcal{I}_n$ and σ_n on which it fails (as promised by Lemma 6), and include that in $\mathcal{I}$ and σ. However, we cannot do this directly, as the set of all protocols is not countable. Instead, we will do this for a countable set of protocols and show that for any potential SZK protocol, there is a protocol in this set that computes the same problem. This countable set will be the set of protocols with simulation-based provers [For87].

Definition 10 (Simulation-based Protocols). *Given (oracle) algorithms A and Sim, the* simulation-based protocol *defined by these is the protocol $\langle P_{\mathsf{Sim}}, A \rangle$, where P_{Sim} is the* simulation-based prover *that behaves as follows: to compute the prover's message at any point in the protocol, sample from the distribution of this message in the output of Sim, conditioned on this output matching the protocol transcript so far (if this conditional distribution is not defined, set the message to be $\perp$).*

The following lemma follows immediately from the statistical zero-knowledge property. (Roughly this statement is also proven as part of the proof of Theorem 5.)

Lemma 8. *Suppose* $\langle \mathsf{P}, \mathsf{A} \rangle$ *is an honest-verifier SZK proof system for a promise problem* Π *with simulator* Sim, *all with respect to some oracle* $\mathcal{O}$. *Then the simulation-based protocol* $\langle \mathsf{P}_{\mathsf{Sim}}, \mathsf{A} \rangle$ *is also an honest-verifier SZK proof for* Π *with simulator* Sim, *with respect to oracle* $\mathcal{O}$.

Given this lemma, we only need to enumerate over pairs of polynomial-time algorithms $(\mathsf{A}, \mathsf{Sim})$ in our diagonalization argument, and this is indeed a countable set. Together, Lemma 8, 9 and 5 prove Theorem 6.

Lemma 9. *There exist* $\mathcal{I} = \{\mathcal{I}_n\}$ *and* $\sigma = \{\sigma_n\}$ *such that no simulation-based protocol is a valid SZK proof system for* $\Pi^{\mathcal{I}, \sigma}$ *with respect to oracles* $(\mathcal{I}, \mathcal{G}_\sigma)$.

3.5   Instance-Hiding Delegation Schemes

In this section, we extend the study to a setting in which a machine A, given an private input x, delegates the computational task of computing a function $f(x)$ to a computationally stronger machine P. We seek solutions in which the prover P does this without learning x, but without asking for any guarantees in case P does not follow the protocol. We further generalize the definition to allow the prover to learn leakage $\ell(x)$ of instance x defined by some PSPACE function ℓ. We note that because some results (e.g. Theorem 2, Theorem 3, Theorem 4, Theorem 5) about IHIP in previous sections rely solely on its correctness of honest prover and hiding properties (and do not need the soundness property), these can be generalized to this setting. We further show strong connections between the existence of such delegation schemes and of IHIP's, and then use these connections together with closure properties of these schemes to show the closure properties of IHIP's stated in Sect. 3.1. Below, as before, for any set S, S_n denotes its intersection with $\{0,1\}^n$. For any promise problem $\Pi = (\text{YES}, \text{No})$, we define its characteristic function to be the partial function that maps inputs in YES to 1, inputs in No to 0, and is undefined on other inputs.

Definition 11 (Instance-Hiding Delegation Scheme (IHD) [FO91]). *Consider a function* $f : \mathcal{X} \to \mathcal{Y}$, *and functions* $\delta, \epsilon : \mathbb{N} \to [0,1]$ *and* $\ell : \mathcal{X} \to \{0,1\}^*$. *A* (δ, ϵ, ℓ)-*Instance-Hiding Delegation Scheme (IHD) for* f *is a protocol* $\langle \mathsf{P}, \mathsf{A} \rangle$ *in which a probabilistic polynomial-time verifier* A *interacts with a computationally unbounded prover* P. *For some* $n \in \mathbb{N}$, A *gets a private input* $x \in \mathcal{X}_n$, *while* P *gets the input* n. *At the end of the interaction,* A *outputs* $y \in \mathcal{Y} \cup \{\perp\}$. *The protocol is required to satisfy the following properties for all large enough* $n \in \mathbb{N}$:

- **Correctness:** *For any input* $x \in \mathcal{X}_n$:
$$\Pr\left[\langle \mathsf{P}(n), \mathsf{A}(x) \rangle = f(x)\right] \geq 1 - \delta(n).$$

- **Hiding Against Honest Prover (with leakage):** *There exists a computationally unbounded randomized algorithm* Sim_P *such that for any input* $x \in \mathcal{X}_n$:
$$\Delta\Big(\mathsf{Sim}_\mathsf{P}\big(n, \ell(x)\big), \text{VIEW}_P(\mathsf{P}(n), \mathsf{A}(x))\Big) \leq \epsilon(n).$$

If the simulator Sim$_P$ *is efficient, we call the protocol* Simulatable-Instance-Hiding Delegation *(Simulatable-IHD). The protocol is* perfectly-hiding *if* $\epsilon(n) = 0$. *If left unspecified, we assume* ℓ *is the constant function that always outputs* $\perp$, *corresponding to the absence of leakage.*

The following proposition directly follows the completeness and soundness for the honest prover in IHIP, and ϵ-hiding.

Proposition 1. *Consider a promise problem* Π *with characteristic functions* $f = \{f_n : \{0,1\}^n \rightarrow \{0,1\} \cup \{\perp\}\}_{n\in\mathbb{N}}$, *and let* $\langle P, A \rangle$ *be a* (δ, ϵ)-*IHIP (resp. simulatable IHIP) for* Π, *then* $\langle P, A \rangle$ *is a* (ϵ, δ)-*IHD (resp. simulatable IHD) for* f.

Next, we define a version of instance-hiding delegation schemes that has an additional verifiability property that protects against provers that may deviate from the protocol.

Definition 12 (Verifiable Instance-Hiding Delegation Scheme [FO91]**).** *Consider any function* $f : \mathcal{X} \rightarrow \mathcal{Y}$, *and functions* $\delta, \epsilon : \mathbb{N} \rightarrow [0,1]$, *and* $\ell : \mathcal{X} \rightarrow \mathcal{Z}$. *A* (δ, ϵ, ℓ)-Verifiable Instance-Hiding Delegation Scheme *(VIHD) for* f *is a IHD protocol that additionally achieves verifiability and hiding against malicious provers:*

- **Correctness:** *For any input* $x \in \mathcal{X}_n$:

$$\Pr\left[\langle P(n), A(x) \rangle = f(x)\right] \geq 1 - \delta(n).$$

- **Verifiability:** *For any prover* P^*, *for any input* $x \in \mathcal{X}_n$:

$$\Pr\left[\langle P^*(n), A(x) \rangle \in \{f(x), \perp\}\right] \geq 1 - \delta(n).$$

- **Hiding against malicious prover (with leakage):** *For any prover* P^*, *there exists a computationally unbounded randomized algorithm* Sim$_{P^*}$ *such that for any input* $x \in \mathcal{X}_n$,

$$\Delta\big(\mathsf{Sim}_{P^*}\big(n, \ell(x)\big), \mathrm{VIEW}_{P^*}(P^*, A(x))\big) \leq \epsilon(n).$$

The VIHD is simulatable if the simulator for honest prover Sim$_P$ *is efficient. If left unspecified, we assume* ℓ *is the constant function that always outputs* $\perp$, *corresponding to the absence of leakage.*

We then have the following proposition, which states that VIHD protocols are essentially stronger than IHIP protocols.

Proposition 2. *Let* f *be the characteristic function for a promise problem* Π. *If* $\langle P, A \rangle$ *is a* (δ, ϵ)-*verifiable instance-hiding delegation (resp. simulatable* (δ, ϵ)-*verifiable instance-hiding delegation) for* f, *then there exists a* (δ, ϵ)-*instance-hiding proof (resp. simulatable* (δ, ϵ)-*instance-hiding interactive proof)* $\langle P', A' \rangle$ *for* Π.

Proof (Proof Sketch). We define $P' = P$ and let A' run A as a black box on the same input, and output 1 (Accept) if and only if A outputs 1. The δ-completeness and ϵ-hiding follow the correctness and ϵ-hiding of $\langle P, A \rangle$ respectively. The soundness of $\langle P', A' \rangle$ follows from the correctness and verifiability of $\langle P, A \rangle$.

Verifiable IHD from IHD

It is immediate that any VIHD is also a IHD. If restricting ℓ to be constant function, [FO91] demonstrates that if any function $f \in$ PSPACE has perfect-hiding zero-leakage $(\delta, 0, \perp)$-IHD, then f also has a perfect-hiding $(\delta', 0, \perp)$-VIHD. We extend their theorem to ϵ-hiding schemes with a richer class of leakage function ℓ. The protocol and proof essentially closely follow that of [FO91, Lemma 3.1], with the only difference being in the hiding statements that the prover proves to the verifier in each round. In our case, the prover proves ϵ-hiding with respect to any PSPACE leakage function, whereas in [FO91] the focus is on perfect hiding and only the constant function as leakage. This generalization will also be useful in other context, such as showing interactive randomized encodings defined in [AIK10] is closed under complementation (see [MV24, Appendix C] for details).

Theorem 7. *Suppose that a function f is computable in polynomial space and has a (δ, ϵ, ℓ)-IHD $\langle P, A \rangle$ for some negligible δ, ϵ and $\ell \in$ PSPACE , then there exists negligible δ', ϵ' and $\langle P', A' \rangle$ such that $\langle P', A' \rangle$ is a $(\delta', \epsilon', \ell)$-VIHD for f.*

Corollary 5. *Suppose that a function f is computable in polynomial space and has a (δ, ϵ)-IHD for some negligible δ, ϵ. If f is the characteristic function for a promise problem Π, then Π has a (δ', ϵ')-IHIP for some negligible δ', ϵ'.*

The above corollary follows from Theorem 7 and Proposition 2, and carries over our results from other sections about the implications of IHIP protocols to IHD schemes. Because the protocol format of an IHD is related to IHIP, just with a possibly different output space at the end, we adopt the notations of elements in Sect. 3.2.

Proof (Proof Sketch). Inspired by the proof for perfect-hiding in [FO91], we rely on the fact that both the correctness and the hiding aspects of an execution are statements in PSPACE, and thus can be proven with an appropriate interactive proof protocol following the celebrated IP = PSPACE theorem [LFKN92] [Sha92]. Intuitively, consider a q-round IHD $\langle P, A \rangle$ for a function f, we construct a new protocol $\langle P', A' \rangle$ that ensures verifiability and hiding against a malicious prover. $\langle P', A' \rangle$ runs $\langle P, A \rangle$ in a round-by-round manner. Before A sends a message in each round, P' proves to A' that for any input x, the distribution of A's next message in this round will not reveal much additional information about x. This ensures that hiding against malicious prover. After the execution of $\langle P, A \rangle$, A' has the view of A: (x, r_A, s), which is supposed to achieve correctness if A interacts with honest prover. To enforce verifiability, P' proves to the verifier that for any input $x \in \mathcal{X}_n$, the public view s achieves correctness with high probability. The protocol is presented in Fig. 4, and full proof is deferred to full version [MV24, Section 7].

Verifiable Instance Hiding Delegation: $\langle P', V' \rangle$

Parameters:

- Function $f : \mathcal{X} \to \mathcal{Y}$.
- Input length n.
- Leakage function ℓ.

Inputs: An instance $x \in \mathcal{X}_n$.

Outputs: $y \in \mathcal{Y} \cup \{\perp\}$.

Ingredients:

- $\langle P, V \rangle$ is a q-round (δ, ϵ)-IHD for R as described.
- Consider the public view of protocol $\langle P, V \rangle$ up to ith round $(u_1, y_1, \ldots, u_i, y_i)$, and any input $x \in \mathcal{X}_n$. Define $\beta^x_{(u_1,y_1,\ldots,u_i,y_i)}$ as the set of verifier's randomness consistent with input x and $(u_1, y_1, \ldots, u_i, y_i)$. Denote by $\mathcal{U}_{(u_1,y_1,\ldots,u_i,y_i)}$ the set of the possible next messages of V:

$$\mathcal{U}_{(u_1,y_1,\ldots,u_i,y_i)} = \bigcup_{x \in \mathcal{X}} \{u_{i+1} = V(x, r_V, (u_1, y_1, \ldots, u_i, y_i)) \mid r_V \in \beta^x_{(u_1,y_1,\ldots,u_i,y_i)}\}.$$

Protocol:

1. V' samples a randomness $r_V \leftarrow \mathcal{R}_V$.
2. V' generates its first message $u_1^* \leftarrow V(x, r_V, \phi)$, and sends it to P', and P' responds with the y_1 that is P's response to this message.
3. For $i \in [2, q]$:
   (a) P' and V' execute an interactive proof protocol where P' proves the following hiding statement:

   "For any two inputs $x_1, x_2 \in \mathcal{X}_n$ such that $\ell(x_1) = \ell(x_2)$,

   $$\sum_{u_i \in \mathcal{U}_{(u_1^*,y_1^*,\ldots,y_i^*)}} \left| \frac{\left| \beta^{x_1}_{(u_1^*,y_1^*,\ldots,u_{i-1}^*,y_{i-1}^*,u_i)} \right|}{\left| \beta^{x_1}_{(u_1^*,y_1^*,\ldots,u_{i-1}^*,y_{i-1}^*)} \right|} - \frac{\left| \beta^{x_2}_{(u_1^*,y_1^*,\ldots,u_{i-1}^*,y_{i-1}^*,u_i)} \right|}{\left| \beta^{x_2}_{(u_1^*,y_1^*,\ldots,u_{i-1}^*,y_{i-1}^*)} \right|} \right| \leq 4\epsilon".$$

   The above statement is in PSPACE if $\ell, f \in$ PSPACE and the IP follows from IP = PSPACE.
   (b) **If** the verifier in the above IP rejects, V' rejects immediately.
   Else
      i. V' computes $u_i^* \leftarrow V(x, r_V, (u_1^*, y_1^*, \ldots, u_{i-1}^*, y_{i-1}^*))$ and sends u_i^* to P'.
      ii. P' computes the response y_i^* according to P and sends it to V'.
4. P' and V' execute an interactive proof protocol where P' proves that:

   "For any $x \in \mathcal{X}_n$: $\Pr_{r_V \leftarrow \beta_s^x} \left[V\left(x, r_V, (u_1^*, \ldots, y_q^*)\right) \neq f(x) \right] < \frac{1}{2^{n/2}}$".

5. **If** the verifier in the above protocol rejects, then V' rejects.
   Else V' outputs $V\left(x, r_V, (u_1^*, \ldots, y_q^*)\right)$.

Fig. 4. Transformation from IHD to VIHD

Closure Properties

In this section, we use some obvious closure properties of instance-hiding delegation schemes, together with the connections to IHIP proven so far, to show similar closure properties for IHIP's. Consider any functions $f : \mathcal{X} \to \mathcal{Y}$ and $p : \mathcal{Y}^* \to \mathcal{Z}$. For any function $k : \mathbb{N} \to \mathbb{N}$, we define the composed function $p \circ f^{\otimes k} : \mathcal{X}^* \to \mathcal{Z}$ as the following partial function for each $n \in \mathbb{N}$:

$$(p \circ f^{\otimes k})(x_1, \ldots, x_{k(n)}) = p\left(f(x_1), \ldots, f(x_{k(n)})\right).$$

where each x_i is of size n.

Proposition 3 (Closure of VIHD under Composition with Efficient Functions). *Consider any function f that has a (δ, ϵ)-VIHD for some negligible functions δ and ϵ, and any efficiently computable function p. For any polynomial $k : \mathbb{N} \to \mathbb{N}$, the composed function $p \circ f^{\otimes k}$ also has a (δ', ϵ')-VIHD for some negligible functions δ' and ϵ'.*

Combining Propositions 1 to 3 and Theorem 7, we get the following as corollaries.

Theorem 1 (Closure under Composition with Efficient Functions). *Consider any promise problems Π that has an IHIP protocol, and any efficiently computable function $f : \{0, 1, \perp\}^* \to \{0, 1, \perp\}$ whose output is $\perp$ whenever any of its inputs is $\perp$. For any polynomial $k : \mathbb{N} \to \mathbb{N}$, the composed promise problem $f \circ \Pi^{\otimes k}$ also has an IHIP protocol.*

Lemma 1 (Closure under Complementation). *Suppose, for some negligible functions δ, ϵ, that a problem Π has a (δ, ϵ)-IHIP (possibly with a non-uniform verifier). Then the complement of Π has a (δ', ϵ')-IHIP (resp. with a non-uniform verifier if starting with a non-uniform verifier), where δ', ϵ' are also negligible.*

Finally, we prove the following propositions regarding closure properties of VIHD schemes in the presence of leakage that will be useful in building the connection with Statistical Randomized Encoding [MV24, Appendix C].

Proposition 4. *Consider two functions $\ell, \ell' \in$ PSPACE defined over domain $\mathcal{X}$ such that for any two inputs $x, x' \in \mathcal{X}$, $\ell(x) = \ell(x')$ if and only if $\ell'(x) = \ell'(x')$. For functions δ, ϵ and any function $f : \mathcal{X} \to \mathcal{Y}$, if $\langle \mathsf{P}, \mathsf{A} \rangle$ is a (δ, ϵ, ℓ)-IHD (resp. (δ, ϵ, ℓ)-VIHD) for f, then $\langle \mathsf{P}, \mathsf{A} \rangle$ is a $(\delta, \epsilon, \ell')$-IHD (resp. $(\delta, \epsilon, \ell')$-VIHD) for f. Furthermore, if there is an efficient bijective map between ℓ and ℓ', the transformation holds for simulatable IHD (resp. simulatable VIHD).*

Proof (Proof Sketch). ℓ and ℓ' are renaming of each other and thus a simulator with respect to ℓ' can be made given a simulator with respect to ℓ.

Acknowledgements. We thank anonymous reviewers of this paper for their useful comments and references. Both authors are supported by the National Research Foundation, Singapore, under its NRF Fellowship programme, award no. NRF-NRFF14-2022-0010.

References

AFK89. Abadi, M., Feigenbaum, J., Kilian, J.: On hiding information from an oracle. J. Comput. Syst. Sci. **39**(1), 21–50 (1989)

AH91. Aiello, W., Håstad, J.: Statistical zero-knowledge languages can be recognized in two rounds. J. Comput. Syst. Sci. **42**(3), 327–345 (1991)

AIK04. Applebaum, B., Ishai, Y., Kushilevitz, E.: Cryptography in NC/sup 0/. In: 45th Annual IEEE Symposium on Foundations of Computer Science, pp. 166–175 (2004)

AIK05. Applebaum, B., Ishai, Y., Kushilevitz, E.: Computationally private randomizing polynomials and their applications (extended abstract). In: 20th Annual IEEE Conference on Computational Complexity (CCC'05), pp. 260–274 (2005)

AIK10. Applebaum, B., Ishai, Y., Kushilevitz, E.: From secrecy to soundness: efficient verification via secure computation. In: International Colloquium on Automata, Languages and Programming (2010)

AIKPC15. Agrawal, S., Ishai, Y., Khurana, D., Paskin-Cherniavsky, A.: Statistical randomized encodings: a complexity theoretic view. In: Halldórsson, M.M., Iwama, K., Kobayashi, N., Speckmann, B., editors, Automata, Languages, and Programming, pp. 1–13. Springer, Berlin, Heidelberg (2015)

App14. Applebaum, B.: Cryptography in Constant Parallel Time. Information Security and Cryptography. Springer, Berlin, Heidelberg (2014). https://doi.org/10.1007/978-3-642-17367-7

AR16. Applebaum, B., Raykov, P.: On the relationship between statistical zero-knowledge and statistical randomized encodings. In: Advances in Cryptology – EUROCRYPT 2016, pp. 449–477. Springer-Verlag, Berlin, Heidelberg (2016). https://doi.org/10.1007/978-3-662-53015-3_16

BF90. Beaver, D., Feigenbaum, J.: Hiding instances in multioracle queries. In: Choffrut, C., Lengauer, T., editors, STACS 90, pp. 37–48. Springer, Berlin, Heidelberg (1990). https://doi.org/10.1007/3-540-52282-4_30

BFOS93. Beaver, D., Feigenbaum, J., Ostrovsky, R., Shoup, V.: Instance-hiding proof systems. Work done at Harvard University, supported in part by NSF grant CCR-870-4513 (1993)

BFS90. Beaver, D., Feigenbaum, J., Shoup, V.: Hiding instances in zero-knowledge proof systems. In: Menezes, A.J., Vanstone, S.A. (eds.) Advances in Cryptology-CRYPTO' 90, pp. 326–338. Springer, Berlin, Heidelberg (2001). https://doi.org/10.1007/3-540-38424-3_24

BGG+88. Ben-Or, M., et al.: Everything provable is provable in zero-knowledge. In: Goldwasser, S. (ed.) Advances in Cryptology — CRYPTO' 88: Proceedings, pp. 37–56. Springer, New York, NY (1990). https://doi.org/10.1007/0-387-34799-2_4

BM82. Blum, M., Micali, S.: How to generate cryptographically strong sequences of pseudo random bits. In: 23rd Annual Symposium on Foundations of Computer Science (SFCS 1982), pp. 112–117 (1982)

BM88. Babai, L., Moran, S.: Arthur-Merlin games: a randomized proof system, and a hierarchy of complexity classes. J. Comput. Syst. Sci. **36**(2), 254–276 (1988)

BT03. Bogdanov, A., Trevisan, L.: On worst-case to average-case reductions for np problems. In: 44th Annual IEEE Symposium on Foundations of Computer Science, 2003. Proceedings, pp. 308–317 (2003)

CD96.   Cramer, R., Damgård, I.: On monotone function closure of statistical zero-knowledge. IACR Cryptol. ePrint Arch., p. 3 (1996)

CGK18.   Corrigan-Gibbs, H., Kogan, D.: The discrete-logarithm problem with preprocessing. In: Nielsen, J.B., Rijmen, V., editors, Advances in Cryptology – EUROCRYPT 2018, pp. 415–447. Springer International Publishing, Cham (2018). https://doi.org/10.1007/978-3-319-78375-8_14

DSDCPY08. De Santis, A., Di Crescenzo, G., Persiano, G., Yung, M.: On monotone formula composition of perfect zero-knowledge languages. SIAM J. Comput. **38**, 1300–1329 (2008)

FF91.   Feigenbaum, J., Fortnow, L.: On the random-self-reducibility of complete sets. In: [1991] Proceedings of the Sixth Annual Structure in Complexity Theory Conference, pp. 124–132 (1991)

FKN03.   Feige, U., Kilian, J., Naor, M.: A minimal model for secure computation. In: Conference Proceedings of the Annual ACM Symposium on Theory of Computing (2003)

FO91.   Feigenbaum, J., Ostrovsky, R.: A note on one-prover, instance-hiding zero-knowledge proof systems. In: Imai, H., Rivest, R.L., Matsumoto, T. (eds.) ASIACRYPT 1991. LNCS, vol. 739, pp. 352–359. Springer, Heidelberg (1993). https://doi.org/10.1007/3-540-57332-1_30

For87.   Fortnow, L.: The complexity of perfect zero-knowledge. In: Proceedings of the Nineteenth Annual ACM Symposium on Theory of Computing, STOC '87, pp. 204–209, New York, NY, USA (1987). Association for Computing Machinery

GK96.   Goldreich, O., Krawczyk, H.: On the composition of zero-knowledge proof systems. SIAM J. Comput. **25**(1), 169–192 (1996)

GMR88.   Goldwasser, S., Micali, S., Rivest, R.L.: A digital signature scheme secure against adaptive chosen-message attacks. SIAM J. Comput. **17**(2), 281–308 (1988)

GMR89.   Goldwasser, L., Micali, S., Rackoff, C.: The knowledge complexity of interactive proof-systems. In: Symposium on the Theory of Computing (1989)

GMW91.   Goldreich, O., Micali, S., Wigderson, A.: Proofs that yield nothing but their validity for all languages in NP have zero-knowledge proof systems. J. ACM **38**(3), 691–729 (1991)

GS86.   Goldwasser, S., Sipser, M.: Private coins versus public coins in interactive proof systems. In: Proceedings of the Eighteenth Annual ACM Symposium on Theory of Computing, STOC '86, pp. 59–68, New York, NY, USA (1986). Association for Computing Machinery

IK00.   Ishai, Y., Kushilevitz, E.: Randomizing polynomials: a new representation with applications to round-efficient secure computation. In: Proceedings 41st Annual Symposium on Foundations of Computer Science, pp. 294–304 (2000)

IL89.   Impagliazzo, R., Luby, M.: One-way functions are essential for complexity based cryptography. In: 30th Annual Symposium on Foundations of Computer Science, pp. 230–235 (1989)

Imp95.   Impagliazzo, R.: A personal view of average-case complexity. In: Proceedings of Structure in Complexity Theory. Tenth Annual IEEE Conference, pp. 134–147 (1995)

Kil88. Kilian, J.: Founding crytpography on oblivious transfer. In: Proceedings of the Twentieth Annual ACM Symposium on Theory of Computing, STOC '88, pp. 20–31, New York, NY, USA (1988). Association for Computing Machinery

KY18.   Komargodski, I., Yogev, E.: On distributional collision resistant hashing. In: Shacham, H., Boldyreva, A. (eds.) Advances in Cryptology – CRYPTO 2018: 38th Annual International Cryptology Conference, Santa Barbara, CA, USA, August 19–23, 2018, Proceedings, Part II, pp. 303–327. Springer International Publishing, Cham (2018). https://doi.org/10.1007/978-3-319-96881-0_11

LFKN92. Lund, C., Fortnow, L., Karloff, H., Nisan, N.: Algebraic methods for interactive proof systems. J. ACM **39**(4), 859–868 (1992)

MV24.   Mu, C., Vasudevan, P.N.: Instance-hiding interactive proofs. ECCC, TR24-100 (2024)

Oka00. Okamoto, T.: On relationships between statistical zero-knowledge proofs. J. Comput. Syst. Sci. **60**(1), 47–108 (2000)

Ost91. Ostrovsky, R.: One-way functions, hard on average problems, and statistical zero-knowledge proofs. In: [1991] Proceedings of the Sixth Annual Structure in Complexity Theory Conference, pp. 133–138 (1991)

RV22.   Rothblum, R.D., Vasudevan, P.N.: Collision-resistance from multi-collision-resistance. Cryptology ePrint Archive, Paper 2022/173 (2022). https://eprint.iacr.org/2022/173

Sha92. Shamir, A.: IP = PSPACE. J. ACM **39**(4), 869–877 (1992)

Sho97. Shoup, V.: Lower bounds for discrete logarithms and related problems. In: Fumy, W. (ed.) Advances in Cryptology — EUROCRYPT '97, pp. 256–266. Springer, Berlin, Heidelberg (1997). https://doi.org/10.1007/3-540-69053-0_18

SV97.   Sahai, A., Vadhan, S.P.: A complete promise problem for statistical zero-knowledge. In: Proceedings 38th Annual Symposium on Foundations of Computer Science, pp. 448–457 (1997)

Tha22. Thaler, J.: Proofs, arguments, and zero-knowledge. Found. Trends Priv. Secur. **4**(2–4), 117–660 (2022)

Vad99. Vadhan, S.P.: A study of statistical zero-knowledge proofs. PhD thesis, Harvard University, USA, (1999). AAI0801528

Yao82. Yao, A.C.: Theory and application of trapdoor functions. In: 23rd Annual Symposium on Foundations of Computer Science (SFCS 1982), pp. 80–91 (1982)

Yao86. Yao, A.C.-C.: How to generate and exchange secrets. In: 27th Annual Symposium on Foundations of Computer Science (SFCS 1986), pp. 162–167 (1986)

Yap83. Yap, C.K.: Some consequences of non-uniform conditions on uniform classes. Theor. Comput. Sci. **26**(3), 287–300 (1983)

The Power of NAPs:

Compressing OR-Proofs via Collision-Resistant Hashing

Katharina Boudgoust[1]($\boxtimes$)(iD) and Mark Simkin[2]

[1] CNRS, Univ Montpellier, LIRMM, Montpellier, France
katharina.boudgoust@lirmm.fr
[2] Aarhus, Denmark
mark@univariate.org

Abstract. Proofs of partial knowledge, first considered by Cramer, Damgård and Schoenmakers (CRYPTO'94) and De Santis et al. (FOCS'94), allow for proving the validity of k out of n different statements without revealing which ones those are. In this work, we present a new approach for transforming certain proofs system into new ones that allows for proving partial knowledge. The communication complexity of the resulting proof system only depends logarithmically on the total number of statements n and its security only relies on the existence of collision-resistant hash functions. As an example, we show that our transformation is applicable to the proof systems of Goldreich, Micali, and Wigderson (FOCS'86) for the graph isomorphism and the graph 3-coloring problem.

Our main technical tool, which we believe to be of independent interest, is a new cryptographic primitive called non-adaptively programmable functions (NAPs). Those functions can be seen as pseudorandom functions which allow for re-programming the output at an input point, which must be fixed during key generation. Even when given the re-programmed key, it remains infeasible to find out where re-programming happened. Finally, as an additional technical tool, we also build explainable samplers for any distribution that can be sampled efficiently via rejection sampling and use them to construct NAPs for various output distributions.

1 Introduction

Proofs of partial knowledge, independently first considered by Cramer, Damgård and Schoenmakers [CDS94] and De Santis et al. [DDP+94], allow a prover to convince a verifier that k out of a list of n statements are true, without revealing which ones those are. Such proofs have received significant interest over the years, as they turn out to be simple enough to be constructed efficiently, while at the same time being expressive enough to be applicable to a wide variety of problems. Both the work of Cramer, Damgård and Schoenmakers and that of De Santis et al. [DDP+94] show that one can generically and *information-theoretically*

M. Simkin—Independent Researcher.

E. Boyle and M. Mahmoody (Eds.): TCC 2024, LNCS 15364, pp. 35–66, 2025.
https://doi.org/10.1007/978-3-031-78011-0_2

transform certain separate proof systems for languages $\mathcal{L}_1, \ldots, \mathcal{L}_n$ respectively, into a single new proof system that allows for proving partial knowledge, i.e. for proving that in a given vector of statements $(x_1, \ldots, x_n)$, there is a subset of indices I of size k, such that $x_i \in \mathcal{L}_i$ for all $i \in I$. The resulting proof systems are conceptually simple and can allow for concretely efficient instantiations, but require the prover and verifier to communicate at least $\Omega(n)$ bits.

Subsequent works [GK15, AC20, ACF21, ACK21, GGHA+22] have shown how to construct proofs of partial knowledge (and more) with communication complexities that have sublinear, even logarithmic, dependencies on n, but rely on *number-theoretic hardness assumptions*, such as the discrete logarithm problem. To the best of our knowledge, despite 30 years of research, there are still no direct analogues of the transformations by Cramer, Damgård and Schoenmakers or De Santis et al., which have both an $o(n)$ communication complexity and do not require number-theoretic hardness assumptions. It seems natural to ask, whether such a transformation exists.

1.1   Our Contribution

In this work, we make progress towards addressing the above question. We present a new approach for transforming a large class of proof systems for language $\mathcal{L}$ into one for the language $\mathcal{L}_{\mathsf{OR}}^n := \{(x_1, \ldots, x_n) \mid \exists i \in \{1, \ldots, n\} : x_i \in \mathcal{L}\}$.[1] Our transformation produces a proof system, whose communication complexity only depends logarithmically on n and that only relies on the existence of collision-resistant hash functions. As an example, we compile the famous proof system of Goldreich, Micali, and Wigderson [GMW86] for graph 3-coloring (and thus for all of NP) into a new one for showing the validity of one out of n NP statements, while only incurring asymptotically small overheads on the communication complexity and only relying on unstructured hardness assumptions.

A key technical tool of our work, which we believe to be of independent interest, is what we call non-adaptively programmable functions (NAPs). These can be seen as pseudorandom functions, which allow for dynamically re-programming the output at an input point, which must already be fixed during key generation. Even when given the re-programmed secret key, it should not be feasible to determine where re-programming happened. We formally define this primitive and show how to construct it from one-way functions (which are implied by collision-resistant hashing).

Another technical tool of our work that may also be of independent interest, is the construction of explainable samplers for distribution that can be sampled efficiently via rejection sampling. An explainable sampler takes random coins r as input and produces a sample x from a target distribution $\mathcal{D}$. They are equipped

---

[1] Throughout this work, we restrict our attention to one language and showing the validity of one out of the n statements. We note, however, that this is done merely for the sake of simplicity and clarity and that our approach can easily be generalized to multiple languages and showing the validity of $k \geq 1$ statements, as we discuss in Sect. 4.2.

with an explanation algorithm that, given a sample x from $\mathcal{D}$, can compute the matching random coins r. Given (x, r) it should not be possible to see, whether x was sampled and r was computed from it or vice versa.

1.2   Related Works

A plethora of existing works have studied proof systems from various perspectives. We are far from the first ones to look at minimizing the communication complexity or the required hardness assumptions. In the following, let us highlight in what ways our approach differs from prior ones.

From Number-Theoretic Assumptions. A series of works [BCC+16, BBB+18, AC20, ACK21] considers the task of designing communication-efficient proof systems from number-theoretic hardness assumptions. These approaches express the given statements as arithmetic circuit satisfiability instances and then show how any such instance can be proven with a communication complexity that is logarithmic in the circuit size. These works differ from ours in two aspects. They all rely on hardness assumptions that imply public-key cryptography, whereas our focus is on solely relying on collision-resistant hashing. Furthermore, these approaches focus on building proof systems from scratch, which can be used to generically transform an instance of $\mathcal{L}_{\mathsf{OR}}^n$ into an arithmetic circuit. While this is in principle possible, it would result in large circuits and also not make any use of a potentially given proof system for language $\mathcal{L}$. In our work, we focus on a more direct approach that transforms a given proof system for $\mathcal{L}$ into one for $\mathcal{L}_{\mathsf{OR}}^n$ efficiently.

Another line of recent works [GK15, ACF21, GGHA+22, WW22] specifically focuses on languages of the same form as $\mathcal{L}_{\mathsf{OR}}^n$. These works either aim for building proof systems for it from scratch or transforming proof systems for $\mathcal{L}$ into ones for $\mathcal{L}_{\mathsf{OR}}^n$ like we do. All of these approaches crucially rely on structured hardness assumptions and it is not clear how one could modify these results to obtain something from collision-resistant hashing alone.

From One-Way or Collision-Resistant Hash Functions. Several known approaches would allow for constructing proof systems from the sole existence of one-way functions. Goldreich, Micali, and Wigderson [GMW86] show how a prover can convince a verifier that a given graph is 3-colorable. Their construction relies on the existence of commitments, which can be constructed from one-way functions [Nao90, HIL+99]. Alternatively, it is also possible to use MPC-in-the-head paradigm of Ishai, Kushilevitz, Ostrovsky, and Sahai [IKO+09], which allows for proving satisfiability of arbitrary statements, expressed as boolean or arithmetic circuits, while only relying on one-way functions. These approaches would result in communication complexities that are at least $\Omega(\sqrt{n})$, whereas we aim for a logarithmic dependency on n. Finally, using probabilistically checkable proofs [AS92, Kil92] or interactive oracle proofs [BCS16, RRR16, BBH+18], it is possible to construct proof systems from collision-resistant hashing, which have communication complexities that are poly-logarithmic in the statement size.

These approaches work yet again by generically transforming an arbitrary statement into a computation expressed in their respective computational model, which depending on the type of statement can result in concretely very large communication complexities and computational overheads. Furthermore, these approaches are conceptually rather involved and complex. Contrary to them, we aim for directly transforming proof systems for $\mathcal{L}$ into ones for $\mathcal{L}_{\mathsf{OR}}^n$ via an efficient and conceptually much simpler transformation.

1.3   Technical Overview

The starting point of our work, is that of Cramer, Damgård and Schoenmakers [CDS94], which transforms proof systems known as Σ-protocols for language $\mathcal{L}$ into ones for $\mathcal{L}_{\mathsf{OR}}^n$. Before presenting our approach, let us recall what Σ-protocols are and how the aforementioned transformation works.

Languages and Relations. Throughout this work, we consider a prover that aims to convince a verifier that some statement x is in the language $\mathcal{L}$. The prover holds a witness w, which attests of x being in $\mathcal{L}$. More formally, we assume there exists an efficiently checkable relation $\mathcal{R}_{\mathcal{L}}$, such that $x \in \mathcal{L}$, if and only if there exists a witness w, such that $(x, w) \in \mathcal{R}_{\mathcal{L}}$.

Σ-Protocols. A three-move public-coin interactive proof system that satisfies completeness, special soundness, and honest verifier zero-knowledge is known as a Σ-protocol. Here, three-move public-coin refers to the fixed communication pattern that these protocols have: the prover sends a message a to the verifier, receives a random challenge e from the verifier back, and sends a response z to the verifier, who then either accepts or rejects the proof transcript (a, e, z). Completeness dictates that an honest interaction between the prover and verifier for a statement $x \in \mathcal{L}$, results in the verifier accepting the proof. Special soundness requires that there exists an efficient extractor Ext, which can extract w with $(x, w) \in \mathcal{R}_{\mathcal{L}}$ from two accepting transcripts (a, e, z) and (a, e', z'), where $e \neq e'$. Honest verifier zero-knowledge requires that there exists a simulator Sim, which is given a uniformly random challenge e and outputs a, z, such that (a, e, z) is indistinguishable from a real interaction for $x \in \mathcal{L}$.

The Approach of Cramer, Damgård and Schoenmakers. Now assume we are given a Σ-protocol for language $\mathcal{L}$ that we would like to transform into one for language $\mathcal{L}_{\mathsf{OR}}^n$. The prover and verifier are given a vector of statements $(x_1, \ldots, x_n)$ and additionally the prover holds a witness w, such that $(x_i, w) \in \mathcal{R}_{\mathcal{L}}$ for some $i \in \{1, \ldots, n\}$. Their approach proceeds as follows: The prover picks challenges e_j uniformly at random and uses the simulator Sim to compute the corresponding messages (a_j, z_j) for all $j \neq i$. The prover honestly compute a_i and sends the vector $(a_1, \ldots, a_n)$ to the verifier, who responds with a uniformly random challenge e. The prover computes e_i, such that $\sum_{j=1}^n e_j = e$, honestly computes the message z_i corresponding to the partial transcript (a_i, e_i), and sends both $(e_1, \ldots, e_n)$ and $(z_1, \ldots, z_n)$ to the verifier, who checks that all challenges sum to the right value and that all n received transcripts are accepting.

This approach does not reveal which witness the prover was holding, because all challenges are uniformly random, conditioned on summing to e, and because honest verifier zero-knowledge guarantees that the transcripts produced by Sim are indistinguishable from real ones.

Our High-Level Idea. Conceptually, our work closely follows the blueprint of Cramer, Damgård and Schoenmakers, but modifies it in a way that allows us to compress all three vectors $(a_1, \ldots, a_n)$, $(e_1, \ldots, e_n)$, and $(z_1, \ldots, z_n)$, which are sent between the prover and the verifier. For this, let us make two additional assumptions. First, let us assume that the given Σ-protocol is not only honest verifier zero-knowledge, but *strongly* honest verifier zero-knowledge, which means that the simulator Sim is given a uniformly random challenge e as well as an independently chosen, uniformly random response z and is asked to compute the corresponding first message a deterministically, such that (a, e, z) is indistinguishable from a real transcript. Secondly, let us assume that we are given a privately programmable pseudorandom function $F : \mathcal{K} \times \{1, \ldots, n\} \to \{0, 1\}^*$, which takes a secret key msk and point x as input and returns a random looking outputs y. We require F to be programmable in the sense that a key msk should allow for obtaining a key psk that produces the same evaluations on all inputs, apart from some chosen point $i \in \{1, \ldots, n\}$, where it returns a re-programmed value y^*. It should be privately programmable in the sense that psk should not reveal any information about where the key was re-programmed.

Equipped with these tools, our approach works as follows: The prover picks uniformly random keys msk_e and msk_z, computes $e_j := F(\mathsf{msk}_e, j)$ and $z_j := F(\mathsf{msk}_z, j)$, and uses simulator Sim to compute the corresponding messages a_j deterministically for all $j \neq i$. The prover then picks the first message a_i honestly and sends $a = H(a_1, \ldots, a_n)$ to the verifier, where H is a collision-resistant hash function. The verifier sends a challenge e to the prover, who computes e_i, such that $\sum_{j=1}^n e_j = e$, then computes z_i honestly. Now the prover computes keys psk_e and psk_z by re-programming keys msk_e and msk_z, such that they return e_i and z_i on input i respectively. Finally, the prover sends back psk_e and psk_z to the verifier, who expands them to the corresponding vectors $(e_1, \ldots, e_n)$ and $(z_1, \ldots, z_n)$ and then computes $(a_1, \ldots, a_n)$ using the deterministic simulator Sim. The verifier checks that all challenges sum to e, that the hash value a matches the hash of the computed vector $(a_1, \ldots, a_n)$ and that all transcripts are accepting.

Why should this be a sensible protocol on an intuitively level? The private programmability of F ensures that the verifier cannot see which location i was re-programmed. The collision-resistant hash ensures that without explicitly sending the vector $(a_1, \ldots, a_n)$, the prover is committing themselves to a fixed first message before seeing the challenge. The simulator Sim computing the first messages deterministically and the fact that simulated and real transcripts are indistinguishable, ensures that the verifier computes the correct values $a_1, \ldots, a_n$, without the prover ever having sent them explicitly.

The communication between prover and verifier is comprised of sending one hash value, one challenge, and two programmed keys. If the key sizes are logarithmic in n, then so is the communication complexity of the resulting Σ-protocol.

The Difficulty with Privately Programmable Pseudorandom Functions. To realize the above idea, we need to construct the privately programmable functions we need. Since our goal is a Σ-protocol from collision-resistant hashing, the privately programmable functions also better be based on a similar assumption. Unfortunately, such constructions currently seem to be out of reach. The only known constructions either rely on indistinguishability obfuscation [BLW17] or lattice-based cryptography [PS18,PS20]. Luckily, we observe that we do not actually need the full power of these programmable functions. In our case, we already know during key generation at which point we would like to program the keys later on, namely at the index for which we have the witness. As it turns out, this makes constructing such functions much simpler, in fact so simple that we can construct them from just one-way functions. We call these functions non-adaptively (privately) programmable functions or NAPs and we believe that they may be of independent interest.

Constructing NAPs. To construct our new primitive, we make use of distributed point functions, originally introduced by Gilboa and Ishai [GI14]. A point function $f_{x^*} : \mathcal{X} \to \{0, 1\}$ evaluates to zero on all points from domain $\mathcal{X}$, apart from a single point $x^* \in \mathcal{X}$, where it evaluates to one. A distributed point function is a pair of functions f_0, f_1 that satisfies correctness and privacy. Correctness requires that for any $x \in \mathcal{X}$, it holds that $f(x) = f_0(x) \oplus f_1(x)$. Privacy requires that f_0 and f_1 constitute an additive secret sharing of f, i.e. that neither share in isolation provides any information about which point function was secret shared. It was shown by Boyle, Gilboa, and Ishai [BGI15] that distributed point functions, where each share is of size $\mathcal{O}(\lambda \cdot \log |\mathcal{X}|)$, can be constructed from one-way functions, where λ is the computational security parameter.

Towards constructing NAPs, we make a simple, but important observation. For any $x \neq x^*$, we have that $f_0(x) \oplus f_1(x) = 0$ and thus $f_0(x) = f_1(x)$. For x^* on the other hand, we have that $f_0(x^*) \oplus f_1(x^*) = 1$ and thus $(f_0(x^*), f_1(x^*)) \in \{(0, 1), (1, 0)\}$. Now we can simply view f_0 as the key of our NAP (with one bit outputs) and evaluating it at point j can be done by returning $f_0(j)$. Furthermore, programming a key at x^* to value $y^* \in \{0, 1\}$, can be done by returning f_b with $f_b(x^*) = y^*$ as the programmed key. Note that seeing the programmed key, is the same as seeing a single share of a 2-out-of-2 secret sharing of f and thus it does not reveal anything about the point x^*. Also, note that this approach crucially relies on the fact that the point at which programming will happen is known during key generation, as it defines the point function that will be shared. To obtain a NAP with t bits of output, we can simply append t many NAPs with single bit outputs. The resulting key size is $\mathcal{O}(t \cdot \lambda \cdot \log |\mathcal{X}|)$.

We note that the same insights we use here to construct NAPs from distributed point functions, have previously been used Hemenway et al. [HJO+16] to construct a notion they call somewhere equivocal encryption. There, the authors use their notion of an encryption scheme to allow programming the plaintext *within the security proof.* In our work on the other hand, we use NAPs and the ability to program them as part of the proof systems we construct.

Constructing NAPs for the Correct Distributions. In the discussion above, we have made an implicit assumption that is not actually valid. The NAPs we have so far constructed, return bit strings, but the second and third round messages of a given Σ-protocol may be completely different objects. As an example, in the proof system of Goldreich, Micali, and Wigderson [GMW86] for the graph isomorphism problem, the challenge e is a bit, but the prover's response z is a permutation. More generally, it may not even be the case that the response is a uniformly random element from the set of all responses.

To overcome this issue, we make use of explainable samplers, which were formally defined by Lu and Waters [LW22]. Such samplers take random coins r as input and produce outputs x that are sampled accordingly to some target distribution $\mathcal{D}$. The samplers have an associated explanation algorithm that first takes sample x from the target distribution and then finds appropriate random coins r for the sampling algorithm, i.e. coins that would produce that sample. Explainable sampler guarantee that, given (x, r), one cannot distinguish whether r was sampled and x was computed or vice versa. Given an explainable sampler for a desired target distribution, we can combine it with our NAP that produces uniformly random looking bits, to obtain a NAP that produces pseudorandom samples from the desired target distribution.

What remains to show is that we can construct efficient explainable samplers for the distributions we care about. Lu and Waters construct explainable samplers for several classes of distribution. We extend their results and show that anything that can be sampled efficiently via a method known as rejection sampling, can also be explained. Using this result, we construct NAPs that output third round messages of well-known Σ-protocols, such as the graph 3-coloring or the graph isomorphism protocols of Goldreich, Micali, and Wigderson.

On the Strong Honest Verifier Zero-Knowledge Requirement. We note that our construction starts with a Σ-protocol that satisfies strong honest verifier zero-knowledge. Many of the existing Σ-protocols either already satisfy this property or can be made to have it via minimal changes. More generally, it was shown by Goel, Green, Hall-Andersen, and Kaptchuk [GGHA+22] that any Σ-protocol with honest verifier zero-knowledge can be transformed into one that satisfies the strong version of this property.[2] Thus our approach is in principle applicable to any Σ-protocol for which we can construct NAPs for the appropriate distributions of the second and third round messages.

---

[2] In the work of Goel, Green, Hall-Andersen, and Kaptchuk [GGHA+22], the terminology *challenge-independent extended* honest verifier zero-knowledge was used, but their notion is identical to the notion of strong honest verifier zero-knowledge of Bellare and Ristov [BR08].

Proofs vs. Arguments. Throughout the introduction and throughout the rest of this paper, we are not making an explicit distinction between proofs and arguments. Commonly, proofs provide soundness against an unbounded adversary, whereas arguments only provide soundness against a computationally bounded adversary. We note that the soundness of the Σ-protocols we construct in this work, relies on collision-resistant hash functions and thus these are arguments, not proofs. For the remainder of the paper, we use these terms interchangeably.

2   Preliminaries

Notation. We write $y \leftarrow A(x)$ to denote the output y of algorithm A, when run on input x. If A is randomized, we assume that uniformly random coins are chosen implicitly, unless stated otherwise. If we want to make random coins r explicit, we write $A(x; r)$.

For a distribution $\mathcal{D}$, we write $x \leftarrow \mathcal{D}$ to denote sampling a value from $\mathcal{D}$ and assigning the value to x. We implicitly assume that all distribution of interest in this work are efficiently samplable. We write $\mathsf{Supp}(\mathcal{D})$ to denote the set of elements that are sampled with a non-zero probability. For $a, b \in \mathbb{R}$ with $a \leq b$, we write $\mathcal{U}[a, b]$ to denote the continuous uniform distribution over the range $[a, b]$. For a set $S = \{s_1, \ldots, s_n\}$, we write $\mathcal{U}\{s_1, \ldots, s_n\}$ or $\mathcal{U}_S$ to denote the discrete uniform distribution over the set S. For a set S, we write $x \leftarrow S$ to denote sampling from the uniform distribution over S. By $(\mathcal{S}_n, \circ)$ we denote the group of permutations $\pi \colon [n] \to [n]$ with $\circ$ the composition of permutations as group operation. We use λ to denote the security parameter. For a language $\mathcal{L} \subseteq \{0, 1\}^*$ we let $\mathcal{R}_{\mathcal{L}}$ be the corresponding relation. That is, $x \in \mathcal{L}$ if and only if there exists a witness w such that $(x, w) \in \mathcal{R}_{\mathcal{L}}$.

We call two distributions $\mathcal{P}$ and $\mathcal{Q}$ statistically close, if for any adversary $\mathcal{A}$, it holds that $|\Pr[1 \leftarrow \mathcal{A}(x) \colon x \leftarrow \mathcal{P}] - [1 \leftarrow \mathcal{A}(x) \colon x \leftarrow \mathcal{Q}]| \leq \mathsf{negl}(\lambda)$, and computationally close if the same holds for any PPT adversary $\mathcal{A}$.

2.1 Σ-Protocols

We recall the definition of Σ-protocols and some of their properties.

Definition 1 (Σ-Protocols). *A Σ-protocol is a three-move protocol with challenge space $\mathcal{E}$ and response distribution $\mathcal{Z}$ for a language $\mathcal{L}$, given by a tuple of PPT algorithms $(\mathsf{P}_1, \mathsf{P}_2, \mathsf{V})$, which are defined as follows:*

$(a, \mathsf{aux}) \leftarrow \mathsf{P}_1(x, w)$**:** *The commitment algorithm takes statement $x \in \mathcal{L}$ and a witness w as input and produces message a and auxiliary output aux.*

$z \leftarrow \mathsf{P}_2(\mathsf{aux}, e)$**:** *The response algorithm takes challenge $e \in \mathcal{E}$ and auxiliary input aux as input and returns response $z \in \mathsf{Supp}(\mathcal{Z})$.*

$b \leftarrow \mathsf{V}(x, a, e, z)$**:** *The verification algorithm takes statement x and transcript (a, e, z) as input and outputs bit b.*

Correctness states that during an honest execution, the verifier all but a negligible fraction of times.

Definition 2 (Correctness). *We say Σ-protocol $(\mathsf{P}_1, \mathsf{P}_2, \mathsf{V})$ with challenge space $\mathcal{E}$ and response distribution $\mathcal{Z}$ for language $\mathcal{L}$ is correct, if for any $\lambda \in \mathbb{N}$, and any (x, w) with $\mathcal{R}_{\mathcal{L}}(x, w) = 1$, it holds that*

$$\Pr\left[\mathsf{V}(x, a, e, z) = 1 : \begin{array}{c} (a, \mathsf{aux}) \leftarrow \mathsf{P}_1(x, w) \\ e \leftarrow \mathcal{E} \\ z \leftarrow \mathsf{P}_2(\mathsf{aux}, e) \end{array}\right] \geq 1 - \mathsf{negl}(\lambda),$$

where the probability is taken over the random coins of the algorithms.

Special soundness guarantees for statements outside the language, no two valid transcripts with the same first message but different challenges exist.

Definition 3 (Special Soundness). *We say Σ-protocol $(\mathsf{P}_1, \mathsf{P}_2, \mathsf{V})$ with challenge space $\mathcal{E}$ and response distribution $\mathcal{Z}$ for language $\mathcal{L}$ is special sound, if there exists a PPT extractor Ext, such that for any $x \in \{0,1\}^*$, any two transcripts (a, e, z) and (a, e', z') with $\mathsf{V}(x, a, e, z) = 1$ and $\mathsf{V}(x, a, e', z') = 1$ and with $e \neq e'$, it holds that*

$$\Pr\left[\mathcal{R}_{\mathcal{L}}(x, w) = 1 : w \leftarrow \mathsf{Ext}(x, a, e, z, e', z')\right] = 1,$$

where the probability is taken over the random coins of the extractor.

Computational special soundness allows such pairs of transcripts to exist, but requires them to be computationally hard to find.

Definition 4 (Computational Special Soundness). *We say Σ-protocol $(\mathsf{P}_1, \mathsf{P}_2, \mathsf{V})$ with challenge space $\mathcal{E}$ and response distribution $\mathcal{Z}$ for language $\mathcal{L}$ is computationally special sound, if for any $\lambda \in \mathbb{N}$ and any PPT adversary $\mathcal{A}$, it holds that*

$$\Pr[\mathsf{Expt}_{\mathcal{A},\mathcal{L}}^{\mathsf{sound}}(1^\lambda) = 1] := \Pr\left[\begin{array}{c} e \neq e' \wedge x \notin \mathcal{L} \\ \mathsf{V}(x, a, e', z') = 1 : (x, a, e, z, e', z') \leftarrow \mathcal{A}(1^\lambda) \\ \mathsf{V}(x, a, e, z) = 1 \end{array}\right] \leq \mathsf{negl}(\lambda),$$

where the probability is taken over the random coins of the experiment.

Honest verifier zero-knowledge guarantees a simulator which, on input a random challenge, can simulate valid transcripts.

Definition 5 (Honest Verifier Zero-Knowledge). *We say Σ-protocol $(\mathsf{P}_1, \mathsf{P}_2, \mathsf{V})$ with challenge space $\mathcal{E}$ and response distribution $\mathcal{Z}$ for language $\mathcal{L}$ is honest verifier zero-knowledge, if there exists a PPT simulator Sim, such that for all $\lambda \in \mathbb{N}$, all PPT adversaries $\mathcal{A}$, all $x \in \mathcal{L}$ and all witnesses w with $\mathcal{R}_{\mathcal{L}}(x, w) = 1$, it holds that*

$$\left|\Pr\left[\mathsf{Expt}_{\mathcal{A}}^{\mathsf{Real}\Sigma}(1^\lambda, x, w) = 1\right] - \Pr\left[\mathsf{Expt}_{\mathcal{A},\mathsf{Sim}}^{\mathsf{Sim}\Sigma}(1^\lambda, x) = 1\right]\right| \leq \mathsf{negl}(\lambda),$$

where the probability is taken over the random coins of the adversary and the experiments defined in Fig. 1.

Remark 1. We remark that our definition of honest verifier zero-knowledge is sometimes also called *special* honest verifier zero-knowledge.

The property below strengthens honest verifier zero-knowledge in the sense that the simulator now gets as input a random challenge and a random response and is required to be deterministic.

Definition 6 (Strong Honest Verifier Zero-Knowledge [BR08]). *We say* Σ*-protocol* $(\mathsf{P}_1, \mathsf{P}_2, \mathsf{V})$ *with challenge space* $\mathcal{E}$ *and response distribution* $\mathcal{Z}$ *for language* $\mathcal{L}$ *is* strong honest verifier zero-knowledge, *if there exists a deterministic polynomial time simulator* Sim, *such that for all* $\lambda \in \mathbb{N}$, *all PPT adversaries* $\mathcal{A}$, *all* $x \in \mathcal{L}$ *and all witnesses* w *with* $\mathcal{R}_{\mathcal{L}}(x, w) = 1$, *it holds that*

$$\left| \Pr\left[\mathsf{Expt}_{\mathcal{A}}^{\mathsf{stReal}\Sigma}(1^{\lambda}, x, w) = 1 \right] - \Pr\left[\mathsf{Expt}_{\mathcal{A},\mathsf{Sim}}^{\mathsf{stSim}\Sigma}(1^{\lambda}, x) = 1 \right] \right| \leq \mathsf{negl}(\lambda),$$

where the probability is taken over the random coins of the adversary and the experiments defined in Fig. 2.

$\underline{\mathsf{Expt}_{\mathcal{A}}^{\mathsf{Real}\Sigma}(1^{\lambda}, x, w)}$

1 : $(a, \mathsf{aux}) \leftarrow \mathsf{P}_1(x, w)$
2 : $e \leftarrow \mathcal{E}$
3 : $z \leftarrow \mathsf{P}_2(\mathsf{aux}, e)$
4 : $b \leftarrow \mathcal{A}(a, e, z)$
5 : **return** b

$\underline{\mathsf{Expt}_{\mathcal{A},\mathsf{Sim}}^{\mathsf{Sim}\Sigma}(1^{\lambda}, x)}$

1 : $e \leftarrow \mathcal{E}$
2 : $(a, z) \leftarrow \mathsf{Sim}(e)$
3 : $b \leftarrow \mathcal{A}(a, e, z)$
4 : **return** b

$\mathsf{Expt}_{\mathcal{A}}^{\mathsf{stReal}\Sigma}(1^{\lambda}, x, w)$

$\overline{\phantom{\mathsf{Expt}_{\mathcal{A}}^{\mathsf{stReal}\Sigma}(1^{\lambda}, x, w)}}$

1 : $(a, \mathsf{aux}) \leftarrow \mathsf{P}_1(x, w)$
2 : $e \leftarrow \mathcal{E}$
3 : $z \leftarrow \mathsf{P}_2(\mathsf{aux}, e)$
4 : $b \leftarrow \mathcal{A}(a, e, z)$
5 : **return** b

$\underline{\mathsf{Expt}_{\mathcal{A},\mathsf{Sim}}^{\mathsf{stSim}\Sigma}(1^{\lambda}, x)}$

1 : $e \leftarrow \mathcal{E}$
2 : $z \leftarrow \mathcal{Z}$
3 : $a \leftarrow \mathsf{Sim}(e, z)$
4 : $b \leftarrow \mathcal{A}(a, e, z)$
5 : **return** b

Fig. 1. Honest verifier zero-knowledge.

Fig. 2. Strong honest verifier zero-knowledge.

Remark 2. In some cases, we will assume that our Σ-protocols run in the presence of a honestly sampled common reference string. This string will, for instance, contain the description of a hash function or a commitment scheme. If a Σ-protocol requires such a string, then throughout the paper, we will assume that this string is sampled honestly at the start of any experiment and all probabilities are taken over the random coins that were used to sampled this string as well.

2.2   Distributed Point Functions [GI14]

We recall the definition of (distributed) point functions.

Definition 7 (Point Functions). *For $x \in \mathcal{X}$ and $y \in \mathcal{Y}$, a point function $f_{x,y}$ with domain $\mathcal{X}$ and range $\mathcal{Y}$ is defined as*

$$f_{x,y}(z) = \begin{cases} y & \text{if } z = x \\ 0 & \text{else} \end{cases}.$$

Let $\mathcal{F}(\mathcal{X}, \mathcal{Y})$ be the set of point functions with domain $\mathcal{X}$ and range $\mathcal{Y}$.

Definition 8 (Distributed Point Functions). *A* distributed point function *for domain $\mathcal{X}$ and range $\mathcal{Y}$ is a pair of PPT algorithms $\mathsf{DPF} = (\mathsf{Share}, \mathsf{Eval})$ that are defined as follows:*

$(f_0, f_1) \leftarrow \mathsf{Share}(1^\lambda, f)$: *The share generation algorithm takes the security parameter λ and point function $f \in \mathcal{F}(\mathcal{X}, \mathcal{Y})$ as input and returns function shares f_0 and f_1.*

$y \leftarrow \mathsf{Eval}(f_b, x)$: *The evaluation algorithm takes function share f_b for $b \in \{0, 1\}$ and $x \in \mathcal{X}$ as input and returns evaluation $y \in \mathcal{Y}$.*

Correctness states that combining the evaluations of both shares gives the original value.

Definition 9 (Correctness). *We say a $\mathsf{DPF} = (\mathsf{Share}, \mathsf{Eval})$ for domain $\mathcal{X}$ and range $\mathcal{Y}$, where $\mathcal{Y}$ is an abelian group with addition, is* correct, *if for any $\lambda \in \mathbb{N}$, any function $f \in \mathcal{F}(\mathcal{X}, \mathcal{Y})$ and any $z \in \mathcal{X}$, it holds that*

$$\Pr\left[\mathsf{Eval}(f_0, z) + \mathsf{Eval}(f_1, z) = f(z) \colon (f_0, f_1) \leftarrow \mathsf{Gen}(1^\lambda, f)\right] = 1.$$

Privacy guarantees that shares do not leak any information about the function they are derived from.

Definition 10 (Privacy). *We say a $\mathsf{DPF} = (\mathsf{Share}, \mathsf{Eval})$ for domain $\mathcal{X}$ and range $\mathcal{Y}$, is* private, *if for any $\lambda \in \mathbb{N}$, any PPT adversary $\mathcal{A}$, it holds that*

$$\mathsf{Adv}^{\mathsf{priv}}(\mathcal{A}) := \left| \Pr\left[\mathsf{Expt}_{\mathcal{A}}^{\mathsf{priv}}(1^\lambda) = 1\right] - \frac{1}{2} \right| \leq \mathsf{negl}(\lambda),$$

where $\mathsf{Expt}_{\mathcal{A}}^{\mathsf{priv}}$ is the experiment in Fig. 3.

We use the following result which shows that one can obtain DPFs from pseudorandom generators, which can themselves be obtained from one-way functions [HIL+99].

Theorem 1 ([BGI15]). *Let $\lambda, \ell \in \mathbb{N}$. Assuming the existence of a pseudorandom generators, there exists a correct and private DPF for domain $\mathcal{X} = \{0, 1\}^\ell$ and range $\mathcal{Y} = \{0, 1\}$ with shares of bit size $\mathcal{O}(\lambda \log |\mathcal{X}|)$.*

2.3 Explainable Samplers [LW22]

Our definition of explainable samplers slightly differs from that of Lu and Waters [LW22]. Their definition assumes that the random coins provided to the sampling algorithm come from a uniformly random distribution. In our definition, we allow the coins to come from other distributions. In their definition, a separate precision parameter specifies how "well" the explain algorithm works. In our definition, we will not have a separate precision parameter, but instead assume that the advantage of the adversary in each security experiment will be negligible in the same security parameter λ.

$\underline{\mathsf{Expt}_{\mathcal{A}}^{\mathsf{RealS}}(1^{\lambda})}$

1 : $r \leftarrow \mathcal{R}$

2 : $x \leftarrow \mathsf{Sample}(1^{\lambda}; r)$

3 : $b \leftarrow \mathcal{A}(r, x)$

4 : **return** b

$\underline{\mathsf{Expt}_{\mathcal{A}}^{\mathsf{priv}}(1^{\lambda})}$

1 : $f^0, f^1 \leftarrow \mathcal{A}(1^{\lambda})$

2 : $b, \tilde{b} \leftarrow \{0, 1\}$

3 : $(f_0^b, f_1^b) \leftarrow \mathsf{Share}(1^{\lambda}, f^b)$

4 : $b' \leftarrow \mathcal{A}(f_{\tilde{b}}^b)$

5 : **return** $b = b'$

$\underline{\mathsf{Expt}_{\mathcal{A}}^{\mathsf{ExplainS}}(1^{\lambda})}$

1 : $r' \leftarrow \mathcal{R}$

2 : $x \leftarrow \mathsf{Sample}(1^{\lambda}; r')$

3 : $r \leftarrow \mathsf{Explain}(1^{\lambda}, x)$

4 : $b \leftarrow \mathcal{A}(r, x)$

5 : **return** b

Fig. 3. The privacy experiment for DPFs.

Fig. 4. The explainability experiments for samplers.

Definition 11 (Samplers). *Let $\lambda \in \mathbb{N}$. A sampler for distribution $\mathcal{D} = \mathcal{D}(\lambda)$ with randomness distribution $\mathcal{R} = \mathcal{R}(\lambda)$ is a pair of PPT algorithms* ES = (Sample, Explain) *that are defined as follows:*

$x \leftarrow$ Sample(1^{λ}): *The sampling algorithm takes the security parameter λ as input and returns a sample x.*

$r \leftarrow$ Explain$(1^{\lambda}, x)$: *The explaining algorithm takes security parameter λ and sample $x \in$ Supp$(\mathcal{D})$ as input and returns random coins r.*

An explainable sampler should be correct in the sense that the samples returned by Sample should be statistically close to samples from the real distribution.

Definition 12 (Correctness). *Let $\lambda \in \mathbb{N}$. A sampler for distribution $\mathcal{D} = \mathcal{D}(\lambda)$ with randomness distribution $\mathcal{R} = \mathcal{R}(\lambda)$ is correct, if for any λ and any adversary $\mathcal{A}$, it holds that*

$$\left| \Pr\left[\mathcal{A}(x) = 1 : x \leftarrow \mathsf{Sample}(1^{\lambda}; r);\ r \leftarrow \mathcal{R}\right] - \Pr\left[\mathcal{A}(x) = 1 : x \leftarrow \mathcal{D}\right] \right| \leq \mathsf{negl}(\lambda),$$

where the probability is taken over the random coins of all algorithms.

An explainable sampler should be explainable in the sense that first sampling an element $x \in \mathsf{Supp}(\mathcal{D})$ and then finding random coins $r \in \mathsf{Supp}(\mathcal{R})$, such that $\mathsf{Sample}(1^\lambda; r) = x$, should be statistically indistinguishable from first sampling $r \leftarrow \mathcal{R}$ and then computing $x \leftarrow \mathsf{Sample}(1^\lambda; r)$.

Definition 13 (Explainability). *Let* $\lambda \in \mathbb{N}$. *A sampler for distribution* $\mathcal{D} = \mathcal{D}(\lambda)$ *with randomness distribution* $\mathcal{R} = \mathcal{R}(\lambda)$ *is* explainable, *if for any* λ *and adversary* $\mathcal{A}$, *it holds that*

$$\left| \Pr\left[\mathsf{Expt}_{\mathcal{A}}^{\mathsf{RealS}}(1^\lambda) = 1 \right] - \Pr\left[\mathsf{Expt}_{\mathcal{A}}^{\mathsf{ExplainS}}(1^\lambda) = 1 \right] \right| \leq \mathsf{negl}(\lambda),$$

where $\mathsf{Expt}_{\mathcal{A}}^{\mathsf{RealS}}$ *and* $\mathsf{Expt}_{\mathcal{A}}^{\mathsf{ExplainS}}$ *are the experiments defined in Fig. 4 and the probability is taken over the random coins of all algorithms.*

3   Non-Adaptively Privately Programmable Functions (NAPs)

This section introduces our new cryptographic primitive, which we call non-adaptive programmable functions (NAPs). These NAPs will be the main tool that allows us to construct our compressed OR-proofs in the next section.

3.1   Definitions

We start by introducing the syntax of NAPs. On a high level, they can be seen as keyed pseudorandom functions, which allow for programming the secret key.

Definition 14 (Non-Adaptively Programmable Functions). *A* non-adaptively programmable function *with domain* $\mathcal{X}$ *and range* $\mathcal{Y}$ *with output distribution* $\mathcal{D}_\mathcal{Y}$ *is a tuple of PPT algorithms* $\mathsf{NAP} = (\mathsf{Gen}, \mathsf{Eval}, \mathsf{Prog}, \mathsf{PEval})$ *that are defined as follows:*

$\mathsf{msk} \leftarrow \mathsf{Gen}(1^\lambda, x^*)$: *They key generation algorithm takes the security parameter* 1^λ *and evaluation point* $x^* \in \mathcal{X}$ *as input and returns a master secret key* msk.

$y \leftarrow \mathsf{Eval}(\mathsf{msk}, x)$: *The evaluation algorithm takes the master secret key* msk *and an evaluation point* $x \in \mathcal{X}$ *and returns an evaluation* $y \in \mathcal{Y}$.

$\mathsf{psk} \leftarrow \mathsf{Prog}(\mathsf{msk}, y^*)$: *The programming algorithm takes as input the master secret key* msk *and an evaluation* $y^* \in \mathcal{Y}$, *and returns a programmed secret key* psk.

$y \leftarrow \mathsf{PEval}(\mathsf{psk}, x)$: *The evaluation algorithm for programmed keys takes the programmed secret key* psk *and an evaluation point* $x \in \mathcal{X}$ *as input and returns the evaluation* $y \in \mathcal{Y}$.

We now define two properties that we would like our NAPs to satisfy. The first one is correctness, which requires that programming works as one would expect. At the programmed location, the programmed key should return the programmed output value and on all other inputs, it should return the same values as the original master secret key.

Definition 15 (Correctness). *We say* NAP *for domain* $\mathcal{X}$ *and output distribution* $\mathcal{D_Y}$ *is correct, if for all* $\lambda \in \mathbb{N}$*, all* $x^* \in \mathcal{X}$ *we have*

$$\Pr \left[\begin{array}{ll} \mathsf{PEval}(\mathsf{psk}, x^*) = y^* & \mathsf{msk} \leftarrow \mathsf{Gen}(1^\lambda, x^*) \\ \wedge \, \forall x \in \mathcal{X} \setminus \{x^*\} & : \qquad\qquad y^* \leftarrow \mathcal{D_Y} \\ \mathsf{PEval}(\mathsf{psk}, x) = \mathsf{Eval}(\mathsf{msk}, x) & \mathsf{psk} \leftarrow \mathsf{Prog}(\mathsf{msk}, y^*) \end{array} \right] \geq 1 - \mathsf{negl}(\lambda),$$

where the probability is taken over the random coins of all algorithms and the choice of y^**.*

The second property is private programmability, which requires the programmed key to hide the location at which it was programmed. This should hold in a strong sense, where the adversary is allowed to choose location x^*, is then either given a key programmed at that location or a simulated key, and should not be able to tell in which of those two cases they are.

Definition 16 (Private Programmability). *We say* NAP *for domain* $\mathcal{X}$ *and output distribution* $\mathcal{D_Y}$ *is privately programmable, if there is a PPT simulator* Sim *such that for all* $\lambda \in \mathbb{N}$ *and every PPT adversary* $\mathcal{A}$*, it holds that*

$$\left| \Pr \left[\mathsf{Expt}_{\mathcal{A}}^{\mathsf{RealPP}}(1^\lambda) = 1 \right] - \Pr \left[\mathsf{Expt}_{\mathcal{A}}^{\mathsf{IdealPP}}(1^\lambda) = 1 \right] \right| \leq \mathsf{negl}(\lambda),$$

where RealPP *and* IdealPP *are the experiments defined in Fig. 5.*

$\mathsf{Expt}_{\mathcal{A}}^{\mathsf{RealPP}}(1^\lambda)$	$\mathsf{Expt}_{\mathcal{A}}^{\mathsf{IdealPP}}(1^\lambda)$
$1: \quad x^* \leftarrow \mathcal{A}(1^\lambda)$	$1: \quad x^* \leftarrow \mathcal{A}(1^\lambda)$
$2: \quad y^* \leftarrow \mathcal{D_Y}$	$2: \quad \mathsf{psk} \leftarrow \mathsf{Sim}(1^\lambda)$
$3: \quad \mathsf{msk} \leftarrow \mathsf{Gen}(1^\lambda, x^*)$	$3: \quad b \leftarrow \mathcal{A}(\mathsf{psk})$
$4: \quad \mathsf{psk} \leftarrow \mathsf{Prog}(\mathsf{msk}, y^*)$	$4: \quad \textbf{return } b$
$5: \quad b \leftarrow \mathcal{A}(\mathsf{psk})$	
$6: \quad \textbf{return } b$	

Fig. 5. The private programmability experiment for NAPs.

3.2   Constructions

We start with building our first NAP whose output are uniformly random bits, from distributed point functions.

Theorem 2. *Let* DPF = (Share, Eval) *be a correct and private distributed point function for domain* $\mathcal{X}$ *and range* $\mathcal{Y} := \{0, 1\}$*. Then the construction* NAP = (Gen, Prog, Eval, PEval) *in Fig. 6 is a correct and privately programmable NAP for domain* $\mathcal{X}$ *and output distribution* $\mathcal{U_Y}$*.*

Proof. To prove the theorem statement, let us consider each property of a NAP separately:

Correctness. Note that $\mathcal{Y}$ with the xor-operation $\oplus$ defines an abelian group. We observe that for any $u, v \in \{0, 1\}$ the two simple implications hold. If $u \oplus v = 0$, then $u = v$ and if $u \oplus v = 1$, then $u \neq v$ and thus in this case $(u, v) \in \{(1, 0), (0, 1)\}$. Now for any $x^* \in \mathcal{X}$, let

$$f(x) := \begin{cases} 1 \text{ if } x = x^* \\ 0 \text{ else} \end{cases}$$

and let $(f_0, f_1) \leftarrow \mathsf{DPF.Share}(1^\lambda, f)$. Correctness of the distributed point function tells us that for any $x \in \mathcal{X}$ with $x \neq x^*$, it holds that $\mathsf{DPF.Eval}(f_0, x) \oplus \mathsf{DPF.Eval}(f_1, x) = 0$ and thus $\mathsf{DPF.Eval}(f_0, x) = \mathsf{DPF.Eval}(f_1, x)$, whereas for x^* we have that $\mathsf{DPF.Eval}(f_0, x^*) \oplus \mathsf{DPF.Eval}(f_1, x^*) = 1$ and thus $(\mathsf{DPF.Eval}(f_0, x^*), \mathsf{DPF.Eval}(f_1, x^*)) \in \{(0, 1), (1, 0)\}$. Since for any $y^* \in \{0, 1\}$, there exists a $b \in \{0, 1\}$ with $\mathsf{DPF.Eval}(f_b, x^*) = y^*$, the correctness of our NAP construction follows.

Private Programmability. Fix an arbitrary $\tilde{x} \in \mathcal{X}$ and let f be the point function that evaluates to one at $\tilde{x}$. We define $\mathsf{Sim}(1^\lambda)$ to be the algorithm that generates $(f_0, f_1) \leftarrow \mathsf{Share}(1^\lambda, f)$ and then returns $f_{b'}$ for a uniformly random b'. Note that returning a uniformly random share is the same as programming the output at $\tilde{x}$ to a uniformly random value. Let $\mathcal{A}$ be an arbitrary PPT adversary with

$$\epsilon := \left| \Pr\left[\mathsf{Expt}_\mathcal{A}^{\mathsf{IdealPP}}(1^\lambda) = 1 \right] - \Pr\left[\mathsf{Expt}_\mathcal{A}^{\mathsf{RealPP}}(1^\lambda) = 1 \right] \right|.$$

We construct a PPT adversary $\mathcal{B}$ against the privacy property of the distributed point function, i.e., an adversary that has advantage $\epsilon/2$ in the experiment $\mathsf{Expt}_\mathcal{B}^{\mathsf{priv}}(1^\lambda)$. The reduction $\mathcal{B}$ works as follows: They initialize $\mathcal{A}$ with fresh random coins, provide them with the security parameter and obtain x^*. They then define

$$f^0(x) := \begin{cases} 1 \text{ if } x = x^* \\ 0 \text{ else} \end{cases} \quad \text{and} \quad f^1(x) := \begin{cases} 1 \text{ if } x = \tilde{x} \\ 0 \text{ else} \end{cases}$$

and provide f^0 and f^1 to their challenger, who returns f_0^b. Adversary $\mathcal{B}$ forwards f_0^b to $\mathcal{A}$ and then returns whatever bit $\mathcal{A}$ returns.

We now observe that when $b = 0$ in the privacy experiment of the distributed point function, then $\mathcal{B}$ perfectly simulates $\mathsf{Expt}_\mathcal{A}^{\mathsf{RealPP}}(1^\lambda)$ towards $\mathcal{A}$, as they are receiving $f_{\tilde{b}}^0$ for a uniformly random $\tilde{b} \in \{0, 1\}$ as expected. When $b = 1$, then $\mathcal{B}$ perfectly simulates $\mathsf{Expt}_\mathcal{A}^{\mathsf{IdealPP}}(1^\lambda)$ towards $\mathcal{A}$, they obtain the expected $f_{\tilde{b}}^1$ for uniformly random $\tilde{b}$. Let $\mathsf{Expt}_\mathcal{A}^{\mathsf{priv}, b}(1^\lambda)$ be the privacy experiment for the distributed point function, where the challenger chooses bit b. From the above observations, we can conclude that

$$2 \cdot \mathsf{Adv}^{\mathsf{priv}}(\mathcal{B}) = \left| \Pr \left[\mathsf{Expt}_{\mathcal{B}}^{\mathsf{priv}}(1^{\lambda}) = 1 \right] - \frac{1}{2} \right| \cdot 2$$

$$= \left| \frac{1}{2} \cdot \Pr \left[\mathsf{Expt}_{\mathcal{B}}^{\mathsf{priv},0}(1^{\lambda}) = 1 \right] + \frac{1}{2} \cdot \Pr \left[\mathsf{Expt}_{\mathcal{B}}^{\mathsf{priv},1}(1^{\lambda}) = 1 \right] - \frac{1}{2} \right| \cdot 2$$

$$= \left| \Pr \left[\mathsf{Expt}_{\mathcal{B}}^{\mathsf{priv},1}(1^{\lambda}) = 1 \right] - \Pr \left[\mathsf{Expt}_{\mathcal{B}}^{\mathsf{priv},0}(1^{\lambda}) = 0 \right] \right|$$

$$= \left| \Pr \left[\mathsf{Expt}_{\mathcal{A}}^{\mathsf{IdealPP}}(1^{\lambda}) = 1 \right] - \Pr \left[\mathsf{Expt}_{\mathcal{A}}^{\mathsf{RealPP}}(1^{\lambda}) = 1 \right] \right| = \epsilon.$$

Since the distributed point function is private, it means that $2 \cdot \mathsf{Adv}^{\mathsf{priv}}(\mathcal{B})$ is negligible in λ and thus so is ϵ.   □

Concatenating the outputs of several NAPs with one bit outputs, we can obtain a NAP with multiple output bits. This is captured formally in the next theorem statement, whose proof uses a standard hybrid argument and we thus defer to the full version of this paper.

Theorem 3. *Let $\lambda, t \in \mathbb{N}$ with $t \in \mathsf{poly}(\lambda)$. Let NAP$'$ be a correct and privately programmable NAP for domain $\mathcal{X}$ and output distribution $\mathcal{U}\{0,1\}$. Then there exists a correct and privately programmable NAP for domain $\mathcal{X}$ and output distribution $\mathcal{U}\{0,1\}^t$.*

$\underline{\mathsf{Gen}(1^{\lambda}, x^{*})}$

1 : $f(x) := \begin{cases} 1 \text{ if } x = x^{*} \\ 0 \text{ else} \end{cases}$

2 : $(f_0, f_1) \leftarrow \mathsf{DPF.Share}(1^{\lambda}, f)$

3 : $\mathsf{msk} := (f_0, f_1, x^{*})$

4 : **return** msk

$\underline{\mathsf{Eval}(\mathsf{msk}, x)}$

1 : parse msk as (f_0, f_1, x^{*})

2 : **return** $\mathsf{DPF.Eval}(f_0, x)$

$\underline{\mathsf{Prog}(\mathsf{msk}, y^{*})}$

1 : parse msk as (f_0, f_1, x^{*})

2 : **if** $\mathsf{DPF.Eval}(f_0, x^{*}) = y^{*}$:

3 : $\mathsf{psk} := f_0$

4 : **else**

5 : $\mathsf{psk} := f_1$

6 : **return** psk

$\underline{\mathsf{PEval}(\mathsf{psk}, x)}$

1 : parse psk as f_b

2 : **return** $\mathsf{DPF.Eval}(f_b, x)$

Fig. 6. NAP for uniform single bit outputs.

$\underline{\mathsf{Gen}(1^{\lambda}, x^{*})}$

1 : $\mathsf{msk} \leftarrow \mathsf{NAP}'.\mathsf{Gen}(1^{\lambda}, x^{*})$

2 : **return** msk

$\underline{\mathsf{Eval}(\mathsf{msk}, x)}$

1 : $r \leftarrow \mathsf{NAP}'.\mathsf{Eval}(\mathsf{msk}, x)$

2 : **return** $\mathsf{ES.Sample}(1^{\lambda}; r)$

$\underline{\mathsf{Prog}(\mathsf{msk}, y^{*})}$

1 : $r^{*} \leftarrow \mathsf{ES.Explain}(1^{\lambda}, y^{*})$

2 : $\mathsf{psk} \leftarrow \mathsf{NAP}'.\mathsf{Prog}(\mathsf{msk}, r^{*})$

3 : **return** psk

$\underline{\mathsf{PEval}(\mathsf{psk}, x)}$

1 : $r \leftarrow \mathsf{NAP}'.\mathsf{PEval}(\mathsf{psk}, x)$

2 : **return** $\mathsf{ES.Sample}(1^{\lambda}; r)$

Fig. 7. NAP for explainable output distributions.

Next, we show that a NAP for one output distribution can be transformed into a NAP for a different distribution by using an appropriate explainable sampler. A bit more concretely, given a NAP with output distribution $\mathcal{R}$ and an explainable sampler with randomness distribution $\mathcal{R}$ and output distribution $\mathcal{X}$, we obtain a NAP with output distribution $\mathcal{X}$. Towards this goal, we use the NAP's output be the input random coins of the sampling algorithm and the output of the sampling algorithm is then defined to be the output of our newly constructed NAP. Programmability of the new NAP will follow from the programmability of the underlying NAP and the explainability of the used sampler. We defer the proof of the following theorem to the full version of this paper.

Theorem 4. *Let* $\lambda \in \mathbb{N}$. *Let* NAP$'$ *be a correct and privately programmable NAP for domain* $\mathcal{X}$ *and output distribution* $\mathcal{R}$. *Let* ES = (Sample, Explain) *be a correct and explainable sampler with randomness distribution* $\mathcal{R}$ *and output distribution* $\mathcal{D}$. *Then the construction* NAP = (Gen, Eval, Prog, PEval) *in Fig. 7 is a correct and privately programmable NAP for domain* $\mathcal{X}$ *and output distribution* $\mathcal{D}$.

3.3   The Sizes of NAP Keys

At this point, let us take a moment to reflect on the sizes of our NAP keys. In the construction from Theorem 2, both master secret and programmed keys are composed of distributed point function shares. Using the construction from Theorem 1, this would result in a NAP key size of $\mathcal{O}(\lambda \log |\mathcal{X}|)$. Plugging this construction into the multiple bit construction from Theorem 3, we get a NAP for uniformly random t-bit outputs and a key size of $\mathcal{O}(t\lambda \log |\mathcal{X}|)$. Alternatively, using this construction in combination with Theorem 4 and an explainable sampler with a randomness distribution that is the uniform distribution over t-bit strings and output distribution $\mathcal{D}$, we get a NAP with key size $\mathcal{O}(t\lambda \log |\mathcal{X}|)$ and output distribution $\mathcal{D}$.

4   Compressing OR-Proofs from NAPs

We now present our main contribution: compressed OR-proofs for Σ-protocols using NAPs. We start by recalling the definition of OR languages, then present our construction with security proofs in Sect. 4.1, sketch how to extend the OR-proof to the more general k-out-of-n setting in Sect. 4.2 and conclude with providing two concrete instantiations in Sect. 4.3.

Definition 17 (OR Languages $\mathcal{L}_{\mathsf{OR}}$). *Let* $n \in \mathbb{N}$ *and let* $\mathcal{L}$ *be a language. We define*

$$\mathcal{L}_{\mathsf{OR}}^n := \{(x_1, \ldots, x_n) \subset \{0,1\}^* \mid \exists i \in [n] : x_i \in \mathcal{L}\}$$

to be the vector of statements of length n, *where at least one entry is in the language* $\mathcal{L}$.

4.1   Construction

Theorem 5. *Let $\lambda, n \in \mathbb{N}$. Let $\mathcal{H} = \mathcal{H}(\lambda)$ be a family of collision-resistant hash functions, mapping from $\{0,1\}^*$ to $\{0,1\}^{\Theta(\lambda)}$. Let Σ-protocol $(\mathsf{P}_1', \mathsf{P}_2', \mathsf{V}')$ with challenge space $\mathcal{E}$, which is an abelian group equipped with addition, and response distribution $\mathcal{Z}$ for language $\mathcal{L}$ be correct, special sound, and strong honest verifier zero-knowledge. Let Sim' be the corresponding strong honest verifier zero-knowledge simulator. Let $\mathsf{NAP}_\mathcal{E}$ be a correct and privately programmable NAP for domain $[n]$ and output distribution $\mathcal{U}_\mathcal{E}$. Let $\mathsf{NAP}_\mathcal{Z}$ be a correct and privately programmable NAP for domain $[n]$ and output distribution $\mathcal{Z}$. Then the construction from Fig. 8 is a correct, computationally special sound, honest verifier zero-knowledge sigma protocol for the language $\mathcal{L}_{\mathsf{OR}}^n$ in the common reference string model.*

$\mathsf{P}_1\left((x_1,\ldots,x_n),(i,w)\right)$

1 : $\mathsf{msk}_e \leftarrow \mathsf{NAP}_\mathcal{E}.\mathsf{Gen}(1^\lambda, i)$
2 : $\mathsf{msk}_z \leftarrow \mathsf{NAP}_\mathcal{Z}.\mathsf{Gen}(1^\lambda, i)$
3 : **for** $j \in [n] \setminus \{i\}$:
4 : $e_j \leftarrow \mathsf{NAP}_\mathcal{E}.\mathsf{Eval}(\mathsf{msk}_e, j)$
5 : $z_j \leftarrow \mathsf{NAP}_\mathcal{Z}.\mathsf{Eval}(\mathsf{msk}_z, j)$
6 : $a_j \leftarrow \mathsf{Sim}'(e_j, z_j)$
7 : $(a_i, \mathsf{aux}_i) \leftarrow \mathsf{P}_1'(x_i, w)$
8 : $a \leftarrow H(a_1, \ldots, a_n)$
9 : $\mathsf{aux} = (\mathsf{msk}_e, \mathsf{msk}_z, \mathsf{aux}_i)$
10 : **return** (a, aux)

$\mathsf{P}_2(\mathsf{aux}, e)$

1 : **parse** aux as $(\mathsf{msk}_e, \mathsf{msk}_z, \mathsf{aux}_i)$
2 : **for** $j \in [n] \setminus \{i\}$:
3 : $e_j \leftarrow \mathsf{NAP}_\mathcal{E}.\mathsf{Eval}(\mathsf{msk}_e, j)$
4 : $e_i := e - \sum_{j \neq i} e_j$
5 : $z_i \leftarrow \mathsf{P}_2'(\mathsf{aux}_i, e_i)$
6 : $\mathsf{psk}_e \leftarrow \mathsf{NAP}_\mathcal{E}.\mathsf{Prog}(\mathsf{msk}_e, e_i)$
7 : $\mathsf{psk}_z \leftarrow \mathsf{NAP}_\mathcal{Z}.\mathsf{Prog}(\mathsf{msk}_z, z_i)$
8 : **return** $(\mathsf{psk}_e, \mathsf{psk}_z)$

$\mathsf{V}(a, e, z)$

1 : **parse** z as $(\mathsf{psk}_e, \mathsf{psk}_z)$
2 : **for** $j \in [n]$:
3 : $e_j \leftarrow \mathsf{NAP}_\mathcal{E}.\mathsf{PEval}(\mathsf{psk}_e, j)$
4 : $z_j \leftarrow \mathsf{NAP}_\mathcal{Z}.\mathsf{PEval}(\mathsf{psk}_z, j)$
5 : $a_j \leftarrow \mathsf{Sim}'(e_j, z_j)$
6 : **if** $\left(\sum_{j=1}^{n} e_j \neq e\right) \vee (H(a_1, \ldots, a_n) \neq a)$:
7 :   **return** 0
8 : **if** $\exists j \in [n]$ s.t. $\mathsf{V}'(x_j, a_j, e_j, z_j) = 0$:
9 :   **return** 0
10 : **return** 1

$\mathsf{Setup}(1^\lambda)$

1 : $H \leftarrow \mathcal{H}$
2 : **return** $\mathsf{crs} := H$

Fig. 8. OR-proof from NAPs.

Proof. To prove the theorem statement, we need to show correctness, computational special-soundness, and honest verifier zero-knowledge. In the following, let us look at each of these separately.

Correctness. The fact that our protocol is correct (with overwhelming probability), follows by inspection.

Computational Special Soundness. Let $\mathcal{A}$ be a PPT adversary, such that

$$\Pr[\mathsf{Expt}^{\mathsf{sound}}_{\mathcal{A},\mathcal{L}^n_{\mathsf{OR}}}(1^\lambda) = 1] = \epsilon.$$

Recall that the winning condition of the experiment requires $\mathcal{A}$ to return a vector (x, a, e, z, e', z'), such that both $\mathsf{V}(x, a, e, z) = 1$ and $\mathsf{V}(x, a, e', z') = 1$, while at the same time $e \neq e'$ and $x \notin \mathcal{L}^n_{\mathsf{OR}}$.

During the verification of (x, a, e, z) and (x, a, e', z'), at step 2 of V in Fig. 8, for each $j \in [n]$, the verifier computes transcripts (a_j, e_j, z_j) and (a'_j, e'_j, z'_j) respectively. Let COLL be the event that $H(a_1, \ldots, a_n) = H(a'_1, \ldots, a'_n)$, but $(a_1, \ldots, a_n) \neq (a'_1, \ldots, a'_n)$. We observe that

$$\Pr[\mathsf{Expt}^{\mathsf{sound}}_{\mathcal{A},\mathcal{L}^n_{\mathsf{OR}}}(1^\lambda) = 1]$$

$$= \Pr[\mathsf{Expt}^{\mathsf{sound}}_{\mathcal{A},\mathcal{L}^n_{\mathsf{OR}}}(1^\lambda) = 1 \mid \mathsf{COLL}] \cdot \Pr[\mathsf{COLL}] + \Pr[\mathsf{Expt}^{\mathsf{sound}}_{\mathcal{A},\mathcal{L}^n_{\mathsf{OR}}}(1^\lambda) = 1 \mid \neg\mathsf{COLL}] \cdot \Pr[\neg\mathsf{COLL}]$$

$$\leq \Pr[\mathsf{COLL}] + \Pr[\mathsf{Expt}^{\mathsf{sound}}_{\mathcal{A},\mathcal{L}^n_{\mathsf{OR}}}(1^\lambda) = 1 \mid \neg\mathsf{COLL}].$$

From the collision-resistance of $\mathcal{H}$, it follows that $\Pr[\mathsf{COLL}] \leq \mathsf{negl}(\lambda)$. More precisely, let $\mathcal{B}$ be an adversary against the collision-resistance of $\mathcal{H}$. Given H, the adversary $\mathcal{B}$ sets $\mathsf{crs} := H$ and honestly simulates the computational special soundness experiment towards $\mathcal{A}$. When $\mathcal{A}$ outputs (x, a, e, z, e', z'), we let $\mathcal{B}$ compute the corresponding vectors $(a_1, \ldots, a_n)$ and $(a'_1, \ldots, a'_n)$ and return them in their experiment. It is easy to see that $\mathcal{B}$ wins, whenever COLL happens and thus $\Pr[\mathsf{COLL}] \leq \mathsf{negl}(\lambda)$.

Now let us assume that COLL did not happen. Then, since the verifier checks $a = H(a_1, \ldots, a_n)$ and $a = H(a'_1, \ldots, a'_n)$ respectively in step 6 of V, and since both verifications are successful, it follows that $(a_1, \ldots, a_n) = (a'_1, \ldots, a'_n)$. However, note that $e \neq e'$ and that the verifier also checks that $\sum^n_{j=1} e_j = e$ and $\sum^n_{j=1} e'_j = e'$ respectively. It must therefore exist an index $j^* \in [n]$, such that $e_{j^*} \neq e'_{j^*}$. Since all transcripts are accepting in step 8 of V, it follows that there exists an x_{j^*} and two accepting transcripts $(a_{j^*}, e_{j^*}, z_{j^*})$ and $(a_{j^*}, e'_{j^*}, z'_{j^*})$, which agree in their first messages, but have different second messages. By assumption, the Σ-protocol $(\mathsf{P}'_1, \mathsf{P}'_2, \mathsf{V}')$ is special sound and thus it must either hold that $x_{j^*} \in \mathcal{L}$ (as the extractor from special soundness successfully extracts a witness for x_{j^*}) and thus $x \in \mathcal{L}^n_{\mathsf{OR}}$ or

$$\Pr[\mathsf{Expt}^{\mathsf{sound}}_{\mathcal{A},\mathcal{L}^n_{\mathsf{OR}}}(1^\lambda) = 1 \mid \neg\mathsf{COLL}] = 0.$$

We can conclude that the adversary's success probability ϵ is negligible in λ.

Honest Verifier Zero-Knowledge. To show honest verifier zero-knowledge, we need to provide a simulator Sim, such that for all $\lambda \in \mathbb{N}$, all PPT adversaries $\mathcal{A}$, all $x \in \mathcal{L}_{\mathsf{OR}}^n$ and its witnesses w, it holds that

$$\left| \Pr\left[\mathsf{Expt}_{\mathcal{A}}^{\mathsf{Real}\Sigma}(1^\lambda, x, w) = 1 \right] - \Pr\left[\mathsf{Expt}_{\mathcal{A},\mathsf{Sim}}^{\mathsf{Sim}\Sigma}(1^\lambda, x) = 1 \right] \right| \leq \mathsf{negl}(\lambda).$$

Our simulator is depicted in Fig. 9.

$$\underline{\mathsf{Sim}(e)}$$

1 : $\mathsf{msk}_e \leftarrow \mathsf{NAP}_{\mathcal{E}}.\mathsf{Gen}(1^\lambda, 1)$

2 : $\mathsf{msk}_z \leftarrow \mathsf{NAP}_{\mathcal{Z}}.\mathsf{Gen}(1^\lambda, 1)$

3 : **for** $j \in [n] \setminus \{1\}$:

4 : $e_j \leftarrow \mathsf{NAP}_{\mathcal{E}}.\mathsf{Eval}(\mathsf{msk}_e, j)$

5 : $z_j \leftarrow \mathsf{NAP}_{\mathcal{Z}}.\mathsf{Eval}(\mathsf{msk}_z, j)$

6 : $e_1 := e - \sum_{j=2}^{n} e_j$

7 : $z_1 \leftarrow \mathcal{Z}$

8 : $\mathsf{psk}_e \leftarrow \mathsf{NAP}.\mathsf{Prog}(\mathsf{msk}_e, e_1)$

9 : $\mathsf{psk}_z \leftarrow \mathsf{NAP}.\mathsf{Prog}(\mathsf{msk}_z, z_1)$

10 : **for** $j \in [n]$:

11 : $a_j \leftarrow \mathsf{Sim}'(e_j, z_j)$

12 : $a := H(a_1, \ldots, a_n)$

13 : $z := (\mathsf{psk}_e, \mathsf{psk}_z)$

14 : **return** (a, z)

Fig. 9. Honest verifier zero-knowledge simulator for the OR-proof.

What remains to do is to argue that our constructed simulator produces transcripts that are indistinguishable from real ones. Since both $\mathsf{NAP}_{\mathcal{E}}$ and $\mathsf{NAP}_{\mathcal{Z}}$ are privately programmable, there exist simulators $\mathsf{Sim}_{\mathcal{E}}$ and $\mathsf{Sim}_{\mathcal{Z}}$ respectively. Since honest verifier zero-knowledge only has to hold for $x \in \mathcal{L}_{\mathsf{OR}}^n$, there exists an index $i \in [n]$ with $x_i \in \mathcal{L}$. We consider the following sequence of hybrids.

Let Hybrid_0 be the experiment $\mathsf{Expt}_{\mathcal{A},\mathsf{Sim}}^{\mathsf{Sim}\Sigma}(1^\lambda, x)$. Let Hybrid_1 be identical to Hybrid_0, apart from how the challenge e is chosen. Instead of letting the challenger pick e and provide it to the simulator, we now let the simulator pick e_1 uniformly at random and define $e = \sum_{j=1}^{n} e_j$. Since the challenge space $\mathcal{E}$ is an abelian group, it follows that it makes no difference, whether we first pick e_1 or e and thus the two hybrids are perfectly indistinguishable from the adversary's perspective.

Let Hybrid_2 be identical to Hybrid_1, apart from how msk_e is chosen. Instead of computing it honestly, we directly compute $\mathsf{psk}_e \leftarrow \mathsf{Sim}_{\mathcal{E}}(1^\lambda)$ and define $e_1 :=$

$\mathsf{NAP}_{\mathcal{E}}.\mathsf{PEval}(\mathsf{psk}_e, 1)$. Indistinguishability of the two hybrids follows from the private programmability of $\mathsf{NAP}_{\mathcal{E}}$. More concretely, we use $\mathcal{A}$ to construct an adversary $\mathcal{B}$ against the private programmability of $\mathsf{NAP}_{\mathcal{E}}$ as follows: Initially, $\mathcal{B}$ outputs $x^* = 1$ and receives psk from the challenger. For $j \in [n]$, adversary $\mathcal{B}$ defines $e_j \leftarrow \mathsf{NAP}_{\mathcal{E}}.\mathsf{PEval}(\mathsf{psk}, j)$. Next, $\mathcal{B}$ computes the values $\mathsf{psk}_z, z_1, e, a$ the same way as Hybrid_1 would and defines $z := (\mathsf{psk}, \mathsf{psk}_z)$. Finally, $\mathcal{B}$ calls $\mathcal{A}$ on input (a, e, z). When $\mathcal{A}$ returns bit b, we let $\mathcal{B}$ output the same bit. If $\mathcal{B}$ was in $\mathsf{Expt}_{\mathcal{A}}^{\mathsf{IdealPP}}(1^\lambda)$, then the view of $\mathcal{A}$ is identical to Hybrid_2. If $\mathcal{B}$ was in $\mathsf{Expt}_{\mathcal{A}}^{\mathsf{RealPP}}(1^\lambda)$, then the view of $\mathcal{A}$ is identical to Hybrid_1. Thus by private programmability, indistinguishability of the two hybrids follows.

Let Hybrid_3 be identical to Hybrid_2, apart from how msk_z is chosen. Instead of computing it honestly, we directly compute $\mathsf{psk}_z \leftarrow \mathsf{Sim}_{\mathcal{Z}}(1^\lambda)$ and define $z_1 := \mathsf{NAP}_{\mathcal{Z}}.\mathsf{PEval}(\mathsf{psk}_z, 1)$. Indistinguishability of Hybrid_2 and Hybrid_3 follows from the private programmability of $\mathsf{NAP}_{\mathcal{Z}}$, similarly to the argument made for the previous pair of hybrids.

Let Hybrid_4 be identical to Hybrid_3, apart from now choosing $\mathsf{msk}_z \leftarrow \mathsf{NAP}_{\mathcal{Z}}.\mathsf{Gen}(1^\lambda, i)$, sampling $z_i \leftarrow \mathcal{Z}$, and computing $\mathsf{psk}_z \leftarrow \mathsf{NAP}_{\mathcal{Z}}.\mathsf{Prog}(\mathsf{msk}_z, z_i)$. Here, $i \in [n]$ is the index such that $x_i \in \mathcal{L}$. Indistinguishability of Hybrid_3 and Hybrid_4 follows from the private programmability of $\mathsf{NAP}_{\mathcal{Z}}$.

Let Hybrid_5 be identical to Hybrid_4, apart from now choosing $\mathsf{msk}_e \leftarrow \mathsf{NAP}_{\mathcal{E}}.\mathsf{Gen}(1^\lambda, i)$, sampling $e_i \leftarrow \mathcal{E}$, and computing $\mathsf{psk}_e \leftarrow \mathsf{NAP}_{\mathcal{E}}.\mathsf{Prog}(\mathsf{msk}_e, e_i)$. Indistinguishability of Hybrid_4 and Hybrid_5 follows from the private programmability of $\mathsf{NAP}_{\mathcal{E}}$.

Let Hybrid_6 be identical to Hybrid_5, apart from now choosing $e \leftarrow \mathcal{E}$ and defining $e_i \leftarrow \sum_{j \neq i} e_j$. Indistinguishability of Hybrid_5 and Hybrid_6 follows from the fact that $\mathcal{E}$ is an abelian group. At this point, we arrived at a hybrid that is identical to the original simulator, but using index i, instead of index 1.

Let Hybrid_7 now be a real execution of the prover using witness (i, w), where $(x_i, w) \in \mathcal{R}_{\mathcal{L}}$. Indistinguishability of Hybrid_6 and Hybrid_7 follows from the strong honest verifier zero-knowledge property of Σ. More concretely, we use $\mathcal{A}$ to construct an adversary $\mathcal{B}$ against the strong honest verifier zero-knowledge property of Σ as follows: Initially, $\mathcal{B}$ receives (a', e', z') from the challenger. They set $a_i = a'$, $e_i = e'$ and $z_i = z'$. Then they compute $\mathsf{msk}_e, \mathsf{msk}_z$ as well as (a_j, e_j, z_j) for $j \neq i$ as specified by Hybrid_6 (which is the same in Hybrid_7). They set $a = H(a_1, \ldots, a_n)$, program both NAPs at the corresponding entries of e_i and z_i to derive programmed keys psk_e and psk_z, defining $z = (\mathsf{psk}_e, \mathsf{psk}_z)$. Again, this process is the same in both hybrids. Finally, $\mathcal{B}$ sets $e = \sum_{j=1}^n e_j$ and forwards (a, e, z) to $\mathcal{A}$. On output bit b by $\mathcal{A}$, we let $\mathcal{B}$ forward the bit as their output. Note that $\mathcal{E}$ is an abelian group, so e again has the correct distribution. If $\mathcal{B}$ was in $\mathsf{Expt}_{\mathcal{B},\mathsf{Sim}'}^{\mathsf{stSim}\Sigma}(1^\lambda, x_i)$, then the view of $\mathcal{A}$ is identical to Hybrid_6. If $\mathcal{B}$ was in $\mathsf{Expt}_{\mathcal{B},\mathsf{Sim}}^{\mathsf{stReal}\Sigma}(1^\lambda, x_i, w)$, then the view of $\mathcal{A}$ is identical to Hybrid_7 (which is identical to the real experiment of strong honest verifier zero-knowledge). Thus by strong honest verifier zero-knowledge, the two hybrids are indistinguishable.

Having shown correctness, computational special soundness, and honest verifier zero-knowledge, concludes the proof. $\qed$

4.2   Extensions

Theorem 5 allows for showing that one out of n statements is in the language $\mathcal{L}$. More generally, it may be desirable to show that there exists a subset I of size k, such that $x_i \in \mathcal{L}_i$ for all $i \in I$. That is, we would like to show that multiple statements are valid in the a setting where we deal with multiple languages. Let us shortly outline, how our approach can easily be extended to this setting.

Showing the Validity of k Out of n Statements for One Language $\mathcal{L}$. To construct such proofs of partial knowledge, we can again directly follow the blueprint of Cramer, Damgård and Schoenmakers [CDS94]. If the prover has witnesses for k statements, then they still need to simulate $n - k$ many Σ-protocol executions. Rather than requiring that all challenges sum to e, we will now require that they all lie on the same polynomial of degree $n - k$. The polynomial will be uniquely defined by the $n - k$ simulated and the received additional challenge. The challenges for the honest executions will be interpolated from this polynomial.

This approach requires us to program our NAPs at multiple points, but luckily such NAPs can easily be constructed from distributed point functions. Rather than viewing the NAP outputs as the evaluation of one function share, we can view them as the xor of the evaluation of multiple shares (for different point functions). The resulting key sizes would all increase by a multiplicative factor of k.

Dealing with Multiple Languages. When dealing with multiple languages, we may have to handle multiple response distributions, but we assume that all challenge sets are the same. Assume we have explainable samplers for all of these response distributions and assume that all of these samplers have the same randomness distribution $\mathcal{R}$. Then we can use a NAP with output distribution $\mathcal{R}$ to construct a NAP, where the output for each $j \in [n]$ comes from a different distribution.

4.3   Examples

Having established our generic transformation in the previous section, let us now look at two prominent examples of Σ-protocols that can be compiled with it. Without loss of generality, we assume throughout this section that n and m are powers of two and hence their corresponding logarithm is a positive integer. Moreover, we use every explainable rejection sampler with precision λ, as detailed in Corollary 10.

Graph Isomorphism. One of the arguably most well-known Σ-protocols is that of Goldreich, Micali, and Wigderson [GMW86], which allows for showing that two graphs are isomorphic without revealing the secret isomorphism between them. More precisely, the statement is $x = (G_0, G_1)$, where G_0 and G_1 are two graphs each of which having m nodes, and the witness w is a permutation $\pi : [m] \to [m]$ which defines the isomorphism. We say $x \in \mathcal{L}^{\mathsf{GI}}$, if $\pi(G_0) = G_1$,

$P_1((G_0, G_1), \pi)$	$P_2(\mathsf{aux}, e)$	$V(a, e, z)$	$\mathsf{Sim}(e, z)$
1 : $\tau \leftarrow S_m$	1 : **parse** aux as τ	1 : **if** $z(G_e) = a$:	1 : $a = z(G_e)$
2 : $G_2 := \tau(G_0)$	2 : $z_0 := \tau$	2 : **return** 1	2 : **return** a
3 : $a := G_2$	3 : $z_1 := \tau \circ \pi^{-1}$	3 : **else** :	
4 : $\mathsf{aux} = \tau$	4 : **return** $z := z_e$	4 : **return** 0	
5 : **return** (a, aux)			

Fig. 10. Σ-Protocol for the graph isomorphism problem by Goldreich, Micali, and Wigderson [GMW86].

where applying a permutation to a graph is interpreted as relabeling node i into node $\pi(i)$. We recall the protocol of Goldreich, Micali, and Wigderson in Fig. 10.

Besides being correct and special sound, we note that their protocol is also strong honest verifier zero-knowledge. To see this, we observe that the simulator, receiving a uniformly random challenge e and a uniformly random permutation $z : [m] \rightarrow [m]$, can deterministically compute $a = z(G_e)$. Furthermore, we observe that the challenge space is $\mathcal{E} = \{0, 1\}$ and the response distribution is the uniform distribution over the group of permutations S_m. Using Theorem 5 in combination with our NAPs from Theorem 4, instantiated with the distributed point functions from Theorem 1, and using the explainable sampler from Corollary 12, we get the following theorem.

Theorem 6. *Let* $\lambda, n, m \in \mathbb{N}$. *Assuming the existence of collision-resistant hash functions, there exists a correct, computationally special sound, and honest verifier zero-knowledge* Σ-*protocol for the language* $\mathcal{L}_{\mathsf{OR}}^{\mathsf{GI}, n}$. *The communication complexity of the protocol is* $\mathcal{O}(m\lambda^3 \log n)$, *where* m *denotes the number of nodes of the graphs in the statement.*

Let us explain how we arrive at the stated communication complexity. The transcript (a, e, z) of the constructed Σ-protocol is comprised of a hash $a \in \{0, 1\}^{\Theta(\lambda)}$, a challenge $e \in \mathcal{E} = \{0, 1\}$, and a response $z = (\mathsf{psk}_e, \mathsf{psk}_z)$, which is a pair of programmed NAP keys for input domain $\mathcal{X} = [n]$. To bound the bit length of the NAP keys, we use the bounds from Sect. 3.3. The bit length of psk_e for the output distribution $\mathcal{U}\{0, 1\}$ is in $\mathcal{O}(\lambda \log n)$. The bit length of psk_z is $\mathcal{O}(t\lambda \log n)$, where t is the number of randomness bits needed for the explainable sampler. To sample a uniformly random permutation from S_m, we use the procedure described in Corollary 12 which requires rejection sampling of the uniform distribution over $[i]$ for $i \in \{2, \ldots, m\}$. We upper bound this by sampling m times over $[m]$. With λ bits of precision and constant M, we need at most $\lambda M(\log m + \lambda) \in \mathcal{O}(\lambda^2)$ many randomness bits for sampling over $[m]$. Here, we used that the number of nodes m is polynomial in λ. Hence, $t \in \mathcal{O}(m\lambda^2)$ and therefore the total bit length of psk_z is in $\mathcal{O}(m\lambda^3 \log n)$, which dominates the overall communication complexity.

Our theorem statement shows that one can prove the validity of one out of n instances of the graph isomorphism problem with a protocol that has a communication complexity that only depends logarithmically on n and that only relies on the existence of collision-resistant hashing.

$P_1(G, \phi)$	$P_2(\text{aux}, e)$
1 : $\tau \leftarrow S_3$	1 : **parse** aux as $(\tau, r_1, \ldots, r_m)$
2 : **for** $\ell \in [m]$:	2 : **parse** e as (i, j)
3 : $r_\ell \leftarrow \{0,1\}^\lambda$	3 : **for** $\ell \in [m] \setminus \{i, j\}$:
4 : $c_\ell \leftarrow \mathsf{Commit}(\tau(\phi(\ell)); r_\ell)$	4 : $c_\ell \leftarrow \mathsf{Commit}(\tau(\phi(\ell)); r_\ell)$
5 : $a := (c_1, \ldots, c_m)$	5 : $z := (r_i, r_j, \tau(\phi(i)), \tau(\phi(j)), (c_\ell)_{\ell \in [m] \setminus \{i,j\}})$
6 : $\mathsf{aux} = (\tau, r_1, \ldots, r_m)$	6 : **return** z
7 : **return** (a, aux)	

$V(a, e, z)$	$\mathsf{Sim}(e, z)$
1 : **parse** a as $(c_1, \ldots, c_m)$	1 : **parse** e as (i, j)
2 : **parse** e as (i, j)	2 : **parse** z as $(r_i, r_j, g_i, g_j, (c_\ell)_{\ell \in [n] \setminus \{i,j\}})$
3 : **parse** z as $(r_i, r_j, g_i, g_j, (c'_\ell)_{\ell \in [m] \setminus \{i,j\}})$	3 : $c_i \leftarrow \mathsf{Commit}(g_i; r_i)$
4 : $c'_i \leftarrow \mathsf{Commit}(g_i; r_i)$	4 : $c_j \leftarrow \mathsf{Commit}(g_j; r_j)$
5 : $c'_j \leftarrow \mathsf{Commit}(g_j; r_j)$	5 : $a = (c_1, \ldots, c_m)$
6 : **if** $g_i = g_j \vee (c_1, \ldots, c_m) \neq (c'_1, \ldots, c'_m)$:	6 : **return** a
7 : **return** 0	
8 : **else** :	
9 : **return** 1	

Fig. 11. A variant of the Σ-Protocol for graph 3-coloring by Goldreich, Micali, and Wigderson [GMW86].

Graph 3-Coloring. Another well-known Σ-protocol that was also presented by Goldreich, Micali, and Wigderson [GMW86] allows for showing that a given graph G is 3-colorable, i.e. that there exists a function ϕ, which assigns one of three colors to each node in a way that no two neighbours share a color. Here, $x = G$ is the statement and $w = \phi$ is the witness. More formally, let G be a graph with m nodes and E its set of edges. A 3-coloring of G is a function $\phi \colon [m] \to \{0, 1, 2\}$ such that for every edge $(i, j) \in E$ with $i, j \in [m]$, it yields $\phi(i) \neq \phi(j)$. We say $x \in \mathcal{L}^{\mathsf{G3C}}$, if there exists a 3-coloring ϕ of G. A slightly modified version of the original protocol is recalled in Fig. 11. In the original protocol, the response z only contains the commitment openings of the two nodes specified by the challenge. The modification appends to the response z the commitments from the other edges (which can be recomputed with the help of the auxiliary information). This change is important to guarantee strong honest verifier zero-knowledge. The protocol involves a hiding and binding commitment scheme $\mathsf{Commit} \colon \{0, 1, 2\} \times \{0, 1\}^\lambda \to \{0, 1\}^{\Theta(\lambda)}$. In the following, we assume that the produced commitments of Commit are pseudorandom bit strings, i.e. computationally indistinguishable from uniformly random bit strings. Such commitment schemes can be build from one-way functions, as shown by Naor [Nao90].[3]

In this setting, the protocol is not only correct and special sound, but also strong honest verifier zero-knowledge. To see the latter, we observe that the simulator, on input a uniformly random challenge e and a uniformly random response z, can deterministically compute the commitments for the i-th and j-th node (using the provided color and randomness in z) and output the full list of commitments (using the other commitments provided in z). The produced transcript is indistinguishable from a real one and due to the pseudorandomness of the commitment scheme, we can simulate those commitments by just picking uniformly random bit strings. The challenge space is given as $\mathcal{E} = E$. The response distribution is a product distribution of twice the uniform distribution over $\{0,1\}^\lambda$ (for the two commitment randomnesses), the uniform distribution over $[6]$ (for the two non-equal colors) and $n-2$ many uniform distributions over $\{0,1\}^{\Theta(\lambda)}$ (for the commitments). Overall, we obtain the following result.

Theorem 7. *Let $\lambda, n, m \in \mathbb{N}$. Assuming the existence of collision-resistant hash functions, there exists a correct, computationally special sound, and honest verifier zero-knowledge Σ-protocol for the language $\mathcal{L}_{\mathsf{OR}}^{\mathsf{G3C},n}$. The communication complexity of the protocol is $\mathcal{O}(m\lambda^3 \log n)$, where m denotes the number of nodes of the graphs in the statement.*

Let us again look at how we arrive at the stated communication complexity. Let (a, e, z) again be a transcript of the protocol. As before, the bit length of the hash a is $\mathcal{O}(\lambda)$, the bit length of e is $\log |E| \leq 2 \log m$. Regarding the bit length of z, we observe that we need $t_1 = 2\lambda + (m-2)\mathcal{O}(\lambda) \in \mathcal{O}(m\lambda)$ many uniform output bits (covering the commitment randomness and the other commitments) and $t_2 = M\lambda(3 + \lambda)$ many bits for the explainable sampler with constant M and λ bits of precision (for sampling over $[6]$). Thus, the total bit size of z is $\mathcal{O}(m\lambda^3 \cdot \log n)$, dominating the overall communication complexity.

5   Explainable Rejection Sampling

Previous works, such as that of Agrawal, Wichs, and Yamada [AWY20], showed that sampling (truncated) discrete gaussians via rejection sampling, as specified by Gentry, Peikert, and Vaikuntanathan [GPV08], is explainable[4]. Lu and Waters [LW22] formalized the concept of explainable samplers and show that large classes of distributions can be sampled in an explainable way. Here, we extend upon their result and show that anything that can be sampled efficiently

---

[3] The interactive commitment scheme originally presented in [Nao90] can be made non-interactive in the common reference string model by interpreting the verifier's (reusable) first message, which is a random bit string, as a crs.

[4] In the work of Agrawal, Wichs, and Yamada [AWY20], the terminology *reversible* sampling was used.

via rejection sampling, can also be explained. Throughout this section, we assume that all involved distributions have efficiently computable probability density functions, i.e. that for any distribution $\mathcal{D}$ and any element x in $\mathsf{Supp}(\mathcal{D})$, we can compute the probability of x being sampled.

5.1 Textbook Rejection Sampling

Before presenting our new results, let us first recall textbook rejection sampling, depicted in Fig. 12, along with the corresponding theorem statement in Theorem 8. For the sake of completeness, we provide a proof of this theorem in the full version of this paper. We note that this proof is not new to our work.

$\mathsf{TextbookRejSample}(\mathcal{P}, \mathcal{Q}, M)$

---

1 : $\rho \leftarrow \mathcal{U}[0, 1]$

2 : $x \leftarrow \mathcal{Q}$

3 :   **if** $\rho \leq \mathcal{P}(x)/(M \cdot \mathcal{Q}(x))$:

4 :   **return** x

5 :   **else** :

6 :   go to Step 1

Fig. 12. Textbook rejection sampling.

Theorem 8 (Rejection Sampling). *Let $\mathcal{P}, \mathcal{Q}$ be two discrete probability distributions such that $\mathsf{Supp}(\mathcal{P}) \subseteq \mathsf{Supp}(\mathcal{Q})$, where $\mathcal{Q}$ is the starting and $\mathcal{P}$ the target distribution. Further, let $M \in \mathbb{N}$ such that $\mathcal{P}(x)/\mathcal{Q}(x) \leq M$ for all $x \in \mathsf{Supp}(\mathcal{P})$. Then, the output of $\mathsf{RejSample}(\mathcal{P}, \mathcal{Q}, M)$ as defined in Fig. 12 is distributed as $\mathcal{P}$. In expectation, the algorithm terminates after M trails.*

5.2 From Rejection Sampling to Explainable Samplers

Let us now see how rejection sampling can be used to construct explainable samplers. Recall, that rejection sampling repeatedly picks pairs (x, ρ), where $x \leftarrow \mathcal{Q}$ and $\rho \leftarrow \mathcal{U}[0, 1]$, and then accepts x, if ρ is in some appropriate interval of $[0, 1]$. As we have shown in the proof of Theorem 8, during each of these iterations, the algorithm will be terminating with probability $1/M$. Thus, the probability of not having terminated after $\lambda \cdot M$ iterations is bounded by

$$\left(1 - \frac{1}{M}\right)^{\lambda \cdot M} = \left(\left(1 - \frac{1}{M}\right)^{M}\right)^{\lambda} \leq e^{-\lambda}, \tag{1}$$

which is a negligible function in λ.

The explainable sampler we construct, outputs samples from some target distribution $\mathcal{P}$ and has randomness distribution $\mathcal{R} := (\mathcal{Q} \times \mathcal{U}[0,1])^{\lambda \cdot M}$ for some starting distribution $\mathcal{Q}$. In other words, our sampler takes $\kappa := \lambda \cdot M$ pairs as input, which are sufficient for simulating a real rejection sampling execution with overwhelming probability.

RejSample($1^\lambda, r$)	RejExplain($1^\lambda, x$)
1: parse r as $(x_i, \rho_i)_{i \in [\kappa]}$	1: $r \leftarrow \mathcal{R}$
2: **for** i **in** $\{1, \ldots, \kappa\}$:	2: parse r as $(x_i, \rho_i)_{i \in [\kappa]}$
3: **if** $\rho_i \leq \mathcal{P}(x_i)/(M \cdot \mathcal{Q}(x_i))$:	3: **for** i **in** $\{1, \ldots, \kappa\}$:
4: **return** x_i	4: **if** $\rho_i \leq \mathcal{P}(x_i)/(M \cdot \mathcal{Q}(x_i))$:
5: **return** $\perp$	5: $x_i := x$
	6: $\rho \leftarrow \mathcal{U}[0, \mathcal{P}(x_i)/(M \cdot \mathcal{Q}(x_i))]$
	7: $\rho_i := \rho$
	8: **return** r
	9: **return** $\perp$

Fig. 13. Explainable sampler via rejection sampling.

Theorem 9. *Let $\lambda \in \mathbb{N}$. Let $\mathcal{P} = \mathcal{P}(\lambda)$ and $\mathcal{Q} = \mathcal{Q}(\lambda)$ be two discrete probability distributions for which $\mathsf{Supp}(\mathcal{P}) \subseteq \mathsf{Supp}(\mathcal{Q})$ and for which there exists an $M = M(\lambda) \in \mathsf{poly}(\lambda)$, such that $\mathcal{P}(x)/\mathcal{Q}(x) \leq M$ for all $x \in \mathsf{Supp}(\mathcal{P})$. Then, the construction in Fig. 13 defines a correct and explainable sampler for distribution $\mathcal{P}$ with randomness distribution $\mathcal{R}$, where $\mathcal{R} := (\mathcal{Q} \times \mathcal{U}[0,1])^{\lambda \cdot M}$.*

Proof. Let $\kappa := \lambda \cdot M$. Since both M and κ are polynomially bounded in λ, it directly follows that both RejSample and RejExplain are efficiently computable. Let us proceed to showing that our sampler is correct and explainable separately.

Correctness. To show correctness, we observe that for all $\lambda \in \mathbb{N}$ and all adversaries $\mathcal{A}$, it holds that

$$\left| \Pr\left[\mathcal{A}(x) = 1 : r \leftarrow \mathcal{R}, x \leftarrow \mathsf{RejSample}(1^\lambda; r) \right] - \Pr\left[\mathcal{A}(x) = 1 : x \leftarrow \mathcal{P} \right] \right|$$

$$\leq \Pr\left[x = \perp : r \leftarrow \mathcal{R}, x \leftarrow \mathsf{RejSample}(1^\lambda; r) \right]$$

$$+ \left| \Pr\left[\mathcal{A}(x) = 1 : r \leftarrow \mathcal{R}, x \leftarrow \mathsf{RejSample}(1^\lambda; r) \mid x \neq \perp \right] - \Pr\left[\mathcal{A}(x) = 1 : x \leftarrow \mathcal{P} \right] \right|$$

$$= \mathsf{negl}(\lambda) + \left| \Pr\left[\mathcal{A}(x) = 1 : r \leftarrow \mathcal{R}, x \leftarrow \mathsf{RejSample}(1^\lambda; r) \mid x \neq \perp \right] - \Pr\left[\mathcal{A}(x) = 1 : x \leftarrow \mathcal{P} \right] \right|,$$

since RejSample returns $\perp$ with negligible probability (cf. Equation 1). By Theorem 8, it holds that RejSample perfectly simulates sampling from $\mathcal{P}$, whenever it does not output $\perp$. Thus, it holds that

$$\left| \Pr\left[\mathcal{A}(x) = 1 : r \leftarrow \mathcal{R}, x \leftarrow \mathsf{RejSample}(1^\lambda; r) \mid x \neq \perp \right] - \Pr\left[\mathcal{A}(x) = 1 : x \leftarrow \mathcal{P} \right] \right| = 0.$$

Therefore, the sampler is correct.

Explainability. Let $R \subset \mathsf{Supp}(\mathcal{R})$ be the set of random tapes on which RejSample successfully produces an output. That is, for all $r \in R$, it holds that $\mathsf{RejSample}(1^\lambda; r) \neq \bot$. Since, RejSample outputs $\bot$ with negligible probability, it follows that $|R| \geq (1 - \mathsf{negl}(\lambda)) \cdot |\mathsf{Supp}(\mathcal{P})|$, meaning that sampled random tapes from distribution $\mathcal{R}$ will be in R with overwhelming probability. Thus,

$$
\left| \Pr \left[\mathcal{A}(x, r) : \begin{array}{c} r \leftarrow \mathcal{R} \\ x \leftarrow \mathsf{RejSample}(1^\lambda; r) \end{array} \right] - \Pr \left[\mathcal{A}(x, \mathrm{r}) : \begin{array}{c} r' \leftarrow \mathcal{R} \\ x \leftarrow \mathsf{RejSample}(1^\lambda; r') \\ r \leftarrow \mathsf{RejExplain}(1^\lambda, x) \end{array} \right] \right|
$$

$$
\leq \left| \Pr \left[\mathcal{A}(x, \mathrm{r}) : \begin{array}{c} r \leftarrow \mathcal{R} \\ x \leftarrow \mathsf{RejSample}(1^\lambda; r) \end{array} \middle| r \in \mathrm{R} \right] - \Pr \left[\mathcal{A}(x, \mathrm{r}) : \begin{array}{c} r' \leftarrow \mathcal{R} \\ x \leftarrow \mathsf{RejSample}(1^\lambda; r') \\ r \leftarrow \mathsf{RejExplain}(1^\lambda, x) \end{array} \middle| r' \in \mathrm{R} \right] \right|
$$

$+\mathsf{negl}(\lambda)$

$$
\leq \left| \Pr \left[\mathcal{A}(x, \mathrm{r}) : \begin{array}{c} r \leftarrow \mathcal{R} \\ x \leftarrow \mathsf{RejSample}(1^\lambda; r) \end{array} \middle| r \in \mathrm{R} \right] - \Pr \left[\mathcal{A}(x, \mathrm{r}) : \begin{array}{c} x \leftarrow \mathcal{P} \\ r \leftarrow \mathsf{RejExplain}(1^\lambda, x) \end{array} \right] \right|
$$

$+\mathsf{negl}(\lambda)$,

where the last inequality follows from the correctness of our sampler.

For $r \in \mathsf{Supp}(\mathcal{R})$, let $\mathsf{Indx}(r) \in [\kappa] \cup \{\bot\}$ be the function that either outputs the first index $j \in [\kappa]$ that is accepted, i.e. such that $\rho_j \leq \mathcal{P}(x_j)/(M \cdot \mathcal{Q}(x_j))$, or, if no index is accepted, outputs $\bot$. By the definition of RejExplain, we observe that

$$
\Pr \left[\mathcal{A}(x, r) : \begin{array}{c} x \leftarrow \mathcal{P} \\ r \leftarrow \mathsf{RejExplain}(1^\lambda, x) \end{array} \right]
$$

$$
= \Pr \left[\mathcal{A}(x, \mathrm{r}) : \begin{array}{c} r' := ((x_1, \rho_1), \ldots, (x_\kappa, \rho_\kappa)) \leftarrow \mathcal{R} \\ j = \mathsf{Indx}(r') \\ x \leftarrow \mathcal{P} \\ \rho \leftarrow \mathcal{U}[0, \mathcal{P}(x_j)/(M \cdot \mathcal{Q}(x_j))] \\ r := ((x_1, \rho_1), \ldots, (x_{j-1}, \rho_{j-1}), (x, \rho), (x_{j+1}, \rho_{j+1}), \ldots, (x_\kappa, \rho_\kappa)) \end{array} \middle| j \neq \bot \right] \pm \mathsf{negl}(\lambda).
$$

Looking at the experiment in the last equation, we note that $\mathcal{R}$ is a product distribution and from the guarantees of rejection sampling it follows that x_j with $j = \mathsf{Indx}(r')$ is a sample from $\mathcal{P}$. The corresponding ρ_j is uniform conditioned on $\rho_j \leq \mathcal{P}(x_j)/(M \cdot \mathcal{Q}(x_j))$. Now, picking a fresh element $x \leftarrow \mathcal{P}$ along with $\rho \leftarrow \mathcal{U}[\mathcal{P}(x^*)/(M \cdot \mathcal{Q}(x^*))]$ is just the process of sampling a new pair from the same distribution as that of (x_j, ρ_j). Replacing one pair by the other does not affect the output distribution and therefore

$$
\left| \Pr \left[\mathcal{A}(x, r) : \begin{array}{c} r \leftarrow \mathcal{R} \\ x \leftarrow \mathsf{RejSample}(1^\lambda; r) \end{array} \right] - \Pr \left[\mathcal{A}(x, \mathrm{r}) : \begin{array}{c} r' \leftarrow \mathcal{R} \\ x \leftarrow \mathsf{RejSample}(1^\lambda; r') \\ r \leftarrow \mathsf{RejExplain}(1^\lambda, x) \end{array} \right] \right| \leq \mathsf{negl}(\lambda),
$$

which shows explainability. $\square$

5.3   Handling Finite Precision

In the above, we assumed that we can sample from the continuous distribution $\mathcal{U}[0, 1]$, but in reality[5] we can clearly only sample from a discrete distribution. Let us note that sampling uniform p-bit integers allows for simulating rejection sampling and our explainable sampler with an additive error of $\mathcal{O}(2^{-p})$. We will not provide a formal proof here, but still provide an intuition of how the statement can be proven easily.

To see that the above claim is true, note that sampling ρ from $\mathcal{U}[0, 1]$ and checking $\rho \leq t$ for threshold $t \in [0, 1]$, where $1/t$ divides 2^p, can be perfectly simulated by sampling ρ' from $\{0, \dots, 2^p - 1\}$ and checking whether $\rho' \leq t \cdot 2^p$. Furthermore, note that any arbitrary threshold $t \in [0, 1]$ is at most an additive factor away from a threshold t' that divides 2^p. The outcome between using the two thresholds only differs for $\rho \in [t, t']$, which happens with probability $\mathcal{O}(2^{-p})$.

Corollary 10. *Let $\lambda, p \in \mathbb{N}$ with $p = \Omega(\lambda)$. Let $\mathcal{P} = \mathcal{P}(\lambda)$ and $\mathcal{Q} = \mathcal{Q}(\lambda)$ be two discrete probability distributions for which $\mathsf{Supp}(\mathcal{P}) \subseteq \mathsf{Supp}(\mathcal{Q})$ and for which there exists an $M = M(\lambda) \in \mathsf{poly}(\lambda)$, such that $\mathcal{P}(x)/\mathcal{Q}(x) \leq M$ for all $x \in \mathsf{Supp}(\mathcal{P})$. Then, there exists a correct and explainable sampler for distribution $\mathcal{P}$ with randomness distribution $\mathcal{R}$, where $\mathcal{R} := (\mathcal{Q} \times \mathcal{U}\{0, \dots, 2^p - 1\})^{\lambda \cdot M}$.*

5.4   Explainable Samplers for Product Distributions and Permutations

Given explainable samplers for distributions $\mathcal{P}_1, \dots, \mathcal{P}_m$ for $m \in \mathsf{poly}(\lambda)$ with randomness distributions $\mathcal{R}_1, \dots, \mathcal{R}_m$ respectively, one can easily construct an explainable sampler for the product distribution $\mathcal{P}_1 \times \dots \times \mathcal{P}_m$ with randomness domain $\mathcal{R}_1 \times \dots \times \mathcal{R}_m$ by simply running all individual explainable samplers in parallel. Correctness and explainability of this sampler follows via a standard hybrid argument.

Corollary 11. *Let $\lambda, m \in \mathbb{N}$ with $m = \mathsf{poly}(\lambda)$. For $i \in [m]$, let ES_i be a correct and explainable sampler for distribution $\mathcal{P}_i = \mathcal{P}_i(\lambda)$ with randomness distribution $\mathcal{R}_i = \mathcal{R}_i(\lambda)$. Then there exists a correct and explainable sampler for distribution $\mathcal{P}_1 \times \dots \times \mathcal{P}_m$ with randomness distribution $\mathcal{R}_1 \times \dots \times \mathcal{R}_m$.*

This corollary is particularly useful, as it allows us to construct an explainable sampler for the uniform distribution over $\mathcal{S}_m$, i.e., uniformly random permutations over $[m]$. To see how, let us first recall the Fisher-Yates shuffle, which takes a list of input values $(a_1, \dots, a_m)$ as input and returns a uniformly random permutation $(b_1, \dots, b_m)$ thereof. The shuffle initializes a set $A = \{a_1, \dots, a_m\}$ and a counter $c = 1$. It then repeatedly picks a uniformly random element $a \in A$, assigns $b_c := a$, removes a from A, and increments c by one until $A = \emptyset$. In other words, in the first step, it selects a uniformly random index $i \in [m]$ and assigns

---

[5] In particular, this is the case in our NAP constructions from Sect. 3.

$b_1 := a_i$, then it selects a uniformly random index j in $[m-1]$ and assigns b_2 to be the j-th elements among the remaining ones and so on.

From the above, we can see that any permutation over $[m]$, corresponds to exactly one element from the set $[m] \times \cdots \times [2]$. Thus, the task of sampling a uniformly random permutation is identical to the task of sampling a uniformly random element in $[m] \times \cdots \times [2]$. We show in the full version how to use rejection sampling to obtain an explainable sampler for the uniform distributions over $[i]$, where $i \in [m]$ is not a power of two. Using Corollary 11, we can then obtain an explainable sampler for permutations from explainable samplers for uniform distributions over the sets $[i]$ for $i \in [m]$.

Corollary 12. *Let* $\lambda, m \in \mathbb{N}$ *with* $m = \mathsf{poly}(\lambda)$. *For* $i \in [m] \setminus \{1\}$, *let* ES_i *be a correct and explainable sampler for the uniform distribution over* $[i]$ *with randomness distribution* $\mathcal{R}_i = \mathcal{R}_i(\lambda)$. *Then there exists a correct and explainable sampler for the uniform distribution over the set* $\mathcal{S}_m$ *of all permutations* π : $[m] \to [m]$ *with randomness distribution* $\mathcal{R}_2 \times \cdots \times \mathcal{R}_m$.

Acknowledgement. We thank Rafail Ostrovsky for pointing us to the works of De Santis et al. [DDP+94] and Hemenway et al. [HJO+16], which we had missed.

References

[AC20]   Attema, T., Cramer, R.: Compressed Σ-protocol theory and practical application to plug & play secure algorithmics. In: Micciancio, D., Ristenpart, T. (eds) Advances in Cryptology – CRYPTO 2020, Part III, vol. 12172. LNCS, pp. 513–543. Springer, Heidelberg (2020). https://doi.org/10.1007/978-3-030-56877-1_18

[ACF21] Attema, T., Cramer, R., Fehr, S.: Compressing proofs of k-out-of-n partial knowledge. In: Malkin, T., Peikert, C. (eds) Advances in Cryptology – CRYPTO 2021, Part IV, vol. 12828. LNCS. Virtual Event, pp. 65–91. Springer, Heidelberg (2021). https://doi.org/10.1007/978-3-030-84259-8_3

[ACK21] Attema, T., Cramer, R., Kohl, L.: A compressed Σ-protocol theory for lattices. In: Malkin, T., Peikert, C. (eds) Advances in Cryptology – CRYPTO 2021, Part II, vol. 12826. LNCS. Virtual Event, pp. 549–579. Springer, Heidelberg (2021). https://doi.org/10.1007/978-3-030-84245-1_19

[AS92]   Arora, S., Safra, S.: Probabilistic Checking of Proofs; a new characterization of NP. In: 33rd FOCS. IEEE Computer Society Press, pp. 2–13 (1992). https://doi.org/10.1109/SFCS.1992.267824

[AWY20] Agrawal, S., Wichs, D., Yamada, S.: Optimal broadcast encryption from LWE and pairings in the standard model. In: Pass, R., Pietrzak, K. (eds) Theory of Cryptography. TCC 2020, Part I, vol. 12550. LNCS, pp. 149–178. Springer, Heidelberg (2020). https://doi.org/10.1007/978-3-030-64375-1_6

[BBB+18] Bünz, B., Bootle, J., Boneh, D., Poelstra, A., Wuille, P., Maxwell, G.: Bulletproofs: short proofs for confidential transactions and more. In: 2018 IEEE Symposium on Security and Privacy. IEEE Computer Society Press, pp. 315–334 (2018). https://doi.org/10.1109/SP.2018.00020

[BBH+18]   Ben-Sasson, E., Bentov, I., Horesh, Y., Riabzev, M.: Scalable, transparent, and post-quantum secure computational integrity. Cryptology ePrint Archive, Report 2018/046 (2018). https://eprint.iacr.org/2018/046

[BCC+16]   Bootle, J., Cerulli, A., Chaidos, P., Groth, J., Petit, C.: Efficient zero-knowledge arguments for arithmetic circuits in the discrete log setting. In: Fischlin, M., Coron, JS. (eds) Advances in Cryptology – EUROCRYPT 2016, Part II, vol. 9666. LNCS, pp. 327–357. Springer, Heidelberg (2016). https://doi.org/10.1007/978-3-662-49896-5_12

[BCS16]   Ben-Sasson, E., Chiesa, A., Spooner, N.: Interactive oracle proofs. In: Hirt, M., Smith, A. (eds.) Theory of Cryptography: 14th International Conference, TCC 2016-B, Beijing, China, October 31-November 3, 2016, Proceedings, Part II, pp. 31–60. Springer, Berlin, Heidelberg (2016). https://doi.org/10.1007/978-3-662-53644-5_2

[BGI15]   Boyle, E., Gilboa, N., Ishai, Y.: Function secret sharing. In: Oswald, E., Fischlin, M. (eds.) Advances in Cryptology - EUROCRYPT 2015: 34th Annual International Conference on the Theory and Applications of Cryptographic Techniques, Sofia, Bulgaria, April 26-30, 2015, Proceedings, Part II, pp. 337–367. Springer, Berlin, Heidelberg (2015). https://doi.org/10.1007/978-3-662-46803-6_12

[BLW17]   Boneh, D., Lewi, K., Wu, D.J.: Constraining pseudorandom functions privately. In: Fehr, S. (eds) Public-Key Cryptography – PKC 2017. PKC 2017. Lecture Notes in Computer Science(), Part II, vol. 10175. LNCS, pp. 494–524. Springer, Heidelberg (2017). https://doi.org/10.1007/978-3-662-54388-7_17

[BR08]   Bellare, M., Ristov, T.: Hash functions from sigma protocols and improvements to VSH. In: Pieprzyk, J. (eds) Advances in Cryptology - ASIACRYPT 2008, vol. 5350. LNCS, pp. 125–142. Springer, Heidelberg (2008). https://doi.org/10.1007/978-3-540-89255-7_9

[CDS94]   Cramer, R., Damgård, I., Schoenmakers, B.: Proofs of partial knowledge and simplified design of witness hiding protocols. In: Desmedt, Y.G. (eds) Advances in Cryptology — CRYPTO'94, vol. 839. LNCS, pp. 174–187. Springer, Heidelberg (1994). https://doi.org/10.1007/3-540-48658-5_19

[DDP+94]   De Santis, A., Di Crescenzo, G., Persiano, G., Yung, M.: On monotone formula closure of SZK. In: 35th FOCS. IEEE Computer Society Press, pp. 454–465 (1994). https://doi.org/10.1109/SFCS.1994.365745

[GGHA+22] Goel, A., Green, M., Hall-Andersen, M., Kaptchuk, G.: Stacking Sigmas: a framework to compose Σ-protocols for disjunctions. In: Dunkelman, O., Dziembowski, S. (eds) Advances in Cryptology – EUROCRYPT 2022, Part II, vol. 13276. LNCS, pp. 458–487. Springer, Heidelberg (2022). https://doi.org/10.1007/978-3-031-07085-3_16

[GI14]   Gilboa, N., Ishai, Y.: Distributed point functions and their applications. In: Nguyen, P.Q., Oswald, E. (eds) Advances in Cryptology – EUROCRYPT 2014. EUROCRYPT 2014, vol. 8441. LNCS, pp. 640–658. Springer, Heidelberg (2014). https://doi.org/10.1007/978-3-642-55220-5_35

[GK15]   Groth, J., Kohlweiss, M.: One-Out-of-Many Proofs: or how to leak a secret and spend a coin. In: Oswald, E., Fischlin, M. (eds) Advances in Cryptology - EUROCRYPT 2015. EUROCRYPT 2015, Part II, vol. 9057. LNCS, pp. 253–280. Springer, Heidelberg (2015). https://doi.org/10.1007/978-3-662-46803-6_9

[GMW86] Goldreich, O., Micali, S., Wigderson, A.: Proofs that yield nothing but their validity and a methodology of cryptographic protocol design (Extended Abstract). In: 27th FOCS. IEEE Computer Society Press, pp. 174–187 (1986). https://doi.org/10.1109/SFCS.1986.47

[GPV08] Gentry, C., Peikert, C., Vaikuntanathan, V.: Trapdoors for hard lattices and new cryptographic constructions. In: Ladner, R.E., Dwork, C. (eds) 40th ACM STOC. ACM Press, pp. 197–206 (2008). https://doi.org/10.1145/1374376.1374407

[HIL+99] Håstad, J., Impagliazzo, R., Levin, L.A., Luby, M.: A pseudorandom generator from any one-way function. SIAM J. Comput. **28**(4), 1364–1396 (1999)

[HJO+16] Hemenway, B., Jafargholi, Z., Ostrovsky, R., Scafuro, A., Wichs, D.: Adaptively secure garbled circuits from one-way functions. In: Robshaw, M., Katz, J. (eds) Advances in Cryptology – CRYPTO 2016, Part III, vol. 9816. LNCS, pp. 149–178. Springer, Heidelberg (2016). https://doi.org/10.1007/978-3-662-53015-3_6

[IKO+09] Ishai, Y., Kushilevitz, E., Ostrovsky, R., Sahai, A.: Zero-knowledge proofs from secure multiparty computation. SIAM J. Comput. **39**(3), 1121–1152 (2009)

[Kil92] Kilian, J.: A note on efficient zero-knowledge proofs and arguments (Extended Abstract). In: 24th ACM STOC. ACM Press, pp. 723–732 (1992). https://doi.org/10.1145/129712.129782

[LW22] Lu, G., Waters, B.: How to Sample a Discrete Gaussian (and more) from a random oracle. In: Kiltz, E., Vaikuntanathan, V. (eds) Theory of Cryptography. TCC 2022, Part II. LNCS, pp. 653–682. Springer, Heidelberg (2022). https://doi.org/10.1007/978-3-031-22365-5_23

[Nao90] Naor, M.: Bit commitment using pseudo-randomness. In: Brassard, G. (ed) CRYPTO'89, vol. 435. LNCS, pp. 128–136. Springer, Heidelberg (1990). https://doi.org/10.1007/0-387-34805-0_13

[PS18] Peikert, C., Shiehian, S.: privately constraining and programming PRFs, the LWE way. In: Abdalla, M., Dahab, R., (eds) PKC 2018, Part II, vol. 10770. LNCS, pp. 675–701. Springer, Heidelberg (2018). https://doi.org/10.1007/978-3-319-76581-5_23.

[PS20] Peikert, C., Shiehian, S.: Constraining and watermarking PRFs from milder assumptions. In: Kiayias, A., Kohlweiss, M., Wallden, P., Zikas, V. (eds) PKC 2020, Part I, vol. 12110. LNCS, pp. 431–461. Springer, Heidelberg (2020). https://doi.org/10.1007/978-3-030-45374-9_15

[RRR16] Reingold, O., Rothblum, G.N., Rothblum, R.D.: Constantround interactive proofs for delegating computation. In: Wichs, D., Mansour, Y. (ed.) 48th ACM STOC. ACM Press, pp. 49–62 (2016). https://doi.org/10.1145/2897518.2897652

[WW22] Waters, B., Wu, D.J.: Batch arguments for NP and more from standard bilinear group assumptions. In: Dodis, Y., Shrimpton, T. (eds) Advances in Cryptology – CRYPTO 2022. CRYPTO 2022, Part II. LNCS, pp. 433–463. Springer, Heidelberg (2022). https://doi.org/10.1007/978-3-031-15979-4_15

zkSNARKs in the ROM with Unconditional UC-Security

Alessandro Chiesa and Giacomo Fenzi[✉][iD]

EPFL, Lausanne, Switzerland
{alessandro.chiesa,giacomo.fenzi}@epfl.ch

Abstract. The universal composability (UC) framework is a "gold standard" for security in cryptography. UC-secure protocols achieve strong security guarantees against powerful adaptive adversaries, and retain these guarantees when used as part of larger protocols. Zero knowledge succinct non-interactive arguments of knowledge (zkSNARKs) are a popular cryptographic primitive that are often used within larger protocols deployed in dynamic environments, and so UC-security is a highly desirable, if not necessary, goal.

In this paper we prove that there exist zkSNARKs in the random oracle model (ROM) that unconditionally achieve UC-security. Here, "unconditionally" means that security holds against adversaries that make a bounded number of queries to the random oracle, but are otherwise computationally unbounded.

Prior work studying UC-security for zkSNARKs obtains transformations that rely on computational assumptions and, in many cases, lose most of the succinctness property of the zkSNARK. Moreover, these transformations make the resulting zkSNARK more expensive and complicated.

In contrast, we prove that widely used zkSNARKs in the ROM are UC-secure without modifications. We prove that the Micali construction, which is the canonical construction of a zkSNARK, is UC-secure. Moreover, we prove that the BCS construction, which many zkSNARKs deployed in practice are based on, is UC-secure. Our results confirm the intuition that these natural zkSNARKs do not need to be augmented to achieve UC-security, and give confidence that their use in larger real-world systems is secure.

Keywords: succinct arguments · random oracle model · universal composability

1 Introduction

The universal composability (UC) framework [Can01] is a "gold standard" for security in cryptography. UC-secure protocols achieve strong security guarantees in the presence of powerful adaptive adversaries, and retain their security when used as part of larger protocols, thereby enabling a modular analysis of these larger protocols. Informally, security in the UC framework is shown by arguing that an adversary (the environment) cannot distinguish between a real execution of the protocol and an "ideal" execution,

For the full version of this extended abstract, see [CF24].

© International Association for Cryptologic Research 2025
E. Boyle and M. Mahmoody (Eds.): TCC 2024, LNCS 15364, pp. 67–89, 2025.
https://doi.org/10.1007/978-3-031-78011-0_3

where the protocol is replaced by an ideal functionality. In a larger protocol then one can argue, via a result known as the composition theorem, that instances of the former protocol can be replaced by this ideal functionality.

Zero knowledge succinct non-interactive arguments of knowledge (zkSNARKs) are a powerful cryptographic primitive that has seen widespread adoption. zkSNARKs are often used within larger protocols deployed in dynamic environments, and so UC-security is a highly desirable (if not necessary) goal.

Achieving UC-security for a zkSNARK is challenging. Security of a zkSNARK is often established via techniques that are problematic, and at times impossible, to use in the UC framework. These techniques include non-black-box extraction and black-box rewinding extraction. In contrast, UC-security prescribes a black-box security proof in a game consisting of polynomially-many interactions with the adversary, and such security proofs are almost exclusively achieved through the use of straightline (non-rewinding) extractors.

UC-security has been studied in the zkSNARK literature, via transformations that "lift" a given zkSNARK into a UC-secure non-interactive argument. In most cases the transformation *increases the argument size to linear in the witness* (of the proved nondeterministic computation) [KZM+15, ARS20, BS21, AGRS24]; the result is a non-interactive argument that is not succinct in the usual desirable sense (the argument size is succinct in the circuit size but not the witness size). One exception is [GKO+23], which achieves UC-secure zkSNARKs by combining a simulation-extractable zkSNARK and a straightline-extractable polynomial commitment scheme. A downside is that this transformation incurs computational overheads, and the resulting zkSNARKs do not reflect ones used in practice. We elaborate further on prior work in Sect. 1.2. Overall, the takeaway is that the desirable goal of UC-secure zkSNARKs has been notably elusive and the known results come with considerable limitations or caveats.

UC-Security with Random Oracles. The focus of this paper is zkSNARKs constructed in the "pure" random oracle model (ROM), where (honest and malicious) parties have query access to a random function and where security holds unconditionally against adversaries that query the random function a bounded number of times.

The ROM is notable for multiple reasons. The elegant Micali construction [Mic00], the "canonical" construction of a zkSNARK, is realized in the ROM. Moreover, many zkSNARKs used in practice follow the BCS construction [BCS16], which is also realized in the ROM.[1] Both constructions are secure in the quantum ROM [CMS19]; in fact, the ROM supports the most efficient post-quantum zkSNARKs to date. Yet, the UC-security of these seminal zkSNARK constructions has, surprisingly, not been investigated so far.

In the context of UC-security, several basic questions arise.

Do zkSNARKs that are (unconditionally) UC-secure in the ROM exist?
Is the Micali construction UC-secure? What about the BCS construction?

---

[1] In practice the random oracle is heuristically instantiated via a suitable cryptographic hash function. This leads to zkSNARKs that are lightweight (no public-key cryptography is used) and easy to deploy (users only need to agree on which hash function to use).

More generally, when does a given zkSNARK in the ROM achieve UC-security?

In this paper we investigate these questions. This requires specifying what is meant by "UC-secure in the ROM". Briefly, this involves specifying an ideal functionality GRO that models a **global random oracle model** (GROM). There are several flavors of GROM [CDG+18]; the most relevant to our setting is the GROM that is *observable* and *(restricted) programmable*. Establishing UC-security then demands arguing, in a hybrid model in which every party has access to GRO, that an adversary cannot distinguish between two cases:(i) a real execution of the given zkSNARK protocol; and (ii) an ideal functionality $\mathcal{F}_{\mathrm{ARG}}$ for zero knowledge non-interactive arguments of knowledge (which equals the ideal functionality in [LR22b], therein called NIZKPoK ideal functionality). Using techniques from UC with Global Subroutines (UCGS) [BCH+20] we then lift the hybrid-model analysis to achieve security in the plain UC framework.

1.1 Our Results

We prove that there exist zkSNARKs that unconditionally achieve UC-security in the GROM, positively answering a basic question about the feasibility of UC-secure zkSNARKs in the information-theoretic setting of random oracles. In fact, we prove something stronger (and far more useful), namely, we prove that two seminal constructions of zkSNARKs with random oracles are UC-secure: the Micali construction and the BCS construction. (In particular, we do not construct new zkSNARKs or modify existing ones). This provides formal evidence that supports the intuition that these seminal constructions of zkSNARKs satisfy far stronger security properties than previously shown, and are suitable for secure use within larger protocols.

Definition 1 (informal). *Let $\mathcal{F}_{\mathrm{ARG}}$ be the non-interactive argument ideal functionality in [LR22b] (therein called NIZKPoK ideal functionality), and let GRO be the ideal functionality for the (observable and restricted programmable) GROM in [CDG+18]. A zkSNARK **unconditionally achieves UC-security in the GROM** if the zkSNARK unconditionally UC-realizes $\mathcal{F}_{\mathrm{ARG}}$ in the GRO-hybrid model. ("Unconditionally" means that security holds against adversaries that are computationally unbounded and that make a bounded number of queries to the ideal functionality GRO).*

Theorem 1 (informal). *There exists a zkSNARK that unconditionally achieves UC-security in the GROM.*

The above result follows from the following theorem. Recall that the Micali construction compiles a given PCP (probabilistically checkable proof) with suitable properties into a zkSNARK, and the BCS construction compiles a given public-coin IOP (interactive oracle proof) with suitable properties into a zkSNARK.

Theorem 2 (informal)

- *The Micali construction unconditionally achieves UC-security in the GROM, provided that the underlying PCP is honest-verifier zero knowledge and knowledge sound.*

- *The BCS construction unconditionally achieves UC-security in the GROM, provided that the underlying IOP is honest-verifier zero knowledge and (state-restoration) knowledge sound with a straightline extractor.*

The properties required of the underlying PCP and IOP for UC-security in Theorem 2 are essentially the same as those typically used in the Micali and BCS constructions.[2] We only additionally require the extractor of the IOP to be straightline, a property satisfied by most IOPs in the literature.

As we elaborate further in Sect. 2, our results are achieved by showing that the given non-interactive argument satisfies certain "UC-friendly" notions of completeness, zero knowledge, and knowledge soundness in the ROM, which in turn we show imply UC-security in the GROM.

Achieving UC-security is a notoriously challenging goal, even for simple cryptographic protocols. As we outline in Sect. 2, establishing UC-security of the Micali construction is distinctly more involved compared to merely establishing its standalone knowledge soundness or zero knowledge (as done in prior work). Even more involved is establishing the UC-security of the BCS construction, which is used in practice.

Adaptive Security. Our results also cover the *adaptive flavor* of UC-security, where the adversary can corrupt parties in the protocol at any time (rather than only at the start of the protocol). This stronger, and more realistic, flavor of UC-security demands additional work both in terms of definitions and analyses.

Concrete Security Bounds. Throughout our work we provide concrete security bounds, parametrized on security parameters and the capabilities of the adversary (e.g., queries to the global random oracle). This ultimately leads to explicit expressions for the UC-security error of the zkSNARKs that we study. Similarly to the ROM, the GROM can be (heuristically) instantiated via a suitable cryptographic hash function, and these expressions enable practitioners to set parameters for the desired security level for UC-security.

1.2 Related Work

We provide references for the model of global random oracle that we use. Then we summarize prior work studying UC-security for non-interactive arguments that are not succinct and for those that are succinct.

Global Random Oracle. The random oracle model is widely used to analyze the security of cryptographic protocols. The generalized UC (GUC) framework in [CDPW07] extends the basic UC framework in [Can01] to allow for *globally shared* ideal functionalities, such as a global random oracle. Subsequently, [BCH+20] identifies a subtle inconsistency in the GUC formulation, and shows a mechanism to model and prove the security of protocols interacting with shared functionalities in the *plain* UC model; this

---

[2] State-restoration knowledge soundness is a natural strengthening of knowledge soundness that is required for the security of the BCS transformation. See [BCS16,CY24] for more details.

is the framework of UC with Global Subroutines (UCGS) that we use to accommodate for a random oracle functionality. There are multiple flavors of a *global random oracle model* (GROM) in the UC framework: [CJS14] propose a GROM where queries can be observed, but not programmed, by the adversary; and [CDG+18] introduce a GROM where queries can be observed as well as programmed by the adversary (with some restrictions). We use the latter flavor in this paper (see [CF24, Sect. 3.3] in the full version of this paper), since it is usually appropriate for constructions in the "pure" ROM (with no cryptography). For example, the simple commitment scheme $f((m,r))$, where m is a message and r a random salt, can be shown to be UC-secure in the latter GROM flavor, but not in the former.

Non-succinct zkNARKs. Several works study UC-security for zero knowledge non-interactive arguments of knowledge (zkNARKs) that are *not* succinct (the size of the argument string is at least the size of the witness for the proved nondeterministic computation).

- *From game-based simulation-secure knowledge soundness.* [Gro06] achieves UC-secure zero-knowledge proofs in the CRS model (assuming cryptographic hardness assumptions), using the observation that straightline knowledge extraction that is secure in the presence of a simulation oracle is crucial for UC-security. The proof size in [Gro06] is linear in the circuit size. In this work we also rely on game-based notions of simulation-secure straightline knowledge soundness (in the ROM setting).
- *Encrypt the witness.* A standard approach to achieve UC-security is to have the argument string include an encryption of the witness and a zero knowledge proof that the encrypted message is a valid witness [DDO+01]. This approach is adopted in various works studying UC-security in the zkSNARK community, including the C∅C∅ framework [KZM+15], LAMASSU [ARS20], TIRAMISU [BS21], and [AGRS24]. All non-interactive arguments following this approach are not succinct since the argument string contains the encryption of a witness. (The argument size can be smaller than the proved circuit but not the witness).
- *Compile a Σ-protocol.* Other works study UC-security for non-interactive arguments obtained from Σ-protocols: [LR22b] shows that a randomized variant of the Fischlin construction [Fis05, Ks22] applied to a Σ-protocol yields a zkNARK that achieves UC-security in the observable programmable GROM, and with a global reference string the construction can be modified to rely only on an observable GROM; then [LR22a] shows how to extend these results to achieve security against adaptive corruptions, assuming a minor property of the Σ-protocol.

While the constructions studied in [LR22b, LR22a] and in this paper are different (non-interactive arguments obtained from Σ-protocols versus from probabilistic proofs), our work is inspired by the ideas in [LR22b, LR22a]. Specifically, we use "UC-friendly" definitions of completeness, zero knowledge, and knowledge soundness in the ROM that suffice (and are necessary) for UC-security in the GROM, which reduces the goal of UC-security to proving that the relevant zkSNARK constructions satisfy these simpler properties. The definitions that we use (which can be found in [CF24, Sect. 5] of the full version of this paper) are variants of those in [LR22b, LR22a], adapted to our pure ROM setting and to facilitate concrete security bounds.

Succinct zkNARKs. [GKO+23] construct zkSNARKs that are computationally UC-secure in a model that provides a global reference string and a global random oracle (that is observable but not programmable). Their approach is a compiler that combines any simulation-extractable zkSNARK and a polynomial commitment scheme with certain properties (each comes with its own reference string), leveraging the random oracle to achieve straightline extraction via proof-of-work ideas inspired by [Fis05].[3] Our work is complementary in that we study a setting without any computational assumptions: we achieve unconditional UC-security for well-known zkSNARKs (without modifications) via a global random oracle (that is observable and programmable). Moreover, the zkSNARKs that we consider are not susceptible to quantum attacks whereas the compiler in [GKO+23] uses a polynomial commitment scheme that is insecure against quantum attacks (and whether there is a suitable post-quantum replacement is an open question).

2 Techniques

We outline the main ideas behind our results.

- In Sect. 2.1 we describe how to adapt the UC-security framework to our setting of unconditional security in the ROM (and with the additional goal of achieving concrete security bounds).
- In Sect. 2.2 we describe how we reduce UC-security in the GROM to three simpler properties in the ROM: *UC-friendly completeness*; *UC-friendly zero knowledge*; and *UC-friendly knowledge soundness*.
- In Sect. 2.3 we discuss the Merkle commitment scheme in the ROM (a component of the zkSNARKs that we study), for which we prove several "UC-friendly" properties that we introduce and rely on.
- In Sect. 2.4 we discuss UC-security of the Micali construction, and then in Sect. 2.5 we discuss UC-security of the BCS construction. In both cases we do so by showing the above UC-friendly properties.
- In Sect. 2.6 we discuss how we achieve UC-security against adaptive corruptions.

2.1 Unconditional UC-Security

We consider UC-security for protocols in the "pure" ROM, where parties have query access to a random function and where security holds unconditionally against adversaries that query the random function a bounded number of times. This setting is not considered in prior work studying UC-security for zkSNARKs and, more generally,

---

[3] Informally, the argument prover, instead of providing an encryption of the witness as in [DDO+01] (which makes argument strings non-succinct), uses a polynomial commitment scheme to commit to a polynomial whose coefficients are the witness; to achieve straight-line extraction, the argument prover also provides a Fischlin-style proof-of-work that requires querying the random oracle on many evaluations of the committed polynomial. The extractor can then use polynomial interpolation to reconstruct the witness from the query-answer trace of a malicious argument prover.

there is no off-the-shelf model of UC-security for this setting. Below we explain how we adapt the UC framework [Can01,Can20] to our needs, and how our goals can be expressed in this adaptation.

UC-Security Against Unbounded Adversaries. We consider adversaries that are computationally unbounded, and are limited only in their access to certain resources, such as queries to a random oracle, queries to a prover oracle, and others. As discussed in detail in [CF24, Sect. 3.2] of the full version of this work, we model this setting by modifying the mechanism of import and time budget described in [Can20, Sect. 3.2] to work with a generalized notion of budget. We endow the environment (and the protocol) with a budget represented as a numeric vector. Each message sent specifies how much budget is deducted from the sender budget and added to the receiver budget, and the budget can be spent on a certain set of actions. With this, we can define the notion of budget-emulation.

Definition 2 (informal). *Let $\mathcal{B}$ be a tuple of non-negative integers. An environment is $\mathcal{B}$-budget if its starting budget is $\mathcal{B}$. A protocol π $\mathcal{B}$-emulates a protocol φ with simulation error σ if π UC-emulates φ with simulation error σ in the presence of any environment that is $\mathcal{B}$-budget.*

GROM and Shared Functionalities. The analogue of the ROM in our setting is a shared global subroutine: the observable and (restricted) programmable GROM introduced in [CDG+18]. The GROM interface allows four types of queries:(i) random oracle; (ii) programming; (iii) observation; (iv) and is-programmed. The random oracle query interface is familiar: each query is consistently answered with a random answer. The programming interface enables setting the answer to arbitrary queries, while the is-programmed interface enables parties *in the session* to detect whether a point has been programmed.[4] Finally, the observation interface allows queriers to receive a list of *illegitimate* queries made to the oracle thus far (queries with prefix sid made by the adversary or parties outside the session sid). The programming interface is used to argue zero knowledge, while the observable and is-programmed interfaces are used to argue knowledge soundness.

We use the approach of *UC with Global Subroutines* [BCH+20] to argue that UC-security in the presence of a global shared functionality implies standard UC-security. Informally, if the shared functionality and the protocols satisfy some mild requirements, then showing UC-emulation in the hybrid model suffices to show (standard) UC-security. See [CF24, Sect 3.2] for more details.

The ARG Functionality. We study UC-security for (succinct) non-interactive arguments. The ideal functionality that we use is the *ARG ideal functionality* $\mathcal{F}_{\mathrm{ARG}}$ from [LR22b] (therein called NIZKPoK ideal functionality), given in [CF24, Sect. 4.1] in the full

---

[4] Here "in the session" refers to the fact that the environment cannot directly ask is-programmed queries to the GROM, but only through the adversary or a corrupted party. This enables the UC simulator to intercept these queries and choose their answers.

version of this paper.[5] Briefly, $\mathcal{F}_{\mathrm{ARG}}$ has a proving interface that produces simulated proofs (to capture zero knowledge) and a verification interface that extracts a witness (to capture knowledge soundness).

Any non-interactive argument ARG in the ROM directly induces a corresponding protocol $\Pi[\mathrm{ARG}]$ in the GROM that matches the proving and verification interface of $\mathcal{F}_{\mathrm{ARG}}$. The protocol $\Pi[\mathrm{ARG}]$, which is described in [CF24, Sect. 4.2] of the full version of this paper, consists of two parties, a prover party M_P and a verifier party M_V.

- The prover party M_P, on input an instance-witness pair, runs $\Pi[\mathrm{ARG}]$'s proving interface, which runs ARG's prover using the GROM, and outputs the resulting argument string.
- The verifier party M_V, on input an instance-proof pair, runs $\Pi[\mathrm{ARG}]$'s verification interface, which runs ARG's verifier using the GROM and checks that none of the verifier queries involves programmed points, and outputs the resulting decision bit (or simply rejects if one of the verifier queries was programmed).[6]

We use the generalized budget mechanism to keep track of the resources used by the environment. Since we consider non-interactive arguments in the ROM, security will depend on the number of queries that the environment makes to the GROM; in our setting, these queries include both random oracle queries and programming queries.[7] Moreover, the environment may query the proving and verification interfaces, which can aid an attack; hence we keep track of such queries as well. Overall, a $(t_{\mathsf{q}}, t_{\mathsf{p}}, \ell_{\mathsf{p}}, \ell_{\mathsf{v}})$-budget environment is an environment that can make: (1) t_{q} random oracle queries to the GROM; (2) t_{p} programming queries to the GROM; (3) ℓ_{p} prover queries; and (4) ℓ_{v} verifier queries.

The above enables us to state our first result in slightly more detail.

Theorem 3 (restatement of Theorem 1). *There exists a non-interactive argument ARG in the ROM for which the protocol $\Pi[\mathrm{ARG}]$ $(t_{\mathsf{q}}, t_{\mathsf{p}}, \ell_{\mathsf{p}}, \ell_{\mathsf{v}})$-emulates the ideal functionality $\mathcal{F}_{\mathrm{ARG}}$ with simulation error*

$$\sigma(\lambda, t_{\mathsf{q}}, t_{\mathsf{p}}, \ell_{\mathsf{p}}, \ell_{\mathsf{v}}) = \frac{\mathsf{poly}(t_{\mathsf{q}}, t_{\mathsf{p}}, \ell_{\mathsf{p}}, \ell_{\mathsf{v}})}{2^{\lambda}} \quad .$$

---

[5] One could extend the ideal functionality $\mathcal{F}_{\mathrm{ARG}}$ to one that models *preprocessing* non-interactive arguments. Our belief is that all results in this paper straightforwardly extend to this case (we believe that the preprocessing variants of the Micali construction and BCS construction, when based on suitable holographic probabilistic proofs, are unconditionally UC-secure in the GROM).

[6] An honest party does not program the GROM. In contrast, an adversary might instead attempt to produce an argument string accepted by the verification interface by running the zero knowledge simulator of the non-interactive argument (and programming the GROM accordingly). Rejecting argument strings whose verification involves programmed points disallows this.

[7] Observation and is-programmed queries do not affect security bounds. The environment knows its own queries to the random oracle and the points that it has programmed, so it does not need to obtain this information from the GROM. Moreover, observation and is-programmed queries do not change the state of the GROM, and thus do not affect other parties in the execution.

We show that natural constructions of zkSNARKs in the ROM suffice for the above theorem: ARG can be the Micali construction or the BCS construction (instantiated over appropriate probabilistic proofs). Moreover, for these constructions we derive explicit expressions for the simulation error $\sigma(\lambda, t_q, t_p, \ell_p, \ell_v)$, which in particular enables setting parameters to achieve concrete UC-security bounds.

Next we describe how we prove such results.

2.2 UC-Friendly Properties

We informally describe three properties about a non-interactive argument ARG that are sufficient and necessary for (unconditional) UC-security in the GROM:

- **UC-friendly completeness** (sketched in Sect. 2.2);
- **UC-friendly zero knowledge** (sketched in Sect. 2.2); and
- **UC-friendly knowledge soundness** (sketched in Sect. 2.2).

These properties are described in detail in the full version of this paper [CF24, Sect. 5]. Intuitively, each property protects against a natural class of attacks against the UC-security of the protocol $\Pi[\mathsf{ARG}]$, which we outline in the corresponding section.

This approach is analogous to the approach taken in [LR22b, LR22a], where the authors rely on somewhat dissimilar security definitions that are sufficient and necessary for UC-security in their setting (NIZKPoKs obtained from Σ-protocols).[8] In particular, the above properties can be viewed as adaptations of their three properties: *overwhelming completeness*; *non-interactive multiple special honest-verifier zero knowledge*; and *non-interactive special simulation soundness*.

The main differences in our definitions include: (a) we target unconditional security, while the previous definitions target computational security; and (b) we allow the adversary to additionally program the random oracle (which is necessary in our "pure" ROM setting). The second difference has important ramifications that we discuss further below.

UC-Friendly Completeness. The ideal functionality $\mathcal{F}_{\mathsf{ARG}}$ that we consider has a verification interface that, to model completeness, accepts any proof that was generated by its proving interface. This might not be the case for the protocol $\Pi[\mathsf{ARG}]$: one attack against UC-security is, for the environment, to invoke the proving interface on inputs that maximize the probability that the resulting proofs are not accepted by the verification interface, which would distinguish the real-world and the ideal-world. UC-friendly completeness bounds the success probability of such an attack.

Definition 3 (informal). ARG *has* **UC-friendly completeness with error** ϵ_{ARG} *if every adversary that*

- *queries the random oracle t_q times,*

---

[8] More precisely, [LR22b, LR22a] discuss properties of a compiler for Σ-protocols, but those properties can be straightforwardly defined for the non-interactive argument output by the compiler.

- *programs the random oracle t_p times,*
- *requests ℓ_p proofs for instances of length at most n, and*
- *requests ℓ_v verifications for instance-proof pairs with instances of length at most n*

causes the verification interface to reject a instance-proof pair generated by the honest prover with probability at most $\epsilon_{ARG}(\lambda, n, t_q, t_p, \ell_p, \ell_v)$.

One may guess that perfect completeness of the given non-interactive argument ARG implies UC-friendly completeness with zero error. However this is not the case because the verification interface rejects proofs whose verification causes the argument verifier to query points programmed by the adversary. Hence if there are queries by the argument verifier that the adversary can predict (and program in advance) then the adversary can induce a rejection despite the perfect completeness of ARG.

Nevertheless we show that the two natural notions below suffice, together with perfect completeness of the non-interactive argument, to achieve UC-friendly completeness with small error.

Definition 4 (informal). ARG *has:*

- **monotone proofs** *if the argument verifier, on input an honestly produced proof, queries the random oracle only at points that have been queried by the honest argument prover that produced that proof; and*
- **unpredictable queries with error** ϵ_P *if every adversary that queries the random oracle t_q times and programs the random oracle t_p times cannot produce an instance-witness pair (with instance length at most n) that causes the honest argument prover to query one of the points previously programmed by the adversary with probability more than $\epsilon_P(\lambda, n, t_q, t_p)$.*

Lemma 1 (informal). *A non-interactive argument with perfect completeness, monotone proofs, and unpredictable queries with error ϵ_P has UC-friendly completeness with error (roughly) $\epsilon_{ARG} = \ell_p \cdot \epsilon_P$.*

UC-Friendly Zero Knowledge

Definition 5 (informal). ARG *has **UC-friendly zero knowledge with error** ζ_{ARG} if every adversary that*

- *queries the random oracle t_q times,*
- *programs the random oracle t_p times, and*
- *requests ℓ_p proofs for instances of length at most n*
- *requests ℓ_v verifications for instance-proof pairs with instances of length at most n*

cannot distinguish between the game in which the returned proofs are generated by the honest argument prover and the game in which they are generated by the zero knowledge simulator (which can also program the random oracle) with an advantage better than $\zeta_{ARG}(\lambda, n, t_q, t_p, \ell_p, \ell_v)$.

Informally, UC-friendly zero knowledge is a version of adaptive multi-instance zero knowledge wherein the adversary can adaptively program the random oracle.[9] Indeed, every party can program the GROM, so we need a zero knowledge property that accounts for this capability. In the real-world the protocol generates proofs using the honest argument prover and in the ideal-world the ideal functionality generates proofs using a simulator, so UC-friendly zero knowledge bounds the probability that an adversary distinguishes between these two worlds based on this difference.

First, since the adversary can query the random oracle, we show that queries to the verifier do not help the adversary, and thus show that UC-friendly zero knowledge is implied by a simplified notion where this oracle is not present. Next, since the adversary can generate simulated proofs (and thus simulate the proof oracle), we can use a hybrid argument to reduce the case of multiple simulated proofs to the case of a single simulated proof. We rely on these simplifications to more conveniently establish UC-friendly zero knowledge for the Micali construction and the BCS construction.

Lemma 2 (informal). *If* ARG *has UC-friendly zero knowledge with error* ζ_{ARG} *against adversaries that request a single proof and no verifications, then* ARG *has UC-friendly zero knowledge with error (roughly)* $\ell_{\mathrm{p}} \cdot \zeta_{\mathrm{ARG}}$ *against adversaries that request* ℓ_{p} *proofs and make* ℓ_{v} *verifier queries.*

UC-Friendly Knowledge Soundness

Definition 6 (informal). ARG *has* **UC-friendly knowledge soundness with error** κ_{ARG} *if there exists a deterministic polynomial-time straightline extractor such that every adversary that*

- *queries the random oracle* t_{q} *times,*
- *programs the random oracle* t_{p} *times,*
- *requests* ℓ_{p} *simulated proofs for instances of length at most* n, *and*
- *outputs* ℓ_{v} *instance-proofs pairs with instances of length at most* n

wins with probability at most $\kappa_{\mathrm{ARG}}(\lambda, n, t_{\mathrm{q}}, t_{\mathrm{p}}, \ell_{\mathrm{p}}, \ell_{\mathrm{v}})$. *Here "winning" means that one of the instance-proof pairs that the adversary output (a) was for an instance not queried to the simulation oracle, (b) convinces the argument verifier (without querying programmed points), and (c) causes the extractor to fail to extract a valid witness for the instance.*

UC-friendly knowledge soundness can be viewed as a variant of simulation extractability wherein the adversary can adaptively program the random oracle, as allowed by the GROM. Since the difference between the ideal-world verification interface and the real-world counterpart is the additional attempt at extraction on proofs that successfully verify, UC-friendly knowledge soundness upper bounds the probability that an adversary is able to distinguish between the two worlds by outputting proofs on which extraction fails. The protocol (and ideal functionality) rejects proofs

---

[9] As shown in the full version of this paper [CF24, Sect. 5.2], UC-friendly zero knowledge is *strictly* stronger: there are non-interactive arguments that are adaptive multi-instance zero knowledge but not UC-friendly zero knowledge.

whose verification involves points programmed by the environment. This is to disallow the environment from submitting proofs generated using the zero knowledge simulator (and programming accordingly), from which it would be (likely) impossible to extract.

Moreover, while not shown in the above informal definition, UC-friendly knowledge soundness mandates that the extractor be *straightline*: the extractor receives as input the instance, argument string, query-answer trace of the adversary with the oracle (as well as the query-answer trace of the simulator with the oracle),[10] but not the adversary itself; in particular, the extractor cannot rewind the adversary. Straightline extraction is required by the UC-security experiment (in which the ideal functionality also performs straightline extraction).

Similarly to the case of UC-friendly zero knowledge, we generically reduce UC-friendly knowledge soundness to a simpler property, in which the adversary outputs only a single instance-proof pair.

UC-Secure ZkSNARKs from UC-Friendly Properties

Lemma 3 (informal). *If a non-interactive argument* ARG *satisfies*

- *UC-friendly completeness with error* ϵ_{ARG},
- *UC-friendly zero knowledge with error* ζ_{ARG}, *and*
- *UC-friendly knowledge soundness with error* κ_{ARG}

then the protocol $\Pi[ARG]$ $(t_q, t_p, \ell_p, \ell_v)$-*emulates the ideal functionality* $\mathcal{F}_{ARG}$ *with simulation error (roughly)*

$$\epsilon_{ARG} + \zeta_{ARG} + \kappa_{ARG} .$$

The proof of Lemma 3 is given in the full version of this paper [CF24, Sect. 6], and follows a game-hopping approach in a GRO-hybrid model. We rely on an observation of [CDG+18] that, in the setting of the restricted programmable GROM, the simulator can program points undetectably. We can then perform three game hops, one for each of our UC-friendly notions. Finally, we lift the result in the GRO-hybrid model to full UC-security by using the UC with Global Subroutines theorem [BCH+20].

UC-Friendliness is Necessary. We show that the UC-friendly properties that we describe are *necessary* for a non-interactive argument ARG in the ROM to unconditionally achieve UC-security. This gives confidence that the UC-friendly properties that we describe are the "right ones" for UC-security in our setting. Moreover, we learn that the upper bound in Lemma 3 is almost tight. Specifically, while the upper bound can plausibly be improved in certain cases (e.g., in the Micali and BCS constructions, establishing UC-friendly completeness and UC-friendly zero knowledge involves separately upper bounding overlapping "bad events"), the improvement is limited. Indeed, the necessity of the UC-friendly properties implies that the simulation error of a non-interactive argument ARG is at least $\max\{\epsilon_{ARG}, \zeta_{ARG}, \kappa_{ARG}\} \geq \frac{1}{3} \cdot (\epsilon_{ARG} + \zeta_{ARG} + \kappa_{ARG})$, at most a factor of 3 (i.e., less than 2 bits of security) away from the upper bound in Lemma 3.

---

[10] More accurately, matching the ideal functionality, the extractor receives a query-answer trace that includes queries performed by the adversary and the simulator but *not* including queries whose answer was previously programmed by the adversary.

On Tightness. We make an effort, throughout this paper, to obtain concrete security bounds that are relatively tight (e.g., as noted for Lemma 3 in the paragraph above). Nevertheless, modest improvements are possible. For example, Lemma 2 reduces UC-friendly zero knowledge to a simpler property (where the adversary requests a single proof and no verifications) at a minor but noticeable cost; this cost can be reduced by directly establishing UC-friendly zero knowledge for the Micali and BCS constructions, avoiding the use of Lemma 2. Similarly for UC-friendly knowledge soundness. These choices reflect striking a balance between aiming for good concrete security bounds, and a modular presentation.

2.3   The Merkle Commitment Scheme is UC-Friendly

The Merkle commitment scheme is a key ingredient in the Micali and BCS constructions (the zkSNARKs that we study), where it acts as unconditionally secure vector commitment scheme. In order to show that said constructions satisfy the UC-friendly security notions sketched in Sect. 2.2, we establish corresponding properties for Merkle commitments. Below we denote by $\mathsf{MT} := \mathsf{MT}[\lambda, \mathsf{l}, \mathsf{r}_{\mathsf{MT}}]$ the Merkle commitment scheme for messages of length l (a power of 2) with salt size r_{MT}, for a random oracle with output size λ.

Completeness. We formulate notions of monotone proofs and unpredictable queries for vector commitments schemes (in analogy to the notions in Definition 4 for ARG), and show that the Merkle commitment scheme satisfies them. This facilitates proving that the Micali and BCS constructions satisfy UC-friendly completeness.

Lemma 4. MT *has monotone proofs, and unpredictable queries with error* $\epsilon_{\mathsf{MT}} = t_{\mathsf{p}} \cdot \mathsf{l} \cdot \left(\frac{1}{2^{\mathsf{r}_{\mathsf{MT}}}} + \frac{1}{2^{\lambda}} \right)$.

Hiding. We formulate a notion of UC-friendly hiding for vector commitment schemes, and show that the Merkle commitment scheme satisfies this property. This contributes towards proving UC-friendly zero knowledge for the Micali and BCS constructions.

Definition 7   (informal). MT *has **UC-friendly hiding with error** ζ_{MT} if every adversary that*

- *queries the random oracle* t_{q} *times,*
- *programs the random oracle* t_{p} *times, and*
- *requests* ℓ_{p} *commitments for messages of size at most* l *and corresponding openings for sets of size at most* q

cannot distinguish between the game in which the returned commitments and openings are real and the game in which they are generated by a simulator (that can also program the random oracle) with an advantage better than $\zeta_{\mathsf{MT}}(\lambda, \mathsf{l}, q, t_{\mathsf{q}}, t_{\mathsf{p}}, \ell_{\mathsf{p}})$.

Lemma 5   (informal). MT *has UC-friendly hiding with error (roughly)* $\zeta_{\mathsf{MT}} = \ell_{\mathsf{p}} \cdot q \cdot \mathsf{l} \cdot \frac{t_{\mathsf{q}} + t_{\mathsf{p}}}{2^{\mathsf{r}_{\mathsf{MT}}}}$.

The proof of Lemma 5 is similar to the hiding proof for the Merkle commitment scheme in the ROM, but adapted to reflect the additional programming capabilities of the adversary.

Extraction. The Merkle commitment scheme in the ROM is known to satisfy strong notions of extraction [BCS16,CY24]. Any adversary that outputs a Merkle commitment and subsequently outputs a valid opening proof must have "known" the opening at commitment time; moreover, this holds even when the adversary outputs multiple commitments and openings at different times. In the definition below we extend extraction to be UC-friendly, considering adversaries that can program the random oracle. We prove that the Merkle commitment scheme satisfies this stronger property.

Definition 8 (informal). MT *has **UC-friendly extraction with error** κ_{MT} if every adversary that*

- *queries the random oracle t_q times,*
- *programs the random oracle t_p times,*
- *requests ℓ_p simulated commitments for messages of size at most l and corresponding simulated openings for sets of size at most q,*
- *submits n commitments, and*
- *finally outputs k opening proofs for submitted commitments.*

wins with probability at most $\kappa_{\mathsf{MT}}(\lambda, \mathsf{l}, q, t_q, t_p, \ell_p, n, k)$. Here "winning" means to: (i) submit a list of commitments such that the extractor outputs different messages for duplicate elements in the list; or (ii) output opening proofs that verify successfully on whose commitment the extractor outputs inconsistent messages.

Lemma 6. MT *has UC-friendly extraction with error (roughly)* $\kappa_{\mathsf{MT}} = \frac{3}{2} \cdot \frac{(t_q + 2\ell_p\mathsf{l})^2}{2^\lambda} + \frac{2k(\mathsf{d}+1) \cdot (t_q + 2\ell_p\mathsf{l})}{2^\lambda}$.

We do not prove Lemma 6; it straightforwardly follows from the extraction property shown in [CY24]. Instead, we prove that the Merkle commitment scheme satisfies an *even stronger* extraction property (i.e., which implies Lemma 6) that we use to achieve adaptive security and we discuss later in Sect. 2.6.

Definition 8 already incorporates some notions on non-malleability that will be crucial for establishing UC-friendly knowledge soundness of the Micali and BCS constructions. UC-friendly extraction allows the adversary to submit simulated commitments (as those obtained from the simulation oracle), and guarantees that the Merkle commitment scheme extractor outputs consistent messages on those simulated commitments.

2.4   The Micali Construction is UC-Secure

We show that the Micali construction unconditionally achieves UC-security in the GROM, when instantiated with suitable ingredients. By Lemma 3, it suffices to show that the Micali construction satisfies UC-friendly completeness, zero knowledge, and knowledge soundness, which we now discuss in turn. After that, we explain how this leads to a proof of Theorem 1.

Review of the Micali Construction. A probabilistically checkable proof (PCP) is a proof system in which the prover sends a (long) proof string, which the verifier checks by probabilistically reading a few locations of it. The Micali construction compiles a (suitable) PCP into a zkSNARK, by using the Merkle commitment scheme in the ROM and the Fiat–Shamir transformation with salt size r. We denote this construction as Micali[PCP, r], and sketch it next.

- The argument prover runs the PCP prover, and commits to the resulting PCP string using the Merkle commitment scheme. Then the argument prover queries the random oracle with the instance, the Merkle commitment, and a random r-bit salt, to obtain PCP randomness. Finally, the argument prover emulates the PCP verifier on the obtained PCP randomness, which induces queries to the PCP string. The argument string output by the argument prover consists of the Merkle commitment, the salt, the queries, their answers, and an opening proof for the queries and answers.
- The argument verifier checks the opening proof, derives PCP randomness like the argument prover did, and checks that the PCP verifier accepts when run with that randomness on the given queries and answers.

UC-Friendly Completeness. We use Lemma 4 to show that the Micali construction has monotone proofs and unpredictable queries. Then by Lemma 1 we deduce that the Micali construction satisfies UC-friendly completeness.

Lemma 7 (informal). Micali[PCP, r] *has monotone proofs and unpredictable queries with error* $\epsilon_{\mathrm{MT}} + \frac{t_{\mathrm{p}}}{2^r}$ *(ϵ_{MT} is from Lemma 4). By Lemma 1,* Micali[PCP, r] *has UC-friendly completeness with error (roughly)* $\epsilon_{\mathrm{ARG}} = \ell_{\mathrm{p}} \cdot (\epsilon_{\mathrm{MT}} + \frac{t_{\mathrm{p}}}{2^r})$.

UC-Friendly Zero Knowledge. We show that the Micali construction satisfies UC-friendly zero knowledge.

Lemma 8 (informal). *Let* PCP *be an honest-verifier zero knowledge PCP with error* ζ_{PCP}. *Let* ζ_{MT} *be the UC-friendly hiding error in Lemma 5. Then* Micali[PCP, r] *has UC-friendly zero knowledge with error (roughly)* $\zeta_{\mathrm{ARG}} = \ell_{\mathrm{p}} \cdot (\frac{t_{\mathrm{q}}+t_{\mathrm{p}}}{2^r} + \zeta_{\mathrm{PCP}} + \zeta_{\mathrm{MT}})$.

The proof of this statement uses Lemma 2 to reduce UC-friendly zero knowledge to a game in which the adversary makes only a single query to the prover oracle. Then we use a sequence of game hops, relying among other things on the UC-friendly hiding property of the Merkle commitment scheme (Lemma 5).

UC-Friendly Knowledge Soundness. We show that the Micali construction satisfies UC-friendly knowledge soundness.

Lemma 9 (informal). *Let* PCP *be a knowledge sound PCP with error* κ_{PCP}. *Let* κ_{MT} *be the UC-friendly extraction error in Lemma 6. Then* Micali[PCP, r] *has UC-friendly knowledge soundness with error (roughly)* $\kappa_{\mathrm{ARG}} = \ell_{\mathrm{v}} \cdot ((t_{\mathrm{q}} + 1) \cdot \kappa_{\mathrm{PCP}} + \kappa_{\mathrm{MT}})$.

Note that Lemma 9 imposes no additional requirements on the PCP compared to what is usually required for regular knowledge soundness of $\mathsf{Micali}[\mathsf{PCP}, \mathsf{r}]$. Yet we achieve the UC-friendly strengthening.

The proof of Lemma 9 informally works as follows. We reduce to the state-restoration knowledge soundness of the PCP (a notion implied by the PCP's knowledge soundness) and to the UC-friendly extraction property of the Merkle commitment scheme. This is similar to prior work [BCS16, CY24] except that in our setting the adversary has access to a simulation oracle, so part of the work in our analysis is showing that simulated proofs do not help the adversary.

In the reduction to the PCP's state-restoration knowledge soundness, the adversary's queries to the Fiat–Shamir oracle are translated to moves in the state-restoration game. The simulator has an advantage over the adversary in its ability to undetectably program the Fiat–Shamir query (the point used to derive the PCP randomness used for PCP verification). In order for the reduction to succeed, we must argue that this additional capability does not help the adversary. This is because points programmed by the simulator are domain-separated by instance, and the adversary wins the UC-friendly knowledge soundness game only by outputting "fresh" instance-proof pairs (the instance was not previously submitted to the simulator oracle). Thus, the instance-proof pair that the adversary outputs must not have been produced by the simulator oracle.

Having made this observation, the state-restoration knowledge soundness adversary runs the UC-friendly knowledge soundness adversary, simulating the simulator oracle and extracting (in a straightline fashion) PCP strings from instance-root-salt triples submitted to the Fiat–Shamir oracle using the Merkle commitment extractor guaranteed by UC-friendly extraction (Definition 8). The analysis of the reduction follows then similarly to that of state-restoration knowledge soundness in the ROM.

Conclusion. Lemma 7, Lemma 8, and Lemma 9 together show that the Micali construction satisfies UC-friendly completeness, UC-friendly zero knowledge, and UC-friendly knowledge soundness, provided that the underlying PCP is honest-verifier zero knowledge and knowledge sound. In turn, Lemma 3 implies that, under these conditions, the Micali construction is unconditionally UC-secure. Both steps provide concrete security bounds, leading to an overall concrete security bound for the UC-security of the Micali construction.

2.5   The BCS Construction is UC-Secure

We follow a similar approach to show that the BCS construction is unconditionally UC-secure: we prove that the BCS construction satisfies UC-friendly completeness, zero knowledge, and knowledge soundness. Recall that the BCS construction underlies many zkSNARKs that are concretely efficient (and widely deployed). We achieve concrete UC-security bounds for this notable class of zkSNARKs.

Review of the BCS Construction. The BCS construction extends the Micali construction to work with interactive oracle proofs (IOPs), a multi-round generalization of PCPs. It compiles a (suitable) public-coin IOP into a zkSNARK, by using Merkle commitment schemes in the ROM, and the (multi-round) Fiat–Shamir transformation with salt size r. We denote this construction as $\mathsf{BCS}[\mathsf{IOP}, \mathsf{r}]$, and sketch it next.

– The argument prover runs the IOP prover, using the random oracle to simulate an interaction with the (public-coin) IOP verifier. For each round, the argument prover computes the round's IOP string, commits to it using the Merkle commitment scheme, and derives the next IOP verifier message using the random oracle (in a certain way that depends on the Merkle commitment and a salt, and either the instance or the previous Merkle commitment). Once the interaction is complete, the argument prover deduces the queries to the IOP strings and corresponding answers, and outputs an argument string containing the Merkle commitments, the salts, the query-answer pairs, and opening proofs of the commitments for those queries.
– The argument verifier checks the opening proofs, re-derives the IOP verifier randomness, and checks that the IOP verifier accepts when run with that randomness on the given queries and answers.

Remark 1 (BCS variant). We consider a minor simplification of the BCS construction where the IOP verifier messages are derived by querying the random oracle at a point consisting of the instance and all Merkle commitment and salts so far. This simplifies the knowledge soundness analysis compared to the more common approach of querying at a point consisting of the last computed IOP verifier message, and the current Merkle commitment and salt. All results that we present directly extend to this more common approach.

UC-Friendly Completeness. We show that the BCS construction has monotone proofs and unpredictable queries, by building on Lemma 4 (which states that the Merkle commitment scheme has monotone proofs and unpredictable queries). Then by Lemma 1 we conclude that the BCS construction satisfies UC-friendly completeness.

Lemma 10 (informal). $\mathsf{BCS}[\mathsf{IOP}, \mathsf{r}]$ *has monotone proofs and unpredictable queries with error* $\mathsf{k} \cdot (\epsilon_{\mathsf{MT}} + \frac{t_{\mathsf{p}}}{2^{\mathsf{r}}})$ *(ϵ_{MT} is from Lemma 4). By Lemma 1, $\mathsf{BCS}[\mathsf{IOP}, \mathsf{r}]$ has UC-friendly completeness with error (roughly)* $\epsilon_{\mathsf{ARG}} = \ell_{\mathsf{p}} \cdot \mathsf{k} \cdot (\epsilon_{\mathsf{MT}} + \frac{t_{\mathsf{p}}}{2^{\mathsf{r}}})$.

UC-Friendly Zero Knowledge. We prove that the BCS construction satisfies UC-friendly zero knowledge, using a strategy similar to the case of the Micali construction (which is captured in Lemma 8). The proof of the lemma is similar, with the main difference being that we need the UC-friendly hiding property of the Merkle commitment scheme to hold for k commitment-openings pairs rather than a single one.

Lemma 11 (informal). *Let* IOP *be a* k*-round public-coin IOP that has honest-verifier zero knowledge with error* ζ_{IOP}. *Let* ζ_{MT} *be the UC-friendly hiding error in Lemma 5. Then* $\mathsf{BCS}[\mathsf{IOP}, \mathsf{r}]$ *has UC-friendly zero knowledge with error (roughly)* $\zeta_{\mathrm{ARG}} := \ell_{\mathsf{p}} \cdot (\frac{t_{\mathsf{q}} + t_{\mathsf{p}}}{2^{\mathsf{r}}} + \zeta_{\mathrm{IOP}} + \zeta_{\mathsf{MT}})$.

UC-Friendly Knowledge Soundness. The BCS construction, when instantiated with an IOP that is state-restoration knowledge sound (with a straightline extractor), satisfies straightline knowledge soundness in the ROM [BCS16,CY24]. We prove a much stronger statement: the BCS construction satisfies UC-friendly knowledge soundness.

Lemma 12 (informal). *Let* IOP *be an IOP with straightline state-restoration knowledge soundness with error* κ_{sr}. *Let* κ_{MT} *be the UC-friendly extraction error in Lemma 6. Then* BCS[IOP, r] *has UC-friendly knowledge soundness with error (roughly)* $\kappa_{ARG} = \ell_v \cdot (\kappa_{sr} + \kappa_{MT})$.

We prove Lemma 12 similarly to Lemma 9, making use of the fact that in that analysis we can reduce to the state-restoration knowledge soundness of the underlying PCP. In the case of the BCS construction, we reduce to the IOP version of state-restoration knowledge soundness. We again have to ensure that the adversary cannot use the simulation oracle in order to obtain an advantage, and an argument similar to that in Lemma 9 readily establishes that.

Conclusion. Lemma 10, Lemma 11, and Lemma 12 together show that the BCS construction satisfies UC-friendly completeness, UC-friendly zero knowledge, and UC-friendly knowledge soundness, provided that the underlying IOP is honest-verifier zero knowledge and (straightline) state-restoration knowledge sound. In turn, Lemma 3 implies that, under these conditions, the BCS construction is unconditionally UC-secure. Both steps provide concrete security bounds, leading to an overall concrete security bound for the UC-security of the BCS construction. This directly shows that existing zkSNARKs constructed from (state-restoration) knowledge sound and honest-verifier zero knowledge IOPs (e.g. [BCR+19, BBHR19] and similar constructions) are unconditionally UC-secure.

2.6   Adaptive Corruptions and Strong UC-Friendly Properties

The previous sections consider UC-security against *non-adaptive* corruptions. Here we outline how we additionally achieve UC-security against *adaptive* corruptions.

In the setting of UC-security against adaptive corruptions, the environment (through the adversary) may corrupt parties at *any time* during the protocol execution. When a party becomes corrupted, it reveals to the environment its private randomness (i.e., its private state). In the real-world the corrupted party directly reveals its own private randomness, while in the ideal-world the UC simulator must somehow sample randomness that "explains" a posteriori the past behavior of the party (possibly up to some error). Specifically, the challenge is that this randomness must be consistent with the input-output behavior of the party until this point of the execution. (The environment can send inputs to any party and receive corresponding outputs).

Depending on the role of the corrupted party, simulating such randomness presents different challenges. If the corrupted party is the verifier, simulating its private randomness is easy, since it is the same in both the real-world and ideal-world. In contrast, if the corrupted party is the prover party then simulating its private randomness is more challenging. Indeed, the prover party invokes the proving interface, which is different in the two worlds: (i) in the real-world the proving interface runs the honest argument prover; and (ii) in the ideal-world the proving interface forwards its input to the ideal functionality, which in turn runs the zero knowledge simulator. In the ideal-world then, if the prover party is corrupted, the UC simulator must be able to produce, a posteriori, argument prover randomness that is consistent with all argument strings produced by the proving interface so far. More explicitly, the UC simulator must output randomness that the honest argument prover would have used to produce the argument strings that were output by the prover party thus far, *despite those argument strings being sampled by the zero knowledge simulator*. These additional capabilities must be explicitly accounted for in the UC-friendly properties.

Therefore, inspired by [LR22a], we consider "strong" variants of the UC-friendly properties in Sect. 2.2, which we obtain by adding a *corruption oracle* that returns the (possibly reconstructed) prover randomness used by the proving oracle of the game. Once the corruption oracle has been queried, we forbid further queries to the corruption oracle (and to the proving oracle), modeling how in the UC-security experiment control of a newly corrupted party (in this case the prover party) is relinquished to the environment.

By using these strong properties, Lemma 3 can be extended to provide emulation in the setting of adaptive corruptions.

Lemma 13 (informal). *If the non-interactive argument* ARG *in Lemma 3 satisfies strong UC-friendly completeness, strong UC-friendly zero knowledge, and strong UC-friendly knowledge soundness, the conclusion of Lemma 3 holds even in the setting of adaptive corruptions (with the same error bound).*

The challenge is to show that the additional capability conferred to the adversary (by the new corruption oracles) in these strong UC-friendly experiments is not a problem. We focus on the steps required to satisfy these properties for the Micali construction; the strategy for the BCS construction is similar.

Strong UC-Friendly Completeness. Strong UC-friendly completeness is, conveniently, already implied by the three properties of perfect completeness, monotone proofs, and unpredictable queries, with the same error bounds. In other words, the Micali construction has strong UC-friendly completeness for free.

Lemma 14 (informal). Micali[PCP, r] *has strong UC-friendly completeness with the same error as in Lemma 7.*

Strong UC-Friendly Zero Knowledge. Establishing strong UC-friendly zero knowledge for the Micali construction is more involved. We show that if the PCP underlying the Micali construction satisfies a natural notion that we call strong honest-verifier zero knowledge, the Micali construction satisfies strong UC-friendly zero knowledge.

Lemma 15 (informal). *Let* PCP *be a strong honest-verifier zero knowledge PCP with error* ζ_{PCP}. *Then* Micali[PCP, r] *has strong UC-friendly zero knowledge with the same error as in Lemma 8.*

The strong UC-friendly zero knowledge simulator is required to sample randomness that "explains" a simulated Micali argument string. This randomness has three components: (i) the PCP prover randomness; (ii) the Merkle commitment randomness; and (iii) the Fiat–Shamir randomness.

The strong honest-verifier zero knowledge property of the PCP is used to reconstruct the first piece of randomness. Roughly, strong honest-verifier zero knowledge PCPs are honest-verifier zero knowledge PCPs where the simulator additionally can, a posteriori, sample randomness that "explains" the sampled PCP local view. (Later, in Sect. 2.6, we show PCPs that satisfy this notion). In order to reconstruct the Merkle commitment randomness, we show that Merkle commitment schemes satisfy a notion of strong UC-friendly hiding (briefly, this property extends Definition 7 with a corruption oracle). Finally, the Fiat–Shamir randomness is included in the Micali argument string, and thus the simulator has no need to reconstruct it. The combination of these three observations yields Lemma 15.

Strong UC-Friendly Knowledge Soundness. Showing strong UC-friendly knowledge soundness for the Micali construction also requires some additional work. We strengthen the UC-friendly extraction property for the Merkle commitment scheme by adding a corruption oracle, and prove that the Merkle commitment scheme satisfies this stronger property.

Lemma 16. MT *has strong UC-friendly extraction with error (roughly)* $\kappa_{\mathsf{MT}} = \frac{3}{2} \cdot \frac{(t_q + 2\ell_p|)^2}{2^\lambda} + \frac{2k(d+1) \cdot (t_q + 2\ell_p|)}{2^\lambda}$.

Lemma 16 directly implies Lemma 6. Our proof of Lemma 16 closely follows the proof of multi-extraction for the Merkle commitment scheme in [CY24], adapted to reflect the additional programming capabilities of the adversary and the presence of simulation and corruption oracles.

We adapt the proof of Lemma 9 to rely on strong UC-friendly extraction, and directly show that the Micali construction satisfies strong UC-friendly knowledge soundness. (Without any additional requirements on the underlying PCP).

Lemma 17 (informal). *Let* PCP *be a knowledge sound PCP with error* κ_{PCP}. *Then* Micali[PCP, r] *has strong UC-friendly knowledge sound with the same error as in Lemma 9.*

Conclusion

UC-Secure zkSNARKs from PCPs. The properties required of the underlying PCP are the ones that one would naturally expect to need for the adaptive UC-security of the Micali construction. Yet to our knowledge the PCP literature does not explicitly provide an off-the-shelf PCP with these properties.

We address this gap, by revisiting a transformation in [IW14] that combines a PCP and a zero knowledge PCP of proximity (PCPP) to obtain a zero knowledge PCP. We show that: (a) if the given PCP is knowledge sound then the resulting PCP is also knowledge sound; and (b) if the PCPP is strong honest-verifier zero knowledge then the resulting PCP is also strong honest-verifier zero knowledge. Then we construct a strong honest-verifier zero knowledge PCPP, and apply the transformation to any knowledge sound PCP (e.g., [BFLS91]) and this PCPP, concluding the proof of Theorem 1.

UC-Secure zkSNARKs from IOPs. As mentioned before, we can prove analogues of Lemmas 15 and 17 for the BCS construction.

Lemma 18 (informal). *Let* IOP *be an IOP.*

- *If* IOP *is strong honest-verifier zero knowledge IOP with error* ζ_{IOP}, *then* BCS[IOP, r] *is strong UC-friendly zero knowledge with the same error as in Lemma 11.*
- *If* IOP *is a state-restoration knowledge sound IOP with error* κ_{IOP}, *then* BCS[IOP, r] *is strong UC-friendly knowledge sound with the same error as in Lemma 12.*

By inspection, we see that many IOPs used in practice satisfy these properties, and thus lead to UC-secure zkSNARKs. We sketch how the masked univariate sumcheck protocol [BCR+19, BCF+17], a core building block of many honest-verifier zero knowledge IOPs is strong honest-verifier zero knowledge. Let $\hat{p}$ be a polynomial, which the verifier has oracle access to, and $H \subseteq \mathbb{F}$ be a domain. The unmasked univariate sumcheck protocol allows the verifier to check that $\sum_{h \in H} \hat{p}(h) = \beta$ for some claimed value β. In the masked version, to achieve zero knowledge, the prover sends (as an oracle) a masking polynomial $\hat{q}$ and the value $\beta' = \sum_{h \in H} \hat{q}(h)$, the verifier samples a challenge c and then both parties run a unmasked univariate sumcheck to check the claim $\sum_{h \in H} (c \cdot \hat{p} + \hat{q})(h) = c \cdot \beta + \beta'$, which ultimately requires the verifier to query $\hat{p}, \hat{q}$ at a single location. The strong honest verifier zero knowledge simulator can reconstruct the prover randomness by sampling $\hat{q}$ uniformly at random, conditioned on the sum equaling β' and on the value of the query to $\hat{q}$ as determined during the honest verifier zero knowledge simulation phase. (The conditioning consists of linear constraints on the coefficients, so this sampling can be done efficiently).

Acknowledgments. We thank Ran Canetti, Megan Chen, Anna Lysyanskaya and Leah Namisa Rosenbloom for insightful discussions on the UCGS framework, the ARG (i.e., NIZKPoK) ideal functionality, and global random oracles. We also thank Francesco Intoci, Giorgio Seguini, Kien Tuong Truong, Eylon Yogev for valuable feedback and suggestions on earlier drafts of this paper. The authors are partially supported by the Ethereum Foundation.

References

[AGRS24] Abdolmaleki, B., Glaeser, N., Ramacher, S., Slamanig, D.: Circuit-succinct universally composable NIZKs with updatable CRS. In: Proceedings of the 37th IEEE Computer Security Foundations Symposium, CSF 2024 (2024)

[ARS20] Abdolmaleki, B., Ramacher, S., Slamanig, D.: Lift-and-Shift: obtaining simulation extractable subversion and updatable SNARKs generically. In: Proceedings of the 27th ACM Conference on Computer and Communications Security, CCS 2020, pp. 1987–2005 (2020)

[BBHR19] Ben-Sasson, E., Bentov, I., Horesh, Y., Riabzev, M.: Scalable zero knowledge with no trusted setup. In: Boldyreva, A., Micciancio, D. (eds.) CRYPTO 2019. LNCS, vol. 11694, pp. 701–732. Springer, Cham (2019). https://doi.org/10.1007/978-3-030-26954-8_23

[BCF+17] Ben-Sasson, E., Chiesa, A., Forbes, M.A., Gabizon, A., Riabzev, M., Spooner, N.: Zero knowledge protocols from succinct constraint detection. In: Kalai, Y., Reyzin, L. (eds.) TCC 2017. LNCS, vol. 10678, pp. 172–206. Springer, Cham (2017). https://doi.org/10.1007/978-3-319-70503-3_6

[BCH+20] Badertscher, C., Canetti, R., Hesse, J., Tackmann, B., Zikas, V.: Universal composition with global subroutines: capturing global setup within plain UC. In: Pass, R., Pietrzak, K. (eds.) TCC 2020. LNCS, vol. 12552, pp. 1–30. Springer, Cham (2020). https://doi.org/10.1007/978-3-030-64381-2_1

[BCR+19] Ben-Sasson, E., Chiesa, A., Riabzev, M., Spooner, N., Virza, M., Ward, N.P.: Aurora: transparent succinct arguments for R1CS. In: Ishai, Y., Rijmen, V. (eds.) EUROCRYPT 2019. LNCS, vol. 11476, pp. 103–128. Springer, Cham (2019). https://doi.org/10.1007/978-3-030-17653-2_4

[BCS16] Ben-Sasson, E., Chiesa, A., Spooner, N.: Interactive oracle proofs. In: Hirt, M., Smith, A. (eds.) TCC 2016. LNCS, vol. 9986, pp. 31–60. Springer, Heidelberg (2016). https://doi.org/10.1007/978-3-662-53644-5_2

[BFLS91] Babai, L., Fortnow, L., Levin, L.A., Szegedy, M.: Checking computations in polylogarithmic time. In: Proceedings of the 23rd Annual ACM Symposium on Theory of Computing, STOC 1991, pp. 21–32 (1991)

[BS21] Baghery, K., Sedaghat, M.: TIRAMISU: black-box simulation extractable NIZKs in the updatable CRS model. In: Conti, M., Stevens, M., Krenn, S. (eds.) CANS 2021. LNCS, vol. 13099, pp. 531–551. Springer, Cham (2021). https://doi.org/10.1007/978-3-030-92548-2_28

[Can01] Canetti, R.: Universally composable security: a new paradigm for cryptographic protocols. In: Proceedings of the 42nd Annual IEEE Symposium on Foundations of Computer Science, FOCS 2001, pp. 136–145 (2001)

[Can20] Canetti, R.: Universally composable security. J. ACM **67**, 1–94 (2020)

[CDG+18] Camenisch, J., Drijvers, M., Gagliardoni, T., Lehmann, A., Neven, G.: The wonderful world of global random oracles. In: Nielsen, J.B., Rijmen, V. (eds.) EUROCRYPT 2018. LNCS, vol. 10820, pp. 280–312. Springer, Cham (2018). https://doi.org/10.1007/978-3-319-78381-9_11

[CDPW07] Canetti, R., Dodis, Y., Pass, R., Walfish, S.: Universally composable security with global setup. In: Vadhan, S.P. (ed.) TCC 2007. LNCS, vol. 4392, pp. 61–85. Springer, Heidelberg (2007). https://doi.org/10.1007/978-3-540-70936-7_4

[CF24] Chiesa, A., Fenzi, G.: zkSNARKs in the ROM with unconditional UC-security. Cryptology ePrint Archive, Paper 2023/724 (2024). https://eprint.iacr.org/2024/724

[CJS14] Canetti, R., Jain, A., Scafuro, A.: Practical UC security with a Global Random Oracle. In: Proceedings of the 21st ACM Conference on Computer and Communications Security, CCS 2014, pp. 597–608 (2014)

[CMS19] Chiesa, A., Manohar, P., Spooner, N.: Succinct arguments in the quantum random oracle model. In: Hofheinz, D., Rosen, A. (eds.) TCC 2019. LNCS, vol. 11892, pp. 1–29. Springer, Cham (2019). https://doi.org/10.1007/978-3-030-36033-7_1

[CY24] Chiesa, A., Yogev, E.: Building Cryptographic Proofs from Hash Functions (2024). https://github.com/hash-based-snargs-book

[DDO+01] De Santis, A., Di Crescenzo, G., Ostrovsky, R., Persiano, G., Sahai, A.: Robust non-interactive zero knowledge. In: Kilian, J. (ed.) CRYPTO 2001. LNCS, vol. 2139, pp. 566–598. Springer, Heidelberg (2001). https://doi.org/10.1007/3-540-44647-8_33

[Fis05] Fischlin, M.: Communication-efficient non-interactive proofs of knowledge with online extractors. In: Shoup, V. (ed.) CRYPTO 2005. LNCS, vol. 3621, pp. 152–168. Springer, Heidelberg (2005). https://doi.org/10.1007/11535218_10

[GKO+23] Ganesh, C., Kondi, Y., Orlandi, C., Pancholi, M., Takahashi, A., Tschudi, D.: Witness-succinct universally-composable SNARKs. In: Hazay, C., Stam, M. (eds.) Proceedings of the 42nd Annual International Conference on Theory and Application of Cryptographic Techniques. EUROCRYPT 2023, pp. 315–346. Springer, Cham (2023). https://doi.org/10.1007/978-3-031-30617-4_11

[Gro06] Groth, J.: Simulation-sound NIZK proofs for a practical language and constant size group signatures. In: Proceedings of the 12th International Conference on Theory and Application of Cryptology and Information Security, ASIACRYPT 2006, pp. 444–459 (2006). http://www0.cs.ucl.ac.uk/staff/J.Groth/NIZKGroupSignFull.pdf

[IW14] Ishai, Y., Weiss, M.: Probabilistically checkable proofs of proximity with zero-knowledge. In: Lindell, Y. (ed.) TCC 2014. LNCS, vol. 8349, pp. 121–145. Springer, Heidelberg (2014). https://doi.org/10.1007/978-3-642-54242-8_6

[Ks22] Kondi, Y., Shelat, A.: Improved straight-line extraction in the random oracle model with applications to signature aggregation. In: Agrawal, S., Lin, D. (eds.) Advances in Cryptology – ASIACRYPT 2022. ASIACRYPT 2022. LNCS, vol. 13792, pp. 279–309. Springer, Cham (2023). https://doi.org/10.1007/978-3-031-22966-4_10

[KZM+15] Kosba, A., et al.: C∅C∅: a framework for building composable zero-knowledge proofs. Cryptology ePrint Archive, Paper 2015/1093 (2015)

[LR22a] Lysyanskaya, A., Rosenbloom, L.N.: Efficient and universally composable non-interactive zero-knowledge proofs of knowledge with security against adaptive corruptions. Cryptology ePrint Archive, Paper 2022/1484 (2022)

[LR22b] Lysyanskaya, A., Rosenbloom, L.N.: Universally composable Σ-protocols in the "Global Random-Oracle Model". In: Proceedings of the 20th Theory of Cryptography Conference, TCC'2022, pp. 203–233 (2022)

[Mic00] Micali, S.: Computationally sound proofs. SIAM J. Comput. **30**(4), 1253–1298 (2000). Preliminary version appeared in FOCS 1994

The Brave New World of Global Generic Groups and UC-Secure Zero-Overhead SNARKs

Jan Bobolz[1], Pooya Farshim[2,3], Markulf Kohlweiss[1,4],
and Akira Takahashi[5(✉)]

[1] University of Edinburgh, Edinburgh, UK
[2] IOG, Zurich, Switzerland
[3] Durham University, Durham, UK
[4] IOG, Edinburgh, UK
[5] JPMorgan AI Research and AlgoCRYPT CoE, New York, USA
takahashi.akira.58s@gmail.com

Abstract. The universal composability (UC) model provides strong security guarantees for protocols used in arbitrary contexts. While these guarantees are highly desirable, in practice, schemes with a standalone proof of security, such as the Groth16 proof system, are preferred. This is because UC security typically comes with undesirable *overhead*, sometimes making UC-secure schemes significantly less efficient than their standalone counterparts.

We establish the UC security of Groth16 without any significant overhead. In the spirit of global random oracles, we design a *global (restricted) observable generic group* functionality that models a natural notion of observability: computations that trace back to group elements derived from generators of other sessions are observable. This notion turns out to be surprisingly subtle to formalize. We provide a general framework for proving protocols secure in the presence of global generic groups, which we then apply to Groth16.

1 Introduction

Composable treatments of cryptosystems measure the security of the system under arbitrary attacks relative to those on an ideal version of the system. Various composition theorems then show that if these systems are sufficiently close, the ideal system can be safely replaced by the real system in a wide variety of contexts. A notable framework that formalizes this approach is that of Universal Composability (UC) [17,18], which has been widely used in the literature, although other approaches also exist [13,42,50,54].

Unfortunately, to date such composable treatments of security due to their complexity often result in complex and less efficient protocols. This is somewhat dissatisfying as it is exactly simple and efficient cryptosystems (proven in stand-alone models of security) that are widely deployed and thus in need

E. Boyle and M. Mahmoody (Eds.): TCC 2024, LNCS 15364, pp. 90–124, 2025.
https://doi.org/10.1007/978-3-031-78011-0_4

of composable security guarantees. This state of affairs necessitates composable treatment of practical cryptosystems with minimal, preferably no, overhead.

A notable example is that of succinct non-interactive arguments of knowledge (SNARKs), which exactly fall into this gap between composition and usage in complex environments: practical SNARKs are either analyzed under property-based definitions, or else need to be modified or compiled, which increase overheads both in terms of proof sizes and prover/verifier time. Such overheads potentially prevent adoption in practice.

Practical SNARKs are typically proven secure in idealized models of computation, such as the random-oracle model or the generic-group model.[1]

While simple and elegant, these proof techniques do not necessarily lend themselves to composable treatments. The central conflict is that both systems' security proofs require exclusive access to the same idealized resource. For instance, it may be that the extractors for two SNARK systems may want to program $\mathcal{H}(0)$ to different conflicting values, or that the knowledge extractor for one system needs to observe all random oracle queries, while that for another needs to keep its oracle queries/programming secret for an indistinguishable simulation [26,53]. In such scenarios, we cannot say anything meaningful about the security of either SNARK when composed with the other.

The examples above demonstrate the need for appropriate formalization of idealized models that are compatible with composability. Here we adopt Canetti's UC framework [17,18]. For random oracles, this question has been largely solved in the form of the *restricted observable global random oracle* functionality [15,21], as well as its programmable version $\mathcal{G}\text{-rpoRO}$ [15]. The functionality $\mathcal{G}\text{-roRO}$ works like a globally accessible random oracle and is not exclusively controlled by any UC simulator (as would be the case for a local version). Instead, $\mathcal{G}\text{-roRO}$ implements an interface through which UC simulators can *partially* control the functionality in the form of observability: the simulator for the protocol running in session *sid* is able to observe all random oracle queries $\mathcal{H}(sid, \cdot)$ prefixed with *sid* that are made in protocol sessions $sid' \neq sid$. ($\mathcal{G}\text{-rpoRO}$ comes with an analogous programming interface.)

With this mechanism, the single random-oracle resource can be shared among multiple protocols in a way that still gives appropriate control over the resource to the UC simulator (observations, or, in the case of $\mathcal{G}\text{-rpoRO}$, programming) to enable UC simulation, and in turn composition with other protocols.

In this case, every protocol session *sid* gets its own hash prefix *sid*, and while every protocol session is using the same resource $\mathcal{G}\text{-roRO}$, they can do so with sufficient domain separation so as to not interfere with each other. As a result, we can prove many proof systems and SNARK constructions UC-secure in the presence of $\mathcal{G}\text{-roRO}$ [26,38,52,53].

In contrast to RO-based proof systems, the state of affairs for systems whose proofs of knowledge extraction rely on idealized groups is much less clear. For example, the popular Groth16 SNARK [40], has a security proof that is "close" to

---

[1] Alternatively, they are proven using knowledge assumptions or in the algebraic-group model (AGM).

UC in the sense it has the prerequisite simulation-extractability and straight-line extraction properties. Despite this, its extraction strategy is not easily compatible with composable frameworks such as the UC framework.

This has led to the strategy of applying some transformation or compilation to SNARKs in order to render their extraction strategy UC-compatible. The cost, however, is increased overhead: one has to accept a noticeable loss in computational efficiency [38], or sometimes even forgo succinctness [48].

Our goal is to avoid such overheads and prove practical SNARKs such as Groth16 secure in a composable framework as-is, while using their native extraction strategies. For Groth16-style SNARKs specifically, we have standalone (non-composable) analyses in the GGM [40], in the AGM [5,36], and under knowledge assumptions [8,41]. However, it is unclear how these analyses apply to a composable setting. Even worse, in contrast to the random-oracle model, it is not even a settled question how to model composable versions of group-related idealized resources. One may consider the following existing approaches:

1. Prove Groth16 secure in the $\mathcal{F}$-GG-hybrid model, where $\mathcal{F}$-GG (e.g., [30]) is simply an ideal functionality implementing a (local) generic group.

2. Prove Groth16 secure in the UC-AGM [1] framework, which is a composable version of the algebraic-group model. UC-AGM is implemented as a modification of the UC framework whereby adversaries are required to output the discrete-logarithm representations of the group elements that they output in terms of input elements they have received so far.

3. Prove Groth16 secure through [46], which is a composable version of knowledge assumptions. It is implemented as a variant of the Constructive Cryptography [54] framework, where all parties are forced to register the discrete-logarithm representations in terms of their input elements with a global registry whenever they output a group element.

The first option is certainly feasible and a Groth16 proof in the $\mathcal{F}$-GG-hybrid model would be considered a folklore adaptation of the standalone Groth16 generic-group security proof [40]. However, the interpretation of $\mathcal{F}$-GG in practice is that every instance of Groth16 (and any other protocol) needs its own independent (generic) group. Of course, this is far from practice, where a few standard groups (such as BLS12-381) are shared among all sessions for many protocols. It is also not desirable from a design standpoint, as the building blocks of complex protocols usually share the same group for compatibility reasons.

The second option, using the UC-AGM [1], is more reasonable: multiple UC-AGM protocols can share the same group. One of the central conflicts that arise when composing multiple protocols over the same group occurs when group elements output by one protocol or session are used as input to another protocol or session. The outputting protocol is interested in hiding the element's discrete-logarithm representation from the environment (e.g., as part of a simulation strategy), while the receiving protocol is interested in learning the element's discrete-logarithm representation (e.g., for proof of knowledge extraction).

This conflict manifests in two different ways in the UC-AGM. First, the *environment* in the UC-AGM is *not* required to output a discrete-logarithm representation when it provides input to honest parties, say an honest Groth16 verifier. For our interests, this means that the environment can submit a Groth16 proof to the ideal functionality $\mathcal{F}$-NIZK for verification without having to provide a representation. The lack of a representation makes it impossible for the UC simulator to extract a witness, even if the proof was computed honestly by the environment. As a consequence, the UC-AGM is too lenient on the environment, making it unsuitable for *non-interactive* proof systems. In particular, it is unclear how to use it to prove Groth16 UC-secure. Second, the *adversary* in the UC-AGM *is* required to output representations whenever it provides input to any functionality (e.g., sending a network message). This leads to situations where the framework is *too strict*: the adversary may want to use a group element output by one protocol to attack another protocol, but because the adversary (usually) does not know an appropriate discrete-logarithm representation, it is prohibited from using the group element. This means that the framework effectively forbids adversaries from mounting cross-session attacks, meaning taking a group element from one session/protocol to mount an attack against another session/protocol. As a consequence, the UC-AGM is not able to adequately model arbitrary environment/attacker behavior, which is a major downside. The original UC-AGM paper discusses and explores the shortcomings of the AGM when it comes to composability [1, Section 1.1], noting that cross-session attacks seem to be an inherent limitation of the AGM rather than a modeling artifact of the UC-AGM.

The third option [46] is similar to the UC-AGM in spirit in that it models algebraic behavior. While [46] is highly configurable and supports a range of different settings, the authors identify inherent conflicts when it comes to composing multiple knowledge assumptions, which roughly correspond to cross-session attacks mentioned above. They conclude that group reuse between multiple protocols remains an open challenge.

This leaves open the question of formulating an adequate framework for composable treatment of security which (1) permits modeling multiple protocols using the same group, (2) does not unnaturally restrict the environment's/adversary's ability to take elements output by one protocol, optionally operate on them, and use the result to attack another protocol, and (3) is suitable to prove modern SNARKs in idealized models for groups, such as Groth16, secure.

1.1 Our Contributions

Driven by the fact that the UC-AGM framework (as well as the work of [46] which follows a similar approach to the AGM) have inherent composability shortcomings, we turn our attention to the generic-group model. We propose a new ideal functionality $\mathcal{G}$-oGG (Sect. 3), in the standard UC framework without modifications, that formalizes access to a *restricted observable global generic (bilinear) group* resource. Similar to its random-oracle counterpart [15,21], $\mathcal{G}$-oGG works like a globally accessible generic group, but additionally offers an observability interface, which allows simulators, based on domain separation, to observe certain group operations. $\mathcal{G}$-oGG allows for group reuse among multiple protocols, and it does not restrict the environment from using group elements output by one protocol as input to another. Additionally, $\mathcal{G}$-oGG naturally features oblivious sampling of group elements with unknown discrete logarithms. As observed in the literature [8,51], this is an important feature of real-world groups, realized, e.g., via hashing into a group [11], and needs to be appropriately reflected in idealized models, particularly in the context of knowledge extraction.

For protocol designers relying on $\mathcal{G}$-oGG, we provide a series of lemmas (Sect. 4) that simplify the process of writing proofs by enabling a transition to a *symbolic* functionality. Symbolic treatment of group exponents is a technique that is at the core of many GGM proofs.

Using our security proof framework, we prove (Sect. 5) that Groth16 UC-realizes the weak ideal functionality $\mathcal{F}$-wNIZK in the presence of $\mathcal{G}$-oGG.[2] We stress that Groth16 is proven secure as-is.

In particular, we achieve UC security without the overhead associated with UC SNARK compilers (e.g., [2,3,6,23,38,48,53]). To the best of our knowledge, (simulation) extractability of Groth16 has been concretely analyzed only in the AGM [5,36], but not in the GGM. Along the way, our analysis (Theorem 1) explicitly provides a concrete upper-bound on the distinguishing advantage of any environment, depending on its query complexity, the size of the group, and the size of the circuit, as well as the simulator query complexity.

Finally, we propose a way (Sect. 6) to deal with composition of protocols sharing a generic group in cases where *some* protocols cannot tolerate their group operations being observed.

1.2 Overview of Our Techniques

The Restricted Observable Global Generic Group Functionality. Observability of generic group operations should be sufficiently broad to allow a UC simulator to extract useful information from the adversary and environment, but it should not allow the environment to learn secret-dependent operations performed by honest parties. This tension goes to the core of compositional proofs: we need to strike a balance between information available to the security proof (UC simulator) for one protocol in a way that does not reveal too much about *other* protocols (UC environment) that would impact *their* security proofs. For random oracles $\mathcal{G}$-roRO, where observability is also used, this balance is easy to achieve via domain separation[3]: hashes of (sid, x) belong to session sid, and they become observable if computed in some session $sid' \neq sid$.

---

[2] Here *weak* refers to the fact that proofs may be re-randomizable, but are otherwise non-malleable. As observed by Kosba et al. [48,49] this weak version suffices in typical applications. As an analogy, many use cases of signatures only require existential unforgeability rather than full-fledged strong unforgeability.

[3] For the reader unfamiliar with domain separation approaches for global UC functionalities, our full version [10] offers an explanation.

While domain separation for random oracles is easily modeled, designing the right domain separation mechanism for generic groups is far less obvious. A natural idea is to implement domain separation for groups via session-specific group generators, by assigning session sid a random generator g_{sid}. Intuitively, all operations done on g_{sid} or group elements derived from it belong to session sid. Operating on elements from a foreign session is deemed "illegal" and such operations are observable. However, compared to random oracles, there are additional difficulties: one can take two group elements g_{sid} and $g_{sid'}$ in two different sessions and meaningfully operate on them. This raises the question of whether cross-session operations such as $g_{sid} + g_{sid'}$ are observable, which session the resulting group element belongs to, and how we keep track of the sessions each group element belongs to.

Roughly speaking, in our approach, $\mathcal{G}$-oGG keeps track of the components of a group element in a symbolic way. Every generator g_{sid} corresponds to a formal (polynomial) variable X_{sid}. A group element such as $g_{sid} + g_{sid'}$ is associated with the polynomial $\mathsf{X}_{sid} + \mathsf{X}_{sid'}$. A group operation in protocol session sid is *illegal* (and hence observable) if the polynomial associated to the operation's result contains any foreign-session variables $\mathsf{X}_{sid'}$ (or a constant term). In other words, operations that involve other sessions' generators (as kept track of via polynomials) are observable. The formalization with polynomials avoids subtle issues with simpler approaches, where an element computed as $g_{sid} + g_{sid'} - g_{sid'}$ is incorrectly associated with both sessions sid and sid', which causes issues with either too much or too little observability.

In the explanation above, every session sid only has a single generator g_{sid}. In our final formulation of $\mathcal{G}$-oGG (Sect. 3), a protocol can simply also call a TOUCH interface on any group element not already belonging to other sessions to declare it as an additional generator for its session. Hence every session can have multiple generators $g_{sid,1}, g_{sid,2}, \ldots$ and the observability mechanism generalizes naturally (the explanation above applies verbatim to the multiple-generator setting).

Cross-Session Element Reuse. Note that in the $\mathcal{G}$-oGG model, the environment/adversary is not restricted in the way it can use group elements. In contrast to the UC-AGM, we allow the environment/adversary to take a group element output by some protocol, and use it to attack another protocol without any restriction. The crucial difference is how the knowledge of discrete logarithms is managed in UC-AGM vs. $\mathcal{G}$-oGG. In the UC-AGM, providing knowledge of discrete logarithms is the task of the environment/adversary. This is unfortunate because we also need to hide certain discrete-logarithm representations from the environment/adversary, e.g., as part of a simulation strategy. Additionally, different protocols have different AGM representation bases, and the environment is typically not able to convert a representation from one basis to another. In the UC-AGM, this leads to the adversary being effectively forbidden to use foreign group elements to attack another protocol.

With $\mathcal{G}$-oGG, there is no burden on the environment/adversary to keep track of representations. The knowledge of discrete-logarithm representations is effectively maintained by $\mathcal{G}$-oGG through observations: certain group operations are observable, and from those observations, anyone can compute (partial[4]) discrete-logarithm representations. As a consequence, the environment/adversary *is* allowed to take group elements from one session and use them to attack another session. The only "restriction" here is that group operations on foreign group elements are *observable*. That "restriction" makes it so protocols have to contend with observability, which makes it harder to prove constructions secure. It does not unnaturally impact the ability of the adversary to execute a wide range of real-world attacks.

Hashing and Oblivious Sampling. The encodings of group elements in our $\mathcal{G}$-oGG functionality belong to fixed sets that are of the same size as the group order. This is a closer modeling of how groups are used in practice (compared to, say, random encoding sets, where one does not even know in advance which of the encodings actually correspond to group elements). Crucially, this choice also allows adversaries and protocols to sample group elements in arbitrary ways, and thus allows us to avoid explicit modeling of oblivious sampling or hashing. (Such modeling is introduced for AGM in [8,51], though to the best of our knowledge not yet ported to UC-AGM.) Fixing the sets of valid group encodings also allows hashing into groups via an independent (possibly global) random oracle functionality in parallel to a group functionality. (And whether or not this hashing is extractable or programmable is left to that functionality [15].) Conveniently, this means that we do not have to explicitly model a "hash-into-group" interface for generic groups: this functionality can be emulated using an external random oracle hashing into the set of valid group encodings.

Embedding Generic Groups into UC. Technically speaking, our $\mathcal{G}$-oGG is simply a *standard* UC functionality. It is *global*, meaning that instead of being a subroutine to a single protocol session, it accepts queries from *all* protocols as well as the environment in arbitrary sessions. For the notion of composability in the presence of global functionalities such as $\mathcal{G}$-oGG, we refer to the UCGS (UC with global subroutines) framework of [4], whose composition theorem shows how to use the *original* UC composition theorem in the presence of global functionalities. (This work also points out certain gaps and shortcomings with the traditional GUC framework [20].) One of the advantages of modeling generic groups as a standard UC global functionality $\mathcal{G}$-oGG is that we do not require any modifications to the UC framework (we simply refer to the UCGS composition theorem for composition in the presence of $\mathcal{G}$-oGG). This is in contrast to other modeling approaches, such as the UC-AGM.

---

[4] "Partial" in the sense that observations are sufficient for the simulator of session *sid* to learn the parts of the representation that pertain to the generators of *sid*; see Sect. 4.3 for the details.

UC-SNARKs Without Overhead. Observable global generic groups are a practical means to study the UC security of efficient constructions. As a concrete application of relevance, we show that the Groth16 SNARK, without any modifications, UC-realizes the weak NIZK functionality $\mathcal{F}$-wNIZK in the $\mathcal{F}$-CRS-hybrid model and in the presence of $\mathcal{G}$-oGG (Theorem 1). To the best of our knowledge, this is the first result to establish the UC security of Groth16 with zero overhead.

Following [48,49], our goal is to UC-realize a slightly relaxed NIZK functionality which allows an adversary to maul an existing proof string π into a new one π^* but for the same statement x. This relaxation is necessary for Groth16 as its proof string can be re-randomized to obtain another valid proof [41]. Crucially, it still remains hard to obtain forged proof π^* for a new statement $x^* \neq x$. We analyze Groth16 as a canonical example due to its popularity in a number of deployed systems, and we believe our analysis should extend to its non-rerandomizable variants such as Groth–Maller [41] and Bowe–Gabizon [12] to show they UC-realize the strong NIZK functionality.

As part of our analysis, we introduce a set of technical lemmas, which provide a reusable template for formal analyses in the presence of global groups. These lemmas essentially allow one to operate with respect to a cleaner global functionality $\mathcal{G}$-oSG that is purely symbolic. In effect, they allow using the Schwartz–Zippel lemma (and in particular extraction of representations of group elements) in the UC setting. In more detail, we introduce a "fully symbolic" counterpart of the aforementioned $\mathcal{G}$-oGG, where every encoded group element maps to a formal polynomial instead of a $\mathbb{Z}_p$ element. In this way, one can guarantee perfect domain separation by ruling out exceptional events in which two group operations occurring in different sessions accidentally output the same group element. Our general lemma shows that one can switch to a hybrid UC experiment in the presence of the symbolic generic group functionality $\mathcal{G}$-oSG accepting a negligible loss in security.

Moreover, we provide a lemma that introduces a routine which makes a given *simulator* fully symbolic as well. Typically, a simulator for UC-NIZK uses secret random exponents (known as simulation trapdoor) to simulate the CRS and proof strings. After invoking this lemma, one can treat these random exponents as formal variables. We then apply these lemmas to analyze UC security of Groth16. The combination of our technical lemmas allows for clean and modular analysis of Groth16 in the UC setting. In particular, once we view all the random exponents in the current session as formal variables, we can reuse the existing weak simulation-extractability analysis of Groth16 [5] almost as is.

Composition when Unobservability is Required. The issue with using group elements from one protocol to attack another (as described above) in the UC-AGM is not unnatural, but rather points to an inherent conflict for composability in algebraic/generic group settings. $\mathcal{G}$-oGG tackles this issue not by restricting the environment (and hence the space of allowed attacks), but by making security proofs harder, essentially erring on the safe side. It does not, on its own, solve the inherent conflict. The observation rules of $\mathcal{G}$-oGG are well-suited for applications that can largely follow domain separation, such as SNARKs, where the prover only operates on CRS elements. However, in other protocols, when a party applies a secret to group elements *not* necessarily in its session, those operations are observable and the secret is effectively leaked. For example, a party in the ElGamal encryption scheme[5] would receive a ciphertext (c_1, c_2) from the environment and compute the plaintext $c_2 - sk \cdot c_1$. If the environment supplies c_1 that does not belong to the ElGamal protocol's session (e.g., a Groth16 CRS element), then the operation $sk \cdot c_1$ becomes observable, leaking the secret key to everyone. This is an inherent conflict with composition. The ElGamal protocol is interested in having unobservable operations on foreign elements. Conflicting with this, Groth16 *requires* that operations on its CRS by ElGamal are observable. Concretely, if decryption were afforded unobservability, then the decryption operation can effectively be used to compute a part of a valid Groth16 proof that the Groth16 UC simulator cannot trace, making extraction impossible.

We suggest a way to resolve this conflict by adapting a slight tweak to UC composition proofs. On a high level, when proving the composition of ElGamal and Groth16, one would *first* replace $\mathcal{F}$-wNIZK by the concrete Groth16 protocol. After that, observability is not needed anymore (as it is only used by the Groth16 simulator in the ideal world, not by the real-world protocol itself) and can be removed (conceptually). *Then*, one would replace $\mathcal{F}$-Enc by ElGamal. This replacement now happens in a setting where observation does not exist anymore. We sketch this approach in Sect. 6, but leave details for future work.

Painting the big picture, attacks involving cross-session use of group elements in the UC-AGM are partially disallowed, making it easy to prove a wide range of applications secure but restricting the class of covered attacks. Cross-session attacks are fully allowed with $\mathcal{G}$-oGG, meaning that we allow for all possible attacks, but such cross-session use results in observable operations, which rules out certain applications. However, this issue is mitigated with the approach described in Sect. 6. So overall, we get the best of both worlds: We can prove composition for a wide range of applications, in a model that does not restrict the environment.

Paper Organization. The rest of the paper is organized as follows. Section 2 summarizes technical preliminaries. In Sect. 3, we formally introduce the restricted observable global generic group functionality $\mathcal{G}$-oGG. Section 4 states useful technical lemmas which provide a reusable template for formal analyses in the presence of global groups. In Sect. 5, we formally analyze UC security of the Groth16 SNARK in the presence of $\mathcal{G}$-oGG. Section 6 provides a tweak to UC composition proofs when unobservability is required. We conclude the paper with future work suggestions in Sect. 7.

---

[5] ElGamal is not a UC-secure encryption scheme. We are using it here for the sake of simplicity of illustration. The same principle applies to CCA2 secure variants of ElGamal, such as Cramer-Shoup [29].

1.3   Related Work

Criticism and Alternatives to the Generic-Group Model. The generic-group model (GGM) is not without criticism. First, similar to random oracles, one can prove (artificial) schemes secure in the GGM that become provably insecure when instantiated with any concrete group [32]. Furthermore, applying the GGM in certain (non-generic) scenarios can lead to spurious security proofs [62].

In addition, the GGM only provides security guarantees against *generic* adversaries. However, we know that the fastest attacks on the discrete-logarithm problem in elliptic curve pairing groups make use of the specific structure of $\mathbb{G}_t$ via index calculus methods. As a result, the guarantees provided by the GGM are somewhat less meaningful. The semi-generic group model [43] addresses this weakness by modeling $\mathbb{G}_t$ as non-generic (while $\mathbb{G}_1, \mathbb{G}_2$ are still generic groups). In practice, even with index-calculus methods, breaking the discrete-logarithm assumption (or any reasonable related assumption) is infeasible. So while there is some speed-up between the generic and non-generic attackers, the speed-up is not meaningful for suitably chosen pairing groups.

Finally, obliviously sampling a group element (or hashing into the group) is a widely used feature, which is often not supported by the GGM, causing issues [8,51]. The generic-group modeling in our paper enables oblivious sampling as discussed above.

Overall, while there is criticism of the generic-group model, it is still widely used as a useful tool to establish security guarantees in the absence of stronger formal evidence.

The algebraic-group model (AGM) [36] was born out of criticism of the GGM. Security in the AGM is established with respect to a restricted class of *algebraic* adversaries, which are required to always supply the (discrete-log) representations of their output group elements in terms of the input elements that they have seen so far. This means that intuitively, because an AGM adversary gets to see proper group element encodings rather than random ones, the AGM is a weaker (less severely restricting) model than the GGM (though depending on the exact AGM/GGM formalization, this intuition is not necessarily formally true [64]). The AGM does not support oblivious hashing, but can be extended to do so [51].

The UC-AGM [1] excludes cross-session group element attacks, as explained above. For this reason, despite the AGM *usually* being the better model than the GGM, the same does not seem to hold true when it comes to questions of composability.

UC-Secure Proof Systems. Although a number of papers study generic transformations that lift NIZK proof systems in the stand-alone setting into a UC-secure one [2,3,6,23,38,48,53], they end up with proof sizes that are linear in the witness size, sacrificing succinctness, or else introduce significant overheads in the proving time. To realize the ideal functionality, these UC-lifting compilers typically output a proof system satisfying the simulation-extractability property [31,35,39,59]. While Groth16 and its variants already have proof of simulation-extractability in the GGM/AGM [5,12,41], their implications to composable security have been unclear prior to our work. So far, there is little work on SNARKs being UC-secure as is, i.e., without having to apply a transformation, which is the state of the art. The exception to this is a recent concurrent work [26] that proves Micali's SNARK [56] and certain IOP-based SNARKs obtained via the BCS transform [9] proven UC-secure in the presence of $\mathcal{G}$-rpoRO, i.e., in the random-oracle setting.

2   Preliminaries

2.1   Notation

Functions and Pseudocode. For a (partial) function $\tau : A \rightarrow B$, define the image $\mathrm{im}(\tau) = \{y \mid \exists x : \tau(x) = y\} \subseteq B$ and the domain $\mathrm{dom}(\tau) = \{x \mid \tau(x) \neq \bot\} \subseteq A$. We write "assert ϕ" as a shorthand for "if $\neg\phi$, then return $\bot$". List concatenation is denoted by colon $(A : B)$.

Sets and Polynomials. For subsets $A, B \subseteq R$ of a ring R, $r \in R$, define $A + B := \{a + b \mid a \in A, b \in B\}$, $r \cdot A := \{r \cdot a \mid a \in A\}$, and $A \cdot B := \{a \cdot b \mid a \in A, b \in B\}$. Still, $A^n = A \times A \times \cdots \times A$ denotes the n-fold Cartesian product.

We denote scalars by lower-case letters (e.g., $a \in \mathbb{Z}_p$), and formal variables/polynomials in sans-serif font (e.g., $\mathsf{A} \in \mathbb{Z}_p[\mathsf{X}]$). We also consider polynomials and variable with negative degree, e.g. $2\mathsf{X} + 3\mathsf{X}^{-1} \in \mathbb{Z}_p[\mathsf{X}, \mathsf{X}^{-1}]$. Sets or maps involving scalars are generally written as S, if they involve polynomials, they are written as S. For a Var a set of variables, we let $\mathsf{Var}^{\pm 1} := \mathsf{Var} \cup \mathsf{Var}^{-1}$, where Var^{-1} is a set containing the inversion of variables in Var.

Let R be a ring of polynomials, $\mathsf{A}, \mathsf{B} \in \mathsf{R}$, and $\mathsf{L} \subseteq \mathsf{R}$ be a finite list of ring elements. Then $\langle \mathsf{L} \rangle_{\mathsf{R}} = \sum_{\mathsf{x} \in \mathsf{L}} \mathsf{x} \cdot \mathsf{R} \subseteq \mathsf{R}$ is the ideal generated by L.

Lemma 1 (Schwartz–Zippel). *Let $\mathbb{F}$ be a finite field, let $\mathsf{Var} = (\mathsf{X}_1, \ldots, \mathsf{X}_n)$ be a list of formal variables. Let $\mathsf{f} \in \mathbb{F}[\mathsf{Var}]$, $\mathsf{f} \neq 0$. Then*

$$\Pr[\mathsf{f}(x_1, \ldots, x_n) = 0] \leq \deg(\mathsf{f})/p \ ,$$

where the probability is over $x_1, \ldots, x_n \xleftarrow{\$} \mathbb{F}$.

Lemma 2 (Schwartz–Zippel for Laurent polynomials). *Let $\mathbb{F}$ be a finite field of order $p > 1$, let $\mathsf{Var} = (\mathsf{Y}_1, \ldots, \mathsf{Y}_n)$ be a list of formal variables. Let $\mathsf{f} \in \mathbb{F}[\mathsf{Var}^{\pm 1}]$ be a Laurent polynomial, $\mathsf{f} \neq 0$. Then*

$$\Pr[\mathsf{f}(y_1, \ldots, y_n) = 0] \leq 2\deg(\mathsf{f})/(p - 1) \ ,$$

where the degree of a Laurent polynomial is defined as the maximal absolute value of the exponent of any term, and the probability is over $y_1, \ldots, y_n \xleftarrow{\$} \mathbb{F}^*$.

2.2   Generic Bilinear Groups

Philosophically, the generic group model represents an idealization of a bilinear group, where protocols and attackers can only (meaningfully) interact with the group by executing group operations. They cannot exploit any additional structure of the group. The generic group model has been formulated in two majors forms: One due to Shoup and Nachaev [57,60] that idealizes element encodings as random strings, and the other due to Maurer [55] that treat group elements as abstract handles. (See also [63] for a more modern perspective and comparisons.) In this work we focus on Shoup's model adopted to the case of bilinear groups.

The bilinear generic-group model is parameterized by (p, S_1, S_2, S_t), consisting of two (carrier) sets of size p corresponding to source groups S_1 and S_2, and another, also of size p, corresponding to the target group S_t. All parties, honest or otherwise, are given oracle access to three random injections $\tau_i \xleftarrow{\$} \mathrm{Inj}(\mathbb{Z}_p, S_i)$ for $i = 1, 2, t$ as well as $(\tau_1(1), \tau_2(1), \tau_t(1))$.

In this model, parties also get oracle access to three compatibly defined group operation oracles which invert a given element via τ_i^{-1}, perform addition over $\mathbb{Z}_p$, and re-encode via τ_i. Finally, a pairing operation allows "multiplying" two elements, one in S_1 and the other in S_2, via inversions under τ_1 and τ_2 respectively, multiplication over $\mathbb{Z}_p$, and encoding via τ_t.

There are three prominent types of bilinear groups that are commonly used in practice, corresponding to whether the groups are different or if there is an isomorphism between the groups. From a generic-group perspective, in type-I groups $S_1 = S_2$ and their corresponding injections τ_1 and τ_2 are also identified. In type-II and type-III groups the injections remain independent, though for type-II groups one also provides oracle access to an isomorphism from the second source group to the first, implemented via inversion under τ_2^{-1} and re-encoding under τ_1. Here we focus on type-III bilinear groups (with no isomorphism in either direction) as these are most commonly used in practice. Throughout, we use additive notations for operations performed in all three groups.

A final distinction made in use of generic groups is whether (honest) group operations are performed with respect to the given set of "canonical" generators $(\tau_1(1), \tau_2(1), \tau_t(1))$ or whether random generators are used. This choice has security implications as shown in [7]. As we shall see, for our UC security proofs, it is critical that protocols use random generators.

2.3   The UC Framework and Its Execution Model

We rely on the Universal Composability (UC) framework [17]. However, our results could also be expressed using the concepts of other comparable frameworks [13,42,50,54]. Historically, the treatment of global resources required a more general and complex compositional framework [20,22]. Badertscher et al. [4] show how to view global functionalities as *global subroutines*, a concept that can be made precise within the latest installment of the plain UC framework [19]. Here, we provide a summary of [19] and refer interested readers to the original works for further details.

Formalism. In the UC framework, protocols are modeled as a system of *Interactive Turing Machines (ITM)*. While ITM itself is just a static piece of code, for each *session identifier sid* $\in \mathbb{N}$, we consider a collection of *ITM instances (ITI)* sharing the same *sid*. Each ITI is an instance of some ITM for a specific session and together they form the runtime notion of a protocol session. Each ITI in a given protocol session is also called a *party*.

The execution of a protocol Π involves a set of parties $\mathcal{P}$, the environment $\mathcal{Z}$ (which essentially behaves like an interactive distinguisher), and the *adversary* $\mathcal{A}$. The environment controls the flow of execution by interacting with the *adversary* $\mathcal{A}$ and choosing inputs to the parties involved in Π and receiving their outputs. An *identity bound* ξ places restrictions on whom $\mathcal{Z}$ can provide input to (e.g., to ensure the environment cannot make calls to subroutines of Π on behalf of Π). The execution terminates when the environment finally terminates with an output 0 or 1.

During an execution of Π, the adversary $\mathcal{A}$ may *corrupt* a subset of parties as defined by the security model in order to learn their internal states and gain control over these parties. In this paper, we focus on static corruption meaning that $\mathcal{A}$ chooses which party to be corrupted in the beginning of the execution.

We denote by $\mathsf{EXEC}_{\Pi,\mathcal{A},\mathcal{Z}}(\lambda, z)$ the distribution of a binary output by $\mathcal{Z}$ after an execution of Π in the presence of $\mathcal{A}$, where $\lambda \in \mathbb{N}$ is a security parameter, $z \in \{0,1\}^*$ is an auxiliary input to $\mathcal{Z}$, and the randomness for all ITMs are assumed to be sampled uniformly at random. We define the family (or ensemble) of random variables $\{\mathsf{EXEC}_{\Pi,\mathcal{A},\mathcal{Z}}(\lambda, z)\}_{\lambda \in \mathbb{N}, z \in \{0,1\}^*}$.

Recall that two binary distribution families X, Y indexed by $\lambda \in \mathbb{N}$, and $z \in \{0,1\}^*$ are called *indistinguishable* (denoted $X \approx Y$) if for all $c, d \in \mathbb{N}$, there exists a $\lambda_0 \in \mathbb{N}$ such that for all $\lambda > \lambda_0$ and all $z \in \cup_{\kappa \leq \lambda^d} \{0,1\}^\kappa$, $|\Pr[X(\lambda, z) = 1] - \Pr[Y(\lambda, z) = 1]| < \lambda^{-c}$.

UC Security. Intuitively, we consider that a protocol Π in the presence of an adversary $\mathcal{A}$ successfully UC-emulates another (typically more idealized) protocol Φ if there exists another adversary (aka. *simulator*) $\mathcal{S}$ such that no environment $\mathcal{Z}$ can distinguish the execution of Φ with $\mathcal{S}$ from that of Π with $\mathcal{A}$.

Definition 1 (UC emulation). *A protocol Π is said to UC-emulate Φ if for any PPT adversary $\mathcal{A}$ there exists a PPT adversary $\mathcal{S}$ such that for all PPT environment $\mathcal{Z}$*

$$\{\mathsf{EXEC}_{\Pi,\mathcal{A},\mathcal{Z}}(\lambda, z)\}_{\lambda \in \mathbb{N}, z \in \{0,1\}^*} \approx \{\mathsf{EXEC}_{\Phi,\mathcal{S},\mathcal{Z}}(\lambda, z)\}_{\lambda \in \mathbb{N}, z \in \{0,1\}^*} .$$

To define the security of protocol Π in the UC framework, one describes an ideal functionality $\mathcal{F}$ which captures the desired functionality of the task in hand in the form of an ITM. One then defines Π UC-secure if Π UC-emulates the *ideal protocol* $\Phi = \mathsf{IDEAL}_{\mathcal{F}}$. The ideal protocol $\mathsf{IDEAL}_{\mathcal{F}}$ models an idealized run of protocol execution: the *simulator* $\mathcal{S}$ only interacts with $\mathcal{Z}$ and influences the execution through the prescribed interfaces of $\mathcal{F}$, and the parties $\mathcal{P}$ are replaced with the so-called *dummy parties* $\tilde{\mathcal{P}}$ which merely forward the inputs from $\mathcal{Z}$ to $\mathcal{F}$ and the responses back from $\mathcal{F}$ to $\mathcal{Z}$.

Syntax for Ideal Functionalities and Protocols. In this paper, we use the following syntax to enable more precise (code-based) specifications of ideal functionalities. We describe $\mathcal{F}$ as a collection of *internal states* and *interfaces*. As usual, upon the first invocation of $\mathcal{F}$ within session *sid* its instance gets created with initial internal states. We model this routine by introducing $\mathcal{F}.\textsc{Init}_{sid}()$, which can be called only once. Once an instance of $\mathcal{F}$ is created within *sid*, the subsequent calls to $\textsc{Init}_{sid}()$ are ignored. If $\mathcal{F}$ comes with interface $\textsc{Interface}$, the (co-)routine "$\mathcal{F}.\textsc{Interface}_{sid}(\text{in})$" defines the behavior of the interface for session *sid* on input in, and returns the resulting output, potentially after interacting with the simulator. Every invocation of $\textsc{Interface}_{sid}$ may update the internal state of an instance of $\mathcal{F}$.

UC with Global Functionalities. [4] model *global functionalities* within the basic UC framework described above. Unlike a (local) functionality $\mathcal{F}$, a single instance of a global functionality $\mathcal{G}$ may take input from and provide outputs to multiple instances of protocols and local functionalities. Moreover, the environment $\mathcal{Z}$ can directly interact with $\mathcal{G}$ without going through spawned instances of the adversary. The definition of security can be naturally extended in the presence of a global functionality as we define next.

Definition 2 (UC emulation with global setup). *Let $\mathcal{G}$ be a global functionality. A protocol Π is said to* UC-emulate Φ *in the presence of $\mathcal{G}$, if for any PPT adversary $\mathcal{A}$, there exists a PPT simulator $\mathcal{S}$ such that for all PPT environment $\mathcal{Z}$,*

$$\{\mathsf{EXEC}_{\Pi,\mathcal{G},\mathcal{A},\mathcal{Z}}(\lambda, z)\}_{\lambda \in \mathbb{N}, z \in \{0,1\}^*} \approx \{\mathsf{EXEC}_{\Phi,\mathcal{G},\mathcal{S},\mathcal{Z}}(\lambda, z)\}_{\lambda \in \mathbb{N}, z \in \{0,1\}^*} .$$

Here, $\mathsf{EXEC}_{\Pi,\mathcal{G},\mathcal{A},\mathcal{Z}}(\lambda, z)$ is defined in terms of $\mathsf{EXEC}_{\mu[\Pi,\mathcal{G}],\mathcal{A},\mathcal{Z}}(\lambda, z)$, where the so-called management protocol μ allows Π to interact with $\mathcal{G}$ but additionally grants access to $\mathcal{G}$ to $\mathcal{Z}$.

In [4], the authors present a *composition theorem (UCGS theorem)*, which states the following: if a protocol Π UC-realizes $\mathcal{F}$ in the presence of $\mathcal{G}$, then the protocol $\rho^{\Pi,\mathcal{G}}$ that is identical to $\rho^{\mathcal{F},\mathcal{G}}$ except that all instances of the ideal functionality $\mathcal{F}$ are replaced by instances of the real protocol Π, UC-emulates $\rho^{\mathcal{F},\mathcal{G}}$ in the presence of $\mathcal{G}$.

2.4 Weak NIZK Functionality

In Functionality 1 we formalize $\mathcal{F}$-wNIZK, the *weak* NIZK ideal functionality that we will be realizing. $\mathcal{F}$-wNIZK is parameterized by polynomial-time relation $\mathcal{R}$, and runs with parties $\mathcal{P}$ and an ideal process adversary $\mathcal{S}$. It stores a proof table T which is initially empty. "Weak" refers to the fact that proofs may be malleable. Our formalization slightly differs from [48, Figure 3] in that mauling of proofs is performed by the simulator and not via an explicit maul interface. We note that with Line 9 removed, we obtain an ideal functionality for a standard ("strong") NIZK.

Functionality 1: $\mathcal{F}$-wNIZK

$\underline{\text{INIT}_{sid}()}$
  1: $T \leftarrow []$

$\underline{\text{PROVE}_{sid}(x, w)}$
  2: **if** $(x, w) \notin \mathcal{R}$ **then return**
     $\perp$
  3: $\pi \leftarrow \mathcal{S}.\text{SIMULATE}_{sid}(x)$
  4: $T \leftarrow T \cup (x, \pi)$
  5: **return** π

$\underline{\text{VERIFY}_{sid}(x, \pi)}$
  6: **if** $(x, \pi) \in T$ **then return** 1
  7: $w \leftarrow \mathcal{S}.\text{EXTRACT}_{sid}(x, \pi)$
  8: **if** $(x, w) \in \mathcal{R}$ **then** $T \leftarrow T \cup (x, \pi)$
  9: **if** $(w = \text{maul} \wedge (x, *) \in T)$ **then** $T \leftarrow T \cup (x, \pi)$
  10: **if** $(x, \pi) \in T$ **then**
  11:     **return** 1
  12: **else**
  13:     **return** 0

Functionality 2: $\mathcal{G}$-GG

$\underline{\text{INIT}()}$
  1: **for** $i \in \{1, 2, t\}$ **do**
  2: $\quad \tau_i \xleftarrow{\$} \text{Inj}(\mathbb{Z}_p, S_i)$

$\underline{\text{OP}_{sid}(i, g_1, g_2, a_1, a_2)}$
  3: **assert** $(g_1, g_2, a_1, a_2) \in S_i^2 \times \mathbb{Z}_p^2$
  4: $h \leftarrow \tau_i(a_1 \tau_i^{-1}(g_1) + a_2 \tau_i^{-1}(g_2))$
  5: **return** h

$\underline{\text{CANONICALGEN}_{sid}(i)}$
  6: **return** $\tau_i(1)$

$\underline{\text{PAIR}_{sid}(g_1, g_2)}$
  7: **assert** $(g_1, g_2) \in S_1 \times S_2$
  8: $h \leftarrow \tau_t(\tau_1^{-1}(g_1) \cdot \tau_2^{-1}(g_2))$
  9: **return** h

Here we consider the case of static corruption. This is sufficiently strong to also give adaptive corruption for $\mathcal{F}$-wNIZK (where the all queried (x, w) are returned upon corruption) assuming secure erasure (of randomness). In order to have a simpler functionality, we do not model that a previously invalid proof must not subsequently become valid. Note, however, that Groth16 enjoys full consistency.

3 The Global Observable Generic Group Functionality

In this section, we first go over the (strict) global generic group model as a warm-up, and then introduce the restricted observable global generic group model, which is what we are going to use to prove UC security of Groth16.

3.1 Warm-Up: The (strict) Global Generic Group Functionality

We focus on type-3 bilinear groups and Shoup's style of generic groups with random encodings (cf. Sect. 2.2). We can easily model such (unobservable) generic bilinear groups as a (global) UC functionality $\mathcal{G}$-GG as in Functionality 2 (similar to, for example, [30]). As in standard generic type-III bilinear groups, $\mathcal{G}$-GG is parameterized by a prime p and three sets S_i for $i \in \{1, 2, t\}$ each of size p. $\mathcal{G}$-GG starts by initializing three random injections $\tau_i : \mathbb{Z}_p \to S_i$ for $i \in \{1, 2, t\}$. (This choice can be made efficient in the standard way, via lazy sampling.)

The functionality $\mathcal{G}$-GG offers three interfaces to protocols. They can use $\mathcal{G}$-GG to access the "canonical" generators $\tau_i(1)$ via CANONICALGEN. As with standard generic groups, $\mathcal{G}$-GG also offers an OP and a PAIR interface. We slightly extend OP to compute an arbitrary linear operation $a_1 \cdot g_1 + a_2 \cdot g_2$ (rather than just $g_1 + g_2$). This is without loss of generality and is used to spare algorithms from implementing double and add.

Because the sets S_i are public and of size p, protocols (and adversaries) can (obliviously) sample group elements of their choice. This could be via an arbitrary algorithm that has an unspecified output distribution. (Some formalizations allow S_i to be a much larger set than $\mathbb{Z}_p$, which prevents these powers.) Moreover this choice better conforms to practical groups (where the carrier sets of a bilinear group are fixed and publicly known).

This feature, when combined with an external random oracle functionality, also enables hashing into the group via random oracle. For this reason, and in contrast to, say, [30], we do not explicitly model a "hash-into-group" interface

As such, $\mathcal{G}$-GG can be seen as the generic-group equivalent of the "strict" global *random-oracle* functionality [15]. It can be used, for example, to analyze the UC security algebraic schemes like ElGamal when they share a generic group.

3.2   The (Restricted) Observable Global Generic Group Functionality

The ability to observe generic-group (and random-oracle) queries forms the basis of many proofs in cryptography. Functionally, $\mathcal{G}$-GG as defined has limited applicability, because it does not offer the UC simulator any "cheating power". This is in contrast to a local group [30] where the simulator takes over the group.

To enable applications where simulators need to observe queries made to the group, we augment $\mathcal{G}$-GG with *observation* capabilities. As seen in the analogous restricted observable global *random oracle* (e.g., [15]), these observation capabilities need to be appropriately *restricted* so as to not render all applications insecure.

Our global *restricted observable generic group* functionality $\mathcal{G}$-oGG is defined in Functionality 3. It contains all interfaces of $\mathcal{G}$-GG, together with two additional ones, OBSERVE and TOUCH. If OBSERVE and TOUCH are never called, then $\mathcal{G}$-oGG behaves identically to $\mathcal{G}$-GG. In particular, $\mathcal{G}$-oGG.OP$_{sid}(i, g_1, g_2, a_1, a_2)$ still effectively returns $h = \tau_i(a_1\tau_i^{-1}(g_1) + a_2\tau_i^{-1}(g_2))$, and the only difference to its counterpart in $\mathcal{G}$-GG is that the operation additionally keeps track of the way group elements are computed, which we discuss below. Similarly, $\mathcal{G}$-oGG.PAIR differs from $\mathcal{G}$-GG.PAIR only in maintaining some additional bookkeeping.

Our strategy to restrict observability is similar to (restricted) observable random oracles [15] in that we deploy a form of "domain separation".[6] $\mathcal{G}$-oGG introduces a notion of group elements belonging to certain sessions, which informs the

---

[6] In our full version [10] we give an overview of domain-separation approaches in global observable functionalities.

Functionality 3: $\mathcal{G}$-oGG

$\mathcal{G}$-oGG is (implicitly) parameterized with
- A prime number p
- Sets $S_1, S_2, S_t \subseteq \{0,1\}^*$ with $|S_i| = p$ for all $i \in \{1, 2, t\}$.

$\mathcal{G}$-oGG maintains the following state:
- $\tau_i : \mathbb{Z}_p \to S_i$ three random encoding functions, mapping discrete logs $x \in \mathbb{Z}_p$ to their randomly encoded group elements $h \in S_i$.
- $\mathsf{Var}_{i,sid}$ initially empty lists of formal variables. // Keeps track of the group i formal variables belonging to session sid.
- $\mathsf{R}_i[h]$ for $i \in \{1, 2, t\}, h \in S_i$ initially empty sets of polynomials // Keep track of polynomial representations corresponding to $h \in S_i$.
- Ob initially empty list of observable actions.

Furthermore, we use the following terms derived from the current state
- We write $\mathsf{Var}_{sid} = \mathsf{Var}_{1,sid} : \mathsf{Var}_{2,sid} : \mathsf{Var}_{t,sid}$ to refer to all variables of session sid (irrespective of which group).
- We write Var to refer to the concatenation of all Var_{sid} (i.e. over all sid).
- $\mathsf{Legal}_{sid} = \langle \mathsf{Var}_{sid} \rangle_{\mathbb{Z}_p[\mathsf{Var}_{sid}]} = \sum_{X \in \mathsf{Var}_{sid}} X \cdot \mathbb{Z}_p[\mathsf{Var}_{sid}]$. // Legal_{sid} is the set of polynomials that contain only this session's variables $X \in \mathsf{Var}_{sid}$, and whose constant term is 0. For example, $15X_{sid} + 7Y_{sid} \in \mathsf{Legal}_{sid}$ and $3X_{sid}Y_{sid} \in \mathsf{Legal}_{sid}$, but $X_{sid} + 3 \notin \mathsf{Legal}_{sid}$ and $X_{sid} + X_{sid'} \notin \mathsf{Legal}_{sid}$.

$\underline{\text{INIT}()}$ // Invoked only upon creation
1: **for** $i \in \{1, 2, t\}$ **do**
2: $\quad \tau_i \xleftarrow{\$} \mathrm{Inj}(\mathbb{Z}_p, S_i)$
3: $\quad \mathsf{R}_i[\tau_i(1)] \leftarrow \{1\}$

$\underline{\text{CANONICALGEN}_{sid}(i)}$
4: **return** $\tau_i(1)$

$\underline{\text{OBSERVE}_{sid}()}$
5: **return** Ob

$\underline{\text{OP}_{sid}(i, g_1, g_2, a_1, a_2)}$
6: assert $(g_1, g_2, a_1, a_2) \in S_i^2 \times \mathbb{Z}_p^2$
7: **for** $j \in \{1, 2\}$ **do**
8: $\quad \text{TOUCH}_{sid}(i, g_j)$
9: $h \leftarrow \tau_i(a_1\tau_i^{-1}(g_1) + a_2\tau_i^{-1}(g_2))$
10: $\mathsf{R}_i[h] \leftarrow \mathsf{R}_i[h] \cup (a_1\mathsf{R}_i[g_1] + a_2\mathsf{R}_i[g_2])$
11: **if** $\exists \mathsf{f} \in \mathsf{R}_i[h] : \mathsf{f} \notin \mathsf{Legal}_{sid}$ **then**
12: $\quad Ob \leftarrow Ob : [(\text{OP}, i, g_1, g_2, a_1, a_2, h)]$

13: **return** h

$\underline{\text{TOUCH}_{sid}(i, g)}$
14: **if** $\mathsf{R}_i[g] = \varnothing$ **then**
15: $\quad$ Initialize fresh variable X
16: $\quad \mathsf{Var}_{i,sid} \leftarrow \mathsf{Var}_{i,sid} : [X]$
17: $\quad \mathsf{R}_i[g] \leftarrow \{X\}$

$\underline{\text{PAIR}_{sid}(g_1, g_2)}$
18: assert $(g_1, g_2) \in S_1 \times S_2$
19: **for** $i \in \{1, 2\}$ **do**
20: $\quad \text{TOUCH}_{sid}(i, g_i)$
21: $h \leftarrow \tau_t(\tau_1^{-1}(g_1) \cdot \tau_2^{-1}(g_2))$
22: $\mathsf{R}_t[h] \leftarrow \mathsf{R}_t[h] \cup (\mathsf{R}_1[g_1] \cdot \mathsf{R}_2[g_2])$
23: **if** $\exists \mathsf{f} \in \mathsf{R}_t[h] : \mathsf{f} \notin \mathsf{Legal}_{sid}$ **then**
24: $\quad Ob \leftarrow Ob :$
$\quad\quad [(\text{PAIR}, t, g_1, g_2, h)]$
25: **return** h

observation rules. This notion, however, is somewhat nontrivial—after all, the entire group is shared equally among all sessions, with no algebraic differentiation between any two group elements. To associate group elements with sessions, we keep track of *polynomial representations* of group elements with respect to certain generators.

Generators. To start, protocols can claim (random) generators $g \in S_i$ for each group in their session by simply calling the $\text{TOUCH}_{sid}(i, g)$ procedure. Reminiscent of the Unix `touch` command, if g is already in use, nothing happens. Otherwise, g becomes a generator of the caller's session sid. (Protocols can choose g randomly to ensure that g is unused with overwhelming probability.) A formal variable X is associated with every touched generator g. The functionality keeps track of each session's generators in terms of their formal variables using lists $\mathsf{Var}_{i,sid}$ (to which X is appended). The canonical generators $\tau_i(1)$ do not belong to any particular session. Looking slightly ahead, every group element $h \in S_i$ will be associated with a (set of) polynomials $\mathsf{R}_i[h]$ that explain how the group element has been computed. For a touched generator g with associated formal variable X, the polynomial representation is simply $\mathsf{R}_i[h] = \{\mathsf{X}\}$. The canonical generators are represented with constant polynomials, $\mathsf{R}_i[\tau_i(1)] = \{1\}$.

Group Operations. When executing group operations, $\mathcal{G}\text{-oGG}$ keeps track of the polynomial representations corresponding to the resulting group element. Whenever two group elements are added, their polynomial representations are summed up to form the corresponding polynomial representation (Line 10 of Functionality 3). Whenever the pairing operation is applied, polynomial representations are multiplied (Line 22). For example, let g_1, g_2 be generators associated with formal variables $\mathsf{R}_i[g_1] = \{\mathsf{X}_1\}, \mathsf{R}_i[g_2] = \{\mathsf{X}_2\}$. If we compute "$h = 1 \cdot g_1 + 3 \cdot g_2$", then the corresponding polynomial is $\mathsf{R}_i[h] = \{\mathsf{X}_1 + 3\mathsf{X}_2\}$. If we further compute "$h' = 2 \cdot h + 50 \cdot g_1$", then $\mathsf{R}_i[h'] = \{52\mathsf{X}_1 + 6\mathsf{X}_2\}$. Note that by design, polynomials in R_1 and R_2 are of degree 1 or 0, and polynomials in R_t for the target group are of degree at most 2.

It may happen that there are two polynomial representations $\mathsf{f} \neq \mathsf{f}'$ for the same group element h. For this reason, $\mathsf{R}_i[h]$ is formally modeled as a *set* containing all known representations. However, by Schwartz–Zippel (Lemma 1), for sufficiently large groups, $\mathsf{R}_i[h]$ will be a singleton set with overwhelming probability (we formally establish this in the UC setting in the proof of Lemma 3).

Observation Rules. With the above bookkeeping mechanisms, we have polynomials $\mathsf{f} \in \mathsf{R}_i[h]$ associated to each group element h, and sessions to each polynomial variable $\mathsf{X} \in \mathsf{Var}_{sid}$. This now allows us to establish the observation rules. For this, we say that a group element h is *legal* in session sid if its associated polynomial(s) $\mathsf{f} \in \mathsf{R}_i[h]$ do not contain variables $\mathsf{X}_{sid'} \in \mathsf{Var}_{sid'}$ of foreign sessions $sid' \neq sid$ (and no constant terms, which correspond to the canonical generators). This the set Legal_{sid} in Functionality 3 formally defines the set of legal polynomials for session sid. A group operation or pairing operation is *observable* if its result is not legal in the caller's session. If an operation is observable, then the input to the operation is added to a global list Ob in Line 12 and 24. Ob can be read by anyone (environment, simulator, adversary, even, theoretically, protocol entities) by calling OBSERVE.

Intuitively, in order to not be observed, the protocol in session sid must only operate with group elements that were derived from its session's generators, with no involvement of generators from other sessions sid'. To comply with domain separation, protocols in session sid must only operate with group elements that were derived from their session's generators, with no involvement of generators from other sessions sid'. For example, if $R_i[h] = \{4X_{sid} + 3X'_{sid}\}$, where $X_{sid}, X'_{sid} \in Var_{i,sid}$ are associated with session sid, then clearly, h belongs to session sid. An OP_{sid} operation called by a party in session sid, resulting in h is an example of an *unobservable* operation. However, if $R_i[h] = \{4X_{sid} + 3Y_{sid'}\}$, where $Y_{sid'} \in Var_{i,sid'}$ belongs to session $sid' \neq sid$, then h does not belong to either session. An OP_{sid} operation called by a party in session sid (or indeed any other session), resulting in h is an example of an *observable* operation. For a pairing operation $PAIR_{sid}(h_1, h_2) = h$, we naturally get that if, say, $R_1[h_1] = \{X_{sid}\}$ and $R_2[h_2] = \{3Z_{sid}\}$, then for the result h, we get $R_t[h] = \{3X_{sid}Z_{sid}\}$, which indicates that h is legal (unobservable). If, however, instead $R_2[h_2] = \{3Z_{sid'}\}$ with $Z_{sid'} \in Legal_{2,sid'}$, then the result is illegal (hence observable), since $R_t[h] = \{3X_{sid}Z_{sid'}\} \not\subseteq Legal_{sid}$.

Using $\mathcal{G}$-oGG in Protocols. A protocol can set up its set of generators by sampling random group elements $g_1 \xleftarrow{\$} S_1, g_2 \xleftarrow{\$} S_2$, and TOUCHing them to make them part of the protocol's session. The protocol can then proceed naturally, performing group and pairing operations as usual. For example, Groth16 can choose a common reference string (CRS) based on g_1, g_2 (see Functionality 6).

With the observation rules in place, the simulator for session sid can be sure that it gets observation information pertaining to all group elements h whose polynomial $f \in R_i[h]$ involves any variable $X \in Var_{sid}$.

If the protocol stays within elements derived from its generators g_1, g_2 (e.g., the CRS and Groth16 proofs computed from it), those operations will, with overwhelming probability, not be observable. See Sect. 4 for a discussion on unlikely error events. A protocol *may* sometimes violate domain separation. For example, this is necessary in Groth16 when verifying a proof π received from the environment, which can potentially contain adversarially generated group elements belonging to other sessions. In this case, operations are observable, hence care must be taken that they do not leak any important information (which is not an issue for Groth16, as the verifier does not hold any secret information). We discuss handling protocols where this is an issue in Sect. 6.

Protocols can hash into the group (similarly to what we described in Sect. 3) by hashing into S_i (e.g., with a random oracle) and then TOUCHing the hash output. If there is sufficient entropy in the hashed element, it is likely that the hash output will belong to the hasher's session, making it safe to perform secret operations on it.

Canonical Generators. The canonical generators g_1, g_2, g_t, available via interface CANONICALGEN correspond to discrete logarithms $\tau_i^{-1}(g_i) = 1$ and the constant polynomials $R_i[g] = \{1\}$. In principle, they can be used by any protocol (session). However, operations involving the canonical generator will all be observable (any polynomial with a non-zero constant term is observable). This is a somewhat arbitrary choice, but makes for nicer algebraic properties of observability (e.g., the set $\mathsf{Legal}_{sid} = \langle \mathsf{Var}_{sid} \rangle_{\mathbb{Z}_p[\mathsf{Var}_{sid}]}$ corresponding to unobservable polynomials can be written as an ideal).

Efficiency. Similar to $\mathcal{G}$-GG, the observable $\mathcal{G}$-oGG is also not efficient. In addition to sampling the random encoding functions τ_i at the start, the sets $R_i[g]$ in $\mathcal{G}$-oGG can also blow up to superpoly sizes in the worst case. However, as we argue in Lemma 3, with overwhelming probability, $R_i[g]$ will be a singleton. To make $\mathcal{G}$-oGG efficient, one can sample τ_i values lazily, and if any set $R_i[g]$ ever gets larger than a single element (which happens only with negligible probability), one can switch to an arbitrary error mode (e.g., stop maintaining R and instead make everything observable).

4   Switching to Symbolic Groups

The restricted global observable generic group functionality $\mathcal{G}$-oGG faithfully models a generic group (as in $\mathcal{G}$-GG) with tacked-on observation capabilities. However, an issue of $\mathcal{G}$-oGG when doing security proofs is that the session separation in $\mathcal{G}$-oGG is imperfect. It *can* happen that some group element belongs to two sessions in $\mathcal{G}$-oGG, and both sessions will be able to observe operations involving it. This is not desirable and will be an error event for most applications. In this section, we present the *symbolic* (restricted observable) generic group model $\mathcal{G}$-oSG, where session separation is *perfect* by definition and this error event cannot happen. Lemma 3 shows that $\mathcal{G}$-oGG can be securely replaced by $\mathcal{G}$-oSG.

In addition to that, $\mathcal{G}$-oSG will also support typical security proof techniques. Many typical (game-based) generic group model security proofs follow roughly (at least in spirit) this template:

1. Run the generic adversary, while the reduction answers its generic group oracle queries.

2. Argue that instead of sampling random discrete logarithm secrets $\alpha, \beta \xleftarrow{\$} \mathbb{Z}_p^*$, the reduction can play the role of the generic group oracle using formal variables X_α, X_β. Applying Schwartz–Zippel shows that this is undetectable to the generic adversary.

3. Argue that the adversary only makes linear (or pairing) operations, so whenever the adversary outputs a group element h^* corresponding to $a \cdot X_\alpha + b X_\beta$, the reduction algorithm can extract the discrete logarithm representation $(a, b) \in \mathbb{Z}_p^2$ of that group element by looking at the generic group oracle queries the adversary made.

4. Argue that the group elements output by the adversary do not threaten security because they are only linear combinations of the (polynomials corresponding to the) elements the reduction has provided (e.g., the adversary cannot output X if we only give it $X + Y$, but not Y).

The last step is highly dependent on the concrete scheme to be proven secure. For example, it can take the form of "We only give $\mathcal{A}$ the public key $[X_x, X_y]_2$ and signatures $\sigma_i = [X_{r_i}, X_{r_i}(X_x + m_i X_y)]_1$, so when the adversary outputs a forgery (in the first group), it must be of the form $[\sum a_i \cdot X_{r_i} + \sum b_i \cdot X_{r_i}(X_x + m_i X_y)]_1$, and hence cannot be forgery" [58]. These arguments are inherently *symbolic*, i.e. in the last step, X_x, X_y, X_{r_i} are formal variables, and the verification equation is an equation over polynomials in those variables. There are no concrete values anymore, and hence we are discussing the values and equations symbolically. In particular, this guarantees that there cannot be any accidental guesses of secret keys or randomness, meaning that proofs at this stage are usually *perfect*.

In this section, we extend $\mathcal{G}$-oSG in Functionality 5 to enable the proof strategy above as follows (the steps here correspond to the steps above).

1. Run the UC environment/adversary with $\mathcal{G}$-oGG replaced by $\mathcal{G}$-oSG.

2. Instead of choosing random secrets $\alpha, \beta \xleftarrow{\$} \mathbb{Z}_p^*$, then have the UC simulator ask (the extended) $\mathcal{G}$-oSG for corresponding formal variables $X_\alpha, X_\beta \leftarrow$ GetRnd(), and use ComputeSymbolic$_{sid}$ to output group elements relative to the secrets. Lemma 4 shows that this switch is undetectable.

3. Have the UC simulator use the algorithm FindRep to extract the discrete logarithm representation (a, b) from element h^*. In contrast to the typical generic group proofs, the UC simulator does not see all generic group operations, but Lemma 5 shows that the restricted observations are enough to get meaningful guarantees.

4. Argue that the group elements output by the adversary do not threaten security. This part is essentially the same as in standard generic group proofs. It is supported by $\mathcal{G}$-oSG (+ extensions), which automatically keeps track of the polynomial $\tau_i^{-1}(h)$ corresponding to each group element h.

The symbolic $\mathcal{G}$-oSG with extensions (Functionality 5) will allow most security proofs to conveniently hop to a setting where secrets are formal variables, group elements correspond one-to-one to polynomials (enabling *symbolic* analysis of group elements/operations), and the simulator can extract discrete logarithm representations. Most proofs can simply invoke our Lemmas 3 to 5 without ever applying Schwartz–Zippel themselves. We use this framework when proving Groth16 secure in Sect. 5.

4.1 The Restricted Observable Global Symbolic Group Model with Perfect Session Separation

We introduce the restricted observable global symbolic group model $\mathcal{G}$-oSG in Functionality 4, which, in contrast to $\mathcal{G}$-oGG, has perfect separation of sessions. This separation is modeled similarly to $\mathcal{G}$-oGG, with polynomials. In contrast to

$\mathcal{G}$-oGG, the polynomials will not only be some bookkeeping artifacts R alongside the actual $\mathcal{G}$-GG functionality, but rather the main driver behind group operations. More concretely, the random encoding function $\tau_i : \mathbb{Z}_p[\mathsf{Var}, \mathsf{SimVar}^{\pm 1}] \to S_i{}^7$ now injectively maps *polynomials* f to random encodings h, rather than concrete discrete logarithms. In particular, this means that any group element (encoding) $h \in S_i$ has a unique polynomial $\tau_i^{-1}(h)$ associated with it, which also directly determines its behavior w.r.t. OP, PAIR. In this sense, the polynomial mapping τ_i serves two purposes now: It manages the algebraic properties of group elements (managed by τ_i over $\mathbb{Z}_p$ in $\mathcal{G}$-oGG) *and* it is used to decide observability (used to be managed by R in $\mathcal{G}$-oGG).

A consequence of having τ_i map *polynomials* to S_i is that there exist no injective $\tau_i : \mathbb{Z}_p[\mathsf{Var}, \mathsf{SimVar}^{\pm 1}] \to S_i$. We cannot choose τ_i randomly at the beginning, anymore. For this reason, images of τ_i are lazily sampled via TAU. Because the adversary is computationally bounded, we will not run out of fresh unused images in $S_i \setminus \mathrm{im}(\tau_i)$ to use in Line 23.

The following lemma establishes that we can replace the procedures of $\mathcal{G}$-oGG with their idealized versions from $\mathcal{G}$-oSG (ignoring the "extra" procedures that $\mathcal{G}$-oSG carries).

Lemma 3. *Let* $\mathcal{O}_{\mathrm{real}} = \mathcal{G}$-oGG.[CANONICALGEN, OBSERVE, TOUCH, OP, PAIR]. *Let* $\mathcal{O}_{\mathrm{symb}} = \mathcal{G}$-oSG.[CANONICALGEN, OBSERVE, TOUCH, OP, PAIR].

For all algorithms $\mathcal{B}$ that make at most q oracle queries, it holds that

$$\left| \Pr\left[\mathcal{B}^{\mathcal{O}_{\mathrm{real}}} = 1 \right] - \Pr\left[\mathcal{B}^{\mathcal{O}_{\mathrm{symb}}} = 1 \right] \right| \le \binom{3q+1}{2} \cdot 2/p \le (9q^2 + 3q)/p$$

When treating interfaces INTERFACE as oracles, this means that the caller specifies session *sid* and input x, then gets the result of $\text{INTERFACE}_{sid}(x)$. The oracles share state. The proof can be found in the full version of this paper [10].

Overall, as the first step in any $\mathcal{G}$-oGG proof, we expect $\mathcal{G}$-oGG to be replaced by $\mathcal{G}$-oSG, which is more convenient to handle in security proofs, and will enable powerful symbolic analysis using its extensions.

4.2   Extending $\mathcal{G}$-oSG with Support for Symbolic Analysis

As sketched at the beginning of Sect. 4, our goal is to support typical GGM proof techniques in the $\mathcal{G}$-oSG UC setting. For this, we extend $\mathcal{G}$-oSG with additional interfaces in Functionality 5.

We direct our attention at Functionality 5's GETRND, COMPUTECONCRETE, COMPUTEATOMIC, and COMPUTESYMBOLIC. They model interaction of an algorithm $\mathcal{B}$ (usually the UC simulator) with hidden variables. They will allow us to make statements about changes in $\mathcal{B}$'s behavior as long as $\mathcal{B}$ does not use those hidden variables other than for group operations. The interfaces are to be used as follows: Whenever $\mathcal{B}$ generates a secret $\alpha \leftarrow \mathbb{Z}_p^*$, this can be modeled as a

---

[7] For now, ignore the list SimVar of formal variables. It is empty and will only be used in the $\mathcal{G}$-oSG extensions (Functionality 5).

Functionality 4: $\mathcal{G}$-oSG

Differences with $\mathcal{G}$-oGG are highlighted in purple. Values relevant only in the $\mathcal{G}$-oSG extensions (Functionality 5) are highlighted in yellow (can be ignored on first read).

- τ_i now maps polynomials ($\mathbb{Z}_p[\mathsf{Var}, \mathsf{SimVar}^{\pm 1}]$ instead of $\mathbb{Z}_p$) to random encodings S_i
- $\mathsf{Var}_{i,sid}$ initially empty lists of polynomial variables
- SimVar_{sid} empty lists of polynomial variables $\mathsf{X}_{\mathrm{rnd}}$. Only used in Functionality 5
- $SimVal_{sid}$ empty lists of random scalars $x_{\mathrm{rnd}} \in \mathbb{Z}_p$ corresponding to SimVar_{sid}
- Ob initially empty list of (globally) observable actions
- Ob_{sid} initially empty lists of all actions observable in specific session sid, including actions of parties *in* session sid (only read in the $\mathcal{G}$-oSG extensions)
- C_i initially empty sets $C_i \subseteq S_i$ of group elements that can be the basis for extraction (only read in the $\mathcal{G}$-oSG extensions)

Furthermore, we use the following terms derived from the current state

- We write Var_{sid}, Var as before. Similarly, SimVar is the concatenation of all SimVar_{sid}. Var_{-sid} is the concatenation of all $\mathsf{Var}_{sid'}$, where $sid' \neq sid$.
- $\mathsf{Legal}_{sid} = \langle \mathsf{Var}_{sid} \rangle_{\mathbb{Z}_p[\mathsf{Var}_{sid}, \mathsf{SimVar}_{sid}^{\pm 1}]} = \sum_{\mathsf{X} \in \mathsf{Var}_{sid}} \mathsf{X} \cdot \mathbb{Z}_p[\mathsf{Var}_{sid}, \mathsf{SimVar}_{sid}^{\pm 1}]$. // Legal_{sid} is the set of (Laurent) polynomials that contain only variables from Var_{sid} and SimVar_{sid} (with potentially negative exponents), where every nonzero term has some factor $\mathsf{X} \in \mathsf{Var}_{sid}$.

$\underline{\mathrm{INIT}()}$ // Invoked only upon creation
1: **for** $i \in \{1, 2, t\}$ **do**
2:      $\tau_i \leftarrow \{\}$
3:      $\mathrm{TAU}(i, 1)$
4:      $C_i \leftarrow C_i \cup \{1\}$

$\underline{\mathrm{CANONICALGEN}_{sid}(i)}$
5: **return** $\mathrm{TAU}(i, 1)$

$\underline{\mathrm{OBSERVE}_{sid}()}$
6: **return** Ob

$\underline{\mathrm{OP}_{sid}(i, g_1, g_2, a_1, a_2)}$
7: assert $(g_1, g_2, a_1, a_2) \in S_i^2 \times \mathbb{Z}_p^2$
8: **for** $j \in \{1, 2\}$ **do**
9:      $\mathrm{TOUCH}_{sid}(i, g_j)$
10: $\mathsf{f} \leftarrow a_1 \tau_i^{-1}(g_1) + a_2 \tau_i^{-1}(g_2)$
11: $h \leftarrow \mathrm{TAU}(i, \mathsf{f})$
12: **if** $\mathsf{f} \notin \mathsf{Legal}_{sid}$ **then**
13:      $Ob \leftarrow Ob : [(\mathrm{OP}, i, g_1, g_2, a_1, a_2, h)]$

14: $Ob_{sid'} \leftarrow Ob_{sid'} : [(\mathrm{OP}, i, g_1, g_2, a_1, a_2, h)]$ for all sid' (incl. sid)
15: $Ob_{sid} \leftarrow Ob_{sid} : [(\mathrm{OP}, i, g_1, g_2, a_1, a_2, h)]$
16: **return** h

$\underline{\mathrm{TOUCH}_{sid}(i, g)}$
17: **if** $g \notin \mathrm{im}(\tau_i)$ **then**
18:      Initialize a fresh variable X
19:      $\mathsf{Var}_{i,sid} \leftarrow \mathsf{Var}_{i,sid} : [\mathsf{X}]$
20:      $\tau_i(\mathsf{X}) \leftarrow g$
21:      $C_i \leftarrow C_i \cup \{g\}$

$\underline{\mathrm{TAU}(i, \mathsf{f})}$ // internal
22: **if** $\tau_i(\mathsf{f}) = \bot$ **then**
23:      $\tau_i(\mathsf{f}) \xleftarrow{\$} S_i \setminus \mathrm{im}(\tau_i)$
24: **return** $\tau_i(\mathsf{f})$

$\underline{\mathrm{PAIR}_{sid}(g_1, g_2)}$
25: assert $(g_1, g_2) \in S_1 \times S_2$
26: **for** $i \in \{1, 2\}$ **do**
27:      $\mathrm{TOUCH}_{sid}(i, g_i)$
28: $\mathsf{f} \leftarrow \tau_1^{-1}(g_1) \cdot \tau_2^{-1}(g_2)$
29: $h \leftarrow \mathrm{TAU}(t, \mathsf{f})$
30: **if** $\mathsf{f} \notin \mathsf{Legal}_{sid}$ **then**
31:      $Ob \leftarrow Ob : [(\mathrm{PAIR}, t, g_1, g_2, h)]$
32: $Ob_{sid'} \leftarrow Ob_{sid'} : [(\mathrm{PAIR}, t, g_1, g_2, h)]$ for all sid' (incl. sid)
33: $Ob_{sid} \leftarrow Ob_{sid} : [(\mathrm{PAIR}, t, g_1, g_2, h)]$
34: **return** h

Functionality 5: $\mathcal{G}$-oSG extensions

This box contains interfaces in addition to the ones shown in Functionality 4. These interfaces are artifacts for security proofs rather than publicly available interfaces. They model interaction with unknown random values/variables and the discrete logarithm representation extraction process via FINDREP. See Lemmas 3 to 5 for how these interfaces are used.

GETRND$_{sid}()$

35: Initialize a new variable X
36: SimVar$_{sid}$ ← SimVar$_{sid}$: [X]
37: $x \xleftarrow{\$} \mathbb{Z}_p^*$
38: $SimVal_{sid}$ ← $SimVal_{sid}$: [x]
39: **return** X

COMPUTESYMBOLIC$_{sid}(i, (h_j, f_j)_{j=1}^n)$

40: assert $\tau_i^{-1}(h_j) \in$ Legal$_{sid}$ // h_j belongs to session sid and $f_j \in \mathbb{Z}_p[\text{SimVar}_{sid}^{\pm 1}]$ for all $j \in [n]$.
41: $f \leftarrow \sum_j \tau_i^{-1}(h_j) \cdot f_j$ // $\in \mathbb{Z}_p[\text{Var}_{sid}, \text{SimVar}_{sid}^{\pm 1}]$
42: $h \leftarrow \text{TAU}(i, f)$
43: $C_i \leftarrow C_i \cup \{h\}$
44: **return** h

COMPUTEATOMIC$_{sid}(i, (h_j, f_j)_{j=1}^n)$

45: assert $\tau_i^{-1}(h_j) \in$ Legal$_{sid}$ // h_j belongs to session sid and $f_j \in \mathbb{Z}_p[\text{SimVar}_{sid}^{\pm 1}]$ for all $j \in [n]$.
46: $f \leftarrow \sum_j \tau_i^{-1}(h_j) \cdot f_j(SimVal_{sid})$ // $\in \mathbb{Z}_p[\text{Var}_{sid}]$
47: $h \leftarrow \text{TAU}(i, f)$
48: **return** h

COMPUTECONCRETE$_{sid}(i, (h_j, f_j)_{j=1}^n)$

49: assert $\tau_i^{-1}(h_j) \in$ Legal$_{sid}$ // h_j belongs to session sid and $f_j \in \mathbb{Z}_p[\text{SimVar}_{sid}^{\pm 1}]$ for all $j \in [n]$.
50: $h \leftarrow \text{TAU}(i, 0)$ // $h = 0$ neutral element
51: **for** $j \in [n]$ **do**
52: $a_j \leftarrow f_j(SimVal_{sid})$ // $\in \mathbb{Z}_p$. Compute exponent a_j from secrets $SimVal_{sid}$
53: $h \leftarrow \text{OP}_{sid}(i, h, h_j, 1, a_j)$ // $h \leftarrow h + a_j \cdot h_j$
54: **return** h

GETREP$_{sid}(i, h^*, B)$

55: assert $i \in \{1, 2\}, h^* \in \text{im}(\tau_i), B \in (C_i)^n$ with $B_j \neq B_\ell$ for $j \neq \ell$.
56: $(a_j)_{j=1}^n \leftarrow \text{FINDREP}(i, h^*, Ob_{sid}, B)$
57: $V = \sum_{j=1}^n a_j \cdot \tau_i^{-1}(B_j)$ // Result as polynomial $V \in \mathbb{Z}_p[\text{Var}, \text{SimVar}^{\pm 1}]$
58: assert $\exists b_j, c_j \in \mathbb{Z}_p[\text{SimVar}^{\pm 1}]$: $V = \tau_i^{-1}(h^*) + \text{foreign} + \text{missing}$, where $\text{foreign} = \sum_{X_j \in \text{Var}_{-sid}} b_j X_j$ and $\text{missing} = \sum_{j : C_i[j] \notin B} c_j \cdot \tau_i^{-1}(C_i[j])$, where $C_i[j]$ is the jth element of the set C_i with some canonical ordering.
59: **return** $a_1, \ldots, a_n$

---

call to GETRND, which samples α for $\mathcal{B}$, and returns a handle (in the form of a formal variable) X_α. $\mathcal{G}$-oSG keeps a list of these variables X_α in SimVar and the corresponding values (hidden from $\mathcal{B}$) in $SimVal$. In the following, $\mathcal{B}$ will use the handle X_α to describe computations involving α using Laurent polynomials $f_j \in \mathbb{Z}_p[\text{SimVar}^{\pm 1}]$. Whenever $\mathcal{B}$ would use α to compute some group element g, we can model this as a call to COMPUTECONCRETE. It passes the description of the sum it wants to compute in the form of pairs $(h_j, f_j) \in S_i \times \mathbb{Z}_p[\text{SimVar}^{\pm 1}]$ as input to COMPUTECONCRETE, which then uses its knowledge of the concrete values $SimVal$ to compute "$h = \sum h_j \cdot f_j(Val)$" using the OP oracle.

COMPUTECONCRETE is indistinguishable from COMPUTESYMBOLIC. In the latter, the computation is done both *atomically* in a single step, and, more importantly, *symbolically*, meaning that COMPUTESYMBOLIC does not access the concrete values *SimVal* at all. Instead, it simply computes the result f in terms of polynomials, and then returns TAU(i, f). This functionality heavily uses the fact that the encoding functions τ_i already work over polynomials. In the original $\mathcal{G}$-oSG, this capability is only used for the sake of domain separation (with the Var variables), but in the presence of COMPUTESYMBOLIC, it is also used to make computations directly over formal variables X_α corresponding to secrets of $\mathcal{B}$. For example, if g is a generator corresponding to $X_g \in$ Var, and the computation is "$h \leftarrow \alpha^{-2} \cdot g$", then the result h will be internally associated with the polynomial $f = X_\alpha^{-2} \cdot X_g = \tau_i^{-1}(h) \in \mathbb{Z}_p[\text{Var}, \text{SimVar}^{\pm 1}]$, and it will algebraically behave like f.

As an intermediate step between the interfaces COMPUTECONCRETE and COMPUTESYMBOLIC, the interface COMPUTEATOMIC does the computation in COMPUTECONCRETE, but using only a single query to TAU.

Overall, this enables the security proof to talk about group elements h by their polynomial representation $\tau_i^{-1}(h)$, which is a powerful analysis tool. The following lemma establishes indistinguishability between the three computation methods.

Lemma 4. *Define $\mathcal{O} = \mathcal{G}$-oSG.[CANONICALGEN, OBSERVE, TOUCH, OP, PAIR, GETRND].*
Let $\mathcal{B}^{\mathcal{O},\text{COMPUTEX}}$ be an algorithm that makes at most q oracle queries. For oracle queries

$$\text{COMPUTEX}(i, (h_{\ell,j}, f_{\ell,j})_{j=1}^{n_\ell}),$$

let $q' \geq \sum_{\ell=1}^{q} n_\ell$ be (an upper bound for) the number of supplied polynomials to the last oracle. Let $d \geq \max_{i,h}(\deg(\tau_i^{-1}(h)))$ be (an upper bound for) the maximum degree of (Laurent) polynomials in the execution of $\mathcal{B}^{\mathcal{O},\text{COMPUTESYMBOLIC}}$ If $3q + q' + 1 \leq p$, then

$$\left| \begin{array}{l} \Pr\left[\mathcal{B}^{\mathcal{O},\text{COMPUTECONCRETE}} = 1\right] \\ - \Pr\left[\mathcal{B}^{\mathcal{O},\text{COMPUTEATOMIC}} = 1\right] \end{array} \right| \leq (2q + q') \cdot q'/(p - q)$$

$$\left| \begin{array}{l} \Pr\left[\mathcal{B}^{\mathcal{O},\text{COMPUTEATOMIC}} = 1\right] \\ - \Pr\left[\mathcal{B}^{\mathcal{O},\text{COMPUTESYMBOLIC}} = 1\right] \end{array} \right| \leq \binom{3q + 1}{2} \cdot 2d/(p - 1)$$

As a consequence of the lemma, we get this bound for applicable $\mathcal{B}$:

$$\left| \begin{array}{l} \Pr\left[\mathcal{B}^{\mathcal{O},\text{COMPUTECONCRETE}} = 1\right] \\ - \Pr\left[\mathcal{B}^{\mathcal{O},\text{COMPUTESYMBOLIC}} = 1\right] \end{array} \right| \leq (2q + q') \cdot \frac{3q'}{2p} + (9q^2 + 3q)d/(p - 1).$$

The proof of Lemma 4 can be found in the full version of this paper [10].

4.3 Extracting Discrete Logarithm Representations

Finally, in generic group model proofs, one usually wants to extract the discrete logarithm representations of certain group elements. In the UC setting with a global generic group, this is complicated by the fact that the UC simulator for session *sid* does not have access to *all* GGM queries, but only to "illegal" queries

---

Function 1: FINDREP

FINDREP(i, h^*, Ob_{sid}, B)

1: // Finds representation of $h^* \in S_i$ w.r.t. basis $B \in S_i^n$. Requires observations Ob_{sid} of globally observable operations and the simulator's operations (see Functionality 5)

2: // Returns a (partial) representation $Rep[h^*] \in \mathbb{Z}_p^n$ in the form of coefficients for basis elements

3: **assert** $i \in \{1, 2\}$ // FINDREP for target group in [10]

4: Parse $B = (B_1, \ldots, B_n) \in S_i^n$ // Basis elements for the representation

5: $Rep[h] \leftarrow 0^n \in \mathbb{Z}_p^n$ initially for all h

6: **for** $j \in [n]$ **do** $Rep[B_j] \leftarrow (\text{Kronecker}_{\ell,j})_{\ell=1}^n$ // $\in \mathbb{Z}_p^n$

7: **for** $ob = (\text{OP}, i, g_1, g_2, a_1, a_2, h) \in Ob_{sid}$ **do** // Observed operations in order of Ob_{sid} (filtered by OP, i)

8:    $Rep[h] \leftarrow a_1 \cdot Rep[g_1] + a_2 \cdot Rep[g_2]$ // Update representation of h w.r.t. to operation result "$h = a_1 g_1 + a_2 g_2$"
   return $Rep[h^*]$ // Return representation for the h^* we were interested in

---

made in foreign sessions $sid' \neq sid$ (Line 12 and 24 in Functionality 3), and to queries made by the adversary in session sid (by design of UC / the default identity bound ξ). The list of observations available to the simulator is modeled in Line 15, 14 and Line 33 and 32 of Functionality 4. Some operations are, by design, unobservable. For example, if a protocol (embodied by the environment) in session sid' computes an element $\mathsf{f} = 3\mathsf{X} \in \mathsf{Legal}_{sid'}$, then the simulator in session sid does not get any information about that computation, and will consequently not be able to extract the coefficient 3.

The GETREP interface (Functionality 5), defines in Line 58 what we can expect from the algorithm FINDREP given the limited observation information: When extracting a representation for h^*, the algorithm FINDREP outputs coefficients that (together with the basis) *almost* sum up to the polynomial $\tau_i^{-1}(h^*)$. What is *missing* from that sum can only be (1) foreign terms, that contain foreign variables X_j from another session (because those terms may be subject to unobservable computations), and (2) missing terms, which contain a variable X not supplied to FINDREP as a basis (because FINDREP has no starting point to find coefficients for X from). When doing security proofs, one would usually argue that those terms are not required for the simulator to successfully do its job. For example, the Groth16 simulator, when extracting a Groth16 proof, is only interested in (1) elements on the correct basis (proofs containing another basis are rejected by the verification equation), and (2) coefficients of one specific term of the proof's polynomial representation, which correspond to the witness.

The FINDREP algorithm (Functionality 1) itself is quite simple: it linearly scans the list of observations and keeps track of their representations Rep in terms of the basis B supplied.

The following lemma states that FINDREP works correctly. This is defined in terms of the symbolic computation setting and the interface GETREP, which runs

FINDREP with the expected input (in particular with the correct observation list Ob_{sid}) and then checks the output.

Lemma 5. *Define* $\mathcal{O} = \mathcal{G}\text{-oSG}.[\text{CANONICALGEN}, \text{OBSERVE}, \text{TOUCH}, \text{OP}, \text{PAIR},$ $\text{GETRND}, \underline{\text{COMPUTESYMBOLIC}}, \underline{\text{GETREP}}].$ *Let* $\mathcal{B}$ *be an algorithm that makes at most* p *queries. Then*

$$\Pr\left[\mathcal{B}^{\mathcal{O}} \text{ has assertion in Line 58 of Functionality 5 fail}\right] = 0$$

The proof can be found in the full version [10].

5   UC Security of Groth16

In Protocol 1, we present the Groth16 protocol Π-G16 in the presence of our global observable generic group functionality $\mathcal{G}$-oGG. The protocol is described in the $\mathcal{F}$-CRS-hybrid model (Functionality 6). The crucial operation is for-loop starting at Line 1, in which $\mathcal{F}$-CRS registers uniformly random session-specific generators $g_{sid,i}$. In this way, all of the group operations performed by honest provers are confined to the domain of the current session and thus unobservable by the environment (except if $\mathcal{F}$-CRS or prover accidentally operates on group elements that are already reserved for another session, which occurs with negligible probability). We defer detailed hybrids for Theorem 1 to the full version [10].

Theorem 1. Π-G16 *UC-realizes* $\mathcal{F}$-wNIZK *in the* $\mathcal{F}$-CRS-*hybrid model in the presence of* $\mathcal{G}$-oGG. *Concretely, for any PPT adversary* $\mathcal{A}$, *there exists a PPT simulator* $\mathcal{S}_{G16}$ *such that for every* $\mathcal{Z}$ *that makes at most* $q_{\mathcal{Z}}$ *queries to* $\mathcal{G}$-oGG, $q_{\mathcal{P}}$ *queries to the* PROVE *interface, and* $q_{\mathcal{V}}$ *queries to the* VERIFY *interface,*

$$|\Pr[\text{EXEC}_{\mathcal{F}\text{-wNIZK},\mathcal{Z},\mathcal{S}_{G16},\mathcal{G}\text{-oGG}}(\lambda, z) = 1] - \Pr[\text{EXEC}_{\Pi\text{-G16},\mathcal{Z},\mathcal{A},\mathcal{G}\text{-oGG}}(\lambda, z) = 1]|$$
$$\leq 72 \cdot d \cdot (m + d + q_{\mathcal{Z}} + (m+d)q_{\mathcal{P}} + \ell q_{\mathcal{V}} + 1)^2/(p-1)$$

and $\mathcal{S}_{G16}$ *performs in total the following operations:*
- *at most* $3q_{\mathcal{P}} + 9q_{\mathcal{V}} + 2q_{\mathcal{Z}} + 3d + m + 8$ *queries to* $\mathcal{G}$-oGG
- *at most* $(2\ell + 8)q_{\mathcal{P}} + (3q_{\mathcal{Z}} + 2\ell + 2)q_{\mathcal{V}} + (d+1)(3m+11)$ *field operations where* d, m, ℓ *depend on the circuit size (see Functionality 6).*

6   Composition When Unobservability Is Required

The observable G-GGM is well suited for proving succinct arguments such as Groth16. In such schemes honest parties do not execute secret-dependent computations on adversarial group elements. As honest provers only compute on group elements originating from their own session, observability does not pose any privacy challenges, e.g. for the proof of the zero-knowledge property.

This situation is significantly different for other cryptographic schemes. For instance for the PAKE proof of [30] the authors assume that no information

---

Functionality 6: $\mathcal{F}$-CRS

$\mathcal{F}$-CRS has access to $\mathcal{G}$-oGG.

$\mathcal{F}$-CRS is parameterized by an NP-relation determined by QAP $(u_i, v_i, w_i)_{i=0}^m \in \mathbb{F}_p^{d-1}[X]$ and $t \in \mathbb{F}_p^d[X]$, where d is the number of multiplication gates and $a_0 = 1$:

$$\mathcal{R}_{\mathsf{QAP}} = \left\{ (\{a_i\}_{i=1}^\ell, \{a_i\}_{i=\ell+1}^m) \ : \ (\textstyle\sum_{i=0}^m a_i u_i)(\sum_{i=0}^m a_i v_i) \equiv (\sum_{i=0}^m a_i w_i) \bmod t \right\}$$

To simplify notation we denote $q_i(\alpha, \beta, x) := \beta u_i(x) + \alpha v_i(x) + w_i(x)$.

$\mathcal{F}$-CRS stores state:

- σ, labels for common reference string

We use the following compact notation for a vector of encoded group elements with known discrete logs:

- $[x, y, \ldots]_{sid,i} := (\mathcal{G}\text{-oGG.}\mathrm{OP}_{sid}(i, g_{sid,i}, g_{sid,i}, x, 0), \mathcal{G}\text{-oGG.}\mathrm{OP}_{sid}(i, g_{sid,i}, g_{sid,i}, y, 0), \ldots)$

$\underline{\mathrm{INIT}_{sid}()}$ // Invoked only upon creation

1: **for** $i = 1, 2$ **do**
2:    $g_{sid,i} \xleftarrow{\$} S_i$
3:    $\mathcal{G}\text{-oGG.}\mathrm{TOUCH}_{sid}(i, g_{sid,i})$
4: $x, \alpha, \beta, \gamma, \delta \xleftarrow{\$} \mathbb{Z}_p$
5: $\sigma_1 \leftarrow [\alpha, \beta, \delta, \{x^i\}_{i=0}^{d-1}, \{q_i(\alpha, \beta, x)\gamma^{-1}\}_{i=0}^\ell, \{q_i(\alpha, \beta, x)\delta^{-1}\}_{i=\ell+1}^m, \{x^i t(x)\delta^{-1}\}_{i=0}^{d-2}]_{sid,1}$
6: $\sigma_2 \leftarrow [\beta, \gamma, \delta, \{x^i\}_{i=0}^{d-1}]_{sid,2}$
7: $\sigma \leftarrow (\sigma_1, \sigma_2)$

$\underline{\mathrm{GETCRS}_{sid}()}$

8: **return** σ

Protocol 1: Π-G16

The protocol has access to $\mathcal{F}$-CRS and $\mathcal{G}$-oGG.

$\underline{\mathrm{PROVE}_{sid}(x = \{a_i\}_{i=1}^\ell, w = \{a_i\}_{i=\ell+1}^m)}$

1: **if** $(x, w) \notin \mathcal{R}_{\mathsf{QAP}}$ **then return** $\bot$
2: $\sigma \leftarrow \mathcal{F}\text{-CRS}[\mathcal{G}\text{-oGG}, \mathcal{R}_{\mathsf{QAP}}].\mathrm{GETCRS}_{sid}()$
3: $r, s \xleftarrow{\$} \mathbb{Z}_p$
4: Compute $h \in \mathbb{F}^{d-2}[X]$ such that $ht = (\sum_{i=0}^m a_i u_i)(\sum_{i=0}^m a_i v_i) - (\sum_{i=0}^m a_i w_i)$
5: $A := [a]_{sid,1} \leftarrow \left[\sum_{i=0}^m a_i u_i(x) + \alpha + r\delta\right]_{sid,1}$ // Computed by calling $\mathcal{G}\text{-oGG.}\mathrm{OP}_{sid}$ on $[x^i]_{sid,1}, [\alpha]_{sid,1}, [\delta]_{sid,1}$
6: $B := [b]_{sid,2} \leftarrow \left[\sum_{i=0}^m a_i v_i(x) + \beta + s\delta\right]_{sid,2}$ // Computed by calling $\mathcal{G}\text{-oGG.}\mathrm{OP}_{sid}$ on $[x^i]_{sid,2}, [\beta]_{sid,2}, [\delta]_{sid,2}$
7: $C := [c]_{sid,1} \leftarrow \left[\sum_{i=\ell+1}^m a_i q_i(\alpha, \beta, x)\delta^{-1} + h(x)t(x)\delta^{-1} + sa + rb - rs\delta\right]_{sid,1}$
   // Computed by calling $\mathcal{G}\text{-oGG.}\mathrm{OP}_{sid}$ on $[q_i(\alpha, \beta, x)\delta^{-1}]_{sid,1}, [x^i t(x)\delta^{-1}]_{sid,1}, [a]_{sid,1}, [\beta]_{sid,1}, [\delta]_{sid,1}$
8: **return** (A, B, C)

$\underline{\mathrm{VERIFY}_{sid}(x = \{a_i\}_{i=1}^\ell, \pi = (A, B, C))}$

9: $\sigma \leftarrow \mathcal{F}\text{-CRS}[\mathcal{G}\text{-oGG}, \mathcal{R}_{\mathsf{QAP}}].\mathrm{GETCRS}_{sid}()$
10: $C_{\mathrm{pub}} \leftarrow \left[\sum_{i=0}^\ell a_i q_i(\alpha, \beta, x)\gamma^{-1}\right]_{sid,1}$ // Computed by calling $\mathcal{G}\text{-oGG.}\mathrm{OP}_{sid}$ on $[q_i(\alpha, \beta, x)\gamma^{-1}]_{sid,1}$
11: **return** $A \cdot B = C_{\mathrm{pub}} \cdot [\gamma]_{sid,2} + C \cdot [\delta]_{sid,2} + [\alpha]_{sid,1} \cdot [\beta]_{sid,2}$ // Computed by calling $\mathcal{G}\text{-oGG.}\mathrm{OP}_{sid}$ and $\mathcal{G}\text{-oGG.}\mathrm{PAIR}_{sid}$

about oracle usage is disclosed between parties. Similar issues arise for public-key encryption and oblivious PRFs [44] when modeled with $\mathcal{G}$-oGG. The security proofs of such schemes fail when using $\mathcal{G}$-oGG, because the environment can send group elements—ciphertexts or blinded evaluation points—that originate from a foreign session. As an honest party applies their secret key to them, this leaks the key.

Note that this is inherent for any observable model of generic groups, as long as sessions are treated "symmetrically". That is, the OBSERVE$_{sid}$ oracle can either be called by the simulator to prove session sid secure, or by the environment to model another protocol in session sid' composed in parallel, and prove overall security when reusing the same group.

Consider two cryptographic schemes: G16 in session sid and in session sid' a CCA2-secure variant of ElGamal, which we refer to as EG2, e.g. ECIES [61] or Cramer-Shoup [29]. The distinguishing environment against G16 can make calls to OP$_{sid'}$. The OBSERVE$_{sid}$ oracle must include OP$_{sid'}$ operations on group elements that originated in session sid, such as those used to generate a reference string for G16. Otherwise the extractor for G16 would fail to extract the witness. However, a distinguishing environment against EG2 (which can call OBSERVE$_{sid}$) must *not* observe OP$_{sid'}$ operations on group elements that originated in session sid. Otherwise it would obtain leaked information about the EG2 secret key.

The crucial step to escape this conundrum is to observe that OBSERVE$_{sid}$ is only called by the Groth16 simulator in the *ideal* world. Thus conceptually, we can work with a non-observable generic group (and apply the standard UCGS composition theorem to protocols like Π-EG2 in that setting). Only when we want to switch from the concrete protocol Π-G16 to the ideal $\mathcal{F}$-wNIZK, we switch to observable groups (as required by the Groth16 ideal world simulator). We develop details in the full version of this paper [10].

7   Conclusion and Future Work

In this paper, we have established the restricted observable global generic group functionality $\mathcal{G}$-oGG and, as an important application to a widespread SNARK, we have proven Groth16 UC-secure in the $\mathcal{F}$-CRS hybrid model in the presence of $\mathcal{G}$-oGG. We expect the functionality $\mathcal{G}$-oGG to find additional applications, in particular for proving other SNARKs UC-secure, especially ones based on polynomial interactive oracle proofs (PIOPs) [14, 16, 27], such as PLONK [37]. In fact, recent works show that SNARKs obtained from PIOP and the KZG polynomial commitment [45] are already simulation-extractable without modification in the AGM and (programmable) ROM [33, 34, 47]. Thus, a natural follow-up question is whether these SNARKs are UC-secure in the presence of $\mathcal{G}$-oGG and (restricted programmable) global random oracle functionalities.

Another exciting research opportunity is to establish a "UC lifting theorem" that allows practitioners to analyze the security of their constructions in the (simpler) game-based generic-group model, and then automatically obtain UC security via lifting. Section 4 already establishes that in spirit, standard GGM proof techniques carry over to the UC setting. Our proof of Groth16 security is a good indicator that the protocol-specific part of the proof mostly boils down to symbolic analysis of polynomials, which is already available from the original paper, or from proofs in the AGM. Establishing formal requirements for a game-based proof to carry over to UC, would be a powerful bridge between game-based "standalone" proofs and UC proofs.

While our paper addresses reuse of the group (multiple protocols using the same group), we leave open the question of a reusable CRS for Groth16, or more generally, the question of reusing (parts of the) CRS across multiple sessions for NIZK in UC. Our Groth16 works in the $\mathcal{F}$-CRS-hybrid model, which means that every session of Groth16 needs its own CRS (which can be "reused" only insofar that parties in the same session can compute multiple proofs from it). The same limitation applies to essentially all existing results on CRS-based NIZK in UC [2,3,6,23,24,28,38,39,48,53], which also rely on non-reusable, local CRS functionalities.

We have focused on the strict and observable versions of the global generic group functionalities. Similarly to random oracles [15], one could envision various levels of programmability for generic groups. While programmability of generic groups is seldomly exploited in game-based proofs (and, to our knowledge, has not been used for NIZK constructions), it is a possibility (e.g., [25]) and deserves formal UC treatment.

While the generic group model seems to have inherent advantages when it comes to compositional proofs, as discussed in the introduction, the algebraic group model (with oblivious sampling [51]) is the more conservative model (in the sense of restricting the adversary and protocols) in general. An interesting question is whether there is a composable model in the spirit of the AGM that does not restrict the environment from using group elements across sessions.

Finally, we have provided a concrete security analysis of Groth16, giving concrete bounds in Theorem 1. It can be interesting to revisit the tightness of this analysis, especially compared to the game-based setting. However, we are not aware of any GGM-based concrete parameter treatment of Groth16 in the literature, even in the game-based setting. Another interesting direction is to explore what this concrete guarantee means for compositions using Groth16 since concrete security of simulation-based security and of the UC theorem is not well-studied in the literature.

Acknowledgments. We thank Sabine Oechsner for insightful discussions on the connection between this work and State Separating Proofs.

Pooya Farshim was supported in part by EPSRC grant EP/V034065/1. This work was supported by Input Output (iohk.io) through their funding of the Edinburgh ZK-Lab.

This paper was prepared in part for information purposes by the Artificial Intelligence Research group of JPMorgan Chase & Co and its affiliates ("JP Morgan"), and is not a product of the Research Department of JP Morgan. JP Morgan makes no representation and warranty whatsoever and disclaims all liability, for the completeness, accuracy or reliability of the information contained herein. This document is not intended as investment research or investment advice, or a recommendation, offer or solicitation for the purchase or sale of any security, financial instrument, financial product or service, or to be used in any way for evaluating the merits of participating in any transaction, and shall not constitute a solicitation under any jurisdiction or to any person, if such solicitation under such jurisdiction or to such person would be unlawful.

References

1. Abdalla, M., Barbosa, M., Katz, J., Loss, J., Xu, J.: Algebraic adversaries in the universal composability framework. In: Tibouchi, M., Wang, H. (eds.) ASIACRYPT 2021. LNCS, vol. 13092, pp. 311–341. Springer, Cham (2021). https://doi.org/10.1007/978-3-030-92078-4_11
2. Abdolmaleki, B., Glaeser, N., Ramacher, S., Slamanig, D.: Universally composable NIZKs: Circuit-succinct, non-malleable and CRS-updatable. Cryptology ePrint Archive, Report 2023/097 (2023). https://eprint.iacr.org/2023/097
3. Abdolmaleki, B., Ramacher, S., Slamanig, D.: Lift-and-shift: obtaining simulation extractable subversion and updatable SNARKs generically. In: Ligatti, J., Ou, X., Katz, J., Vigna, G. (eds.) ACM CCS 2020, pp. 1987–2005. ACM Press (2020). https://doi.org/10.1145/3372297.3417228
4. Badertscher, C., Canetti, R., Hesse, J., Tackmann, B., Zikas, V.: Universal composition with global subroutines: capturing global setup within plain UC. In: Pass, R., Pietrzak, K. (eds.) TCC 2020. LNCS, vol. 12552, pp. 1–30. Springer, Cham (2020). https://doi.org/10.1007/978-3-030-64381-2_1
5. Baghery, K., Kohlweiss, M., Siim, J., Volkhov, M.: Another look at extraction and randomization of Groth's zk-SNARK. In: Borisov, N., Diaz, C. (eds.) FC 2021. LNCS, vol. 12674, pp. 457–475. Springer, Heidelberg (2021). https://doi.org/10.1007/978-3-662-64322-8_22
6. Baghery, K., Sedaghat, M.: Tiramisu: black-box simulation extractable NIZKs in the updatable CRS model. In: Conti, M., Stevens, M., Krenn, S. (eds.) CANS 2021. LNCS, vol. 13099, pp. 531–551. Springer, Cham (2021). https://doi.org/10.1007/978-3-030-92548-2_28
7. Bartusek, J., Ma, F., Zhandry, M.: The distinction between fixed and random generators in group-based assumptions. In: Boldyreva, A., Micciancio, D. (eds.) CRYPTO 2019. LNCS, vol. 11693, pp. 801–830. Springer, Cham (2019). https://doi.org/10.1007/978-3-030-26951-7_27
8. Bauer, B., Farshim, P., Harasser, P., Kohlweiss, M.: The uber-knowledge assumption: a bridge to the agm. Cryptology ePrint Archive, Paper 2023/1601 (2023). https://eprint.iacr.org/2023/1601
9. Ben-Sasson, E., Chiesa, A., Spooner, N.: Interactive oracle proofs. In: Hirt, M., Smith, A. (eds.) TCC 2016. LNCS, vol. 9986, pp. 31–60. Springer, Heidelberg (2016). https://doi.org/10.1007/978-3-662-53644-5_2
10. Bobolz, J., Farshim, P., Kohlweiss, M., Takahashi, A.: The brave new world of global generic groups and UC-secure zero-overhead SNARKs. Cryptology ePrint Archive, Paper 2024/818 (2024). https://eprint.iacr.org/2024/818
11. Boneh, D., Lynn, B., Shacham, H.: Short signatures from the weil pairing. In: Boyd, C. (ed.) ASIACRYPT 2001. LNCS, vol. 2248, pp. 514–532. Springer, Heidelberg (2001). https://doi.org/10.1007/3-540-45682-1_30
12. Bowe, S., Gabizon, A.: Making groth's zk-SNARK simulation extractable in the random oracle model. Cryptology ePrint Archive, Report 2018/187 (2018). https://eprint.iacr.org/2018/187

13. Brzuska, C., Delignat-Lavaud, A., Fournet, C., Kohbrok, K., Kohlweiss, M.: State separation for code-based game-playing proofs. In: Peyrin, T., Galbraith, S. (eds.) ASIACRYPT 2018. LNCS, vol. 11274, pp. 222–249. Springer, Cham (2018). https://doi.org/10.1007/978-3-030-03332-3_9

14. Bünz, B., Fisch, B., Szepieniec, A.: Transparent SNARKs from DARK compilers. In: Canteaut, A., Ishai, Y. (eds.) EUROCRYPT 2020. LNCS, vol. 12105, pp. 677–706. Springer, Cham (2020). https://doi.org/10.1007/978-3-030-45721-1_24

15. Camenisch, J., Drijvers, M., Gagliardoni, T., Lehmann, A., Neven, G.: The wonderful world of global random oracles. In: Nielsen, J.B., Rijmen, V. (eds.) EUROCRYPT 2018. LNCS, vol. 10820, pp. 280–312. Springer, Cham (2018). https://doi.org/10.1007/978-3-319-78381-9_11

16. Campanelli, M., Faonio, A., Fiore, D., Querol, A., Rodríguez, H.: Lunar: a toolbox for more efficient universal and updatable zkSNARKs and commit-and-prove extensions. In: Tibouchi, M., Wang, H. (eds.) ASIACRYPT 2021. LNCS, vol. 13092, pp. 3–33. Springer, Cham (2021). https://doi.org/10.1007/978-3-030-92078-4_1

17. Canetti, R.: Universally composable security: a new paradigm for cryptographic protocols. In: 42nd FOCS, pp. 136–145. IEEE Computer Society Press (2001). https://doi.org/10.1109/SFCS.2001.959888

18. Canetti, R.: Universally composable security. J. ACM **67**(5), 28:1–28:94 (2020). https://doi.org/10.1145/3402457

19. Canetti, R.: Universally composable security: a new paradigm for cryptographic protocols. Cryptology ePrint Archive, Paper 2000/067 (2020). https://eprint.iacr.org/2000/067, https://eprint.iacr.org/2000/067

20. Canetti, R., Dodis, Y., Pass, R., Walfish, S.: Universally composable security with global setup. In: Vadhan, S.P. (ed.) TCC 2007. LNCS, vol. 4392, pp. 61–85. Springer, Heidelberg (2007). https://doi.org/10.1007/978-3-540-70936-7_4

21. Canetti, R., Jain, A., Scafuro, A.: Practical UC security with a global random oracle. In: Ahn, G.J., Yung, M., Li, N. (eds.) ACM CCS 2014, pp. 597–608. ACM Press (2014). https://doi.org/10.1145/2660267.2660374

22. Canetti, R., Rabin, T.: Universal composition with joint state. In: Boneh, D. (ed.) CRYPTO 2003. LNCS, vol. 2729, pp. 265–281. Springer, Heidelberg (2003). https://doi.org/10.1007/978-3-540-45146-4_16

23. Canetti, R., Sarkar, P., Wang, X.: Triply adaptive UC NIZK. In: Agrawal, S., Lin, D. (eds.) ASIACRYPT 2022, Part II. LNCS, vol. 13792, pp. 466–495. Springer, Heidelberg (2022). https://doi.org/10.1007/978-3-031-22966-4_16

24. Chase, M., Lysyanskaya, A.: On Signatures of Knowledge. In: Dwork, C. (ed.) CRYPTO 2006. LNCS, vol. 4117, pp. 78–96. Springer, Heidelberg (2006). https://doi.org/10.1007/11818175_5

25. Chen, B., et al.: Rotatable zero knowledge sets - post compromise secure auditable dictionaries with application to key transparency. In: Agrawal, S., Lin, D. (eds.) ASIACRYPT 2022, Part III. LNCS, vol. 13793, pp. 547–580. Springer, Heidelberg (2022). https://doi.org/10.1007/978-3-031-22969-5_19

26. Chiesa, A., Fenzi, G.: zksnarks in the rom with unconditional uc-security. Cryptology ePrint Archive, Paper 2024/724 (2024). https://eprint.iacr.org/2024/724

27. Chiesa, A., Hu, Y., Maller, M., Mishra, P., Vesely, N., Ward, N.: Marlin: preprocessing zkSNARKs with universal and updatable SRS. In: Canteaut, A., Ishai, Y. (eds.) EUROCRYPT 2020. LNCS, vol. 12105, pp. 738–768. Springer, Cham (2020). https://doi.org/10.1007/978-3-030-45721-1_26

28. Cohen, R., Shelat, A., Wichs, D.: Adaptively secure MPC with sublinear communication complexity. In: Boldyreva, A., Micciancio, D. (eds.) CRYPTO 2019. LNCS, vol. 11693, pp. 30–60. Springer, Cham (2019). https://doi.org/10.1007/978-3-030-26951-7_2

29. Cramer, R., Shoup, V.: A practical public key cryptosystem provably secure against adaptive chosen ciphertext attack. In: Krawczyk, H. (ed.) CRYPTO 1998. LNCS, vol. 1462, pp. 13–25. Springer, Heidelberg (1998). https://doi.org/10.1007/BFb0055717

30. Cremers, C., Naor, M., Paz, S., Ronen, E.: CHIP and CRISP: Protecting all parties against compromise through identity-binding PAKEs. In: Dodis, Y., Shrimpton, T. (eds.) CRYPTO 2022, Part II. LNCS, vol. 13508, pp. 668–698. Springer, Heidelberg (2022). https://doi.org/10.1007/978-3-031-15979-4_23

31. De Santis, A., Di Crescenzo, G., Ostrovsky, R., Persiano, G., Sahai, A.: Robust noninteractive zero knowledge. In: Kilian, J. (ed.) CRYPTO 2001. LNCS, vol. 2139, pp. 566–598. Springer, Heidelberg (2001). https://doi.org/10.1007/3-540-44647-8_33

32. Dent, A.W.: Adapting the weaknesses of the random oracle model to the generic group model. In: Zheng, Y. (ed.) ASIACRYPT 2002. LNCS, vol. 2501, pp. 100–109. Springer, Heidelberg (2002). https://doi.org/10.1007/3-540-36178-2_6

33. Faonio, A., Fiore, D., Kohlweiss, M., Russo, L., Zajac, M.: From polynomial IOP and commitments to non-malleable zkSNARKs. In: Rothblum, G.N., Wee, H. (eds.) TCC 2023, Part III. LNCS, vol. 14371, pp. 455–485. Springer, Heidelberg (2023). https://doi.org/10.1007/978-3-031-48621-0_16

34. Faonio, A., Fiore, D., Russo, L.: Real-world universal zksnarks are non-malleable. Cryptology ePrint Archive, Paper 2024/721 (2024). https://eprint.iacr.org/2024/721

35. Faust, S., Kohlweiss, M., Marson, G.A., Venturi, D.: On the non-malleability of the fiat-shamir transform. In: Galbraith, S., Nandi, M. (eds.) INDOCRYPT 2012. LNCS, vol. 7668, pp. 60–79. Springer, Heidelberg (2012). https://doi.org/10.1007/978-3-642-34931-7_5

36. Fuchsbauer, G., Kiltz, E., Loss, J.: The algebraic group model and its applications. In: Shacham, H., Boldyreva, A. (eds.) CRYPTO 2018. LNCS, vol. 10992, pp. 33–62. Springer, Cham (2018). https://doi.org/10.1007/978-3-319-96881-0_2

37. Gabizon, A., Williamson, Z.J., Ciobotaru, O.: PLONK: permutations over lagrange-bases for oecumenical noninteractive arguments of knowledge. Cryptology ePrint Archive, Report 2019/953 (2019). https://eprint.iacr.org/2019/953

38. Ganesh, C., Kondi, Y., Orlandi, C., Pancholi, M., Takahashi, A., Tschudi, D.: Witness-succinct universally-composable SNARKs. In: Hazay, C., Stam, M. (eds.) EUROCRYPT 2023, Part II. LNCS, vol. 14005, pp. 315–346. Springer, Heidelberg (2023). https://doi.org/10.1007/978-3-031-30617-4_11

39. Groth, J.: Simulation-Sound NIZK proofs for a practical language and constant size group signatures. In: Lai, X., Chen, K. (eds.) ASIACRYPT 2006. LNCS, vol. 4284, pp. 444–459. Springer, Heidelberg (2006). https://doi.org/10.1007/11935230_29

40. Groth, J.: On the size of pairing-based non-interactive arguments. In: Fischlin, M., Coron, J.-S. (eds.) EUROCRYPT 2016. LNCS, vol. 9666, pp. 305–326. Springer, Heidelberg (2016). https://doi.org/10.1007/978-3-662-49896-5_11

41. Groth, J., Maller, M.: Snarky signatures: minimal signatures of knowledge from simulation-extractable SNARKs. In: Katz, J., Shacham, H. (eds.) CRYPTO 2017. LNCS, vol. 10402, pp. 581–612. Springer, Cham (2017). https://doi.org/10.1007/978-3-319-63715-0_20

42. Hofheinz, D., Shoup, V.: GNUC: a new universal composability framework. J. Cryptol. **28**(3), 423–508 (2015). https://doi.org/10.1007/s00145-013-9160-y

43. Jager, T., Rupp, A.: The semi-generic group model and applications to pairing-based cryptography. In: Abe, M. (ed.) ASIACRYPT 2010. LNCS, vol. 6477, pp. 539–556. Springer, Heidelberg (2010). https://doi.org/10.1007/978-3-642-17373-8_31

44. Jarecki, S., Kiayias, A., Krawczyk, H.: Round-optimal password-protected secret sharing and T-PAKE in the password-only model. In: Sarkar, P., Iwata, T. (eds.) ASIACRYPT 2014. LNCS, vol. 8874, pp. 233–253. Springer, Heidelberg (2014). https://doi.org/10.1007/978-3-662-45608-8_13

45. Kate, A., Zaverucha, G.M., Goldberg, I.: Constant-size commitments to polynomials and their applications. In: Abe, M. (ed.) ASIACRYPT 2010. LNCS, vol. 6477, pp. 177–194. Springer, Heidelberg (2010). https://doi.org/10.1007/978-3-642-17373-8_11

46. Kerber, T., Kiayias, A., Kohlweiss, M.: Composition with knowledge assumptions. In: Malkin, T., Peikert, C. (eds.) CRYPTO 2021. LNCS, vol. 12828, pp. 364–393. Springer, Cham (2021). https://doi.org/10.1007/978-3-030-84259-8_13

47. Kohlweiss, M., Pancholi, M., Takahashi, A.: How to compile polynomial IOP into simulation-extractable SNARKs: a modular approach. In: Rothblum, G.N., Wee, H. (eds.) TCC 2023, Part III. LNCS, vol. 14371, pp. 486–512. Springer, Heidelberg (2023). https://doi.org/10.1007/978-3-031-48621-0_17

48. Kosba, A., et al.: C∅c∅: a framework for building composable zero-knowledge proofs. Cryptology ePrint Archive, Report 2015/1093 (2015). https://eprint.iacr.org/2015/1093

49. Kosba, A.E., Miller, A., Shi, E., Wen, Z., Papamanthou, C.: Hawk: the blockchain model of cryptography and privacy-preserving smart contracts. In: 2016 IEEE Symposium on Security and Privacy, pp. 839–858. IEEE Computer Society Press (2016). https://doi.org/10.1109/SP.2016.55

50. Küsters, R.: Simulation-based security with inexhaustible interactive Turing machines. Cryptology ePrint Archive, Report 2006/151 (2006). https://eprint.iacr.org/2006/151

51. Lipmaa, H., Parisella, R., Siim, J.: Algebraic group model with oblivious sampling. In: Rothblum, G.N., Wee, H. (eds.) Theory of Cryptography - 21st International Conference, TCC 2023, Taipei, Taiwan, 29 November–2 December 2023, Proceedings, Part IV. LNCS, vol. 14372, pp. 363–392. Springer, Heidelbegr (2023). https://doi.org/10.1007/978-3-031-48624-1_14

52. Lysyanskaya, A., Rosenbloom, L.N.: Efficient and universally composable non-interactive zero-knowledge proofs of knowledge with security against adaptive corruptions. Cryptology ePrint Archive, Report 2022/1484 (2022). https://eprint.iacr.org/2022/1484

53. Lysyanskaya, A., Rosenbloom, L.N.: Universally composable Σ-protocols in the global random-oracle model. In: Kiltz, E., Vaikuntanathan, V. (eds.) TCC 2022, Part I. LNCS, vol. 13747, pp. 203–233. Springer, Heidelberg (2022). https://doi.org/10.1007/978-3-031-22318-1_8

54. Maurer, U.: Constructive Cryptography – A Primer. In: Sion, R. (ed.) FC 2010. LNCS, vol. 6052, p. 1. Springer, Heidelberg (2010). https://doi.org/10.1007/978-3-642-14577-3_1

55. Maurer, U.M.: Abstract models of computation in cryptography (invited paper). In: Smart, N.P. (ed.) 10th IMA International Conference on Cryptography and Coding. LNCS, vol. 3796, pp. 1–12. Springer, Heidelberg (2005)

56. Micali, S.: Computationally sound proofs. SIAM J. Comput. **30**(4), 1253–1298 (2000). https://doi.org/10.1137/S0097539795284959

57. Nechaev, V.I.: Complexity of a determinate algorithm for the discrete logarithm. Math. Notes **55**(2), 165–172 (1994)
58. Pointcheval, D., Sanders, O.: Short randomizable signatures. In: Sako, K. (ed.) CT-RSA 2016. LNCS, vol. 9610, pp. 111–126. Springer, Heidelberg (2016). https://doi.org/10.1007/978-3-319-29485-8_7
59. Sahai, A.: Non-malleable non-interactive zero knowledge and adaptive chosen-ciphertext security. In: 40th FOCS, pp. 543–553. IEEE Computer Society Press (1999). https://doi.org/10.1109/SFFCS.1999.814628
60. Shoup, V.: Lower bounds for discrete logarithms and related problems. In: Fumy, W. (ed.) EUROCRYPT'97. LNCS, vol. 1233, pp. 256–266. Springer, Heidelberg (1997). https://doi.org/10.1007/3-540-69053-0_18
61. Smart, N.P.: The exact security of ECIES in the generic group model. In: Honary, B. (ed.) 8th IMA International Conference on Cryptography and Coding. LNCS, vol. 2260, pp. 73–84. Springer, Heidelberg (2001)
62. Stern, J., Pointcheval, D., Malone-Lee, J., Smart, N.P.: Flaws in applying proof methodologies to signature schemes. In: Yung, M. (ed.) CRYPTO 2002. LNCS, vol. 2442, pp. 93–110. Springer, Heidelberg (2002). https://doi.org/10.1007/3-540-45708-9_7
63. Zhandry, M.: To label, or not to label (in generic groups). In: Dodis, Y., Shrimpton, T. (eds.) CRYPTO 2022, Part III. LNCS, vol. 13509, pp. 66–96. Springer, Heidelberg (2022). https://doi.org/10.1007/978-3-031-15982-4_3
64. Zhang, C., Zhou, H.S., Katz, J.: An analysis of the algebraic group model. In: Agrawal, S., Lin, D. (eds.) ASIACRYPT 2022, Part IV. LNCS, vol. 13794, pp. 310–322. Springer, Heidelberg (2022). https://doi.org/10.1007/978-3-031-22972-5_11

Hamming Weight Proofs of Proximity with One-Sided Error

Gal Arnon[1] , Shany Ben-David[2]($\boxtimes$) , and Eylon Yogev[2]

[1] Weizmann Institute, Rehovot, Israel
gal.arnon@weizmann.ac.il
[2] Bar-Ilan University, Ramat Gan, Israel
{shany.ben-david,eylon.yogev}@biu.ac.il

Abstract. We provide a wide systematic study of proximity proofs with one-sided error for the Hamming weight problem Ham_α (the language of bit vectors with Hamming weight at least α), surpassing previously known results for this problem. We demonstrate the usefulness of the one-sided error property in applications: no malicious party can frame an honest prover as cheating by presenting verifier randomness that leads to a rejection.

We show proofs of proximity for Ham_α with one-sided error and sublinear proof length in three models (MA, PCP, IOP), where stronger models allow for smaller query complexity. For n-bit input vectors, highlighting input query complexity, our MA has $O(\log n)$ query complexity, the PCP makes $O(\log\log n)$ queries, and the IOP makes a single input query. The prover in all of our applications runs in expected quasi-linear time. Additionally, we show that any perfectly complete IP of proximity for Ham_α with input query complexity $n^{1-\epsilon}$ has proof length $\Omega(\log n)$.

Furthermore, we study PCPs of proximity where the verifier is restricted to making a single input query (SIQ). We show that any SIQ-PCP for Ham_α must have a linear proof length, and complement this by presenting a SIQ-PCP with proof length $n + o(n)$.

As an application, we provide new methods that transform PCPs (and IOPs) for arbitrary languages with nonzero completeness error into PCPs (and IOPs) that exhibit perfect completeness. These transformations achieve parameters previously unattained.

Keywords: Hamming weight problem · interactive proofs of proximity · interactive oracle proofs

1 Introduction

A Motivating Example. On April 14, 2022, businessman Elon Musk made an unsolicited and non-binding offer to purchase the social media company "Twitter, Inc." for \$43 billion and take it private, which the board reluctantly accepted. In July, Musk announced his intention to terminate the agreement in the wake of reports that, despite the board's assurance, 5% of Twitter's daily active users

© International Association for Cryptologic Research 2025
E. Boyle and M. Mahmoody (Eds.): TCC 2024, LNCS 15364, pp. 125–157, 2025.
https://doi.org/10.1007/978-3-031-78011-0_5

were *spambot* accounts. In order to collect data, Musk posted a Twitter poll asking followers about the amount of spambots. In response, Twitter pursued legal action against Musk, which eventually led to the completion of the acquisition on October 27, 2022.

The acquisition was messy, involved extensive litigation, dropped the share price, affected many individuals, and was expensive and time-consuming. The process could have been more straightforward had the parties had the tools to build mutual trust. Specifically, they lacked a method for Twitter to efficiently *prove* to Musk, beyond a reasonable doubt, that the number of spambots is indeed lower than 5%. Musk could have hired experts to examine whether a handful of *specific* users are spambots, but exploring all of the ~350 million users is impractical. The appropriate tool to remedy the situation is a *proof of proximity*.

Proofs of Proximity. Proofs of proximity are probabilistic proofs with a sublinear time verifier. Since the verifier runs in sublinear time, it cannot even read the entire input. Following work on sublinear time algorithms and property testing [RS96, GGR98], the verifier is given *query access* to the input: the input x is treated as an oracle and, on query i, the verifier receives $x[i]$. The goal is to construct probabilistic proofs with sublinear query complexity while minimizing parameters such as verifier running time and communication complexity. Proofs of proximity were first introduced by Ergun, Kumar, and Rubinfeld [EKR04] and further studied by Rothblum, Vadhan, and Wigderson [RVW13] and Gur and Rothblum [GR18], motivated by applications to delegation of computation. Since then, there has been considerable research on proofs of proximity across various models.

The Hamming Weight Problem. This work focuses on probabilistic proofs of proximity for the *Hamming weight* problem. Here, the task is to decide whether a given string $x \in \{0,1\}^n$ has Hamming weight at least $\alpha(n)$ or is far from it: it has Hamming weight less than $\alpha(n) - \delta(n)$, for a proximity parameter δ.

A proof of proximity for this problem would have been useful in the context of the Twitter acquisition. Twitter's network can be represented as a binary vector x whose length corresponds to the number of Twitter accounts with a value of 1 indicating the non-spambot users. Twitter would submit a proof of the vector's Hamming weight, and Musk, or any other interested party, could efficiently verify the proof while performing only a few queries. A query to the input vector is translated to the expensive task of determining whether a given user is a spambot, which fuels the desire for small query complexity.

Beyond our motivating example, proofs of proximity for the Hamming weight problem have many applications, as the primary tool in other proximity tests. For example, testing whether an n-vertex graph contains many k-cliques can be directly reduced to the Hamming weight of a corresponding vector of size n^k (where 1 indicates a k-clique). Furthermore, proofs of proximity for Hamming weight (with one-sided error) can be used to transform standard proof systems for arbitrary languages to achieve perfect completeness (we demonstrate this in Sect. 1.2).

Framing-Free Security. There is a subtle but crucial property we need from our probabilistic proof in the form of one-sided error. To motivate this property, we return to the Twitter saga. Suppose that the proof of proximity has two-sided error. This means that even if Twitter generates a proof honestly, a malicious party could find a choice of randomness that makes the verifier reject this proof. Musk could leverage this by presenting such choice of randomness to a (resource-limited) judge, claiming that Twitter is lying, which might lead to the revocation of the acquisition. In order for Twitter to be willing to post a proof of their claims, we must ensure the system is "framing-free", which is obtained when the proximity proof has a one-sided error (perfect completeness). In other words: *One-sided error guarantees framing-free security, where honest parties cannot be accused of wrongdoing.*

On top of the above, there are also concrete benefits in the parameters of protocols with one-sided error. These protocols can be more efficiently amplified compared to their two-sided error counterparts. Repeating a protocol k times maintains the one-sided error property of a protocol and reduces the soundness error from ϵ to ϵ^k. For protocols with two-sided error, the soundness error only reduces to $\epsilon^{\Omega(k)}$, which means that to get the same soundness error, one needs more repetitions (and thus higher query complexity).

A Brief History of Hamming Weight Proximity Testing. There are several different proofs of proximity of the Hamming weight problem[1] in various models. Without the aid of a prover (i.e., property testing), known sampling lower bounds (see, e.g., [Gol11, Theorem 2.1], or [BKS01, Theorem 15]) tell us that the query complexity of any property tester for the Hamming weight problem is $\Omega(\min\{n, \delta^{-2}\})$, where n is the vector length and δ is the proximity parameter (with constant soundness error). A simple test achieves this bound but does not have perfect completeness (i.e., it has two-sided error).

In striking contrast to the above bounds, we observe that the query complexity of any property tester with perfect completeness (and without a prover) is significantly higher; specifically, it must be $\Omega(n)$, effectively rendering the test trivial.[2]

In [RVW13], an IP of proximity was given (without perfect completeness), with query and communication complexities $O(\delta^{-1} \cdot \mathrm{polylog}(n))$, and $O(\log n)$ many rounds. Alternatively, they construct a 2-message version of their protocol

---

[1] The Hamming weight problem in previous work usually refers to the problem of *exact* Hamming weight α, whereas we define the constraint to be *at least* weight α. However, the two problems have (almost) tight reductions between each other. We show this reduction in the full version of this paper.

[2] Consider $\alpha = 2/3$, and suppose towards contradiction that the query complexity is $q = o(n)$. By soundness with respect to the all-zeroes vector, we know that there exists verifier randomness ρ for which the verifier rejects upon querying only zeros. Construct a vector with all ones except for these q places; then the verifier rejects it with nonzero probability. On the other hand, the vector has weight $1 - q/n$ which is more than α since $q = o(n)$, so by perfect completeness the verifier accepts the vector with probability 1.

but with a much higher query and communication complexity of $O(n^{1/3} \cdot \delta^{-2/3} \cdot$ polylog$(n))$. In [GGR18, RR20b], an IP of proximity for a larger complexity classes was given (which include the Hamming problem) with similar round and communication complexity, with constant query complexity.

A *non-interactive* proof of proximity (MAPs) for the Hamming weight problem was given in [GR18]. They showed that for every constant $\alpha \in (0, 1)$ there is a MAP (with two-sided error) for Hamming weight with proof length $\widetilde{O}(n^\alpha)$, and query complexity $\widetilde{O}(\sqrt{n^{1-\alpha}} \cdot \delta^{-1})$. For example, for $\alpha = 2/3$, the proof length is $\widetilde{O}(n^{2/3})$ and the query complexity is $\widetilde{O}(n^{1/6} \cdot \delta^{-1})$. They also showed that their results can be transformed to have perfect completeness while incurring a poly-logarithmic overhead to the query and proof complexities [GR18, Lemma 4.5]. Applying this transformation to the simple tester (without a prover) yields a one-sided error MAP with proof length $O(\delta^{-4} \cdot \log^2 n \cdot \log(\delta^{-1} \cdot \log n))$ and query complexity $O(\delta^{-4} \cdot \log n \cdot \log(\delta^{-1} \cdot \log n))$.

The work of [AGRR23] studied distribution-free proofs of proximity for the Hamming weight problem, where the verifier receives input samples from an unknown distribution. They showed a distribution-free protocol with perfect completeness, $O(\delta^{-1} \cdot \log n)$ rounds, $O(\delta^{-1} \cdot \log^2 n)$ communication complexity and δ^{-1} samples. [KSY20] studied the Hamming weight of social graphs, where instance samples are given via random walks in the graph. Finally, departing from information-theoretic security, [KR15] introduced the notion of interactive *arguments* of proximity. Roughly, they showed that all P has a 2-message argument with communication and query complexity $o(n)$ (assuming sub-exponentially secure FHE).

PCPs and IOPs of Proximity. PCPs of proximity (PCPPs) were studied in [BGH+06, DR04]. They are non-interactive proof of proximity systems where the verifier has *oracle access* to both the input and the given proof. In contrast to MAPs (where the verifier reads the entire proof), the proof string in PCPPs is typically of super-linear length (but the verifier reads only a few bits from it). Quoting [GR18], PCPPs may be thought of as the PCP analog of property testing, whereas MAPs are the NP analog of property testing. We are unaware of explicit works of PCPPs for the Hamming weight problem (beyond general PCPPs that are applicable for all languages in P). Applying a general purpose theorem for PCPPs (e.g., [Mie09]), one can obtain a PCPP for the Hamming weight problem with constant query complexity (for constant distance δ) but with a super-linear proof length and a relatively slow prover (however, still polynomial time).

IOPs of proximity (IOPP) are a combination of IPs and PCPs of proximity [BCS16, RRR16]. Here, the prover and verifier interact in multiple rounds, but the verifier has only oracle access to the prover's messages in addition to its oracle access to the input. IOPs leverage interaction to overcome barriers that arise with PCPs. For instance, known IOPs achieve linear proof length as well as other desirable properties such as fast provers, zero knowledge, and concrete efficiency [BCGV16, BBC+17, BCG+17a, BBHR18, BCG+17b, XZZ+19, BCG20, BCL22, RR20a, ACY22b, ACY23, ACFY24, BN22, RR22]. We are unaware of explicit IOPPs for the Hamming weight language.

One additional advantage of constructing PCPPs and IOPPs is that they serve as the underlying building block for an interactive *arguments* with small communication complexity. For example, one can use the Kilian construction [Kil92] while relying on collision-resistant hash functions to commit to the prover message and only reveal the locations queries by the verifier. This is how hash-based arguments and SNARKs are constructed (see also [Mic00, BCS16, CY20, CY21a, CY21b]).

1.1   Main Results

We provide a systematic study of the Hamming weight problem, presenting new protocols in various models (MAP, PCPP, IOPP) with sublinear communication, surpassing all known results for testing proximity to the Hamming weight. We also present new lower bounds, pointing to the limits of this problem. Let Ham_α be the language of all binary vectors of Hamming weight at least α. Recall that without a prover, $\Omega(n)$ queries are required for one-sided error.

In all our results, we distinguish between the proof query complexity (queries performed to the prover messages) and the input query complexity (queries performed to the input). The reason is that, depending on the application, each query might incur different costs. This is exemplified in the Twitter example where a proof query is relatively cheap (a query to a position in some file sitting on a server), while a query to the input is rather expensive (verifying that a specific user is not a spambot). Thus, it is typically most desirable to minimize the input query complexity.

Sublinear Proofs of Proximity. For each model (MAP, PCPP, IOPP), we give a protocol with one-sided error, sublinear communication, while also providing small query complexity. Focusing on the input query complexity, our MAP has $O(\log n)$ query complexity, the PCPP makes $O(\log\log n)$ queries, and the IOPP makes a single input query (where n is the vector length). The following theorem is an informal summary of these results presented for constant α, constant distance δ, and constant soundness error. For simplicity, in the theorem we hide dependencies on α and δ.

Theorem 1 (Informal). *For every constant $\alpha \in (0, 1]$ there are MAP, PCPP, and IOPP protocols for Ham_α with perfect completeness and parameters summarized below:*

Model	Queries to input	Queries to proof	Proof length	Rounds
MAP	$O(\log n)$	-	$O(\log^2 n)$	-
PCPP	$O(\log\log n)$	$O(\log n \cdot \log\log n)$	$O(n/\log^2 n)$	-
IOPP	1	$O(\log n)$	$O(\log^2 n)$	2

The precise theorem statement and dependencies on all parameters can be found in Theorem 6 for the MAP protocol, in Theorem 8 for the PCPP protocol, and in the full version for the IOPP protocol.

The MAP described in Theorem 1 improves upon the one described in [GR18] by removing a loglog n factor; the input complexity is $O(\log n)$ and the proof length is $O(\log^2 n)$, compared to $O(\log n \cdot \log\log n)$ and $O(\log^2 n \cdot \log\log n)$ respectively. Our PCPP improves on this by reducing the input query complexity dramatically to $O(\log\log n)$, while also allowing the verifier to read fewer bits from the prover message. We are unaware of any other PCPP for the Hamming problem beyond the one described in Theorem 1. The IOPP, when compared to the IPP derived from [GGR18] yields an improvement in the number of rounds, which is reduced from $O(\log n)$ to 2, and the verifier only needs to query $O(\log n)$ bits from the prover messages, rather than reading the entire messages of size polylog n.[3]

Lower Bound. We continue our systematic study with a lower bound for the Hamming weight problem. [GR18] shows a lower bound for MAPs for the Hamming weight problem: roughly speaking, a protocol with proof complexity $\mathsf{l} = \Omega(\log n)$ and query complexity q must satisfy $\mathsf{l} \cdot \mathsf{q} = \Omega(\min\{n, \delta^{-2}\})$.

We give lower bounds for perfectly complete IPPs and IOPPs for the Hamming weight problem regardless of the number of rounds. Our IOPP lower bound applies to protocols in which the verifier is semi-adaptive, meaning that the verifier decides which queries to perform to the i-th prover message based on the first i prover/verifier messages (i.e., including the randomness sampled right after the i-th message). Note that PCPPs and IPPs are special cases of semi-adaptive IOPPs.

Theorem 2 (informal). *For every constant $\alpha \in (0,1)$ the following hold:*

1. *Any perfectly complete IPP for Ham_α with total proof length l and input query complexity q_{x} has $\mathsf{l} = \Omega(\log(n/\mathsf{q}_{\mathsf{x}}))$.*
2. *Any semi-adaptive perfectly complete IOPP for Ham_α with total length l, input query complexity q_{x} and proof query complexity q_π has $\mathsf{q}_\pi \cdot \log \mathsf{l} = \Omega(\log(n/\mathsf{q}_{\mathsf{x}}))$.*

The above theorem has the following consequence: IPPs (regardless of the number of rounds) with query complexity $\mathsf{q}_{\mathsf{x}} = n^{1-\epsilon}$ for any constant $\epsilon > 0$, must have at least a logarithmic proof length. This lower bound implies that our MAP construction in Theorem 1 has proof length that is optimal up to a $O(\log n)$ factor. For (semi-adaptive) IOPPs, it shows that any IOPP with length polylog(n) and constant input query complexity must have proof query complexity $\Omega(\log(n)/\log\log n)$. The challenge of proving a lower bound for (fully) adaptive IOPPs remains as an open problem.

---

[3] The protocol from [GGR18] is described with constant query complexity but can be naturally modified to have a single input query [Rot24].

Single Input Query (SIQ). Our IOPP, as described in Theorem 1, has the remarkable property that, in addition to having a one-sided error, the verifier performs only a *single query to the input.* We denote such protocols as SIQ protocols (single input query). However, the cost of our SIQ-IOPP relative to its PCP counterpart is having additional rounds. Thus, we ask: can we achieve SIQ-PCPPs with sublinear proof length?

We give a negative answer to this question and show that no perfectly complete proof of proximity (for the Hamming weight problem) can simultaneously have a single input query, sublinear length, and be non-interactive.

Theorem 3. *For any $\alpha \in (0.5, 0.77)$, any perfectly complete PCP (or MA) of proximity for Ham_α with input query complexity 1 has proof length $\Omega(n)$.*

On the positive side, we show that with proof length $n + o(n)$, we can construct perfectly complete SIQ-PCPPs with small proof query complexity.

Theorem 4 (Informal). *For every constant $\alpha \in (0, 1]$, there exists a perfectly complete SIQ-PCPP of proximity for Ham_α with proof length $n + O(\log^2 n)$ and proof query complexity $O(\log^2 n)$.*

Prover Running Time. We further strengthen the protocols described in Theorems 1 and 4 by showing efficient algorithms for the honest prover strategies, making our protocols doubly-efficient. In particular, the honest prover in both theorems runs in expected time $O(n \log n)$, where perfect completeness always holds when the prover outputs a message. This holds also for the first message of the IOPP in Theorem 1, and its second message can be computed in deterministic time polylog(n). We further remark that, given a Nisan–Wigderson type PRG [NW94], the prover in all of the protocols can be made to run in deterministic time poly(n). All prior works on proofs of proximity for Hamming weight did not explicitly analyze the honest prover running time.

1.2   Application: Perfect Completeness for PCPs and IOPs

The problem of transforming proof systems with imperfect completeness to ones with perfect completeness was first studied in the context of interactive proofs by [FGM+89] and is considered a cornerstone of research into IPs. Perfect completeness for PCPs and IOPs began to be explored only recently, with the goals of improving hardness of approximation results [BV19, ACY22a, ACY22b], and as a tool for proving barriers for proof systems [ABCY22].

We observe that proofs of proximity for Hamming weight can be utilized in this application. Using the techniques developed in the previous sections, we show new ways to transform PCPs and IOPs with nonzero completeness error into ones with perfect completeness. The following theorem is an informal summary of our results, presented for constant completeness and soundness errors, both for the original proof system, and for the resultant perfectly complete proof system.

Theorem 5 (informal). *Every language L that has a PCP (resp. IOP) with constant completeness error has a perfectly complete PCP (resp. IOP) with parameters given in Table 1.*

Table 1. A comparison of our PCP to perfectly complete PCP and IOP to perfectly complete IOP transformations with prior work. Above, q, l, r, and k denote the query complexity, proof length, randomness complexity, and number of rounds of the original PCP/IOP being transformed, and n is the instance size. Each of our results is derived by taking one of our upper bounds an using it to transform a PCP/IOP with imperfect completeness into one with perfect completeness.

	Model	Queries	Proof length	Rounds
[BV19]	PCP	$q + O(r)$	$l + O(2^r)$	-
[This work]	PCP	$O(q \cdot r + r^2)$	$l + O(r^2)$	-
[This work]	PCP	$O((q + r) \cdot \log r)$	$l + O(2^r/r^2)$	-
[This work]	PCP	$q + O(r^2)$	$l + 2^r + O(r^2)$	-
[ACY22a, ACY22b]	IOP	$O(\max\{1, k/\log n\})$	$poly(n, l, r)$	k
[ABCY22]	IOP	$O(q \cdot \log r + r \cdot \log r)$	$O(l \cdot r \cdot \log r)$	k + 1
[This work]	IOP	$q + O(r)$	$O(l \cdot r)$	k + 1

2   Techniques

In this section, we give an overview of our techniques. Throughout, we denote weight(x) $:= \frac{1}{n} \sum_{i \in [n]} x[i]$ to be the Hamming weight of $x \in \{0,1\}^n$ and use the shorthand $x[i + j]$ to mean $x[i + j \mod n]$. For simplicity, unless stated otherwise we consider all parameters (e.g., α, etc.) apart from n to be constant.

2.1   PCPP for Hamming Weight with Sublinear Proof Length

In this section, we sketch the proof of the PCPP of Theorem 1 in which our focus is on minimizing query complexity while maintaining sublinear proof length. We construct a PCPP for Hamming weight α that for vectors of length n has: (1) length $o(n)$ (2) input query complexity $O(\log\log n)$, and (3) proof query complexity $O(\log n \cdot \log\log n)$. Moreover, the honest prover runs in (expected) time $O(n \log n)$.

Our construction relies on the concept of "good shifts" and is achieved by combining an "outer protocol" and an "inner protocol". We start by defining good shifts, which will be the cornerstone of the honest prover strategies throughout this paper. This technique is inspired by the beautiful "reverse randomization" method, which can be traced back to Lautemann's proof that BPP is in the polynomial hierarchy [Lau83], and has been useful for other applications as well (e.g., [FGM+89, Nao89, DNR04, HNY17, BV22]).

Good Shifts. We say that the "shifts" $z_1, \ldots, z_t \in [n]$ are "good" for a vector $x \in \{0,1\}^n$ if for every $\rho \in [n]$ it holds that the induced vector $x_\rho := (x[\rho + z_1], \ldots, x[\rho + z_t]) \in \{0,1\}^t$ has Hamming weight at least $0.95 \cdot \alpha$. We show that for $t := \Theta(\frac{1}{\alpha} \cdot \log n)$ the following hold:

1. *Large Hamming weight.* For every x with $\mathsf{weight}(x) \geq \alpha$, there exist shifts $z_1, \ldots, z_t$ that are good for x, i.e., where for every ρ, it holds that $\mathsf{weight}(x_\rho) \geq 0.95 \cdot \alpha$. Moreover, these shifts can be found in expected time $O(n \cdot \log n)$.
2. *Small Hamming weight.* For every x with $\mathsf{weight}(x) = \alpha - \delta$ where $\delta \in (0, \alpha)$, and any choice of $z_1, \ldots, z_t$:
   (a) $\Pr_\rho[\mathsf{weight}(x_\rho) \geq 0.95 \cdot \alpha] \leq 1.1 \cdot \frac{\alpha - \delta}{\alpha}$, and
   (b) $\mathbb{E}_\rho[\mathsf{weight}(x_\rho)] = \alpha - \delta$.

Discussion. Following the definition of good shifts, a natural strategy emerges for verifying the Hamming weight of a vector x: the prover sends good shifts $z_1, \ldots, z_t$, and the verifier needs to check that the shifts are indeed good (with perfect completeness). Recall that in the honest case, the induced vector x_ρ has large Hamming weight for every ρ, whereas if x has small Hamming weight, then x_ρ has small Hamming weight for most choices of ρ. Thus it is natural to sample $\rho \leftarrow [n]$ and check that the vector $x_\rho := (x[\rho + z_1], \ldots, x[\rho + z_t])$ has high Hamming weight by querying x at all t locations. While perfectly complete and sound, this PCPP has bad parameters: it results in the verifier reading $O(t \cdot \log n) = O(\log^2 n)$ queries from the proof and making $O(t) = O(\log n)$ queries to the input.

In order to lower the query complexities, we would like to apply a PCPP for the claim that all of the vectors in $(x_\rho)_{\rho \in [n]} \subseteq \{0,1\}^t$ have large Hamming weight. Naively, we could solve this by having the prover supply a separate proof showing that x_ρ has large Hamming weight for each $\rho \in [n]$. Alas, we cannot afford this since there would be $O(n)$ such proofs; even if each proof was one bit in length, we would miss our target of sublinear length. To overcome this challenge the prover will provide a proof that applies multiple choices of ρ simultaneously.

The Protocol. For $a = O(\log^3 n)$,[4] let $(X_s)_{s \in [n/a]}$ be a partition of the induced vectors $(x_\rho)_{\rho \in [n]}$ into n/a sets of size a. Our protocol, given $x \in \{0,1\}^n$, is as follows:

1. Prover: Send shifts $z_1, \ldots, z_t$ which are good for x. Then, for every $s \in [n/a]$ write an inner proof π_s claiming that all vectors in X_s have high Hamming weight (i.e., Hamming weight at least $0.95 \cdot \alpha$).
2. Verifier: Choose $s \leftarrow [n/a]$ uniformly at random. Run the inner proof verifier for the claim that all vectors in X_s have high Hamming weight, and accept if the inner proof verifier accepts.

We analyze the PCPP we constructed and derive properties which, if they are held by the inner protocol, are sufficient for our needs:

---

[4] This value for a is chosen for convenience. In the full protocol, it is left as a parameter which allows for tuning properties of the proof.

1. *Perfect completeness:* Following Item 1, it holds that if x has high Hamming weight, then, for every s, all vectors in X_s have high Hamming weight. Consequently, if the inner protocol has perfect completeness then this holds also for the final PCPP.
2. *Soundness:* Fix $x \in \{0,1\}^n$ with Hamming weight $\alpha - \delta$, where $\delta \in (0, \alpha)$, and a prover message $z_1, \ldots, z_t, (\pi_s)_{s \in [n/a]}$. Let $\beta_s := \frac{1}{a} \sum_{i=1}^{a} \mathsf{weight}(X_s[i])$ be the average weight in X_s. By construction:

$$\Pr[\mathbf{V} \text{ accepts}] = \Pr_s [\, \mathbf{V}^{\mathrm{in}} \text{ accepts } X_s \text{ given } \pi_s \,]$$

$$= \sum_{\beta} \Pr_s [\, \beta_s = \beta \,] \cdot \Pr_s [\, \mathbf{V}^{\mathrm{in}} \text{ accepts } X_s \text{ given } \pi_s \mid \beta_s = \beta \,] \ .$$

In order to bound the error, it suffices that $\Pr_s [\, \mathbf{V}^{\mathrm{in}} \text{ accepts } X_s \text{ given } \pi_s \mid \beta_s = \beta \,] \leq \beta \cdot \varepsilon$ for ε that does not depend on s and β (and this is what we will later achieve):

$$\Pr[\mathbf{V} \text{ accepts}] \leq \sum_{\beta} \Pr_s [\, \beta_s = \beta \,] \cdot \beta \cdot \varepsilon = \mathbb{E}[\beta_s] \cdot \varepsilon = (\alpha - \delta) \cdot \varepsilon \ .$$

The final equality follows from Item 2b, which posits that $\mathbb{E}[\beta_s] = \frac{1}{a} \sum_{i=1}^{a} \mathbb{E}_\rho[\mathsf{weight}(x_\rho)] = \alpha - \delta$. In our construction of the inner protocol, $\varepsilon \approx \frac{1}{\alpha}$, so that the soundness error is approximately $(\alpha - \delta)/\alpha$.
3. *Complexity parameters:* Let l^{in}, $\mathsf{q}_x^{\mathrm{in}}$, and $\mathsf{q}_\pi^{\mathrm{in}}$ denote the proof length, input query complexity, and proof query complexity of the inner proof, respectively. Then the PCPP has proof length $t \cdot \log n + \frac{n}{a} \cdot \mathsf{l}^{\mathrm{in}}$, and so to achieve sublinear proof length we require $\mathsf{l}^{\mathrm{in}} = o(a) = o(\log^3 n)$. The input query complexity is $\mathsf{q}_x^{\mathrm{in}}$ and the proof query complexity is $\mathsf{q}_\pi^{\mathrm{in}} + O(\mathsf{q}_x^{\mathrm{in}} \cdot \log n)$: each query to X_s induces a query to $x_\rho[i] = x[\rho + z_i]$ for some i and ρ which, in turn, induces an input query, and the reading of z_i (which has length $O(\log n)$). Finally, the verifier must read $\mathsf{q}_\pi^{\mathrm{in}}$ bits from π_s. Thus, to achieve the parameters of the PCPP described in Theorem 1, we require $\mathsf{q}_x^{\mathrm{in}} = O(\log\log n)$ and $\mathsf{q}_\pi^{\mathrm{in}} = O(\log n \cdot \log\log n)$.

The Inner Protocol. The inner protocol works on similar ideas to the outer protocol: the prover sends good shifts, and the verifier needs to check that these shifts are, indeed, good. This requires us to change the definition of good shifts to apply also to sets of vectors $X_s = (x_1, \ldots, x_a) \subseteq \{0,1\}^t$. Indeed, we show that, provided that $t' := \Theta(\frac{1}{\alpha} \cdot \log(a \cdot t)) = \Theta(\log\log n)$, the following hold:

1. *Large Hamming weight.* For every $x_1, \ldots, x_a$ such that $\mathsf{weight}(x_i) \geq \alpha$ for every $i \in [t]$, there exist shifts $z_1, \ldots, z_{t'} \in [t]$ that are good for all the vectors in the set simultaneously. Moreover, these shifts can be found in expected time $O(t \cdot a \cdot \log(t \cdot a)) = \mathrm{polylog}(n)$.
2. *Small average Hamming weight.* For every $x_1, \ldots, x_a$ with $\frac{1}{a} \sum_{i \in [a]} \mathsf{weight}(x_i) = \alpha - \delta$ where $\delta \in (0, \alpha)$, and any choice of $z_1, \ldots, z_{t'} \in [t]$: $\Pr_{i,\rho}[\mathsf{weight}(x_{i,\rho}) \geq 0.95 \cdot \alpha] \leq 1.1 \cdot \frac{\alpha - \delta}{\alpha}$, where $x_{i,\rho} := (x_i[\rho + z_1], \ldots, x_i[\rho + z_{t'}])$.

This extended definition allows us to construct our inner protocol. The protocol proceeds as follows on input $X_s = (\mathbf{x}_1, \ldots, \mathbf{x}_a) \subseteq \{0,1\}^t$:

1. Prover: Send shifts $z_1, \ldots, z_{t'} \in [t]$ which are good for X_s.
2. Verifier: Read all of $z_1, \ldots, z_{t'}$, choose $i \leftarrow [a]$ and $\rho \leftarrow [t]$ uniformly at random, and check that $\mathsf{weight}(\mathbf{x}_i[\rho+z_1], \ldots, \mathbf{x}_i[\rho+z_{t'}]) \geq 0.95 \cdot \alpha$ by querying $\mathbf{x}_i$ at the appropriate locations.

The length of the proof is $\mathsf{l}^{\mathsf{in}} = t' \cdot \log n = O(\log n \cdot \log\log n) = o(a)$. The verifier reads this proof in its entirety, so $\mathsf{q}_\pi^{\mathsf{in}} = \mathsf{l}^{\mathsf{in}} = O(\log n \cdot \log\log n)$ bits. The input query complexity is $\mathsf{q}_\mathbf{x}^{\mathsf{in}} = t' = O(\log\log n)$.

Completeness follows from Item 1 of the adapted definition of good shifts. For soundness, recall that we wanted:

$$\Pr\left[\mathbf{V}^{\mathsf{in}} \text{ accepts } \mid \frac{1}{a} \sum_{i \in [a]} \mathsf{weight}(\mathbf{x}_i) = \beta \right] \leq \beta \cdot \varepsilon \ ,$$

for ε that does not depend on β. The verifier accepts only if $\mathsf{weight}(\mathbf{x}_i[\rho + z_1], \ldots, \mathbf{x}_i[\rho + z_{t'}]) \geq 0.95 \cdot \alpha$. It follows from Item 2 of the adapted definition of good shifts that the probability of this occurring when the average Hamming weight of the vectors in X_s is β is $1.1 \cdot \frac{\beta}{\alpha}$, which concludes the proof of soundness (here, $\varepsilon = \frac{1.1}{\alpha}$).

Finally, we observe that the inner protocol is useful in its own right. In fact, by choosing $a = 1$ (and replacing t with n) we get the MAP for Hamming weight described in Theorem 1.

2.2 SIQ-PCPP for Hamming Weight

In this section, we focus on perfectly complete PCPPs for the Hamming weight problem, where the verifier makes a single input query (SIQ). In Sect. 2.2, we sketch the proof of Theorem 3, showing a lower bound on the proof length for SIQ MAPs (which induces a bound also for PCPPs). In Sect. 2.2, we give a construction of a SIQ PCPP with linear proof size (Theorem 4).

Lower Bound. In this section, we sketch the proof of Theorem 3, showing that any perfectly complete MAP for Hamming weight with a single input query must have a large proof length. Let $\alpha = 2/3$ and $\delta = 1/3$.

Consider a MAP with message length l, and input query complexity 1, where for inputs of distance δ from Hamming weight has nontrivial soundness error. Let $\mathsf{Exact\text{-}Ham}_{\alpha,n} \subseteq \mathsf{Ham}_\alpha$ be the set of all vectors of size n that have Hamming weight exactly α. For a prover message π, let S_π be the set of all vectors in $\mathsf{Exact\text{-}Ham}_{\alpha,n}$ for which π is the honest prover message. By an averaging argument, since there are at most 2^l different prover messages, there must exist some proof π with $|S_\pi| \geq |\mathsf{Exact\text{-}Ham}_{\alpha,n}|/2^\mathsf{l}$. Since each vector in $\mathsf{Exact\text{-}Ham}_{\alpha,n}$ has exactly $(1 - \alpha) \cdot n$ zeros, $|\mathsf{Exact\text{-}Ham}_{\alpha,n}| = \binom{n}{(1-\alpha) \cdot n}$. However, the number of vectors that the honest prover can prove with the same proof is small: Claim 1 shows that $|S_\pi| \leq \binom{(1-\alpha+\delta)\cdot n}{(1-\alpha)\cdot n}$. By rearranging the terms and taking a logarithm, we get that $l \geq \log \binom{n}{(1-\alpha)\cdot n} - \log \binom{(1-\alpha+\delta)\cdot n}{(1-\alpha)\cdot n} = \Omega(n)$ (the final equality follows since $\alpha = 2/3$ and $\delta = 1/3$).

Claim 1. $|S_\pi| \leq \binom{(1-\alpha+\delta)\cdot n}{(1-\alpha)\cdot n}$.

Proof Sketch. Let x be the bitwise AND of all the vectors in S_π and let I_0 be the indices where x is zero. By the definition of x, for every $v \in S_\pi$ and $j \in [n]$ where $v[j] = 0$, it must hold that $j \in I_0$ (i.e., $x[j] = 0$). Thus, we can bound the size S_π by the number of vectors that have zeroes only within I_0. Since $S_\pi \subseteq$ Exact-Ham$_{\alpha,n}$, every $v \in S_\pi$ has exactly $(1-\alpha) \cdot n$ zeroes. The maximal number of vectors with exactly $(1-\alpha)\cdot n$ zeroes that have zeroes only within I_0 is $\binom{|I_0|}{(1-\alpha)\cdot n}$. It follows that $|S_\pi| \leq \binom{|I_0|}{(1-\alpha)\cdot n}$. We now show that $|I_0| < (1-\alpha+\delta)\cdot n$, which completes the proof.

Assume towards contradiction that $|I_0| \geq (1-\alpha+\delta) \cdot n$, meaning that x is δ far from Ham$_\alpha$. By the soundness property of the protocol, there exists some randomness ρ for which the verifier rejects. Let $j \in [n]$ be the index of the single bit of x queried by the verifier given access to π and randomness ρ. Since x is the bitwise AND of the vectors in S_π, there exists some vector $v \in S_\pi$ with $v[j] = x[j]$. Fix such vector v. Since j is the only index queried by the verifier when given the proof π and the randomness ρ, the verifier will reject v. This contradicts the perfect completeness of the protocol as $v \in S_\pi \subseteq$ Exact-Ham$_{\alpha,n} \subseteq$ Ham$_\alpha$, and since π is the honest prover's message for v (by definition of S_π). $\square$

Upper Bound. In this section, we describe our construction of a PCPP for Hamming weight where the verifier makes a single input query, and the proof length is $n + O(\log^2 n)$, as described in Theorem 4.

The Protocol. The basic idea underlying how our protocol achieves single input query complexity is that the prover copies the vector x into the proof and writes a proof that this copy has large Hamming weight. The verifier then checks that the copy has large Hamming weight and that the copy is consistent with x. On input $x \in \{0,1\}^n$, the protocol proceeds as follows:

1. Prover: Send $x' := x$ and additionally send shifts $z_1, \ldots, z_t \in [n]$ which are good for x.
2. Verifier: Read all of $z_1, \ldots, z_t$ and accept if the following checks pass:
   (a) Choose $\rho_1, \ldots, \rho_m \leftarrow [n]$ for $m = O(\log n)$ and check that for every ℓ, the induced vector $x_{\rho_\ell} := (x'[\rho_i + z_1], \ldots, x'[\rho_i + z_t])$ has Hamming weight $\geq 0.95 \cdot \alpha$ by querying x' at the appropriate locations.
   (b) Choose $r_1, \ldots, r_q \leftarrow [n]$ for $q = O(\log n)$ and query $x'[r_i]$. If $x'[r_i] = 0$ for every i, then we consider the check to have passed. Otherwise, let ℓ be the minimal index so that $x'[r_\ell] = 1$. Check that $x[r_\ell] = 1$ by querying x.

Analysis. We begin by assessing the complexity parameters. The proof length is $n + t \cdot \log n = n + O(\log^2 n)$, and the verifier makes at most one query to x, and $O(\log^2 n)$ queries to the proof string. Perfect completeness follows from Item 1 of the definition of good shifts and from the fact that the honest vector sets $x' = x$. All that remains is to show soundness.

Fix $x \in \{0,1\}^n$ that is δ-far from Ham_α and a prover message $\pi = (x', z_1, \ldots, z_t)$. Intuitively, if the Hamming weight of the copied vector is close to the Hamming weight of the input vector, then the verifier's check in Item 2a will fail with high probability. On the other hand, if the Hamming weight of the copied vector is much larger than the Hamming weight of the input vector, then there is a large disparity between x and x' so the verifier's check in Item 2b will fail with high probability. We now formalize this intuition.

For every $\rho \in [n]$, let $x'_\rho := (x'[\rho_i + z_1], \ldots, x'[\rho_i + z_t])$, and let $\mathcal{H} := \{\rho \mid \mathsf{weight}(x'_\rho) \geq 0.95 \cdot \alpha\}$ be the set of all ρ such that the vector x'_ρ has Hamming weight $\geq 0.95 \cdot \alpha$. We split the analysis into two cases: $|\mathcal{H}| < n/2$, and $|\mathcal{H}| \geq n/2$. If $|\mathcal{H}| < n/2$ then by the definition of $\mathcal{H}$, the verifier's check in Item 2a will pass with probability at most $(1/2)^m = (1/n)^{O(1)}$. If $|\mathcal{H}| \geq n/2$ then the verifier accepts with probability at most $1.1 \cdot \frac{\alpha - \delta}{\alpha} + \frac{1}{n^{O(1)}}$, as exemplified in Lemma 1. Overall, we conclude that the verifier accepts with probability at most $1.1 \cdot \frac{\alpha - \delta}{\alpha} + \frac{1}{n^{O(1)}}$ as described in Theorem 4.

Lemma 1. *If $|\mathcal{H}| \geq n/2$ then the verifier accepts with probability at most $1.1 \cdot \frac{\alpha - \delta}{\alpha} + \frac{1}{n^{O(1)}}$.*

Proof Sketch. Let $\beta' := \mathsf{weight}(x')$ be the Hamming weight of x'. To begin with, we show that $\beta' \geq 0.95 \cdot \alpha/2$ by observing that, by the definition of good shifts (specifically Item 2b), $\mathsf{weight}(x') = \mathbb{E}_\rho[x'_\rho]$. Since $|\mathcal{H}| \geq n/2$, at least half of the vectors x'_ρ have weight at least $0.95 \cdot \alpha$, and so $\mathbb{E}_\rho[x'_\rho] \geq 0.95 \cdot \alpha/2$.

Define the following events: E_{weight} is the event that the verifier's check in Item 2a passes, E_0 is the event that the verifier's check in Item 2b passes because the verifier read only zeros from x', and E_1 is the event that the verifier's check in Item 2b passes and the verifier has read a nonzero entry of x'. Using this notation,

$$\Pr[\text{Verifier accepts}] = \Pr[E_{\mathsf{weight}} \wedge (E_0 \vee E_1)]$$

Since the two checks of the verifier are independent, and by using the union-bound:

$$\Pr[E_{\mathsf{weight}} \wedge (E_0 \vee E_1)] = \Pr[E_{\mathsf{weight}}] \cdot \Pr[E_0 \vee E_1] \leq \Pr[E_{\mathsf{weight}}] \cdot (\Pr[E_0] + \Pr[E_1]) \ .$$

We bound the probabilities that E_0 and E_1 occur:

- $\Pr[E_0]$: Since $\beta' \geq 0.95 \cdot \alpha/2$, the probability that all of the samples r_i are to locations where x' contains 0 is at most: $(1 - 0.95 \cdot \alpha/2)^q = 1/n^{O(1)}$.
- $\Pr[E_1]$: Conditioned on sampling a nonzero index in x', the smallest such index is distributed uniformly over the nonzero entries of x'. The fraction of ones in x' is β' and the fraction of ones in x is $\alpha - \delta$, and so sampling a random nonzero entry in x' is nonzero in x with probability at most $(\alpha - \delta)/\beta'$. Consequently: $\Pr[E_1] \leq \Pr[E_1 \mid \text{sampled nonzero location}] \leq (\alpha - \delta)/\beta'$.

Therefore, $\Pr[\text{Verifier accepts}] \leq \Pr[E_{\text{weight}}] \cdot (\Pr[E_0] + \Pr[E_1]) \leq \Pr[E_{\text{weight}}] \cdot$ $(\frac{\alpha-\delta}{\beta'} + \frac{1}{n^{O(1)}})$. We now split the argument into two cases. In both cases, we show that the verifier accepts with probability at most $1.1 \cdot (\alpha - \delta)/\alpha + 1/n^{O(1)}$, which concludes this proof sketch.

1. If $\alpha < 1.1 \cdot \beta'$: then $\Pr[\text{Verifier accepts}] \leq \frac{\alpha-\delta}{\beta'} + \frac{1}{n^{O(1)}} < 1.1 \cdot \frac{\alpha-\delta}{\alpha} + \frac{1}{n^{O(1)}}$.
2. If $\alpha \geq 1.1 \cdot \beta'$: then $\Pr_\rho[\text{weight}(\mathsf{x}'_\rho) \geq 0.95 \cdot \alpha] \leq 1.1 \cdot \frac{\beta'}{\alpha}$ by Item 2a in the properties of good shifts. Therefore, the probability that the verifier's check in Item 2a passes is $\left(1.1 \cdot \frac{\beta'}{\alpha}\right)^m$. Thus, the verifier accepts with probability at most:

$$\Pr[\text{Verifier accepts}] \leq \left(1.1 \cdot \frac{\beta'}{\alpha}\right)^m \cdot \left(\frac{\alpha-\delta}{\beta'} + \frac{1}{n^{O(1)}}\right) \leq 1.1 \cdot \frac{\alpha-\delta}{\alpha} + \frac{1}{n^{O(1)}} \ .$$

$\square$

2.3   A SIQ-IOPP for Hamming Weight with Sublinear Proof Length

In this section, we show that by utilizing interaction, perfect completeness, sublinear proof length, and input query complexity 1 are all simultaneously achievable. This is in stark contrast to the non-interactive (i.e., PCPP) case where, as shown in Sect. 2.2, achieving all three properties together is impossible.

Recall that an IOP is a generalization of PCPs, where the prover and verifier interact over multiple rounds. Similarly to a PCP, the verifier is given oracle access to the messages supplied by the prover. We sketch the construction of the IOPP in Theorem 1, showing an IOPP for the Hamming weight problem with perfect completeness, input query complexity 1, four messages, proof length polylog(n) and proof query complexity $O(\log n)$.

Discussion. The IOPP utilizes the ideas developed in Sect. 2.1. Specifically, recall the initial construction proposed: The prover generates good shifts $z_1, \ldots, z_t$ for $t = \text{polylog}(n)$, the verifier chooses ρ, and needs to verify that $\mathsf{x}_\rho := (\mathsf{x}[\rho + z_1], \ldots, \mathsf{x}[\rho + z_t])$ has at least a $0.95 \cdot \alpha$ fraction of ones. In the non-interactive case, we ran into the problem that we could not write a proof of this fact for every possible x_ρ, i.e., for every choice of ρ. Our observation is that if the protocol is allowed to be interactive, it suffices for the prover to give an "inner proof" that x_ρ has high Hamming weight only for the single ρ chosen by the verifier.

Since this inner statement itself has size polylog(n), which is the communication complexity that we are already willing to afford, a simple proof will suffice: the prover will send x_ρ to the verifier, who will check that it has high Hamming weight. It then checks that x_ρ matches the restriction of the real vector x. While we could do this by simply comparing the two on a random location, since we are only really interested in the restriction of x having many nonzero entries, we get better soundness error by choosing a random nonzero location j of x_ρ and checking that $\mathsf{x}[\rho + z_j] = 1$.

The Protocol. Given $x \in \{0, 1\}^n$, the protocol proceeds as follows:

1. Prover: Send good shifts $z_1, \ldots, z_t \in [n]$.
2. Verifier: Choose $\rho \leftarrow [n]$ uniformly at random.
3. Prover: Send $x_\rho \in \{0, 1\}^t$, where in the honest case $x_\rho := (x[\rho + z_1], \ldots, x[\rho + z_t])$.
4. Verifier: Read x_ρ in its entirety, and (a) check that $\mathsf{weight}(x_\rho) \geq 0.95 \cdot \alpha$, and (b) choose a random j from the indices where x_ρ is nonzero, and check that $x[\rho + z_j] = 1$.

Completeness and soundness follow straightforwardly from the analysis done in Sect. 2.1 regarding good shifts, and a simple probabilistic argument showing that if the prover did not send the correct x_ρ, then it will be caught by the verifier with high probability.

2.4   A Lower Bound for IPPs and Semi-adaptive IOPPs

In this section, we discuss the proof of Theorem 2, showing a trade-off between the length, input query complexity and proof query complexity of IPPs and *semi-adaptive* IOPPs. IPPs are a special case of semi-adaptive IOPPs, and so in this overview we consider semi-adaptive IOPPs unless stated otherwise. In the full proof a minor optimization is utilized to give better bounds for IPPs.

We prove our lower-bound in two steps: (1) in Sect. 2.4 we introduce a communication complexity problem which we call HitOne, and prove a lower bound for it, and (2) in Sect. 2.4 we show that any semi-adaptive IOPP for Hamming weight with one-sided error can be used as a strategy to solve the HitOne problem. Together, these introduce bounds on the parameters of the IOPP.

Semi-adaptive IOPPs. A k-round IOPP is *semi-adaptive* if the locations of the verifier's queries made to the prover's i-th message π_i (also known as the verifier's *view* of this oracle) depend only on $\rho_1, \ldots, \rho_i$ and the verifier's view of the prover's messages π_1 through π_i.[5] See the full version of this paper for a formal definition.

The HitOne Problem. In the HitOne problem, Alice, given a binary vector $x \in \{0, 1\}^n$ with at least $\alpha(n)$ fraction of ones, must communicate to Bob the location of a single 1 (for this sketch we consider constant α). In more detail, Alice is given x and outputs a message m. Bob then reads this message and makes q queries to x. The goal is for Bob to query a nonzero location of x (with probability 1) while minimizing the size of the message m and the number of queries made to x (indeed, the task is trivial if $|m| = \log n$ or $q > (1 - \alpha) \cdot n$).

We show that $|m| = \Omega(\log(n/q))$. To see why, suppose towards contradiction that $m = o(\log(n/q))$. We construct a vector of length n with Hamming weight α for which Bob queries only zeroes, which contradicts the correctness of the

---

[5] Adaptivity with respect to π_i is allowed: the verifier's j-th query π_i can depend on the previous $j - 1$ queries to made to π_i.

protocol. For every one of the $2^m = o(n/q)$ possible verifier messages, set the q locations queried by Bob to be 0. Set the rest of the vector to be all ones. The vector contains at most $2^m \cdot q = o(n)$ zeroes, and so has an α-fraction of ones (recall that in this sketch, we are assuming that α is constant). On the other hand, by how we defined the vector, no matter what message Alice sends, Bob will always query the vector at locations that all contain zeroes.

IOPP to HitOne. We show how to transform any semi-adaptive IOPP $(\mathbf{P}, \mathbf{V})$ for Hamming weight α with perfect completeness into a strategy for HitOne (as in the rest of this technical overview, we consider constant α). Specifically, we show that given an IOPP for Hamming weight with perfect completeness, it can be converted into a strategy for HitOne where Alice sends a message of length $O(q_\pi \cdot \log l)$ and Bob makes q_x queries, where q_π, l and q_x are the proof query complexity, length and input query complexity of the IOPP respectively. When put together with the lower-bound for HitOne described in Sect. 2.4, we conclude that $O(q_\pi \cdot \log l) > \log(n/q_x)$. For constant q_x and polylogarithmic proof length, we conclude that $q_\pi = \Omega(\log n / \log\log n)$.

In this section, fix $x \in \{0,1\}^n$ to be a vector with at least $\alpha \cdot n$ ones for the HitOne problem. We describe the transformation for 4-message IOPPs for Hamming weight of $\alpha \cdot n$. This can be readily generalized for any number of messages.

Warm Up. We start with a transformation where Alice's message length is linear in the verifier's randomness complexity. We define notions of *useful* random strings: (a) (ρ_1, ρ_2) are useful if for $\pi_1 := \mathbf{P}(x)$ and $\pi_2 := \mathbf{P}(x, \rho_1)$ it is the case that the IOPP verifier rejects the all zeroes vector, i.e., $\mathbf{V}^{\vec{0},\pi_1,\pi_2}(\rho_1, \rho_2) = 0$, and (b) ρ_1 is useful if there exists ρ_2 such that (ρ_1, ρ_2) are useful. The definition of useful strings is exemplified by the following claim:

Claim 2. *If* $\mathbf{V}^{\vec{0},\pi_1,\pi_2}(\rho_1, \rho_2) = 0$ *where* $\pi_1 := \mathbf{P}(x)$ *and* $\pi_2 := \mathbf{P}(x, \rho_1)$, *then* $\mathbf{V}^{x,\pi_1,\pi_2}(\rho_1, \rho_2)$ *queries* x *at a nonzero location.*

Proof Sketch. By the perfect completeness of the IOPP, we have that $\mathbf{V}^{x,\pi_1,\pi_2}(\rho_1, \rho_2) = 1$ since π_1 and π_2 were generated honestly with respect to x. On the other hand by the claim statement, it holds that $\mathbf{V}^{\vec{0},\pi_1,\pi_2}(\rho_1, \rho_2) = 0$. The only difference between the executions is the existence of ones in the vector x, and these are only accessed via verifier queries. Therefore, $\mathbf{V}$ must query x at a nonzero location. □

Claim 2 yields a natural strategy for HitOne: Alice computes $\pi_1 := \mathbf{P}(x)$, finds the (lexicographically) smallest ρ_1 that is useful, computes $\pi_2 := \mathbf{P}(x, \rho_1)$, and chooses the smallest ρ_2 so that (ρ_1, ρ_2) are useful (such a choice exists since ρ_1 is useful). Finally she outputs as her message $m = (\pi_1, \rho_1, \pi_2, \rho_2)$. Bob runs $\mathbf{V}^{x,\pi_1,\pi_2}(\rho_1, \rho_2)$ making the same queries to x as made by $\mathbf{V}$.

Alice's message has length $O(r + l)$ and Bob makes q_x queries, where r, l and q_x are the randomness, length, and input query complexity of the IOPP respectively. As mentioned in Sect. 2.4, the HitOne problem is trivial if Alice's message is allowed to have length $\log n$. Both r and l are commonly at least logarithmic in n, and so we need to reduce the dependency on r and l. We lower the dependency on l by observing that $\mathbf{V}$ reads π_1 and π_2 only at a few locations. It therefore suffices for Alice to send Bob the views w_1 and w_2 of π_1 and π_2 respectively their stead (where each view contains both the query locations and the values read from its respective proof), getting us to length $O(\mathsf{r} + \mathsf{q}_\pi \cdot \log \mathsf{l})$ where q_π is the proof query complexity of the IOPP.

We are left with the goal of reducing the dependency on r. In fact, we will completely eliminate it by removing ρ_1 and ρ_2 from Alice's message, and having Bob *infer* them given only w_1 and w_2.

Second Attempt. We would like for Bob to mimic the way that Alice chooses ρ_1 and ρ_2. In order to do so, naively Bob would have to compute π_1 and π_2, which requires knowledge of x that Bob does not have. While Bob does not have access to π_1 and π_2, he knows that the randomness chosen by Alice is consistent with w_1 and w_2, i.e., ρ_1 and ρ_2 never cause $\mathbf{V}$ to query outside of w_1 and w_2. Thus we have the following strategy for Bob: choose the smallest ρ_1 that is consistent with w_1 and w_2 where there exists a consistent ρ_2 such that $\mathbf{V}^{\vec{0},\mathsf{w}_1,\mathsf{w}_2}(\rho_1, \rho_2) = 0$, where, by oracle access to w_1 and w_2 we mean that Bob emulates the verifier's access to π_1 and π_2 using the information in w_1 and w_2. Since ρ_1 and ρ_2 are consistent with $\mathsf{w}_1, \mathsf{w}_2$ the verifier only queries inside the views, and so this operation is well-defined. This choice of ρ_1 immediately also gives Bob a choice of a consistent ρ_2.

Alas, this does guarantee that (ρ_1, ρ_2) are useful due to a circular dependency: Bob's choice of ρ_1 depends on w_2, whereas the honestly generated w_2 depends on ρ_1 (since $\pi_2 := \mathbf{P}(\mathsf{x}, \rho_1)$). In order to exemplify this we give a (contrived) example of this issue. Consider an IOPP where the honest proof $\pi_2 := \mathbf{P}(\mathsf{x}, \rho_1)$ contains at its first index the first bit of ρ_1. Following the interaction, the verifier queries $\pi_2[1]$ and checks that $\rho_1[1] = \pi_2[1]$. If this does not hold, the verifier immediately rejects without querying x.

Alice chooses ρ_1^{A} and ρ_2^{A} as above and uses them to generate $(\mathsf{w}_1, \mathsf{w}_2)$. For any ρ_1^{B} and ρ_2^{B} that Bob may choose where $\rho_1^{\mathsf{B}}[1] \neq \rho_1^{\mathsf{A}}[1]$, it holds that $\mathbf{V}^{\vec{0},\mathsf{w}_1,\mathsf{w}_2}(\rho_1^{\mathsf{B}}, \rho_2^{\mathsf{B}}) = 0$. Since ρ_1^{B} is inconsistent with w_2, the verifier does not query x and, consequently, Bob will also not query x (let alone at a nonzero location).

To resolve this issue, we need to remove this circular dependency.

The Transformation. To resolve the circular dependency, we choose ρ_1 using a property that is stronger than being useful: we choose ρ_1 if, given $\pi_1 := \mathbf{P}(\mathsf{x})$, for *every* π_2 there exists some ρ_2 so that $\mathbf{V}^{\vec{0},\pi_1,\pi_2}(\rho_1, \rho_2) = 0$. We show that this definition suffices, beginning with the protocol:

- Alice, given x:
  1. Compute $\pi_1 := \mathbf{P}(\mathsf{x})$.
  2. Let ρ_1 be the (lexicographically) smallest string so that for every π_2' there exists ρ_2' such that $\mathbf{V}^{\vec{0},\pi_1,\pi_2'}(\rho_1, \rho_2') = 0$.

3. Compute $\pi_2 := \mathbf{P}(\mathrm{x}, \rho_1)$.
4. Let ρ_2 be the smallest string so that $\mathbf{V}^{\vec{0},\pi_1,\pi_2}(\rho_1,\rho_2) = 0$.
5. Send $(\mathsf{w}_1, \mathsf{w}_2)$, which are $\mathbf{V}$'s views of π_1 and π_2 (respectively) in the execution $\mathbf{V}^{\mathrm{x},\pi_1,\pi_2}(\rho_1,\rho_2)$.

- Bob, given $(\mathsf{w}_1, \mathsf{w}_2)$ and oracle access to x:
    1. Let ρ_1 be the smallest string that is consistent with w_1 and for every π_2' there exists ρ_2' such that $\mathbf{V}^{\vec{0},\mathsf{w}_1,\pi_2'}(\rho_1,\rho_2') = 0$.
    2. Let ρ_2 be the smallest string that is consistent with w_2 so that $\mathbf{V}^{\vec{0},\mathsf{w}_1,\mathsf{w}_2}(\rho_1,\rho_2) = 0$.
    3. Run $\mathbf{V}^{\mathrm{x},\mathsf{w}_1,\mathsf{w}_2}(\rho_1,\rho_2)$ making the same queries that it makes to x.

Alice sends $O(\mathsf{q}_\pi \cdot \log \mathsf{l})$ bits to Bob, who makes q_x queries. Theorem 2 follows by applying this transformation to the bound derived in Sect. 2.4. If the IOPP is an IPP (i.e., $\mathsf{q}_\pi = \mathsf{l}$), then the verifier's view contains the entire proof, so Alice does not need to send indices in the proof and her message length can be decreased to l. This optimization yields the improved bound for IPPs described in Theorem 2. We sketch the proof showing that Bob must query a nonzero index of x.

Lemma 2. *Bob queries a nonzero index of* x.

Proof Sketch. We show that Alice is able to find (ρ_1, ρ_2), and that Bob derives the same (ρ_1, ρ_2). Since these strings are such that $\mathbf{V}^{\vec{0},\pi_1,\pi_2}(\rho_1,\rho_2) = \mathbf{V}^{\vec{0},\mathsf{w}_1,\mathsf{w}_2}(\rho_1,\rho_2) = 0$, it follows by Claim 2 that Bob queries x at a nonzero location.

- *Alice finds some* (ρ_1, ρ_2). We first show that Alice will have a choice of ρ_1: indeed, suppose towards contradiction that for every ρ_1 there exists π_2' such that for every ρ_2' it holds that $\mathbf{V}^{\vec{0},\pi_1,\pi_2'}(\rho_1,\rho_2') = 1$. If this is the case, then a malicious Prover could convince the verifier to accept the all-zeroes vector with probability 1 by sending π_1, getting challenge ρ_1, and then following the strategy to get a π_2' that is accepted by the verifier for every ρ_2'. This contradicts the soundness of the IOPP. Once ρ_1 has been chosen, $\pi_2 := \mathbf{P}(\mathrm{x}, \rho_1)$ is defined. Then, since ρ_1 was chosen, it must be the case that there exists ρ_2 for Alice to choose where $\mathbf{V}^{\vec{0},\pi_1,\pi_2}(\rho_1,\rho_2) = 0$.

- *Bob chooses the same* (ρ_1, ρ_2). We show that Alice and Bob agree on ρ_1. Agreement on ρ_2 follows by a similar argument. Bob goes over ρ_1^* in lexicographic order. We show that Bob does not choose $\rho_1^* < \rho_1$ (this is where we will use the fact that the IOPP is semi-adaptive) and that when it reaches $\rho_1^* = \rho_1$ it chooses this string.

    • $\rho_1^* < \rho_1$: Suppose towards contradiction that Bob chooses $\rho_1^* < \rho_1$. Since Alice did not choose ρ_1^*, it holds that there exists π_2' such that for every ρ_2, $\mathbf{V}^{\pi_1,\pi_2'}(\rho_1^*,\rho_2) = 1$. Furthermore, since Bob chose ρ_1^*, it holds that ρ_1^* is consistent with w_1. Since the IOPP is semi-adaptive, the view of the verifier of π_1 depends only on its first randomness ρ_1^*. Thus, ρ_1 and ρ_1^* induce the same view w_1 from π_1, and they do so regardless of π_2' and ρ_2'. We conclude that there exists π_2' such that for every ρ_2' it holds that

$\mathbf{V}^{w_1,\pi'_2}(\rho^*_1,\rho'_2) = \mathbf{V}^{\pi_1,\pi'_2}(\rho^*_1,\rho'_2) = 1$. This is a contradiction to the fact that, since Bob has chosen ρ^*_1, it holds that for every π'_2 there exists ρ'_2 so that $\mathbf{V}^{w_1,\pi'_2}(\rho^*_1,\rho'_2) = 0$.

- $\rho^*_1 = \rho_1$: Since Alice chose ρ_1, it holds that for every π'_2 there exists a ρ'_2 so that $\mathbf{V}^{\pi_1,\pi'_2}(\rho_1,\rho'_2) = 1$. Moreover, by definition ρ_1 is consistent with w_1. It follows that for every π'_2 there exists ρ'_2 so that $\mathbf{V}^{w_1,\pi'_2}(\rho_1,\rho'_2) = 0$. Therefore Bob will choose $\rho^*_1 = \rho_1$ when it is reached. □

2.5 Application: Perfect Completeness for PCPs and IOPs

In this section, we show, as an application of our main results, how to transform PCPs and IOPs for arbitrary languages with two-sided error into ones with perfect completeness.

Perfect Completeness for PCPs. Consider a PCP system for a language L with completeness error c and soundness error s where the verifier uses r bits of randomness. We reduce the completeness error to 0 using any of the PCPPs (or the MAP) for the Hamming weight problem described in previous sections.

Given an instance x and the honest prover's proof π, we can define a binary vector x of length 2^r where at index $\rho \in \{0,1\}^r$ the vector x is equal to 1 if and only if the PCP verifier accepts given x, randomness ρ and oracle access to π. If $x \in L$ then x has at least $(1-c) \cdot 2^r$ ones, and if $x \notin L$ then x has at most $s \cdot 2^r$ ones. Given a perfectly complete PCPP (or MAP) for asserting that x has at least a $1-c$ fraction of ones, we produce a PCP for L with perfect completeness: The new PCP contains the original PCP proof and the PCPP proof that x has many ones. The new PCP verifier runs the PCPP verifier, where in order to query x at ρ, the verifier runs the original PCP verifier on randomness ρ, and outputs the PCP verifier decision as the value in $x[\rho]$. Perfect completeness and soundness follow from the completeness and soundness of the PCPP.

Perfect Completeness for IOPs. One would hope that the above approach for PCPs would also work to eliminate completeness error in IOPs. Unfortunately, this does not seem to be the case: defining a static x relying on verifier randomness in all rounds combined seems incompatible with the reliance of IOPs on interaction to achieve soundness. Due to this difficulty, we do not give a generic transformation for achieving perfect completeness in IOPs given an IOPP for the Hamming weight problem. Nonetheless, we show that the IOPP described in Sect. 2.3 can be adapted to transform any IOP with two-side error into one with perfect completeness.

3 Preliminaries

For a vector $x \in \{0,1\}^n$ and an index $i \in \mathbb{N}$, we let $x[i] := x[i \mod n]$. For interactive (oracle) algorithms $\mathbf{A}$ and $\mathbf{B}$, we denote by $\langle \mathbf{A}(a), \mathbf{B}(b) \rangle(c)$ the random variable describing the output of $\mathbf{B}$ following the interaction between $\mathbf{A}$ and $\mathbf{B}$.

where $\mathbf{A}$ is given private input a, $\mathbf{B}$ is given private input b and both parties are given joint input c. We define a function $f : \mathbb{N} \to (0,1]$ to be *computable in linear time* if the time to compute $f(x)$ is linear in the size of the binary representation of x. Moreover, for any two functions $f, f' : \mathbb{N} \to (0,1]$, we say that $f < f'$ if for any $x \in \mathbb{N}$, $f(x) < f'(x)$.

3.1   Hamming Weight Problem and Hamming Distance

In this paper, we consider the relative hamming weight of bit vectors:

Definition 1 ((Relative) Hamming weight). *The relative Hamming weight of a bit vector* $\mathrm{x} \in \{0,1\}^n$, *denoted* $\mathsf{weight}(\mathrm{x})$, *is the fraction of ones in* x:

$$\mathsf{weight}(\mathrm{x}) = \frac{1}{n} \cdot |\{i \in [n] \mid \mathrm{x}[i] = 1\}| \ .$$

The main language that we consider in this paper is α-Hamming-weight, which consists of all bit vectors of weight at least α:

Definition 2 (α-Hamming-weight language). *For* $\alpha : \mathbb{N} \to (0,1]$, *the* α-*Hamming-weight language,* Ham_α, *is the set of all bit vectors with Hamming weight at least* $\alpha(\cdot)$, *where* α *is a function on the size of the vector:*

$$\mathsf{Ham}_\alpha := \bigcup_{n \in \mathbb{N}} \{\mathrm{x} \mid \mathrm{x} \in \{0,1\}^n \wedge \mathsf{weight}(\mathrm{x}) \geq \alpha(n)\} \ .$$

We define a language that k-Ham_α contains all lists of k vectors that all have Hamming weight α. The language is defined so that 1-$\mathsf{Ham}_\alpha \equiv \mathsf{Ham}_\alpha$.

Definition 3 ((k,α)-list-Hamming-weight language). *For* $k \in \mathbb{N}$ *and* $\alpha \in (0,1]$, *the* (k,α)-*list-Hamming-weight language,* k-Ham_α, *is the language of all lists of* k *vectors of identical length, each of which has Hamming weight at least* α:

$$k\text{-}\mathsf{Ham}_\alpha := \bigcup_{n \in \mathbb{N}} \{\mathrm{x}_1, \ldots, \mathrm{x}_k \in \{0,1\}^n \mid \forall i \in [k], \ \mathsf{weight}(\mathrm{x}_i) \geq \alpha(n)\} \ .$$

We use Hamming distance as our measure of distance from the α-Hamming-weight language:

Definition 4 (Hamming distance). *Let* n, k *be parameters in* $\mathbb{N}$. *For any two bit vectors* $\mathrm{x}, \mathrm{x}' \in \{0,1\}^n$, *denote* $\Delta(\mathrm{x}, \mathrm{x}')$ *as the Hamming distance between* x *and* x'. *Formally,*

$$\Delta(\mathrm{x}, \mathrm{x}') := \frac{1}{n} \cdot \sum_{i \in [n]} |\mathrm{x}[i] - \mathrm{x}'[i]| \ .$$

Moreover, for any $\mathrm{x} \in \{0,1\}^n$ *and a language* $L \subseteq \{0,1\}^n$, *denote* $\Delta(\mathrm{x}, L)$ *as the Hamming distance between* x *and* L. *Formally,*

$$\Delta(\mathrm{x}, L) := \min_{\mathrm{x}' \in L \cap \{0,1\}^n} \Delta(\mathrm{x}, \mathrm{x}') \ .$$

3.2   Probabilistic Proof Systems

In this paper we consider a number of models of proof systems, such as IOPs, PCPs, MA proofs, their "proximity" variants, and variants where the error function may depend arbitrarily on the inputs. We choose to define them through the lens of a general object which we call "generalized IOPs", which includes explicit and implicit inputs, a witness, and arbitrary errors.

A *generalized* k-round (public-coin) IOP [BCS16, RRR16], works as follows. The verifier is given explicit input y and oracle access to implicit input x. The (honest) prover is additionally given a witness w. In every round $i \in [k]$, the verifier sends a uniformly random message ρ_i to the prover; then the prover sends a proof string π_i to the verifier. After k rounds of interaction, the verifier reads explicit input y, makes some queries to the implicit input x and to the proof strings $\pi_1, \ldots, \pi_k$ sent by the prover and then decides if to accept or to reject. The following definition discusses the error parameters of a generalized IOP:

Definition 5 (Generalized IOPP). *Let* $(\mathbf{P}, \mathbf{V})$ *be a tuple where* $\mathbf{P}$ *is an interactive algorithm, and* $\mathbf{V}$ *is an interactive oracle algorithm. We say that* $(\mathbf{P}, \mathbf{V})$ *is a public-coin* **generalized IOP** *for a relation* $R := \{((x, y), w)\}$ *with* k *rounds, completeness error* c, *and soundness error* s *if the following holds.*

- **Completeness.** *For every* $((x, y), w) \in R$,

$$\Pr_{\rho_1, \ldots, \rho_k} \left[\mathbf{V}^{x, \pi_1, \ldots, \pi_k}(|x|, y, \rho_1, \ldots, \rho_k) = 1 \,\middle|\, \begin{matrix} \pi_1 \leftarrow \mathbf{P}(x, y, w) \\ \vdots \\ \pi_k \leftarrow \mathbf{P}(x, y, w, \rho_1, \ldots, \rho_k) \end{matrix} \right] \geq 1 - c(x, y) \ .$$

If $c(x, y) = 0$ *for every* $(x, y) \in L(R)$, *we say that the IOPP has* perfect completeness.

- **Soundness.** *For every* $(x, y) \notin L(R)$ *and unbounded malicious prover* $\tilde{\mathbf{P}}$,

$$\Pr_{\rho_1, \ldots, \rho_k} \left[\mathbf{V}^{x, \pi_1, \ldots, \pi_k}(|x|, y, \rho_1, \ldots, \rho_k) = 1 \,\middle|\, \begin{matrix} \pi_1 \leftarrow \tilde{\mathbf{P}} \\ \vdots \\ \pi_k \leftarrow \tilde{\mathbf{P}}(\rho_1, \ldots, \rho_k) \end{matrix} \right] \leq s(x, y) \ .$$

Above, $L(R) := \{(x, y) \mid \exists w, ((x, y), w) \in R\}$.

In the rest of this paper, we sometimes omit explicitly writing the verifier's input $|x|$, but this is always assumed to be given to the verifier.

Efficiency Measures. We study several efficiency measures. All of these complexity measures are implicitly functions of the instance (x, y).

- *Rounds* k: The IOP has k rounds of interaction.
- *Proof length* l: the combined number of bits in the proofs π_i.
- *Queries to (implicit) input* q_x: the number of bits read by the verifier from x.
- *Queries to proof* q_π: the number of bits read by the verifier from $\pi_1, \ldots, \pi_k$.

- *Randomness* r: the combined number of bits in the verifier messages ρ_i.
- *Verifier time* vt: **V** runs in time vt.
- *Prover time* pt: The prover runs in time pt. In some cases we will have *expected* prover running time, in which case this will be stated explicitly.

We use generalized versions of PCPs and MA proofs:

Definition 6 (Generalized PCP and generalized MA). *A **generalized probabilistically checkable proof** (generalized PCP) is a generalized IOP with no interaction rounds (only a single prover message, after which the verifier may choose random coins). A **generalized MA proof** is a generalized PCP in which the verifier queries the entire (single) prover message.*

An IOP of proximity is a generalized IOP where the completeness error depends only on the length of the inputs, and the soundness error can be described as a function of the distance of the implicit instance x from an implicit input in the language. Formally:

Definition 7 (Proofs of proximity). *An **IOP of proximity** (IOPP) with respect to distance function Δ is a generalized IOP where there exist functions c' and s' such that $c(x, y) = c'(|x|, y)$ and $s(x, y) = s'(|x|, y, \delta)$ where $\delta := \Delta(x, L_y(R) \cap \{0, 1\}^{|x|})$ for $L_y(R) := \{x' \in \{0, 1\}^* \mid \exists w, ((x', y), w) \in R\}$.*

PCPs of proximity (PCPPs) and MA proofs of proximity (MAPs) are similarly defined as variants of generalized PCPs and generalized MA proofs respectively.

Whenever the distance function Δ is not explicitly specified, we implicitly refer to Hamming distance. It is common for proofs of proximity to be defined for relations with no explicit input y or witness w. Indeed, this is the case for the Hamming relation Ham_α which is the focus of this work. In this case we will omit y and w from all notation.

Finally, we define standard IOPs, PCPs and MA proofs:

Definition 8 (Standard IOP/PCP/MA proofs). *A (standard) IOP (respectively standard PCP or standard MA proof) is an IOPP (respectively PCPP or MAP proof) for a relation $R := \{((\bot, y), w)\}$ (i.e., there is no x in the relation).*

For the standard variants of probabilistic proof systems, we will omit x from notation, as it is always set to $\bot$. Moreover, we will sometimes denote the input by x and witness by w (instead of y and w) as is standard for IOPs.

Remark 1 (Computability of error functions). In this work we assume unless stated otherwise that c and s are computable in polynomial time given the implicit input, x, explicit input y, and the proximity δ (as defined in Definition 7).

3.3 Probabilistic Inequalities

We use the multiplicative Chernoff bound.

Theorem 1 (Multiplicative Chernoff Bound). *Let* $X = \sum_{i \in [n]} X_i$, *where* $X_1, \ldots, X_n$ *are independent random variables in* $\{0, 1\}$, *with* $\mathbb{E}[X] = \mu$. *Then for any* $\epsilon \geq 0$,

$$\Pr[X \leq (1 - \epsilon)\mu] \leq e^{-\left(\epsilon^2 \mu / 2\right)},$$
$$\Pr[X \geq (1 + \epsilon)\mu] \leq e^{-\left(\epsilon^2 \mu / 3\right)} \ .$$

4 Finding Good Shifts

In this section, we define the concept of "good" shifts and prove that such shifts can be found efficiently in expected probabilistic time. These good shifts will be helpful for us throughout the paper, generally for showing perfect completeness of protocols and for bounding the (expected) running time of the honest prover.

We define good shifts for a set of vectors:

Definition 9 (Good shifts). *For every* $n, k, t \in \mathbb{N}$, $\epsilon \in (0, 1]$, *and for every list of bit vectors* $\mathrm{x}_1, \ldots, \mathrm{x}_k \in \{0, 1\}^n$ *we define the set* $\mathsf{Good}_{t,\epsilon}(\mathrm{x}_1, \ldots, \mathrm{x}_k)$ *to be the set of shifts* $(z_1, \ldots, z_t) \in \{0, 1\}^{t \cdot n}$ *such that*

$$\forall i \in [k], \rho \in [n] \quad \sum_{j \in [t]} \mathrm{x}_i[\rho + z_j] \geq \epsilon \cdot t \ .$$

We give a probabilistic algorithm that, given a list of vectors, outputs a set of good shifts in small (expected) time:

Construction 2 (Shift finding algorithm). The algorithm $\mathbf{A}$ is given as input α, η, and $(\mathrm{x}_1, \ldots, \mathrm{x}_k)$. It proceeds as follows:

– Repeat the following until shifts are output:
  1. Sample $z_1, \ldots, z_t \leftarrow [n]$ uniformly at random.
  2. For every $i \in [k]$:
     (a) Set $\mathsf{counter}_i := 0$ and let bucket_i be the all zeros array of size n.
     (b) For every $\rho \in [n]$: if $\mathsf{counter}_i < \alpha \cdot n$ and $x_i[\rho] = 1$ then update: $\mathsf{counter}_i := \mathsf{counter}_i + 1$ and, for every $j \in [t]$, update $\mathsf{bucket}_i[\rho - z_j] := \mathsf{bucket}_i[\rho - z_j] + 1$.
     (c) Check that $\mathsf{bucket}_i[\rho] \geq (\alpha - \eta) \cdot t$ for every $\rho \in [n]$.
  3. Output $z_1, \ldots, z_t$ if the previous checks passed for every $i \in [k]$.

The following lemma shows that $\mathbf{A}$ finds good shifts and gives a bound on its running:

Lemma 1. *Fix parameters* $n \in \mathbb{N}$, $\alpha \in (0, 1]$ *and* $\eta \in (0, \alpha)$, *and let* $t := 2 \cdot \log(k \cdot n)/\eta^2$. *For every set of bit vectors* $\mathrm{x}_1, \ldots, \mathrm{x}_k \in \mathsf{Ham}_\alpha \cap \{0, 1\}^n$, *there exist* $(z_1, \ldots, z_t) \in \mathsf{Good}_{t,\alpha-\eta}(\mathrm{x}_1, \ldots, \mathrm{x}_k)$ *and the algorithm* $\mathbf{A}(\alpha, \eta, \mathrm{x}_1, \ldots, \mathrm{x}_k)$, *described in Construction 2, outputs a set of such shifts in expected time:* $O\left(\frac{\alpha}{\alpha-\eta} \cdot n \cdot k \cdot \log(n \cdot k)\right)$.

Proof. Fix bit vectors $x_1, \ldots, x_k \in \mathsf{Ham}_\alpha$, and for each i let x'_i be x_i where all but the first $\alpha \cdot n$ ones are flipped to 0 (note that $\mathsf{weight}(x'_i) = \alpha \cdot n \leq \mathsf{weight}(x_i)$). In Claim 2 we show that $\mathbf{A}$ outputs shifts if and only if they are good for $(x'_1, \ldots, x'_k)$. Then, in Claim 3, we show that the probability that a randomly sampled set of shifts is good for $(x'_1, \ldots, x'_k)$ is at least 0.2. Observe that $\mathsf{Good}_{t,\alpha-\eta}(x'_1, \ldots, x'_t) \subseteq \mathsf{Good}_{t,\alpha-\eta}(x_1, \ldots, x_t)$ since for every i and ρ:

$$\sum_{j \in [t]} x[\rho + z_j] \geq \sum_{j \in [t]} x'[\rho + z_j] \ .$$

Therefore, the expected number of times that $z_1, \ldots, z_t$ are sampled until $\mathbf{A}$ outputs $(z_1, \ldots, z_t) \in \mathsf{Good}_{t,\alpha-\eta}(x_1, \ldots, x_t)$ is 5.

Each sample takes time $O(t)$. The algorithm then iterates over all of the vectors and their values and, for each vector x_i, updates bucket_i for every j for at most $\alpha \cdot n$ times due to the counter $\mathsf{counter}_i$. Each update takes time $O(t)$. Thus, the computation for each vectors takes time $O(n + \alpha \cdot n \cdot t)$.

Overall, the expected running time of $\mathbf{A}$ is

$$O(t + k \cdot (n + \alpha \cdot n \cdot t)) = O\left(k \cdot (n + \alpha \cdot n \cdot \frac{\log(n \cdot k)}{\alpha - \eta})\right)$$

$$= O\left(\frac{\alpha}{\alpha - \eta} \cdot n \cdot k \cdot \log(n \cdot k)\right) \ ,$$

where the second equality holds since $\alpha/(\alpha - \eta) \geq O(1)$.

We now prove our first claim, showing that $\mathbf{A}$ outputs $z_1, \ldots, z_t$ if and only if they are good.

Claim 2. $\mathbf{A}$ outputs the sampled shifts $z_1, \ldots, z_t$ if and only if $(z_1, \ldots, z_t) \in \mathsf{Good}_{t,\alpha-\eta}(x'_1, \ldots, x'_k)$.

Proof. Consider a set of shifts $z_1, \ldots, z_t$. For a set index $i \in [k]$, $\mathsf{counter}_i$ begins at 0 and, for every ρ with $x_i[\rho] = 1$, $\mathsf{counter}_i$ is increased by 1. Once $\mathsf{counter}_i = (\alpha - \eta) \cdot n$ (i.e., once the first $(\alpha - \eta) \cdot n$ ones of x_i are seen), $\mathsf{counter}_i$ and bucket_i do not change. Therefore, the algorithm acts identically for $x_1, \ldots, x_k$ and $x'_1, \ldots, x'_k$.

Now note that for every ρ with $x'_i[\rho] = 1$, we add 1 to $\mathsf{bucket}_i[\rho - z_j]$ for every $j \in [t]$. Thus

$$\mathsf{bucket}_i[\rho] = |\{j \in [t] : x'_i[\rho + z_j] = 1\}| = \sum_j x'_i[\rho + z_j] \ .$$

Thus, by the end of the iteration, $\mathsf{bucket}_i[\rho] = \sum_j x'_i[\rho + z_j]$. The algorithm outputs $z_1, \ldots, z_t$ if and only if for every $i \in [k]$, and every $\rho \in [n]$:

$$\sum_j x'_i[\rho + z_j] \geq \mathsf{bucket}_i[\rho] \geq (\alpha - \eta) \cdot k \ ,$$

which precisely means that $z_1, \ldots, z_t$ is output if and only if $(z_1, \ldots, z_t) \in \mathsf{Good}_{t,\alpha-\eta}(x'_1, \ldots, x'_k)$. □

We now show that by uniformly sampling shifts, one hits a good set with constant probability:

Claim 3. $\Pr_{z_1,\ldots,z_t}\left[\,(z_1,\ldots,z_t) \in \mathsf{Good}_{t,\alpha-\eta}(x'_1,\ldots,x'_k)\,\right] > 0.2$.

Proof. Recall that

$$\Pr_{z_1,\ldots,z_t}\left[\,(z_1,\ldots,z_t) \in \mathsf{Good}_{t,\alpha-\eta}(x'_1,\ldots,x'_k)\,\right]$$

$$= \Pr_{z_1,\ldots,z_t}\left[\forall i \in [k], \rho \in [n]\ \sum_{j\in[t]} x'_i[\rho+z_j] \geq (\alpha-\eta)\cdot t\right] .$$

Notice that for every i and ρ:

$$\Pr_{z_j\leftarrow[n]}[x'_i[\rho+z_j]=1] = \Pr_{z_j\leftarrow[n]}[x'_i[z_j]=1] .$$

Thus, by applying the union bound, we have that:

$$\Pr_{z_1,\ldots,z_t}\left[\exists\rho\in[n].\ \sum_{j\in[t]} x'_i[\rho+z_j] < (\alpha-\eta)\cdot t\right]$$

$$\leq \sum_{\rho\in[n]}\left(\Pr_{z_1,\ldots,z_t}\left[\sum_{j\in[t]} x'_i[\rho+z_j] < (\alpha-\eta)\cdot t\right]\right)$$

$$= n\cdot \Pr_{z_1,\ldots,z_t}\left[\sum_{j\in[t]} x'_i[z_j] < (\alpha-\eta)\cdot t\right] .$$

Notice that for every j:

$$\mathbb{E}_{z_j}[x'_i[z_j]] = \Pr_{z_j}[x'_i[z_j]=1] = (\alpha-\eta)\cdot t .$$

Thus, by applying the Chernoff bound with $\epsilon := \alpha-\eta$, we have that

$$\Pr_{z_1,\ldots,z_t}\left[\sum_{j\in[t]} x'_i[z_j] < (\alpha-\eta)\cdot t\right] \leq e^{-\frac{\eta^2}{2\alpha}\cdot t} ,$$

Therefore,

$$\Pr_{z_1,\ldots,z_t}\left[\exists\rho\in[n]\ \sum_{j\in[t]} x'_i[\rho+z_j] < (\alpha-\eta)\cdot t\right] \leq n\cdot e^{-\frac{\eta^2}{2\alpha}\cdot t} .$$

By applying the union bound, we have that:

$$\Pr_{z_1,\dots,z_t}\left[\exists\, i \in [k], \rho \in [n] \sum_{j\in[t]} \mathrm{x}'_i[\rho + z_j] < (\alpha - \eta)\cdot t\right] \le k\cdot n\cdot e^{-\frac{\eta^2}{2\alpha}\cdot t}$$

$$= 2^{\log(k\cdot n)}\cdot e^{-\frac{\log(k\cdot n)}{\alpha}}$$

$$\le (2/e)^{\log(k\cdot n)}$$

$$< 0.8\ ,$$

where the equality follows from the definition of $t := 2\cdot \log(k\cdot n)/\eta^2$. Therefore,

$$\Pr_{z_1,\dots,z_t}\left[\forall\, i \in [k], \rho \in [n] \sum_{j\in[t]} \mathrm{x}'_i[\rho + z_j] \ge (\alpha - \eta)\cdot t\right] > 0.2\ .$$

□

5   Non-interactive Proofs for Hamming Weight with Sublinear Communication

In this section, we develop an MA proof and a PCPP with sublinear communication complexity for the Hamming weight problem. We begin by describing the MAP:

Theorem 3. *For every $\alpha, \eta : \mathbb{N} \to (0,1]$ such that $0 < \eta < \alpha$ (that are computable in linear time), there exists a perfectly complete MAP for Ham_α with the following parameters,*

MAP for Ham_α	
Soundness error	$\mathsf{s}(\delta) = \frac{\alpha-\delta}{\alpha-\eta}$
Communication length	$2\cdot \log^2 n/\eta^2$
Queries to input	$2\cdot \log n/\eta^2$
Randomness	$\log n$
Verifier running time	$O(\log n/\eta^2)$
Prover expected running time	$O\left(\alpha/(\alpha-\eta)\cdot n\cdot \log n\right)$

where $n \in \mathbb{N}$ is the input size, $\alpha := \alpha(n)$, and $\eta := \eta(n)$.

The PCPP is as follows:

Theorem 4. *For every $\alpha, \eta : \mathbb{N} \to (0,1]$ such that $0 < \eta < \frac{2}{3}\cdot \alpha$ (that are computable in linear time), there exists a perfectly complete PCPP for Ham_α with the following parameters,*
where $n \in \mathbb{N}$ is the input size, $\alpha := \alpha(n)$, and $\eta := \eta(n)$.

PCPP for Ham$_\alpha$	
Soundness error	$s(\delta) = \frac{\alpha - \delta}{\alpha - 1.5\eta}$
Proof length	$O\left(\frac{n}{\log^2 n} \cdot (-\log^2 \eta)/\eta^2\right)$
Queries to input	$O\left((\log\log n - \log \eta)/\eta^2\right)$
Queries to proof	$O\left(\log n \cdot (\log\log n - \log^2 \eta)/\eta^2\right)$
Randomness	$\log n + \log\log n - 2\log \eta + 1$
Verifier running time	$O\left(\log n \cdot (\log\log n - \log^2 \eta)/\eta^2\right)$
Prover expected running time	$O\left(\frac{\alpha}{\alpha - 1.5\eta} \cdot n \cdot \log n \cdot (\log\log n - \log \eta)/\eta^2\right)$

This section is organized as follows:

- In Sect. 5.1 we construct a generalized MA for list-Hamming. Theorem 3 follows as a corollary from this construction.
- In Sect. 5.2 we introduce a transformation from generalized PCP for list-Hamming with specific error structure (which the generalized MA constructed in the previous section has) to a PCPP for Hamming.
- In Sect. 5.3 we construct a PCPP for Hamming by plugging in the result from Sect. 5.1, which provides a generalized MA for list-Hamming, into the transformation described in Sect. 5.2. Note that MAs can be used in this transformation since MAs are a specific case of PCPs. This step directly implies Theorem 4.

5.1 MA Proof of Proximity

We construct a generalized MA proof for k-Ham$_\alpha$ with sublinear communication complexity. The resultant generalized MA proof will directly imply an MAP for Ham$_\alpha$.

Theorem 5. *For every $k \in \mathbb{N}$, $\alpha, \eta : \mathbb{N} \to (0,1]$ such that $0 < \eta < \alpha$ (that are computable in linear time), Construction 7 yields a perfectly complete generalized MA proof for k-Ham$_\alpha$ with the following parameters:*

Generalized MA for k-Ham$_\alpha$	
Soundness error	$\frac{1}{k \cdot (\alpha - \eta)} \cdot \sum_{i=1}^{k} \text{weight}(x_i)$
Proof length	$2 \cdot \log n \cdot \log(k \cdot n)/\eta^2$
Queries to input	$2 \cdot \log(k \cdot n)/\eta^2$
Randomness	$\log(k \cdot n)$
Verifier running time	$O(\log(k \cdot n)/\eta^2)$
Prover expected running time	$O\left(\alpha/(\alpha - \eta) \cdot n \cdot k \cdot \log(n \cdot k)\right)$

where $(x_1, \ldots, x_k) \in (\{0,1\}^n)^k$ is the input, $\alpha := \alpha(n)$, and $\eta := \eta(n)$.

Note that for $k = 1$, we have that $1\text{-}\mathsf{Ham}_\alpha \equiv \mathsf{Ham}_\alpha$. Moreover, the soundness error of the protocol is a function of the distance from the language: $\frac{1}{\alpha - \eta} \cdot$ $\mathsf{weight}(\mathbf{x}) = \frac{1}{\alpha - \eta} \cdot (\alpha - \Delta(\mathbf{x}, \mathsf{Ham}_\alpha))$. Therefore, Theorem 5, when fixing $k = 1$, directly implies the following theorem.

Theorem 6. *For every $\alpha, \eta : \mathbb{N} \to (0,1]$ such that $0 < \eta < \alpha$ (that are computable in linear time), Construction 7 yields a perfectly complete oracle MAP for $k\text{-}\mathsf{Ham}_\alpha$ with the following parameters:*

MAP for Ham_α	
Soundness error	$\mathsf{s}(\delta) = \frac{\alpha - \delta}{\alpha - \eta}$
Proof length	$2 \cdot \log^2 n / \eta^2$
Queries to input	$2 \cdot \log n / \eta^2$
Randomness	$\log n$
Verifier running time	$O(\log n / \eta^2)$
Prover expected running time	$O\left(\alpha/(\alpha - \eta) \cdot n \cdot \log n\right)$

where $n \in \mathbb{N}$ is the input size, $\alpha := \alpha(n)$, and $\eta := \eta(n)$.

Theorem 5 follows from the construction below:

Construction 7. Let $t := 2 \cdot \log(k \cdot n)/\eta^2$. The prover $\mathbf{P}$ receives as input bit vector $\mathbf{x}_1, \ldots, \mathbf{x}_k \in \{0,1\}^n$, while the verifier $\mathbf{V}$ has oracle access to the vector $\mathbf{x}_1, \ldots, \mathbf{x}_k$. They interact as follows.

- $\mathbf{P}(\mathbf{x}_1, \ldots, \mathbf{x}_k)$: The prover sends $z_1, \ldots, z_t \in [n]$.
- $\mathbf{V}^{\mathbf{x}_1, \ldots, \mathbf{x}_k}(n', z_1, \ldots, z_t)$:
  1. Set $n := n'/k$.
  2. Choose $i \leftarrow [k]$, $\rho \leftarrow [n]$ uniformly.
  3. Query $\mathbf{x}_i[\rho + z_1], \ldots, \mathbf{x}_i[\rho + z_t]$.
  4. Accept if $\mathsf{weight}(\mathbf{x}_i[\rho + z_1], \ldots, \mathbf{x}_i[\rho + z_t]) \geq (\alpha - \eta)$ and reject otherwise.

The full proof for the above construction is in the full version of this paper.

5.2   PCP for List-Hamming to PCPP for Hamming

We construct a PCPP for Hamming from a (generalized) PCP for list-Hamming.

Theorem 8. *Suppose that for every $\alpha', \eta' : \mathbb{N} \to (0,1]$ such that $0 < \eta' < \alpha'$ (that are computable in linear time), there is perfectly complete generalized PCP $(\mathbf{P}_{\mathsf{PCP}}, \mathbf{V}_{\mathsf{PCP}})$ for $k'\text{-}\mathsf{Ham}_{\alpha'}$ such that for input $(\mathbf{x}_1, \ldots, \mathbf{x}_{k'}) \in (\{0,1\}^{n'})^{k'}$ has soundness error of the form $\epsilon(\alpha', \eta') \cdot \frac{1}{k'} \cdot \sum_{i=1}^{k'} \mathsf{weight}(\mathbf{x}_i)$. Then for every $a \in \mathbb{N}$, $\alpha, \eta : \mathbb{N} \to (0,1]$ such that $0 < \eta' < \alpha'$ (that are computable in linear* *time), Construction 9 yields a PCPP* $(\mathbf{P}_{\mathsf{PCPP}}, \mathbf{V}'_{\mathsf{PCPP}})$ *for* Ham_α *with the following parameters:*

Generalized PCP $(\mathbf{P}, \mathbf{V})$ for k'-$\mathsf{Ham}_{\alpha'}$	
Soundness error	$\epsilon(\alpha, \eta) \cdot \frac{1}{k'} \cdot \sum_{i=1}^{k'} \mathsf{weight}(\mathbf{x}_i)$
Proof length	$\mathsf{l}_\mathbf{P} := \mathsf{l}_\mathbf{P}(n', k', \eta')$
Queries to input	$\mathsf{q}_\mathbf{x} := \mathsf{q}_\mathbf{x}(n', k', \eta')$
Queries to proof	$\mathsf{q}_\pi := \mathsf{q}_\pi(n', k', \eta')$
Randomness	$\mathsf{r} := \mathsf{r}(n', k', \eta')$
Verifier running time	$\mathsf{vt} := \mathsf{vt}(n', k', \eta')$
Prover expected running time $\mathsf{pt} := \mathsf{pt}(n', k', \alpha', \eta')$	

$\longrightarrow$

PCPP $(\mathbf{P}', \mathbf{V}')$ for Ham_α	
Soundness error	$\mathsf{s}(\delta, \alpha, \eta) = \epsilon(\alpha', \eta') \cdot (\alpha - \delta)$
Proof length	$n' \cdot \log n + \frac{n}{a} \cdot \mathsf{l}_\mathbf{P}$
Queries to input	$\mathsf{q}_\mathbf{x}$
Queries to proof	$\log n \cdot \mathsf{q}_\mathbf{x} + \mathsf{q}_\pi$
Randomness	$\log(n/a) + \mathsf{r}$
Verifier running time	$\mathsf{vt} + O(\mathsf{q}_\mathbf{x})$
Prover expected running time $O\left(\left(\frac{1}{\eta^2} + \frac{\alpha}{\alpha - \frac{\eta}{2}}\right) \cdot n \cdot \log n + \frac{n}{a} \cdot \mathsf{pt}\right)$	

where $n' = 2 \cdot \log n / \eta^2(n)$, $k' = a$, $\eta' = \eta(n)/2$, $\alpha' = \alpha(n) - \eta(n)/2$.

Construction 9. Let $t := 8 \cdot \log n / \eta^2$, and for every $s \in [n/a]$ let $I_s := ((s-1) \cdot a + 1, \ldots, s \cdot a)$ be a list of a indices. Let $(\mathbf{P}_{\mathsf{PCP}}, \mathbf{V}_{\mathsf{PCP}})$ be a perfectly complete PCP for k'-$\mathsf{Ham}_{\alpha'}$ with vectors of size $n' := t$, and $\eta' := \eta/2$. The prover $\mathbf{P}_{\mathsf{PCPP}}$ receives as input the bit vector $\mathbf{x}$, while the verifier $\mathbf{V}_{\mathsf{PCPP}}$ has oracle access to the bit vector $\mathbf{x}$. They interact as follows.

- $\mathbf{P}_{\mathsf{PCPP}}(\mathbf{x})$:
    1. Set bit vectors $z_1, \ldots, z_t \in [n]$.
    2. For every $\rho \in [n]$, set $\mathbf{x}_\rho := (\mathbf{x}[\rho + z_1], \ldots, \mathbf{x}[\rho + z_t])$.
    3. For every $s \in [n/a]$, set $X_s := (\mathbf{x}_\rho)_{\rho \in I_s}$, and compute $\pi_s := \mathbf{P}_{\mathsf{PCP}}(X_s)$.
    4. Output $((z_1, \ldots, z_t), (\pi_1, \ldots, \pi_{n/a}))$.
- $\mathbf{V}_{\mathsf{PCPP}}^{\mathbf{x}, \pi}(n)$:
    0. *Notation:*
        (a) For every $\rho \in [n]$, let $\mathbf{x}_\rho := (\mathbf{x}[\rho + z_1], \ldots, \mathbf{x}[\rho + z_t])$.
        (b) For every $s \in [n/a]$, let $X_s := (\mathbf{x}_\rho)_{\rho \in I_s}$.
        (Note that the verifier does not compute the above.)
    1. Parse $\pi := ((z_1, \ldots, z_t), (\tilde{\pi}_1, \ldots, \tilde{\pi}_{n/a}))$.
    2. Choose $s \leftarrow [n/a]$ uniformly.
    3. Emulate $\mathbf{V}_{\mathsf{PCP}}^{X_s, \tilde{\pi}_s}(a \cdot t)$, where for every input query $\mathbf{x}_j[i]$, query z_i, $\mathbf{x}[I_s[j] + z_i]$, and answer accordingly.
    4. Accept if and only if $\mathbf{V}^{X_s, \tilde{\pi}_s}(a \cdot t)$ accepts.

The full proof for the above construction can be found in the full version of this paper.

5.3   PCP of Proximity

The following theorem follows by plugging in Theorem 5 into Theorem 8.

Theorem 10. *For every $\alpha, \eta : \mathbb{N} \to (0,1]$ such that $\eta \in (0,\alpha)$ (that are computable in linear time), there exists a perfectly complete PCPP $(\mathbf{P}, \mathbf{V})$ for Ham_α with the following parameters:*

PCPP $(\mathbf{P}, \mathbf{V})$	
Completeness error	0
Soundness error	$\mathsf{s}(\delta, \alpha, \eta) = \frac{\alpha - \delta}{\alpha - \eta}$
Proof length	$O\left(\frac{n}{\eta^2 \cdot \log^2 n} \cdot (-\log^2 \eta)\right)$
Queries to input	$O\left((\log\log n - \log \eta)/\eta^2\right)$
Queries to proof	$O\left(\log n \cdot (\log\log n - \log^2 \eta)/\eta^2\right)$
Randomness	$\log n + \log\log n - 2\log \eta + 1$
Verifier running time	$O\left(\log n \cdot (\log\log n - \log^2 \eta)/\eta^2\right)$
Prover expected running time	$O\left(\frac{\alpha}{\alpha - \eta} \cdot n \cdot \log n \cdot (\log\log n - \log \eta)/\eta^2\right)$

where $n \in \mathbb{N}$ is the input size, $\alpha := \alpha(n)$, and $\eta := \eta(n)$.

The proof of this theorem appears in the full version of the paper.

Acknowledgments. We are grateful to Ron Rothblum for valuable discussions and for directing us to related work.

Gal Arnon is supported in part by a grant from the Israel Science Foundation (no. 2686/20) and by the Simons Foundation Collaboration on the Theory of Algorithmic Fairness. Shany Ben-David is supported by the Israel Science Foundation (Grant no. 2302/22), and by the Clore Israel Foundation. Eylon Yogev is supported by the Israel Science Foundation (Grant No. 2302/22), European Research Union (ERC, CRYPTO-PROOF, 101164375), and by an Alon Young Faculty Fellowship. Views and opinions expressed are however those of the author(s) only and do not necessarily reflect those of the European Union or the European Research Council. Neither the European Union nor the granting authority can be held responsible for them.

References

[ABCY22] Arnon, G., Bhangale, A., Chiesa, A., Yogev, E.: A toolbox for barriers on interactive oracle proofs. In: Kiltz, E., Vaikuntanathan, V. (eds.) TCC 2022. LNCS, vol. 13747, pp. 447–466. Springer, Cham (2022). https://doi.org/10.1007/978-3-031-22318-1_16

[ACFY24] Arnon, G., Chiesa, A., Fenzi, G., Yogev, E.: STIR: ReedSolomon proximity testing with fewer queries. Cryptology ePrint Archive, Paper 2024/390 (2024)

[ACY22a]   Arnon, G., Chiesa, A., Yogev, E.: A PCP theorem for interactive proofs.
           In: Dunkelman, O., Dziembowski, S. (eds.) EUROCRYPT 2022. LNCS, vol.
           13276, pp. 64–94. Springer, Cham (2022). https://doi.org/10.1007/978-3-
           031-07085-3_3
[ACY22b]   Arnon, G., Chiesa, A., Yogev, E.: Hardness of approximation for stochastic
           problems via interactive oracle proofs. In: CCC 2022 (2022)
[ACY23]   Arnon, G., Chiesa, A., Yogev, E.: IOPs with inverse polynomial soundness
           error. IEEE (2023)
[AGRR23]   Aaronson, H., Gur, T., Rajgopal, N., Rothblum, R.: Distribution-free proofs
           of proximity. In: Electronic Colloquium on Computational Complexity
           (2023)
[BBC+17]   Ben-Sasson, E.: Computational integrity with a public random string from
           quasi-linear PCPs. In: Coron, J.-S., Nielsen, J.B., et al. (eds.) EURO-
           CRYPT 2017. LNCS, vol. 10212, pp. 551–579. Springer, Cham (2017).
           https://doi.org/10.1007/978-3-319-56617-7_19
[BBHR18]   Ben-Sasson, E., Bentov, I., Horesh, Y., Riabzev, M.: Fast reed–solomon
           interactive oracle proofs of proximity. In: ICALP 2018 (2018)
[BCG+17a] Ben-Sasson, E., Chiesa, A., Gabizon, A., Riabzev, M., Spooner, N.: Inter-
           active oracle proofs with constant rate and query complexity. In: ICALP
           2017 (2017)
[BCG+17b] Bootle, J., Cerulli, A., Ghadafi, E., Groth, J., Hajiabadi, M., Jakobsen,
           S.K.: Linear-time zero-knowledge proofs for arithmetic circuit satisfiability.
           In: ASIACRYPT 2017 (2017)
[BCG20]   Bootle, J., Chiesa, A., Groth, J.: Linear-time arguments with sublinear
           verification from tensor codes. In: Pass, R., Pietrzak, K. (eds.) TCC 2020.
           LNCS, vol. 12551, pp. 19–46. Springer, Cham (2020). https://doi.org/10.
           1007/978-3-030-64378-2_2
[BCGV16]   Ben-Sasson, E., Chiesa, A., Gabizon, A., Virza, M.: Quasi-linear size zero
           knowledge from linear-algebraic PCPs. In: Kushilevitz, E., Malkin, T.
           (eds.) TCC 2016. LNCS, vol. 9563, pp. 33–64. Springer, Heidelberg (2016).
           https://doi.org/10.1007/978-3-662-49099-0_2
[BCL22]   Bootle, J., Chiesa, A., Liu, S.: Zero-knowledge IOPs with linear- time
           prover and polylogarithmic-time verifier. In: Dunkelman, O., Dziembowski,
           S. (eds.) EUROCRYPT 2022. LNCS, vol. 13276, pp. 275–304. Springer,
           Cham (2022). https://doi.org/10.1007/978-3-031-07085-3_10
[BCS16]   Ben-Sasson, E., Chiesa, A., Spooner, N.: Interactive oracle proofs. In: Hirt,
           M., Smith, A. (eds.) TCC 2016. LNCS, vol. 9986, pp. 31–60. Springer,
           Heidelberg (2016). https://doi.org/10.1007/978-3-662-53644-5_2
[BGH+06]   Ben-Sasson, E., Goldreich, O., Harsha, P., Sudan, M., Vadhan, S.P.: Robust
           PCPs of proximity, shorter PCPs, and applications to coding. SIAM J.
           Comput. (2006)
[BKS01]   Bar-Yossef, Z., Kumar, R., Sivakumar, D.: Sampling algorithms: lower
           bounds and applications. In: Vitter, J.S., Spirakis, P.G., Yannakakis, M.
           (eds.) ACM (2001)
[BN22]   Bordage, S., Nardi, J.: Interactive oracle proofs of proximity to algebraic
           geometry codes. In: CCC 2022 (2022)
[BV19]   Bafna, M., Vyas, N.: Imperfect gaps in gap-ETH and PCPs. In: Shpilka,
           A. (eds.) LIPIcs. Schloss Dagstuhl - Leibniz-Zentrum für Informatik, vol.
           137 (2019)
[BV22]   Bitansky, N., Vaikuntanathan, V.: A note on perfect correctness by deran-
           domization. J. Cryptol. (2022)

[CY20]   Chiesa, A., Yogev, E.: Barriers for succinct arguments in the random oracle model. In: Pass, R., Pietrzak, K. (eds.) TCC 2020. LNCS, vol. 12551, pp. 47–76. Springer, Cham (2020). https://doi.org/10.1007/978-3-030-64378-2_3

[CY21a] Chiesa, A., Yogev, E.: Subquadratic SNARGs in the random oracle model. In: Malkin, T., Peikert, C. (eds.) CRYPTO 2021. LNCS, vol. 12825, pp. 711–741. Springer, Cham (2021). https://doi.org/10.1007/978-3-030-84242-0_25

[CY21b] Chiesa, A., Yogev, E.: Tight security bounds for Micali's SNARGs. In: Nissim, K., Waters, B. (eds.) TCC 2021. LNCS, vol. 13042, pp. 401–434. Springer, Cham (2021). https://doi.org/10.1007/978-3-030-90459-3_14

[DNR04] Dwork, C., Naor, M., Reingold, O.: Immunizing encryption schemes from decryption errors. In: Cachin, C., Camenisch, J.L. (eds.) EUROCRYPT 2004. LNCS, vol. 3027, pp. 342–360. Springer, Heidelberg (2004). https://doi.org/10.1007/978-3-540-24676-3_21

[DR04]   Dinur, I., Reingold, O.: Assignment testers: towards a combinatorial proof of the PCP theorem. In: FOCS 2004 (2004)

[EKR04] Ergün, F., Kumar, R., Rubinfeld, R.: Fast approximate probabilistically checkable proofs. In: Information and Computation (2004)

[FGM+89] Fürer, M., Goldreich, O., Mansour, Y., Sipser, M., Zachos, S.: On completeness and soundness in interactive proof systems. In: Advances in Computing Research (1989)

[GGR18] Goldreich, O., Gur, T., Rothblum, R.D.: Proofs of proximity for context-free languages and read-once branching programs. Inf. Comput. (2018)

[GGR98] Goldreich, O., Goldwasser, S., Ron, D.: Property testing and its connection to learning and approximation. J. ACM (1998)

[Gol11] Goldreich, O.: A sample of samplers: a computational perspective on sampling. In: Goldreich, O. (ed.) Studies in Complexity and Cryptography. Miscellanea on the Interplay between Randomness and Computation. LNCS, vol. 6650, pp. 302–332. Springer, Heidelberg (2011). https://doi.org/10.1007/978-3-642-22670-0_24

[GR18]   Gur, T., Rothblum, R.D.: Non-interactive proofs of proximity. Comput. Complex. (2018)

[HNY17] Hubácek, P., Naor, M., Yogev, E.: The journey from NP to TFNP hardness. In: Papadimitriou, vol. 67. LIPIcs. Schloss Dagstuhl - Leibniz-Zentrum für Informatik (2017)

[Kil92] Kilian, J.: A note on efficient zero-knowledge proofs and arguments. In: STOC 1992 (1992)

[KR15]   Kalai, Y.T., Rothblum, R.D.: Arguments of proximity. In: Gennaro, R., Robshaw, M. (eds.) CRYPTO 2015. LNCS, vol. 9216, pp. 422–442. Springer, Heidelberg (2015). https://doi.org/10.1007/978-3-662-48000-7_21

[KSY20] Katzir, L., Shikhelman, C., Yogev, E.: Interactive proofs for social graphs. In: Micciancio, D., Ristenpart, T. (eds.) CRYPTO 2020. LNCS, vol. 12172, pp. 574–601. Springer, Cham (2020). https://doi.org/10.1007/978-3-030-56877-1_20

[Lau83] Lautemann, C.: BPP and the polynomial hierarchy. Inf. Process. Lett. (1983)

[Mic00] Micali, S.: Computationally sound proofs. SIAM J. Comput. (2000). Preliminary version appeared in FOCS 1994

[Mie09] Mie, T.: Short PCPPs verifiable in polylogarithmic time with O(1) queries. Ann. Math. Artif. Intell. (2009)

[Nao89] Naor, M.: Bit commitment using pseudo-randomness. In: Brassard, G. (ed.) CRYPTO 1989. LNCS, vol. 435, pp. 128–136. Springer, New York (1990). https://doi.org/10.1007/0-387-34805-0_13

[NW94] Nisan, N., Wigderson, A.: Hardness vs randomness. J. Comput. Syst. Sci. (1994)

[Rot24] Rothblum, R.: Private communication

[RR20a] Ron-Zewi, N., Rothblum, R.: Local proofs approaching the witness length. In: FOCS 2020 (2020)

[RR20b] Rothblum, G.N., Rothblum, R.D.: Batch verification and proofs of proximity with polylog overhead. In: Pass, R., Pietrzak, K. (eds.) TCC 2020. LNCS, vol. 12551, pp. 108–138. Springer, Cham (2020). https://doi.org/10.1007/978-3-030-64378-2_5

[RR22] Ron-Zewi, N., Rothblum, R.D.: Proving as fast as computing: succinct arguments with constant prover overhead. In: STOC 2022 (2022)

[RRR16] Reingold, O., Rothblum, R., Rothblum, G.: Constant-round interactive proofs for delegating computation. In: STOC 2016 (2016)

[RS96] Rubinfeld, R., Sudan, M.: Robust characterizations of polynomials with applications to program testing. SIAM J. Comput. (1996)

[RVW13] Rothblum, G.N., Vadhan, S.P., Wigderson, A.: Interactive proofs of proximity: delegating computation in sublinear time. In: STOC 2013 (2013)

[XZZ+19] Xie, T., Zhang, J., Zhang, Y., Papamanthou, C., Song, D.: Libra: succinct zero-knowledge proofs with optimal prover computation. In: Boldyreva, A., Micciancio, D. (eds.) CRYPTO 2019. LNCS, vol. 11694, pp. 733–764. Springer, Cham (2019). https://doi.org/10.1007/978-3-030-26954-8_24

Untangling the Security of Kilian's Protocol: Upper and Lower Bounds

Alessandro Chiesa[1], Marcel Dall'Agnol[2], Ziyi Guan[1(✉)], Nicholas Spooner[3,4], and Eylon Yogev[5]

[1] EPFL, Lausanne, Switzerland
{alessandro.chiesa,ziyi.guan}@epfl.ch
[2] Princeton University, Princeton, USA
dallagnol@princeton.edu
[3] University of Warwick, Coventry, UK
nicholas.spooner@warwick.ac.uk
[4] NYU, New York, USA
[5] Bar-Ilan University, Ramat Gan, Israel
eylon.yogev@biu.ac.il

Abstract. Sigma protocols are elegant cryptographic proofs that have become a cornerstone of modern cryptography. A notable example is Schnorr's protocol, a zero-knowledge proof-of-knowledge of a discrete logarithm. Despite extensive research, the security of Schnorr's protocol in the standard model is not fully understood.

In this paper we study *Kilian's protocol*, an influential public-coin interactive protocol that, while not a sigma protocol, shares striking similarities with sigma protocols. The first example of a succinct argument, Kilian's protocol is proved secure via *rewinding*, the same idea used to prove sigma protocols secure. In this paper we show how, similar to Schnorr's protocol, a precise understanding of the security of Kilian's protocol remains elusive. We contribute new insights via upper bounds and lower bounds.

- *Upper bounds.* We establish the tightest known bounds on the security of Kilian's protocol in the standard model, via strict-time reductions and via expected-time reductions. Prior analyses are strict-time reductions that incur large overheads or assume restrictive properties of the PCP underlying Kilian's protocol.
- *Lower bounds.* We prove that significantly improving on the bounds that we establish for Kilian's protocol would imply improving the security analysis of Schnorr's protocol beyond the current state-of-the-art (an open problem). This partly explains the difficulties in obtaining tight bounds for Kilian's protocol.

Keywords: succinct interactive arguments · vector commitment schemes

1 Introduction

Sigma protocols are a fundamental class of cryptographic proofs with notable applications in cryptography (see [25] and references therein). A sigma protocol is a public-coin interactive protocol that satisfies strong zero knowledge and soundness properties, and enjoys a simple structure. The prover sends a commitment, then the verifier

© International Association for Cryptologic Research 2025
E. Boyle and M. Mahmoody (Eds.): TCC 2024, LNCS 15364, pp. 158–188, 2025.
https://doi.org/10.1007/978-3-031-78011-0_6

responds with a random challenge, and finally, the prover sends an opening; the verifier computes a decision bit based on the instance and the interaction transcript. Perhaps the most prominent example of a sigma protocol is Schnorr's protocol [33, 34], which proves, in zero knowledge, the knowledge of the discrete logarithm of a given group element (for a given cyclic group and base group element). Numerous works study in detail Schnorr's protocol (and its derivates), establishing upper and lower bounds on its security in different settings [5, 6, 20, 29, 30, 35, 36]. Remarkably, gaps remain in our understanding of the security of Schnorr's protocol, and closing these gaps remains a challenging open problem.

In this paper we study *Kilian's protocol* [23], a public-coin interactive protocol that, while not a sigma protocol, shares striking similarities with sigma protocols. This protocol is historically significant as the first example of a *succinct argument*, a computationally-sound interactive proof for nondeterministic relations where the communication complexity is much smaller than the size of the relation's witness. Kilian's protocol is also the simplest example of a succinct interactive argument obtained via the VC-based approach, a fundamental paradigm for constructing succinct arguments from a probabilistic proof and a vector commitment (VC) scheme.

The shared structure with a sigma protocol is evident. The argument prover commits to a probabilistically checkable proof (PCP) string via a VC scheme (Kilian's presentation uses a Merkle commitment scheme, a VC scheme obtained from collision-resistant hash functions), and sends the resulting commitment to the argument verifier; the argument verifier sends PCP verifier randomness to the argument prover; and finally the argument prover reveals the values of the queried locations of the PCP string and accompanies these values with opening information. The argument verifier accepts if the opening information is valid and the PCP verifier accepts.

Succinct arguments are a rare example of an "advanced" cryptographic primitive that can be achieved from simple cryptography. Indeed, it is remarkable that, based solely on the existence of a collision resistant hash function (even given as a black box), one can achieve cryptographic proof systems with such remarkable efficiency. On the other hand, the security reduction of a succinct argument is tasked with a challenging goal: find a "long" witness when given a malicious argument prover that only outputs "short" messages in any given interaction. This naturally leads to *rewinding*, a fundamental method of analysis in cryptography.

While Kilian [23] gives only an informal analysis, the security of Kilian's protocol via rewinding is studied in later works. Barak and Goldreich [4] give a detailed analysis, but with limitations: their analysis incurs overheads and applies only to PCPs that satisfy restrictive properties. Other works [15, 21, 26, 27] provide brief analyses in the setting of negligible errors, without quantifying security bounds in terms of the underlying ingredients. We further elaborate on prior work in Sect. 1.3.

Motivated by the surge of interest in succinct arguments (e.g., in the context of blockchains [31, 32]), we revisit the security of Kilian's protocol. As we discuss shortly, we expose a fine structure and open problems, much alike to the state of affairs for arguably simpler protocols such as Schnorr's protocol. This challenges the commonly-held belief that Kilian's protocol is "understood". We now turn to discuss our results.

1.1   Our Results

Kilian's protocol [23] combines a PCP system PCP and a vector commitment scheme VC to obtain a succinct (public-coin) interactive argument. Throughout this section, we fix these ingredients (unless otherwise specified).

- PCP is a PCP system for a relation R with proof length ℓ, query complexity q, and soundness error ϵ_{PCP}. (These may depend on the given instance x.)
- VC is a vector commitment scheme VC and we denote by ϵ_{VC} its *position binding error*, which bounds the probability that an adversary outputs valid openings for the same commitment that disagree in at least one position. In general, ϵ_{VC} is a function of the security parameter λ, length ℓ of the committed vector, number s of opened entries of the vector, and bound t_{VC} on the adversary running time.

Soundness. We provide the tightest known bounds for the soundness error of Kilian's protocol.

Theorem 1 (Informal). *The soundness error ϵ_{ARG} of* Kilian[PCP, VC] *satisfies the following for every security parameter λ, instance* $x \notin L(R)$, *adversary time bound t_{ARG}, and error tolerance $\epsilon > 0$:*

$$\epsilon_{\mathsf{ARG}}(\lambda, x, t_{\mathsf{ARG}}) \leq \epsilon_{\mathsf{PCP}}(x) + \epsilon_{\mathsf{VC}}(\lambda, \ell, q, t_{\mathsf{VC}}) + \epsilon, \text{ where } t_{\mathsf{VC}} = O\left(\frac{\ell}{\epsilon} \cdot t_{\mathsf{ARG}}\right) .$$

The above bound for Kilian's protocol has an intuitive explanation. An adversary that commits to the PCP string $\widetilde{\Pi}$ with maximal acceptance probability (and opens accordingly) convinces the argument verifier with probability at least ϵ_{PCP}. Moreover, an adversary that then tries to find a collision when $\widetilde{\Pi}$ is rejected achieves (under some mild conditions) a convincing probability of $\epsilon_{\mathsf{PCP}} + (1 - \epsilon_{\mathsf{PCP}}) \cdot \epsilon_{\mathsf{VC}}$. The $\frac{\ell}{\epsilon}$ multiplicative loss in t_{VC} compared to t_{ARG} expresses the *price of rewinding*: to reconstruct an almost full PCP string from small fragments revealed in each (valid) opening, we rewind the malicious argument prover sufficiently many times. Improving this multiplicative factor remains an open problem. Nevertheless, we show an exponential improvement when VC satisfies *expected*-time position binding, via an expected-time reduction that we discuss next.

Expected-Time Adversaries. We use $\epsilon_{\mathsf{VC}}^{\star}$ to denote the *expected-time* position binding error of VC, in which case we use $t_{\mathsf{VC}}^{\star}$ to denote a bound on the *expected* running time of the adversary. Namely, $\epsilon_{\mathsf{VC}}^{\star}$ is the error probability given an adversary that runs in *expected-time* $t_{\mathsf{VC}}^{\star}$.

We provide the first soundness analysis of Kilian's protocol against adversaries with bounded expected running time. Since the (strict-time) soundness error of Kilian's protocol is upper-bounded by its expected-time soundness error, the following theorem gives an alternative upper bound on the (strict-time) soundness error in terms of the expected-time position binding error $\epsilon_{\mathsf{VC}}^{\star}$ of VC.

Theorem 2 (Informal). *If* PCP *has a non-adaptive verifier with running time t_{V}, the expected-time soundness error $\epsilon_{\mathsf{ARG}}^{\star}$ of* Kilian[PCP, VC] *satisfies the following for every security parameter λ, instance* $x \notin L(R)$, *adversary expected time bound $t_{\mathsf{ARG}}^{\star}$, and error tolerance $\epsilon > 0$:*

$$\epsilon_{\mathsf{ARG}}^{\star}(\lambda, x, t_{\mathsf{ARG}}^{\star}) \leq \epsilon_{\mathsf{PCP}}(x) + q \cdot \epsilon_{\mathsf{VC}}^{\star}(\lambda, \ell, q, t_{\mathsf{VC}}^{\star}) + \epsilon, \text{ where } t_{\mathsf{VC}}^{\star} = O\left(\log\frac{q}{\epsilon} \cdot (t_{\mathsf{ARG}}^{\star} + \ell \cdot t_{\mathsf{V}})\right).$$

This is an *exponential improvement* in the dependency of ϵ compared to the strict-time setting (Theorem 1). Note that Theorem 2 assumes that the PCP underlying Kilian's protocol has a *non-adaptive verifier* (its queries are determined by the instance $\mathbb{x}$ and the PCP verifier randomness). For PCPs with an adaptive verifier, we prove an alternative statement that achieves the same bound except with $t_{VC}^\star = O\left(\log\frac{q}{\epsilon} \cdot \ell \cdot t_{ARG}^\star\right)$.

Lower Bounds on Soundness. Kilian's protocol shares certain structural resemblances to a sigma protocol: both start with a prover's commitment, followed by a verifier's challenge, and end with an opening to the commitment. However, sigma protocols are special sound while Kilian's protocol is not (see Sect. 1.3). Hence, it is unclear whether there is any formal connection between Kilian's protocol and sigma protocols.

We obtain the first lower bound on the soundness error of Kilian's protocol by showing that bounding the soundness of Kilian's protocol is *as hard as that of the Schnorr identification scheme*, a sigma protocol obtained from Schorr's protocol whose security, despite significant research efforts, remains only partially understood.

Theorem 3 (Informal). *There exists* PCP *for a relation* R *and* VC *such that, for every security parameter* λ, *instance* $\mathbb{x} \notin L(R)$, *Schnorr adversary time bound* $t_{ID} \in \mathbb{N}$, *and Schnorr adversary expected time bound* $t_{ID}^\star \in \mathbb{N}$,

$$\epsilon_{Schnorr}(\lambda, t_{ID}) \leq \epsilon_{ARG}(\lambda, \mathbb{x}, t_{ARG}) \ , \ and$$
$$\epsilon_{Schnorr}^\star(\lambda, t_{ID}^\star) \leq \epsilon_{ARG}^\star(\lambda, \mathbb{x}, t_{ARG}^\star) \ .$$

Above, ϵ_{ARG} *and* $\epsilon_{ARG}^\star$ *are the soundness error and the expected-time soundness error of* ARG $:=$ Kilian[PCP, VC], *respectively;* $\epsilon_{Schnorr}$ *and* $\epsilon_{Schnorr}^\star$ *are the security against passive impersonation attacks of the Schnorr identification scheme and its expected-time analogue, respectively. Moreover,* $t_{ARG} = O(t_{ID})$, *and* $t_{ARG}^\star = O(t_{ID}^\star)$.

In Sect. 1.2 we discuss how Theorem 3 tells us that in the strict-time setting there is a polynomial gap between upper and lower bounds, whereas in the expected-time setting there is essentially no gap.

Knowledge Soundness. The above discussion focuses only on the soundness error of Kilian's protocol. Recall that the soundness error is an upper bound on the probability that a time-bounded adversary convinces the argument verifier to accept an instance not in the language. Another important security notion is the *knowledge soundness error*, which bounds the probability that a time-bounded adversary convinces the verifier but a corresponding extractor, given that adversary, fails to find a valid witness for the instance. The knowledge soundness error is an upper bound on the soundness error because any extractor cannot find a valid witness for an instance not in the language (there are no valid witnesses).

We construct an extractor for Kilian's protocol that runs in time $O\left(\frac{\ell}{\epsilon} \cdot t_{ARG}\right)$, and similarly to Theorem 1, prove that its knowledge soundness error satisfies

$$\kappa_{ARG}(\lambda, \mathbb{x}, t_{ARG}) \leq \kappa_{PCP}(\mathbb{x}) + \epsilon_{VC}(\lambda, \ell, q, t_{VC}) + \epsilon, \text{ where } t_{VC} = O\left(\frac{\ell}{\epsilon} \cdot t_{ARG}\right) \ .$$

We prove this bound by making explicit, in the proof of Theorem 1, a subroutine with running time $O\left(\frac{\ell}{\epsilon} \cdot t_{ARG}\right)$ that outputs a "good" PCP (after which we rely on the PCP knowledge extractor to obtain a witness).

What can we say about the setting of expected-time adversaries?

A similar bound as the above can straightforwardly be proved, but this would not take advantage of an expected-time reduction to achieve a smaller upper bound. Ideally, we would convert the bound on soundness error in Theorem 2 into a similar bound on knowledge soundness error; however, this does *not* work. Indeed, while the proofs behind Theorems 1 and 2 both use rewinding arguments, they are qualitatively different (more details in Sects. 2.2 and 2.3). Obtaining a knowledge soundness bound from the proof of Theorem 1 is straightforward because the extractor for the PCP and the collision finder for the VC are similar algorithms. However, the proof of Theorem 2 leverages extra efficiency by breaking this symmetry: only the VC collision finder is efficient, while the extractor that constructs a PCP is not. Hence, obtaining better bounds for the expected-time knowledge soundness of Kilian's protocol remains open.

We conclude by noting that similar considerations apply for proving the security of Kilian's protocol when based on a probabilistically checkable *argument* (PCA) [7, 12, 22] rather than a probabilistically checkable *proof*. Since a PCA is computationally sound, the running time to generate the PCA string is essential. Hence, our work yields a strict-time reduction that is compatible with PCAs, while our expected-time reduction is not compatible with PCAs.

Remark 1 (Adaptive Choice of x*).* The results of Theorems 1 to 3 are stated, for simplicity, in the plain model (no trusted setups), where the argument verifier is responsible for sampling and sending public parameters pp for VC to the argument prover. However, we actually *prove* these results in the (adaptive) common reference string model, wherein public parameters pp for VC are sampled by a trusted party and *a malicious argument prover may adaptively choose the instance* x *after learning* pp. Since in these stronger theorems there is no pre-set instance x, the analogous statements (for corresponding security properties) in the common reference model replace x with a size bound n (and hold for all instances such that $|x| \leq n$). The plain model variants are straightforwardly implied (see Sect. 2.6 and Remark 7).

1.2 Discussion

How Tight are the Soundness Bounds? We discuss the tightness of the soundness upper bounds in Theorems 1 and 2. The takeaway is that, for the setting in Theorem 3: (i) there is a polynomial gap between Theorem 1 and the best strict-time analysis of the security of the Schnorr identification scheme; and (ii) there is essentially no gap between Theorem 2 and the best expected-time analysis of the security of the Schnorr identification scheme. This mirrors the state of the affairs for the Schnorr identification scheme, as we now elaborate.

The security of the Schnorr identification scheme relies on the hardness of the discrete logarithm problem. In the strict-time setting, the best analysis shows (roughly) a square-root loss in the error:

$$\epsilon_{\mathsf{Schnorr}}(\lambda, \mathsf{t}_{\mathsf{ID}}) \leq \sqrt{\epsilon_{\mathsf{DLOG}}(\lambda, O(\mathsf{t}_{\mathsf{ID}}))} \ ,$$

On the other hand, in the expected-time setting, it is straightforward to show that there is essentially no loss:

$$\epsilon^{\star}_{\mathsf{Schnorr}}(\lambda, t^{\star}_{\mathsf{ID}}) \leq \epsilon^{\star}_{\mathsf{DLOG}}(\lambda, O(t^{\star}_{\mathsf{ID}})) \ .$$

Above $\epsilon_{\text{DLOG}} = \epsilon_{\text{DLOG}}(\lambda, t_{\text{DLOG}})$ and $\epsilon^\star_{\text{DLOG}} = \epsilon^\star_{\text{DLOG}}(\lambda, t^\star_{\text{DLOG}})$ are the discrete logarithm error and the expected-time discrete logarithm error, respectively for a given group. That is, for every $t_{\text{DLOG}} \in \mathbb{N}$ and t_{DLOG}-time adversary, given random y, the probability of finding x such that $y = g^x$ is bounded by $\epsilon_{\text{DLOG}}(\lambda, t_{\text{DLOG}})$. Similarly, the success probability of any adversary that has expected running time $t^\star_{\text{DLOG}}$ is bounded by $\epsilon^\star_{\text{DLOG}}(\lambda, t^\star_{\text{DLOG}})$.

Below we only state the bounds, the detailed calculation can be found in [14, Sects. 8.3 and 8.4].

- *Tightness of Theorem 1:* Consider the PCP and VC from Theorem 3. Let $\text{ARG} := \text{Kilian}[\text{PCP}, \text{VC}]$. Theorem 1 implies that

$$\epsilon_{\text{ARG}}(\lambda, \mathbb{x}, t_{\text{ARG}}) \leq 2^{-\lambda} + \epsilon_{\text{DLOG}}\left(\lambda, \frac{\ell}{\epsilon} \cdot t_{\text{ARG}}\right) + \epsilon .$$

For a natural setting of parameters, we can instantiate the bounds of $\epsilon_{\text{Schnorr}}$ and ϵ_{ARG} as follows:

$$\epsilon_{\text{Schnorr}}(\lambda, t_{\text{ID}}) \leq O\left(\sqrt{\frac{t^2_{\text{ID}}}{2^\lambda}}\right) , \text{ and}$$

$$\epsilon_{\text{ARG}}(\lambda, \mathbb{x}, t_{\text{ARG}}) \leq 2^{-\lambda} + \ell^{2/3} \cdot \Theta\left(\sqrt[3]{\frac{t^2_{\text{ARG}}}{2^\lambda}}\right) .$$

This shows a polynomial gap between the best analysis of the Schnorr identification scheme and our analysis of Kilian's protocol. Closing this gap remains an open problem.

- *Tightness of Theorem 2:* From Theorem 2, $\text{ARG} := \text{Kilian}[\text{PCP}, \text{VC}]$ has expected-time soundness error $\epsilon^\star_{\text{ARG}}$ where

$$\epsilon^\star_{\text{ARG}}(\lambda, \mathbb{x}, t^\star_{\text{ARG}}) \leq 2^{-\lambda} + \epsilon^\star_{\text{DLOG}}\left(\lambda, O\left(\log \frac{q}{\epsilon} \cdot t^\star_{\text{ARG}}\right)\right) + \epsilon .$$

This upper bound almost matches with the best known expected-time upper bound for the security of the Schnorr identification scheme, except for a polylogarithmic loss in the adversary running time.

Why Not Use a Random Oracle? One method of analyzing Kilian's protocol is relying on idealized models such as the random oracle model. Here, the need to rewind the adversary is obviated as the PCP can be extracted directly by observing the queries performed by the adversary to the random oracle. This approach yields an analysis with tight bounds (see e.g., [19]) but is not applicable in the standard model.

In applications, practitioners replace the random oracle with a specific hash function, choosing parameters based on the idealized model's analysis. However, this limits the choice of hash functions to those presumed to sufficiently mimic a random oracle, excluding hash functions that offer notable benefits but cannot replace a random oracle. This includes, for example, hash functions with an algebraic structure (e.g., Pedersen hash), which can be fast to compute or friendly for recursive composition. Understanding the trade-offs in security bounds when using a rewinding-based analysis instead of the random oracle model is meaningful and valuable.

On the Price of Rewinding. We compare the soundness of Kilian's protocol when analyzed via: (i) a rewinding extractor when VC is based on a collision resistant hash function; or (ii) a straightline extractor when VC is based on an ideal hash function (a random oracle). This highlights the "price of rewinding": the cost of a more expensive security reduction that works under weaker assumptions on the underlying cryptography.

(i) *Rewinding extractor.* Suppose that the vector commitment scheme VC is a Merkle commitment scheme obtained from a collision-resistant hash function with security $\epsilon_{\mathsf{CRH}}(\lambda, t_{\mathsf{CRH}})$. By Remark 2,

$$\epsilon_{\mathsf{VC}}(\lambda, \ell, s, t_{\mathsf{VC}}) \leq \epsilon_{\mathsf{CRH}}\left(\lambda, t_{\mathsf{CRH}} = t_{\mathsf{VC}} + O(t_{h_\lambda} \cdot \mathsf{q} \cdot \log \ell)\right) \ .$$

Suppose that $\epsilon_{\mathsf{CRH}}(\lambda, t_{\mathsf{CRH}}) \leq t_{\mathsf{CRH}}^2 / 2^\lambda$, which is what would be achieved by an ideal hash function. In this case, Theorem 1 gives the following upper bound on the soundness error for $\mathsf{Kilian}[\mathsf{PCP}, \mathsf{VC}]$:

$$\epsilon_{\mathsf{ARG}}(\lambda, \mathbb{x}, t_{\mathsf{ARG}}) \leq \epsilon_{\mathsf{PCP}}(\mathbb{x}) + O\left(\frac{1}{2^\lambda} \cdot \left(\frac{\ell}{\epsilon} \cdot t_{\mathsf{ARG}} + t_{h_\lambda} \cdot \mathsf{q} \cdot \log \ell\right)^2\right) + \epsilon \ .$$

Setting $\epsilon = \Theta((\ell \cdot t_{\mathsf{ARG}})^{2/3} \cdot 2^{-\lambda/3})$ minimizes the right-hand side at $\epsilon_{\mathsf{PCP}}(\mathbb{x}) + \Theta(\ell^{2/3} \cdot (t_{\mathsf{ARG}}^2 \cdot 2^{-\lambda})^{1/3})$.[1]

(ii) *Straightline extractor.* Suppose that we model the collision-resistant hash function as an ideal hash function, and analyze $\mathsf{Kilian}[\mathsf{PCP}, \mathsf{VC}]$ in the random oracle model. Then [19] shows that:

$$\epsilon_{\mathsf{ARG}}(\lambda, \mathbb{x}, t_{\mathsf{ARG}}) \leq \epsilon_{\mathsf{PCP}}(\mathbb{x}) + \Theta(t_{\mathsf{ARG}}^2 \cdot 2^{-\lambda}) \ .$$

This smaller upper bound is achieved thanks to a straightline (i.e., non-rewinding) extractor for the vector commitment scheme, which is a Merkle commitment scheme in the random oracle model.

Remark 2 (security of underlying components). We derive security bounds for argument systems *as a function of the security bounds of the underlying components*. In short, we take ϵ_{VC}, ϵ_{PCP}, κ_{PCP} as given. While statistical soundness bounds on PCPs can be calculated (they are information-theoretic components), the position binding errors for VC must be derived from some (concrete) computational assumption.

For example, if VC is a Merkle commitment scheme obtained from a collision-resistant hash function $h_\lambda : \{0,1\}^{2\lambda} \to \{0,1\}^\lambda$ computable in time t_{h_λ} whose collision probability against t_{CRH}-size adversaries is bounded by $\epsilon_{\mathsf{CRH}}(\lambda, t_{\mathsf{CRH}})$ then VC has binding error $\epsilon_{\mathsf{VC}}(\lambda, \ell, s, t_{\mathsf{VC}}) \leq \epsilon_{\mathsf{CRH}}(\lambda, t_{\mathsf{CRH}})$ where $t_{\mathsf{CRH}} = t_{\mathsf{VC}} + O(t_{h_\lambda} \cdot \mathsf{q} \cdot \log \ell)$ for a small hidden constant that can be derived from the security reduction. (The reduction transforms a t_{VC}-size adversary A_{VC} against the Merkle commitment scheme into a t_{CRH}-size adversary A_{CRH} against the collision-resistant hash function. Briefly, A_{CRH} runs A_{VC} and then looks for a collision among the authentication paths output by A_{VC}, resulting in the additive increase of $O(t_{h_\lambda} \cdot \mathsf{q} \cdot \log \ell)$ in size.)

---

[1] Ignoring the lower-order term $t_{h_\lambda} \cdot \mathsf{q} \cdot \log \ell$.

1.3   Related Work

The literature on succinct arguments presents a vast landscape of constructions exhibiting complex tradeoffs between efficiency, expressiveness, and security. The goal of this work is to study the security of Kilian's protocol, which is a succinct *interactive* argument. Below we summarize only the most relevant prior work.

Succinct Arguments from Collision-Resistant Functions. The first construction of a succinct argument is due to Kilian [23], and follows the VC-based approach (the underlying vector commitment is a Merkle commitment scheme based on a collision-resistant hash function). The security reduction in [23] is informal, and does not provide any asymptotic (nor explicit) security bounds.

Barak and Goldreich [4] provide a formal analysis of a variant of Kilian's construction, towards their goal of constructing zero-knowledge arguments with a non-black-box simulator. Due to their setting, they restrict their result to the case where the PCP is *non-adaptive* and *reverse-samplable*. While the former restriction is mild (many known PCP constructions are non-adaptive, with few exceptions such as [24]), the latter restriction is a non-standard strong property of the PCP query algorithm, which has not been shown to hold for a number of PCP constructions of interest (e.g., the short PCPs in [9,10]). Under these conditions, they establish that Kilian's protocol achieves non-adaptive knowledge soundness, with a constant multiplicative factor loss in soundness versus the PCP soundness. In contrast, our work applies to *all* PCPs (including adaptive PCPs) and establishes the tightest known bound for adaptive knowledge soundness.[2]

Ishai, Mahmoody, Sahai, and Xiao [21] provide a soundness analysis for Kilian's protocol instantiated with a PCP with negligible soundness error and a Merkle commitment scheme with negligible position binding error; they do not quantify the security of the succinct argument in terms of the security of the underlying cryptography. Lai and Malavolta [26, Appendix C] prove secure a variant of Kilian's protocol, realized with any *linear PCP* and *linear map commitment*; this generality can lead to shorter proofs.

Chiesa, Ma, Spooner, and Zhandry [15] prove *post-quantum* security of Kilian's protocol. As part of their analysis, they give a proof of security for Kilian that also applies to the classical setting. Their analysis differs significantly from ours due to challenges unique to the quantum setting, and incurs a multiplicative soundness loss. In this work we consider soundness against classical adversaries only.

Succinct Arguments from Ideal Hash Functions. A line of work studies security reductions for succinct *non-interactive* arguments in the random oracle model (ROM) [8,11,16–19,28,37]. They take advantage of the ROM in two key ways. First, they use the observability of oracle queries to construct a vector commitment scheme with a *straightline* (i.e., non-rewinding) extractor: a Merkle commitment scheme in the ROM. As noted in Sect. 1.2, this leads to tighter security bounds. In fact, since these constructions are *unconditionally* secure in the ROM, it is often possible to compute their *exact* soundness. Second, these constructions use the Fiat–Shamir transformation to convert

---

[2] Formally, our result is incomparable with the one of Barak and Goldreich. In more detail, they use the reverse samplability property of the PCP to obtain a collision-finder whose running time does not depend on the PCP length. This is necessary in their setting, as there the size of an extracted PCP is not *a priori* bounded by any polynomial. It is open whether such a reduction is possible for (even polynomial-size) PCPs that are not reverse samplable.

an underlying *interactive* argument into a *non-interactive* one; the general security of this transformation has been shown only in the ROM.

Special-Sound Protocols. Interactive protocols with *special soundness* are an important and well-studied family of public-coin protocols. In the sigma protocol setting (three-message public-coin protocols), k-special soundness means that a witness can be efficiently extracted from any k accepting protocol transcripts with distinct verifier challenges. A line of works extends this notion to multiple rounds [1–3]. The concrete security of general special sound protocols is relatively well-understood.

As noted in [15], for reasonable choices of PCP, Kilian's protocol is *not* k-special sound for any polynomial k (for example, one can find a set of transcripts that includes only queries to a small fraction of the PCP).[3] We are therefore not able to apply results about special soundness directly.

2   Techniques

We overview the main ideas underlying our results. In Sect. 2.1 we review Kilian's protocol. In Sect. 2.2 we sketch our proof of Theorem 1. In Sect. 2.3 we sketch our proof of Theorem 2. In Section 2.4 we sketch our proof of Theorem 3. In Section 2.5 we explain how to show the strict-time knowledge soundness of Kilian's protocol. In Section 2.6 we discuss adaptive security.

Vector Commitment Schemes. We fix a vector commitment scheme VC throughout this technical overview, whose interface and properties are sketched below; see Sect. 3.2 for formal definitions. Here we omit the algorithm that samples public parameters (and suppress these parameters in the interfaces of VC).[4]

– VC.Commit: On input a message m, VC.Commit outputs a commitment cm and auxiliary state aux.
– VC.Open: On input the auxiliary state aux and a query set $\mathcal{Q}$, VC.Open outputs an opening proof pf.
– VC.Check: On input a commitment cm, query set $\mathcal{Q}$, answers ans, and opening proof pf, VC.Check determines if pf is valid for ans being the restriction to $\mathcal{Q}$ of the message committed in cm.

The property of *perfect completeness* ensures that VC.Check always accepts if pf is output by VC.Open given the auxiliary information produced by VC.Commit. The security property of VC is *position binding*: VC has *position binding error* $\epsilon_{vc}(\lambda, \ell, s, t_{vc})$ if, when VC is instantiated with security parameter λ for messages of length ℓ, every t_{vc}-time adversary that outputs (cm, ans, ans', $\mathcal{Q}$, $\mathcal{Q}'$, pf, pf') with $|\mathcal{Q}| = |\mathcal{Q}'| = s$ satisfies the following predicate with probability at most $\epsilon_{vc}(\lambda, \ell, s, t_{vc})$ (over VC's public parameters):

---

[3] Towards a tighter security proof for Kilian in the post-quantum setting, Lombardi, Ma, and Spooner [27] introduce the notion of *probabilistic special soundness* (PSS), a relaxation of special soundness, and show that Kilian's protocol is PSS. We do not follow this approach, as we do not expect it to yield tight security bounds in the classical setting.

[4] For example, if VC is based on a Merkle commitment scheme, the public parameters are the (randomly sampled) collision-resistant function to be used for hashing the given message down to the Merkle root.

$$\exists i \in \mathcal{Q} \cap \mathcal{Q}' : \mathsf{ans}[i] \neq \mathsf{ans}'[i]$$
$$\wedge \ \mathsf{VC.Check}(\mathsf{cm}, \mathcal{Q}, \mathsf{ans}, \mathsf{pf}) = 1$$
$$\wedge \ \mathsf{VC.Check}(\mathsf{cm}, \mathcal{Q}', \mathsf{ans}', \mathsf{pf}') = 1$$

In other words, position binding makes it hard to produce two incompatible openings to the same commitment. Moreover, we also consider *expected-time position binding*: the expected-time position binding error $\epsilon_{\mathsf{VC}}^\star = \epsilon_{\mathsf{VC}}^\star(\lambda, \ell, s, t_{\mathsf{VC}}^\star)$ is the position binding property against adversaries whose expected running time is at most $t_{\mathsf{VC}}^\star$.

Stateful Algorithms. Throughout this section, the interactive algorithms that participate in protocols are stateful. When it is important to distinguish different computation phases of a stateful algorithm, we make explicit the state passed from one phase to the next.

2.1 Kilian's Protocol

We review Kilian's protocol that compiles a PCP and a VC scheme to a succinct interactive argument.

Kilian's protocol [23] obtains a succinct interactive argument by combining two ingredients: a probabilistically checkable proof (PCP) and a vector commitment scheme VC (fixed above). Let $\mathsf{PCP} = (\mathbf{P}, \mathbf{V})$ be a PCP system for a relation R with alphabet Σ, proof length ℓ, query complexity q, and verifier randomness complexity r. Kilian[PCP, VC] is an interactive argument $\mathsf{ARG} = (\mathcal{P}, \mathcal{V})$ in which the argument prover $\mathcal{P}$ receives an instance $\mathbb{x}$ and a witness $\mathbb{w}$, and the argument verifier $\mathcal{V}$ receives the instance $\mathbb{x}$. Then $\mathcal{P}$ and $\mathcal{V}$ interact, exchanging 3 messages, as follows.

1. $\mathcal{P}$ computes the PCP string $\Pi \leftarrow \mathbf{P}(\mathbb{x}, \mathbb{w})$, computes the commitment $(\mathsf{cm}, \mathsf{aux}) \leftarrow \mathsf{VC.Commit}(\Pi)$, and sends cm to $\mathcal{V}$.
2. $\mathcal{V}$ samples PCP verifier randomness $\rho \leftarrow \{0, 1\}^r$ and sends it to $\mathcal{P}$.
3. $\mathcal{P}$ deduces the set $\mathcal{Q}$ of queries that $\mathbf{V}(\mathbb{x}; \rho)$ makes to Π, sets the query answers $\mathsf{ans} := \Pi[\mathcal{Q}]$, generates an opening proof $\mathsf{pf} \leftarrow \mathsf{VC.Open}(\mathsf{aux}, \mathcal{Q})$, and sends the tuple $(\mathcal{Q}, \mathsf{ans}, \mathsf{pf})$ to $\mathcal{V}$.
4. $\mathcal{V}$ performs the following checks.
   (a) $\mathsf{VC.Check}(\mathsf{pp}, \mathsf{cm}, \mathcal{Q}, \mathsf{ans}, \mathsf{pf}) = 1$ (i.e., ans are valid answers for positions $\mathcal{Q}$ relative to cm);
   (b) $\mathbf{V}^{[\mathcal{Q}, \mathsf{ans}]}(\mathbb{x}; \rho) = 1$ (i.e., the PCP verifier $\mathbf{V}(\mathbb{x}; \rho)$ accepts the answers ans on $\mathcal{Q}$).

Above, the notation $\mathbf{V}^{[\mathcal{Q}, \mathsf{ans}]}(\mathbb{x}; \rho)$ refers to the decision bit of the PCP verifier $\mathbf{V}$, given instance $\mathbb{x}$ and PCP randomness ρ, when each query $j \in \mathcal{Q}$ is answered with $\mathsf{ans}[j] \in \Sigma$. (If $\mathbf{V}$ queries outside the set $\mathcal{Q}$ then $\mathbf{V}^{[\mathcal{Q}, \mathsf{ans}]}(\mathbb{x}; \rho) = 0$.)

2.2 Soundness Analysis of Kilian's Protocol

We discuss the proof idea for Theorem 1.

Security Reduction. Intuitively, the soundness error of Kilian[PCP, VC] should be at most the (statistical) soundness error of PCP plus the position binding error of VC. The key lemma below formalizes this intuition.

Consider a malicious argument prover $\widetilde{\mathcal{P}}$ whose first message is the commitment cm. Intuitively, by the position binding property of VC, $\widetilde{\mathcal{P}}$ is "bound" to open locations of at most a single underlying PCP string $\widetilde{\Pi}$. By *rewinding* $\widetilde{\mathcal{P}}$ sufficiently many times to recover the underlying PCP string $\widetilde{\Pi}$, we can relate the probability of $\widetilde{\mathcal{P}}$ convincing the argument verifier $\mathcal{V}$ to the probability of $\widetilde{\Pi}$ convincing the PCP verifier $\mathbf{V}$.

Lemma 1 (Informal). *There exists a probabilistic algorithm $\mathcal{R}$ (the **reductor**) that, for every instance $\mathbb{x}$, error parameter $\epsilon > 0$, adversary time bound $t_{\mathsf{ARG}} \in \mathbb{N}$, and t_{ARG}-size adversary $\widetilde{\mathcal{P}}$, satisfies*

$$
\Pr\left[
\begin{array}{l}
\mathbf{V}^{[\widetilde{\mathcal{Q}},\widetilde{\Pi}]}(\mathbb{x};\rho) \neq 1 \\
\wedge\, \mathbf{V}^{[\mathcal{Q},\mathsf{ans}]}(\mathbb{x};\rho) = 1 \\
\wedge\, \mathsf{VC.Check}(\mathsf{cm}, \mathcal{Q}, \mathsf{ans}, \mathsf{pf}) = 1
\end{array}
\middle|
\begin{array}{l}
\mathsf{cm} \leftarrow \widetilde{\mathcal{P}} \\
(\widetilde{\mathcal{Q}}, \widetilde{\Pi}) \leftarrow \mathcal{R}^{\widetilde{\mathcal{P}}}(\mathsf{cm}, \epsilon) \\
\rho \leftarrow \{0,1\}^r \\
(\mathcal{Q}, \mathsf{ans}, \mathsf{pf}) \leftarrow \widetilde{\mathcal{P}}(\rho)
\end{array}
\right] \leq \epsilon_{\mathsf{vc}}(\lambda, \ell, \mathsf{q}, t_{\mathsf{vc}}) + \epsilon,
$$

where $t_{\mathsf{vc}} = O\left(\frac{\ell}{\epsilon} \cdot t_{\mathsf{ARG}}\right)$.

The reductor $\mathcal{R}$ handles the aforementioned rewinding process: $\mathcal{R}$ constructs a proof string $\widetilde{\Pi} \in \Sigma^\ell$ whose convincing probability is approximately the same as that of the argument prover $\widetilde{\mathcal{P}}$ (up to the position binding error of VC and an arbitrary error term ϵ). Note that $\mathcal{R}$ requires only black-box access to $\widetilde{\mathcal{P}}$.

In the lemma above, the PCP verifier and the argument verifier are "coupled" in that they receive the same randomness ρ. The lemma states that it is unlikely, for a randomly-chosen ρ, that the argument verifier $\mathcal{V}$ accepts the answers provided by $\widetilde{\mathcal{P}}$ but the PCP verifier $\mathbf{V}$ rejects $\widetilde{\Pi}$ under the same randomness. Intuitively, this allows us to approximately equate the probability that $\widetilde{\mathcal{P}}$ convinces the argument verifier $\mathcal{V}$ to the probability that $\widetilde{\Pi}$ convinces the PCP verifier $\mathbf{V}$.

First we discuss how to use Lemma 1 to establish soundness error of Kilian[PCP, VC] in Sect. 2.2. Then in Sect. 2.2 we sketch the proof of Lemma 1. For simplicity, all probability statements in this section are with respect to the experiment in Lemma 1 unless otherwise specified.

Soundness Analysis. We wish to upper bound the soundness error of Kilian[PCP, VC]. As claimed in Theorem 1, we argue that for every instance $\mathbb{x} \notin L(R)$, time bound $t_{\mathsf{ARG}} \in \mathbb{N}$, and t_{ARG}-size adversary $\widetilde{\mathcal{P}}$,

$$
\Pr\left[\langle \widetilde{\mathcal{P}}, \mathcal{V}(\mathbb{x})\rangle = 1\right] \leq \epsilon_{\mathsf{PCP}}(\mathbb{x}) + \epsilon_{\mathsf{vc}}(\lambda, \ell, \mathsf{q}, t_{\mathsf{vc}}) + \epsilon .
$$

The above probability can be bounded with the following by the law of total probability:

$$
\Pr\left[
\begin{array}{l}
\mathbf{V}^{[\widetilde{\mathcal{Q}},\widetilde{\Pi}]}(\mathbb{x};\rho) = 1 \\
\wedge\, \mathbf{V}^{[\mathcal{Q},\mathsf{ans}]}(\mathbb{x};\rho) = 1 \\
\wedge\, \mathsf{VC.Check}(\mathsf{cm}, \mathcal{Q}, \mathsf{ans}, \mathsf{pf}) = 1
\end{array}
\right]
+ \Pr\left[
\begin{array}{l}
\mathbf{V}^{[\widetilde{\mathcal{Q}},\widetilde{\Pi}]}(\mathbb{x};\rho) \neq 1 \\
\wedge\, \mathbf{V}^{[\mathcal{Q},\mathsf{ans}]}(\mathbb{x};\rho) = 1 \\
\wedge\, \mathsf{VC.Check}(\mathsf{cm}, \mathcal{Q}, \mathsf{ans}, \mathsf{pf}) = 1
\end{array}
\right] .
$$

The term on the right is bounded from above by $\epsilon_{\mathsf{VC}}(\lambda, \ell, \mathsf{q}, t_{\mathsf{VC}}) + \epsilon$, due to Lemma 1.

The term on the left is bounded by $\epsilon_{\mathsf{PCP}}(\mathbb{x})$ (the soundness error of PCP). Indeed, we can view the first message of $\widetilde{\mathcal{P}}$ (cm in the experiment above) and the reductor $\mathcal{R}$ as a malicious PCP prover $\widetilde{\mathbf{P}}$ that outputs a PCP string $\widetilde{\Pi}$. Since $\mathbb{x} \notin L(R)$, by the definition of soundness error of PCP,

$$\Pr\left[\begin{array}{l}\mathbf{V}^{[\widetilde{\mathcal{Q}},\widetilde{\Pi}]}(\mathbb{x}; \rho) = 1 \\ \wedge\ \mathbf{V}^{[\mathcal{Q},\mathsf{ans}]}(\mathbb{x}; \rho) = 1 \\ \wedge\ \mathsf{VC.Check}(\mathsf{cm}, \mathcal{Q}, \mathsf{ans}, \mathsf{pf}) = 1\end{array}\right] \le \Pr\left[\mathbf{V}^{\widetilde{\Pi}}(\mathbb{x}) = 1\right] \le \epsilon_{\mathsf{PCP}}(\mathbb{x}) \ .$$

Proof Sketch of Lemma 1. We are left to sketch the proof of Lemma 1. To do so, we present a reductor algorithm $\mathcal{R}$.

The goal of $\mathcal{R}$ is to piece together a PCP string $\widetilde{\Pi}$ obtained from the argument prover $\widetilde{\mathcal{P}}$. Intuitively, $\widetilde{\Pi}$ is "fixed" after $\widetilde{\mathcal{P}}$ outputs a commitment cm, and $\mathcal{R}$ attempts to obtain information about $\widetilde{\Pi}$ by *rewinding* the second phase of $\widetilde{\mathcal{P}}$, when given freshly sampled choices of PCP randomness ρ. Each such execution (if it outputs a valid opening) reveals a fragment of $\widetilde{\Pi}$. By repeating this process sufficiently many times, $\mathcal{R}$ obtains enough locations of the string $\widetilde{\Pi}$. Below we denote by $\mathsf{N} = \mathsf{N}(\epsilon)$ the number of samples (set later).

$\mathcal{R}^{\widetilde{\mathcal{P}}(\mathsf{aux},\cdot)}(\mathsf{cm}, \epsilon)$:
1. Initialize a proof string: $\widetilde{\Pi} := (\sigma)^{\ell}$, where σ is an arbitrary element in Σ.
2. Initialize an empty set $\widetilde{\mathcal{Q}}$ to track which locations of $\widetilde{\Pi}$ are filled in.
3. Repeat the following N times:
   (a) Sample PCP verifier randomness $\rho \leftarrow \{0, 1\}^{\mathsf{r}}$.
   (b) Ask $\widetilde{\mathcal{P}}$ for answers to this randomness: $(\mathcal{Q}, \mathsf{ans}, \mathsf{pf}) \leftarrow \widetilde{\mathcal{P}}(\mathsf{aux}, \rho)$.
   (c) If $\mathsf{VC.Check}(\mathsf{pp}, \mathsf{cm}, \mathcal{Q}, \mathsf{ans}, \mathsf{pf}) = 1$, set $\widetilde{\Pi}[\mathcal{Q}] := \mathsf{ans}$ and update $\widetilde{\mathcal{Q}} := \widetilde{\mathcal{Q}} \cup \mathcal{Q}$.
4. Output $(\widetilde{\mathcal{Q}}, \widetilde{\Pi})$.

We make explicit the two computation phases of the (stateful) malicious argument prover $\widetilde{\mathcal{P}}$:

$$(\mathsf{cm}, \mathsf{aux}) \leftarrow \widetilde{\mathcal{P}} \quad \text{and} \quad (\mathcal{Q}, \mathsf{ans}, \mathsf{pf}) \leftarrow \widetilde{\mathcal{P}}(\mathsf{aux}, \rho) \ ,$$

where aux is the auxiliary state passed across the two computation phases of $\widetilde{\mathcal{P}}$. The reductor $\mathcal{R}$ needs to rerun only the second phase of $\widetilde{\mathcal{P}}$, so the oracle for $\mathcal{R}$ is $\widetilde{\mathcal{P}}(\mathsf{aux}, \cdot)$.

As stated in Lemma 1, with the above notation we wish to bound the following probability:

$$\Pr\left[\begin{array}{l}\mathbf{V}^{[\widetilde{\mathcal{Q}},\widetilde{\Pi}]}(\mathbb{x}; \rho) \ne 1 \\ \wedge\ \mathbf{V}^{[\mathcal{Q},\mathsf{ans}]}(\mathbb{x}; \rho) = 1 \\ \wedge\ \mathsf{VC.Check}(\mathsf{cm}, \mathcal{Q}, \mathsf{ans}, \mathsf{pf}) = 1\end{array}\right] \ .$$

If $\mathsf{VC.Check}(\mathsf{cm}, \mathcal{Q}, \mathsf{ans}, \mathsf{pf}) = 1$ then $\mathbf{V}^{\widetilde{\Pi}}(\mathbb{x}; \rho) \ne 1 \wedge \mathbf{V}^{[\mathcal{Q},\mathsf{ans}]}(\mathbb{x}; \rho) = 1$ implies either: (i) $\widetilde{\Pi}$ and ans disagree at a position $q \in \mathcal{Q} \cap \widetilde{\mathcal{Q}}$; or (ii) there is query q in $\mathcal{Q}$ but not in $\widetilde{\mathcal{Q}}$. We analyze the two events separately, which bounds the probability above by a union bound. We suppress the probability experiment in the derivations below.

(i) Valid openings with disagreeing answers We informally argue that

$$\Pr\left[\begin{matrix} \exists q \in \mathcal{Q} \cap \widetilde{\mathcal{Q}} : \mathsf{ans}[q] \neq \widetilde{\Pi}[q] \\ \wedge\, \mathsf{VC.Check}(\mathsf{cm}, \mathcal{Q}, \mathsf{ans}, \mathsf{pf}) = 1 \end{matrix}\right] \leq \epsilon_{\mathsf{vc}}(\lambda, \ell, \mathsf{q}, t_{\mathsf{vc}})\ .$$

The reductor $\mathcal{R}$ checks the validity of the opening for each position it fills into $\widetilde{\Pi}$. Hence the event above implies that there are valid openings to two different values at the same query position; equivalently, one can construct an adversary $\mathcal{A}_{\mathsf{vc}}$ that runs the reductor $\mathcal{R}$ and executes $\langle \widetilde{\mathcal{P}}, \mathcal{V}(\mathbb{x}, \rho) \rangle$ for some verifier randomness ρ that breaks VC's position binding. Since $\mathcal{A}_{\mathsf{vc}}$ has running time $t_{\mathsf{vc}} = O(\mathsf{N} \cdot t_{\mathsf{ARG}})$ (its running time is dominated by the running time of $\mathcal{R}$), the target probability is at most $\epsilon_{\mathsf{vc}}(\lambda, \ell, \mathsf{q}, t_{\mathsf{vc}})$ by the position binding property of the VC.

(ii) Missing position in $\widetilde{\Pi}$ We show that

$$\Pr\left[\begin{matrix} \mathcal{Q} \setminus \widetilde{\mathcal{Q}} \neq \emptyset \\ \wedge\, \mathsf{VC.Check}(\mathsf{pp}, \mathsf{cm}, \mathcal{Q}, \mathsf{ans}, \mathsf{pf}) = 1 \end{matrix}\right] \leq \frac{\ell}{\mathsf{N}}\ .$$

To upper bound the probability of a query $q \in \mathcal{Q}$ not having been filled in by $\mathcal{R}$, we use the probability that a given position $q \in [\ell]$ is queried. The *weight* $\delta(q)$ of a query $q \in [\ell]$ is the probability that it is queried by the argument verifier with uniformly sampled randomness. We can write:

$$\Pr\left[\mathcal{Q} \setminus \widetilde{\mathcal{Q}} \neq \emptyset\right] = \Pr\left[\exists q \in [\ell] : q \in \mathcal{Q} \wedge q \notin \widetilde{\mathcal{Q}}\right] \leq \sum_{q \in [\ell]} \delta(q) \cdot (1 - \delta(q))^{\mathsf{N}}\ ,$$

where the inequality follows from the fact that $\mathcal{Q}$ and all query sets used to generate $\widetilde{\mathcal{Q}}$ correspond to independently sampled verifier randomness. Note that, for every $\delta \in [0, 1]$, $\delta \cdot (1 - \delta)^{\mathsf{N}} \leq 1/\mathsf{N}$.[5] Hence, the target probability is upper bounded by $\frac{\ell}{\mathsf{N}}$.

In fact, the proof for this case is more delicate than sketched above. If a position $q \in [\ell]$ has weight $\delta(q)$, we cannot conclude that $q \notin \widetilde{\mathcal{Q}}$ with probability at most $(1 - \delta(q))^{\mathsf{N}}$, because $\widetilde{\mathcal{P}}$ may often output invalid openings for q while $\mathcal{R}$ only includes valid openings. To fix this issue, we use a refined notion: $\delta(q)$ is the probability that during the execution of the interactive argument, the verifier $\mathcal{V}$ samples randomness that corresponds to a query set containing q *and the prover $\mathcal{P}$ outputs a valid VC opening for the query set*.

Setting Parameters. By an union bound, the desired probability can be upper bounded by $\epsilon_{\mathsf{vc}}(\lambda, \ell, \mathsf{q}, t_{\mathsf{vc}}) + \frac{\ell}{\mathsf{N}}$. Setting $\mathsf{N} := \frac{\ell}{\epsilon}$, we get $t_{\mathsf{vc}} = O(\mathsf{N} \cdot t_{\mathsf{ARG}}) = O\left(\frac{\ell}{\epsilon} \cdot t_{\mathsf{ARG}}\right)$ and $\frac{\ell}{\mathsf{N}} = \epsilon$, yielding the bound stated in Lemma 1.

Remark 3. Superficially one might hope for an improved analysis showing that one only needs $\frac{\ell}{\mathsf{q} \cdot \epsilon}$ rewindings rather than $\frac{\ell}{\epsilon}$. Indeed, each rewinding that leads to an accepting transcript yields a freshly sampled fragment of the PCP containing q locations. However such a bound is unrealistic because, in general, a PCP may have dummy queries. For example, consider a PCP where only $O(1)$ of the q queries are "real",

---

[5] A simple derivation of the inequality is the following: with $f(x) = x \cdot (1 - x)^{\mathsf{N}}$, we have $\frac{d}{dx} f(\delta) = 0 \iff \delta = \frac{1}{\mathsf{N}+1}$. As $f(0) = f(1) = 0$ and δ is the only critical point in $[0, 1]$, it achieves the maximum: $\max_{x \in [0,1]} \{f(x)\} = f(\delta) \leq 1/\mathsf{N}$.

while all others are dummy queries to fixed locations of the PCP string. That said, there may be other metrics through which the factor $\frac{\ell}{\epsilon}$ can be improved, for example, our Theorem 2 considers VC schemes with expected-time position binding and avoids this multiplicative factor.

2.3 Expected-Time Soundness Analysis of Kilian's Protocol

We provide an alternative analysis for the expected-time soundness of Kilian's protocol (Theorem 2) to avoid the blowup of $\frac{\ell}{\epsilon}$ in the VC adversary running time.

Recall that in the previous analysis, we "coupled" the reductor $\mathcal{R}$ and the VC adversary A_{vc}: they are essentially the same algorithm. However, notice the running time of A_{vc} affects the soundness error, while the running time of $\mathcal{R}$ does not. This leads us to the following new security reduction lemma, which "decouples" the two algorithms:

Lemma 2 (Informal). *There exists a probabilistic algorithm $\mathcal{R}$ (the **reductor**) and algorithms $A_{vc}^{(i)}$ (the **VC adversaries**) for each $i \in [q]$ that, for every instance $\mathbb{x}$, error tolerance $\epsilon > 0$, adversary time bound $t_{ARG} \in \mathbb{N}$, and t_{ARG}-time adversary $\widetilde{\mathcal{P}}$, satisfies*

$$
\Pr\left[
\begin{array}{l|l}
\mathbf{V}^{\widetilde{\Pi}^\star}(\mathbb{x}; \rho) \neq 1 & cm \leftarrow \widetilde{\mathcal{P}} \\
\wedge\, \mathbf{V}^{[\mathcal{Q}, ans]}(\mathbb{x}; \rho) = 1 & \widetilde{\Pi}^\star \leftarrow \mathcal{R}^{\widetilde{\mathcal{P}}}(cm, \epsilon) \\
\wedge\, \mathsf{VC.Check}(cm, \mathcal{Q}, ans, pf) = 1 & \rho \leftarrow \{0,1\}^r \\
\wedge\, \forall i \in [q], ans[\mathcal{Q}[i]] = ans^{(i)}[\mathcal{Q}[i]] & (\mathcal{Q}, ans, pf) \leftarrow \widetilde{\mathcal{P}}(\rho) \\
& \textit{For } i \in [q]: \\
& (cm, \mathcal{Q}, ans, pf, \mathcal{Q}^{(i)}, ans^{(i)}, pf^{(i)}) \leftarrow A_{vc}^{(i)}(\rho)
\end{array}
\right] \leq \epsilon,
$$

where the expected running time of $A_{vc}^{(i)}$ is $t_{vc}^\star = O\left(\log \frac{q}{\epsilon} \cdot (t_{ARG} + \ell \cdot t_{\mathbf{v}})\right)$ for every $i \in [q]$.

For simplicity, all probability statements in the rest of this section are with respect to the experiment in Lemma 2 unless otherwise specified.

Construction of the Reductor. Similar to the reductor in Sect. 2.2, our new reductor $\mathcal{R}$ rewinds to extract the PCP string committed by the adversary $\widetilde{\mathcal{P}}$. In fact, $\mathcal{R}$ rewinds over all possible verifier randomness to extract the "best" PCP string.

$\mathcal{R}^{\widetilde{\mathcal{P}}}(cm)$:
1. Initialize a proof string: $\widetilde{\Pi}^\star := (\bot)^\ell$.
2. For every PCP verifier randomness $\rho \in \{0,1\}^r$:
   (a) Run $(\mathcal{Q}, ans, pf) \leftarrow \widetilde{\mathcal{P}}(\rho)$.
   (b) If $\mathsf{VC.Check}(cm, \mathcal{Q}, ans, pf) = 0$, skip to next iteration.
   (c) Record the answer for each location for later.
3. For every location $i \in [\ell]$, set $\widetilde{\Pi}^\star[i]$ to be the most frequently appeared answer in the loop (break ties with the lexicographic order).
4. Output $\widetilde{\Pi}^\star$.

Constructions of the VC Adversaries. Let C be some constant to be specified later. For every $q \in [\ell]$, we define $\mathcal{S}_q$ to be the following set:

$$\mathcal{S}_q := \{\rho \in \{0,1\}^r : q \in \mathcal{Q} \text{ where } \mathcal{Q} \text{ is the set of queries make by } \mathbf{V}(\mathbb{x}; \rho)\}\ .$$

We first introduce a subroutine of the VC adversaries, the reverse sampler Samp. On input a query $q \in [\ell]$, Samp outputs a randomness ρ sampled uniformly from $\mathcal{S}_q$. We can implement Samp as follows.

Samp(q):
1. Repeat the following:
   (a) Sample $\rho \leftarrow \{0,1\}^r$.
   (b) Compute the query set $\mathcal{Q}$ corresponding to ρ by running the PCP verifier $\mathbf{V}(\mathbb{x}; \rho)$.
   (c) If $q \in \mathcal{Q}$, output ρ.

For every $i \in [\mathsf{q}]$, we construct the VC adversary $A_{\mathsf{vc}}^{(i)}$. In particular, given a randomness ρ with corresponding query set is $\mathcal{Q}$, $A_{\mathsf{vc}}^{(i)}$ tries to find inconsistent answers for the i-th query in $\mathcal{Q}$.

$A_{\mathsf{vc}}^{(i)}(\rho)$:
1. Run $\mathsf{cm} \leftarrow \widetilde{\mathcal{P}}(\mathbb{x})$ and $(\mathcal{Q}, \mathsf{ans}, \mathsf{pf}) \leftarrow \widetilde{\mathcal{P}}(\rho)$.
2. Check that $\mathsf{VC.Check}(\mathsf{cm}, \mathcal{Q}, \mathsf{ans}, \mathsf{pf}) = 1$. If not, output $(\mathsf{cm}, \mathsf{ans}, \mathsf{ans}, \mathcal{Q}, \mathcal{Q}, \mathsf{pf}, \mathsf{pf})$.
3. Define $q := \mathcal{Q}(i)$ and set $j := 0$.
4. Repeat the following:
   (a) Run $\rho' \leftarrow \mathsf{Samp}(q)$.
   (b) Run $(\mathcal{Q}', \mathsf{ans}', \mathsf{pf}') \leftarrow \widetilde{\mathcal{P}}(\rho')$.
   (c) If $\mathsf{VC.Check}(\mathsf{cm}, \mathcal{Q}', \mathsf{ans}', \mathsf{pf}') = 1$:
      i. If $\mathsf{ans}[q] \neq \mathsf{ans}'[q]$, output $(\mathsf{cm}, \mathcal{Q}, \mathsf{ans}, \mathsf{pf}, \mathcal{Q}', \mathsf{ans}', \mathsf{pf}')$.
      ii. If $\mathsf{ans}[q] = \mathsf{ans}'[q]$, set $j := j + 1$. Further, if $j = C$, output $(\mathsf{cm}, \mathsf{ans}, \mathsf{ans}, \mathcal{Q}, \mathcal{Q}, \mathsf{pf}, \mathsf{pf})$.

We compute the expected running time of $A_{\mathsf{vc}}^{(i)}$. For every $q \in [\ell]$, let $p_{i,q}$ be the probability that the i-th query is q for a uniformly sampled randomness:

$$p_{i,q} := \Pr\left[\mathcal{Q}(i) = q \;\middle|\; \begin{array}{l} \mathsf{cm} \leftarrow \widetilde{\mathcal{P}} \\ \rho \leftarrow \{0,1\}^r \\ (\mathcal{Q}, \mathsf{ans}, \mathsf{pf}) \leftarrow \widetilde{\mathcal{P}}(\rho) \end{array}\right].$$

Let X be the running time of the reverse sampler Samp. Then,

$$\mathbb{E}[X] \leq \sum_{q \in [\ell]} p_{i,q} \cdot \frac{1}{p_{i,q}} \cdot t_{\mathbf{V}} = \ell \cdot t_{\mathbf{V}} \ .$$

For every $q \in [\ell]$, let ξ_q be the probability that $\widetilde{\mathcal{P}}$ gives a valid opening to a query set given that the i-th query is q:

$$\xi_q := \Pr\left[\begin{array}{l} \mathsf{VC.Check}(\mathsf{cm}, \mathcal{Q}, \mathsf{ans}, \mathsf{pf}) = 1 \\ \text{conditioned on} \\ \mathcal{Q}(i) = q \end{array} \;\middle|\; \begin{array}{l} \mathsf{cm} \leftarrow \widetilde{\mathcal{P}} \\ \rho \leftarrow \{0,1\}^r \\ (\mathcal{Q}, \mathsf{ans}, \mathsf{pf}) \leftarrow \widetilde{\mathcal{P}}(\rho) \end{array}\right].$$

Let I be the random variable that equals to 1 if the check in Step 2 passes and equals to 0 otherwise. Let Y be the random variable for the running time of Step 4. The expected running time of $A_{\mathsf{VC}}^{(i)}$ can be computed as follows:

$$
\begin{aligned}
t_{\mathsf{VC}}^* &= t_{\mathsf{ARG}}^* + \mathbb{E}\left[Y\right] \\
&= t_{\mathsf{ARG}}^* + 0 \cdot \mathbb{E}\left[Y \mid I = 0\right] \cdot \Pr\left[I = 0\right] + \mathbb{E}\left[Y \mid I = 1\right] \cdot \Pr\left[I = 1\right] \\
&\leq t_{\mathsf{ARG}}^* + C \cdot \mathbb{E}\left[X\right] + \sum_{q \in [\ell]} C \cdot p_{i,q} \cdot \frac{1}{\xi_q} \cdot t_{\mathsf{ARG}}^* \cdot \xi_q \\
&= t_{\mathsf{ARG}}^* + C \cdot (t_{\mathsf{ARG}}^* + \ell \cdot t_{\mathsf{V}}) \ .
\end{aligned}
$$

Proof Sketch of Security Reduction Lemma. We wish to bound the following probability:

$$
\Pr\left[
\begin{array}{l}
\mathbf{V}^{\widetilde{\Pi}^*}(\mathbf{x}; \rho) \neq 1 \\
\wedge \mathbf{V}^{[\mathcal{Q}, \mathsf{ans}]}(\mathbf{x}; \rho) = 1 \\
\wedge \mathsf{VC.Check}(\mathsf{cm}, \mathcal{Q}, \mathsf{ans}, \mathsf{pf}) = 1 \\
\wedge \forall i \in [\mathsf{q}], \mathsf{ans}[\mathcal{Q}[i]] = \mathsf{ans}^{(i)}[\mathcal{Q}[i]]
\end{array}
\right] \ .
$$

Similar to Sect. 2.2, if $\mathsf{VC.Check}(\mathsf{cm}, \mathcal{Q}, \mathsf{ans}, \mathsf{pf}) = 1$, then $\mathbf{V}^{\widetilde{\Pi}^*}(\mathbf{x}; \rho) \neq 1$ and $\mathbf{V}^{[\mathcal{Q}, \mathsf{ans}]}(\mathbf{x}; \rho) = 1$ implies that $\widetilde{\Pi}^*$ and ans disagree at a position $q \in \mathcal{Q}$. Unlike before, here there is no case of missing queries, because the reductor $\mathcal{R}$, by construction, exhausts all verifier randomness. On the other hand, we have a new condition, $\forall i \in [\mathsf{q}], \mathsf{ans}[\mathcal{Q}[i]] = \mathsf{ans}^{(i)}[\mathcal{Q}[i]]$, which means that none of the VC adversaries successfully find inconsistent openings to the same location. Hence, we focus on the following event:

$$
\exists i \in [\mathsf{q}], \mathsf{ans}[\mathcal{Q}[i]] = \mathsf{ans}^{(i)}[\mathcal{Q}[i]] \neq \widetilde{\Pi}^*[\mathcal{Q}[i]] \ .
$$

For every $q \in [\ell]$, $\widetilde{\Pi}^*[q]$ consists of the symbol that $\widetilde{\mathcal{P}}$ opens to with highest probability. In other words, let $p(q, \sigma)$ be defined as follows:

$$
p(q, \sigma) := \Pr\left[
\begin{array}{l}
q \in \mathcal{Q} \\
\wedge \mathsf{ans}[q] = \sigma \\
\wedge \mathsf{VC.Check}(\mathsf{cm}, \mathcal{Q}, \mathsf{ans}, \mathsf{pf}) = 1
\end{array}
\left|
\begin{array}{l}
\mathsf{cm} \leftarrow \widetilde{\mathcal{P}} \\
\rho \leftarrow \{0,1\}^r \\
(\mathcal{Q}, \mathsf{ans}, \mathsf{pf}) \leftarrow \widetilde{\mathcal{P}}(\rho)
\end{array}
\right.
\right] \ .
$$

Then, by construction of $\mathcal{R}$,

$$
\widetilde{\Pi}^*[q] = \arg\max_{\sigma \in \Sigma} \{p(q, \sigma)\} \ ,
$$

with ties broken lexicographically.

Therefore, let $q \in \mathcal{Q}$ be the location such that $\widetilde{\Pi}^*[q] \neq \mathsf{ans}[q]$, and $p(q, \mathsf{ans}[q]) \leq \frac{1}{2}$, as otherwise, $p(q, \widetilde{\Pi}^*[q]) \geq p(q, \mathsf{ans}[q]) > \frac{1}{2}$, which implies that $p(q, \widetilde{\Pi}^*[q]) + p(q, \mathsf{ans}[q]) > 1$, a contradiction.

Since $A_{\mathsf{VC}}^{(i)}$ samples C randomness ρ' such that for $(\mathcal{Q}', \mathsf{ans}', \mathsf{pf}') \leftarrow \widetilde{\mathcal{P}}(\rho')$ (i) $\mathcal{Q}[i] \in \mathcal{Q}'$, (ii) $\mathsf{ans}[\mathcal{Q}[i]] = \mathsf{ans}'[\mathcal{Q}[i]]$, and (iii) $\mathsf{VC.Check}(\mathsf{cm}, \mathcal{Q}', \mathsf{ans}', \mathsf{pf}') = 1$, we can conclude that for every $i \in [\mathsf{q}]$,

$$
\Pr\left[\mathsf{ans}[\mathcal{Q}[i]] = \mathsf{ans}^{(i)}[\mathcal{Q}[i]] \neq \widetilde{\Pi}^*[\mathcal{Q}[i]]\right] \leq 2^{-C} \ .
$$

Hence,

$$\Pr\left[\exists i \in [\mathsf{q}], \mathsf{ans}[\mathcal{Q}[i]] = \mathsf{ans}^{(i)}[\mathcal{Q}[i]] \neq \widetilde{\varPi}^\star[\mathcal{Q}[i]]\right] \leq \mathsf{q} \cdot 2^{-C}\ .$$

Setting $C = \log \frac{\mathsf{q}}{\epsilon}$ gives us the desired bound.

Soundness Analysis From Lemma 2. Similar to Sect. 2.2, we wish to upper bound the soundness error of $\mathsf{Kilian}[\mathsf{PCP}, \mathsf{VC}]$. As claimed in Theorem 2, we argue that for every instance $\mathbb{x} \notin L(R)$, time bound $t_{\mathsf{ARG}} \in \mathbb{N}$, and t_{ARG}-size adversary $\widetilde{\mathcal{P}}$,

$$\Pr\left[\langle \widetilde{\mathcal{P}}, \mathcal{V}(\mathbb{x})\rangle = 1\right] \leq \epsilon_{\mathsf{PCP}}(\mathbb{x}) + \epsilon_{\mathsf{VC}}^\star(\lambda, \ell, \mathsf{q}, t_{\mathsf{VC}}^\star) + \epsilon\ .$$

Using the law of total probability, the above probability can be bounded by

$$\Pr\left[\begin{matrix} \mathbf{V}^{\widetilde{\varPi}^\star}(\mathbb{x}; \rho) = 1 \\ \wedge\, \mathbf{V}^{[\mathcal{Q}, \mathsf{ans}]}(\mathbb{x}; \rho) = 1 \\ \wedge\, \mathsf{VC.Check}(\mathsf{cm}, \mathcal{Q}, \mathsf{ans}, \mathsf{pf}) = 1 \end{matrix}\right] + \Pr\left[\begin{matrix} \mathbf{V}^{\widetilde{\varPi}^\star}(\mathbb{x}; \rho) \neq 1 \\ \wedge\, \mathbf{V}^{[\mathcal{Q}, \mathsf{ans}]}(\mathbb{x}; \rho) = 1 \\ \wedge\, \mathsf{VC.Check}(\mathsf{cm}, \mathcal{Q}, \mathsf{ans}, \mathsf{pf}) = 1 \end{matrix}\right]\ .$$

The term on the left is bounded by $\epsilon_{\mathsf{PCP}}(\mathbb{x})$ (the soundness error of PCP) using similar reasoning as in Sect. 2.2.

The term on the right can be bounded by Lemma 2 and the expected-time position binding error of the VC. Another application of the law of total probability gives

$$\Pr\left[\begin{matrix} \mathbf{V}^{\widetilde{\varPi}^\star}(\mathbb{x}; \rho) \neq 1 \\ \wedge\, \mathbf{V}^{[\mathcal{Q}, \mathsf{ans}]}(\mathbb{x}; \rho) = 1 \\ \wedge\, \mathsf{VC.Check}(\mathsf{cm}, \mathcal{Q}, \mathsf{ans}, \mathsf{pf}) = 1 \end{matrix}\right]$$

$$= \Pr\left[\begin{matrix} \mathbf{V}^{\widetilde{\varPi}^\star}(\mathbb{x}; \rho) \neq 1 \\ \wedge\, \mathbf{V}^{[\mathcal{Q}, \mathsf{ans}]}(\mathbb{x}; \rho) = 1 \\ \wedge\, \mathsf{VC.Check}(\mathsf{cm}, \mathcal{Q}, \mathsf{ans}, \mathsf{pf}) = 1 \\ \wedge\, \forall i \in [\mathsf{q}], \mathsf{ans}[\mathcal{Q}[i]] = \mathsf{ans}^{(i)}[\mathcal{Q}[i]] \end{matrix}\right] + \Pr\left[\begin{matrix} \mathbf{V}^{\widetilde{\varPi}^\star}(\mathbb{x}; \rho) \neq 1 \\ \wedge\, \mathbf{V}^{[\mathcal{Q}, \mathsf{ans}]}(\mathbb{x}; \rho) = 1 \\ \wedge\, \mathsf{VC.Check}(\mathsf{cm}, \mathcal{Q}, \mathsf{ans}, \mathsf{pf}) = 1 \\ \wedge\, \exists\, i \in [\mathsf{q}], \mathsf{ans}[\mathcal{Q}[i]] \neq \mathsf{ans}^{(i)}[\mathcal{Q}[i]] \end{matrix}\right]$$

$$\leq \epsilon + \sum_{i \in [\mathsf{q}]} \Pr\left[\mathsf{ans}[\mathcal{Q}[i]] \neq \mathsf{ans}^{(i)}[\mathcal{Q}[i]]\right]\ .$$

The term on the right can be bounded by $\mathsf{q} \cdot \epsilon_{\mathsf{VC}}^\star(\lambda, \ell, \mathsf{q}, t_{\mathsf{VC}}^\star) = O(\log \frac{\mathsf{q}}{\epsilon} \cdot (t_{\mathsf{ARG}}^\star + \ell \cdot t_{\mathbf{v}})))$ from the expected-time position binding property of the VC.

Extension to PCPs with Adaptive Verifiers. The above $A_{\mathsf{VC}}^{(i)}$ construction only works for PCPs with non-adaptive verifiers because we cannot compute the query set as in Item 4a for adaptive PCP verifiers. However, we can adapt the construction of $A_{\mathsf{VC}}^{(i)}$ to work for adaptive PCP verifiers as follows.

$A_{\mathsf{VC}}^{(i)}(\rho)$:
1. Run $\mathsf{cm} \leftarrow \widetilde{\mathcal{P}}(\mathbb{x})$ and $(\mathcal{Q}, \mathsf{ans}, \mathsf{pf}) \leftarrow \widetilde{\mathcal{P}}(\rho)$.
2. Check that $\mathsf{VC.Check}(\mathsf{cm}, \mathcal{Q}, \mathsf{ans}, \mathsf{pf}) = 1$. If not, output $(\mathsf{cm}, \mathsf{ans}, \mathsf{ans}, \mathcal{Q}, \mathcal{Q}, \mathsf{pf}, \mathsf{pf})$.
3. Define $q := \mathcal{Q}(i)$ and set $j := 0$.
4. Repeat the following:

(a) Repeatedly sample $\rho' \leftarrow \{0,1\}^r$ and run $(\mathcal{Q}', \mathsf{ans}', \mathsf{pf}') \leftarrow \widetilde{\mathcal{P}}(\rho')$ until the following holds:
    i. $q \in \mathcal{Q}'$, and
    ii. $\mathsf{VC.Check}(\mathsf{cm}, \mathcal{Q}', \mathsf{ans}', \mathsf{pf}') = 1$.
(b) Run $(\mathcal{Q}', \mathsf{ans}', \mathsf{pf}') \leftarrow \widetilde{\mathcal{P}}(\rho')$.
(c) If $\mathsf{ans}[q] \neq \mathsf{ans}'[q]$, output $(\mathsf{cm}, \mathcal{Q}, \mathsf{ans}, \mathsf{pf}, \mathcal{Q}', \mathsf{ans}', \mathsf{pf}')$.
(d) If $\mathsf{ans}[q] = \mathsf{ans}'[q]$, set $j := j + 1$. Further, if $j = C$, output $(\mathsf{cm}, \mathsf{ans}, \mathsf{ans}, \mathcal{Q}, \mathcal{Q}, \mathsf{pf}, \mathsf{pf})$.

By a similar analysis (details in Section [14, Sect. 6.1]), we can conclude that, for the above $A_{\mathsf{VC}}^{(i)}$,

$$t_{\mathsf{VC}}^{\star} = C \cdot \ell \cdot t_{\mathsf{ARG}}^{\star} \ .$$

The rest of the analysis can be directly applied to the new construction of $A_{\mathsf{VC}}^{(i)}$.

Remark 4. When the underlying PCP has an adaptive verifier, the expected running time of $A_{\mathsf{VC}}^{(i)}$ cannot be better than $C \cdot \ell \cdot t_{\mathsf{ARG}}^{\star}$. Consider a PCP with proof length ℓ and query complexity q. Assume that the PCP verifier is adaptive and the query distribution is almost uniform. Then, in order to sample a randomness that queries a fix location q as in Item 4a, the expected number of iterations is roughly ℓ. Since each iteration runs the argument adversary $\widetilde{\mathcal{P}}$, $A_{\mathsf{VC}}^{(i)}$ has expected running time $C \cdot \ell \cdot t_{\mathsf{ARG}}^{\star}$ for this PCP.

Remark 5 (Comparison with [4]). [4] gives a formal analysis of a variant of Kilian's protocol based on a *non-adaptive* and *reverse-samplable* PCP and a collision-resistance hash function. Their analysis shares similarities with our analysis in this section; both analyses construct the adversaries to the vector commitment scheme and to the PCP separately, contrary to the approach in Sect. 2.2. Nevertheless, our analysis in this section deviates from the analysis in [4] (and other previous analyses) due to the differences below.

- Our analysis considers VC adversaries that run in expected running time while [4] considers strict running time. As a result, [4] crucially relies on the PCP's non-adaptivity and reverse sampler, as they cannot construct an efficient strict-time collision finder without these. Instead, our analysis works for all PCPs.
- The rewinding algorithm in [4] uses the PCP reverse sampler. For every location $q \in [\ell]$, they reverse sample several PCP randomness strings that query q and record an answer only if $\widetilde{\mathcal{P}}$ opens to it sufficiently often. This construction has a tradeoff between the running time and error probability similar to our reductor in Sect. 2.2 (the $\frac{1}{\epsilon}$ blowup in the VC adversary time versus the additive error ϵ). In contrast, our reductor in this section searches over all PCP randomness strings to find the "best" PCP string according to $\widetilde{\mathcal{P}}$'s answers. This difference allows us to significantly mediate this tradeoff: to achieve an additive error of ϵ, the expected running time of our VC adversary only has a blowup of $\log \frac{1}{\epsilon}$. Unfortunately, while [4]'s analysis gives knowledge soundness guarantee, ours in this section does not. We discuss in Sect. 2.5 how to extend our strict-time soundness analysis in Sect. 2.2 to prove knowledge soundness.

2.4 Lower Bounds from the Schnorr Identification Scheme

We discuss how to prove Theorem 3, and the connection to Schnorr's protocol

Review: The Schnorr Identification Scheme. Let GroupGen be a group generation algorithm that, given a security parameter λ, samples a tuple $(\mathbb{G}, p, g)$ where $\mathbb{G}$ is a group of prime order $p \geq 2^\lambda$ and g is a generator of the group. The Schnorr identification scheme [33, 34] is of a tuple of algorithms $\mathsf{ID}_{\mathsf{Schnorr}} = (\mathsf{P}, \mathsf{V})$ where, for a random w in $\mathbb{Z}_p$, the prover P receives the instance $\mathrm{x} = ((\mathbb{G}, p, g), h = g^{\mathrm{w}} \in \mathbb{G})$ and witness w, and the verifier V receives the instance x. Then P and V interact as follows.

1. P samples a random element $r \leftarrow \mathbb{Z}_p$, computes its first message $\alpha := g^r \in \mathbb{G}$, and sends α to V.
2. V samples a random challenge $\beta \leftarrow \mathbb{Z}_p$ and sends it to P.
3. P computes its second message $\gamma := \mathrm{w} \cdot \beta + r \bmod p$ and sends it to V.
4. V checks that $g^\gamma = \alpha \cdot h^\beta$.

We say that $\mathsf{ID}_{\mathsf{Schnorr}}$ has error $\epsilon_{\mathsf{Schnorr}}$ if for every time bound $t_{\mathsf{ID}} \in \mathbb{N}$ and t_{ID}-time adversary $\widetilde{\mathsf{P}}$,

$$
\Pr \left[\langle \widetilde{\mathsf{P}}(\mathrm{x}), \mathsf{V}(\mathrm{x}) \rangle = 1 \;\middle|\; \begin{array}{l} (\mathbb{G}, p, g) \leftarrow \mathsf{GroupGen}(1^\lambda) \\ \mathrm{w} \leftarrow \mathbb{Z}_p \\ h := g^{\mathrm{w}} \\ \mathrm{x} := ((\mathbb{G}, p, g), h) \end{array} \right] \leq \epsilon_{\mathsf{Schnorr}}(\lambda, t_{\mathsf{ID}}) \ .
$$

The security of the Schnorr identification scheme is based on the hardness of the *discrete logarithm problem* (it is hard for any time-bounded adversary, given a random $y \in \mathbb{G}$, to find $x \in \mathbb{Z}_p$ such that $y = g^x$). The protocol has special soundness meaning that one can efficiently compute the discrete logarithm when given two valid interaction transcripts. Thus, given a transcript of the protocol, the security reduction rewinds the adversary in order to obtain an additional accepting transcript and then extracts a witness. The analysis uses the *forking lemma* [29] to bound the success probability of the second invocation of the adversary (conditioned on a successful first invocation).

VC Scheme From the Schnorr Identification Scheme. While Kilian's protocol shares a similar structure with sigma protocols like the Schnorr identification scheme (prover's commitment, verifier's challenge, and prover's opening), Kilian's protocol is *not* a sigma protocol. Nevertheless, we show how to construct a VC scheme whose security is based on that of the Schnorr identification scheme, and later we will see how to connect this to the security of Kilian's protocol.

Recall that the position binding property ensures that the probability for any time-bounded adversary to find two inconsistent openings for the same location is bounded. On the other hand, the security of the Schnorr identification scheme relies on the fact that the it is hard for any time-bounded adversary to find two accepting transcripts of the protocol.

Therefore, the VC scheme we construct reduces finding inconsistent answers to finding accepting Schnorr transcripts, which ensures position binding from the hardness of discrete logarithm.

We construct $\mathsf{VC} = (\mathsf{VC.Commit}, \mathsf{VC.Open}, \mathsf{VC.Check})$ as follows. (Our VC only supports messages of length 1.) Recall that in this section, we omit the algorithm for VC that samples the public parameters. For this construction, the public parameter consists of a description $(\mathbb{G}, p, g)$ of a group generated by GroupGen given the security parameter λ, and a random group element $h \in \mathbb{G}$.

- VC.Commit(m):
    1. Sample $r \leftarrow \mathbb{Z}_p$.
    2. Set cm $:= g^r$.
    3. Set aux $:= (r, m)$.
    4. Output (cm, aux).
- VC.Open(aux $= (r, m), \{1\}$): Output pf $:= r + m$.
- VC.Check(cm, $\{1\}$, ans, pf): Check that $g^{\mathsf{pf}} = $ cm $\cdot h^{\mathsf{ans}}$.

Consider a VC adversary A_{VC} that outputs (cm, $\mathcal{Q} = \{1\}, \mathcal{Q}' = \{1\}$, ans, ans', pf, pf') such that

- ans $\neq$ ans',
- $g^{\mathsf{pf}} = $ cm $\cdot h^{\mathsf{ans}}$, and
- $g^{\mathsf{pf}'} = $ cm $\cdot h^{\mathsf{ans}'}$.

Then, one can recover $x \in \mathbb{Z}_p$ such that $h = g^x$:

$$x := (\mathsf{pf}' - \mathsf{pf}) \cdot (\mathsf{ans}' - \mathsf{ans})^{-1} \ .$$

We can conclude that VC has position binding error ϵ_{VC} such that

$$\epsilon_{\mathsf{VC}}(\lambda, 1, 1, t_{\mathsf{VC}}) \leq \epsilon_{\mathsf{DLOG}}(\lambda, O(t_{\mathsf{VC}})) \ .$$

Security Reduction from Kilian to Schnorr. We explain how to connect the security of Kilian's protocol to the security of the Schnorr identification scheme. The VC scheme that we consider is described above. We are left to fix a PCP.

Since the VC scheme works for messages of length 1, the PCP we consider has proof length 1. Moreover, we ensure that the PCP has very small soundness error, so that the dominant term will come from the VC scheme. In more detail, we consider a PCP system PCP for the empty relation $R = \emptyset$ with alphabet $\Sigma = \{0, 1\}^\lambda$, proof length $\ell = 1$, query complexity q $= 1$, and verifier randomness complexity r $= \lambda$. For every instance $\mathbb{x}$, given a PCP proof $\widetilde{\Pi} \in \Sigma$, the PCP verifier **V** works as follows:

$\mathbf{V}^{\widetilde{\Pi}}(\mathbb{x})$:
   1. Sample randomness $\rho \leftarrow \{0, 1\}^\lambda$.
   2. Check that $\widetilde{\Pi} = \rho$.

The soundness error of PCP is $\epsilon_{\mathsf{PCP}} = 2^{-\lambda}$.

Let ARG $:=$ Kilian[PCP, VC]. Consider the optimal adversary $\widetilde{\mathsf{P}}$ for the Schnorr identification scheme. We construct an argument adversary $\widetilde{\mathcal{P}}$ against the argument verifier for Kilian's protocol. Note that the argument adversary $\widetilde{\mathcal{P}}$ has access to the public parameter for the VC scheme in Sect. 2.4, which consists of $((\mathbb{G}, p, g), h)$ where $(\mathbb{G}, p, g)$ is sampled by GroupGen and $h \in \mathbb{G}$ is a random group element.

$\widetilde{\mathcal{P}}$:
1. $\widetilde{\mathcal{P}}$'s commitment:
    (a) Set the instance $\mathbb{x}_{\mathsf{Schnorr}} := ((\mathbb{G}, p, g), h)$ (using the public parameter of VC).
    (b) Run $(\alpha, \mathbf{aux}) \leftarrow \widetilde{\mathsf{P}}(\mathbb{x}_{\mathsf{Schnorr}})$.
    (c) Output $(\mathsf{cm}, \mathsf{aux}) := (\alpha, \mathbf{aux})$.
2. $\widetilde{\mathcal{P}}$'s opening given verifier challenge ρ:
    (a) Run $\gamma \leftarrow \widetilde{\mathsf{P}}(\mathbf{aux}, \rho)$.
    (b) Output $(\mathcal{Q} := \{1\}, \mathsf{ans} := \rho, \mathsf{pf} = \gamma)$.

The running time of $\widetilde{\mathcal{P}}$ is $O(\mathsf{t}_{\mathsf{ID}})$, where t_{ID} is the running time of $\widetilde{\mathsf{P}}$. Moreover, $\langle \widetilde{\mathcal{P}}, \mathcal{V}(\mathbb{x}) \rangle = 1$ if and only if $\langle \widetilde{\mathsf{P}}(\mathbb{x}_{\mathsf{Schnorr}}), \mathsf{V}(\mathbb{x}_{\mathsf{Schnorr}}) \rangle = 1$. Hence, we conclude that for every instance $\mathbb{x} \notin L(R)$ the following holds:

$$\epsilon_{\mathsf{Schnorr}}(\lambda, \mathsf{t}_{\mathsf{ID}}) \leq \epsilon_{\mathsf{ARG}}(\lambda, \mathbb{x}, O(\mathsf{t}_{\mathsf{ID}})) \ .$$

Similarly, in the expected-time setting, we can show that

$$\epsilon_{\mathsf{Schnorr}}^{*}(\lambda, t_{\mathsf{ID}}^{*}) \leq \epsilon_{\mathsf{ARG}}^{*}(\lambda, \mathbb{x}, O(t_{\mathsf{ID}}^{*})) \ .$$

2.5   Knowledge Soundness Analysis of Kilian's Protocol

We wish to upper bound the knowledge soundness error of Kilian[PCP, VC]. As claimed in Sect. 1.1, we argue that, for every $\epsilon > 0$, there exists a probabilistic extractor $\mathcal{E}$ that runs in time $O\left(\frac{\ell}{\epsilon} \cdot t_{\mathsf{ARG}}\right)$ such that, for every instance $\mathbb{x}$, time bound $t_{\mathsf{ARG}} \in \mathbb{N}$, and t_{ARG}-size adversary $\widetilde{\mathcal{P}}$,

$$\Pr \left[\begin{array}{l} b = 1 \\ \wedge \ (\mathbb{x}, \mathbb{w}) \notin R \end{array} \middle| \begin{array}{l} b \leftarrow \langle \widetilde{\mathcal{P}}, \mathcal{V}(\mathbb{x}) \rangle \\ \mathbb{w} \leftarrow \mathcal{E}^{\widetilde{\mathcal{P}}}(\mathbb{x}) \end{array} \right] \leq \kappa_{\mathsf{PCP}}(\mathbb{x}) + \epsilon_{\mathsf{VC}}(\lambda, \ell, \mathsf{q}, t_{\mathsf{VC}}) + \epsilon \ .$$

By construction of the argument verifier $\mathcal{V}$, the above probability is equivalent to the following:

$$\Pr \left[\begin{array}{l} \mathbf{V}^{[\mathcal{Q}, \mathsf{ans}]}(\mathbb{x}; \rho) = 1 \\ \wedge \ \mathsf{VC.Check}(\mathsf{pp}, \mathsf{cm}, \mathcal{Q}, \mathsf{ans}, \mathsf{pf}) = 1 \\ \wedge \ (\mathbb{x}, \mathbb{w}) \notin R \end{array} \middle| \begin{array}{l} \mathsf{cm} \leftarrow \widetilde{\mathcal{P}} \\ \rho \leftarrow \{0, 1\}^{\mathsf{r}} \\ (\mathcal{Q}, \mathsf{ans}, \mathsf{pf}) \leftarrow \widetilde{\mathcal{P}}(\rho) \\ \mathbb{w} \leftarrow \mathcal{E}^{\widetilde{\mathcal{P}}}(\mathbb{x}) \end{array} \right] \ .$$

We construct $\mathcal{E}$ using the PCP prover $\widetilde{\mathsf{P}}$ described in Sect. 2.2 and the PCP extractor $\mathbf{E}$ (which is given by the underlying PCP system):

$\mathcal{E}^{\widetilde{\mathcal{P}}}(\mathbb{x})$:
1. Run $\widetilde{\Pi} \leftarrow \widetilde{\mathsf{P}}$.
2. Output $\mathbb{w} \leftarrow \mathbf{E}(\mathbb{x}, \widetilde{\Pi})$.

Using the law of total probability,

$$
\Pr\left[\begin{array}{l} \mathbf{V}^{[\mathcal{Q},\,\text{ans}]}(\mathbb{x};\rho)=1 \\ \wedge\,\text{VC.Check}(\text{pp},\text{cm},\mathcal{Q},\text{ans},\text{pf})=1 \\ \wedge\,(\mathbb{x},\mathbb{w})\notin R \end{array}\middle|\begin{array}{l} \text{cm}\leftarrow\widetilde{\mathcal{P}} \\ \rho\leftarrow\{0,1\}^r \\ (\mathcal{Q},\text{ans},\text{pf})\leftarrow\widetilde{\mathcal{P}}(\rho) \\ \mathbb{w}\leftarrow\mathcal{E}^{\widetilde{\mathcal{P}}}(\mathbb{x}) \end{array}\right]
$$

$$
=\Pr\left[\begin{array}{l} \mathbf{V}^{[\widetilde{\mathcal{Q}},\,\widetilde{\Pi}]}(\mathbb{x};\rho)=1 \\ \wedge\,\mathbf{V}^{[\mathcal{Q},\,\text{ans}]}(\mathbb{x};\rho)=1 \\ \wedge\,\text{VC.Check}(\text{pp},\text{cm},\mathcal{Q},\text{ans},\text{pf})=1 \\ \wedge\,(\mathbb{x},\mathbb{w})\notin R \end{array}\right]+\Pr\left[\begin{array}{l} \mathbf{V}^{[\widetilde{\mathcal{Q}},\,\widetilde{\Pi}]}(\mathbb{x};\rho)\neq 1 \\ \wedge\,\mathbf{V}^{[\mathcal{Q},\,\text{ans}]}(\mathbb{x};\rho)=1 \\ \wedge\,\text{VC.Check}(\text{pp},\text{cm},\mathcal{Q},\text{ans},\text{pf})=1 \\ \wedge\,(\mathbb{x},\mathbb{w})\notin R \end{array}\right],
$$

where the last two probabilities are with respect to the experiment

$$
\left[\begin{array}{l} \text{cm}\leftarrow\widetilde{\mathcal{P}} \\ \rho\leftarrow\{0,1\}^r \\ (\mathcal{Q},\text{ans},\text{pf})\leftarrow\widetilde{\mathcal{P}}(\rho) \\ \widetilde{\Pi}\leftarrow\widetilde{\mathbf{P}} \\ \mathbb{w}\leftarrow\mathbf{E}(\mathbb{x},\widetilde{\Pi}) \end{array}\right].
$$

The term on the right is bounded by $\epsilon_{\text{vc}}(\lambda,\ell,\text{q},t_{\text{vc}})+\epsilon$ due to Lemma 1.

The term on the left is bounded by $\kappa_{\text{PCP}}(\mathbb{x})$ (the knowledge soundness error of PCP) as shown below:

$$
\Pr\left[\begin{array}{l} \mathbf{V}^{[\widetilde{\mathcal{Q}},\,\widetilde{\Pi}]}(\mathbb{x};\rho)=1 \\ \wedge\,\mathbf{V}^{[\mathcal{Q},\,\text{ans}]}(\mathbb{x};\rho)=1 \\ \wedge\,\text{VC.Check}(\text{pp},\text{cm},\mathcal{Q},\text{ans},\text{pf})=1 \\ \wedge\,(\mathbb{x},\mathbb{w})\notin R \end{array}\right]\leq\Pr\left[\begin{array}{l} \mathbf{V}^{\widetilde{\Pi}}(\mathbb{x};\rho)=1 \\ \wedge\,(\mathbb{x},\mathbb{w})\notin R \end{array}\middle|\begin{array}{l} \rho\leftarrow\{0,1\}^r \\ \widetilde{\Pi}\leftarrow\widetilde{\mathbf{P}} \\ \mathbb{w}\leftarrow\mathbf{E}(\mathbb{x},\widetilde{\Pi}) \end{array}\right]\leq\kappa_{\text{PCP}}(\mathbb{x}).
$$

2.6   Succinct Interactive Arguments with Adaptive Security

For simplicity, we described our security analyses in the *plain model*, where there are no public parameters available to all parties; in particular, the argument verifier is responsible for sampling and sending VC's public parameters to the argument prover. However, in the technical sections [14, Sects. 5 to 7] we prove stronger versions of Theorems 1 and 2 that hold *with adaptive security in the common reference string (CRS) model*.

An interactive argument in the CRS model includes an additional algorithm: a trusted *generator algorithm* that samples public parameters pp for the argument prover and argument verifier (which can be used any number of times across different interactions). After that, based on pp, a malicious argument prover can choose the instance on which to interact with the argument verifier. This setting necessitates appropriate definitions of *adaptive* soundness and knowledge soundness (see Sect. 3.1), which require error bounds to hold for any instance $\mathbb{x}$ chosen by the malicious argument prover up to an instance size bound n.[6] In particular, the (soundness and knowledge soundness) error bounds depend on n rather than $\mathbb{x}$.

---

[6] For convenience, we use soundness and knowledge notions for the PCPs in which the malicious prover chooses the instance (see Sect. 3.3). In to the information-theoretic setting, these definitions are equivalent to the standard ones with fixed instances.

We achieve adaptive security in the CRS model by following the structure sketched in the sections above, with only syntactic modifications due to the different target definitions. (E.g., modifying experiments to replace a fixed instance x with an instance size bound n, and letting the malicious argument prover choose the instance.)

Overall, the (formal) statements provided in the technical sections [14, Sects. 5 to 7] are stronger than the (informal) statements in Theorems 1 and 2 because we achieve adaptive security in the CRS model.[7]

For consistency, the formal statement of Theorem 3 (our lower bounds for Kilian's protocol) in the technical section [14, Sect. 8] is also proved in the setting of adaptive security in the CRS model. Nevertheless, as noted in [14, Remark 8.12], the results hold even for non-adaptive security, which is an even stronger statement.

3   Preliminaries

Definition 1. *A **relation** R is a set of pairs (x, w) where x is an instance and w a witness. The corresponding **language** $L(R)$ is the set of instances x for which there exists a witness w such that $(x, w) \in R$.*

3.1   Interactive Arguments

An *interactive argument* (in the common reference string model) for a relation R is a tuple of polynomial-time algorithms $\mathsf{ARG} = (\mathcal{G}, \mathcal{P}, \mathcal{V})$ that satisfies the following properties.

Definition 2 (Perfect Completeness). $\mathsf{ARG} = (\mathcal{G}, \mathcal{P}, \mathcal{V})$ *for a relation R has **perfect completeness** if for every security parameter $\lambda \in \mathbb{N}$, instance size bound $n \in \mathbb{N}$, public parameter $\mathsf{pp} \in \mathcal{G}(1^\lambda, n)$, and instance-witness pair $(x, w) \in R$ with $|x| \leq n$,*

$$\Pr\left[\langle \mathcal{P}(\mathsf{pp}, x, w), \mathcal{V}(\mathsf{pp}, x)\rangle = 1\right] = 1 .$$

Definition 3 (Adaptive Soundness). $\mathsf{ARG} = (\mathcal{G}, \mathcal{P}, \mathcal{V})$ *for a relation R has **(adaptive strict-time) soundness error** ϵ_{ARG} if for every security parameter $\lambda \in \mathbb{N}$, instance size bound $n \in \mathbb{N}$, auxiliary input distribution $\mathcal{D}$, adversary time bound $t_{\mathsf{ARG}} \in \mathbb{N}$, and t_{ARG}-time algorithm $\widetilde{\mathcal{P}}$,*

$$\Pr\left[\begin{array}{l|l} |x| \leq n & \mathsf{pp} \leftarrow \mathcal{G}(1^\lambda, n) \\ \wedge\, x \notin L(R) & \eta \leftarrow \mathcal{D} \\ \wedge\, b = 1 & (x, \mathsf{aux}) \leftarrow \widetilde{\mathcal{P}}(\mathsf{pp}, \eta) \\ & b \leftarrow \langle \widetilde{\mathcal{P}}(\mathsf{aux}), \mathcal{V}(\mathsf{pp}, x)\rangle \end{array}\right] \leq \epsilon_{\mathsf{ARG}}(\lambda, n, t_{\mathsf{ARG}}) .$$

---

[7] Adaptive security in the CRS model directly implies security in the plain model. Since no CRS is allowed, the argument verifier can begin the interaction by running itself the generator algorithm and sending the public parameters for the argument system to the argument prover. See Remark 7.

Definition 4 (Adaptive Expected-Time Soundness). $\mathsf{ARG} = (\mathcal{G}, \mathcal{P}, \mathcal{V})$ *for a relation* R *has (adaptive) expected-time soundness error* ϵ_{ARG} *if for every security parameter* $\lambda \in \mathbb{N}$, *instance size bound* $n \in \mathbb{N}$, *auxiliary input distribution* $\mathcal{D}$, *adversary time bound* $t_{\mathsf{ARG}} \in \mathbb{N}$, *and algorithm* $\widetilde{\mathcal{P}}$ *with expected running time* $t^\star_{\mathsf{ARG}}$,

$$
\Pr \left[\begin{array}{l} |\mathbb{x}| \leq n \\ \wedge\, \mathbb{x} \notin L(R) \\ \wedge\, b = 1 \end{array} \,\middle|\, \begin{array}{l} \mathsf{pp} \leftarrow \mathcal{G}(1^\lambda, n) \\ \eta \leftarrow \mathcal{D} \\ (\mathbb{x}, \mathsf{aux}) \leftarrow \widetilde{\mathcal{P}}(\mathsf{pp}, \eta) \\ b \leftarrow \langle \widetilde{\mathcal{P}}(\mathsf{aux}), \mathcal{V}(\mathsf{pp}, \mathbb{x}) \rangle \end{array} \right] \leq \epsilon^\star_{\mathsf{ARG}}(\lambda, n, t^\star_{\mathsf{ARG}}) \ .
$$

Definition 5 (Adaptive Knowledge Soundness). $\mathsf{ARG} = (\mathcal{G}, \mathcal{P}, \mathcal{V})$ *for a relation* R *has (adaptive) knowledge soundness error* κ_{ARG} *with extraction time* $t_\mathcal{E}$ *if there exists a probabilistic algorithm* $\mathcal{E}$ *such that for every security parameter* $\lambda \in \mathbb{N}$, *instance size bound* $n \in \mathbb{N}$, *auxiliary input distribution* $\mathcal{D}$, *adversary time bound* $t_{\mathsf{ARG}} \in \mathbb{N}$, *and* t_{ARG}*-time algorithm* $\widetilde{\mathcal{P}}$,

$$
\Pr \left[\begin{array}{l} |\mathbb{x}| \leq n \\ \wedge\, (\mathbb{x}, \mathbb{w}) \notin R \\ \wedge\, b = 1 \end{array} \,\middle|\, \begin{array}{l} \mathsf{pp} \leftarrow \mathcal{G}(1^\lambda, n) \\ \eta \leftarrow \mathcal{D} \\ (\mathbb{x}, \mathsf{aux}) \leftarrow \widetilde{\mathcal{P}}(\mathsf{pp}, \eta) \\ b \xleftarrow{\mathsf{tr}} \langle \widetilde{\mathcal{P}}(\mathsf{aux}), \mathcal{V}(\mathsf{pp}, \mathbb{x}) \rangle \\ \mathbb{w} \leftarrow \mathcal{E}^{\widetilde{\mathcal{P}}(\mathsf{aux})}(\mathsf{pp}, \mathbb{x}, \mathsf{tr}) \end{array} \right] \leq \kappa_{\mathsf{ARG}}(\lambda, n, t_{\mathsf{ARG}}) \ ;
$$

moreover, $\mathcal{E}$ *runs in time* $t_\mathcal{E}(\lambda, n, t_{\mathsf{ARG}})$.

Above, $b \xleftarrow{\mathsf{tr}} \langle \widetilde{\mathcal{P}}(\mathsf{aux}), \mathcal{V}(\mathsf{pp}, \mathbb{x}) \rangle$ denotes the fact that tr is the transcript of the interaction (i.e., public parameters and messages exchanged between $\widetilde{\mathcal{P}}$ and $\mathcal{V}$). Moreover, $\mathcal{E}^{\widetilde{\mathcal{P}}}$ means that $\mathcal{E}$ has black-box access to (each next-message function of) $\widetilde{\mathcal{P}}$; in particular $\mathcal{E}$ can send verifier messages to $\widetilde{\mathcal{P}}$ in order to obtain the next message of $\widetilde{\mathcal{P}}$ (for a partial interaction where $\mathcal{V}$ sent those messages).

Moreover, we can assume, without loss of generality, that $\widetilde{\mathcal{P}}$ is deterministic relative to auxiliary input η (as the internal coin flips of a probabilistic $\widetilde{\mathcal{P}}$ can be incorporated into the auxiliary input distribution $\mathcal{D}$).

Remark 6. The argument generator $\mathcal{G}$ receives two inputs: the security parameter λ and an instance size bound n. This means that the public parameter sampled by $\mathcal{G}$ may work only for instances of size at most n. However, one could consider the stronger notion where the sampled public parameter works for all instance sizes; in this case $\mathcal{G}$ receives only λ as input. Our analysis works for both cases; see Remark 9.

Remark 7 (plain model variant). The above definitions consider interactive arguments in the *common reference string model*, where a generator samples a public parameter used by the argument prover and the argument verifier. One could also consider interactive arguments in the *plain model*, where there is no generator. This latter notion is implied, at the cost of an additional verifier message, as we now explain.

Suppose that $(\mathcal{G}, \mathcal{P}, \mathcal{V})$ is an interactive argument in the common reference string model. We describe an interactive argument $(\mathcal{P}', \mathcal{V}')$ in the plain model with an additional verifier message. The argument prover $\mathcal{P}'$ receives as input an instance $\mathbb{x}$ and witness $\mathbb{w}$, and the argument verifier $\mathcal{V}'$ receives as input the instance $\mathbb{x}$; both also receive as input the security parameter λ (in unary). They interact as follows:

- $\mathcal{V}'$ samples a public parameter $\mathsf{pp} \leftarrow \mathcal{G}(1^\lambda, |\mathbb{x}|)$ and sends pp to $\mathcal{P}'$;
- $\mathcal{P}'$ and $\mathcal{V}'$ simulate an interaction of $\mathcal{P}(\mathsf{pp}, \mathbb{x}, \mathbb{w})$ and $\mathcal{V}(\mathsf{pp}, \mathbb{x})$.

It is straightforward to see that $(\mathcal{P}', \mathcal{V}')$ satisfies the standard definitions of completeness, soundness, and knowledge soundness for interactive arguments in the plain model.[8] In fact, it would suffice for $(\mathcal{G}, \mathcal{P}, \mathcal{V})$ to satisfy the non-adaptive relaxations of soundness and knowledge soundness.

3.2 Vector Commitments

A (static) *vector commitment scheme* [13] over alphabet Σ is a tuple of algorithms

$$\mathsf{VC} = (\mathsf{Gen}, \mathsf{Commit}, \mathsf{Open}, \mathsf{Check})$$

with the following syntax.

- $\mathsf{VC.Gen}(1^\lambda, \ell) \to \mathsf{pp}$: On input a security parameter $\lambda \in \mathbb{N}$ and message size bound $\ell \in \mathbb{N}$, $\mathsf{VC.Gen}$ samples public parameter pp.
- $\mathsf{VC.Commit}(\mathsf{pp}, m) \to (\mathsf{cm}, \mathsf{aux})$: On input a public parameter pp and a message $m \in \Sigma^\ell$, $\mathsf{VC.Commit}$ produces a commitment cm and the corresponding auxiliary state aux.
- $\mathsf{VC.Open}(\mathsf{pp}, \mathsf{aux}, \mathcal{Q}) \to \mathsf{pf}$: On input a public parameter pp, an auxiliary state aux, and a query set $\mathcal{Q} \subseteq [\ell]$, $\mathsf{VC.Open}$ outputs an opening proof string pf attesting that $m[\mathcal{Q}]$ is a restriction of m to $\mathcal{Q}$.
- $\mathsf{VC.Check}(\mathsf{pp}, \mathsf{cm}, \mathcal{Q}, \mathsf{ans}, \mathsf{pf}) \to \{0, 1\}$: On input a public parameter pp, a commitment cm, a query set $\mathcal{Q} \subseteq [\ell]$, an answer string $\mathsf{ans} \in \Sigma^\mathcal{Q}$, and an opening proof string pf, $\mathsf{VC.Check}$ determines if pf is a valid proof for $\mathsf{ans} \in \Sigma^\mathcal{Q}$ being a restriction of the message committed in cm to $\mathcal{Q}$.

The vector commitment scheme VC must satisfy perfect completeness and position binding.

Definition 6 (Completeness). $\mathsf{VC} = (\mathsf{Gen}, \mathsf{Commit}, \mathsf{Open}, \mathsf{Check})$ *has **perfect completeness** if for every security parameter* $\lambda \in \mathbb{N}$, *message length* $\ell \in \mathbb{N}$, *message* $m \in \Sigma^\ell$, *and query set* $\mathcal{Q} \subseteq [\ell]$,

$$\Pr\left[\mathsf{VC.Check}(\mathsf{pp}, \mathsf{cm}, \mathcal{Q}, m[\mathcal{Q}], \mathsf{pf}) = 1 \;\middle|\; \begin{array}{l} \mathsf{pp} \leftarrow \mathsf{VC.Gen}(1^\lambda, \ell) \\ (\mathsf{cm}, \mathsf{aux}) \leftarrow \mathsf{VC.Commit}(\mathsf{pp}, m) \\ \mathsf{pf} \leftarrow \mathsf{VC.Open}(\mathsf{pp}, \mathsf{aux}, \mathcal{Q}) \end{array}\right] = 1 \;.$$

Definition 7 (Position Binding). $\mathsf{VC} = (\mathsf{Gen}, \mathsf{Commit}, \mathsf{Open}, \mathsf{Check})$ *has **(stricttime) position binding error*** ϵ_{vc} *if for every security parameter* $\lambda \in \mathbb{N}$, *message length*

---

[8] These standard definitions can be derived from Definitions 2, 3 and 5 by setting pp to be empty.

$\ell \in \mathbb{N}$, *query set size* $s \in \mathbb{N}$ *with* $s \leq \ell$, *auxiliary input distribution* $\mathcal{D}$, *adversary time bound* $t_{VC} \in \mathbb{N}$, *and* t_{VC}-*time algorithm* A_{VC},

$$\Pr \left[\begin{array}{l} |\mathcal{Q}| = |\mathcal{Q}'| = s \\ \wedge\ \exists\, i \in \mathcal{Q} \cap \mathcal{Q}' : \mathsf{ans}[i] \neq \mathsf{ans}'[i] \\ \wedge\ \mathsf{VC.Check}(\mathsf{pp}, \mathsf{cm}, \mathcal{Q}, \mathsf{ans}, \mathsf{pf}) = 1 \\ \wedge\ \mathsf{VC.Check}(\mathsf{pp}, \mathsf{cm}, \mathcal{Q}', \mathsf{ans}', \mathsf{pf}') = 1 \end{array} \middle| \begin{array}{l} \mathsf{pp} \leftarrow \mathsf{VC.Gen}(1^\lambda, \ell) \\ \eta \leftarrow \mathcal{D} \\ \binom{\mathsf{cm}, \mathsf{ans}, \mathsf{ans}',}{\mathcal{Q}, \mathcal{Q}', \mathsf{pf}, \mathsf{pf}'} \leftarrow A_{VC}(\mathsf{pp}, \eta) \end{array} \right] \leq \epsilon_{VC}(\lambda, \ell, s, t_{VC}).$$

Definition 8 (Expected-Time Position Binding). $\mathsf{VC} = (\mathsf{Gen}, \mathsf{Commit}, \mathsf{Open}, \mathsf{Check})$ *has **expected-time position binding error** $\epsilon_{VC}^\star$ if for every security parameter* $\lambda \in \mathbb{N}$, *message length* $\ell \in \mathbb{N}$, *query set size* $s \in \mathbb{N}$ *with* $s \leq \ell$, *auxiliary input distribution* $\mathcal{D}$, *adversary time bound* $t_{VC}^\star \in \mathbb{N}$, *and an algorithm* A_{VC} *with expected running time* $t_{VC}^\star$,

$$\Pr \left[\begin{array}{l} |\mathcal{Q}| = |\mathcal{Q}'| = s \\ \wedge\ \exists\, i \in \mathcal{Q} \cap \mathcal{Q}' : \mathsf{ans}[i] \neq \mathsf{ans}'[i] \\ \wedge\ \mathsf{VC.Check}(\mathsf{pp}, \mathsf{cm}, \mathcal{Q}, \mathsf{ans}, \mathsf{pf}) = 1 \\ \wedge\ \mathsf{VC.Check}(\mathsf{pp}, \mathsf{cm}, \mathcal{Q}', \mathsf{ans}', \mathsf{pf}') = 1 \end{array} \middle| \begin{array}{l} \mathsf{pp} \leftarrow \mathsf{VC.Gen}(1^\lambda, \ell) \\ \eta \leftarrow \mathcal{D} \\ \binom{\mathsf{cm}, \mathsf{ans}, \mathsf{ans}',}{\mathcal{Q}, \mathcal{Q}', \mathsf{pf}, \mathsf{pf}'} \leftarrow A_{VC}(\mathsf{pp}, \eta) \end{array} \right] \leq \epsilon_{VC}^\star(\lambda, \ell, s, t_{VC}^\star) .$$

Remark 8 (Monotonicity of ϵ_{VC}). We assume hereafter that the position binding error ϵ_{VC} is monotone in each coordinate in the natural direction:

- $\epsilon_{VC}(\cdot, \ell, s, t_{VC})$ is non-increasing (larger security parameters decrease an adversary's success);
- $\epsilon_{VC}(\lambda, \cdot, s, t_{VC})$ is non-decreasing (opening some set in a string is easier than opening in a substring);
- $\epsilon_{VC}(\lambda, \ell, \cdot, t_{VC})$ is non-decreasing (finding a collision in a set is easier than finding one in a subset); and
- $\epsilon_{VC}(\lambda, \ell, s, \cdot)$ is non-decreasing (the success of an adversary increases with its computational power).

The last condition is trivially satisfied, while the first should also hold in any reasonable commitment scheme. The remaining two are natural (and satisfied in the case of Merkle commitment schemes); in any case, otherwise one may replace, in our computations, expressions of the type $\epsilon_{VC}(\lambda, \ell_{max}, s_{max}, t_{VC})$, when $\ell_{max} = \max_i \{\ell_i\}$ and $s_{max} = \max_j \{s_j\}$, with

$$\max_{i,j} \{\epsilon_{VC}(\lambda, \ell_i, s_j, t_{VC})\} .$$

Analogously, we assume the expected-time position binding error $\epsilon_{VC}^\star$ has monotonicity as well.

3.3   Probabilistically Checkable Proofs

A *probabilistically checkable proof* (PCP) is an information-theoretic proof system where a probabilistic verifier has oracle access to a proof string.

Definition 9 (Completeness). $\mathsf{PCP} = (\mathbf{P}, \mathbf{V})$ *for a relation R has **perfect completeness** if, for every instance-witness pair* $(x, w) \in R$,

$$\Pr \left[\mathbf{V}^\Pi(x; \rho) = 1 \middle| \begin{array}{l} \Pi \leftarrow \mathbf{P}(x, w) \\ \rho \leftarrow \{0, 1\}^r \end{array} \right] = 1 .$$

Definition 10 (Soundness). PCP $= (\mathbf{P}, \mathbf{V})$ *for a relation* R *has* **soundness error** ϵ_{PCP} *if, for every (unbounded) circuit* $\tilde{\mathbf{P}}$ *and auxiliary input distribution* $\mathbf{D}$,

$$\Pr \begin{bmatrix} |x| \le n \\ \wedge\, x \notin L(R) \\ \wedge\, \mathbf{V}^{\tilde{\varPi}}(x; \rho) = 1 \end{bmatrix} \begin{matrix} \mathbf{ai} \leftarrow \mathbf{D} \\ (x, \tilde{\varPi}) \leftarrow \tilde{\mathbf{P}}(\mathbf{ai}) \\ \rho \leftarrow \{0,1\}^r \end{matrix} \le \epsilon_{\mathsf{PCP}}(n) \ .$$

Definition 11 (Knowledge Soundness). PCP $= (\mathbf{P}, \mathbf{V})$ *for a relation* R *has* **knowledge soundness error** κ_{PCP} **with extraction time** $t_{\mathbf{E}}$ *if there exists a probabilistic algorithm* $\mathbf{E}$ *such that, for every adversary* $\tilde{\mathbf{P}}$ *and auxiliary input distribution* $\mathbf{D}$,

$$\Pr \begin{bmatrix} |x| \le n \\ \wedge\, (x, w) \notin R \\ \wedge\, \mathbf{V}^{\tilde{\varPi}}(x; \rho) = 1 \end{bmatrix} \begin{matrix} \mathbf{ai} \leftarrow \mathbf{D} \\ (x, \tilde{\varPi}) \leftarrow \tilde{\mathbf{P}}(\mathbf{ai}) \\ \rho \leftarrow \{0,1\}^r \\ w \leftarrow \mathbf{E}(x, \tilde{\varPi}) \end{matrix} \le \kappa_{\mathsf{PCP}}(n) \ ;$$

moreover, $\mathbf{E}$ *runs in time* $t_{\mathbf{E}}(n)$.

We consider several efficiency measures for a PCP:

- the *proof alphabet* Σ is the alphabet over which a PCP string is written;
- the *proof length* ℓ is the number of alphabet symbols in the PCP string;
- the *query complexity* $\mathsf{q} \in [\ell]$ is the number of queries that the PCP verifier makes to the PCP string (each query is an index in $[\ell]$ and is answered by the corresponding symbol in Σ in the PCP string);
- the *randomness complexity* r is the number of random bits used by the PCP verifier.

An efficiency measure may be a function of the instance x (e.g., of its size $|x|$).

4 Kilian's Protocol

The construction of $(\mathcal{G}, \mathcal{P}, \mathcal{V}) := \mathsf{Kilian}[\mathsf{PCP}, \mathsf{VC}]$ is specified below.

Construction 4 *The argument generator* $\mathcal{G}$ *receives as input a security parameter* $\lambda \in \mathbb{N}$ *and an instance size bound* $n \in \mathbb{N}$, *and works as follows.*

$\mathcal{G}(\lambda, n)$:
  1. *Sample public parameter for the VC scheme:* $\mathsf{pp}_{\mathsf{VC}} \leftarrow \mathsf{VC.Gen}(1^\lambda, \ell(n))$.
  2. *Set public parameter for the interactive argument:* $\mathsf{pp} := \mathsf{pp}_{\mathsf{VC}}$.
  3. *Output* pp.

The argument prover $\mathcal{P}$ *receives as input the public parameter* pp, *an instance* x *and a witness* w, *and the argument verifier* $\mathcal{V}$ *receives as input the public parameter* pp *and the instance* x. *Then* $\mathcal{P}$ *and* $\mathcal{V}$ *interact as follows.*

1. $\mathcal{P}$'s *commitment.*
   (a) *Compute a PCP string:* $\varPi \leftarrow \mathbf{P}(x, w)$.

   (b) *Compute a vector commitment to the PCP string:* $(\mathsf{cm}, \mathsf{aux}) \leftarrow$ VC.Commit(pp, Π).
   (c) *Send* cm *to* $\mathcal{V}$.
2. $\mathcal{V}$*'s challenge.*
   (a) *Sample PCP verifier randomness:* $\rho \leftarrow \{0, 1\}^r$.
   (b) *Send* ρ *to* $\mathcal{P}$.
3. $\mathcal{P}$*'s response.*
   (a) *Run the PCP verifier* $\mathbf{V}^\Pi(\mathbb{x}; \rho)$ *to deduce its query set* $\mathcal{Q} \subseteq [\ell]$.
   (b) *Compute a VC opening proof:* pf $\leftarrow$ VC.Open$(\mathsf{pp}, \mathsf{aux}, \mathcal{Q})$.
   (c) *Set* ans $:= \Pi[\mathcal{Q}]$.
   (d) *Send* $(\mathcal{Q}, \mathsf{ans}, \mathsf{pf})$ *to* $\mathcal{V}$.
4. $\mathcal{V}$*'s decision: check that* $\mathbf{V}^{[\mathcal{Q}, \mathsf{ans}]}(\mathbb{x}; \rho) = 1$ *and* VC.Check$(\mathsf{pp}, \mathsf{cm}, \mathcal{Q}, \mathsf{ans}, \mathsf{pf}) = 1$.

The interactive argument consists of three messages: a prover message; a verifier message; and a prover message. The interactive argument is public-coin since the verifier's (only) message is a uniform random string. The efficiency measures of interactive arguments are as follows:

- the generator outputs public parameter of size $|\mathsf{pp}_{\mathsf{VC}}|$ bits;
- the prover-to-verifier communication consists of $|\mathsf{cm}| + \mathsf{q} \cdot (\log \ell + \log|\Sigma|) + |\mathsf{pf}|$ bits;
- the verifier-to-prover communication consists of r bits;
- the time complexity of the argument generator is $t_{\mathsf{VC.Gen}}$.
- the time complexity of the argument prover is $t_{\mathbf{P}} + t_{\mathsf{VC.Commit}} + t_{\mathbf{V}} + t_{\mathsf{VC.Open}}$;
- the time complexity of the argument verifier is $t_{\mathbf{V}} + t_{\mathsf{VC.Check}}$.

Remark 9. There are vector commitments for which VC.Gen needs only the security parameter λ as input (i.e., VC.Gen works for every message size); for example, Merkle commitment schemes are vector commitment schemes with this property, because the public parameter consists of (the description of) a hash function, which suffices for every message size. In this case, the argument generator $\mathcal{G}$ in Theorem 4 requires only λ as input and works for every instance size. This leads the notion of an interactive argument discussed in Remark 6.

Remark 10. In the plain-model variant of Theorem 4 (see Remark 7), the public parameters pp $:= \mathsf{pp}_{\mathsf{VC}}$ are sampled and sent by the argument verifier (resulting in a four-message protocol). Hence the plain-model variant is public-coin if (and only if) VC.Gen is a public-coin algorithm (its output includes all of its randomness).

Acknowledgments. Alessandro Chiesa and Ziyi Guan are partially supported by the Ethereum Foundation. We thank Fermi Ma and Julius Vering for valuable discussions and participating in early stages of this work. We thank Zijing Di for valuable feedback and comments on earlier drafts of this paper. Eylon Yogev is supported by the Israel Science Foundation (Grant No. 2302/22), European Research Union (ERC, CRYPTOPROOF, 101164375), and by an Alon Young Faculty Fellowship. Views and opinions expressed are however those of the author(s) only and do not necessarily reflect those of the European Union or the European Research Council. Neither the European Union nor the granting authority can be held responsible for them.

Disclosure of Interests. The authors have no competing interests to declare that are relevant to the content of this article.

References

1. Attema, T., Cramer, R.: Compressed σ-protocol theory and practical application to plug & play secure algorithmics. In: Proceedings of the 40th Annual International Cryptology Conference, pp. 513–543. CRYPTO 2020 (2020)
2. Attema, T., Cramer, R., Kohl, L.: A compressed σ-protocol theory for lattices. In: Proceedings of the 41st Annual International Cryptology Conference, pp. 549–579. CRYPTO 2021 (2022)
3. Attema, T., Fehr, S.: Parallel repetition of $(k_1, \ldots, k_\mu)$-special-sound multi-round interactive proofs. In: Proceedings of the 42nd Annual International Cryptology Conference, pp. 415–443. CRYPTO 2022 (2022)
4. Barak, B., Goldreich, O.: Universal arguments and their applications. SIAM J. Comput. **38**(5), 1661–1694 (2008). preliminary version appeared in CCC 2002
5. Bellare, M., Dai, W.: The multi-base discrete logarithm problem: tight reductions and non-rewinding proofs for Schnorr identification and signatures. In: Progress in Cryptology – INDOCRYPT 2020. pp. 529–552 (2020)
6. Bellare, M., Palacio, A.: GQ and schnorr identification schemes: Proofs of security against impersonation under active and concurrent attacks. In: Yung, M. (ed.) Advances in Cryptology - CRYPTO 2002, 22nd Annual International Cryptology Conference, Santa Barbara, California, USA, 18-22 August 2002, Proceedings. Lecture Notes in Computer Science, vol. 2442, pp. 162–177. Springer (2002). https://doi.org/10.1007/3-540-45708-9_11
7. Ben-David, S.: Probabilistically checkable arguments for all NP. In: Joye, M., Leander, G. (eds.) Advances in Cryptology - EUROCRYPT 2024 - 43rd Annual International Conference on the Theory and Applications of Cryptographic Techniques, Zurich, Switzerland, 26-30 May 2024, Proceedings, Part III. Lecture Notes in Computer Science, vol. 14653, pp. 345–374. Springer (2024). https://doi.org/10.1007/978-3-031-58734-4_12
8. Ben-Sasson, E., Chiesa, A., Spooner, N.: Interactive oracle proofs. In: Proceedings of the 14th Theory of Cryptography Conference, pp. 31–60. TCC 2016-B (2016)
9. Ben-Sasson, E., Kaplan, Y., Kopparty, S., Meir, O., Stichtenoth, H.: Constant rate PCPs for Circuit-SAT with sublinear query complexity. In: Proceedings of the 54th Annual IEEE Symposium on Foundations of Computer Science, pp. 320–329. FOCS 2013 (2013)
10. Ben-Sasson, E., Sudan, M.: Robust locally testable codes and products of codes. Random Struct. Algorithms **28**(4), 387–402 (2006)
11. Block, A.R., Garreta, A., Tiwari, P.R., Zajac, M.: On soundness notions for interactive oracle proofs, p. 1256 (2023)
12. Bronfman, L., Rothblum, R.D.: PCPS and instance compression from a cryptographic lens. In: Braverman, M. (ed.) 13th Innovations in Theoretical Computer Science Conference, ITCS 2022, January 31 - February 3, 2022, Berkeley, CA, USA. LIPIcs, vol. 215, pp. 30:1–30:19. Schloss Dagstuhl - Leibniz-Zentrum für Informatik (2022)
13. Catalano, D., Fiore, D.: Vector commitments and their applications. In: Proceedings of the 16th International Conference on Practice and Theory in Public Key Cryptography, pp. 55–72. PKC 2013 (2013)
14. Chiesa, A., Dall'Agnol, M., Guan, Z., Spooner, N., Yogev, E.: Untangling the security of Kilian's protocol: upper and lower bounds. IACR Cryptol. ePrint Arch., 1434 (2024). https://eprint.iacr.org/2024/1434
15. Chiesa, A., Ma, F., Spooner, N., Zhandry, M.: Post-quantum succinct arguments: breaking the quantum rewinding barrier. In: Proceedings of the 62nd Annual IEEE Symposium on Foundations of Computer Science, pp. 49–58. FOCS 2021 (2021)
16. Chiesa, A., Manohar, P., Spooner, N.: Succinct arguments in the quantum random oracle model. In: Proceedings of the 17th Theory of Cryptography Conference, pp. 1–29. TCC 2019 (2019), available as Cryptology ePrint Archive, Report 2019/834

17. Chiesa, A., Yogev, E.: In: Proceedings of the 41st Annual International Cryptology Conference, pp. 711–741. CRYPTO 2021 (2021)
18. Chiesa, A., Yogev, E.: Tight security bounds for micali's SNARGs. In: Proceedings of the 19th Theory of Cryptography Conference, pp. 401–434. TCC 2021 (2021)
19. Chiesa, A., Yogev, E.: Building cryptographic proofs from hash functions (2024). https://github.com/hash-based-snargs-book
20. Fuchsbauer, G., Plouviez, A., Seurin, Y.: Blind Schnorr signatures and signed ElGamal encryption in the algebraic group model. In: Advances in Cryptology – EUROCRYPT 2020, pp. 63–95 (2020)
21. Ishai, Y., Mahmoody, M., Sahai, A., Xiao, D.: On zero-knowledge PCPs: limitations, simplifications, and applications (2015). http://www.cs.virginia.edu/~mohammad/files/papers/ZKPCPs-Full.pdf
22. Kalai, Y.T., Raz, R.: Probabilistically checkable arguments. In: Proceedings of the 29th Annual International Cryptology Conference, pp. 143–159. CRYPTO 2009 (2009)
23. Kilian, J.: A note on efficient zero-knowledge proofs and arguments. In: Proceedings of the 24th Annual ACM Symposium on Theory of Computing, pp. 723–732. STOC 1992 (1992)
24. Kilian, J., Petrank, E., Tardos, G.: Probabilistically checkable proofs with zero knowledge. In: Proceedings of the 29th Annual ACM Symposium on Theory of Computing, pp. 496–505. STOC 1997 (1997)
25. Krenn, S., Orrù, M.: Proposal: σ-protocols (2021). https://docs.zkproof.org/pages/standards/accepted-workshop4/proposal-sigma.pdf
26. Lai, R.W.F., Malavolta, G.: Subvector commitments with application to succinct arguments. In: Proceedings of the 39th Annual International Cryptology Conference, pp. 530–560. CRYPTO 2019 (2019)
27. Lombardi, A., Ma, F., Spooner, N.: Post-quantum zero knowledge, revisited or: how to do quantum rewinding undetectably. In: Proceedings of the 63rd Annual IEEE Symposium on Foundations of Computer Science, pp. 851–859. FOCS 2022 (2022)
28. Micali, S.: Computationally sound proofs. SIAM J. Comput. **30**(4), 1253–1298 (2000. preliminary version appeared in FOCS 1994
29. Pointcheval, D., Stern, J.: Security arguments for digital signatures and blind signatures. J. Cryptol. **13**, 361–396 (2000)
30. Rotem, L., Segev, G.: Tighter security for schnorr identification and signatures: a high-moment forking lemma for σ-protocols. In: Proceedings of the 41st Annual International Cryptology Conference, pp. 222–250. CRYPTO 2021 (2021)
31. Scafuro, A., Siniscalchi, L., Visconti, I.: Publicly verifiable proofs from blockchains. In: Lin, D., Sako, K. (eds.) PKC 2019. LNCS, vol. 11442, pp. 374–401. Springer, Cham (2019). https://doi.org/10.1007/978-3-030-17253-4_13
32. Scafuro, A., Siniscalchi, L., Visconti, I.: Publicly verifiable zero knowledge from (collapsing) blockchains. In: Garay, J.A. (ed.) Public-Key Cryptography - PKC 2021 - 24th IACR International Conference on Practice and Theory of Public Key Cryptography, Virtual Event, 10-13 May 2021, Proceedings, Part II. LNCS, vol. 12711, pp. 469–498. Springer (2021). https://doi.org/10.1007/978-3-030-75248-4_17
33. Schnorr, C.P.: Efficient identification and signatures for smart cards. In: Proceedings of the 9th Annual International Cryptology Conference, pp. 239–252. CRYPTO '89 (1989)
34. Schnorr, C.P.: Efficient signature generation by smart cards. J. Cryptol. **4**(3), 161–174 (1991)
35. Segev, G., Sharabi, A., Yogev, E.: Rogue-instance security for batch knowledge proofs. In: Proceedings of the 23th Theory of Cryptography Conference, pp. 121–157. TCC 2023 (2023)

36. Shoup, V.: Lower bounds for discrete logarithms and related problems. In: Proceedings of the 16th International Conference on the Theory and Application of Cryptographic Techniques, pp. 256–266. EUROCRYPT 1997 (1997)
37. Valiant, P.: Incrementally verifiable computation or proofs of knowledge imply time/space efficiency. In: Proceedings of the 5th Theory of Cryptography Conference, pp. 1–18. TCC 2008 (2008)

Kolmogorov and One-Way Functions

Lower Bounds for Levin–Kolmogorov Complexity

Nicholas Brandt$^{(\boxtimes)}$ [iD]

Department of Computer Science, ETH Zurich, Zurich, Switzerland
nicholas.brandt@inf.ethz.ch

Abstract. The hardness of Kolmogorov complexity is intricately connected to the existence of one-way functions and derandomization. An important and elegant notion is Levin's version of Kolmogorov complexity, Kt, and its decisional variant, MKtP. The question whether MKtP can be computed in polynomial time is particularly interesting because it is not subject to known technical barriers such as algebrization or natural proofs that would explain the lack of a proof for MKtP $\notin$ P.

We take a major step towards proving MKtP $\notin$ P by developing a novel yet simple diagonalization technique to show *unconditionally* that MKtP $\notin$ DTIME $[\mathcal{O}(n)]$, i.e., no deterministic linear-time algorithm can solve MKtP on every instance. This allows us to affirm a conjecture by Ren and Santhanam [64] about a non-halting variant of Kt complexity.

Additionally, we give *conditional* lower bounds for MKtP that tolerate either more runtime or one-sided error. If the underlying computational model has a linear-time universal simulation, e.g. random-access machines, then we obtain a quadratic lower bound, i.e., MKtP $\notin$ DTIME $[\mathcal{O}(n^2)]$.

1 Introduction

The formal concept of "complexity" was spearheaded in the 1960's by Solomonoff [68–70], Kolmogorov [42,43], and Chaitin [16,17]. Ideas and techniques from meta-complexity—the computational hardness of complexity—have diffused into adjacent subfields like learning theory, derandomization and cryptography (see Sect. 2 for related work). We refer to Trakhtenbrot [71] for a historical survey of complexity and to the more recent survey by Allender [2].

In this work we focus on Levin's notion of Kolmogorov complexity Kt [44], which elegantly incorporates a time bound and thus evades the undecidability of the original Kolmogorov complexity. The Levin–Kolmogorov complexity of a given string x is the minimum over all programs that produce x of the sum of the program's length plus the logarithm of its runtime, i.e., $Kt(x) = \min_{\Pi \mapsto x}(|\Pi| + \lceil \log_2(t) \rceil)$ where Π computes the string x in time t. Its decisional problem is defined as MKtP $:= \{(x, k) \mid Kt(x) \leq k\}$. For an in-depth introduction to meta-complexity problems we refer the reader to [46].

© International Association for Cryptologic Research 2025
E. Boyle and M. Mahmoody (Eds.): TCC 2024, LNCS 15364, pp. 191–221, 2025.
https://doi.org/10.1007/978-3-031-78011-0_7

In fascinating works Liu and Pass [49,52] uncover a surprising connection between derandomization and the existence of one-way functions (OWF) through Kt complexity. On the one hand, they show that (weak) derandomization BPP $\neq$ EXP is equivalent to the *zero*-sided average-case hardness of MKtP, and on the other that the existence of OWFs is equivalent to the *two*-sided average-case hardness of MKtP. One-way functions are central to modern cryptography: they characterize *symmetric* cryptography, dubbed "Minicrypt" by Impagliazzo [38]. They are necessary and sufficient for: digital signatures [66], (cryptographic) pseudorandom generators [13,25], pseudorandom functions [21], private-key encryption [22], commitment schemes [60] and much more. Moreover, the existence of OWFs is itself equivalent to the hardness of many other meta-complexity problems (see at the end of Sect. 2).

These cross connections add to the importance of understanding the hardness of Kolmogorov complexity. While most variants of complexity have (reasonable) unconditional lower bounds (again see Sect. 2 for related work) and despite the plausible conjecture MKtP $\notin$ NP, only a comparatively weak *unconditional* lower bound for Kt complexity is known. Namely, Hirahara [32] shows that the Kt-random strings $R_{Kt} := \{x \mid Kt(x) \geq |x|\}$ are immune[1] to the circuit class P-uniform ACC^0 (constant depth circuits with constant-modulo gates). Now, one might ask:

Why are there no stronger lower bounds for Kt complexity?

The reason that Hirahara's approach fails for stronger classes is that it requires a satisfiability (SAT) solver of the given class. In fact, Hirahara shows that immunity of R_{Kt} for class C result is indeed equivalent to a SAT solver for C—which explains the lack of a stronger immunity lower bound. However, even considering a weaker (compared to immunity) *worst-case* lower bound, the EXP-completeness of MKtP under BPP reductions [52] explains why there is no worst-case lower bound against probabilistic polynomial-time algorithms (BPP) because it would imply BPP $\neq$ EXP which itself is subject to the relativization barrier [11]. In the face of this barrier we might ask about an even weaker worst-case lower bound against a deterministic polynomial-time algorithms (P). Even proving the comparatively weaker statement MKtP $\notin$ P (mentioned e.g. in [32,61]) is a longstanding open problem at least since Allender et al. [7] posed it explicitly in 2002. This is particularly interesting because MKtP $\notin$ P is *not*[2] subject to technical barriers like algebrization [1,10,39] or natural proofs [63]. Given the lack of barriers it is not clear whether relativizing techniques suffice to prove MKtP $\notin$ P. That our lower bounds relativize can be taken as a hint that relativizing techniques might in fact be strong enough to prove MKtP $\notin$ P.

---

[1] No infinite subset of R_{Kt} is in P-uniform ACC^0.

[2] Ren and Santhanam [64] show that the relativization barrier applies to the problem of approximating MKtP.

2   Contributions and Related Work

Our main contribution is a new diagonalization technique tailored to Kt complexity. Using our technique we give the first unconditional lower bound of Kt complexity against a uniform time class. This constitutes a significant step towards proving MKtP $\notin$ P.

While our diagonalization strategy is fairly simple, its analysis is somewhat involved and simplifying it would be interesting on its own. We stress that our approach differs strongly from all previous approaches like the one of Hirahara [32] or for randomized complexity notions [31,61]. A major technical difficulty for Kt lower bounds based on diagonalization is that the diagonalization algorithm for Kt needs to be *deterministic*, and thus no probabilistic tools from complexity theory are available. In Sect. 3 we explain why this leads to a black-box barrier for diagonalization-based proofs and how our technique overcomes it. Also, note that derandomization is not useful here because a) we are interested in an *unconditional* bound, and b) Liu and Pass [52] already show that (weak) derandomization implies a stronger zero-sided lower bound. Our main result is summarized as follows:

Theorem 1. *The Levin–Kolmogorov complexity cannot be decided in deterministic linear time in the worst-case, i.e.,* MKtP $\notin$ DTIME $[\mathcal{O}(n)]$.

On the $\widetilde{Kt}$ notion of Ren and Santhanam. Because our lower bound relativizes we can partially affirm a conjecture (Open Problem 4.7.) by Ren and Santhanam [64]. They introduce a "non-halting" variant $\widetilde{Kt}$ of Levin–Kolmogorov complexity whose definition[3] is almost identical to the standard Kt complexity except that the witness program producing a given string need not halt after writing the string on its tape. Ren and Santhanam conjecture that—despite their close definitions—the two notions behave quite differently in that infinitely many strings x have $\widetilde{Kt}(x) \lneq Kt(x)$. By analyzing the proof of Theorem 1 we can give a concrete example affirming their conjecture. Concretely, infinitely many prefixes of Chaitin's constant Ω have $\widetilde{Kt}(\Omega_1||...||\Omega_\ell) <_{\mathsf{io}} K(\Omega_1||...||\Omega_\ell) \leq Kt(\Omega_1||...||\Omega_\ell)$. To see this assume the opposite (all-but-finitely many prefixes have $\widetilde{Kt}(\Omega_1||...||\Omega_\ell) \geq_{\mathsf{abf}} Kt(\Omega_1||...||\Omega_\ell)$), then our proof of Theorem 1 allows us to prove the linear-time hardness of $\widetilde{Kt}$ relative to any oracle. However, Ren and Santhanam [64] already give an oracle relative to which $\widetilde{Kt}$ is computable in linear time. Pushing the limits of our technique we find $\widetilde{Kt}(\Omega_1||...||\Omega_\ell) \leq_{\mathsf{io}} Kt(\Omega_1||...||\Omega_\ell) - \Theta(\ln\ln(\ell))$ falling short of the stronger conjecture $\widetilde{Kt}(\Omega_1||...||\Omega_\ell) \leq_{\mathsf{io}} Kt(\Omega_1||...||\Omega_\ell)/\Theta(1)$ as required by Ren and Santhanam.

In particular, relative to their oracle Kt can be approximated in linear time to within a multiplicative factor of $2 + \epsilon$ for any $\epsilon > 0$. Our relativizing result

---

[3]   Formally, Ren and Santhanam [64] define their $\widetilde{Kt}$ notion not relative to any UTM but more informally "over all machines". We thus consider a $\widetilde{Kt}$ notion that is defined formally analogously to our notion Definition 2.

is compatible with [64] because Ren and Santhanam only show that proving hardness of Kt for small thresholds $\lesssim n/\left(2+\epsilon\right)$ requires a non-relativizing proof but we show hardness of Kt for a large threshold $\gtrsim n$. Consequently, showing (worst-case) hardness of Kt for small thresholds seems qualitatively harder than for large thresholds. This should be contrasted with recent developments [48,51] where the worst-case hardness (of a conditioned version) of K^t for different thresholds between n^δ and $n-2$ is equivalent (Thm 1.1. in [51]).

Comparison to Hirahara's Lower Bound. Hirahara [32] shows an incomparable unconditional lower bound for Kt complexity, namely, that the Kt-random strings R_{Kt} are immune to P-uniform ACC^0 (see [2] for a nice description of Hirahara's approach). Compared to Hirahara's immunity lower bound (no infinite subset can be decided), our result is weaker in that it only provides worst-case hardness (no algorithm can decide correctly for *every* string). On the other hand, our lower bound holds against deterministic linear time $\mathsf{DTIME}\left[\mathcal{O}\left(n\right)\right]$ which—we argue—is closer to P than the rather weak circuit class P-uniform ACC^0 for which Hirahara's lower bound holds. The only case in which our result would be subsumed by [32] is the implausible case that $\mathsf{P} = $ P-uniform ACC^0 which would already imply $\mathsf{MKtP} \notin \mathsf{P}$ and in fact a nontrivial SAT solver for P.

We emphasize that our proof strategy differs conceptually from the one in [32]. The approach of Hirahara is based on the "algorithmic method" of Williams [72,73] where a nontrivial satisfiability algorithm for a circuit class yields a lower bound against that class. Obtaining a stronger immunity of R_{Kt} using the Hirahara–Williams approach is equivalent to satisfiability algorithms for stronger circuit classes which may be subject to known barriers such as algebrization [1,10,39] or natural proofs [63]. In comparison, our approach opens new avenues for improved lower bounds that possibly evade these barriers. See Sect. 3 for a discussion of the limitations of our technique and possible ways to overcome them.

Stronger Conditional Bounds. By analyzing our approach for the proof of Theorem 1 we are able to give conditional lower bounds which either tolerate larger runtime or one-sided error.

Theorem 2. *For each time bound* $\mathsf{t}\left(n\right) \geq n$ *at least one of the following is true:*

1. $\mathsf{MKtP} \notin \mathsf{DTIME}\left[\mathsf{t}\right]$,
2. $\mathsf{MKtP} \notin \mathsf{Heur}_{\gamma_{\mathsf{fp}},\gamma_{\mathsf{fn}}}\mathsf{DTIME}\left[\mathcal{O}\left(n\right)\right]$ *with no false positive error* $\gamma_{\mathsf{fp}}\left(n\right) := 0$ *and false negative error* $\gamma_{\mathsf{fn}}\left(n\right) := {}^1\!/2n\mathsf{t}(2n) - 2/2^n$,

More Related Work. In recent years there has been a flurry of meta-complexity results—too many to discuss here ([4,12,23,28–30,32–34,36,37,47,50,53–56,58, 59,61,65] to name only a few). Here, we restrict ourselves to some Kt-related notions and their resp. lower bounds to contextualize our lower bound for MKtP.

The canonical time-bounded variant $\mathsf{MK}^t\mathsf{P}$ [24,41,42,67] of Kolmogorov complexity is parameterized over some time bound t and limits the witness program of a given string x to run in time at most $\mathsf{t}\left(|x|\right)$. Limiting the witness program's runtime makes this notion computable, opposed to standard Kolmogorov complexity. For exponential time bounds t Hirahara [32] shows that $\mathsf{MK^t P}$ is EXP-complete under ZPP reductions and even that the set of K^t-random strings is immune to P (no infinitely large subset of K^t-random strings is in P).

Allender et al. [8] show that the Levin–Kolmogorov complexity MKtP is EXP-complete under P/poly or NP reductions, i.e., $\mathsf{MKtP} \in \mathsf{P/poly} \iff \mathsf{EXP} \subseteq \mathsf{P/poly}$. Liu and Pass [52] improve this to BPP reductions, i.e., $\mathsf{MKtP} \in \mathsf{BPP} \iff \mathsf{EXP} = \mathsf{BPP}$. Thus, any nontrivial derandomization $\mathsf{BPP} \neq \mathsf{EXP}$ is equivalent to a lower bound $\mathsf{MKtP} \notin \mathsf{BPP}$ against bounded-error probabilistic TMs. In turn, this means that any barrier preventing us from proving $\mathsf{BPP} \neq \mathsf{EXP}$ also prevents us from proving the randomized lower bound $\mathsf{MKtP} \notin \mathsf{BPP}$. In contrast, our lower bound $\mathsf{MKtP} \notin \mathsf{DTIME}\left[\mathcal{O}(n)\right]$ is much weaker both in the quantitative runtime (linear vs. polynomial) as well as the computational model (deterministic vs. probabilistic)—and thus evades known barriers.

Oliveira [61] introduces rKt—a randomized version of Levin–Kolmogorov complexity—where the witness program of a given string x must produce that string x on at least a 2/3-fraction of randomnesses. This randomized complexity is BPE-complete (Lemma 12 in [61]) and Oliveira shows hardness of his notion against quasipolynomial time bounded-error TMs, i.e., $\mathsf{MrKtP} \notin \mathsf{BPTIME}\left[n^{\log(n)^{\Theta(1)}}\right]$. Later Later Hirahara [31] improves that bound to $\mathsf{GapMrKtP} \notin \text{io-}\mathsf{BPTIME}\left[2^{\epsilon n}\right]$ for any $\epsilon \gtrless 0$. Oliveira [61] also gives a potential avenue toward proving $\mathsf{MKtP} \notin \mathsf{P}$ via the implication $\mathsf{MrKtP} \in \mathsf{Promise\text{-}EXP} \implies \mathsf{MKtP} \notin \mathsf{P}$.

For a nondeterministic NEXP-complete complexity notion KNt Allender et al. [9] show unconditionally that the set of KNt-random strings is not in NP ∩ co-NP.

The canonical problem for circuit complexity is nowadays called the minimum circuit size problem (MCSP) [40]. It has been previously considered by Trakhtenbrot [71] (Task 4), and Levin reportedly delayed the publication of his work on NP-completeness to include MCSP. Since $\mathsf{MCSP} \in \mathsf{NP}$ an unconditional lower bound seems unlikely; the question is rather whether MCSP is NP-complete which is related to major open questions in theoretical computer science. We refer the interested reader to [2,5] and references therein for more details about the NP-completeness of MCSP.

Oliveira, Pich, and Santhanam [62] give "hardness magnification" results for gap versions of MKtP and MCSP. They establish that slightly improved lower bounds for these problems can be "magnified" to strong lower bounds. The reason why we cannot use their result to magnify our linear-time lower bound is a difference in the parameter regime (similar to [64]). They consider the hardness of distinguishing strings of low complexity from string of even lower complexity (e.g. $n^\epsilon + \Theta(\log n)$ vs. n^ϵ). On the other hand, we crucially use the fact (as our counter assumption) that we are able to exactly compute the complexity of a given string $x \in \{0,1\}^n$ even when $Kt(x) \approx n$.

Huang, Ilango, and Ren [35] show unconditional hardness of an oracle variant of the minimum circuit size problem (MOCSP) using a cryptographic tool called witness encryption [19].

Connection to One-Way Functions. In recent years there has emerged a research effort to characterize one-way functions (OWF) by the hardness of meta-complexity problems. As an incomplete list: OWFs are equivalent to the mild two-sided hardness of $\mathsf{MK^tP}$ [49], the two-sided hardness of MKtP [52], the two-sided hardness[4] of an (NP-complete) conditional variant McKTP [6] of Allender's KT complexity [3], the mild two-sided hardness of (parameterized versions of) $\mathsf{MK^tP}$ against sublinear time over a smooth range of parameters [48], the mild average-case hardness of the probabilistic $\mathsf{MpK^tP}$ (introduced in [20]) for polynomial t [53], the *worst-case* hardness of a promise version of $\mathsf{MK^tP}$ (with small computational depth) [51], the hardness of a distributional variant of Kolmogorov complexity under the assumption $\mathsf{NP} \not\subseteq \mathsf{io\text{-}P/poly}$ [27].

3   Technical Overview

To simplify this overview, we assume that the UTM $\mathcal{U}$ simulates any given program Π without any overhead. In the formal proof we will account for the logarithmic overhead of the UTM.

A natural approach to proving lower bounds for a given meta-complexity problem is to assume that the problem is easy and then leverage an efficient solver for that problem to quickly construct a highly complex string (w.r.t. to the given complexity measure). The historical proof of the undecidability of standard Kolmogorov complexity as well as Hirahara's much more sophisticated lower bound for Kt complexity [32] are instantiations of this approach.

To directly apply this approach to Kt complexity it is useful to define what we call the "critical threshold" $\theta_{\Pi,t} := |\Pi| + \lceil \log_2(t) \rceil$ of a given TM Π after t steps of its execution. We will assume that the decision problem MKtP can be worst-case decided by a TM Π_{Kt} in linear time. Then we construct a TM $\Pi_\sharp$ (using Π_{Kt} as a subroutine) that quickly outputs a Kt-random string z (i.e., $Kt(z) \geq |z|$). To reach a formal contradiction, our TM $\Pi_\sharp$ must in t steps produce a Kt-random string z that is strictly longer than the critical threshold $\theta_{\Pi_\sharp,t}$, i.e., $\theta_{\Pi_\sharp,t} \geq Kt(z) \geq |z| \gtrsim \theta_{\Pi_\sharp,t}$ where the first inequality is by the definition of Kt complexity and the fact that Π outputs z in t steps, the second inequality is the Kt-randomness of z, and the last inequality is by assumption. (In this overview, we gloss over some minor definitional details that are rigorously taken care of in the formal proof.)

Black-Box Barrier. A conceptual problem to the algorithmic approach for a lower bound for MKtP is that we know little about the *structure* of the Kt-random strings $R_{Kt} := \{x \mid Kt(x) \geq |x|\}$. We say a TM Π_{BB} yields a contradiction in a *black-box* way, if given access to *any* set of potentially Kt-random

---

[4] Here, the error probabilities are not equal for both directions.

strings $R \neq \{0,1\}^*$ it produces a string $z \notin R$ in t steps such that $\theta_{\Pi_{\mathsf{BB}},t} \lesssim |z|$. Intuitively, a potential TM Π_{BB} ignores the structure of the set R since it works for any arbitrary R. Such a Π_{BB} cannot exist because we can define $R_{\Pi_{\mathsf{BB}}} := \{0,1\}^* \setminus \{z \mid \Pi_{\mathsf{BB}}$ queries z to its oracle or outputs z in t steps and $\theta_{\Pi_{\mathsf{BB}},t} \lesssim |z|\}$ that breaks Π_{BB}. This black-box barrier explains why a lower bound for *deterministic* Kt is so hard to obtain (as opposed to randomized rKt[5]). So, for our algorithmic approach to succeed we need to exploit some property exhibited by the *actual* set of Kt-random strings R_{Kt} but not by any set $R_{\Pi_{\mathsf{BB}}}$. Before we explain how, let us first present our rather simple strategy for a TM Π_{ℓ}.

Our Search Strategy. As a first step we use the length-monotonic depth-first-search described in Fig. 1. The high-level idea is to traverse the binary tree of finite strings starting with the string 0.[6] Whenever the i-th string z_i is visited our search algorithm TRAVERSE queries z_i to its oracle R_{Kt} and if $z_i \in R_{Kt}$ descends to the next length with $z_{i+1} := z_i || 0$ (the left child of z_i), otherwise it continues with the lexicographically next string of the same length $z_{i+1} := \mathrm{next}(z_i)$ (the right neighbor of z_i). See Fig. 2 for an exemplary run of TRAVERSE. Crucially, the length of the visited strings is non-decreasing. We note that our TRAVERSE algorithm doesn't terminate and hence does not suffice for a proper contradiction (even if it visits a Kt-random string quickly enough). To actually reach a contradiction we have to a) construct a TM Π_{TRA} implementing TRAVERSE that at some point visits a string $\check{z}$ within $\hat{t}$ steps s.t. $\theta_{\Pi_{\mathsf{TRA}},\hat{t}} \lesssim |\check{z}|$, and b) implement a mechanism s.t. Π_{TRA} also recognizes this fact—so that it can terminate and output $\check{z}$.

As a stepping stone it will be useful to see that TRAVERSE visits infinitely many different strings $(z_i)_{i \in \mathbb{N}}$. This follows from the existence of at least one Kt-random string of each length on which TRAVERSE descends to the next length. Moreover, we observe that TRAVERSE never "wraps around". That is TRAVERSE never reaches an all 1s string at the right border of the binary tree. Assuming an infinite (1-random) string s whose every prefix is Kt-random, this is also easy to see. Whenever TRAVERSE visits a prefix $z_i = s_1 || ... || s_\ell$ it descends to the next string $z_{i+1} := s_1 || ... || s_\ell || 0$—thus always staying "to the left" of the infinite string s in the binary tree. Glossing over a minor technical issue, we can take Chaitin's constant Ω (encoded in binary) to be such an infinite 1-random string. In fact, the 1-randomness of Ω is the crucial information about the actual set of Kt-random strings R_{Kt} that allows our TRAVERSE algorithm to sidestep the aforementioned black-box barrier.

Analysis. Next, we analyze the behavior of TRAVERSE to prove that after some $\hat{t}$ steps TRAVERSE visits some Kt-random string $z_{\hat{i}}$ s.t. $\theta_{\Pi_{\mathsf{TRA}},\hat{t}} \lesssim |z_{\hat{i}}|$. Let $Z := \{z_i \mid i \in \mathbb{N}\}$ be the set of visited strings. Let $i_\ell := \left| Z \cap \{0,1\}^{\leq \ell} \right|$ be the number of strings visited of length at most ℓ. Let $Z_\ell := Z \cap \{0,1\}^\ell =$

---

[5] It is not even clear how $R_{\Pi_{\mathsf{BB}}}$ would be defined for probabilistic Π_{BB}.

[6] We choose to start with 0 instead of ε because it simplifies some edge cases.

TRAVERSE
_____

1 : $z_1 := 0 \in \{0,1\}^*$

2 :   **for** $i \in \mathbb{N}_{\geq 1}$

3 :   **if** $Kt(z_i) \geq |z_i|$ **then** $z_{i+1} := z_i||0$

4 :   **else** $z_{i+1} := \text{next}(z_i)$

Fig. 1. Our (simplified) traversal algorithm.

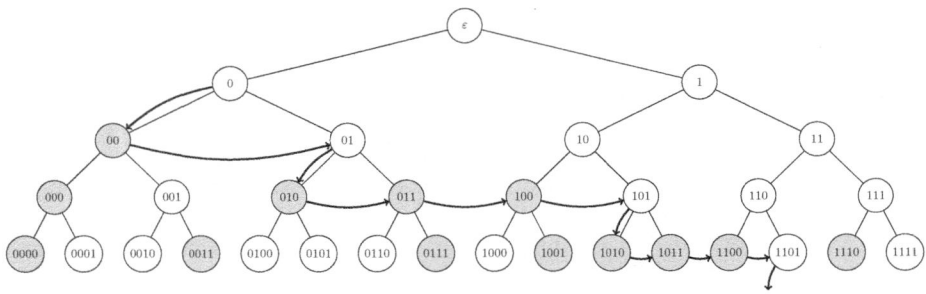

Fig. 2. Exemplary run of TRAVERSE: white strings are Kt-random.

$\{z_{i_{\ell-1}}||0,...,z_{i_\ell}\}$ be the set of visited strings of length exactly ℓ. Let $S_\ell := \{z \in \{0,1\}^\ell \mid int(z) \geq int(z_{i_\ell})\} \subset \{0,1\}^\ell$ be the lexicographical successors of Z_ℓ (the right neighbors of Z_ℓ). Now, note that because TRAVERSE doesn't wrap around, it holds that $Z_{\ell+1} \cup S_{\ell+1} = (\{z_{i_\ell}\} \cup S_\ell)||\{0,1\}$ and thus $|Z_{\ell+1}| - |S_{\ell+1}| = 2|S_\ell| + 2$. Let $\gamma_\ell := |Z_\ell|/|Z_\ell \cup S_\ell|$ be the fraction of strings of length ℓ that TRAVERSE actually visits to the strings that it could potentially visit. By recursion the number of visited strings of length ℓ can be expressed as $|Z_\ell| = \gamma_\ell \sum_{\kappa=1}^{\ell} 2^\kappa \prod_{i=\ell-\kappa+1}^{\ell} (1 - \gamma_i)$. For our approach we'd like i_ℓ and thus $|Z_\ell|$ to be asymptotically small. An informal argument for this is that the formula for $|Z_\ell|$ expresses a "self-limiting" behavior that emerges from our TRAVERSE algorithm. Namely, the faster γ_i goes to 0 the smaller $|Z_\ell|$ because $|Z_\ell|$ depends linearly on γ_ℓ. On the other hand, $|Z_\ell|$ depends on the product $\prod_{i=j-\kappa+1}^{\kappa} (1 - \gamma_i)$ which is closer to 1 the faster γ_i goes to 0. These antagonistic influences suggest there is some asymptotic rate of γ_i that leads to an asymptotically maximal $|Z_\ell|$. This behavior of $|Z_\ell|$ can also be captured informally from the algorithmic view of TRAVERSE. Whenever $|Z_{\ell-1}|$ is large this means that TRAVERSE moves far to the right, forcing the next $|Z_\ell|$ to be small because only few strings remain to the right. In this manner, there cannot be many successive $|Z_j|$ that are large. Turning back to the more formal analysis, we can bound the number of visited strings of length at most ℓ by

$$i_\ell := \sum_{j=1}^{\ell} |Z_j| = \sum_{j=1}^{\ell} \gamma_j \sum_{\kappa=1}^{j} 2^\kappa \prod_{i=j-\kappa+1}^{j} (1 - \gamma_i) \leq \sum_{j=1}^{\ell} \gamma_j \sum_{\kappa=1}^{j} 2^\kappa e^{\sigma_j - \kappa - \sigma_j} \quad (1)$$

where $\sigma_j := \sum_{i=1}^{j} \gamma_i$. Using the following technical lemma we can bound this quantity.

Lemma 1 (Infinitely-often bound). *For any sequence $(\gamma_j)_{j \in \mathbb{N}}$ with $\gamma_j \in [0,1]$ and $\sigma_\ell := \sum_{i=1}^{\ell} \gamma_i$ it holds that infinitely often $\sum_{j=1}^{\ell} \gamma_j \sum_{\kappa=1}^{j} 2^\kappa e^{\sigma_j - \kappa - \sigma_j} \leq_{\text{io}} 2^\ell / \ell \ln(\ell)$.*

The rigorous proof of Lemma 1 is contained in the full version [14]. This means that for infinitely many "critical" lengths $\hat{\ell}$ when TRAVERSE visits the last string $z_{i_{\hat{\ell}}} \in \{0,1\}^{\hat{\ell}} \cap R_{Kt}$ it took at most $\mathcal{O}\left(i_{\hat{\ell}} \cdot \hat{\ell}\right)$ steps to do so—assuming MKtP $\in$ DTIME $[\mathcal{O}(n)]$. Recall that for any length ℓ it holds that $z_{i_\ell} \in R_{Kt}$ because z_{i_ℓ} is the last string of length ℓ that TRAVERSE visits from which it descends to the next length. Now, if TRAVERSE were to output any such $z_{i_{\hat{\ell}}}$, then we would reach the contradiction

$$\hat{\ell} \leq Kt\left(z_{i_{\hat{\ell}}}\right) \leq |\Pi_{\text{TRA}}| + \left\lceil \log_2\left(\mathcal{O}\left(i_{\hat{\ell}} \cdot \hat{\ell}\right)\right) \right\rceil \leq \hat{\ell} - \ln \ln\left(\hat{\ell}\right) + \mathcal{O}(1) . \quad (2)$$

The missing piece is hence to construct a TM Π'_{TRA} that implements TRAVERSE such that it is aware of its own critical threshold—so it knows when to output a string $z_{i_{\hat{\ell}}}$. A generic approach is to simply simulate TRAVERSE with a $\mathcal{O}(n \ln(n))$ slowdown. However, this would result in

$$\hat{\ell} \leq Kt\left(z_{i_{\hat{\ell}}}\right) \leq |\Pi_{\text{TRA}}| + \left\lceil \log_2\left(\mathcal{O}\left(i_{\hat{\ell}} \cdot \hat{\ell} \cdot \ln\left(i_{\hat{\ell}} \cdot \hat{\ell}\right)\right)\right) \right\rceil \quad (3)$$

$$\leq \hat{\ell} + \ln\left(\hat{\ell}\right) - \ln \ln\left(\hat{\ell}\right) + \mathcal{O}(1) \quad (4)$$

which does not suffice for a contradiction. Hence, we let Π'_{TRA} count the size $|Z_\ell|$ not one-by-one but only once it reaches a Kt-random string (the last string of each length). This way, each length ℓ incurs an additive runtime overhead of $\mathcal{O}(\ell)$ instead of $\Omega(|Z_\ell| \ell \ln(\ell))$. Due to space restrictions and because the details of the step-counting don't provide much conceptual insight, we defer these details to the formal proof of Theorem 1.

On Lemma 1. In the previous paragraph we have bounded the runtime of our contradicting TM Π'_{TRA} in terms of the number of visited strings i_ℓ which in turn can be bounded by the term in Lemma 1. As alluded to earlier the specific term in Lemma 1 arises from the "self-limiting" behavior of our TRAVERSE algorithm. Recall that on the binary tree TRAVERSE only moves to the right neighbor or the left child of the current string. Fix some length $\hat{\ell}$. If for many of the previous lengths $\ell \lesssim \hat{\ell}$ the TM TRAVERSE visited few strings, then the number $i_{\hat{\ell}}$ of visited strings at length $\hat{\ell}$ will be small by definition. On the other hand, if TRAVERSE visits many strings of length ℓ, then TRAVERSE moves farther to the right, leaving fewer strings of subsequent lengths to be potentially visited. With this intuition in mind, it remains to prove Lemma 1 formally, though we defer the rigorous proof of Lemma 1 to the full version [14]. Instead, here we give a superficial sketch of our proof.

The basic idea is to prove Lemma 1 by contradiction, hence we may assume

$$\sum_{j=1}^{\ell} \gamma_j \sum_{\kappa=1}^{j} 2^{\kappa-\ell} e^{\sigma_{j-\kappa}-\sigma_j} \geq 1/\ell \ln(\ell) \tag{5}$$

for all $\ell \in \mathbb{N}$. We sum this inequality and bound the inner sum on the left-hand side of Eq. (5) by $2^{j-\ell+1}$ (using the trivial inequality $\sigma_j - \sigma_{j-\kappa} \geq 0$) to obtain a first lower bound for $\sigma_{\hat{\ell}}$, i.e.,

$$2\sigma_{\hat{\ell}} \geq \sum_{\ell=1}^{\hat{\ell}} \sum_{j=1}^{\ell} \gamma_j 2^{j-\ell+1} \geq 2 \sum_{\ell=1}^{\hat{\ell}} \frac{1}{\ell \ln(\ell)} \approx \int \frac{1}{\hat{\ell} \ln\left(\hat{\ell}\right)} d\hat{\ell} \in \Omega\left(\ln \ln\left(\hat{\ell}\right)\right) . \tag{6}$$

Here, we use the crucial property that the antiderivative of $1/x \ln(x)$ is superconstant.

In the next steps we reuse the same strategy. Instead of bounding the inner sum on the left-hand side of Eq. (5) trivially by $2^{j-\ell+1}$ we use the stronger bound from Eq. (6) to obtain an even stronger bound $\sigma_{\hat{\ell}} \in \Omega(\ln(\hat{\ell})^{1/17})$. Reapplying the same strategy a third time finally yields the lower bound $\sigma_{\hat{\ell}} \in \Omega(\ln(\hat{\ell})^3)$ which is strong enough to yield a contradiction to Eq. (5). In this brief sketch we glossed over many details and refer the interested reader to the formal proof in Sect. 6. However, a quick sanity check may be in order at this point. If $\gamma_j \leq 1/j \ln(j)$, then Lemma 1 holds trivially. Considering slightly larger $\gamma_j := \epsilon/j$ for any constant $\epsilon > 0$ (thus $\sigma_j \approx \epsilon \ln(j)$) yields $\mathcal{O}(\sum_{j=1}^{\ell} \gamma_j \sum_{\kappa=1}^{j} 2^{\kappa} e^{\sigma_{j-\kappa}-\sigma_j}) = \mathcal{O}(\sum_{j=1}^{\ell} \frac{1}{j} \sum_{\kappa=1}^{j} 2^{\kappa} (1 - \kappa/j)^{\epsilon}) = \mathcal{O}(2^{\ell}/\ell^{1+\epsilon})$ which is also consistent with Lemma 1.

Robustness. While (unbounded) Kolmogorov complexity is quite robust against definitional changes (by invariance theorems), resource-bounded notions of complexity are more sensitive. There are many ways of defining Kt complexity formally: representative variations include [32,52,64]. Our Definition 2 essentially corresponds to the one in [32]. In general, the notion of Kt complexity depends—aside from the underlying computational model—on whether

- the runtime is measure in terms of the number of steps of the *simulated* program Π (direct time) or the *simulating* universal machine $\mathcal{U}$ (universal time),
- the witness program Π produces the entire string x (global compression) on the empty input or outputs the i-th bit on input $bin(i)$ (local compression).

Lower bound	Global compression	Local compression
Direct time	DTIME $\left[\mathcal{O}\left(n^2\right)\right]$	DTIME $\left[\mathcal{O}\left(n\right)\right]$
Universal time + const. overhead	DTIME $\left[\mathcal{O}\left(n^2\right)\right]$	DTIME $\left[\mathcal{O}\left(n\right)\right]$
Universal time + log. overhead	DTIME $\left[\mathcal{O}\left(n\right)\right]$ $^{(*)}$	–

Fig. 3. Our lower bounds for several definitional variantions of Kt complexity. As a rule of thumb going from global to local, or from constant to logarithmic simulation overhead decreases the lower bound by a linear factor. Our results are formally stated for the setting $(*)$.

- the universal machine is "prefix-free" (Kt) or "plain" (Ct).

First, we state that currently our technique only works for prefix-free complexity because it requires an (infinite) strings whose prefixes are Kt-random, and we only know such a string for prefix-free complexity (there is no plain 1-random string; Sect. 6.1 in [18]). Though, conceivably one might find another way of arguing the "no-wrap-around" property of our search algorithm, to extend our result to plain Ct complexity.

Second, we remark that resource-bounded *universal time* complexity is a somewhat fragile notion that does not enjoy an invariance theorem. The reason is that one can always modify a universal machine to artificially run an arbitrary amount of time to increase the $\lceil \log_2 (t_{\mathcal{U}} (\Pi)) \rceil$ term arbitrarily, yet the machine remains universal. So, to remain a meaningful notion we only consider universal machines with at most logarithmic overhead.

All of our formal results are stated for the setting of global compression, universal time measurement and logarithmic simulation overhead. Each result can be adapted to other settings as follows: When considering direct time measurement or models with constant simulation overhead[7], we can actually strenghen our lower bound to DTIME $\left[\mathcal{O}\left(n^2\right)\right]$ because (to reach a contradiction) our search algorithm saves a factor of roughly ℓ on level ℓ in runtime—which can be spend on an (assumed) more expensive DTIME $\left[\mathcal{O}\left(\ell^2\right)\right]$ solver for MKtP. Independently, if we consider local compression, we have to reduce the lower bound for global compression by a linear factor. The reason is that witness programs for global compression are required to run for at least $|x|$ steps but witness programs for local compression are only required to run for $\mathcal{O}\left(\log_2 |x|\right)$ steps. We summarize the instantiations of our main result in different settings in Fig. 3.

Limitations and Stronger Conditional Lower Bounds. As presented, our strategy using Π'_{TRA} cannot (unconditionally) tolerate any errors because

- if Π'_{TRA} obtains a false negative query response (false high complexity), then it outputs a string that is not actually Kt-random which does not violate the definition of Kt-randomness, and

---

[7] E.g. random-access machines and Kolmogorov–Uspensky machines.

- if Π'_{TRA} obtains a false positive query response (false low complexity), then it may skip (from left to right) the separating line defined by Chaitin's 1-random constant, thus potentially increasing the runtime prohibitively.

However, we can conditionally tolerate some (false negative) one-sided errors. For example, suppose $\mathsf{MKtP} \in \mathsf{DTIME}\left[\mathcal{O}\left(n^2\right)\right]$ can be worst-case decided in quadratic time by a TM Π_{Kt,n^2}, and $\mathsf{MKtP} \in \mathsf{Heur}_{0,\gamma_{\mathsf{fn}}}\mathsf{DTIME}\left[\mathcal{O}\left(n\right)\right]$ can be decided in linear time with false negative probability $\gamma_{\mathsf{fn}}\left(n\right) \in o\left(1/n^2\right)$ (and no false positives) by a TM $\widetilde{\Pi}_{Kt,n}$. Then we can construct a modified TM Π''_{TRA} which for each visited string z_i first queries z_i to the quicker linear-time heuristic $\widetilde{\Pi}_{Kt,n}$. If $\widetilde{\Pi}_{Kt,n}$ outputs $\widetilde{b} = 0$ (high complexity), Π''_{TRA} queries z_i to the slower Π_{Kt,n^2} to obtain the definitive answer $b = 0 \iff z_i \in R_{Kt}$. If $\widetilde{b} = 0 \wedge b = 0$, then Π''_{TRA} descends to $z_{i+1} := z_i||0$, otherwise $z_{i+1} := \text{next}\left(z_i\right)$. First, note that Π''_{TRA} visits exactly the same set of strings (in the same order) as TRAVERSE. In contrast to the unconditional case, however, we find that whenever Π''_{TRA} visits a string $z_{i_{\hat{\ell}}}$ of critical length $\hat{\ell}$ it took at most

$$\mathcal{O}\left(\sum_{\ell=1}^{\hat{\ell}} |Z_\ell| \cdot \ell + 2^\ell \gamma_{\mathsf{fn}}\left(\ell\right) \cdot \ell^2\right) = \mathcal{O}\left(i_{\hat{\ell}} \cdot \hat{\ell} + 2^{\hat{\ell}} \gamma_{\mathsf{fn}}\left(\hat{\ell}\right) \cdot \hat{\ell}^2\right) \subseteq o\left(2^{\hat{\ell}}\right) \quad (7)$$

steps because at length ℓ there are at most $2^\ell \gamma_{\mathsf{fn}}\left(\ell\right)$ strings on which $\widetilde{\Pi}_{Kt,n}$ gives a false negative answer.[8] Consequently, when Π''_{TRA} visits and outputs such a string $z_{i_{\hat{\ell}}}$ it yields the contradiction

$$\hat{\ell} \leq Kt\left(z_{i_{\hat{\ell}}}\right) \leq |\Pi_{\mathsf{TRA}}| + \left\lceil \log_2\left(o\left(2^{\hat{\ell}}\right)\right)\right\rceil \leq \hat{\ell} - \omega\left(1\right) + \mathcal{O}\left(1\right) . \quad (8)$$

On Overcoming the Limitations. First, we want to point out a curious effect reminiscent of Williams's algorithmic method where a computational upper bound implies another lower bound. Namely, any nontrivial *worst-case* upper bound for MKtP (Item 1 in Theorem 2 is false) implies an improved linear-time lower bound for MKtP with one-sided error (Item 2 in Theorem 2 is true).

Above we state that—at first glance—our approach cannot tolerate any errors unconditionally. In truth, our approach actually tolerates some false positive error, e.g. $\gamma_{\mathsf{fp}}\left(n\right) \leq 1/4n\ln(n+1)^2$. Recall that the reason given above for not tolerating false positive errors is because then our algorithm might "skip" Chaitin's 1-random constant and thus the recursion formula $Z_{\ell+1} \cup S_{\ell+1} = \left(\{z_{i_\ell}\} \cup S_\ell\right) || \{0, 1\}$ no longer holds. In turns out[9] that there are many Kt-random strings of each length, in fact, they have an arbitrary (constant) density. Thus, it is fine for our algorithm to skip some prefixes of 1-random strings in each length, because as long as we only skip a few, there will always be sufficiently many remaining "'to the right" of our algorithm's current position.

---

[8] Here, we naturally assume that $2^\ell \gamma_{\mathsf{fn}}\left(\ell\right)$ is non-decreasing.
[9] See the full version [14].

Corollary 1. *Let γ_{fp} be a false positive error rate s.t. $\sum_{\ell=1}^{\infty} \gamma_{\mathsf{fp}}(\ell) \lesssim 1$,[10] and let $\gamma_{\mathsf{fn}}(n) := 0$ be no false negative error. The Levin–Kolmogorov complexity cannot be decided in deterministic linear time even with some false positive error, i.e.,* $\mathsf{MKtP} \notin \mathsf{Heur}_{\gamma_{\mathsf{fp}},\gamma_{\mathsf{fn}}} \mathsf{DTIME}\left[\mathcal{O}(n)\right].$

The requirement $\sum_{\ell=1}^{\infty} \gamma_{\mathsf{fp}}(\ell) \lesssim 1$ is sufficient because in length ℓ we skip up to $2^{\ell}\gamma_{\mathsf{fp}}(\ell)$ strings. This means that at length $\hat{\ell}$ we might have skipped up to $\sum_{\ell=1}^{\hat{\ell}} 2^{\hat{\ell}-\ell} \cdot 2^{\ell}\gamma_{\mathsf{fp}}(\ell)$ strings (all strings of length $\hat{\ell}$ that have a skipped string as a prefix) whereas we have at least $2^{\hat{\ell}}(1-\hat{\epsilon})$ many (prefixes of) 1-random strings in length $\hat{\ell}$ (for any $\hat{\epsilon} \in \mathbb{R}_{\geq 0}$). Thus, $\sum_{\ell=1}^{\infty} \gamma_{\mathsf{fp}}(\ell) \lesssim 1$ ensures that in each length there are always more prefixes of 1-random strings than are potentially skipped for $\hat{\epsilon} := (1 - \sum_{\ell=1}^{\infty} \gamma_{\mathsf{fp}}(\ell))/2$.

Another obvious question is whether our technique is capable of proving a worst-case bound beyond linear time. By an improved analysis of the proof of Lemma 1 we can push our bound to slightly superlinear time (resp. superquadratic for the corresponding settings in Fig. 3).

Corollary 2. *The Levin–Kolmogorov complexity cannot be decided in deterministic slightly superlinear time in the worst-case, i.e.,* $\mathsf{MKtP} \notin \bigcup_{k\in\mathbb{N}} \mathsf{DTIME}\left[\prod_{i=0}^{k} \ln^{(i)}(n)\right]$ *where $\ln^{(i)}$ is the i times iterated logarithm (with $\ln^{(0)}(n) := n$).*

Corollaries 1 and 2 can be combined. The reason for this somewhat peculiar time bound $\mathfrak{t}(n) := \prod_{i=0}^{k} \ln^{(i)}(n)$ is that the antiderivative (of its reciprocal) $\int 1/\mathfrak{t}(x)\mathrm{d}x = \ln^{(k+1)}(x) \in \omega(1)$ is superconstant which is the property that we need to get our proof of Lemma 1 going.

In contrast, going to some polynomial lower bound, i.e., $\mathsf{MKtP} \notin \mathsf{DTIME}\left[n^{1+\epsilon}\right]$ for some $\epsilon > 0$ seems challenging. With our current proof strategy this would require a stronger version of Lemma 1 in the form of $\sum_{j=1}^{\ell} \gamma_j \sum_{\kappa=1}^{j} 2^{\kappa}/e^{\sigma_j - \sigma_{j-\kappa}} \leq 2^{\ell}/\ell^{1+\epsilon}$ for some $\epsilon > 0$. However, this cannot hold for *arbitrary* γ_j because of the following counter example: $\gamma_j := \epsilon/j$ implies $\sum_{j=1}^{\ell} \gamma_j \sum_{\kappa=1}^{j} 2^{\kappa}/e^{\sigma_j - \sigma_{j-\kappa}} \in \Theta\left(2^{\ell}/\ell^{1+\epsilon}\right)$.

Nonetheless, there is a possibility to achieve such a stronger bound by leveraging more structure of R_{Kt} to restrict the space of possible γ_j (as we did by integrating Chaitin's constant in our analysis). We hope that our new technique inspires further research into even better diagonalization approaches. For example, it could be that adding multiple 0's to a high-complexity string or moving more steps to the right on a low-complexity string might yield a better lower bound with an adapted analysis.

4   Preliminaries

Notation. Real functions are usually denoted by Greek letters γ, θ, ε, etc., while natural/bit functions by Fraktur script $\mathfrak{t}$, $\mathfrak{f}$, etc. Languages are denoted by the

---

[10] That is, there exists some constant c such that $\sum_{\ell=1}^{\infty} \gamma_{\mathsf{fp}}(\ell) \leq c \lesssim 1$.

uppercase letter L. The empty string is denoted by ε. Integers related to sizes are denoted by lowercase Latin letters n, m, c, while indices are denoted by i, j, k, κ. Strings are denoted by lowercase Latin letters x, y, z, etc. Turing machines (TM) are denoted by caligraphic letters $\mathcal{U}$, $\mathcal{M}$ as well as Π for the code of a TM. Complexity classes are denoted in sans-serif letters P, NP, EXP, etc.

For convenience we add $\boxed{\text{framed boxes}}$ with explanations of relevant (in-)equalities.

Notation 1 (Functional inequalities). *Let* $\mathfrak{f}, \mathfrak{g} : \mathbb{N} \to \mathbb{R}$ *be two functions. We write*

$$\mathfrak{f} \leq \mathfrak{g} \iff \forall n \in \mathbb{N} : \qquad \mathfrak{f}(n) \leq \mathfrak{g}(n) \tag{9}$$

$$\mathfrak{f} \leq_{\mathsf{abf}} \mathfrak{g} \iff \exists n_0 \in \mathbb{N} \; \forall n \geq n_0 : \; \mathfrak{f}(n) \leq \mathfrak{g}(n) \tag{10}$$

$$\mathfrak{f} \leq_{\mathsf{io}} \mathfrak{g} \iff \forall n_0 \in \mathbb{N} \; \exists n \geq n_0 : \; \mathfrak{f}(n) \leq \mathfrak{g}(n) \tag{11}$$

when $\mathfrak{f}$ *is less or equal to* $\mathfrak{g}$ *on all inputs, on all but finitely many inputs, or on infinitely many inputs. Note that*

$$\mathfrak{f} \leq \mathfrak{g} \implies \mathfrak{f} \leq_{\mathsf{abf}} \mathfrak{g} \iff \overline{\mathfrak{f} >_{\mathsf{io}} \mathfrak{g}} \implies \mathfrak{f} \leq_{\mathsf{io}} \mathfrak{g} \; . \tag{12}$$

It may be that $\mathfrak{g} \leq_{\mathsf{io}} \mathfrak{f}$ *while simultaneously* $\mathfrak{g} \geq_{\mathsf{io}} \mathfrak{f}$. *Sometimes we abuse notation and write* $\mathfrak{f}(n) \leq_{\mathsf{abf}} \mathfrak{g}(n)$ *to mean* $(n \mapsto \mathfrak{f}(n)) \leq_{\mathsf{abf}} (n \mapsto \mathfrak{g}(n))$.

Notation 2 (Languages). *Let* $L \subseteq \{0,1\}^*$, *then for any* $x \in \{0,1\}^*$ *we use the abbreviated notation* $L(x) = 1 \iff x \in L$ *and* $L(x) = 0 \iff x \notin L$.

Notation 3 (Integers and strings). *Let* $int : \{0,1\}^* \to \mathbb{N} : x \mapsto 2^{|x|+1} + \sum_{i=1}^{|x|} 2^{i-1} x_i$ *be the canonical lexicographical bijection between strings and integers. Let* $bin := int^{-1}$ *be its inverse operation. Let* $next(x) := bin\left((int(x)+1) \mod 2^{|x|} + 2^{|x|}\right)$ *be the function that returns the lexicographically next string of the same length.*

Computational Model. We present our result for Turing machines but they carry over to over computational models. We discuss this in more detail in Sect. 3.

We generally assume a Turing machine (TM) has fixed number of tapes, one of which is a read-only the input tape, one a write-only output tape, and the rest are read-write work tapes. This naturally extends to oracle machine with a dedicated oracle tape, although we will not need it in this work.

Let $\mathcal{M}$ be a deterministic Turing machine (TM). For any $x \in \{0,1\}^*$ denote by $\mathcal{M}(x) \in \{0,1\}^* \cup \{\bot\}$ the content of the output tape after $\mathcal{M}$ has entered a terminal state, or $\bot$ if $\mathcal{M}$ does not terminate on input x. In particular, if $\mathcal{M}$ halts with a string $y \in \{0,1\}^n$ then it must have run for at least n steps.

Throughout the paper let $\mathcal{U}$ denote a prefix-free universal Turing machine (UTM). For any string $\Pi \in \{0,1\}^*$ let $\mathfrak{t}_{\mathcal{U}}(\Pi)$ be the (minimum) number of steps after which $\mathcal{U}$ halts on input Π. We assume that $\mathcal{U}$ simulates any given TM with (multiplicative) logarithmic overhead [26]. That is, there exists some universal constant $c_{\mathcal{U}} \in \mathbb{N}$ such that if the TM encoded by Π halts in t steps on input ε, then $\mathcal{U}$ halts on input Π in $t_{\mathcal{U}}(\Pi) \leq c_{\mathcal{U}} t \log_2(t)$ steps. Let $t : \mathbb{N} \to \mathbb{N}$ be a time bound. Let $\mathsf{DTM}[t]$ be the set of deterministic TMs that halt within $t(n)$ steps on inputs of length $n \in \mathbb{N}$. For any TM $\mathcal{M}$ let $L_{\mathcal{M}} := \{x \in \{0,1\}^* \mid \mathcal{M}(x) = 1\}$ be its (characteristic) language. Throughout, we require a time bound t to be time-constructible, i.e., there exists a TM $\mathcal{M}_t \in \mathsf{DTM}[\mathcal{O}(t)]$ that computes t. Let

$$\mathsf{DTIME}[t] := \{L \subseteq \{0,1\}^* \mid \exists \mathcal{M} \in \mathsf{DTM}[t] : L = L_{\mathcal{M}}\} \tag{13}$$

be the class of languages decided by some DTM in time t. Let $\mathsf{DTIME}[\mathcal{O}(t)] := \bigcup_{d \in \mathbb{N}} \mathsf{DTIME}[d \cdot t]$ be the class of languages decided by some DTM in time $\mathcal{O}(t)$. In the following let C be some class of languages that is closed under intersection. Let

$$\mathsf{Heur}_{\gamma_{\mathsf{fp}}, \gamma_{\mathsf{fn}}} \mathsf{C} := \left\{ L \subseteq \{0,1\}^* \;\middle|\; \exists L' \in \mathsf{C} : \begin{array}{l} \left| (L \setminus L') \cap \{0,1\}^\lambda \right| \leq_{\mathsf{abf}} \gamma_{\mathsf{fp}}(\lambda) 2^\lambda \\ \left| (L' \setminus L) \cap \{0,1\}^\lambda \right| \leq_{\mathsf{abf}} \gamma_{\mathsf{fn}}(\lambda) 2^\lambda \end{array} \right\} \tag{14}$$

be the class of languages with a C-heuristic with false-positive error at most γ_{fp} and false-negative error at most γ_{fn}.

Complexity Measures. The most basic notion of Kolmogorov complexity is the length of the smallest program (witness program) that produces a given string w.r.t. some UTM.

Definition 1 (Solomonoff–Kolmogorov–Chaitin complexity [17,42,72]). *Let $\mathcal{U}$ be a (prefix-free) UTM. For any string $x \in \{0,1\}^*$ we say*

$$K_{\mathcal{U}}(x) := \min\{|\Pi| \mid \Pi \in \{0,1\}^* : \mathcal{U}(\Pi) = x\} \tag{15}$$

is the (prefix-free) Kolmogorov complexity[11].

While a powerful notion, it is not computable, hence Levin [44] came up with an alternative definition which charges an additional logarithmic term for the runtime of the witness program that produces the given string.

Definition 2 (Levin–Kolmogorov complexity [44,71]). *Let $\mathcal{U}$ be a (prefix-free) UTM. For any string $x \in \{0,1\}^*$ we say*

$$Kt_{\mathcal{U}}(x) := \min\{|\Pi| + \lceil \log_2(t) \rceil \mid \Pi \in \{0,1\}^*, t \in \mathbb{N} : \mathcal{U}(\Pi) = x \wedge t_{\mathcal{U}}(\Pi) \leq t\} \tag{16}$$

is the (prefix-free global) Levin–Kolmogorov complexity. Let

$$\mathsf{MKtP}_{\mathcal{U}} := \{(y,k) \in \{0,1\}^m \times [m] \mid m \in \mathbb{N} : Kt(y) \leq k\} \tag{17}$$

---

[11] For brevity and in accord with the literature [46] we simply use the term "Kolmogorov complexity".

be the decisional minimum Kt-problem. This version is called "global compression" because the witness program outputs the entire string y.

For reference, we also define the "local compression" version where the witness program outputs each bit of the string y separately. For any string $x \in \{0,1\}^*$ we say

$$\ddot{K}t_{\mathcal{U}}(x) := \min \left\{ |\Pi| + \lceil \log_2(t) \rceil \;\middle|\; \begin{matrix} \Pi \in \{0,1\}^*, t \in \mathbb{N} : \forall i \in \{1,...,|x|\} : \\ \mathcal{U}(\Pi, i) = x_i \wedge t_{\mathcal{U}}(\Pi, i) \leq t \end{matrix} \right\} \tag{18}$$

is the (prefix-free local) Levin–Kolmogorov complexity.

We mainly focus on the global version and discuss various definitional subtleties in Sect. 3.

Fact 1 (Relation between K and Kt). *For any string $x \in \{0,1\}^*$ it holds that $Kt(x) \geq K(x) + \lceil \log_2(|x|) \rceil$.*

Proof This is because even the shortest (global witness) program for x must run for at least $|x|$ steps.[12]   □

Definition 3 (1-/ Martin-Löf-randomness ([18] referring to [15,45,57])). *Let $\mathcal{U}$ be a (prefix-free) UTM. An infinite sequence of bits $w = (w_i)_{i \in \mathbb{N}}$ is called 1-random, iff there exists some constant $\hat{c}_{\mathcal{U},w} \in \mathbb{N}$ such that for each $n \in \mathbb{N}$ it holds that $K(w_1||...||w_n) \geq n - \hat{c}_{\mathcal{U},w}$.*

Analogously, an infinite sequence of bits $w = (w_i)_{i \in \mathbb{N}}$ is called 1-Kt-random, iff there exists some constant $\hat{c}_{\mathcal{U},w} \in \mathbb{N}$ such that for each $n \in \mathbb{N}$ it holds that $Kt(w_1||...||w_n) \geq n + \lceil \log_2(n) \rceil - \hat{c}_{\mathcal{U},w}$.

Going forward we fix some arbitrary UTM $\mathcal{U}$ but omit it in our notation and simply write K, Kt, MKtP, etc. By Fact 1 K-randomness implies Kt-randomness.

Fact 2 (Chaitin's Ω constant is 1-random [15]). *Let Ω_i be the i-th bit of Chaitin's constant [15] in binary representation. Then the sequence $\Omega = (\Omega_i)_{i \in \mathbb{N}}$ is 1-random and thus 1-Kt-random with constant $\hat{c}_{\Omega}$.*

5   Formal Results

Lemma 2. *The algorithm* TRAVERSE$_{\hat{c}_{\Omega}, c_{Kt}}$ *in Fig. 4 visits infinitely many different strings $(z_i)_{i \in \mathbb{N}}$.*

Proof. First note that the lengths of z_i are non-decreasing, i.e., $|z_{i+1}| \geq |z_i|$. Suppose for contradiction that there exists some maximal length $\hat{\ell} \in \mathbb{N}$ such that all strings $|z_i| \leq \hat{\ell}$ for all $i \in \mathbb{N}$. By inspection it is apparent that from some point onward TRAVERSE$_{\hat{c}_{\Omega}, c_{Kt}}$ cycles through all strings of length $\hat{\ell}$.

---

[12]   Here, we presume the global compression version of Kt, and add $\lceil \log_2(|x|) \rceil$.

Because the prefixes of Chaitin's constant $\Omega = (\Omega_i)_{i \in \mathbb{N}}$ are a 1-Kt-random sequence, for each length $\ell \in \mathbb{N}$ the string $\Omega_1||...||\Omega_\ell \in \{0,1\}^\ell$ has complexity $Kt(\Omega_1||...||\Omega_\ell) \geq K(\Omega_1||...||\Omega_\ell) \geq \ell + \lceil \log_2(\ell) \rceil - \hat{c}_\Omega$. Thus, once TRAVERSE$_{\hat{c}_\Omega, c_{Kt}}$ visits the string $z_i = \Omega_1||...||\Omega_{\hat{\ell}}$ the next string is $z_{i+1} = \Omega_1|...||\Omega_{\hat{\ell}}||0$ due to line 3. This contradicts $\hat{\ell} + 1 = |z_i| + 1 \leq \hat{\ell}$. □

Now, we prove our main result.

Theorem 1. The Levin–Kolmogorov complexity cannot be decided in deterministic linear time in the worst-case, i.e., MKtP $\notin$ DTIME$[\mathcal{O}(n)]$.

Proof. The intuition of this proof is already outlined in Sect. 3. The high-level idea is to assume that Kt can be computed quickly, and then construct a sufficiently fast TM that produces a highly complex string. This then contradicts the definition of a complex string needing a large or slow program to compute. Key properties of our constructed TM is that it finds a complex string sufficiently fast and that the TM is aware of its own runtime. For the latter property we use a counter variable in our TM to upper bound its runtime by counting the number of visited strings of a given length. This counter needs to be larger than the actual runtime of the TM (Claim 1) so it is guaranteed to output a string larger than its own critical threshold. On the other hand, the counter must not be too large (Claim 3), for otherwise it would not output critical strings that would actually suffice for a contradiction.

Suppose for contradiction MKtP $\in$ DTIME$[\mathcal{O}(n)]$, then there exists some $c_{Kt} \in \mathbb{N}$ such that MKtP $\in$ DTIME$[2^{c_{Kt}}n]$, i.e., there exists some TM Π_{Kt} that decides $Kt(z) \leq k$ in time at most $\mathsf{t}(n + \lceil \log_2(n) \rceil) \leq \mathsf{t}(2n) := 2^{c_{Kt}+1}n$ on any instance $(z, k) \in \{0,1\}^n \times [n]$. Later, we will choose a sufficiently large c_{Kt}.

Fix the constant $\hat{c}_\Omega$ from Fact 2. For any c_{Kt} let $\mathcal{M}_{\hat{c}_\Omega, c_{Kt}}$ be the smallest TM implementing the TRAVERSE$_{\hat{c}_\Omega, c_{Kt}}$ algorithm from Fig. 4. There exists some universal[13] constant $c_{\mathsf{fix}} \in \mathbb{N}$ such that for any integer $c_{Kt} \in \mathbb{N}$ the TM $\mathcal{M}_{\hat{c}_\Omega, c_{Kt}}$ has size $|\mathcal{M}_{\hat{c}_\Omega, c_{Kt}}| \leq c_{\mathsf{fix}} + 2 \lfloor \log_2(c_{Kt}) + 1 \rfloor$ by storing c_{Kt} prefix-free. In particular, for any $c_{Kt} \geq 2(c_{\mathsf{fix}} + c_\mathcal{U}) + 8$ the TM's size is bounded by $|\mathcal{M}_{\hat{c}_\Omega, c_{Kt}}| \leq c_{Kt} - c_\mathcal{U}$ (recall that $c_\mathcal{U}$ is the universal simulation constant). We derive a contradiction through a series of claims about the TM $\mathcal{M}_{\hat{c}_\Omega, c_{Kt}}$.

The TM $\mathcal{M}_{\hat{c}_\Omega, c_{Kt}}$ visits the sequence $(z_i)_{i \in \mathbb{N}}$ of strings. Let $Z := \{z_i \mid i \in \mathbb{N}\}$. For each length $\ell \in \mathbb{N}$ let $\mathsf{v}Z_\ell := Z \cap \{0,1\}^\ell = \{\hat{z}_\ell, ..., \check{z}_\ell\}]$ where $\hat{z}_\ell$ and $\check{z}_\ell$ are the lexicographically first resp. last string in Z_ℓ. Our first claim establishes that—whenever $\mathcal{M}_{\hat{c}_\Omega, c_{Kt}}$ checks whether to output a visited string in line 10— its variable t_ℓ is larger than the number of steps that $\mathcal{M}_{\hat{c}_\Omega, c_{Kt}}$ took so far. This means that $\mathcal{M}_{\hat{c}_\Omega, c_{Kt}}$ can use the variable t_ℓ to effectively bound its own critical threshold.

Claim 1 (Time counter lower bound). For any length ℓ let $\tilde{t}_\ell$ be the number of steps that $\mathcal{M}_{\hat{c}_\Omega, c_{Kt}}$ takes to reach line 10 with length ℓ. It holds that $t_\ell \geq \tilde{t}_\ell$.

---
[13] Independent of c_{Kt}.

TRAVERSE$_{\hat{c}_\Omega, c_{Kt}}$

---

1 : $z_1 := 0 \in \{0,1\}^*$

2 : $t_0 := 0 \in \mathbb{N}$

3 : $\ell := 1 \in \mathbb{N}$

4 : $\hat{z}_1 := 1 \in \{0,1\}^*$

5 :   **for** $i \in \mathbb{N}_{\geq 1}$

6 :   **if** $Kt(z_i) \gtrsim \ell + \lceil \log_2(\ell) \rceil - \hat{c}_\Omega$ // in $2^{c_{Kt}+1}\ell$ steps

7 : $z_{i+1} := z_i \| 0 \in \{0,1\}^{\ell+1}$ // in 4ℓ steps

8 : $\hat{z}_{\ell+1} := z_{i+1} \in \{0,1\}^{\ell+1}$ // store the starting node of length $\ell + 1$

9 : $t_\ell := t_{\ell-1} + (int(z_i) - int(\hat{z}_\ell) + 1) 2^{c_{Kt}+2}\ell + 2^{2c_{Kt}+\ell-\lceil \log_2(\ell) \rceil+1}$

10 :   **if** $Kt(z_i) \gtrsim c_{Kt} + \lceil \log_2(t_\ell \log_2(t_\ell)) \rceil$

11 :   **return** z_i

12 :   **endif**

13 : $\ell := \ell + 1$ // in 4ℓ steps

14 :   **else**

15 : $z_{i+1} := next(z_i) \in \{0,1\}^\ell$ // in 4ℓ steps

16 :   **endif**

17 : **endfor**

Fig. 4. Our search algorithm with runtime bounds under the assumption MKtP $\in$ DTIME$[2^{c_{Kt}}n]$. The parameters $\hat{c}_\Omega, c_{Kt} \in \mathbb{N}$ are hardcoded. It might not be obvious why line 9 can be executed in $c_{Kt}^3\ell^2$ steps, the reason is fleshed out in the proof of Claim 1.

Proof. First, under the assumption MKtP $\in$ DTIME$[2^{c_{Kt}}n]$ we argue that $\mathcal{M}_{\hat{c}_\Omega, c_{Kt}}$ takes at most $c_{Kt}^3\ell^2$ steps to execute line 9. Our first goal is to bound the time needed to execute line 9.

First, we recursively bound the variable t_ℓ by

$$t_\ell := t_{\ell-1} + (int(z_i) - int(\hat{z}_\ell) + 2) 2^{c_{Kt}+1}\ell + 2^{2c_{Kt}+\ell-\lceil \log_2(\ell) \rceil+1} \tag{19}$$

$$= t_{\ell-1} + 2^{c_{Kt}+2} |Z_\ell| \ell + 2^{2c_{Kt}+\ell-\lceil \log_2(\ell) \rceil+1} \tag{20}$$

$$\leq t_{\ell-1} + 2^{4\ell+4c_{Kt}} \tag{21}$$

for sufficiently large c_{Kt}. Resolving this recursive upper bound for sufficiently large c_{Kt} it follows that $t_\ell \leq 2^{4\ell+4c_{Kt}} + t_0$ where $t_0 := 0$.

Now, the value t_ℓ can be computed by simple arithmetic (addition, multiplication) and bit shifting operations taking at most quadratic time in the maximal bit length $\mathcal{O}(\ell)$ of the operands ℓ, t_ℓ $int(\hat{z}_\ell)$, $int(z_i) = int(\hat{z}_\ell)$ and c_{Kt}. That means there is some $c' \in \mathbb{N}$ (independent of c_{Kt}) such that t_ℓ can be computed in time $c' \log_2(t_\ell)^2 \leq c'(4\ell + 4c_{Kt})^2 \leq c_{Kt}^3\ell^2$ for sufficiently large c_{Kt}.

Taking a step back we observe that the TM $\mathcal{M}_{\hat{c}_\Omega, c_{Kt}}$ takes at most $\widetilde{\Delta}_\ell :=$ $\widetilde{t}_\ell - \widetilde{t}_{\ell-1}$ actual steps to iterate over the strings Z_ℓ of length ℓ (lines 6 through 13). We see through

$$\widetilde{\Delta}_\ell := \widetilde{t}_\ell - \widetilde{t}_{\ell-1} \tag{22}$$

$$\leq \underbrace{|Z_\ell| \left(2^{c_{Kt}+1}\ell + 4\ell \right)}_{\text{steps for } Z_\ell \setminus \{\check{z}_\ell\} \text{ in lines } 6 \text{ and } 15} + \underbrace{2^{c_{Kt}+1}\ell + 4\ell + c_{Kt}^3 \ell^2 + 2^{c_{Kt}+1}\ell + c_{Kt}\ell + 4\ell}_{\text{steps for } \check{z}_\ell \text{ in lines } 6\text{--}13} \tag{23}$$

$$\leq \left(2^{c_{Kt}+1} + 4 \right) |Z_\ell| \ell + \left(2^{c_{Kt}+2} + 8 + c_{Kt}^3 + c_{Kt} \right) \ell^2 \tag{24}$$

$$\leq 2^{c_{Kt}+2} |Z_\ell| \ell + 2^{2c_{Kt}+\ell - \lceil \log_2(\ell) \rceil + 1} \tag{25}$$

$$= \Delta_\ell \tag{26}$$

that the variable t_ℓ grows more quickly than $\widetilde{t}_\ell$ and since $t_0 = 0 = \widetilde{t}_0$, it follows that $t_\ell \geq \widetilde{t}_\ell$ for any $\ell \in \mathbb{N}$.   ■

Claim 2 (Non-termination).   The   TM $\mathcal{M}_{\hat{c}_\Omega, c_{Kt}}$ never   halts,   thus $\text{TRAVERSE}_{\hat{c}_\Omega, c_{Kt}}$ never halts.

Proof. If $\mathcal{M}_{\hat{c}_\Omega, c_{Kt}}$ halted and produced a string $\hat{z} \in \{0,1\}^{\hat{\ell}}$ within $\widetilde{t}_{\hat{\ell}}$ steps, then by definition of the (prefix-free global) Levin–Kolmogorov complexity

$$Kt(\hat{z}) \leq |\mathcal{M}_{\hat{c}_\Omega, c_{Kt}}| + \lceil \log_2(t_\mathcal{U}(\mathcal{M}_{\hat{c}_\Omega, c_{Kt}})) \rceil \tag{27}$$

$$\leq |\mathcal{M}_{\hat{c}_\Omega, c_{Kt}}| + \lceil \log_2(c_\mathcal{U} \widetilde{t}_{\hat{\ell}} \log_2(\widetilde{t}_{\hat{\ell}})) \rceil \tag{28}$$

$$\leq c_{Kt} - c_\mathcal{U} + \lceil \log_2(c_\mathcal{U} \widetilde{t}_{\hat{\ell}} \log_2(\widetilde{t}_{\hat{\ell}})) \rceil \tag{29}$$

$$\leq c_{Kt} + \lceil \log_2(\widetilde{t}_{\hat{\ell}} \log_2(\widetilde{t}_{\hat{\ell}})) \rceil \tag{30}$$

$$\leq c_{Kt} + \lceil \log_2(t_{\hat{\ell}} \log_2(t_{\hat{\ell}})) \rceil \tag{31}$$

by the fact that $|\mathcal{M}_{\hat{c}_\Omega, c_{Kt}}| \leq c_{Kt} - c_\mathcal{U}$ and Claim 1. However, the only way $\mathcal{M}_{\hat{c}_\Omega, c_{Kt}}$ returns a string is in line 11, thus the condition in line 10 must be fulfilled, namely $Kt(\hat{z}) \gtrsim c_{Kt} + \lceil \log_2(t_{\hat{\ell}} \log_2(t_{\hat{\ell}})) \rceil$. This contradicts Eq. (27). Consequently, under the hypothesis $\text{MKtP} \in \text{DTIME}[2^{c_{Kt}}n]$ the TM $\mathcal{M}_{\hat{c}_\Omega, c_{Kt}}$ never halts.   □

Because of Claim 2 the TM $\mathcal{M}_{\hat{c}_\Omega, c_{Kt}}$ visits the same sequence of strings $(z_i)_{i \in \mathbb{N}}$ as $\text{TRAVERSE}_{\hat{c}_\Omega, c_{Kt}}$. For any length ℓ let $i_\ell := \sum_{j=1}^{\ell} |Z_j|$ be number of visited string of length at most ℓ.

Claim 3 (Time counter upper bound). For any length ℓ it holds that $t_\ell \leq 2^{2c_{Kt}+4} \left(i_\ell \ell + 2^\ell / \ell \right)$.

Proof. Using Eqs. (19) and (26) we can bound the telescope sum

$$t_\ell = t_0 + \sum_{j=1}^{\ell} \Delta_j \tag{32}$$

$$= \sum_{j=1}^{\ell} \left(2^{c_{K\ell}+2} |Z_j| \, j + 2^{2c_{K\ell}+j-\lceil \log_2(j)\rceil+1} \right) \tag{33}$$

$$\leq 2^{c_{K\ell}+2} \ell \left(\sum_{j=1}^{\ell} |Z_j| \right) + 2^{2c_{K\ell}+3+\ell}/\ell \tag{34}$$

$$= 2^{c_{K\ell}+2} i_\ell \ell + 2^{2c_{K\ell}+3+\ell}/\ell \tag{35}$$

$$\leq 2^{2c_{K\ell}+4} \left(i_\ell \ell + 2^\ell/\ell \right) . \tag{36}$$

∎

Now we have upper bounded the counter variable t_ℓ in terms of the number i_ℓ of visited strings of length at most ℓ. It remains to argue that for infinitely many ℓ the value i_ℓ is sufficiently small, to reach a contradiction. To this end, we will reexpress i_ℓ in a different form. Let $S_\ell \subset \{0,1\}^\ell$ be the lexicographical successors of Z_ℓ (the right neighbors of Z_ℓ). Now, note that because TRAVERSE$_{\hat{c}_\Omega, c_{K\ell}}$ doesn't wrap around (staying to the left of Chaitin's constant), it holds that $Z_{\ell+1} \cup S_{\ell+1} = (\{z_{i_\ell}\} \cup S_\ell) \, || \, \{0,1\}$ and thus $|Z_{\ell+1}| + |S_{\ell+1}| = 2\,|S_\ell| + 2$. Let $\gamma_\ell := |Z_\ell|/|Z_\ell \cup S_\ell|$ be the fraction of strings of length ℓ that TRAVERSE$_{\hat{c}_\Omega, c_{K\ell}}$ actually visits to the strings that it could potentially visit. Using this expression for γ_ℓ we can rewrite the previous equality as a recursive formula for $|S_\ell|$ (depending on γ_ℓ), i.e.,

$$2\,|S_\ell| + 2 = |Z_{\ell+1}| + |S_{\ell+1}| \tag{37}$$

$$= \left(|Z_{\ell+1}| + |S_{\ell+1}| \right) \gamma_{\ell+1} + |S_{\ell+1}| \tag{38}$$

$$= 2 \left(|S_\ell| + 1 \right) \gamma_{\ell+1} + |S_{\ell+1}| \tag{39}$$

$$\implies |S_{\ell+1}| = 2 \left(|S_\ell| + 1 \right) \left(1 - \gamma_{\ell+1} \right) \tag{40}$$

By solving this recursion with $|S_1| := 1$ we can express the number of successor strings as

$$|S_\ell| = \sum_{\kappa=1}^{\ell} 2^\kappa \prod_{i=\ell-\kappa+1}^{\ell} (1 - \gamma_i) . \tag{41}$$

In turn, we can use the definition of γ_ℓ to express the number of visited strings of length exactly ℓ as

$$|Z_\ell| = 2 \left(|S_{\ell-1}| + 1 \right) \gamma_\ell = \gamma_\ell \sum_{\kappa=1}^{\ell} 2^\kappa \prod_{i=\ell-\kappa+1}^{\ell-1} (1 - \gamma_i) . \tag{42}$$

Lastly, we can sum over all lengths to obtain

$$i_\ell := \sum_{j=1}^{\ell} |Z_j| \tag{43}$$

$$= \sum_{j=1}^{\ell} \gamma_j \sum_{\kappa=1}^{j} 2^\kappa \prod_{i=j-\kappa+1}^{j} (1 - \gamma_i) \tag{44}$$

$$= \sum_{j=1}^{\ell} \gamma_j \sum_{\kappa=1}^{j} 2^\kappa e^{\sum_{i=j-\kappa+1}^{j} \ln(1-\gamma_i)} \tag{45}$$

$$\leq \sum_{j=1}^{\ell} \gamma_j \sum_{\kappa=1}^{j} 2^\kappa e^{-\sum_{i=j-\kappa+1}^{j} \gamma_i} \tag{46}$$

$$= \sum_{j=1}^{\ell} \gamma_j \sum_{\kappa=1}^{j} 2^\kappa e^{\sigma_{j-\kappa} - \sigma_j} \tag{47}$$

where $\sigma_\ell := \sum_{i=1}^{\ell} \gamma_i$. This expression is bounded by Lemma 1.

Conclusion. Using Lemma 1 let $\hat{\ell} \geq e^{2^{3c_{Kt} + \hat{c}_\Omega + 6}}$ be an arbitrarily large integer such that $i_{\hat{\ell}} \leq 2^{\hat{\ell}}/\hat{\ell}\ln(\hat{\ell})$. Let $z_{i_{\hat{\ell}}} \in \{0,1\}^{\hat{\ell}}$ be the last string of length $\hat{\ell}$ visited by $\text{TRAVERSE}_{\hat{c}_\Omega, c_{Kt}}$. Because $z_{i_{\hat{\ell}}}$ is the last string of length $\hat{\ell}$ the condition $Kt\left(z_{i_{\hat{\ell}}}\right) \gtrless |z_{i_{\hat{\ell}}}| + \lceil\log_2\left(|z_{i_{\hat{\ell}}}|\right)\rceil - \hat{c}_\Omega = \hat{\ell} + \lceil\log_2\left(\hat{\ell}\right)\rceil - \hat{c}_\Omega$ in line 6 in $\text{TRAVERSE}_{\hat{c}_\Omega, c_{Kt}}$ must be fulfilled. Moreover, because $\text{TRAVERSE}_{\hat{c}_\Omega, c_{Kt}}$ never halts—according to Claim 2—the violated return condition in line 10 in $\text{TRAVERSE}_{\hat{c}_\Omega, c_{Kt}}$ dictates $Kt\left(z_{i_{\hat{\ell}}}\right) \leq c_{Kt} + \lceil\log_2\left(t_{\hat{\ell}} \log_2\left(t_{\hat{\ell}}\right)\right)\rceil$. Thus we arrive at the contradiction

$$\hat{\ell} + \lceil\log_2\left(\hat{\ell}\right)\rceil - \hat{c}_\Omega \lessgtr Kt\left(z_{i_{\hat{\ell}}}\right) \tag{48}$$

$$\leq c_{Kt} + \lceil\log_2\left(t_{\hat{\ell}} \log_2\left(t_{\hat{\ell}}\right)\right)\rceil \tag{49}$$

$$\leq c_{Kt} + \lceil\log_2\left(t_{\hat{\ell}}\right)\rceil + \log_2\left(\hat{\ell}\right) \tag{50}$$

$$\leq c_{Kt} + \left\lceil(2c_{Kt} + 4) + \log_2\left(i_{\hat{\ell}}\hat{\ell} + 2^{\hat{\ell}}/\hat{\ell}\right)\right\rceil + \log_2\left(\hat{\ell}\right) \tag{51}$$

$$\leq c_{Kt} + \left\lceil(2c_{Kt} + 4) + \log_2\left(2^{\hat{\ell}}/\ln\left(\hat{\ell}\right) + 2^{\hat{\ell}}/\hat{\ell}\right)\right\rceil + \log_2\left(\hat{\ell}\right) \tag{52}$$

$$\leq c_{Kt} + 2c_{Kt} + 6 + \log_2\left(2^{\hat{\ell}}/\ln\left(\hat{\ell}\right)\right) + \log_2\left(\hat{\ell}\right) \tag{53}$$

$$= c_{Kt} + 2c_{Kt} + 6 + \hat{\ell} - \log_2\ln\left(\hat{\ell}\right) + \log_2\left(\hat{\ell}\right) \tag{54}$$

$$\leq c_{Kt} + 2c_{Kt} + 6 + \hat{\ell} - (3c_{Kt} + \hat{c}_\Omega + 6) + \log_2\left(\hat{\ell}\right) \tag{55}$$

$$= \hat{\ell} + \log_2\left(\hat{\ell}\right) - \hat{c}_\Omega . \tag{56}$$

□

The proof of Theorem 1 relativizes. By adapting it we can show analogous results for various definitions of Kt complexity.

Corollary 3. *Assume a computational model with constant universal simulation overhead, e.g. random-access machines. The (global compression) Levin–Kolmogorov complexity cannot be decided in deterministic quadratic time in the worst-case, i.e.,* $\mathsf{MKtP} \notin \mathsf{DTIME}\left[\mathcal{O}\left(n^2\right)\right]$*. The (local compression) Levin–Kolmogorov complexity cannot be decided in deterministic linear time in the worst-case, i.e.,* $\mathsf{M\ddot{K}tP} \notin \mathsf{DTIME}\left[\mathcal{O}\left(n\right)\right]$*.*

Next, we prove our conditional lower bounds.

Theorem 2. *For each time bound* $\mathsf{t}\left(n\right) \geq n$ *at least one of the following is true:*

1. $\mathsf{MKtP} \notin \mathsf{DTIME}\left[\mathsf{t}\right]$,
2. $\mathsf{MKtP} \notin \mathsf{Heur}_{\gamma_{\mathsf{fp}},\gamma_{\mathsf{fn}}}\mathsf{DTIME}\left[\mathcal{O}\left(n\right)\right]$ *with no false positive error* $\gamma_{\mathsf{fp}}\left(n\right) := 0$ *and false negative error* $\gamma_{\mathsf{fn}}\left(n\right) := 1/2n\mathsf{t}(2n) - 2/2^n$,

Proof. This proof is a slight modification of the proof of Theorem 1, thus we only include the relevant changes. For contradiction assume $\mathsf{MKtP} \in \mathsf{DTIME}\left[\mathsf{t}\right]$ (by a TM Π_{Kt}) and $\mathsf{MKtP} \in \mathsf{Heur}_{0,\gamma_{\mathsf{fn}}}\mathsf{DTIME}\left[\mathcal{O}\left(n\right)\right]$ with false negative error probability $\gamma_{\mathsf{fn}}\left(n\right) := 1/2n\mathsf{t}(2n) - 2/2^n$ (by a TM $\widetilde{\Pi}_{Kt}$). See Fig. 5 for the modified traversal algorithm $\mathsf{TRAVERSE}'_{\hat{c}_\Omega, c_{Kt}, \Pi_{\mathsf{t}}, \Pi_{Kt}, \widetilde{\Pi}_{Kt}}$. Let $\mathcal{M}'_{\hat{c}_\Omega, c_{Kt}, \Pi_{\mathsf{t}}, \Pi_{Kt}, \widetilde{\Pi}_{Kt}}$ be a TM implementing the modified $\mathsf{TRAVERSE}'_{\hat{c}_\Omega, c_{Kt}, \Pi_{\mathsf{t}}, \Pi_{Kt}, \widetilde{\Pi}_{Kt}}$. Clearly, if the analog of Claim 1 holds, then $\mathcal{M}'_{\hat{c}_\Omega, c_{Kt}, \Pi_{\mathsf{t}}, \Pi_{Kt}, \widetilde{\Pi}_{Kt}}$ does not terminate for the same reason as in Claim 2 (note there that the check in line 14 is an errorless check). Because the definition of the counter variable t_ℓ is identical to $\mathsf{TRAVERSE}_{\hat{c}_\Omega, c_{Kt}, \Pi_{\mathsf{t}}, \Pi_{Kt}, \widetilde{\Pi}_{Kt}}$ the analog of Claim 3 also holds.

It remains to argue the analog of Claim 1. As before we observe that the TM $\mathcal{M}'_{\hat{c}_\Omega, c_{Kt}, \Pi_{\mathsf{t}}, \Pi_{Kt}, \widetilde{\Pi}_{Kt}}$ takes at most $\widetilde{\Delta}_\ell := \widetilde{t}_\ell - \widetilde{t}_{\ell-1}$ actual steps to iterate over the strings Z_ℓ of length ℓ (lines 6 through 17). Though, note here that we incur an additional cost for the exact check using time $\mathsf{t}(2\ell)$ on at most $2^\ell \gamma_{\mathsf{fn}}\left(\ell\right)$ strings of length ℓ, plus one exact check at in line 14. Thus, we see through

$$\widetilde{\Delta}_\ell := \widetilde{t}_\ell - \widetilde{t}_{\ell-1} \tag{57}$$

$$\leq \underbrace{|Z_\ell|\left(2^{cKt+1}\ell + 4\ell\right) + 2^\ell \gamma_{\mathsf{fn}}\left(\ell\right)\mathsf{t}(2\ell)}_{\text{steps for } Z_\ell \setminus \{\tilde{z}_\ell\} \text{ in lines } 6,8,9} \tag{58}$$

$$\underbrace{2^{cKt+1}\ell + \mathsf{t}(2\ell) + 4\ell + c_{Kt}^3\ell^2 + c_{Kt}\ell + \mathsf{t}(2\ell) + 4\ell}_{\text{steps for } \tilde{z}_\ell \text{ in lines } 6-17} \tag{59}$$

$$\leq \left(2^{cKt+1} + 4\right)|Z_\ell|\ell + \left(2^\ell \gamma_{\mathsf{fn}}\left(\ell\right) + 2\right)\mathsf{t}(2\ell) + \left(2^{cKt+1} + 8 + c_{Kt}^3 + c_{Kt}\right)\ell^2 \tag{60}$$

$$\leq 2^{cKt+2}|Z_\ell|\ell + \left(2^\ell \gamma_{\mathsf{fn}}\left(\ell\right) + 2\right)\mathsf{t}(2\ell) + 2^{2cKt+\ell-\lceil\log_2(\ell)\rceil} \tag{61}$$

$$\leq 2^{cKt+2}|Z_\ell|\ell + 2^{2cKt+\ell-\lceil\log_2(\ell)\rceil+1} \tag{62}$$

$$= t_\ell - t_{\ell-1} \tag{63}$$

$$=: \Delta_\ell \tag{64}$$

□

TRAVERSE$'_{\hat{c}_\Omega, c_{Kt}, \Pi_t, \Pi_{Kt}, \tilde{\Pi}_{Kt}}$

1 : $z_1 := 0 \in \{0,1\}^*$

2 : $t_0 := 0 \in \mathbb{N}$

3 : $\ell := 1 \in \mathbb{N}$

4 : $\hat{z}_1 := 1 \in \{0,1\}^*$

5 :   **for** $i \in \mathbb{N}_{\geq 1}$

6 : $b := \tilde{\Pi}_{Kt}\left(z_i, \ell + \lceil \log_2(\ell) \rceil - \hat{c}_\Omega\right)$ $/\!/$ in $2^{c'+1}\ell$ steps / quick error-prone check

7 :   **if** $b = 1$

8 : $b := \Pi_{Kt}\left(z_i, \ell + \lceil \log_2(\ell) \rceil - \hat{c}_\Omega\right)$ $/\!/$ in $t(2\ell)$ steps / slower exact check

9 :   **fi**

10 :   **if** $b = 0$ $/\!/$ assert $Kt(z_i) \geq \ell + \lceil \log_2(\ell) \rceil - \hat{c}_\Omega$

11 : $z_{i+1} := z_i || 0 \in \{0,1\}^{\ell+1}$ $/\!/$ in 4ℓ steps

12 : $\hat{z}_{\ell+1} := z_{i+1} \in \{0,1\}^{\ell+1}$ $/\!/$ store the starting node of length $\ell + 1$

13 : $t'_\ell := t_{\ell-1} + (int(z_i) - int(\hat{z}_\ell) + 2)\, 2^{c_{Kt}+1}\ell + 2^{2c_{Kt}+\ell-\lceil \log_2(\ell)\rceil+1}$

14 :   **if** $\Pi_{Kt}\left(z_i, c_{Kt} + \lceil \log_2(t_\ell \log_2(t_\ell)) \rceil\right) = 0$

15 :   **return** z_i

16 :   **endif**

17 : $\ell := \ell + 1$ $/\!/$ in 4ℓ steps

18 :   **else**

19 : $z_{i+1} := next(z_i) \in \{0,1\}^{\ell}$ $/\!/$ in 4ℓ

20 :   **endif**

21 :   **endfor**

Fig. 5. Our search algorithm with runtime bounds under the assumption MKtP $\notin$ DTIME $[t]$ and MKtP $\notin$ Heur$_{\gamma_{\mathrm{fp}},0}$DTIME $[\mathcal{O}(n)]$ where t is assumed to be time-constructible. The parameters $\hat{c}_\Omega, c_{Kt} \in \mathbb{N}$, the TM Π_t computing t, the t-time TM Π_{Kt} and the linear-time TM $\tilde{\Pi}_{Kt}$ are hardcoded. Changes to Fig. 4 are marked in gray.

that the variable t_ℓ grows more quickly than $\tilde{t}_\ell$ and since $t_0 = 0 = \tilde{t}_0$, it follows that $t_\ell \geq \tilde{t}_\ell$ for any $\ell \in \mathbb{N}$ which establishes Claim 3. The concluding part of the proof works exactly as in the proof of Theorem 1.

The reason why our proof can tolerate the additional runtime cost caused by the exact Kt solver Π_{Kt} is because the safety margin that we add to the counter in line 13 is more than we actually need for Theorem 1.

6   Proof of Lemma 1

Due to space restrictions we only include an abbreviated proof of Lemma 1 in the main body of this work. We refere the interested reader to the full proof in the full version [14].

Lemma 1 (Infinitely-often bound). *For any sequence* $(\gamma_j)_{j \in \mathbb{N}}$ *with* $\gamma_j \in [0, 1]$ *and* $\sigma_\ell := \sum_{i=1}^\ell \gamma_i$ *it holds that infinitely often* $\sum_{j=1}^\ell \gamma_j \sum_{\kappa=1}^j 2^\kappa e^{\sigma_j - \kappa - \sigma_j} \leq_{\text{io}} 2^\ell / \ell \ln(\ell)$.

Proof. Our proof of this claim is quite technical and somewhat tedious although it fundamentally only requires analytic Riemann integration bounds . A high-level intuition for our bound may best be explained by looking at the double sum

$$\mathfrak{s}(\ell) := \sum_{j=1}^\ell \gamma_j \sum_{\kappa=1}^j \frac{2^\kappa}{e^{\sigma_j - \sigma_{j-\kappa}}} \tag{65}$$

where $\sigma_\ell := \sum_{i=1}^\ell \gamma_i$. We don't know the exact values of $\gamma_j \in [0, 1]$ but we see that the summands of the outer sum depend on γ_j in two ways. The faster γ_j grows the faster the outer summands grow because the j-th summand depends linearly on γ_j. On the other hand, the faster γ_j grows the faster σ_j grows and thus the slower the inner summands grow because of the e^{σ_j} term in the denominator of the κ-th inner summand. So, there is a "sweet spot" for the asymptotic growth rate of γ_j that maximizes the growth rate of $\mathfrak{s}$. The maximal growth rate is close to $\Theta\left(\sum_{j=1}^\ell \frac{1}{j} \sum_{\kappa=1}^j 2^\kappa \left(1 - \frac{\kappa}{j}\right)^\epsilon\right) = \Theta\left(2^\ell / \ell^{1+\epsilon}\right)$ for small $\epsilon > 0$ and $\gamma_j = \epsilon / j$, thus $\sigma_j \approx \epsilon \ln(j)$. Thus we cannot hope to prove $\mathfrak{s}(\ell) \in \mathcal{O}\left(2^\ell / \ell^{1+\epsilon}\right)$ without further restrictions on γ_j. However, we can prove a weaker bound $\mathfrak{s}(\ell) \leq_{\text{io}} \mathcal{O}\left(2^\ell / \ell \ln(\ell)\right)$. The way we prove this bound is by establishing increasingly stronger lower bounds for the sum σ_ℓ. The first bound will be of the rough form $\sigma_\ell \in \Omega(\ln \ln(\ell))$, the second one $\sigma_\ell \in \Omega\left(\ln(\ell)^{1/17}\right)$ and the third one $\sigma_\ell \in \Omega\left(\ln(\ell)^3\right)$. The last bound then yields a contradiction to the counter assumption $2^\ell / \ell \ln(\ell) \leq_{\text{abf}} \mathfrak{s}(\ell)$.

Let us proceed with the formal proof. We use the convention that for any $b < a$ the sum $\sum_{i=a}^b \mathfrak{f}(i) := 0$. Suppose for contradiction

$$\frac{2^\ell}{\ell \ln(\ell)} \leq_{\text{abf}} \mathfrak{s}(\ell) := \sum_{j=1}^\ell \gamma_j \sum_{\kappa=1}^j \frac{2^\kappa}{e^{\sigma_j - \sigma_{j-\kappa}}} , \tag{66}$$

then there exists some $\ell_1 \in \mathbb{N}$ such that for all $\ell \geq \ell_1$

$$\frac{1}{\ell \ln(\ell)} \leq \sum_{j=1}^{\ell} \gamma_j \sum_{\kappa=1}^{j} \frac{2^{\kappa-\ell}}{e^{\sigma_j - \sigma_{j-\kappa}}} \tag{67}$$

$$\leq \sum_{j=1}^{\ell} \gamma_j \sum_{\kappa=1}^{j} 2^{\kappa-\ell} \tag{68}$$

$$\leq \sum_{j=1}^{\ell} 2^{j+1-\ell} \gamma_j \tag{69}$$

where Eq. (68) trivially uses $\sigma_j \geq \sigma_{j-k}$ and Eq. (69) uses $\sum_{\kappa=1}^{j} 2^{\kappa} = 2^{j+1}-2$. For convenience, we define a helper variable $\delta_\ell := \max(0, \lceil \ln\ln(\ell+1)/8 - \ln\ln(\ell_1)/4 \rceil) \leq \ell$. Note that $\delta_\ell \geq \log_2 \ln(\ell)/16$ for $\ell \geq \ell_1$ if ℓ_1 is sufficiently large (which is without loss of generality). Using a Riemann bound on the sum of Eq. (67) from ℓ_1 to ℓ yields

$$\frac{1}{4} \ln\ln(\ell+1) - \frac{1}{4} \ln\ln(\ell_1) \leq \sigma_\ell - \sigma_{\delta_\ell} + \delta_\ell . \tag{70}$$

Reordering the terms yields

$$\sigma_\ell - \sigma_{\delta_\ell} \geq \ln\ln(\ell+1)/8 \geq \ln\ln(\ell)/16 \tag{71}$$

for all $\ell \geq \ell_1$. To get this bound we started Eq. (67) off with the trivial bound $\sigma_j \geq \sigma_{j-\kappa}$. Now, we can use our new nontrivial bound for σ_j repeat the previous procedure and obtain an even better bound.

Plugging Eq. (71) back into a weighted sum of Eq. (67) gives the better bound on σ_ℓ for $\ell \geq \ell_1$, i.e.,

$$\ln(\ell+1) - \ln(\ell_1) \leq 2^{\ell_1+1} + 16\sigma_\ell \ln(\ell)^{15/16} . \tag{72}$$

Let $\delta'_\ell := \left\lceil \log_2(e) \ln(\ell)^{1/17} \right\rceil$. Thus there exists some sufficiently large $\ell_2 \in \mathbb{N}$ s.t. for all $\ell \geq \ell_2$ it holds that

$$\sigma_\ell - \sigma_{\delta'_\ell} \geq \sigma_\ell - \delta'_\ell \tag{73}$$

$$\geq \left(\ln(\ell+1) - \ln(\ell_1) - 2^{\ell_1+1}\right) / \left(16 \ln(\ell)^{15/16}\right) - \log_2(e) \ln(\ell)^{1/17} - 1 \tag{74}$$

$$\geq \ln(\ell)^{1/17} . \tag{75}$$

Now, we repeat the previous strategy for a third time to reach the final sufficient bound $\sigma_\ell \in \Omega\left(\ln(\ell)^3\right)$. Plugging Eq. (73) back into a weighted sum of Eq. (67) gives the better bound on σ_ℓ for $\ell \geq \ell_2$

$$2(\ell+1)^{1/2} - 2\ell_2^{1/2} \leq 2^{\ell_2+1} + 16\sigma_\ell \frac{\ell^{1/2} \ln(\ell)}{e^{\ln(\ell)^{1/17}}} . \tag{76}$$

Let $\delta_\ell'' := \left\lceil \log_2{(e)} \ln{(\ell)}^3 \right\rceil$. Thus there exists some sufficiently large $\ell_3 \in \mathbb{N}$ s.t. for all $\ell \geq \ell_3$ it holds that

$$\sigma_\ell - \sigma_{\delta_\ell''} \geq \sigma_\ell - \delta_\ell'' \tag{77}$$

$$\geq \left((\ell+1)^{1/2} - (\ell_2)^{1/2} - 2^{\ell_2+1}\right) \frac{e^{\ln(\ell)^{1/17}}}{16\ell^{1/2} \ln{(\ell)}} - \log_2{(e)} \ln{(\ell)}^3 - 1 \tag{78}$$

$$\geq \ln{(\ell)}^3 . \tag{79}$$

Finally, we can use our last bound to obtain a contradiction. Plugging Eq. (77) into Eq. (67) yields

$$\frac{1}{\ell \ln{(\ell)}} \leq 2^{\ell_3+1-\ell} + \frac{2\ell^2}{e^{\ln(\ell)^3}} \tag{80}$$

or equivalently the contradiction

$$1 \leq \frac{\ell \ln{(\ell)}}{2^{\ell-\ell_3-1}} + \frac{2\ell^3 \ln{(\ell)}}{e^{\ln(\ell)^3}} \to 0 \tag{81}$$

for $\ell \to \infty$. $\square$

To the valiant reader that has retraced the full proof of Lemma 1 we want to put the proposition that the proof can be carried out so long as the right-hand side of the lemma has the form $2^\ell / \prod_{i=0}^k \ln^{(i)}(\ell)$ for some fixed $k \in \mathbb{N}$ where $\ln^{(i)}$ is the i-th times iterated logarithm. Towards this, we assume a slight simplification of the form $\sum_{j=1}^\ell \gamma_j \sum_{\kappa=1}^j 2^\kappa / e^{\sigma_j - \sigma_{j-\kappa}} \approx \sum_{j=1}^\ell 2^j \gamma_j / e^{\sigma_j} \leq_{\mathrm{io}} 2^\ell / \prod_{i=0}^k \ln^{(i)}(\ell)$. We sketch a proof by induction where we go from a bound $\sigma_\ell \in \Omega\left(\ln^{(k+1)}(\ell)\right)$ to $\sigma_\ell \in \Omega\left(\ln^{(k)}(\ell)\right)$.

Starting out with the counter assumption $\sum_{j=1}^\ell 2^j \gamma_j / e^{\sigma_j} \geq_{\mathrm{abf}} 2^\ell / \prod_{i=0}^k \ln^{(i)}(\ell)$ we find that the first repetition of Eq. (70) is of the form $\Theta\left(\ln^{(k+1)}(\ell)\right) = \Theta\left(\int 1/\prod_{i=0}^k \ln^{(i)}(\ell) d\ell\right) \leq \Theta(\sigma_\ell)$. Inserting this bound into the counter assumption gives

$$\sum_{j=1}^\ell 2^j \gamma_j / e^{\ln^{(k+1)}(j) \cdot \Theta(1)} = \sum_{j=1}^\ell 2^j \gamma_j / \ln^{(k)}(j)^{\Theta(1)} \geq 2^\ell / \prod_{i=0}^k \ln^{(i)}(\ell) \tag{82}$$

$$\implies \sigma_\ell \geq \ln^{(k)}(j)^{\Theta(1)} / \prod_{i=0}^k \ln^{(i)}(\ell) \tag{83}$$

The second repetition of Eq. (70) takes the form

$$\Theta\left(\ln^{(k)}(\ell)\right) = \Theta\left(\int \frac{\ln^{(k)}(\ell)}{\prod_{i=0}^{k}\ln^{(i)}(\ell)}d\ell\right) \tag{84}$$

$$\leq \Theta\left(\sum_{\ell'=1}^{\ell}\ln^{(k)}(\ell')\sum_{j=1}^{\ell'}2^{j-\ell}\gamma_j/\ln^{(k)}(j)^{\Theta(1)}\right) \tag{85}$$

$$\leq \Theta\left(\ln^{(k)}(\ell)^{1-\Theta(1)}\sigma_\ell\right) \tag{86}$$

$$\implies \sigma_\ell \in \Omega\left(\ln^{(k)}(\ell)^{\Theta(1)}\right) \tag{87}$$

which is already a better bound than from the first repetition, although not quite $\Theta(\sigma_\ell) \geq \Theta\left(\ln^{(k)}(\ell)\right)$. The third repetition of Eq. (70) takes the form

$$\Theta\left(\ln^{(k)}(\ell)\right) = \Theta\left(\int \frac{\ln^{(k)}(\ell)}{\prod_{i=0}^{k}\ln^{(i)}(\ell)}d\ell\right) \tag{88}$$

$$\leq \Theta\left(\sum_{\ell'=1}^{\ell}\ln^{(k)}(\ell')\sum_{j=1}^{\ell'}2^{j-\ell}\gamma_j/e^{\ln^{(k)}(j)^{\Theta(1)}}\right) \tag{89}$$

$$\leq \Theta\left(\ln^{(k)}(\ell)/e^{\ln^{(k)}(j)^{\Theta(1)}}\cdot\sigma_\ell\right) \tag{90}$$

$$\implies \sigma_\ell \in \Omega\left(e^{\ln^{(k)}(\ell)^{\Theta(1)}}\right) \geq \Theta\left(\ln^{(k)}(\ell)\right) \tag{91}$$

which concludes the induction step.

Acknowledgments. The author would like to thank the anonymous reviewers for their helpful comments. Moreover, the author expresses his gratitude to Rafael Pass for suggesting the problem of an unconditional lower bound for Kt, Yanyi Liu for many helpful discussions about meta-complexity, Akın Ünal for checking the proof of a previous version of Lemma 1, and Chris Brzuska for a helpful discussion about the density of 1-random prefixes.

References

1. Aaronson, S., Wigderson, A.: Algebrization: a new barrier in complexity theory. In: Ladner, R.E., Dwork, C. (eds.) 40th ACM STOC, pp. 731–740. ACM Press (2008)
2. Allender, E., Vaughan, J.: Kolmogorov complexity, and the new complexity landscape around circuit minimization. New Zealand J. Math. **52**, 585–604 (2021)
3. Allender, E.: When worlds collide: derandomization, lower bounds, and kolmogorov complexity. In: Hariharan, R., Vinay, V., Mukund, M. (eds.) FSTTCS 2001. LNCS, vol. 2245, pp. 1–15. Springer, Heidelberg (2001). https://doi.org/10.1007/3-540-45294-X_1

4. Allender, E., Hirahara, S., Tirumala, H.: Kolmogorov complexity characterizes statistical zero knowledge. In: Kalai, Y.T. (ed.) ITCS 2023. LIPIcs, vol. 251, pp. 3:1-3:19 (2023)
5. Allender, E., Ilango, R., Vafa, N.: The non-hardness of approximating circuit size. Theory Comput. Syst. **65**, 559–578 (2021)
6. Allender, E., et al.: One-way functions and a conditional variant of MKTP. In: Bojańczy, M., Chekuri, C. (eds.) 41st IARCS Annual Conference on Foundations of Software Technology and Theoretical Computer Science (FSTTCS 2021). Leibniz International Proceedings in Informatics (LIPIcs), vol. 213, pp. 7:1–7:19. Schloss Dagstuhl - Leibniz-Zentrum für Informatik, Dagstuhl (2021)
7. Allender, E., et al.: Power from random strings. In: 43rd FOCS, pp. 669–678. IEEE Computer Society Press (2002)
8. Allender, E., et al.: Power from random strings. SIAM J. Comput. **35**(6), 1467–1493 (2006). https://doi.org/10.1137/050628994
9. Allender, E., et al.: The pervasive reach of resource-bounded Kolmogorov complexity in computational complexity theory. J. Comput. Syst. Sci. **77**(1), 14–40 (2011)
10. Aydinlioğlu, B., Bach, E.: Affine relativization: unifying the algebrization and relativization barriers. ACM Trans. Comput. Theory **10**(1), 1–67 (2018)
11. Baker, T., Gill, J., Solovay, R.: Relativizations of the $\mathcal{P} =?\mathcal{NP}$ Question. SIAM J. Comput. **4**(4), 431–442 (1975). https://doi.org/10.1137/0204037
12. Ball, M., et al.: Kolmogorov comes to cryptomania: on interactive kolmogorov complexity and key-agreement. In: 2023 IEEE 64th Annual Symposium on Foundations of Computer Science (FOCS), pp. 458–483 (2023)
13. Blum, M., Micali, S.: How to generate cryptographically strong sequences of pseudo random bits. In: 23rd FOCS, pp. 112–117. IEEE Computer Society Press (1982)
14. Brandt, N.: Lower bounds for levin-kolmogorov complexity. Cryptology ePrint Archive, Report 2024/687 (2024)
15. Chaitin, G.J.: A theory of program size formally identical to information theory. J. ACM **22**(3), 329–340 (1975)
16. Chaitin, G.J.: On the length of programs for computing finite binary sequences. J. ACM **13**(4), 547–569 (1966)
17. Chaitin, G.J.: On the simplicity and speed of programs for computing infinite sets of natural numbers. J. ACM **16**(3), 407–422 (1969)
18. Downey, R., Hirschfeldt, D.: Algorithmic Randomness and Complexity (2010)
19. Garg, S., et al.: Witness encryption and its applications. In: Boneh, D., Roughgarden, T., Feigenbaum, J. (eds.) 45th ACM STOC, pp. 467–476. ACM Press (2013)
20. Goldberg, H., et al.: Probabilistic kolmogorov complexity with applications to average-case complexity. In: Lovett, S. (ed.) 37th Computational Complexity Conference (CCC 2022). Leibniz International Proceedings in Informatics (LIPIcs), vol. 234, pp. 16:1–16:60. Schloss Dagstuhl – Leibniz-Zentrum für Informatik, Dagstuhl (2022)
21. Goldreich, O., Goldwasser, S., Micali, S.: On the cryptographic applications of random functions (extended abstract). In: Blakley, G.R., Chaum, D. (eds.) CRYPTO 1984. LNCS, vol. 196, pp. 276–288. Springer, Heidelberg (1985). https://doi.org/10.1007/3-540-39568-7_22
22. Goldwasser, S., Micali, S.: Probabilistic Encryption. J. Comput. Syst. Sci. **28**(2), 270–299 (1984)
23. Golovnev, A., et al.: $AC^0[p]$ lower bounds against MCSP via the coin problem. In: Baier, C., et al. (eds.) ICALP 2019. LIPIcs, vol. 132, pp. 66:1–66:15. Schloss Dagstuhl (2019)

24. Hartmanis, J.: Generalized kolmogorov complexity and the structure of feasible computations (preliminary report). In: 24th FOCS, pp. 439–445. IEEE Computer Society Press (1983)

25. Håstad, J., et al.: A pseudorandom generator from any one-way function. SIAM J. Comput. **28**(4), 1364–1396 (1999)

26. Hennie, F.C., Stearns, R.E.: Two-tape simulation of multitape turing machines. J. ACM **13**(4), 533–546 (1966)

27. Hirahara, S.: Capturing one-way functions via NP-hardness of meta-complexity. In: Proceedings of the 55th Annual ACM Symposium on Theory of Computing. STOC 2023, pp. 1027–1038. Association for Computing Machinery, New York (2023)

28. Hirahara, S.: Characterizing average-case complexity of PH by worst-case meta-complexity. In: 61st FOCS, pp. 50–60. IEEE Computer Society Press (2020)

29. Hirahara, S.: Non-black-box worst-case to average-case reductions within NP. In: Thorup, M. (ed.) 59th FOCS, pp. 247–258. IEEE Computer Society Press (2018)

30. Hirahara, S.: NP-hardness of learning programs and partial MCSP. In: 63rd FOCS, pp. 968–979. IEEE Computer Society Press (2022)

31. Hirahara, S.: Symmetry of information from meta-complexity. In: Lovett, S. (ed.) 37th Computational Complexity Conference (CCC 2022). Leibniz International Proceedings in Informatics (LIPIcs), vol. 234, pp. 26:1–26:41. Schloss Dagstuhl - Leibniz-Zentrum für Informatik, Dagstuhl (2022)

32. Hirahara, S.: Unexpected hardness results for Kolmogorov complexity under uniform reductions. In: Makarychev, K., et al. (ed.) 52nd ACM STOC, pp. 1038–1050. ACM Press (2020)

33. Hirahara, S.: Unexpected power of random strings. In: Vidick, T. (ed.) ITCS 2020. LIPIcs, vol. 151, pp. 41:1–41:13 (2020)

34. Hirahara, S., Nanashima, M.: On worst-case learning in relativized heuristica. In: 62nd FOCS, pp. 751–758. IEEE Computer Society Press (2022)

35. Huang, Y., Ilango, R., Ren, H.: NP-hardness of approximating meta-complexity: a cryptographic approach. In: Proceedings of the 55th Annual ACM Symposium on Theory of Computing. STOC 2023, pp. 1067–1075. Association for Computing Machinery, New York (2023)

36. Ilango, R.: Approaching MCSP from above and below: hardness for a conditional variant and $AC^0[p]$. In: Vidick, T. (ed.) ITCS 2020. LIPIcs, vol. 151, pp. 34:1–34:26 (2020)

37. Ilango, R.: Constant depth formula and partial function versions of MCSP are hard. In: 61st FOCS, pp. 424–433. IEEE Computer Society Press (2020)

38. Impagliazzo, R.: A personal view of average-case complexity. In: Proceedings of Structure in Complexity Theory. Tenth Annual IEEE Conference, pp. 134–147 (1995)

39. Impagliazzo, R., Kabanets, V., Kolokolova, A.: An axiomatic approach to algebrization. In: Mitzenmacher, M. (ed.) 41st ACM STOC, pp. 695–704. ACM Press (2009)

40. Kabanets, V., Cai, J.: Circuit minimization problem. In: 32nd ACM STOC, pp. 73–79. ACM Press (2000)

41. Ko, K.-I.: On the notion of infinite pseudorandom sequences. Theor. Comput. Sci. **48**, 9–33 (1986)

42. Kolmogorov, A.N.: On tables of random numbers. Sankhyā: Indian J. Stat. Ser. A (1961–2002) **25**(4), 369–376 (1963)

43. Kolmogorov, A.: Three approaches to the quantitative definition of information. Problemy Peredachi Informatsii **1**, 3–11 (1965)

44. Levin, L.A.: Randomness conservation inequalities; information and independence in mathematical theories. Inf. Control **61**(1), 15–37 (1984)
45. Levin, L.A.: Laws of information conservation (nongrowth) and aspects of the foundation of probability theory. Problemy Peredachi Informatsii **10**(3), 30–35 (1974)
46. Li, M., Vitányi, P.: An Introduction to Kolmogorov Complexity and its Applications. Springer, New York (2008). https://doi.org/10.1007/978-3-030-11298-1
47. Liu, Y., Pass, R.: A direct PRF construction from kolmogorov complexity. In: Joye, M., Leander, G. EUROCRYPT 2024, Part IV. LNCS, vol. 14654, pp. 375–406. Springer, Cham (2024). DOI: https://doi.org/10.1007/978-3-031-58737-5_14
48. Liu, Y., Pass, R.: Cryptography from sublinear-time average-case hardness of time-bounded Kolmogorov complexity. In: Khuller, S., Williams, V.V. (eds.) 53rd ACM STOC, pp. 722–735. ACM Press (2021)
49. Liu, Y., Pass, R.: On one-way functions and kolmogorov complexity. In: 61st FOCS, pp. 1243–1254. IEEE Computer Society Press (2020)
50. Liu, Y., Pass, R.: On one-way functions and sparse languages. In: Rothblum, G.N., Wee, H. (eds.) TCC 2023, Part I. LNCS, vol. 14369, pp. 219–237. Springer, Cham (2023). https://doi.org/10.1007/978-3-031-48615-9_8
51. Liu, Y., Pass, R.: On one-way functions and the worst-case hardness of time-bounded kolmogorov complexity. Cryptology ePrint Archive, Paper 2023/1086 (2023). https://eprint.iacr.org/2023/1086
52. Liu, Y., Pass, R.: On the possibility of basing cryptography on EXP$\neq$ BPP. In: Malkin, T., Peikert, C. (eds.) CRYPTO 2021. LNCS, vol. 12825, pp. 11–40. Springer, Cham (2021). https://doi.org/10.1007/978-3-030-84242-0_2
53. Liu, Y., Pass, R.: One-way functions and the hardness of (probabilistic) time-bounded kolmogorov complexity w.r.t. samplable distributions. In: Handschuh, H., Lysyanskaya, A. (eds.) CRYPTO 2023, Part II. LNCS, vol. 14082, pp. 645–673. Springer, Cham (2023). https://doi.org/10.1007/978-3-031-38545-2_21
54. Lu, Z., Oliveira, I.C.: Theory and Applications of Probabilistic Kolmogorov Complexity (2022). arXiv: 2205.14718 [cs.CC]
55. Lu, Z., Oliveira, I.C., Santhanam, R.: Pseudodeterministic algorithms and the structure of probabilistic time. In: Khuller, S., Williams, V.V. (eds.) 53rd ACM STOC, pp. 303–316. ACM Press (2021)
56. Lu, Z., Oliveira, I.C., Zimand, M.: Optimal coding theorems in time- bounded kolmogorov complexity. In: Bojanczyk, M., Merelli, E., Woodruff, D.P. (eds.) ICALP 2022. LIPIcs, vol. 229, pp. 92:1– 92:14. Schloss Dagstuhl (2022)
57. Martin-Löf, P.: The definition of random sequences. Inf. Control **9**(6), 602–619 (1966)
58. Mazor, N., Pass, R.: Gap MCSP is not (levin) NP-complete in obfustopia. In: Santhanam, R. (ed.) 39th Computational Complexity Conference (CCC 2024). Leibniz International Proceedings in Informatics (LIPIcs), vol. 300, pp. 36:1-36:21. Schloss Dagstuhl – Leibniz-Zentrum für Informatik, Dagstuhl (2024)
59. Mazor, N., Pass, R.: The non-uniform perebor conjecture for time-bounded kolmogorov complexity is false. In: Guruswami, V. (ed.) 15th Innovations in Theoretical Computer Science Conference (ITCS 2024), vol. 287, pp. 80:1–80:20. Leibniz International Proceedings in Informatics (LIPIcs). Schloss Dagstuhl - Leibniz-Zentrum für Informatik, Dagstuhl (2024)
60. Naor, M.: Bit commitment using pseudorandomness. J. Cryptol. **4**(2), 151–158 (1991)
61. Oliveira, I.C.: Randomness and intractability in kolmogorov complexity. In: Baier, C., et al. (eds.) ICALP 2019. LIPIcs, vol. 132, pp. , 32:1–32:14. Schloss Dagstuhl (2019)

62. Oliveira, I.C., Pich, J., Santhanam, R.: Hardness magnification near state- of-the-art lower bounds. In: Shpilka, A. (ed.) 34th Computational Complexity Conference (CCC 2019). Leibniz International Proceedings in Informatics (LIPIcs), vol. 137, pp. 27:1–27:29. Schloss Dagstuhl–Leibniz-Zentrum fuer Informatik, Dagstuhl (2019)

63. Razborov, A.A., Rudich, S.: Natural Proofs. J. Comput. Syst. Sci. **55**(1), 24–35 (1997)

64. Ren, H., Santhanam, R.: A relativization perspective on meta-complexity. In: Berenbrink, P., Monmege, B. (eds.) 39th International Symposium on Theoretical Aspects of Computer Science (STACS 2022). Leibniz International Proceedings in Informatics (LIPIcs), vol. 219, pp. 54:1–54:13. Schloss Dagstuhl - Leibniz-Zentrum für Informatik, Dagstuhl (2022)

65. Ren, H., Santhanam, R.: Hardness of KT characterizes parallel cryptography. In: Proceedings of the 36th Computational Complexity Conference. CCC 2021. Schloss Dagstuhl–Leibniz-Zentrum fuer Informatik, Dagstuhl (2021)

66. Rompel, J.: One-way functions are necessary and sufficient for secure signatures. In: 22nd ACM STOC, pp. 387–394. ACM Press (1990)

67. Sipser, M.: A complexity theoretic approach to randomness. In: 15th ACM STOC, pp. 330–335. ACM Press (1983)

68. Solomonoff, R.: A formal theory of inductive inference. Part I. Inf. Control **7**(1), 1-22 (1964)

69. Solomonoff, R.: A formal theory of inductive inference. Part II. Inf. Control **7**(2), 224–254 (1964)

70. Solomonoff, R.: A Preliminary Report on a General Theory of Inductive Inference. AFOSR TN-60-1459. United States Air Force, Office of Scientific Research (1960)

71. Trakhtenbrot, B.: A survey of Russian approaches to perebor (brute-force searches) algorithms. Ann. Hist. Comput. **6**(4), 384–400 (1984)

72. Williams, R.: Improving exhaustive search implies superpolynomial lower bounds. SIAM J. Comput. **42**(3), 1218–1244 (2013). https://doi.org/10.1137/10080703X

73. Williams, R.: Nonuniform ACC circuit lower bounds. J. ACM **61**(1) (2014)

On One-Way Functions, the Worst-Case Hardness of Time-Bounded Kolmogorov Complexity, and Computational Depth

Yanyi Liu[1]([✉]) and Rafael Pass[2]

[1] Cornell Tech, New York, USA
yl2866@cornell.edu
[2] Cornell Tech, Technion, TAU, New York, USA
rafael@cs.cornell.edu

Abstract. Whether one-way functions (OWF) exist is arguably the most important problem in Cryptography, and beyond. While lots of candidate constructions of one-way functions are known, and recently also problems whose average-case hardness characterize the existence of OWFs have been demonstrated, the question of whether there exists some *worst-case hard problem* that characterizes the existence of one-way functions has remained open since their introduction in 1976.

In this work, we present the first "OWF-complete" promise problem— a promise problem whose worst-case hardness w.r.t. BPP (resp. P/poly) is *equivalent* to the existence of OWFs secure against PPT (resp. nuPPT) algorithms. The problem is a variant of the Minimum Time-bounded Kolmogorov Complexity problem ($\mathsf{MK}^t\mathsf{P}[s]$ with a threshold s), where we condition on instances having small "computational depth".

We furthermore show that depending on the choice of the threshold s, this problem characterizes either "standard" (polynomially-hard) OWFs, or quasi polynomially- or subexponentially-hard OWFs. Additionally, when the threshold is sufficiently small (e.g., $2^{O(\sqrt{\log n})}$ or $\mathrm{poly}\log n$) then *sublinear* hardness of this problem suffices to characterize quasi-polynomial/sub-exponential OWFs.

While our constructions are black-box, our analysis is *non-black box*; we additionally demonstrate that fully black-box constructions of OWF from the worst-case hardness of this problem are impossible. We finally show that, under Rudich's conjecture, and standard derandomization assumptions, our problem is not inside coAM; as such, it yields the first candidate problem believed to be outside of AM ∩ coAM, or even **SZK**, whose worst case hardness implies the existence of OWFs.

Y. Liu—Supported by a JP Morgan Fellowship. Part of work done while visiting the Simons Institute.

R. Pass—Part of work done while visiting the Simons Institute. Supported in part by NSF Award CNS 2149305, NSF Award CNS-2128519, NSF Award RI-1703846, AFOSR Award FA9550-18-1-0267, FA9550-23-1-0312, AFOSR Award FA9550-23-1-0387, a JP Morgan Faculty Award, the Algorand Centres of Excellence programme managed by Algorand Foundation, and DARPA under Agreement No. HR00110C0086. Any opinions, findings and conclusions or recommendations expressed in this material are those of the author(s) and do not necessarily reflect the views of the United States Government, DARPA or the Algorand Foundation.

E. Boyle and M. Mahmoody (Eds.): TCC 2024, LNCS 15364, pp. 222–252, 2025.
https://doi.org/10.1007/978-3-031-78011-0_8

1   Introduction

A *one-way function* [DH76] (OWF) is a function f that can be efficiently computed (in polynomial time), yet no probabilistic polynomial-time (PPT) algorithm can invert f with inverse polynomial probability for infinitely many input lengths n. Whether one-way functions exist is unequivocally the most important open problem in Cryptography (and arguably the most important open problem in the theory of computation, see e.g., [Lev03]): OWFs are both necessary [IL89] and sufficient for many of the most central cryptographic primitives and protocols (e.g., pseudorandom generators [BM84,HILL99], pseudorandom functions [GGM84], private-key encryption [GM84], digital signatures [Rom90], commitment schemes [Nao91], identification protocols [FS90], coin-flipping protocols [Blu82], and more). These primitives and protocols are often referred to as *private-key primitives*, or "Minicrypt" primitives [Imp95] as they exclude the notable task of public-key encryption [DH76,RSA83]. Additionally, as observed by Impagliazzo [Gur89,Imp95], the existence of a OWF is equivalent to the existence of polynomial-time method for sampling hard *solved* instances for an NP language (i.e., hard instances together with their witnesses).

Cryptography from Worst-case Hardness and the "coAM Barrier": A long standing question, dating back to the original work by Diffie and Hellman [DH76], is whether OWFs can be based on the *worst-case hardness* of some NP problem; ideally, this problem should be NP-complete which would yield the existence of OWFs based on the assumption that NP $\not\subseteq$ BPP (which trivially is implied by the existence of OWFs). This question is usually referred to as the "holy grail" of Cryptography, and is still wide open.

Following the breakthrough result of Ajtai in 1996 [Ajt96], there has been an explosion of cryptography based on the worst-case hardness of lattice problems (see e.g., [AD97,Reg04]); these problems, however, are all in AM $\cap$ coAM [GG00] and are thus unlikely to be NP-complete. Indeed, starting in the early 1980's, works by Brassard [Bra83], Bogdanov and Trevisan [BT03] and Akavia, Goldreich, Goldwasser and Moshkovitz [AGGM06] show that such containment in AM $\cap$ coAM may be necessary—at least w.r.t. *black-box reductions*[1]. The work by Akavia et al., however, explicitly mention the possibility that non-black box techniques, although "uncommon" in complexity theory, may be useful in overcoming these barriers:

Can OWFs be based on the worst-case hardness of some promise problem
$\Pi \not\subseteq$ coAM?

OWF-Complete Problems. More generally, we may ask whether some NP problem can be used to *characterize* the existence of OWFs—namely, do "OWF-complete" problems exist?

---

[1] We highlight that these results actually do not manage to fully rule out all black-box reductions; they either apply to so-called *non-adaptive* black-box reductions, or only to restricted types of one-way functions.

As we will explain in more detail shortly, the above coAM black-box barriers also extend to OWF-completeness, and as such, we will here focus on defining a notion of OWF-completeness w.r.t. *non black-box* reductions—in fact, for generality, we will allow even non explicit reductions (although the actual reduction presented in this paper will be explicit).

Define the class OWF of promise problems Π having the property that there exists some polynomial-time computable function f such that if there exists some "efficient attacker" that can invert f with probability (say $1/2$) for infinitely many n, then Π can be decided on infinitely many input lengths by some "efficient attacker". Additionally, we refer to a problem Π as being OWF-hard if it holds that if Π can be decided (in the worst-case) for infinitely many input lengths by "efficient attackers", then all poly-time functions can be inverted with probability $1/2$ by "efficient attackers". Finally, Π is OWF-complete if $\Pi \in$ OWF and Π is OWF-hard.

To prevent artificial complete problems (e.g., $L = SAT$ if polynomially-secure OWF exists and empty otherwise[2]), and to capture intuitions similar to those of black-box reductions (which also prevent artificial complete problems), we require the above to *simultaneously* hold for any "natural" class $\mathcal{C}$ of "efficient adversaries".[3] For simplicity of notation, we here focus on $\mathcal{C} = \{\text{PPT}, \text{nuPPT}\}$, but our result directly extends also to any uniform (resp. non-uniform) class of adversaries whose running time is closed under polynomial composition (e.g., poly-time, quasi-polynomial-time or subexponential-time). With the above concrete choice of "efficient attacker" (i.e., the above class $\mathcal{C}$), we have that a promise problem Π is OWF-complete if it holds that $\Pi \notin$ ioBPP (resp. $\Pi \notin$ ioP/poly) if and only if OWFs secure against PPT (resp. secure against non-uniform polynomial-time algorithms) exist.

Given this notion of completeness, an natural question is whether there is some promise problem that characterizes the existence of OWFs:

Does there exist some promise problem in NP that is OWF complete? That is, $\Pi \notin$ ioBPP (resp. $\Pi \notin$ ioP/poly) if and only if OWFs secure against PPT (resp. nuPPT) exist?

Black-box Barriers to OWF-Complete Problems. As alluded to above, the barriers established by Bogdanov and Trevisan [BT03] and Akavia, Goldreich, Goldwasser and Moshkovitz [AGGM06] also yield limitations of OWF-complete problem. These works demonstrate that *non-adaptive black-box reductions* can only be used to reduce OWFs to the worst-case hardness of languages in AM∩coAM, which under standard derandomization assumptions equals NP ∩ coNP. In other words, under standard derandomization assumptions, only languages in NP ∩ coNP would exist in OWF in case we only considered Karp,

---

[2] We thank an anonymous reviewer for pointing out this "trivial" complete problem.

[3] That is, the problem is "uniform" w.r.t. the attack class. This is needed to prevent the "complete" problem from simply encoding that OWF exists w.r.t. to a specific attack model; uniformity/obliviousness w.r.t. the attack class ensures that the problem captures the "essence" of the notion of one-wayness.

or even non-adaptive black-box, reductions when defining the class OWF. But it was shown already by Blum-Impagliazzo [BI87] and Rudich [Rud88] in the 1980s that there are no so-called "fully black-box" constructions of a hard language in NP∩coNP based on the existence of OWFs; in fact, recently, Bitansky, Degwekar and Vaikuntanathan [BDV17] strengthened this result to show impossibility of fully black-box constructions of a hard problem in NP∩coNP from a host of standard cryptographic primitives, including injective OWFs and indistinguishability obfuscation [BDV17].

Of course, these results do not show that obtaining a OWF-complete problem is impossible—only that it will require using either adaptive black-box techniques, or to use non black-box techniques, but either of these are rare, at least for the analysis of the most basic cryptographic building blocks.

1.1 Our Results

In this paper, we demonstrate the existence of a OWF-complete problem. Our problem will be natural variant of the standard time-bounded Kolmogorov complexity problem and will be based on a recent thread of literature demonstrating the existence of natural problems whose *average-case* hardness characterize the existence of OWFs. As we shall see, we will show how to use *non-black box techniques* to extend these results to also work in the worst-case regime.

In a bit more detail, we will present a promise version of the time-bounded Kolmogorov complexity problem, parametrized by a threshold s. When the threshold is large, worst-case hardness of this problem will characterize "plain" OWFs, when it is "intermediate", it will characterize quasi-polynomially secure OWFs, and when it is "small", it will characterize subexponentially secure OWFs. In other words, we identify not only a OWF-complete problem, but the same problem, with a different threshold is also complete for quasi-polynomial/subexponential OWFs. Additionally, as we shall see, in the regime of quasi-polynomial/subexponential OWFs, it will suffice to assume that the promise problem is (worst-case) hard w.r.t. sublinear time algorithms.

Before turning to the formal statement of our results, let us first review the recent literature connecting OWFs and Kolmogorov complexity.

On OWFs and Kolmogorov Complexity: The MK^tP Problem. Given a truthtable $x \in \{0,1\}^n$ of a Boolean function, what is the size of the smallest "program" that computes x? This problem has fascinated researchers since the 1950 [Tra84, Yab59a, Yab59b], and various variants of it have been considered depending on how the notion of a program is formalized. For instance, when the notion of a program is taken to be circuits (e.g., with AND,OR,NOT gates), then it corresponds to the Minimum Circuit Size problem (MCSP) [KC00, Tra84], and when the notion of a program is taken to be a time-bounded Turing machine, then it corresponds to the Minimum Time-Bounded Kolmogorov complexity problem (MKTP) [Kol68, Ko86, Sip83, Har83, All01, ABK+06]. Our focus here is on the latter scenario. Given a string x describing a truthtable, let $K^t(x)$ denote the t-bounded Kolmogorov complexity of x—that is, the length of the shortest string Π such that for every $i \in [n]$, $U(\Pi, i) = x_i$ within time $t(|\Pi|)$, where U is a fixed Universal Turing machine.[4]

Given a threshold, $s(\cdot)$, and a polynomial time-bound, $t(\cdot)$, let $\mathsf{MK}^t\mathsf{P}[s]$ denote the language consisting of strings x such that $K^t(x) \leq s(|x|)$; $\mathsf{MK}^t\mathsf{P}[s]$ is clearly in NP, but it is unknown whether it is NP-complete—indeed, this is a long-standing open problem. In [LP20], Liu and Pass recently showed that when the threshold $s(\cdot)$ is "large" (more precisely, when $s(n) = n - c \log n$, for some constant c), then mild *average-case hardness* of this language w.r.t., the uniform distribution of instances is equivalent to the existence of one-way functions (OWF).[5]

Even more recently, a different work by Liu and Pass [LP21a] demonstrated that when the threshold is smaller, and if we consider a notion called *mild average-case* hardness* (which roughly speaking requires average-case hardness conditioned on both YES and NO instances), then this problem characterizes also quasi-polynomial or sub-exponential one-way functions. In particular, quasi-polynomially secure and subexponentially-secure OWFs are characterized by mild average-case* hardness of $\mathsf{MK}^t\mathsf{P}[s]$ where the threshold are $s(n) = 2^{O(\sqrt{\log n})}$ and $s(n) = \mathsf{poly} \log n$ respectively. Intriguingly, their result—following a literature on so-called *hardness magnification* [OS18, MMW19, CT19, OPS19, CMMW19] [Oli19, CJW19, CHO+20] shows that it suffices to assume *sublinear* hardness of these problems to provide those characterizations (when the threshold is sublinear). We mention one caveat in these results—whereas the original result of [LP20] characterizing standard OWFs applies both in the uniform and non-uniform regime, the small threshold characterization (which only require sublinear hardness) only applies in the non-uniform regime (i.e., they characterize hardness of $\mathsf{MK}^t\mathsf{P}[s]$ with respect to non-uniform algorithms through OWFs secure against non-uniform algorithms).

Roughly speaking, our main results will show that if we consider a promise-problem variant of the $\mathsf{MK}^t\mathsf{P}[s]$ problem, then we can demonstrate the above characterization but in terms of simply worst-case hardness of the problem. Additionally, our characterizations simultaneously holds in both the non-uniform and uniform regime, as required by our definition of OWF-completeness.[6]

---

[4] There are many ways to define time-bounded Kolmogorov complexity. We here consider the "local compression" version—which corresponds to the above truthtable compression problem—and where the running-time bound is a function of the length of the program. A different version of (time-bounded) Kolmogorov complexity instead considers the size of the shortest program that outputs the *whole* string x. This other notion refers to a "global compression" notion, but is less appealing from the point of view of truthtable compression, as the running-time of the program can never be smaller than the length of the truthtable x.

[5] Strictly speaking, [LP20] considered the "global compression" version of Kolmogorov complexity, but when the threshold is large, these notion are essentially equivalent, and the result from [LP20] directly applies also the "local compression" notion of Kolmogorov complexity considered here.

[6] In fact, our techniques could also be applied to the average-case setting and show that the results in [LP21a] actually also work in the uniform regime.

Computational Depth and "Natural" Instances. To state our results, let us first (abuse the notations and) let $\mathsf{MK}^t\mathsf{P}[s]$ denote the promise problem where:

– **YES**-instances consist of strings x such that $K^t(x) \leq s(|x|)$;
– **NO**-instances consist of string x such that $K^t(x) \geq n - 1$;

Note that the only difference between the $\mathsf{MK}^t\mathsf{P}[s]$ language defined above and this promise problem is we restrict the NO-instances to have very high K^t-complexity (i.e., they are "K^t-random"). Ideally, we would like to show that worst-case hardness of this standard problem characterizes OWFs. We will, however, need to consider a somewhat stronger hardness assumption. Roughly speaking, we will require this problem to be hard even when we restrict the inputs to be of a certain "natural" form (i.e., we require that every algorithm fails on some natural input), where naturality will be defined in a precise mathematical way.

Given a promise problem $\Pi = (\Pi_{\mathsf{YES}}, \Pi_{\mathsf{NO}})$, and an event $Q \subseteq \{0,1\}^*$, we define the "conditioned" promise problem $\Pi|_Q \overset{\text{def}}{=} (\Pi_{\mathsf{YES}} \cap Q, \Pi_{\mathsf{NO}} \cap Q)$. To define naturality, we will consider the notion of *computational depth* [AFvMV06]. Recall that the computational depth of a string x is defined as $CD^t(x) = K^t(x) - K(x)$. For every function t and constant β, define the following event

$$Q^t_\beta = \{x \in \{0,1\}^* : K^t(x) - K(x) \leq \beta \log K(x)\}$$

That is, the event that the computational depth is "small" relative to $K(x)$. Intuitively, the notion of computational depth is thought of a measure of "unnaturality" of strings: arguably, only "unnatural" strings have a large gap between how much they can be efficiently and non efficiently compressed. Thus, by conditioning on strings with (relatively) small computational depth, it means that we require the problem to be hard on "natural" inputs. In other words, hardness of a promise problem conditioned on the event Q^t_β requires every algorithm to fail on some "natural" string.

We remark that the event Q^t_β is not *computable* as $K(x)$ is not computable. We mention, however, that all the result of this paper would still remain valid if replacing $K(x)$ by $K^{\mathsf{EXP}}(x) = K^{t'}(x)$ where $t'(n) = 2^{\mathsf{poly}(n)}$.

The Work of Antunes and Fortnow [AF09]. We highlight that Antunes and Fortnow [AF09] elegantly used computational depth to connect worst-case hardness of a problem when restricting attention to elements with small computational depth and average-case hardness on sampleable distributions. We will rely on some of the same intuitions, but emphasize a crucial difference. [AF09] only connects the notion of *errorless* average-case hardness (i.e., average-case hardness w.r.t. algorithms that never make mistake—they either give the right answer or output $\perp$) and worst-case hardness, and their proof techniques are tailored to this notion. And for the particular problem that we consider (i.e., $\mathsf{MK}^t\mathsf{P}[s]$), it is already known [Hir18,LP21b], that worst-case hardness directly (without considering computational depth) implies errorless average-case hardness with respect to the uniform distribution, so it would seem that computational depth is not helpful. Nevertheless, as we shall see, we will be able to essentially connect worst-case hardness conditioned on instances with small computational depth and also *two-sided* error average-case hardness (and thus be able to rely on results like [LP20,LP21a]).

We are now ready to state our main theorems.

Characterizing OWFs. Our first result demonstrates the first OWF-complete problem, thus providing a positive answer to the second question in the introduction:

Theorem 1 (Characterizing OWFs) *For every polynomial* $t(n) \geq 2n$, *all constant* $\beta > 0, \delta > 0$, *and any threshold function* $s(\cdot)$, $n^\delta \leq s(n) < n - 1$, *the following are equivalent:*

- *OWF (resp. non-uniformly secure OWF) exists;*
- $\mathsf{MK}^t\mathsf{P}[n-2]|_{Q_\beta^t} \notin$ ioBPP *(resp.* $\mathsf{MK}^t\mathsf{P}[n-2]|_{Q_\beta^t} \notin$ ioP/poly*)*
- $\mathsf{MK}^t\mathsf{P}[s]|_{Q_\beta^t} \notin$ ioBPP *(resp.* $\mathsf{MK}^t\mathsf{P}[s]|_{Q_\beta^t} \notin$ ioP/poly*).*

As mentioned above, the above problem is robust in the sense that completeness holds also when considering more general classes of "efficient adversaries" such as probabilistic/non-uniform quasi-polynomal, or probabilistic/non-uniform subexponential, attackers.[7]

Computational Depth and Average-Case Hardness. As mentioned above, the work of Antunes and Fortnow [AF09] demonstrates that worst-case hardness of a language L conditioned on instances with small computational depth implies *errorless* average-case hardness on sampleable distributions.

One may, however, wonder whether a similar result can be shown also for two-sided error average-case hardness—which for the particular $\mathsf{MK}^t\mathsf{P}$ problem has been shown to be equivalent to OWFs (when considering average-case hardness w.r.t. the uniform distribution) [LP20]. We do not know a proof of this for general languages L (and thus the proof of Theorem 1 relies on a different approach), but note that as a direct corollary of Theorem 1 and the main results of [LP20], we have that worst-case hardness of $\mathsf{MK}^t\mathsf{P}[n - O(\log n)]$ conditioned on instances with small computational depth is equivalent to average-case hardness of $\mathsf{MK}^t\mathsf{P}[n - O(\log n)]$ w.r.t. the *uniform distribution* (since by our results, the former is equivalent to OWFs, and by [LP20] the latter is equivalent to OWFs). In fact, under standard derandomization assumptions, we can also get average-case hardness under samplable distributions (as long as t is sufficiently bigger than the running time of the sampler)—this follows since [LP22a] recently showed (under derandomization assumptions) the equivalence between OWFs and average-case hardness of $\mathsf{MK}^t\mathsf{P}[n - O(\log n)]$ under sampleable distributions (when t is sufficiently big).

The Complexity of $\mathsf{MK}^t\mathsf{P}[n-2]|_{Q_\beta^t}$ and Going Beyond the coAM barrier. An interesting consequence of Theorem 1 is the equivalence of bullet 2 and 3— that is, the hardness of the problem remains the same when the thresholds is

---

[7] We remark that this result also holds for the "global compression" version of time-bounded Kolmogorov complexity, as in [LP20].

anywhere from $n^{\Omega(1)}$ to $n - 2$; as we shall see shortly, this will (likely) not be the case when the threshold is significantly smaller (as the same problem will characterize quasi-polynomial/sub-exponential OWFs).

We additionally remark that under reasonable assumptions—in particular, under Rudich's assumption [Rud97] regarding the existence of cryptographic PRGs secure against coNP algorithms, and standard derandomization assumptions (i.e., the same ones used to traditionally argue that $\mathsf{MK}^t\mathsf{P}[s]$ is not inside coAM [ABK+06,Hir18]) —$\mathsf{MK}^t\mathsf{P}[s]|_{Q^t_\beta}$ is not inside coAM when t, β are sufficiently big; as such, Theorem 1 yields the first problem believed to be outside of AM ∩ coAM whose worst-case hardness (even just) *implies* the existence of OWFs, providing a positive answer to question 1 in the introduction (under computational assumptions). In more detail, we will show that the problem (at least in some parameter regime that suffices to characterize OWFs) is not in io-coNP/poly, which contains coAM.

Theorem 2 (Informally Stated). *There exists some $\beta > 0$ such that under Rudich's conjecture and standard derandomization assumption, it holds that for all sufficiently large polynomials $t(n)$,*

$$\mathsf{MK}^t\mathsf{P}[n - 2]|_{Q^t_\beta} \not\subseteq \text{io-coNP/poly}$$

Impossibility of Fully Black-Box Constructions. As mentioned above, the proof of our main theorems rely on *non-black box techniques*. In particular, in contrast to the construction of OWFs from the average-case hardness of $\mathsf{MK}^t\mathsf{P}[s]$ of [LP20] which is *fully black-box*, we make use of the code of the attacker in analyzing the security of the OWFs. We show that this non-black box usage is needed, by demonstrating the impossibility of fully black-box constructions of OWF from the hardness of $\mathsf{MK}^t\mathsf{P}[s]|_{Q^t_\beta}$ when β is sufficiently big. Roughly speaking, we here refer to a reduction to $\mathsf{MK}^t\mathsf{P}$ as being *fully black-box* if both the construction and the reduction treats the universal Turing machine in the definition of K^t in a black-box way, and additionally the reduction only gets black-box access to the attacker. We note that we here also rule out *adaptive* black reductions (c.f. the results of [BT03,AGGM06] that only deal with non-adaptive ones).

Theorem 3. *For all sufficiently large $\beta > 0$, for all polynomials $t(n) \geq 2n$, there does not exists a fully black-box construction of OWFs from $\mathsf{MK}^t\mathsf{P}[n - 2]|_{Q^t_\beta} \not\subseteq$ ioP/poly.*

We highlight that perhaps surprisingly, the proof of the black-box impossibility result heavily relies on the proof techniques developed to show Theorem 1 (i.e., our main characterization).

Characterizing Qpoly/Subexponential OWFs. We show that $\mathsf{MK}^t\mathsf{P}[s]|_{Q^t_\beta}$ becomes "easier" when the threshold is smaller by showing that its hardness characterizes quasi-polynomially/sub-exponentially secure OWFs when the threshold is smaller. We here additionally show that *sublinear* hardness of the same problem also characterizes the same primitive.

To simplify notation, we state these results for the setting of uniform security, but emphasize that these results (just as Theorem 1 where we did it explicitly) also work in the setting on non-uniform security. We highlight that this is not immediate since we are employing non-black box techniques.

Theorem 4 (Characterizing Quasi-Polynomially Secure OWFs). *For every polynomial $t(n) \geq 2n$, every constant $\beta > 0, \delta > 0$, the following are equivalent,*

- *Quasi-polynomially secure OWFs exist;*
- $\mathsf{MK}^t\mathsf{P}[2^{O(\sqrt{\log n})}]|_{Q^t_\beta} \notin \mathsf{ioBPTIME}[n^\delta]$

Theorem 5 (Characterizing Subexponentially Secure OWFs). *For every polynomial $t(n) \geq 2n$, every constant $\beta > 0, \delta > 0$, the following are equivalent,*

- *Subexponentially secure OWFs exists;*
- $\mathsf{MK}^t\mathsf{P}[\mathrm{poly}\log n]|_{Q^t_\beta} \notin \mathsf{ioBPTIME}[n^\delta]$

Theorems 4 and 5 follow from a more general theorem characterizing T-secure OWF through the worst-case hardness of $\mathsf{MK}^t\mathsf{P}[s]|_{Q^t_\beta}$ where s is polynomially related to T^{-1} (see Theorem 15 in Sect. 3).

1.2 Perspective

Taken together, our results demonstrate that worst-case hardness of the *same* natural problem—that is, i.e., $\mathsf{MK}^t\mathsf{P}[s]$ conditioned on inputs being "natural" (i.e., of small computational depth) characterizes all of OWFs, quasi-polynomially secure OWFs and subexponentionally secure OWFs, depending on how the threshold is set. There are several interesting consequences one can draw from this:

- **Characterizing the "holy grail"**: As mentioned above, the holy grail of Cryptography is basing OWFs on the assumption that $\mathsf{NP} \nsubseteq \mathsf{BPP}$ (or more precisely $\mathsf{NP} \nsubseteq \mathsf{ioBPP}$). By our results, solving this problem is *equivalent* to showing that our promise problem is NP complete (perhaps with a non-black box reduction). As far as we know, there are no barriers to this since as argued above, the problem is unlikely to be inside coAM. There has been lots of recent progress (see e.g. [Ila20, ILO20, Ila21, Ila22, LP22b, Hir22]) on showing that $\mathsf{MK}^t\mathsf{P}[s]$ may be NP complete (for various variants of the problems), so there is hope that this can be done.
- **Characterizing Hardness Magnification for OWFs**: Could it be that plain OWFs imply quasi-polynomially secure (or even subexponentially secure OWFs)? Our results demonstrate that this is equivalent to demonstrating a reduction—in the *worst-case regime*—from the low threshold case to the high threshold case for our promise problem.

– **Towards** NP ≠ P, **or even** NP ⊄ BPTIME(2^{n^ϵ}) As far as we know, Theorem 4 and 5 yield the first problem whose *sublinear* worst-case hardness implies that NP ≠ P (and in fact, they yield even the stronger consequence that NP cannot be solved in quasi-polynomial or subexponential time). Worst-case hardness w.r.t. sublinear time algorithms is typically easy to show for natural problem (e.g., [LP21a] even showed it for a different variant of the $MK^tP[s]$ problem) so there is hope that our results yield a new path toward solving the NP v.s. P problem.

– **Beyond OWFs:** Our work introduces a new non black-box technique to analyze protocols based on the hardness of Kolmogorov complexity problems. We believe these techniques will be useful also outside the realm of just OWFs. Indeed, a very recent paper [BLMP23] which follows up on ours, demonstrates how to use these techniques (and in particular how restricting attention to an appropriate analog of computational depth) can be used to get a characterization of *key-exchange agreement* [DH76] using the worst-case hardness of a Kolmogorov complexity-style problem.

Concurrent and Independent Work: A concurrent and independent elegant work by Hirahara and Nanashima [HN23] also provides a worst-case characterization of OWFs.[8] There are some conceptual similarities: both works consider worst-case hardness of a language/promise problem conditioned on instances with small computational depth.

There are also some significant differences:

– [HN23] does not actually characterize OWF but rather only so-called *infinitely-often* OWFs (which are less relevant for cryptography). Their proof technique seemingly does not extend to deal with "standard" OWFs. (In contrast, ours directly extends to also characterize infinitely-often OWFs.)
– For our problem, changing the threshold enables performing "hardness magnification" (i.e., characterizing stronger OWFs and enabling using simply sublinear worst-case hardness in the small threshold case.) Their problem/proof approach is seemingly not amenable to this.
– The actual problem they consider is less standard/more complicated ("estimating the probability that a random program outputs a certain string") than the one we consider (i.e., the standard MK^tP problem). Additionally, they also do not rely on the standard notion of computational depth but a variant of it related to the above problem.
  As a consequence, whereas our problem is (trivially) in NP, theirs is only shown to be in AM (and even this requires some work).
– The problem in [HN23] is not proven to be OWF-complete according to our notion of completeness as the characterization only holds in the *uniform* setting (since a non black-box proof is used, security in the uniform setting does not imply security in the non-uniform setting). In contrast, we show equivalence in both the uniform and the non-uniform setting. (Conceivably

---

[8] Both papers were submitted to FOCS'23. Theirs was accepted, ours not.

however, our new proof technique for dealing with non-uniformity may also be applicable to their problem.)
- Finally, [HN23] do not show that their problem is not contained coAM; conceivably, however, our proof technique may be applicable to show that theirs also is not in coAM.

(Of course, [HN23] also contains other intriguing results, but we are here simply comparing the characterization of OWFs.)

Despite all these differences, the results of [HN23] indicate that a conceptually different type of a OWF-complete problem may be within reach, and consequently that the class of OWF-complete promise problems may contain conceptually different types of problem (similar to NP-complete problems)—we interpret this as exciting evidence of the richness of the OWF class.

1.3 Proof Overview

We here provide a proof overview of Theorem 1, 4 and 5.

The Key Idea In a Nutshell. To explain our approach, let us start by a simple but powerful observation. Let Π denote some decidable promise problem and let $\mathbf{KR}_c$ denote the event that $K(x) \geq n - c \log n$ (i.e., x is asymptotically "Kolmogorov Random"). Then, for every $c > 1$, worst-case hardness of the conditional promise problem $\Pi|_{\mathbf{KR}_c}$ implies mild average-case hardness of Π with respect to the uniform distribution. To see this, assume for contradiction that some *uniform* polynomial-time attacker A manages to solve Π on average with probability $1 - 1/n^{c'}$ for some sufficiently big $c' > c$. In other words, there are at most $3 \times 2^n/n^{c'}$ instances on which A fails with probability $\geq 1/3$ over its randomness. But then all those instances must have Kolmogorov complexity bounded by $\log(2^n/n^{c'}) + O(\log n)$ (to index the instance among the list of elements on which A fails with probability $\geq 1/3$, plus the additional $O(\log n)$ to describe n as well as to provide the *constant-size* description of A). But for a sufficiently large c', this is strictly smaller than $n - c \log n$, so A can *only* fail on instances outside of the promise $\mathbf{KR}_c$. Note that the above argument is *non-black box*: we rely on the fact that we have a short description of the attacker A. In fact, the above argument seemingly only shows average-case hardness w.r.t *uniform* algorithms A. However, by an additional trick we can extend it to work also for non-uniform algorithms (assuming worst-case hardness of $\Pi|_{\mathbf{KR}_c}$ with respect to non-uniform polynomial-time algorithms). Assume for contradiction that there exists some non-uniform polynomial-time algorithm with size/time bounded by n^d that breaks the average-case hardness of Π. Then, given d (which can be described in $O(1)$ bits), we can simply enumerate all possible non-uniform attackers of size up to n^d and pick the one who solves the promise problem with the highest probability, and do the rest of the argument with respect to this attacker (which now can be described using $O(1)$ bits). Note that we here need to rely on the decidability of the promise problem.

Characterizing OWF Through KR: A Warm-Up. We note that although the above observation is simple, it is   quite powerful. It can already be used, combined with the results of [LP20], to demonstrate that worst-case hardness of $\mathsf{MK}^t\mathsf{P}[n - c \log n]|_{\mathbf{KR}_{2c}}$ characterizes the existence of OWF for every sufficiently large c. Roughly speaking, this follows from the fact that [LP20] showed that mild average-case hardness of $\mathsf{MK}^t\mathsf{P}[n - c \log n]$ is equivalent to the existence of OWF (for every sufficiently large c); in fact, by observing the proof of [LP20], it turns out that for all sufficiently big c, the equivalence holds w.r.t. $\mathsf{MK}^t\mathsf{P}[n - c \log n]$ being $1 - 1/n^{c+3}$-average-case hard (i.e., no PPT attacker can solve the problem with probability better than $1 - 1/n^{c+3}$), which is implied by the worst-case hardness of $\mathsf{MK}^t\mathsf{P}[n - c \log n]|_{\mathbf{KR}_{2c}}$ by the above argument (since c is sufficiently big). In other words, worst-case hardness of $\mathsf{MK}^t\mathsf{P}[n - c \log n]|_{\mathbf{KR}_{2c}}$ implies the existence of OWFs. Furthermore, by [LP20], the existence of OWFs imply that $\mathsf{MK}^t\mathsf{P}[n - c \log n]$ is mildly hard on average, which by a standard averaging argument implies worst-case hardness of $\mathsf{MK}^t\mathsf{P}[n - c \log n]|_{\mathbf{KR}_{2c}}$ since the probability of $\mathbf{KR}_{2c}$ is $1 - O(1/n^{2c})$.

The reader may wonder why we need to through the result of [LP20] at all here: the "key-observation" shows that worst-case hardness conditioned on $\mathbf{KR}_{2c}$ yields average-case hardness w.r.t. the uniform distribution. And as noted in the previous sentence, average-case hardness w.r.t. the uniform distribution implies worst-case hardness conditioned on $\mathbf{KR}_{2c}$, so it would seem that two-sided error average-case and worst-case hardness conditioned on $\mathbf{KR}_{2c}$ are equivalent! (and then we can just rely [LP20] in a black-box way to get a OWF-complete problem). There is an important issue with this approach: worst-case hardness conditioned on $\mathbf{KR}_{2c}$ only implies a weak form of average-case hardness, but in the other direction we require a quantitatively stronger form of average-case hardness to get back worst-case hardness conditioned on $\mathbf{KR}_{2c}$. Going through [LP20], and its cryptographic machinery, enables doing this amplification. (So, at the end of the day, with respect to the particular $\mathsf{MK}^t\mathsf{P}$ problem, it is the case that two-sided error average-case and worst-case hardness conditioned on high K-complexity are equivalent, but proving so relies on going through OWFs and cryptographic machinery).

Characterizing OWFs Through CD. While the above yields a simple characterization of OWFs, it requires tightly calibrating the constant c in the definition of $\mathbf{KR}_c$ to the threshold of the $\mathsf{MK}^t\mathsf{P}$ problem, so it makes for a somewhat brittle characterization. Furthermore, the simple argument above only works to considering hardness of $\mathsf{MK}^t\mathsf{P}[s]$ where $s = n - O(\log n)$, and as such will not be helpful when wanting to characterize quasi-polynomially/subexponentially secure OWFs.

It turns out that instead conditioning on strings having small *computational depth* [AFvMV06, AF09] enables us to deal with these issues and provides for a clean characterization where we can simply condition on the *same* event (namely Q^t_β for any $\beta > 0$), and consider $\mathsf{MK}^t\mathsf{P}[s]$ with respect to any threshold s.

The forward direction of our proof, follows similar intuition to the above, but requires going deeper into the constructions and proofs in [LP20, LP21a], and combining the high-level ideas in those proofs with intuitions similar to the ones use above. We can then show that for any constant β, worst-case hardness of

$\mathsf{MK}^t\mathsf{P}[s]|_{Q_\beta^t}$ implies OWF or even quasi-polynomially/subexponentially secure OWF when the threshold is sufficiently small, and additionally, in the small threshold case, it suffices to just require *sublinear* time (worst-case) hardness.

For the backward direction, we may again rely on the proofs in [LP20, LP21a] combined the with the above observation to show that OWFs (resp T-secure OWFs) imply worst-case hardness of $\mathsf{MK}^t\mathsf{P}[s]|_{Q_\beta^t}$. While the high-level ideas here are similar to [LP20, LP21a], we are required to provide a tighter analysis to deal with the fact that we here consider hardness of the *promise* problem $\mathsf{MK}^t\mathsf{P}[s]$, where for NO-instances, x, requires $K^t(x) \geq n - 1$. As such, the actual technical details here are somewhat different than those in [LP20, LP21a]. Additionally, [LP21a] (which considered the small threshold case in the average-case setting) unfortunately only works for non-uniform attackers. To deal with uniform attacker, we develop a new proof technique (that also ought to work in the average-case setting and may be of independent interest). Without getting too deep in the details, the key obstacle is that [LP21a] relies on the security of a primitive (called an conditionally-secure entropy-preserving PRF (cond EP-PRF) for which it is (seemingly) hard to check if an attacker manages to break its security, and non-uniformity was used to provide the input lengths on which the attacker succeeds. We here show how to also deal with this obstacle without non-uniform advice.

Roughly speaking, the key idea is to leverage the fact that in [LP21a], a cond EP-PRF was constructed based on the existence of a PRG and a PRF (primitives for which we efficiently check whether an attacker succeeds) using an explicit (efficient) *black-box* reduction having the property that any attacker that breaks the cond EP-PRF on some specific inputs length n can be used to break the PRG (or the PRF) on some specific (and efficiently computable) input length n'. We can next use this reduction to efficiently find the input lengths on which the attacker succeeds in breaking the cond EP-PRF.

2   Preliminaries

For any string $x \in \{0,1\}^*$, we let $[x]_n$ denote the first n-bit prefix of x. For any functions $s(\cdot)$, we refer to it as a *threshold function* if s is time-constructible and strictly increasing.

Sublinear-Time Algorithms. If an algorithm M runs in time n^δ for some $\delta < 1$, we refer to M as a sublinear-time algorithm. Notice that sublinear-time algorithms cannot read the whole input. In this work, we assume that a (uniform) sublinear-time algorithm, when running on some input, will be additionally provided with the length of the input.

2.1   Promise Problems and "Conditioned" Problems

In this work, we focus on promise problems $\Pi = (\Pi_{\mathsf{YES}}, \Pi_{\mathsf{NO}})$, and algorithms that decides Π on infinitely many input lengths. We say that an algorithm

M decides Π infinitely often if there exists infinitely many $n \in \mathbb{N}$ such that $(\Pi_{\mathsf{YES}} \cup \Pi_{\mathsf{NO}}) \cap \{0,1\}^n \neq \emptyset$ and M decides Π on input length n.

We consider the promise variant of standard infinitely often complexity classes. Let ioBPP (resp ioP/poly, io-coNP/poly) denote the class of promise problems where for any promise problem Π, $\Pi \in$ ioBPP (resp ioP/poly, io-coNP/poly) if and only if there exists a probabilistic (resp non-uniform, non-uniform co-non deterministic) polynomial time algorithm M that decides Π infinitely often. For any running time bound T, we define ioBPTIME$[T]$, ioSIZE$[T]$ in a similar way (but allowing M to run in time T).

Let us introduce what it means by *"conditioned"* promise problems. For any promise problem Π, and any event $Q \subseteq \{0,1\}^*$, we define the promise problem

$$\Pi|_Q \overset{\text{def}}{=} (\Pi_{\mathsf{YES}} \cap Q, \Pi_{\mathsf{NO}} \cap Q)$$

Note that for any Q, Q', $Q \subseteq Q'$, we have that $\Pi|_Q \subseteq \Pi|_{Q'}$. (And therefore, $\Pi|_{Q'}$ is "harder" than $\Pi|_Q$. Namely, if $\Pi|_Q \notin$ ioBPP, $\Pi|_{Q'} \notin$ ioBPP.)

2.2 One-Way Functions

We recall the standard definitions of one-way functions (with security w.r.t. uniform or non-uniform attackers).

Definition 6. Let $f : \{0,1\}^* \to \{0,1\}^*$ be a polynomial-time computable function. f is said to be a (T, ε)-*one-way function* if for any probabilistic algorithm $\mathcal{A}$ of running time $T(n)$, for all sufficiently large $n \in \mathbb{N}$,

$$\Pr[x \leftarrow \{0,1\}^n; y = f(x) : \mathcal{A}(1^n, y) \in f^{-1}(f(x))] < \varepsilon(n)$$

We say that f is *non-uniformly secure* if the above holds for all non-uniform algorithm $\mathcal{A}$.

We say that f is $T(n)$-one-way (or is a T-hard one-way function) if f is $(T(n), 1/T(n))$-one-way. We say that f is $\varepsilon(n)$-weak $T(n)$-one-way if f is $(T(n), 1 - \varepsilon(n))$-one-way. If $\varepsilon(n)$ is the inverse of a (monotonically increasing) polynomial, we say f is *weak* $T(n)$-one-way. We say that f is simply *one-way* if f is $T(n)$-one-way for all polynomials $T(n)$. When $T(n)$ is a super-polynomial function, we refer to f as being *subexponentially-secure* (resp *quasi-polynomially-secure*) if there exists a constant $c > 0$ such that f is 2^{n^c}-one-way (resp $n^{c \log n}$-one-way).

We recall the hardness amplification lemma [Yao82] which was originally stated for (polynomially-hard) OWFs; we here extend it to work for T-one-way functions.

Lemma 7 (Hardness Amplification [Yao82]). *Assume that there exists a weak $T(n)$-one-way function for an arbitrary function $T(\cdot)$. Then, there exists a $(T'(n))$-one-way function where $T'(n) = \sqrt{\frac{T(n^{\Omega(1)})}{n^{O(1)}}} - n^{O(1)}$.*

We refer the read to [LP21a] for a proof of the above Lemma.

2.3   The OWF Class

We turn to defining, OWF, the class of promise problems Π whose worst-case hardness imply the existence of OWFs. Formally, $\Pi \in$ OWF if and only if there exists a efficiently computable function f such that the following holds: If there exists a PPT (resp. a nuPPT algorithm $\mathcal{A}$) such that $\mathcal{A}$ inverts f infinitely often—that is, for infinitely many $n \in \mathbb{N}$,

$$\Pr[x \leftarrow \{0,1\}^n, y = f(x) : \mathcal{A}(1^n, y) \in f^{-1}(f(x))] \geq \frac{1}{2}$$

then, $\Pi \in$ ioBPP (resp. $\Pi \in$ ioP/poly).

We highlight that containment in OWF requires the problem to be "as hard as" the efficient function f (is to invert) *simultaneously* w.r.t. uniform PPT as well as non-uniform polynomial-time algorithm. This uniformity is a "proxy" for the uniformity imposed by standard definitions of black-box reductions which also provide this guarantee. (One could also extend this uniformity to hold with respect to attackers with larger, e.g., subexponential running time; while this indeed is the case for our results, we simply stick to uniform/non-uniform PPT, for simplicity of notation.)

Let us turn to define OWF-hardness. We say that Π is OWF-hard if the following holds: If $\Pi \in$ ioBPP (resp. ioP/poly), then any efficient function f can be inverted w.p. $1/2$ for infinitely many input length in probabilistic polynomial time (resp. non-uniform polynomial time).

Finally, we say that Π is OWF-complete if $\Pi \in$ OWF and Π is OWF-hard. In other words, Π being OWF-complete means that $\Pi \in$ ioBPP (resp. $\Pi \in$ ioP/poly) iff all efficient functions can be inverted for infinitely many input lengths by PPT algorithms (resp. non uniform polynomial-time algorithms).

2.4   Time-Bounded Kolmogorov Complexity

We define the notion of t-time-bounded Kolmogorov complexity that we rely on. We consider some universal Turing machines U that can emulate any Turing machine M with polynomial overhead. The universal Turing machine U receives as input a description/program $\Pi \in \{0,1\}^* = (M, w)$ where M is a Turing machine and $w \in \{0,1\}^*$ is an input to M; we let $U(\Pi(i), 1^{t(|\Pi|)})$ denote the output of $M(w, i)$ when emulated on U for $t(|\Pi|)$ steps.

Definition 8. Let U be a universal Turing machine and $t(\cdot)$ be a polynomial. Define
$$K^t(x) = \min_{\Pi \in \{0,1\}^*} \{|\Pi| : \forall i \in [|x|], U(\Pi(i), 1^{t(|\Pi|)}) = x_i\}.$$

We remark that the notion of time-bounded Kolmogorov complexity has been defined in a lot of different ways [Kol68, Sip83, Tra84, Ko86, ABK+06]; the definition we consider here is the "local compression" version (see e.g., [ABK+06, LP21a]) where the program Π is required to efficiently output each individual bit x_i of the string x, given i as input.

A basic computational problem regarding t-time-bounded Kolmogorov complexity is the minimum K^t-complexity problem $\mathsf{MK}^t\mathsf{P}$. In this work, we consider its decisional version, which is parameterized by a threshold $s(\cdot)$, and the goal is to distinguish strings x with small K^t-complexity ($\leq s(|x|)$) from those with large K^t-complexity $\geq n - 1$.

Definition 9. ($\mathsf{MK}^t\mathsf{P}$) Let $\mathsf{MK}^t\mathsf{P}[s]$ denote the following promise problem:

- YES: $x \in \{0,1\}^*$, $K^t(x) \leq s(|x|)$.
- NO: $x \in \{0,1\}^*$, $K^t(x) \geq n - 1$.

Computational Depth. We will focus our attention on $\mathsf{MK}^t\mathsf{P}$ with instances having small computational depth [AFvMV06]. Roughly speaking, the computational depth of a string x is the difference between its K^t-complexity and its (time-unbounded) K-complexity. Recall that for any string $x \in \{0,1\}^*$, its (time-unbounded) K-complexity, $K(x)$, is defined to be the length of the shortest program that produces x. Formally,

$$K(x) = \min_{\Pi \in \{0,1\}^*} \{|\Pi| : \exists t \in \mathbb{N}, U(\Pi, 1^t) = x\}$$

And we refer to $K^t(x) - K(x)$ as the computational depth of x. Throughout this work, for any polynomial t, any constant $\beta > 0$, we define

$$Q_\beta^t \overset{\text{def}}{=} \{x \in \{0,1\}^* : K^t(x) - K(x) \leq \beta \log K(x)\}$$

be the set of strings with computational depth logarithmic in $K(x)$. (And recall that $\mathsf{MK}^t\mathsf{P}|_{Q_\beta^t}$ is the promise variant of $\mathsf{MK}^t\mathsf{P}$ where we condition on instances $\in Q_\beta^t$.) As argued in the introduction, Q_β^t is the set of "natural" instances. Observe that for any polynomial $t_0, t_1, t_1(n) \geq t_0(n)$, for any constant $\beta_1 \geq \beta_0 > 0$, we have that

$$Q_{\beta_0}^{t_0} \subseteq Q_{\beta_0}^{t_1}, Q_{\beta_0}^{t_0} \subseteq Q_{\beta_1}^{t_0}$$

We recall the following fact about (time-bounded) Kolmogorov complexity (and we refer to [LP21a] for a short proof).

Fact 10. *There exists a constant c such that for every polynomial $t(n) \geq (1 + \varepsilon)n, \varepsilon > 0$, the following holds:*

(1) For every $x \in \{0,1\}^*$, $K^t(x) \leq |x| + c$;
(2) For every integer $n \in \mathbb{N}$, every function $0 < s(n) < n$, $2^{\lfloor s(n) \rfloor - c} \leq |\mathsf{MK}^t\mathsf{P}[s(n)] \cap \{0,1\}^n| \leq 2^{\lfloor s(n) \rfloor + 1}$.

2.5 Distributions, Random Variables, and Entropy

Let $\mathcal{D}$ be a distribution. We let $\mathsf{supp}(\mathcal{D})$ denote the support of $\mathcal{D}$. For any $x \in \mathsf{supp}(\mathcal{D})$, we let $\mathcal{D}(x)$ denote $\Pr[\mathcal{D} = x]$.

For a random variable X, let $H(X) = \mathsf{E}[\log \frac{1}{\Pr[X=x]}]$ denote the (Shannon) entropy of X. The following lemma will be useful for us.

Lemma 11 (Implicit in [LP20, IRS21]). *Let X be a random variable distributed over $S \subseteq \{0,1\}^n$, E be an set $\subseteq S$. It holds that*

$$\Pr[x \leftarrow X : x \in E] \le \frac{\log|S| + 1 - H(X)}{\log|S| - \log|E|}$$

Proof: Let flag be a binary random variable (jointly distributed with $x \sim X$) such that flag $= 1$ if $x \in E$, and flag $= 0$ if $x \notin E$. Let α denote the value of $\Pr_{x \sim X}[x \in E]$, and assume for contradiction that $\alpha > \frac{\log|S| + 1 - H(X)}{\log|S| - \log|E|}$. Note that by the chain rule of entropy:

$$H(X) \le H(X, \text{flag}) = H(\text{flag}) + \alpha H(X | x \in E) + (1 - \alpha) H(X | x \notin E)$$

Note that on the RHS, $H(\text{flag}) \le 1$ since flag is binary. $H(X | x \in E) \le \log|E|$, and $H(X | x \notin E) \le \log|S|$ (since X is distributed over S). So the RHS is at most

$$\begin{aligned} \text{RHS} &\le 1 + \alpha \log|E| + (1 - \alpha) \log|S| \\ &= 1 + \log|S| - \alpha(\log|S| - \log|E|) \\ &< 1 + \log|S| - \frac{\log|S| + 1 - H(X)}{\log|S| - \log|E|}(\log|S| - \log|E|) \\ &= H(X) \end{aligned}$$

which is a contradiction. ∎

2.6 "Nice" Function Classes

We consider "nice" classes of function families, where the class of functions $\mathcal{F}$ is said to be "nice" if

- for every function $T \in \mathcal{F}$, T is time-constructible and strictly increasing.
- $\mathcal{F}$ is closed under (sublinear) polynomial compositions: for any $T \in \mathcal{F}$, for all $0 < \varepsilon_1, \varepsilon_2 < 1$, $(T(n^{\varepsilon_1}))^{\varepsilon_2} \in \mathcal{F}$.

Given a class of functions, let $\mathcal{F}^{-1}$ denote the class of inverse function: $\mathcal{F}^{-1} = \{f \text{ s.t. } f^{-1} \in \mathcal{F}\}$. Several examples of "nice" classes of super-polynomial functions (and their inverse classes) are (a) $\mathcal{F}_{\text{subexp}} = \{2^{cn^\varepsilon}\}_{c>0, 0<\varepsilon<1}$ and $\mathcal{F}_{\text{subexp}}^{-1} = \{c \log^\beta n\}_{c>0, \beta>1}$, (b) $\mathcal{F}_{\text{qpoly}} = \{n^{c \log n}\}_{c>0}$ and $\mathcal{F}_{\text{qpoly}}^{-1} = \{2^{c\sqrt{\log n}}\}_{c>0}$.

The notion of "nice" function classes has the important property that "polynomial-time" reductions "preserve $\mathcal{F}$-hardness". Roughly speaking, almost all the reductions (considered in this work) are of form "if A is $T(n)$-hard, B is $(T(n^{\Omega(1)})^{\Omega(1)}/n^{O(1)} - n^{O(1)})$-hard". When A is a promise problem, we refer to A as being $T(n)$-hard if A is hard for $T(n)$-time algorithms. When A is a cryptographic primitive, we refer to A as being $T(n)$-hard if A is secure against all $T(n)$-time attackers. The following fact shows that such reductions actually prove the following statement: "if there exists $T_1 \in \mathcal{F}$ such that A is $T_1(n)$-hard, then there exists $T_2 \in \mathcal{F}$ such that B is $T_2(n)$-hard".

Fact 12. *Let $\mathcal{F}$ be a nice class of super-polynomial functions. For every $T \in \mathcal{F}$, for all $0 < \varepsilon_1, \varepsilon_2 < 1, c_1, c_2 > 1$, there exists a function $T' \in \mathcal{F}$ such that for all sufficiently large n, $T'(n) \leq T(n^{\varepsilon_1})^{\varepsilon_2}/n^{c_1} - n^{c_2}$.*

We refer the reader to [LP21a] for a proof of this fact.

3   Our Results

Our first result is an equivalence between OWFs and the hardness of $\mathsf{MK}^t\mathsf{P}[s]$ on the natural instances, where the threshold s is moderately large and t is a polynomial.

Theorem 13 (Characterizing OWFs). *For any threshold function $s(\cdot)$, $n^\varepsilon \leq s(n) < n-1, \varepsilon > 0$, any polynomial $t(n) \geq 2n$, any constant $\beta > 0$, the following are equivalent:*

(a) $\mathsf{MK}^t\mathsf{P}[s]|_{Q^t_\beta} \notin \mathsf{ioBPP}$ (resp. $\mathsf{MK}^t\mathsf{P}[s]|_{Q^t_\beta} \notin \mathsf{ioP/poly}$).
(b) One-way functions (resp. non-uniformly secure one-way functions) exist.

Proof: (a) $\Rightarrow$ (b) follows from Theorem 16 (stated and proved in Sect. 4) and Lemma 7. The non-uniform version of the implication (b) $\Rightarrow$ (a) follows from Theorem 19, and Lemma 21 (stated and proved in Sect. 5). The uniform version of the implication follows from Theorem 19, Proposition 22, and Lemma 24 (stated and proved in Sect. 5). ∎

We remark that Theorem 1 (stated in the introduction) follows from Theorem 13 by taking $s = n^{\Omega(1)}$ or $s = n - 2$. In addition, this yields the first OWF-complete problem.

Corollary 14. *Let s, t, β as in Theorem 13. $\mathsf{MK}^t\mathsf{P}[s]|_{Q^t_\beta}$ is OWF-complete.*

Our second result demonstrates that the hardness of the same problem, $\mathsf{MK}^t\mathsf{P}[s]|_{Q^t_\beta}$, with respect to polynomial time (or even sublinear-time) algorithms, will characterize quasi-polynomially or subexponentially secure OWF when the threshold s is small. We rely on the notion of "nice" classes of functions, which captures classes of "polynomially-related" functions. We refer the reader to Sect. 2.6 for more on "nice" classes and we here proceed to our theorem statement.

Theorem 15 (Characterizing T-hard OWFs). *Let $\mathcal{F}$ be a "nice" class of super-polynomial functions. For any polynomial $t(n) \geq 2n$, any constant $\beta > 0, \delta > 0$, the following are equivalent:*

(a) There exists a function $T \in \mathcal{F}$ such that T-hard (resp. non-uniformly T-hard) one-way functions exist.
(b) There exists a function $s \in \mathcal{F}^{-1}$ such that $\mathsf{MK}^t\mathsf{P}[s]|_{Q^t_\beta} \notin \mathsf{ioBPTIME}[n^\delta]$ (resp. $\mathsf{MK}^t\mathsf{P}[s]|_{Q^t_\beta} \notin \mathsf{ioSIZE}[n^\delta]$).

Proof: (b) ⇒ (a) follows from Theorem 17 (stated and proved in Sect. 4) and Lemma 7. The non-uniform version of the implication (a) ⇒ (b) follows from Theorem 19, and Lemma 20 (stated and proved in Sect. 5). Its uniform version follows from Theorem 19, Proposition 22, and Lemma 23 (stated and proved in Sect. 5). ∎

Taking $\mathcal{F} = \{n^{c\log n}\}_{c>0}$ to be the class of quasi-polynomial functions, we obtain Theorem 4 (stated in the introduction), and taking $\mathcal{F} = \{2^{cn^{\varepsilon}}\}_{c>0,0<\varepsilon<1}$ to be the class of subexponential functions, we obtain Theorem 5 (stated in the introduction). Furthermore, we can take $\mathcal{F}$ to be any nice class of super-polynomial functions (such as $\mathcal{F} = \{n^{c\log\log n}\}_{c>0}$) and we obtain equivalence between $\mathcal{F}$-hard OWFs and the hardness of $\mathsf{MK}^t\mathsf{P}[\mathcal{F}^{-1}]$ on natural instances.

4   OWFs from Worst-Case Hardness of $\mathsf{MK}^t\mathsf{P}|_Q$

We start by proving that if there exist a polynomial t and a constant $\beta > 0$ such that $\mathsf{MK}^t\mathsf{P}|_{Q^t_\beta}$ is hard, then standard (weak) OWFs exist.

Theorem 16. *If there exist a constant $\beta > 0$, a threshold function s, $0 < s(n) < n - 1$, and a polynomial t such that $\mathsf{MK}^t\mathsf{P}[s]|_{Q^t_\beta} \notin \mathsf{ioBPP}$ (resp. $\mathsf{ioP/poly}$), then weak one-way (resp. weak non-uniformly secure one-way) functions exist.*

Proof: Consider the function $f : \{0,1\}^{n+\lceil\log(n)\rceil} \to \{0,1\}^*$, which given an input $\ell\|\Pi'$ where $|\ell| = \lceil\log(n)\rceil$ and $|\Pi'| = n$, outputs

$$\ell\|U(\Pi(1), 1^{t(\ell)})\|U(\Pi(2), 1^{t(\ell)})\|\ldots\|U(\Pi(n-1), 1^{t(\ell)})\|U(\Pi(n), 1^{t(\ell)})$$

where Π is the ℓ-bit prefix of Π'. Note that U only has polynomial overhead, so f can be computed in polynomial time.

This function is only defined over some input lengths, but by an easy padding trick, it can be transformed into a function f' defined over all input lengths, such that if f is weak one-way (over the restricted input lengths), then f' will be weak one-way (over all input lengths): $f'(x')$ simply truncates its input x' (as little as possible) so that the (truncated) input x now becomes of length $n' = n + \lceil\log(n)\rceil$ for some n and outputs $f(x)$.

Assume for contradiction that f is not $\frac{1}{q(n)}$-weak one-way (resp non-uniformly $\frac{1}{q(n)}$-weak one-way) where $q(n) = n^{\beta+4}$. There exists a polynomial $p(\cdot)$ and a p-time attacker $\mathcal{A}$ such that the attacker $\mathcal{A}$ inverts the function f with probability at least $1 - \frac{1}{q(n)}$ for infinitely many n. We can assume without loss of generality that there exists a constant γ such that for all sufficiently large n, $\mathcal{A}$ (on input length n) can be described using γ bits given n: If $\mathcal{A}$ is a uniform attacker, we can let γ be the length of the code of $\mathcal{A}$; if $\mathcal{A} = \{A_n\}_{n\in\mathbb{N}}$ is a non-uniform attacker, on input length n, we can consider A_n as being the lexicographically smallest $p(n)$-time non-uniform attacker such that A_n inverts f with probability at least $1 - \frac{1}{q(n)}$. (If there is no such attacker on input length n, we let A_n be simply an outputting $\perp$ attacker.) Note that A_n can be described using the code of f, the polynomial $p(\cdot)$, and the polynomial $q(\cdot)$, so the attacker $\mathcal{A}$ can be described in constant bits. Fix some n such that $\mathcal{A}$ succeeds with probability at least $1 - \frac{1}{q(n)}$ on input length n.

We turn to constructing a polynomial-time uniform (resp non-uniform) algorithm M to decide $\mathsf{MK}^t\mathsf{P}[s]$ on inputs $z \in \{0,1\}^n \cap Q_\beta^t$. Our algorithm M, on input z, runs $\mathcal{A}(i\|z)$ for every $i \in [n]$ where i is represented as a $\lceil \log(n) \rceil$-bit string, and outputs 1 if and only if the length of the shortest program Π output by $\mathcal{A}$, which produces each bit in the string z within $t(|\Pi|)$ steps, is at most $s(n)$. Since $\mathcal{A}$ runs in polynomial time, our algorithm will also terminate in polynomial time.

We next show that our algorithm will output 1 with probability at least $2/3$ on input z if $K^t(z) \le s(n)$ and $z \in Q_\beta^t$. Assume for contradiction that M outputs 1 with probability $< 2/3$. Let $w = K^t(z)$. Consider any string y such that $K^t(y) = w$, and L_w be the set of "bad" strings such that

$$L_w \overset{\text{def}}{=} \{y \in \{0,1\}^n : K^t(y) = w, \Pr[M(y) = 1] < 2/3\}$$

It follows that $z \in L_w$. We rely on the following claim on the Kolmogorov complexity of strings in L_w.   ∎

Claim 1. *For all* $y \in L_w$, $K(y) < w - \beta \log n$.

Proof: We first argue that

$$|L_w| \le 3 \cdot 2^{w-(\beta+3)\log n}$$

Consider any $y \in L_w$. Note that $K^t(y) = w$, there must exist a program Π of size w such that Π outputs each bit of y in time $t(|\Pi|)$. And (w, Π) will be sampled with probability

$$\frac{1}{n} 2^{-w}$$

in the one-way function experiment. However, since $\Pr[M(y) = 1] < 2/3$, $\mathcal{A}$ must fail to invert f on input $(w\|y)$ with probability at least $1/3$. So $\mathcal{A}$ will fail to invert f in the one-way function experiment with probability at least

$$1/3 |L_w| \cdot \frac{1}{n} 2^{-w}$$

which is at most $\frac{1}{q(n)} = \frac{1}{n^{\beta+4}}$ since $\mathcal{A}$ is a good inverter. We conclude that

$$|L_w| \le 3 \cdot 2^{w+\log(n)-(\beta+4)\log n} \le 3 \cdot 2^{w-(\beta+3)\log n}.$$

We turn to showing how to obtain a short description for each string $\in L_w$. For any $y \in L_w$, consider the following program with n, w, t, the code of M (which as shown before, is of constant length), and the location of y (in L_w) hardwired in it. The program first generate the set L_w by enumerating all strings in $\{0,1\}^n$, and writing down the string if its K^t-complexity is w and the probability that $M(z) = 1$ is $< 2/3$. The program can be described using $2 \log n + O(\log \log n) + \log |L|$ bits. So it follows that for any $y \in L_w$,

$$K(y) \leq 2 \log n + O(\log \log n) + w - (\beta + 3) \log n + O(1) < w - \beta \log n.$$

■

Therefore, $K(z) < w - \beta \log n$. However, recall that $K^t(z) = w$ and $z \in Q_\beta^t$, it holds that $K(z) \geq w - \beta \log K(z) > w - \beta \log n$, which is a contradiction.

We finally prove that if $K^t(z) > n - 1$, $M(z)$ will never output 1. Note that $M(z)$ will output 1 only when it finds a K^t-witness of length no more than s, and there is no such witness if $K^t(z) > n - 1$. It follows that $M(z)$ will never output 1.

We turn to showing that the smaller the threshold in Theorem 16 is, the stronger the OWF we deduce. And we only require sublinear-time hardness.

Theorem 17. *Let $\mathcal{F}$ be a nice class of super-polynomial functions. Assume that there exist a function $s \in \mathcal{F}^{-1}$, constants $\beta, \delta > 0$, and a polynomial $t > 0$ such that $\mathsf{MK}^t\mathsf{P}[s]|_{Q_\beta^t} \notin \mathsf{ioBPTIME}[n^\delta]$ (resp $\mathsf{ioSIZE}[n^\delta]$). Then, there exist $T \in \mathcal{F}$ and a weak T-one-way (resp weak non-uniform T-one-way) function.*

We defer the proof of Theorem 17 to the full version.

5   Worst-Case Hardness of $\mathsf{MK}^t\mathsf{P}|_Q$ from OWFs

In this section, we prove that the existence of OWFs implies worst-case hardness of $\mathsf{MK}^t\mathsf{P}|_Q$. To simplify the presentation, we first prove this in the non-uniform setting where the reduction has access to some non-uniform advice. We will later remove the non-uniform advice and prove it in the uniform setting.

5.1   Conditionally-Secure Entropy-Preserving Pseudorandom Functions

We start by recalling the notion of a non-uniform conditionally-secure entropy-preserving pseudorandom function [LP21a], which will be an important tool in our proof.

Definition 18. *An efficiently computable function $f : \{0,1\}^n \times \{0,1\}^{k(n)} \to \{0,1\}$ is a non-uniform $(T(\cdot), \varepsilon(\cdot))$-conditionally-secure α-entropy-preserving pseudorandom function $((T, \varepsilon)$-cond α-EP-PRF$)$ if there exist a sequence of events $= \{E_n\}_{n \in \mathbb{N}}$ such that the following conditions hold:*

- **(pseudorandomness):** *For every non-uniform $T(n)$-time attacker $\mathcal{A}$ and sufficiently large $n \in \mathbb{N}$,*

$$|\Pr[s \leftarrow \{0,1\}^n; \mathcal{A}^{f(s,\cdot)}(1^n) = 1 | E_n] - \Pr[f' \leftarrow \mathcal{F}; \mathcal{A}^{f'(\cdot)}(1^n) = 1]| < \varepsilon(n), \quad (1)$$

where $\mathcal{F} = \{f' : \{0,1\}^{k(n)} \to \{0,1\}\}$.

- **(entropy-preserving):** For all sufficiently large $n \in \mathbb{N}$, $H(\mathsf{tt}_n(f(\mathcal{U}_n|E_n, \cdot)))$ $\geq n - \alpha \log n$, where $\mathsf{tt}_n(\cdot)$ denote the n-bit prefix of the truthtable of the function.

We refer to the constant α as the *entropy-loss constant*. We say that f is a *cond EP-PRF* (without mentioning "non-uniform") if the pseudorandomness condition holds just w.r.t. all probabilistic T-time attackers. We refer to f as a (non-uniform) ε-cond α-EP-PRF if f is secure w.r.t. all (non-uniform) PPT attackers.

We say that $f : \{0,1\}^n \times \{0,1\}^{k(n)} \to \{0,1\}$ has rate-1 efficiency if for all $n \in \mathbb{N}, x \in \{0,1\}^n, i \in \{0,1\}^{k(n)}$, $f(x,i)$ runs in $n + O(n^\varepsilon)$ time for some constant $\varepsilon < 1$. Recall that a rate-1 efficient cond EP-PRF can be constructed from OWFs [LP21a]. We notice that if the OWF we start with is T-hard, then we obtain a T-hard cond EP-PRF. If the OWF is of (plain) polynomial security, we obtain a cond EP-PRF that is polynomially secure.

Theorem 19 (Cond EP-PRF from OWFs [LP21a]. *The following statement holds.*

- *(T-hard cond EP-PRF) Let $\mathcal{F}$ be a nice class of super-polynomial functions. Assume that there exists $T \in \mathcal{F}$ and a T-hard (resp non-uniform T-hard) OWF. Then, for any constant $\alpha > 0, \delta \geq 1$, there exist $T_1 \in F$ and a rate-1 efficient $(T_1^\delta, 0.1)$-cond α-EP-PRF (resp non-uniformly secure cond EP-PRF) $f : \{0,1\}^n \times [T_1(n)] \to \{0,1\}$.*
- *(Polynomially hard cond EP-PRF) Assume that there exists a OWF (resp non-uniform OWF). Then, for any constant $\alpha > 0$ and any polynomial $d(n) \geq n$, there exists a rate-1 efficient 0.1-cond α-EP PRF (resp non-uniformly secure cond EP-PRF) $f : \{0,1\}^n \times [d(n)] \to \{0,1\}$.*

[LP21a] only proved a weaker version of the above theorem (in which they showed the existence of a cond α-EP-PRF for some constant α). A standard padding argument will be needed to prove the stronger version stated above, and we include a proof for Theorem 19 in the full version.

5.2 (Non-uniform) Worst-Case Hardness of $\mathsf{MK}^t\mathsf{P}|_Q$ from (Non-uniform) OWFs

We turn to showing that the existence of cond EP-PRFs implies hardness of $\mathsf{MK}^t\mathsf{P}$, even when conditioned on the event Q_β^t. We will first present the proof in the non-uniform setting.

Lemma 20 (Hardness of $\mathsf{MK}^t\mathsf{P}[T^{-1}]$ from T-hard Cond EP-PRF). *Let $\mathcal{F}$ be a nice class of super-polynomial functions, $\delta > 1, \beta > 0$ be some constants. Assume that there exist $T_1 \in \mathcal{F}$ and a non-uniformly secure rate-1 efficient $(T_1^\delta, 0.1)$-cond $(\beta/10)$-EP-PRF $h : \{0,1\}^n \times [T_1(n)] \to \{0,1\}$. Then, for every constant $\varepsilon' > 0, 0 < \delta' < \delta$, every polynomial $t(n) \geq 2n$, every $T_2 \in \mathcal{F}$ satisfying $T_2(n) \leq T_1(n/2)$, $\mathsf{MK}^t\mathsf{P}[T_2^{-1}]|_{Q_\beta^t} \notin \mathsf{ioSIZE}[n^{\delta'}]$.*

Proof: Consider any polynomial $t(n) \geq 2n$, and any constant $0 < \delta' < \delta$. Let $\varepsilon = 0.1$. We will show that for any $T_2 \in \mathcal{F}, T_2(n) \leq T_1(n/2)$, $\mathsf{MK}^t\mathsf{P}[T_2^{-1}]|_{Q_\beta^t} \notin$ ioSIZE$[n^{\delta'}]$.

Note that the truthtable of the PRF h is of length $T_1(n)$ (for seeds of length n). For any function $T_2 \in \mathcal{F}$ satisfying $T_2(n) \leq T_1(n/2)$, we will truncate the cond EP-PRF h to another cond EP-PRF f that is easier to work with (so that the truthtable of f is of length roughly $T_2(n)$). Note that both h and T_2 can be computed by uniform algorithms, let γ be a (sufficiently large) constant such that h together with T_2 can be described within $\gamma/4$ bits. Let $f : \{0,1\}^n \times [T_2(n + \gamma)] \rightarrow \{0,1\}$ be the function obtained by truncating h to the first $T_2(n + \gamma)$ entries. Note that $T_2(n + \gamma) < T_2(2n) \leq T_1(n)$ (due to our choice of T_2 and that T_2 is strictly increasing), so the truncation is always possible. Also notice that f is still a rate-1 efficient $(T_1^\delta, \varepsilon)$-cond $(\beta/10)$-EP-PRF (as h is). In addition, the code of f can be described in $\gamma/2$ bits.

We assume for contradiction that there exists some $m^{\delta'}$-time non-uniform algorithm that decides each instance of $\mathsf{MK}^t\mathsf{P}[T_2^{-1}]$ in Q_β^t with probability $\frac{2}{3}$. By a Chernoff-type argument, we can show that there exists an algorithm M that succeeds with probability 0.99 and runs in $O(m^{\delta'})$ time (by using constant-fold parallel repetition and taking a majority vote). We will use the algorithm M to build a non-uniform attacker $\mathcal{A}(1^n)$ that breaks the cond EP-PRF f.

Note that f is a function that given a seed of length n, maps an integer $\in [T_2(n + \gamma)]$ to either '0' or '1'. For any fixed seed $x \in \{0,1\}^n$, let $\mathsf{tt}_m(f(x, \cdot))$ denote the first m bits of the truth table of $f(x, \cdot)$. Consider any integer $m \leq T_2(n + \gamma)$. Note that for any $x \in \{0,1\}^n$, $\mathsf{tt}_m(f(x, \cdot))$ has low K^t-complexity (with probability 1):

$$K^t(\mathsf{tt}_m(f(x, \cdot))) \leq n + \gamma - 1$$

since a Turing machine that contains the code of f (of length $\gamma/2$, as argued above) and the seed x (of length n) can output each bit i on the truth table in $t(n)$ time (since f is rate-1 efficient). However, a random string of length m has high K^t-complexity with high probability:

$$\Pr_{y \in \{0,1\}^m}[K^t(y) \geq m - 1] \geq 1 - \frac{1}{2},$$

since there are at most 2^{m-1} Turing machines with description length no longer than $m-2$, and each of them can produce at most a single truth table of length m.

With the above observations, we are ready to construct $\mathcal{A}$ (which breaks f). On input length n, let m be an integer such that $m \in [T_2(n+\gamma-1), T_2(n+\gamma)-1]$ and the algorithm M succeeds in deciding $\mathsf{MK}^t\mathsf{P}[T_2^{-1}]|_{Q_\beta^t}$ on input length m. We will provide our attacker $\mathcal{A}$ with the integer m as non-uniform advice. (Since M only succeeds infinite often, $\mathcal{A}$ simply aborts if such m doesn't exist.) With the advice m, the attacker (denoted by $\mathcal{A}_m$) proceeds as follows. Given black-box access to a function $f' : [T_2(n + \gamma)] \rightarrow \{0,1\}$, $\mathcal{A}_m(1^n)$ first queries f' on every input $i \in [m]$ and obtains the first m bits of the truth table of f', $\mathsf{tt}_m(f')$. Then $\mathcal{A}_m(1^n)$ feeds $\mathsf{tt}_m(f')$ to the algorithm M and outputs $M(\mathsf{tt}_m(f'))$. Note that the attacker $\mathcal{A}_m(1^n)$ runs in time $O(m) + m^{\delta'} < T_1(n)^\delta$.

Since M decides $\mathsf{MK}^t\mathsf{P}[T_2^{-1}]$ on each instances $\in Q_\beta^t$ with probability 0.99 on infinitely many input lengths m, we will show that the attacker $\mathcal{A}$ succeeds in distinguishing the cond EP-PRF f from random functions on infinitely many input lengths (which is a contradiction). Fix some input length m on which M succeeds. Let n be the integer such that

$$T_2(n + \gamma - 1) \leq m < T_2(n + \gamma)$$

(guaranteed to exist since T_2 is strictly increasing). The following two claims will show that $\mathcal{A}_m$ will distinguish f from random with probability at least 2ε, which conclude the proof. ∎

Claim 2. $\mathcal{A}_m(1^n)$ *will output 0 with probability at least* $\frac{1}{2} - 0.02$ *when given access to* f_r, *where* f_r *is uniformly sampled from* $\mathcal{F} = \{f_r : [T_2(n+\gamma)] \to \{0, 1\}\}$.

Proof: Note that for a random f_r, the probability that $K^t(\mathsf{tt}_m(f_r)) \geq m-1$ is at least $\frac{1}{2}$. Note that $K(\mathsf{tt}_m(f_r))$ is at least $m - \beta \log m$ with probability 0.01, so it follows that $\mathsf{tt}_m(f_r) \in Q_\beta^t$ if $K^t(\mathsf{tt}_m(f_r)) \geq m-1$. Since M decides $\mathsf{MK}^t\mathsf{P}[T_2^{-1}]|_{Q_\beta^t}$ with probability 0.99 on input length m, by a Union bound, $\mathcal{A}_m(1^n)$ will output 0 with probability $\frac{1}{2} - 0.02$. ∎

Claim 3. $\mathcal{A}_m(1^n)$ *will output 0 with probability at most* $0.2 + 0.01$ *when given access to* $f \leftarrow f(\mathcal{U}_n|E_n, \cdot)$, *where* E_n *is the event associated with* f.

Proof: Recall that M decides each instance of $\mathsf{MK}^t\mathsf{P}[T_2^{-1}]$ in Q_β^t with probability 0.99 on input length m. Let $s = \lfloor T_2^{-1}(m) \rfloor$ and notice that

$$s = n + \gamma - 1$$

(by the choice of n). Let

$$X = \mathsf{tt}_m(f(\mathcal{U}_n|E_n, \cdot))$$

be the random variable of the first m bits of the truth table of f. Recall that any string x in the support of X will have K^t-complexity at most $n + \gamma - 1 = s$. Since f is entropy preserving, the entropy of X is at least

$$H(X) \geq n - 0.1\beta \log n$$

Let

$$S = \mathsf{supp}(X)$$

be the set of pseudorandom truth tables. It follows that $2^{H(X)} \leq |S| \leq 2^n$. Let

$$Z = \{z \in S : z \notin Q_\beta^t\}$$

be the set of pseudorandom truth tables that are outside of Q_β^t. Recall that the algorithm M is only guaranteed to work if the input is in Q_β^t, so we can think of Z as the set of "bad" strings. For any $z \in Z$, since $z \in S$ and $z \notin Q_\beta^t$, it holds that $K(z) < K^t(z) - \beta \log K(z) \leq s - \beta \log s$. By a standard counting argument w.r.t. K-complexity, it follows that $|Z| \leq 2^{s-\beta \log s+1}$. Recall that X is a random variable distributed over S, and $Z \subseteq S$. By Lemma 11, it follows that the probability that $X \in Z$ is at most

$$\Pr[X \in Z] \leq \frac{\log |S| + 1 - H(X)}{\log |S| - \log |Z|} \leq \frac{n + 1 - (n - 0.1\beta \log n)}{n - 0.1\beta \log n - (s - \beta \log s)} \leq 0.2$$

when n is sufficiently large. Therefore, the probability that $M(X)$ outputs 0 is at most

$$\begin{aligned}
\Pr[M(X) = 0] &= \Pr[X \in Z]\Pr[M(X) = 0|X \in Z] + \Pr[X \notin Z]\Pr[M(X) = 0|X \notin Z] \\
&\leq \Pr[X \in Z] + \Pr[M(X) = 0|X \notin Z] \\
&\leq 0.2 + \Pr[M(X) = 0|X \in Q_\beta^t] \\
&\leq 0.2 + 0.01
\end{aligned}$$

where the last step follows from the correctness of M. ∎

While in the above theorems, we assume super polynomial hardness, the reduction runs in polynomial time. So the statement will also hold in the polynomial hardness region.

Lemma 21 (Hardness of $\mathsf{MK}^t\mathsf{P}[n^{\Omega(1)}]$ from poly-hard Cond EP-PRF). *Let $s(\cdot)$ be a threshold function, $n^\varepsilon \leq s(n) \leq n - 2$, $\varepsilon > 0$. Let $d(\cdot)$ be a polynomial such that $s^{-1}(n) \leq d(n/2)$, and $\beta > 0$ be a constant. Assume that there exists a rate-1 efficient non-uniformly secure $(\mathsf{poly}, 0.1)$-cond $(\beta/10)$-EP-PRF $f : \{0,1\}^n \times [d(n)] \rightarrow \{0,1\}$. Then, for every constant $\varepsilon' > 0$, every polynomial $t(n) \geq (1 + \varepsilon')n$, $\mathsf{MK}^t\mathsf{P}[s]|_{Q_\beta^t} \notin \mathsf{ioP/poly}$.*

Proof: This lemma follows from the proof of Lemma 20 by considering T_1 being d and T_2 being s^{-1}. ∎

5.3 Eliminating the Non-uniform Advice

The key observation we rely on in this section is that the security of our cond EP-PRF is established through *black-box* reductions to standard cryptographic primitives. Let us introduce the notion of black-box reductions we rely on.

We say that a (T, ε)-cond EP-PRF f has a *polynomial-time black-box security reduction* to a $(T_{\mathsf{prg}}, \varepsilon_{\mathsf{prg}})$-PRG f_{prg} and a $(T_{\mathsf{prf}}, \varepsilon_{\mathsf{prf}})$-PRF f_{prf} if there exist functions $l_{\mathsf{prg}}, l_{\mathsf{prf}}$ (referred to as *input length functions*)[9] , polynomials $p_{\mathsf{prg}}, p_{\mathsf{prf}}$ (referred to as *security loss functions*), and oracle machines $R_{\mathsf{prg}}, R_{\mathsf{prf}}$ (referred to as *reductions*) such that the following are satisfied:

---

[9] Note that we consider reductions that establish almost-everywhere security, so it is important for the reduction to specify on which input lengths it works.

- $l_{\mathsf{prg}}, l_{\mathsf{prf}}$ are time-constructible and increasing.
- For any T-time probabilistic adversary $\mathcal{A}$, and any input length n (for f), let n_{prg} (resp n_{prf}) be the input length for PRG (resp PRF) such that

$$l_{\mathsf{prg}}(n_{\mathsf{prg}}) \le n < l_{\mathsf{prg}}(n_{\mathsf{prg}} + 1), l_{\mathsf{prf}}(n_{\mathsf{prf}}) \le n < l_{\mathsf{prf}}(n_{\mathsf{prf}} + 1)$$

(Note that such $n_{\mathsf{prg}}, n_{\mathsf{prf}}$ always exist since $l_{\mathsf{prg}}, l_{\mathsf{prf}}$ are increasing.) If $\mathcal{A}(1^n)$ distinguishes the cond EP-PRF f from random functions on input length n with advantage $\varepsilon(n)$, then

(a) either $R_{\mathsf{prg}}^{\mathcal{A}}(1^{n_{\mathsf{prg}}})$ distinguishes f_{prg} from random with advantage $\frac{1}{p_{\mathsf{prg}}(n_{\mathsf{prg}}, 1/\varepsilon(n))} \ge 4\varepsilon_{\mathsf{prg}}(n_{\mathsf{prg}})$ on input length n_{prg} in time $T_{\mathsf{prg}}(n_{\mathsf{prg}})$;

(b) or $R_{\mathsf{prf}}^{\mathcal{A}}(1^{n_{\mathsf{prf}}})$ distinguishes f_{prf} from random functions with advantage $\frac{1}{p_{\mathsf{prf}}(n_{\mathsf{prf}}, 1/\varepsilon(n))} \ge 4\varepsilon_{\mathsf{prf}}(n_{\mathsf{prf}})$ on input length n_{prf} in time $T_{\mathsf{prf}}(n_{\mathsf{prf}})$.

In other words, if $\mathcal{A}$ breaks f on input length n, either we break f_{prg} on input length n_{prg}, or we break f_{prf} on input length n_{prf}.

If such a black-box reduction exists, we can prove that f is indeed a (T, ε)-cond EP-PRF if f_{prg} is a $(T_{\mathsf{prg}}, \varepsilon_{\mathsf{prg}})$-PRG and f_{prf} a $(T_{\mathsf{prf}}, \varepsilon_{\mathsf{prf}})$-PRF. Note that the security parameters $T_{\mathsf{prg}}, \varepsilon_{\mathsf{prg}}$ (and $T_{\mathsf{prf}}, \varepsilon_{\mathsf{prf}}$) for the PRG (and the PRF) will usually be implicit in (but can be inferred from) the reduction itself, and we sometimes simply omit them if they will be clear from the reduction.

As mentioned before, we observe that the cond EP-PRF we obtain in Theorem 19 has a black-box security reduction.

Proposition 22. *Let f be the cond EP-PRF in Theorem 19. f has a black-box security reduction to a PRG and a PRF.*

(In the full version, we will formally state and prove that f indeed has a black-box reduction.)

We proceed to proving the uniform version of Lemma 20.

Lemma 23. *Let $\mathcal{F}$ be a nice class of super-polynomial functions, $\delta > 2, \beta > 0$ be any constants. Assume that there exist $T_1 \in \mathcal{F}$ and a rate-1 efficient $(T_1^{\delta}, 0.1)$-cond $(\beta/10)$-EP-PRF $h : \{0,1\}^n \times [T_1(n)] \to \{0,1\}$ with a poly-time black-box security reduction to a $(T_{\mathsf{prg}}, \varepsilon_{\mathsf{prg}})$-PRG f_{prg} and a $(T_{\mathsf{prf}}, \varepsilon_{\mathsf{prf}})$-PRF f_{prf}. Then, for every constant $0 < \delta' < \delta - 1$, every polynomial $t(n) \ge 2n$, every $T_2 \in \mathcal{F}$ satisfying $T_2(n) \le T_1(n/2)$, $\mathsf{MK}^t\mathsf{P}[T_2^{-1}]|_{Q_{\beta}^t} \notin \mathsf{ioBPP}$.*

The proof of Lemma 23 is deferred to the full version.

We notice that Lemma 23 also holds w.r.t. polynomial hardness (since the reduction runs in polynomial time).

Lemma 24. *Let $s(\cdot)$ be a threshold function, $n^{\varepsilon} \le s(n) \le n - 2$, $\varepsilon > 0$. Let $d(\cdot)$ be a polynomial such that $s^{-1}(n) \le d(n/2)$, and $\beta > 0$ be a constant. Assume that there exists a rate-1 efficient $(\mathsf{poly}, 0.1)$-cond $(\beta/10)$-EP-PRF $f : \{0,1\}^n \times [d(n)] \to \{0,1\}$ with a black-box security reduction to a $(\mathsf{poly}, \varepsilon_{\mathsf{prg}})$-PRG f_{prg} and a $(\mathsf{poly}, \varepsilon_{\mathsf{prf}})$-PRF f_{prf}. Then, for every constant $\varepsilon' > 0$, every polynomial $t(n) \ge (1 + \varepsilon')n$, $\mathsf{MK}^t\mathsf{P}[s]|_{Q_{\beta}^t} \notin \mathsf{ioBPP}$.*

6   Rudich's Conjecture and Non-containment in coAM

In this section, we show that the promise problem that characterized OWFs is unlikely to be in coAM. As such, it yields the first example of problem outside of AM ∩ coAM whose worst-case hardness even just implies the existence of OWFs.

We will rely on Rudich's conjecture as well as standard derandomization assumptions. Rudich [Rud97] conjectured the existence of a pseudorandom generator secure against (co-)non deterministic attackers. Let us recall the definition of such PRGs.

Definition 25 ([Rud97]). Let $g : \{0,1\}^n \to \{0,1\}^{n+1}$ be an efficiently computable function. We say that g is a *pseudorandom generator with non-deterministic hardness* if for all poly-time non-uniform non-deterministic machine $\mathcal{A}$, there exists a negligible function μ such that for all $n \in \mathbb{N}$,

$$\Pr[\mathcal{A}(1^n, \mathcal{U}_{n+1}) = 1] - \Pr[\mathcal{A}(1^n, g(\mathcal{U}_n)) = 1] \le \mu(n)$$

In other words, no non-uniform attacker can prove random strings are "random" with higher probability than pseudorandom strings. Notice that the order of the probabilities is important – there exists a trivial attacker (by just guessing the seed) if the order is switched.

We are now ready to state the Rudich's conjecture that we rely on.

Conjecture 26 (Implied by [Rud97, Conjecture 4]). *There exists a PRG* $g : \{0,1\}^n \to \{0,1\}^{n+1}$ *with non-deterministic hardness.*

We proceed to showing that under Rudich's conjecture (and assuming an appropriate derandomization assumption), the promise problem we consider is not contained in coAM. (In more detail, we will show that it is not in io-coNP/poly, which contains coAM.)

Theorem 27. *Assume that Conjecture 26 holds and* $\mathsf{E} \not\subseteq \mathsf{ioNSIZE}[2^{\Omega(n)}]$. *Then, there exists a constant* $\beta > 0$, *a polynomial* $t_1(n)$, *such that for all polynomials* $t(n) \ge t_1(n)$, $\mathsf{MK}^t\mathsf{P}[n-2]|_{Q_\beta^t} \not\in \mathsf{io\text{-}coNP/poly}$.

Due to space limit, we defer the proof of Theorem 27 to the full version.

Deferred Content. We defer our result on impossibility of Fully Black-box Constructions to the full version.

Acknowledgements. We thank the anonymous FOCS and TCC reviewers for their helpful comments.

References

[ABK+06] Allender, E., Buhrman, H., Kouckỳ, M., Van Melkebeek, D., Ronneburger, D.: Power from random strings. SIAM J. Comput. **35**(6), 1467–1493 (2006)

[AD97] Ajtai, M. and Dwork, C.: A public-key cryptosystem with worst-case/average-case equivalence. In: Leighton, F.T., Shor, P.W. (eds.) Proceedings of the Twenty-Ninth Annual ACM Symposium on the Theory of Computing, El Paso, Texas, USA, May 4-6, 1997, pp. 284–293. ACM (1997)

[AF09] Antunes, L., Fortnow, L.: Worst-case running times for average-case algorithms. In: 2009 24th Annual IEEE Conference on Computational Complexity, pp. 298–303. IEEE (2009)

[AFvMV06] Antunes, L., Fortnow, L., Van Melkebeek, D., Vinodchandran, N.V.: Computational depth: concept and applications. Theor. Comput. Sci. **354**(3), 391–404 (2006)

[AGGM06] Akavia, A., Goldreich, O., Goldwasser, S., Moshkovitz, D.: On basing one-way functions on NP-hardness. In: STOC 2006, pp. 701–710 (2006)

[Ajt96] Ajtai, M.: Generating hard instances of lattice problems (extended abstract). In: Gary L. Miller (ed.) Proceedings of the Twenty-Eighth Annual ACM Symposium on the Theory of Computing, Philadelphia, Pennsylvania, USA, May 22-24, 1996, pp. 99–108. ACM (1996)

[All01] Allender, E.: When worlds collide: derandomization, lower bounds, and kolmogorov complexity. In: Hariharan, R., Vinay, V., Mukund, M. (eds.) FSTTCS 2001. LNCS, vol. 2245, pp. 1–15. Springer, Heidelberg (2001). https://doi.org/10.1007/3-540-45294-X_1

[BDV17] Bitansky, N., Degwekar, A., Vaikuntanathan, V.: Structure vs. hardness through the obfuscation lens. In: Katz, J., Shacham, H. (eds.) CRYPTO 2017. LNCS, vol. 10401, pp. 696–723. Springer, Cham (2017). https://doi.org/10.1007/978-3-319-63688-7_23

[BI87] Blum, M., Impagliazzo, R.: Generic oracles and oracle classes. In: 28th Annual Symposium on Foundations of Computer Science (SFCS 1987), pp. 118–126. IEEE (1987)

[BLMP23] Ball, M., Liu, Y., Mazor, N., Pass, R.: On interactive Kolmogorov complexity and key-agreement, Kolmogorov comes to cryptomania (2023)

[Blu82] Blum, M.: Coin flipping by telephone - a protocol for solving impossible problems. In: COMPCON 1982, Digest of Papers, Twenty-Fourth IEEE Computer Society International Conference, San Francisco, California, USA, February 22-25, 1982, pp. 133–137. IEEE Computer Society (1982)

[BM84] Blum, M., Micali, S.: How to generate cryptographically strong sequences of pseudo-random bits. SIAM J. Comput. **13**(4), 850–864 (1984)

[Bra83] Brassard, G.: Relativized cryptography. IEEE Trans. Inf. Theory **29**(6), 877–893 (1983)

[BT03] Bogdanov, A., Trevisan, L.: On worst-case to average-case reductions for np problems. In: FOCS 2003, pp. 308–317 (2003)

[CHO+20] Chen, L., Hirahara, S., Oliveira, I.C., Pich, J., Rajgopal, N., Santhanam, R.: Beyond natural proofs: Hardness magnification and locality. In: 11th Innovations in Theoretical Computer Science Conference (ITCS 2020). Schloss Dagstuhl-Leibniz-Zentrum für Informatik (2020)

[CJW19] Chen, L., Jin, C., Williams, R.R.: Hardness magnification for all sparse NP languages. In: 2019 IEEE 60th Annual Symposium on Foundations of Computer Science (FOCS), pp. 1240–1255. IEEE, (2019)

[CMMW19] Chen, L., McKay, D.M., Murray, C.D., Williams, R.R.: Relations and equivalences between circuit lower bounds and karp-lipton theorems. In: 34th Computational Complexity Conference (CCC 2019). Schloss Dagstuhl-Leibniz-Zentrum fuer Informatik (2019)

[CT19] Chen, L., Tell, R.: Bootstrapping results for threshold circuits "just beyond" known lower bounds. In: Proceedings of the 51st Annual ACM SIGACT Symposium on Theory of Computing, pp. 34–41 (2019)

[DH76] Diffie, W., Hellman, M.: New directions in cryptography. IEEE Trans. Inf. Theory **22**(6), 644–654 (1976)

[FS90] Feige, U., Shamir, A.: Witness indistinguishable and witness hiding protocols. In: STOC 1990, pp. 416–426 (1990)

[GG00] Goldreich, O., Goldwasser, S.: On the limits of nonapproximability of lattice problems. J. Comput. Syst. Sci. **60**(3), 540–563 (2000)

[GGM84] Goldreich, O., Goldwasser, S., Micali, S.: How to construct random functions. In: FOCS (1984)

[GM84] Goldwasser, S., Micali, S.: Probabilistic encryption. J. Comput. Syst. Sci. **28**(2), 270–299 (1984)

[Gur89] Gurevich, Y.: The Challenger-solver Game: Variations on the Theme of P = NP. In Logic in Computer Science Column, The Bulletin of EATCS (1989)

[Har83] Hartmanis, J.: Generalized kolmogorov complexity and the structure of feasible computations. In: 24th Annual Symposium on Foundations of Computer Science (SFCS 1983), pp. 439–445 (1983)

[HILL99] Håstad, J., Impagliazzo, R., Levin, L.A., Luby, M.: A pseudorandom generator from any one-way function. SIAM J. Comput. **28**(4), 1364–1396 (1999)

[Hir18] Hirahara, S.: Non-black-box worst-case to average-case reductions within NP. In: 59th IEEE Annual Symposium on Foundations of Computer Science, FOCS 2018, pp. 247–258 (2018)

[Hir22] Hirahara, S.: Np-hardness of learning programs and partial MCSP. In: 2022 IEEE 63rd Annual Symposium on Foundations of Computer Science (FOCS), pp. 968–979. IEEE (2022)

[HN23] Hirahara, S., Nanashima, M.: Learning in pessiland via inductive inference (2023)

[IL89] Impagliazzo, R., Luby, M.: One-way functions are essential for complexity based cryptography (extended abstract). In: 30th Annual Symposium on Foundations of Computer Science, Research Triangle Park, North Carolina, USA, 30 October - 1 November 1989, pp. 230–235 (1989)

[Ila20] Ilango, R.: Approaching MCSP from above and below: hardness for a conditional variant and $AC^0[p]$. In: 11th Innovations in Theoretical Computer Science Conference, ITCS 2020, pp. 34:1–34:26 (2020)

[Ila21] Ilango, R.: The minimum formula size problem is (eth) hard. In: 2021 IEEE 62nd Annual Symposium on Foundations of Computer Science (FOCS), pp. 427–432. IEEE (2021)

[Ila22] Ilango, R.: Constant depth formula and partial function versions of MCSP are hard. SIAM J. Comput. (0), FOCS20–317 (2022)

[ILO20] Ilango, R., Loff, B., Carboni Oliveira, I.: NP-hardness of circuit mini-mization for multi-output functions. In: 35th Computational Complexity Conference, CCC 2020, pp. 22:1–22:36 (2020)

[Imp95] Impagliazzo, R.: A personal view of average-case complexity. In: Structure in Complexity Theory 1995, pp. 134–147 (1995)

[IRS21] Ilango, R., Ren, H., Santhanam, R.: Hardness on any samplable dis-tribution suffices: new characterizations of one-way functions by meta-complexity. Electron. Colloquium Comput. Complex. **28**, 82 (2021)

[KC00] Kabanets, V., Cai, J.Y.: Circuit minimization problem. In: Proceedings of the Thirty-Second Annual ACM Symposium on Theory of Computing, 21-23 May 2000, Portland, OR, USA, pp. 73–79 (2000)

[Ko86] Ko, K.-I.: On the notion of infinite pseudorandom sequences. Theor. Comput. Sci. **48**(3), 9–33 (1986)

[Kol68] Kolmogorov, A.N.: Three approaches to the quantitative definition of information. Int. J. Comput. Math. **2**(1–4), 157–168 (1968)

[Lev03] Levin, L.A.: The tale of one-way functions. Probl. Inf. Transm. **39**(1), 92–103 (2003)

[LP20] Liu, Y., Pass, R.: On one-way functions and Kolmogorov complexity. In: 61st IEEE Annual Symposium on Foundations of Computer Science, FOCS 2020, Durham, NC, USA, November 16-19, 2020, pp. 1243–1254. IEEE (2020)

[LP21a] Liu, Y., Pass, R.: Cryptography from sublinear time hardness of time-bounded kolmogorov complexity. In: STOC (2021)

[LP21b] Liu, Y., Pass, R.:. On the possibility of basing cryptography on EXP $\neq$ BPP. In: CRYPTO (2021)

[LP22a] Liu, Y., Pass, R.: Leakage-resilient hardness vs randomness. Electron. Colloquium Comput. Complexity (2022). https://eccc.weizmann.ac.il/report/2022/113/

[LP22b] Liu, Y., Pass, R.: On one-way functions from NP-complete problems. In: Proceedings of the 37th Computational Complexity Conference, pp. 1–24 (2022)

[MMW19] McKay, D.M., Murray, C.D., Williams, R.R.: Weak lower bounds on resource-bounded compression imply strong separations of complexity classes. In: Proceedings of the 51st Annual ACM SIGACT Symposium on Theory of Computing, pp. 1215–1225 (2019)

[Nao91] Naor, M.: Bit commitment using pseudorandomness. J. Cryptology **4**(2), 151–158 (1991)

[Oli19] Oliveira, I.C.: Randomness and intractability in kolmogorov complexity. In: 46th International Colloquium on Automata, Languages, and Programming (ICALP 2019). Schloss Dagstuhl-Leibniz-Zentrum fuer Informatik (2019)

[OPS19] Oliveira, I.C., Pich, J., Santhanam, R.: Hardness magnification near state-of-the-art lower bounds (2019)

[OS18] Oliveira, I.C., Santhanam, R.: Hardness magnification for natural problems. In: 2018 IEEE 59th Annual Symposium on Foundations of Computer Science (FOCS), pp. 65–76. IEEE (2018)

[Reg04] Regev, O.: New lattice based cryptographic constructions. J. ACM **51**(6), 899–942 (2004)

[Rom90] Rompel, J.: One-way functions are necessary and sufficient for secure signatures. In: STOC, pp. 387–394 (1990)

[RSA83]   Rivest, R.L., Shamir, A., Adleman, L.M.: A method for obtaining digital signatures and public-key cryptosystems (reprint). Commun. ACM **26**(1), 96–99 (1983)

[Rud88]   Rudich, S.: Limits on the Provable Consequences of One-Way Functions. University of California at Berkeley (1988)

[Rud97]   Rudich, S.: Super-bits, demi-bits, and *NP/qpoly*-natural proofs. In: Rolim, J. (ed.) RANDOM 1997. LNCS, vol. 1269, pp. 85–93. Springer, Heidelberg (1997). https://doi.org/10.1007/3-540-63248-4_8

[Sip83]   Sipser, M.: A complexity theoretic approach to randomness. In: Proceedings of the 15th Annual ACM Symposium on Theory of Computing, 25-27 April, 1983, Boston, Massachusetts, USA, pp. 330–335. ACM (1983)

[Tra84]   Trakhtenbrot, B.A.: A survey of Russian approaches to perebor (brute-force searches) algorithms. Ann. Hist. Comput. **6**(4), 384–400 (1984)

[Yab59a]   Yablonski, S.: The algorithmic difficulties of synthesizing minimal switching circuits. Problemy Kibernetiki **2**(1), 75–121 (1959)

[Yab59b]   Yablonski, S.V.: On the impossibility of eliminating perebor in solving some problems of circuit theory. Doklady Akademii Nauk SSSR **124**(1), 44–47 (1959)

[Yao82]   Yao, A.C.: Theory and applications of trapdoor functions (extended abstract). In: 23rd Annual Symposium on Foundations of Computer Science, Chicago, Illinois, USA, 3-5 November 1982, pp. 80–91 (1982)

One-Way Functions and pKt Complexity

Shuichi Hirahara[1], Zhenjian Lu[2]([✉]), and Igor C. Oliveira[2]

[1] National Institute of Informatics, Chiyoda, Japan
s_hirahara@nii.ac.jp
[2] University of Warwick, Coventry, UK
{zhenjian.lu,igor.oliveira}@warwick.ac.uk

Abstract. We introduce pKt complexity, a new notion of time-bounded Kolmogorov complexity that can be seen as a probabilistic analogue of Levin's Kt complexity. Using pKt complexity, we upgrade two recent frameworks that characterize one-way functions (OWF) via symmetry of information and meta-complexity, respectively. Among other contributions, we establish the following results:

(i) OWF can be based on the worst-case assumption that BPEXP is not contained infinitely often in P/poly if the failure of symmetry of information for pKt in the *worst-case* implies its failure on *average*.

(ii) (Infinitely-often) OWF exist if and only if the average-case easiness of approximating pKt with *two-sided* error implies its (mild) average-case easiness with *one-sided* error.

Previously, in a celebrated result, Liu and Pass (CRYPTO 2021 and CACM 2023) proved that one can base (infinitely-often) OWF on the assumption that EXP $\not\subseteq$ BPP if and only if there is a reduction from computing Kt on average with *zero* error to computing Kt on average with *two-sided* error. In contrast, our second result shows that closing the gap between two-sided error and one-sided error average-case algorithms for approximating pKt is both necessary and sufficient to *unconditionally* establish the existence of OWF.

Keywords: one-way functions · Kolmogorov complexity · average-case complexity · symmetry of information.

1 Introduction

1.1 Context and Motivation

This paper is primarily concerned with research directions **(1)** and **(2)** described next:

(1) Existence of one-way functions.
A one-way function is a function that is easy to compute but hard to invert on average [11]. Due to its equivalence to several basic cryptographic primitives, such as private-key encryption [14], pseudorandom generators [15], digital signatures [48], and commitment schemes [43], the existence of one-way functions is widely regarded as the most important open problem in Cryptography. In order

© International Association for Cryptologic Research 2025
E. Boyle and M. Mahmoody (Eds.): TCC 2024, LNCS 15364, pp. 253–286, 2025.
https://doi.org/10.1007/978-3-031-78011-0_9

to be precise in our subsequent discussion, we capture the question of the existence of one-way functions through the following formal statement:

∃OWF: There is a function $f = \{f_n\} \in$ FP, where each $f_n \colon \{0,1\}^n \to \{0,1\}^{\text{poly}(n)}$, such that for every probabilistic polynomial time (PPT) algorithm A, and for every large enough n,

$$\Pr_{A,\ x \sim \{0,1\}^n} [A(f_n(x)) \in f_n^{-1}(f_n(x))] \leq \frac{1}{n^{\omega(1)}}.$$

(2) Base one-way functions on a natural worst-case computational assumption.
Since a proof of the existence of one-way functions would imply that P $\neq$ NP, a less ambitious problem is whether we can base their existence on a widely believed worst-case complexity assumption. This question has also received significant attention over the past several decades (see, e.g., [1,7–9,21,25,36,42] and references therein).

Recently, there have been attempts to investigate directions **(1)** and **(2)** through the lens of the theory of (time-bounded) Kolmogorov complexity, which studies the minimum encoding length of binary strings according to different measures of complexity. Interestingly, the new approaches are complete, in the sense that they provide both necessary and sufficient conditions to achieve **(1)** and **(2)**. We can categorize these approaches into two strands of research:

(A) Structural theory of time-bounded Kolmogorov complexity.
This research direction relates the existence of one-way functions to the failure of key properties of (time-unbounded) Kolmogorov complexity in the time-bounded setting, such as language compression, conditional coding, and symmetry of information.

(B) Complexity of computing time-bounded Kolmogorov complexity.
This research direction, often referred to as meta-complexity, connects one-way functions to the computational hardness of estimating the time-bounded Kolmogorov complexity of a given string.

In both **(A)** and **(B)**, several measures of (time-bounded) Kolmogorov complexity have been considered, such as K^{poly}, pK^{poly} and rK^{poly} in **(A)**, as in [18,38,39], and K, K^{poly}, pK^{poly}, Kt, KT, and cK^{poly} in **(B)**, as in [24,33–35,37,47].

In this work, we advance this area of research by proposing a new measure of time-bounded Kolmogorov complexity that offers significant benefits for the investigation of connections between **(A)** and **(B)** and directions **(1)** and **(2)**. We describe our contributions in detail next.

1.2   Our Contributions

pKt: A Probabilistic Analogue of Levin's Kt Complexity. Recall that the Kolmogorov complexity of a string $x \in \{0,1\}^*$, denoted $\mathsf{K}(x)$, is the description length $|p| \in \mathbb{N}$ of the shortest program p that prints x. Formally, we fix a universal machine U, and minimize over the length of all strings p such that $U(p) = x$.

Despite the numerous applications of Kolmogorov complexity, its inherent uncomputability becomes an important issue in situations where an upper bound on the running time of algorithms is relevant. To mitigate this issue, Levin [31] introduced a time-bounded variant of Kolmogorov complexity called Kt. In Levin's definition, the complexity of a string x considers both the length of a program p generating x and its running time. Formally, $\mathsf{Kt}(x)$ denotes the minimum over $|p| + \lceil \log t \rceil$, where p is a string such that $U(p) = x$ when U computes for at most t steps over the input string p. It is also possible to consider the conditional Kt complexity of a string x given y, denoted $\mathsf{Kt}(x \mid y)$. In this case, in addition to the input string p, we assume that the universal machine U has random access to the string y. While the $\log t$ term might seem arbitrary at first, it leads to a close relationship between Kt complexity and optimal search algorithms. For this and other reasons, Levin's definition has been highly influential in algorithms and complexity theory (see, e.g., [2–4]).

In this work, we put forward a *probabilistic* variant of Kt complexity called pKt. Informally, the new definition is simply Kt in the presence of public randomness, i.e., x has "small" pKt complexity if with probability at least $2/3$ over the randomness r, x has "small" Kt complexity given access to r (think of it as Kt in the "Common Random String" (CRS) model). Formally, for a string $x \in \{0,1\}^*$,

$$\mathsf{pKt}(x) := \min \left\{ k \in \mathbb{N} \;\middle|\; \Pr_{r \sim \{0,1\}^{2^k}} \left[\mathsf{Kt}(x \mid r) \leq k \right] \geq \frac{2}{3} \right\}.$$

Thus bounded pKt complexity means that in the presence of a typical random string r, x has bounded Kt complexity. A key advantage of pKt over Kt is that the former considers randomized computations, which provides a much more suitable setting for cryptography.

Our definition of pKt is inspired by rKt, a variant of Kt complexity considered in [44], and $\mathsf{pK}^{\mathsf{poly}}$, a similar probabilistic notion of Kolmogorov complexity for fixed time bounds considered in [13] (see Section 2 for the corresponding definitions). More information about probabilistic notions of time-bounded Kolmogorov complexity is available in [40].

OWF from BPEXP Lower Bounds via Worst-Case to Average-Case Failure of SoI. We explore the possibility of basing one-way functions on a mild worst-case computational assumption. We consider the widely believed hypothesis that $\mathsf{BPEXP} \not\subseteq \text{i.o.SIZE}[\mathsf{poly}]$, i.e., that there is a language computable in probabilistic time $2^{\mathsf{poly}(n)}$ that requires super-polynomial size Boolean circuits on all large enough input lengths. (Note that this is significantly weaker than the standard hypothesis from derandomization that $\mathsf{E} \not\subseteq \text{i.o.SIZE}[2^{o(n)}]$ [28].) In order to state our result, we first need to review a central notion from the theory of Kolmogorov complexity.

Symmetry of Information (SoI) is a fundamental property of Kolmogorov complexity [53] that has found applications in a number of areas (see, e.g., [32, 50]). It states that for every pair of strings $x, y \in \{0,1\}^n$,

$$\mathsf{K}(x,y) \approx \mathsf{K}(y) + \mathsf{K}(x \mid y) \approx \mathsf{K}(x) + \mathsf{K}(y \mid x),$$

up to an additive factor of order $\pm O(\log n)$ in each equation. In other words, SoI says that: (i) to describe both x and y it is sufficient to describe x optimally without considering y, then describe y optimally assuming access to a description of x; and (ii) there is no significantly better way to describe the pair x, y. While (i) is easily seen to hold, (ii) is non-trivial and states that

$$\mathsf{K}(x,y) \geq \mathsf{K}(x) + \mathsf{K}(y \mid x) - O(\log n).$$

Interestingly, while SoI holds for time-unbounded Kolmogorov complexity, it is known that it fails for Levin's Kt complexity. More precisely, [49] established that for every large n, there is a pair of strings $x, y \in \{0,1\}^n$ such that

$$\mathsf{Kt}(x,y) < \mathsf{Kt}(x) + \mathsf{Kt}(y \mid x) - \omega(\log n).$$

In contrast, whether SoI fails for other measures of time-bounded Kolmogorov complexity remains open. It is known that this must be the case under the existence of one-way functions [38,39]. More recently, [18] proved that SoI fails for $\mathsf{pK}^{\mathsf{poly}}$ in a certain average-case sense *if and only if* one-way functions exist. In other words, it is not only sufficient but also necessary to understand SoI in time-bounded Kolmogorov complexity in order to determine the existence of one-way functions. Unfortunately, while SoI fails for Kt (unconditionally), we appear to be far from establishing the failure of SoI for polynomial-time measures such as $\mathsf{pK}^{\mathsf{poly}}$.

This motivates the consideration of the failure of SoI for pKt complexity, which is merely a variant of Kt in the presence of a random string. To investigate this question and its connections to cryptography, we introduce the following statements.

Worst-Case-Asymmetry-pKt: For every constant $c > 0$, if n is large enough then there exist $x, y \in \{0,1\}^n$ such that

$$\mathsf{pKt}(x,y) < \mathsf{pKt}(x) + \mathsf{pKt}(y \mid x) - c \cdot \log n.$$

Average-Case-Asymmetry-pKt: There is a polynomial-time samplable distribution family $\{\mathcal{D}_n\}$, where each $\mathcal{D}_n$ is supported over $\{0,1\}^n \times \{0,1\}^n$, and a polynomial q such that for every constant $c > 0$ and for every large enough n,

$$\Pr_{(x,y)\sim\mathcal{D}_n} [\mathsf{pKt}(x,y) < \mathsf{pKt}(x) + \mathsf{pKt}(y \mid x) - c \cdot \log n] \geq \frac{1}{q(n)}.$$

We are now ready to state the main result of this section.

Theorem 1 (Conditional Equivalence Between OWF and Worst-to-Average-Case Failure of SoI). *Assume that* BPEXP $\not\subseteq$ i.o.SIZE[poly]. *The following equivalence holds:*

(Worst-Case-Asymmetry-pKt $\Rightarrow$ Average-Case-Asymmetry-pKt) $\iff$ $\exists$OWF

Additionally, we have

$$\text{Average-Case-Asymmetry-pKt} \iff \exists\text{OWF}$$

$$\text{BPEXP} \not\subseteq \text{i.o.SIZE[poly]} \implies \text{Worst-Case-Asymmetry-pKt}$$

As a consequence of Theorem 1, we can base one-way functions on the worst-case hardness assumption BPEXP $\not\subseteq$ i.o.SIZE[poly] if the failure of SoI for pKt in the worst case implies its failure on average. Note that the assumption that BPEXP $\not\subseteq$ i.o.SIZE[poly] is significantly weaker than NP $\not\subseteq$ i.o.SIZE[poly].

Corollary 1. *Suppose*

$$\text{Worst-Case-Asymmetry-pKt} \Rightarrow \text{Average-Case-Asymmetry-pKt}.$$

Then BPEXP $\not\subseteq$ i.o.SIZE[poly] $\Rightarrow$ $\exists$OWF.

In fact, we show that Average-Case-Asymmetry-pKt is equivalent to a *worst-case* version of asymmetry of information with some additive error: $\mathsf{pKt}(x, y) < \mathsf{pKt}(x) + \mathsf{pKt}(y \mid x) - O(\mathsf{cd}^t(x, y) + \log t)$ for some $x, y \in \{0, 1\}^n$, and some $t \geq \mathrm{poly}(n)$, where $\mathsf{cd}^t(x, y) := \mathsf{pK}^t(x, y) - \mathsf{K}(x, y)$ is called *computational depth*. Thus, we can base one-way functions on BPEXP $\not\subseteq$ i.o.SIZE[poly] if the failure of SoI for pKt in the worst case is witnessed by a pair (x, y) of strings with small computational depth. We refer to the full version [19] for details.

We note that the relation between worst-case and average-case complexity is well understood in certain settings, such as with respect to computational hardness against non-uniform circuits (see, e.g., [10,51] and references therein). Whether similar "amplification" techniques can be developed in the context of (a)symmetry of information is an intriguing research direction.

It would be very interesting to remove the assumption BPEXP $\not\subseteq$ i.o.SIZE[poly] from Theorem 1. Towards showing that the implication

$$\text{Worst-Case-Asymmetry-pKt} \Rightarrow \text{Average-Case-Asymmetry-pKt}$$

yields one-way functions, we prove, without the lower bound assumption, that if the implication Worst-Case-Asymmetry-pKt $\Rightarrow$ Average-Case-Asymmetry-pKt is true, then *natural properties* [46] against sub-exponential size circuits do not exist. (The latter statement about natural properties is closely related to the existence of one-way functions of quasi-polynomial security.) We refer to the full version [19] for more details about this result.

OWF via One-Sided to Two-Sided Error Reductions for Approximating pKt. In this section, we consider the more ambitious goal of unconditionally proving the existence of one-way functions. As mentioned above, several recent results have shown that to achieve this goal it is sufficient to prove that certain meta-computational problems about time-bounded Kolmogorov complexity are computationally hard [24,33–35,37,47].

We upgrade this approach by showing that obtaining a reduction from two-sided average-case approximations of pKt to one-sided average-case approximations of pKt suffices to show the existence of one-way functions. In other words, instead of proving an unconditional lower bound, as in previous papers, designing a reduction between two notions of average-case complexity is enough.

To formalize this result, we will need a couple of definitions. For a function $\tau \colon \mathbb{N} \to \mathbb{N}$, let $\mathsf{GapMpKtP}[\tau]$ be the following promise problem ($\mathsf{YES}, \mathsf{NO}$):

$$\mathsf{YES} := \{(x, 1^s) \mid \mathsf{pKt}(x) \leq s\},$$
$$\mathsf{NO} := \{(x, 1^s) \mid \mathsf{pKt}(x) > s + \tau(|x|)\}.$$

For an algorithm A, $x \in \{0,1\}^*$, and $s \in \mathbb{N}$, we say that A *decides* $\mathsf{GapMpKtP}[\tau]$ *on* $(x, 1^s)$ if the following holds:

$$A(x, 1^s) = \begin{cases} 1 & \text{if } \mathsf{pKt}(x) \leq s, \\ 0 & \text{if } \mathsf{pKt}(x) > s + \tau(|x|), \\ \textbf{either } 0 \textbf{ or } 1 & \text{otherwise.} \end{cases}$$

We will also need the following statements.

2-Sided-Error-Approx-pKt: For every polynomial-time samplable distribution family $\{\mathcal{D}_n\}_n$ supported over $\{0,1\}^n$, and every polynomial q, there exist a PPT algorithm A and a constant $c > 0$ such that for all sufficiently large n and all $1 \leq s \leq n + O(\log n)$,

$$\Pr_{x \sim \mathcal{D}_n, A}[A \text{ decides } \mathsf{GapMpKtP}[\tau] \text{ on } (x, 1^s)] \geq 1 - \frac{1}{q(n)},$$

where $\tau(n) = c \cdot \log n$.

Mild-1-Sided-Error-Approx-pKt: There is $\varepsilon > 0$ and a PPT algorithm B such that, for every large enough n, the following holds:

(1) If $x \in \{0,1\}^n$ and $\mathsf{pKt}(x) \leq n^\varepsilon$, then $\Pr_B[B(x) = 1] \geq \frac{2}{3}$.

(2) With probability at least $1/n$ over $x \sim \{0,1\}^n$, $\Pr_B[B(x) = 0] \geq \frac{2}{3}$.

(Note that, while 2-Sided-Error-Approx-pKt considers an arbitrary polynomial-time samplable distribution, Mild-1-Sided-Error-Approx-pKt is only concerned with the uniform distribution.)

A remark about terminology is in order. We note that any PPT algorithm B that accepts every string x with pKt complexity at most n^ε and rejects every string x with pKt complexity at least $0.99n$ satisfies conditions (1) and (2) above. This is because one can show that the overwhelming majority of n-bit strings have pKt complexity close to n. Since (2) significantly relaxes the correctness requirement of B on strings of large complexity, we can think of the algorithm B as a mild approximator for pKt. Regarding the error, if we think of strings x with pKt complexity at most n^ε as positive instances, and strings x with pKt complexity at least $0.99n$ as negative instances, then B makes mistakes only on negative instances. On the other hand, the algorithm A in the statement 2-Sided-Error-Approx-pKt can make mistakes on both negative and positive instances. Therefore, A is a two-sided error algorithm, while B is one-sided. (In Section 1.3 below, we discuss a proof that Mild-1-Sided-Error-Approx-pKt $\Rightarrow$ 2-Sided-Error-Approx-pKt.)

Similarly to the statement $\exists$OWF defined above, we can consider the weaker statement $\exists$i.o.OWF, which postulates the existence of one-way functions that are hard to invert on infinitely many input lengths. (The precise definition of $\exists$i.o.OWF appears in Section 2.)

We are ready to state the main result of this section.

Theorem 2. (Equivalence Between OWF and One-Sided to Two-Sided Error Reductions for pKt). *The following equivalence holds:*

(2-Sided-Error-Approx-pKt $\Rightarrow$ Mild-1-Sided-Error-Approx-pKt) $\iff$ $\exists$i.o.OWF

Additionally, we have[1]

$\neg$ 2-Sided-Error-Approx-pKt $\iff$ $\exists$i.o.OWF

$\neg$Mild-1-Sided-Error-Approx-pKt holds unconditionally

Previously, in a celebrated result, Liu and Pass [34] proved that one can base (infinitely-often) OWF on the assumption that EXP $\not\subseteq$ BPP if and only if there is a reduction from computing Kt on average with zero error under the uniform distribution to computing Kt on average with two-sided error. In contrast, as a consequence of Theorem 2, (infinitely-often) one-way functions exist *unconditionally* if there is a probabilistic average-case polynomial-time reduction from mildly approximating pKt with one-sided error to approximating pKt with two-sided error.[2] Moreover, the existence of a quasi-polynomial-time reduction suffices, due to the proof of a slightly stronger result in Section 1.3 below. Therefore, this result shows that the hardness needed for one-way functions comes from

---

[1] We state the result in this way to allow for a direct comparison with prior work.

[2] It is also possible to define zero-error and one-sided error (as opposed to mildly one-sided error) average-case notions of approximating pKt. However, employing them in Theorem 2 would make the result weaker (i.e., it is easier to obtain a mild one-sided error algorithm from a two-sided error algorithm than to obtain a zero-error algorithm from a two-sided error algorithm). For completeness, we provide a comprehensive discussion of these notions in the full version [19].

the difference between 1-sided and 2-sided error, and not from the assumption that $\mathsf{EXP} \not\subseteq \mathsf{BPP}$.

Theorem 2 suggests a tantalizing possibility: the existence of one-way functions would follow from the design of an efficient reduction involving different notions of average-case complexity for the same computational task.[3] For instance, a reduction of this nature is known for $\mathsf{UP} \cap \mathsf{coUP}$ and can be constructed from an instance checker [22].

Given the stakes, it is natural to consider potential barriers that one might need to overcome when attempting to obtain such a reduction. In our next result, we establish that a reduction cannot be obtained through the use of *relativizing* techniques (in the sense of [6]). More precisely, we consider a scenario where an oracle $\mathcal{O}$ is available to all computations, i.e., the universal machine defining pKt, the samplers defining the polynomial-time samplable distributions, and the algorithms that attempt to approximate $\mathsf{pKt}^{\mathcal{O}}$. We prove the following result.

Theorem 3. *There exists an oracle* $\mathcal{O} \in$ PSPACE *relative to which* 2-Sided-Error-Approx-pKt *is true, but* Mild-1-Sided-Error-Approx-pKt *is false.*

In other words, techniques that hold in the presence of an arbitrary oracle cannot be used to obtain a one-sided to two-sided error reduction for approximating pKt. Indeed, Theorem 3 provides an even stronger PSPACE-relativization barrier in the sense of [20]. We refer to the full version [19] for further discussions on this barrier.

We remark that many techniques employed in the investigation of time-bounded Kolmogorov complexity and meta-complexity relativize, but not all of them (see [16] for a striking recent example). For this reason, we view Theorem 3 more as a guiding principle than a strong negative result suggesting that one should not investigate such reductions.

1.3   Techniques

In this section, we discuss the proofs of Theorem 1 and Theorem 2, which rely on some intermediate results that might be of independent interest. Since our arguments make use of a number of techniques from time-bounded Kolmogorov complexity and rely on several ideas from previous papers, we only provide a high-level exposition, referring to the main body of the paper for further technical details. After this discussion, we summarise some advantages of pKt complexity over other time-bounded Kolmogorov complexity measures.

OWF and Worst-Case to Average-Case Failure of SoI for pKt (Theorem 1). First, a careful adaptation of the techniques from [18] and [39] allows us to establish an equivalence between the failure of SoI for pKt on average and the existence of one-way functions.

---

[3] In a sense, one can think of the result as an *algorithmic* approach to establish the existence of one-way functions.

Theorem 4. *The following equivalence holds:*

$$\text{Average-Case-Asymmetry-pKt} \iff \exists\text{OWF}.$$

However, the more complex notion of pKt introduces additional technicalities, as we explain next. Using ideas from [39], it can be shown that if SoI for $\mathsf{K}^{\mathsf{poly}}$ holds on average, then for an average image y of the candidate one-way function, one can upper bound the $\mathsf{K}^{\mathsf{poly}}$ complexity of most (say, at least $1/2$) of the pre-images x of y as follows.

$$\mathsf{K}^{\mathsf{poly}}(x \mid y) \lesssim \log |f^{-1}(y)| =: k.$$

Then by defining a sampling procedure that randomly picks a program of size k and run it for *polynomially many* steps (conditional on y), x can be obtained with probability roughly 2^{-k}, which is $1/|f^{-1}(y)|$. Since this holds for at least $|f^{-1}(y)|/2$ pre-images, it follows that we obtain *some* pre-image with decent probability. (Contrapositively, if $\exists$OWF then asymmetry of information for K^t holds on average.)

Using similar ideas, we can show that if *average-case* SoI for pKt holds, then for an average image y of the candidate one-way function, one can upper bound the pKt complexity of most of its pre-images x as follows.

$$\mathsf{pKt}(x \mid y) \lesssim \log |f^{-1}(y)| =: k.$$

Now since we can only upper bound the pKt complexity of a pre-image (instead of $\mathsf{pK}^{\mathsf{poly}}$), the previously mentioned sampling procedure no longer works. This is because, by the definition of pKt, the above only implies that for a uniformly random string $r \in \{0,1\}^{2^k}$, there are integers s and t such that $s + \log t \leq k$ and there is a program of size s that, given y and r, runs in time t and outputs x. In particular, t may not be bounded by $\mathsf{poly}(n)$ in this case.

To cope with this issue, we further observe that for most of the pre-images x, *with high probability* over $r \sim \{0,1\}^{2^k}$, any program that generates x, given r and y, must be large in the sense that

$$\mathsf{K}(x \mid y, r) \geq |f^{-1}(y)| - O(\log n).$$

This can by shown by using a counting argument. Now given the above, we can say that for a uniformly random string $r \in \{0,1\}^{2^k}$, there are integers s and t such that $s + \log t \leq k$ and there is a program of size s that, given y and r, runs in time t and outputs x. Moreover, s must be at least $k - O(\log n)$. Note that this implies $t = \mathsf{poly}(n)$.

At this point, it seems we can carry out the previous argument and show that we can obtain a pre-image of y in polynomial time, by randomly picking a string $r \in \{0,1\}^{2^k}$, a program $p \in \{0,1\}^{\leq k}$ and running p for $\mathsf{poly}(n)$ steps, while given oracle access to r and y. However, there is one more issue. To perform this sampling procedure, we need to pick a uniformly random string r of length 2^k, which is not necessarily $\mathsf{poly}(n)$. Fortunately, since we only need to run our programs for $\mathsf{poly}(n)$ steps, we do not need to keep the entire random string. Instead, we can generate random bits on-the-fly and maintain the same behavior of our program as if it were running with a pre-generated random string.

Next, complementing Theorem 4, we explore the failure of SoI for pKt in the worst case. We are able to show that the latter holds under a worst-case circuit lower bound assumption for a language in BPEXP. This is a key result which allows us to link a worst-case lower bound in the complexity-theoretic regime to the cryptographic regime in Theorem 1.

Theorem 5. *If* $\mathsf{BPEXP} \not\subseteq \mathsf{i.o.SIZE}[\mathsf{poly}]$ *then* $\mathsf{Worst\text{-}Case\text{-}Asymmetry\text{-}pKt}$ *holds.*

To our knowledge, this is the first result showing the failure of symmetry of information for a probabilistic notion of time-bounded Kolmogorov complexity under a lower bound assumption in the complexity-theoretic regime, as opposed to a lower bound assumption in the cryptographic regime (e.g., [18,39]).

In Theorem 5 the goal is to construct a pair (x, y) of n-bit strings witnessing the asymmetry of information of this pair with respect to pKt complexity. Inspired by the unconditional construction of such a pair with respect to Kt complexity [49], we attempt a generalization of the argument to the probabilistic setting of pKt. The construction of [49] relies on a simple (deterministic) exhaustive search that defines an appropriate pair (x, y) and certifies the necessary Kt bounds for the strings. Unfortunately, in a probabilistic setting, it is unclear if a similar (probabilistic) exhaustive search specifies a *canonical* pair (x, y) with the desired properties, which is needed in order to obtain upper bounds on probabilistic Kolmogorov complexity.

In more detail, a key step in the proof from [49] is to compute given a string y the set $S_y^{\mathsf{Kt}} \subseteq \{0,1\}^n$ of strings of conditional Kt complexity at most s, for some threshold s. This is done in time $O(2^s)$ using a deterministic algorithm A that decides whether $\mathsf{Kt}(x \mid y) \leq s$ for a given x. In our case, we are only able to use a corresponding *randomized* algorithm B that checks whether $\mathsf{pKt}(x \mid y) \leq s$ or $\mathsf{pKt}(x \mid y) \geq 2s$, with no guarantee on the remaining instances. Unfortunately, the exhaustive search over all strings performed with the help of B will not produce a fixed set S_y^{pKt}, since its behaviour outside the promise region means that on different executions a different set of strings could be added to S_y^{pKt}, according to the internal randomness of B.

We attempt to fix this issue under the assumption that $\mathsf{BPEXP} \not\subseteq \mathsf{i.o.SIZE}[\mathsf{poly}]$, which is sufficient for the construction of a non-trivial *pseudodeterministic* pseudorandom generator. The latter allows us to perform an exhaustive search over probabilistic algorithms in a way that produces a canonical pair (x, y) with high probability.

It turns out that this is not quite enough to finish the proof, because under the weak lower bound assumption $\mathsf{BPEXP} \not\subseteq \mathsf{i.o.SIZE}[\mathsf{poly}]$ we are only able to construct strings of conditional pKt complexity larger than s in time roughly $2^{2^{o(s)}}$. This is an important issue that is not present in [49]. To address this difficulty, we show via a more sophisticated *iterative process* for constructing strings that symmetry of information is indeed violated for *some pair* (x, y)

specified during the process. Since this is somewhat delicate and technical to describe, we refer the reader to Section 4.2.

It is easy to see that Theorem 1 follows from Theorem 4 and Theorem 5 (see Section 4.3).[4]

OWF and 1-Sided to 2-Sided Error Reductions for Approximating pKt (Theorem 2). To establish this result, we first obtain an equivalence between the existence of (infinitely-often) one way functions and the average-case hardness of approximating pKt complexity with two-sided error.

Theorem 6. *The following equivalence holds:*

$$\neg\,2\text{-Sided-Error-Approx-pKt} \iff \exists\text{i.o.OWF}.$$

The proof of Theorem 6 makes use of a connection between one-way functions and the hardness of approximating (time-unbounded) Kolmogorov complexity K [24], which can be adapted to pKt by investigating the relation between K and pKt for strings generated by a polynomial-time samplable distribution. In more detail, the argument in [24] relied on the use of the *coding theorem* for time-unbounded Kolmogorov complexity. Here, we extend their approach and employ a recently discovered efficient coding theorem for pK^{poly} [41], which also applies to pKt.

Next, we establish an unconditional lower bound against probabilistic algorithms that mildly approximate pKt on average with one-sided error.

Theorem 7. Mild-1-Sided-Error-Approx-pKt *is false. Moreover, the corresponding lower bound holds against randomized algorithms running in time* $n^{poly(\log n)}$

Theorem 7 highlights an important difference between pKt and Kt that plays a central role in the proof of Theorem 2: we can establish *unconditional* complexity lower bounds for computing pKt, while the same result is unknown for Kt The proof of Theorem 7 modifies an argument employed to show a complexity lower bound of a similar nature for estimating rKt complexity [44]. It can be described as an indirect diagonalization that heavily relies on techniques from computational pseudorandomness. The proof relies on the following key lemmas

1. If pKt can be approximated on average with mild-one-sided error in time $n^{poly(\log n)}$, then $\mathsf{BPE} \subseteq \mathsf{SIZE}[n^{poly(\log n)}]$.

2. If pKt can be approximated on average with mild-one-sided error in time $n^{poly(\log n)}$, then $\mathsf{PSPACE} \subseteq \mathsf{BPTIME}[n^{poly(\log n)}]$. In particular, under this assumption $\mathsf{DSPACE}[2^{n^{o(1)}}] \subseteq \mathsf{BPE}$. (We observe that this step is problematic

---

[4] We note that the proof that there are strings (x, y) for which symmetry of information fails is by constructing such strings for which the running time t of the pKt witness is *exponential*. On the other hand, the proof that average-case symmetry of information implies that we can break any one-way function uses the fact that on any samplable distribution, with high probability on the sample y, the pKt witness has *polynomial* running time. Bridging this gap is a very interesting research direction.

in the setting of Kt, as it relies on techniques from pseudorandomness whose underlying algorithms are *randomized*.)

These two lemmas, which require the analysis of different pseudorandom generators and of the time-bounded Kolmogorov complexity of their output strings, use that pKt is both "probabilistic" and "exponential" (as opposed to Kt, which is "deterministic", and pK^{poly}, which is "polynomial").

3. There is a language in DSPACE$[2^{n^{o(1)}}]\backslash$SIZE$[n^{\text{poly}(\log n)}]$.

The proof of this third lemma uses a standard diagonalization technique.

Assuming Mild-1-Sided-Error-Approx-pKt holds, we obtain from Items 1 and 2 that DSPACE$[2^{n^{o(1)}}] \subseteq$ BPE $\subseteq$ SIZE$[n^{\text{poly}(\log n)}]$, in contradiction with Item 3.

Finally, Theorem 2 easily follows from Theorem 6 and Theorem 7 (see Section 5.3).

We note in passing that Theorem 6 can be used to give a reduction from the task of approximating pKt with two-sided error over *any polynomial-time samplable distribution* to the task of approximating pKt with one-sided error over the *uniform distribution* and, in particular, can be used to prove

$$\text{Mild-1-Sided-Error-Approx-pKt} \Rightarrow \text{2-Sided-Error-Approx-pKt}.$$

Indeed, under Mild-1-Sided-Error-Approx-pKt it is not hard to show that every candidate cryptographic pseudorandom generator can be broken. Since the latter is equivalent to the non-existence of (infinitely-often) one-way functions [15] (i.e., ¬∃i.o.OWF), we immediately derive 2-Sided-Error-Approx-pKt from Theorem 6.

The benefits of pKt complexity. We summarize here some advantages of pKt over other time-bounded Kolmogorov complexity measures:

- An optimal coding theorem is known to hold unconditionally for pK^{poly} [41] and for pKt. This is a key principle in Kolmogorov complexity and a very useful tool in applications. The same result is not known to hold unconditionally for other complexity measures.
- A central aspect in recent investigations of meta-complexity and its applications is the advice complexity and time-bounded Kolmogorov complexity measure associated with the reconstruction procedure of pseudorandom generators. When using pK^{poly} and pKt, existing generators offer superior bounds, which allow results to be more easily established in the polynomial-time regime as opposed to the quasi-polynomial time regime and above.
- In contrast to the situation for pK^{poly} and other polynomial-time complexity measures, we have unconditional super-polynomial complexity lower bounds for approximating pKt (as in Theorem 7).
- The unconditional failure of symmetry of information is only known to hold for an exponential-time measure (Kt), which suggests that it will be easier to resolve this question for pKt and rKt as opposed to polynomial-time measures such as pK^{poly}. Indeed, showing the failure of symmetry of information for certain polynomial-time measures would imply that P $\neq$ NP [17], while no consequence of a similar form is known in the case of pKt.

The first two bullets highlight advantages of the probabilistic measures pK^{poly} and pKt over deterministic complexity measures such as K^t and Kt, while the last two bullets highlight the advantages of pKt over polynomial-time measures (such as pK^{poly}). We also note that, while pKt is closely related to Kt, super-polynomial complexity lower bounds are not known for the problem of computing Kt. Overall, the aforementioned features make pKt complexity an attractive complexity measure for the investigation of connections between one-way functions and the theory of time-bounded Kolmogorov complexity.

1.4   Directions and Open Problems

There are a few directions to be explored that would advance this research program. Moreover, to our knowledge the concrete problems listed below might all be within the reach of existing techniques.

Theorem 5 establishes the failure of SoI for pKt under a circuit lower bound assumption. In contrast, as mentioned above, it is known unconditionally that SoI fails for Kt. Can the same be done for pKt? If not, can we connect this question to major open problems about the power of randomness in computation?

Easiness assumptions can often be used to establish symmetry of information for different complexity measures [12,13,17]. Is it possible to prove that if $BPEXP \subseteq i.o.SIZE[poly]$ then SoI holds for pKt on infinitely many input lengths (i.e., ¬Worst-Case-Asymmetry-pKt)? This would allow us to strengthen Theorem 2 and obtain the following equivalence:

$$(\text{Worst-Case-Asymmetry-pKt} \implies \text{Average-Case-Asymmetry-pKt})$$

$$\Updownarrow$$

$$(\text{BPEXP} \nsubseteq \text{i.o.SIZE[poly]} \implies \exists \text{OWF})$$

In other words, we would obtain that connecting the failure of SoI for pKt in the worst case and in the average case is not only sufficient but also necessary to base one-way functions on a worst-case non-uniform lower bound for $BPEXP$. Given the techniques developed in previous papers, the main difficulty in showing SoI for pKt from the assumption $BPEXP \subseteq i.o.SIZE[poly]$ seems to be that it states a non-uniform upper bound instead of a uniform one.

We obtained an unconditional lower bound against probabilistic quasi-poly-time algorithms for the task of estimating pKt complexity (Theorem 7). If one could show a sub-exponential time lower bound, this would relax even more the running time of the reduction from two-sided approximation to mild one-sided approximation needed to establish the existence of one-way functions in Theorem 2.

Finally, there would be significant consequences to complexity theory and cryptography if one could show that

$$\text{2-Sided-Error-Approx-pKt} \Rightarrow \text{Mild-1-Sided-Error-Approx-pKt}.$$

Are there additional difficulties that must be overcome beyond the relativization barrier established in Theorem 3?

Acknowledgements. We are thankful to Eric Allender for suggesting the investigation of the failure of symmetry of information for Kt and its connections to cryptography in light of the results in [18]. We also appreciate the anonymous reviewers for their valuable feedback on the presentation. This work received support from the Royal Society University Research Fellowship URF\R1\191059; the UKRI Frontier Research Guarantee Grant EP/Y007999/1; and the Centre for Discrete Mathematics and its Applications (DIMAP) at the University of Warwick.

Remainder of the paper. We give the necessary background in Section 2. In Section 3, we formally define pKt and state some useful properties. We prove Theorem 1 in Section 4, and Theorem 2 in Section 5. Due to space constraints, we omit many proofs in this extended abstract. The full version of the paper is available at [19].

2   Preliminaries

For a probability distribution $\mathcal{D}$ and a string $x \in \{0,1\}^*$, we use $\mathcal{D}(x)$ to denote the probability that x is sampled from $\mathcal{D}$. For a distribution $\mathcal{D}$ over $\{0,1\}^n \times \{0,1\}^n$ and a string $y \in \{0,1\}^n$, we let $\mathcal{D}(\cdot \mid y)$ denote the conditional distribution of $\mathcal{D}$ on the first half given that the second half is y.

One-Way Functions. Let FP denote the set of functions that can be computed in deterministic polynomial time.

Definition 1 (One-Way Function). *We say that a function $f = \{f_n\} \in \mathsf{FP}$, where $f_n \colon \{0,1\}^n \to \{0,1\}^{\mathsf{poly}(n)}$, is a one-way function if for every probabilistic polynomial time (PPT) algorithm A, and for every large enough n,*

$$\Pr_{A,\, x \sim \{0,1\}^n} [A(f(x)) \in f^{-1}(f(x))] \leq \frac{1}{n^{\omega(1)}}.$$

Definition 2 (Infinitely-Often One-Way Function). *We say that a function $f = \{f_n\} \in \mathsf{FP}$, where $f_n \colon \{0,1\}^n \to \{0,1\}^{\mathsf{poly}(n)}$, is an infinitely-often one-way function if for every probabilistic polynomial time (PPT) algorithm A, there is an infinite set $S_A \subseteq \mathbb{N}$ such that for every $n \in S_A$,*

$$\Pr_{A,\, x \sim \{0,1\}^n} [A(f_n(x)) \in f_n^{-1}(f_n(x))] \leq \frac{1}{n^{\omega(1)}}.$$

Note that the set S_A of inputs can depend on A. It is possible to show that this definition implies that for every k there is an infinite set $S_k \subseteq \mathbb{N}$ such that every PPT algorithm A that runs in time $O(n^k)$ only succeeds to invert f with negligible probability on large input lengths $n \in S_A$. (This is because one can define a "universal" PPT algorithm B that runs every algorithm of time bound n^{k+1} and description length $\log n$ while trying to invert f_n.)

Theorem 8 ([26,27]). *Assume infinitely-often one-way functions do not exist. Let $\{\mathcal{D}_n\}_n$ be a family of polynomial-time samplable distributions, and let q be any polynomial. There exists a probabilistic polynomial-time algorithm B such that for all $n \in \mathbb{N}$,*

$$\Pr_{x \sim \mathcal{D}_n, B}\left[\frac{\mathcal{D}_n(x)}{2} \leq B(1^n, x) \leq \mathcal{D}_n(x)\right] \geq 1 - \frac{1}{q(n)}.$$

Kolmogorov Complexity. We fix a universal Turing machine U. We write $U(p)$ to indicate the output of U on an input string p, where p is written on the input tape. For a string y, we write U^y to indicate that U has random access to y. In other words, y is written on an oracle tape, and U can query the i-th bit of y by specifying the index i on a query tape.

Definition 3 (Kt [31]). *For $x, y \in \{0,1\}^*$, the* time-bounded Kolmogorov complexity *of x given y is defined as*

$$\mathsf{Kt}(x \mid y) := \min_{p \in \{0,1\}^*, \, t \in \mathbb{N}} \left\{|p| + \lceil \log t \rceil \mid U^y(p) \text{ outputs } x \text{ within } t \text{ steps}\right\}.$$

Definition 4 (pK^t [13]). *Let $x, y \in \{0,1\}^*$ and $t \in \mathbb{N}$. The* probabilistic t-time-bounded Kolmogorov complexity *of x given y is defined as*

$$\mathsf{pK}^t(x \mid y) := \min\left\{k \in \mathbb{N} \;\middle|\; \Pr_{r \sim \{0,1\}^t}\left[\begin{array}{l}\exists p \in \{0,1\}^k \text{ s.t. } U^{y,r}(p) \\ \text{outputs } x \text{ within } t \text{ steps}\end{array}\right] \geq \frac{2}{3}\right\}.$$

We recall some useful results regarding Kolmogorov complexity.

Lemma 1 (See, e.g., [18, **Lemma 9**]). *There exists a universal constant $b > 0$ such that for every distribution family $\{\mathcal{E}_n\}_n$, where each $\mathcal{E}_n$ is over $\{0,1\}^n$, and for all $n \in \mathbb{N}$,*

$$\Pr_{x \sim \mathcal{E}_n}\left[\mathsf{K}(x) < \log \frac{1}{\mathcal{E}_n(x)} - \alpha\right] < \frac{n^b}{2^\alpha}.$$

Theorem 9 (**Coding Theorem** [30]). *Let $\mathcal{E}$ be a distribution whose cumulative distribution function can be computed by some program p. Then for every $x \in \mathsf{Support}(\mathcal{E})$,*

$$\mathsf{K}(x \mid p) \leq \log \frac{1}{\mathcal{E}(x)} + O(1).$$

Theorem 10 (**Efficient Coding Theorem** [41]). *For every distribution family $\{\mathcal{D}_n\}_n$ samplable in polynomial time, where each $\mathcal{D}_n$ is supported over $\{0,1\}^n$, there exists a polynomial p such that for every $x \in \mathsf{Support}(\mathcal{D}_n)$,*

$$\mathsf{pK}^{p(n)}(x) \leq \log \frac{1}{\mathcal{D}_n(x)} + \log p(n).$$

Theorem 11 ([18]). *The following are equivalent.*

1. *There exist no (resp. infinitely-often) one-way functions.*
2. **(Average-Case Conditional Coding)** *For every polynomial-time sam-plable distribution family $\{\mathcal{D}_n\}_{n \in \mathbb{N}}$ supported over $\{0,1\}^n \times \{0,1\}^n$ and every polynomial q, there exists a polynomial p such that for infinitely many (resp. all) n,*

$$\Pr_{(x,y) \sim \mathcal{D}_n} \left[\mathsf{pK}^{p(n)}(x \mid y) \leq \log \frac{1}{\mathcal{D}_n(x \mid y)} + \log p(n) \right] \geq 1 - \frac{1}{q(n)}.$$

Pseudorandomness. We will need the following results in pseudorandomness.

Lemma 2 ([28,45]).*] Suppose* $\mathsf{BPEXP} \not\subseteq$ *i.o.$\mathsf{SIZE}[\mathrm{poly}]$ (resp. $\mathsf{BPEXP} \not\subseteq$ $\mathsf{SIZE}[\mathrm{poly}]$). Then for every $\varepsilon > 0$, there is a pseudorandom generator map-ping $r := s^\varepsilon$ bits to s bits, computable in pseudodeterministic time $2^{O(r)}$, that fools circuit of size s with error $1/s$, for all but finitely many (resp. for infinitely many) s.*

Theorem 12 ([5,29]).* For every constant $0 < \lambda < 1$, there is a pseudoran-dom generator $\left\{ G_n^{(-)} \colon \{0,1\}^{n^\lambda} \to \{0,1\}^n \right\}_n$ such that the following holds. Let $f \colon \{0,1\}^* \to \{0,1\}$.*

1. *G_n^f can be can be computed in deterministic time $\exp\left(O(n^\lambda)\right)$ given oracle access to f on inputs of length at most n^λ.*
2. *For every function $D \colon \{0,1\}^n \to \{0,1\}$, if*

$$\left| \Pr_{r \sim \{0,1\}^{n^\lambda}} \left[D(G_n^f(r)) = 1 \right] - \Pr_{x \sim \{0,1\}^n} \left[D(x) = 1 \right] \right| \geq \frac{1}{O(n)}$$

for every large enough n, then there is a sequence $\{C_n\}_n$ of polynomial-size D-oracle circuits that computes f on input length n.

Theorem 13 ([28]).* For every constant $0 < \lambda < 1$, there is a pseudoran-dom generator $\left\{ \mathsf{IW}_n^{(-)} \colon \{0,1\}^{n^\lambda} \to \{0,1\}^n \right\}_n$ such that the following holds. Let $f \colon \{0,1\}^* \to \{0,1\}$ be a function that is both random self-reducible and down-ward self-reducible.*

1. *IW_n^f can be can be computed in deterministic time $\exp\left(O(n^\lambda)\right)$ given oracle access to f on inputs of length at most n^λ.*
2. *For every oracle $\mathcal{O}$, if there is a probabilistic $\mathcal{O}$-oracle algorithm D with run-ning time $t(n)$ such that*

$$\left| \Pr_{r \sim \{0,1\}^{n^\lambda}, D} \left[D(\mathsf{IW}_n^f(r)) = 1 \right] - \Pr_{x \sim \{0,1\}^n, D} \left[D(x) = 1 \right] \right| \geq \frac{1}{O(n)}$$

for every large enough n, then there is a randomized $\mathcal{O}$-oracle algorithm with running time $\mathrm{poly}(n) \cdot t(n)$ that on every input x outputs $f(x)$ with high proba-bility.

Theorem 14 ([52]).* There is a language $L_{\mathsf{TV}} \in \mathsf{DSPACE}[O(n)]$ that is PSPACE-hard, random self-reducible, and downward self-reducible.*

3   pKt: Probabilistic Levin Complexity

In this section, we formally define pKt and state some useful properties which will be used in the proofs of our results.

We start with the definition of pKt.

Definition 5 (pKt). *For $x \in \{0,1\}^*$ and $0 < \lambda \leq 1$, the λ-probabilistic time-bounded Kolmogorov complexity of x, denoted by $\mathsf{pKt}_\lambda(x)$, is defined to be the minimum $k \in \mathbb{N}$ such that with probability at least λ over $r \sim \{0,1\}^{2^k}$, there exist a program $p \in \{0,1\}^*$ and a time bound $t \in \mathbb{N}$ that satisfy $|p| + t \leq k$ and $U^r(p)$ outputs x within t steps. Equivalently*

$$\mathsf{pKt}_\lambda(x) := \min \left\{ k \in \mathbb{N} \mid \Pr_{r \sim \{0,1\}^{2^k}} [\mathsf{Kt}(x \mid r) \leq k] \geq \lambda \right\}.$$

We omit the subscript λ when $\lambda = 2/3$.

This definition can be extended to *conditional* Kolmogorov complexity in the natural way. More specifically, in $\mathsf{pKt}(x \mid y)$ the machine U is also given oracle access to the string y.

Proposition 1. *There is a universal constant $b > 0$ such that for every $x, y \in \{0,1\}^*$ and $t \in \mathbb{N}$,*

1. $\mathsf{pKt}(x \mid y) \leq \mathsf{pK}^t(x \mid y) + \log t$, and
2. $\mathsf{K}(x \mid y) \leq \mathsf{pKt}(x \mid y) + b \log |x|$.

Next, we state a relation between Kt and pKt. The proof of this fact follows by an easy adaptation of results from [12, Appendix A.2].

Proposition 2. *If $\mathsf{E} \not\subseteq \mathrm{i.o.NSIZE}[2^{\Omega(n)}]$, then there is a constant $c > 0$ such that for every string $x \in \{0,1\}^*$, $\mathsf{pKt}(x) \leq \mathsf{Kt}(x) \leq c \cdot \mathsf{pKt}(x)$.*

Note that the relation between Kt and pKt from Proposition 2 is not as tight as the relation between $\mathsf{K}^{\mathsf{poly}}$ and $\mathsf{pK}^{\mathsf{poly}}$ described in [12, Appendix A.2]. This is due to the polynomial time overhead in the simulation, which can incur a constant factor in the description complexity due to the $\log t$ term. In particular, for this reason, we cannot easily derive the failure of SoI for pKt from the failure of SoI for Kt under a lower bound assumption.

Lemma 3 (Success Amplification; following [13]). *For any string $x \in \{0,1\}^n$, $y \in \{0,1\}^*$, and $0 \leq \alpha < \beta \leq 1$, we have*

$$\mathsf{pKt}_\beta(x \mid y) \leq \mathsf{pKt}_\alpha(x \mid y) + O\left(\log(q/\alpha) + \log n\right),$$

where $q := \ln(1/(1 - \beta))$.

We define a gap version of the minimum pKt problem, GapMpKtP, which can be viewed as the decision version of the problem of approximating pKt. For $\tau \colon \mathbb{N} \to \mathbb{N}$, let GapMpKtP$[\tau]$ be the following promise problem (YES, NO).

$$\text{YES} := \{(x, 1^s) \mid \mathsf{pKt}(x) \leq s\},$$
$$\text{NO} := \{(x, 1^s) \mid \mathsf{pKt}(x) > s + \tau(|x|)\}.$$

Lemma 4. *There is a constant $c > 0$ such that for every $\tau(n) \geq c \log n$, GapMpKtP$[\tau] \in$ prBPE.*

The following lemma will be convenient for us.

Lemma 5. *There is a probabilistic algorithm B such that given $x \in \{0,1\}^m$ and $y \in \{0,1\}^{\leq 2^m}$, $B(x, y)$ runs in time $2^{O(m)}$, rejects (with high probability) if $\mathsf{pKt}(x \mid y) < m/2$ and accepts (with high probability) if $\mathsf{pKt}(x \mid y) \geq 2m/3$.*

The following relates the problem of computing GapMpKtP and that of approximating pKt.

Proposition 3. *The following are equivalent.*

1. 2-Sided-Error-Approx-pKt.
2. *For every polynomial-time samplable distribution family $\{\mathcal{D}_n\}_n$ supported over $\{0,1\}^n$ and every polynomial q there exist a probabilistic polynomial-time algorithm A and a polynomial p such that for all $n \in \mathbb{N}$,*

$$\Pr_{x \sim \mathcal{D}_n, A} [\mathsf{pKt}(x) - \log p(n) \leq A(x) \leq \mathsf{pKt}(x)] \geq 1 - \frac{1}{q(n)}.$$

4   One-Way Functions and Asymmetry of Information for pKt

4.1   Equivalence of OWF and Average-Case Asymmetry of Information

We show the following which implies Theorem 4.

Theorem 15. *The following are equivalent.*

1. *There exist no (resp. infinitely-often) one-way functions.*
2. *(**Infinitely-Often (resp. Almost-Everywhere) Average-Case Symmetry of Information for pKt**) For every polynomial-time samplable distribution family $\{\mathcal{D}_n\}_n$ supported over $\{0,1\}^n \times \{0,1\}^n$ and every polynomial q, there exists a constant c such that for infinitely many (resp. all) $n \in \mathbb{N}$,*

$$\Pr_{(x,y) \sim \mathcal{D}_n} [\mathsf{pKt}(x, y) \geq \mathsf{pKt}(x) + \mathsf{pKt}(y \mid x) - c \cdot \log n] \geq 1 - \frac{1}{q(n)}.$$

Lemma 6. *We have (Item 1 ⇒ Item 2) in Theorem 15.*

To show Lemma 6, we need the following technical lemma.

Lemma 7. *If one-way functions do not exist, then for every polynomial-time samplable distribution family $\{\mathcal{E}_n\}_n$ supported over $\{0,1\}^n \times \{0,1\}^n$ and for every polynomial q, there exists a polynomial p such that for infinitely many $n \in \mathbb{N}$,*

$$\Pr_{(a,b)\sim\mathcal{E}_n}\left[\mathsf{pKt}(a \mid b) \leq \log \frac{1}{\mathcal{E}_n(a \mid b)} + 2\log p(n)\right] \geq 1 - \frac{1}{q(n)}.$$

Proof. The lemma follows directly from Theorem 11 and Proposition 1.   □

We are now ready to show Lemma 6.

Proof. Let $\{\mathcal{D}_n\}_n$ be a polynomial-time samplable distribution family and q be a polynomial.

Let $\{\mathcal{E}_n\}_n$ be the polynomial-time samplable distribution family that is dual to $\{\mathcal{D}_n\}_n$ in the following sense: To sample $\mathcal{E}_n$, we sample (x, y) from $\mathcal{D}_n$ and output (y, x). To show the lemma, it suffices to show that there exists a constant c such that for infinitely many $n \in \mathbb{N}$,

$$\Pr_{(a,b)\sim\mathcal{E}_n}\left[\mathsf{pKt}(b,a) \geq \mathsf{pKt}(b) + \mathsf{pKt}(a \mid b) - c \cdot \log n\right] \geq 1 - \frac{1}{q(n)}.$$

Since we assume that one-way function do not exist, then by Lemma 7, there exists a polynomial p such that for infinitely many $n \in \mathbb{N}$,

$$\Pr_{(a,b)\sim\mathcal{E}_n}\left[\mathsf{pKt}(a \mid b) \leq \log \frac{1}{\mathcal{E}_n(a \mid b)} + 2\log p(n)\right] \geq 1 - \frac{1}{2q(n)}.$$

Let $\mathcal{E}_n^{'}$ be the marginal distribution of $\mathcal{E}_n$ on the second half. Note that

$$\mathsf{pKt}(a \mid b) \leq \log \frac{1}{\mathcal{E}_n(a \mid b)} + 2\log p(n)$$

$$= \log \frac{\mathcal{E}_n(a,b)}{\mathcal{E}_n'(b)} + 2\log p(n)$$

$$= \log \frac{1}{\mathcal{E}_n(a,b)} - \log \frac{1}{\mathcal{E}_n'(b)} + 2\log p(n). \tag{1}$$

On the one hand, by Lemma 1, we get that for every n, with probability at least $1 - 1/(2q(n))$ over $(a, b) \sim \mathcal{E}_n$,

$$\mathsf{K}(b,a) \geq \log \frac{1}{\mathcal{E}_n(a,b)} - \log 2q(n) - O(\log n).$$

Then by Proposition 1, with the same probability we get

$$\mathsf{pKt}(b,a) \geq \mathsf{K}(b,a) - O(\log n) \geq \log \frac{1}{\mathcal{E}_n(a,b)} - \log 2q(n) - O(\log n). \tag{2}$$

On the other hand, by Theorem 10, there exists a polynomial p' such that for every n and $b \in \mathsf{Support}(\mathcal{E}'_n)$,

$$\mathsf{pKt}(b) \leq \mathsf{pK}^{p'(n)}(b) + \log p'(n) \leq \log \frac{1}{\mathcal{E}'_n(y)} + 2\log p'(n). \tag{3}$$

By plugging Equations (2) and (3) into Equation (1), and by a union bound, we get that for infinitely many $n \in \mathbb{N}$, with probability at least $1 - 1/q(n)$ over $(a, b) \sim \mathcal{E}_n$,

$$\mathsf{pKt}(a \mid b) \leq \mathsf{pKt}(b, a) - \mathsf{pKt}(b) + 2\log p(n) + \log 2q(n) + 2\log p'(n) + O(\log n),$$

as desired. □

Lemma 8. *We have (Item 2 $\Rightarrow$ Item 1) in Theorem 15.*

Proof. Let $f \colon \{0,1\}^n \to \{0,1\}^n$ be any candidate one-way function that is supposed to be infinitely-often secure. Let q be any polynomial. We will construct a polynomial-time algorithm that inverts f with probability at least $1 - 1/q(n)$. We first show a few useful claims. □

Claim 1 *([39, Lemma 3.5]). For every n and every $x \in \{0,1\}^n$, we have*

$$\mathsf{K}(f(x)) \geq \mathsf{K}(x) - \log|f^{-1}(f(x))| - O(\log n).$$

Proof of Claim 1. Note that for every $x \in \{0,1\}^n$, we have

$$\mathsf{K}(x \mid f(x)) \leq \log|f^{-1}(f(x))| + O(\log n). \tag{4}$$

This is because given $f(x)$, we can recover x knowing the index of x in the set $f^{-1}(f(x))$. Also, we have

$$\mathsf{K}(x) \leq \mathsf{K}(x \mid f(x)) + \mathsf{K}(f(x)),$$

which combined with Equation (4) yields

$$\begin{aligned}
\mathsf{K}(f(x)) &\geq \mathsf{K}(x) - \mathsf{K}(x \mid f(x)) \\
&\geq \mathsf{K}(x) - \log|f^{-1}(f(x))| - O(\log n).
\end{aligned}$$

This completes the proof of Claim 1. ◇

Claim 2. *For infinitely many $n \in \mathbb{N}$, with probability at least $1 - 1/q(n)^2$ over $x \sim \{0,1\}^n$, we have*

$$\mathsf{pKt}(x \mid f(x)) \leq \log|f^{-1}(f(x))| + O(\log q(n)).$$

Proof of Claim 2. Consider the polynomial-time samplable distribution family $\{\mathcal{D}_n\}$ where each $\mathcal{D}_n$ samples $x \sim \{0,1\}^n$ and outputs $(f(x), x)$.

By the assumption that infinitely-often average-case symmetry of information for pKt holds, there is a constant $c > 0$ such that for infinitely many $n \in \mathbb{N}$, with probability at least $1 - 1/(2q(n)^2)$ over $x \sim \{0,1\}^n$,

$$
\begin{aligned}
\mathsf{pKt}(x \mid f(x)) &\leq \mathsf{pKt}(f(x), x) - \mathsf{pKt}(f(x)) + c \log n \\
&\leq \mathsf{pKt}(x) - \mathsf{pKt}(f(x)) + c \log n + O(\log n) \\
&\leq \mathsf{pKt}(x) - \mathsf{K}(f(x)) + c \log n + O(\log n) \\
&\leq \mathsf{pKt}(x) - \big(\mathsf{K}(x) - \log |f^{-1}(f(x))| - O(\log n)\big) + c \log n + O(\log n) \\
&\leq \mathsf{pKt}(x) - \mathsf{K}(x) + \log |f^{-1}(f(x))| + c \log n + O(\log n), \quad (5)
\end{aligned}
$$

where the second inequality uses the fact that given x we can compute $f(x)$ efficiently and the second last inequality is by Claim 1.

Also, note that by a counting argument, with probability at least $1 - 1/(2q(n)^2)$ over $x \sim \{0,1\}^n$, we have

$$
\mathsf{K}(x) \geq n - O(\log q(n)),
$$

which implies

$$
\mathsf{pKt}(x) - \mathsf{K}(x) \leq O(\log q(n)).
$$

Plugging this into Equation (5), we get, by a union bound, that with probability at least $1 - 1/q(n)^2$ over $x \sim \{0,1\}^n$

$$
\mathsf{pKt}(x \mid f(x)) \leq \log |f^{-1}(f(x))| + O(\log q(n)),
$$

as desired.   ◇

Claim 3. *For every $n \in \mathbb{N}$, every image y of f and $k \leq 2n$, with probability at least $1 - 1/q(n)$ over $x \sim f^{-1}(y)$, we have*

$$
\Pr_{r \sim \{0,1\}^{2^k}} \big[\mathsf{K}(x \mid y, r) \geq \log |f^{-1}(y)| - O(\log q(n))\big] \geq 1 - \frac{1}{n}.
$$

Proof of Claim 3 By a simple counting argument, for every fixed image y of f and every fixed $r \in \{0,1\}^{2^k}$, we have

$$
\Pr_{x \sim f^{-1}(y)} \big[\mathsf{K}(x \mid y, r) \geq \log |f^{-1}(y)| - O(\log q(n))\big] \geq 1 - \frac{1}{n \cdot q(n)}.
$$

This implies that every image y, we have

$$
\Pr_{\substack{x \sim f^{-1}(y) \\ r \sim \{0,1\}^{2^k}}} \big[\mathsf{K}(x \mid y, r) \geq \log |f^{-1}(y)| - O(\log q(n)]\big] \geq 1 - \frac{1}{n \cdot q(n)}.
$$

Finally, by an averaging argument, we have that with probability at least $1 - 1/q(n)$ over $x \sim f^{-1}(y)$, it holds that

$$
\Pr_{r \sim \{0,1\}^{2^k}} \big[\mathsf{K}(x \mid y, r) \geq \log |f^{-1}(y)| - O(\log q(n)]\big] \geq \frac{1}{n},
$$

as desired.   ◇

By Claim 2, we get that for infinitely many $n \in \mathbb{N}$, with probability at least $1 - 1/q(n)^2$ over $x \sim \{0,1\}^n$, we have

$$\mathsf{pKt}(x \mid f(x)) \leq \log|f^{-1}(f(x))| + O(\log q(n)). \qquad (6)$$

In what follows, we fix n so that Equation (6) holds.

Now observe the following equivalent way of sampling $(x, f(x))$ while x is uniformly at random: We first sample $y := f(z)$ for a uniformly random z and then sample $x \sim f^{-1}(y)$. By an averaging argument, Equation (6) yields that with probability at least $1 - 1/q(n)$ over y sample this way, for at least $1 - 1/q(n)$ fraction of the $x \in f^{-1}(y)$, we have

$$\mathsf{pKt}(x \mid y) \leq \log|f^{-1}(y)| + O(\log q(n)). \qquad (7)$$

Consider any *good* y such that Equation (7) holds. By Claim 3, we get that for at least $1 - 1/q(n)$ fraction of the $x \in f^{-1}(y)$, it holds that

$$\Pr_{r \sim \{0,1\}^{2^k}} \left[\mathsf{K}(x \mid y, r) \geq \log|f^{-1}(y)| - O(\log q(n)) \right] \geq 1 - \frac{1}{n}, \qquad (8)$$

where $k := \mathsf{pKt}(x \mid y)$.

let S_y be the set of $x \in f^{-1}(y)$ such that both Equations (7) and (8) hold. Note that by a union bound,

$$|S_y| \geq (1 - 2/q(n)) \cdot |f^{-1}(y)|.$$

Let $d > 0$ be a sufficiently large constant. Consider the following procedure A that takes n and y as input and does the following.

1. Pick a uniformly random $k \sim [O(n)]$,
2. Pick a uniformly random $r \sim \{0,1\}^{2^k}$,
3. Pick uniformly at random $\ell \sim [O(n)]$ and $p \sim \{0,1\}^\ell$,
4. Run $U^{y,r}(p)$ for n^d steps and return its output.

Claim 4. *For every $x \in S_y$, A$(1^n, y)$ outputs x with probability at least*

$$\frac{1}{\mathsf{poly}(n) \cdot |f^{-1}(y)|}.$$

Proof of Claim 4. Fix $x \in S_y$. Note that we have

$$\mathsf{pKt}(x \mid y) \leq \log|f^{-1}(y)| + O(\log q(n)).$$

In other words, for $k := \mathsf{pKt}(x \mid y) \leq \log|f^{-1}(y)| + O(\log n)$, with probability at least $2/3$ over $r \sim \{0,1\}^{2^k}$, there exist a program of p and a running time $t \in \mathbb{N}$ such that $|p| + \log t \leq k$ and $U^{y,r}(p)$ outputs x within t steps. Note that t may not be upper bounded by $\mathsf{poly}(n)$. However, if for that r we also have that

$$\mathsf{K}(x \mid y, r) \geq \log|f^{-1}(y)| - O(\log q(n)), \qquad (9)$$

then it must be the case that $|p| \geq \log |f^{-1}(y)| - O(\log q(n))$. The condition $|p| + \log t \leq \log |f^{-1}(y)| + O(\log q(n))$ then implies that $t \leq n^d$ for some sufficiently large constant d.

Note that Equation (9) also holds with probability at least $1 - 1/n$ over $r \sim \{0,1\}^{2^k}$. It follows that with probability at least $2/3 - 1/n$ over $r \sim \{0,1\}^{2^k}$, there is a program p of size at most $\log |f^{-1}(y)| + O(\log q(n))$ such that $U^{y,r}(p)$ outputs x within n^d steps.

Therefore, after performing the first 3 steps in the procedure, we get such a program p with probability at least

$$\frac{1}{O(n)} \cdot \left(\frac{2}{3} - \frac{1}{n}\right) \cdot \frac{1}{O(n)} \cdot \frac{1}{2^{\log |f^{-1}(y)| + O(\log q(n))}} \geq \frac{1}{\mathsf{poly}(n) \cdot |f^{-1}(y)|},$$

as desired.   ◇

Now consider the following procedure A′ that can *simulate* A.

1. Pick a uniformly random $k \sim [O(n)]$,
2. Pick uniformly at random $\ell \sim [O(n)]$ and $p \sim \{0,1\}^\ell$,
3. Run $U^{y,(-)}(p)$ for n^d steps while answering its queries to the second oracle string (which is of length 2^k) as follows. For any valid query, if it did not appear before, pick a random bit b, record the query as well as the bit b, and return b; otherwise, return the corresponding bit recorded.

Denote the above procedure by A′. Note that $\mathsf{A}(1^n, y)$ has running time $\mathsf{poly}(n)$. Also, by Claim 4 the probability that $\mathsf{A'}(1^n, y)$ outputs *some* $x \in S_y$ is at least

$$|S_y| \cdot \frac{1}{\mathsf{poly}(n) \cdot |f^{-1}(y)|} \geq \frac{1}{\mathsf{poly}(n)}.$$

In other words, with probability at least $1/q(n)$ over $x \sim \{0,1\}^n$ (in which case $f(x)$ is good), $\mathsf{A'}(1^n, y)$ outputs some pre-image of $f(x)$ with probability at least $1/\mathsf{poly}(n)$. This breaks the one-way-ness of f.   □

Finally, we complete the proof of Theorem 15.

Proof of Theorem 15. Each direction of the theorem follows directly from Lemmas 6 and 8, respectively.

Also, we note that while those lemmas only show the equivalence between the non-existence of one-way functions and infinitely-often average-case symmetry of information for pKt, it is straightforward to adapt the proofs to show the equivalence between the non-existence of infinitely-often one-way functions and almost-everywhere average-case symmetry of information for pKt.   □

4.2 Asymmetry of Information from Circuit Lower Bounds

In this subsection, we show the following which implies Theorem 5.

Theorem 16. *Suppose* BPEXP $\not\subseteq$ i.o.SIZE[poly] *(resp.* BPEXP $\not\subseteq$ SIZE[poly]*). Then for every constant $c > 0$, there exist $x, y \in \{0, 1\}^n$ such that*

$$\mathsf{pKt}(x, y) < \mathsf{pKt}(x) + \mathsf{pKt}(y \mid x) - c \cdot \log n,$$

for all but finitely many (resp. infinitely many) n.

We first show the following technical lemma.

Lemma 9. *Suppose* BPEXP $\not\subseteq$ i.o.SIZE[poly] *(resp.* BPEXP $\not\subseteq$ SIZE[poly]*). Then for every constant $c > 0$, the following holds for all but finitely many (resp. infinitely many) m. There exist $v \in \{0, 1\}^m$ and $u \in \{0, 1\}^{m'}$, where $m \leq m' \leq 2^{m/(8c)}$, such that*

$$\mathsf{pKt}(u, v) < \mathsf{pKt}(u) + \mathsf{pKt}(v \mid u) - m/4,$$

Proof. We first show the case for BPEXP $\not\subseteq$ i.o.SIZE[poly].

For the sake of contradiction, suppose there is a constant $c > 0$ such that the following holds for infinitely many m. For all $v \in \{0, 1\}^m$ and all $u \in \{0, 1\}^{m'}$, where $m' \leq 2^{m/(8c)}$,

$$\mathsf{pKt}(u, v) \geq \mathsf{pKt}(u) + \mathsf{pKt}(v \mid u) - m/4.$$

Fix any (sufficiently large) m such that the above holds. For $x \in \{0, 1\}^m$ and $y \in \{0, 1\}^{\leq 2^m}$, let $C_{(x,y)} \colon \{0, 1\}^{2^{bm}} \to \{0, 1\}$ be a circuit of size 2^{bm} that views its input as internal randomness and computes $B(x, y)$, where B is the algorithm in Lemma 5 and $b \geq 0$ is a constant.

Let $\varepsilon := 1/(32bc)$ and let $G_s \colon \{0, 1\}^r \to \{0, 1\}^s$ be the PRG in Lemma 2, where $s := 2^{bm}$ and $r := s^\varepsilon$. We assume without loss of generality, using amplification if necessary, that the pseudodeterministic algorithm that computes G_s outputs the correct answer except with exponentially small probability. We abuse notation and use G_s to denote the algorithm that computes the PRG G_s.   □

Consider the following algorithm.

Algorithm 1. Pseudodeterministic Constructions of Large pKt-Complexity Strings

---

1: **procedure** $A(1^m, y)$
2:     **for** $x \in \{0, 1\}^m$ **do**
3:         $\mu_x := \Pr_{z \sim \{0,1\}^r}[C_{(x,y)}(G_s(z)) = 1]$
4:         **if** $\mu_x > 1/3 + 1/10$ **then**
5:             output x
6:     Output $\perp$

Claim 5. *The above algorithm A, on input 1^m and $y \in \{0,1\}^{\leq 2^m}$, runs in time $2^{2^{m/(16c)}}$ and outputs, with high probability, a fixed m-bit string x such that $\mathsf{pKt}(x \mid y) \geq m/2$.*

Proof of Claim 5 We first argue the running time. It is easy to that the algorithm runs in time

$$2^m \cdot 2^{O(s^\varepsilon)} \leq 2^{2^{m/(16c)}}.$$

Also, since G_s can be computed pseudodeterministically with error $1/\exp(s)$, by a union bound over $x \in \{0,1\}^m$ and $z \in \{0,1\}^{s^\varepsilon}$, the algorithm will output a fixed answer with high probability.

We now argue the correctness. Note that since G_s $(1/10)$-fools $C_{(x,y)}$ on *every* $x \in \{0,1\}^m$ and $y \in \{0,1\}^{\leq 2^m}$, for every x, (the canonical) μ_x is a good estimate of $\Pr_B[B(x,y) = 1]$. Then an output x of the algorithm cannot be that $\mathsf{pKt}(x \mid y) < m/2$. This is because in that case the algorithm $\Pr_B[B(x,y) = 1] < 1/3$ and μ_x should be less than $1/3 + 1/10$. Also, since we enumerate every x in $\{0,1\}^m$, $B(-,y)$ must accept at least one x, and in this case we have $\mu_x \geq 2/3 - 1/10 \geq 1/3 + 1/10$. This completes the proof of Claim 5.   ◇

Let $t := 2^{m/(10c)}$. We define $z_1, z_2, \ldots, z_t \in \{0,1\}^m$ as follows.

- z_1 is the canonical output of $A(1^m, \emptyset)$.
- z_i is the canonical output of $A(1^m, z_1, \ldots, z_{i-1})$ for $i = 2, 3. \ldots, t$.

On the one hand, by our assumption and by Claim 5, we have

$$\begin{aligned}
\mathsf{pKt}(z_1, z_2, \ldots, z_t) &\geq \mathsf{pKt}(z_1, z_2, \ldots, z_{t-1}) + \mathsf{pKt}(z_t \mid z_1, z_2, \ldots, z_{t-1}) - m/4 \\
&\geq \mathsf{pKt}(z_1, z_2, \ldots, z_{t-1}) + m/2 - m/4 \\
&\geq \mathsf{pKt}(z_1, z_2, \ldots, z_{t-1}) + m/4.
\end{aligned}$$

We can repeat the above for $\mathsf{pKt}(z_1, z_2, \ldots, z_{t-1})$ and so on. As a result we get

$$\mathsf{pKt}(z_1, z_2, \ldots, z_t) \geq tm/4 \geq 2^{m/(10c)}. \tag{10}$$

On the other hand, since A is pseudodeterministic (and hence outputs the same value with very high probability) and runs in time $2^{2^{m/(16c)}}$, given the numbers m and t, we can obtain $z_1, z_2, \ldots, z_t$ (with high probability) in time

$$O\left(t \cdot 2^{2^{m/(16c)}}\right).$$

Therefore, we have

$$\mathsf{pKt}(z_1, z_2, \ldots, z_t) \leq O(\log m) + O(\log t) + 2^{m/(16c)} < 2^{m/(8c)},$$

which contradicts Equation (10).

The case for $\mathsf{BPEXP} \not\subseteq \mathsf{SIZE}[\text{poly}]$ can be shown similarly. We assume, for contradiction, that there is a constant $c > 0$ such that the following holds for all but finitely many m. For all $v \in \{0,1\}^m$ and all $u \in \{0,1\}^{m'}$, where $m \leq m' \leq 2^{m/(8c)}$,

$$\mathsf{pKt}(u, v) \geq \mathsf{pKt}(u) + \mathsf{pKt}(v \mid u) - m/4.$$

We then consider any (sufficiently large) s such that G_s is a good PRG, and let m be the largest integer such that $2^{bm} \leq s$. The remainder of the argument is essentially the same. □

We are now ready to show Theorem 16.

Proof of Theorem 16. We first show the case for $\mathsf{BPEXP} \not\subseteq \mathsf{i.o.SIZE[poly]}$.

Let $c > 0$ be a sufficiently large constant, and let n be any large enough integer. We let m be such that

$$2^{m/(8c)} \leq n < 2^{(m+1)/(8c)}. \tag{11}$$

By Lemma 9, there exist $v \in \{0,1\}^m$ and $u \in \{0,1\}^{m'}$, where $m \leq m' \leq 2^{m/(8c)}$, such that

$$\mathsf{pKt}(u,v) < \mathsf{pKt}(u) + \mathsf{pKt}(v \mid u) - m/4. \tag{12}$$

We let

$$x := u0^{n-|u|} \quad \text{and} \quad y := v0^{n-|v|}. \tag{13}$$

Then we have

$$
\begin{aligned}
\mathsf{pKt}(x,y) &\leq \mathsf{pKt}(u,v) + O(\log n) && \text{(by Equation (13))}\\
&\leq \mathsf{pKt}(u) + \mathsf{pKt}(v \mid u) - m/4 + O(\log n) && \text{(by Claim 12)}\\
&< \mathsf{pKt}(x) + \mathsf{pKt}(y \mid x) + O(\log n) - m/4 + O(\log n) && \\
& && \text{(by Equation (13))}\\
&\leq \mathsf{pKt}(x) + \mathsf{pKt}(y \mid x) + O(m/c) - m/4 && \text{(by Equation (11))}\\
&\leq \mathsf{pKt}(x) + \mathsf{pKt}(y \mid x) - m/5 && \\
&\leq \mathsf{pKt}(x) + \mathsf{pKt}(y \mid x) - c\log n, && \text{(by Equation (11))}
\end{aligned}
$$

where for the second last inequality we use that c is a sufficiently large constant.

The case for $\mathsf{BPEXP} \not\subseteq \mathsf{SIZE[poly]}$ can be shown similarly. By Lemma 9, for infinitely many m, there exist $v \in \{0,1\}^m$ and $u \in \{0,1\}^{m'}$, where $m' \leq 2^{m/(8c)}$, such that

$$\mathsf{pKt}(u,v) < \mathsf{pKt}(u) + \mathsf{pKt}(v \mid u) - m/4.$$

We can then let $x := v0^{m'-|v|}$ and $y := u$, and the remainder of the argument is essentially the same as in the case for $\mathsf{BPEXP} \not\subseteq \mathsf{i.o.SIZE[poly]}$ described above. □

4.3   Proof of Theorem 1

In this subsection, we prove Theorem 1.

Proof of Theorem 1. Suppose it holds that

Worst-Case-Asymmetry-pKt $\Rightarrow$ Average-Case-Asymmetry-pKt.

Assuming $\mathsf{BPEXP} \not\subseteq \mathsf{i.o.SIZE[poly]}$, by Theorem 16, Worst-Case-Asymmetry-pKt holds, which then implies that Average-Case-Asymmetry-pKt also holds. By Theorem 4, this implies that one-way functions exist.

On the other hand, suppose one-way functions exist. Then by Theorem 4 Average-Case-Asymmetry-pKt holds. This trivially implies that

$$\text{Worst-Case-Asymmetry-pKt} \Rightarrow \text{Average-Case-Asymmetry-pKt},$$

as desired.   □

5   One-Way Functions and Hardness of Approximating pKt

5.1   Equivalence of OWF and Average-Case Hardness of Approximating pKt

We show the following which, by Proposition 3, implies Theorem 6.

Theorem 17. *The following are equivalent.*

1. *Infinitely-often one-way functions do not exist.*
2. **(Average-Case Easiness of Approximating** pKt**)** *For every polynomial-time samplable distribution family $\{\mathcal{D}_n\}_n$ supported over $\{0,1\}^n$, there exist a probabilistic polynomial-time algorithm A and a polynomial τ such that for all $n \in \mathbb{N}$,*

$$\Pr_{x \sim \mathcal{D}_n, A} \left[\mathsf{pKt}(x) - \log \tau(n) \le A(x) \le \mathsf{pKt}(x) \right] \ge 1 - \frac{1}{q(n)}.$$

Lemma 10. *We have (Item 1 $\Rightarrow$ Item 2) in Theorem 17.*

Proof. Let $\{\mathcal{D}_n\}_n$ be a polynomial-time samplable distribution family, where each $\mathcal{D}_n$ is over $\{0,1\}^n$. Let q be any polynomial. Let τ be a polynomial specified later.

First of all, by Theorem 10 and Proposition 1, there is a polynomial p such that for all $x \in \mathsf{Support}(\mathcal{D}_n)$,

$$\mathsf{pKt}(x) \le \mathsf{pK}^{p(n)}(x) + \log p(n) \le \log \frac{1}{\mathcal{D}_n(x)} + 2 \log p(n). \tag{14}$$

On the other hand, by Lemma 1, we get

$$\Pr_{x \sim \mathcal{D}_x} \left[\mathsf{K}(x) > \log \frac{1}{\mathcal{D}_n(x)} - b \cdot \log n - 2 \log q(n) \right] \ge 1 - \frac{1}{q(n)^2},$$

for some large constant b. Note that by Proposition 1,

$$\mathsf{K}(x) \le \mathsf{pKt}(x) + b \cdot \log n.$$

Then the above implies that with probability at least $1 - 1/q(n)^2$ over $x \sim \mathcal{D}_n$, it holds that

$$\mathsf{pKt}(x) > \log \frac{1}{\mathcal{D}_n(x)} - 2b \cdot \log n - 2 \log q(n). \tag{15}$$

Let B be the algorithm in Theorem 8, instantiated with the polynomial $q'(n) := q(n)^2$. Then by Theorem 8, we get that at least $1 - 1/q(n)^2$ over $x \sim \mathcal{D}_n$ and the internal randomness of B,

$$\frac{\mathcal{D}_n(x)}{2} \leq B(1^n, x) \leq \mathcal{D}_n(x). \tag{16}$$

Our algorithm A works as follows: On $(x, 1^s)$, output

$$\beta := \log \frac{1}{B(1^n, x)} - 2b \cdot \log n - 2 \log q(n) - 1.$$

It is easy to see that A runs in polynomial time. Next, we show its correctness.

Note that if both Equation (15) and Equation (16) hold, which happens with probability at least $1 - 1/q(n)$ over $x \sim \mathcal{D}_n$ and the internal randomness of A, we have both

$$\beta := \log \frac{1}{B(1^n, x)} - 2b \cdot \log n - 2 \log q(n) - 1$$

$$\leq \log \frac{1}{\mathcal{D}_n(x)} + 1 - 2b \cdot \log n - 2 \log q(n) - 1 \qquad \text{(by Equation (16))}$$

$$\leq \mathsf{pKt}(x). \qquad \text{(by Equation (15))}$$

and

$$\beta := \log \frac{1}{B(1^n, x)} - 2b \cdot \log n - 2 \log q(n) - 1$$

$$\geq \log \frac{1}{\mathcal{D}_n(x)} - 1 - 2b \cdot \log n - 2 \log q(n) - 1 \qquad \text{(by Equation (16))}$$

$$\geq \mathsf{pKt}(x) - 2 - 2b \cdot \log n - 2 \log q(n) - 2 \log p(n) \qquad \text{(by Equation (14))}$$

$$\geq \mathsf{pKt}(x) - \log \tau(n),$$

where the last inequality holds if we let τ be a sufficiently large polynomial. This completes the proof of the lemma. □

Lemma 11. *We have (Item 2 ⇒ Item 1) in Theorem 17.*

Proof Sketch The proof follows that of [23, Theorem 36]. At a higher level, the idea is that if we have an efficient algorithm for approximating pKt on average over polynomial-time samplable distributions, then we can construct a function that distinguishes the output distribution of a cryptographic pseudorandom generator from the uniform distribution. This is because the outputs of such a generator have low pKt complexity while a uniformly random string has high pKt complexity. By [15], this implies that infinitely-often one-way functions do not exist. □

We now complete the proof of Theorem 17.

Proof of Theorem 17. The theorem follows directly from Lemmas 10 and 11. □

5.2   Hardness of Approximating pKt with Mild-One-Sided Error

In this subsection, we prove Theorem 7. We will need the following lemmas.

Lemma 12. *If* pKt *can be approximated on average with mild-one-sided error in time* $n^{\mathsf{poly}(\log n)}$, *then* BPE $\subseteq$ SIZE$[n^{\mathsf{poly}(\log n)}]$.

Proof. Let $L \in$ BPE. we identify L with a function from $\{0,1\}^*$ to $\{0,1\}$.

Since pKt can be approximated on average with mild-one-sided error in time $n^{\mathsf{poly}(\log n)}$, by standard amplification techniques, there exist a constant $0 < \varepsilon < 1$ and a probabilistic polynomial-time A such that for all sufficiently large n,

$$\Pr_{x \sim \{0,1\}^n} \left[\Pr_A [A(x) = 0] \geq 1 - \frac{1}{n^2} \right] \geq \frac{1}{n},$$

Note that this implies

$$\Pr_{x \sim \{0,1\}^n, A} [A(x) = 0] \geq \frac{1}{2n}.$$

Also, for every $x \in \{0,1\}^n$ with $\mathsf{pKt}(x) \leq n^\varepsilon$,

$$\Pr_A [A(x) = 1] \geq 1 - \frac{1}{n^2}.$$

Now let $\left\{ G_n^{(-)} \colon \{0,1\}^{n^\lambda} \to \{0,1\} \right\}_n$ be the pseudorandom generator from Theorem 12 instantiated with parameter $\lambda := \varepsilon/2$.

Firstly, note that for every $r \in \{0,1\}^{n^\lambda}$, $G_n^L(r)$ can be computed in deterministic time $\exp\left(O(n^\lambda)\right)$ given oracle access to L on inputs of length at most n^λ. Since L on inputs of length at most n^λ can be computed in *randomized* time $\exp(O(n^\lambda))$, it follows that $G_n^L(r)$ can be obtained (with high probability) in randomized time $\exp(O(n^\lambda))$, which implies

$$\mathsf{pKt}(G_n^L(r)) \leq O(n^\lambda) \leq n^\varepsilon. \tag{17}$$

We remark that since G_n^L can only be computed in a randomized manner, in the above we can only upper-bound the pKt complexity of the output strings of G_n^L, rather than the Kt complexity.[5]

It follows by the properties of the algorithm A that

$$\Pr_{r \sim \{0,1\}^{n^\lambda}, A} \left[A(G_n^L(r)) = 1 \right] \geq 1 - \frac{1}{n^2} \quad \text{and} \quad \Pr_{x \sim \{0,1\}^n, A} [A(x) = 1] \leq 1 - \frac{1}{2n}.$$

Now by averaging, there exists some fixing of the internal randomness of A, which gives a quasi-polynomial-size $\mathcal{O}$-oracle circuit A', so that A' can distinguish the output of G_n^L from the uniform distribution with advantage at least $1/(3n)$. By Theorem 12, we get that L can be computed by polynomial-size A'-oracle circuits, and hence by a quasi-polynomial-size $\mathcal{O}$-oracle circuit.   □

---

[5] We would be able to upper bound Kt complexity if we started with a language in E instead of BPE, but the resulting inclusion E $\subseteq$ SIZE$[n^{\mathsf{poly}(\log n)}]$ would be insufficient for the proof of a deterministic variant of Theorem 7, since a deterministic analogue of Lemma 13 is unknown.

Lemma 13. *If* pKt *can be approximated on average with mild-one-sided error in time* $n^{\text{poly}(\log n)}$, *then* PSPACE $\subseteq$ BPTIME$[n^{\text{poly}(\log n)}]$.

Proof Sketch. The proof is similar to that of Lemma 12. We consider the pseudorandom generator $\text{IW}_n^{(-)}$ from Theorem 13, instantiated with the PSPACE-hard language L_{TV} in Theorem 14. Then using an algorithm that approximates pKt with mild-one-sided error, we can distinguish the output distribution of $\text{IW}_n^{L_{\text{TV}}}$ from the uniform distribution. This yields a quasi-polynomial-time randomized algorithm for computing L_{TV}.   □

Finally, we need the following lemma.

Lemma 14. *There is a language in* DSPACE$[2^{n^{o(1)}}]\backslash$SIZE$[n^{\text{poly}(\log n)}]$.

We are now ready to show Theorem 7.

Proof of Theorem 7. Suppose, for the sake of contradiction, pKt can be approximated on average with mild-one-sided error in time $n^{\text{poly}(\log n)}$. First of all, by Lemma 12, we get that BPE $\subseteq$ SIZE$[n^{\text{poly}(\log n)}]$.

By Lemma 14, there is a language $L \in$ DSPACE$[2^{n^{o(1)}}]\backslash$SIZE$[n^{\text{poly}(\log n)}]$. Now by Lemma 13, we get that PSPACE $\subseteq$ BPTIME$[n^{\text{poly}(\log n)}]$. Then by a padding argument, we get that $L \in$ BPE. However, this means that BPE $\not\subseteq$ SIZE$[n^{\text{poly}(\log n)}]$. A contradiction.   □

5.3   Proof of Theorem 2

In this subsection, we show Theorem 2.

Proof of Theorem 2. Suppose it holds that

2-Sided-Error-Approx-pKt $\Rightarrow$ Mild-1-Sided-Error-Approx-pKt.

By Theorem 7, we have that $\neg$ Mild-1-Sided-Error-Approx-pKt holds, which by the above implication yields that $\neg$ 2-Sided-Error-Approx-pKt holds. Then by Theorem 6, we get that infinitely-often one-way functions exist.

On the other hand, suppose infinitely-often one-way functions exist. It follows from Theorem 6 that 2-Sided-Error-Approx-pKt does not hold. This trivially implies that

2-Sided-Error-Approx-pKt $\Rightarrow$ Mild-1-Sided-Error-Approx-pKt,

as desired.   □

References

1. Akavia, A., Goldreich, O., Goldwasser, S., Moshkovitz, D.: On basing one-way functions on NP-hardness. In: Symposium on Theory of Computing (STOC). pp. 701–710 (2006). https://doi.org/10.1145/1132516.1132614

2. Allender, E.: Applications of time-bounded Kolmogorov complexity in complexity theory. In: Kolmogorov complexity and computational complexity, pp. 4–22. Springer (1992). https://doi.org/10.1007/978-3-642-77735-6_2

3. Allender, E.: When worlds collide: Derandomization, lower bounds, and kolmogorov complexity. In: Conference on Foundations of Software Technology and Theoretical Computer Science (FSTTCS). pp. 1–15 (2001). https://doi.org/10.1007/3-540-45294-X_1

4. Allender, E.: The complexity of complexity. In: Computability and Complexity. pp. 79–94. Springer (2017). https://doi.org/10.1007/978-3-319-50062-1_6

5. Babai, L., Fortnow, L., Nisan, N., Wigderson, A.: BPP has subexponential time simulations unless EXPTIME has publishable proofs. Comput. Complex. **3**, 307–318 (1993). https://doi.org/10.1007/BF01275486

6. Baker, T.P., Gill, J., Solovay, R.: Relativizatons of the P =? NP Question. SIAM J. Comput. **4**(4), 431–442 (1975). https://doi.org/10.1137/0204037

7. Ball, M., Liu, Y., Mazor, N., Pass, R.: Kolmogorov comes to cryptomania: On interactive Kolmogorov complexity and key-agreement. In: Symposium on Foundations of Computer Science (FOCS). pp. 458–483 (2023). https://doi.org/10.1109/FOCS57990.2023.00034

8. Bogdanov, A., Brzuska, C.: On basing size-verifiable one-way functions on NP-hardness. In: Theory of Cryptography Conference (TCC). pp. 1–6 (2015). https://doi.org/10.1007/978-3-662-46494-6_1

9. Bogdanov, A., Trevisan, L.: Average-case complexity. Found. Trends Theor. Comput. Sci. **2**(1) (2006). https://doi.org/10.1561/0400000004

10. Chen, L., Lu, Z., Lyu, X., Oliveira, I.C.: Majority vs. approximate linear sum and average-case complexity below NC^1. In: International Colloquium on Automata, Languages, and Programming (ICALP). pp. 51:1–51:20 (2021). https://doi.org/10.4230/LIPIcs.ICALP.2021.51

11. Diffie, W., Hellman, M.E.: New directions in cryptography. IEEE Trans. Inf. Theory **22**(6), 644–654 (1976). https://doi.org/10.1109/TIT.1976.1055638

12. Goldberg, H., Kabanets, V.: A simpler proof of the worst-case to average-case reduction for polynomial hierarchy via symmetry of information. Electron. Colloquium Comput. Complex. **TR22-007** (2022), https://eccc.weizmann.ac.il/report/2022/007

13. Goldberg, H., Kabanets, V., Lu, Z., Oliveira, I.C.: Probabilistic Kolmogorov complexity with applications to average-case complexity. In: Computational Complexity Conference (CCC). pp. 16:1–16:60 (2022). https://doi.org/10.4230/LIPIcs.CCC.2022.16

14. Goldwasser, S., Micali, S.: Probabilistic encryption. J. Comput. Syst. Sci. **28**(2), 270–299 (1984). https://doi.org/10.1016/0022-0000(84)90070-9

15. Håstad, J., Impagliazzo, R., Levin, L.A., Luby, M.: A pseudorandom generator from any one-way function. SIAM J. Comput. **28**(4), 1364–1396 (1999). https://doi.org/10.1137/S0097539793244708

16. Hirahara, S.: Np-hardness of learning programs and partial MCSP. In: Symposium on Foundations of Computer Science (FOCS). pp. 968–979 (2022). https://doi.org/10.1109/FOCS54457.2022.00095

17. Hirahara, S.: Symmetry of information from meta-complexity. In: Computational Complexity Conference (CCC). pp. 26:1–26:41 (2022). https://doi.org/10.4230/LIPIcs.CCC.2022.26

18. Hirahara, S., Ilango, R., Lu, Z., Nanashima, M., Oliveira, I.C.: A duality between one-way functions and average-case symmetry of information. In: Symposium on Theory of Computing (STOC). pp. 1039–1050 (2023). https://doi.org/10.1145/3564246.3585138

19. Hirahara, S., Lu, Z., Oliveira, I.C.: One-way functions and pKt complexity. Cryptology ePrint Archive, Paper 2024/1388 (2024), https://eprint.iacr.org/2024/1388

20. Hirahara, S., Lu, Z., Ren, H.: Bounded relativization. In: Conference on Computational Complexity (CCC). pp. 6:1–6:45 (2023). https://doi.org/10.4230/LIPIcs.CCC.2023.6

21. Hirahara, S., Nanashima, M.: Learning in pessiland via inductive inference. In: Symposium on Foundations of Computer Science (FOCS). pp. 447–457 (2023). https://doi.org/10.1109/FOCS57990.2023.00033

22. Hirahara, S., Santhanam, R.: Errorless versus error-prone average-case complexity. In: Innovations in Theoretical Computer Science Conference (ITCS). pp. 84:1–84:23 (2022). https://doi.org/10.4230/LIPIcs.ITCS.2022.84

23. Ilango, R., Ren, H., Santhanam, R.: Hardness on any samplable distribution suffices: New characterizations of one-way functions by meta-complexity. Electron. Colloquium Comput. Complex. **TR21-082** (2021), https://eccc.weizmann.ac.il/report/2021/082

24. Ilango, R., Ren, H., Santhanam, R.: Robustness of average-case meta-complexity via pseudorandomness. In: Symposium on Theory of Computing (STOC). pp. 1575–1583 (2022). https://doi.org/10.1145/3519935.3520051

25. Impagliazzo, R.: A personal view of average-case complexity. In: Proceedings of Structure in Complexity Theory (CCC). pp. 134–147 (1995). https://doi.org/10.1109/SCT.1995.514853

26. Impagliazzo, R., Levin, L.A.: No better ways to generate hard NP instances than picking uniformly at random. In: Symposium on Theory of Computing (STOC). pp. 812–821 (1990). https://doi.org/10.1109/FSCS.1990.89604

27. Impagliazzo, R., Luby, M.: One-way functions are essential for complexity based cryptography (extended abstract). In: Symposium on Theory of Computing (STOC). pp. 230–235 (1989). https://doi.org/10.1109/SFCS.1989.63483

28. Impagliazzo, R., Wigderson, A.: $P = BPP$ if E requires exponential circuits: Derandomizing the XOR lemma. In: Leighton, F.T., Shor, P.W. (eds.) Symposium on Theory of Computing (STOC). pp. 220–229 (1997). https://doi.org/10.1145/258533.258590

29. Klivans, A.R., van Melkebeek, D.: Graph nonisomorphism has subexponential size proofs unless the polynomial-time hierarchy collapses. SIAM J. Comput. **31**(5), 1501–1526 (2002). https://doi.org/10.1137/S0097539700389652

30. Levin, L.A.: Laws of information conservation (nongrowth) and aspects of the foundation of probability theory. Problemy Peredachi Informatsii **10**(3), 30–35 (1974)

31. Levin, L.A.: Randomness conservation inequalities; information and independence in mathematical theories. Inf. Control **61**(1), 15–37 (1984). https://doi.org/10.1016/S0019-9958(84)80060-1

32. Li, M., Vitányi, P.M.B.: An Introduction to Kolmogorov Complexity and Its Applications, 4th Edition. Texts in Computer Science, Springer (2019). https://doi.org/10.1007/978-3-030-11298-1

33. Liu, Y., Pass, R.: On one-way functions and Kolmogorov complexity. In: Symposium on Foundations of Computer Science (FOCS). pp. 1243–1254 (2020). https://doi.org/10.1109/FOCS46700.2020.00118

34. Liu, Y., Pass, R.: On the possibility of basing cryptography on EXP≠BPP. In International Cryptology Conference (CRYPTO). pp. 11–40 (2021). https://doi org/10.1007/978-3-030-84242-0_2

35. Liu, Y., Pass, R.: On one-way functions from NP-complete problems. In: Conference on Computational Complexity (CCC). pp. 36:1–36:24 (2022). https://doi org/10.4230/LIPIcs.CCC.2022.36

36. Liu, Y., Pass, R.: On one-way functions and the worst-case hardness of time-bounded Kolmogorov complexity. Electron. Colloquium Comput. Complex. **TR23-103** (2023), https://eccc.weizmann.ac.il/report/2023/103

37. Liu, Y., Pass, R.: One-way functions and the hardness of (probabilistic) time-bounded Kolmogorov complexity w.r.t. samplable distributions. In: International Cryptology Conference (CRYPTO). pp. 645–673 (2023). https://doi.org/10.1007/978-3-031-38545-2_21

38. Longpré, L., Mocas, S.: Symmetry of information and one-way functions. Inf. Process. Lett. **46**(2), 95–100 (1993). https://doi.org/10.1016/0020-0190(93)90204-M

39. Longpré, L., Watanabe, O.: On symmetry of information and polynomial time invertibility. Inf. Comput. **121**(1), 14–22 (1995). https://doi.org/10.1006/inco.1995.1120

40. Lu, Z., Oliveira, I.C.: Theory and applications of probabilistic Kolmogorov complexity. Bull. EATCS **137** (2022), http://bulletin.eatcs.org/index.php/beatcs/article/view/700

41. Lu, Z., Oliveira, I.C., Zimand, M.: Optimal coding theorems in time-bounded Kolmogorov complexity. In: International Colloquium on Automata, Languages, and Programming (ICALP). pp. 92:1–92:14 (2022). https://doi.org/10.4230/LIPIcs.ICALP.2022.92

42. Nanashima, M.: On basing auxiliary-input cryptography on np-hardness via non-adaptive black-box reductions. In: Innovations in Theoretical Computer Science (ITCS). pp. 29:1–29:15 (2021). https://doi.org/10.4230/LIPIcs.ITCS.2021.29

43. Naor, M.: Bit commitment using pseudorandomness. J. Cryptol. 4(2), 151–158 (1991). https://doi.org/10.1007/BF00196774

44. Oliveira, I.C.: Randomness and intractability in Kolmogorov complexity. In: International Colloquium on Automata, Languages, and Programming (ICALP). pp. 32:1–32:14 (2019). https://doi.org/10.4230/LIPIcs.ICALP.2019.32

45. Oliveira, I.C., Santhanam, R.: Pseudodeterministic constructions in subexponential time. In: Symposium on Theory of Computing (STOC). pp. 665–677 (2017). https://doi.org/10.1145/3055399.3055500

46. Razborov, A.A., Rudich, S.: Natural proofs. J. Comput. Syst. Sci. **55**(1), 24–35 (1997). https://doi.org/10.1006/jcss.1997.1494

47. Ren, H., Santhanam, R.: Hardness of KT characterizes parallel cryptography. In: Computational Complexity Conference (CCC). pp. 35:1–35:58 (2021). https://doi.org/10.4230/LIPIcs.CCC.2021.35

48. Rompel, J.: One-way functions are necessary and sufficient for secure signatures. In: Symposium on Theory of Computing (STOC). pp. 387–394 (1990). https://doi.org/10.1145/100216.100269

49. Ronneburger, D.: Kolmogorov Complexity and Derandomization. Ph.D. thesis. Rutgers University (2004)

50. Shen, A., Uspensky, V.A., Vereshchagin, N.: Kolmogorov complexity and algorithmic randomness. American Mathematical Society (2017)

51. Sudan, M., Trevisan, L., Vadhan, S.P.: Pseudorandom generators without the XOR lemma. J. Comput. Syst. Sci. **62**(2), 236–266 (2001). https://doi.org/10.1006/jcss.2000.1730

52. Trevisan, L., Vadhan, S.P.: Pseudorandomness and average-case complexity via uniform reductions. Comput. Complex. **16**(4), 331–364 (2007). https://doi.org/10.1007/s00037-007-0233-x

53. Zvonkin, A.K., Levin, L.A.: The complexity of finite objects and the algorithmic concepts of randomness and information. UMN (Russian Math. Surveys) **25**(6), 83–124 (1970). https://doi.org/10.1070/rm1970v025n06abeh001269

On Bounded Storage Key Agreement and One-Way Functions

Chris Brzuska[1(✉)], Geoffroy Couteau[2], Christoph Egger[2], and Willy Quach[3]

[1] Aalto University, Espoo, Finland
chris.brzuska@aalto.fi
[2] Université Paris Cité, CNRS, IRIF, Paris, France
[3] Weizmann Institute of Science, Rehovot, Israel

Abstract. We study key agreement in the bounded-storage model, where the participants and the adversary can use an a priori fixed bounded amount of space, and receive a large stream of data. While key agreement is known to exist unconditionally in this model (Cachin and Maurer, Crypto'97), there are strong lower bounds on the space complexity of the participants, round complexity, and communication complexity that unconditional protocols can achieve.

In this work, we explore how a minimal use of cryptographic assumptions can help circumvent these lower bounds. We obtain several contributions:

- Assuming one-way functions, we construct a one-round key agreement in the bounded-storage model, with arbitrary polynomial space gap between the participants and the adversary, and communication slightly larger than the adversarial storage. Additionally, our protocol can achieve everlasting security using a second streaming round.
- In the other direction, we show that one-way functions are *necessary* for key agreement in the bounded-storage model with large space gaps. We further extend our results to the setting of *fully-streaming* adversaries, and to the setting of key agreement with multiple streaming rounds.

Our results rely on a combination of information-theoretic arguments and technical ingredients such as pseudorandom generators for space-bounded computation, and a tight characterization of the space efficiency of known reductions between standard Minicrypt primitives (from distributional one-way functions to pseudorandom functions), which might be of independent interest.

1 Introduction

Perhaps surprisingly, while cryptographic primitives must typically rely on hardness assumptions in the time-bounded setting (and proving their security unconditionally would entail proving $P \neq NP$), several cryptographic primitives of interest are known to exist *unconditionally* in the bounded-storage model (BSM). In this model, introduced by Maurer [Mau92], the participants and adversary are *space-bounded* (with a gap between the space s honest parties need and the space a the adversary needs) and have one-time read access to a huge random

E. Boyle and M. Mahmoody (Eds.): TCC 2024, LNCS 15364, pp. 287–318, 2025.
https://doi.org/10.1007/978-3-031-78011-0_10

string (of length $\gg a$). In the BSM, symmetric key encryption [Mau92], signatures [DQW22], key agreement [CM97], and oblivious transfer [Din01], all exist unconditionally. Yet, unconditional constructions of "public-key-style" primitives in the bounded-storage model typically suffer from strong efficiency limitations regarding the space gap between honest parties and adversaries, round complexity, and communication complexity. For example, the bounded-storage model key agreement (from now on, BSM-KA) of [CM97] requires the honest parties to use $s = \omega(\sqrt{a})$ bits of storage. More recently, the work of [DQW23] circumvented this limitation, but at the cost of requiring $r = \omega(a/s^2)$ streaming rounds and $C = \omega((a/s)^2)$ bits of communication. Unfortunately, these limitations are known to be inherent: the protocol of [CM97] was shown in [DM08] to achieve an optimal space gap $a = \tilde{\Theta}(s^2)$ when the BSM-KA uses a single streaming round, and [DQW23] further proved that the number of rounds must grow with a, and the communication must grow superlinearly with a, whenever $a \gg s^2$. Therefore, achieving unconditional security for BSM-KA requires paying a significant price either in honest parties space or in rounds and communication.

In this work, we initiate the study of cryptography in the bounded-storage model beyond the regime where the impossibility results of [DM08, DQW23] apply. That is, we ask:

Is it possible to circumvent known lower bounds on key agreements in the bounded-storage model by making a minimal use of cryptographic assumptions?

To study this question, we place ourselves in the *streaming* variant of the BSM, introduced in [DQW23], where the participants themselves can stream long strings (of length $C \gg a \gg s$) to each other. In [DQW23], it was argued that this captures more adequately the properties one wants from cryptography with bounded-storage.

1.1   Our Contributions

We provide an affirmative answer to the question. As our first contribution, we exhibit a key agreement in the streaming model tolerating an arbitrary (polynomial) gap between the space s of the honest parties and the space a of the adversary, using a single streaming round and $C = \tilde{O}(a)$ bits of communication, assuming the existence of one-way functions (OWFs).

Theorem 1 (Informal). *Let λ be a security parameter and $a = a(\lambda)$ be an arbitrary polynomial in λ. Assuming the existence of one-way functions, there is an BSM-KA protocol in the streaming model secure against an eavesdropper with space a that uses a single long stream of length $a \cdot \mathsf{poly}(\lambda)$ (followed by a single $\mathsf{poly}(\lambda)$-sized short message in the other direction), and where the honest parties use $s = \mathsf{poly}(\lambda)$ storage.*

In the Theorem above, $\mathsf{poly}(\lambda)$ denotes a fixed polynomial independent of a. The BSM-KA uses two rounds of communication with one stream; it can alternatively use a single simultaneous round of streaming (in both directions), yielding a non-interactive key agreement in the streaming model. Eventually, the security of the BSM-KA can be strengthened to everlasting security (the shared key remains protected even if the adversary becomes all powerful after the completion of the protocol) at the cost of using an additional round of streaming.

Theorem 1 shows that OWFs are sufficient to obtain an (everlasting-secure) key agreement in the streaming model, which is essentially optimal regarding space gaps and round complexity. Then, we ask:

> *Are one-way functions also necessary for obtaining key agreement in the streaming model in the regime where it cannot exist unconditionally?*

To approach this question, we initiate a systematic study of the relations between various forms of key agreements in the streaming model and the existence of one-way functions. We make significant progress towards answering the above question affirmatively. Our work also leaves several natural and intriguing questions open; we hope that our preliminary findings will motivate their study in future works.

In the course of our analysis, we observe that answering this question requires tightly characterizing the space efficiency of reductions between various Minicrypt primitives such as distributional OWFs, weak OWFs, standard OWFs, pseudorandom generators, and variants of pseudorandom functions. We provide some preliminary investigation in this direction, characterizing the space efficiency of existing reductions between these primitives, which we believe might be of independent interest. We believe that our work provides some additional motivation for the question of designing space-tight reduction between Minicrypt primitives, a natural question which has not received much attention so far.

Answering the question turns out to require careful considerations regarding the type of protocols and the type of adversaries that are considered. Before stating our results, we provide a brief outline of these considerations:

- key agreements in the streaming model can have a single long stream (and multiple short rounds), or multiple long streams. The distinction between these two settings was traditionally made on the basis of the desirability of minimizing the number of long rounds (see for example the discussion on the "desirable property (a)" in [DQW23]). For the question we raise, it turns out that another important distinction for single-long-stream protocols is whether the protocol starts with the long stream (a setting called the "traditional bounded-storage model" in [DQW23]), or whether it starts with short rounds.
- One can consider two types of space-bounded adversaries (we follow the naming conventions of [DQW23] for these two models and refers the reader to [DQW23] for further discussions on the distinction): "fully streaming adversaries" have space bounded by a throughout the entire protocol, while adversaries in the "unbounded processing model" are allowed unlimited short-term storage, and are only subject to keeping an a-bit state in between long rounds. Of course, building key agreement in the unbounded processing model is more

desirable (our construction of Theorem 1 is in this model), while proving impossibility results in the full streaming model yields a stronger result.

We note that our notion of unbounded processing differs from that of [DQW23] due to our use of computational assumptions: in [DQW23], an unbounded processing adversary has bounded storage during the streaming rounds, unbounded storage otherwise, and unbounded computational power throughout. We consider here a variant where the adversary remains probabilistic polynomial time (hence, in particular, always uses a polynomial amount of storage) but has no further storage bound inbetween the streaming rounds (but can only store an a-bit state after a long round). To avoid confusion, we will sometime use the terminologies "fully-streaming PPT adversary" and "unbounded-processing PPT adversary", where PPT refers to probabilistic polynomial-time. Eventually, we also consider *everlasting* security, where the adversary are (fully-streaming or unbounded-processing) PPT throughout the protocol, but become all powerful after the protocol.

In the following, we will write SM-KA to denote key agreement in the streaming model for a fully-streaming PPT adversary, and UP-KA to denote key agreement in the streaming model for an adversary in the unbounded processing PPT model. With this terminology in mind, our protocol in Theorem 1 is actually an UP-KA, secure in the unbounded-processing PPT model (the strongest adversarial model we consider). We complement this result by showing that *space-bounded* OWFs (*i.e.*, functions which are one-way against PPT adversaries with a fixed polynomially-bounded amount of storage) actually suffice for constructing SM-KA (where the adversary is fully streaming) via our construction. This requires in particular carefully tracking the space efficiency of the traditional constructions of pseudorandom generators from OWFs [HILL99], and of pseudorandom functions from pseudorandom generators [GGM84].

Corollary 2 (Informal). *Let λ be a security parameter and $a = a(\lambda)$ be an arbitrary polynomial in λ. Assuming the existence of space-bounded one-way functions with space bound $\mathsf{poly}(a)$, there is an SM-KA protocol secure against a fully-streaming PPT eavesdropper with space a that uses a single long stream of length $a \cdot \mathsf{poly}(\lambda)$ (followed by a single $\mathsf{poly}(\lambda)$-sized short message in the other direction), and where the honest parties use $s = \mathsf{poly}(\lambda)$ storage.*

We now state our main results towards showing the necessity of OWFs for streaming key agreement beyond the unconditional regime. We first focus on protocols which involve a single streaming message and a short answer.

Theorem 3 (Informal). *Assume that there exists a streaming key agreement* KA *against space-a PPT adversaries consisting of a single long stream from Alice to Bianca and a short message from Bianca to Alice and using $s \ll \sqrt{a}$ space for the honest parties. Then,*

- *if* KA *is an UP-KA, there exists one-way functions;*
- *if* KA *is an SM-KA, there exists space-bounded one-way functions.*

The conclusion of Theorem 3 is the best possible, as it matches exactly our positive results of Theorem 1 and Corollary 2. However, one may ask whether it could be possible to relax the requirement of one-way functions if we either restrict the adversary to be fully streaming, and/or if the protocol can have additional streaming rounds and short rounds. In this more general setting, we prove the following theorem:

Theorem 4 (Informal). *Assume that there exists a streaming key agreement against space-a (fully-streaming or unbounded-processing) PPT adversary with r rounds using $s \ll a^{1/\mathsf{polylog}(r)^r}$ space for the honest parties, for a suitably large* polylog. *Then,*

- *if* KA *is an UP-KA, there exists non-uniform, infinitely-often one-way functions;*
- *if* KA *is an SM-KA, there exists non-uniform, infinitely-often space-bounded one-way functions $f : \{0,1\}^n \rightarrow \{0,1\}^n$ with space bound $n^{\Omega(\mathsf{polylog}(r)^r)}$.*

The conclusions of Theorem 4 are weaker than that of Theorem 3 on two aspects: first we only get infinitely-often secure OWFs, and second, the conclusion requires assuming a larger space gap. The first limitation (infinitely-often security) is an unfortunate but standard consequence of the use of a disjunction argument based on the existence of a OWF inverter (a similar limitation appears in many previous works). As for the last limitation, we observe that when the number of long streams is 1, assuming only $a \gg s^2$ (up to polylog factor) suffices to achieve the weaker conclusion of space-bounded *distributional* OWFs. We view as an interesting open question the goal of obtaining space-bounded OWFs from streaming key agreement with a smaller space gap (ideally $a \gg s^2$). A natural starting point to solve this question would be to find a space-tight reduction from (space-bounded) distributional OWFs to OWFs, a question which we believe to be also of independent interest. Additionally, we note that the one-way functions obtained in Theorem 4 are non-uniform; our result can be strengthened to provide uniform one-way functions in the special case of a single long stream.

Due to the exponential dependency in r, Theorem 4 is only meaningful in the setting where r is a constant. We leave as an intriguing open question to prove (or disprove) that SM-KA with a superconstant number of rounds imply OWFs.

1.2 Discussions

One-way functions are known to be a necessary assumption for most cryptographic primitives [IL89]. Several lines of work have investigated the necessity of one-way functions for various types of cryptographic *protocols*, notably in the setting of zero-knowledge interactive proofs for NP [OW93], single-server private information retrieval [BIKM99], and constant-bias coin flipping [MPS10, HO11, BHT14]. In each case, unconditionally secure variants of these protocols can be obtained by relaxing the constraints, such as using multiple parties or servers [BOL85, CGKS95] or restricting the class of languages to SZK.

Our work fits in this broad program by studying another example of crypto-graphic protocol, streaming-model key-agreements, in the regime where it cannot exist unconditionally. Similar to constant-bias coin flipping and zero-knowledge for NP, we actually show that one-way functions are essentially *equivalent* to streaming key agreement. Our results nevertheless leave several gaps in the space gap between the honest parties and the adversary, most notably for protocols with a large numbers of streaming rounds. Whether these gaps can be closed, or whether some non-trivial forms of streaming key agreement beyond the uncon-ditional regime could possibly exist without one-way functions remains an inter-esting open question, the main one left open by our work.

Turning to our positive result, the efficiency achieved by our protocol is essentially the best possible regarding space requirement for the honest parties (concretely, using a pseudorandom function with 128 bit keys to instantiate the protocol, the parties only need a few hundreds bits of storage) and round com-plexity (a single long round). However, it still requires a large amount of com-munication, larger than the space bound a of the adversary. A natural question is whether communicating more than a remains necessary if we assume one-way functions.[1] While this is somewhat orthogonal to our work, we still discuss it briefly.

Intuitively, if the adversary can store the entire stream, we would expect them to break the key agreement by virtue of the inexistence of key agreement from one-way functions [IR89]. And indeed, if the total communication c is below $\sqrt{a}$, the protocol can be broken in time roughly quadratic in the honest parties' runtime by the attack of Barak and Mahmoody [BM09] (the attack is only efficient in the number of oracle queries, but it can be made concretely efficient given a one-way function inverter, see e.g. [CFM21]). However, if the total communication c is much closer to a (e.g. $\delta \cdot a$ for some constant $\delta < 1$), the question becomes equivalent to the following problem: is it possible to build key agreement from one-way functions against polynomial-time *linear space* adversaries? Interestingly, this question remains wide open as of today, even if we model the one-way function with a random oracle: all known attacks on key agreements from random oracles [IR89, BM09] appear to inherently require a quadratic amount of space (in the runtime of the honest parties, hence in particular in the communication overhead of the protocol), yet all known variants of Merkle's seminal key agreement protocol in the ROM [Mer74, Mer78] can be broken in linear space.

1.3   Our Techniques

OWFs are Sufficient for Streaming Key Agreement. We start with our construc-tive results. Our construction of gap-optimal and round-optimal UP-KA from

---

[1] Of course, in the unbounded processing model, the question is meaningless as the adversary can store everything and get unbounded space afterwards, which makes it essentially an unbounded-space polytime adversary. The question makes sense, however, in the fully-streaming model where the adversarial storage remains bounded after the computation.

OWFs is suprisingly simple and conceptually quite natural in hindsight. Our starting point is the unconditional key agreement protocol of Cachin and Maurer [CM97]: in this protocol, Alice streams $C > a$ bits to Bianca, who stores $s \approx \sqrt{C}$ bits of the stream while Alice does the same. By the birthday paradox, the parties get a collision with noticeable probability, and after exchanging the positions of the bits they stored, agree on a key.

We observe that if Alice has the ability to *recompute* the stream, then the parties can store considerably less data: Bianca can store $s \approx \lambda$ bits (where λ is a fixed security parameter) and send her positions to Alice, who recomputes the stream and stores the same bits. The common key is extracted from these bits. This suggests a simple methodology: in our protocol, Alice stores a pseudorandom function (PRF) key $k \in \{0,1\}^\lambda$ and then streams $C > a$ many bits $\mathsf{PRF}(k,1),..,\mathsf{PRF}(k,C)$. Bianca receives the stream and stores λ many of the bits at random locations $\ell_1,..,\ell_\lambda$ which she sends to Alice once her streaming phases ended. They both set their key to be

$$\mathsf{key} := \mathsf{Ext}(\mathsf{PRF}(k,\ell_1)\|..\|\mathsf{PRF}(k,\ell_\lambda)). \tag{1}$$

Except for an additional game-hop based on the PRF, the security analysis of this protocol is analogous to [CM97] and, conceptually, captures that in space $a \ll C$, the adversary only has a small probability p to have stored the information about $\mathsf{PRF}(k,\ell_i)$ and thus, its advantage is upper-bounded by p^λ. Furthermore, the protocol can be made everlasting secure using the bounded storage extractor of Vadhan [Vad04]: instead of outputting the key, Alice creates a stream of length $2a$ and both parties use the key k obtained from the computational protocol as extraction seed.[2]

Eventually, in the fully-streaming PPT model (where the adversary remains space-bounded after the protocol), it is clear that it suffices for the PRF above to be secure against space-bounded PPT adversaries. However, while PRFs are known to be equivalent to OWFs [HILL99,GGM84], it is not immediately obvious that *space-bounded* PRFs should be equivalent to *space-bounded* OWFs – and indeed, this does not appear to follow from existing reductions! Nevertheless, by carefully tracking down the space efficiency of the OWF-to-PRG and PRG-to-PRF reductions, we observe that space-bounded OWFs are actually sufficient (albeit with a loss in space) to build space-bounded *consecutive* PRFs, a simple variant of PRF which restricts the queries to be consecutive integers (which clearly suffices to instantiate our protocol above).

OWFs are Necessary for Stream-First UP-KA. Conversely, we show that the existence of UP-KA beyond the unconditional

---

[2] This is very close in spirit to the hybrid-BSM approach discussed in [DM04], where a similar idea is used to convert a "standard" computational key exchange into an everlasting one. However, several works [DM04,HN06] have pointed out that this strategy fails in general. Our setting is slightly different, and is in particular not captured by the impossibility results in [DM04,HN06], and our concrete instantiation can actually be proven secure formally.

regime implies a one-way function. We start with
stream-first UP-KA, and show that any such protocol implies a OWF. Our OWF construction
follows Impagliazzo and Luby's approach [IL89]
who, given a key agreement protocol KA, construct a distributional OWF (dOWF), i.e., a
OWF where it is hard to sample a uniformly
random pre-image, see Fig. 1. f_{IL} generates a
(transcript, key) from the distribution induced by

$$f_{\text{IL}}(b, r_A, r_B, \text{key}')$$

$$\overline{\text{(transcript, key)} \leftarrow \text{KA}(r_A, r_B)}$$

if $b = 1$:

  key $\leftarrow$ key$'$

return (transcript, key)

Fig. 1. f_{IL}

the key agreement protocol, and then replaces key with a uniform key with probability $\frac{1}{2}$. f_{IL} is a dOWF because a uniformly random pre-image of (transcript, key)
would reveal the bit b, i.e., whether the key key is real or random. Unfortunately,
when KA is a streaming key agreement, we cannot claim that f_{IL} is a dOWF,
since accessing the entire protocol transcript might allow trivial inversion attacks:
For example, in our protocol, described in and before Eq. (1), given the entire
transcript, one can simply take the indices $\ell_1, .., \ell_\lambda$ which Bianca sent to Alice
and then look up the values of $\text{PRF}(k, \ell_i)$ for all $1 \leq i \leq \lambda$ in Alice's message.

To circumvent this issue, we rely on the information-theoretic attacker of
Dziembowski and Maurer [DM08] (we call it Eve). At a high level, the attacker
sample $\mathcal{O}(s)$ views for Bianca consistent with the long stream. The main Theorem of Dziembowski and Maurer (stated in a re-phrased, weaker version as
Theorem 21 in our work) states that the view of Eve has large mutual information with the shared key. Equivalently, the distributions induced by the sampling
of Eve's view (for a random stream) together with the *short* message (after the
long stream) and *either* the shared key or the random key are statistically far. If
the protocol is secure, these distributions must be computationally indistinguishable; this suggests a modified distributional OWF f_{DM} (represented on Fig. 2)
that replaces Alice's stream by the adversary's $\mathcal{E}'_{\text{DM}}s$ view. Here, short-transcript
denotes the short message from Bianca to Alice.

By Dziembowski-Maurer,
when state and key come
from a real protocol exe-
cution, $f(0, r_A, r_B, (r_{B,1}, ..,$
$r_{B,400s}), \text{key}')$ and $f(1, ..)$
are statistically far from
one another, so that a uni-
form inverter of f_{DM} directly
yields a distinguisher for
the key agreement protocol.
Now, given a dOWF, we

$$f_{\text{DM}}(b, r_A, r_B, (r_{B,1}, .., r_{B,s}), \text{key}')$$

$$\overline{\text{(stream, short-transcript, key)} \leftarrow \text{KA}(r_A, r_B)}$$

for $i = 1..400s$:

  state$_{B,i} \leftarrow B_1(\text{stream}, r_{B,i})$

if $b = 1$:

  key $\leftarrow$ key$'$

return (short-transcript, key, state$_{B,1}, ..,$ state$_{B,400s}$)

Fig. 2. The dOWF candidate f_{DM}

obtain a PRF via a sequence of MiniCrypt reductions:

$$\text{distributional OWF} \overset{[\text{IL89,Yao82}]}{\Rightarrow} \text{OWF} \overset{[\text{HILL99}]}{\Rightarrow} \text{PRG} \overset{[\text{GGM84}]}{\Rightarrow} \text{PRF}$$

It remains to argue that the resulting PRF is *space-efficient*, e.g., in addition to
storing the key k, the PRF uses only uses $|k|$ bits additional space. Since the

original dOWF internally computes the stream of an UP-KA, a straightforward implementation of dOWF might indeed consume a lot of space and so might the PRF constructed from it. However, given any pseudorandom function PRF with key length λ, we know that it consumes at most space $\mathsf{poly}(\lambda)$ for some fixed polynomial poly. Now, based on PRF, define the following space-efficient $\mathsf{PRF_{SE}}$ with key-length $\lambda_{\mathsf{SE}} := \lambda + \mathsf{poly}(\lambda)$

$$\mathsf{PRF_{SE}}(k, x) := \mathsf{PRF}(k_{1..\lambda}, x),$$

where $k_{1..\lambda}$ are the first bits of key k. In addition to space $|k|$ to store the key k, $\mathsf{PRF_{SE}}$ indeed only uses space $|k| \geq \mathsf{poly}(\lambda)$.

To obtain SM-KA (*i.e.* KA in the fully-streaming PPT model), it suffices to assume a *space-bounded* one-way function (SB-OWF) that is secure against space-bounded PPT adversaries. In order to prove that SM-KA implies SB-OWF, we need to further modify f_{DM} once more for this purpose. Namely, if Alice and Bianca use a lot of randomness, they receive this randomness as a stream[3] However, the function f_{DM} needs to take all of this randomness as input – which can be potentially larger than the space bound a of the adversary! In contrast, a SB-OWF should be computable using much less space than the space a allocated to the adversary.

A natural idea to circumvent this limitation is to derandomize the input of f_{DM} via a pseudorandom generator. Of course, since we seek to prove the existence of a SB-OWF, we cannot assume a PRG which is already a stronger primitive. Fortunately, it turns out that in this setting, it suffices to rely on a *non-cryptographic* pseudorandom generator for space-bounded algorithms, such as Nisan's PRG for read-once branching programs [Nis90]. A slight technicality remains: we need to argue that the distribution $\{f_{\mathsf{DM}}(b, r_A, r_B, (r_{B,1}, .., r_{B,400s}), \mathsf{key}') : (r_A, r_B) \leftarrow \$ \{0,1\}^*\}$ is statistically close to the distribution obtained by replacing (r_A, r_B) by the output of a PRG for space-bounded algorithms. Unfortunately, this is not implied by the security of the PRG, since PRG security only implies that it fools distinguishers outputting a *single bit* – that is, it only guarantees that the marginal distributions of each of the output bits are statistically close, but not that the distributions themselves are statistically close (a property called *non-boolean* pseudorandomness in [DI06]). Fortunately, a closer look at the security analysis of Nisan's PRG [Nis90] (with minor modifications of the parameters of the proof) reveals that it actually already is an unconditionally secure non-boolean PRG for space-bounded algorithm, which allows us to conclude.

OWFs versus General Streaming Key Agreement. Eventually, we turn to our last result, summarized in Theorem 4. We follow the round-reduction method introduced in DQW [DQW23] to prove a lower bound on multi-round streaming protocols. Essentially, their approach recursively uses (a variant of) the unconditional attacker of Dziembowski and Maurer [DM08] to convert an ℓ-long-round

---

[3] This is equivalent to having one-time read access to their random tape, which is the standard way to model probabilistic space-bounded algorithms.

UP-KA KA_ℓ into an $(\ell - 1)$-long-round streaming key agreement $\mathsf{KA}_{\ell-1}$, as follows:

- One party, say, Bianca, locally samples $s+1$ states $(\mathsf{st}_1^B, \cdots, \mathsf{st}_s^B, \mathsf{st}_{s+1}^B)$ consistent with her state after the first long round of KA_ℓ. She sends $(\mathsf{st}_1^B, \cdots, \mathsf{st}_s^B)$ to Alice.
- Alice samples an "Alice view" st^A of KA_ℓ consistent with the s states $(\mathsf{st}_1^B, \cdots, \mathsf{st}_s^B)$ received from Bianca.
- Both parties execute the rest of KA_ℓ using st^A and st_{s+1}^B as their state.

It is easy to see that the above yields a correct $(\ell - 1)$-long-round protocol $\mathsf{KA}_{\ell-1}$; the crux in the analysis of DQW lies in showing that this round-reduction also preserves security.

Now, to show that a streaming key agreement beyond the unconditional regime implies OWFs, we show that a one-way function inverter can be used to make the DQW round-reduction efficient. At a high level,

- Bianca locally samples a valid transcript T for all the short rounds of KA_ℓ. Then, she samples $(s + 1)$ pre-long-round states $(\mathsf{prestate}_1^B, \cdots, \mathsf{prestate}_{s+1}^B)$ consistant with T (using the efficient inverter for distributional OWFs), locally simulates the long stream, and computes in parallel the $s+1$ resulting states $(\mathsf{st}_1^B, \cdots, \mathsf{st}_s^B, \mathsf{st}_{s+1}^B)$, and sends the s first states to Alice.
- Alice samples st^A consistent with $(\mathsf{st}_1^B, \cdots, \mathsf{st}_s^B)$, using again the distributional OWF inverter, and both parties execute the rest of KA_ℓ using st^A and st_{s+1}^B as their state.

Using a dedicated analysis (building upon the methods of DQW), we prove that the above protocol is an $(\ell - 1)$-long-round secure streaming key agreement $\mathsf{KA}_{\ell-1}$, with the same adversarial space bound. However, there is a degradation in the honest parties space, which increased from s in KA_ℓ to $\Omega(s^2)$ in $\mathsf{KA}_{\ell-1}$. After ℓ rounds of round-reduction, we obtain a protocol KA_0 with space bound $s' = s^{2^\ell}$ and no long rounds. If $s' < a$, this yields a contradiction. One intuitively expects this strategy to rule out the existence of KA_ℓ with adversarial storage $a > s^{2^\ell}$, which is polynomial as long as ℓ is a constant.

The above high-level sketch leaves several important details under the rug. In particular, for technical reasons, the space loss of our reduction actually grows with the total number r of rounds of the protocol rather than the number ℓ of long rounds; the loss is of the form $s^{\mathsf{polylog}(r)^r} < a$, which remains polynomial as long as r is a constant. Eventually, in the fully-streaming setting, we rely on the inexistence of *space-bounded* OWFs to perform the round-reduction and use in addition an information-theoretic PRG of Nisan [Nis90] to derandomize the space-bounded OWF constructed, which introduces additional technicalities and yields a worse gap (though still polynomial when r is a constant).

1.4   Related Works

The bounded storage model has received significant attention since its introduction by Maurer [Mau92], both in the symmetric setting [Lu02, DR02, ADR02,

DM02, Vad04] and in the public-key setting [CM97, CCM98, Din01, DHRS04, HCR02, DQW23]. Recently, a breakthrough result of Raz on space lower bounds for learning parities [Raz16, Raz17] has led to a renewal of interest for the model [KRT17, GRT18, GZ19, DQW22].

A closely-related, but distinct model compared to our work is the hybrid bounded-storage model (hybrid BSM), introduced in [DM04] and further studied in [HN06]. In the hybrid BSM as in our model, the adversary is space-bounded *and* computationally bounded throughout the execution of the protocol. However, the setting and goal are quite different: in the hybrid BSM, the parties first agree on a shared key via a "standard" computational key-exchange (e.g. the Diffie-Hellman key exchange), and then use the shared key K to agree on which positions to read from a long stream to generate a new key K'. The hope is that even if the standard key-exchange is only computationally secure, since the long stream disappears afterwards, the scheme will enjoy everlasting security, and K' will remain private even if the adversary becomes all powerful afterwards. The work of [DM04] showed (via a contrived counter-example) that this intuition fails to hold in general, and [HN06] proved a general black-box impossibility result for the hybrid-BSM, as well as a positive result in the bounded-storage + random oracle models. We note that, while we also consider everlasting security and computationally bounded adversaries, our setting is different in that we do not use a classical (computational) key agreement combined with an unconditional BSM key agreement; rather, we directly build a streaming key agreement from one-way functions. Other works that discuss combinations of the bounded-storage model with computational assumptions in a different setting include [MST04] (on timestamping in the BSM), [GZ21] (achieving primitives that are impossible to achieve classically by combining the BSM with computational assumptions), and [BS23] (combining BSM with grey-box obfuscation to obtain simulation-secure functional encryption).

Eventually, as we discussed earlier, our work fits in the general program of demonstrating the necessity of one-way functions for various cryptographic protocols in the regime where they cannot exist unconditionally, such as zero-knowledge interactive proofs for NP [OW93] and constant-bias coin flipping [MPS10, HO11, BHT14].

1.5   Organization

In Sect. 2, we introduce some technical definitions and lemmas. Section 3 introduces our models for streaming key agreement, with either fully-streaming PPT adversaries (SM-KA) or unbounded processing PPT adversaries (UP-KA). Section 4 introduces our construction of UP-KA with small honest space requirement from pseudorandom functions, using a single streaming round, and extends this construction to show a stream-first SM-KA from space-bounded (consecutive) pseudorandom functions. Section 5 provides two converse of our construction, showing that *stream-first* UP-KA beyond the unconditional regime implies one-way functions, and that general UP-KA with a constant number of streaming rounds imply infinitely-often OWFs. Section 6 extends our analysis to SM-KA using information-theoretic pseudorandom generators for space-bounded computations, obtaining space-bounded OWFs and infinitely-often space-bounded OWFs for stream-first and general SM-KA respectively; it relies on a derandomization lemma which had been observed before, but without a precise quantitative statement. A self-contained proof of this derandomization lemma is included in Appendix C of the full version of this paper Eventually, in Sect. 7, we fill the remaining gap with respect to our construction by proving that space-bounded one-way functions imply space-bounded consecutive pseudorandom functions.

2   Preliminaries

Definition 5 (Infinitely Often Distributional One-Way Functions). *A function f is a ε infinitely often distributional one-way functions (ε-io-dOWF), if it can be computed in time polynomial in its input size and for infinitely many $\lambda_1 < \lambda_2 < ..$, it holds that for all PPT algorithms $\mathcal{A}$ and large enough j*

$$\mathsf{SD}\left((U_{\lambda_j}, f(U_{\lambda_j})), (\mathcal{A}(1^{\lambda_j}, f(U_{\lambda_j})), f(U_{\lambda_j}))\right) > \varepsilon(\lambda_j),$$

where U_{λ_j} denotes the uniform distribution over $\{0,1\}^{\lambda_j}$.

Remark. We will also use non-uniform ε-io-dOWFs where f can be computed by a non-uniform sequence of polynomial-size circuits.

2.1   Information-Theoretic Tools

Definition 6 (Extractor [NZ96]). *We say that an efficient function Ext : $\{0,1\}^{\mathsf{SEED}} \times \{0,1\}^n \rightarrow \{0,1\}^\ell$ is an (α, ϵ)-extractor if for all random variables (X, Z) such that X is supported over $\{0,1\}^n$ and $\mathrm{H}_\infty(X \mid Z) \geq \alpha$ we have $\mathsf{SD}((Z, S, \mathsf{Ext}(S; X)), (Z, S, U_\ell)) \leq \epsilon$ where S, U_ℓ are uniformly random and independent bit-strings of length d, ℓ respectively.*

Lemma 7 (Extractor [ILL89]). *For $\alpha \geq \ell + 2\log(1/\epsilon)$ and $\mathsf{SEED} \geq n + \ell$, there exist an (α, ϵ)-extractor $\mathsf{Ext} : \{0,1\}^{\mathsf{SEED}} \times \{0,1\}^n \rightarrow \{0,1\}^\ell$. Furthermore, such an extractor can be computed in $\mathcal{O}(n)$ time and space.*

Let $h(p)$ be the binary entropy function and h^{-1} its inverse s.th. $p \geq \frac{1}{2}$

Lemma 8 (Bit-Entropy [DQW23] Lemma 3.1). *For $1 \leq \delta \leq 1$, assume X, Y are random variables, where X is distributed over $\{0,1\}^k$. Let $X[i]$ denote the i'th bit of X. If $\mathrm{H}_\infty(X \mid Y) \geq \delta k$, and I is uniformly random over $[k]$ and independent of X, Y then $\mathrm{H}_\infty(X[I] \mid Y, I) \geq -\log(h^{-1}(\delta))$*

Lemma 9 (Jensen). *For all random variables X, $\mathbb{E}[X^2] \geq \mathbb{E}[X]^2$.*

3   Key Agreement in the Streaming Model

In this section, we will introduce the notion of key agreement in the streaming model. We start by introducing the notion of streaming algorithm we will use throughout the paper as well as some notational conventions. We further provide security notions both in the fully streaming setting—all parties remain space-restricted at all times—and the unbounded processing setting where parties may temporarily use arbitrary (polynomial) space for processing messages.

Notation and Conventions. An algorithm $\mathcal{A}$ may have input to one or more streamed inputs. We write $\mathcal{A}(a, b)$ to indicate (streaming) access to the ordered tuple (a, b) and $\mathcal{A}(a; b)$ if $\mathcal{A}$ can read independently from streams a and b. Concretely, $\mathcal{A}(\mathsf{st}, x; r)$ indicates that $\mathcal{A}$ can read from a stream containing first the state st and then the transcript x as well as independently read random coins

Table 1. Conventions on variable names

λ	: security parameter
s	: space bound for honest parties
C	: Communication stream length
r	: rounds, i.e., nbr. of messages
a	: adversary's space bound

from r. Additionally, we annotate inputs which exceed the memory limit and thus need to be read in a streaming fashion by superscript ^{str}, e.g., r^{str}. We write $\mathsf{str}^{\mathsf{str}}.\mathsf{read}(\mathsf{len})$ for reading len bits from a stream and $\mathsf{str}^{\mathsf{str}}.\mathsf{write}(\mathsf{val})$ for writing the value val to the stream. Finally, throughout this paper we stick to the conventions on variable names outlined in Table 1. As is the tradition in key agreement, we denote the adversary by $\mathcal{E}$ (Eve) to avoid confusion with Alice who is abbreviated with A. Note that we often omit the security parameter for succinctness of notation.

3.1   Fully Streaming Model

In the streaming model, algorithms are restricted in the space they use throughout their executions. They can still read from input streams and write to output streams larger than their space bound.

Definition 10 (Streaming algorithm). *Let $s : \mathbb{N} \to \mathbb{N}$ and $c : \mathbb{N} \to \mathbb{N}$ be polynomials in λ. An algorithm $\mathcal{A}$ is an (s, C)-streaming PPT, if it gets the security parameter 1^λ, some input x with $|x| \leq C(\lambda)$ as well as two parallel streams $(\mathsf{str}^{\mathsf{str}}; r^{\mathsf{str}})$ with $|\mathsf{str}^{\mathsf{str}}| \leq C(\lambda)$, outputs a value y and a stream $\mathsf{str}_{\mathcal{A}}^{\mathsf{str}}$ such that*

Efficiency. *$\mathcal{A}$ runs in time polynomial in λ,*
Space-bound. *$\mathcal{A}$ uses at most $s(\lambda)$ bits of storage at any point of time and, in particular, $|y| \leq s(\lambda)$, and*
Stream-bound. *$|\mathsf{str}_{\mathcal{A}}^{\mathsf{str}}| \leq C(\lambda)$.*

Note that $\mathcal{A}$ does not have further randomness beyond the randomness received as a r^{str}. Further, as $\mathcal{A}$ receives multiple streams as input, it can independently read from the randomness and is not required to fully read any of the streams it receives.

Definition 11 (Key Agreement in the Streaming Model (SM-KA)). *Let* s, C, *and* r *be polynomials in* λ. *A* (s, C, r)-*SM-KA protocol* KA *consists of* r (s, C)-*streaming PPT* $(A_1, B_1, \ldots, A_{r/2}, B_{r/2})$, *such that each of the PPT* P *has syntax*

$$(\mathsf{st}', x'^{\mathsf{str}}, \mathsf{key}) \leftarrow P(\mathsf{st}, x^{\mathsf{str}}; r^{\mathsf{str}})$$

with $|\mathsf{key}| = \lambda$ *and together, they satisfy correctness (cf. Definition 12).*

When running a (s, C, r)-SM-KA protocol, A_1 and B_2 take as input an empty state, and since A_1 sends the first message, A_1 also takes as input an empty x^{str}. Only the last stages $A_{r/2}$ and $B_{r/2}$ return a key, but for uniformity of syntax and w.l.o.g., we let all protocol stages return a key. With this understanding of the syntax, we define a protocol as follows:

$$
\begin{aligned}
&\underline{\mathsf{KA}(r_A{}^{\mathsf{str}}, r_B{}^{\mathsf{str}}) = (r_{A,1}^{\mathsf{str}}, .. r_{A,r/2}^{\mathsf{str}}, r_{B,1}^{\mathsf{str}}, ..., r_{B,r/2}^{\mathsf{str}})}\\
&\mathsf{st}_A \leftarrow [\,]; \quad \mathsf{st}_B \leftarrow [\,]; \quad x_{B,0}^{\mathsf{str}} \leftarrow [\,]\\
&\textbf{for } i = 1, .., r/2 \textbf{ do}\\
&\quad (\mathsf{st}_A, x_{A,i}^{\mathsf{str}}, \mathsf{key}_{A,i}) \leftarrow A_i(\mathsf{st}_A, x_{B,i}^{\mathsf{str}}; r_{A,i}^{\mathsf{str}})\\
&\quad (\mathsf{st}_B, x_{B,i}^{\mathsf{str}}, \mathsf{key}_{B,i}) \leftarrow B_i(\mathsf{st}_B, x_{A,i}^{\mathsf{str}}; r_{B,i}^{\mathsf{str}})\\
&\mathsf{key}_A \leftarrow \mathsf{key}_{A,r/2}\\
&\mathsf{key}_B \leftarrow \mathsf{key}_{B,r/2}\\
&x^{\mathsf{str}} \leftarrow (x_{A,1}^{\mathsf{str}}, x_{B,1}^{\mathsf{str}}, .., x_{A,r/2}^{\mathsf{str}}, x_{B,r/2}^{\mathsf{str}})\\
&\textbf{return } (x^{\mathsf{str}}, \mathsf{key}_A, \mathsf{key}_B)
\end{aligned}
$$

Definition 12 (Correctness). *Let* s, C, *and* r *be polynomials in* λ. *An* (s, C, r)-*SM-KA is* ϵ_{KA}-*correct if for all but finitely many* λ

$$\Pr_{r^{\mathsf{str}}}\left[\mathsf{key}_A = \mathsf{key}_B : (x^{\mathsf{str}}, \mathsf{key}_A, \mathsf{key}_B) \leftarrow \mathsf{KA}(r^{\mathsf{str}})\right] = 1 - \epsilon_{\mathsf{KA}}.$$

If ϵ_{KA} *is* negl *we sometimes omit it.*

Security of a (s, C, r)-SM-KA protocol has an additional parameter a which bounds the length of the adversary's storage and requires that Alice's key is indistinguishable from random (and thus, by correctness, so is Bianca's key).

Definition 13 (Fully Streaming Security). *Let* s, C, r *and* a *be polynomials in* λ. KA *is a* (s, C, r, a)-*SM-KA* δ_{KA}-*secure protocol if it is a* (s, C, r)-*SM-KA and for all but finitely many* λ *and all* (a, Cr)-*streaming PPT* $\mathcal{E}$, *the advantage* $\mathsf{Adv}_{\mathsf{KA}, \mathcal{E}}^{\mathsf{stream}}(\lambda) :=$

$$
\left|
\begin{aligned}
&\Pr_{r^{\mathsf{str}}, r_{\mathcal{E}}{}^{\mathsf{str}}}\left[1 = \mathcal{E}(1^\lambda, \mathsf{key}_A; x^{\mathsf{str}}; r_{\mathcal{E}}) : (x^{\mathsf{str}}, \mathsf{key}_A, \mathsf{key}_B) \leftarrow \mathsf{KA}(r^{\mathsf{str}})\right]\\
&- \Pr_{r^{\mathsf{str}}, r_{\mathcal{E}}{}^{\mathsf{str}}, \mathsf{key}}\left[1 = \mathcal{E}(1^\lambda, \mathsf{key}; x^{\mathsf{str}}; r_{\mathcal{E}}) : (x^{\mathsf{str}}, \mathsf{key}_A, \mathsf{key}_B) \leftarrow \mathsf{KA}(r^{\mathsf{str}})\right]
\end{aligned}
\right|
$$

is upper bounded by δ_{KA}. *If* δ_{KA} *is* negl *in* λ *we sometimes omit it.*

3.2   Unbounded Processing Model

In addition, we relax the space-bound and define *unbounded processing* algorithms. Unbounded processing algorithms may use arbitrary (polynomial in λ) space, however their output y still has to satisfy $|y| \leq s(\lambda)$.

Definition 14 (Unbounded Processing Protocol). *Let* $s : \mathbb{N} \to \mathbb{N}$ *and* $c : \mathbb{N} \to \mathbb{N}$ *be polynomials in* λ. *An protocol* Π *is an* (s, C)-*unbounded-processing PPT, if it consists of rounds* $(\mathsf{st}, \mathsf{str}^{\mathsf{str}}, x) \leftarrow \mathsf{send}(1^\lambda, \mathsf{st})$, $(\mathsf{st}, x) \leftarrow$ *$\mathsf{receive}(1^\lambda, \mathsf{st}, \mathsf{str}^{\mathsf{str}})$ where Alice and Bianca alternate in running the* send *and* $\mathsf{receive}$ *algorithms such that*

Efficiency. send *and* $\mathsf{receive}$ *run in time polynomial in* λ,
Stream-bound. $|\mathsf{str}^{\mathsf{str}}| \leq C(\lambda)$.
Small State and Output. *The state* st *and output* x *is bounded by* $s(\lambda)$

Definition 15 (Key Agreement in the Unbounded Processing (UP-KA)). *Let* s, C, *and* r *be polynomials in* λ. *A* (s, C, r)-*UP-KA protocol* KA *consists of* r *UP round functions PPT* $(\mathsf{send}_{A,1}, \mathsf{receive}_{B,1}), \ldots, (\mathsf{send}_{B,r}, \mathsf{receive}_{A,r})$, *with syntax*

$$(\mathsf{st}', x'^{\mathsf{str}}, \mathsf{key}) \leftarrow \mathsf{send}(\mathsf{st}; r^{\mathsf{str}})$$
$$(\mathsf{st}', \mathsf{key}) \leftarrow \mathsf{receive}(\mathsf{st}, x^{\mathsf{str}}; r^{\mathsf{str}})$$

with $|\mathsf{key}| = \lambda$ *and together, they satisfy correctness (cf. Definition 12). Regrouping, we also consider the sequence* $(A_1 := (\mathsf{receive}_{A,1}, \mathsf{send}_{A,1}), B_1 := (\mathsf{receive}_{B,1}, \mathsf{send}_{B,1})), \ldots, (A_{r/2} := (\mathsf{receive}_{A,r/2}, \mathsf{send}_{A,r/2}), B_{r/2} := (\mathsf{receive}_{B,r/2}, \mathsf{send}_{B,r/2}))$ *where the first receive algorithm and the last send algorithm is empty.*

For security in the Unbounded Processing setting, we need to split the adversary in one instance per round $\mathcal{E}_1, \ldots, \mathcal{E}_r$ and final distinguishing adversary $\mathcal{E}$. Similarly to the round algorithms, $\mathcal{E}$ are required to be PPT in λ and follow the syntax $\mathsf{st} \leftarrow \mathcal{E}(\mathsf{st}, \mathsf{str}^{\mathsf{str}}; r^{\mathsf{str}})$ where $|\mathsf{st}| \leq a(\lambda)$.

Definition 16 (Unbounded Processing (UP-KA) security). *Let* s, C, *and* r *be polynomials in* λ. KA *is a* (s, C, r, a)-*UP-KA* δ_{KA} *secure protocol if it is a* (s, C, r)-*UP-KA and for all but finitely many* λ *and for all PPT* $\mathcal{E}_1, \ldots, \mathcal{E}_r$ *outputting a state* $\mathsf{st}_{\mathcal{E}_i}$ *with* $|\mathsf{st}_{\mathcal{E}_i}| \leq a(\lambda)$ *and all PPT* $\mathcal{E}$, *the advantage*

$$\mathsf{Adv}^{\mathsf{unbound}}_{\mathsf{KA}, \mathcal{E}_r, \mathcal{E}}(\lambda) := |\Pr[1 = \mathcal{E}(1^\lambda, \mathsf{key}_A; \mathsf{st}_{\mathcal{E}_r}; r_{\mathcal{E}})] \Pr[1 = \mathcal{E}(1^\lambda, \mathsf{key}; \mathsf{st}_{\mathcal{E}_r}; r_{\mathcal{E}})]|$$

is upper bounded by δ_{KA}, *where the probabilities are taken over sampling* r^{str}, *the (implicit) randomness of* $\mathcal{E}, \mathcal{E}_1, \ldots, \mathcal{E}_r$ *and, for the second probability,* key, $x^{\mathsf{str}}, \mathsf{key}_A, \mathsf{key}_B) \leftarrow \mathsf{KA}(r^{\mathsf{str}})$ *and* $\mathsf{st}^{\mathsf{str}}_{\mathcal{E}_i} \leftarrow \mathcal{E}_i(\mathsf{st}_{\mathcal{E}_{i-1}}, x^{\mathsf{str}}_i)$ *and* $(x^{\mathsf{str}}_1, \cdots, x^{\mathsf{str}}_{2r}) \leftarrow x^{\mathsf{str}}$). *If* δ_{KA} *is negl in* λ *we sometimes omit it.*

Normal Form

We additionally place the following additional constraints on protocols in both the fully streaming and unbounded processing model:

Short Rounds are Short. In particular, all short messages in a protocol fit within honest parties space $s(\lambda)$

No Consecutive Long Rounds. Between two long (streaming) messages, we require at least one short message

4   Constructing Key Agreement

In this section we present our $(s, C, r = 2)$-SM-KA and $(s, C, r = 2)$-UP-KA protocols. Recall, that in contrast to [CM97] the stream is generated by Alice using a PRF. Consequently, Bianca can choose a single index and send it to Alice who can reconstruct the bit using the (small) PRF key. To produce a large, uniform key, we parallel compose the basic protocol $\widetilde{\mathcal{O}}(\lambda)$ times and extract the key using a seed chosen by Bianca. In our proof, we rely on consecutive PRFs—a weaker notion of PRFs which can only be accessed on consecutive values—as this notion suffices for our proofs and can be constructed *space efficient* from one-way functions.

4.1   Consecutive PRFs

While the reduction for the GGM construction of PRFS [GGM84] requires space linear in the number of queries, the reduction can be made space-efficient under the restriction of only allowing sequential queries. We formally discuss this reduction in the last section of the full version and use consecutive PRFs in our construction.

Definition 17. *A function* $f : \{0,1\}^\lambda \times \{0,1\}^\lambda \to \{0,1\}$ *is a sequential PRF if for all probabilistic adversaries* $\mathcal{A}$ *running in time* $\mathsf{poly}(\lambda)$

$$\left| \begin{array}{l} \Pr_{k \leftarrow \$\{0,1\}^\lambda} \left[1 = \mathcal{A}^{\mathsf{EVAL}^0_{f,k}(\cdot)}(1^\lambda) \right] \\ - \Pr_{k \leftarrow \$\{0,1\}^\lambda} \left[1 = \mathcal{A}^{\mathsf{EVAL}^1_{f,k}(\cdot)}(1^\lambda) \right] \end{array} \right| \leq \mathsf{negl}(\lambda)$$

$\underline{\mathsf{EVAL}^b_{f,k}(i)}$

if ctr $= \perp$ then ctr $\leftarrow 0$

assert $i = \mathsf{ctr} + 1$

ctr $\leftarrow i$

if $b = 0$ then $y \leftarrow f(k, i)$

else $y \leftarrow \$\{0,1\}$

return y

4.2   SB-PRF $\Rightarrow$ Fully Streaming Key-Agreement

For simplicity we set the desired length of the produced keys to λ matching the security parameter of the consecutive PRF.

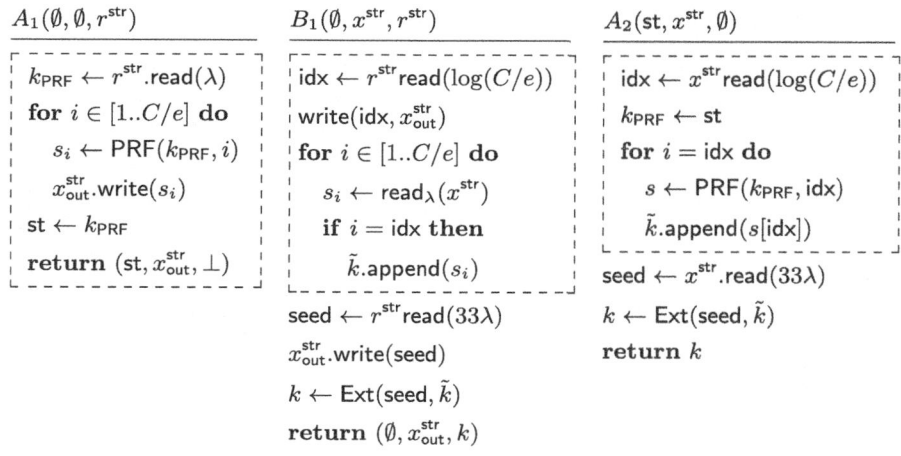

Fig. 3. Honest Protocol $\mathsf{KA} := ((A_1, B_1), (A_2))$ where ⌐boxed parts¬ are repeated $e :=$ 30λ times in parallel

Theorem 18 (SB-PRFs $\Rightarrow$ fully streaming key-agreement (SM-KA)). *Let* PRF *be a Consecutive SB-PRF* $\{0,1\}^\lambda \times \{0,1\}^\lambda \to \{0,1\}$ *which can be evaluated in space* s_{PRF} *and* Ext *and* $(3\lambda, \lambda)$-*extractor* $\{0,1\}^{30\lambda} \times \{0,1\}^{31\lambda} \to \{0,1\}^\lambda$. *Then* KA *Fig.* 3 *is a* $(s, C, r = 2)$-*SM-KA protocol with perfect correctness and honest user space* $s = \mathcal{O}(\lambda \cdot \log(C) + s_{\mathsf{PRF}})$ *and* $(s, C, r = 2, a = \frac{C}{60\lambda})$-*SM-KA security*

The proof is fairly standard and omitted in the conference version but included in the full version of this paper.

4.3   PRF $\Rightarrow$ Unbounded Processing Key-Agreement

Theorem 19 (PRFs $\Rightarrow$ unbounded processing key-agreement (UP-KA)). *Let* PRF *be a PRF* $\{0,1\}^\lambda \times \{0,1\}^\lambda \to \{0,1\}$ *and* Ext *and* $(3\lambda, \lambda)$-*extractor* $\{0,1\}^{30\lambda} \times \{0,1\}^{31\lambda} \to \{0,1\}^\lambda$. *Then* KA *Fig.3 is a* $(s, C, r = 2)$-*UP-KA protocol with perfect correctness and honest user space* $s = \mathcal{O}(\lambda)$ *and* $(s, C, r = 2, a = \frac{C}{60\lambda})$-*UP-KA security*

Proof Sketch. The unbounded processing model places fewer restrictions on the honest parties, and thus we can avoid the requirement for the PRF to allow evaluation in restricted space. For security, observe that the only point where we used the space restriction on the adversary was to bound the size of the adversary's space after receiving the stream from Alice. As Eve is space bounded between rounds in the unbounded processing model as well, the same argument applies. □

4.4   Arbitrary Output Length and Everlasting Security

[DQW23] show that it is possible to obtain large keys at the cost of one additional round: Alice streams C uniform bits and both parties use their derived key k as seed to extract a large key K using a bounded storage extractor [Vad04] with good locality. This transformation applies directly to our construction as well, with additional space cost $\mathcal{O}(|K|)$ for the honest parties. We further observe that this step is secure against unbounded adversaries and the seed k can be published after the protocol terminates thus resulting in a protocol with *everlasting* security.

5   Unbounded Processing: UP-KA Implies dOWFs

5.1   Stream-First Key Agreement $\Rightarrow$ dOWF

We start by considering the *stream first* setting, where Alice first sends a long streaming message to Bianca, and afterwards, Bianca sends a short message to Alice. As outlined in Sect. 1.3, if KA is a strong stream-first UP-KA protocol that is secure against adversaries with large enough space, then f_{DM} (cf. Figure 2) is a dOWF.

Theorem 20 (Stream-first UP-KA $\Rightarrow$ dOWF). *Let* KA *be a stream-first* (s, C, r, a)-*UP-KA protocol with* $a \geq 400s^2$, *correctness error* $\epsilon_{\mathsf{KA}} \leq \frac{1}{400}$ *and security gap* $\delta_{\mathsf{KA}} \leq \frac{1}{5}$, *then* f_{DM} *is an* $\epsilon_{\mathcal{I}}$-*dOWF for any constant* $\epsilon_{\mathcal{I}} \leq \frac{1}{10}$.

The proof of Theorem 20 builds on the following Dziembowski-Maurer (DM) theorem on the function f_{DM} which is induced by a key agreement protocol KA. For $b \in \{0, 1\}$, we define the distributions $f_{\mathsf{DM}}(b, R)$ by sampling $r = (r_A, r_B, r_{B,1}, .., r_{B,s}, \mathsf{key}')$ uniformly at random and returning $f_{\mathsf{DM}}(b, r)$.

Theorem 21 (Dziembowski-Maurer). *If* KA *is a stream-first* (s, C, r, a)-*UP-KA or SM-KA protocol with* $\epsilon_{\mathsf{KA}} \leq \frac{1}{400}$-*correctness error. Then for all large enough* λ,

$$\mathsf{SD}(f_{\mathsf{DM}}(0, R), f_{\mathsf{DM}}(1, R)) \geq \frac{9}{10}$$

Remark. Dziembowski and Maurer prove a stronger version of Theorem 21 which precisely characterizes the entropy of the key rather than only its statistical distance from a uniformly random key. The above is a re-statement of Dziembowski-Maurer (DM) in the DQW fully streaming/unbounded processing model, simplified for our application. A self-contained proof of Theorem 21 is included in Appendix A of the full version of this paper

In addition to DM, we will use the following useful claim throughout this and the next section to lower bound the advantage of a distinguisher induced by a uniform inverter.

Claim 1. *For* $b \in \{0, 1\}$, *let* X^b *be two arbitrary distributions, and let* Y *be the distribution which samples* b *uniformly and then returns* $z \leftarrow_{\$} X^b$. *Then,*

$$\mathbb{E}_{b, z \leftarrow_{\$} Y}[\Pr_{b', z' \leftarrow_{\$} Y}[b' = b \mid z' = z]] \geq (\mathsf{SD}(X^0, X^1))^2$$

We prove Claim 1 in Appendix B of the full version and now use Claim 1 to prove Theorem 20.

Proof of Theorem 20. Assume towards contradiction that f_{DM} is not an $\epsilon_{\mathcal{I}}$-dOWF for $\epsilon_{\mathcal{I}} = \frac{1}{10}$. Then, there exists a PPT inverter $\mathcal{I}$ such that for infinitely many security parameters

$$\mathsf{SD}((B, R, f_{\mathsf{DM}}(B, R)), (\mathcal{I}(f_{\mathsf{DM}}(B, R)), f_{\mathsf{DM}}(B, R))) < \epsilon_{\mathcal{I}}, \tag{2}$$

where R is the uniform input $(r_A^{\mathsf{str}}, r_B^{\mathsf{str}}, (r_{B,1}^{\mathsf{str}}, .., r_{B,400s}^{\mathsf{str}}), \mathsf{key}')$. Let $\mathcal{E}_{\mathcal{I}}$ be the distinguisher which given z, runs

$$(b, r) \leftarrow \$ \mathcal{I}(z); \textbf{ return } b.$$

We construct the following adversary $\mathcal{E}_{\mathcal{I}}$ against the stream-first (s, C, r, a)-UP-KA protocol KA: Adversary $\mathcal{E}_{\mathcal{I}}$ prepares the running of $400s$ different copies of Bianca, each with its own randomness stream $r_{B,j}^{\mathsf{str}}$ which $\mathcal{E}_{\mathcal{I}}$ does not store, but instead generates (in parallel) on the fly as needed. When $\mathcal{E}_{\mathcal{I}}$ receives stream, adversary $\mathcal{E}_{\mathcal{I}}$ computes $\mathsf{st}_{B,j} \leftarrow B_1(\mathsf{stream}, r_{B,j}^{\mathsf{stream}})$ in parallel for all $1 \leq j \leq 400s$ and stores $\mathsf{st}_{B,1}, .., \mathsf{st}_{B,400s}$. Next, $\mathcal{E}_{\mathcal{I}}$ receives short-transcript, key, runs

$$(b^*, r) \leftarrow \$ \mathcal{I}(\mathsf{st}_{B,1}, .., \mathsf{st}_{B,400s}, \mathsf{short\text{-}transcript}, \mathsf{key})$$

and returns b^*. In the proof, we denote by $\mathcal{E}_{\mathcal{U}}$ the analogous (inefficient) adversary which, instead of the (efficient) $\mathcal{I}$, runs $\mathcal{U}$ that returns a *perfectly* uniform pre-image of z under f_{DM}.

Space. The adversary $\mathcal{E}_{\mathcal{I}}$ samples $400s$ Bianca states, each of which requires space s. Thus, in the streaming phase, $\mathcal{E}_{\mathcal{I}}$ runs in space $400s^2$. Note that $\mathcal{I}$ is run after receiving the stream has terminated, so that its space consumption does not affect $\mathcal{E}$'s space limitation while receiving.

Advantage. Now, we can lower bound the advantage $\mathsf{Adv}_{\mathsf{KA}, \mathcal{E}_{\mathcal{I}}}^{\mathsf{unbound}}(\lambda)$ as follows:

$$\Big| \Pr_{r_A^{\mathsf{str}}, r_B^{\mathsf{str}}, r_{\mathcal{E}_{\mathcal{I}}}^{\mathsf{str}}, \mathsf{key}} \big[1 = \mathcal{E}_{\mathcal{I}}(1^\lambda, \mathsf{key}; x^{\mathsf{str}}; r_{\mathcal{E}_{\mathcal{I}}}) : (x^{\mathsf{str}}, \mathsf{key}_A, \mathsf{key}_B) \leftarrow \mathsf{KA}(r_A^{\mathsf{str}}, r_B^{\mathsf{str}}) \big]$$

$$- \Pr_{r_A^{\mathsf{str}}, r_B^{\mathsf{str}}, r_{\mathcal{E}_{\mathcal{I}}}^{\mathsf{str}}} \big[1 = \mathcal{E}_{\mathcal{I}}(1^\lambda, \mathsf{key}_A; x^{\mathsf{str}}; r_{\mathcal{E}_{\mathcal{I}}}) : (x^{\mathsf{str}}, \mathsf{key}_A, \mathsf{key}_B) \leftarrow \mathsf{KA}(r_A^{\mathsf{str}}, r_B^{\mathsf{str}}) \big] \Big|$$

$$= \big| \Pr_{r, \mathcal{I}}[(1, *) = \mathcal{I}(f_{\mathsf{DM}}(1, r))] - \Pr_{r, \mathcal{I}}[(1, *) = \mathcal{I}(f_{\mathsf{DM}}(0, r))] \big|$$

$$\overset{(\dagger)}{\geq} \big| \Pr_{r, \mathcal{U}}[(1, *) = \mathcal{U}(f_{\mathsf{DM}}(1, r))] - \Pr_{r, \mathcal{U}}[(1, *) = \mathcal{U}(f_{\mathsf{DM}}(0, r))] \big| - 4\epsilon$$

$$= \big| \Pr_{r, \mathcal{U}}[(1, *) = \mathcal{U}(f_{\mathsf{DM}}(1, r))] + \Pr_{r, \mathcal{U}}[(0, *) = \mathcal{U}(f_{\mathsf{DM}}(0, r))] - 1 \big| - 4\epsilon$$

$$\geq 2\mathbb{E}_{b, r}[\Pr_{r', b'}[b' = b \mid f_{\mathsf{DM}}(b', r') = f_{\mathsf{DM}}(b, r)]] - 1 - 4\epsilon_{\mathcal{I}}$$

$$\overset{\text{Cl. 1}}{\geq} 2\mathsf{SD}(f_{\mathsf{DM}}(1, R), f_{\mathsf{DM}}(0, R))^2 - 1 - 4\epsilon_{\mathcal{I}}$$

$$\overset{\text{T. 21}}{\geq} 2\left(\frac{9}{10}\right)^2 - 1 - 4\epsilon_{\mathcal{I}} > 2\left(\frac{9}{10}\right)^2 - 1 - \frac{4}{10} > \frac{3}{5} - \frac{2}{5} = \frac{1}{5} \geq \delta_{\mathsf{KA}}$$

where $(\dagger)$ follows, because $\mathcal{I}$ approximates the uniform distribution ϵ well, but since the statistical distance in (2) is over the choice of b as well, the loss is doubled, and then, it is further doubled since we have a loss for each term. $\square$

5.2   Sampling st Conditioned on q Copies of Itself

Let us open up one of the ideas of Dziembowski-Maurer (DM) underlying their proof of Theorem 21, since it is a useful tool for generalizing Sect. 5.1 to key agreement protocols with multiple streaming rounds.

DM show that q equally distributed Bianca states already contain most of the information of Bianca's *actual* state. Using DM's ideas, Dodis, Quach and Wichs (DQW) strengthen the lemma into stating that, in fact, *sampling* a Bianca state conditioned on q of his own states will yield an almost equally distributed state. Both DM and DQW state their lemmas in more general terms and we follow their tradition here. Namely, consider a pair of *jointly* distributed random variables (Z, Y). First sample Y and then q random variables $Z_1, .., Z_q$, each of which is sampled according to the distribution of Z conditioned on Y. Now, the claim is that if we sample Z' according to Z conditioned on $Z_1, .., Z_i$ (rather than on Y) for a suitable $1 \le i \le q$, then these two distribution are close. In the lemma below, X is equal to $f(Y)$ for some (potentially probabilistic) function f.

Lemma 22 (DQW). $\exists i : 1 \le i \le q$ such that

$$\mathsf{SD}((X, Z, Z_1, .., Z_i), (X, Z', Z_1, .., Z_i)) \le \sqrt{\frac{H(X)}{2(q+1)}}$$

Remark. Intuitively, sampling Z' conditioned on *more* information about Y should be useful to decrease the statistical distance and hence, one might think that choosing $i = q$ is always a valid choice. However, the proof of Lemma 22 currently just relies on the chain rule for mutual information and only shows that such an i *exists*. Note that we stated Theorem 21 with $400s$ instead of i, because statistical distance can only increase when adding more variables, but the same argument does not directly apply here.[4]

When we apply Lemma 22 in Sect. 5.3, X is Alice's state, $Z_1, .., Z_q$ are Bianca states and Z and Z' are also Bianca states. Since Alice's state size is upper-bounded by s, we also have $H(X) \le s$, and choosing $q = \frac{s^{1+2m}}{2}$ yields an upper bound of $\sqrt{\frac{H(X)}{2(q+1)}} \le \sqrt{\frac{s}{s^{1+2m}}} \le \frac{1}{s^m}$.

5.3   dOWFs via Round Reduction

Section 5.1 shows that stream-first UP-KA (with large enough space gap) implies a dOWF. This result is of interest on its own and didactically meaningful, since all subsequent analyses of success probability follow a similar template, but have additional steps or additional conceptual ideas. Nevertheless, the most important

---

[4] More precisely, for any function g, $\mathsf{SD}((X, X'), (Y, Y')) \ge \mathsf{SD}(g(X, X'), g(Y, Y'))$ and choosing g to be a projection on the first variable shows $\mathsf{SD}((X, X'), (Y, Y')) \ge \mathsf{SD}(X, Y)$. Unfortunately, $(X, Z', Z_1, .., Z_i)$ is not a projection of $(X, Z', Z_1, .., Z_q)$, since Z' is conditioned on $Z_1, .., Z_i$ and $Z_1, .., Z_q$, respectively.

role of the result for stream-first UP-KA is that it establishes as *base case* for an inductive argument that we carry out in this section.

Concretely, we follow the DQW round reduction template: DQW prove that if there is an r-message UP-KA/SM-KA protocol, then there is also an $r - 1$-message UP-KA/SM-KA protocol with slightly worse parameters. Arguing by induction, we then obtain that any r-message UP-KA/SM-KA protocol with large enough parameters implies a stream-first UP-KA/SM-KA protocol (possibly with an empty first stream, if all messages end up being short), which we already know implies a dOWF.

The DQW round reduction technique operates in the information-theoretic setting, and we would like to adopt their technique to the computational setting. Unfortunately, several sampling operations in the DQW round reduction are inefficient. Thus, we prove that an r-message UP-KA/SM-KA protocol can be transformed into an $r - 1$-message SM-KA protocol with slightly worse parameters *or* that an infinitely-often dOWF exists. Applying the argument iteratively, we obtain that an r-message UP-KA/SM-KA protocol implies an *or* statement over $r + 1$ possible candidates for an infinitely often (io) dOWF.

Conceptual Idea. To present the conceptual idea behind the DQW round reduction technique and our variant of it, we now describe the protocol transformation using inefficient reverse sampling and then subsequently replace inefficient reverse sampling by an inverter $\mathcal{I}$ similarly as in the previous section.

We denote $A_1, B_1, A_2, B_2, ..$ the code of Alice and Bianca in the original protocol and add an overline for the transformed protocol $\overline{A}_1, \overline{B}_1, \overline{A}_2, \overline{B}_2, ...$ Assume w.l.o.g. that Alice sends the first message x_A.

Short Messages. If the message x_A is short, then we can just "move it into Bianca's computation" and have Alice perform reverse sampling to compute her state later, i.e., we obtain a protocol where Bianca sends the following first message:

$\overline{B}_1$	$\overline{A}_1(\overline{x_B})$	$A_1^{\mathsf{mess}}(r_A{}^{\mathsf{str}})$
$(\mathsf{st}_A, x_A) \leftarrow \$ A_1$	parse $(x_A, x_B) \leftarrow \overline{x_B}$	$(\mathsf{st}_A, x_A) \leftarrow A_1(r_A{}^{\mathsf{str}})$
$/\!\!/$ The randomness r_A is implicit.	$r_A{}^{\mathsf{str}} \leftarrow \$ (A_1^{\mathsf{mess}})^{-1}(x_A)$	return x_A
$(\mathsf{st}_B, x_B) \leftarrow \$ B_1(x_A)$	$(\mathsf{st}_A, x_A) \leftarrow A_1(r_A)$	
$\overline{x_B} \leftarrow (x_A, x_B)$	$(\mathsf{st}'_A, x'_A) \leftarrow \$ A_2(\mathsf{st}_A, x_B)$	
return $(\mathsf{st}_B, \overline{x_B})$	return (st'_A, x'_A)	

We now prove that the function A_1^{mess} which maps Alice's randomness to Alice's message x_A is a dOWF—or that we have a protocol with one round less. Namely, if A_1^{mess} is *not* a dOWF, then we obtain a new $r - 1$ message protocol where we replace the inefficient inverse sampling $r_A{}^{\mathsf{str}} \leftarrow \$ (A_1^{\mathsf{mess}})^{-1}(x_A)$ of Alice's state by an efficient sampler. W.l.o.g., we consider protocols in a normal form, where no two streaming rounds follow onto each other, but rather, there are always short rounds in between.

Lemma 23 (Short messages). *Let $m > 0$ be a constant. Let KA be a (s, C, r, a)-UP-KA with $a > \frac{s^{2+2m}}{2}$, correctness error ϵ_{KA}, security δ_{KA}, where the length of the first message is bounded by $\frac{s^{2+2m}}{2}$. Then, either A_1^{mess} is an $\epsilon_{\mathcal{I}}$-io-dOWF, or there exists an inverter $\mathcal{I}$ for A_1^{mess} such that for all but finitely many λ,*

$$\mathsf{SD}((A_1^{\mathsf{mess}}(R), R), (A_1^{\mathsf{mess}}(R), \mathcal{I}(A_1^{\mathsf{mess}}(R)))) < \epsilon_{\mathcal{I}}, \tag{3}$$

where R is a uniform sample of r_A^{str}. Moreover, $\overline{\mathsf{KA}}$ defined by $\overline{A_1}$ (replacing $(A_1^{\mathsf{mess}})^{-1}$ by $\mathcal{I}$), $\overline{B_1}$ and $\overline{A_j} := A_{j+1}$, $\overline{B_j} := B_j$ for $j > 1$ is a $(s^{2+2m}, C, r-1, a)$-UP-KA with correctness error $\epsilon_{\overline{\mathsf{KA}}} = \epsilon_{\mathsf{KA}} + \epsilon_{\mathcal{I}}$ and security $\delta_{\overline{\mathsf{KA}}} = \delta_{\mathsf{KA}} + \epsilon_{\mathcal{I}}$.

Remark. We only obtain an infinitely often (io) dOWF rather than a dOWF, because we need $\mathcal{I}$ to successfully invert A_1^{mess} on all but finitely many λ for security and correctness to hold.

Proof. Communication length C. Note that for $\overline{\mathsf{KA}}$, the transcript

$$(\overline{x_{B,1}}, \overline{x_{A,1}}, \overline{x_{B,2}}, ..)$$

is equal to

$$((x_{A,1}, x_{B,1}), x_{A,2}, x_{B,2}, ..)$$

and thus, the communication complexity of the two protocols are identical (we omit constant costs for bracketing $(x_{A,1}, x_{B,1})$).

Normal Form. The protocol is still in normal form: If $x_{B,1}$ in KA was a stream, then $x_{A,2}$ is short. Now, $\overline{x_{B,1}} = (x_{A,1}, x_{B,1})$ is a stream, too, and $\overline{x_{A,1}} = x_{A,2}$ is still short. If $x_{B,1}$ in KA was short, then $\overline{x_{B,1}} = (x_{A,1}, x_{B,1})$ is still short, since $|x_{A,1}| + |x_{B,1}| \le \frac{s^{2+2m}}{2} + s < s^{2+2m}$.

Space Bounds of Honest Parties. Since we only modified the behaviour of the parties on non-streaming rounds, their behaviour in streaming rounds remains the same, using the same space bounds as before. Moreover, the $\overline{B_1}$ only stores a state $\overline{\mathsf{st}_B} = \mathsf{st}_B$ of size s. Finally, for $\overline{A_1}$, the receive$_{\overline{A_1}}$ can just store the message $\overline{x_{B,1}} = (x_{A,1}, x_{B,1})$ because $|x_{A,1}| + |x_{B,1}| \le \frac{s^{2+2m}}{2} + s < s^{2+2m}$ is lower than its space bound.

Correctness. The distribution of Bianca's key in KA and $\overline{\mathsf{KA}}$ is identical, but the distribution of Alice's key might change by at most $\epsilon_{\mathcal{I}}$ due to the statistical distance of the sampler.

Security. Let $\mathcal{E}$ be a PPT adversary against $\overline{\mathsf{KA}}$ and assume towards contradiction that $\mathcal{E}$'s advantage $\delta_{\mathcal{E}} > \delta_{\mathsf{KA}} + \epsilon_{\mathcal{I}}$. Since the transcript $(\overline{x_{B,1}}, \overline{x_{A,1}}, \overline{x_{B,2}}, ..)$ of $\overline{\mathsf{KA}}$ is equal to $((x_{A,1}, x_{B,1}), x_{A,2}, x_{B,2}, ..)$ and since $|x_{A,1}| \le a$, the reduction $\mathcal{R}_{\mathcal{E}}$ against KA can store $x_{A,1}$ and then run the first stage of $\mathcal{E}$ only once $\mathcal{R}_{\mathcal{E}}$ also receives $x_{B,1}$. Subsequently, $\mathcal{R}_{\mathcal{E}}$ proceeds exactly as $\mathcal{E}$.

$\mathcal{R}_{\mathcal{E}}$'s simulation of KA is up to $\epsilon_{\mathcal{I}}$-far from the distribution of $\overline{\mathsf{KA}}$, since Alice's state in $\overline{\mathsf{KA}}$ has statistical distance at most $\epsilon_{\mathcal{I}}$ from her state in KA. Hence, we obtain that $\mathcal{R}_{\mathcal{E}}$ has advantage

$$\delta_{\mathcal{R}_{\mathcal{E}}} \ge \delta_{\mathcal{E}} - \epsilon_{\mathcal{I}} > \delta_{\mathsf{KA}} - \epsilon_{\mathcal{I}} + \epsilon_{\mathcal{I}} = \delta_{\mathsf{KA}}$$

against KA and we reach a contradiction.   □

Long Messages. Now, in the case that Alice's first message x_A is long, Bianca cannot generate Alice's first message x_A, send it to her together with his own message x_B and then Alice performs reverse sampling given x_A, because this would destroy the normal form of the protocol, since x_B is a short message and might be followed by a long message. Therefore, we would like to replace x_B by a message which is also *short*.

Lemma 22 gives us a tool how Alice can sample an almost well-distributed state given something short, namely s copies of her own state. Indeed, Bianca could sample s copies of Alice's state in the unbounded pre-processing model (and assuming a suitably efficient inverter). However, for consistency with the next section, we implement a different strategy here that will also work in the fully streaming setting.

As we have already seen in f_{DM}, Bianca can efficiently sample several of *her own* states. Very surprisingly, DQW show that if Alice samples her state conditioned on i copies of *Bianca's* state $\mathsf{st}_{B,1},..,\mathsf{st}_{B,i}$, her state is actually well-distributed, yielding the following transformed protocol, where i is the index guaranteed by Lemma 22.

$\overline{B}_1$	$\overline{A}_1(\overline{x_B})$
$(\mathsf{st}_A, x_A^{\mathsf{str}}) {\leftarrow}\$ A_1$	$(z, x_B) \leftarrow \mathsf{parse}\ \overline{x_B}$
$\ /\!/$ Running Alice.	$(r_A^{\mathsf{str}}, \_) {\leftarrow}\$ (\mathbf{B_1} \circ A_1)^{-1}(z)\quad /\!/$ Re-sample cond.
for $j = 1..i$:	$/\!/$ rand. for Alice.
$\quad (\mathsf{st}_{B,j}, x_{B,j}) {\leftarrow}\$ B_1(x_A^{\mathsf{str}})$	$(\mathsf{st}_A, x_A^{\mathsf{str}}) \leftarrow A_1(r_A^{\mathsf{str}})\qquad /\!/$ Running Alice.
$\quad /\!/$ Sampling $i \leq s^{a+2c}$ Bianca states.	$(\mathsf{st}'_A, x'_A) {\leftarrow}\$ A_2(\mathsf{st}_A, x_B)$
$z \leftarrow (\mathsf{st}_{B,1}, x_{B,1}, .., \mathsf{st}_{B,i}, x_{B,i})$	$\overline{\mathsf{st}_A} \leftarrow \mathsf{st}'_A$
$(r_A^{\mathsf{str}}, \_) {\leftarrow}\$ (\mathbf{B_1} \circ A_1)^{-1}(z)$	$\overline{x_A} \leftarrow x'_A$
$\quad /\!/$ Re-sample conditional	**return** $(\overline{\mathsf{st}_A}, \overline{x_A})$
$\quad /\!/$ randomness for Alice.	
$(\mathsf{st}'_A, x_A^{'\,\mathsf{str}}) \leftarrow A_1(r_A^{\mathsf{str}})$	$(\mathbf{B_1} \circ A_1)(r_A^{\mathsf{str}}, (r_{B,1}, .., r_{B,i}))$
$\quad /\!/$ Running Alice.	$(\mathsf{st}_A, x_A^{\mathsf{str}}) \leftarrow A_1(r_A^{\mathsf{str}})\quad /\!/$ Running Alice.
$(\overline{\mathsf{st}_B}, x_B) {\leftarrow}\$ B_1(x_A^{'\,\mathsf{str}})$	**for** $j = 1..i$:
$\quad /\!/$ Sampling a fresh Bianca state.	$\quad (\mathsf{st}_{B,j}^{\mathsf{str}}, x_{B,j}^{\mathsf{str}}) \leftarrow B_1(x_A^{\mathsf{str}}; r_{B,j})$
$\overline{x_B} \leftarrow (z, x_B)$	$\quad /\!/$ Computing $i \leq s^{1+2m}$ Bianca states.
return $(\overline{\mathsf{st}_B}, \overline{x_B})$	**return** $(\mathsf{st}_{B,1}, x_{B,1}, .., \mathsf{st}_{B,i}, x_{B,i})$

The function $(\mathbf{B_1} \circ A_1)$ is a natural candidate for a dOWF since the above protocol transformation only works if $(\mathbf{B_1} \circ A_1)$ is *not* an (infinitely often) dOWF. Before turning to an efficient implementation of the protocol using an efficient inverter for $\mathbf{B_1} \circ A_1$, let us briefly consider why these inefficient versions of $\overline{A}_1$ and $\overline{B}_1$ would yield a good *joint* distribution of Alice and Bianca states. The DQW key idea here is that *both* Alice and Bianca, sample their state conditioned on

$x_{B,1}, \mathsf{st}_{B,1},..,x_{B,i}, \mathsf{st}_{B,i}$ *only*. Therefore, Alice's state is *perfectly* distributed as in the original protocol by the definition of conditional sampling. Now, to argue that the *joint* distribution of Alice's and Bianca's state is close to the original distribution, we invoke Lemma 22 on Bianca's state to conclude that sampling conditioned on $x_{B,1}, \mathsf{st}_{B,1},..,x_{B,i}, \mathsf{st}_{B,i}$ yields a sample that is statistically close to the original distribution. We now make these arguments formal.

Lemma 24 (Long messages). *Let* $m > 0$ *be a constant. Let* KA *be a* (s, C, r, a)-*UP-KA with* $a > s^{2+2m}$, *correctness error* ϵ_{KA} *and security* δ_{KA}, *where the length of the first message is greater than* $\frac{s^{2+2m}}{2}$. $\mathbf{B_1} \circ A_1$ *is a non-uniform* $\epsilon_{\mathcal{I}}$-*io-dOWF, or there exists an inverter* $\mathcal{I}$ *for* $\mathbf{B_1} \circ A_1$ *such that for all but finitely many* λ,

$$\mathsf{SD}((\mathbf{B_1} \circ A_1(R), R), (\mathbf{B_1} \circ A_1(R), \mathcal{I}(\mathbf{B_1} \circ A_1(R)))) < \epsilon_{\mathcal{I}}, \qquad (4)$$

where R *is a uniform sample of* r_A^{str}, $(r_{B,1}, .., r_{B,i})$ *and* i *is the index guaranteed by Lemma 22. Moreover,* $\overline{\mathsf{KA}}$ *defined by* $\overline{A_1}$ *(replacing* $(\mathbf{B_1} \circ A_1)^{-1}$ *by* $\mathcal{I}$), $\overline{B_1}$ *and* $\overline{A_j} := A_{j+1}, \overline{B_j} := B_j$ *for* $j > 1$ *is a* $(s^{2+2m}, C, r-1, a)$-*UP-KA with correctness error* $\epsilon_{\overline{\mathsf{KA}}} = \epsilon_{\mathsf{KA}} + 2\epsilon_{\mathcal{I}} + \frac{1}{s^m}$ *and security* $\delta_{\overline{\mathsf{KA}}} = \delta_{\mathsf{KA}} + 2\epsilon_{\mathcal{I}} + \frac{1}{s^m}$.

Remark. The non-uniformity is induced by the need to know the index i, which cannot be computed efficiently and which might be a different index for each security parameter. Thus, the non-uniform advice is $\mathcal{O}(\log \lambda)$ when Lemma 24 is applied once and $\mathcal{O}(r \log \lambda)$ when Lemma 24 is applied recursively r times.

Proof. Communication Length C. Since we assumed that $|x_A| > \frac{s^{2+2m}}{2}$, the communication complexity of the protocol decreased, since instead of x_A, we now send up to $\frac{s^{1+2m}}{2}$ Bianca states each of which has size at most s, so overall, we replaced a message of size $|x_A| > \frac{s^{2+2m}}{2}$ by a message of size $\leq \frac{s^{2+2m}}{2}$.

Normal Form. The protocol is still in normal form. Since $x_{A,1}$ is long, $x_{B,1}$ in KA is short. Now, $\overline{x_{B,1}}$ is still short, since it contains $|x_{B,1}| \leq s$ bits as well as up to $\frac{s^{1+2m}}{2}$ many Bianca states, each of which are of size at most s, so the overall length of $\overline{x_{B,1}}$ is bounded by $\frac{s^{2+2m}}{2} + s < s^{2+2m}$ and thus below the new space bound for honest parties.

Space Bounds of Honest Parties. Analogously to the short message case, the parties' behaviour in rounds other than the first remains the same, using the same space bounds as before. Moreover, $\overline{B_1}$ only stores a state $\overline{\mathsf{st}_B} = \mathsf{st}_B$ of size s. And similarly to before, for $\overline{A_1}$, the receive$_{\overline{A_1}}$ can just store the message $\overline{x_{B,1}} = (x_{A,1}, x_{B,1})$ because $\frac{s^{2+2m}}{2} + s < s^{2+2m}$ is lower than its space bound.

Security. Let $\mathcal{E}$ a PPT adversary with space-bound a against $\overline{\mathsf{KA}}$ and assume towards contradiction that $\mathcal{E}$ has advantage $\delta_{\overline{\mathsf{KA}}} > \delta_{\mathsf{KA}} + 2\epsilon_{\mathcal{I}} + \frac{1}{s^m}$. We construct a new PPT adversary $\mathcal{R}_{\mathcal{E}}$ against KA. As in the previous section, after the first message of $\overline{\mathsf{KA}}$, the reduction $\mathcal{R}_{\mathcal{E}}$ just runs $\mathcal{E}$, we thus now focus on $\mathcal{R}_{\mathcal{E}}$'s simulation of the first message $\overline{x_{B,1}}$ of $\overline{\mathsf{KA}}$. Upon receiving x_A^{str} as a stream, $\mathcal{R}_{\mathcal{E}}$ computes $\frac{s^{1+2m}}{2}$ many Bianca states in parallel as follows:

$$\mathcal{D}_1(\lambda) \xrightarrow{\quad \frac{1}{s^m} \quad} \mathcal{D}_2(\lambda) \xrightarrow{\quad \text{perfect} \quad}$$

$\mathcal{D}_1(\lambda)$	$\mathcal{D}_2(\lambda)$
$(\mathsf{st}_{A,1}, x_{A,1}^{\mathsf{str}}) \leftarrow\!\!\$\ A_1$	$(\mathsf{st}_{A,1}, x_{A,1}^{\mathsf{str}}) \leftarrow\!\!\$\ A_1$
$\textbf{for } j = 1..i :$	$\textbf{for } j = 1..i :$
$\quad (\mathsf{st}_{B,j}, x_{B,j}) \leftarrow\!\!\$\ B_1(x_{A,1}^{\mathsf{str}})$	$\quad (\mathsf{st}_{B,j}, x_{B,j}) \leftarrow\!\!\$\ B_1(x_{A,1}^{\mathsf{str}})$
$z \leftarrow (\mathsf{st}_{B,1}, x_{B,1}, .., \mathsf{st}_{B,i}, x_{B,i})$	$z \leftarrow (\mathsf{st}_{B,1}, x_{B,1}, .., \mathsf{st}_{B,i}, x_{B,i})$
	$(r_{A,1}^{\mathsf{str}}, \_) \leftarrow\!\!\$\ (\mathbf{B_1} \circ A_1)^{-1}(z)$
	$(\_, x_{A,1}^{\mathsf{str}\prime}) \leftarrow A_1(r_{A,1}^{\mathsf{str}})$
$(\mathsf{st}_B, x_B) \leftarrow\!\!\$\ B_1(x_{A,1}^{\mathsf{str}})$	$(\mathsf{st}_B, x_B) \leftarrow\!\!\$\ B_1(x_{A,1}^{\mathsf{str}\prime})$
$(\mathsf{st}_{A,2}, x_{A,2}) \leftarrow\!\!\$\ A_2(\mathsf{st}_{A,1}, x_B)$	$(\mathsf{st}_{A,2}, x_{A,2}) \leftarrow\!\!\$\ A_2(\mathsf{st}_{A,1}, x_B)$
$\textbf{return } (z, x_B, \mathsf{st}_{B,1}, \mathsf{st}_{A,2})$	$\textbf{return } (z, x_B, \mathsf{st}_{B,1}, \mathsf{st}_{A,2})$

$$\xrightarrow{\quad \text{perfect} \quad} \mathcal{D}_3(\lambda) \xrightarrow{\quad 2\epsilon_{\mathcal{I}} \quad} \mathcal{D}_4(\lambda)$$

$\mathcal{D}_3(\lambda)$	$\mathcal{D}_4(\lambda)$
$(\mathsf{st}_{A,1}, x_{A,1}^{\mathsf{str}}) \leftarrow\!\!\$\ A_1$	$(\mathsf{st}_{A,1}, x_{A,1}^{\mathsf{str}}) \leftarrow\!\!\$\ A_1$
$\textbf{for } j = 1..i :$	$\textbf{for } j = 1..i :$
$\quad (\mathsf{st}_{B,j}, x_{B,j}) \leftarrow\!\!\$\ B_1(x_{A,1}^{\mathsf{str}})$	$\quad (\mathsf{st}_{B,j}, x_{B,j}) \leftarrow\!\!\$\ B_1(x_{A,1}^{\mathsf{str}})$
$z \leftarrow (\mathsf{st}_{B,1}, x_{B,1}, .., \mathsf{st}_{B,i}, x_{B,i})$	$z \leftarrow (\mathsf{st}_{B,1}, x_{B,1}, .., \mathsf{st}_{B,i}, x_{B,i})$
$(r_{A,1}^{\mathsf{str}}, \_) \leftarrow\!\!\$\ (\mathbf{B_1} \circ A_1)^{-1}(z)$	$(r_{A,1}^{\mathsf{str}}, \_) \leftarrow\!\!\$\ \mathcal{I}(z)$
$(\_, x_{A,1}^{\mathsf{str}\prime}) \leftarrow A_1(r_{A,1}^{\mathsf{str}})$	$(\_, x_{A,1}^{\mathsf{str}\prime}) \leftarrow A_1(r_{A,1}^{\mathsf{str}})$
$(\mathsf{st}_B, x_B) \leftarrow\!\!\$\ B_1(x_{A,1}^{\mathsf{str}\prime})$	$(\mathsf{st}_B, x_B) \leftarrow\!\!\$\ B_1(x_{A,1}^{\mathsf{str}\prime})$
$(r_{A,1}^{\mathsf{str}\prime}, \_) \leftarrow\!\!\$\ (\mathbf{B_1} \circ A_1)^{-1}(z)$	$(r_{A,1}^{\mathsf{str}\prime}, \_) \leftarrow\!\!\$\ \mathcal{I}(z)$
$(\mathsf{st}_{A,1}', x_{A,1}^{\mathsf{str}\prime\prime}) \leftarrow A_1(r_{A,1}^{\mathsf{str}\prime})$	$(\mathsf{st}_{A,1}', x_{A,1}^{\mathsf{str}\prime\prime}) \leftarrow A_1(r_{A,1}^{\mathsf{str}\prime})$
$(\mathsf{st}_{A,2}, x_{A,2}) \leftarrow\!\!\$\ A_2(\mathsf{st}_{A,1}', x_B)$	$(\mathsf{st}_{A,2}, x_{A,2}) \leftarrow\!\!\$\ A_2(\mathsf{st}_{A,1}', x_B)$
$\textbf{return } (z, x_B, \mathsf{st}_{B,1}, \mathsf{st}_{A,2})$	$\textbf{return } (z, x_B, \mathsf{st}_{B,1}, \mathsf{st}_{A,2})$

Fig. 4. Hybrids for Lemma 24

$$\textbf{for } j=1..i:$$
$$(\mathsf{st}_{B,j}, x_{B,j}) \leftarrow\!\!\$\ B_1(x_A^{\mathsf{str}})$$
$$/\!/ \text{ Sampling } i \leq s^{1+2m} \text{ Bianca states.}$$
$$z \leftarrow (\mathsf{st}_{B,1}, x_{B,1}, .., \mathsf{st}_{B,i}, x_{B,i})$$

Since $a > \frac{s^{2+2m}}{2}$, $\mathcal{R}_{\mathcal{E}}$ can store those. Next, upon receiving receiving Bianca's message x_B, $\mathcal{R}_{\mathcal{E}}$ runs $\mathcal{E}$ on (z, x_B), and from there just runs $\mathcal{E}$. We argue about the statistical distance of $\mathcal{R}_{\mathcal{E}}$'s simulation by game-hopping. In Fig. 4, the upper-left column describes how the joint distribution of $(z, x_B, \mathsf{st}_B, \mathsf{st}_{A,2})$ is generated in $\mathcal{E}$'s simulation, and the lower-right column describes how the joint distribution of $(z, x_B, \mathsf{st}_B, \mathsf{st}_{A,2})$ is generated in $\overline{\mathsf{KA}}$.

From the 1st to 2nd column, we replace sampling of Bianca's state and message by conditional inverse sampling. By Lemma 22, the statistical distance is at most $\frac{1}{s^m}$, cf. discussion in Sect. 5.2. From the 2nd to 3rd column, we sample Alice's state conditionally. This step is perfect. Finally, from the 3rd to 4th column, we replace the 2 perfect inverse samplings by inverse samplings by $\mathcal{I}$; the statistical distance is $< 2\epsilon_\mathcal{I}$. Thus, we obtain that $\mathcal{R_E}$ has advantage greater than

$$\delta_{\overline{\mathsf{KA}}} - \frac{1}{s^m} - 2\epsilon_\mathcal{I} > \delta_{\mathsf{KA}} + \frac{1}{s^m} + 2\epsilon_\mathcal{I} - \frac{1}{s^m} - 2\epsilon_\mathcal{I} = \delta_{\mathsf{KA}}$$

and we reach a contradiction.

Correctness. As we analyzed security via a *statistical* sequence of game-hops, the analysis implies that the overall distribution of the protocol's behaviour changes by $2\epsilon_\mathcal{I} + \frac{1}{s^m}$ and thus, the correctness error increases by the same amount.

□

5.4   Conclusion

We proved in the unbounded processing PPT model that, when space gaps are large enough, r-message UP-KA can be transformed into $r-1$-message UP-KA, or an io-dOWF exists. Moreover, we proved that stream-first UP-KA implies dOWFs. Now, we put these transformations together into the following theorem which states that r-message UP-KA with large enough space gaps implies io-dOWF. Note that for the following theorem, no efforts have been made to optimize the parameters.

Theorem 25 (UP-KA $\Rightarrow$ io-dOWF). *Let r be a constant. Let* KA *be a (s, C, r, a)-UP-KA with $a \geq s^{(3m)^r}$, where m is a constant such that $m \geq \log_s 10^4 r$ for large enough security parameters. Then, there exists a non-uniform ϵ-io-dOWF with $\epsilon = \frac{1}{10^4 r}$.*

Proof. Space of Honest Parties. Lemma 23 and Lemma 24 both increase the space of honest parties from s to s^{2+2m}. Thus, after $r-1$ applications of either of the lemmas, we obtain space $s^{(2+2\,m)^{r-1}} \leq s^{(3\,m)^{r-1}}$. Now, Theorem 20 requires the adversary to have space at least $(s^{(3m)^{r-1}})^2$. which is indeed lower than $a = s^{(3m)^r}$.

Correctness and Security. Each application of Lemma 23 and Lemma 24 reduces correctness and security by at most $2\epsilon_\mathcal{I} + \frac{1}{s^m}$. Theorem 20 requires the correctness error of the stream-first protocol to be at most $\frac{1}{400}$ and the security gap to be at most $\frac{1}{5}$. The increase of the correctness error and security gap are both dominated by $2r \cdot \epsilon_\mathcal{I} = \frac{2}{10^4}$. Additionally, we get a term that is upper bounded by $r \cdot \frac{1}{s^m} \leq \frac{1}{10^4}$, and $\frac{3}{10^4} < \frac{1}{400}$, which is also smaller than $\frac{1}{5}$.   □

6   Fully Streaming: SM-KA Implies SB-dOWFs

6.1   A Derandomization Lemma

We start by stating a derandomization lemma, which states (in essence) that if an algorithm $\mathcal{A}$ takes as input a random stream r of length $|r| \gg s$ (and possibly some additional short input), runs in time t, uses space at most s, and returns an output of size s, then this algorithm can be derandomized into an algorithm $\mathsf{Der}(\mathcal{A})$ that uses slightly larger space $\Theta(s \cdot \log t)$ but takes as input only $O(s \cdot \log t)$ bits of randomness, such that the output distribution of $\mathsf{Der}(\mathcal{A})$ is statistically close to that of $\mathcal{A}$. Looking ahead, our results in the fully-streaming model will build upon this lemma to convert the OWFs constructed in Sect. 5 into SB-OWFs.

Lemma 26 (Derandomization). *There exist a global constant c and a transformation* Der *such that the following holds: Let $\mathcal{A}$ be a deterministic algorithm, taking as input a uniformly random string $r \in \{0,1\}^t$ (its randomness), running in time t and space s and producing an output of length $\leq s$. Then if $2^s \geq 8t^2 \log t$,*

$$\mathsf{SD}(\mathcal{A}(r), \mathsf{Der}(\mathcal{A})(r_{\mathsf{short}})) \leq 2^{-s},$$

where $r \leftarrow\!\!\$\{0,1\}^t$, $r_{\mathsf{short}} \leftarrow\!\!\$\{0,1\}^{s(\log t + c)}$, *and* $\mathsf{Der}(\mathcal{A})$ *runs in time at most* $c \cdot t \cdot \log t \cdot s^2$ *and uses space at most* $56 \log t \cdot s + c \cdot s$

In Appendix C of the full version, we prove Lemma 26. We stress that the proof is not from us: it basically follows the analysis of Nisan from [Nis90]. However, Lemma 26 does not follow from any Theorem in Nisan's paper, but rather follows from the *proof* of Theorem 1 in Nisan's paper. For completeness, we therefore reproduce this proof here, following the presentation given in the lecture notes of Ryan O'Donnell[5], with some suitable adaptation of the parameters to derive Lemma 26. In essence, the core observation is that Nisan's pseudorandom generator for low-space algorithms satisfies a stronger property: it fools *non-boolean distinguishers* that output a string $x \in \{0,1\}^s$ (where fooling means that the output distribution of the distinguishers given outputs of Nisan's PRG is statistically close to their output distribution given true random coins). We also note that this property has been observed before: it was mentioned in passing in the works of Nisan and Zuckerman [NZ96] and of Dubrov and Ishai [DI06].

6.2 Stream-First Key Agreement ⇒ SB-dOWF

We now adapt the proof of Theorem 20 to the fully streaming setting. Naturally, the resulting dOWF is only secure against space-bounded adversaries.

Definition 27 (Space-bounded Distributional One-Way Functions). *A function $f : \{0,1\}^n \to \{0,1\}^m$ is a (s, a, ε)-space-bounded distributional one way function (SB-dOWF), if the following conditions hold.*

Space-bounded Efficiency. *f can be computed in time polynomial in λ and in space $s(\lambda)$. Furthermore, we impose $m(\lambda) \leq s(\lambda)$.*

Security. *For every polynomial-time adversary $\mathcal{A}$ which uses at most $s(\lambda)$ bits of storage, we have that for all large enough λ,*

$$\mathsf{SD}\left((U_n, f(U_n)), (\mathcal{A}(1^\lambda, f(U_n)), f(U_n))\right) \geq \varepsilon(\lambda). \tag{5}$$

---

[5] https://www.cs.cmu.edu/~odonnell/complexity/docs/lecture16.pdf.

Remark. Analogously to infinitely often OWFs (Definition 5), we will later also use (s, a, ε)-io-SB-dOWFs, where (5) only holds for infinitely many λ. Jumping ahead, the infinitely often property will later be needed In the long message lemma (included in the full version), which is the analogous statement to Lemma 24. Again, we will use a dOWF inverter to construct a protocol, and correctness requires the inverter to invert correctly on all but finitely many λ. We will also consider non-uniform versions of (s, a, ε)-io-SB-dOWFs, where f can be computed by a non-uniform sequence of polynomial-size circuits of width $\leq a$. Again, as for Lemma 24, the non-uniform advice will be the index i guaranteed by Lemma 22.

Different from Theorem 20, we first need to modify f_{DM}, since it encodes the protocol into a deterministic function and the participants could use (much) more randomness than space, increasing the input length of f_{DM} beyond the adversary's space bound. We thus invoke Lemma 26 (derandomization) and, instead consider $f_{\text{stream}-1\text{st}}(b, r_{\text{short}})$ which is a derandomized version of f_{DM} and has (almost) the same output distribution despite using significantly less randomness.

Theorem 28 (Stream-first SM-KA $\Rightarrow$ SB-dOWF). *Let* KA *be a stream-first* (s, C, r, a) *SM-KA in with* $a = \mathcal{O}(s^{4+k})$ *for some constant* $k > 0$, *correctness error* $\epsilon_{\text{KA}} \leq \frac{1}{400}$, *security gap* $\delta_{\text{KA}} < \frac{1}{10^3}$ *and A and B running in overall time t. Additionally, we assume (for convenience) that* $56 \cdot 400 \log(400ts) + 400c \leq s$, *and* $400^3 c \log(400st) \leq s$. *Then,*

$$
f_{\text{stream}-1\text{st}}(b, r_{\text{short}}) := \begin{cases} \mathsf{Der}(f_{\text{DM}}(0, \cdot))(r_{\text{short}}) & \text{if } b = 0 \\ \mathsf{Der}(f_{\text{DM}}(1, \cdot))(r_{\text{short}}) & \text{if } b = 1 \end{cases}
$$

with $r_{\text{short}} \in \{0,1\}^{s^3}$, *is an* $(s', a, \epsilon_{\mathcal{I}})$*-SB-dOWF with space* $s' = s^3$, *time* ts^3 *for any* $\epsilon_{\mathcal{I}} \leq \frac{1}{5}$.

The proof of Theorem 28 is analogous to the proof of Theorem 20, with an additional (small) loss for the derandomization inaccuracy as well as an additional increase in space due to the derandomization. The details can be found in the full version of this paper.

6.3 Conclusion

We proved in the fully streaming PPT model that, when space gaps are large enough, r-message SM-KA can be transformed into $r - 1$-message SM-KA, or a non-uniform io-SB-dOWF exists. Moreover, we proved that stream-first SM-KA implies SB-dOWFs. Now, analogously to Theorem 25, we put these transformations together into the following theorem which states that r-message SM-KA with large enough space gaps implies a non-uniform io-SB-dOWF. Note that for the following theorem, no efforts have been made to optimize the parameters.

Theorem 29 (SM-KA $\Rightarrow$ io-SB-dOWF). *Let r and w be constants. Let* KA *be a* (s, C, r, a)*-SM-KA with* $a \geq s^{(3mw)^r}$, *where m is a constant such that* $m \geq \log_s 10^4 wr$ *for large enough security parameters. Then, there exists a non-uniform* (s_f, a_f, ϵ_f)*-io-SB-dOWF f with* $a_f = s_f^w$ *and with* $\epsilon_f = \frac{1}{10^4 r}$.

Discussion. DQW use a (short) common reference string (CRS) as a technical tool in their round reduction arguments for the fully streaming protocol, which allows them to rely on setup routines that are not necessarily space-bounded—note that this is the only reason that the CRS is useful, because else, the CRS could just be generated and sent by the party who generates the first message. In addition to being a technical tool, including a CRS makes their result stronger, since DQW also rule out protocols where the CRS is not (space-)efficiently computable. We, in turn, do not achieve such a stronger result, since we seek to build (space-)efficiently computable SB-dOWF. Thus, we cannot use a CRS as a technical tool where we move (space-)inefficient computations that the transformation incurs. However, using derandomization (Lemma 26) as well as efficient inverters (which exist assuming that a certain function is *not* an SB-dOWF), our results also show that in our setting, all transformations can be implemented in a space-efficient manner. It is conceivable that analogous derandomization arguments also apply to DQW (using inefficient inverters), but we did not investigate this question in sufficient depth to make this claim.

7 SB-dOWFs Implies SB-PRFs

Impagliazzo and Luby (IL [IL89]) show that distributional OWFs imply weak OWFs via universal hashing, and that Yao shows that weak OWFs imply standard OWFs via parallel repetition, cf. [Yao82, Gol01], then several constructions transform OWFs into PRGs [HILL99, HRV13, VZ12], and finally, Goldreich, Goldwasser and Micali transform PRGs into PRFs [GGM84]. The goal of this section is to show that the aforementioned reductions are sufficiently tight in space so that, together with Theorem 29, we obtain the following theorem for SM-KA.

Theorem 30 SM-KA ⇒ SB-PRFs). *There exists a universal constant u such that the following holds: let r and w be arbitrary constants. Let KA be a (s, C, r, a)-SM-KA with $a \geq s^{u \cdot (3mw)^r}$, where m is a constant such that $m \geq \log_s 10^4 wr$ for large enough security parameters. Then, there exists a non-uniform (s_f, a_f)-io-SB-consecutive-PRF F with $a_f = s_f^w$.*

Theorem 30 follows mainly by inspection, and observing that the reductions mentioned above preserve the fine-grained space hardness of the notions pretty well. Due to space constraints the proof is only included in the full version of the paper.

Acknowledgments. Chris Brzuska was supported by the Research Council of Finland grant No. 358950. Geoffroy Couteau was supported by the French Agence Nationale de la Recherche (ANR), under grant ANR-20-CE39-0001 (project SCENE), by the France 2030 ANR Project ANR22-PECY-003 SecureCompute, and by ERC project OBELiSC (Grant 101115790). Christoph Egger was supported by the European Commission under the Horizon2020 research and innovation programme, Marie Sklodowska-Curie grant agreement No 101034255. Willy Quach was supported by the Israel Science Foundation (Grant No. 3426/21), and by the Horizon Europe Research and Innovation Program via ERC Project ACQUA (Grant 101087742).

References

[ADR02] Aumann, Y., Ding, Y.Z., Rabin, M.O.: Everlasting security in the bounded storage model. IEEE Trans. Inf. Theory **48**(6), 1668–1680 (2002)

[BHT14] Berman, I., Haitner, I., Tentes, A.: Coin flipping of *any* constant bias implies one-way functions. In: Shmoys, D.B. (ed.) 46th ACM STOC, pp. 398–407. ACM Press, May/June 2014

[BIKM99] Beimel, A., Ishai, Y., Kushilevitz, E., Malkin, T.: One-way functions are essential for single-server private information retrieval. In: 31st ACM STOC, pp. 89–98. ACM Press, May 1999

[BM09] Barak, B., Mahmoody-Ghidary, M.: Merkle puzzles are optimal — an $O(n^2)$-query attack on any key exchange from a random oracle. In: Halevi, S. (ed.) CRYPTO 2009. LNCS, vol. 5677, pp. 374–390. Springer, Heidelberg (2009). https://doi.org/10.1007/978-3-642-03356-8_22

[BOL85] Ben-Or, M., Linial, N.: Collective coin flipping, robust voting schemes and minima of Banzhaf values. In: 26th Annual Symposium on Foundations of Computer Science (SFCS 1985), pp. 408–416. IEEE (1985)

[BS23] Barhoush, M., Salvail, L.: Functional encryption in the bounded storage models. CoRR, abs/2309.06702 (2023)

[CCM98] Cachin, C., Crépeau, C., Marcil, J.: Oblivious transfer with a memory-bounded receiver. In: 39th FOCS, pp. 493–502. IEEE Computer Society Press, November 1998

[CFM21] Couteau, G., Farshim, P., Mahmoody, M.: Black-box uselessness: composing separations in cryptography. In: Lee, J.R. (ed.) ITCS 2021, vol. 185, pp. 47:1–47:20. LIPIcs, January 2021

[CGKS95] Chor, B., Goldreich, O., Kushilevitz, E., Sudan, M.: Private information retrieval. In: 36th FOCS, pp. 41–50. IEEE Computer Society Press, October 1995

[CM97] Cachin, C., Maurer, U.: Unconditional security against memory-bounded adversaries. In: Kaliski, B.S. (ed.) CRYPTO 1997. LNCS, vol. 1294, pp. 292–306. Springer, Heidelberg (1997). https://doi.org/10.1007/BFb0052243

[DHRS04] Ding, Y.Z., Harnik, D., Rosen, A., Shaltiel, R.: Constant-round oblivious transfer in the bounded storage model. In: Naor, M. (ed.) TCC 2004. LNCS, vol. 2951, pp. 446–472. Springer, Heidelberg (2004). https://doi.org/10.1007/978-3-540-24638-1_25

[DI06] Dubrov, B., Ishai, Y.: On the randomness complexity of efficient sampling. In: Kleinberg, J.M. (ed.) 38th ACM STOC, pp. 711–720. ACM Press, May 2006

[Din01] Ding, Y.Z.: Oblivious transfer in the bounded storage model. In: Kilian, J. (ed.) CRYPTO 2001. LNCS, vol. 2139, pp. 155–170. Springer, Heidelberg (2001). https://doi.org/10.1007/3-540-44647-8_9

[DM02] Dziembowski, S., Maurer, U.M.: Tight security proofs for the bounded-storage model. In: 34th ACM STOC, pp. 341–350. ACM Press, May 2002

[DM04] Dziembowski, S., Maurer, U.: On generating the initial key in the bounded-storage model. In: Cachin, C., Camenisch, J.L. (eds.) EUROCRYPT 2004. LNCS, vol. 3027, pp. 126–137. Springer, Heidelberg (2004). https://doi.org/10.1007/978-3-540-24676-3_8

[DM08] Dziembowski, S., Maurer, U.: The bare bounded-storage model: the tight bound on the storage requirement for key agreement. IEEE Trans. Inf. Theory **54**(6), 2790–2792 (2008)

[DQW22] Dodis, Y., Quach, W., Wichs, D.: Authentication in the bounded storage model. In: Dunkelman, O., Dziembowski, S. (eds.) EUROCRYPT 2022, Part III. LNCS, vol. 13277, pp. 737–766. Springer, Cham (2022). https://doi.org/10.1007/978-3-031-07082-2_26

[DQW23] Dodis, Y., Quach, W., Wichs, D.: Speak much, remember little: cryptography in the bounded storage model, revisited. In: Hazay, C., Stam, M. (eds.) EUROCRYPT 2023, Part I. LNCS, vol. 14004, pp. 86–116. Springer, Heidelberg (2023). https://doi.org/10.1007/978-3-031-30545-0_4

[DR02] Ding, Y.Z., Rabin, M.O.: Hyper-encryption and everlasting security. In: Alt, H., Ferreira, A. (eds.) STACS 2002. LNCS, vol. 2285, pp. 1–26. Springer, Heidelberg (2002). https://doi.org/10.1007/3-540-45841-7_1

[GGM84] Goldreich, O., Goldwasser, S., Micali, S.: How to construct random functions (extended abstract). In: 25th FOCS, pp. 464–479. IEEE Computer Society Press, October 1984

[Gol01] Goldreich, O.: Foundations of Cryptography: Basic Tools, vol. 1. Cambridge University Press, Cambridge (2001)

[GRT18] Garg, S., Raz, R., Tal, A.: Extractor-based time-space lower bounds for learning. In: Diakonikolas, I., Kempe, D., Henzinger, M.: (eds.) 50th ACM STOC, pp. 990–1002. ACM Press, June 2018

[GZ19] Guan, J., Zhandary, M.: Simple schemes in the bounded storage model. In: Ishai, Y., Rijmen, V. (eds.) EUROCRYPT 2019. LNCS, vol. 11478, pp. 500–524. Springer, Cham (2019). https://doi.org/10.1007/978-3-030-17659-4_17

[GZ21] Guan, J., Zhandry, M.: Disappearing cryptography in the bounded storage model. In: Nissim, K., Waters, B. (eds.) TCC 2021. LNCS, vol. 13043, pp. 365–396. Springer, Cham (2021). https://doi.org/10.1007/978-3-030-90453-1_13

[HCR02] Hong, D., Chang, K.-Y., Ryu, H.: Efficient oblivious transfer in the bounded-storage model. In: Zheng, Y. (ed.) ASIACRYPT 2002. LNCS, vol. 2501, pp. 143–159. Springer, Heidelberg (2002). https://doi.org/10.1007/3-540-36178-2_9

[HILL99] Håstad, J., Impagliazzo, R., Levin, L.A., Luby, M.: A pseudorandom generator from any one-way function. SIAM J. Comput. 28(4), 1364–1396 (1999)

[HN06] Harnik, D., Naor, M.: On everlasting security in the hybrid bounded storage model. In: Bugliesi, M., Preneel, B., Sassone, V., Wegener, I. (eds.) ICALP 2006. LNCS, vol. 4052, pp. 192–203. Springer, Heidelberg (2006). https://doi.org/10.1007/11787006_17

[HO11] Haitner, I., Omri, E.: Coin flipping with constant bias implies one-way functions. In: Ostrovsky, R. (ed.) 52nd FOCS, pp. 110–119. IEEE Computer Society Press, October 2011

[HRV13] Haitner, I., Reingold, O., Vadhan, S.P.: Efficiency improvements in constructing pseudorandom generators from one-way functions. SIAM J. Comput. 42(3), 1405–1430 (2013)

[IL89] Impagliazzo, R., Luby, M.: One-way functions are essential for complexity based cryptography (extended abstract). In: 30th FOCS, pp. 230–235. IEEE Computer Society Press, October/November 1989

[ILL89] Impagliazzo, R., Levin, L.A., Luby, M.: Pseudo-random generation from one-way functions (extended abstracts). In: 21st ACM STOC, pp. 12–24. ACM Press, May 1989

[IR89] Impagliazzo, R., Rudich, S.: Limits on the provable consequences of one-way permutations. In: 21st ACM STOC, pp. 44–61. ACM Press, May 1989

[KRT17] Kol, G., Raz, R., Tal, A.: Time-space hardness of learning sparse parities. In: Hatami, H., McKenzie, P., King, V. (eds.) 49th ACM STOC, pp. 1067–1080. ACM Press, June 2017

[Lu02]   Lu, C.-J.: Hyper-encryption against space-bounded adversaries from online strong extractors. In: Yung, M. (ed.) CRYPTO 2002. LNCS, vol. 2442, pp. 257–271. Springer, Heidelberg (2002). https://doi.org/10.1007/3-540-45708-9_17

[Mau92] Maurer, U.M.: Conditionally-perfect secrecy and a provably-secure randomized cipher. J. Cryptol. **5**(1), 53–66 (1992)

[Mer74] Merkle, R.: C.s. 244 project proposal. In: Facsimile (1974). http://www.merkle.com/1974

[Mer78] Merkle, R.C.: Secure communications over insecure channels. Commun. ACM **21**(4), 294–299 (1978)

[MPS10] Maji, H.K., Prabhakaran, M., Sahai, A.: On the computational complexity of coin flipping. In: 51st FOCS, pp. 613–622. IEEE Computer Society Press, October 2010

[MST04] Moran, T., Shaltiel, R., Ta-Shma, A.: Non-interactive timestamping in the bounded storage model. In: Franklin, M. (ed.) CRYPTO 2004. LNCS, vol. 3152, pp. 460–476. Springer, Heidelberg (2004). https://doi.org/10.1007/978-3-540-28628-8_28

[Nis90] Nisan, N.: Psuedorandom generators for space-bounded computation. In: 22nd ACM STOC, pp. 204–212. ACM Press, May 1990

[NZ96]   Nisan, N., Zuckerman, D.: Randomness is linear in space. J. Comput. Syst. Sci. **52**(1), 43–52 (1996)

[OW93]   Ostrovsky, R., Wigderson, A.: One-way functions are essential for nontrivial zero-knowledge. : [1993] The 2nd Israel Symposium on Theory and Computing Systems, pp. 3–17. IEEE (1993)

[Raz16] Raz, R.: Fast learning requires good memory: a time-space lower bound for parity learning. In: Dinur, I. (ed.) 57th FOCS, pp. 266–275. IEEE Computer Society Press, October 2016

[Raz17] Raz, R.: A time-space lower bound for a large class of learning problems. In: Umans, C. (ed.) 58th FOCS, pp. 732–742. IEEE Computer Society Press, October 2017

[Vad04] Vadhan, S.P.: Constructing locally computable extractors and cryptosystems in the bounded-storage model. J. Cryptol. **17**(1), 43–77 (2004)

[VZ12]   Vadhan, S.P., Zheng, C.J.: Characterizing pseudoentropy and simplifying pseudorandom generator constructions. In: Karloff, H.J., Pitassi, T. (eds.) 44th ACM STOC, pp. 817–836. ACM Press, May 2012

[Yao82] Yao, A.C.-C.: Theory and applications of trapdoor functions (extended abstract). In: 23rd FOCS, pp. 80–91. IEEE Computer Society Press, November 1982

Rate-1 Zero-Knowledge Proofs from One-Way Functions

Noor Athamnah$^{(\boxtimes)}$, Eden Florentz – Konopnicki, and Ron D. Rothblum

Taub Faculty of Computer Science, Technion, Haifa, Israel
noor.athamnah@gmail.com, edenko@campus.technion.ac.il,
rothblum@cs.technion.ac.il

Abstract. We show that every NP relation that can be verified by a bounded-depth polynomial-sized circuit, or a bounded-space polynomial-time algorithm, has a computational zero-knowledge proof (with statistical soundness) with communication that is only *additively larger* than the witness length. Our construction relies only on the minimal assumption that one-way functions exist.

In more detail, assuming one-way functions, we show that every NP relation that can be verified in NC has a zero-knowledge proof with communication $|w| + \text{poly}(\lambda, \log(|x|))$ and relations that can be verified in SC have a zero-knowledge proof with communication $|w| + |x|^\varepsilon \cdot \text{poly}(\lambda)$. Here $\varepsilon > 0$ is an arbitrarily small constant and λ denotes the security parameter. As an immediate corollary, we also get that *any* NP relation, with a size S verification circuit (using unbounded fan-in XOR, AND and OR gates), has a zero-knowledge proof with communication $S + \text{poly}(\lambda, \log(S))$.

Our result improves on a recent result of Nassar and Rothblum (Crypto, 2022), which achieves length $(1 + \varepsilon) \cdot |w| + |x|^\varepsilon \cdot \text{poly}(\lambda)$ for bounded-space computations, and is also considerably simpler. Building on a work of Hazay et al. (TCC 2023), we also give a more complicated version of our result in which the parties only make a *black-box* use of the one-way function, but in this case we achieve only an inverse polynomial soundness error.

1 Introduction

Zero-knowledge proofs, introduced in the groundbreaking work of Goldwasser Micali and Rackoff [GMR89], are interactive protocols in which a powerful but untrusted prover convinces a verifier of the validity of a computational statement, in such a way, that no additional information is revealed. Different notions of zero-knowledge have been studied in the literature. In this work we focus exclusively on proofs offering *statistical soundness* and *computational zero-knowledge*, and refer to this notion whenever we say zero-knowledge proof (see Remark 4 for a discussion of related variants).

In their seminal work, Goldreich, Micali and Wigderson [GMW86] constructed a zero-knowledge proof for checking that a given graph is 3-colorable

© International Association for Cryptologic Research 2025
E. Boyle and M. Mahmoody (Eds.): TCC 2024, LNCS 15364, pp. 319–350, 2025.
https://doi.org/10.1007/978-3-031-78011-0_11

(assuming the existence of one-way functions). As 3-coloring is NP-complete, their result yielded the amazing fact that every problem in NP (i.e., every problem possessing a classical proof) also has a zero-knowledge proof.

The protocol of [GMW86], henceforth referred to as GMW, proceeds by having the prover commit to a random 3-coloring of the graph $G = (V, E)$, the verifier chooses an edge and the prover decommits to the colors of the two endpoints. In order to get soundness error $2^{-\lambda}$, this base protocol is repeated sequentially[1] $\Theta(|E| \cdot \lambda)$ times.

Thus, the overall communication in the GMW protocol is $|V| \cdot |E| \cdot \text{poly}(\lambda)$. This should be contrasted with the direct NP proof which has length $|V| \cdot \log_2(3)$.[2] Things becomes even worse when considering general NP languages – for such languages, due to the Karp reduction to 3-coloring, the GMW protocol gives communication that is (a relatively large) polynomial in the complexity of the NP verification circuit rather than the length of the raw witness. A similar overhead is incurred by other classical approaches such as Blum's [Blu86] Hamiltonicity protocol.

It is natural to wonder whether the overhead incurred by these protocols is inherent. This question has been studied in several works that show that it is possible to achieve communication that is polynomial in the witness length, rather than the size of the verification circuit, for a large subclass[3] of NP relations [IKOS09, KR08, GKR15, RRR21, NR22, HVW23]. Similarly to the original GMW protocol, the protocols in this line of work all rely on the existence of one-way functions, an assumption that is also known to be necessary for the construction of zero-knowledge proofs for NP [OW93, HN24]. A different approach, proposed by Gentry *et al.* [GGI+15], constructs zero-knowledge proofs with communication $m + \text{poly}(\lambda)$, where m is the size of the witness and λ is the security parameter, but relies on the existence of a *fully homomorphic encryption scheme* (FHE), which is (believed to be) a much stronger assumption (and is currently only known to be instantiable assuming the circular security of LWE [Gen09, BV11, MV24], or via indistinguishibility obfuscation [CLTV15]).[4]

All the aforementioned results that rely on one-way functions incur at the very least a large multiplicative blowup over the witness size. In a recent work, Nassar and Rothblum [NR22], relying only on the existence of one-way functions, showed that any bounded space NP relation, has a zero-knowledge proof with length $(1 + \gamma) \cdot m + n^{\beta} \cdot \text{poly}(\lambda)$, where m is the witness length, n is the instance length, λ is the security parameter and $\gamma, \beta > 0$ are arbitrarily small constants.

---

[1] While it may seem natural to repeat the protocol in parallel, this is insecure, see [HLR21].

[2] For this high-level discussion, we ignore minor issues arising from rounding and efficient bit-representation of trits.

[3] The results obtained in this line of work differ, but loosely speaking, other than [GGI+15], all known results hold for NP relations that can be decided by either bounded depth circuits or by bounded space algorithms.

[4] Gentry *et al.* [GGI+15] focus on *non-interactive* zero-knowledge proofs, but note that their approach is also applicable to interactive zero-knowledge.

1.1   Our Results

As our main result, we construct zero-knowledge proofs, with communication that is *only additively larger than the witness length*, for any NP relation that can be verified either by a bounded space algorithm or by a bounded-depth circuit. Our constructions rely only on the minimal assumption of one-way functions.

Theorem 1 (Succinct Zero-Knowledge for Bounded Depth). *Assume that one-way functions exist. Let R be an NP relation with input size n and witness size m, that can be decided by a polynomial-size circuit with depth D and assume $n \leq \text{poly}(m)$. Then, R has a zero-knowledge proof with soundness error $2^{-\lambda}$ and communication complexity $m + \text{poly}(\lambda, \log(m), D)$ where λ denotes the security parameter.*

Furthermore, the prover and verifier run in time $\text{poly}(n, \lambda)$, the protocol is public-coin and the number of rounds is $\text{poly}(\lambda, \log(m), D)$.

Theorem 2 (Succinct Zero-Knowledge for Bounded Space). *Assume that one-way functions exist. Let R be an NP relation with input size n and witness size m that can be decided by a polynomial-time and space S algorithm and assume $n \leq \text{poly}(m)$. Then, for every constant $\delta > 0$, the relation R has a zero-knowledge proof with soundness error $2^{-\lambda}$, and communication complexity $m + n^{\delta} \cdot \text{poly}(S, \lambda)$, where λ denotes the security parameter.*

Furthermore, the prover and verifier run in time $\text{poly}(m, \lambda)$, the protocol is public-coin and the number of rounds is $\text{poly}(\lambda)$.

Theorems 1 and 2 improve on the result in [NR22] in that they achieve a truly *additive* overhead in communication over the raw witness length (in contrast to the the $(1 + \gamma)$ multiplicative overhead in [NR22]).[5] For example, Theorem 1 implies that satisfiability of a polynomial-size formula on n-variables has a zero-knowledge proof with communication $n + \text{poly}(\lambda, \log n)$, and 3-colorability of an n-vertex graph has a zero-knowledge proof with communication $n \cdot \log_2(3) + \text{poly}(\lambda, \log n)$.

These results are optimal in two ways. First, in terms of assumptions, they only rely on the minimal assumption that one-way functions exist [OW93,HN24]. Second, in terms of communication, assuming the strong exponential-time hypothesis (SETH) [IP99], the witness length is a lower bound on communication (up-to additive terms), due to known limitations on so-called "laconic" provers [GH98,GVW02]. Given the above, we refer to zero-knowledge proofs with a strictly additive overhead over the witness as having *rate-1*.

The proofs of Theorems 1 and 2 are also significantly simpler than that of [NR22] (which relied on recent non-trivial results on high-rate interactive oracle proofs (IOPs) [RR20]). The key idea, on which we elaborate in Sect. 1.2, is a form of "hybrid zero-knowledge" and is inspired by the construction in [GGI+15]

---

[5] Our result is also more general than that of [NR22] in that it holds also for bounded depth circuits, whereas [NR22] is explicitly only stated for bounded space algorithms. Nevertheless, by relying on [RR20, Remark 1.5], the techniques of [NR22] could also yield proofs with communication roughly $(1 + \gamma) \cdot m$ for bounded-depth circuits.

(and can be further traced back to hybrid encryption). In a nutshell, we give a simple reduction from constructing a rate-1 zero-knowledge proof, to constructing a zero-knowledge with communication that can depend polynomially on the *witness length* (rather than the size of the verification circuit). Theorems 1 and 2 then follow by combining our reduction with known zero-knowledge proofs from the literature.

It is worth pointing out some second order differences between Theorem 1 and Theorem 2, which are inherited from doubly-efficient interactive-proofs on which they rely. The additive term in the communication in Theorem 1 depends only poly-logarithmically on the input-size, whereas in Theorem 2 the dependence has the form n^δ. On the other hand, the round complexity in Theorem 2 is $\text{poly}(\lambda)$ whereas in Theorem 1 the number of rounds also depends poly-logarithmically on the witness size and linearly on the depth.

Circuit-size Communication for General NP *Relations.* Theorem 1 also yields a new zero-knowledge proof for *general* NP relations with communication that is only additively larger than the *size* of the verification circuit. This essentially follows from the NP completeness of SAT: any NP relation can be verified in (poly-)logarithmic depth, if the witness includes the values obtained by all of the gates in the evaluation of the verification circuit (indeed, this "extended witness" can be checked by verifying that each gate is separately satisfied by the assignment).

Corollary 3 (Succinct Zero-Knowledge for General Relations).
Assume that one-way functions exist. Let R be an NP relation that can be verified by a circuit of size S with unbounded fan-in XOR, AND and OR gates. Then, R has a zero-knowledge proof with soundness error $2^{-\lambda}$ and communication complexity $S + \text{poly}(\lambda, \log(S))$, where λ is the security parameter.

Corollary 3 improves over a similar result for general circuits obtained by [IKOS09], which had a constant multiplicative overhead, and a result that can be derived from [NR22], which gives $(1 + \varepsilon)$ multiplicative overhead.

Remark 4 (On Computationally Sounds Proofs). In contrast to the statistically sound proofs considered in this work, it is well-known that (assuming the existence of collision-resistant hash functions) there exist zero-knowledge *arguments* (aka computationally sound proofs) in which the communication is *substantially smaller than the witness length* [Kil92].

Our focus however is on the case of statistical soundness. In this case, assuming reasonable hardness assumptions, the witness length poses a barrier on the communication [GH98, GVW02].

1.1.1   Zero-Knowledge with Black-Box Use of the OWF

Many of the aforementioned constructions of succinct zero-knowledge proofs, including the protocols establishing Theorems 1 and 2, make a *non black-box* use of the one-way function. This means that the implementation of the prover and the verifier depends on the actual *code* of the one-way function. This is in contrast to a black-box construction in which it suffices for the parties to receive oracle access to the one-way function (in other words, the one-way function is merely used as a sub-routine). Non black-box constructions are usually considered less efficient than their black-box counterparts and it is therefore desirable to construct protocols that avoid such a non black-box use of the one-way function. Such constructions are also more modular, enabling applications that may not be possible otherwise (see [KRV24] for a recent example).

The MPC-in-the-head framework of Ishai *et al.* [IKOS09] gives an alternate approach that enables a black-box use of the one-way function. In particular, a very recent work by Hazay, Venkitasubramaniam and Weiss [HVW23] builds on this framework to construct *black-box* zero-knowledge proofs with communication roughly $(1 + \varepsilon) \cdot m$, thereby matching the non black-box result of [NR22]. A downside of their result, compared to [NR22], is that they only achieve a constant soundness error (which cannot be reduced by repetition unless we blowup the communication).

Our second set of results are zero-knowledge proofs with a black-box use of the one-way function, that improve on the result of [HVW23] in two ways. Our main improvement is that we obtain proof length that is only additively larger than m – i.e., a rate-1 zero-knowledge proof (improving on the $(1 + \varepsilon)$ multiplicative overhead in [HVW23]). The second improvement is that we obtain soundness error that is polynomial in the (reciprocal of) the security parameter, thereby improving on the constant error achieved in [HVW23]. Our construction also avoids the use of the relatively heavy hammer of high-rate IOPs used by [HVW23] and relies on more basic tools (e.g., the doubly-efficient interactive proof of [GKR15]).

Theorem 5. *Assume that one-way functions exist. Let R be an NP relation with input size n and witness size m, that is computable by a (non-uniform) circuit family C of size $S = S(n)$ and depth $D = D(n)$ and assume $n \leq \text{poly}(m)$. Then, for any $\varepsilon > 0$ the relation R has a zero-knowledge proof with perfect completeness, and soundness error ε, in which the verifier, prover and simulator all only make a black-box use of the one-way function. The communication complexity is $m + \text{poly}\left(\frac{1}{\varepsilon}, \lambda, D, \log(S)\right)$, where λ is the security parameter.*

Furthermore, the prover and verifier run in polynomial time, the protocol is public-coin and the number of rounds is $\text{poly}(D, \log(S))$.

We remark that a similar result to Theorem 5 for bounded space computations can also be obtained, see discussion in Sect. 1.2.2.

1.2   Techniques

In this section we give an overview of our techniques.

1.2.1   Rate-1 Zero-Knowledge: Proving Theorems 1 and 2

As mentioned above, the proofs of Theorems 1 and 2 are surprisingly simple. The key idea behind the protocols, which is inspired by [GGI+15], is to reduce the construction of rate-1 zero-knowledge proofs, to constructing zero-knowledge proofs whose communication depends polynomially only on the witness length.

The protocol proceed as follows. Given an input x and its witness w, the prover randomly samples a short seed $s \in \{0,1\}^\lambda$ for a pseudorandom generator (PRG) G and then uses it to mask the witness. That is, the prover computes and sends $u = G(s) \oplus w$ to the verifier.

At this point, we view the PRG seed s as playing the role of a new witness, in the sense that if the verifier knew s then she could verify that x is indeed in the language. Needless to say, sending s in the clear would violate the zero-knowledge property, but we observe that it now suffices for the the prover to prove, in zero-knowledge, that it could have revealed an s that would have made the verifier accept. The key benefit is that s, which serves as the new witness, is much shorter than the original witness. Hence, we can afford to use one of the pre-existing zero-knowledge proofs that have a *polynomial overhead* in the witness. Thus, while the first message sent has length exactly $m = |w|$, the length of the messages sent afterwards is polynomial in the length of the seed s.

In more detail, given an NP relation R, the prover generates $u = G(s) \oplus w$ and we consider the relation $R'_G = \{ ((x,u),s) \mid (x, G(s) \oplus u) \in R \}$. Observe that the tuple $((x,u),s)$ is in R'_G if and only if $(x, G(s) \oplus u) \in R$. So by sending u, we have reduced the problem to one with a smaller witness.

The relation R'_G is in NP, since given s we can compute $G(s)$ in polynomial time in $|w|$, and then run the NP verifier on $(x, G(s) \oplus u)$, which can also be done in $\mathrm{poly}(|x|)$ time. Moreover, we observe that if R can be decided in small depth then so can R'_G – this follows from the fact that, assuming one-way functions, there exists a PRG $G : \{0,1\}^\lambda \to \{0,1\}^m$ computable by depth $\log(m) \cdot \mathrm{poly}(\lambda)$ (and size $\mathrm{poly}(m, \lambda)$) circuits. Indeed such a PRG follows by using a stretch-doubling PRG (which can be constructed from a one-way function [HILL99]) and applying the [GGM86] tree-based construction for $\log(m)$ levels. Therefore, since the relation R'_G is verifiable in small depth, using pre-existing results from the literature[6] [GKR15], this relation has a zero-knowledge proof with a communication complexity $\mathrm{poly}(\lambda, \log(n), D)$, where D denotes the depth of the original verification circuit.

Overall, we obtain a zero-knowledge proof for R with communication complexity that is larger than the witness length only by an additive $\mathrm{poly}(\lambda, \log(n), D)$ factor.

For relations R that can be verified in small space we follow a similar approach, using a zero-knowledge proof for small space relations with polynomial overhead in the witness size [RRR21] and using a PRG computable in small space

---

[6] The main result in [GKR15] is a doubly-efficient interactive proof for bounded-depth computations, which is not zero-knowledge. We use here a corollary [GKR15, Theorem 1.6] that obtains *computationally* zero-knowledge proofs for bounded depth NP relations.

(such a PRG follows essentially by the textbook stretch increasing construction of a PRG, see [Gol01, Construction 3.3.2]).

1.2.2   Rate-1 Zero-Knowledge: The Black-Box Way A downside of the approach described in Sect. 1.2.1 is that the prover and verifier make a non black-box use of the one-way function. This is due to the fact that the new relation R'_G has the PRG G encoded as part of its specification circuit. All known general purpose zero-knowledge proofs need an explicit representation of the NP verification circuit (and this is inherent, see [Ros12]). Thus, a zero-knowledge proof for R'_G has to use the code of the PRG, which translates into a non black-box use of the one-way function that G is based on.

In this section we present a different approach in which the prover, verifier and simulator all make a black-box use of the one-way function. A caveat of this alternate approach is that we only get a soundness error that is polynomially related to the (reciprocal of the) security parameter, rather than an exponentially small soundness error as in Theorems 1 and 2. Nevertheless, this already significantly improves on the constant soundness error achieved by the previous black-box construction of Hazay *et al.* [HVW23].

We continue with the idea of hiding the witness by masking it with a PRG, but rather than employing an off-the-shelf zero-knowledge protocol to prove that the masked witness can be opened, we use a general interactive protocol, which is not zero-knowledge, and make it zero-knowledge by applying multi-party computation (MPC) techniques, details follow.

Following [HVW23] (although their idea is not quite articulated in the same way), our main step is constructing a form of "distributed zero-knowledge", in which we have a single prover and k verifiers. The goal is for the verifiers to each be convinced that the prover holds a valid witness, but in such a way that a subset $t < k$ of the verifiers does not learn anything else. The distributed zero-knowledge protocol can then be compiled into a standard one (i.e., with a single monolithic verifier), using the MPC-in-the head approach: the prover emulates the interaction between the k verifiers via an MPC protocol, and sends commitments to their views. The monolithic verifier can now request that some of these views be opened to check that the MPC protocol was executed correctly.

In order to get our desired communication complexity, we therefore need for the overall communication in the k-party distributed protocol to be roughly $m + \mathrm{poly}(\lambda)$, and for the MPC-in-the-head emulation to only increase this additively.

The Distributed Zero-Knowledge Protocol. We start by secret sharing the witness w to the k verifiers, where, for $i \in [k-1]$ the share is a PRG seed s_i and the remaining k-th share is set to $w \oplus (\bigoplus_{i=1}^{k-1}(G(s_i)))$. Note that this is indeed a secret sharing of the witness w, since by expanding the seed and XORing, we can recover the witness. Also, the overall communication of this step is at most $m + k \cdot \mathrm{poly}(\lambda)$ as desired.

Assume that the NP relation is decidable in small depth. The prover now starts an execution of the doubly-efficient GKR protocol for bounded-depth computations [GKR15] to prove that $(x, w) \in R$. In each round in the protocol, rather than sending the next GKR prover message in the clear, the prover secret shares it between the parties. Since the GKR protocol is public-coin, the GKR verifier's messages can be generated by some global source of randomness. Note that for circuits verifiable in NC, the communication in this part is just $k \cdot \text{polylog}(n)$.

At the end of the interactive phase, the GKR verifier needs to check some predicate on (x, w) and the interaction transcript. Since our verifier is distributed, we perform this task via an off-the-shelf (semi-honest secure) MPC protocol.

The idea so far yields a zero-knowledge proof, but hides a somewhat subtle flaw. The circuit which the parties emulate via the MPC protocol needs to fully expand the k PRG seeds, recover the witness and then check that the witness is valid. This means that the size of the circuit is at least $k \cdot m$, which increases the complexity of the MPC protocol beyond what we can afford.

Holography to the Rescue. To resolve this difficulty, we recall an extremely useful property of the GKR protocol (as well as related protocols in the literature) – it is a *holographic proof* [BFLS91,GR17]. Namely, the GKR verifier does not need full access to its input w but rather only to compute a single point in the low degree extension of w.[7] Moreover, the desired point depends only on the verifier's randomness.

Given this, rather than applying the MPC protocol on the full shares of w, we have each of the k verifiers compute its local contribution to the low degree extension at the desired point. Here we crucially use the fact that both the secret-sharing and low-degree extension are computed as linear[8] functions, and so the sum of contributions of the shares is indeed equal to the low degree extension of w at the desired point.

Thus, the MPC protocol only needs to recombine these small shares and then run the GKR verification step.

Compiling into a Monolithic Verifier. We now compile the distributed protocol to one with a single monolithic verifier. The prover simply sends commitments to all of the shares of the witness and the messages that were sent to the k parties, and then runs the MPC "in the head". To maintain short communication, for the last share of w, which has length m, we use a commitment scheme with only

---

[7] Recall that a low degree extension of a string $w \in \{0,1\}^m$ is a low degree multivariate polynomial that agrees with w on a prescribed sub-domain (see Sect. 2.2 for details) For our purposes it will only be important that the low-degree extension is a *linear* function.

[8] It is important here that these procedures are linear over the same field. To do this, we employ the GKR protocol over a characteristic 2 fields, in which case the additive secret sharing can be via an XOR (a linear function over such fields). Also, the secret sharing is not quite linear, because the k-th share is a PRG seed that first needs to be expanded, but this suffices for our approach.

additive overhead (which can be achieved similarly to our original construction by XORing with the output of a PRG).

After the prover simulates the MPC, it sends commitments to the parties views. The verifier then chooses t parties at random and asks the prover to decommit to everything concerning these parties. Assuming the MPC protocol has perfect correctness, the only way for the prover to cheat is by providing one of the players with an incorrect view or a pair of players with inconsistent views. The former case is caught with probability at least t/k and the latter with probability at least $\frac{t \cdot (t-1)}{k \cdot (k-1)}$. So the last thing for the verifier to do is to check the validity of all decommitments and that all revealed parties behaved consistently with the protocol.

In order to get a polynomially small soundness error, we set $k = \text{poly}(\lambda)$ and use as our MPC protocol the semi-honest GMW protocol [GMW87] in the OT-hybrid model, which offers perfect semi-honest security against $t = k - 1$ parties. This yields a soundness error of $O(1/k)$.

We remark that an analogous result for bounded space computations can also be obtained by replacing the [GKR15] that we used with the [RRR21] protocol for bounded space computations, which is also holographic.

Remark 6 (On Negligible Soundness via Malicious MPC]). Following [IKOS09], it is natural to try to improve the above and obtain a negligible soundness error by relying on an MPC protocol with *malicious security*. Recall that in malicious MPC the computation is robust even if a constant fraction of the parties are corrupt. The idea would then be for the verifier to request to a open a constant fraction of the parties views such that either she will identify one of the corrupt parties and reject or, if all the opened views are consistent, the computation should be correct.

The reason why this attempt fails is that malicious MPC robustness holds at the condition that the function has the same output no matter the input of the corrupted parties. In the case where the function being computed by the parties is the NP verification of the relation, this attempt would work, since no matter what the witness is, the function should reject. However, we apply the MPC on a much simple function (which recover the low degree extension at just a single point) and changing the input of even just one party can change the result of the computation.

1.3   Open Questions

The main open question left by our work is constructing rate-1 zero-knowledge proofs for *all* NP relations. By the aforementioned result of [GGI+15], such proofs are known to exist assuming (full-fledged) FHE, but the question is whether a similar result can be established from a weaker assumption; ideally, just from the minimal assumption of one-way functions. We remark that, using our hybrid zero-knowledge approach, such a rate-1 zero-knowledge proof would follow from the existence of a zero-knowledge proof for NP that has an arbitrary polynomial dependence on the witness length (but does not scale linearly with the size of the verification circuit).

A second question left open by our work is whether we can construct succinct zero-knowledge proofs that use the one-way function as a black-box, but achieve a negligible soundness error (in contrast to the inverse polynomial soundness error achieved by our construction). We remark that [IKOS09], building on [DI06], give such a result with communication $O(|C|) + \mathrm{poly}(\lambda, \log(|C|))$, where C is the size of the NP verification circuit. This falls short of our goal of additive overhead over the NP *witness*. Actually, to the best of our knowledge it is not even known how to construct such protocols (i.e., with black box use of the one-way function and negligible soundness error) with communication $\mathrm{poly}(m) + \mathrm{poly}(\lambda, \log(m))$ (even for NP relations that are decidable in NC).

1.4   Organization

Preliminaries are in Sect. 2. In Sect. 3 we construct the succinct zero-knowledge proofs that establish Theorems 1 and 2. The constructions that make a blackbox use of the one-way function, proving Theorem 5, are in Sect. 4.

2   Preliminaries

For an NP relation R, we denote by L_R the language $L_R = \{x : \exists w, \text{ s.t. } (x, w) \in R\}$. Throughout this work we use n to denote the instance size $|x|$, and m to denote the witness size $|w|$.

2.1   Computational Indistinguishably

Definition 7. *Let* $D = \{D_\lambda\}_{\lambda \in \mathbb{N}}, E = \{E_\lambda\}_{\lambda \in \mathbb{N}}$ *be two distribution ensembles indexed by a security parameter* λ. *We say that the ensembles are computationally indistinguishable, denoted* $D \overset{c}{\approx} E$, *if for any family of polynomial size circuits* $\{C_\lambda\}_{\lambda \in \mathbb{N}}$, *the following quantity is a negligible function in* λ:

$$\left| \Pr_{x \leftarrow D_\lambda} [C_\lambda(x) = 1] - \Pr_{x \leftarrow E_\lambda} [C_\lambda(x) = 1] \right|.$$

Fact 8 (Computational Data-Processing Inequality). *If the distributions* D *and* E *are computationally indistinguishable, and* A *is a PPT algorithm, then* $A(D)$ *and* $A(E)$ *are also computationally indistinguishable.*

2.2   Interactive Proofs

Definition 9 (Interactive Proof). *A pair of interactive machines* (P, V) *is called an* interactive proof system *for a language* L, *if* V *is a probabilistic polynomial-time machines, and the following conditions hold for every security parameter* $\lambda \in \mathbb{N}$:

– **Completeness:** *For every* $x \in L$, V *accepts with probability* 1 *when interacting with* P *on common input* $(x, 1^\lambda)$.
– **Soundness:** *For every* $x \notin L$, *and every prover* P^*, V *accepts with probability at most* $\varepsilon(\lambda)$ *when interacting with* P^* *on common input* $(x, 1^\lambda)$.

We say that an interactive proof has an efficient prover *if* P *can be implemented in (probabilistic) polynomial-time. In the context of an interactive proof for an* NP *relation, we allow the prover access to an* NP *witness.*

We remark that all proofs that we construct in this work will have an efficient prover.

The Interactive Proof-System of [GKR15]. Our construction will build on the interactive proof-system of [GKR15]. This protocol relies on the *multi-linear extension encoding*, which we recall next. Let $\mathbb{F}$ be a finite field and d an integer. The multi-linear extension of a function $f : \{0,1\}^d \to \mathbb{F}$ is the unique multi-linear polynomial (over $\mathbb{F}$) such that $\hat{f}(x) = f(x)$, for all $x \in \{0,1\}^d$. A multi-linear extension of a string $w \in \{0,1\}^d$ can be defined by viewing the string as the truth-table of a function $f_w : \{0,1\}^{\log(d)} \to \{0,1\}$. The multi-linear extension can be explicitly written as:

$$\hat{f}(x) = \sum_{h \in \{0,1\}^d} f(h) \cdot I(x, h)$$

where

$$I(x, h) = \prod_{j \in [d]} \left(x_j \cdot h_j + (1 - x_j) \cdot (1 - h_j) \right).$$

This formula also directly shows that the multi-linear extension at a given point $x \in \mathbb{F}^d$ can be computed in time $2^d \cdot \mathrm{poly}(\log(\mathbb{F}))$.

Theorem 10 (Follows from [GKR15, Theorem 1.5]). *Let* L *be a language computable by a (non-uniform) circuit family* C *of size* $S = S(n)$ *and depth* $D = D(n)$. *Let* $\mathbb{F} = \mathbb{F}(n)$ *be a constructible field ensemble. Then, there exists a two phase public-coin interactive proof* $(P, V_{interactive}, V_{post})$ *with the following properties*

1. *In the interactive phase* $(P, V_{interactive})$, P *gets as input* (C, x) *and* $V_{interactive}$ *gets only* $S = |C|$. *The prover* P *runs in time* $\mathrm{poly}(S)$, *and* $V_{interactive}$ *runs in time* $D \cdot \mathrm{poly}(\log(S), \log(|\mathbb{F}|))$. *Denote by* transcript *all messages sent between the parties. The communication complexity of the interactive phase is* $\mathrm{poly}(D, \log(S), \log(|\mathbb{F}|))$.
2. *From* transcript *and the circuit* C *we can derive* $z \in \mathbb{F}^d$, $\alpha \in \mathbb{F}$ *and* $\langle C \rangle \in \{0,1\}^{\mathrm{poly}(D, \log(S), \log(|\mathbb{F}|))}$ *in time* $\mathrm{poly}(S)$.
3. V_{post} *gets as input* $(\text{transcript}, \langle C \rangle, \hat{x}(z))$ *and either accepts or rejects.* V_{post} *performs a test on* $(\text{transcript}, \langle C \rangle)$ *and checks the claim* $\hat{x}(z) = \alpha$. V_{post} *runs in time* $\mathrm{poly}(D, \log(S), \log(|\mathbb{F}|)$.

The interactive protocol obtained by first running the interactive phase, then having the verifies derive $\langle C \rangle, \hat{x}(z)$ and finally running V_{post}, has perfect completeness and soundness error $O\left(\frac{D \log S}{|\mathbb{F}|}\right)$.

We remark that [GKR15, Theorem 1.5] does not separate the proof-system into two phases as above. However, such a separation follows easily using the fact that the GKR protocol is *holographic*, meaning that the verifier's only needs to preprocess some queries to the low degree extension of the input prior to the interaction, and subsequently runs in $\text{poly}(D, \log(S))$ time.

2.3   Zero-Knowledge Proofs

Next, we recall the definition of zero-knowledge proofs. For sake of simplicity we focus on the basic standalone definition but note that our constructions also achieve the stronger notion of *auxilary-input zero-knowledge*.

Definition 11 (Zero-Knowledge Proofs). *Let (P, V) be an interactive proof system for an NP relation R with security parameter λ. The proof-system (P, V) is computational zero-knowledge if for every polynomial-time interactive machine $\hat{V}$ there exists a probabilistic polynomial-time machine Sim, called the simulator, such that for every ensemble $(x, w) = (x_\lambda, w_\lambda)_\lambda$, with $(x_\lambda, w_\lambda) \in R$ the following distribution ensembles are computationally indistinguishable:*

- $\left\{ View_{\hat{V}}^{P(w)}\left(x, 1^\lambda\right) \right\}_{\lambda \in \mathbb{N}}$, and
- $\left\{ Sim\left(x, 1^\lambda\right) \right\}_{\lambda \in \mathbb{N}}$.

Succinct Zero-Knowledge Proofs. Next, we state two prior works obtaining succinct zero-knowledge proofs for bounded depth and bounded space computations. In contrast to our results, these prior works have a large multiplicative overhead over the witness length.

Theorem 12 ([GKR15, Theorem 1.6]). *Assume one-way functions exist, and let $\lambda = \lambda(n) \geq \log(n)$ be a security parameter. Let L be a language in NP/poly, whose relation R can be computed on inputs of length n with witnesses of length $m = m(n)$ by Boolean circuits of size $\text{poly}(n)$ and depth $d(n)$. Then L has a zero-knowledge interactive proof:*

1. *The prover runs in time $\text{poly}(n, \lambda)$ (given an NP witness), the verifier runs in time $\text{poly}(n, \lambda)$ and number of rounds is $\text{poly}(\lambda, d(n))$.*
2. *The protocol has perfect completeness and soundness error $2^{-\lambda}$.*
3. *The protocol is public-coin, with communication complexity $m \cdot \text{poly}(\lambda, d(n))$.*

Remark 13. The theorem statement in [GKR15] (i.e., [GKR15, Theorem 1.6]) does not explicitly state the number of rounds, but it can be inferred in a straightforward manner from the protocol. Additionally, the stated soundness error there is $\frac{1}{2}$, but the protocol can be repeated λ times (sequentially) to achieve a soundness error of $2^{-\lambda}$.

Theorem 14 ([RRR21, Theorem 2]). *Assume one-way functions exist, and let $\delta > 0$ be a constant. Let R be an* NP *relation, with instance length n, and witness length m that can be verified by a* $\mathrm{poly}(m)$*-time and space $S = S(m)$ Turing Machine, where $n \leq \mathrm{poly}(m)$. Then, the relation R has a public-coin zero-knowledge interactive proof with perfect completeness, constant soundness error, and communication complexity $(m + S(m)) \cdot m^{\varepsilon} \cdot \mathrm{poly}(\lambda)$. The (honest) prover, given a valid witness, runs in time $\mathrm{poly}(m, \lambda)$. The verifier runs in time $\mathrm{poly}(m, \lambda)$.*

2.4 Pseudorandom Generator

Definition 15 (Pseudorandom Generator). *A pseudorandom generator (PRG) is a deterministic polynomial-time algorithm G satisfying the following two conditions:*

1. **Expansion:** *There exists a function $\ell : \mathbb{N} \to \mathbb{N}$ such that $\ell(\lambda) > \lambda$ for all $\lambda \in \mathbb{N}$, and $|G(s)| = \ell(|s|)$ for all $s \in \{0,1\}^{*}$.*
2. **Pseudorandomness:** *The ensembles $\{G(U_{\lambda})\}_{\lambda}$ and $\{U_{\ell(\lambda)}\}_{\lambda}$ are computationally indistinguishable.*

Proposition 16. *Assuming one-way functions exist, for every polynomial $\ell = \ell(\lambda)$, there exist a PRG $G : \{0,1\}^{\lambda} \to \{0,1\}^{\ell}$ computable by circuits of size $\mathrm{poly}(\lambda, \ell)$ and depth $\mathrm{poly}(\lambda) \cdot \log(\ell)$.*

We emphasize that here (as well as in Theorem 17 below) poly refers to a fixed polynomial that is independent of ℓ.

Theorem 16 follows from the tree based PRF construction of Goldreich *et al.* [GGM86] (see also [Gol01, Construction 3.6.5]), where we simply output the $\log(\ell)$-th layer of the tree (where the root is at layer 0).

Proposition 17. *Assuming one-way functions exist, for every polynomial $\ell = \ell(\lambda)$, there exists a PRG $G : \{0,1\}^{\lambda} \to \{0,1\}^{\ell}$ computable by a time $\mathrm{poly}(\lambda, \ell)$ and space $\mathrm{poly}(\lambda) + \log(\ell)$ Turing machine.*

Theorem 17 follows from the standard stretch-increasing PRG construction (see [Gol01, Construction 3.3.2]).

2.5 Commitment Scheme

Next, we define commitment schemes. We focus on non-interactive statistically binding commitments in the common random string (CRS) model, which can be constructed from one-way functions.

Definition 18 (Commitment Scheme). *A commitment scheme in the CRS model is a tuple of probabilistic polynomial-time algorithms (Gen, Com, Ver) with the following semantics:*

1. *$crs \leftarrow Gen(1^{\lambda})$, where crs is referred to as the common reference string.*

2. *For any string* $m \in \{0,1\}^* : (com, dec) \leftarrow Com(crs, m)$.
3. *For any* $com, dec, m \in \{0,1\}^* : \{0,1\} \leftarrow Ver(crs, com, m, dec)$.

The scheme must satisfy the following requirements:

1. **Correctness:** *Ver always accepts in an honest execution, i.e., for any string m and any security parameter λ,*

$$\Pr_{\substack{crs \leftarrow Gen(1^\lambda) \\ (com, dec) \leftarrow Com(crs, m)}} \left[Ver(crs, com, m, dec) = 1 \right] = 1.$$

2. **Hiding:** *For any two strings $m_1, m_2 \in \{0,1\}^*$ and any common reference string crs, the distribution of the commitment of m_1 and m_2 are computationally indistinguishable, i.e., if we denote by Com_c only the commitment part of Com then:* $\{Com_c(crs, m_1)\}_{\lambda \in \mathbb{N}} \overset{c}{\approx} \{Com_c(1^\lambda, crs, m_2)\}_{\lambda \in \mathbb{N}}$.

3. **Binding:** *For every $\lambda \in \mathbb{N}$, with probability at least $1 - 2^{-\lambda}$ over the common reference string, any commitment com^* has at most one value m that can be accepted by Ver, i.e.,*

$$\Pr_{crs \leftarrow Gen(1^\lambda)} \left[\exists m_1, m_2, dec_1, dec_2 \in \{0,1\}^* : \begin{matrix} m_0 \neq m_1, \\ Ver(crs, com^*, m_1, dec_1) = 1, \\ Ver(crs, com^*, m_2, dec_2) = 1 \end{matrix} \right] < 2^{-\lambda}.$$

Theorem 19 ([Nao91,HILL99]). *Assuming the existence of a one-way function, there exists a commitment scheme in the CRS model. Furthermore, the commitment scheme only makes a black-box use of the one-way function.*

Fact 20. *Let D a distribution over strings of length λ, f a function and com a commitment scheme. Then $(D, com(f(D)))$ and $(D, com(0^\lambda))$ are computationally indistinguishable.*

2.6   Multi-party Computation

We consider the following multi party computation model: n parties wish to evaluate a function defined jointly on their n private inputs. While there are many variations of this model, we focus on the one where the output of all of the parties should be the same (aka "secure function evaluation"). The communication between parties is synchronous and all pairwise communication channels are secure. Additionally, following [IKOS09],we also allow an OT-channel between every two parties. In each round, each party can perform local computations on all its view (input and all messages seen up to that round), send messages to any other party and read all its incoming messages. A protocol in this setting, is a specification for each of the n parties.

For this setting we define the notion of privacy and robustness as given by [IKOS09]:

Definition 21 (Correctness). *Given a deterministic n-party functionality $f(w_1, ..., w_n)$ (where input w_i belongs to party i), we say that Π realizes f with perfect correctness if for all inputs $w_1, \ldots, w_n$, the probability that the output of some party is different from the output of f is 0, where the probability is over the randomness of all of the parties.*

Definition 22 (t-Privacy). *Let* $1 \leq t < n$. *We say that* Π *realizes* f *with perfect t-privacy if there exists a PPT simulator Sim such that for any inputs* $w_1, \ldots, w_n$, *and every set of corrupted parties* $T \subset [n]$, *where* $|T| \leq t$, *the joint views of parties in* T *(which includes their inputs, randomness and received messages) is distributed identically to* $Sim(T, (w_i)_{i \in T}, f(w_1, \ldots, w_n))$.

We will rely on the classical construction of a secure MPC protocol against $t \leq n - 1$ corruptions, which has perfect semi-honest security in the OT-hybrid model, due to Goldreich, Micali and Wigderson [GMW87].

Theorem 23 ([GMW87]). *For any n-input functionality* f, *computable by a circuit of size* S, *there is an n-party protocol in the OT-hybrid model with perfect correctness and perfect* $(n - 1)$*-privacy. The parties run in time* $\text{poly}(S, n)$.

3   Succinct Zero-Knowledge Proofs

In this section we prove our main results: zero-knowledge proofs for any NP relation that can be verified either in bounded space or by a bounded depth circuits. We start with a technical definition, which, for any NP relation R gives a related relation R' with a shorter witness (but while increasing the length of the input and complexity of verifying the relation). For an NP relation R, recall that we use n to denote the input length, m to denote the witness length and λ to denote the security parameter.

Definition 24. *Let* R *be an* NP *relation, and* G *be a PRG, then we define the* NP *relation* $R'_G \triangleq \{ ((x, u), s) : (x, G(s) \oplus u) \in R \}$.

Our main technical lemma shows how to covert a zero-knowledge proof for R'_G to one for R (where we benefit if the protocol for R'_G mainly depends on the witness length).

Lemma 25. *Let* R *be an* NP *relation with input size* n *and witness size* m, G *be a PRG, and* λ *a security parameter. If* R'_G *has a zero-knowledge proof with communication complexity* $cc(m, n, \lambda)$ *and soundness error* ε, *then* R *has a zero-knowledge proof with communication complexity* $m + cc(m, n, \lambda)$ *and soundness error* ε.

Before proving Lemma 25, we first show how to use it to derive our main results.

Deriving Theorems 1 and 2 from Lemma 25. Let R be an NP relation by depth $D = D(n)$ polynomial-sized circuits. Assuming the existence of one-way function, by Theorem 16, there exists a PRG $G : \{0,1\}^\lambda \to \{0,1\}^m$ computable by depth $\log(m) \cdot \text{poly}(\lambda)$ and size $\text{poly}(m, \lambda)$ circuits. This implies that the relation R'_G can be decided by a depth $D + \log(m) \cdot \text{poly}(\lambda)$ and size $\text{poly}(n, m, \lambda)$ circuit. By Theorem 12 (and once again using the assumption that one-way functions exist), we have that R'_G has a zero-knowledge proof with communication complexity

$cc(m, n, \lambda) = \text{poly}(\log(m), \lambda, D)$, and soundness error $2^{-\lambda}$ (and a polynomial-time prover and verifier). Theorem 1 now follows directly from Lemma 25.

Theorem 2 follows similarly, by combining the small space PRG of Theorem 17 with the succinct zero-knowledge proof for bounded space computations of Theorem 14.

3.1   Proof of Lemma 25

Let R be an NP relation. The zero-knowledge proof for R, which establishes Lemma 25, is presented in Fig. 1.

Common Input: $x \in \{0,1\}^n$ and security parameter 1^λ.
Prover's Additional Input: witness $w \in \{0,1\}^m$, such that $(x, w) \in R$.

The Protocol:

1. P generates a random PRG seed $s \in \{0,1\}^\lambda$.
2. P sends $u = G(s) \oplus w$ to V.
3. P and V emulate (P', V') with (x, u) as the common input, s as the witness and wrt security parameter λ.

Fig. 1. Succinct Zero-Knowledge Proof for NP Relation R

Let R'_G be the related NP relation (see Definition 24) and assume that (P', V') is a zero-knowledge proof for R'_G.

Completeness. Let $(x, w) \in R$. For any $s \in \{0,1\}^\lambda$, by construction, it holds that $\big((x, u), s\big) \in R'_G$, where $u = G(s) \oplus w$. Thus, the protocol (P', V') is run on a YES instance. Perfect completeness now follows immediately from the perfect completeness of (P', V').

Soundness. Let $x \notin L_R$ and let P^* be a cheating prover strategy. Without loss of generality we assume that P^* is deterministic. We denote P^*'s first message in the protocol by u^*. Assume toward a contradiction that $(x, u^*) \in L'_R$. By definition, there exists an s s.t. $(x, u^* \oplus G(s)) \in R$, but that contradicts our assumption that $x \notin L_R$. Therefore $(x, u^*) \notin L'_R$ and so, the protocol (P', V') is run on a NO instance. By the soundness of the latter protocol, the verifier accepts with probability at most ε.

Complexity. The prover sends u to V, where $u = G(s) \oplus w$ so $|u| = |w|$. Then, the parties emulate (P', V') to prove that $((x, u), s) \in R'$. The communication complexity for R'_G from the given zero-knowledge protocol is $cc(m, n, \lambda)$. Thus, overall we get communication complexity $|w| + cc(m, n, \lambda)$. In addition, assuming P' and V' are polynomial-time, then so are P and V.

Computational Zero-Knowledge. Computational zero-knowledge follows from the computational zero-knowledge of (P', V') and the pseudorandomness of G. details follow.

Given a malicious verifier $\hat{V}$ we show how to simulate its view. We note that after P sends the first message, the parties run the zero-knowledge protocol for R'_G, hence we can view the behavior of $\hat{V}$ from that point on as the behavior of a malicious verifier in the (P', V') protocol. We denote this residual cheating verifier behavior by $\hat{V}'$. Since (P', V') is zero-knowledge, $\hat{V}'$ has a simulator S' that can simulate its view. We use S' to construct an S for $\hat{V}$:

$S(x, 1^\lambda)$:

1. Choose $u^* \in \{0,1\}^m$.
2. Run S' on input $((x, u^*), 1^\lambda)$ and output $(x, u^*, S'(x, u^*))$.

Claim. For every ensemble $(x, w) \in R$ it holds that $\left\{View_{\hat{V}}^{P(w)}(x, 1^\lambda)\right\}_{\lambda \in \mathbb{N}} \overset{c}{\approx} \left\{S(x, 1^\lambda)\right\}_{\lambda \in \mathbb{N}}.$

Proof. The proof is via a hybrid argument. Define the following hybrid distributions (to avoid cluttering the notation we omit the 1^λ from all distributions):

$$H_0 := \left(x, u, View_{\hat{V}'}(x, u)\right),$$
$$H_1 := \left(x, u, S'(x, u)\right),$$
$$H_2 := \left(x, u^*, S'(x, u^*)\right),$$

where $s \in_R \{0,1\}^\lambda$ is a random seed, $u = G(s) \oplus w$ and $u^* \in_R \{0,1\}^m$. Note that $H_0 = View_{\hat{V}}^{P(w)}(x)$ and that $H_2 = S(x)$ and so it suffices to show that H_0 and H_2 are both computationally indistinguishable from H_1.

$H_0 \overset{c}{\approx} H_1$: Assume towards a contradiction that the distributions are computationally distinguishable. Then, there exists a distinguisher D that distinguishes between H_0 and H_1 with non-negligible advantage δ. By an averaging argument, there is some $s = (s_\lambda)_{\lambda \in \mathbb{N}}$ such that D has a distinguishing δ advantage conditioned on choosing s as the PRG seed. We hardwire this choice of s into the distinguisher D as non-uniform advice and denote the resulting distinguisher by D_s. We use D_s to build a distinguisher D' between $View_{\hat{V}'}((x, u))$ and $S'(x, u)$ (recall that $u = G(s) \oplus w$ with the aforementioned s) in contradiction to the zero-knowledge property of (P', V'). Since (x, u) is the input of the protocol (P', V') they already exists in the view of $\hat{V}'$, so D' will take them from the view, concatenate everything to $(x, u, View_{\hat{V}'(z)}(x, u))$, then use D and achieve the same distinguishing probability δ.

$H_1 \overset{c}{\approx} H_2$: Assume towards a contradiction that there exists a non-uniform distinguisher D that distinguishes between the hybrids for some (x, w). We build D' that distinguishes between U_n and $G(U_{|\lambda|})$. We give D' the non-uniform advice (x, w). Given as input $r \in \{0, 1\}^m$, the distinguisher D' runs D on input $(x, w \oplus r, S'(x, w \oplus r))$ and outputs the result. If r is sampled from U_n, then $w \oplus r$ will also be a random element of U_n and thus $(x, w \oplus r, S'(x, w \oplus r))$ will be of the same distribution as $(x, u^*, S'(x, u^*))$. On the other hand, if r is sampled from $G(U_{|\lambda|})$ then $(x, w \oplus r, S'(x, w \oplus r))$ is the same distribution as $(x, u, S'(x, u))$. So D' will be able to distinguish with the same probability as D, in contradiction to the pseudorandomness of G.

4 Zero-Knowledge with Black-Box Use of the OWF

Recall that the proof of Theorems 1 and 2 relies on a protocol in which the prover and verifier make a non black-box use of the one-way function (see Lemma 25 for details). In this section, we prove Theorem 5 which gives a different construction that only makes black-box use of the one-way function. A caveat however is that here we only achieve an inverse polynomial soundness error, whereas Theorem 1 and Theorem 2 had an exponentially small error.

As mentioned in the introduction, the proof of Theorem 5 is inspired by, and improves upon the aforementioned work of Hazay, Venkitasubramaniam and Weiss [HVW23]. Similarly to their work, we utilize the MPC-in-the-head [IKOS09] techniques in order to avoid the non black-box use of the one way function.

4.1 Proof of Theorem 5

Let R be an NP relation. We denote by n the instance length and m the witness length, we denote with $S = S(n)$ the size of the verification circuit and $D = D(n)$ its depth. Let λ be a security parameter and ε the desired soundness error. To construct the protocol establishing Theorem 5, we will use the following ingredients, all of which either exist unconditionally or can be constructed (via a fully black-box construction) from a one-way function:

- A pseudorandom generator (PRG) $G : \{0, 1\}^\lambda \to \{0, 1\}^m$ (e.g., the one from Theorem 17, but any PRG with a similar stretch would do – the depth bound is not needed) with security parameter $\lambda' = \lambda + \log(3/\varepsilon)$
- The non-interactive statistically binding CRS commitment scheme from Theorem 19, which we denote by com.
- The interactive protocol from Theorem 10, denoted $(P_{GKR}, V_{interactive}, V_{post})$. We denote the number or rounds in the interactive part by $r = O(D \cdot \log(S))$. We choose a field with characteristic 2 and size $\Theta\left(\frac{D \cdot \log(S)}{\varepsilon}\right)$, where all operations below will be done over this field.
- An MPC protocol from Theorem 23 with perfect security and $(k - 1)$-privacy with k parties, where $k = \Theta(1/\varepsilon)$.

Using these components, the zero-knowledge proof for R that establishes Theorem 5 is presented in Fig. 2.

We proceed to show that the protocol satisfies the desired properties.

Complexity. First, the verifier sends to P a reference string of size poly(λ). Then, P sends to V commitments to all random seeds and w_{com}. Each commitment is of size poly(λ), and $|w_{com}| = m$. The prover and verifier run the interactive phase that has communication complexity poly($D, \log(S), \log(|\mathbb{F}|)$), and since it is secret shared among k parties, we have communication $k \cdot$ poly($D, \log(S), \log(|\mathbb{F}|)$).

The prover P then sends commitments to the views of all k parties in the MPC. The MPC's input for each party consists of the multi-linear extension at point z, which has size $\log(\mathbb{F})$, and b_j (where $b_j = (m_{i,j})_{i \in [r]}$, the messages from Step Item 4), each of size poly($D, \log(S), \log(|\mathbb{F}|)$). The size of the circuit computed by the MPC is poly($D, \log(S), \log(|\mathbb{F}|)$), as derived from the complexity of V_{post} in Theorem 10.

By Theorem 23, the parties run in time polynomial in the size of the input and the circuit, so the size of the view is at most poly($k, D, \log(S), \log(\mathbb{F})$). The size of the commitment to the view is there poly($\lambda, k, D, \log(S), \log(|\mathbb{F}|)$). Finally, P sends the $O(k)$ decommitments of size poly(λ) each.

Overall, the communication complexity is therefore $m + $ poly($\lambda, k, D, \log(S)$, $\log(|\mathbb{F}|)$). The communication complexity stated in the theorem statement now follows by taking $k = \Theta(\frac{1}{\varepsilon})$ and $\mathbb{F}$ as mentioned above. In addition since the commitment, PRG, GKR protocol and the MPC protocol are computable in polynomial-time, then so are P and V.

Completeness. Let $(x, w) \in R$. If (P, V) follow the protocol specification, the input of V_{post} in Step 5c is: $\left(coins_V, \left(\bigoplus_{j \in [k]} b_j \right) \right)$, where by construction

$\bigoplus_{j \in [k]} b_j = (m_i)_{i \in [r]}$. Hence, $\left(coins_V, \left(\bigoplus_{j \in [k]} b_j \right) \right)$ is the transcript of the interaction between $(P_{GKR}, V_{interactive})$. Also note that $\langle C \rangle$ is the circuit "hash" for the GKR protocol. Lastly, $\bigoplus_{j \in [k]} a_j = \left(\bigoplus_{j \in [k-1]} \widehat{G(s_j)}[z] \right) \oplus \widehat{w_s}[z] = \widehat{w}[z]$, where the last equality stems from the fact that the low degree extension is a linear function and the addition is done bit-wise over a field of characteristic two.

Thus, V_{post}'s input in Step 5c is a valid run of the GKR protocol and by its perfect completeness, the verifier will accepts. Hence, from the (perfect) completeness of the MPC protocol, the run of the MPC protocol will be an accepting one. Since P behaved according to the protocol, P should be able to open all the commitments correctly, and all checks in Step 8 will pass and therefore V accepts.

Soundness. Let $x \notin L_R$ and let P^* be a cheating prover strategy. Without loss of generality we assume that P^* is deterministic.

Common Input: $x \in \{0,1\}^n$ and security parameter 1^λ.
Prover's Additional Input: witness $w \in \{0,1\}^m$, such that $(x,w) \in R$.

The Protocol:

1. V generates a reference string for the commitment scheme and sends it to P using security parameter $\lambda' = \lambda + \log(3/\varepsilon)$. All commitments in the protocol are done using the commitment scheme com with respect to this reference string, which we omit to avoid cluttering the notation.
2. P generates k random PRG seeds $s_1, \ldots, s_k \in \{0,1\}^\lambda$.
3. P sends commitments $\{com(s_i)\}_{i \in [k]}$ to all the seeds. In addition, it sends $w_{com} = w_s \oplus G(s_k)$, where $w_s = (w \oplus G(s_1) \oplus \cdots \oplus G(s_{k-1}))$. (The pair $(w_{com}, com(s_k))$ should be interpreted as a commitment to w_s).
4. P and V emulate the interactive phase of the GKR protocol (see Theorem 10) on input (C_x, w) (where C_x denotes the circuit that computes the relation R with x hardcoded). However, in every round $i \in [r]$, whenever P_{GKR} wants to send a message m_i, the prover does not forward the message directly, but rather generates an additive secret sharing of the message s.t $m_{i,1} \oplus \cdots \oplus m_{i,k} = m_i$, and sends to V commitments to $m_{i,1}, \ldots, m_{i,k}$. (We denote the coins sent from V to P in this stage as $coins_V$).
5. (a) P derives $z \in \mathbb{F}^d$ and $\langle C \rangle$ (He can do it from Item 4 as explained in Theorem 10).
   (b) P computes the multi-linear extension of $G(s_1), \ldots, G(s_{k-1})$ and w_s at the point z. That is, for every $j \in [k-1]$, it computes $a_j = \widehat{G(s_j)}[z]$, and additionally computes $a_k = \widehat{w_s}[z]$ (see Sect. 2.2 for details).
   (c) P executes ("in its head") the k-party MPC protocol with the following inputs. For party $j \in [k-1]$, the input is $input_j = (a_j, b_j)$, where $b_j := (m_{i,j})_{i \in [r]}$. For the last party $input_k = (a_k, b_k)$, where $b_k := (m_{i,k})_{i \in [r]}$. The MPC is executed relative to the functionality
   $$V_{post}\left(\left(coins_V, \bigoplus_{j \in [k]} (b_j)\right), \langle C \rangle, \bigoplus_{j \in [k]} a_j\right). \text{ Where } b_j = (m_{i,j})_{i \in [r]}.$$
   (a) P sends commitments to the views of the k parties in the MPC protocol.
6. V randomly chooses a subset of size $t = k - 1$ of the parties, denoted by $T_q = [k] \backslash \{q\}$, and sends it to P.
7. For every $j \in T_q$, the prover P decommits to everything related to j, namely s_j, $(m_{i,j})_{i \in [r]}$, and the view of party j.
8. V verifies that (1) all inputs of the parties in T_q were computed correctly, (2) all their views are consistent (3) all parties properly followed the specification of the MPC protocol (4) all of the parties accepted. If all tests pass then V accepts, otherwise it rejects.

Fig. 2. Succinct Zero-Knowledge Proof for NP Relation R

By Definition 18, since we used security parameter $\lambda' \geq \log(3/\varepsilon)$, with probability at least $1 - \varepsilon/3$ the reference string generated in Step 1 produces a perfectly binding commitment. We continue the analysis under the assumption that the CRS is indeed perfectly binding, while noting that this can only increase the soundness error by $\varepsilon/3$.

Consider the following possible behaviors of P^*:

1. It produces an invalid decommitment.
2. The behavior of one of the parties in the MPC protocol transcript, that is defined by the commitment (since they are perfectly binding), does not follow the protocol specification.
3. A pair of views is inconsistent (i.e., messages sent by one party are not received correctly by the other parties).

In the first case the verifier when checking the decommitments. In the second case, with probability $1 - \frac{1}{k}$, the verifier V will choose the relevant party and reject. In the third case, with probability at least $1 - \frac{2}{k}$ the relevant pair of parties is selected and the verifier rejects.

Additionally, if P calculates $\langle C \rangle$ incorrectly then this either does not change the outcome of the MPC or it changes (at least) one of the parties' behavior, or creates an inconsistency between the views of two parties, then once again with probability $1 - \frac{2}{k}$, V will choose the relevant party/parties and reject. Thus, we can continue the analysis assuming the MPC protocol computes the intended function on the defined inputs while adding at most $\frac{2}{k}$ to the soundness error.

Assuming all commitments can be opened and in one way, and assuming P simulates the MPC protocol correctly and on the inputs derived from the opening of the commitments as defined in the protocol, then from the perfect correctness of the MPC protocol, we get that the MPC protocol calculates the output of $V_{post}(coins_V, \{m_i\}_{i \in [r]}), \langle C \rangle, \hat{w}_*[z]$. For some w_* (derived from the unique de-commitment and recombining of the messages in Item 5b), and $(coins_V, \{m_i\}_{i \in [r]}), \langle C \rangle$ derived of a possible run of the GKR protocol. Since $x \notin L_R$, for any such w_* it holds that $(x, w_*) \notin R$ and so the circuit C_x does not accept w_*. By fixing the field size to be $\Theta(\frac{D \cdot \text{polylog}(S)}{\varepsilon})$ for a sufficiently large constant in the Θ-notation, by Theorem 10, the GKR protocol has a soundness error of $\varepsilon/3$.

Overall, the probability that V accepts is at most $\frac{\varepsilon}{3} + \frac{2}{k} + \frac{\varepsilon}{3}$. By choosing $k := \lceil \frac{6}{\varepsilon} \rceil$ we can get the desired soundness error of ε.

Computational Zero-knowledge. Let V^* be a malicious verifier, which we assume without loss of generality to be deterministic. For a given input $(x, w) \in R$, we denote V^*'s first message on input x (which should specify a reference string for the commitment) by ref. By Definition 18, the commitment is hiding when using *any* reference string, in particular ref. For clarity of notation we therefore omit ref below, but note that all commitments are done relative to this fixed reference string.

Our proof of zero-knowledge follows the outline of the textbook proof of zero-knowledge of the 3-coloring protocol [Gol01, Section 4.4.2.3]. In particular, we will present a simulator S that is allowed to output a special abort symbol $\perp$ and analyze it via two key propositions:

- In Proposition 26 we show that the probability that $S(x)$ outputs $\perp$ is at most $1 - O(\frac{1}{k})$.
- In Proposition 27 we show that conditioned on not outputting $\perp$, the output of $S(x)$ is computationally indistinguishable from the verifier's view in a real execution of the protocol.

These two properties, combined with rejection sampling, yield the desired simulator (see [Gol01, Definition 4.3.2] for details). The base simulator (which is allowed to abort) is presented in Fig. 3.

Proposition 26. *The probability that S outputs $\perp$ is at most $1 - O(1/k)$.*

Proof. Recall that V^* is deterministic. We assume without loss of generality that V^* always specifies a valid set T_{q^*} (i.e. $T_{q^*} \subseteq [k]$ is a subset of size $k-1$) in Step 6 (since otherwise we can just interpret its message as some fixed T_{q^*}).

We view two strings $m = (s, \alpha, \beta), m' = (s', \alpha', \beta')$, where s, s' represent some choice of seeds for the PRG (in Step 3), α, α' two randomness choices for the secret sharing (in Step 4) and β, β' two randomness choices for the MPC simulator (in Step 5d). These randomness choices, together with a choice of $q \in [k]$ (in Step 5c) and randomness of the commitments, define all the randomness of the simulator.

Denote by $\Pr[V_{q^*}^*(m, q)]$ the probability, taken over the randomness only of the commitment, that the verifier V^* requests q^* given simulator behavior corresponding to randomness (m, q). For any different choices (m, q) and (m', q'), due to the hiding property of the commitment, the difference between the probabilities of the verifier making the choice q^* for these two interactions is negligible (otherwise there exist two distinct messages that we can distinguish between using V^*).

Thus, for every polynomial p_1 and every choice q^* it holds that $|\Pr[V_{q^*}^*(m, q)] - \Pr[V_{q^*}^*(m', q')]| < \frac{1}{p_1(n)}$. Using this inequality, we prove the claim.

The simple idea is that if the choice of the verifier for T_{q^*} is made regardless (up to negligible probability) of the messages sent by the prover, then with probability close to $\frac{1}{k}$ the verifier will choose the same set and there will be no abort. The rigorous proof that follows is with elementary manipulations over the probabilities.

The Simulator for V^*

Input: main input $x \in L$ and security parameter 1^λ.

1. The simulator S starts emulating V^* on input x and obtain in response a reference string ref. All commitments in the protocol are done using this reference string, which we omit similarly to the protocol.

2. S chooses $\tilde{w} \in \{0,1\}^m$ and generates k random PRG seeds $s_1, \ldots, s_k \in \{0,1\}^\lambda$.

3. S sends to V^* commitments to all random seeds $\{s_i\}_{i \in [k]}$. In addition, it sends $\tilde{w}_{com} = \tilde{w}_s \oplus G(s_k)$, where $\tilde{w}_s = (\tilde{w} \oplus G(s_1) \oplus \cdots \oplus G(s_{k-1}))$.

4. S emulates with V^* the interactive phase of the GKR protocol as follows: In every round $i \in [r]$, the simulator S randomly chooses $\tilde{m}_i$, and secret shares the message to k shares s.t $\tilde{m}_{i,1} \oplus \cdots \oplus \tilde{m}_{i,k} = \tilde{m}_i$, and sends to V^* commitments to $\tilde{m}_{i,1} \ldots \tilde{m}_{i,k}$. We denote the coins sent from V to P in this stage by $coins_{V^*}$, and the entire interaction in this stage (the commitments to all shares as well as the verifier's coins) by $\widetilde{tr_{GKR}}$.

5. (a) Based on the interaction, S computes $z \in \mathbb{F}^d$ and $\langle C \rangle$ as described in Theorem 10.

   (b) S computes the multi-linear extension of $G(s_1), \ldots, G(s_{k-1})$ and $\tilde{w}_s$ at the point z. That is, for every $j \in [k-1]$, it computes $a_j = \widehat{G(s_j)}[z]$, and additionally computes $a_k = \widehat{\tilde{w}_s}[z]$.

   (c) S chooses a random subset $T_q = [k] \backslash \{q\}$ of $k-1$ parties.

   (d) S computes the inputs for the selected parties as in the protocol, and runs the MPC simulator denoted S_{MPC} on the selected parties' inputs. The MPC simulation is executed wrt the function
   $$V_{post}\left(\left(coins_{V^*}, \bigoplus_{j \in [k]} b_j \right), \langle C \rangle, \bigoplus_{j \in [k]} a_j \right), \text{ where } b_j = (\tilde{m}_{i,j})_{i \in [r]}. \text{ We denote}$$
   S_{MPC}'s output for party $i \in T_q$ by $\widetilde{view}_i$.

   (e) S sets the view of the remaining party q, to a default value, $\widetilde{view}_q = 0^{|view|}$, and sends to V^* commitments to the $k-1$ views generated by S_{MPC} and the view of the remainder party q and all communication channels. Denote these commitments by $com(\widetilde{view}_i)_{i \in [k]}$.

6. V^* responds with a set T_{q*}.

7. If $T_q \neq T_{q*}$, then S outputs $\perp$ and terminates. Otherwise, S outputs $(x, ref, \bar{c}, \tilde{w}_{com}, \widetilde{tr_{GKR}}, \{com(\widetilde{view}_i)\}_{i \in [k]}, T_q, \{dec_S(i), dec_m(i), dec_v(i)s\}_{i \in T})$, where (1) $\bar{c} = com(s_1), \ldots, com(s_k)$, (2) $dec_s(i), dec_m(i), dec_v(i)$ respectively the decommitments to s_i, $\tilde{m}_i$ and party i's view.

Fig. 3. Zero-Knowledge Simulator

We note that all randomness choices are independent, hence using elementary manipulations:

$$\Pr[S = \bot] = \underset{\bar{s},\alpha,\beta,q}{\mathbb{E}} \left[\sum_{q^* \neq q} \Pr\left[V_{q^*}^*(m_{\bar{s},\alpha,\beta}, q)\right] \right]$$

$$\leq \underset{\bar{s},\alpha,\beta,q}{\mathbb{E}} \left[\sum_{q^* \neq q} \left(\Pr[V_{q^*}^*(\bar{0},0)] + \frac{1}{2k^2} \right) \right]$$

$$\leq \underset{\bar{s},\alpha,\beta}{\mathbb{E}} \left[\underset{q}{\mathbb{E}} \left[\sum_{q^* \neq q} \Pr[V_{q^*}^*(\bar{0},0)] \right] \right] + \frac{1}{2k}$$

$$= \underset{\bar{s},\alpha,\beta}{\mathbb{E}} \left[\underset{q^*}{\mathbb{E}} \left[\sum_{q \neq q^*} \Pr\left[V_{q^*}^*(\bar{0},0)\right] \right] \right] + \frac{1}{2k}$$

$$= \underset{\bar{s},\alpha,\beta}{\mathbb{E}} \left[(k-1) \underset{q^*}{\mathbb{E}} \left[\Pr[V_{q^*}^*(\bar{0},0)] \right] \right] + \frac{1}{2k}$$

$$= \underset{\bar{s},\alpha,\beta}{\mathbb{E}} \left[\frac{(k-1)}{k} \right] + \frac{1}{2k}$$

$$= 1 - \frac{1}{2k},$$

and the proposition follows.

Denote by $\bar{S}(x)$ the distribution of $S(x)$ conditioned on $S(x) \neq \bot$ (i.e., conditioned on $T_q = T_{q^*}$).

Proposition 27. *The ensembles $\bar{S}(x)$ and $\{View_{V_*}^{P(w)}(x, \lambda)\}_{x \in L}$ are computationally indistinguishable.*

Proof. Let $T_q \subseteq [k]$ denote the set of parties that the verifier selects, both with respect to the simulator and the prover (note that T_q depends on the previous messages that the prover/simulator sent). For $x \in L$, both $\bar{S}(x)$ and $View_{V_*}^{P(w)}(x, \lambda)_{x \in L}$ are sequences of the following form:

$$\left(x, ref, \bar{c}, w_{com}, \mathrm{tr_{GKR}}, \{com(view_i)\}_{i \in [k]}, T_q, \{dec_S(i), dec_m(i), dec_v(i)\}_{i \in T} \right).$$

Since we fixed (x, w) and ref we omit them from the notation when analyzing these two distributions.

We define for each subset $T_q = [k] \backslash q$ two random variables describing, respectively, the output of $\bar{S}$ and the view of V^* in a real interaction, in the case that the verifier's request equals T_q:

1. Let $\mu_q(x)$ denote the output of $\bar{S}(x)$ conditioned on having the verifier's request in Step 6 equal T_q when interacting with V^*. Let $p_q(x)$ denote the probability that the verifier requests the set T_q when interacting with $\bar{S}(x)$.

2. Let $\nu_q(x)$ denote $View_{V^*}^{P(w)}(x)$ conditioned on $View_{V^*}^{P(w)}(x)$ having the verifier's request in Step 6 in the protocol (i.e., when interacting with $P(x,w)$) equal T_q. Let $f_q(x)$ denote the probability that V^* selects T_q when interacting with $P(x,w)$ in the protocol.

Assume toward a contradiction that the two ensembles in the statement of the claim are distinguishible. Then one of the following cases must occur.

Case 1: There exists $q \in [k]$ such that $|p_q - f_q|$ is non-negligible. To show that Case 1 leads to a contradiction, we first argue that the part of the interaction up to the opening of the commitment is computationally indistinguishible. This is is captured by the following claim.

Claim. It holds that $(\bar{c}, \tilde{w}_{com}, \widetilde{tr_{GKR}}, com(\widetilde{view}_i)_{i\in[k]}) \stackrel{c}{\approx} (\bar{c}, w_{com}, tr_{GKR}, com(view_i)_{i\in[k]})$, where $\bar{c} = (com(s_1), \ldots, com(s_k))$.

Section 4.1 follows in a straightforward manner from hiding property of the commitment scheme and so we defer its proof to Sect. 4.1.1.

Assuming Case 1 occurs, we can build a (non-uniform) distinguisher between the two distributions by feeding V^* with the distribution and seeing whether it outputs q, the distinguisher output 1 if q was chosen and 0 otherwise thus case 1 leads to contradiction.

Case 2: If we are not in Case 1, then, loosely speaking, for every q it holds that

$$|p_q(x) - f_q(x)| \le \frac{1}{\text{poly}(|x|)}.$$

Since we assumed the ensembles are distinguisible, by an averaging argument, there exists some $q \in [k]$ for which p_q and f_q are close and yet the distinguisher is able to distinguish even conditioned on this value of q. Formally, there exists a probabilistic polynomial-time algorithm A, a polynomial $p(\cdot)$, and an infinite sequence of integers such that for each integer n (in the sequence) there exists an $x, |x| = n$ and a set of parties T_q such that the following conditions hold[9]:

1. $f_q(x) > \frac{1}{2 \cdot p(n)}$,
2. $|p_q(x) - f_q(x)| < \frac{1}{8 \cdot p(n)^2}$,
3. $|\Pr[A(\mu_q(x)) = 1] - \Pr[A(\nu_q(x)) = 1]| > \frac{1}{2 \cdot p(n)}$.

We proceed to show that Case 2 leads to a contradiction to the following claim,

---

[9] The conditions follows from the fact that A distinguishes the two distributions and that Case 1 does not hold. From an averaging argument, there exist a player $q \in [k]$ s.t $\left| f_q(x) \cdot \Pr[A(\mu_q(x))] - p_q(x) \cdot \Pr[A(\nu_q(x))] \right| \ge \frac{1}{p(n)}$. Now for Item 2 we use the fact that Case 1 does not hold, using a suitably large polynomial. Now we conclude that $\left| f_q(x) \cdot \Pr[A(\mu_q(x))] - f_q(x) \cdot \Pr[A(\nu_q(x))] \right| \ge \frac{1}{2 \cdot p(n)}$ and Items 1 and 3 follow.

Claim. Let $T_q = [k] \setminus \{q\}$ be a fixed set of parties, denote:

H_0

$$= \left(\bar{c}, \tilde{w}_{com}, \widetilde{\mathsf{tr}_{\mathsf{GKR}}}, \{com(\widetilde{view}_i)\}_{i \in [T_q]}, com(\widetilde{view}_q), T_q, \{dec_S(i), dec_m(i), dec_v(i)\}_{i \in T_q} \right)$$

H_1

$$= \left(\bar{c}, w_{com}, \widetilde{\mathsf{tr}_{\mathsf{GKR}}}, \{com(\widetilde{view}_i)\}_{i \in [T_q]}, com(view_q), T_q, \{dec_S(i), dec_m(i), dec_v(i)\}_{i \in T_q} \right)$$

then, $H_0 \overset{c}{\approx} H_1$.

We yet again defer the proof of the claim to Sect. 4.1.2 and proceed directly to showing why it leads to a contradiction. Namely, we use A to construct a distinguisher A' that distinguishes between H_0 and H_1 thereby contradicting Sect. 4.1. Consider A' that emulates the simulator and checks if T_q was chosen by V^*. If so A' runs A on its input (which is sampled either from H_0 or H_1). Otherwise A' outputs 0.

We proceed to show that A' indeed distinguishes between these two distributions:

$$\left| \Pr[A'(H_0)] - \Pr[A'(H_1)] \right|$$
$$= \left| f_q(x) \cdot \Pr[A(\mu_q(x))] - p_q(x) \cdot \Pr[A(\nu_q(x))] \right|$$
$$\geq f_q(x) \cdot \left| \Pr[A(\mu_q(x))] - \Pr[A(\nu_q(x))] \right| - \Pr[A(\nu_q(x))] \cdot \left| p_q(x) - f_q(x) \right|$$
$$\geq f_q(x) \cdot \left| \Pr[A(\mu_q(x))] - \Pr[A(\nu_q(x))] \right| - \left| p_q(x) - f_q(x) \right|$$
$$> \frac{1}{2 \cdot p(n)} \cdot \frac{1}{2 \cdot p(n)} - \frac{1}{8 \cdot p(n)^2}$$
$$= \frac{1}{8 \cdot p(n)^2},$$

where the first inequality follows from the (reverse) triangle inequality and the third inequality from the above distance bound on p_q vs. f_q. Thus, A' distinguishes between H_0 and H_1 with non-negligible probability, in contradiction to Sect. 4.1.

This concludes the proof of Proposition 27.

4.1.1   Proof of Section 4.1

The proof is via a hybrid argument. Define:

$$H_0 := \left(\bar{c}, \tilde{w}_{com}, \widetilde{\mathsf{tr}_{\mathsf{GKR}}}, com(\widetilde{view}_i)_{i \in [k]} \right),$$
$$H_1 := \left(\bar{c}, w_{com}, \widetilde{\mathsf{tr}_{\mathsf{GKR}}}, com(\widetilde{view}_i)_{i \in [k]} \right),$$
$$H_2 := \left(\bar{c}, w_{com}, \mathsf{tr}_{\mathsf{GKR}}, com(view_i)_{i \in [k]} \right).$$

We show that H_0 and H_2 are both indistinguishable from H_1, from which the claim follows.

$H_0 \overset{c}{\approx} H_1$: Assume towards a contradiction that the distributions are computationally distinguishable. Then, since the only difference between the hybrids lies in $\tilde{w}_{com}$ versus w_{com}, there exists a distinguisher D that distinguishes between $(\tilde{w}_{com})$ and w_{com}. (recall $w_{com} = w_s \oplus G(s_k)$, where $w_s = (w \oplus G(s_1) \oplus \cdots \oplus G(s_{k-1}))$, and $\tilde{w}_{com} = \tilde{w}_s \oplus G(s_k)$, where $\tilde{w}_s = (\tilde{w} \oplus G(s_1) \oplus \cdots \oplus G(s_{k-1}))$. We construct D' that distinguishes between U_n and $G(U_{|\lambda|})$. We give D' the non-uniform advice (x, w).

The distinguisher D', given an input $r \in \{0,1\}^m$, chooses $s_1, \ldots, s_{k-1}$, and runs D on the input $\hat{w}_{com} = r \oplus (w \oplus G(s_1) \oplus \cdots \oplus G(s_{k-1}))$ and outputs the result. If r is sampled from U_n, then $\hat{w}_{com}$ will also be a random element of U_n and thus $\hat{w}_{com}$ will be of the same distribution as $\tilde{w}_{com}$. On the other hand, if r is sampled from $G(U_{|\lambda|})$ then $\hat{w}_{com}$ is the same distribution as w_{com}. So D' will be able to distinguish with the same probability as D, in contradiction to the pseudorandomness of G.

$H_1 \overset{c}{\approx} H_2$: Due to the hiding property of the commitment, for any two strings $m_1, m_2 \in \{0,1\}^*$ and any common reference string ref, the distribution of the commitment of m_1 and m_2 are computationally indistinguishable. Thus the commitments of the simulator are computationally indistinguishable from the commitments to in the real interaction.

4.1.2   Proof of Section 4.1

We first show that the inputs and views of the parties selected in the set T_q are computationally indistinguishable in the two cases: that is, when V^* interacts with P vs. its interaction with S.

For simplicity of notation we will assume without loss of generality that $q = 1$ and we use T to denote the selected set $T = \{2, \ldots, k\}$. Thus, we need to show that

$$\left((s_i)_{i \in T}, \tilde{w}_s, (\tilde{m}_i)_{i \in T}, \widetilde{(view_i)}_{i \in [T]} \right) \overset{c}{\approx} \left((s_i)_{i \in t}, w_s, (m_i)_{i \in T}, (view_i)_{i \in [T]} \right),$$

where recall that for $i \in T$:

- m_i is the share for party i of the GKR message in the real interaction (Fig. 2, Step 4) and $\tilde{m}_i$ is is the corresponding share of a random message, in the simulation (Fig. 3, Step 4).
- $\widetilde{input}_i$ is the input to party i in the MPC protocol, derived by the simulator in Fig. 3, Step 5d . That is, $\widetilde{input}_i = \left(\widetilde{G(s_i)}(z), \tilde{m}_i \right)$, for $i \neq k$ and $\widetilde{input}_k = \left(\widetilde{\tilde{w}_s}(z), \tilde{m}_k \right)$.
- $\widetilde{view}_i$ consists of the input for party i followed by the output of S_{MPC} for the party i. Thus, $\left\{ \widetilde{(view_i)} \right\}_{i \in [T]} = \left(\widetilde{(input_i)}_{i \in T}, S_{MPC}\left(\widetilde{(input_i)}_{i \in T} \right) \right)$.
- $input_i$ is the input to party i in the MPC protocol in the real interation, Fig. 2, Step 5c . Thus, $input_i = \left(s\widetilde{(G(s_i)}(z), m_i \right)$ for $i \neq k$, and $input_k = \left(\widetilde{w_s}(z), m_k \right)$.
- $view_i$ is $input_i$ followed by the view of that party in the MPC protocol (all in the real interaction).

We first show the distribution of the inputs and views of the parties in T are computationally indistinguishable in the two cases. We then conclude that the commitment and decommitment to those distributions are also computationally indistinguishable. Finally, we show we can add to those distributions the commitment of the remaining party and $coins_{V^*}$ sent by V^* in Step 4 and the claim follows.

The proof is via a hybrid argument. Consider the following hybrid distributions:

$$H_0 := \left((s_i)_{i \in T}, \tilde{w}_s, (\tilde{m}_i)_{i \in T}, \{ \widetilde{(view_i)} \}_{i \in [T]} \right)$$

$$= \left((s_i)_{i \in T}, \tilde{w}_s, (\tilde{m}_i)_{i \in T}, ((\widetilde{input_i})_{i \in T}, S_{MPC}((\widetilde{input_i})_{i \in T})) \right)$$

$$H_1 := \left((s_i)_{i \in T}, w_s, (\tilde{m}_i)_{i \in T}, ((\overline{input_i})_{i \in T}, S_{MPC}((\overline{input_i})_{i \in T})) \right),$$

where for $i \neq k$, $(\overline{input_i}) = \left(\widehat{G(s_i)}(z)), \tilde{m}_i \right)$, and $(\overline{input_k}) = \left(\widehat{w_s}(z)), \tilde{m}_k \right)$

$$H_2 := \left((s_i)_{i \in T}, w_s, (m_i)_{i \in T}, ((input_i)_{i \in T}, S_{MPC}((input_i)_{i \in T})) \right),$$

$$H_3 := \left((s_i)_{i \in T}, w_s, (m_i)_{i \in T}, \{ (view_i) \}_{i \in [T]} \right).$$

$H_0 \overset{c}{\approx} H_1$: We first show that $(s_2, \ldots, s_{k-1}, \tilde{w}_s) \overset{c}{\approx} (s_2, \ldots, s_{k-1}, w_s)$. Assume there exists a distinguisher D that distinguishes between $(s_2, \ldots, s_{k-1}, \tilde{w}_s)$ and $(s_2, \ldots, s_{k-1}, w_s)$ with non-negligible advantage. Recall that $\tilde{w}_s = (\tilde{w} \oplus G(s_1) \oplus \cdots \oplus G(s_{k-1}))$ and $w_s = (w \oplus G(s_1) \oplus \cdots \oplus G(s_{k-1}))$.

We construct D' that distinguishes between U_n and $G(U_{|\lambda|})$. We give D' the non-uniform advice (x, w). The distinguisher D', given as input $r \in \{0, 1\}^m$, generates $s_2, \ldots, s_{k-1} \in \{0, 1\}^{\{|\lambda|\}}$, then computes $G(s_2) \ldots G(s_{k-1})$ and runs D on input $(s_2 \ldots, s_{k-1}, \bar{w}_s)$, where $\bar{w}_s = r \oplus (w \oplus G(s_2) \oplus \cdots \oplus G(s_{k-1}))$ and outputs the result. If r is sampled from U_n, then $\bar{w}_s$ will also be a random element of U_n and thus $\bar{w}_s$ will be of the same distribution as $\tilde{w}_s$. On the other hand, if r is sampled from $G(U_{|\lambda|})$ then $\bar{w}_s$ is the same distribution as w_s. So D' will be able to distinguish with the same probability as D, in contradiction to the pseudorandomness of G.

Observe that H_0 and H_1 are obtained from the two distributions above via the same procedure. Namely, $(\widetilde{input_i})_{i \in T}$ and $(\overline{input_i})_{i \in T}$ are computed by applying G on the seeds and computing the multi-linear extension at the point z, followed by, either $\tilde{w}_s(z), (\tilde{m}_i)_{i \in T}$ or $\widehat{w_s}(z), (\tilde{m}_i)_{i \in T}$. Then, in the same way run S_{MPC} on $(\widetilde{input_i})_{i \in T}$ and $(\overline{input_i})_{i \in T}$). Hence, using Theorem 8, since G, the multi-linear extension and S_{MPC} are PPT algorithms, we conclude that $H_0 \overset{c}{\approx} H_1$.

$H_1 \equiv H_2$: Recall $(m_i)_{i \in [k]}$ is the distribution of the additive secret sharing of the GKR messages as in Fig. 2, Step 4 , whereas $(\tilde{m}_i)_{i \in [k]}$ is the distribution of a secret sharing of a random message in Fig. 3, Step 4 .

Since the restriction of an additive secret sharing to any set of $k - 1$ shares is uniformly random, it follows that $(m_i)_{i \in T}$ is distributed identically to $(\tilde{m}_i)_{i \in T}$.

Thus, since the rest of the distributions are simply computed in the same manner for both distributions similarly to the previous case, we conclude $H_1 \equiv H_2$.

$H_2 \equiv H_3$ By the $(k-1)$-privacy of the MPC protocol (see Definition 22 and Theorem 23), it holds that $\{(view_i)\}_{i \in [T]}$ is distributed identically to $S_{MPC}((input_i)_{i \in T})$. Thus, since the input and the rest of the hybrids are identical in the two cases, we have that $H_2 \equiv H_3$.

Thus, we conclude that $H_0 \overset{c}{\approx} H_3$. Denote:

$$C_0 := \left(com(s_2), \ldots \tilde{w}_{com}, com(s_k), com(\tilde{m}_2) \ldots com(\tilde{m}_k), \{com(\widetilde{view_i})\}_{i \in [T]}, \overline{dec} \right)$$

$$C_1 := \left(com(s_2), \ldots w_{com}, com(s_k), com(m_2) \ldots com(m_k), \{com(view_i)\}_{i \in [T]}, \overline{dec} \right),$$

where $\overline{dec} = \{dec_S(i), dec_m(i), dec_v(i)\}_{i \in T}$ and $dec_s(i)$, $dec_m(i)$, $dec_v(i)$ are the decommitments to s_i, $\tilde{m}_i$ and party i's view, respectively.

Observe that C_0 (resp., C_1) is computed from H_0 (resp., H_3) by the same procedure – namely, committing to the seeds, $(\tilde{m}_i)_{i \in T}$ (resp., $(m_i)_{i \in T}$) and $(\widetilde{view_i})_{i \in T}$ (resp., $(view_i)_{i \in T}$), generating a random seed s_k and computing $\tilde{w}_{com} = \tilde{w}_s \oplus G(s_k)$ (resp., $w_{com} = w_s \oplus G(s_k)$). Thus, by Theorem 8, we conclude that $C_0 \overset{c}{\approx} C_1$.

Finally, from Theorem 20 we can add the commitment to the input of the remaining party $j = 1$, i.e.:

$$(C_0, com(s_1), com(\tilde{m}_1), com(\widetilde{view_1})) \overset{c}{\approx} (C_1, com(s_1), com(m_1), com(view_1)).$$

The remaining difference between the claim and what we have proved are $\mathsf{tr}_{\mathsf{GKR}}$ and $\widetilde{\mathsf{tr}_{\mathsf{GKR}}}$. Recall that $\mathsf{tr}_{\mathsf{GKR}} = (com(m_1), \ldots, com(m_k), coins_{V^*})$, and $\widetilde{\mathsf{tr}_{\mathsf{GKR}}} = (com(\tilde{m}_1), \ldots, com(\tilde{m}_k), coins_{V^*})$, where $coins_{V^*}$ are the strings sent by V^* in step 4 . From Section 4.1, the interaction up to the opening of the commitment is computationally indistinguishable between the interaction with P and $\bar{S}$. Therefore, $coins_{V^*}$ are also indistinguishable between the interaction of V^* with P and $\bar{S}$. Hence, we can add $coins_{V^*}$ to the distributions, and the claim follows.

Acknowledgements. We thank Yuval Ishai for useful discussions, and the anonymous reviewers insightful comments.

Noor Athamnah and Ron Rothblum are funded by the European Union (ERC, FASTPROOF, 101041208). Views and opinions expressed are however those of the author(s) only and do not necessarily reflect those of the European Union or the European Research Council. Neither the European Union nor the granting authority can be held responsible for them.

References

[BFLS91] Babai, L., Fortnow, L., Levin, L.A., Szegedy, M.: Checking computations in polylogarithmic time. In: Koutsougeras, C., Vitter, J.S. (eds.) Proceedings of the 23rd Annual ACM Symposium on Theory of Computing, 5-8 May 1991, New Orleans, Louisiana, USA, pp. 21–31. ACM (1991)

[Blu86] Blum, M.: How to prove a theorem so no one else can claim it. In: Proceedings of the International Congress of Mathematicians, vol. 1, p. 2. Citeseer (1986)

[BV11] Brakerski, Z., Vaikuntanathan, V.: Efficient fully homomorphic encryption from (standard) LWE. In: Ostrovsky, R. (ed.) IEEE 52nd Annual Symposium on Foundations of Computer Science, FOCS 2011, Palm Springs, CA, USA, 22-25 October 2011, pp. 97–106. IEEE Computer Society (2011)

[CLTV15] Canetti, R., Lin, H., Tessaro, S., Vaikuntanathan, V.: Obfuscation of probabilistic circuits and applications. In: Dodis, Y., Nielsen, J.B. (eds.) TCC 2015. LNCS, vol. 9015, pp. 468–497. Springer, Heidelberg (2015). https://doi.org/10.1007/978-3-662-46497-7_19

[DI06] Damgård, I., Ishai, Y.: Scalable secure multiparty computation. In: Dwork, C. (ed.) CRYPTO 2006. LNCS, vol. 4117, pp. 501–520. Springer, Heidelberg (2006). https://doi.org/10.1007/11818175_30

[Gen09] Gentry, C.: A fully homomorphic encryption scheme. PhD thesis, Stanford University, USA (2009)

[GGI+15] Gentry, C., Groth, J., Ishai, Y., Peikert, C., Sahai, A., Smith, A.D.: Using fully homomorphic hybrid encryption to minimize non-interactive zero-knowledge proofs. J. Cryptol. 28(4), 820–843 (2015)

[GGM86] Goldreich, O., Goldwasser, S., Micali, S.: How to construct random functions. J. ACM 33(4), 792–807 (1986)

[GH98] Goldreich, O., Håstad, J.: On the complexity of interactive proofs with bounded communication. Inf. Process. Lett. 67(4), 205–214 (1998)

[GKR15] Goldwasser, S., Kalai, Y.T., Rothblum, G.N.: Delegating computation: interactive proofs for Muggles. J. ACM 62(4), 27:1–27:64 (2015)

[GMR89] Goldwasser, S., Micali, S., Rackoff, C.: The knowledge complexity of interactive proof systems. SIAM J. Comput. 18(1), 186–208 (1989)

[GMW86] Goldreich, O., Micali, S., Wigderson, A.: How to prove all NP-statements in zero-knowledge, and a methodology of cryptographic protocol design. In: Odlyzko, A.M. (ed.) Advances in Cryptology - CRYPTO '86, Santa Barbara, California, USA, 1986, Proceedings, vol. 263 of LNCS, pp. 171–185. Springer, Heidelberg(1986)

[GMW87] Goldreich, O., Micali, S., Wigderson, A.: How to play any mental game or A completeness theorem for protocols with honest majority. In: Aho, A.V. (ed.) Proceedings of the 19th Annual ACM Symposium on Theory of Computing, 1987, New York, New York, USA, pp. 218–229. ACM (1987)

[Gol01] Goldreich, O.: The Foundations of Cryptography - Volume 1: Basic Techniques. Cambridge University Press (2001)

[GR17] Gur, T., Rothblum, R.D.: A hierarchy theorem for interactive proofs of proximity. In: Papadimitriou, C.H. (ed.) 8th Innovations in Theoretical Computer Science Conference, ITCS 2017, 9-11 January 2017, Berkeley, CA, USA, vol. 67 of LIPIcs, pp. 39:1–39:43. Schloss Dagstuhl - Leibniz-Zentrum für Informatik (2017)

[GVW02] Goldreich, O., Vadhan, S.P., Wigderson, A.: On interactive proofs with a laconic prover. Comput. Complex. **11**(1–2), 1–53 (2002)

[HILL99] Håstad, J., Impagliazzo, R., Levin, L.A., Luby, M.: A pseudorandom generator from any one-way function. SIAM J. Comput. **28**(4), 1364–1396 (1999)

[HLR21] Justin Holmgren, Alex Lombardi, and Ron D. Rothblum. Fiat-Shamir via list-recoverable codes (or: parallel repetition of GMW is not zero-knowledge). In: Khuller, S., Williams, V.V. (eds.) STOC 2021: 53rd Annual ACM SIGACT Symposium on Theory of Computing, Virtual Event, Italy, 21-25 June 2021, pp. 750–760. ACM (2021)

[HN24] Hirahara, S., Nanashima, M.: One-way functions and zero knowledge (2024)

[HVW23] Hazay, C., Venkitasubramaniam, M., Weiss, M.: Beyond MPC-in-the-head: black-box constructions of short zero-knowledge proofs. In: Rothblum, G.N., Wee, H. (eds.) Theory of Cryptography - 21st International Conference, TCC 2023, Taipei, Taiwan, November 29 - December 2, 2023, Proceedings, Part I, vol. 14369 of LNCS, pp. 3–33. Springer, Cham (2023). https://doi.org/10.1007/978-3-031-48615-9_1

[IKOS09] Ishai, Y., Kushilevitz, E., Ostrovsky, R., Sahai, A.: Zero-knowledge proofs from secure multiparty computation. SIAM J. Comput. **39**(3), 1121–1152 (2009)

[IP99] Impagliazzo, R. and Paturi, R.: Complexity of k-SAT. In: Proceedings of the 14th Annual IEEE Conference on Computational Complexity, Atlanta, Georgia, USA, May 4-6, 1999, pp. 237–240. IEEE Computer Society (1999)

[Kil92] Kilian, J.: A note on efficient zero-knowledge proofs and arguments (extended abstract). In: Kosaraju, S.R., Fellows, M., Wigderson, A., Ellis, J.A. (eds.) Proceedings of the 24th Annual ACM Symposium on Theory of Computing, May 4-6, 1992, Victoria, British Columbia, Canada, pp. 723–732. ACM (1992)

[KR08] Kalai, Y.T., Raz, R.: Interactive PCP. In: Aceto, L., Damgård, I., Goldberg, L.A., Halldórsson, M.M., Ingólfsdóttir, A., Walukiewicz, I. (eds.) ICALP 2008. LNCS, vol. 5126, pp. 536–547. Springer, Heidelberg (2008). https://doi.org/10.1007/978-3-540-70583-3_44

[KRV24] Keret, O., Rothblum, R.D., Vasudevan, P.N.: Doubly-efficient batch verification in statistical zero-knowledge. IACR Cryptol. ePrint Arch., p. 781 (2024)

[MV24] Micciancio, D., Vaikuntanathan, V.: SoK: learning with errors, circular security, and fully homomorphic encryption. In: Tang Q., Teague, V. (eds.) Public-Key Cryptography - PKC 2024 - 27th IACR International Conference on Practice and Theory of Public-Key Cryptography, Sydney, NSW, Australia, April 15-17, 2024, Proceedings, Part IV, vol. 14604 of LNCS, pp. 291–321. Springer (2024). https://doi.org/10.1007/978-3-031-57728-4_10

[Nao91] Naor, M.: Bit commitment using pseudorandomness. J. Cryptol. **4**(2), 151–158 (1991). https://doi.org/10.1007/BF00196774

[NR22] Nassar, S., Rothblum, R.D.: Succinct interactive oracle proofs: applications and limitations. In: Dodis, Y., Shrimpton, T. (eds.) Advances in Cryptology - CRYPTO 2022 - 42nd Annual International Cryptology Conference, CRYPTO 2022, Santa Barbara, CA, USA, 15-18 August 2022, Proceedings, Part I, volume 13507 of LNCS, pp. 504–532. Springer (2022). https://doi.org/10.1007/978-3-031-15802-5_18

[OW93] Ostrovsky, R., Wigderson, A.: One-way functions are essential for non-trivial zero-knowledge. In: Second Israel Symposium on Theory of Computing Systems, ISTCS 1993, Natanya, Israel, 7-9 June 1993, Proceedings, pp. 3–17. IEEE Computer Society (1993)

[Ros12] Rosulek, M.: Must you know the code of f to securely compute f? In: Safavi-Naini, R., Canetti, R. (eds.) CRYPTO 2012. LNCS, vol. 7417, pp. 87–104. Springer, Heidelberg (2012). https://doi.org/10.1007/978-3-642-32009-5_7

[RR20] Ron-Zewi, N., Rothblum, R.: Local proofs approaching the witness length. In: Irani, S. (ed.) 61st IEEE Annual Symposium on Foundations of Computer Science, FOCS 2020, Durham, NC, USA, November 16-19, 2020, pp. 846–857. IEEE (2020)

[RRR21] Reingold, O., Rothblum, G.N., Rothblum, R.D.: Constant-round interactive proofs for delegating computation. SIAM J. Comput. **50**(3), 49–62 (2021)

Consensus and Messaging

Consensus in the Presence of Overlapping Faults and Total Omission

Julian Loss[1], Kecheng Shi[1,3], and Gilad Stern[2]

[1] CISPA Helmholtz Center for Information Security, Saarbrücken, Germany
[2] Tel Aviv University, Tel Aviv, Israel
gilad.stern@mail.huji.ac.il
[3] Saarland University, Saarbrücken, Germany

Abstract. Understanding the fault tolerance of Byzantine Agreement protocols is an important question in distributed computing. While the setting of Byzantine faults has been thoroughly explored in the literature, the (arguably more realistic) omission fault setting is far less studied. In this paper, we revisit the recent work of Loss and Stern who gave the first protocol in the mixed fault model tolerating t Byzantine faults, s send faults, and r receive faults, when $2t + r + s < n$ and omission faults do not overlap. We observe that their protocol makes no guarantees when omission faults can overlap, i.e., when parties can simultaneously have send and receive faults. We give the first protocol that overcomes this limitation and tolerates the same number of potentially overlapping faults. We then study, for the first time, the *total omission setting* where all parties can become omission faulty. This setting is motivated by real-world scenarios where every party may experience connectivity issues from time to time, yet agreement should still hold for the parties who manage to output values. We show the first agreement protocol in this setting with parameters $s < n$ and $s+r = n$. On the other hand, we prove that there is no consensus protocol for the total omission setting which tolerates even a single overlapping omission fault, i.e., where $s+r = n+1$ and $s > 2$, or a broadcast protocol for $s + r = n$ and $s > 1$ even without overlapping faults.

1 Introduction

Consensus is a fundamental problem in distributed computing that asks a set of n parties to agree on a common output. Their task is complicated by a subset of faulty parties who interfere with the honest parties' execution of the consensus protocol by sending incorrect messages or simply crashing. Consensus serves as a key building block in various applications such as verifiable secret sharing, MPC, state-machine replication, and more. The overwhelming majority of the literature considers protocols for the fully malicious (a.k.a. Byzantine) setting, where nodes can exhibit arbitrary behaviour. These protocols offer a high degree of security, which may be justified in high-stakes applications such as blockchain systems or reliable databases. On the other hand, the fault tolerance of such

E. Boyle and M. Mahmoody (Eds.): TCC 2024, LNCS 15364, pp. 353–382, 2025.
https://doi.org/10.1007/978-3-031-78011-0_12

protocols is also inherently limited. Indeed, it is well-known that in the plain model without setup, consensus can be solved if and only if the number t of (maliciously) faulty parties satisfies $t < n/3$. While this can be ameliorated by relying on cryptographic setup such as digital signatures, it can be shown that even given these additional tools, consensus can be achieved if and only if $t < n/2$. A natural question is therefore whether a higher fault tolerance can be achieved if the faulty parties' deviant behaviour is restricted in some manner. One of the most important types of faults one can consider in this context are *omission faults*. Omission faults are parties who run the protocol code honestly, but for which some of the protocol messages may get lost during sending (send omission) or during receiving (receive omission). On one hand, omission faults model a realistic network setting where intermittent failures may occur. On the other hand, consensus can be solved for any number of omission faults $o < n$ (assuming a synchronous network). Moreover, under some conditions, it is even possible to guarantee *uniformity*, meaning that any omission faulty party that does output, does so in agreement with honest parties [21,23,29]. In this work, we significantly advance our understanding of the omission fault setting by showing the following results:

- We begin by revisiting the recent work of Loss and Stern [19] who consider a model with mixed types of faults. More precisely, their work gives the first protocol tolerating (simultaneously) t Byzantine faults, r receive faults (for whom the adversary can drop arbitrary incoming messages), and s send faults (for whom the adversary can drop arbitrary outgoing messages), s.t. $2t + r + s < n$. We observe that their protocol does not work when faults can be *overlapping*, i.e., when a party can become both receive and send faulty at the same time. To overcome this limitation, we give a novel consensus protocol which tolerates the same number of faults, but allows to count overlapping faults twice (i.e., as both send- and receive faulty) in the above formula.
- In the second part of our paper, we study consensus in a setting where *every party* can be *either* send faulty *or* receive faulty, i.e., $r + s \leq n$. This setting is motivated by the fact that, from time to time, every party may experience connectivity issues and lose messages. In this case, we would still like to guarantee that for parties who successfully complete the protocol, their output satisfies the usual requirements of a consensus protocol. On the positive side, we give the first protocol in this setting achieving consensus. An interesting feature of our protocol is that it runs in only $O(s)$ many rounds and achieves perfect security. On the negative side, we show that there is no broadcast protocol in this setting when $s > 1$. Additionally, whenever $s > 2$ there is no protocol tolerating even a *single overlapping omission fault*, i.e., where $s + r = n + 1$.

1.1   Our Techniques

We now give a technical overview of our results. '

Zombies and Ghosts. Our work builds on the ideas of Zikas, Hauser and Maurer [29] and of Loss and Stern [19]. Zikas *et al.* constructed an information theoretic consensus protocol resilient to t Byzantine corruptions, s send corruptions and r receive corruptions when $n > 3t + r + s$. At the base of their constructions, they utilized the idea of *self-detection*. When a party s sends a message m directly to some party p, p might not receive m for two possible reasons: p might be receive faulty or s might be Byzantine or send faulty (or both). In order to help party p self-detect as receive faulty in the above scenario, s instead relays m to p through every other party in the network. If p is *not* receive faulty, it receives messages from many other parties containing either m or a notification that s did not send a message to p. On the other hand, if p *is* receive faulty, it may receive only very few messages. In the latter scenario, p can detect that it is receive faulty. It then becomes a *zombie*, and stops participating in the protocol in order to make sure it does not harm the rest of network by propagating messages that are inconsistent with honest parties' protocol states.

The work of Loss and Stern generalizes these ideas to the cryptographic setting, assuming $n > 2t + r + s$. The novelty of their construction is a means for send faulty parties to detect themselves, upon which they become *ghosts* and stop participating in the protocol. As before, parties in their protocol send messages to each other through the whole network in order to allow for receive faulty parties to detect themselves as zombies. However, in their protocol, parties also reply to the sender, allowing it to learn whether it succeeded in sending its message or whether it should abort by becoming a ghost. If a sender s receives very few of these abort messages, it knows that its message was delivered to at least one non-faulty party p, who will then be able to propagate it to the rest of the network. These ideas are used in their most basic primitive, a weak multicast protocol (WMC). In WMC, the sender s either successfully delivers its message m to at least one non-faulty party or detects itself as send-faulty.

Additional Challenges with Full-Omission Faults. We notice that the WMC protocol of Loss and Stern (and by extension, all protocols building on top of it) does not cover the most general type of omission fault which cause a party to become simultaneously send- *and* receive faulty, i.e., full-omission faulty. Specifically, when the sender s in their WMC protocol is full-omission faulty, it may not receive the abort messages that non-faulty parties send back to s when they did not receive its message. This prevents s from detecting itself as faulty and becoming a ghost. Dealing with this issue turns out to be very subtle. We devise a novel WMC protocol that leverages additional communication among the receivers, so as to help the sender s detect itself as faulty.

In more detail, parties that do not receive messages from s inform each other of this fact in the form of "abort" messages. Now any party p that is *exclusively* send faulty must have received all abort messages from all non-faulty parties. In the last step of our protocol parties then forward a list of *all* of the abort messages they received back to s. This allows us to modify the conditions under which s turns itself a ghost compared to the protocol of Loss and Stern. Namely, our protocol counts the *total number* of abort messages received directly *or* indirectly through the above mechanism. In this manner, we force the adversary into the following dilemma. Either, it drops a large number of messages to s in the last step of the protocol. This causes the sender to infer that it must be receive faulty and turn itself a zombie. Alternatively, the adversary delivers the collection of abort messages assembled by at least one party that received all abort messages from all non-faulty parties back to s. This, on the other hand, will make s detect itself as send-faulty and turn itself a ghost. In summary, our WMC allows even a full-omission faulty sender to either send its message to at least one non-faulty party, or turn detect itself as send or receive faulty by the end of the protocol. Using our new protocol, it is possible to construct an undead graded multicast protocol, as defined in Loss and Stern's work [19]. The construction is provided Appendix C and is very similar to the construction in [19], with very slight changes to the validity condition. The undead graded multicast protocol can be used as a drop in replacement for calls to GMC in the protocols of Loss and Stern. In this manner, we can easily carry over the their consensus protocol to the full-omission setting.

Total Omission Setting. In the second technical part of our work, we initiate the study of a setting in which *all parties* could be omission faulty. This is a very realistic setting that is based on the observation that in practice, it may be very difficult to guarantee permanent connectivity of any of the individual protocol participants. In this case, we would still like a protocol that ensures uniformity, i.e., that parties who output are in consensus with each other. We design a uniform consensus protocol resilient to any s send faults and r receive faults s.t. $s + r = n$ and $s < n$. For completeness, we also show that no such protocol exists if $s = n$. This slighlty strengthens a previous result of Hadzilacos [15]who showed that no broadcast protocol exists when $s = n$. We remark that one could imagine a setting where $s + r > n$ without overlapping faults, in which the adversary has the flexibility to choose the *actual* number of corrupted parties of each kind. We do not address this setting in our paper, but believe that this is a very interesting direction for future work.

An interesting question that arises as a consequence of studying the total omission setting is how it relates to the work of Eldefrawy *et al.* [11]. Their work includes a lower bound showing that $n > 2t + r + s$ is a necessary condition for consensus. Namely, their bound is stated in a model which allows the adversary to forcibly "zombify" receive faulty parties at the onset of the protocol, upon which they cease any subsequent participation.

This severely limits the generality of protocols covered by this lower bound, since some protocols might have parties send messages even after detecting their own faults. In particular, our protocol for the total omission setting heavily relies on parties who have detected themselves as zombies to continue assisting in the rest of the protocol.

Impossibility Results. We complement our study of the total omission setting by proving two impossibility results. This helps us fill in some of the gaps in our current understanding of the task of consensus.

- Although we construct a uniform consensus protocol with in the total omissions setting, surprisingly, we show that it is impossible to construct a broadcast protocol in this setting whenever $s > 1$. We briefly illustrate why this is the case. Our consensus protocol relies heavily on the capability of the receive faulty parties to distribute their initial inputs to the non-receive faulty protocol parties. This approach fails completely for a broadcast protocol, since only the sender has input.
- Our second impossibility result shows that it is generally impossible to construct a uniform consensus protocol if $s + r > n$ and $s > 2$. This shows our protocol has the optimal corruption threshold.

1.2   Related Work

The study of consensus protocols, and the related study of broadcast protocols, has a long history [9,12,16,20]. Early results dealt with constructing protocols for systems with a single type of failure. For example, Hadzilacos [15] showed that broadcast is possible in a system of s send faulty parties if and only if $n > s$. Following that, Perry and Toueg [22] shows that broadcast is possible in systems with o general omission faults if $n > o$, while not requiring uniformity, i.e., where omission faulty parties output the correct values. When considering protocols that do require uniformity of outputs, works by Raynal and Parvédy [21,23] showed that consensus is possible if and only if $n > 2o$. Dolev and Strong [9] showed that a similar result holds for Byzantine authenticated broadcast (i.e. with a PKI setup) can be solved in the presence of t Byzantine faults if $n > t+1$. On the other hand, Lamport, Shostak and Pease [16] showed that Byzantine consensus can be solved if $n > 3t$ in the unauthenticated setting and $n > 2t$ in the authenticated setting.

Later work also dealt with constructing such protocols in networks of mixed faults. Garay and Perry [13] constructed a consensus protocol resilient to t Byzantine parties and c crash faulty parties that can crash in any point in time and stop participating in the protocol, assuming that $n > 3t + c$. Siu, Chin and Yang [26] strengthened this result and constructed a consensus protocol resilient to t Byzantine parties and k parties with arbitrary non-malicious faults if $n > 3t + k$. Additional more specialized models dealt with t malicious parties, k non-malicious parties and f parties that can act maliciously, but cannot send different messages to different parties. Protocols such as those of Thambidurai and Park [27] and of Lincoln and Rushby [18] are correct as long as $n > 3t + 2f + k$. The more recent work of Hauser, Maurer and Zikas [29] showed that consensus, broadcast and MPC constructions are possible in networks with t Byzantine parties, s send faulty parties and r receive faulty parties, assuming that $n > 3t + r + s$. Recently, Konstantinos and Zikas [3] provided a tight characterization of feasibility for information theoretically secure consensus and MPC with in networks with Byzantine and full-omission faults in the general adversary structure.

Using many of these ideas, the recent work of Eldefrawy, Loss and Terner [11] Abraham, Dolev, Kagan and Stern [1] and Loss and Stern [19] construct mixed-fault protocols in the authenticated setting. Abraham *et al.* [1] construct an authenticated consensus protocol if $n > 2t + c$ Eldefrawy *et al.* construct such a protocol if $n > 2t + 2s + r$, or if $n > 2t + r + s$ and send faulty parties can either successfully send all messages in a given round, or no messages. The followup work by Loss *et al.* removes this requirement on send faulty parties and achieves consensus if $n > 2t + r + s$. One approach to achieving high resilience is to limit the adversary's actions, and only allow it to act Byzantine in certain parts of the code. This means that in some sense, faulty parties have mixed faults: Byzantine in some code sections, but only non-malicious in others. For example, the works of [5,7,8,17,28] use trusted execution environments (or similar abstractions) to enforce such behaviour from Byzantine parties. Alternatively, some protocols only allow specific parties to be Byzantine [25] or only allow one type of corruption at a time [2].

Similar results have been shown in partially synchronous systems that start as asynchronous networks, and eventually stabilize and become synchronous. For example, the Scrooge [24] protocol is secure if $n > 4t + 2c$. On the other hand, theUpright [6] and SBFT [14] protocols are secure as long if $n > 3t + 2k$ and $n > 3t + 2c$ respectively. Note that like results in synchronous networks, the latter two protocols also "naturally" combine the resilience of protocols for a single faulty type. That is, we know that $n > 3t$ or $n > 2k$ is required for partially synchronous protocols when allowing only Byzantine or non-malicious faults respectively [10].

2   Models, Definitions and Notations

2.1   Network Model

Throughout this work we deal with a fully-connected network of n parties. This means that each pair of parties has a direct channel between them, allowing parties to send messages to each other. The channels are authenticated, meaning that when parties receive a message they know the identity of the sender. In addition, when dealing with Byzantine corruptions, we assume a PKI setup, which allows parties to sign messages and verify each other's messages. We follow the standard approach of modelling the signature scheme as perfectly unforgeable. When replacing these signatures with existentially unforgeable signatures, the guarantees of the protocols hold when considering computationally bounded adversaries. We use the notation $\langle m \rangle_i$ to mean the message m, accompanied by i's signature on the message. The network is assumed to be synchronous. This means that the parties have access to synchronized clocks and run protocol proceeds in well-defined rounds. Parties can send messages in the beginning of a round, and all message that aren't dropped by the adversary (see below) are delivered at the end of the round. Messages can be delivered within each round in whichever order the adversary chooses. Parties can then choose which messages to send in a certain round based on the messages received from the previous round. Our protocols are described in steps of fixed duration (i.e., number of rounds) that are executed in lock-step one after another.

2.2   Adversary Model

Our work aims to design protocols with mixed-fault networks. There are four types of corruption in our work, and we will mention which types are included at the beginning of each section.

- **Send-Omission Faults.** Send faulty parties follow the protocol description. For any message sent from a send faulty party, the adversary can choose to drop that message. We assume there are at most s send omission faults.
- **Receive-Omission Faults.** Receive faulty parties follow the protocol description. For any message sent to a receive faulty party, the adversary can choose to drop that message. We assume that there are at most r send omission faults.
- **Full-Omission Faults.** Full omission faulty parties follow the protocol description and are both send faulty and receive faulty. This means that the adversary can drop any message sent by or to full omission faulty parties.
- **Byzantine/Malicious Faults.** Byzantine/Malicious parties can deviate arbitrarily from the protocol. We assume there are at most t Byzantine parties.

In this work we consider a strongly adaptive adversary that can corrupt parties at any time throughout the protocol, and can drop messages to receive faulty parties, drop messages to send faulty parties and replace messages sent by Byzantine parties in the same round they are corrupted. When corrupting a party, the adversary learns its entire state. On the other hand, the lower bounds of this paper work for a static adversary that chooses which parties to corrupt in the beginning of the protocol.

2.3   Definitions

In this section we define the tasks to be solved in the paper. We follow the ideas and notation presented by Loss *et al.* [19] in the definitions. In their protocols, parties always receive two flags z, g as inputs, in addition to any inputs they receive in the protocol. In all of the protocols, parties may not receive $\perp$ as an input, and indeed never receive that input in our protocols. One could allow such inputs by having distinct $\perp$ values for each protocol. The flags z and g indicate whether the party is already a zombie or a ghost respectively in the beginning of the protocol, and parties store these values in the beginning of each protocol. This allows parties to exclude themselves from protocols if they already know they are zombies or ghosts. A party that is not a zombie or a ghost is said to be *alive*. Parties then output a value x along with two flags z, g. The outputs z and g indicate whether the party is a zombie or a ghost respectively by the end of the protocol. When dealing with mixed faults with the presence of Byzantine faults we keep this notation in order to be consistent with previous work. However, in protocols for the total omission setting, parties might be required to participate even if they detect their own faults. In addition, in this setting our protocols do not allow for parties to detect their send faults and become ghosts. This means that inputting the flags Z, G and outputting the flag g are not meaningful in this setting, and for simplicity we remove these flags. Standard definitions of the tasks are also provided in Appendix A. The standard definitions are the same as the undead versions, except parties do not become zombies or ghosts. The lower bounds in this paper hold for the standard definitions, which also imply lower bounds for the undead versions.

Undead Weak Multicast. An undead weak multicast protocol, defined in the work of Loss et al. [19], allows parties to attempt to send their values to all other parties in the presence of Byzantine, send and receive faults. This is done in such a way that receive faulty parties can detect that they did not receive the message, and send faulty parties can detect that no non-faulty party received the message. In their work, Loss *et al.*, construct an undead uniform consensus protocol in such a network by first constructing an undead multicast protocol. They then construct a stack of protocols culminating in a consensus protocol. In this work we adapt the undead weak multicast protocol and only very slightly adapt the undead graded multicast protocol. Therefore, an undead weak multicast definition is provided below, and the definition and adaptation of the undead graded multicast protocol is provided in Appendix C.

Definition 1. *Let Π be a protocol executed by parties $1, \ldots, n$, with a designated sender i^* starting with an input $m \neq \bot$. In addition, every party i has two values $z_i, g_i \in \{\mathsf{True}, \mathsf{False}\}$ as input. Every party outputs a triplet (x, z, g) such that x is either a possible message or $\bot$, and z, g are boolean values.*

- **Validity.** *If i^* is non-faulty or receive faulty and is alive in the beginning of the protocol, every non-Byzantine party j either outputs (x, z, g) such that $x = m$, or such that $z = \mathsf{True}$. In addition, if i^* is send faulty, no non-Byzantine party outputs (x, z, g) such that $x \notin \{m, \bot\}$.*
- **Detection.** *If i^* is send faulty and it is alive at the end of the protocol, at least one non-faulty party output (x, z, g) such that $x = m$.*
- **Termination.** *All non-Byzantine parties complete the protocol and output a value.*
- **No Living Undead.** *If a non-Byzantine party j outputs (x, z, g) such that $z = \mathsf{True}$ (resp. $g = \mathsf{True}$), then it is receive faulty (resp. send faulty).*

If Π has the Validity, Detection, Termination and No Living Undead properties whenever at most t parties are Byzantine, s parties are send faulty and r parties are receive faulty, we say that it is a (t, s, r)-secure undead weak multicast protocol.

Very Weak Multicast. In order to construct a consensus protocol in the total omission setting, we start by constructing a rudimentary multicast primitive which we call a very weak multicast protocol. This protocol has a designated sender that attempts to multicast its message. Informally, the multicast must succeed if the sender is receive faulty, or if it is send faulty and there are fewer than r receive faulty parties. Parties that do not receive the message due to their own receive faults must become zombies. Formally, the protocol is defined as follows:

Definition 2. *Let Π be a protocol executed by parties $1, \ldots, n$, where i^* is the designated sender starting with an input $m \neq \perp$. Every party $j \in [n]$ outputs (x, Z_j) at the end of the protocol, where x is either a possible message or $\perp$, Z_j is a boolean value.*

- **Validity.** *Every party outputs (x, Z) such that $x \in \{m, \perp\}$. In addition, if i^* is non-faulty and there are at most $r - 1$ receive faulty parties or if i^* is a receive faulty party, then every party j either outputs (m, False), or outputs $(\perp, \mathsf{True})$ by the end of the protocol.*
- **Termination.** *All parties terminate and output a value at the end of the protocol.*
- **No Living Undead.** *If some party j outputs (x, True), then j is receive faulty.*

If Π has the Validity, Termination and No Living Undead properties whenever at most t parties are Byzantine, s parties are send faulty and r parties are receive faulty, we say that it is a (t, s, r)-secure very weak multicast protocol.

Undead Uniform Consensus. In a uniform consensus protocol, all parties have an input and they are required to output the same value, or possibly output $\perp$ if they are receive faulty. Importantly, in "normal" consensus protocols, the output of receive faulty parties is not required to be consistent with other parties' outputs. In a uniform consensus protocol, even faulty parties must output the same value as all other values, unless they can detect their own faults and output $\perp$. Similarly to above, parties also output a boolean flag z, indicating whether they detected their own receive faults and became zombies. For a definition of a uniform consensus protocol without the notion of undead parties, see Appendix A.

Definition 3. *Let Π be a protocol executed by parties $1, \ldots, n$, where each party $j \in [n]$ starts with input $m_j \neq \perp$. Every party j outputs (x_j, Z_j) at the end of the protocol.*

- **Validity.** *If each party j starts with the same value $m_j = m$, all parties output (m, False) or $(\perp, \mathsf{True})$ at the end of the protocol.*
- **Consistency.** *All non-faulty parties and send faulty parties output $x_j = m$ for the same value m at the end of the protocol. In addition, every receive faulty party either outputs m or $\perp$.*
- **Termination.** *Each party j terminates and outputs (x_j, Z_j) at the end of the protocol.*
- **No Living Undead.** *If $Z_j = \mathsf{True}$ at the end of the protocol, j must be a receive faulty.*

If Π has the Validity, Consistency, Termination and No Living Undead properties whenever at most t parties are Byzantine, s parties are send faulty and r parties are receive faulty, we say that it is a (t, s, r)-secure undead uniform consensus protocol.

Broadcast. The task of broadcast is highly related to the task of consensus, and has been shown to be equivalent in some network settings [4,15]. In this task, one designated sender has an input m and all parties output the same value x in the end of the protocol. If the sender does not exhibit faults that prevent it from sending its input (i.e. send or Byzantine faults), all parties should output $x = m$ as well. For a formal definition see Appendix A.

3   Byzantine Agreement with Overlapping Omission Faults

This section deals with the construction of a Byzantine Agreement protocol in the presence of t Byzantine faults, r receive faults and s send faults when $n > 2t + r + s$ and the faults can overlap. The lower bound of [11] shows that this is the optimal resilience for protocols in which the adversary is allowed to forcibly zombify receive-faulty parties, causing them to stop communicating. While in this section we construct a protocol achieving this resilience, showing a tight lower bound in the general case or a tighter upper bound for protocols in which the adversary cannot force receive-faulty parties to remain silent is an interesting open problem. The work of [19] constructs a protocol with such resilience when disallowing overlapping omission faults. In this section we adapt their protocol to the overlapping fault setting. Their protocol is constructed from a stack of four protocols: undead weak multicast, undead graded multicast, undead weak consensus and finally undead consensus.

The most basic protocol in the stack, the undead weak multicast protocol, heavily relies on send faulty parties receiving an indication that others did not hear their message. This allows them to become ghosts and stop participating in the protocol. This mechanism does not work when these parties can also exhibit receive faults. In order to remedy this, parties also send these indications to each other, which are then forwarded back to the faulty sender. If a sender receives enough of these messages it will be able to detect its own send faults and become a ghost. On the other hand, if a party receives too few of these forwarded messages (or messages indicating that no error occurred), they will detect their receive faults and become zombies instead. The protocol is presented in Fig. 1.

The rest of the stack is nearly identical to the original construction. Very slight adaptations to the undead graded multicast definition and protocol are presented in Appendix C. In the original construction, if a party is receive faulty, it must succeed in sending its message. This property is actually not needed for the rest of the constructions and the proofs, as they only rely on fully non-faulty parties succeeding in sending their messages. In that sense, that property is "too strong" and is used in the original work only because it is possible to achieve. Since the rest of the constructions and proofs remain exactly the same in the mixed-fault setting, Appendix C only contains adaptations to the undead graded multicast protocol.

Protocol Π_{WMC}

Input and Initialization: Each party $j \in [n]$ has inputs Z_j, G_j, the designated sender i^* inputs m additionally. Every party j initializes $m_j = \bot$.

Parties execute the following steps:

1. The sender $i^* \in [n]$ sends $\langle m \rangle_{i^*}$ to all other parties if $Z_{i^*} = \mathsf{False}$ and $G_{i^*} = \mathsf{False}$.
2. Every party $j \neq i^*$ sets $m_j = m'$, upon receiving a message m' with a valid signature from i^* in Step 1. If no message was received from i^*, j sets $m_j = \bot$. If $m_j \neq \bot$, j sends $\langle m_j \rangle_{i^*}$ to all other parties. Otherwise, it sends $\langle \bot \rangle_j$.
3. Every party j that has $m_j = \bot$ and received a forwarded message $\langle m' \rangle_{i^*}$ with a verifying signature from i^* sets $m_j = m'$ (if more than one such message is received, choose one arbitrarily). Every party j who did not receive any message with i^*'s signature (either directly in Step 1 or indirectly in Step 2) does as follows.
   - If j received $\langle \bot \rangle_p$ from at least $n - t - s$ different parties p in Step 2, j sends $\langle \mathsf{Abort} \rangle_j$ to all other parties.
   - Otherwise, if party j received $\langle \bot \rangle_p$ from less than $n - t - s$ many parties p, it sends "$Z_j = \mathsf{True}$" to the sender and sets $Z_j = \mathsf{True}$.
4. Each party j gathers all $\langle \mathsf{Abort} \rangle_j$ messages it received from distinct parties j in Step 3 with verifying signatures into a *report* and sends them to the sender. If j receives no such messages, it sends $\langle \mathsf{NoMsg} \rangle_j$ to the sender instead.

Output Determination: If the sender i^* received $\langle \mathsf{Abort} \rangle_j$ with verifying signatures from at least $t + 1$ distinct parties (either directly in Step 3 or through reports in step 4), it sets $G_{i^*} = \mathsf{True}$. If i^* received messages from less than $n - t - s$ different parties in Step 4, it sets $Z_{i^*} = \mathsf{True}$ and $m_{i^*} = \bot$. Each party j outputs (m_j, Z_j, G_j) and terminates.

Fig. 1. An undead weak multicast protocol

Proofs of the following two claims are provided in Appendix B.1.

Lemma 1. *Assume at most t parties are Byzantine, s parties are send faulty and r parties are receive faulty, where $2t + r + s < n$. No non-Byzantine party j will send $\langle \mathsf{Abort} \rangle_j$ in step 3 of Π_{WMC} unless the designated sender has Byzantine or send faults.*

Theorem 1. *Protocol Π_{WMC} is a (t, s, r)-secure undead weak multicast protocol resilient to overlapping faults if $n > 2t + s + r$.*

4 Undead Uniform Consensus in the Total Omission Setting

This section deals with constructing a uniform consensus protocol in the total omission setting. That is, we construct an (s, r)-*secure* uniform consensus protocol that is resilient to s send faults and r receive faults when $s + r = n$. Constructing this protocol fills in a gap left by the lower bound presented in [11]. Their lower bound showed that in a setting where Byzantine failures are also allowed, $n > 2t + r + s$ must hold in order to solve the task. Setting $t = 0$, this would seem to imply that $n > r + s$ is required in the total omission setting. However, their lower bound assumes that the adversary is also allowed to actively "zombify" receive faulty parties throughout the protocol. This means that it can force them to stop participating in the protocol. While in some protocols [19,29] parties do stop participating if they detect their own faults, this assumption limits the generality of the result. In the protocol presented in this section, parties do detect their own faults in order to be able to output $\perp$ when required, but do not necessarily stop participating in the protocol. In fact, since this model does not consider mixed faults, a party can act upon finding out that it is receive faulty. By that we mean that such a party knows that its message will arrive at all parties that aren't receive faulty, and thus it can use that power to help push forward consensus. This work extends ideas of [22,23] to the total omission model, while using the syntax of [19,29] regarding zombification.

4.1 Very Weak Multicast

We first construct an (s, r)-*secure* very weak multicast protocol in the synchronous setting resilient to s send faults and r receive faults, where $s < n$ and $s + r = n$. In the protocol, the sender sends its message to all parties. Parties then forward the received message, or $\perp$ if no message was received. Finally, every party that received a small number of messages (fewer than $n - s$) becomes a zombie. Every other party outputs the message received or forwarded from i^* if such a message exists, and $\perp$ otherwise. This protocol is described fully in Fig. 2.

A proof of the following claim is provided in Appendix B.2.

Lemma 2. *Protocol* Π_{VWMC} *is an* (s, r)-secure *very weak multicast protocol for any* s, r *such that* $s < n, s + r \leq n$ *without overlapping faults.*

Note that generally when we say parties send messages to all parties, for simplicity we also assume that they send messages to themselves. Parties (including i^*) can choose not to send messages to themselves and slightly adjust the counting in order to account for one fewer message being received.

4.2 Optimal Uniform Consensus

Now we construct an (s, r)-*secure* undead uniform consensus protocol Π_{TOC} in the total omission setting, i.e. with $n = s + r$. The protocol proceeds in $s +$

Protocol Π_{VWMC}

Input and Initialization: Each party $j \in [n]$ sets $Z_j :=$ False, the designated sender i^* has input m. Every party j sets $m_j = \bot$.

Parties execute the following steps:

1. The sender $i^* \in [n]$ sends its input m to all other parties.
2. Every party j that has received a message m in the first step sets $m_j = m$. Party j sends m_j to all parties.

Output Determination: If party j has received messages from less than $n - s$ parties (in total) in Step 1 and 2, it sets $Z_j =$ True. If party j receives a message $m \neq \bot$ in either round 1 or round 2 and $Z_j =$ False, it sets $m_j = m$. Party j outputs (m_j, Z_j).

Fig. 2. A Very Weak Multicast Protocol

1 rounds. Each round has a designated sender, which is rotated in a round robin fashion. Each sender invokes the very weak multicast protocol with its current value and zombie flags one by one. Parties simply adopt any non-$\bot$ value they receive and continue propagating it in the next rounds. Intuitively, having $s + 1$ such rounds guarantees that at least one of the rounds has a leader that is not send faulty. Every party will either receive that leader's message or become a zombie. Considering the latest such leader, all following leaders are only send faulty, and thus receive its message. This means that they will continue propagating its message in the following rounds, and thus its message will be all parties' output from the protocol. The protocol is provided in Fig. 3.

Protocol Π_{TOC}

Input and Initialization: Each party $j \in [n]$ inputs v_j, Z_j and sets $Z_j :=$ False, $I_j = v_j$.

Parties execute the following steps, for every $i \in [s + 1]$:

- Party i becomes the leader and invokes Π_{VWMC} on the input I_i. Let (m_j^i, Z_j^i) denote the output of party j in the i'th invocation of Π_{VWMC}. If $Z_j^i =$ True, j sets $Z_j =$ True. Then, if $Z_j =$ False and $m_j^i \neq \bot$, j sets $I_j = m_j^i$.

Output Determination: If $Z_j =$ True, j terminates with output $(\bot, Z_j)$. Otherwise, it terminates with output (I_j, Z_j).

Fig. 3. A consensus protocol for $s + r \leq n$.

A proof of the following theorem is provided in Appendix B.3.

Theorem 2. *Protocol Π_{TOC} is an (s, r)-secure undead uniform consensus protocol for any s, r such that $s < n, s + r \leq n$ without overlapping faults.*

5   Lower Bounds

This section provide several new lower bounds that show the optimality of the presented uniform consensus protocol. We also show the impossibility of broadcast in the total omission conditions, despite being able to construct a uniform consensus protocol in this setting.

5.1   Total Send Corruption

The protocol in Sect. 4 works when $s + r \leq n$, as long as $s < n$. We start by showing that $s < n$ is a necessary condition in order to construct a uniform consensus protocol. Intuitively, we partition the parties into 2 groups and only allow parties to communicate within the groups. If one group receives one input and the other receives another, they would be forced to output different values and the protocol would not remain consistent. A proof of the following theorem is provided in Appendix D.1

Theorem 3. *There does not exist an $(n, 0)$-secure uniform consensus protocol.*

5.2   Total Omission Broadcast

One might expect that since uniform consensus can be solved in the total omission setting, broadcast would be solvable as well. Note that the uniform consensus construction in this paper uses the fact the receive faulty parties can push their inputs to all other parties, which can then be used to achieve consensus. However, in a broadcast protocol only one party's input is taken into consideration. If that party is send faulty, it will not be able to successfully push its value to all other parties, making this approach fail.

We formalize this by constructing a broadcast lower bound in the total omission setting. In this lower bound, we have the designated sender i^* communicate with a set A of $s - 1$ parties freely. The rest of the parties, denoted by a set B, do not hear anything from i^* or from A, either due to them being receive faulty, or due to the rest being send faulty. Parties in B must output some value, even without hearing anything from i^*, while the rest of the parties hear all sent messages and must be consistent with i^*'s input because the parties in B might simply be receive faulty. Since this can be made to take place even when parties in B are non faulty the rest are send faulty, we immediately break the consistency of the protocol. A proof of the following theorem is provided in Appendix D.2.

Theorem 4. *There is no (s, r)-secure broadcast protocol resilient to s send faults and r receive faults for any s, r such that $s \geq 1, s + r = n$ without overlapping faults.*

5.3   Consensus with Overlapping Faults

In this section, we prove that the threshold $s + r \leq n$ is necessary to achieve uniform consensus as long as $s > 2$. This shows the optimal corruption tolerance of our uniform consensus protocol. The basic idea in the proof of Theorem 4 relies on the fact that hearing one party's messages (in that proof, the sender) is not reliable, because it could be send faulty and thus only a subset of the parties hear those messages. In the following proof, we use this idea to show that one could "switch" one party's input without changing the outputs of all parties. After switching all of the parties' inputs, we finally find either a validity violation or a consistency violation.

Below we prove the lower bound for the minimal case in which $s > 2$ and $s \neq n$, i.e. $n = 4$, $s = 3$ and $r = 2$. A proof of the general case is provided in Appendix D.3. In the lower bound for the minimal case, we have 4 parties, R_1, R_2, S_1, S_2. In all of the executions S_1, S_2 are send faulty and R_1, R_2 are receive faulty. R_1 and R_2 sometimes also exhibit overlapping send faults. In addition, R_1, R_2 hear nothing in all executions, and S_1, S_2 only hear messages from R_1, R_2, but not necessarily all of these message. We start off with all four parties having the input 1, and use the previous intuition to show that one could switch the inputs of R_1, R_2 gradually by making them send faulty as well. This is done in a series of executions, with each pair of consecutive executions having at least one party with the same view, forcing the same value to be output. Finally, after switching the inputs of R_1, R_2, it is easy to switch the two final inputs and reach either a consistency violation or a validity violation. Figure 4 illustrates the executions used in the lower bound. The proof in Appendix D.3 uses the same strategy, simply switching all receive faulty parties' inputs one-by-one, and then switching the send faulty parties' inputs.

Theorem 5. *There is no (s, r)-secure uniform consensus protocol resilient to overlapping faults for any s, r s.t. $s > 2$ and $s + r > n$.*

Proof. We prove the lower bound holds for $n = 4, s = 3, r = 2$, and a proof for the general case is provided in Appendix D.3. Note that when $r < 2$, all parties can be send faulty, which was already proven impossible in Theorem 3. Assume there are four parties, R_1, R_2, S_1 and S_2. R_1 and R_2 are receive faulty in all executions, and have overlapping send faults in some of the executions. S_1 and S_2 are send faulty in all executions. The adversary drops all messages sent to R_1, R_2 and all messages sent from S_1, S_2 in all executions. This means that in all executions R_1 and R_2 hear no messages, and S_1, S_2 hear only messages from R_1 and R_2, but might not hear some in executions where they have overlapping send faults as well. In all of the following descriptions, parties S_1, S_2 hear all messages sent by R_1, R_2, unless explicitly stated otherwise.

1. In the first execution, all parties start with input 1 and no parties has overlapping faults.
2. In the second execution, R_1 has overlapping send faults. All parties start with input 1. The adversary drops all message sent from R_1 to S_2, but delivers messages from R_1 to S_1.

368   J. Loss et al.

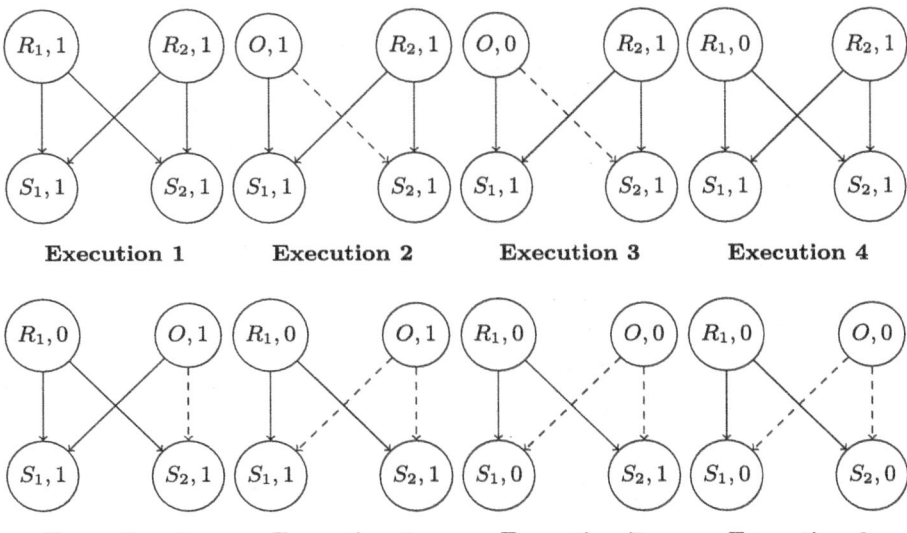

Fig. 4. Lower Bound Executions. A node with the text P, b indicates that party P has input b. Parties named R_i are receive faulty, parties named S_i are send faulty, and parties named O have overlapping faults. Arrows indicate messages are successfully sent, dashed arrows indicate that message are dropped. Parties whose names are colored red have views indistinguishable from the previous execution. (Color figure online)

3. In the third execution, R_1 has overlapping send faults. R_1 starts with input 0 and all other parties have the input 1. The adversary drops all messages sent from R_1 to S_2, but delivers messages from R_1 to S_1.
4. In the forth execution, R_1 starts with input 0 and all other parties have input 1. All messages from R_1, R_2 are delivered to S_1, S_2.
5. In the fifth execution, R_2 has overlapping send faults. All messages sent from R_2 to S_2 are dropped, but messages from R_2 to S_1 are delivered. R_1 starts with input 0, and all other parties start with input 1.
6. In the sixth execution, R_2 has overlapping send faults. All messages sent from R_2 are dropped by the adversary. R_1 and R_2 start with input 0, while S_1 and S_2 starts with input 1.
7. In the seventh execution, R_2 has overlapping send faults. All messages sent from R_2 are dropped by the adversary. S_2 starts with input 1 and all other parties start with input 0.
8. In the eighth execution, R_2 has overlapping send faults. All messages sent from R_2 are dropped by the adversary. All parties start with input 0.

By the validity requirements, parties S_1 and S_2 must output 1 in execution 1. S_1 has indistinguishable views in executions 1 and 2, so it outputs 1 in execution 2. Since the protocol is consistent, S_2 does so as well. On the other hand, S_2 has indistinguishable views in executions 2 and 3 since it hears nothing from R_1 in both. Therefore, it outputs 1 in execution 3 and therefore S_1 does so too. S_1's view is identical in executions 3 and 4 and thus it outputs 1 in execution 4, and S_2 outputs 1 as well due to consistency. Executions 4 and 5 are indistinguishable from S_1's point of view, so it outputs 1 in execution 5. From consistency, S_2 outputs 1 too in execution 5. S_2 has identical views in executions 5 and 6, so it must output 1, and so does S_1 from consistency. S_2's views in execution 7 is indistinguishable from its view in execution 6, so it outputs 1, and so does S_1. Finally, S_1's views in executions 7 and 8 are indistinguishable, and thus it outputs 1 in both. However, all parties have the input 0 in execution 8. This means that from validity, S_1 must output 0 in execution 8, reaching a contradiction.

Note 1. Execution 4 and 6 can be removed from the proof, but are kept in the proof in order to have a small number of changes between consecutive executions.

Acknowledgements. Julian Loss was supported by the European Union, ERC-2023-STG, Project ID: 101116713. Views and opinions expressed are however those of the author(s) only and do not necessarily reflect those of the European Union. Neither the European Union nor the granting authority can be held responsible for them.

Gilad Stern was Supported in part by ISF 2338/23, AFOSR Award FA9550-23-1-0387, AFOSR Award FA9550-23-1-0312, and an Algorand Foundation grant. Any opinions, findings and conclusions or recommendations expressed in this material are those of the author(s) and do not necessarily reflect the views of the United States Government, AFOSR or the Algorand Foundation.

The authors would like to express their sincere gratitude to the anonymous reviewers for their valuable feedback and constructive comments.

A   Standard Task Definitions

A.1   Uniform Consensus

Definition 4. *Let Π be a protocol executed by parties $1, \ldots, n$, where each party $j \in [n]$ starts with input $m_j \neq \bot$. Every party j outputs x_j at the end of the protocol.*

- *Validity. If each party j starts with the same value $m_j = m$, all parties that are not receive faulty output m, and receive faulty parties output m or $\bot$ at the end of the protocol.*
- *Consistency. All non-faulty parties and send faulty parties output $x_j = m$ for the same value m at the end of the protocol. In addition, every receive faulty party either outputs m or $\bot$.*
- *Termination. Each party j terminates and outputs x_j at the end of the protocol.*

If Π has the Validity, Consistency and Termination properties whenever at most s parties are send faulty and r parties are receive faulty, we say that it is an (s, r)-secure uniform consensus protocol.

A.2   Broadcast

Definition 5. *Let Π be a protocol executed by parties $1, \ldots, n$, where i^* is the designated sender starting with an input $m \neq \bot$. Every party j outputs x_j at the end of the protocol.*

- *Validity. If the sender is non-faulty or receive faulty, every party that isn't receive faulty outputs m and receive faulty parties output m or $\bot$ at the end of the protocol.*
- *Consistency. Every non-faulty or send faulty party j outputs $x_j = v$ for the same value $v \in \{m, \bot\}$ at the end of the protocol. In addition, every receive faulty party outputs $x_j = v$ or $x_j = \bot$.*
- *Termination. Each party j terminates and outputs x_j at the end of the protocol.*

If Π has the Validity, Consistency and Termination properties whenever at most s parties are send faulty and r parties are receive faulty, we say that it is an (s, r)-secure broadcast protocol.

B   Proofs of Protocols

B.1   Proofs for Undead Weak Multicast

Lemma 1. *Assume at most t parties are Byzantine, s parties are send faulty and r parties are receive faulty, where $2t + r + s < n$. No non-Byzantine party j will send $\langle \mathsf{Abort} \rangle_j$ in step 3 of Π_{WMC} unless the designated sender has Byzantine or send faults.*

Proof. Assume there is a non-Byzantine party j that sends $\langle \mathsf{Abort} \rangle_j$. It must have received $\langle \bot \rangle$ from at least $n - t - s \geq t + r + 1$ different parties, and at least one of those messages is from a party without receive omission or Byzantine faults. That party would have received the message if the designated sender is neither send faulty nor Byzantine.

Theorem 1. *Protocol Π_{WMC} is a (t, s, r)-secure undead weak multicast protocol resilient to overlapping faults if $n > 2t + s + r$.*

Proof. **Validity.** We will start by showing the first part of the property: if i^* is non-faulty or is receive faulty and alive in the beginning of the protocol, all non-Byzantine parties either output m or become zombies. If that is the case, i^* sends $\langle m \rangle_{i^*}$ to every party and all non-faulty parties receive it and forward it. Since i^* is non-Byzantine, it only sends one verifying signature and thus every party that isn't Byzantine either outputs m or $\bot$. Furthermore, every party that is neither receive faulty nor Byzantine, receives i^*'s message and outputs m. It is only left to show that receive faulty parties output (x, z, g) such that $x = m$ or $z = \mathsf{True}$. If a receive-faulty party j sets $Z_j = \mathsf{True}$ then it outputs $z = Z_j = \mathsf{True}$ and we are done. If that is not the case, then it receives messages from at least

$n - t - s \geq 2t + s + r + 1 - t - s = t + r + 1$ different parties. Since at most $t + r$ parties are either Byzantine or receive-faulty, at least one of the messages j received was from a party that is neither Byzantine nor receive faulty. Those parties receive the message m from i^* and forward it, and thus every $j \neq i^*$ that hasn't become a zombie, outputs m. In addition, if $Z_{i^*} \neq$ True by the end of the protocol, it outputs (m, Z_{i^*}, G_{i^*}) as well.

For the second part of the property, we will assume that i^* is send faulty. Party i^* only signs the message m and thus no party receives another signed message from i^*. This means that every non-Byzantine party either outputs m or $\bot$.

Detection. If $Z_{i^*} =$ False and $G_{i^*} =$ False at the end of the protocol, i^* receives messages from at least $n-t-s$ parties in step 4 with and receives Abort messages from at most t parties. Since $n-t-s \geq t+r+1$, i^* received the report sent by at least one party that is neither Byzantine nor receive faulty. This party heard all Abort messages sent by all non-faulty parties. In other words, i^* either directly or indirectly heard all Abort messages sent by non-faulty parties. Since in total it received Abort messages from at most t parties, at least one non-faulty party did not send such a message. This party received i^*'s message and will output it in the end of the protocol.

Termination. All parties terminate after exactly 4 rounds.

No Living Undead. In the end of the protocol, every party j outputs (m_j, Z_j, G_j). This means that we need to argue that only receive faulty parties set $Z_j =$ True and only send faulty parties set $G_j =$ True.

- NLU of the designated sender: If the sender is non-faulty, by Lemma 1, at most t parties p send $\langle \text{Abort} \rangle_p$ messages, and thus i^* does not set $G_{i^*} =$ True. In addition, it will receive at least $n - t - s$ many messages in the step 4, so it won't set $Z_{i^*} =$ True either.
- NLU of all other parties: Each non-receive-faulty party j must receive at least $n - t - s$ messages in the step 3, so they won't set $Z_j =$ True and they don't set $G_j =$ True anywhere in the protocol.

B.2 Proofs for Very Weak Multicast

Lemma 2. *Protocol* Π_{VWMC} *is an* (s,r)-*secure very weak multicast protocol for any* s,r *such that* $s < n, s + r \leq n$ *without overlapping faults.*

Proof. **Validity.** For the first part of the property, note that parties only output a value other than $\bot$ if they received i^*'s message containing m, or another party's message forwarding m. In either case, parties only send i^*'s input. For the second part of the property, we start by considering a non-faulty sender i^* and assuming that there are fewer than r receive faulty parties. If some party j output (x, Z_j) with $Z_j =$ False, it must have received messages from at least $n - s > r - 1$ many parties. By assumption, at most $r - 1$ parties are receive faulty, so at least one of the messages comes was received from a party that is not receive faulty. Those receive i^*'s message in round 1 and forward it, and thus in both cases j receives the sender's input, sets $m_j = m$ and outputs this value.

Now assume the sender is receive faulty. If some party j output (x, Z_j) with $Z_j =$ False, it must have received messages from at least $n - s \geq r$ many parties. If it received messages from all receive faulty parties, by the non-overlapping assumption, it must have received one from i^* as well and set $m_j = m$. Otherwise, it received at least one message from a send-faulty party. That party does not exhibit any receive faults, so it received m from i^* and forwarded that message to j. In either case j sets $m_j = m$ and outputs that value.

Termination. The protocol Π_{VWMC} terminates in exactly 2 rounds.

No Living Undead. Assume that some party j outputs $Z_j =$ True. It only sets Z_j to True if it receives messages from a total of less than $n - s$ many different parties in Steps 2 and 3 of Π_{VWMC}. This means that j did not receive a message from at least one party that is not send faulty. This implies that j must be a receive faulty party, as required.

B.3   Proofs for Total Omission Consensus

Theorem 2. *Protocol Π_{TOC} is an (s, r)-secure undead uniform consensus protocol for any s, r such that $s < n, s + r \leq n$ without overlapping faults.*

Proof. **Validity.** Assume all parties start with the same input m. This means that they all set $I_j = m$ in the beginning of the protocol. We will show that if all parties have $I_j = m$ in the beginning of a round, this will continue to hold in the end of the round. Following a simple inductive argument, this means that all parties have $I_j = m$ in the end of round $s + 1$, and thus either output (I_j, False) if $Z_j =$ False or $(\bot, \mathsf{True})$ otherwise. Assume that all parties have $I_j = m$ in the beginning of round r. This means that the round's leader sends (m, Z_r) in the Π_{VWMC} protocol. From the validity property of the protocol, all parties receive (m', Z) such that $m' \in \{m, \bot\}$. This means that each j either updates I_j to m if it output $m' = m$, or does not update I_j at all otherwise. Therefore all parties have $I_j = m$ in the end of the round as well.

Consistency. First assume that at least one of the first $s + 1$ leaders is receive faulty, and let l be the maximal such party. If that is not the case, then there are no receive faulty parties among the first $s + 1$ leaders. Since there are at most s send faulty parties, at least one of these parties is non-faulty. In addition, if at least $s + 1$ parties are not receive faulty, then there are at most $n - (s+1) \leq r - 1$ receive faulty parties. Let l be the nonfaulty leader with the maximal index such that $l \leq s + 1$. In either case, let m' be the message sent by the leader l. From the validity property of Π_{VWMC}, every party j either receives the message m' and sets $I_j = m'$ or sets $Z_j =$ True at the end of round l.

We will show that in every subsequent round (if such a round exists), every party is either receive faulty with $Z_j =$ True or has $I_j = m'$. Note that in both of the above cases, there are no receive faulty leaders after round l. That is, parties $l + 1, \ldots, s + 1$ are not receive faulty. First, since parties $l + 1, \ldots, s + 1$ are not receive faulty, from the Validity and No Living Undead properties of Π_{VWMC}, each such j outputs m', False from the protocol in round l and updates $I_j = m'$. Therefore, in the beginning of round $l + 1$, the leader sends the value $I_{l+1} = m'$ in the Π_{VWMC} protocol and thus from the Validity property, every party either outputs m' or $\bot$. This means that every party that updates its I_j variable in round $l+1$ updates it to m'. Following identical logic, the same holds for rounds $l + 2, \ldots, s + 1$, and thus parties don't update I_j to any value other than m' following round l. Finally, every party that has $Z_j = $ True outputs $(\bot, \mathsf{True})$ from the protocol. Every other party updated $I_j = m'$ in round l, and possibly in following rounds as well, and finally output (m', False).

Termination. The protocol terminates after $s + 1$ rounds and each party j will output (m_j, Z_j).

No Living Undead. Parties only set $Z_j = $ True in the protocol if they output (x, True) in one of the invocations of Π_{VWMC}. From no living undead property of Π_{VWMC}, only receive faulty parties do so, as required.

C   Undead Graded Multicast

C.1   Definition

An undead graded multicast protocol has a designated sender i^* with input m. Every party i also has two flags $z_i, g_i \in \{\mathsf{True}, \mathsf{False}\}$ as input indicating whether it is already a zombie or a ghost when starting the protocol. Every party outputs a value, as well as grade $y \in \{0, 1, 2\}$, indicating whether it thinks that the sender succeeded in propagating its message. If some party thinks that a non Byzantine sender definitely succeeded in sending its message (outputs $y = 2$), then all parties actually received that message or became zombies. The protocol is formally defined bellow.

Definition 6. *Let Π be a protocol executed by parties $1, \ldots, n$, with a designated sender i^* starting with an input $m \neq \bot$. In addition, every party i has two values $z_i, g_i \in \{\mathsf{True}, \mathsf{False}\}$ as input. Every party outputs a tuple (x, y, z, g) such that x is either a possible message or $\bot$, $y \in \{0, 1, 2\}$ and z, g are boolean values.*

- **Validity.** *If i^* is non-faulty, every non-Byzantine party j outputs (x, y, z, g) such that either $x = m, y = 2$, or such that $z = \mathsf{True}$. In addition, if i^* is send faulty, no non-Byzantine party outputs (x, y, z, g) such that $x \notin \{m, \bot\}$.*
- **Detection.** *If i^* is send faulty and it is alive at the end of the protocol, every non-faulty party output (x, y, z, g) such that $x = m$ and $y \geq 1$.*
- **Consistency.** *If i^* is non-Byzantine, for every two non-Byzantine parties j, k that output (x_j, y_j, z_j, g_j) and (x_k, y_k, z_k, g_k) respectively, either $|y_j - y_k| \leq 1$, or at least one of z_j, z_k equals True. In addition, either $x_j = \bot$ and $y_j = 0$, or $x_j = m$.*
- **Termination.** *All parties complete the protocol and output a value.*
- **No Living Undead.** *If a non-Byzantine party j outputs (x, y, z, g) such that $z = \mathsf{True}$ (resp. $g = \mathsf{True}$), then it is receive faulty (resp. send faulty).*

If Π has the Validity, Detection, Consistency, Termination and No Living Undead properties whenever at most t parties are Byzantine, s parties are send faulty and r parties are receive faulty, we say that it is a (t,s,r)-secure undead graded multicast protocol.

The only difference from the original definition, provided in [19], is in the validity property. In the original property, validity was required to hold when i^* is either receive faulty or non-faulty. This is much harder to achieve if overlapping faults are allowed. That is because originally, a zombie could send a message and know that it will arrive even after finding out it is receive faulty. However, a party with overlapping omission faults might become a zombie instead of becoming a ghost and thus won't know whether its future messages will arrive at their destination. Therefore, in this definition we only require the validity to hold when the sender is non-faulty. Thankfully this is enough, as the proofs of [19] only rely on non-faulty parties successfully sending their messages.

C.2   Construction

In the protocol, the sender starts by sending its input to all parties in an undead weak multicast protocol. Following that, every party that is still alive forwards the received message in an undead weak multicast protocol as well. If a party received a message from i^* in both rounds it knows that it did not become a ghost, and thus at least one non-faulty party received its message in the first round. This means that it can output $m, 2$ and be assured that all other parties will receive the message from that non-faulty party and be able to output m with a grade of at least 1, or become zombies (Fig. 5).

C.3   Security Proof

Theorem 6. *Protocol Π_{GMC} is a (t,s,r)-secure undead graded multicast protocol resilient to overlapping faults if $n > 2t + s + r$.*

Proof. **Validity.** If i^* is non-faulty, then from the Validity of the Π_{WMC} protocol, every non-Byzantine party j outputs $\langle m \rangle_{i^*}$ in the weak multicast instances with i^* as sender in both rounds or outputs either $Z'_j = \mathsf{True}$ or $Z_{j,i^*} = \mathsf{True}$. In the first case, j outputs $m, 2, z, g$ in the end of the protocol, and in the second it outputs $\perp, 0, \mathsf{True}, g$. Note that from the no living undead property of Π_{WMC}, i^* has $Z'_{i^*} = G'_{i^*} = \mathsf{False}$ so it does send $\langle m \rangle_{i^*}$ in the second round as well.

Detection. Assume i^* is send faulty and is alive in the end of the protocol. This means that it has $Z_{i^*} = G_{i^*} = \mathsf{False}$ in the end of the protocol and outputs these flags. It did not set $Z_{i^*} = \mathsf{True}$ or $G_{i^*}\mathsf{True}$ in the beginning of round 2, so it output $Z'_{i^*} = G'_{i^*} = \mathsf{False}$. From the detection and no living undead properties of the Π_{WMC} protocol, some non-faulty party k output $\langle m \rangle_{i^*}, \mathsf{False}, \mathsf{False}$ from the first call to Π_{WMC}. Party j then sent that message in the Π_{WMC} protocol, and from the validity and detection properties of the protocol every non-Byzantine party outputs $x_{j,k}, Z_{j,k}, G_{j,k}$ such that either $x_{j,k} = \langle m \rangle_{i^*}$ or has $Z_{j,k} = \mathsf{True}$.

Protocol Π_{GMC}

Input and Initialization: Each party $j \in [n]$ has inputs z_j, g_j, the designated sender i^* also has input m. Every party j initializes $m_j = \bot$, $Z_j = z_j$ and $G_j = g_j$.

Parties execute the following steps:

1. The sender i^* sends $\langle m \rangle_{i^*}$ to all other parties using Π_{WMC} if $Z_{i^*} = \mathsf{False}$ and $G_{i^*} = \mathsf{False}$.
2. Let x_j, Z'_j, G'_j be j's output in the previous round. If $Z'_j = \mathsf{True}$, j sets $Z_j = \mathsf{True}$, and if $G'_j = \mathsf{True}$, j sets $G_j = \mathsf{True}$. Every party that receives $x = \langle m' \rangle_{i^*}$ (i.e. a message m' with a verifying signature from i^*) sets $m_j = \langle m' \rangle_{i^*}$. Every party j that has $Z_j = G_j = \mathsf{False}$ sends m_j using Π_{WMC}.

Output Determination: For every pair j, k, define $x_{j,k}, Z_{j,k}, G_{j,k}$ to be j's output in the Π_{WMC} protocol with k as sender. If there exists a k such that $Z_{j,k} = \mathsf{True}$, j sets $Z_j = \mathsf{True}$. In addition, if there exists a k such that $G_{j,k} = \mathsf{True}$, j sets $G_j = \mathsf{True}$. If $Z_j = \mathsf{False}$, $m_j = \langle m' \rangle_{i^*} \neq \bot$ and $x_{j,i^*} = m_j$, j outputs $(m', 2, Z_j, G_j)$. Otherwise, if $Z_j = \mathsf{False}$ and for some k, $x_{j,k} = \langle m' \rangle_{i^*}$ with a verifying signature from i^*, j outputs $m', 1, Z_j, G_j$ (choose one arbitrarily if more than one exists). Finally, if j did not output a value in either of the previous cases, it outputs $\bot, 0, Z_j, G_j$.

Fig. 5. An undead graded multicast protocol

If $Z_{j,k}$, then j sets $Z_j = \mathsf{True}$ and outputs $\bot, 0, \mathsf{True}, G_j$. From the no living undead property, this only takes place if j is receive faulty. On the other hand, if $x_{j,k} = \langle m \rangle_{i^*}$, then j received m with a valid signature from i^*. Since i^* only signs one message, m is the only message j will receive with a valid signature, and thus j outputs m, y, z, g with $y = 1$ if it hasn't done so with $y = 2$ already.

Consistency. Assume i^* is not Byzantine and let j, k be two non-Byzantine parties that output (x_j, y_j, z_j, g_j) and (x_k, y_k, z_k, g_k) respectively. If either $z_j = \mathsf{True}$ or $z_k = \mathsf{True}$, then the first part of the property holds. The first part of the property also holds if neither party outputs a grade of 2, i.e. if $y_j \neq 2$ and $y_k \neq 2$, In order to prove the final case, assume w.l.o.g that $y_j = 2$. If that is the case, it received the same message $\langle m' \rangle_{i^*}$ from i^* in both calls to Π_{WMC}. Since i^* is not Byzantine and from the validity of the Π_{WMC} protocol, i^* sent the message m' in both of these calls. If i^* is either non-faulty or receive faulty, from the validity of the Π_{WMC} protocol, every nonfaulty party received that message in the first call to Π_{WMC}. If i^* is send faulty, from the detection of the protocol, at least one non-faulty party l receive the message. Following that, l sent the message in the second round. By assumption, k outputs $z_k = \mathsf{False}$. This means that it output $Z_{k,l} = \mathsf{False}$ as well, because otherwise it would have become a zombie and output $z_k = \mathsf{True}$. By validity, this means that it also output $x_{k,l} = \langle m' \rangle_{i^*}$. Finally, during the output determination, if k doesn't output $(m', 2, z_k, g_k)$, it will reach the second condition and output $(m', 1, z_k, z_k)$ instead. For the second part of the property, if j receives some message $\langle m' \rangle_{i^*}$ with a verifying signature by i^*, it outputs $x_j = m'$. Since i^* is not Byzantine it only signs its input m, so $x_j = m$. If j does not receive such a message, then it output $\perp, 0, Z_j, G_j$, as required.

Termination. The protocol after exactly two calls to Π_{WMC}.

No Living Undead. Party j outputs the flags Z_j, G_j in the end of the protocol. It sets $Z_j = \mathsf{True}$ if $Z'_j = \mathsf{True}$ or $Z_{j,k} = \mathsf{True}$ for some k. Similarly, it only sets $G_j = \mathsf{True}$ if $G'_j = \mathsf{True}$ or $G_{j,k} = \mathsf{True}$ for some k. The values Z'_j, G'_j as well as $Z_{j,k}, G_{j,k}$ are the flags output from the Π_{WMC} protocol. From the no living undead property of Π_{WMC}, Z'_j or $Z_{j,k}$ only equal True if j is receive faulty. Similarly, G'_j or $G_{j,k}$ only equal True if j is send faulty, as required.

D   Lower Bound Proofs

D.1   Total Send Corruption Uniform Consensus

Theorem 3. *There does not exist an $(n, 0)$-secure uniform consensus protocol.*

Proof. Assume there exists an $(n, 0)$-secure uniform consensus protocol. Let $A, B \subseteq [n]$ be an arbitrary partition of $[n]$ to non-empty sets. That is $A \cup B = [n]$, $A \cap B = \emptyset$ and neither A nor B are empty. We build three executions as follows.

1. In the first execution, all parties start with the input 1. The parties in A are non-faulty and the parties in B are send faulty. The adversary drops all messages sent from parties in group B to parties in group A. By the validity requirements, all parties in group A must output 1.
2. In the first execution, all parties start with the input 0. The parties in A are send faulty and the parties in B are non-faulty. The adversary drops all messages sent from parties in group A to parties in group B.
3. In the third execution, all parties are send faulty. Parties in A start with input 1 and parties in group B start with input 0. The adversary drop all messages sent between parties in group A and in group B, but delivers all messages within each of the groups.

All parties in group A have indistinguishable views in execution 1 and in execution 3, and thus must output 1 in both. On the other hand, all parties in group B have indistinguishable views in execution 2 and execution 3 and thus must output 0 in both. Parties in execution 3 output different values, and thus the protocol does not have the consistency property, reaching a contradiction.

D.2   Total Omission Broadcast

Theorem 4. *There is no (s, r)-secure broadcast protocol resilient to s send faults and r receive faults for any s, r such that $s \geq 1, s + r = n$ without overlapping faults.*

Proof. Assume there exists an (s, r)-*secure* broadcast protocol for $s \geq 1, s + r = n$. Let i^* be the index of the designated sender, and let A, B be an arbitrary partition of $[n] \setminus \{i^*\}$ such that $|A| = s - 1$ and $|B| = r$. For example, let A be the $s - 1$ minimal indices that are not i^*, and let $B = [n] \setminus (A \cup \{i^*\})$. In all of the following executions i^* and parties in A successfully communicate with each other and within A, and hear messages sent by parties in B. On the other hand, parties in B hear nothing from i^* or from parties in A, but communicate successfully among themselves. We construct four executions as follows.

1. In the first execution, i^* has the input 0. Parties in A and i^* are send faulty, but parties in B are non faulty. Parties in A and i^* communicate among themselves, but due to their send faults all messages to B are dropped. In addition, parties in B communicate among themselves, and any messages they send arrive at A and i^*.
2. In the second execution, i^* has the input 1. Parties in A and i^* are send faulty, but parties in B are non faulty. Parties in A and i^* communicate among themselves, but due to their send faults all messages to B are dropped. In addition, parties in B communicate among themselves, and any messages they send arrive at A and i^*.
3. In the third execution, i^* has the input 0. Parties in A and i^* are non-faulty, but parties in B are receive faulty. Parties in A and i^* communicate among themselves, but all messages to B are dropped due to their receive faults. In addition, parties in B communicate among themselves, and any messages they send arrive at A and i^*.
4. In the fourth execution, i^* has the input 1. Parties in A and i^* are non-faulty, but parties in B are receive faulty. Parties in A and i^* communicate among themselves, but all messages to B are dropped due to their receive faults. In addition, parties in B communicate among themselves, and any messages they send arrive at A and i^*.

Note that in the third and fourth executions, i^* and parties in A are non-faulty. From validity they must all output 0 and 1 in executions 3 and 4 respectively. In addition, the view of these parties in executions 1 and 3 are indistinguishable, as well as their views in executions 2 and 4. This means that they must also output 0 and 1 in executions 1 and 2 respectively. On the other hand, parties in B have identical views in all 4 executions, and thus act the same in all of them. These parties are non-faulty in executions 1 and 2 and thus must output consistent values. If parties in B output a value $v \neq 0^1$ in all executions, then this leads to a consistency violation in execution 1. Similarly, if they output a value $v \neq 1$ in all executions, then this leads to a consistency violation in execution 2.

---

[1] Technically, in probabilistic protocols there might not be only one possible output in this case. Since this proof deals with perfectly secure protocols, it is enough that there is a positive probability they output $v \neq 0$.

D.3 Generalizing Theorem 5

The technique in Theorem 5 showed that it is possible to take one receive faulty party and switch its input, but all parties must still output the same value. In order to prove the general result, one could start with all parties having the input 1, and then switching their inputs one-by-one until all of them have the input 0. Finally, if the send faulty parties' messages are all dropped, their inputs can also be switched without other parties noticing. Finally, we will find that all parties have the input 0, but output the value 1, which will contradict the validity of the protocol. A formal proof of the general case of Theorem 5 is provided below.

Theorem 5. *There is no (s,r)-secure uniform consensus protocol resilient to overlapping faults for any s, r s.t. $s > 2$ and $s + r > n$.*

Proof. Assume there exists an (s,r)-secure uniform consensus protocol resilient to overlapping faults for some s, r such that $s > 2$ and $s + r > n$. For every $i \in [r]$ let $R_i = i$ and for every $j \in [s]$ let $S_j = r + j$. In all of the executions, parties $R_1, \ldots, R_r$ will be receive faulty (and one possibly send faulty as well) and parties $S_1, \ldots, S_s$ will be send faulty. In all of the executions Parties $R_1, \ldots, R_r$ will receive no message due to their receive faults, and the messages sent by $S_1, \ldots, S_s$ will be dropped. This means that the S_j parties will hear from every party R_i, except for possibly those that are also send faulty in particular executions. Messages sent from every R_i in all executions must be identical since all receive faulty parties hear nothing in all executions. We will show inductively on $i \in \{0, \ldots, r\}$ that in the following conditions all send faulty parties must output 1:

– parties $R_1, \ldots, R_r$ are receive faulty, parties $S_1, \ldots, S_s$ are send faulty, and no party has full omission faults,
– parties $R_1, \ldots, R_i$ have the input 0 and all other parties have the input 1, and
– parties $R_1, \ldots, R_r$ receive no messages and parties $S_1, \ldots, S_s$ receive all messages from parties $R_1, \ldots, R_r$ but no messages from each other.

For $i = 0$, this immediately holds because all parties have input 1 and thus the send faulty parties must output 1 due to validity. We assume this is the case for $i < r$ and will show that this holds for $i + 1$ as well. We will do so by constructing 5 executions:

1. $R_1, \ldots, R_i$ have input 0 and all other parties have input 1. $R_1, \ldots R_r$ are receive faulty and receive no messages, $S_1, \ldots, S_s$ are send faulty and only receive messages sent by $R_1, \ldots, R_r$.
2. $R_1, \ldots, R_i$ have input 0 and all other parties have input 1. $R_1, \ldots R_r$ are receive faulty and $S_1, \ldots, S_s$ are send faulty. R_{i+1} also has send omissions, i.e. it has full omission faults. $R_1, \ldots, R_r$ hear no messages. R_{i+1}'s messages are not delivered to S_1. $S_1, \ldots, S_s$ hear all other messages from $R_1, \ldots, R_r$ and hear no message sent by each other.

3. $R_1, \ldots, R_i$ have input 0 and all other parties have input 1. $R_1, \ldots R_r$ are receive faulty and parties $S_1, \ldots, S_s$ are send faulty. R_{i+1} also has send omissions, i.e. it has full omission faults. $R_1, \ldots, R_r$ hear no messages. R_i's messages are not delivered to $S_1, \ldots, S_s$. $S_1, \ldots, S_s$ hear all other messages from $R_1, \ldots, R_r$ and hear no message sent by each other.

4. $R_1, \ldots, R_{i+1}$ have input 0 and all other parties have input 1. $R_1, \ldots R_r$ are receive faulty and parties $S_1, \ldots, S_s$ are send faulty. R_i also has send omissions, i.e. it has full omission faults. $R_1, \ldots, R_r$ hear no messages. R_i's messages are not delivered to $S_1, \ldots, S_s$. $S_1, \ldots, S_s$ hear all other messages from $R_1, \ldots, R_r$ and hear no message sent by each other.

5. $R_1, \ldots, R_{i+1}$ have input 0 and all other parties have input 1. $R_1, \ldots R_r$ are receive faulty and receive no messages, $S_1, \ldots, S_s$ are send faulty and only receive messages sent by $R_1, \ldots, R_r$.

The first execution is the one described in the induction hypothesis, and thus $S_1, \ldots, S_s$ output 1. $S_2, \ldots, S_n$'s views in executions 1 and 2 are indistinguishable and thus they output 1 in execution 2 as well[2]. From the consistency of the protocol, S_1 outputs 1 as well. S_1 has an identical view in executions 2 and 3, so it outputs 1 in execution 3. From the consistency of the protocol, $S_2, \ldots, S_s$ outputs 1 as well. $S_2, \ldots, S_s$'s views in executions 3 and 4 are indistinguishable, so they output 1 in execution 4. From the consistency of the protocol, S_1 outputs 1 as well. Finally, S_1's has identical views in executions 4 and 5 and thus it outputs 1 in execution 5, and so do $S_2, \ldots, S_s$. Note that execution 5 is one in which $R_1, \ldots, R_r$ are receive faulty, $S_1, \ldots, S_s$ are send faulty. In addition, parties $R_1, \ldots, R_{i+1}$ have the input 0 and the rest of the parties have the input 1. In other words, we proved the claim for $i + 1$.

Applying this claim to $i = r$, we find that if $R_1, \ldots, R_r$ have the input 0 and $S_1, \ldots, S_s$ have the input 1, and the only message delivered are those from $R_1, \ldots, R_r$ to $S_1, \ldots, S_s$, all parties output 1. We now construct three final executions to show that all parties output 1 even when they all have the input 0, which would contradict the validity of the protocol.

1. $R_1, \ldots, R_r$ have input 0 and $S_1, \ldots, S_s$ have input 1. $R_1, \ldots R_r$ are receive faulty and receive no messages, $S_1, \ldots, S_s$ are send faulty and only receive messages sent by $R_1, \ldots, R_r$.

2. $R_1, \ldots, R_r, S_1$ have input 0 and $S_2, \ldots, S_s$ have input 1. $R_1, \ldots R_r$ are receive faulty and receive no messages, $S_1, \ldots, S_s$ are send faulty and only receive messages sent by $R_1, \ldots, R_r$.

3. All parties have the input 0. $R_1, \ldots R_r$ are receive faulty and receive no messages, $S_1, \ldots, S_s$ are send faulty and only receive messages sent by $R_1, \ldots, R_r$.

Execution 1 is the execution described in the induction above with $i = r$. As shown, all parties output 1. $S_2, \ldots, S_s$ have indistinguishable views in executions 1 and 2 and thus they output 1 in execution 2 as well. From the consistency of

---

[2] The assumption that $s > 2$ is used here to guarantee that S_2 exists.

the protocol, S_1 does so as well. S_1's views in executions 2 and 3 are indistinguishable, so it outputs 1 in execution 3. From consistency, $S_2, \ldots, S_s$ also output 1. However, all parties have the input 0, so this violates the validity of the protocol, reaching a contradiction.

Note that in the definitions used in this paper, receive faulty parties are allowed to output $\perp$, but send faulty parties must output a correct value. This proof can be adjusted to show that in execution 3 parties $S_1, \ldots, S_s$ must output non-$\perp$ values even if we allow send faulty parties to output $\perp$. In order to show that S_i must output non-$\perp$ values in execution 3 above, we can construct another execution which is identical to execution 3, except S_i is non-faulty, but receives no messages from the rest of the send faulty parties. S_i's view is identical in execution 3 and this new execution, and thus it must output non-$\perp$ values in both since it is non-faulty in one of them. Since this is true for an arbitrary S_i, this is true for all of them.

References

1. Abraham, I., Dolev, D., Kagan, A., Stern, G.: Brief announcement: authenticated consensus in synchronous systems with mixed faults. In: Scheideler, C. (ed.) 36th International Symposium on Distributed Computing, DISC 2022, 25-27 October 2022, Augusta, Georgia, USA. LIPIcs, vol. 246, pp. 38:1–38:3. Schloss Dagstuhl - Leibniz-Zentrum für Informatik (2022). https://doi.org/10.4230/LIPIcs.DISC.2022.38
2. Bessani, A.N., Sousa, J., Alchieri, E.A.P.: State machine replication for the masses with BFT-SMART. In: 44th Annual IEEE/IFIP International Conference on Dependable Systems and Networks, DSN 2014, Atlanta, GA, USA, June 23–26, 2014, pp. 355–362. IEEE Computer Society (2014). https://doi.org/10.1109/DSN.2014.43
3. Brazitikos, K., Zikas, V.: General adversary structures in byzantine agreement and multi-party computation with active and omission corruption. Cryptology ePrint Archive (2024)
4. Chandra, T.D., Toueg, S.: Unreliable failure detectors for reliable distributed systems. J. ACM **43**(2), 225–267 (1996). https://doi.org/10.1145/226643.226647
5. Chun, B., Maniatis, P., Shenker, S., Kubiatowicz, J.: Attested append-only memory: making adversaries stick to their word. In: Bressoud, T.C., Kaashoek, M.F. (eds.) Proceedings of the 21st ACM Symposium on Operating Systems Principles 2007, SOSP 2007, Stevenson, Washington, USA, 14-17 October 2007, pp. 189–204. ACM (2007). https://doi.org/10.1145/1294261.1294280
6. Clement, A., et al.: Upright cluster services. In: Matthews, J.N., Anderson, T.E. (eds.) Proceedings of the 22nd ACM Symposium on Operating Systems Principles 2009, SOSP 2009, Big Sky, Montana, USA, October 11-14, 2009. pp. 277–290. ACM (2009). https://doi.org/10.1145/1629575.1629602
7. Correia, M., Lung, L.C., Neves, N.F., Veríssimo, P.: Efficient byzantine-resilient reliable multicast on a hybrid failure model. In: 21st Symposium on Reliable Distributed Systems (SRDS 2002), 13-16 October 2002, Osaka, Japan, pp. 2–11. IEEE Computer Society (2002). https://doi.org/10.1109/RELDIS.2002.1180168
8. Correia, M., Neves, N.F., Veríssimo, P.: How to tolerate half less one byzantine nodes in practical distributed systems. In: 23rd International Symposium on Reliable Distributed Systems (SRDS 2004), 18-20 October 2004, Florianopolis, Brazil,

pp. 174–183. IEEE Computer Society (2004). https://doi.org/10.1109/RELDIS. 2004.1353018

9. Dolev, D., Strong, H.R.: Authenticated algorithms for byzantine agreement. SIAM J. Comput. **12**(4), 656–666 (1983). https://doi.org/10.1137/0212045

10. Dwork, C., Lynch, N., Stockmeyer, L.: Consensus in the presence of partial synchrony. J. ACM (JACM) **35**(2), 288–323 (1988)

11. Eldefrawy, K., Loss, J., Terner, B.: How byzantine is a send corruption? In: Applied Cryptography and Network Security: 20th International Conference, ACNS 2022, Rome, Italy, June 20-23, 2022, Proceedings, pp. 684–704. Springer-Verlag, Heidelberg (2022). https://doi.org/10.1007/978-3-031-09234-3_34

12. Fitzi, M., Maurer, U.: Efficient Byzantine agreement secure against general adversaries. In: Kutten, S. (ed.) DISC 1998. LNCS, vol. 1499, pp. 134–148. Springer, Heidelberg (1998). https://doi.org/10.1007/BFb0056479

13. Garay, J.A., Perry, K.J.: A continuum of failure models for distributed computing. In: Segall, A., Zaks, S. (eds.) WDAG 1992. LNCS, vol. 647, pp. 153–165. Springer, Heidelberg (1992). https://doi.org/10.1007/3-540-56188-9_11

14. Golan-Gueta, G., et al.: SBFT: a scalable and decentralized trust infrastructure. In: 49th Annual IEEE/IFIP International Conference on Dependable Systems and Networks, DSN 2019, Portland, OR, USA, June 24-27, 2019, pp. 568–580. IEEE (2019). https://doi.org/10.1109/DSN.2019.00063

15. Hadzilacos, V.: Issues of fault tolerance in concurrent computations (databases, reliability, transactions, agreement protocols, distributed computing). Ph.D. thesis, Harvard University (1985)

16. Lamport, L., Shostak, R.E., Pease, M.C.: The byzantine generals problem. ACM Trans. Program. Lang. Syst. **4**(3), 382–401 (1982). https://doi.org/10.1145/357172.357176

17. Levin, D., Douceur, J.R., Lorch, J.R., Moscibroda, T.: TrInc: small trusted hardware for large distributed systems. In: Rexford, J., Sirer, E.G. (eds.) Proceedings of the 6th USENIX Symposium on Networked Systems Design and Implementation, NSDI 2009, 22-24 April 2009, Boston, MA, USA. pp. 1–14. USENIX Association (2009). http://www.usenix.org/events/nsdi09/tech/full_papers/levin/levin.pdf

18. Lincoln, P., Rushby, J.M.: A formally verified algorithm for interactive consistency under a hybrid fault model. In: Digest of Papers: FTCS-23, The Twenty-Third Annual International Symposium on Fault-Tolerant Computing, Toulouse, France, 22-24 June 1993. pp. 402–411. IEEE Computer Society (1993). https://doi.org/10.1109/FTCS.1993.627343

19. Loss, J., Stern, G.: Zombies and ghosts: optimal byzantine agreement in the presence of omission faults. In: Rothblum, G., Wee, H. (eds.) Theory of Cryptography Conference, pp. 395–421. Springer (2023). https://doi.org/10.1007/978-3-031-48624-1_15

20. Micali, S., Rogaway, P.: Secure Computation. Springer, Heidelberg (1992). https://doi.org/10.1007/3-540-46766-1_32

21. Parvédy, P.R., Raynal, M.: Uniform agreement despite process omission failures. In: 17th International Parallel and Distributed Processing Symposium (IPDPS 2003), 22-26 April 2003, Nice, France, CD-ROM/Abstracts Proceedings, p. 212. IEEE Computer Society (2003). https://doi.org/10.1109/IPDPS.2003.1213388

22. Perry, K.J., Toueg, S.: Distributed agreement in the presence of processor and communication faults. IEEE Trans. Software Eng. **12**(3), 477–482 (1986). https://doi.org/10.1109/TSE.1986.6312888

23. Raynal, M.: Consensus in synchronous systems: a concise guided tour. In: 2002 Pacific Rim International Symposium on Dependable Computing, 2002. Proceedings, pp. 221–228. IEEE (2002)
24. Serafini, M., Bokor, P., Dobre, D., Majuntke, M., Suri, N.: Scrooge: reducing the costs of fast byzantine replication in presence of unresponsive replicas. In: Proceedings of the 2010 IEEE/IFIP International Conference on Dependable Systems and Networks, DSN 2010, Chicago, IL, USA, June 28 - July 1 2010, pp. 353–362. IEEE Computer Society (2010). https://doi.org/10.1109/DSN.2010.5544295
25. Serafini, M., Suri, N.: The fail-heterogeneous architectural model. In: 26th IEEE Symposium on Reliable Distributed Systems (SRDS 2007), Beijing, China, 10-12 October 2007, pp. 103–113. IEEE Computer Society (2007). https://doi.org/10.1109/SRDS.2007.33
26. Siu, H.S., Chin, Y.H., Yang, W.P.: Byzantine agreement in the presence of mixed faults on processors and links. IEEE Trans. Parallel Distrib. Syst. **9**(4), 335–345 (1998). https://doi.org/10.1109/71.667895
27. Thambidurai, P.M., Park, Y.: Interactive consistency with multiple failure modes. In: Seventh Symposium on Reliable Distributed Systems, SRDS 1988, Columbus, Ohio, USA, October 10-12, 1988, Proceedings, pp. 93–100. IEEE Computer Society (1988). https://doi.org/10.1109/RELDIS.1988.25784
28. Veronese, G.S., Correia, M., Bessani, A.N., Lung, L.C., Veríssimo, P.: Efficient byzantine fault-tolerance. IEEE Trans. Computers **62**(1), 16–30 (2013). https://doi.org/10.1109/TC.2011.221
29. Zikas, V., Hauser, S., Maurer, U.: Realistic failures in secure multi-party computation. In: Reingold, O. (ed.) TCC 2009. LNCS, vol. 5444, pp. 274–293. Springer, Heidelberg (2009). https://doi.org/10.1007/978-3-642-00457-5_17

On the (Im)possibility of Game-Theoretically Fair Leader Election Protocols

Ohad Klein[1]([✉])[iD], Ilan Komargodski[1,2][iD], and Chenzhi Zhu[3][iD]

[1] Hebrew University of Jerusalem, Jerusalem, Israel
ohadkel@gmail.com, ilank@cs.huji.ac.il
[2] NTT Research, Sunnyvale, CA, USA
[3] Paul G. Allen School of Computer Science & Engineering,
University of Washington, Seattle, WA, USA
zhucz20@cs.washington.edu

Abstract. We consider the problem of electing a leader among n parties with the guarantee that each (honest) party has a reasonable probability of being elected, even in the presence of a coalition that controls a subset of parties, trying to bias the output. This notion is called "game-theoretic fairness" because such protocols ensure that following the honest behavior is an equilibrium and also the best response for every party and coalition. In the two-party case, Blum's commit-and-reveal protocol (where if one party aborts, then the other is declared the leader) satisfies this notion and it is also known that one-way functions are necessary. Recent works study this problem in the multi-party setting. They show that composing Blum's 2-party protocol for $\log n$ rounds in a tournament-tree-style manner results with perfect game-theoretic fairness: each honest party has probability $\geqslant 1/n$ of being elected as leader, no matter how large the coalition is. Logarithmic round complexity is also shown to be necessary if we require perfect fairness against a coalition of size $n-1$. Relaxing the above two requirements, i.e., settling for approximate game-theoretic fairness and guaranteeing fairness against only constant fraction size coalitions, it is known that there are $O(\log^* n)$ round protocols.

This leaves many open problems, in particular, whether one can go below logarithmic round complexity by relaxing only one of the strong requirements from above. We manage to resolve this problem for commit-and-reveal style protocols, showing that
- $\Omega(\log n/\log \log n)$ rounds are necessary if we settle for approximate fairness against very large (more than constant fraction) coalitions;
- $\Omega(\log n)$ rounds are necessary if we settle for perfect fairness against n^ε size coalitions (for any constant $\varepsilon > 0$).

These show that both relaxations made in prior works are necessary to go below logarithmic round complexity. Lastly, we provide several additional upper and lower bounds for the case of single-round commit-and-reveal style protocols.

© International Association for Cryptologic Research 2025
E. Boyle and M. Mahmoody (Eds.): TCC 2024, LNCS 15364, pp. 383–412, 2025.
https://doi.org/10.1007/978-3-031-78011-0_13

1   Introduction

Suppose that Rivest, Shamir, and Adleman win yet another important award for the invention of their groundbreaking RSA crypto-system. The award committee announces that all of them are invited to the ceremony but only one of them can deliver a presentation. Since they all want to present and they all reside in different parts of the world, they need to run a leader election protocol over the internet. Of course, they are aware of Cleve's famous lower bound [5] stating that *strongly fair* protocols do not exist, i.e., in any protocol, there exists a strategy for half of the parties to bias the output. However, not all hope is lost because for their application the classical notion of fairness is overly stringent. Indeed, a recent line of works [3,4,8,12,17] observed that a relaxed notion of fairness, called *game-theoretic fairness*, in the context of leader election is often sufficient and also possible to achieve even when an arbitrary number of parties may be corrupt.

To exemplify the notion and possibility of game-theoretic fairness we recall Blum's original 2-party coin flipping protocol [2]: each party first commits to a random coin, they then open their coin, and the XOR of the two bits is used to elect the winner. If one party fails to commit or correctly open, it is eliminated and the remaining party is declared the winner. Blum's protocol satisfies game-theoretic fairness in the following sense. As long as the commitment scheme is not broken, a corrupt party cannot bias the coin to its own favor no matter how it deviates from the protocol. Note that Blum's protocol is not strongly fair since a corrupt party can indeed bias the coin, but only to the other party's advantage.

The above 2-party protocol can be generalized to handle n parties via a tournament-tree protocol, as follows. Suppose that n is a power of 2 for simplicity. We first divide the n parties into $n/2$ pairs, and each pair elects a winner using Blum's protocol. The winner survives to the next round, where we again divide the surviving $n/2$ parties into $n/4$ pairs. The protocol continues in the same manner for $\log_2 n$ rounds when a final winner is elected.[1] At any point in the protocol, if a party fails to commit or correctly open its commitment, it is eliminated and its opponent survives to the next round.

The recent work of Chung et al. [3] proved that the above tournament-tree protocol satisfies a strong notion of game-theoretic fairness, as explained below. Suppose that the winner obtains a utility of 1 and everyone else obtains a utility of 0. As long as the commitment scheme is not broken, the tournament tree protocol guarantees that:

- No coalition of any size can *increase its own expected utilty* no matter what strategy it adopts.
- No coalition of any size can *harm any individual honest player's expected utility*, no matter what strategy it adopts.

---

[1] By default, throughout this paper log stands for $\log_2$.

Recent work in this space [3,4,8,17] calls the former notion cooperative-strategy-proofness (or *CSP-fairness* for short), and calls the latter notion *maximin fairness*. Philosophically, CSP-fairness guarantees that any rational, profit-seeking individual or coalition has no incentive to deviate from the honest protocol; and maximin fairness ensures that any paranoid individual who wants to maximally protect itself in the worst-case scenario has no incentive to deviate either. In summary, the honest protocol is an equilibrium and also the best response for every player and coalition. Therefore, prior works [3,4,8,17] argue that game-theoretic notions of fairness are compelling and worth investigating because (1) they are arguably more natural (albeit strictly weaker) than the classical strong fairness notion in practical applications; and (2) the game-theoretic relaxation allows us to circumvent classical impossibility results pertaining to strong fairness in the presence of majority coalitions [5].

Since we know that the tournament tree protocol satisfies game-theoretic fairness, a natural question is whether logarithmic round complexity is necessary. A protocol of [12] (following up on [3]) showed that if we settle for an approximate notion of game-theoretic fairness, then the answer is no: there are $O(\log^* n)$-round protocols.[2] In approximate fairness we require to satisfy the above notions of game theoretic fairness (i.e., CSP-fairness and maximin fairness) up to an ε slack. More specifically, we say that a protocol is $(1 - \varepsilon)$-fair if every coalition's expected utility cannot exceed $1/(n(1 - \varepsilon))$ times the size of the coalition and if any honest individual's expected utility cannot drop below $(1 - \varepsilon)/n$. Perfect fairness holds when $(1 - \varepsilon)$-fairness holds with $\varepsilon = 0$.

While the above works provide feasibility of round-efficient protocols for game-theoretically fair leader election, it is still widely open to characterize the minimal round complexity needed. This is a major problem left open in the works of [3,12]. Most strikingly, it is not even known if single-round commit-and-reveal style protocols exist. This seemingly simple setting with minimal interaction already turns out to be quite challenging to analyze and our work is the first to address this problem with various possibility and impossibility results.

Single-Round Protocols. We start by focusing on single-round "commit-and-reveal" protocols which consist of two phases: in the first phase each party commits to a value. In the second phase, each party either opens their commitment or sends a special abort symbol. Finally, a publicly known function is applied to the revealed values, specifying the identity of a leader. To simplify, we assume an ideal commitment scheme; this has the advantage of separating the computational issue regarding cryptography from the game-theoretic aspects of the problem. Note that this will only make our lower bounds stronger.

Before stating our main results, we want to illustrate the non-triviality of the problem by going back to the Rivest-Shamir-Adleman conundrum. As men-

---

[2] In fact, their protocol enables a smooth trade-off between the round complexity and the resilience to strategic behavior, but their framework requires at least $\Omega(\log^* n)$ rounds to provide any meaningful fairness guarantee. Here $\log^* n$ denotes the minimum number of times the logarithm function must be iteratively applied to n before the result is less 1.

tioned, they can fairly decide who will deliver the presentation using a "depth-two" tournament tree (commit-and-reveal-commit-and-reveal). Can they do it using only commit-and-reveal? We answer this question by showing the following results:

1. *An upper bound*: there is a commit-and-reveal protocol achieving (3/4)-fairness.
2. *A lower bound*: there is no commit-and-reveal protocol achieving $(1 - \varepsilon)$-fairness for any $\varepsilon < 1/4$.

The upper bound is obtained via the following simple protocol: every pair runs Blum's perfectly fair leader election protocol. A party is declared as the leader if it wins both of its tournaments. If no party won both tournaments, we simply declare party 1 as the leader. Because the pair-wise protocol is perfectly fair, any fixed party will be declared as leader with probability at least 1/4. Thus, the protocol is $(1/4)/(1/3) = (3/4)$-fair. The more surprising aspect of the above result is the lower bound, showing that this protocol is optimal. Our proof relies on a non-trivial application of the minimax principle. More generally, we prove the following theorem for any number of parties:

Theorem 1 (Fairness of single-round protocols; informal). *For protocols on n parties, even in the presence of a corrupted coalition of size $n - 1$:*

– *There exists $(n/2^{n-1})$-fair single-round "commit-and-reveal" protocol.*
– *Any α-fair single-round "commit-and-reveal" protocol satisfies $\alpha \leqslant n/2^{n-1}$.*

Extensions. By a "grouping" argument we extend the above impossibility result to the setting where the honest set of parties consists of a constant β fraction of parties. For instance, when $\beta = 1/3$, our result shows that there is no (8/9)-fair leader election protocol. See Theorem 18 for the exact statement. Lastly, we consider the low-corruption regime, i.e., when the coalition is of size say 1 or 2 and $n \geqslant 3$ is arbitrarily large. We show (in Theorem 25) that in this setting there are no perfectly fair leader election protocols.

Multiple-Round Protocols. It was shown in [3, Theorem 8.1] that $\Omega(\log n)$ rounds are required for perfectly fair leader election among n parties. When the protocol is required to be only approximately fair, the number of rounds can be reduced to $O(\log^* n)$ by [12].

This gap is due to two differences between the regimes. First, perfect fairness is more stringent, requiring $\varepsilon = 0$ in the fairness definition. Second, the $\Omega(\log n)$ lower bound implicitly assumes protection against a corrupted coalition of size $n - 1$ (which we abbreviate as $(n - 1)$-corruption), while the $O(\log^* n)$-round protocol assumes a constant fraction (i.e. $n - \Omega(n)$) of corrupted parties.

Therefore, there are two cases in which the round complexity is undetermined (in addition to the question of whether the $O(\log^* n)$ protocol is most round-efficient), giving rise to the following questions:

– **Question 1**: Is there a $o(\log n)$-round protocol with guaranteed approximate fairness against coalitions of size $n - o(n)$?

– **Question 2**: Is there a $o(\log n)$-round protocol with guaranteed perfect fairness against coalitions of size less than $n - 1$?

We answer both of the above questions by providing nearly tight lower bounds on the number of rounds in both cases. At a high level, we show that for every $\varepsilon \in (0, 1)$, perfect fairness in the presence of n^ε corrupted parties requires $\Omega(\log n)$ rounds. We proceed with a more precise statement of our results.

Approximate Fairness. We show that $\Omega(\log n / \log \log n)$ rounds are necessary even in a weak $(1/n)$-fairness requirement by extending an argument of [3]. The protocols we consider are as in [3], and are composed of a sequence of r rounds, each of which is a "commit-and-reveal" sub-protocol, as described earlier. Specifically, we prove the following theorem in Sect. 5.

Theorem 2 (Approximate fairness against large coalitions requires at least $\log(n) / \log \log(n)$ **rounds).** *A leader election protocol on n parties, having r "commit-and-reveal" rounds, in which each honest party has a chance of $1/n^2$ to be elected (i.e. $1/n$-fairness), even in the presence of a corrupted coalition of size $n - k$, must satisfy*

$$r > \frac{\log(n) - \log(k)}{\log \log(n) + 3}.$$

We further extend this result to the case of committee election, where a small set of t parties is to be elected; see Sect. 5 for detail.

Perfect Fairness. We also show a logarithmic lower bound on the round complexity of any perfectly fair leader election protocol in the presence of sub-$(n-1)$ corrupted parties. Specifically, we prove the following theorem in Sect. 6.2.

Theorem 3 (Perfect fairness against size-k coalitions requires at least $\log k$ **rounds).** *A leader election protocol on n parties, having r "commit-and-reveal" rounds, which is perfectly fair in the presence of a corrupted coalition of size k, must satisfy*

$$r \geqslant \lceil \log(\min(n, 2k)) \rceil.$$

Organization. In Sect. 2, we provide a technical overview of our proofs. In Sect. 3, we define fairness, committee-election protocols, and prove an n-party minimax theorem. In Sect. 4, we give a tight bound on the fairness of single-round protocols. In Sect. 5, we apply this bound to bound the round-efficiency of reasonably-fair protocols. Finally, in Sect. 6, we lower bound the number of rounds of perfectly fair protocols.

1.1 Additional Related Work

There are several prior results on lower bounds of coin flipping protocols that imply certain impossiblity results of leader election protocols. In the information-theoretical regime, Russel, Saks and Zuckerman [14] showed that for any n-party coin flipping protocols with $r = o(\log^* n)$ rounds where each party can only send one bit per round, a coalition of a constant fraction of parties can bias the outcome. Later, Filmus et al. [7] extended the results to protocols where each party is allowed to send arbitrary messages. In the setting where a constant fraction of parties are corrupted, since a fair n-party r-round leader election protocol implies an n-party $(r + 1)$-round coin flipping protocol safe against a constant bias, the results imply that there is no fair n-party leader election protocol with $r = o(\log^* n)$ rounds in the information-theoretical regime. The $(\log^* n + O(1))$-round protocol by Russell and Zuckerman [15] and Feige's famous lightest bin protocol [6] show that the above lower bounds are tight.

A result by Berman, Haitner and Tentes [1] (improving on [11]) shows that any 2-party weak coin flipping protocol safe against any constant bias implies the existence of one-way functions. Here the security of 2-party weak coin flipping guarantees that the adversary cannot bias the outcome towards 1 by corrupting party one and cannot bias the outcome towards 0 by corrupting party two. The result implies that any fair n-party leader election protocol in the dishonest majority setting implies the existence of one-way functions, since such an n-party leader election protocol implies a 2-party weak coin flipping protocol safe against a constant bias.

We also note that there is a line of work on random selection protocols in the information-theoretical regime [9,10,16], wherein n parties want to agree on a random value sampled from a output universe of size p and the security goal is to prevent the corrupted parties from causing the output to lie in some small subset of the output universe. Although one can view a random selection protocol as a leader election protocol for $p = n$, we emphasize that their security goal is very different from our fairness notion. In particular, they do not prevent an attacker that controls $n - 1$ parties from always making sure that the output is one of the corrupted $n - 1$ parties, which is exactly the setting that we are interested in. As another evidence of the difference, Gradwohl, Vadhan and Zuckerman [10] give a $\log^*(n)$-round random selection protocol in the dishonest majority setting without using any cryptography/ideal model commitments, while for our notion of fairness this is impossible [1] (as mentioned above).

1.2   Open Problems

One limitation of our impossibility results is that we only consider the commit-and-reveal style protocols, and it is unclear whether we can generalize our impossibility results to stronger models (e.g., only assuming one-way functions or oblivious transfer).

Another main open problem is whether we can extend our lower bounds on the number of rounds to the setting where the number of honest parties is greater than $n/\log n$. For example, when a constant fraction of parties are honest, the protocol of [12] needs $O(\log^* n)$ rounds, but we do not know whether this is optimal.

Regarding upper bounds, for the $(n - 1)$-corruption case, we only know that there are perfectly fair protocols with $\log n$ rounds, but it is unclear whether we can do slightly better than $\log n$ rounds for approximate fairness. Our lower bound shows that a fair protocol needs at least $\frac{\log n}{\log \log n + O(1)}$ rounds. It is interesting to see whether we can close this gap.

In the regime of perfect fairness, it is unclear whether our lower bound is tight. Even if the adversary only corrupts a single party, it is unclear whether we can construct a *perfectly fair* leader election protocol with $r < \log n$ rounds or show it is impossible. Also, for single-round protocols, we only show there is no perfect leader election protocol, but it is unclear whether it can be extended to committee election protocol. For example, it is unclear whether we can elect 2 out of 5 parties by a single round protocol with perfect fairness assuming only one party is malicious.

2   Technical Overview

In this section we describe the technical methods underlying the proofs of our main results. In Sect. 2.1 we explain the ideas behind the proof of the single-round setting Theorem 1, and in Sect. 2.2 we explain how to obtain our results in the multi-round setting, i.e., Theorems 2 and 3.

For the lower bounds of approximate fairness, we focus on the $(n-1)$-corruption case in the following explanations. Our results for $(n-k)$-corruption follow by "grouping" various sets of parties together and treating them as one, as follows: Roughly, given a fair n-party protocol against $(n-k)$-corruptions, we construct a fair n/k-party protocol against $(n/k-1)$-corruptions by partitioning n parties into n/k groups of size k and viewing each group as a single party. We refer to Sects. 4.3 and 5.1 for details on this reduction.

2.1   Lower Bounds for Single-Round Commit-and-Reveal Protocols

Given a single-round n-party commit-and-reveal leader election protocol, we show that there exists an adversary corrupting $n-1$ parties such that the probability that the honest party is the leader is at most $2^{-(n-1)}$. Since the protocol is commit-and-reveal, the adversary must choose the inputs for all corrupted parties before seeing the honest party's input. After receiving the honest party's input, the only strategy of the adversary is to let some corrupt parties abort.

The idea of our attack is to let all but one corrupted party abort. After receiving the input of the honest party, the adversary checks whether there exists a corrupted party i such that party i wins against the honest party if all corrupted parties except party i abort. Denote the event that the honest party j wins against party i as Loss_i. The intuition that this attack works is that, on average, the probability that Loss_i occurs should be at most $1/2$, and therefore, since there are $n-1$ corrupted parties, the probability that no corrupted party wins against the honest party should be at most $2^{-(n-1)}$.

However, this simple argument does not work. The main issue is that the two events Loss_i and Loss_k for two corrupted parties i and k are not independent. In fact, they both depend on the input of the honest party j. The idea to address this is to fix the input of the honest party in our analysis. Since Loss_i depends only on the inputs of party i and the honest party, assuming the adversary chooses the input of each corrupted party independently, the events Loss_i and Loss_k are independent given the input of the honest party x_j. Therefore, the probability that the honest party is the leader is at most $\max_x \prod_i \Pr[\mathsf{Loss}_i|x]$, where $\Pr[\mathsf{Loss}_i|x]$ denotes as the probability that Loss_i occurs given that x is input of the honest party.

The problem then reduces to bounding $\max_x \prod_i \Pr[\mathsf{Loss}_i|x]$. To this end, we define a few notations for describing the adversary's strategy. We use $\mathcal{S}_i$ to denote a (mixed) strategy for choosing the input of party i. We denote $p_{i,j}(\mathcal{S}_i, x_j)$ as the probability that Loss_i occurs under the strategy $\mathcal{S}_i$ given that party j is the honest party and the input of party j is x_j. Then, the probability that the honest party j wins and elected as the leader is upper bounded by

$$W_j = \min_{\{\mathcal{S}_i\}_{i \in [n] \setminus \{j\}}} \max_{x_j} \prod_i p_{i,j}(\mathcal{S}_i, x_j). \tag{1}$$

Recall that the protocol is 'not fair' even if for one specific j the value W_j is too small. We will even show that the expected value of $\log(W_j)$ over uniformly random $j \sim [n]$ is small.

To bound (1), we use the minimax theorem from game theory. The minimax theorem shows that for any two parties i and j, $\min_{\mathcal{S}_i} \max_{x_j} p_{i,j}(\mathcal{S}_i, x_j) + \min_{\mathcal{S}_j} \max_{x_i} p_{j,i}(\mathcal{S}_j, x_i) = 1$. Therefore, denoting $p_{i,j} := \min_{\mathcal{S}_i} \max_{x_j} p_{i,j}(\mathcal{S}_i, x_j)$, we rewrite the minimax equation as $p_{i,j} + p_{j,i} = 1$ for all $i \neq j \in [n]$. Also, the probability that the honest party is the leader is bounded by $\prod_{i \in [n] \setminus \{j\}} p_{i,j}$.

Overall, we converted the problem to the following question: given $0 \leqslant p_{i,j} \leqslant 1$ and $p_{i,j} + p_{j,i} = 1$ for all $i \neq j \in [n]$, show that there exists j such that $\prod_{i \in [n] \setminus \{j\}} p_{i,j} \leqslant 2^{-(n-1)}$. To show this, we take the logarithm of both sides, which converts products to sums. Since $p_{i,j} + p_{j,i} = 1$, by Jensen's inequality, we have $\log p_{i,j} + \log p_{j,i} \leqslant 2\log(p_{i,j}/2 + p_{j,i}/2) = -2$. It remains to show that there exists j such that $\sum_{i \in [n] \setminus \{j\}} \log p_{i,j} \leqslant -(n-1)$. For simplicity, we demonstrate the proof for $n = 3$. By summing of all pairs of $i \neq j$, we have

$$\log p_{2,1} + \log p_{3,1} + \log p_{1,2} + \log p_{3,2} + \log p_{1,3} + \log p_{2,3} \leqslant -6 \ .$$

Therefore, one of the followings holds:

$$\log(W_1) = \log p_{2,1} + \log p_{3,1} \leqslant -2,$$
$$\log(W_2) = \log p_{1,2} + \log p_{3,2} \leqslant -2,$$
$$\log(W_3) = \log p_{1,3} + \log p_{2,3} \leqslant -2.$$

This proves that any one-round leader election protocol cannot be α-fair for $\alpha \geqslant 2^{-(n-1)}/(1/n) = n/2^{n-1}$. We refer to Sect. 4.2 for the full proof.

Extending to Committee Election. Committee election protocols are similar to leader election protocols, except that they elect a committee of t parties, instead of just one party. Each party wants to be elected with probability about t/n.

If we wish to show that single-round protocols are not fair, we cannot use the same adversary for committee election protocols, since it aborts all but two parties. This means that the honest party will always be elected once two parties are elected. The adversary is supposed to prevent this from happening.

To address this, the idea is to partition the corrupted parties into groups of size k where k is larger than the committee size. After receiving the honest party's input, the adversary picks a group and lets all other groups abort. Similarly to the leader election case, assuming that party j is the honest party and the input of j is x_j, for a set of parties $T \subset [n] \setminus \{j\}$ and a (mixed) strategy $\mathcal{S}_T$ of parties in T, we denote $p_{T,j}(\mathcal{S}_T, x_j)$ the probability that the honest party is in the committee under the strategy $\mathcal{S}_T$ given that all corrupted parties except those in T abort. Denote $p_{T,j} := \min_{\mathcal{S}_T} \max_{x_j} p_{T,j}(\mathcal{S}_T, x_j)$. By extending the minimax theorem to the $(k+1)$-party case, we can show that $\sum_{j \in T'} p_{T' \setminus \{j\}, j} \leq t$, where $T' \subset [n]$ is a set of size $k+1$. Intuitively, this shows that on average $p_{T,j} \leq t/(k+1)$. Also, given party j as the honest party and a partition $\mathcal{P} = (T_1, \ldots, T_{(n-1)/k})$ of the corrupted parties, the probability that the honest party is in the committee is bounded by $\prod_{T \in \mathcal{P}} p_{T,j}$. Using a similar calculation for the leader election case, we show that there exists party j and a partition $\mathcal{P}$ such that $\sum_{T \in \mathcal{P}} \log p_{T,j} \leq (n-1)/k \log(t/(k+1))$. We refer to Sect. 4.2 for the full proof.

By setting $k = 2t-1$, the probability that the honest party is in the committee is bounded by $2^{-\frac{n-1}{2t-1}}$. We remark that other choices k cannot improve the bound asymptotically. In fact, our upper bound for single-round committee election protocols indicates that the lower bound is tight up to a constant factor in the exponent. Intuitively, the lower bound means that it is not possible to fairly elect a committee of size smaller than $O(n/\log n)$ in one-round, which is a useful fact used in proving the lower bounds of multi-round protocols (that we discuss next).

2.2 Extending to Multi-round Protocols

Here, we shall focus on leader election protocols and note that similar arguments apply to committee election protocols as well. The key step is to show the following inductive argument: given an α-fair r-round n-party commit-and-reveal leader election protocol Π, there exists an α'-fair $(r-1)$-round commit-and-reveal leader election protocol Π' for $\Omega(n/\log n)$ parties, where α' is not significantly lower than α. Intuitively, this means that at each round the number of parties can only shrink by at most a factor of $1/\log n$. Therefore, a fair n-party leader election protocol requires at least $\frac{\log n}{\log\log n + O(1)}$ rounds.

We prove such a reduction as follows. After the first round of commit-and-reveal, we observe that some parties might be "eliminated," making the probability that these parties are elected become small or 0. We first show that the number of parties that are not "eliminated" is $\Omega(n/\log n)$, meaning that the number of parties after the first round does not shrink too much. We show this by viewing the first round as a single-round committee election protocol, where the elected committee is the set of parties that are not "eliminated." Now, we use our lower bound for single-round committee election protocols to conclude that the number of parties that are not "eliminated" is $\Omega(n/\log n)$. Finally, we construct Π' from Π by fixing the first-round execution and grouping all eliminated parties together with one of the remaining parties as one party.

To make the above argument formal, we need to first define the condition under which a party is eliminated formally and show that the condition implies that Π' is α'-fair for some $\alpha' > 0$. Concretely, after the first-round execution, we say a party i is eliminated if and only if there exists an adversary corrupting all but party i such that the probability that i is elected is smaller than $\alpha/n - 2/n^2$. Then, for the resulting $(r - 1)$-round protocol, no matter which parties the adversary corrupts the probability that the honest party is elected is at least $\alpha/n - 2/n^2$, meaning that the $(r-1)$-round protocol is $\Omega((\alpha - 2/n)/\log n)$-fair.

Also, we need to show that there exists a first-round execution such that the number of remaining (non-eliminated) parties is $\Omega(n/\log n)$. We prove it by contradiction. Suppose this is not true. By our lower bound of single-round committee election protocols, there exists an adversary such that the honest party is not eliminated after the first round with probability at most $1/n^2$. Therefore, by the definition of "elimination," we can construct an adversary such that the honest party is elected as the leader with probability at most $\varepsilon/n - 1/n^2$, which contradicts the fact that Π is ε-maximin-fair. The full details are given in Sect. 5.

2.3   Lower Bounds for Perfectly Fair Protocols

The prior result [3] by Chung et al. shows that any perfectly fair n-party leader election protocol against $(n - 1)$-corruption is at least $\lceil \log n \rceil$-round. We extend their result to protocols against k-corruption by showing that the requirement for the number of corrupted parties in the following key step of their proof can be relaxed. Concretely, their proof shows that for any perfectly fair n-party leader election protocol against $(n - 1)$-corruption, there exists a first-round execution such that given the first-round execution, the number of parties left is at least $n/2$, where we say a party is eliminated if the probability that the party is elected is 0. We relax the condition of $(n - 1)$-corruption in the above claim and show that for any perfectly fair n-party leader election protocol against k-corruption, there exists a first-round execution such that given the first-round execution, the number of parties left is at least $\min\{n/2, k\}$. Given the first-round execution, we can view the rest of the execution of the protocol as a protocol for $\min\{n/2, k\}$ parties by fixing the execution for all the eliminated parties arbitrarily. Intuitively, since there are k corrupted parties, the resulting protocol must be perfectly fair even if all but one party are corrupted. Since the prior result indicates that the resulting protocol needs at least $\lceil \log(\min\{n/2, k\}) \rceil$ rounds, the n-party protocol needs at least $\lceil \log(\min\{n/2, k\}) \rceil + 1$ rounds. We refer to Sect. 6 for details.

3   Preliminaries

Notations. We use $[n]$ to denote the set $\{1, \ldots, n\}$ and $[\ell..n]$ to denote the set $\{\ell, \ldots, n\}$. We use $\boldsymbol{x} \in \Omega^n$ to denote a vector and x_i to denote the i-th entry of $\boldsymbol{x}$. We always use $\log x$ to denote the logarithm of x to the base 2.

3.1   Commit-and-Reveal Committee Election Protocols

An (n, r, t)-commit-and-reveal committee election protocol is a $2r$-round interactive protocol among n parties that outputs a committee of size at most t. In this context, we assume that each party has a public identity $1, 2, \ldots, n$, and that the interaction is synchronous, so that the protocol proceeds in rounds. Further, we use the notion of an ideal commitment functionality $\mathcal{F}_{\mathsf{com}}$, as defined in Fig. 1.

$\mathcal{F}_{\mathsf{com}}$ runs with parties $\{1, \ldots, n\}$.

- Upon receiving input (commit, sid, msg) from party i, if $\mathsf{msg}_{(i,\mathsf{sid})}$ is not recorded, $\mathcal{F}_{\mathsf{com}}$ records $\mathsf{msg}_{(i,\mathsf{sid})} := \mathsf{msg}$ and sends (receipt, i, sid) to all parties.
- Upon receiving input (open, sid) from party i, if $\mathsf{msg}_{(i,\mathsf{sid})}$ is recorded, $\mathcal{F}_{\mathsf{com}}$ sends (open, i, sid, msg) to all parties.

Fig. 1. The ideal commitment functionality $\mathcal{F}_{\mathsf{com}}$

For each $i \in [r]$, in the $(2i-1)$-th round, each party j picks an element $x_j^{(i)}$ from Ω and sends (commit, $i, x_j^{(i)}$) to $\mathcal{F}_{\mathsf{com}}$. W.l.o.g., in an honest execution, we assume that $x_j^{(i)}$ is sampled uniformly from Ω. In the $2i$-th round, after receiving (receipt, j', i) for each party j', each party j sends (open, i) to $\mathcal{F}_{\mathsf{com}}$. If the party aborts in either of the two rounds or does not open its commitment, we denote $x_j^{(i')} = \perp$ for $i \leq i' \leq r$. Finally, each party uses a deterministic algorithm which takes $(\boldsymbol{x}^{(1)}, \ldots, \boldsymbol{x}^{(r)})$ as input to compute the selected committee. Since all communication relies on the functionality $\mathcal{F}_{\mathsf{com}}$, which implicitly implies broadcast channels, each party receives the same view during the execution of the protocol, and thus all parties agree on the final selected committee.

For simplicity, we say the protocol is an r-round commit-and-reveal protocol. We call $\boldsymbol{x}^{(i)}$ the input of round i and $x_j^{(i)}$ the input of party j in round i. Formally, the commit-and-reveal committee election protocol can be represented as a function Π, indicating which parties win the election and are included in the committee (see Definition 4).

Definition 4 (Commit-and-Reveal Committee/Leader Election). *For any integers $r \geq 1$ and $1 \leq t \leq n$, an (n, r, t)-commit-and-reveal committee election protocol with input space Ω is a function*

$$\Pi : ((\{\perp\} \cup \Omega)^n)^r \rightarrow (\{0, 1\})^n$$

such that for any $\boldsymbol{x}^{(1)}, \ldots, \boldsymbol{x}^{(r)} \in (\{\perp\} \cup \Omega)^n$, $1 \leq \sum_{i=1}^n \Pi_i(\boldsymbol{x}^{(1)}, \ldots, \boldsymbol{x}^{(r)}) \leq t$, where $\Pi_i(\boldsymbol{x}^{(1)}, \ldots, \boldsymbol{x}^{(r)})$ denotes the i-th entry of the output of Π. In particular, an $(n, r, 1)$-commit-and-reveal committee election protocol is an (n, r)-commit-and-reveal leader election protocol.

394 O. Klein et al.

Remark 5. We note here that for committee election we only require the protocol to select a non-empty committee with size at most t instead of exactly t. This is because we mainly consider impossibility results in this paper, and our definition can cover a wider range of protocols, which makes our impossibility results stronger. Also, for our positive results (see Sect. 4.1), our committee election protocol does always select t parties.

Security. An adversary can corrupt k parties at the beginning, before the rounds begin. Since we use the ideal commitment functionality, during each round, the only strategy of the adversary is to choose the inputs of all corrupt parties independent of all honest parties' inputs (for that round) and decide, for each corrupted party, whether to abort according to the revealed inputs of the honest parties. That is, we assume the adversary is *rushing*, i.e., the adversary can decide whether to abort after observing all honest parties' revealed inputs.

Fairness. We use the same fairness definition as [12]. Maximin-fairness means that the adversary cannot decrease the probability that an honest party is in the committee by a factor of $(1 - \varepsilon)$, and is formally defined in Definition 6. Furthermore, CSP-fairness means that the adversary cannot increase the expected fraction of corrupted parties in the committee by a factor of $\frac{1}{1-\varepsilon}$, and is formally defined in Definition 7.

Definition 6 (Maximin-Fairness). *We say that an (n, r, t)-commit-and-reveal committee election protocol is $(1 - \varepsilon, k)$-maximin-fair if for any adversary $\mathcal{A}$ that corrupts a set $S \subseteq [n]$ of parties of size k, and for any $i \in [n] \setminus S$,*

$$\Pr[i \text{ is in the committee}] \geq \frac{(1 - \varepsilon)t}{n} \,,$$

where the probability is taken over the randomness of $\mathcal{A}$ and all honest parties' inputs $\{x_j^{(\ell)}\}_{j \in [n] \setminus S, \ell \in [r]}$ with $x_j^{(\ell)}$ sampled uniformly from Ω.

Definition 7 (CSP-Fairness). *We say that an (n, r, t)-committee election protocol is $(1 - \varepsilon, k)$-CSP-fair if for any adversary $\mathcal{A}$ that corrupts a set $S \subseteq [n]$ of parties of size k,*

$$\mathbb{E}[\text{the fraction of corrupted parties in the committee}] \leq \frac{k}{n(1 - \varepsilon)} \,,$$

where the expectation is taken over the randomness of $\mathcal{A}$ and all honest parties' inputs $\{x_j^{(\ell)}\}_{j \in [n] \setminus S, \ell \in [r]}$ with $x_j^{(\ell)}$ sampled uniformly from Ω.

Moreover, we say a scheme is $(1 - \varepsilon, k)$-fair if the scheme is both $(1 - \varepsilon, k)$-maximin-fair and $(1 - \varepsilon, k)$-CSP-fair. We say a scheme is perfectly fair against k-corruption if and only if the scheme is $(1, k)$-fair.

3.2 Minimax Theorem

We first recall the minimax theorem from game theory, which was first proved in [13]. Then, we show an n-variable extension of the theorem, which is used in our proofs of lower bounds for single-round protocols. For any n-variable function $f : \Omega^n \to \mathbf{R}$, a (mixed) strategy for a set $S \subseteq [n]$ (of players) is a probability distribution over all inputs $\{x_i \in \Omega\}_{i \in S}$. Such a strategy can be regarded as a function $\mathcal{S} : \Omega^{|S|} \to [0,1]$ such that $\sum_{x \in \Omega^{|S|}} \mathcal{S}(x) = 1$. Given two strategies $\mathcal{S}_1, \mathcal{S}_2$ where $\mathcal{S}_1$ is for $S \subseteq [n]$ and $\mathcal{S}_2$ is for $[n] \setminus S$, we denote

$$f(\mathcal{S}_1, \{x_j\}_{j \in [n] \setminus S}) := \sum_{\{x_i\}_{i \in S} \in \Omega^{|S|}} \mathcal{S}_1(\{x_i\}_{i \in S}) f(x_1, \dots, x_n)$$

and

$$f(\mathcal{S}_1, \mathcal{S}_2) := \sum_{x \in \Omega^n} \mathcal{S}_1(\{x_i\}_{i \in S}) \mathcal{S}_2(\{x_j\}_{j \in [n] \setminus S}) f(x_1, \dots, x_n) \ .$$

Theorem 8 (Minimax Theorem [13]). *For any 2-variable function $f : \Omega^2 \to \mathbf{R}$, we have*

$$\max_{\mathcal{S}_1} \min_{\mathcal{S}_2} f(\mathcal{S}_1, \mathcal{S}_2) = \min_{\mathcal{S}_2} \max_{\mathcal{S}_1} f(\mathcal{S}_1, \mathcal{S}_2) \ ,$$

where $\mathcal{S}_1$ denotes a strategy for the first input and $\mathcal{S}_2$ denotes a strategy for the second input.

Using the above theorem, we deduce the following lemma, which can be viewed as an n-variable extension of the original minimax theorem.

Lemma 9 (n-Party Minimax). *For any $k \in \mathbf{R}$, and any n-variable functions $f_1, \dots, f_n : \Omega^n \to \mathbf{R}$ such that $\sum_{i \in [n]} f_i(x) \leqslant k$ for any $x \in \Omega^n$, we have*

$$\sum_{i \in [n]} \min_{\mathcal{S}_{\hat{i}}} \max_{\mathcal{S}_i} f_i(\mathcal{S}_{\hat{i}}, \mathcal{S}_i) \leqslant k \ ,$$

where $\mathcal{S}_{\hat{i}}$ denotes a strategy for $[n] \setminus \{i\}$ and $\mathcal{S}_i$ denotes a strategy for $\{i\}$.

Remark 10. In order to see that Lemma 9 extends Theorem 8, we can apply the former twice with $(f_1, f_2, k) = (f, -f, 0)$ and with $(f_1, f_2, k) = (-f, f, 0)$ respectively.

Proof. By viewing f_i as a two-variable function and applying Theorem 8, we have

$$\min_{\mathcal{S}_{\hat{i}}} \max_{\mathcal{S}_i} f_i(\mathcal{S}_{\hat{i}}, \mathcal{S}_i) = \max_{\mathcal{S}_i} \min_{\mathcal{S}_{\hat{i}}} f_i(\mathcal{S}_{\hat{i}}, \mathcal{S}_i) \ .$$

For each $i \in [n-1]$, there exists $\mathcal{S}_i^{(0)}$ such that

$$\max_{\mathcal{S}_i} \min_{\mathcal{S}_{\hat{i}}} f_i(\mathcal{S}_{\hat{i}}, \mathcal{S}_i) = \min_{\mathcal{S}_{\hat{i}}} f_i(\mathcal{S}_{\hat{i}}, \mathcal{S}_i^{(0)}) \ .$$

Then, for each $i \in [n-1]$,

$$\min_{\mathcal{S}_n} f_i(\mathcal{S}_1^{(0)}, \dots, \mathcal{S}_{n-1}^{(0)}, \mathcal{S}_n) \geq \min_{\mathcal{S}_{\hat{i}}} f_i(\mathcal{S}_{\hat{i}}, \mathcal{S}_i^{(0)}) = \max_{\mathcal{S}_i} \min_{\mathcal{S}_{\hat{i}}} f_i(\mathcal{S}_{\hat{i}}, \mathcal{S}_i).$$

Therefore,

$$\max_{\mathcal{S}_{\hat{n}}} \min_{\mathcal{S}_n} \sum_{i \in [n-1]} f_i(\mathcal{S}_{\hat{n}}, \mathcal{S}_n) \geq \min_{\mathcal{S}_n} \sum_{i \in [n-1]} f_i(\mathcal{S}_1^{(0)}, \dots, \mathcal{S}_{n-1}^{(0)}, \mathcal{S}_n)$$

$$\geq \sum_{i \in [n-1]} \min_{\mathcal{S}_n} f_i(\mathcal{S}_1^{(0)}, \dots, \mathcal{S}_{n-1}^{(0)}, \mathcal{S}_n) \qquad (2)$$

$$\geq \sum_{i \in [n-1]} \max_{\mathcal{S}_i} \min_{\mathcal{S}_{\hat{i}}} f_i(\mathcal{S}_{\hat{i}}, \mathcal{S}_i).$$

Thus,

$$\sum_{i \in [n]} \min_{\mathcal{S}_{\hat{i}}} \max_{\mathcal{S}_i} f_i(\mathcal{S}_{\hat{i}}, \mathcal{S}_i) = \min_{\mathcal{S}_{\hat{n}}} \max_{\mathcal{S}_n} f_n(\mathcal{S}_{\hat{n}}, \mathcal{S}_n) + \sum_{i \in [n-1]} \max_{\mathcal{S}_i} \min_{\mathcal{S}_{\hat{i}}} f_i(\mathcal{S}_{\hat{i}}, \mathcal{S}_i)$$

$$\leq \min_{\mathcal{S}_{\hat{n}}} \max_{\mathcal{S}_n} \left(k - \sum_{i \in [n-1]} f_i(\mathcal{S}_{\hat{n}}, \mathcal{S}_n) \right) + \max_{\mathcal{S}_{\hat{n}}} \min_{\mathcal{S}_n} \sum_{i \in [n-1]} f_i(\mathcal{S}_{\hat{n}}, \mathcal{S}_n)$$

$$= k - \left(\max_{\mathcal{S}_{\hat{n}}} \min_{\mathcal{S}_n} \sum_{i \in [n-1]} f_i(\mathcal{S}_{\hat{n}}, \mathcal{S}_n) \right) + \max_{\mathcal{S}_{\hat{n}}} \min_{\mathcal{S}_n} \sum_{i \in [n-1]} f_i(\mathcal{S}_{\hat{n}}, \mathcal{S}_n)$$

$$= k,$$

where the first equality is due to the minimax theorem, the first inequality is due to Equation (2), and the next equality is due to the fact that $\min_x -f(x) = -\max_x f(x)$.

4   Upper and Lower Bounds of Single-Round Protocols

In this section, we first show a single-round n-party commit-and-reveal leader election protocol that is $(n/2^{n-1}, n-1)$-fair. Then, we show that the protocol is optimal by proving a tight lower bound for the $(n-1)$-corruption case. Finally, we extend the results to a general corruption setting .

We extend both the upper and lower bounds to committee election protocols. The bounds we get are tight up to a constant factor in the exponent for the $(n-1)$-corruption case. These bounds are used in the next section when we extend our lower bounds to multi-round protocols.

4.1   Optimal Single-Round Leader Election

The protocol works as follows. We let each pair of parties run a 2-party tournament. I.e., each party first commits to a random bit, which is then revealed in

---

The parties are divided into t groups with size at most $\lceil n/t \rceil$. Within each group, we denote the parties as $\{1, \ldots, \ell\}$. The input of each party i is $x_i \in \{0,1\}^\ell \times [\ell]$. Given all parties' inputs $(x_1, \ldots, x_\ell)$, at most one party in $\{1, \ldots, \ell\}$ is selected in the committee as follows.

- For each pair $1 \leqslant i < j \leqslant \ell$, if $x_i[j] \oplus x_j[i] = 1$, we say party i wins against party j. Otherwise, we say party j wins against party i. If one of the parties abort, i.e., $x_i = \perp$ or $x_j = \perp$, then the other party wins against the party that aborts.
- Party i is selected if party i wins against all other parties in the group.
- If such i does not exist, the first party is selected.

Fig. 2. The single-round commit-and-reveal committee election protocol Π_{opt}.

the second round, and the winner of the tournament is indicated by the XOR of the two revealed bits. If one of the two parties aborts, the other party is the winner of the tournament. Finally, if there exists a party that wins all its tournaments, then the party is selected as the leader (note that the winner is unique). Otherwise, we select an arbitrary party.

Remark 11. We note that we can easily make the protocol perfectly fair in honest executions by letting a random party be selected when there is no party that won all its tournaments. More concretely, this can be done by letting party 1 additionaly sample a random index $i \in [n]$ and put it in the input. If there is no party that won all its tournaments, party i will be selected as the leader. We will see that this change will not affect our analysis of fairness, and we only show a version without perfect fairness in honest executions for simplicity of presenting the protocol.

Since the probability that any honest party wins each tournament is at least $1/2$, the probability of any honest party to be selected as the leader is at least $1/2^{n-1}$, no matter how the corrupted parties behave. This implies that the protocol is $(n/2^{n-1}, n-1)$-fair. The above protocol can be extended to select a committee of size t, by dividing the parties into t groups with sizes at most $\lceil n/t \rceil$, and electing a leader inside each group using the previous method. Similarly, the probability of any honest party to be selected is at least $2^{-(\lceil n/t \rceil - 1)}$. This protocol is detailed in Fig. 2, and is denoted by Π_{opt}.

Theorem 12. *For any $n \geqslant 2$ and $1 \leqslant t \leqslant n/2$, there exists a $(n, 1, t)$-commit-and-reveal committee election protocol that is $(2^{-(\lceil n/t \rceil - 1)} \frac{n}{t}, n - 1)$-fair. In particular, for $t = 1$, there exists a $(n, 1)$-commit-and-reveal leader election protocol that is $(2^{-(n-1)} n, n - 1)$-fair.*

Proof. We show that Π_{opt} is $(2^{-(\lceil n/t \rceil - 1)} \frac{n}{t}, n-1)$-fair. Let $\mathcal{A}$ be an adversary that corrupts $n-1$ parties. For any honest party, no matter how $\mathcal{A}$ behaves, the probability that it wins against another party in its group is at least $1/2$. Therefore, the probability that the honest party is in the committee is at least $2^{-(\lceil n/t \rceil - 1)}$, which implies that Π_{opt} is $(\alpha, n-1)$-maximin-fair, where $\alpha := 2^{-(\lceil n/t \rceil - 1)} \frac{n}{t}$. This also implies that the expected fraction of corrupted parties in the committee is at most $\frac{t - 2^{-(\lceil n/t \rceil - 1)}}{t}$, which means Π_{opt} is $(\frac{n-1}{n-\alpha}, n-1)$-CSP-fair. Since $\alpha \leqslant 1$ and $\frac{n-1}{n-\alpha} \geqslant \frac{1}{2-\alpha} \geqslant \alpha$, Π_{opt} is $(\alpha, n-1)$-fair.   □

4.2 Lower Bound for $(n-1)$-Corruption

We show the above leader election protocol has the best possible fairness guarantee by showing the following theorem.

Theorem 13 (Single-Round, $(n-1)$-Corruption). *For any integers $1 \leqslant t \leqslant n/2$, there is no $(n, 1, t)$-commit-and-reveal committee election protocol that is $(\alpha, n-1)$-fair for $\alpha > 2^{-\lfloor \frac{n-1}{2t-1} \rfloor} \frac{n}{t}$.*

Remark 14 Note that in the $t = 1$ case, which corresponds to leader election, Theorem 13 shows that the protocol Π_{opt} is optimally fair when exposed to $n-1$ corruptions.

Remark 15. In the proof, we show a slightly stronger result that there is no $(\alpha, n-1)$-maximin-fair protocol for $\alpha > 2^{-\lfloor \frac{n-1}{2t-1} \rfloor} \frac{n}{t}$.

Proof. Let Π be an $(n, 1, t)$-commit-and-reveal committee election protocol. For any set $T \subseteq [n]$, suppose all parties not in T abort. Denote Π^T as the protocol Π given all parties not in T abort, i.e., $\Pi^T(\{x_i\}_{i \in T}) := \Pi(\{x_i'\}_{i \in [n]})$, where $x_i' = x_i$ if $i \in T$ and $x_i' = \bot$ otherwise.

For each $i \in T$, there exists a strategy $\mathcal{S}_{T,i}$ for the players $T \setminus \{i\}$ that minimizes $\max_{x_i \in \Omega} \Pi_i^T(\mathcal{S}_{T,i}, x_i)$, where $\Pi_i^T(\mathcal{S}_{T,i}, x_i)$ is defined according to Sect. 3.2. By Lemma 9, we have that

$$\sum_{i \in T} \max_{x_i \in \Omega} \Pi_i^T(\mathcal{S}_{T,i}, x_i) \leqslant t . \tag{3}$$

Denote $p_{T,i} := \max_{x_i \in \Omega} \Pi_i^T(\mathcal{S}_{T,i}, x_i)$, which is the maximal probability that party i is in the committee under $\mathcal{S}_{T,i}$. We let $t \leqslant k \leqslant n$ be an arbitrary integer and denote $\ell := \lfloor (n-1)/k \rfloor$. To construct an adversary $\mathcal{A}$, we pick an index $i \in [n]$ as the honest party (the party $\mathcal{A}$ does not corrupt) and pick a partition $P = (T_1, \ldots, T_\ell)$ of $[n] \setminus \{i\}$ such that one of groups is of size $k' = n-1-k(\ell-1)$ and all the other groups are of size k. We note here that $k' \geqslant k$. Denote $\mathcal{P}_i$ as the set of all such partitions.

For each T_j, $\mathcal{A}$ uses the strategy $\mathcal{S}_{T_j \cup \{i\}, i}$ to sample the inputs for the parties in T_j. After $\mathcal{A}$ sees the input of party i, it picks a T_j (if any) such that party i is not in the committee if all corrupted parties not in T_j aborts. Otherwise, $\mathcal{A}$

does nothing. Thus, the probability that party i is in the committee is at most

$$\Pr_{x_i \sim \Omega, \{x'_i\}_{i' \in T_j} \sim \mathcal{S}_{T_j \cup \{i\}, i}} \left[\bigwedge_{j \in [\ell]} \Pi_i^{T_j \cup \{i\}}(\{x'_i\}_{i' \in T_j \cup \{i\}}) = 1 \right]$$

$$\leq \max_{x_i \in \Omega} \Pr_{\{x'_i\}_{i' \in T_j} \sim \mathcal{S}_{T_j \cup \{i\}, i}} \left[\bigwedge_{j \in [\ell]} \Pi_i^{T_j \cup \{i\}}(\{x'_i\}_{i' \in T_j \cup \{i\}}) = 1 \right]$$

$$= \max_{x_i \in \Omega} \prod_{j \in [\ell]} \Pr_{\{x'_i\}_{i' \in T_j} \sim \mathcal{S}_{T_j \cup \{i\}, i}} \left[\Pi_i^{T_j \cup \{i\}}(\{x'_i\}_{i' \in T_j \cup \{i\}}) = 1 \right]$$

$$\leq \prod_{j \in [\ell]} \max_{x_i \in \Omega} \Pi_i^{T_j \cup \{i\}}(\mathcal{S}_{T_j \cup \{i\}, i}, x_i)$$

$$= \prod_{j \in [\ell]} p_{T_j \cup \{i\}, i} ,$$

where the probability is taken over uniform choice of x_i from Ω and the randomness used by $\mathcal{S}_{T_j \cup \{i\}}$. Also, note that the seond equality is due to the fact that the event $\Pi_i^{T_j \cup \{i\}}(\mathcal{S}_{T_j \cup \{i\}, i}, x_i) = 1$ and $\Pi_i^{T_{j'} \cup \{i\}}(\mathcal{S}_{T_{j'} \cup \{i\}, i}, x_i) = 1$ are independent for $j' \neq j$ given a fixed x_i.

It is left to show there exists an index $i \in [n]$ and a partition $P \in \mathcal{P}_i$ such that the above probability is small. By summing over all possible i and partitions,

$$\sum_{i \in [n]} \sum_{P \in \mathcal{P}_i} \log \left(\prod_{T \in P} p_{T \cup \{i\}, i} \right) = \sum_{i \in [n]} \sum_{P \in \mathcal{P}_i} \sum_{T \in P} \log(p_{T \cup \{i\}, i})$$

$$= \sum_{\substack{T' \subseteq [n] \\ |T'| \in \{k+1, k'+1\}}} \sum_{i \in T'} \sum_{(T' \setminus \{i\}) \in P \in \mathcal{P}_i} \log(p_{T', i})$$

$$= \sum_{\substack{T' \subseteq [n] \\ |T'| \in \{k+1, k'+1\}}} \sum_{P \in \mathcal{P}_{T'}} \sum_{i \in T'} \log(p_{T', i})$$

$$\leq \sum_{\substack{T' \subseteq [n] \\ |T'| \in \{k+1, k'+1\}}} \sum_{P \in \mathcal{P}_{T'}} |T'| \log(t/|T'|)$$

$$= \frac{n!}{(k'+1)!(k!)^{\ell-1}(\ell-1)!}(k'+1)\log(t/(k'+1))$$

$$+ \frac{n!}{(k+1)!(k!)^{\ell-2}(k')(\ell-2)!}(k+1)\log(t/(k+1)))$$

$$= \frac{n!}{(k!)^{\ell-1}k'!(\ell-1)!}(\log(t/(k'+1)) + (\ell-1)\log(t/(k+1)))$$

$$\leq \frac{n!}{(k!)^{\ell-1}k'!(\ell-1)!}\ell\log(t/(k+1))) ,$$

where $\mathcal{P}_{T'}$ denotes the set of all partitions of $[n] \setminus T'$ of the form $(T_1, \ldots, T_{\ell-1})$ such that, in case $|T'| = k' + 1$, each group is of size k; in case of $|T'| = k + 1$, one of groups is of size k' and all the other groups are of size k. Also, note that the first inequality is due to Eq. 3 and Jensen's inequality. Since

$$\sum_{i \in [n]} \sum_{P \in \mathcal{P}_i} 1 = \frac{n!}{(k!)^{\ell-1} k'! (\ell - 1)!} \,,$$

there exists $i \in [n]$ and $P \in \mathcal{P}_i$ such that $\log \left(\prod_{T \in P} p_{T \cup \{i\}, i} \right) \leqslant \ell \log(t/(k+1)) = \lfloor \frac{n-1}{k} \rfloor \log(t/(k+1))$. By setting $k = 2t-1$, we get $\log \left(\prod_{T \in P} p_{T \cup \{i\}, i} \right) \leqslant - \lfloor \frac{n-1}{2t-1} \rfloor$, which concludes the proof.   □

4.3   Lower Bounds for $(n - k)$-Corruption

For any $(n, 1, t)$-commit-and-reveal committee election protocol Π that is $(\alpha \frac{n}{t}, n - k)$-maximin-fair, we can construct a $(n/k, 1, t)$-commit-and-reveal committee election protocol from Π by partitioning n parties into n/k groups of size k and viewing each group as a single party. Each group is in the committee if and only if one of the party in the group is in the committee. We can show that the new protocol is $(\alpha \frac{n}{kt}, n/k - 1)$-maximin fair.

Also, for any $(n, 1, t)$-commit-and-reveal committee election protocol Π that is $(\frac{n-k}{n\alpha}, n - k)$-CSP fair, i.e., for any adversary that corrupts at most $n - k$ parties, the expected fraction of corrupted parties in the committee is at most α, we can construct an $(n/k, r, t)$-commit-and-reveal committee election protocol Π that is $(\alpha n/k, n/k - 1)$-CSP fair from Π in the same way as the above.

Combining the above two arguments, we have the following lemma.

Lemma 16. *If there exists a (n, r, t)-commit-and-reveal committee election protocol Π that is $(\alpha, n - k)$-fair, then there exists a $(n/k, r, t)$-commit-and-reveal committee election protocol that is*

$$\left(\max \left\{ \frac{\alpha}{k}, \left(1 - \frac{n - k}{\alpha n} \right) \frac{n}{tk} \right\}, n/k - 1 \right) \text{-maximin fair.}$$

Remark 17. Here we only consider the case k divides n for simplicity of presenting the results as the bound would not change asymptotically for the case k does not divide n. If k does not divide n, similarly to the proof of Theorem 13, we can divide n parties into $\ell = \lfloor n/k \rfloor$ groups with $\ell - 1$ groups of size k and the last group of size $k' = n - k(\ell - 1) \geqslant k$, and get a $(\lfloor n/k \rfloor, r, t)$ committee election protocol Π' from a (n, r, t) committee election protocol Π. The rest of proof goes through since corrupting $\ell - 1$ parties in Π corresponds to corrupting at most $n - k$ parties in Π. The final bound on maximin fairness changes to $\max \{ \alpha \lfloor n/k \rfloor / n, (1 - (n - k)/(\alpha n)) \cdot (\lfloor n/k \rfloor / t) \}$, which is asymptotically the same as the bound in the above lemma.

Proof. For a (n, r, t)-commit-and-reveal committee election protocol Π that is $(\alpha, n - k)$-fair, we construct a $(n/k, r, t)$-commit-and-reveal committee election protocol Π' from Π by partitioning n parties into n/k groups $T_1, \ldots, T_{n/k}$ of size k and letting each party i in Π' simulate the behaviors of parties in T_i such that party i is selected in Π' if and only if one of parties in T_i is selected in Π.

Consider an adversary $\mathcal{A}$ against Π' that corrupts $n/k - 1$ parties. Denote the honest party corresponding to the group T_i. We can view $\mathcal{A}$ as an adversary $\mathcal{A}'$ against Π that corrupts all parties not in T_i, and the number of corrupted party is $n - k$. Since Π is $(\alpha, n-k)$-fair, it holds that (1) the probability that any honest party is selected is at least $\alpha\frac{t}{n}$ and (2) the expected fraction of corrupted parties in the committee is at most $\frac{(n-k)}{n\alpha}$.

Since T_i is selected in Π' if one of the honest parties is selected in Π, by (1), T_i is selected with probability at least $\alpha\frac{t}{n}$, which means Π' is $(\alpha/k, n/k - 1)$-maximin fair. If T_i is not selected, then the fraction of corrupted parties in the committee is 1. By (2), it holds that $1 - \Pr[T_i \text{ is selected}] \leq \frac{(n-k)}{n\alpha}$. Therefore, the probability that T_i is selected is at least $(1 - (n-k)/(n\alpha))$, which means Π' is $((1 - (n-k)/(n\alpha))n/(tk), n/k - 1)$-maximin fair. Therefore, we can conclude the lemma. □

By Theorem 13 and Remark 15, we know there is no $(n/k, 1, t)$-commit-and-reveal committee election protocol that is $(\beta, n/k - 1)$-maximin-fair for $\beta > 2^{-\lfloor \frac{n/k-1}{2t-1} \rfloor} \frac{n}{kt}$. Therefore, by Lemma 16, we have the following theorem.

Theorem 18. *For any integers $1 \leq t \leq k \leq n/2$, there is no $(n, 1, t)$-commit-and-reveal committee election protocol that is $(\alpha, n - k)$-fair for*

$$\alpha > \min\left\{ 2^{-\frac{n-k}{k(2t-1)}} \frac{n}{t}, \frac{n-k}{n\left(1 - 2^{-\frac{n-k}{k(2t-1)}}\right)} \right\}.$$

In particular, for leader election protocols, there is no single-round n-party leader election protocol that is $(\alpha, n - k)$-fair for $\alpha > \min\left\{ 2^{-\frac{n-k}{k}} n, \frac{n-k}{n\left(1-2^{-\frac{n-k}{k}}\right)} \right\}.$

From the above theorem, for $k = \beta n$ where $0 < \beta < 1/2$ is a constant, there is no $(n, 1)$-commit-and-reveal leader election protocol that is $(\alpha, n(1 - \beta))$-fair for $\alpha < \frac{1-\beta}{1-2^{-\frac{1-\beta}{\beta}}}$. For $k \leq \frac{n}{4 \log n}$, there is no $(n, 1)$-commit-and-reveal leader election protocol that is $(1/n, n - k)$-fair.

5 Lower Bounds for Multiple Rounds

We extend the lower bounds for single-round commit-and-reveal protocols to multi-round commit-and-reveal protocols for the $(n - 1)$-corruption case, which is formally stated in Theorem 19. In particular, we show that there is no r-round leader election protocol that achieves constant-fairness against $(n-1)$-corruption for $r \leq \frac{\log n}{\log \log n + 3}$, which is implied by Corollary 20 below.

Theorem 19. *For any $0 < \delta < 1$, any integer $r, t \geqslant 1$, and any integer $n \geqslant t(2\lceil \log 1/\delta \rceil)^r$, there is no (n, r, t)-commit-and-reveal committee election protocol that is $(\alpha, n-1)$-maximin-fair for $\alpha > r\delta n/t$.*

For any $n \geqslant 1$, if we set $\delta = 1/n^3$, for any $r \leqslant \frac{\log(n/t)}{\log(2\lceil \log n^3 \rceil)} \leqslant \frac{\log n - \log t}{\log \log n + 3}$, by applying the above theorem, we get the following corollary.

Corollary 20. *For any integer $1 \leqslant t \leqslant n$, any integer $r \leqslant \frac{\log n - \log t}{\log \log n + 3}$, there is no (n, r, t)-commit-and-reveal committee election protocol that is $\left(\frac{1}{nt}, n-1\right)$-maximin-fair.*

To prove Theorem 19, the key tool is the following inductive argument. Roughly, it shows that a maximin-fair (n, r, t)-commit-and-reveal protocol implies either a maximin-fair $(n, 1, n')$-commit-and-reveal protocol or a maximin-fair $(n', r-1, t)$-commit-and-reveal protocol.

Lemma 21. *For any integers $1 \leqslant t \leqslant n'$ and $n \geqslant 2n'$, any integer $r \geqslant 1$, and $0 < \alpha' < \alpha$, if there exists an (n, r, t)-commit-and-reveal committee election protocol that is $(\alpha n/t, n-1)$-maximin-fair, there exists either an $(n', r-1, t)$-commit-and-reveal committee election protocol that is $((\alpha - \alpha')n'/t, n'-1)$-maximin-fair or an $(n, 1, n')$-commit-and-reveal committee election protocol that is $(\alpha' n/n', n-1)$-maximin-fair.*

We use Lemma 21 through the following corollary. Intuitively, it shows that a maximin-fair (n, r, t)-commit-and-reveal protocol implies a fair $(n', r-1, t)$-commit-and-reveal protocol for $n' = O(n/\log n)$.

Corollary 22. *For any integers $1 \leqslant t \leqslant n'$ and $n \geqslant 2n'$, any integer $r \geqslant 1$, and $0 < \alpha$, if there exists a (n, r, t)-commit-and-reveal committee election protocol that is $(\alpha n/t, n-1)$-maximin-fair, there exists an $(n', r-1, t)$-commit-and-reveal committee election protocol that is $((\alpha - 2^{-\lfloor \frac{n-1}{2n'-1} \rfloor})n'/t, n'-1)$-maximin-fair.*

To prove Corollary 22 we note that Theorem 13 implies that there is no $(n, 1, n')$-commit-and-reveal protocol that is $(2^{-\lfloor \frac{n-1}{2n'-1} \rfloor \frac{n}{n'}}, n-1)$-maximin-fair. Hence, among the two options in Lemma 21, only the first is eligible. This immediately implies Corollary 22.

We now show how to prove Theorem 19 using Corollary 22.

Proof. (Theorem19). For $r = 1$, since $n \geqslant 2t\lceil \log(1/\delta) \rceil$ implies $2^{-\lfloor \frac{n-1}{2t-1} \rfloor} \leqslant 2^{-\lfloor \frac{n}{2t} \rfloor} \leqslant 2^{-\lceil \log(1/\delta) \rceil} \leqslant \delta$, the theorem follows from Theorem 13. For $r > 1$, suppose the theorem holds for $(r-1)$-round protocols. For any $t \geqslant 1$ and $n \geqslant t(2\lceil \log 1/\delta \rceil)^r$, assume there exists an (n, r, t)-commit-and-reveal protocol that is $(\alpha, n-1)$-maximin-fair for $\alpha < r\delta n/t$. Let $n' = n/(2\lceil \log 1/\delta \rceil)$. Since $2^{-\lfloor \frac{n-1}{2n'-1} \rfloor} \leqslant \delta$, by Corollary 22, there exists an $(n', r-1, t)$-commit-and-reveal protocol that is $(\alpha', n'-1)$-maximin-fair, where $\alpha' = \alpha - \delta n/t$. Since $\alpha' < (r-1)\delta n'/t$ and $n' = n/(2\log 1/\delta) \geqslant t(2\log 1/\delta)^{r-1}$, it contradicts with the assumption that the theorem holds for $(r-1)$-round protocols. Therefore, we concludes the theorem by induction. $\square$

Finally, we show how to prove Lemma 21. The key idea of the proof is to consider a fixed first-round input. For an (n, r, t)-committee election protocol that is $(\alpha n/t, n-1)$-maximin-fair, by fixing a first-round input $\boldsymbol{x} \in \Omega^n$, we can view it as an $(n, r-1, t)$-committee election protocol. Then, we look into the probability p_i that each party i is in the committee if the adversary corrupts all parties but i and acts optimally. If, for any $\boldsymbol{x}$, the number of $i \in [n]$ such that $p_i \geqslant \alpha - \alpha'$ is more than n', we can construct an $(n', r-1, t)$-committee election protocol that is $((\alpha - \alpha')n'/t, n'-1)$-maximin-fair. Otherwise, if for all $\boldsymbol{x}$, at most n' of them satisfy $p_i \geqslant \alpha - \alpha'$, then we can construct an $(n, 1, n')$-committee election protocol such that given $\boldsymbol{x}$, party i is in the committee if and only if $p_i \geqslant \alpha - \alpha'$ and we can show this protocol is $(\alpha' n/t, n-1)$-maximin-fair.

Proof. (Lemma 21). Let Π be an (n, r, t)-commit-and-reveal committee election protocol that is $(\alpha n/t, n-1)$-maximin-fair. Suppose there is no $(n', r-1, t)$-committee election protocol that is $((\alpha - \alpha')n'/t, n'-1)$-maximin-fair and no $(n, 1, n')$-commit-and-reveal committee election protocol that is $(\alpha' n/n', n-1)$-maximin-fair. We just need to show that there is an adversary $\mathcal{A}$ against Π corrupting $n-1$ parties such that the probability that the honest party is in the committee is less than α. For any first-round input $\boldsymbol{x} \in (\{\perp\} \cup \Omega)^n$, let $T_{\boldsymbol{x}} := \{i \mid x_i \neq \perp\}$ and denote $\Pi^{\boldsymbol{x}}(\cdot) := \Pi(\boldsymbol{x}, \cdot)$, which is an $(n, r-1, t)$-committee election protocol. Denote $p_{\boldsymbol{x}, i}$ as the minimal probability that party i is in the committee over all adversaries for $\Pi^{\boldsymbol{x}}$ that corrupts all parties but i. Denote $S_{\boldsymbol{x}} := \{i \in T_{\boldsymbol{x}} \mid p_{\boldsymbol{x}, i} \geqslant \alpha - \alpha'\}$.

We first show that $|S_{\boldsymbol{x}}| \leqslant n'$ for all $\boldsymbol{x}$. Suppose $|S_{\boldsymbol{x}}| > n'$. We construct an $(n', r-1, t)$ protocol Π' from $\Pi^{\boldsymbol{x}}$ as follows. We first pick an arbitrary set S' of party of size $|S_{\boldsymbol{x}}| - n' + 1$ from $S_{\boldsymbol{x}}$ and then let Π' be the same as $\Pi^{\boldsymbol{x}}$ except we let a single party (denoted as party i^*) simulate the behaviors of parties in $S' \cup ([n] \setminus S_{\boldsymbol{x}})$, while the rest of parties (i.e., parties in $S_{\boldsymbol{x}} \setminus S'$) acts the same as before. Party i^* is selected in Π' if and only if one of parties in the set corresponding to i^* is selected in $\Pi^{\boldsymbol{x}}$. Then, party i^* would be selected with probability as least $p_{\boldsymbol{x}, j}$ for any $j \in S'$ even if all othe parties are corrupted. Also, for party each $j \in S_{\boldsymbol{x}} \setminus S'$, $p_{\boldsymbol{x}, j}$ is exactly the probability that party j is guaranteed to be elected in Π', given that j is honest and all other $n'-1$ parties are corrupted. Therefore, each honest party among the n' players wins with probability at least $\alpha - \alpha'$. Thus, Π' is $((\alpha - \alpha')n'/t, n'-1)$-maximin-fair, which contradict the impossibility assumption of such protocols.

We continue by describing the adversary $\mathcal{A}$ against the original protocol Π. Consider an $(n, 1, n')$-committee election protocol Γ defined using $S_{\boldsymbol{x}}$ as follows. For any input $\boldsymbol{x}$, party i is elected to be in the committee if and only if $i \in S_{\boldsymbol{x}}$, i.e., $\Gamma_i(\boldsymbol{x}) := \mathbb{1}\{i \in S_{\boldsymbol{x}}\}$. By our assumption, there is no $(n, 1, n')$-committee election protocol that is $(\alpha' n/n', n-1)$-maximin-fair. Therefore, there exists an adversary $\mathcal{B}$ against Γ corrupting $n-1$ parties such that the probability of the honest party to be in the committee is at most α'. We now construct $\mathcal{A}$ using $\mathcal{B}$. In the first-round, $\mathcal{A}$ behaves exactly the same as $\mathcal{B}$. After the first-round, $\mathcal{A}$ uses the best strategy for the rest of the execution. Let party i be the honest party. After the first round, if i is not in $S_{\boldsymbol{x}}$, where $\boldsymbol{x}$ denotes the first-round message, we know the probability that i is in the committee is at most $p_{x,i} < \alpha - \alpha'$. By the definition of $\mathcal{B}$, we have that the probability of $i \in S_x$ is less than α'. Therefore, the probability that party i is in the committee is less than α. This concludes the proof.   □

5.1   Lower Bounds for $(n - k)$-Corruption

By Lemma 16, if there exists a (n, r, t)-commit-and-reveal committee election protocol Π that is $(\alpha, n - k)$-fair, then there exists a $(n/k, r, t)$-commit-and-reveal committee election protocol that is $(\alpha/k, n/k-1)$-maximin-fair. Therefore, by Theorem 19, we have the following corollary.

Corollary 23. *For any* $0 < \delta < 1$, *any integer* $r, t, k \geqslant 1$, *and any integer* $n \geqslant tk(2 \lceil \log 1/\delta \rceil)^r$, *there is no* (n, r, t)-*commit-and-reveal committee election protocol that is* $(\alpha, n - k)$-*maximin-fair for* $\alpha > r\delta n/t$.

For any constant $n \geqslant 1$, if we set $\delta = 1/n^3$, by applying the above corollary, we get the following corollary.

Corollary 24. *For any integer* $1 \leqslant t, k \leqslant n$, *any integer* $r \leqslant \frac{\log n - \log t - \log k}{\log \log n + 3}$, *there is no* (n, r, t)-*commit-and-reveal* $\left(\frac{1}{nt}, n - k\right)$-*maximin-fair committee election protocol.*

6   Lower Bounds for Perfect Fairness

We recall that a n-party leader election protocol is perfectly fair against k-party corruption if and only if it is $(1, k)$-fair, i.e., the probability of any honest party being selected is at least $1/n$ if the number of corrupted party is at most k. We first show that even if only one party is corrupted, there is no single-round perfectly fair leader election protocol. The prior impossibility results [3] by Chung et al. only show it for the $(n-1)$-corruption case. Also, for multi-round protocols, we extend the prior results [3] to the case of k-corruption for $k < n-1$ and show that there is no r-round perfectly fair leader election protocol against k-corruption for $r < \min\{\lceil \log n \rceil, \lceil \log k \rceil + 1\}$.

Notations. We define the following convenient notations to simplify our proofs. For any $x \in (\{\bot\} \cup \Omega)^n$ and $y \in \{\bot\} \cup \Omega$, we use $(x : x_i \leftarrow y)$ to denote a vector which is exactly the same as x except the i-th entry of x is changed to y. If multiple entries are changed, we denote it as $(x : \{x_i \leftarrow y_i\}_{i \in S})$, where S is a subset of $[n]$.

6.1   Impossibility of Single-Round Protocols

Theorem 25. *For any* $n \geqslant 3$ *and* $1 \leqslant k < n$, *there is no perfectly fair single-round commit-and-reveal leader election protocol against k-corruption.*

Proof Sketch. Our proof can be divided in two steps. First, we show that for any $(1, k)$-fair single-round commit-and-reveal leader election protocol Π, Π must be *abort-invariant*, i.e., the resulting leader will not change, if any party other than the leader aborts. Moreover, this implies that if any party i other than the resulting leader changes its input, the leader must be either the original leader or changed to i, which is formally stated in Lemma 26. Then, we show that this property implies that there must exist an input y^* for party i^* and another party $j^* \neq i^*$ such that if the input of party i^* is y^*, party j^* will never be the leader no matter how the other parties choose their inputs. This means that Π is not fair.

To find such (y^*, i^*, j^*), we start from an arbitrary input $\boldsymbol{x}$ of all parties. Suppose party i is selected given $\boldsymbol{x}$. We pick an arbitrary $j \neq i$ and attempt to find another input y of party j such that the leader is changed to party j if party j changes its input to y while the inputs of all other parties remain the same as $\boldsymbol{x}$. If such y does not exist, it means that j would never be selected no matter what input party j picks. Also, due to *abort-invariance* of Π, j would never be selected no matter how parties other than i and j choose their inputs given party i selects x_i. Therefore, $(y^* = x_i, i^* = i, j^* = i)$ is the tuple we want. If such y exists, we repeat the above for input $(\boldsymbol{x} : x_j \leftarrow y)$ until we find such a tuple.

We then show that the above process always terminates. Suppose it does not terminate. Since the input set is finite, we can find a loop of input-party pairs $(\boldsymbol{x}_1, i_1), \ldots, (\boldsymbol{x}_\ell, i_\ell)$ with $(\boldsymbol{x}_1, i_1) = (\boldsymbol{x}_\ell, i_\ell)$ such that $\boldsymbol{x}_k$ is the same as $\boldsymbol{x}_{k-1}$ except that party i_k is selected given $\boldsymbol{x}_k$ and the input of party i_k is changed. To yield a contradiction, the idea is to start from $\boldsymbol{x}_1$ and do all the changes in the loop except that we do not change the input of party i_1. Equivalently, we consider an alternative loop $(\boldsymbol{x}'_1, i_1), \ldots, (\boldsymbol{x}'_\ell, i_\ell)$ where $x'_k := (\boldsymbol{x}_k : x_{k,i_1} \leftarrow x_{1,i_1})$. We show that for $i_k \neq i_1$, given $\boldsymbol{x}'_k$, party i_k is still selected. Then, since $i_{\ell-1} \neq i_\ell = i_1$, it implies that party $i_{\ell-1}$ is selected given $\boldsymbol{x}'_{\ell-1}$. However, since $\boldsymbol{x}_1 = \boldsymbol{x}'_\ell = \boldsymbol{x}'_{\ell-1}$, party i_1 should be selected given $\boldsymbol{x}'_{\ell-1}$, which yields a contradiction.

Lemma 26. *Suppose $\Pi : (\{\bot\} \cup \Omega)^n \to \{0,1\}^n$ is a perfectly maximin-fair n-party single-round commit-and-reveal leader election protocol against a single-party corruption. Π must be* abort-invariant, *i.e., for any $\boldsymbol{x} \in \Omega^n$ and $i \in [n]$ such that $\Pi_i(\boldsymbol{x}) = 0$, it holds that $\Pi_j(\boldsymbol{x} : x_i \leftarrow \bot) = \Pi_j(\boldsymbol{x})$ for any $j \in [n]$. Moreover,* abort-invariant *implies, for any $\boldsymbol{x} \in \Omega^n$, $y \in \Omega$, if $\Pi_i(\boldsymbol{x}) = \Pi_i(\boldsymbol{x} : x_i \leftarrow y) = 0$, i.e., party i is not selected given $\boldsymbol{x}$ or $(\boldsymbol{x} : x_i \leftarrow y)$, then $\Pi_j(\boldsymbol{x} : x_i \leftarrow y) = \Pi_j(\boldsymbol{x})$ for any $j \in [n]$.*

Proof. (Lemma26). Suppose Π is not abort-invariant, which means there exists $\boldsymbol{x} \in \Omega^n$ and $i, j \in [n]$ such that $\Pi_i(\boldsymbol{x}) = 0$, $\Pi_j(\boldsymbol{x}) = 1$, and $\Pi_j(\boldsymbol{x} : x_i \leftarrow \bot) = 0$. We construct an adversary $\mathcal{A}$ as follows. $\mathcal{A}$ corrupts party i and lets party i run the protocol honestly except party i aborts if the inputs of all parties are exactly $\boldsymbol{x}$. Then, the probability that party j is selected as the leader is smaller than the probability that party j is selected when all parties behave honestly, which is exactly $1/n$. Therefore, the protocol is not perfectly fair.

We now show the "moreomver" part. For any $\boldsymbol{x} \in \Omega^n$, $y \in \Omega$, and $i \in [n]$ such that $\Pi_i(\boldsymbol{x} : x_i \leftarrow y) = 0$, since Π is abort-invariant, we have $\Pi_j(\boldsymbol{x} : x_i \leftarrow y) = \Pi_j(\boldsymbol{x} : x_i \leftarrow \bot) = \Pi_j(\boldsymbol{x})$ for any $j \in [n]$. $\qquad\qquad\qquad\square$

Proof. (Theorem 25). Suppose $\Pi : (\{\bot\} \cup \Omega)^n \to \{0,1\}^n$ is a n-party single-round commmit-and-reveal leader election protocol. We just need to show that there exists an input $y^* \in \Omega$ for some party i^* and another party $j^* \neq i^*$ such that $\Pi_{j^*}(\boldsymbol{x}) = 0$ for all $\boldsymbol{x} \in \Omega^n$ with $x_{i^*} = y^*$, which implies that Π is not fair.

We use the following algorithm to find (i^*, y^*, j^*); The algorithm is not efficient, but it is sufficient in order to show the existence of (i^*, y^*, j^*). Initially, the algorithm picks an arbitrary input $\boldsymbol{x}_0 \in \Omega^n$. We denote i_0 as the leader given $\boldsymbol{x}_0$ as the inputs of all parties and $y_0 := x_{0,i_0}$ as the input of party i_0. Then, we keep iterating the following. At the ℓ-th iteration, since $n \geqslant 3$, the algorithm picks an arbitrary $i_\ell \in [n] \setminus \{i_{\ell-1}, i_{\ell-2}\}$. (For the first iteration, the algorithm picks an arbitrary $i_1 \in [n] \setminus \{i_0\}$.) Then, it finds y_ℓ such that party i_ℓ is the leader given $\boldsymbol{x}_\ell := (\boldsymbol{x}_{\ell-1} : x_{\ell-1,i_\ell} \leftarrow y_\ell)$ as the inputs of all parties, i.e., the input of party i_ℓ is changed to y_ℓ while the inputs of all other parties remain the same as $\boldsymbol{x}_{\ell-1}$. If such y_ℓ does not exist, then the algorithm returns $(i^* \leftarrow i_{\ell-1}, y^* \leftarrow y_{\ell-1}, j^* \leftarrow i_\ell)$.

We first show that (i^*, y^*, j^*) returned by the algorithm satisfies the property mentioned at the beginning of the proof. Denote $\boldsymbol{x}^* := \boldsymbol{x}_{\ell-1}$. By the execution of the algorithm, party j^* is not selected given input $\boldsymbol{x}^*$. For any $\boldsymbol{x} \in \Omega^n$ with $x_1 = y^*$, we change $\boldsymbol{x}^*$ step by step to make it equal to $\boldsymbol{x}$ and party j^* remains not the leader. First, we change the input of party j^* in $\boldsymbol{x}^*$ to x_{j^*}. By the execution of the algorithm, party i^* remains the leader. Then, by Lemma 26, the leader is not changed to j^* if party $k \in [n] \setminus \{i^*, j^*\}$ changes its input to x_k, which concludes our claim.

It is left to show the algorithm always returns. Suppose the algorithm does not return. Since the input space is finite, the algorithm must find a loop $(i_\ell, \boldsymbol{x}_\ell, y_\ell), \ldots, (i_m, \boldsymbol{x}_m, y_m)$ such that $(i_\ell, \boldsymbol{x}_\ell, y_\ell) = (i_m, \boldsymbol{x}_m, y_m)$. We now show that such a loop cannot exist. By the execution of the algorithm, it holds that $\boldsymbol{x}_{j+1}$ is the same as $\boldsymbol{x}_j$ except that the input of party i_{j+1} is changed to y_{j+1} for $\ell \leqslant j < m$ and party i_j is leader given the input $\boldsymbol{x}_j$ for $\ell \leqslant j \leqslant m$.

To yield a contradiction, we consider the following loop of inputs $(\tilde{\boldsymbol{x}}_\ell, \ldots, \tilde{\boldsymbol{x}}_m)$, where $\tilde{\boldsymbol{x}}_j$ is the same as $\boldsymbol{x}_j$ except that the input of party i_ℓ is changed to y_ℓ, i.e., $\tilde{\boldsymbol{x}}_j := \boldsymbol{x}_j : x_{j,i_\ell} \leftarrow y_\ell$. We will show that party i_ℓ is not selected as the leader given input $\tilde{\boldsymbol{x}}_j$ for any $\ell < j \leqslant m$. It yields a contradiction since party i_ℓ is selected as the leader given input $\boldsymbol{x}_j = \tilde{\boldsymbol{x}}_\ell = \tilde{\boldsymbol{x}}_m$. More precisely, we are going to show that for any $\ell + 1 \leqslant j \leqslant m$, if $i_j \neq i_\ell$, then party i_j is selected given $\tilde{\boldsymbol{x}}_j$, and if $i_j = i_\ell$, then party $i_{j-1} (\neq i_j = i_\ell)$ is selected given $\tilde{\boldsymbol{x}}_j$.

First, for $j = \ell + 1$, since $i_{\ell+1} \neq i_\ell$, we know $\tilde{\boldsymbol{x}}_{\ell+1} = \boldsymbol{x}_{\ell+1}$. Therefore, party i_j is selected given $\tilde{\boldsymbol{x}}_j$.

For $j > \ell + 1$, there are three cases: (i) $i_{j-1} \neq i_\ell$ and $i_j \neq i_\ell$; (ii) $i_{j-1} \neq i_\ell$ and $i_j = i_\ell$; (iii) $i_{j-1} = i_\ell$. For the first two cases, suppose party i_{j-1} is selected given $\tilde{\boldsymbol{x}}_{j-1}$. If $i_j \neq i_\ell$, since both party i_ℓ and party i_j are not selected given $\tilde{\boldsymbol{x}}_{j-1}$, by Lemma 26, party i_ℓ is also not selected given $\tilde{\boldsymbol{x}}_j = (\tilde{\boldsymbol{x}}_{j-1} : \tilde{x}_{j-1,i_j} \leftarrow y_j)$.

Then, since $\tilde{\boldsymbol{x}}_j = (\boldsymbol{x}_j : x_{j,i_\ell} \leftarrow y_\ell)$, by Lemma 26, we have $\Pi_{i_j}(\tilde{\boldsymbol{x}}_j) = \Pi_{i_j}(\boldsymbol{x}_j) = 1$. Otherwise, if $i_j = i_\ell$, we have $\tilde{\boldsymbol{x}}_{j-1} = \tilde{\boldsymbol{x}}_j$ and thus party i_{j-1} is selected given $\tilde{\boldsymbol{x}}_j$.

For case (iii), suppose party i_{j-2} is selected given $\tilde{\boldsymbol{x}}_{j-1}$. By the execution of the algorithm, we know $i_j, i_{j-1}(= i_\ell), i_{j-2}$ are distinct. Since both party i_ℓ and party i_j are not the leader given the inputs $\tilde{\boldsymbol{x}}_{j-1}$, by Lemma 26, party i_ℓ is not selected either given $\tilde{\boldsymbol{x}}_j = (\tilde{\boldsymbol{x}}_{j-1} : \tilde{x}_{j-1,i_j} \leftarrow y_j)$. Then, since $\tilde{\boldsymbol{x}}_j = (\boldsymbol{x}_j : x_{j,i_\ell} \leftarrow y_\ell)$, by Lemma 26, we have $\Pi_{i_j}(\tilde{\boldsymbol{x}}_j) = \Pi_{i_j}(\boldsymbol{x}_j) = 1$. Therefore, we can conclude the statement by induction. □

6.2 Lower Bounds for Multi-round Protocols

For multi-round protocols, the prior result [3] by Chung et al. shows that there is no perfectly fair ($\lceil \log n \rceil - 1$)-round leader election protocol against $(n-1)$-corruption. We show that their result can be extended to any k-corruption for $k \geqslant n/2$. Also, for $2 \leqslant k < n/2$, we show there is no perfectly fair $\lceil \log k \rceil$-round protocol. Formally, we show Theorem 27. We also note that this result is incomparable to our result for the single-round case since the statement is trivial for $k = 1$.

Theorem 27. *For any* $2 \leqslant k \leqslant n$, *there is no perfectly fair* r-*round commit-and-reveal leader election protocol against* k-*corruption for* $r \leqslant \lceil \log(\min\{n/2, k\}) \rceil$.

We prove a stronger statement: we show that the impossibility result holds even for protocols satisfying a weaker security notion, called *tightness*, which is introduced in [3]. We say a protocol is tight against k-corruption if and only if the winning probability of any honest party given k corrupted parties is as high as in honest executions, which is formally defined as follows. It is clear that a perfectly fair protocol against k-corruption is tight against k-corruption.[3]

Definition 28 ([3]). *A* n-*party leader election protocol* Π *is tight against* k-*corruption if and only if for any adversary* $\mathcal{A}$ *that corrupts at most* k *parties and any honest party* i, *no matter how* $\mathcal{A}$ *behaves,*

$$\Pr[i \text{ is the leader}] \geqslant \mathcal{P}_i \, ,$$

where $\mathcal{P}_i$ *denotes the probability that party* i *is elected in an honest execution.*

The proof technique is similar to [3]. We say that a party is still alive after i rounds if the party still has a chance to be the leader after i rounds. To show a lower bound on round complexity, the idea is to lower bound the number of alive parties. The prior work [3] shows that in a tight protocol against $(n-1)$-corruption, the number of alive parties after the first round is at least $n'/2$, where

---

[3] For a perfectly fair protocol, the winning probability of any party in an honest execution is $1/n$. Therefore, the winning probability of any honest party i given k corrupted parties is at least $\mathcal{P}_i = 1/n$.

n' denotes the alive parties before the first round. Then, by fixing the first round input, one can show the rest of protocol is still tight, and the same argument shows that the number of alive parties after i round is at least $n'/2^i$. Since in the final round, the number of alive parties is 1 and thus the round complexity of a tight protocol is at least $\lceil \log(n') \rceil$.

We extend the prior proof to the case of k-corruption and show that the number of alive parties after the first round is at least $\min\{n'/2, k\}$.[4] By a similar induction, we conclude that the round complexity is at least $\lceil \log(\min\{n'/2, k\}) \rceil$ and for perfectly fair protocols, we have $n' = n$.

Remark 29. We also note that the technique here is different from the previous section on the single-round protocols. The single-round result shows that the number of alive parties after the first round is at least 2 given that one party is corrupted. However, it is unclear how to improve this bound for larger corruptions.

Proof. (Theorem 27) Let $\Pi : (\{\bot\} \cup \Omega)^{nr} \to \{0,1\}^n$ be a r-round commit-and-reveal leader election protocol. For any $x \in (\{\bot\} \cup \Omega)^n$, denote $\mathcal{P}_i(x)$ as the probability that party i is elected in an honest execution given that the first-round inputs of all parties are x. We say that party i is eliminated if $\mathcal{P}_i(x) = 0$. Otherwise, we say that the party i is still alive. Denote $\mathcal{S}(x) := \{i \in [n] \mid \mathcal{P}_i(x) > 0\}$ as the set of the alive parties. Also, we denote $\mathcal{S}_0 := \bigcup_{x \in \Omega^n} \mathcal{S}(x)$, which is the set of parties that are alive before the first round, and denote $n' = |\mathcal{S}_0|$. We say Π is a protocol with n' alive parties.

We first show the the following lemma which generalizes the abort-invariant property of single-round leader election protocols (Lemma 26) to the multi-round case. Roughly, the abort-invariance means that for any first-round input x, an eliminated party i given x, and $j \neq i$, $\mathcal{P}_j(x)$ would not change if party i aborts, and moreover, it implies that if party i changes its input, $\mathcal{P}_j(x)$ would only decrease. The proof is similar to the single-round case and deferred to the end of the section.

Lemma 30. *Suppose* $\Pi : (\{\bot\} \cup \Omega)^n \to \{0,1\}^n$ *is a tight n-party commit-and-reveal leader election protocol against a single-party corruption. Π must be abort-invariant, i.e., for any $x \in \Omega^n$ and $i \in [n]$ such that $\mathcal{P}_i(x) = 0$, it holds that $\mathcal{P}_j(x : x_i \leftarrow \bot) = \mathcal{P}_j(x)$ for any $j \in [n]$. Moreover, for any $y \in \Omega$, $\mathcal{P}_j(x : x_i \leftarrow y) \leqslant \mathcal{P}_j(x)$ for any $j \in [n] \setminus \{i\}$.*

We use the lemma to show the following claim.

Claim. If Π is tight, then there exists $x \in \Omega^n$ such that $|\mathcal{S}(x)| \geqslant \min\{n'/2, k\}$.

Proof. Let $x_0 \in \Omega^n$ be an arbitrary input. Without loss of generality, assume $\mathcal{S}_0 = \{1, ..., n'\}$ and $\mathcal{S}(x_0) = \{1, ..., \ell\}$. The claim holds if $\ell \geqslant \min\{n'/2, k\}$. Otherwise, we run the following algorithm to find x such that $|\mathcal{S}(x)| \geqslant$

---

[4] Note that this statement is only useful when $k \geqslant 2$. For $k = 1$, it means the number of alive parties after the first round is at least 1, which holds trivially.

$\min\{n'/2, k\}$. For $1 \leqslant i \leqslant n' - \ell$, the algorithm finds $y_i \in \Omega$ such that party $\ell + i$ becomes alive after it changes its first round input to y_i, i.e., $\mathcal{P}_{\ell+i}(\boldsymbol{x}_{i-1} : x_{i-1,\ell+i} \leftarrow y_i) > 0$ and sets $\boldsymbol{x}_i := \boldsymbol{x}_{i-1} : x_{i-1,\ell+i} \leftarrow y_i$. The algorithm returns $\boldsymbol{x}_i$ if $|\mathcal{S}(\boldsymbol{x}_i)| \geqslant \min\{n/2, k\}$.

We first show that the algorithm can find y_i for each i. Suppose for any $y \in \Omega$ such that $\mathcal{P}_{\ell+i}(\boldsymbol{x}_{i-1} : x_{i-1,\ell+i} \leftarrow y) = 0$. Since the algorithm did not return, we know $|\mathcal{S}(\boldsymbol{x}_{i-1})| < \min\{n'/2, k\}$. For any $\boldsymbol{x}' \in \Omega^n$ such that $x'_j = x_{i-1,j}$ for each $j \in \mathcal{S}(\boldsymbol{x}_{i-1})$, we show that $\mathcal{P}_{\ell+i}(\boldsymbol{x}') = 0$. First, if we change the input of party $\ell + i$ to $x'_{\ell+i}$, we have $\mathcal{P}_{\ell+i}(\boldsymbol{x}_{i-1} : x_{i-1,\ell+i} \leftarrow x'_{\ell+i}) = 0$. Denote $\boldsymbol{x}'' = \boldsymbol{x}_{i-1} : x_{i-1,\ell+i} \leftarrow x'_{\ell+i}$. By Lemma 30, if we change the input of each party $j \in [n] \setminus (\{\ell + i\} \cup \mathcal{S}(\boldsymbol{x}_{i-1}))$ from x''_j to x'_j, the probability that party $i + \ell$ is the leader is still 0, which implies $\mathcal{P}_{\ell+i}(\boldsymbol{x}') = 0$. This shows that Π is not tight, since the adversary can prevent party $\ell + i$ from being selected by corrupting all parties in $\mathcal{S}(\boldsymbol{x}_{i-1})$ and setting their first-round inputs to be the same as $\boldsymbol{x}_{i-1}$.

We now show that the algorithm always returns. For $1 \leqslant i \leqslant n' - \ell$, we show that $j \in \mathcal{S}(\boldsymbol{x}_i)$ for each $\ell + 1 \leqslant j \leqslant \ell + i$, which implies that the algorithm must returns when $i = \min\{n'/2, k\} \leqslant n' - \ell$. For each $1 \leqslant i \leqslant n' - \ell$, suppose $j \in \mathcal{S}(\boldsymbol{x}_{i-1})$ for each $\ell + 1 \leqslant j \leqslant \ell + i - 1$, which trivially holds for $i = 1$. Denote $\mathcal{D} := \{\boldsymbol{x} \in \Omega^n \mid x_j = x_{0,j} \text{ for } j \in [\ell] \cup \{i + \ell\}\}$. For each $\boldsymbol{x}' \in \mathcal{D}$, since all parties in $[(\ell + 1)..n] \setminus \{\ell + i\}$ are eliminated given x_0, by Lemma 30, we know $\mathcal{P}_{\ell+i}(\boldsymbol{x}') = \mathcal{P}_{\ell+i}(\boldsymbol{x}_0 : \{x_{0,j} \leftarrow x'_j\}_{j \in [(\ell+1)..n] \setminus \{\ell+i\}}) \leqslant \mathcal{P}_{\ell+i}(\boldsymbol{x}_0) = 0$, which means party $\ell + i$ is eliminated given any input $\boldsymbol{x}' \in \mathcal{D}$. Then, by Lemma 30, for any $j \in [n] \setminus \{\ell + i\}$

$$\mathcal{P}_j(\boldsymbol{x}' : x'_{\ell+i} \leftarrow y_i) \leqslant \mathcal{P}_j(\boldsymbol{x}') \ . \tag{4}$$

Since Π is tight, it holds that for any $j \in [(\ell + 1)..n] \setminus \{\ell + i\}$ and any $y \in \Omega$,

$$\mathbb{E}_{\boldsymbol{x}' \sim \mathcal{D}}[\mathcal{P}_j(\boldsymbol{x}')] = \mathbb{E}_{\boldsymbol{x}' \sim \mathcal{D}}[\mathcal{P}_j(\boldsymbol{x}' : x'_{\ell+i} \leftarrow y)] \ ,$$

since otherwise the adversary can decrease the chance that party j is selected by corrupting parties $[\ell] \cup \{\ell + i\}$ (the number of which is at most k) and letting the input of parties $[\ell]$ be that same as $\boldsymbol{x}'$ and the input of party $\ell + i$ be y that gives the worst expectation. Therefore, by Eq. (4), we have $\mathcal{P}_j(\boldsymbol{x}' : x'_{\ell+i} \leftarrow y_i) = \mathcal{P}_j(\boldsymbol{x}')$ for each $\boldsymbol{x}' \in \mathcal{D}$. Since $\boldsymbol{x}_{i-1} \in \mathcal{D}$ and $\mathcal{P}_j(\boldsymbol{x}_{i-1}) > 0$ for each $\ell + 1 \leqslant j \leqslant \ell + i - 1$, we have $\mathcal{P}_j(\boldsymbol{x}_i) = \mathcal{P}_j(\boldsymbol{x}_{i-1} : x_{i-1,\ell+i} \leftarrow y_i) = \mathcal{P}_j(\boldsymbol{x}_{i-1}) > 0$. Also, since $\mathcal{P}_{\ell+i}(\boldsymbol{x}_i) > 0$, we have $j \in \mathcal{S}(\boldsymbol{x}_i)$ for each $\ell + 1 \leqslant j \leqslant \ell + i$. Therefore, we can conclude the statement by induction. $\qquad\square$

We now show that for any tight protocol Π with n' alive parties, the round complexity of Π is at least $\lceil \log(\min\{n'/2, k\}) \rceil$ by doing induction on n'. For $n' = 1$, which means the leader is already determined at the beginning, the statement holds trivially since $r \geqslant 0$. For $n' > 1$, suppose the statement holds for smaller n' and Π is a protocol with n' alive parties and optimal round complexity. By the claim, there exists $\boldsymbol{x} \in \Omega^n$ such that $|\mathcal{S}(\boldsymbol{x})| \geqslant \min\{n'/2, k\}$. Given that the first-round inputs is $\boldsymbol{x}$, we can view the rest of the execution of Π as a $(r - 1)$-round leader election protocol. Denote the resulting protocol as Π'. It is not hard to show that Π' is also tight and the number of alive parties of Π' before the first round is $|\mathcal{S}(\boldsymbol{x})|$. Since Π is round optimal, we have $|\mathcal{S}(\boldsymbol{x})| < n'$. By our assumption, the round complexity of Π' is at least $\lceil \log(\min\{|\mathcal{S}(\boldsymbol{x})|/2, k\}) \rceil \geqslant \lceil \log(\min\{n'/4, k/2, k\}) \rceil = \lceil \log(\min\{n'/2, k\}/2) \rceil = \lceil \log(\min\{n'/2, k\}) \rceil - 1$, which implies the round complexity of Π is at least $\lceil \log(\min\{n'/2, k\}) \rceil$. We can conclude the theorem since a perfectly fair n-party protocol against k-corruption is a tight protocol against k-corruption with n alive parties. $\qquad\square$

Proof. (*Lemma 30*). Suppose Π is not abort-invariant, which means there exists $\boldsymbol{x} \in \Omega^n$ and $i \neq j \in [n]$ such that $\mathcal{P}_i(\boldsymbol{x}) = 0$, $\mathcal{P}_j(\boldsymbol{x}) \neq \mathcal{P}_j(\boldsymbol{x} : x_i \leftarrow \bot)$. Without loss of generality we can assume $\mathcal{P}_j(\boldsymbol{x}) > \mathcal{P}_j(\boldsymbol{x} : x_i \leftarrow \bot)$.[5] We construct an adversary $\mathcal{A}$ as follows. $\mathcal{A}$ corrupts party i and lets party i run the protocol honestly except party i aborts if the inputs of all parties are exactly $\boldsymbol{x}$. Then, the probability that party j is selected as the leader

$$\Pr_{\boldsymbol{x}' \sim \Omega^n}[\boldsymbol{x} = \boldsymbol{x}'] \cdot \mathcal{P}_j(\boldsymbol{x} : x_i \leftarrow \bot) + \sum_{\boldsymbol{z} \neq \boldsymbol{x} \in \Omega^n} \Pr_{\boldsymbol{x}' \sim \Omega^n}[\boldsymbol{z} = \boldsymbol{x}'] \cdot \mathcal{P}_j(\boldsymbol{z})$$

$$< \Pr_{\boldsymbol{x}' \sim \Omega^n}[\boldsymbol{x} = \boldsymbol{x}'] \cdot \mathcal{P}_j(\boldsymbol{x}) + \sum_{\boldsymbol{z} \neq \boldsymbol{x} \in \Omega^n} \Pr_{\boldsymbol{x}' \sim \Omega^n}[\boldsymbol{z} = \boldsymbol{x}'] \cdot \mathcal{P}_j(\boldsymbol{z})$$

$$= \sum_{\boldsymbol{z} \in \Omega^n} \Pr_{\boldsymbol{x}' \sim \Omega^n}[\boldsymbol{z} = \boldsymbol{x}'] \cdot \mathcal{P}_j(\boldsymbol{z}) = \mathcal{P}_j,$$

where $\mathcal{P}_j$ is the probability that party j is selected in an honest execution. Therefore, the protocol is not tight.

For the "moreover" part, suppose there exists $y \in \Omega$ and $j \in [n] \backslash \{i\}$ such that $\mathcal{P}_j(\boldsymbol{x} : x_i \leftarrow y) > \mathcal{P}_j(\boldsymbol{x})$. Since Π is abort-invariant, we have $\mathcal{P}_j(\boldsymbol{x} : x_i \leftarrow y) > \mathcal{P}_j(\boldsymbol{x}) = \mathcal{P}_j(\boldsymbol{x} : x_i \leftarrow \bot)$. Let $\hat{\boldsymbol{x}} := (\boldsymbol{x} : x_i \leftarrow y)$. Then, $\mathcal{P}_j(\hat{\boldsymbol{x}}) < \mathcal{P}_j(\hat{\boldsymbol{x}} : \hat{x}_i \leftarrow \bot)$. Therefore, we can use the same argument from the first part to construct an adversary $\mathcal{A}$ that breaks the tightness of Π. $\qquad\square$

Acknowledgments. Klein and Komargodski were supported in part by an Alon Young Faculty Fellowship, by a grant from the Israel Science Foundation (ISF Grant No. 1774/20), by a grant from the US-Israel Binational Science Foundation and the US National Science Foundation (BSF-NSF Grant No. 2020643), and by the European Union (ERC, SCALE,101162665). Ilan Komargodski is the Incumbent of the Harry & Abe Sherman Senior Lectureship at the School of Computer Science and Engineering at the Hebrew University. Views and opinions expressed are however those of the author(s) only and do not necessarily reflect those of the European Union or the European Research Council. Neither the European Union nor the granting authority can be held responsible for them. Zhu was supported in part by NSF grants CNS-2026774, CNS-2154174, a JP Morgan Faculty Award, a CISCO Faculty Award, and a gift from Microsoft.

---

[5] Otherwise, since $\sum_{k \in [n] \backslash i} \mathcal{P}_k(\boldsymbol{x}) = 1 = \sum_{k \in [n] \backslash i} \mathcal{P}_k(\boldsymbol{x} : x_i \leftarrow \bot)$, if there exists j such that $\mathcal{P}_j(\boldsymbol{x}) < \mathcal{P}_j(\boldsymbol{x} : x_i \leftarrow \bot)$, there also exists j' such that $\mathcal{P}_{j'}(\boldsymbol{x}) > \mathcal{P}_{j'}(\boldsymbol{x} : x_i \leftarrow \bot)$.

References

1. Berman, I., Haitner, I., Tentes, A.: Coin flipping of any constant bias implies one-way functions. J. ACM **65**(3), 1–95 (2018). https://doi.org/10.1145/2979676
2. Blum, M.: Coin flipping by telephone a protocol for solving impossible problems. SIGACT News **15**(1), 23–27 (1983)
3. Chung, K.M., Chan, T.H.H., Wen, T., Shi, E.: Game-theoretic fairness meets multi-party protocols: the case of leader election. In: Malkin, T., Peikert, C. (eds.) CRYPTO 2021, Part II. LNCS, vol. 12826, pp. 3–32. Springer, Cham, Virtual Event (2021). https://doi.org/10.1007/978-3-030-84245-1_1
4. Chung, K.-M., Guo, Y., Lin, W.-K., Pass, R., Shi, E.: Game theoretic notions of fairness in multi-party coin toss. In: Beimel, A., Dziembowski, S. (eds.) TCC 2018. LNCS, vol. 11239, pp. 563–596. Springer, Cham (2018). https://doi.org/10.1007/978-3-030-03807-6_21
5. Cleve, R.: Limits on the security of coin flips when half the processors are faulty (extended abstract). In: 18th ACM STOC, pp. 364–369. ACM Press (1986). https://doi.org/10.1145/12130.12168
6. Feige, U.: Noncryptographic selection protocols. In: 40th FOCS, pp. 142–153. IEEE Computer Society Press (1999). https://doi.org/10.1109/SFFCS.1999.814586
7. Filmus, Y., Hambardzumyan, L., Hatami, H., Hatami, P., Zuckerman, D.: Biasing boolean functions and collective coin-flipping protocols over arbitrary product distributions. CoRR arxiv preprint arxiv: abs/1902.07426 (2019). http://arxiv.org/abs/1902.07426
8. Gelashvili, R., Goren, G., Spiegelman, A.: Short paper: on game-theoretically-fair leader election. In: Eyal, I., Garay, J.A. (eds.) FC 2022. LNCS, vol. 13411, pp. 531–538. Springer, Cham (2022). https://doi.org/10.1007/978-3-031-18283-9_26
9. Goldreich, O., Goldwasser, S., Linial, N.: Fault-tolerant computation in the full information model. SIAM J. Comput. **27**(2), 506–544 (1998)
10. Gradwohl, R., Vadhan, S., Zuckerman, D.: Random selection with an adversarial majority. In: Dwork, C. (ed.) CRYPTO 2006. LNCS, vol. 4117, pp. 409–426. Springer, Heidelberg (2006). https://doi.org/10.1007/11818175_25
11. Haitner, I., Omri, E.: Coin flipping with constant bias implies one-way functions. In: Ostrovsky, R. (ed.) 52nd FOCS, pp. 110–119. IEEE Computer Society Press (2011). https://doi.org/10.1109/FOCS.2011.29
12. Komargodski, I., Matsuo, S., Shi, E., Wu, K.: log*-round game-theoretically-fair leader election. In: Dodis, Y., Shrimpton, T. (eds.) CRYPTO 2022, Part III. LNCS, vol. 13509, pp. 409–438. Springer, Cham (2022). https://doi.org/10.1007/978-3-031-15982-4_14
13. v. Neumann, J.: Zur theorie der gesellschaftsspiele. Mathematische annalen **100**(1), 295–320 (1928)
14. Russell, A., Saks, M.E., Zuckerman, D.: Lower bounds for leader election and collective coin-flipping in the perfect information model. In: 31st ACM STOC, pp. 339–347. ACM Press (1999). https://doi.org/10.1145/301250.301337
15. Russell, A., Zuckerman, D.: Perfect information leader election in log*n + O(1) rounds. In: 39th FOCS, pp. 576–583. IEEE Computer Society Press (1998). https://doi.org/10.1109/SFCS.1998.743508

16. Sanghvi, S., Vadhan, S.P.: The round complexity of two-party random selection. In: Gabow, H.N., Fagin, R. (eds.) 37th ACM STOC, pp. 338–347. ACM Press (2005). https://doi.org/10.1145/1060590.1060641

17. Wu, K., Asharov, G., Shi, E.: A complete characterization of game-theoretically fair, multi-party coin toss. In: Dunkelman, O., Dziembowski, S. (eds.) EURO-CRYPT 2022, Part I. LNCS, vol. 13275, pp. 120–149. Springer, Cham (2022). https://doi.org/10.1007/978-3-031-06944-4_5

The Cost of Maintaining Keys in Dynamic Groups with Applications to Multicast Encryption and Group Messaging

Michael Anastos[1]([✉]) [ID], Benedikt Auerbach[2] [ID], Mirza Ahad Baig[1] [ID],
Miguel Cueto Noval[1] [ID], Matthew Kwan[1] [ID], Guillermo Pascual-Perez[1] [ID],
and Krzysztof Pietrzak[1] [ID]

[1] ISTA, Klosterneuburg, Austria
{michael.anastos,mbaig,mcuetono,matthew.kwan,gpascual,pietrzak,
bauerbac}@ista.ac.at
[2] PQShield, Oxford, UK
benedikt.auerbach@pqshield.com

Abstract. In this work we prove lower bounds on the (communication) cost of maintaining a shared key among a dynamic group of users. Being "dynamic" means one can add and remove users from the group. This captures important protocols like multicast encryption (ME) and continuous group-key agreement (CGKA), which is the primitive underlying many group messaging applications.

We prove our bounds in a combinatorial setting where the state of the protocol progresses in rounds. The state of the protocol in each round is captured by a set system, with each of its elements specifying a set of users who share a secret key. We show this combinatorial model implies bounds in symbolic models for ME and CGKA that capture, as building blocks, PRGs, PRFs, dual PRFs, secret sharing, and symmetric encryption in the setting of ME, and PRGs, PRFs, dual PRFs, secret sharing, public-key encryption, and key-updatable public-key encryption in the setting of CGKA. The models are related to the ones used by Micciancio and Panjwani (Eurocrypt'04) and Bienstock et al. (TCC'20) to analyze ME and CGKA, respectively.

We prove – using the Bollobás' Set Pairs Inequality – that the cost (number of uploaded ciphertexts) for replacing a set of d users in a group of size n is $\Omega(d\ln(n/d))$. Our lower bound is asymptotically tight and both improves on a bound of $\Omega(d)$ by Bienstock et al. (TCC'20), and generalizes a result by Micciancio and Panjwani (Eurocrypt'04), who proved a lower bound of $\Omega(\log(n))$ for $d = 1$.

Benedikt Auerbach conducted part of this work at ISTA.

E. Boyle and M. Mahmoody (Eds.): TCC 2024, LNCS 15364, pp. 413–443, 2025.
https://doi.org/10.1007/978-3-031-78011-0_14

1   Introduction

1.1   Membership Changes in Multicast Encryption and Continuous Group-Key Agreement

Multicast Encryption and CGKA. A prevalent problem in many areas of cryptography involves the agreement on a common key by a group of protocol users. This underpins communication primitives which try to achieve scalability beyond what is offered by point-to-point communication. The problem is made more interesting (and practical) if we further consider a dynamically-changing group of users, i.e., where users get added and removed to and from the group, and which thus requires an ever-evolving common key. The two main primitives capturing this problem are, arguably, Multicast Encryption (ME) and Continuous Group-Key Agreement (CGKA). The former, with constructions dating back to the 1990 s, considers the problem in the presence of a central authority (CA) that has access to all secrets and is in charge of sending protocol messages to users in order to effect group membership changes. In turn, CGKA is a much newer primitive, resulting from the development of end-to-end encrypted messaging systems, such as WhatsApp or Signal, and the recent IETF standard Message Layer Security (MLS). Given that the goal of these systems is the confidentiality of the messages exchanged, the reliance on a central authority to manage key material is naturally out of the question. Instead, group members themselves are the ones who refresh the key material when membership changes take place, with communication taking place over an untrusted server. CGKA has the additional security goal of post-compromise security (PCS), which roughly states users can "heal" from a compromise, so that future keys/messages can become again secure.

As mentioned before, the main goal of these protocols is to provide scalability to large groups, and so it is important that the protocols messages are small. In particular, these should be of size sub-linear in the group size n.

Key-Trees. The main technique employed by efficient ME and CGKA constructions are so-called *key-trees*, which were first used by [16,17] for building multicast protocols. A key-tree is a (usually, though not necessarily, binary) tree graph where each node is associated to a key. In the case of ME, keys typically correspond to a symmetric encryption scheme, whereas for CGKA, they correspond to a key-pair of a public-key encryption scheme. Leaves in the tree are associated to users, and the root of the tree corresponds to the group key. Further, the tree can be seen as a directed graph, with edges capturing the following hierarchical relationship between the keys: knowledge of the (in the CGKA case, secret) key of the source implies knowledge of the (secret) key of the target. It is easy to see that, if we consider the key at each leaf being known to exactly the user associated to it, users know exactly the keys on the path from their leaf to the root. This is known as the *tree invariant*, and the security of the protocol can be seen as ensuring this invariant holds throughout key-material changes.

The benefit of using key-trees is that, by making use of the auxiliary keys corresponding to the internal tree nodes, key material can be refreshed and shared to the rest of the group very efficiently. For the purpose of simplicity, in the following we focus on the communication cost of replacing users, i.e., substituting one user with another, so that the group size remains constant. In practice, this is equivalent to eliminating the keys known to the removed user, including the group key, and communicating the new (freshly sampled) group key to the new user and the remainder of the group.[1] It is clear that the cost of removing a user from the group, i.e., that of communicating a new key to the remainder of the group, is similar to that of a replacement. Thus, we will indistinctly use the term *replacement* throughout the paper except where a distinction is relevant. In particular, due to the tree invariant, key-trees allow to replace (or remove) a user with a cost equal to the length of the path of the replaced (removed) user times the in-degree of the nodes in said path. Indeed, each new key for a node along the path can be communicated to all users (leaves) below it by simply encrypting it to all of its children. If we consider a binary tree, this cost is approximately $2\log(n)$.[2] This was improved upon by multicast protocols using a pseudo-random generator (PRG) [8] to derive the new keys along a path, reducing the communication by a factor of 2. Most CGKA protocols incorporate this technique as well, thus also allowing for a replacement with $\log(n)$ cost.

Batching Replacements for ME. A natural attempt to improve on the efficiency of the above constructions would be to consider batching replacements. Indeed, if we wanted to batch d replacements, we would need to replace only $d(1 + \log(n/d))$ nodes in expectation [13] (those on the intersection of the paths of d uniformly random leaves), as opposed to $d\log(n)$. One would hope that this would translate to protocols with an improved communication cost. And indeed, this is the case, as shown implicitly by [13] and explicitly for ME in [11,14], which propose protocols, using only hashing and encryption as building blocks, that allow batching dynamic operations and, in the case where only replacements are performed, can replace d users in a single round of communication with a communication cost of $d(1 + \log(n/d))$. A further motivation for these works was to alleviate out-of-sync-related issues that can arise in bigger groups where re-keying becomes more frequent.

Batching Replacements for CGKA. Similar approaches can be seen in CGKA constructions, where the situation is more involved due to the absence of a central authority. Indeed the main example of this approach is TreeKEM, the CGKA underlying MLS [4]. Here, d users can be replaced, concurrently in 2 rounds of communication, with a communication cost of $d(1 + \log(n/d))$ at the

---

[1] In CGKA, a so-called *update* operation, designed to provide security against a potential compromise of the issuer, can also be seen as such a replacement, where the old (potentially leaked) state is replaced by a new one.

[2] Computing the amortized cost of removing users is more convoluted, since by removing the key of a node one effectively increases the in-degree of its parent. Whereas replacing this key in ME can be easily done by the central authority, it becomes an issue for CGKA protocols, where removing a sizeable number of users can result in subsequent communication costs degrading to linear in n.

cost of increasing the cost of future group communication.[3] A first round where all d users announce a new key for the leaf will follow by another where one of the d users will sample the new group key. In TreeKEM the keys on the paths of the other $d-1$ users will get deleted and set to null, thus preventing their usage until they are replaced by future operations. Hence, this communication complexity is only achieved under so-called "fair-weather" conditions, i.e., under beneficial sequences of operations that, e.g., contribute towards quickly replacing the removed keys. All of the subsequent protocols based on TreeKEM share the same or very similar issues.

Lower Bounds. Given the upper bounds highlighted above, an interesting question is whether they are optimal. The first steps in this direction were taken in works by Canetti, Malkin and Nissim [9] and Snoeyink, Suri and Varghese [15], both, however, making restricting assumptions on the schemes and, in particular, not allowing for the use of pseudorandom generators. Regarding single (non-batched) replacements in ME, Micciancio and Panjwani [12] showed, in a symbolic model in the style of Dolev and Yao [10], that the protocol by [8] is optimal among those built using encryption and PRGs, proving a worst-case lower bound of $\log(n) + o(1)$.

As a result of the introduction of CGKA and the big amount of constructions proposed in the last years, a new line of work proving similar lower bounds in the symbolic model has been taking shape. Particularly interesting to our setting, Bienstock, Dodis and Rösler [6], in a work on the communication complexity of concurrent recovery from corruption in CGKA, implicitly prove a lower bound of d for batched user replacements, which essentially says that every new leaf key in the group must be addressed separately. In the case $d = 1$ Alwen et al. [1] lift the bound of [12] to an average case bound, and further extend it to CGKAs. This work also generalizes the bound to the case of several, potentially overlapping groups. The recent [3] generalizes [6] to a setting where the condition of recovery from corruption is relaxed a larger number of rounds.

Going beyond bounds in the symbolic model, Bienstock et al. [5], by means of a black-box separation from public-key encryption, analyze the worst-case efficiency of CGKA. The work gives a sustained lower bound that is linear in the group size, i.e., $\Omega(n)$. This is done for a sequence of operations, in which a set of users of size $\Omega(n)$ is added to the group, followed by a sequence of removals and adds of a single user per round. However, the bound does not apply to ME and is worst-case, meaning that it relies on a particular, adversarially chosen sequence of additions and removals of users.

Despite both the ME constructions above and the lower bound of [12] existing for roughly 20 years, neither better constructions nor a matching lower bound considering batching have been proposed since, leaving upper bounds of order $d(1 + \log(n/d))$ and the implicit lower bound of d [6] as the state of the art regarding batched user replacements in ME.

---

[3] If considering only removals, the additive term d would not be present, as this corresponds to the individual encryptions to the new users.

1.2   Our Contributions

A Tight Lower Bound on Batched User Replacements. In this work we close the gap between upper and lower bounds on the communication complexity incurred by batched user replacements in multicast encryption and continuous group-key agreement. On a high level, we prove the following statement.

> In the symbolic model, consider a secure and correct ME (or CGKA) scheme. If a set of d users chosen uniformly at random from a group with n members is replaced with different users, then the protocol messages must have contained at least $\frac{\ln(2)}{3} \cdot d \cdot \log(n/d)$ ciphertexts in expectation.

In the above we allow for symmetric encryption, pseudorandom generators, (dual) pseudorandom functions, and secret sharing as building blocks for ME, and for (key-updatable) public-key encryption, pseudorandom generators, (dual) pseudorandom functions, and secret sharing in the case of CGKA. As there exist constructions of ME [11,14,18] and CGKA [4] (the latter however only with respect to fair-weather complexity, as discussed above) that achieve a communication cost of $d(1 + \log(n/d))$ our bound is tight up to a small multiplicative factor.[4] Intuitively, this shows that existing ME and CGKA constructions are optimal and, in particular, suggests that the way the removal of users is handled in the MLS standard [4] cannot be improved by simple means.

We point out that our bound is an average case bound, as the set of replaced users is chosen uniformly at random (as is the case for the single user bound of [1]), as opposed to ones relying on an adversarially chosen sequences of operations [3,5,12]. Our technical statements regarding ME and CGKA (Corollary 1 for ME and see the full version [2] for CGKA) take *amortized* communication complexity into account. I.e., we consider a game running over $t_{\max}$ rounds where, in every round t, a set of d_t group members, chosen uniformly at random from the current group, is replaced by new users. Then, if we denote the set of ciphertexts and keys sent in round t by M_t, we prove that

$$\mathbb{E}\left[\sum_{t=0}^{t_{\max}} |\mathsf{M}_t|\right] \geq \frac{\ln(2)}{3} \sum_{t=1}^{t_{\max}} d_t \log\left(\frac{n}{d_t}\right).$$

Note that we cannot guarantee that $|\mathsf{M}_t| \geq (\ln(2)/3) \cdot d_t \cdot \log(n/d_t)$ for all t. This is necessary as, in principle, some of the communication required to replace the users in round t might already have happened in prior rounds, as will be discussed in greater detail below.

Proof Overview. Conceptually, we follow the approach of [3], who prove lower bounds on the cost incurred by CGKA schemes recovering from corruption(s) over several rounds. That is, we decouple the combinatorial problem at the core

---

[4] We point out that for typical use cases we have $d \ll n$. Further, the case $\log(n/d) < 1$ in which our bound is not asymptotically optimal implies $d > n/2$. In this case the linear lower bound by Bienstock, Dodis, and Rösler [6] is asymptotically optimal.

of minimizing the cost for batched user replacements from the more technical issues that arise when arguing within the confines of the symbolic model. More precisely, our proof consists of two major parts, the first of which is common to both the case of multicast encryption and CGKA simultaneously. First, in Sect. 3 we capture the problem of securely replacing a batch of users in ME and CGKA in a clean, self-contained combinatorial model, and prove our lower bound within this model. The second step consists of showing that bounds in the combinatorial model imply bounds in the symbolic model. This is done for ME in Sect. 4 in the full version, the proofs being very similar. We discuss these steps in greater detail below.

The Combinatorial Model. Our aim with the combinatorial model is to capture in an intuitive way how the sets of users that share a secure secret evolve over time. Here, 'secret' can be thought of as a symmetric key or secret key depending on whether we want to model ME or CGKA. More precisely, for $n_{\max}, t_{\max} \in \mathbb{N}$, we let $[n_{\max}]$ be the universe of users and, for rounds $t \in [t_{\max}]$, consider a sequence of groups $G_t \subseteq [n_{\max}]$ evolving round-by-round by replacing a set of group members in every round. We then capture the secrets shared by users in each round as a sequence of set systems $\mathcal{S}_t \subseteq 2^{[n_{\max}]}$. A set $S \subseteq [n_{\max}]$ being part of $\mathcal{S}_t$ intuitively means that there exists a secret $\mathbf{r}$ with the following two properties. On the one hand, the set of users in G_t that, in round t (or any round before), are able to recover $\mathbf{r}$ from their internal states and the protocol messages sent so far is exactly given by S; and, on the other hand, $\mathbf{r}$ is secure. The latter means that, even given the protocol messages as well as the current and all prior states of every user *not* in G_t, it is not possible to recover $\mathbf{r}$.

Correctness and security of the corresponding ME or CGKA scheme impose two restrictions on $\mathcal{S}_t$. Namely, for all t we have $G_t \in \mathcal{S}_t$, which corresponds to the existence of a secure group key shared by all the members in G_t. Further, as keys known to non-members of the group are being considered insecure, it must be the case that $S \subseteq G_t$ for all $S \in \mathcal{S}_t$.

The set system $\mathcal{S}_t$ evolves over time. Removing a user u from the group leads to all secrets they had at some point access to being considered insecure. This means that all sets in $\mathcal{S}_{t-1}$ that contained u can no longer be present in $\mathcal{S}_t$. On the other hand, by sending protocol messages, new secrets can be shared with users, meaning that sets can be added to $\mathcal{S}_t$. Adding sets to $\mathcal{S}_t$, however, comes at a communication cost, since the corresponding secrets cannot be simply sent in the clear, but instead must be encrypted under (potentially multiple) secure keys already present in the system. We capture this with a cost function $\text{Cost}(t)$ that, for now, can be thought of as a lower bound on the ciphertexts needed to be sent in the rounds up to t, in order to communicate the secrets corresponding to $\mathcal{S}_t$. While the definition of $\mathcal{S}_t$ can be seen as a natural generalization of the set system introduced for static groups in [3] to the setting of dynamic groups, our definition of the cost function deviates substantially from prior lower bounds in the symbolic model, and we consider it to be one of the main conceptual contributions of this work, as we discuss below.

Defining the Cost Function. Prior works giving lower bounds for ME or CGKA schemes in the symbolic model follow one of two different approaches for counting the number of ciphertexts sent in order to achieve both correctness and security of the scheme. [1,12] for round t use as cost function the amount of ciphertexts that were used to communicate the group key of round $t - 1$, and are no longer of use in round t as they are encryptions of keys that are known by users removed from the group in round t. Each of these ciphertexts can be identified with a particular secret (which is one of the encryption keys used in the ciphertext), and thus in our abstraction this cost metric can be seen as giving a cover of the set $G_{t-1} \setminus D_t$ using sets in S_{t-1}, where D_t denotes the set of users removed from the group in round t. Moreover, it also admits another interpretation, namely, these ciphertexts are encryptions of secrets that are known by users in D_t and this means that the cost metric can be seen as counting some of the sets removed from the set system in round t.

On the other hand, [3,6] consider the number of ciphertexts sent in a particular round t that are necessary to communicate a new secret $\mathbf{r}$ to (some of) the group members. Note that in order to communicate $\mathbf{r}$, it must have been encrypted under secret keys already established by the scheme. Seen through the abstraction of set system S_t, this means if the set S (corresponding to $\mathbf{r}$) is added to S_t, it must have been covered by the union of a collection of sets in S_{t-1}. Accordingly, one can essentially use as cost function the size of a minimum cover of S with respect to S_{t-1}, i.e., the smallest amount of sets in S_{t-1} the union of which covers S. To be a bit more precise, the cover may also include singletons $\{u\}$ for all users $u \in [n_{\max}]$ (corresponding to the users' personal keys). In particular, this is relevant regarding users being added to the group which, by the rules imposed by correctness and security, cannot be part of any set in S_{t-1}.

In this work we define $\mathrm{Cost}(t)$ taking into account both the number of removed sets and the size of a minimum cover of G_t using sets in S_{t-1} and singletons for all users $u \in [n_{\max}]$. Unlike [1,12], which only take into account *some* of the destroyed sets, we generalize their approach and count *every* set removed from the set system. This is motivated by the following observation. When considering a scheme in the combinatorial model, we would like to exploit that, in every round t, the group G_t must be an element of S_t. Following the second cost metric described above, we can argue that the cost of adding the corresponding key to the set system must be at least the size of a minimum cover of G_t with respect to the prior set system S_{t-1}. However, we consider a security experiment running over multiple rounds and do not want to impose unnecessary restrictions on S_{t-1}. In particular, it could be the case that $S_{t-1} = 2^{G_{t-1}}$ is the full power set of the prior group. Thus, if we denote the d users removed from and added to G_{t-1} by D_t and A_t, respectively, we have that $S = (G_{t-1} \setminus D_t) \in S_{t-1}$, and obtain a minimum cover of the new group as

$$G_t = S \cup \bigcup_{u \in A_t} \{u\}.$$

This means that removing the users from the group comes essentially for free, and the only contribution to the cost function stems from adding the users in A_t to the group. As a consequence, using this cost metric we would end up with a cost that is linear in d, in turn recovering the bound already implicitly given in [6].

Note, however, that in the example above the set system $\mathcal{S}_{t-1}$ contains a number of sets that is exponential in the group size n. Further, every set in $\mathcal{S}_{t-1}$ containing at least one of the removed users would no longer be considered secure after round t, and there is an exponential number of sets of this type. Thus, in the first cost metric discussed above, i.e., counting sets removed from the system, maintaining such a huge system would be prohibitively expensive. For this reason, in this paper we use the sum of the two prior approaches as cost metric and define

$$\mathrm{Cost}(t) = \underbrace{|\{S \in \mathcal{S}_{t-1} : S \cap D_t \neq \emptyset\}|}_{\text{sets removed from } \mathcal{S}_{t-1}} + \underbrace{\mathrm{SizeMinCov}(G_t, \mathcal{S}_{t-1} \cup \{\{u\} : u \in G_t\})}_{\text{size of minimum cover of } G_t}.$$

For an illustration of our cost function for a concrete key-tree see Fig. 1. We stress that $\mathrm{Cost}(t)$ is not to be understood as the amount of ciphertexts sent in round t, but instead as a lower bound on the ciphertexts sent up to, and including, that round. Further, our precise definition of the cost function (see Definition 2) also accounts for minor potential savings in terms of ciphertexts, stemming from the following two observations. On the one hand, that adding singletons to $\mathcal{S}_t$ does not necessarily require sending a ciphertext; on the other, that one ciphertext in the second summand of $\mathrm{Cost}(t)$ can be saved by deriving new keys from the output of a pseudorandom generator evaluated on the secret corresponding to one of the sets making up the minimum cover.

Lower Bounding Cost(t) in the Combinatorial Model. The example discussed above suggests a trade-off between the two terms of $\mathrm{Cost}(t)$. Intuitively, the larger the set system $\mathcal{S}_{t-1}$, the cheaper it is to add G_t to $\mathcal{S}_t$. Here, the extreme case is given by the example discussed above, which essentially corresponds to preparing a key for the removal of every possible subset of G_{t-1}, and that leads to a large cost due to the first summand of $\mathrm{Cost}(t)$. The opposite extreme would be $\mathcal{S}_{t-1} = G_{t-1} \cup \{\{u\} : u \in G_{t-1}\}$ where, except for the group key, there is only a personal key for every group member. In this case any cover of G_t with respect to the previous set system would be made up of singletons and thus of size linear in $|G_t|$. Hence, to minimize the overall cost, intuitively it makes sense to balance the two components of $\mathrm{Cost}(t)$, which turns out to also be the case for the best known constructions of ME [11, 14, 18]. In these constructions, based on balanced binary trees, replacing d uniformly random group members requires in expectation to replace $\Theta(d(1 + \log(n/d)))$ keys in the system, each of which comes at the cost of one ciphertext. Further, the expected size of a minimum cover of G_t turns out to be of the same size. Accordingly, both summands of $\mathrm{Cost}(t)$ are of order $\Theta(d(1 + \log(n/d)))$.

We show that these constructions are optimal (up to a small constant factor) by roughly proving in Theorem 1 that, for every choice of $(\mathcal{S}_t)_{t=0}^{t_{\max}}$ satisfying the

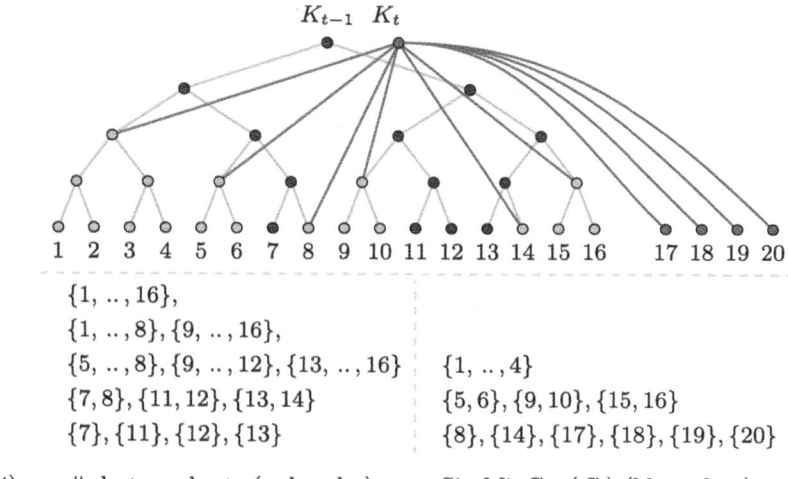

$$\text{Cost}(t) = \quad \# \text{ destroyed sets (red nodes)} \quad + \quad \text{SizeMinCov}(G_t) \text{ (blue edges)}$$

Fig. 1. Example of our cost function on a balanced binary key-graph (top). The set associated to a node (key) is given by all leaves (users) whose path to the root contains the node in question. The figure depicts users 7, 11, 12, 13 in the group $G_{t-1} = \{1, \ldots, 16\}$ being replaced by users 17, 18, 19, and 20, producing group G_t. Gray and blue nodes were already part of the system at time $t-1$, blue nodes are added at time t. Our cost function $\text{Cost}(t)$ counts the sets in $\mathcal{S}_{t-1}$ no longer secure after removing the users (bottom left, corresponding to the red nodes), as well as the size of a minimum cover of the new group with respect to the remaining secure sets and the added users' personal keys (bottom right, corresponding to the blue edges), i.e., the number of ciphertexts that have to be sent in order to establish the new group key K_t. Note that what is described here is a simplification ignoring possible optimizations and special cases (that our formal model does capture). (Color figure online)

requirements of the combinatorial model, it must hold that

$$\mathbb{E}\left[\sum_{t=0}^{t_{\max}} \text{Cost}(t)\right] \geq \sum_{t=1}^{t_{\max}} d_t \ln\left(\frac{n}{d_t}\right),$$

where d_t denotes the amount of users replaced in round t and the set D_t of users replaced is sampled uniformly at random in every round. In the proof we consider two families $(X_{D_t})_{D_t \subseteq G_{t-1}}$ and $(Y_{D_t})_{D_t \subseteq G_{t-1}}$ of set systems $X_{D_t}, Y_{D_t} \subseteq 2^{[n_{\max}]}$, parameterized by all possible choices of D_t. These essentially correspond to the two summands of the cost function. Accordingly, the elements of X_{D_t} capture the sets in $\mathcal{S}_{t-1}$ that are destroyed due to the removal of users in round t, and the elements of Y_{D_t} correspond to a minimum cover of the new group G_t with respect to $\mathcal{S}_{t-1}$. We then observe that the two families of set systems satisfy a disjoint-edness condition required for the Bollobás Set Pairs Inequality [7]. Applying the inequality allows us to lower bound a term related to $\sum_{D_t \subseteq G_{t-1}} |X_{D_t}| + |Y_{D_t}|$ which, after some calculations, yields the desired bound on $\text{Cost}(t)$.

Translation to the Symbolic Model. In the second conceptual step, we prove that lower bounds on $\sum_{t=1}^{t_{\max}} \text{Cost}(t)$ in the combinatorial model imply lower bounds on the amount of ciphertexts sent by a secure and correct ME or CGKA scheme in the symbolic model, albeit at a potential loss of a factor of $1/3$. In the symbolic model [10], one considers ME or CGKA schemes constructed from cryptographic primitives used as building blocks that are essentially modeled to satisfy ideal security. Our lower bound for ME allows for pseudorandom generators (PRGs), pseudorandom functions (PRFs), dual PRFs (dPRFs), secret sharing, and symmetric encryption (SE), and thus in particular covers all building blocks used for the corresponding upper bounds [11,14,18]. Compared to prior lower bounds, it covers more building blocks than the ones considered in [1,12], which do not cover dPRFs. Our lower bound for CGKA uses PRGs, PRFs, dPRFs, secret sharing, public-key encryption (PKE), and key-updatable public-key encryption (kuPKE) as building blocks, and in particular covers all primitives used in important schemes like MLS [4]. Regarding a comparison to prior bounds, while it covers strictly more primitives than the one of [1], it is incomparable to the bound of [6], who do not allow for secret sharing, but additionally consider broadcast encryption (BE). We consider it an interesting open question, whether our bound can be extended to BE, but point out that it is a very powerful primitive, on the one hand, has to the best of our knowledge not been used in practical CGKA constructions, and, on the other hand, implies the existence of a multicast encryption scheme with constant communication complexity As a consequence any such bound would have to substantially differ from the techniques used in this work.

We now describe the translation of our combinatorial bound to the symbolic model in more detail. In every round t, to every secure secret $\mathbf{r}$ present in the symbolic model we associate the set of users that had access to $\mathbf{r}$ in a round up to and including t. Then, we prove that the resulting set systems satisfy the security and correctness properties imposed in the combinatorial model, and further that

$$\sum_{t=0}^{t_{\max}} |\mathsf{M}_t| \geq \frac{1}{3} \sum_{t=0}^{t_{\max}} \text{Cost}(t),$$

where M_t denotes the protocol message sent in the symbolic model in round t. In fact, the inequality holds even if we only take into account the number of ciphertexts sent rather than all protocol messages. In combination with our lower bound in the combinatorial model, this immediately yields the desired bounds on ME and CGKA.

The loss of $1/3$ in our bound is due to the following. Consider the cost function $\text{Cost}(t)$, for some t, in the combinatorial model. Intuitively, each of the two components, i.e., amount of sets removed from the system and size of a minimum cover of G_t, is justified by the requirement that a corresponding amount of ciphertexts is sent to communicate the respective secrets. However, it might be the case that a ciphertext that corresponded to a part of the minimum cover of group G_t in a later round $t' > t$, might be the one being used to justify the cost of a set being removed from $\mathcal{S}_{t'-1}$ following the removal of some users. In this case, the same ciphertext is being counted twice in $\sum_{t=1}^{t_{\max}} \text{Cost}(t)$.

For a minimal example of this, consider the universe of users $\{u_i : i = 0, \ldots, n_{\max}\}$, where each user holds a personal keys $\mathbf{k}_i$, and the sequence of groups is given by $G_t = \{u_0, u_t\}$. I.e., the second user of a group of size 2 is replaced in every round by encrypting the new group key to user u_t's personal key (it is possible to communicate the new group key to user 0 without the need of an additional ciphertext by making a clever use of a pseudorandom generator). Then, the ciphertext accounting for the minimum cover of G_t is the same as the one corresponding to the set $G_t = \{u_0, u_t\}$ that is being removed from the set system $\mathcal{S}_t$ when considering the cost of the following round $t+1$. Accordingly we have that $\text{Cost}(t) = 2$ for every round, while only one ciphertext is being sent per round.

However, we are able to show that this kind of double counting is essentially the only thing that can go wrong in our translation between combinatorial and symbolic models. The idea behind this is to derive separate bounds on the sum over t of each summand of $\text{Cost}(t)$.

We start by studying $\sum_{t=0}^{t_{\max}} (\text{SizeMinCov}(G_t, \mathcal{S}_{t-1} \cup \{\{u\} : u \in G_t\}) - 1)$. In order to find a cover for the set G_t we first cover the subset of users in G_{t-1} that are not removed from the group at time t, i.e., $G_{t-1} \setminus D_t$. Every user in $G_{t-1} \setminus D_t$ must be able to derive the group key of round $t-1$ and do so by decrypting some ciphertexts sent in or before round $t-1$. If for each of these ciphertexts we consider the set of users who know the secret key needed for decryption we obtain a cover $\mathcal{C}_{t,1}$ of $G_{t-1} \setminus D_t$. Moreover, these ciphertext can be chosen so that they are an encryption of a secret that is no longer useful in round t. This guarantees that the ciphertexts used for $\mathcal{C}_{t,1}$ and $\mathcal{C}_{\tilde{t},1}$ are different for $t \neq \tilde{t}$. Therefore $\sum_{t=1}^{t_{\max}} |\mathcal{C}_{t,1}| \leq \sum_{t=0}^{t_{\max}-1} |\mathsf{M}_t|$.

Next we obtain a cover for G_t by considering the singletons $\{u\}$ for each user that is added in round t. Since the users being added at time t do not share any secrets with the users in G_{t-1}, we have $|\mathsf{M}_t| \geq |A_t| - 1$, where the subtraction comes from the possible use of PRGs. However this might introduced some double counting as these ciphertext might be used to obtain the inequality at the end of the previous paragraph. Thus

$$\sum_{t=0}^{t_{\max}} |\mathsf{M}_t| \geq \frac{1}{2} \sum_{t=0}^{t_{\max}} (\text{SizeMinCov}(G_t, \mathcal{S}_{t-1} \cup \{\{u\} : u \in G_t\}) - 1).$$

Regarding our bound on the first summand of $\text{Cost}(t)$, if we consider a set S associated to some secret $\mathbf{r}$ in round $t-1$ that contains at least two users, it must be the case that at least one of them had to decrypt a ciphertext in order to learn $\mathbf{r}$. Now, the additional restriction that $S \cap D_t \neq \emptyset$ guarantees that this ciphertext is not used in future rounds and therefore we obtain

$$\sum_{t=0}^{t_{\max}} |\mathsf{M}_t| \geq \sum_{t=1}^{t_{\max}} |\{S \in \mathcal{S}_{t-1} : S \cap D_t \neq \emptyset \text{ and } |S| > 1\}|.$$

Combining the bounds on both components yields our bound on $\sum_{t=1}^{t_{\max}} \text{Cost}(t)$.

2   Preliminaries

2.1   Definitions and Results from Combinatorics

Definition 1 (Cover and (size of a) minimum cover). *Let* $n \in \mathbb{N}$ *and* $\mathcal{S} \subseteq 2^{[n]}$. *Then for* $X \subseteq [n]$, *a* cover *of* X *with respect to* $\mathcal{S}$ *is a set* $\mathcal{T} \subseteq \mathcal{S}$ *satisfying* $X = \bigcup_{T \in \mathcal{T}} T$. *A cover of* X *with respect to* $\mathcal{S}$ *of minimal cardinality is referred to as a* minimum cover. *We will use the notation* $\text{SizeMinCov}(X, \mathcal{S})$ *to denote the cardinality of a minimum cover of* X *with respect to* $\mathcal{S}$.

We now recall two results from combinatorics; the well-known inequality of arithmetic and geometric means and the *Bollobás Set Pairs Inequality*.

Proposition 1 (Inequality of arithmetic and geometric means). *For* $k \in \mathbb{N}$ *let* $x_1, \ldots, x_k \in \mathbb{R}$ *be non-negative. Then*

$$\prod_{i=1}^{k} x_i \leq \left(\frac{1}{k} \sum_{i=1}^{k} x_i \right)^k.$$

Lemma 1 (Bollobás Set Pairs Inequality [7]). *Let* $m \in \mathbb{N}$ *and consider families of finite sets* $\mathcal{X} = \{X_1, X_2, \ldots, X_m\}$ *and* $\mathcal{Y} = \{Y_1, Y_2, \ldots, Y_m\}$ *such that* $X_i \cap Y_j = \emptyset$ *if and only if* $i, j \in [m]$ *are equal. Then*

$$\sum_{i=1}^{m} \binom{|X_i| + |Y_i|}{|X_i|}^{-1} \leq 1.$$

3   Lower Bounds in the Combinatorial Model

In this section we present a simple combinatorial model for the batched replacement of users in multicast encryption and continuous group-key agreement (in Sect. 3.1) and then use it to derive a lower bound on the communication required to replace sets of users picked uniformly at random from the group members (in Sect. 3.2).

3.1   The Combinatorial Model

In this section we present a simple, purely combinatorial model that aims to capture the communication cost of batched replacements of users in multicast-encryption (ME) and continuous group-key agreement (CGKA) schemes. In both settings, a group of users evolving through rounds wants to agree on a sequence of group-keys by sending and processing protocol messages. In the case of ME, these are generated and sent by a central authority, whereas in the case of CGKA they are generated by the users themselves and distributed via an untrusted server.

Security essentially requires that, even given access to all protocol messages and the current and prior internal states of all users not currently in the group, it is not possible to gain any information on the current group key. Our model closely resembles the one of [3] but extends it to dynamic groups, and further differs in some aspects such as, for example, the cost metric (see Remark 1). Looking ahead, in Sect. 4 we show that lower bounds in the combinatorial model imply lower bounds on the number of ciphertexts sent in ME schemes in the symbolic model.

High-level Structure and Evolution of the Group. An instantiation of the combinatorial model consists of two integers $n_{\max}, t_{\max} \in \mathbb{N}$, a set $G_0 \subseteq [n_{\max}]$, sequences of sets $(D_t, A_t)_{t=1}^{t_{\max}}$, and a sequence of collections of sets $(\mathcal{S}_t)_{t=0}^{t_{\max}}$. Here $[n_{\max}]$ represents the universe of users, $t_{\max}$ the number of rounds, and G_0 the initial group. For $t \in [t_{\max}]$, the sets D_t and A_t represent the users removed and added from and to the group, respectively. Accordingly, for $t \geq 1$ we inductively define the group in round t as

$$G_t := (G_{t-1} \cup A_t) \setminus D_t.$$

To make the additions and removals to and from the group meaningful we impose the requirement that $D_t \subseteq G_{t-1}$ and $A_t \subseteq [n_{\max}] \setminus G_{t-1}$ for all $t \geq 1$. Regarding the removed users, we will even impose the stronger requirement that they are never added back to the group, i.e., that for all $t \in [t_{\max}]$ we have that

$$A_t \subseteq [n_{\max}] \setminus \left(G_{t-1} \cup \bigcup_{t'=1}^{t-1} D_{t'} \right).$$

Looking ahead, this requirement will be necessary to formally justify our cost function. Consider the scenario where every even round user u replaces user v, and vice versa in odd rounds. Then, after the first couple of rounds, no more communication is required, as all users could simply switch between 2 previously established group keys, essentially allowing the repeated replacement of 2 users for free when considering the amortized cost over many rounds. Our restriction above, thus, allows us to get around artificial examples of this kind.

Associated Set System and Cost Function. The final component of the combinatorial model is a sequence $(\mathcal{S}_t)_{t=0}^{t_{\max}}$, where every $\mathcal{S}_t \subseteq 2^{[n_{\max}]}$ is a collection of sets of users. We will refer to $\mathcal{S}_t$ as the set *system* at time t. The intuition behind a set S being part of $\mathcal{S}_t$ is that, in the corresponding ME or CGKA scheme, there exists a key that is secure in round t and known to exactly the users contained in S. More precisely, this means that the key is derivable from the (current or any prior) internal state of every user $u \in S$, but cannot be recovered from the sent protocol messages as well as the current and previous states of users not in S.

To capture the correctness and security of ME and CGKA schemes the set systems $\mathcal{S}_t$ in an instantiation of the combinatorial model must satisfy the following two properties.

(i) $G_t \in \mathcal{S}_t$ for all $t \in [t_{\max}]$. This corresponds to all group members in round t agreeing on a secure key.

(ii) $S \subseteq G_t$ for all sets $S \in \mathcal{S}_t$. This property represents that all keys known to users not in G_t are being considered insecure in round t.

Finally, we associate a cost to each round in an instantiation of the combinatorial model. The cost of round t is given by the sum of two terms; the first essentially being the size of a minimum cover of the new group G_t with respect to set system $\mathcal{S}_{t-1}$ of round $t-1$, and the second essentially being the number of sets in $\mathcal{S}_{t-1}$ no longer present in $\mathcal{S}_t$ due to the removal of the users in D_t. Intuitively, the first summand corresponds to a lower bound on the number of ciphertexts that have to be send in round t in order to establish the group key K_t and the second summand to keys established in previous rounds that are no longer secure, but were established at the cost of sending at least one ciphertext (see Remark 1).

Definition 2. Let $\left((n_{\max}, t_{\max}, G_0), (D_t, A_t)_{t=1}^{t_{\max}}, (\mathcal{S}_t)_{t=0}^{t_{\max}} \right)$ be an instantiation of the combinatorial model. We define the cost of round 0 as

$$\mathrm{Cost}(0) = \mathrm{SizeMinCov}(G_0, \{\{u\} : u \in G_0\}) - 1 = |G_0| - 1,$$

and for $t \geq 1$ we define the cost of round t as

$$\mathrm{Cost}(t) = \mathrm{SizeMinCov}(G_t, \mathcal{S}_{t-1} \cup \{\{u\} : u \in G_t\}) - 1$$
$$+ |\{S \in \mathcal{S}_{t-1} : S \cap D_t \neq \emptyset \text{ and } |S| > 1\}|.$$

Looking ahead, we will show that $\sum_{t=0}^{t_{\max}} \mathrm{Cost}(t)$ in the symbolic model corresponds to a lower bound on the number of ciphertexts sent as part of protocol messages over the whole execution of the experiment, albeit with a loss of a factor of 3. Before proving our lower bound in the combinatorial model we discuss some similarities and differences to the combinatorial model used in [3], which is used to derive lower bounds on the communication cost of recovering from state corruptions in CGKA by means of concurrent key updates.

Remark 1. While the structure of our combinatorial model closely resembles the one of [3], it differs from it in the following aspects.

(a) Our model allows for additions and removals of users to and from the group.
(b) We work with a different cost function. The cost metric used in [3] for set $S \in \mathcal{S}_t \setminus \mathcal{S}_{t-1}$ and round t (following the minimum cover approach discussed in the introduction) essentially quantifies the communication cost required in round t to add S to the set system. The cost function we use in this work additionally takes the cost of sets being eliminated from $\mathcal{S}_{t-1}$ into account. Accordingly $\mathrm{Cost}(t)$ is not to be understood as the communication sent in the current round, but instead also takes communication that already occurred in prior rounds into account.

(c) [3] also connects the cost of adding a set S to $\mathcal{S}_t$ to a minimum cover with respect to the previous set system $\mathcal{S}_{t-1}$, However, [3] uses a relaxed definition of minimum cover, which requires S to be covered by a union of sets, not necessarily to be *equal* to the union. The intuition behind this is that, in this work, instead of security against an adversary corrupting users, we want to protect the group key against the users themselves as soon as they have been removed from the group, even if they stored all keys they previously had access to. Phrased differently, if a secret/symmetric key is communicated to a user at any point in time, we assume it remains known to that user for the remainder of the experiment. Accordingly, in this work we define the set system $\mathcal{S}_t$ by associating to a (secure) key the set of users in G_t which, at any point in time until round t, had access to the key. Since (except for the user generating the key from fresh randomness) all other users in the corresponding set must have learned it from a ciphertext encrypted under a secure key already known to them, the corresponding communication cost must be at least the size of a minimum cover of the set with respect to the previous set system (in the stronger sense of Definition 1).

On the other hand, [3] associated to a key the set of users which are able to recover the key from their states since the last corruption before round t, effectively allowing users to forget keys they knew in some prior round and leading to a relaxed definition of minimum cover.

3.2 Lower Bound for Batched Replacements of Users

We now prove a bound on the communication complexity of batched replacement of users in the combinatorial model. It essentially states that the prior multicast encryption schemes batching dynamic operations [11,14] and the MLS continuous group-key agreement standard [4] (the latter with respect to fair-weather communication complexity) are optimal up to a small constant factor.

On a technical level, we define two families of subsets of G_t, which essentially correspond to the two contributors to the cost function, i.e., the sets forming a minimum cover of the new group G_t with respect to the previous set system, and the sets containing at least one user removed in the current round, respectively. We then observe that said families satisfy the disjointedness condition required to apply the Bollobás Set Pairs Inequality. This allows us to lower bound their sizes, which after some calculations implies the desired bound.

We first prove an implication of the Bollobás Set Pairs Inequality (Lemma 1).

Lemma 2. *Let* $\mathcal{X} = \{X_1, X_2, \ldots, X_m\}$ *and* $\mathcal{Y} = \{Y_1, Y_2, \ldots, Y_m\}$ *be families of subsets of a finite set* Z *such that* $X_i \cap Y_j \neq \emptyset$ *if and only if* $i, j \in [m]$ *are distinct. Then*

$$\sum_{i=1}^{m} (|X_i| + |Y_i|) \geq m \ln m.$$

Proof. The condition of $X_i \cap Y_j \neq \emptyset$ for all $i \neq j$ implies $X_i, Y_i \neq \emptyset \ \forall i \in [m]$. Thus, from Lemma 1 we obtain

$$\sum_{i=1}^{m} \binom{|X_i| + |Y_i|}{|X_i|}^{-1} \leq 1,$$

which, using the bound $\binom{n}{k} \leq \left(\frac{en}{k}\right)^k$, implies

$$1 \geq \sum_{i=1}^{m} \binom{|X_i| + |Y_i|}{|X_i|}^{-1} \geq \sum_{i=1}^{m} \left(\frac{e\,(|X_i| + |Y_i|)}{|X_i|}\right)^{-|X_i|}$$

$$= \sum_{i=1}^{m} e^{-|X_i|} \cdot \left(1 + \frac{|Y_i|}{|X_i|}\right)^{-|X_i|}.$$

Now, using that $(1 + x/n)^{-n} \geq e^{-x}$ and by multiplying by $1/m$ we obtain that

$$\frac{1}{m} \geq \frac{1}{m} \sum_{i=1}^{m} e^{-|Y_i|} \cdot e^{-|X_i|} \geq \frac{1}{m} \sum_{i=1}^{m} e^{-(|Y_i| + |X_i|)}.$$

By the inequality of arithmetic and geometric means (Proposition 1) we have that

$$\frac{1}{m} \geq \left(\prod_{i=1}^{m} e^{-(|X_i| + |Y_i|)}\right)^{1/m} = \left(\prod_{i=1}^{m} e^{(|X_i| + |Y_i|)}\right)^{-1/m},$$

which by taking ln gives the desired result of $\sum_{i=1}^{m} (|X_i| + |Y_i|) \geq m \ln m$. $\square$

We are now able to show that in the combinatorial model replacing a set of d users chosen uniformly at random in a group of size n has cost at least $d \cdot \ln(n/d)$ in expectation. The bound holds in an amortized sense, i.e., even if the experiment is repeated for several rounds. More formally, we obtain the following.

Theorem 1. *Let $n, t_{max}, n_{max} \in \mathbb{N}$ and $(d_t)_{t=1}^{t_{max}}$ such that $d_t \in \mathbb{N}$ with $d_t \leq n$ for all t. Consider an instantiation of the combinatorial model with respect to (n_{max}, t_{max}, G_0) and $(D_t, A_t)_{t=1}^{t_{max}}$ where $|G_0| = n$ and, for all t, the set D_t of removed users is sampled uniformly at random from the set $\{D \subseteq G_{t-1} \mid |D| = d_t\}$, and A_t can be arbitrary according to the restrictions $A_t \subseteq [n_{max}] \setminus (G_{t-1} \cup \bigcup_{t'=1}^{t-1} D_{t'})$ and $|A_t| = |D_t|$. Then it holds that*

$$\mathbb{E}\left[\sum_{t=0}^{t_{max}} \mathrm{Cost}(t)\right] \geq \sum_{t=1}^{t_{max}} \left(d_t \ln\left(\frac{n}{d_t}\right) - 1\right),$$

where the expectation is taken over the choice of $(D_t)_t$. In particular, if $d_t = d$ for all t, then

$$\mathbb{E}\left[\sum_{t=0}^{t_{max}} \mathrm{Cost}(t)\right] \geq t_{max} \cdot \left(d \cdot \log\left(\frac{n}{d}\right) - 1\right).$$

Proof. Since $|D_t| = |A_t| = d_t$ for all $t > 0$, we have $|G_t| = n$ for all $t \geq 0$. We first consider the cost of a single round $t \in [t_{\max}]$. By definition $G_t = (G_{t-1} \cup A_t) \setminus D_t$, where $D_t \subset G_{t-1}$, and $G_{t-1} \cap A_t = \emptyset$. Therefore we get that $G_t \cap G_{t-1} = G_{t-1} \setminus D_t = G_t \setminus A_t$ and

$$
\begin{aligned}
&\text{SizeMinCov}(G_t, \mathcal{S}_{t-1} \cup \{\{u\} : u \in G_t\}) \\
&= \text{SizeMinCov}(G_t \setminus A_t, \mathcal{S}_{t-1} \cup \{\{u\} : u \in G_t \setminus A_t\}) + |\{\{u\} : u \in A_t\}| \\
&= \text{SizeMinCov}(G_t \setminus A_t, \mathcal{S}_{t-1} \cup \{\{u\} : u \in G_t \setminus A_t\}) + d_t \\
&= \text{SizeMinCov}(G_{t-1} \setminus D_t, \mathcal{S}_{t-1} \cup \{\{u\} : u \in G_{t-1} \setminus D_t\}) + d_t
\end{aligned}
\tag{1}
$$

as $S \cap A_t = \emptyset$ for all $S \in \mathcal{S}_{t-1}$ (as $S \subseteq G_{t-1}$ by Property (ii) of the combinatorial model).

Now for each possible subset $D_t \subseteq G_{t-1}$ such that $|D_t| = d_t$, consider the sets

$$
\begin{aligned}
X_{D_t} &= \{S \in \mathcal{S}_{t-1} \mid S \cap D_t \neq \emptyset\} \cup \{\{u\} : u \in D_t\} \\
&= \{S \in \mathcal{S}_{t-1} \mid S \cap D_t \neq \emptyset \text{ and } |S| > 1\} \cup \{\{u\} : u \in D_t\}.
\end{aligned}
\tag{2}
$$

Further, let Y_{D_t} denote any minimum cover of $G_{t-1} \setminus D_t$ with respect to $\mathcal{S}_{t-1} \cup \{\{u\} : u \in G_{t-1} \setminus D_t\}$. Such a minimum cover always exists since $G_{t-1} \setminus D_t$ is actually covered by sets in $\mathcal{S}_{t-1} \cup \{\{u\} : u \in G_{t-1} \setminus D_t\}$. Note that Y_{D_t} also is a minimum cover of $G_{t-1} \setminus D_t$ with respect to $(\mathcal{S}_{t-1} \cup \{\{u\} : u \in G_{t-1} \setminus D_t\}) \setminus X_{D_t}$, and that by Eq. 1 we have that

$$
\text{SizeMinCov}(G_t, \mathcal{S}_{t-1} \cup \{\{u\} : u \in G_t\}) = |Y_{D_t}| + d_t.
\tag{3}
$$

We claim that $X_{D_t} \cap Y_{D_t'} = \emptyset$ if and only if $D_t = D_t'$. Take the case of $D_t = D_t'$; if $S \in Y_{D_t}$, then by definition of Y_{D_t}, $S \notin X_{D_t}$, thus $X_{D_t} \cap Y_{D_t} = \emptyset$. Now for the case of $D_t \neq D_t'$, there must be a user u such that $u \in D_t, u \notin D_t'$. Since $Y_{D_t'}$ covers $G_{t-1} \setminus D_t'$, there must exist $S \in Y_{D_t'}$ such that $u \in S$. Thus $S \in X_{D_t}$. Hence $X_{D_t} \cap Y_{D_t'} \neq \emptyset$.

Using Lemma 2 we obtain

$$
\frac{1}{\binom{n}{d_t}} \sum_{D_t \subseteq G_{t-1}, |D_t| = d_t} |X_{D_t}| + |Y_{D_t}| \geq \frac{1}{\binom{n}{d_t}} \binom{n}{d_t} \ln \binom{n}{d_t} \geq d_t \ln \frac{n}{d_t}.
\tag{4}
$$

Note that Eq. 4 gives a lower bound on the expectation of $|X_{D_t}| + |Y_{D_t}|$ if the set D_t is chosen uniformly at random. To make this formal, given n, $n_{\max}$, $t_{\max}$, $(d_t)_{t=1}^{t_{\max}}$, and G_0, we define a sequence of random variables $(\mathbf{D}_t, \mathbf{A}_t, \mathbf{G}_t)_{t=1}^{t_{\max}}$ all taking values in $2^{[n_{\max}]}$ where $\mathbf{G}_1 := (G_0 \cup \mathbf{A}_1) \setminus \mathbf{D}_1$ and for $t \geq 2$

$$
\mathbf{G}_t := (\mathbf{G}_{t-1} \cup \mathbf{A}_t) \setminus \mathbf{D}_t.
$$

The sequence is distributed as follows. The set $\mathbf{D}_1$ of users removed in the first round is distributed uniformly over $\{D_1 \subseteq G_0 : |D_1| = d_1\}$ and $\mathbf{A}_1$ can distributed arbitrarily over $\{A_1 \subseteq [n_{\max}] \setminus G_0 : |A_1| = d_1\}$. Now, conditioned on $\mathbf{D}_{t'} = D_{t'}$, $\mathbf{A}_{t'} = A_{t'}$, and $\mathbf{G}_{t'} = G_{t'}$ for $t' \in [t-1]$, the random variables $\mathbf{D}_t$ is distributed uniformly over $\{D_t \subseteq G_{t-1} : |D_t| = d_t\}$ and $\mathbf{A}_t$ can be distributed arbitrarily over $\{A_t \subseteq [n_{\max}] \setminus (G_{t-1} \cup \bigcup_{t'=1}^{t-1} D_{t'}) : |A_t| = d_t\}$.

If we consider the expected cost of round t (see Definition 2) with respect to the sequence of adds and removes given by $(\mathbf{D}_t, \mathbf{A}_t)_{t=1}^{t_{\max}}$ we obtain by Eqs. 2, 3, and 4 that

$$
\begin{aligned}
\mathbb{E}[\mathrm{Cost}(t)] &= \mathbb{E}[|\{S \in \mathcal{S}_{t-1} : S \cap \mathbf{D}_t \neq \emptyset \text{ and } |S| > 1\}|] \\
&\quad + \mathbb{E}[\mathrm{SizeMinCov}(\mathbf{G}_t, \mathcal{S}_{t-1} \cup \{\{u\} : u \in \mathbf{G}_t\})] - 1 \\
&\geq \mathbb{E}[|X_{\mathbf{D}_t}| - d_t + |Y_{\mathbf{D}_t}| + d_t] - 1 \\
&\geq d_t \ln \frac{n}{d_t} - 1.
\end{aligned}
$$

Now, the theorem's statement follows by linearity of expectation. □

4 Lower Bound for Batched Replacements in Multicast Encryption

In this section we define multicast encryption in the symbolic model and show that the lower bound on batched replacement of users in the combinatorial model of Sect. 3 carries over. Section 4.1 specifies the symbolic model and provides syntax for multicast encryption, Sect. 4.2 proves the corresponding bound. For the results for CGKA see the full version of this paper [2].

4.1 Multicast Encryption in the Symbolic Model

Considered Building Blocks. We now define syntax for *multicast encryption* (ME) in a symbolic model in the style of Dolev and Yao [10]. In models of this type, keys and ciphertexts of cryptographic primitives are seen as symbolic variables, which are generated according to grammar rules, and can be derived from sets of other symbolic variables according to an entailment relation $\vdash$, which itself models ideal security notions of the used cryptographic building blocks. Throughout this section we will denote symbolic variables in typewriter font to distinguish them from non-symbolic inputs and outputs of algorithms. Further, single variables are depicted using lower case letters, sets of variables using upper case letters.

In our symbolic treatment of multicast encryption we consider symbolic variables of the following two types; (pseudo)random strings denoted by $\mathbf{r}$ and messages $\mathbf{m}$. The former will also serve as keys of symmetric encryption schemes and, in this context, we will often denote them by $\mathbf{k}$. Similarly, ciphertexts of symmetric encryption are of message type and we will often denote them by $\mathbf{c}$. We consider ME schemes constructed from symmetric encryption schemes (SE), pseudorandom generators (PRG), pseudorandom functions (PRF), dual pseudorandom functions (dPRF) and secret sharing defined according to the following syntax.

- A symmetric encryption scheme $SE = (SE.Enc, SE.Dec)$ specifies an encryption algorithm $SE.Enc(k, m)$ that, on input symmetric key k of type r and message m, returns a ciphertext c that is of message type. Deterministic decryption algorithm $SE.Dec(k, c)$, on input symmetric key k and ciphertext c, returns a message m.
  We require perfect correctness, i.e., $SE.Dec(k, SE.Enc(k, m)) = m$ for all k and m.
- A pseudorandom generator $PRG(r)$, on input random string r, returns a value (r_1, r_2), consisting of two pseudorandom strings. For simplicity we restrict ourselves to PRGs with stretch 2. Note that PRGs with larger stretch can easily be built from these using standard methods.
- A pseudorandom function $PRF(r, ad)$, on input random string r and non-symbolic associated data ad, returns a pseudorandom string r'.
- A dual pseudorandom function $dPRF(r_1, r_2)$, takes two random strings r_1, r_2 as input and returns a pseudorandom string $r' = dPRF(r_1, r_2) = dPRF(r_2, r_1)$.
- A secret sharing scheme given by two algorithms S and R. On input a message m, S outputs a set of s many shares $S(m) = \{S_i(m)\}_{i \in [s]}$ of type message and the original message can be recovered given some subset of shares as determined by an access structure $\Gamma \subseteq 2^{[s]}$, namely, for every $I \in \Gamma$, $R(I, \{S_i(m)\}_{i \in I}) = m$.

We now describe the grammar rules and entailment relation.

variable type		grammar rule
r	$\leftarrow$	terminal type, $PRG(r), PRF(r), dPRF(r_1, r_2)$
m	$\leftarrow$	$r, SE.Enc(k, m), S_i(m)$

entailment relation		
$m \in M$	$\Rightarrow$	$M \vdash m$
$M \vdash r$	$\Rightarrow$	$M \vdash PRG(r) = (r_1, r_2)$
$M \vdash r$	$\Rightarrow$	$\forall ad: M \vdash PRF(r, ad)$
$M \vdash r_1, r_2$	$\Rightarrow$	$M \vdash dPRF(r_1, r_2)$
$M \vdash r, m$	$\Rightarrow$	$M \vdash SE.Enc(r, m)$
$M \vdash (r, c) : c = SE.Enc(r, m)$	$\Rightarrow$	$M \vdash m$
$\exists I \in \Gamma: M \vdash \{S_i(m)\}_{i \in I}$	$\Rightarrow$	$M \vdash m$

The grammar rules state that (pseudo)random coins can either be directly sampled or generated using a PRG or be obtained as the image of PRF or dPRF; that the encryption algorithm of SE, on input a key of type r and message m, generates a ciphertext; and that messages can be of arbitrary type. The entailment relation states that every symbolic variable contained in a set M can be recovered from the set. Further, it models ideal PRG security, stating that outputs of a PRG can only be recovered if given access to the respective input. PRF security is also modeled in the same way, which means that there is no significant difference between PRGs and PRFs in the symbolic model. The security of a dPRF is modeled by requiring that outputs of a dPRF can only be recovered given access to both inputs. Similarly, ideal SE security, i.e., that ciphertexts can only be decrypted if given access to the corresponding key. For a more detailed explanation and examples of the symbolic model we refer to [12]. The security of the secret sharing scheme corresponds to the requirement that the original message can be recovered from a set of shares as determined by the access structure. Given a set M of symbolic variables we denote the set of all variables derivable from it using the entailment relation by $\mathsf{Der}(\mathsf{M})$, i.e.,

$$\mathsf{m} \in \mathsf{Der}(\mathsf{M}) \text{ exactly if } \mathsf{M} \vdash \mathsf{m}.$$

If $\mathsf{M}_1, \mathsf{M}_2$ are two sets of symbolic variables, we use the notation $\mathsf{Der}(\mathsf{M}_1, \mathsf{M}_2) = \mathsf{Der}(\mathsf{M}_1 \cup \mathsf{M}_2)$.

Multicast Encryption Syntax. A multicast encryption scheme essentially allows a central authority to provide a dynamically changing group of users with a group key by sending protocol messages via a broadcast channel. The main goal being to use protocol messages that are as small as possible while still achieving correctness and security, i.e., that group members in every round agree on a group key that, however, cannot be recovered from the sent protocol messages even if given access to all previous states of non-members of the group.

As our goal in this work is to prove lower bounds and these are easier to state by keeping the group size constant over all rounds, we work with a simplified syntax only allowing for replacements of users, but not arbitrary removes and adds. We essentially follow [1,12], who analyzed the communication cost of multicast encryption for replacing a single user per round in the setting of a single group and of a system of potentially overlapping groups, respectively. The main difference in this work is that we allow for batched operations, i.e., replacing a set of more than one user at a time. Note that such a replacement can always be implemented by both removing and adding parties and thus our bounds in particular also hold for schemes allowing these operations.

In the following we split the inputs and outputs of algorithms into a symbolic part, i.e., sets of symbolic variables, and a non-symbolic part containing, e.g., user identifiers. As already stated above, the former variables are depicted in typewriter font, the latter in italics.

A multicast encryption scheme ME specifies algorithms ME.Setup, ME.Init, ME.Repl, ME.Proc, ME.Key with the following syntax.[5]

- ME.Setup$(n_{\max}; \mathsf{R})$ takes as input $n_{\max}$, the universe of users, and the set of random coins R. It sets up the initial state $(\mathsf{ST}_u^{-1}, st_u^{-1})$ for every user $u \in [n_{\max}]$. The symbolic part of the initial state, namely, ST_u^{-1} is subject to the requirements that $\mathsf{ST}_u^{-1} = \{\mathsf{k}_u^{-1}\}$ where k_u^{-1} is of type random string and $\mathsf{ST}_u^{-1} \cap \mathsf{Der}(\bigcup_{v \in [n_{\max}] \setminus \{u\}} \mathsf{ST}_v^{-1}) = \emptyset$. Similar assumptions are also made in [1,12]. For instance, in [12] it is assumed that each user is assigned exactly one key that cannot be derived from those assigned to other users, while in [1]

---

[5] One can consider the possibility that some of these algorithms be randomized by also including non-symbolic randomness as an input and the results would hold for any choice of non-symbolic randomness.

users are additionally assigned a key for each subgroup they belong to with the property that they cannot be derived from keys of users that do not belong to the corresponding subgroup. Making this kind of assumption is justified. Otherwise one could consider schemes in which communication is artificially reduced. For instance, generating two keys $k_{S,1}, k_{S,2}$ for each possible subset $S \in 2^{[n_{\max}]}$ during setup and instead of giving users these keys, they would get a ciphertext $c_S = \mathsf{Enc}(k_{S,1}, k_{S,2})$ for each set they are a member of and then the key $k_{S,1}$ would be sent in the clear in a later round.[6]

- ME.Init$(G_0; \mathtt{R})$, on input the first group G_0 and a set of random coins $\mathtt{R}$, outputs a control message $(\mathtt{M}, M)$. Further, it implicitly sets up the initial group key $\mathtt{k}^0$.

- ME.Repl$(A_t, D_t; \mathtt{R})$ allows replacing a set D_t of group members by a set A_t of new users. In round t it takes as input the set $A_t \in [n_{\max}] \setminus G_{t-1}$ of users to be added to the group, $D_t \subseteq G_{t-1}$, the set of users to be removed, and a set of random coins $\mathtt{R}$. We require that $|A_t| = |D_t|$. The output of the algorithm is a control message $(\mathtt{M}, M)$. Further, the algorithm implicitly sets up the tth group key $\mathtt{k}_t$.

- Deterministic algorithm ME.Proc$((\mathtt{ST}_u^{t-1}, st_u^{t-1}), (\mathtt{M}, M))$ takes as input, in round t, a user's internal state $(\mathtt{ST}_u^{t-1}, st_u^{t-1})$ as well as a control message $(\mathtt{M}, M)$ (either output by ME.Init or by ME.Repl). It returns the user's updated state $(\mathtt{ST}_u^t, st_u^t)$.

- Deterministic algorithm ME.Key$(\mathtt{ST}_u^t, st_u^t)$, on input user u's state at the end of round t, returns the tth group key $\mathtt{k}^t$.

The algorithms ME.Setup, ME.Init, ME.Repl are run by the central authority and it is understood that they also take as input all users' states and all messages despite this not being explicitly indicated. We require that symbolic outputs of algorithms are derivable from the symbolic part of their inputs, e.g. if $(\mathtt{ST}_u^t, st_u^t) \leftarrow$ ME.Proc$((\mathtt{ST}_u^{t-1}, st_u^{t-1}), (\mathtt{M}, M))$ then it must hold that $(\mathtt{ST}_u^{t-1}, \mathtt{M}) \vdash \mathtt{ST}_u^t$. Moreover, we also require that only a finite number of derivation steps is needed. Further and for brevity, while in the following we will make the users removed from, and added to, the group explicit, we will often drop the non-symbolic parts of protocol messages and users' states, and simply write $\mathtt{ST}_u^t \leftarrow$ ME.Proc$(\mathtt{ST}_u^{t-1}, \mathtt{M})$.

Correctness and Security. We capture security and correctness of multicast-encryption schemes in the symbolic model simultaneously with the game in Fig. 2. Similar to the experiment in the combinatorial model, the game is parameterized by a tuple $(n_{\max}, t_{\max}, G_0)$ which specifies the initialization of the group and a sequence $(A_t, D_t)_{t=1}^{t_{\max}}$ of users added to, and removed from, the group. In

---

[6] The restriction that $\mathtt{ST}_u^{-1}$ consists of just one element can be weakened if one requires that it only consists of random coins and for all coins $\mathtt{r} \in \mathtt{ST}_u^{-1}$ it holds that $\mathtt{r} \notin \mathsf{Der}((\mathtt{ST}_u^{-1} \setminus \{\mathtt{r}\}) \cup \bigcup_{v \in [n_{\max}] \setminus \{u\}} \mathtt{ST}_v^{-1})$. This is done in the full version in the case of CGKA schemes and it applies, mutatis mutandis, to the case of ME. But it comes at the cost of an additional step in the proof of the lower bound, so we leave it for the appendix.

round 0 the states of all users in $[n_{\max}]$ are set up using ME.Setup and the group G_0 is initialized using ME.Init and ME.Proc. Then security and correctness are verified for the first round, meaning that (a) all users in G_0 have access to the (unique) group key k^0, and (b) the non-members of G_0 are not able to derive k^0 from their internal states and the protocol message M^0 sent in round 0 even if colluding. If both checks succeed, the game proceeds in rounds t. In each of them the users in A_t are added to the group and the users in D_t removed from it using ME.Repl(A_t, D_t), and all current group members are made to process the resulting protocol message M^t with ME.Proc. Again it is checked that the round satisfies correctness and security. The former means that all users in G_t derive the same group key for round t, which can essentially be seen as the requirement that

$$\exists k^t : k^t = \mathsf{ME.Key}(\mathsf{ST}_u^t) \text{ for all } u \in G_t.$$

Note that this in particular implies $k^t \in \mathsf{Der}(\mathsf{ST}_u^t)$ for all $u \in G_t$.

The latter means that, even if all non group-members never deleted their old states and collude, they are not able to recover the current group key, i.e.,

$$k^t \notin \mathsf{Der}\left((M_{t'})_{t'=0}^t, ((\mathsf{ST}_u^{t'})_{t'=-1}^t)_{u \in [n_{\max}] \setminus G_t} \right).$$

This notion of security only asks for post-compromise security and not forward-secrecy since we are not considering the possibility that the group key at time t can be derived from future exposures. This only strengthens our lower-bound. If one of the checks fails, the game aborts and returns 0, else it returns 1. We say that a ME scheme ME is correct and secure, if game SEC with respect to any input $(n_{\max}, t_{\max}, G_0), (A_t, D_t)_{t=1}^{t_{\max}}$ returns 1.

Game $\mathsf{SEC}^{\mathsf{ME}}((n_{\max}, t_{\max}, G_0), (A_t, D_t)_{t=1}^{t_{\max}})$	Oracle $\mathsf{ROUND}(A_t, D_t)$
00 **sample** R_{-1}, R_0	16 **require** $D_t \subseteq G_{t-1} \wedge A_t \subseteq [n_{\max}] \setminus G_{t-1}$
01 $(\mathsf{ST}_u^{-1})_{u \in [n_{\max}]} \leftarrow \mathsf{ME.Setup}(n_{\max}; R_{-1})$	17 $G_t \leftarrow (G_{t-1} \cup A_t) \setminus D_t$
02 $M_0 \leftarrow \mathsf{ME.Init}(G_0; R_0)$	18 **sample** R_t
03 **for** $u \in G_0$:	19 $M_t \leftarrow \mathsf{ME.Repl}(A_t, D_t; R_t)$
04 $\quad \mathsf{ST}_u^0 \leftarrow \mathsf{ME.Proc}(\mathsf{ST}_u^{-1}, M_0)$	20 **for** $u \in G_t$:
05 $\quad k_u^0 \leftarrow \mathsf{ME.Key}(\mathsf{ST}_u^0)$	21 $\quad \mathsf{ST}_u^t \leftarrow \mathsf{ME.Proc}(\mathsf{ST}_u^{t-1}, M_t)$
06 $\quad k^0 \leftarrow k_u^0$	22 $\quad k_u^t \leftarrow \mathsf{ME.Key}(\mathsf{ST}_u^t)$
07 **for** $u \in [n_{\max}] \setminus G_0$:	23 $\quad k^t \leftarrow k_u^t$
08 $\quad \mathsf{ST}_u^0 \leftarrow \mathsf{ST}_u^{-1}$	24 **for** $u \in [n_{\max}] \setminus G_t$:
09 **if** $\exists u \in G_0 : k_u^0 \neq k^0$:	25 $\quad \mathsf{ST}_u^t \leftarrow \mathsf{ST}_u^{t-1}$
10 $\quad$ **return** 0 $\qquad$ \\disagreement on key	26 **if** $\exists u \in G_t : k_u^t \neq k^t$:
11 **if** $k^0 \in \mathsf{Der}(M_0, ((\mathsf{ST}_u^{t'})_{t'=-1}^0)_{u \notin G_0})$:	27 $\quad$ **return** 0 $\qquad$ \\disagreement on key
12 $\quad$ **return** 0 $\qquad$ \\group key insecure	28 **if** $k^t \in \mathsf{Der}((M_{t'})_{t'=0}^t, ((\mathsf{ST}_u^{t'})_{t'=-1}^t)_{u \notin G_t})$:
13 **for** $t = 1, \ldots, t_{\max}$:	29 $\quad$ **return** 0 $\qquad$ \\group key insecure
14 $\quad \mathsf{ROUND}(A_t, D_t)$	
15 **return** 1	

Fig. 2. Symbolic security and correctness game for multicast encryption scheme ME. In Line 16 if the condition after **require** is not met the game aborts and outputs 1, meaning that the execution of the game is considered to have been secure.

Useful Keys and Associated Set System. Consider an execution of game $\mathsf{SEC}^{\mathsf{ME}}$ with respect to $(n_{\max}, t_{\max}, G_0)$ and $(A_t, D_t)_{t=1}^{t_{\max}}$. Let $t \in [t_{\max}]_0 := [t_{\max}] \cup \{0\}$ and consider a random coin $\mathbf{r}$ that was generated in some round up to and including t. We say $\mathbf{r}$ is *useful* at time t, if

$$\mathbf{r} \notin \mathsf{Der}\left((\mathsf{M}_{t'})_{t'=0}^t, ((\mathsf{ST}_u^{t'})_{t'=-1}^t)_{u \in [n_{\max}] \setminus G_t}\right),$$

which means that it cannot be derived from all protocol messages sent so far and all prior and current states of users that are not members of the group at time t. Following [3], we associate to a secure coin $\mathbf{r}$ a set of users, with the important difference, however, that in this work the set contains all users that had access to $\mathbf{r}$ *at any point in time*.

Definition 3. *Consider an execution of security game* $\mathsf{SEC}^{\mathsf{ME}}$ *with respect to input* $(n_{\max}, t_{\max}, G_0)$ *and* $(A_t, D_t)_{t=1}^{t_{\max}}$. *Let* $t \in [t_{\max}]_0$ *and* $\mathbf{r}$ *be a random coin. We define*

$$S(t, \mathbf{r}) := \{u \in [n_{\max}] \mid \mathbf{r} \in \mathsf{Der}(\mathsf{ST}_u^{-1}, (\mathsf{M}_{t'})_{t' \leq t \colon u \in G_{t'}})\}$$

It should be noted that $\mathsf{ST}_u^{t'} \subseteq \mathsf{Der}(\mathsf{ST}_u^{-1}, (\mathsf{M}_{t'})_{t' \leq t \colon u \in G_{t'}})$ *for* $t' \leq t$. *Further, we define the set system at time* t *as*

$$\mathcal{S}_t := \{S \subseteq [n_{\max}] \mid \exists \text{ useful coin } \mathbf{r} : S = S(t, \mathbf{r})\}.$$

We prove two Lemmas that capture how derivation works in the symbolic model and connects it to the sets defined in Definition 3.

Lemma 3. *Let* $\mathbf{r}$ *be of type random coin and useful at time* $t \in [t_{\max}]_0$, *and* u *a user such that* $u \in S(t, \mathbf{r})$. *Then (at least) one of the following cases holds.*

1. *There exist* $\mathbf{r}'$ *with* $\mathsf{PRG}(\mathbf{r}') = (\mathbf{r}_1, \mathbf{r}_2)$ *and* $i \in \{1, 2\}$ *such that* $\mathbf{r} = \mathbf{r}_i$. *Further,* $\mathbf{r}'$ *is useful at time* t *and* $u \in S(t, \mathbf{r}')$.
2. *There exists* $\mathbf{r}'$ *and associated data* ad *such that* $\mathsf{PRF}(\mathbf{r}', ad) = \mathbf{r}$. *Further,* $\mathbf{r}'$ *is useful at time* t *and* $u \in S(t, \mathbf{r}')$.
3. *There exist* $\mathbf{r}_1$ *and* $\mathbf{r}_2$ *such that* $\mathsf{dPRF}(\mathbf{r}_1, \mathbf{r}_2) = \mathbf{r}$, *at least one of* $\mathbf{r}_1$ *and* $\mathbf{r}_2$ *is useful at time* t, *and* $u \in S(t, \mathbf{r}_1) \cap S(t, \mathbf{r}_2)$.
4. $\mathbf{r} \in \mathsf{ST}_u^{-1}$
5. *There exists* $\mathbf{c} = e_0(\cdot) \circ \ldots \circ e_g(\cdot) \circ \ldots \circ e_h(\mathbf{r})$ *where* $e_i = \mathsf{SE.Enc}(\mathbf{r}_i, \cdot)$ *or* $e_i = \mathsf{S}_{i_j}(\cdot)$ *and*
   (a) $\mathbf{c} \in \bigcup_{\tilde{t} \leq t \colon u \in G_{\tilde{t}}} \mathsf{M}_{\tilde{t}}$,
   (b) *if* $e_i = \mathsf{SE.Enc}(\mathbf{r}_i, \cdot)$ *and* $i \geq g + 1$, $\mathbf{r}_i$ *is not useful at time* t,
   (c) *there exists* $i \in \{0, \ldots, h\}$ *such that* $e_i = \mathsf{SE.Enc}(\mathbf{r}_i, \cdot)$,
   (d) $e_g = \mathsf{SE.Enc}(\mathbf{r}_g, \cdot)$ *and* $\mathbf{r}_g$ *is useful at time* t, *and*
   (e) *for all encryptions* $e_i = \mathsf{SE.Enc}(\mathbf{r}_i, \cdot)$, *it holds that* $u \in S(t, \mathbf{r}_i)$.

Proof. If $\mathbf{r}$ admits a PRG pre-image $\mathbf{r}'$, $\mathbf{r}'$ must be useful at time t since $\mathbf{r}$ is. Therefore we have two possible cases depending on whether $u \in S(t, \mathbf{r}')$. If $u \in S(t, \mathbf{r}')$ we are in Case 1. If $u \notin S(t, \mathbf{r}')$, then one of the following holds:

- $\mathbf{r} \in \mathsf{ST}_u^{-1} \cup \bigcup_{t' \leq t:\, u \in G_{t'}} \mathsf{M}_{t'}$ and the fact that $\mathbf{r}$ is useful implies that $\mathbf{r} \in \mathsf{ST}_u^{-1}$.
- Or, by repeatedly applying the last two rules of the entailment relation, there exists a ciphertext $\mathbf{c} \in \mathsf{ST}_u^{-1} \cup \bigcup_{t' \leq t:\, u \in G_{t'}} \mathsf{M}_{t'}$ of the form $e_0(\cdot) \circ \ldots \circ e_g(\cdot) \circ \ldots \circ e_h(\mathbf{r})$ where each e_i is an application of S or SE.Enc such that condition *(e)* holds. By assumption ST_u^{-1} only contains symbols of type random coins, so $\mathbf{c} \in \bigcup_{t' \leq t:\, u \in G_{t'}} \mathsf{M}_{t'}$. Therefore there must exist at least one encryption in $\mathbf{c}$ under a useful key since $\mathbf{r}$ is useful. This shows *(c)* and *(d)*. Condition *(b)* is just a matter of choice.

The two options above correspond to Cases 4 or 5, respectively.

If $\mathbf{r}$ does not admit a PRG pre-image, we consider whether it admits a PRF pre-image $\mathbf{r}'$, which must be useful at time t since $\mathbf{r}$ is. If $u \in S(t, \mathbf{r}')$ we are in Case 2, else we are in Cases 4 or 5. If $\mathbf{r}$ does not admit a PRF pre-image, we study whether there exist $\mathbf{r}_1$ and $\mathbf{r}_2$ such that $\mathsf{dPRF}(\mathbf{r}_1, \mathbf{r}_2) = \mathbf{r}$. In this case at least one of $\mathbf{r}_1$ and $\mathbf{r}_2$ must be useful at time t since $\mathbf{r}$ is. If $u \in S(t, \mathbf{r}_1) \cap S(t, \mathbf{r}_2)$, then we are in Case 3. Else we are in Cases 4 or 5.

Repeatedly applying Lemma 3 one can obtain the following result:

Lemma 4. *Let $\mathbf{r}$ be of type random coin and useful at time $t \in [t_{\max}]_0$, and u a user such that $u \in S(t, \mathbf{r})$. Then there exists a sequence $\{\mathbf{r}_{1,u,t}, \ldots, \mathbf{r}_{\ell_u, u, t}\}$ such that*

6. *for all i the secret $\mathbf{r}_{i,u,t}$ is useful at time t and $u \in S(t, \mathbf{r}_{i,u,t})$,*
7. $\mathbf{r}_{\ell_u, u, t} = \mathbf{r}$,
8. $\mathbf{r}_{1,u,t} \in \mathsf{ST}_u^{-1}$, *and*
9. *for all $i \in \{1, \ldots, \ell_u - 1\}$ one of the following is true*
   (a) $\mathsf{PRG}(\mathbf{r}_{i,u,t}) = (\mathbf{r}_1, \mathbf{r}_2)$ *for some $\mathbf{r}_1$, $\mathbf{r}_2$ such that either $\mathbf{r}_{i+1,u,t} = \mathbf{r}_1$ or $\mathbf{r}_{i+1,u,t} = \mathbf{r}_2$, or*
   (b) *there exists ad such that $\mathsf{PRF}(\mathbf{r}_{i,u,t}, ad) = \mathbf{r}_{i+1,u,t}$, or*
   (c) *there exists $\mathbf{r}_{i,u,t}'$ such that $u \in S(t, \mathbf{r}_{i,u,t}')$ and $\mathsf{dPRF}(\mathbf{r}_{i,u,t}, \mathbf{r}_{i,u,t}') = \mathbf{r}_{i+1,u,t}$, or*
   (d) *there exists a ciphertext $\mathbf{c}_{i,u,t} \in \bigcup_{\tilde{i} \leq t:\, u \in G_{\tilde{i}}} \mathsf{M}_{\tilde{i}}$ such that*

$$\mathbf{c}_{i,u,t} = e_0(\cdot) \circ \ldots \circ e_g(\cdot) \circ \ldots \circ e_h(\mathbf{r}_{i+1,u,t})$$

   where all properties of Case 5 are satisfied and $\mathbf{r}_{i,u,t} = \mathbf{r}_g$ the secret used in $e_g = \mathsf{SE.Enc}(\mathbf{r}_g, \cdot)$.

Observe that ℓ_u depends on u, t and $\mathbf{r}$, so in some cases we make this explicit and write $\ell_{u,t,\mathbf{r}}$ or just $\ell_{u,t}$ if the random coin $\mathbf{r}$ is clear from context.

Proof. Let $\mathbf{r} \leftarrow \mathbf{r}$ and $\mathsf{Seq} \leftarrow \emptyset$. Repeat $(\mathbf{r}, \mathsf{Seq}) \leftarrow f(\mathbf{r}, \mathsf{Seq})$ until $\mathbf{r} = \mathsf{STOP}$ where:

$$f(\mathbf{r}, \mathsf{Seq}) = \begin{cases} \text{if we are in Case 1, do } (\mathbf{r}, \mathsf{Seq}) \leftarrow (\mathbf{r}', \{\mathbf{r}\} \cup \mathsf{Seq}), \\ \text{if we are in Case 2, do } (\mathbf{r}, \mathsf{Seq}) \leftarrow (\mathbf{r}', \{\mathbf{r}\} \cup \mathsf{Seq}), \\ \text{if we are in Case 3 and } \mathbf{r}_i \text{ is useful, do } (\mathbf{r}, \mathsf{Seq}) \leftarrow (\mathbf{r}_i, \{\mathbf{r}\} \cup \mathsf{Seq}), \\ \text{if we are in Case 4, do} (\mathbf{r}, \mathsf{Seq}) \leftarrow (\mathsf{STOP}, \{\mathbf{r}\} \cup \mathsf{Seq}), \\ \text{if we are in Case 5, do} (\mathbf{r}, \mathsf{Seq}) \leftarrow (\mathbf{r}_g, \{\mathbf{r}\} \cup \mathsf{Seq}). \end{cases}$$

By construction, Properties 6, 7, 8, as well as one of Properties 9a to 9d are clearly satisfied by Seq at every point in time. This process must end since we require that only a finite number of derivation steps is made by the ME algorithms.

Now we follow the approach of [12] in order to construct a graph for each round and use it to establish a connection between the sets in $\mathcal{S}_t$ and those in $\mathcal{S}_{t-1}$ obtaining a similar result to the one in [3].

The sequences constructed in Lemma 4 suggest considering the following graph $\mathcal{G}_t = (\mathcal{V}_t, \mathcal{E}_t)$ for $t \in [t_{\max} - 1]_0$. The set of nodes $\mathcal{V}_t$ is a subset of useful random coins at time t which corresponds to the elements of the sequences $\{\mathbf{k}_{1,u,t}^t, \ldots, \mathbf{k}_{\ell_u,u,t}^t\}$ associated to the group key $\mathbf{k}^t = \mathbf{k}_{\ell_u,u,t}^t$ and each user $u \in S(t, \mathbf{k}^t)$. The set of edges $\mathcal{E}_t$ consists of all pairs of the form $(\mathbf{k}_{i,u,t}^t, \mathbf{k}_{i+1,u,t}^t)$.

In the case that an edge $(\mathbf{k}_{i,u,t}^t, \mathbf{k}_{i+1,u,t}^t)$ is obtained from Property 9c, i.e., there exists $\mathbf{r}'_{i,u,t}$ such that $\mathsf{dPRF}(\mathbf{r}_{i,u,t}, \mathbf{r}'_{i,u,t}) = \mathbf{r}_{i+1,u,t}$ and $u \in S(t, \mathbf{r}'_{i,u,t})$, one can construct the sequence from Lemma 4 using the secret $\mathbf{r}'_{i,u,t}$ instead of $\mathbf{r}_{i,u,t}$ when both $\mathbf{r}_{i,u,t}$ and $\mathbf{r}'_{i,u,t}$ are useful at time t. If this happens, we make the same choice for all users in order to guarantee that one dPRF pre-image (Case 9c) does not result in two edges in $\mathcal{E}_t$. This is possible since $u \in S(t, \mathbf{r}_{i,u,t}) \cap S(t, \mathbf{r}'_{i,u,t})$.

If an edge $(\mathbf{k}_{i,u,t}^t, \mathbf{k}_{i+1,u,t}^t)$ satisfies Properties 9a, 9b or 9c we refer to it as a trivial edge, while we refer to an edge that satisfies Property 9d as a communication edge. The graph $\mathcal{G}_t$ has some basic properties which we state in the following result.

Lemma 5. *Let* ME *be a correct and secure ME scheme. Consider an execution of game* $\mathsf{SEC}^{\mathsf{ME}}$ *on input* $(n_{\max}, t_{\max}, G_0)$ *and* $(A_t, D_t)_{t=1}^{t_{\max}}$ *such that* $D_t \subseteq G_{t-1}$ *and* $A_t \subseteq [n_{\max}] \setminus (G_{t-1} \cup \bigcup_{t'=1}^{t-1} D_t)$ *for all* $t \in [t_{\max}]$. *Let* $t \in \{0, \ldots, t_{\max} - 1\}$ *and* $\mathbf{k}^t$ *denote the group key at time* t *output by* ME.Key *in Line 22. Then the following properties of the graph* $\mathcal{G}_t$ *are true.*

10. *For every* $u \in S(t, \mathbf{k}^t)$, *the node* $\mathbf{k}_{1,u,t}^t$ *has no incoming edges and* $\mathbf{k}_{1,u,t}^t \neq \mathbf{k}_{1,v,t}^t$ *for all* $u \neq v$. *Actually it holds that* $S(t, \mathbf{k}_u^{-1}) = \{u\}$.
11. *For every node* $\mathbf{k}_{i,u,t}^t$ *there exists at most one node* $\mathbf{r}$ *such that* $\mathsf{PRG}(\mathbf{r}) = (\mathbf{r}'_1, \mathbf{r}'_2)$ *and* $\mathbf{r}'_j = \mathbf{k}_{i,u,t}^t$ *for some* $j \in \{1, 2\}$, *or that* $\mathsf{PRF}(\mathbf{r}, ad) = \mathbf{k}_{i,u,t}^t$ *for some* ad, *or that* $\mathsf{dPRF}(\mathbf{r}, \mathbf{r}') = \mathbf{k}_{i,u,t}^t$ *or* $\mathsf{dPRF}(\mathbf{r}', \mathbf{r}) = \mathbf{k}_{i,u,t}^t$ *for some* $\mathbf{r}'$ *(where* $\mathbf{r}'$ *may not be in* $\mathcal{V}_t$*).*
12. *There exists at most one user* u *in* $S(t, \mathbf{k}^t)$ *such that for all* $1 \leq i \leq \ell_u - 1$ *the edge* $(\mathbf{r}_{i,u,t}, \mathbf{r}_{i+1,u,t})$ *is a trivial edge.*
13. *If* $D_{t+1} \neq \emptyset$, *then for every* $u \in S(t, \mathbf{k}^t) \setminus D_{t+1}$, *there exists* $j_{u,t}$ *such that* $1 \leq j_{u,t} < \ell_{u,t}$ *and for the corresponding edge* $(\mathbf{k}_{j_{u,t},u,t}^t, \mathbf{k}_{j_{u,t}+1,u,t}^t) \in \mathcal{E}_t$ *there exists a user* $v \in D_{t+1}$ *such that* $v \in S(t, \mathbf{k}_{j_{u,t}+1,u,t}^t)$ *and for all* $w \in D_{t+1}$ *we have* $w \notin S(t, \mathbf{k}_{j_{u,t},u,t}^t)$. *Moreover,* $j_{u,t}$ *will denote the least integer in* $\{1, \ldots, \ell_{u,t} - 1\}$ *with this property.*

Proof. Since $\mathsf{ST}_u^{-1} = \{\mathbf{k}_u^{-1}\}$, it follows from Property 8 that $\mathbf{k}_{1,u,t}^t = \mathbf{k}_u^{-1}$. If there exists $(\mathbf{r}, \mathbf{k}_u^{-1}) \in \mathcal{E}_t$, then there exists a user $v \in S(t, \mathbf{k}^t)$ such that $u \neq v$

and $k_{i,v,t}^t = r$ and $k_{i+1,v,t}^t = k_u^{-1}$ by definition of $\mathcal{G}_t$. By Property 6 applied to $k_{i+1,v,t}^t$, we obtain $v \in S(t, k_u^{-1})$. This would imply that it would not be secure to remove user v in round $t+1$ while maintaining u in the group. Indeed,

$$k^{t+1} \in \mathsf{Der}(\mathsf{ST}_u^{-1}, (M_{t'})_{t' \leq t+1 : \, u \in G_{t'}}) \subseteq \mathsf{Der}\left((M_{t'})_{t'=0}^{t+1}, ((\mathsf{ST}_u^{t'})_{t'=-1}^{t+1})_{u \in [n_{\max}] \setminus G_t}\right).$$

We have actually shown that $v \in S(t, k_u^{-1})$ implies $v = u$. Therefore $S(t, k_u^{-1}) = \{u\}$. This completes the proof of Property 10.

Property 11 follows directly from the properties of the symbolic model and the fact that when constructing $\mathcal{G}_t$ we choose only one edge of the two possible for dPRF evaluations.

Property 12 is a direct consequence of the two previous properties.

Property 13 follows from the observation that the node $k_{\ell_u, u, t} = k^t$ satisfies the first condition for all users in D_{t+1} and the node $k_{1,u,t} = k_u^{-1}$ satisfies the second condition (by Property 10). Since $D_{t+1} \neq \emptyset$ by assumption, there must exist an edge with the required property.

4.2 Lower Bound on Batched Replacements

We now show that a subset $\tilde{\mathcal{S}}_t$ of the set system $\mathcal{S}_t$ defined above satisfies the properties of the combinatorial model regarding correctness and security and, additionally, that the amount of ciphertexts sent in the symbolic model matches the cost function of Sect. 3.1 (with respect to the set system $\tilde{\mathcal{S}}_t$) up to a multiplicative loss of 3. As a consequence, the lower bound derived in Sect. 3.2 applies to batched replacements in multicast in the symbolic model.

Lemma 6. *Let $n_{\max}$ and $t_{\max}$ be in $\mathbb{N}$ and $(d_t)_{t=1}^{t_{\max}}$ such that $d_t \leq n_{\max}$ for all t. Let ME be a correct and secure ME scheme. Consider an execution of game $\mathsf{SEC}^{\mathsf{ME}}$ on input $(n_{\max}, t_{\max}, G_0)$ and $(A_t, D_t)_{t=1}^{t_{\max}}$ such that $D_t \subseteq G_{t-1}$ and $A_t \subseteq [n_{\max}] \setminus (G_{t-1} \cup \bigcup_{t'=1}^{t-1} D_{t'})$ for all $t \in [t_{\max}]$. Let $(\mathcal{S}_t)_{t=0}^{t_{\max}}$ be the associated set system as defined in Definition 3. Further, for $t \in [t_{\max}]_0$ let*

$$\tilde{\mathcal{S}}_t = \left\{ S \in \mathcal{S}_t \,\middle|\, \begin{array}{l} \exists r \text{ such that } S = S(t, r), \, r \text{ is useful at time } t \text{ and} \\ \nexists r_1, r_2 \text{ such that } \mathsf{dPRF}(r_1, r_2) = r \text{ and } S(t, r_1) \cap S(t, r_2) = S(t, r) \end{array} \right\}.$$

Then it holds that

(i) $G_t \in \tilde{\mathcal{S}}_t$ for all $t \in [t_{\max}]_0$,
(ii) $S \subseteq G_t$ for all $S \in \mathcal{S}_t$ and, in particular, $S \subseteq G_t$ for all $S \in \tilde{\mathcal{S}}_t$
(iii) $\sum_{t=0}^{t_{\max}} |M_t| \geq 1/3 \cdot \sum_{t=0}^{t_{\max}} \mathsf{Cost}(t)$, where $\mathsf{Cost}(t)$ is the cost function defined in Sect. 3.1 with respect to $\tilde{\mathcal{S}}_t$, namely:

$$\mathsf{Cost}(t) = (\mathsf{SizeMinCov}(G_t, \tilde{\mathcal{S}}_{t-1} \cup \{\{u\} : u \in G_t\}) - 1) + |\{S \in \tilde{\mathcal{S}}_{t-1} : S \cap D_t \neq \emptyset \text{ and } |S| > 1\}|.$$

The reason for introducing $\tilde{\mathcal{S}}_t$ is that allowing the use of dPRFs means that the original set $\mathcal{S}_t$ also contains the intersection of any pair of sets such that one of the associated secrets is useful and this does not require any additional communication. Before turning to the lemma's proof we state our bound on the communication complexity of batched replacements in multicast encryption, which follows directly by applying Theorem 1 to set system $(\tilde{\mathcal{S}}_t)_{t=0}^{t_{\max}}$ which is possible due to Lemma 6.

Corollary 1. *Let $n \leq n_{\max}$ and $t_{\max}$ be in $\mathbb{N}$ and $(d_t)_{t=1}^{t_{\max}}$ such that $d_t \leq n$ for all t. Let ME be a correct and secure ME scheme. Consider an execution of game $\mathrm{SEC}^{\mathsf{ME}}$ on input $(n_{\max}, t_{\max}, G_0)$ and $(A_t, D_t)_{t=1}^{t_{\max}}$ where $|G_0| = n$ and, for all t, the set D_t of removed users is sampled uniformly at random from the set $\{D \subseteq G_{t-1} \mid |D| = d_t\}$ and A_t can be arbitrary according to the restrictions $A_t \subseteq [n_{\max}] \setminus (G_{t-1} \cup \bigcup_{t'=1}^{t-1} D_{t'})$ and $|A_t| = |D_t|$. Then, it holds that*

$$\mathbb{E}\left[\sum_{t=0}^{t_{\max}} |M_t|\right] \geq \frac{\ln(2)}{3} \sum_{t=1}^{t_{\max}} d_t \log\left(\frac{n}{d_t}\right),$$

where the expectation is taken over the choice of $(D_t)_t$. In particular, if $d_t = d$ for all t, then

$$\mathbb{E}\left[\sum_{t=0}^{t_{\max}} |M_t|\right] \geq \frac{\ln(2)}{3} t_{\max} \cdot d \cdot \log\left(\frac{n}{d}\right).$$

Proof (Proof of Lemma 6). We start proving Property (ii). Let $S = S(t, \mathbf{r}) \in \mathcal{S}_t$ and $u \in S$. By definition of $S(t, \mathbf{r})$ we have that $\mathbf{r} \in \mathsf{Der}(\mathsf{ST}_u^{-1}, (M_{t'})_{t' \leq t: \, u \in G_{t'}})$ and since $\mathbf{r}$ is useful at time t it holds that $\mathbf{r} \notin \mathsf{Der}((M_{t'})_{t'=0}^{t}, ((\mathsf{ST}_u^{t'})_{t'=-1})_{u \notin G_t})$. Thus $u \in G_t$ as claimed in Property (ii).

Now we proceed to show that Property (i) is true. Recall that $\mathsf{ST}_u^t \subseteq \mathsf{Der}(\mathsf{ST}_u^{-1}, (M_{t'})_{t' \leq t: \, u \in G_{t'}})$. By correctness there exists a key $\mathbf{k}^t$ such that $\mathbf{k}^t = \mathsf{ME.Key}(\mathsf{ST}_u^t)$ for all users $u \in G_t$ and by security we have that $\mathbf{k}^t \notin \mathsf{Der}((M_{t'})_{t'=0}^t, ((\mathsf{ST}_u^{t'})_{t'=-1})_{u \notin G_t})$, so $S(t, \mathbf{k}^t) = G_t$ and $S(t, \mathbf{k}^t) \in \mathcal{S}_t$. Moreover, assume that there exist $\mathbf{r}_1, \mathbf{r}_2$ such that $\mathsf{dPRF}(\mathbf{r}_1, \mathbf{r}_2) = \mathbf{k}^t$ and $S(t, \mathbf{r}_1) \cap S(t, \mathbf{r}_2) = S(t, \mathbf{k}^t) = G_t$. Since $\mathbf{k}^t$ is useful at time t, there exists $i \in \{1, 2\}$ such that $\mathbf{r}_i$ is useful at time t. By Property (ii) it must hold that $S(t, \mathbf{r}_i) \subseteq G_t$. The fact that $S(t, \mathbf{r}_1) \cap S(t, \mathbf{r}_2) = S(t, \mathbf{k}^t) = G_t$ implies that we also have $G_t \subseteq S(t, \mathbf{r}_i)$. Therefore $S(t, \mathbf{r}_i) = G_t$. By repeating this process we can find a secret $\mathbf{r}$ that is useful at time t such that $S(t, \mathbf{r}) = G_t$ and that satisfies the property that $\nexists \mathbf{r}_1, \mathbf{r}_2$ such that $\mathsf{dPRF}(\mathbf{r}_1, \mathbf{r}_2) = \mathbf{r}$ and $S(t, \mathbf{r}_1) \cap S(t, \mathbf{r}_2) = S(t, \mathbf{r})$. This shows that $G_t \in \tilde{\mathcal{S}}_t$ as claimed in Property (i). Observe that we have shown $S(t, \mathbf{k}^t) = G_t$ and not just $G_t \in \tilde{\mathcal{S}}_t$.

We now proceed to prove Property (iii). We divide the proof into showing each of the following two equations separately:

$$\sum_{t=0}^{t_{\max}}|M_t| \geq \frac{1}{2}\sum_{t=0}^{t_{\max}}(\text{SizeMinCov}(G_t, \tilde{S}_{t-1} \cup \{\{u\} : u \in G_t\}) - 1) \tag{5}$$

$$\sum_{t=0}^{t_{\max}}|M_t| \geq \sum_{t=1}^{t_{\max}}|\{S \in \tilde{S}_{t-1} : S \cap D_t \neq \emptyset \text{ and } |S| > 1\}|. \tag{6}$$

Let $t \in \{1, \ldots, t_{\max}\}$ and denote by $\mathbf{k}^t$ the group key of round t. If $D_t = \emptyset$, $\text{SizeMinCov}(G_t, \tilde{S}_{t-1} \cup \{\{u\} : u \in G_t\}) - 1 = 0$, so we assume that $D_t \neq \emptyset$. In order to construct a cover of G_t we give a cover of $G_t \setminus A_t$ and a cover of A_t. Observe that $u \in G_t \setminus A_t$ if and only if $u \in G_{t-1} \setminus D_t$.

For each $u \in G_{t-1} \setminus D_t$, we consider the index $j_{u,t-1}$ from Property 13. We claim that

$$\mathcal{C}_{t,1} = \{S(t-1, \mathbf{k}^{t-1}_{j_{u,t-1},u,t-1}) \mid u \in G_{t-1} \setminus D_t\}$$

is a cover of $G_{t-1} \setminus D_t$ and $\mathcal{C}_{t,1} \subseteq \mathcal{S}_{t-1}$. The fact that $u \in S(t-1, \mathbf{k}^{t-1}_{j_{u,t-1},u,t-1})$ and $S(t-1, \mathbf{k}^{t-1}_{j_{u,t-1},u,t-1}) \in \mathcal{S}_{t-1}$ is a consequence of Property 6. It also holds that $S(t-1, \mathbf{k}^{t-1}_{j_{u,t-1},u,t-1}) \subseteq G_{t-1} \setminus D_t$ by Properties 13 and (ii).

Let $d_{j_{u,t-1}+1}$ denote the in-degree of the node $\mathbf{k}^{t-1}_{j_{u,t-1}+1,u,t-1}$ in $\mathcal{G}_{t-1}$ and let $u_1 = u, u_2, \ldots, u_h$ be users such that $\mathbf{k}^{t-1}_{j_{u,t-1}+1,u,t-1} = \mathbf{k}^{t-1}_{j_{u_i,t-1}+1,u_i,t-1}$ for $i = 1, \ldots, h$ and for any user v with $\mathbf{k}^{t-1}_{j_v,t-1+1,v,t-1} = \mathbf{k}^{t-1}_{j_{u,t-1}+1,u,t-1}$, there exists a unique $i \in \{1, \ldots, h\}$ such that $\mathbf{k}^{t-1}_{j_v,t-1,v,t-1} = \mathbf{k}^{t-1}_{j_{u_i,t-1},u_i,t-1}$. I.e., we choose exactly one user u_i for each of the incoming edges of the node $\mathbf{k}^{t-1}_{j_{u,t-1}+1,u,t-1}$ that satisfy Property 13. Therefore $d_{j_{u,t-1}+1} \geq h$. Each node $\mathbf{k}^{t-1}_{j_{u,t-1}+1,u,t-1}$ has at most one incoming trivial edge (Property 11). All the other $d_{j_{u,t-1}+1} - 1$ incoming edges correspond to ciphertexts in $\bigcup_{t'=0}^{t} M_{t'}$. If $d_{j_{u,t-1}+1} \geq h+1$, then the node $\mathbf{k}^{t-1}_{j_{u,t-1}+1,u,t-1}$ contributes to $\mathcal{C}_{t,1}$ with at most $h \leq d_{j_{u,t-1}+1} - 1$ sets. If $d_{j_{u,t-1}+1} = h$, then we can consider the graph we would obtain for the secret $\mathbf{k}^{t-1}_{j_{u,t-1}+1,u,t-1}$ rather than $\mathbf{k}^{t-1}$. Let's denote it $\mathcal{H}$. The set of nodes corresponds to the elements of the sequences constructed in Lemma 4 for the secret $\mathbf{k}^{t-1}_{j_{u,t-1}+1,u,t-1}$ and the set of edges consists of all pairs of consecutive elements in those sequences. Since the node $\mathbf{k}^{t-1}_{j_{u,t-1}+1,u,t-1}$ in $\mathcal{H}$ has at least one additional incoming edge that corresponds to the user $v \in D_t$ guaranteed to exist by Property 13 for $\mathcal{G}_{t-1}$, which does not contribute to $\mathcal{C}_{t,1}$, the node $\mathbf{k}^{t-1}_{j_{u,t-1}+1,u,t-1}$ contributes to $\mathcal{C}_{t,1}$ with at most $h = d_{j_{u,t-1}+1}$ sets and we have at least $d_{j_{u,t-1}+1}$ ciphertexts in $\bigcup_{t'=0}^{t-1} M_{t'}$. Thus $|\mathcal{C}_{t,1}| \leq \sum_{t'=0}^{t-1}|M_{t'}|$.

We observe that $S(t-1, \mathbf{k}^{t-1}_{j_{u,t-1}+1,u,t-1}) \cap D_t \neq \emptyset$. Therefore, $\mathbf{k}^{t-1}_{j_{u,t-1}+1,u,t-1}$ is not a useful random coin at time t. This guarantees that the node $\mathbf{k}^{t-1}_{j_{u,t-1}+1,u,t-1}$ will not be in $\mathcal{G}_{\tilde{t}}$ for $\tilde{t} \geq t$. Therefore $\sum_{t=1}^{t_{\max}}|\mathcal{C}_{t,1}| \leq \sum_{t=0}^{t_{\max}-1}|M_t|$.

Moreover, we can find covers $\mathcal{C}'_{t,1} \subseteq \tilde{S}_{t-1}$ such that $\sum_{t=1}^{t_{\max}}|\mathcal{C}'_{t,1}| \leq \sum_{t=0}^{t_{\max}-1}|M_t|$. We obtain $\mathcal{C}'_{t,1}$ from $\mathcal{C}_{t,1}$ by substituting the sets that are in $\mathcal{S}_{t-1} \setminus \tilde{S}_{t-1}$ for sets in $\tilde{\mathcal{S}}_{t-1}$. Let's assume that there exist $\mathbf{r}_1, \mathbf{r}_2$ such that $\mathsf{dPRF}(\mathbf{r}_1, \mathbf{r}_2) = \mathbf{k}^{t-1}_{j_{u,t-1},u,t-1}$ and $S(t-1, \mathbf{r}_1) \cap S(t-1, \mathbf{r}_2) = S(t-1, \mathbf{k}^{t-1}_{j_{u,t-1},u,t-1})$. Since $\mathbf{k}_{j_{u,t-1},u,t-1}$ is useful at time $t-1$, there exists $i \in \{1,2\}$ such that $\mathbf{r}_i$ is useful at time $t-1$. From $S(t-1, \mathbf{r}_1) \cap S(t-1, \mathbf{r}_2) = S(t-1, \mathbf{k}^{t-1}_{j_{u,t-1},u,t-1})$ and the way sequences are constructed in Lemma 4, it follows that $j_{u,t-1} > 1$, $\mathbf{k}^{t-1}_{j_{u,t-1}-1,u,t-1} = \mathbf{r}_i$. From $S(t-1, \mathbf{r}_1) \cap S(t-1, \mathbf{r}_2) = S(t-1, \mathbf{k}^{t-1}_{j_{u,t-1},u,t-1})$, we obtain $S(t-1, \mathbf{k}^{t-1}_{j_{u,t-1},u,t-1}) \subseteq S(t-1, \mathbf{r}_i) = S(t-1, \mathbf{k}^{t-1}_{j_{u,t-1}-1,u,t-1})$. The minimality condition imposed on $j_{u,t}$ by Property 13 guarantees that $S(t-1, \mathbf{k}^{t-1}_{j_{u,t-1}-1,u,t-1}) \cap D_t = \emptyset$. This shows that $\mathcal{C}'_{t,1} = (\mathcal{C}_{t,1} \setminus \{S(t-1, \mathbf{k}^{t-1}_{j_{u,t-1},u,t-1})\}) \cup \{S(t-1, \mathbf{r}_i)\}$ is also a cover of $G_{t-1} \setminus D_t$ and it has the same size as $\mathcal{C}_{t,1}$. Therefore by repeating this process we obtain a cover of $G_{t-1} \setminus D_t$ with respect to $\tilde{\mathcal{S}}_{t-1}$ and it has at most as many sets as the original $\mathcal{C}_{t,1}$. We denote it $\mathcal{C}'_{t,1}$ and it holds that

$$\sum_{t=1}^{t_{\max}} |\mathcal{C}'_{t,1}| \leq \sum_{t=0}^{t_{\max}-1} |\mathsf{M}_t|. \tag{7}$$

Now we give a cover of A_t. The argument also considers the case where $t = 0$ if we define $A_0 = G_0$. For each $u \in A_t$, let $i_{u,t} \in \{1, \ldots, \ell_{u,t}\}$ be maximal such that for all $1 \leq j < i_{u,t}$, $(\mathbf{k}^t_{j,u,t}, \mathbf{k}^t_{j+1,u,t})$ is a trivial edge. By Property 12, there exists at most one user in A_t such that $i_{u,t} = \ell_{u,t}$. For every user $u \in A_t$ such that $i_{u,t} < \ell_{u,t}$, there exists a ciphertext $c_{i_{u,t},u,t}$ as proven in Property 9d. All these ciphertexts must be different or else there would exist users $u, v \in A_t$ such that $\mathbf{k}^t_{i_{u,t},u,t} = \mathbf{k}^t_{i_{v,t},v,t}$, which would contradict Properties 11 and 10.

Each of the ciphertexts $c_{i_{u,t},u,t}$ belongs to $\bigcup_{\tilde{t} \leq t: \, u \in G_{\tilde{t}}} \mathsf{M}_{\tilde{t}}$. From the condition $A_t \subseteq [n_{\max}] \setminus (G_{t-1} \cup \bigcup_{t'=1}^{t-1} D_t)$, it follows that $c_{i_{u,t},u,t} \in \mathsf{M}_t$. Thus we have at least $|A_t| - 1$ many ciphertexts sent in round t. The cover of A_t, $\mathcal{C}_{t,2} = \{\{u\} \mid u \in A_t\}$ satisfies the inequality $|\mathsf{M}_t| \geq |\mathcal{C}_{t,2}| - 1$. From this inequality and Eq. 7, we obtain

$$\frac{1}{2} \sum_{t=1}^{t_{\max}} |\mathcal{C}_{t,1}| + \frac{1}{2} \sum_{t=0}^{t_{\max}} (|\mathcal{C}_{t,2}| - 1) \leq \frac{1}{2} \sum_{t=0}^{t_{\max}-1} |\mathsf{M}_t| + \frac{1}{2} \sum_{t=0}^{t_{\max}} |\mathsf{M}_t| \leq \sum_{t=0}^{t_{\max}} |\mathsf{M}_t|.$$

This shows Eq. 5 since $|\mathcal{C}'_{t,1}| \leq |\mathcal{C}_{t,1}|$ and $\mathcal{C}'_{t,1} \cup \mathcal{C}_{t,2}$ is a cover of G_t for all $t \in [t_{\max}]_0$ (we take $\mathcal{C}'_{0,1} = \emptyset$).

Now we show Eq. 6. Let $S = S(t-1, \mathbf{r}) \in \tilde{\mathcal{S}}_{t-1}$ such that $S \cap D_t \neq \emptyset$, $|S| > 1$, and $\nexists \mathbf{r}_1, \mathbf{r}_2$ that satisfy the following two properties: $\mathsf{dPRF}(\mathbf{r}_1, \mathbf{r}_2) = \mathbf{r}$ and $S(t-1, \mathbf{r}_1) \cap S(t-1, \mathbf{r}_2) = S(t-1, \mathbf{r})$. We proceed to consider the graph $\mathcal{G}_{t-1,\mathbf{r}} = (\mathcal{V}_{t-1,\mathbf{r}}, \mathcal{E}_{t-1,\mathbf{r}})$ where $\mathcal{V}_{t-1,\mathbf{r}}$ is a subset of useful random coins at time $t-1$ which corresponds to the elements of the sequences $\{\mathbf{r}_{1,u,t-1}, \ldots, \mathbf{r}_{\ell_u,u,t-1}\}$ constructed in Lemma 4 for each user $u \in S(t-1, \mathbf{r})$. The set of edges $\mathcal{E}_{t-1,\mathbf{r}}$ consists of all pairs $(\mathbf{r}_{i,u,t-1}, \mathbf{r}_{i+1,u,t-1})$. From Property 12[7] and the fact that $|S| > 1$, it follows that not all edges in $\mathcal{E}_{t-1,\mathbf{r}}$ are trivial edges. If the node $\mathbf{r}$ only has only

---

[7] Property 12 was shown for the graph $\mathcal{G}_t$ and the same argument shows that this property also holds for $\mathcal{G}_{t-1,\mathbf{r}}$.

one incoming edge of the form $(\mathbf{r}_{\ell_u-1,u,t-1}, \mathbf{r}_{\ell_u,u,t-1} = \mathbf{r})$ for some $u \in S(t-1,\mathbf{r})$ and it is a trivial edge, then $S(t-1,\mathbf{r}_{\ell_u-1,u,t-1}) = S(t-1,\mathbf{r})$. In order to show this we consider two cases:

- if $\nexists \mathbf{r}_1, \mathbf{r}_2$ such that $\mathsf{dPRF}(\mathbf{r}_1,\mathbf{r}_2) = \mathbf{r}$, then $(\mathbf{r}_{\ell_u-1,u,t-1}, \mathbf{r}_{\ell_u,u,t-1} = \mathbf{r})$ must correspond to a PRG or a PRF and $S(t-1,\mathbf{r}_{\ell_u-1,u,t-1}) = S(t-1,\mathbf{r})$,
- if $\exists \mathbf{r}_1, \mathbf{r}_2$ such that $\mathsf{dPRF}(\mathbf{r}_1,\mathbf{r}_2) = \mathbf{r}$, but $S(t-1,\mathbf{r}_1) \cap S(t-1,\mathbf{r}_2) \subsetneq S(t-1,\mathbf{r})$, then there exists a user $v \in S(t-1,\mathbf{r}) \setminus S(t-1,\mathbf{r}_1) \cap S(t-1,\mathbf{r}_2)$ and by Property 9c $\mathbf{r}_{\ell_v-1,v,t-1} \neq \mathbf{r}_1$ and $\mathbf{r}_{\ell_v-1,v,t-1} \neq \mathbf{r}_2$. This contradicts the assumption that $\mathbf{r}$ had only one incoming edge.

As argued in the previous paragraph we may assume without loss of generality that for some user $u \in S(t-1,\mathbf{r}) = S$ the edge $(\mathbf{r}_{\ell_u-1,u,t-1}, \mathbf{r}_{\ell_u,u,t-1} = \mathbf{r})$ corresponds to a ciphertext $c_{\ell_u-1,u,t} \in \bigcup_{t'=0}^{t-1} \mathsf{M}_{t'}$. This shows that $\sum_{t'=0}^{t-1} |\mathsf{M}_{t'}| \geq |\{S \in \tilde{\mathcal{S}}_{t-1} : S \cap D_t \neq \emptyset \text{ and } |S| > 1\}|$. Moreover, the fact that $S \cap D_t \neq \emptyset$ guarantees that $\mathbf{r}$ does not appear in $\mathcal{G}_{\tilde{t}-1,\tilde{\mathbf{r}}}$ for any $\tilde{t} > t$ and useful $\tilde{\mathbf{r}}$ at time $\tilde{t}$ by Property (ii). Thus,

$$\sum_{t=0}^{t_{\max}-1} |\mathsf{M}_t| \geq \sum_{t=1}^{t_{\max}} |\{S \in \tilde{\mathcal{S}}_{t-1} : S \cap D_t \neq \emptyset \text{ and } |S| > 1\}|.$$

Finally we multiply Eq. 5 by $2/3$ and Eq. 6 by $1/3$ and add them together to obtain $\sum_{t=0}^{t_{\max}} |\mathsf{M}_t| \geq 1/3 \cdot \sum_{t=0}^{t_{\max}} \mathsf{Cost}(t)$, as desired.

References

1. Alwen, J., et al.: Grafting key trees: efficient key management for overlapping groups. In: Nissim, K., Waters, B. (eds.) TCC 2021, Part III. LNCS, vol. 13044, pp. 222–253. Springer, Cham (2021). https://doi.org/10.1007/978-3-030-90456-2_8
2. Anastos, M., et al.: The cost of maintaining keys in dynamic groups with applications to multicast encryption and group messaging. Cryptol. ePrint Arch. Paper 2024/1097 (2024). https://eprint.iacr.org/2024/1097
3. Auerbach, B., Cueto Noval, M., Pascual-Perez, G., Pietrzak, K.: On the cost of post-compromise security in concurrent continuous group-key agreement. In: Rothblum, G., Wee, H. (eds.) TCC 2023, Part III. LNCS, vol. 14371, pp. 271–300. Springer, Heidelberg (2023). https://doi.org/10.1007/978-3-031-48621-0_10
4. Barnes, R., Beurdouche, B., Robert, R., Millican, J., Omara, E., Cohn-Gordon, K.: The Messaging Layer Security (MLS) Protocol. RFC 9420 (Jul 2023). https://doi.org/10.17487/RFC9420, https://www.rfc-editor.org/info/rfc9420
5. Bienstock, A., Dodis, Y., Garg, S., Grogan, G., Hajiabadi, M., Rösler, P.: On the worst-case inefficiency of CGKA. In: Kiltz, E., Vaikuntanathan, V. (eds.) TCC 2022, Part II. LNCS, vol. 13748, pp. 213–243. Springer, Cham (2022). https://doi.org/10.1007/978-3-031-22365-5_8
6. Bienstock, A., Dodis, Y., Rösler, P.: On the price of concurrency in group ratcheting protocols. In: Pass, R., Pietrzak, K. (eds.) TCC 2020, Part II. LNCS, vol. 12551, pp. 198–228. Springer, Cham (2020). https://doi.org/10.1007/978-3-030-64378-2_8
7. Bollobás, B.: On generalized graphs. Acta Math. Acad. Scientiarum Hung. **16**(3), 447–452 (1965)

8. Canetti, R., Garay, J., Itkis, G., Micciancio, D., Naor, M., Pinkas, B.: Multicast security: a taxonomy and some efficient constructions. In: IEEE INFOCOM'99. Conference on Computer Communications. Proceedings. Eighteenth Annual Joint Conference of the IEEE Computer and Communications Societies. The Future is Now (Cat. No. 99CH36320), vol. 2, pp. 708–716. IEEE (1999)
9. Canetti, R., Malkin, T., Nissim, K.: Efficient communication-storage tradeoffs for multicast encryption. In: Stern, J. (ed.) EUROCRYPT'99. LNCS, vol. 1592, pp. 459–474. Springer, Berlin, Heidelberg (1999). https://doi.org/10.1007/3-540-48910-X_32
10. Dolev, D., Yao, A.: On the security of public key protocols. IEEE Trans. Inf. Theory 29(2), 198–208 (1983). https://doi.org/10.1109/TIT.1983.1056650
11. Li, X.S., Yang, Y.R., Gouda, M.G., Lam, S.S.: Batch rekeying for secure group communications. In: Proceedings of the 10th International Conference on World Wide Web, pp. 525–534. WWW '01, Association for Computing Machinery, New York, NY, USA (2001). https://doi.org/10.1145/371920.372153, https://doi.org/10.1145/371920.372153
12. Micciancio, D., Panjwani, S.: Optimal communication complexity of generic multicast key distribution. In: Cachin, C., Camenisch, J. (eds.) EUROCRYPT 2004. LNCS, vol. 3027, pp. 153–170. Springer, Berlin, Heidelberg (2004). https://doi.org/10.1007/978-3-540-24676-3_10
13. Naor, D., Naor, M., Lotspiech, J.: Revocation and tracing schemes for stateless receivers. In: Kilian, J. (ed.) CRYPTO 2001. LNCS, vol. 2139, pp. 41–62. Springer, Berlin, Heidelberg (2001). https://doi.org/10.1007/3-540-44647-8_3
14. Sherman, A.T., McGrew, D.A.: Key establishment in large dynamic groups using one-way function trees. IEEE Trans. Software Eng. 29(5), 444–458 (2003)
15. Snoeyink, J., Suri, S., Varghese, G.: A lower bound for multicast key distribution. In: Proceedings IEEE INFOCOM 2001. Conference on Computer Communications. Twentieth Annual Joint Conference of the IEEE Computer and Communications Society (Cat. No.01CH37213), vol. 1, pp. 422–431 (2001). https://doi.org/10.1109/INFCOM.2001.916725
16. Wallner, D., Harder, E., Agee, R.: Key management for multicast: issues and architectures. Request for Comments 2627, Internet Engineering Task Force (1999). https://www.rfc-editor.org/rfc/rfc2627
17. Wong, C.K., Gouda, M., Lam, S.S.: Secure group communications using key graphs. IEEE/ACM Trans. Networking 8(1), 16–30 (2000)
18. Yang, Y., Li, X., Zhang, X., Lam, S.: Reliable group rekeying: a performance analysis. In: ACM SIGCOMM Computer Communication Review (2002). https://doi.org/10.1145/383059.383062

Compact Key Storage in the Standard Model

Yevgeniy Dodis$^{(\boxtimes)}$ and Daniel Jost

New York University, New York, USA
{dodis,daniel.jost}@cs.nyu.edu

Abstract. In recent work [Crypto'24], Dodis, Jost, and Marcedone introduced Compact Key Storage (CKS) as a modern approach to backup for end-to-end (E2E) secure applications. As most E2E-secure applications rely on a sequence of secrets $(s_1, \ldots, s_n)$ from which, together with the ciphertexts sent over the network, all content can be restored, Dodis et al. introduced CKS as a primitive for backing up $(s_1, \ldots, s_n)$. The authors provided definitions as well as two practically efficient schemes (with different functionality-efficiency trade-offs). Both, their security definitions and schemes relied however on the random oracle model (ROM).

In this paper, we first show that this reliance is inherent. More concretely, we argue that in the standard model, one cannot have a general CKS instantiation that is applicable to all "CKS-compatible games", as defined by Dodis et al., and realized by their ROM construction. Therefore, one must restrict the notion of CKS-compatible games to allow for standard model CKS instantiations.

We then introduce an alternative standard-model CKS definition that makes concessions in terms of functionality (thereby circumventing the impossibility). More precisely, we specify CKS which does not recover the original secret s_i but a derived key k_i, and then observe that this still suffices for many real-world applications. We instantiate this new notion based on minimal assumptions. For passive security, we provide an instantiation based on one-way functions only. For stronger notions, we additionally need collision-resistant hash functions and dual-PRFs, which we argue to be minimal.

Finally, we provide a modularization of the CKS protocols of Dodis et al. In particular, we present a unified protocol (and proof) for standard-model equivalents for both protocols introduced in the original work.

1 Introduction

Backup is an essential functionality of any application storing user data. For instance, users of a secure messaging (SM) application may expect cloud backup to be provided such that they do not lose their conversation history or sent

Y. Dodis—Research partially supported by NSF grant CNS-2055578, and gifts from JP Morgan, Protocol Labs, Stellar, and Algorand Foundation.

E. Boyle and M. Mahmoody (Eds.): TCC 2024, LNCS 15364, pp. 444–475, 2025.
https://doi.org/10.1007/978-3-031-78011-0_15

and received attachments, such as photos, in the event their device is broken, lost, or stolen. The existing cryptographic literature on backup heavily focuses on how to secure a cryptographic secret under a human-memorizable secret, such as a low-entropy password. For instance, WhatsApp combines hardware secure modules (HSM) with PAKE such that users can retrieve a cryptographic secret, that is securely stored on WhatsApp's HSMs, based on their password. Various solutions replacing the trust assumption on the HSM with secret sharing have also been proposed. For example password-protected secret sharing (PPSS) [1,11] and more recent solutions such as updatable oblivious key management [12] and DPaSE [6].

In contrast, very little attention has been paid to *what cryptographic secret* should be securely stored or how this interacts with the security of the application under consideration. Indeed, most end-to-end (E2E) secure applications use the rather naive solution of using a static secret key to symmetrically encrypt the user content and upload it to the cloud. This not only can have determinantal effects on the application's (presumed) security as recently demonstrated by Fábrega et al. [9] but also lacks all of the advanced security properties, such as forward secrecy (FS) and post-compromise security (PCS), we have been accustomed to from E2E-secure protocols. Secure messaging furthermore has a clear push toward enabling large groups with potentially thousands of members—such as the recent IETF Message Layer Security (MLS) standard. The naive backup solution, however, cannot take advantage of this inherent redundancy across users for either storage or bandwidth.

Compact Key Storage. In recent work, Dodis et al. [7] introduce the notion of *compact key storage (CKS)*. Essentially, CKS serves as the backup of underlying secrets of an E2E-secure application, rather than the content itself. For instance, for an SM application using the Double Ratchet protocol, CKS would back up the keys from the symmetric ratcheting layer used to encrypt and authenticate the ciphertexts. In addition, the service provider would then need to retain the original Double Ratchet ciphertexts or outsource them to some cloud storage of the users' choice.

CKS uses a compact secret state that evolves whenever a user's application learns or generates a new key, offloading the storage to an untrusted server. Crucially, (1) any users outsourcing the same sequence of keys can use a shared outsourced storage and (2) CKS allows for fine-grained FS and PCS such that every user can restore exactly the set of keys they once knew and have not erased in the meantime. The compact local state can then be backed up using traditional methods such as HSMs or secret sharing. This has several key benefits:

- **PCS/FS:** When using CKS for backup, the combined application inherits the PCS/FS guarantees of the underlying messaging application. In particular, user can efficiently *erase* messages from their storage and the backup by securely replacing their CKS state with an updated one.
- **Deduplication:** All cloud storage (both the CKS storage and the storage of the application ciphertexts) is shared among all users of a given chat.

– **Delegation:** Fine-grained FS enables efficient delegation of parts of the conversation history. The user can create a copy of their CKS state, erase all parts they wish not to share, and then delegate access by sending the CKS state to another party.

In their work, Dodis et al. observe that the natural security notion—key indistinguishability from randomness, conditioned on the outsourced storage—is impossible. Instead, the authors propose a novel security notion of *preservation security* which, roughly speaking, demands that a broad class of applications remains secure when enhanced by CKS. That is, for each given application one needs to show that it is "CKS compatible" to deduce that it can be securely augmented by any secure CKS scheme. They then provide formal definitions of preservation security and present efficient schemes. However, both the security notion and the protocol inherently live in the Random Oracle model (ROM).

1.1   Contributions

In this work, we investigate CKS in the standard model.

Impossibility of Preservation Security. First, we show that the notion of preservation security by Dodis et al. inherently requires an idealized model. More concretely, we show that for any CKS scheme in the standard model, there exists a CKS-compatible game that becomes insecure when enhanced with the CKS scheme.[1]

Standard Model CKS Definitions. While the original CKS notion was aimed at augmenting any (legacy) E2E-secure application, we observe that if the application is designed with CKS in mind, then the aforementioned impossibility can be circumvented. More concretely, we observe the following: if instead of recovering the original secrets $(s_1, \ldots, s_n)$, henceforth called *seed*, each party only needs to recover a derived *key* $(k_1, \ldots, k_n)$ then the impossibility no longer holds. For instance, assume that the seeds are the output of a Continuous Group Agreement (CKA) or Continuous Group Key Agreement (CGKA) protocol. Our proposed notion is compatible with any E2E-secure application that only uses a derived key $k_i = \text{KDF}(s_i)$ instead of the seed. This can either be a new application explicitly with CKS in mind (in which case the standard-model CKA scheme gets to choose the KDF) or a legacy application that already happens to involve an additional key derivation step (under modest assumptions on the KDF).

On a high level, we observe that the impossibility stems from circularity that necessitates an idealized model such as the ROM. Having an explicit key derivation step then resolves this circularity. Indeed, we observe that for this weaker notion of CKA, indistinguishability from randomness is achievable, no longer necessitating the (rather intricate) notion of preservation security. We

---

[1] Note the order of quantifiers. A stronger statement that there exist CKS-compatible applications that are insecure for any CKS scheme is conceivable, but left to future work. Still, our result means we cannot instantiate the definition from [7].

then adapt the CKS notion accordingly. Our standard-model CKS is incomparable with the original ROM-based definition from [7]. On the one hand, we obtain the stronger indistinguishability-based notion. On the other hand, we have to concede in several aspects:

- As mentioned above, standard-model CKS recovers only keys instead of the seeds. This makes it (potentially) unsuitable for some legacy applications.
- Delegation of keys only. Similarly, parties can only delegate keys. This somewhat restricts functionality as the receiving party can no longer equally contribute to the shared outsourced state without the original seeds.
- Selective security only. Fully adaptive security seems to imply non-committing encryption for messages longer than the key, as the compact local state is significantly shorter than the total length of the keys that are outsourced. This is generally known to be impossible in the standard model. We therefore settle for selective security, even though for (some of) our schemes the framework by Kamath et al. [13] should yield at least quasi-polynomial reductions against adaptive adversaries.

Standard-Model CKS Schemes. We present an efficient scheme for standard-model CKA. When targeting outsider security and an honest-but-curious server, our scheme only needs a PRG and one-time secure symmetric encryption. In other words, in its weakest form, it can be constructed purely from one-way functions. When targeting an actively malicious server, we additionally need collision-resistant hash functions. To achieve insider security, where either parties delegate inconsistent keys, or already start with inconsistent seeds, our scheme additionally needs a Dual-PRF [2,4], for which it is an open problem whether they can be constructed from one-way functions.

Modularization. Dodis et al. [7] present two CKS schemes: One which allows all-or-nothing delegation (and all-or-nothing erasure) and which has a constant size local state st_u. The other allows to efficiently delegate any continuous interval of secrets and has a local state that grows logarithmically in the number of epochs. At their core, both schemes use Convergent Encryption (CE) [8] to recursively aggregate the two secrets into one and a ciphertext. Slightly simplified, the former scheme aggregates the old state st_u and the secret s for the next consecutive epoch as:

- Parse $(K, T) \leftarrow st_u$
- Compute a new key $K' \leftarrow H(st_u \| s)$
- Compute $C' \leftarrow SE.Enc(K, (st_u \| s))$
- Compute $T' \leftarrow H(C' \| T)$
- Set $st'_u \leftarrow (K, T)$ and send $C \leftarrow (C, T')$ to the server.

This process is called "derive" in the schematic representation of the all-or-nothing scheme in Fig. 1. The security of the scheme inherently requires the ROM for the key generation in the second step. Moreover, the authors of [7] observe that the abstraction of CE as Message Locked Encryption (MLE) by Bellare et al. [3]

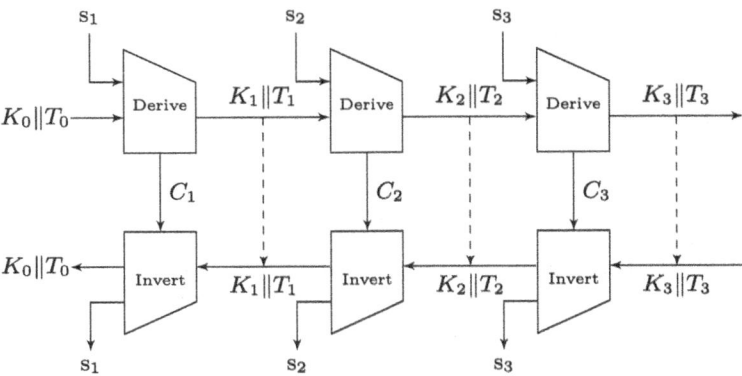

Fig. 1. [7, Fig. 7]. A schematic representation of all-or-nothing CKS scheme from [7]. The top half depicts the parties outsourcing the keys, while the lower half shows the key-recovery process.

does not apply to the recursive application, and the authors instead proved the scheme's security directly based on the security of the symmetric encryption SE. Enc and the ROM. This raises the question: what is the appropriate substitute for the above "derivation box" for standard-model CKS? Observe that while the above construction allows to recover s based on the ciphertext and the local state, whereas standard-model CKS only needs to recover a key that is derived from the seed. We, therefore, answer this question by introducing the abstraction of a *Trapdoor KDF (TKDF)*. A TKDF, in a nutshell, represents a kind of "invertible" KDF that generates a key k and updated state z' from a seed s and previous state z, such that from z a secret *trapdoor* t to invert the operation can be derived.

As a second abstraction, we introduce the notion of *iterative CKS*, which is a class of CKS protocols that encompass both schemes from [7]. This abstraction has several benefits: (1) its definitions are significantly simpler than the ones of fully general CKS; (2) it allows us to formalize and prove the security of a natural unified protocol of which the all-or-nothing and the interval protocol are special cases. In particular, we note that the iterative CKS notion reduces finding the right trade-off between functionality (in terms of delegation and fine-grained erasure) and efficiency of the scheme to a graph theoretic problem. The class of graphs involved is further closely related to graphs studied in pebbling games, for instance, allowing us to link it with the work on adaptive security by Jafargholi et al. [10] and Kamath et al. [13].

1.2   Outline

In Sect. 2, we first argue the impossibility of standard-model CKS, according to the definition of [7], and then introduce an alternative definition with weakened functionality (which still suffices for many practical applications). In Sect. 3, we then introduce the TKDF notion, abstracting over the core component of both constructions from [7], and provide an efficient instantiation from standard-model primitives. In Sect. 4 we introduce a special case of CKS protocols, dubbed iterative CKS, and show how a generic protocol (based on TKDF) abstracts over both protocols from [7]. Finally, in Sect. 5, we sketch how any iterative CKS protocol implies a general (standard model) CKS protocol.

2 Compact Key Storage

2.1 Overview

Recall from Sect. 1 that Compact Key Storage allows a group of users that know a shared set of secrets $(s_1, \ldots, s_n)$ to maintain a shared backup of those secrets. To this end, for every new secret s_i obtained by the users, *at least one* user uploads a ciphertext C_i to the (untrusted) server. Each user u only keeps a small local state st_u and the server storage should not grow in the number of users—hence the name *compact*. All users must then be able to use their local state and the ciphertexts to recover all secrets they once knew (and have not explicitly erased). Importantly, [7] introduced CKS for *dynamic* groups, meaning that not every user necessarily knows all secrets. On the contrary, a user who does not know a certain secret s_i should not be able to derive any information about s_i from the CKS ciphertexts. This, in turn, implies post-compromise security, as st_u before the user u learned s_i together with all ciphertexts $(C_1, \ldots, C_n)$ must not leak information about s_i. Unfortunately, it was shown in [7] that the natural definition of s_i remaining pseudorandom given all ciphertexts $(C_1, \ldots, C_n)$, and a party's initial state, is impossible even in idealized models.

Before recapping the formal CKS notion of [7], let us provide a high-level summary of the desired functionality.

- *Outsourcing secrets.* Each user can append a secret s_i for a new epoch i to their local state. To save bandwidth, this should, intuitively, be an operation done locally by all users except one. As this is infeasible when having users who know substantially different subsets of secrets, [7] relaxed this condition slightly. More precisely, a user U should upload unless another user U', who knew a superset of the secrets of the former, did the upload when learning s_i.
- *Retrieving secrets.* Whenever the user U later wants to retrieve one or more of the secrets they knew at some point, they should be able to use their local state st_u and the help of the server. The notion of [7] imposes *integrity* to ensure that U will never retrieve a different secret than they originally knew. Of course, as for any outsourced storage scheme a malicious server can do a denial-of-service attack. A strong correctness notion, however, ensures that as long as the server is honest other malicious group members cannot prevent U from retrieving their secrets.
- *Key delegation.* A user U should be able to delegate access to the entirety or parts of their secrets by sending a short message msg over a secure channel to any other user U'. Using msg, U' should then be able to recover those secrets with the help of the server.

– *Key erasure.* To securely delete specific content of the application, the user U should be able to delete access to their secrets. In other words, U may wish to erase s_i (or more generally a subset of the secrets) such that afterward their updated state st_U and the ciphertexts $(C_1, \ldots, C_n)$ no longer reveal information about s_i, without requiring the server to securely erase information. This can be seen as a special case of delegation where the user delegates themselves the set of secrets they wish to retain; more efficient implementations are however conceivable.

It is not too hard to see that it is impossible for a scheme to support erasing and delegating arbitrary subsets of the secrets while maintaining a compact local state. Thus, [7] parametrized each concrete CKS in the set of operations that it supports efficiently. Those sets are described as predicates that determine whether an operation is feasible for a set of epochs share given the set of epochs know for which the user currently "knows" the secrets (i.e., learned and not erased them).

Definition 1 ([7, Def. 1]). *A delegation family $\mathcal{G}$ is a predicate $\mathcal{G}\colon \mathcal{P}(\mathbb{N}) \times \mathcal{P}(\mathbb{N}) \to \{0,1\}$, where for a set* know $\subseteq \mathbb{N}$ *of epochs with the respective keys known to a party, $\mathcal{G}(\text{know}, \text{share})$ indicates whether they can delegate* share $\subseteq \mathbb{N}$. *Analogously, a* retrieval family $\mathcal{R}$ *and a* erasure family $\mathcal{E}$ *indicate whether the party can recover* share $\subseteq \mathbb{N}$ *or erase* share $\subseteq \mathbb{N}$, *respectively.*

2.2 CKS Syntax

We now recap the Compact Key Storage notion. The following section is mostly taken verbatim from [7].

Definition 2 ([7, Def. 2]). *A* Compact Key Storage (CKS) *scheme* CKS *for a delegation family $\mathcal{G}$, a retrieval family $\mathcal{R}$, and an erasure family $\mathcal{E}$ (or $(\mathcal{G}, \mathcal{R}, \mathcal{E})$-CKS for short) is an interactive protocol between stateful user U and server S algorithms, respectively, defined by the following sub-algorithms:*

Initialization:

– *The* $st_S \leftarrow \text{S.Init}(1^\kappa)$ *algorithm initializes the server's state.*
– *The* $st \leftarrow \text{U.Init}(1^\kappa)$ *algorithm initializes a user's state.*

Key Management:

– *The non-interactive append algorithm takes the current state* st, *an epoch* e, *a secret* s, *and flag* upload. *The invocation*

$$(st', st_{up}) \leftarrow \text{U.Append}(st, e, s, upload),$$

produces an updated state st' *and, if* upload = true, *an upload state* st_{up}. *(If* upload = false, *then* $st_{up} = \bot$.)

- *The interactive upload algorithm takes the upload state and after the interaction*

$$\bigl(\bot; \mathrm{st}'_S\bigr) \leftarrow \langle \mathrm{U.Upload}(\mathrm{st}_{\mathrm{up}}) \leftrightarrow \mathrm{S.Upload}(\mathrm{st}_S) \rangle,$$

  the server outputs an updated state st'_S.
- *The interactive erase algorithm takes the current state* st *and a set of epochs* share $\subseteq \mathbb{N}$. *After the following interaction*

$$\bigl(\mathrm{st}'; \bot\bigr) \leftarrow \langle \mathrm{U.Erase}(\mathrm{st}, \mathrm{share}) \leftrightarrow \mathrm{S.Erase}(\mathrm{st}_S) \rangle,$$

  both the user outputs an updated state st' *(and the server has no output).*

Delegation:

- *The interactive granting algorithm takes a user* U_1's *state* st_1 *and a set* share $\subseteq \mathbb{N}$ *of keys to be shared with another user* U_2. *After the interaction*

$$\bigl(\mathrm{msg}; \bot\bigr) \leftarrow \langle U_1.\mathrm{Grant}(\mathrm{st}_1, \mathrm{share}) \leftrightarrow \mathrm{S.Grant}(\mathrm{st}_S) \rangle$$

  the user outputs the information msg *to be sent to the other party* U_2.
- *The interactive grant-accepting algorithm extends another user's* U_2 *known key set by processing a grant* msg. *After the interaction*

$$\bigl(\mathrm{st}'_2, \mathrm{st}_{\mathrm{up}}; \bot\bigr) \leftarrow \langle U_2.\mathrm{Accept}(\mathrm{st}_2, \mathrm{share}, \mathrm{msg}, \mathrm{upload}) \leftrightarrow \mathrm{S.Accept}(\mathrm{st}_S) \rangle$$

  the user outputs an updated state st'_2, *as well as (if* upload $=$ **true***) a state for the* Upload *algorithm.*

Retrieval:

- *The interactive key-retrieval algorithm restores the secrets for epochs* share $\subseteq$ $\mathbb{N}$ *with the interaction*

$$\bigl(\mathrm{secrets}; \mathrm{st}'_S\bigr) \leftarrow \langle \mathrm{U.Retrieve}(\mathrm{st}, \mathrm{share}) \leftrightarrow \mathrm{S.Retrieve}(\mathrm{st}_S) \rangle$$

  ending with the user outputting a function secrets: share $\rightarrow$ s, *as well as an updated server state.*

A CKS scheme is considered efficient if all operations work in sublinear—ideally logarithmic—time in the number of epochs n (when secrets are appended in consecutive order). As such, the predicates $(\mathcal{G}, \mathcal{R}, \mathcal{E})$ dictate efficiency requirements: if for instance a party wants to retrieve an arbitrary set $\mathcal{I}$ of epochs, they can find a minimal cover $\mathcal{I} = \mathcal{I}_1 \cup \cdots \cup \mathcal{I}_k$ of subsets consistent with $\mathcal{R}$ and retrieve subset. This leads to an overall efficiency of $\mathcal{O}(k \log(n))$. In terms of client state, we require it to grow at most in the order of $\mathcal{O}(d \log(n))$, with d denoting the number of erasure operations.

In case secrets are appended sparsely (such as odd epochs only), are appended completely out of order, or linearly many erasures have been performed, efficiency may degrade to linear time. The server state must grow at most linearly in the number of overall epochs outsourced by any party, and in particular, must not grow in the number of participating parties.

2.3   Impossibility of Standard-Model CKS

The authors of [7] showed that any non-trivial state compactness guarantee of the user makes it impossible to satisfy the most desirable key indistinguishability property for CKS, even if one only wants to recover all n secrets $(s_1, \ldots, s_n)$ from the latest state st_n of the user, with the help of the CKS server. Concretely, the following probability cannot be upper bounded by $\frac{1}{2} + \mathsf{negl}(\kappa)$ for all efficient attackers $\mathcal{A}$:

$$
\Pr \left[b = b' \left| \begin{array}{r}
b \leftarrow_\$ \{0,1\} \\
st \leftarrow \mathrm{U.Init}(1^\kappa); st_S \leftarrow \mathrm{S.Init}(1^\kappa) \\
s_1^0, s_1^1, s_2^0, s_2^1, \ldots, s_n^0, s_n^1 \leftarrow_\$ \{0,1\}^\kappa \\
\forall i \in [n] : (st, st_{up}) \leftarrow \mathrm{U.Append}(st, i, s_i^0, \mathtt{true}), \\
(\bot; st_S) \leftarrow \langle \mathrm{U.Upload}(st_{up}) \leftrightarrow \mathrm{S.Upload}(st_S) \rangle \\
b' \leftarrow \mathcal{A}(1^\kappa, s_1^b, \ldots, s_n^b, st_S)
\end{array} \right. \right]
$$

Intuitively, one cannot expect that the n secrets $(s_1, \ldots, s_n)$ are still pseudorandom when the attacker gets access to the CKS functionality (in particular, server public storage st_S). This is because CKS provides a testable functionality—(user) state compaction—which is not possible with random unrelated secrets.

To circumvent this result in the random oracle model (ROM), the authors introduced a rather intricate, weaker notion of "CKS-preservation", described below. Note that while the authors of [7] observed that relying on an idealized model for CKS-preservation seemed inherent, no formal result was proven. In the next section, we close this gap, showing that preservation security is impossible *in the standard model*. Since preservation security was meant to be the weakest meaningful security notion for CKS this, in spirit, establishes that CKS recovering the original secrets (as a standalone primitive) is impossible in the standard model.[2]

Impossibility of CKS-Preservation. Intuitively, CKS-preservation relaxes key indistinguishability with the requirement that access to the CKS functionality does not hurt the security of the underlying application Π (originally not designed with CKS in mind). To make this statement non-tautologous, [7] had to define the types of applications Π where this makes sense, without using CKS-syntax inside Π, but still keeping Π as general as possible. They call such games *CKS-compatible*. Below we give a special case of such a CKS-compatible game, which already shows the impossibility of standard-model CKS-presevation.

Concretely, we will concentrate on the (subset of) CKS-compatible games Π where: (1) Π has a sequence of secrets $(s_1, \ldots, s_n)$; (2) Π remains secure even if permits the adversary $\mathcal{A}$ has access to the testing oracle $\mathsf{Test}(i, s)$ which returns 1 if $s = s_i$. The ROM-based construction of [7] worked for all the games in

---

[2] In the standard model, our result is a strict strengthening of the impossibility result of key-indistinguishable CKS from [7], but does not generalize to idealized models.

this class, provided the honest parties do not use the random oracle utilized by the CKS.[3] Thus, to show the standard-model impossibility of instantiating this result, we only need to construct a single game Π which satisfies properties (1) and (2), but where the knowledge of server state st_S will break Π.

Counter-Example Game. We consider the following game Π between the challenger $\mathcal{C}$ and the polynomial-time attacker $\mathcal{A}$, where κ is the security parameter, and n is chosen large enough so that the length of the CKS state st_n after appending n random secrets $s_i \in \{0,1\}^\kappa$ satisfies $|st_n| \leq n(\kappa - \omega(\log \kappa))$.

1. $\mathcal{C}$ samples random $s_1, \ldots, s_n \in \{0,1\}^\kappa$.
2. $\mathcal{C}$ computes the states of the user after appending $s_1, \ldots, s_n$:

$$st_0 \leftarrow \text{U.Init}(1^\kappa)$$
$$\forall i \in [n] : (st_i, \cdot) \leftarrow \text{U.Append}(st_{i-1}, i, s_i, \texttt{false}),$$

3. $\mathcal{C}$ sends st_n to $\mathcal{A}$.
4. $\mathcal{C}$ honestly responds to $\text{Test}(i, s)$ queries of $\mathcal{A}$: return 1 iff $s = s_i$.
5. $\mathcal{A}$ send guess values $s_1', \ldots, s_n'$.
6. $\mathcal{C}$ outputs 1 iff $\forall i \in [n]$ $s_i = s_i'$.

First, we argue that this game is easily won by the attacker if the attacker $\mathcal{A}$ *additionally* gets the server state st_S when the standard-model CKS is applied to $s_1, \ldots, s_n$, as allowed by the CKS-preservation security security definition from [7]. This is true because the correctness of the CKS holds even when the Append and the Upload algorithms are run by the different users. Namely, the adversary can still successfully recover the original secrets $s_1, \ldots, s_n$, by using the "Alice's state" st_n (given to $\mathcal{A}$ by the challenger $\mathcal{C}$ above) and the server state st_S obtained when "another user Bob" (corresponding to the helper in the "CKS-enhanced game" of [7]) uploaded the corresponding ciphertexts to the server. Hence, CKS-preservation does not happen for Π.

Second, we nevertheless argue that the original game Π is "CKS-compatible". Namely, Π is secure against any polynomial time attacker $\mathcal{A}$, who does not get to see the server state st_S in Π, but is allowed to have the Test oracle. To see this, we use a standard compression argument. Let us say that $\mathcal{A}$ made $q = \text{poly}(\kappa)$ queries to the Test oracle. The key observation is to notice that one can compactly encode all q responses using significantly fewer than q bits. Namely, for each $i \in [n]$, we only need to know the first index $j \in [q + 1]$ where the q's query of $\mathcal{A}$ was successful (or set $j = q + 1$ if this never happened). Thus, all q answers obtained by $\mathcal{A}$ take at most $n \log(q + 1) = O(n \log \kappa)$ bits to encode. Now, if the attacker wins Π with non-negligible probability, we can use $\mathcal{A}$ to successfully compress $n\kappa$ truly random bits $s_1, \ldots, s_n$ as follows:

– Include the final state st_n, whose size is assumed to be $|st_n| \leq n(\kappa - \omega(\log \kappa))$.
– Include the encoding of q test queries of $\mathcal{A}$, which takes at most $n \log(q+1) = O(n \log \kappa)$ bits to encode.

---

[3] In practice, this is easy to accomplish with salting.

Combined, this information is enough to run the attacker to produce its guess $s'_1, \ldots, s'_n$. Yet, the compression string has overall length $|st_n| + n \log(q+1) \ll n\kappa$. Which means that the probability that $(s'_1, \ldots, s'_n) = (s_1, \ldots, s_n)$ must be negligible. Which shows that game Π is CKS-compatible.

Discussion. We make several observations. First, our game Π was allowed to depend on the (hypothetical) algorithms of the standard-model CKS. Indeed, unlike ROM, there is no effective mechanism to prevent honest users from (artificially) utilizing the CKS inside the game Π, if Π is only restricted to satisfy very weak properties (1) and (2) for CKS-preservation.[4] Notice, that simple techniques like utilizing the common reference string do not help, since that string should be available to the users to run the CKS, and a general application (even CKS-compatible) could still "trick" the users to use the right common reference string. Second, our counter-example above is extremely artificial, specifically targeting to break CKS-compatibility, while supporting the Test oracle. This is expected, since for most "natural" applications, such as Signal or MLS, we expect the heuristic instantiation of the ROM-based construction of [7] to be secure in the real world. Instead, the counter-example below should be viewed from the lens that "CKS-preservation" does not appear to be the right security notion of CKS for *standard-model* instantiations. Indeed, our standard model solution will go back to the clean and elegant key-indistinguishability, but will slightly change the functionality of the application to circumvent the impossibility result below.

2.4   Weaker Standard Model CKS

In this section, we now introduce our new notion of standard-model CKS. Simply put, we distinguish between *seeds* $(s_1, \ldots, s_n)$ and *keys* $(k_1, \ldots, k_n)$, where each key is (deterministically) derived from its respective seed. More concretely, U.Append appends a seed s_i whilst U.Retrieve later recovers the respective key k_i. In addition, delegation is assumed to only delegate keys rather than seeds. This weaker notion of CKS, of course, is only compatible with applications that distribute seeds, for instance as part of a CGKA, but then use keys for the message encryption layer.

Definition 3. *A* Standard Model Compact Key Storage (CKS) *scheme* CKS *is a CKS scheme for which there is additionally a deterministic algorithm* U.Key$(e, s) \to k$ *which takes an epoch* e *and a seed* s, *and returns the corresponding key* k. *A standard-model CKS scheme is defined with respect to a generalized delegation family* $\mathcal{G}$, *retrieval family* $\mathcal{R}$, *and erasure family* $\mathcal{E}$, *each of which takes two arguments: the set of epochs for which a party knows the seeds (and therefore also the keys) and the set of epochs for which they know the keys only. Finally, for consistency, we denote the output of* U.Retrieve *as keys (instead of* secrets*).*

---

[4] Indeed, we will later observe (cf. Theorem 3 and Corollary 4) that for a special subclass of protocols, we can build provably secure CKS in the standard model, even satisfying key indistinguishability!.

Correctness and Security. We now adapt correctness and security to the standard-model setting. The former remains mostly unchanged from ROM-CKS with the obvious difference that U.Retrieve now must return the correct keys instead of seeds. That is, if a user for epoch e appended a seed s to their CKS state, then correctness requires that U.Retrieve later recovers U.Key(e, s), instead of s as in the ROM-CKS notion.

ROM-CKS formalized security as two properties: preservation security and integrity. Intuitively, the former demands that applying CKS to a so-called "CKS-compatible" application does not undermine that application's security. The latter, on the other hand, requires that the CKS scheme only recovers correct seeds—that is, the ones they initially appended to their state—or an error, for an honest party interacting with a malicious server potentially colluding with other malicious users. Integrity of standard-model CKS also remains mostly unchanged from ROM-CKS, with the obvious changes to accommodate the key derivation. We present both the adapted correctness and integrity games in the full version of this work.

In the remainder of this section, we present the key-indistinguishability notion of standard-model CKS. This notion replaced the preservation-security notion and, intuitively, represents the desired best-possible security.

Definition 4. *We say that a standard-model* $(\mathcal{G}, \mathcal{R}, \mathcal{E})$-*CKS scheme* CKS *is* key indistinguishable, *if the probability of any PPT adversary $\mathcal{A}$ winning the* $(\mathcal{G}, \mathcal{R}, \mathcal{E})$-CKS-KeyIndist$_{\mathsf{CKS}}^{\mathcal{A}}$ *game from Fig. 2 is negligible in κ.*

The goal of the adversary is to guess whether the game uses real keys ($b = 0$) or random ones ($b = 1$). The game follows the template of the preservation-security game from [7], which is very similar to the one of the correctness and integrity games. Notably, the adversary has various oracles mirroring the CKS algorithms. For each of the interactive algorithms, the adversary furthermore assumes the role of the server; that is, the game considers an actively malicious server. (Note that we assume the adversary not to interleave calls of the oracles for the same user.) The game mostly just executes the protocol while keeping track of some additional state. For instance, KnownSeed[U, e] and KnownKey[U, e] keep track whether the user u knows the seed and key for epoch e, respectively. Furthermore, the game uses ActualKey[u, e] to keep track whether the key known by the user for an epoch is the one chosen by the game or one injected by the adversary. The seeds and keys chosen by the game are tracked using Seed[e] and Keys[e].

Observe that the function `sample-if-nec` samples one fresh seed for every epoch e and then uses that one consistently thorough the execution. Furthermore, depending on the bit b, it either derives the respective key or chooses an independent one. Those keys are then output as part of U.Append and U.Retrieve as challenges, whenever the respective user is known to use the proper seed. (If the adversary instead provides a seed for U.Append, by inputting s $\neq \perp$, then `sample-if-nec` just returns keys that are consistent.)

Finally, note that in the Grant oracle the adversary gets to choose whether they receive the message produces by U.Grant or not, using the leak flag. This

---

Game $(\mathcal{G}, \mathcal{R}, \mathcal{E})$-CKS-KeyIndist$_{\text{CKS}}^{\mathcal{A}}$ (Security)

Main

$b \leftarrow\$ \{0, 1\}$
$n \leftarrow 0$
$St[\cdot], Secret[\cdot], Keys[\cdot], GrantInfo[\cdot] \leftarrow \perp$
$KnownSeed[\cdot, \cdot], KnownKey[\cdot, \cdot], ActualKey[\cdot, \cdot] \leftarrow \texttt{false}$
$(st_{\mathcal{A}}, Corr) \leftarrow \mathcal{A}(1^{\kappa})$
$b' \leftarrow \mathcal{A}^{\text{CreateUser},\dots,\text{Accept}}(1^{\kappa}, st_{\mathcal{A}})$
return $b' = b$

Oracle CreateUser

$n \leftarrow n + 1$
$St[n] \leftarrow U.\text{Init}(1^{\kappa})$

Oracle Corrupt

Input: $u \in [n]$
req $ActualKey[u, \cdot] \subseteq Corr$
return $St[u]$

Oracle Append

Input: $(u, e, s) \in [n] \times \mathbb{N} \times \{0, 1\}^{\kappa}$
req $\neg KnownSeed[u, e]$
$(s, k) \leftarrow \texttt{sample-if-nec}(u, e, s)$
$KnownKey[u, e] \leftarrow \texttt{true};$
$KnownSeed[u, e] \leftarrow \texttt{true}$
try $(St[u], st_{up}) \leftarrow U.\text{Append}(St[u], e, s, upload)$
try $\langle U.\text{Upload}(st_{up}) \leftrightarrow \mathcal{A} \rangle$
return k

Oracle Erase

Input: $(u, share) \in [n] \times \mathcal{P}(\mathbb{N})$
req $\mathcal{E}(KnownSeed[u, \cdot], KnownKey[u, \cdot], share)$
try $(St[u]; \perp) \leftarrow \langle U.\text{Erase}(St[u], share) \leftrightarrow \mathcal{A} \rangle$
for $e \in share$ do
  $KnownSeed[u, e] \leftarrow \texttt{false}; KnownKey[u, e] \leftarrow \texttt{false}$
  $ActualKey[u, e] \leftarrow \texttt{false}$

Oracle Retrieve

Input: $(u, share) \in [n] \times \mathcal{P}(\mathbb{N})$
req $\mathcal{R}(KnownSeed[u, \cdot], KnownKey[u, \cdot], share)$
try $(keys; \perp) \leftarrow \langle U.\text{Retrieve}(St[u], share) \leftrightarrow \mathcal{A} \rangle$
for $e \in share$ do
  if $ActualKey[u, e]$ then $keys(e) \leftarrow Keys[e]$
return $keys$

Oracle Grant

Input: $(u, share, leak) \in [n] \times [n] \times \mathcal{P}(\mathbb{N}) \times \{0, 1\}$
req $\mathcal{G}(KnownSeed[u, \cdot], KnownKey[u, \cdot], share)$
$actual \leftarrow \{e \in share \mid ActualKey[u, e]\}$
req $\neg leak \vee actual \subseteq Corr$
try $(msg; \perp) \leftarrow \langle U.\text{Grant}(St[u], share) \leftrightarrow \mathcal{A} \rangle$
if $leak$ then
  $h \leftarrow msg$
else
  $h \leftarrow\$ \{0, 1\}^{\kappa}$ // handle for delivery
  $Msgs[h] \leftarrow (msg, actual)$
return h

Oracle Accept

Input: $(u', share, h) \in [n] \times \mathcal{P}(\mathbb{N}) \times \{0, 1\}^*$
$actual = \perp$
if $Msgs[h] \neq \perp$ then
  $(msg, actual) \leftarrow Msgs[h]$ // Delivery
else
  $msg \leftarrow h$ // Injection
try $(St[u'], st_{up}; \perp)$
  $\leftarrow \langle U.\text{Accept}(St[u'], share, msg, upload) \leftrightarrow \mathcal{A} \rangle$
try $\langle U.\text{Upload}(st_{up}) \leftrightarrow \mathcal{A} \rangle$
if $actual \neq \perp$ then
  for $e \in actual$ do
    if $KnownKey[u', e] = \texttt{false}$ then
      $ActualKey[u', e] \leftarrow \texttt{true}$
for $e \in share$ do
  $KnownKey[u', e] \leftarrow \texttt{true}$

sample-if-nec(U, e, s)

if $s \neq \perp$ then
  $k \leftarrow U.\text{Key}(e, s)$
  return (s, k)
else if $Secret[e] \neq \perp$ then
  $Secret[e] \leftarrow\$ \{0, 1\}^{\kappa}$
  if $b = 0 \vee e \in Corr$ then $Keys[e] \leftarrow U.\text{Key}(e, s)$
  else $Keys[e] \leftarrow\$ \{0, 1\}^{\kappa}$
$ActualKey[U, e] \leftarrow \texttt{true}$
return $(Secret[e], Keys[e])$

Fig. 2. The key-indistinguishability notion for standard-model CKS. We assume the adversary to not interleave calls of the adversarial oracles for the same user.

message is assumed to be transmitted over a secure channel to the recipient; therefore, leaking the message implies leaking the delegated keys. If the message is transmitted securely, then the adversary is given an opaque handle h to the message instead, which they later can use for delivery to another user u'. In the Accept oracle, the adversary can then either input a handle h or a granting message msg. In the former case, the game looks up the actual granting message msg, as well as for which of the granted keys correspond to actual keys chosen by the game (as opposed to keys injected by the adversary).

Note that the game formalizes *selective security* by having the adversary commit to the set *Corr* of all epochs for which the keys can be compromised before starting the interaction. Any type of corruption, whether leaking a user's private set or a grant message, is then predicated all of the keys which can be deduced by correctness being for corruptible epochs. Finally, observe that this formalizes forward secrecy and post-compromise security as corruptions are allowed whenever a user are not supposed to know the epoch's actual key.

3   Trapdoor Key Derivation

3.1   Defining TKDFs

In this section, we introduce the Trapdoor KDF (TKDF) primitive that will serve as the fundamental building block for our standard-model schemes. Recall from Sect. 1.1 that TKDF, in a nutshell, represents a kind of "invertible" KDF that generates a key k and updated state z' from a seed s and previous state z, such that from z a secret *trapdoor* t to invert the operation can be derived.

A schematic representation of a TKDF scheme is presented in Fig. 3. Observe that (to avoid circularity) we only require the inversion to recover the key and trapdoor rather than the seed and state. To be suitable for our CKS construction, we also require certain operations to be deterministic, as expressed as part of the following definition.

Definition 5. *A* Trapdoor Key Derivation Function (TKDF) *scheme is a tuple* (TKDF. Key, TKDF. Derive, TKDF. Trapdoor, TKDF. Invert) *of PPT algorithms with an associated seed space* $\mathcal{S}$, *key space* $\mathcal{K}$, *state space* $\mathcal{Z}$, *trapdoor space* $\mathcal{T}$, *and ciphertext space* $\mathcal{C}$.

- *The deterministic key derivation algorithm* $k_i \leftarrow$ TKDF. Key(s_i) *outputs the key* k_i *corresponding to a seed* s_i
- *The state derivation algorithm* $(z_i, c_i) \leftarrow$ TKDF. Derive(s_i, z_{i-1}) *takes a seed* s_i *and a state* z_{i-1} *as inputs, and outputs the next state* z_i *and a ciphertext* c_i. *The algorithm can be randomized, but* z_i *is a deterministic function of the inputs. Hence, only* c_i *may depend on the algorithm's randomness.*
- *The deterministic* $t_i \leftarrow$ TKDF. Trapdoor(z_i) *algorithm outputs a trapdoor* t_i *based on the state.*
- *The deterministic inversion algorithm* $(k_i, t_{i-1}) \leftarrow$ TKDF. Invert(c_i, t_i) *takes the ciphertext and trapdoor, and outputs the key and the previous trapdoor.*

We generally require the state space $\mathcal{Z}$ *to be small (e.g., about as big as the key space) and in particular to consist only of elements of the same length.*

Let us first define correctness. Correctness requires that TKDF. Invert correctly inverts TKDF. Derive, as formalized by the following definition.

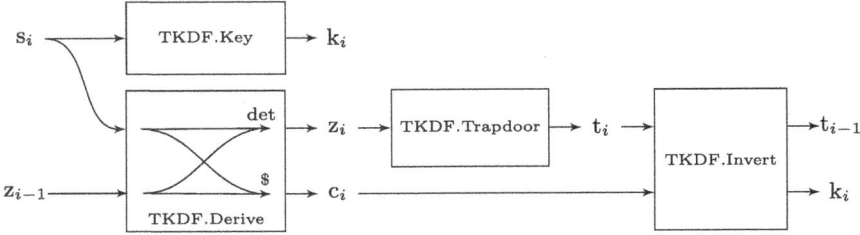

Fig. 3. A schematic representation of our symmetric TKDF scheme.

Definition 6 (Correctness). *We say that a TKDF is correct, if*

$$
\Pr\left[(k_i, t_{i-1}) = \mathrm{TKDF.\,Invert}(c_i,\ t_i)\ \middle|\
\begin{array}{c}
s_i \leftarrow\!\!\$\ \mathcal{S},\ z_{i-1} \leftarrow\!\!\$\ \mathcal{Z}, \\
t_{i-1} \leftarrow \mathrm{TKDF.\,Trapdoor}(z_{i-1}), \\
k_i \leftarrow \mathrm{TKDF.\,Key}(s_i), \\
(z_i, c_i) \leftarrow \mathrm{TKDF.\,Derive}(s_i, z_{i-1}), \\
t_i \leftarrow \mathrm{TKDF.\,Trapdoor}(z_i)
\end{array}
\right] = 1,
$$

where the randomness is taken both over the sampling of z_{i-1} and s_i, as well as over the coins of TKDF. Derive.

For security, we require that the resulting key k_i is indistinguishable from an independent uniform random, for an attacker that does not know the seed s_i. Analogously, we require that the trapdoor t_i is indistinguishable from random for an attacker that does not know the secret state z_i. (This will be important for being able to iterate the TKDF.) Finally, we require the ciphertext c_i to be semantically secure and not reveal any information about either k_i or t_{i-1} to an adversary not knowing t_i. The precise security definitions are a bit subtle. We now first state the formal definition and then discuss some of the intricacies.

Definition 7 (TKDF Security). *A TKDF scheme is said to be secure if there exists a PPT algorithm* $\mathrm{TKDF.\,Sim}(t_i, k_i, t_{i-1}) \rightarrow c_i$ *which simulates ciphertexts such that the following three properties hold:*

1. **Key randomness.** *For any PPT $\mathcal{A}$, the advantage*

$$
\mathsf{Adv}_{\mathsf{G}_{\mathrm{TKDF}}^{\mathrm{KeyRand}}}(\mathcal{A}) := \left| \Pr[\mathsf{G}_{\mathrm{TKDF}}^{\mathrm{KeyRand\text{-}0}}(\mathcal{A}) \Rightarrow 1] - \Pr[\mathsf{G}_{\mathrm{TKDF}}^{\mathrm{KeyRand\text{-}1}}(\mathcal{A}) \Rightarrow 1] \right|
$$

is negligible in the security parameter κ, for the real-or-ideal game from Fig. 4.

2. **Trapdoor randomness.** *For any PPT $\mathcal{A}$, the advantage*

$$
\mathsf{Adv}_{\mathsf{G}_{\mathrm{TKDF}}^{\mathrm{TdRand}}}(\mathcal{A}) := \left| \Pr[\mathsf{G}_{\mathrm{TKDF}}^{\mathrm{TdRand\text{-}0}}(\mathcal{A}) \Rightarrow 1] - \Pr[\mathsf{G}_{\mathrm{TKDF}}^{\mathrm{TdRand\text{-}1}}(\mathcal{A}) \Rightarrow 1] \right|
$$

is negligible in the security parameter κ, for the real-or-ideal game from Fig. 5.

3. **Semantic security.** *For any keys* k_i^0 *and* k_i^1, *and any trapdoors* t_{i-1}^0 *and* t_{i-1}^1, *the following distributions are computationally indistinguishable:*

$$\left\{ \left(k_i^0, k_i^1, t_{i-1}^0, t_{i-1}^1, \text{TKDF. Sim}(t_i, k_i^0, t_{i-1}^0) \right) : t_i \leftarrow_\$ \mathcal{T} \right\}$$
$$\approx_c \left\{ \left(k_i^0, k_i^1, t_{i-1}^0, t_{i-1}^1, \text{TKDF. Sim}(t_i, k_i^1, t_{i-1}^1) \right) : t_i \leftarrow_\$ \mathcal{T} \right\}.$$

We denote with $\text{Adv}_{G_{\text{TKDF}}^{\text{IND-CPA-OT}}}(\mathcal{A})$ *the maximum respective advantage for an adversary* $\mathcal{A}$, *over any challenge.*

We say that the TKDF scheme is one-time *secure if no PPT adversary has non-negligible advantage when restricted to a single* Derive *query in the key-randomness and trapdoor-randomness games.*

Let us consider the key-randomness property. Intuitively, this property requires that k_i is indistinguishable from random when not knowing the seed s_i. However, the property further has to account for leakage from the ciphertext and, especially, the state z_i (which can be used for subsequent evaluations). Therefore, the property demands that k_i and z_i are indistinguishable from independently sampled uniform random values. In any actual scheme, however, those values are related via the ciphertext c_i by correctness: Any attacker can derive t_i from z_i and use this to decrypt c_i, resulting in (t_{i-1}, k_i). Therefore, $G_{\text{TKDF}}^{\text{KeyRand-1}}$ allows the ciphertext to be generated consistently using a simulator TKDF. Sim. Crucially, the simulator ensures that t_i from z_i are only related indirectly via the trapdoor t_i, i.e., that the above check is essentially the only thing an attacker can do to distinguish k_i and z_i from independent uniform random values. Finally, note that the attacker gets multiple TKDF. Derive queries for their prior state z_{i-1} of choice. This will turn out to be vital for active security where several users knowing the same seed s_i are tricked to evaluate the TKDF with different prior states. Indeed, for passive security one-time TKDF security suffices.

Trapdoor randomness is then defined analogously to key randomness. For instance, the attacker gets to do multiple TKDF. Derive to anticipate attacks where to parties with the same secret state z_i are tricked into using different seeds s_i chosen by the adversary.

Finally, consider semantic security. This is essentially one-time IND-CPA security for the ciphertext. Note that as all three security properties use the same simulator, the former ones already imply that the simulated ciphertext is indistinguishable from a real one. Phrasing semantic security in terms of the simulator will turn out to make the definition a bit easier to use in hybrid arguments where either key randomness or trapdoor randomness is applied first.

3.2 Symmetric TKDF

For more CKS schemes with non-trivial delegation and erasure, we need a TKDF that treats its two inputs more interchangeably than the basic TKDF notion introduced above. That is, a TKDF does not strictly distinguish between the

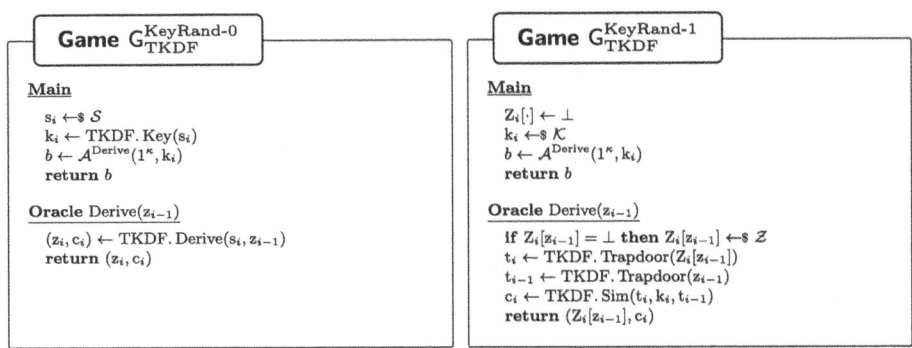

Fig. 4. The games formalizing key-randomness of a TKDF scheme.

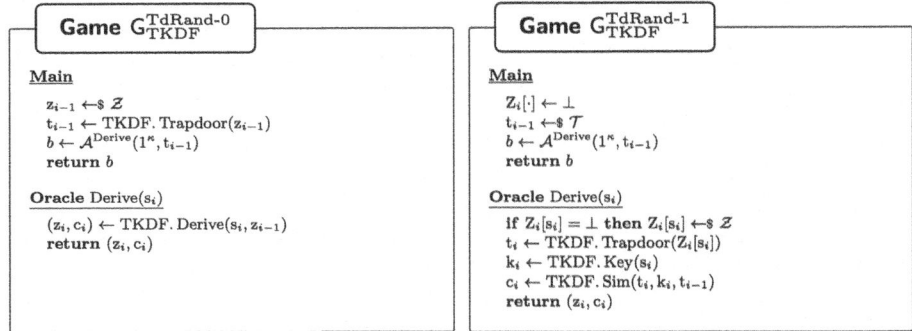

Fig. 5. The games formalizing trapdoor-randomness of a TKDF scheme.

concepts of seeds and states and allows them to be used somewhat interchangeably. In particular, we want (1) a TKDF state z can be used as a seed for a subsequent TKDF call, and (2) that trapdoors are generated analogously to derived keys.

We call such a TKDF a symmetric TKDF. (We remark that unlike the notion of a symmetric PRF [4] we do not necessarily require that such a TKDF treats its argument symmetrically, i.e., $\mathrm{TKDF.Derive}(s, z) = \mathrm{TKDF.Derive}(z, s)$, but simply that the two arguments play the same general role.) We formalize the structural requirement in the following definition.

Definition 8. *A* symmetric TKDF *is a TKDF scheme with the following structural properties:*

- *The seed space is equal to the state space, i.e., $\mathcal{S} = \mathcal{Z}$, and the key space is equal to the trapdoor space, i.e., $\mathcal{K} = \mathcal{T}$.*
- *The key derivation is equivalent to the trapdoor derivation. In other words, that* $\mathrm{TKDF.Key} = \mathrm{TKDF.Trapdoor}$.

The security of a symmetric TKDF is the same as the security of a regular TKDF. Note that key randomness and trapdoor randomness coincide iff TKDF. Derive treats its argument symmetrically.

3.3   A Standard-Model Symmetric-TKDF Construction

We now present a simple construction of a symmetric TKDF. The construction is based on a length-doubling PRG, a dual-PRF [2,4], and a one-time secure symmetric encryption scheme SE. Recall that a dual-PRF is a deterministic algorithm dPRF : $\{0,1\}^\kappa \times \{0,1\}^\kappa \to \{0,1\}^\kappa$ that behaves like a PRF in both arguments, i.e., such that for a uniform random key k, both dPRF$(k, \cdot)$ and dPRF$(\cdot, k)$ are PRFs. The scheme first uses the PRG to expand the seed s_i into the key k_i and an auxiliary value x_i, and to expand the previous z_{i-1} into y_i and the previous trapdoor t_{i-1}. The values x_i and y_i are then combined using the dPRF to obtain the next state z_i. From this state, we moreover derive the current trapdoors t_i as the second part of the output yield from expanding z_i (analogously as for t_{i-1}). t_i then serves as encryption key to encrypt (t_{i-1}, k_i). The trapdoor algorithm simply recomputes t_i from z_i and, finally, the inversion algorithm decrypts the ciphertext to obtain the trapdoor and key.[5] A schematic depiction of the scheme is presented in Fig. 6, whereas for completeness formal definition is given in Fig. 7.

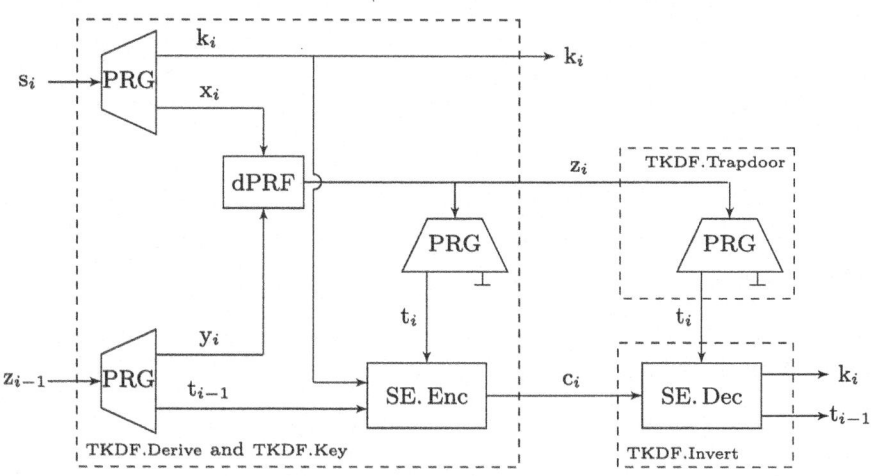

Fig. 6. A schematic representation of the Symmetric TKDF scheme from Fig. 7. The left box shows both TKDF. Key (the upper output only depending on s_i) and TKDF. Derive (the middle and lower outputs).

---

[5] We remark that if a party consecutively computes $z_i \leftarrow$ TKDF. Derive(s_i, z_{i-1}), and $z_{i+1} \leftarrow$ TKDF. Derive(s_{i+1}, z_i), then an actual implementation would not need to expand z_i in both operations separately. Thus, the number of PRG iterations per epoch is actually two instead of three.

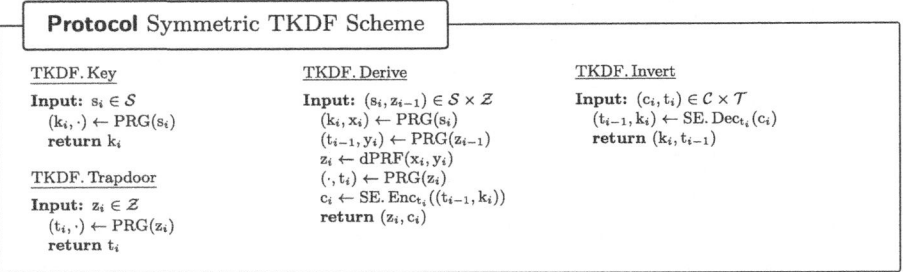

Fig. 7. A simple construction based on a PRG, a dual-PRF, and symmetric encryption. Note that TKDF. Key and TKDF. Trapdoor are the same, as required for a symmetric TKDF.

Note that we assumed here that $\mathcal{Z} = \mathcal{S} = \{0,1\}^\kappa$. Using a length-doubling PRG, we can thus observe that $\mathcal{K} = \mathcal{T} = \{0,1\}^\kappa$ as well, implying that our construction satisfies the structural property of a symmetric TKDF. Correctness then immediately follows by the correctness of the symmetric encryption scheme SE. Security is established by the following theorem.

Theorem 1. *Assume* SE *is a one-time IND-CPA secure symmetric encryption scheme*, PRG *is a secure length-doubling pseudo-random generator, and* dPRF *is a secure dual-PRF. Then, the TKDF from Fig. 7 scheme is secure. More formally, for each of the three properties and every PPT adversary* $\mathcal{A}$*, there exist attackers* $\mathcal{A}_{\mathrm{PRG}}$ *against the PRG security game* $\mathsf{G}_{\mathrm{PRG}}^{\mathrm{IND}}$*, and* $\mathcal{A}_{\mathrm{SE}}$ *against the IND-CPA game* $\mathsf{G}_{\mathrm{SE}}^{\mathrm{IND\text{-}CPA}}$*, that have roughly the same running time, such that*

$$\mathsf{Adv}_{\mathsf{G}_{\mathrm{TKDF}}^{\mathrm{KeyRand}}}(\mathcal{A}) \leq \mathsf{Adv}_{\mathsf{G}_{\mathrm{PRG}}^{\mathrm{IND}}}(\mathcal{A}_{\mathrm{PRG}}) + \mathsf{Adv}_{\mathsf{G}_{\mathrm{dPRF}}^{\mathrm{IND}}}(\mathcal{A}_{\mathrm{dPRF}}) \tag{1}$$

$$\mathsf{Adv}_{\mathsf{G}_{\mathrm{TKDF}}^{\mathrm{TdRand}}}(\mathcal{A}) \leq \mathsf{Adv}_{\mathsf{G}_{\mathrm{PRG}}^{\mathrm{IND}}}(\mathcal{A}_{\mathrm{PRG}}) + \mathsf{Adv}_{\mathsf{G}_{\mathrm{dPRF}}^{\mathrm{IND}}}(\mathcal{A}_{\mathrm{dPRF}}) \tag{2}$$

$$\mathsf{Adv}_{\mathsf{G}_{\mathrm{TKDF}}^{\mathrm{IND\text{-}CPA\text{-}OT}}}(\mathcal{A}) \leq \mathsf{Adv}_{\mathsf{G}_{\mathrm{SE}}^{\mathrm{IND\text{-}CPA\text{-}OT}}}(\mathcal{A}_{\mathrm{SE}}). \tag{3}$$

Proof. We use the following simple simulator that just mimics the encryption performed by the scheme

$$\mathrm{TKDF.\,Sim}(\mathsf{t}_i, \mathsf{k}_i^0, \mathsf{t}_{i-1}^0) := \mathrm{SE.\,Enc}_{\mathsf{t}_i}((\mathsf{t}_{i-1}, \mathsf{k}_i)).$$

First, consider key randomness. Observe that, in the TKDF. Derive computation of $\mathsf{G}_{\mathrm{TKDF}}^{\mathrm{KeyRand\text{-}0}}$, by PRG security k_i and x_i are indistinguishable from independent and uniformly random sampled values as s_i is sampled uniformly at random and not otherwise used. Now, we can apply dual-PRF security to conclude that in the Derive oracle the $\mathrm{dPRF}(\mathsf{x}_i, \mathsf{z}_{i-1})$ evaluation furthermore behaves like a uniform random function in the second argument. Therefore, we can instead replace z_i with the output of a URF, as in $\mathsf{G}_{\mathrm{TKDF}}^{\mathrm{KeyRand\text{-}1}}$. The indistinguishability now follows by observing that TKDF. Derive just computes t_i and t_{i-1} the same way as TKDF. Trapdoor in $G_{TKDF}^{KeyRand-1}$, followed by the same encryption that TKDF. Sim performs.

The trapdoor randomness follows analogously, using that $dPRF(\cdot, z_{i-1})$ behaves like a uniform random function for z_{i-1} chosen uniformly at random. Finally, consider the semantic security. Given the definition of our simulator, this follows directly from the one-time IND-CPA security of SE. Enc.   □

Corollary 1. *Trapdoor KDFs exist if and only if dual-PRFs exist.*

Proof. Dual-PRFs imply the existence of one-way functions and, thus, PRG and (one-time secure) symmetric encryption. Therefore, the first direction follows from Theorem 1. Moreover, observe that key-randomness and trapdoor-randomness games jointly imply dual-PRF security with respect to the first output z_i of TKDF. Derive.

Variants. We now consider some variants of the scheme. First, observe that for one-time TKDF security, we can replace the dual-PRF with a simple XOR operation of x_i and y_i. The proof follows analogously, observing that for a single evaluation $x_i \oplus y_i$ behaves indistinguishable from the dual-PRF. While dPRFs are known to be constructible from standard assumptions [4] it is an open problem whether than can be constructed from one-way functions only.

Theorem 2. *When replacing* $z_i \leftarrow dPRF(x_i, y_i)$ *with* $z_i \leftarrow x_i \oplus y_i$ *in the scheme from Fig. 7, then the modified scheme is one-time TKDF secure, assuming* SE *is a one-time IND-CPA secure symmetric encryption scheme and* PRG *is a secure length-doubling pseudo-random generator.*

Corollary 2. *The existence of one-way functions implies the existence of one-time secure TKDF schemes.*

Second, we observe that the usage of the PRG is just one special case of a key derivation mechanism, expanding a seed s_i or state z_i into two independent secrets. Therefore, if we have a legacy application that already prescribes a key-derivation step, and that allows us to derive one more unrelated secret, then our scheme can be made compatible with the legacy application. For instance, the MLS group messaging protocol already involves a key derivation function (KDF) based on HKDF [5,14]. Our TKDF scheme, could therefore derive k_i according to that key derivation and x_i using the same key derivation but on a different context (and analogously for expanding z_i). As long as the legacy application does not use that context itself, the composed scheme is secure. The proof of the following theorem follows analogous to Theorem 1.

Theorem 3. *For any secure key derivation function (KDF) we can replace the usage of* PRG *in the scheme from Fig. 7 with the* KDF *evaluated twice on two distinct contexts. The resulting scheme is a secure TKDF, assuming the KDF, the dual-PRF are secure and* SE *is a one-time IND-CPA secure symmetric encryption scheme.*

4   Iterative CKS

Recall from Sect. 1.1 that the all-or-nothing scheme by Dodis et al. was built around iteratively applying a "derivation" that aggregates a secret state and a seed into a new secret state (and a ciphertext) as depicted in Fig. 1. The second scheme by Dodis et al.—which allows for efficient delegation and erasure of arbitrary continuous intervals of secrets—follows a similar template. Indeed, the scheme simply arranges the epochs as leaves in a binary tree, where each node aggregates its two children. (We refer to [7] for details on the scheme.)

In this section, we abstract CKS schemes built around this template. We call such a scheme an *iterative* CKS scheme, for which we define the respective notion. The corresponding (security) definitions for this special case turn out to be significantly simpler than the (fully general) CKS notion as introduced in [7]. We then present a unified protocol for the iterative CKS template, based on a TKDF, and prove its security. This essentially allows us to reduce choosing the right trade-off between functionality (in terms of delegation and fine-grained erasure) and efficiency of CKS schemes to a graph theoretic problem.

4.1   Syntax

In this section, we formally introduce the simplified iterative CKS notion. On a high level, the idea is that such a scheme repeatedly aggregates secrets—which could either be seeds or secret states themselves—into a new secret and a ciphertext. Intuitively, the resulting secret should allow to reverse the aggregation. Therefore, recursively, the state when combined with the appropriate ciphertexts should allow recovering any secret that went into the aggregation.

Note that the aggregation essentially forms a directed graph with seeds as sources and each non-source having indegree two. To avoid circularity, we will restrict ourselves to directed acyclic graphs (DAG). The following definition assigns each node the set of epochs that have a path from their source to the node, i.e., the set of seeds they aggregate over.

Definition 9. *We say $\mathfrak{S} \subseteq \mathcal{P}(2^{\mathbb{N}})$ is a set family for an interactive CKS if:*

1. *$\varnothing \notin \mathfrak{S}$*
2. *$\{e\} \in \mathfrak{S}$, for all $e \in \mathbb{N}$*
3. *For each set $\mathcal{S} \in \mathfrak{S}$ with $|\mathcal{S}| > 1$, there exists a unique decomposition $\mathcal{S}_1, \mathcal{S}_2 \in \mathfrak{S}$ such that $\mathcal{S} = \mathcal{S}_1 \cup \mathcal{S}_2$.*

Furthermore, let $\mathcal{D}ag_{\mathfrak{S}}$ denote the respective DAG over the set $\mathfrak{S}$ where an edge $(\mathcal{S}_i, \mathcal{S}_j)$ is present iff there exists $\mathcal{S}' \in \mathfrak{S}$ such that $\mathcal{S}_j = \mathcal{S}_i \cup \mathcal{S}'$. By property 3, each internal node of $\mathcal{D}ag_{\mathfrak{S}}$ has in-degree 2.

We now define iterative CKS for a set family $\mathfrak{S}$. Recursively aggregating seeds according to edges in $\mathcal{D}ag_{\mathfrak{S}}$, such a scheme allows a party knowing all seeds $\{s_e \mid e \in \mathcal{S}\}$ to create a compact *seeds state* $SS_{\mathcal{S}}$ and a compact *keys state* $KS_{\mathcal{S}}$, as well as ciphertext $C_{\mathcal{S}}$. For security, the ciphertexts should not reveal any information about the keys derived from the seeds. For correctness, on the other hand, the keys state KS_S and ciphertext C_S should be sufficient to recover the *keys* by "undoing" the aggregation and, ultimately, recover individual keys k_e.

Definition 10. *An* Iterative Compact Key Storage (I-CKS) *scheme* CKS *consists of the following PPT algorithms:*

- GenPub(1^κ) $\rightarrow$ pub *generates public parameters for the scheme.*
- DeriveKey(pub, s_e, e) $\rightarrow$ k_e *returns the key corresponding to a seed for epoch* e. *This algorithm is assumed to be deterministic.*
- Init(pub, e, s_e) $\rightarrow$ $(SS_{\{e\}}, C_{\{e\}})$ *initializes a secret seeds state for* $S = \{e\}$. *Additionally, output an (optional) ciphertext.*
- Compact($S_1, SS_{S_1}, S_2, SS_{S_2}$) $\rightarrow$ $(SS_{S_1 \cup S_2}, C_{S_1 \cup S_2})$ *takes two seed states and compacts them into a joint one and a ciphertext to be stored. This assumes that* $(S_1 \cup S_2) \in \mathfrak{S}$.
- DeriveKS(S, SS_S) $\rightarrow$ KS_S *computes the keys state corresponding to a seeds state.*
- Expand(S, KS_S, C_S, S_1, S_2) $\rightarrow$ (KS_{S_1}, KS_{S_2}) *obtains the keys state for a subintervals* $S_1 \subset S$ *and* $S_2 \subset S$ *based on the keys state for the joint interval* $S = S_1 \cup S_2$ *and the respective ciphertext.*
- Recover(e, $KS_{\{e\}}, C_{\{e\}}$) $\rightarrow$ k_e *recovers the key* k_e *for an epoch* e.

Correctness. We now formalize the correctness of our notion. Simply put, we require the following two properties:

1. Recover "undoes" Init. Consider an epoch $e \in \mathbb{N}$. Then,
   - $(SS_{\{e\}}, C_{\{e\}}) \leftarrow$ Init(pub, e, s_e)
   - $KS_{\{e\}} \leftarrow$ DeriveKS($\{e\}, SS_{\{e\}}$)
   - $k'_e \leftarrow$ Recover(e, $KS_{\{e\}}, C_{\{e\}}$)
   outputs the correct key, i.e., $k'_e =$ DeriveKey(pub, s_e, e).
2. Expand "undoes" Compact. Consider an epoch sets $S_1, S_2 \in \mathfrak{S}$ such that their union is in $\mathfrak{S}$. Then,
   - $(SS_{S'}, C_{S'}) \leftarrow$ Compact($S_1, SS_{S_1}, S_2, SS_{S_2}$)
   - $KS_{S'} \leftarrow$ DeriveKS($S', SS_{S'}$)
   - $(KS'_{S_1}, KS'_{S_2}) \leftarrow$ Expand($S', KS_{S'}, C_{S'}, S_1, S_2$)
   produces keys states such that KS'_{S_1} is interchangeable with KS_{S_1} obtained via DeriveKS(S_1, SS_{S_1}), and KS'_{S_2} is interchangeable with KS_{S_2}, respectively.

A formal version of correctness is presented in Fig. 8. Note that the game treats any seeds state, keys state, and ciphertext for the same epoch set $S \in \mathfrak{S}$ interchangeably. In a deterministic scheme this is trivially achieved by each being unique—we however only formally require DeriveKey to be deterministic.

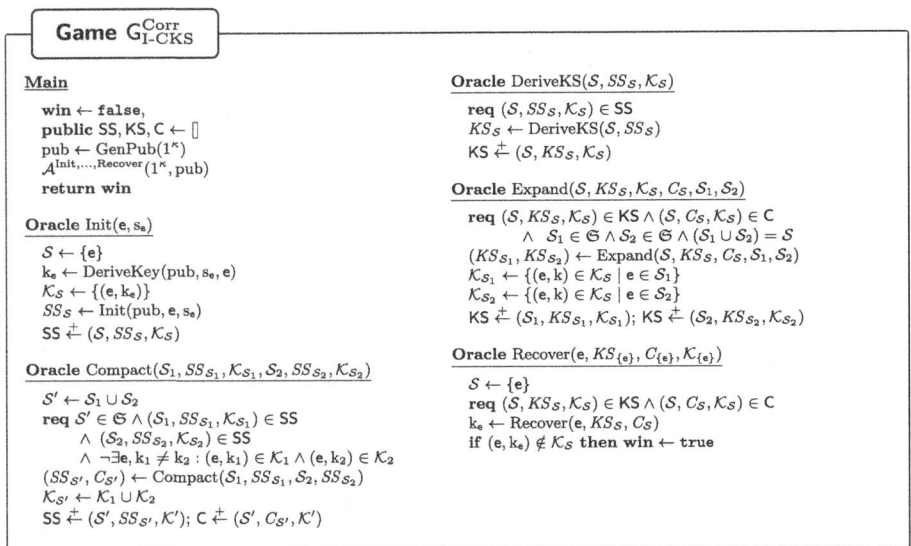

Fig. 8. The Iterative CKS correctness game.

4.2 Security

For security, we consider two games: pseudorandomness and integrity. The pseudorandomness game is depicted in Fig. 9. The game allows the adversary to create an arbitrary number of seed states for a single epoch, using Init, and then to gradually accumulate seeds using Compact, returning the ciphertext to the adversary. For Init, the adversary obtains either the real key k_e, if $b = 0$, or a random one, if $b = 1$. Note that the adversary can also inject their own seed by inputting $s_e \neq \bot$, in which case the real key is used. Finally, note that, for simplicity, the game formalizes selective security, with the adversary having to commit to the set of corruptions $Corr$ ahead of time. However, observe that the structure of our game (and I-CKS in general) is essentially one of a pebbling game on the graph $Dag_{\mathfrak{S}}$. Therefore, the framework on adaptive security by Jafargholi et al. [10] and Kamath et al. [13] should allow us to get (quasi-polynomial) adaptive security for specific graphs $Dag_{\mathfrak{S}}$.

Definition 11. *An I-CKS scheme is secure, if for any set family $\mathcal{S}$, the following advantage*

$$\mathsf{Adv}_{\mathsf{G}_{\text{I-CKS}}^{\text{Keys-RoR}}}(\mathcal{A}) := \Pr[\mathsf{G}_{\text{I-CKS}}^{\text{Keys-RoR}}(\mathcal{A}) \Rightarrow 1]$$

is negligible in κ for any PPT adversary $\mathcal{A}$. We say that the scheme is passively secure if the advantage is negligible for any $\mathcal{A}$ who is restricted to only pass $s_e = \bot$ to the Init oracle.

The integrity is similar to the correctness game in structure. It, however, no longer restricts the adversary to submit honestly generated ciphertexts and, in

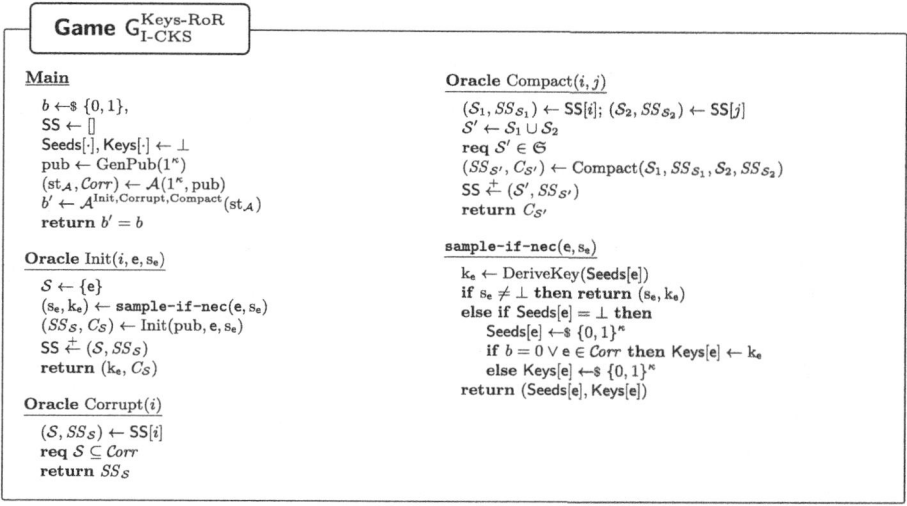

Fig. 9. The real-or-random security game for an Iterative CKS scheme.

turn, allows the algorithms to fail. Integrity then requires that Recover either fails or outputs the same key k_e that was initially aggregated over. In addition, the game can be won if Compact succeeds on seed states that contain conflicting information for the same epoch. Observe that the game formalizes a strong variant of integrity where all states are presumed to be public (analogous to the general CKS integrity game) (Fig. 10).

Definition 12. *An I-CKS scheme is said to satisfy integrity, if for any set family $\mathcal{S}$, the following advantage is negligible in κ for any PPT adversary $\mathcal{A}$:*

$$\mathsf{Adv}_{\mathsf{G}^{\text{Integrity}}_{\text{I-CKS}}}(\mathcal{A}) := \Pr[\mathsf{G}^{\text{Integrity}}_{\text{I-CKS}}(\mathcal{A}) \Rightarrow 1].$$

4.3 Constructing I-CKS from TKDF

We now build a generic iterative CKS scheme based on a (symmetric) TKDF. Recall from Sect. 1.1 that the goal of a TKDF was to provide a standard-model abstraction for the "derive" and "invert" boxes used in the schemes of [7]. See, for example, Fig. 1 for a high-level schematic of the ROM-CKS all-or-nothing scheme—and compare it with the intended analogous for the standard model presented in Fig. 11.

The scheme for a set family $\mathfrak{S}$ is then fairly straightforward. In a nutshell, TKDF states roughly correspond to seed states, and TKDF trapdoors to key states. For each internal node of $\mathcal{Dag}_\mathfrak{S}$ we use TKDF. Derive to compact the seed states of its two child nodes as part of Compact. Conversely, for Expand we use TKDF. Invert to obtain the key states of the node's children. We now discuss the scheme in a bit more detail; see Fig. 12 for a pseudocode description.

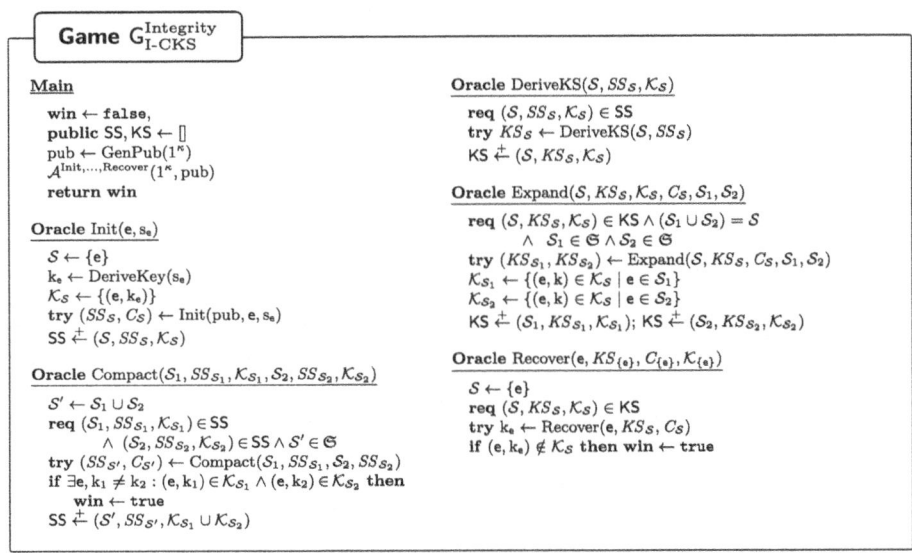

Fig. 10. The integrity game for an Iterative CKS scheme.

Seed states and key states. For now, let us describe a variant of the scheme without integrity. Each seed state SS_S is then of one of two forms: (a) a regular state $SS_S = z_S$ storing a TKDF state, or (b) an immediate state $SS_S = s_e$, in case $S = \{e\}$. (For clarity, we further mark the state with the constant 'seeds'.) Analogously, each keys state KS_S either (a) is a TKDF trapdoor $KS_S = t_S$, if $|S| > 1$, or (b) a key $KS_e = k_e$ if $S = \{e\}$.

Init and Recover. Both Init and Recover are, in principle, extremely simple. The former just outputs $SS_{\{e\}} = s_e$ as seed state, with no ciphertext necessary. The latter takes $KS_{\{e\}} = k_e$ and outputs k_e.

Some complications arise from supporting regular TKDF, for instance for the all-or-nothing scheme depicted in Fig. 11. Observe that here $SS_{\{1\}}$ and $SS_{\{2\}}$ have to behave slightly differently, as the former seed s_1 has the extra derivation with the initial constant state $\tilde{z}$. (Looking slightly ahead, the TKDF. Derive mixing in s_2 will be performed as part of Compact of $SS_{\{1\}}$ and $SS_{\{2\}}$.) To solve this issue, the formal protocol from Fig. 12 solves this issue by introducing a "base set" $\mathcal{B} \subseteq \mathbb{N}$ of epochs, for which such an extra derivation should be performed. Both $\mathcal{B}$ and $\tilde{z}$ are then considered protocol parameters.

Compact, DeriveKS, and Expand. As already mentioned, Compact corresponds directly to TKDF. Derive and Expand to TKDF. Invert. Similarly, DeriveKS corresponds directly to TKDF. Trapdoor, deriving the TKDF trapdoor (= keys state) from the TKDF state (= seeds state). One more subtlety arises, however. We want different users to compact two states in the same order, i.e., they

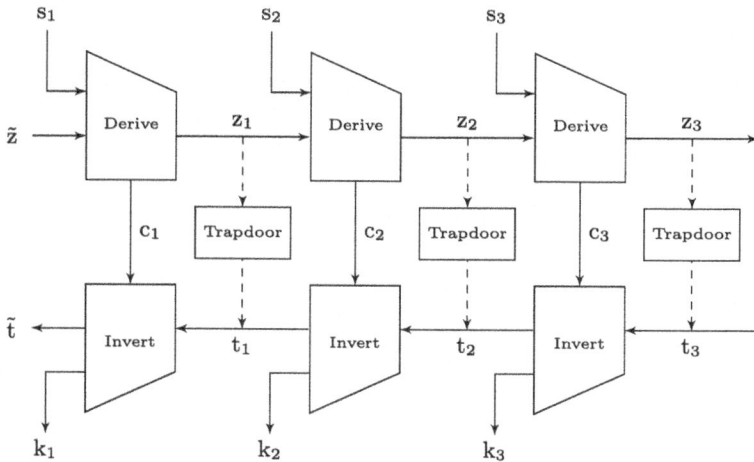

Fig. 11. The all-or-nothing scheme from Fig. 1 adapted to the standard-model CKS setting, using a TKDF instead of convergent encryption. $\tilde{z}$ is some fixed TKDF state used to initialize the iteration. Note that the tags T_i from Fig. 1 are omitted here (which are not to be confused with the trapdoors t_i).

should agree on which of the states $SS_{\mathcal{S}_1}$ or $SS_{\mathcal{S}_2}$ is used as a first and which as a second argument. Otherwise, various parties who may learn the same set of seeds in different orders may still create incompatible outsourcings, undermining the compactness of the server state. In particular, the order must be well defined when using Expand to recover prior trapdoors. We solve this by introducing as a protocol parameter an order $\prec$ on any two sets $\mathcal{S}_1$ and $\mathcal{S}_2$ which can be combined. (Note that this is not required to be a proper order relation among all $\mathfrak{S}$, something like the lexicographic order on the descriptions of $\mathcal{S}_1$ and $\mathcal{S}_2$ would suffice.)

Integrity. Finally, let us enhance our protocol to satisfy integrity. This can be done using a collision-resistant hash function $H_{\mathrm{pub}}(\cdot)$. Each state is enhanced with a hash, where the hash of a combined state is set to $h = H_{\mathrm{pub}}(h_1, h_2, c)$, when computing Compact on seed states with hashes h_1 and h_2, respectively, and c is the TKDF ciphertext produced during Compact. The hashes h_1 and h_2 are then output as part of the ciphertext along c, i.e., we set $C = (h_1, h_2, c)$. For an immediate state $SS_{\{e\}}$ the hash just binds the epoch number e.

Correctness and Security. The correctness of the scheme follows from the correctness of the TKDF and inspection.

Theorem 4. *The iterative CKS scheme from Fig. 12 is correct if the underlying TKDF is correct and has deterministic ciphertexts. More concretely,*

$$\mathsf{Adv}_{\mathsf{G}^{\mathrm{Corr}}_{\mathrm{I-CKS}}}(\mathcal{A}) \leq (q_{\mathrm{Init}} + q_{\mathrm{Compact}}) \cdot \mathsf{Adv}_{\mathsf{G}^{\mathrm{Corr}}_{\mathrm{TKDF}}}(\mathcal{A}'))$$

Protocol I-CKS Scheme

Parameters:
- set family $\mathfrak{S}$;
- ordering of sets $\mathcal{S}_1 \prec \mathcal{S}_2$, for all $\mathcal{S}_1, \mathcal{S}_2$ such that $\mathcal{S}_1 \cup \mathcal{S}_2 \in \mathfrak{S}$;
- set of epochs $\mathcal{B} \subseteq \mathbb{N}$ for which an extra derivation step is applied;
- a constant TKDF state $\bar{z} \in \mathcal{Z}$ to be used for epochs $e \in \mathcal{B}$.

$\underline{\text{GenPub}(1^\kappa)}$

pub $\leftarrow\$ \{0,1\}^\kappa$
return pub

$\underline{\text{DeriveKey}(\text{pub}, s_e, e)}$

$k_e \leftarrow \text{TKDF}.\text{Key}(s_e)$
return k_e

$\underline{\text{Init}(\text{pub}, e, s_e)}$

$h \leftarrow H_{\text{pub}}(e)$
if $e \in \mathcal{B}$ **then**
$\quad (z, c) \leftarrow \text{TKDF}.\text{Derive}(s_e, \bar{z})$
$\quad SS \leftarrow (\text{'seeds'}, z, h)$
$\quad C \leftarrow (h, \bot, c)$
$\quad$**return** (SS, C)
else
$\quad h \leftarrow H_{\text{pub}}(e)$
$\quad SS \leftarrow (\text{'seeds'}, s_e, h)$
$\quad$**return** $(SS, \bot)$

$\underline{\text{Compact}(\mathcal{S}_1, SS_{\mathcal{S}_1}, \mathcal{S}_2, SS_{\mathcal{S}_2})}$

req $\mathcal{S}_1, \mathcal{S}_2 \in \mathfrak{S} \wedge (\mathcal{S}_1 \cup \mathcal{S}_2) \in \mathfrak{S}$
$\qquad \wedge \mathcal{S}_1 \prec \mathcal{S}_2$
parse $(\text{'seeds'}, z_1, h_1) \leftarrow SS_{\mathcal{S}_1}$
parse $(\text{'seeds'}, z_2, h_2) \leftarrow SS_{\mathcal{S}_1}$
$(z, c) \leftarrow \text{TKDF}.\text{Derive}(z_1, z_2)$
$h \leftarrow H_{\text{pub}}(h_1, h_2, c)$
$C \leftarrow (h_1, h_2, c)$
$SS \leftarrow (\text{'seeds'}, z, h)$
return (SS, C)

$\underline{\text{DeriveKS}(\mathcal{S}, SS_{\mathcal{S}})}$

req $\mathcal{S} \in \mathfrak{S}$
if $\exists e \in \mathbb{N} \setminus \mathcal{B} : \mathcal{S} = \{e\}$ **then**
$\quad$**parse** $(\text{'seeds'}, s, h) \leftarrow SS_{\mathcal{S}}$
$\quad k \leftarrow \text{TKDF}.\text{Key}(s)$
$\quad KS_{\mathcal{S}} \leftarrow (\text{'keys'}, k, h)$
else
$\quad$**parse** $(\text{'seeds'}, z, h) \leftarrow SS_{\mathcal{S}}$
$\quad t \leftarrow \text{TKDF}.\text{Trapdoor}(z)$
$\quad KS_{\mathcal{S}} \leftarrow (\text{'keys'}, t, h)$
return $KS_{\mathcal{S}}$

$\underline{\text{Expand}(\mathcal{S}, KS_{\mathcal{S}}, C_{\mathcal{S}}, \mathcal{S}_1, \mathcal{S}_2)}$

req $\mathcal{S}, \mathcal{S}_1, \mathcal{S}_2 \in \mathfrak{S} \wedge (\mathcal{S}_1 \cup \mathcal{S}_2) = \mathcal{S}$
$\qquad \wedge \mathcal{S}_1 \prec \mathcal{S}_2$
parse $(\text{'keys'}, t, h) \leftarrow KS_{\mathcal{S}}$
parse $(h_1, h_2, c) \leftarrow C_{\mathcal{S}}$
req $h = H_{\text{pub}}(h_1, h_2, c)$
$(t_1, t_2) \leftarrow \text{TKDF}.\text{Invert}(c, t)$
$KS_1 \leftarrow (\text{'keys'}, t_1, h_1)$
$KS_2 \leftarrow (\text{'keys'}, t_2, h_2)$
return (KS_1, KS_2)

$\underline{\text{Recover}(e, KS_{\{e\}}, C_{\{e\}})}$

if $e \in \mathcal{B}$ **then**
$\quad$**parse** $(\text{'keys'}, t, h) \leftarrow KS_{\{e\}}$
$\quad$**parse** $(h', \bot, c) \leftarrow C_{\{e\}}$
$\quad$**req** $h' = h \wedge h = H_{\text{pub}}(e)$
$\quad (k, t') \leftarrow \text{TKDF}.\text{Invert}(c, t)$
$\quad$**req** $t' = \text{TKDF}.\text{Trapdoor}(\bar{z})$
else
$\quad$**parse** $(\text{'keys'}, k, h) \leftarrow KS_{\{e\}}$
$\quad$**req** $h = H_{\text{pub}}(e)$
return k

Fig. 12. A description of the I-CKS scheme based on a (symmetric) TKDF. Note that for brevity we did not include the public hash key pub as part of every state. Furthermore, in Compact and Expand we assume $\mathcal{S}_1 \prec \mathcal{S}_2$; the general protocol is obtained by invoking the algorithm with reversed arguments in the other case.

where q_{Init} and q_{Compact} denote bounds on the number of Init *and* Compact *calls.*

We now establish security of the TKDF scheme. A proof of the following theorems is presented in the full version of this work.

Theorem 5. *The iterative CKS scheme from Fig. 12 satisfies real-or-random security of keys if the TKDF is secure. More concretely,*

$$\text{Adv}_{G_{\text{I-CKS}}^{\text{Keys-RoR}}}(\mathcal{A}) \leq (q_{\text{Init}} + q_{\text{Compact}}) \cdot \left(\text{Adv}_{G_{\text{TKDF}}^{\text{KeyRand}}}(\mathcal{A}_1) + \text{Adv}_{G_{\text{TKDF}}^{\text{TdRand}}}(\mathcal{A}_2) \right.$$
$$\left. + \text{Adv}_{G_{\text{TKDF}}^{\text{IND-CPA-OT}}}(\mathcal{A}_3) \right)$$

where q_{Init} and q_{Compact} denote bounds on the number of Init *and* Compact *calls.*

Theorem 6. *The iterative CKS scheme from Fig. 12 satisfies integrity if the hash function $H_{\text{pub}}(\cdot)$ is collision-resistant and the TKDF correct and has deterministic ciphertexts. More concretely,*

$$\text{Adv}_{G_{\text{I-CKS}}^{\text{Integrity}}}(\mathcal{A}) \leq (q_{\text{Init}} + q_{\text{Compact}}) \cdot \left(\text{Adv}_{G_{\text{TKDF}}^{\text{Corr}}}(\mathcal{A}') + \text{Adv}_{G_{\text{H}}^{\text{CR}}}(\mathcal{A}'') \right)$$

where q_{Init} and q_{Compact} denote bounds on the number of Init *and* Compact *calls.*

Variants. The above scheme is secure against an active adversary controlling the server (i.e., delivering wrong ciphertexts) and malicious insiders making parties use inconsistent and adversarially chosen seeds. We state some simple observations about weaker security models. First, we note that hash functions are only needed to protect against an active attacker delivering wrong ciphertexts.

Corollary 3. *Standard-model I-CKS against honest-but-curious servers, i.e., without integrity, can be built from dual-PRFs. Additionally, the TKDF ciphertexts do not need to be deterministic.*

Second, we observe that one-time TKDF security suffices when considering outsider security only.

Lemma 1. *Outsider-secure I-CKS, e.g., when restricting the adversary to submit $s_e = \bot$ for the Init oracle can be built from one-time secure TKDF and, therefore, from one-way function only.*

5   CKS from Iterative CKS

In this section, we sketch how to turn any iterative CKS scheme into a regular (standard model) CKS scheme. This provides a template for how to use iterative CKS for a group of parties to outsource a sequence of keys that are derived from seeds. Note that the key derivation U.Key(e, s) for the standard-model CKS scheme is just the one from the iterative CKS scheme, i.e., DeriveKey(s_e, e). If we target insider security or security against malicious servers, we require the iterative CKS scheme to have deterministic ciphertexts. For the weakest passive security notion, any I-CKS scheme suffices. In the following, we consider the stronger security notion (and briefly discuss the weaker variants).

Server State and Algorithms. The server just implements a bulletin board BB. Each entry stores an I-CKS ciphertext C and is indexed by a collision-resistant hash thereof, i.e., $BB[H_{pub}(C)] = C$. Importantly, the server will compute the hash themselves. This ensures that a malicious insider cannot overwrite a valid ciphertext of another user, or preemptively set a position of the bulletin board to something invalid. For a passively secure CKS protocol, we can index the bulletin board using a description of the set $\mathfrak{S}$ instead, i.e., $BB[\mathcal{S}] = C_{\mathcal{S}}$. The server will then store the first ciphertext sent for each $\mathcal{S}$ and ignore all subsequent ones.

As we will see, U.Upload will just send a set of ciphertexts that the server will store. Similarly, U.Erase, U.Grant, U.Accept, and U.retrieve will query the bulletin board for a subset of positions. We note that for our specific iterative CKS scheme, this could be a bit optimized: as $C = (h_1, h_2, c)$ the user would not need to (iteratively) query for h_1 and h_2 and the server could just (recursively) include all ciphertexts needed by the protocol.

User State. The client state depends on the graph $\mathcal{D}ag_{\mathfrak{S}}$. More specifically, the client stores the seeds state $SS_{\mathcal{S}}$ or the keys state $KS_{\mathcal{S}}$ for a subset of nodes. We say that for a node $\mathcal{S} \in \mathfrak{S}$, we say that $SS_{\mathcal{S}}$ is *derivable* if either (a) $SS_{\mathcal{S}}$ is directly stored or (b) it is derivable for at least one of the parent nodes of $\mathcal{S}$. We say that $KS_{\mathcal{S}}$ is derivable if either (a) $KS_{\mathcal{S}}$ is stored, (b) $SS_{\mathcal{S}}$ is stored, or (c) the keys state is derivable for at least one of the parent nodes of $\mathcal{S}$. We say that $SS_{\mathcal{S}}$ and $KS_{\mathcal{S}}$ are *indirectly* derivable if the respective options (a) do not apply. The user state is then maintained subject to the following invariant, where additional seeds states or keys states are purged.

Invariant 1 (Compactness). *A node $\mathcal{S} \in \mathfrak{S}$ only has the seeds state SS stored if it's not indirectly derivable. Analogously, it only has the keys state KS stored if it's not indirectly derivable. (This in particular means that no node stores both seeds and keys state.)*

Appending Seeds. When appending a seed s_{e} for an epoch e, the algorithm proceeds in three steps:

1. Create a seeds state $SS_{\{e\}} \leftarrow \text{Init}(e, s_e)$ for the leaf node.
2. Iteratively derive seeds along all paths starting at the leaf node using Compact. That is, for any of the nodes along a path, if the seeds states of both children are known, then use Compact to compute the one for this node.
3. Purge any seeds states or keys states that violate compactness.

The upload state st_{up} then contains all ciphertexts produced by Compact. We assume those ciphertexts to be deterministic (which does not violate security; for instance, our TKDF uses a one-time IND-CPA secure encryption scheme) then they can simply be sent to the server.

Retrieving Keys. To retrieve the key k_{e} for an epoch e, U.retrieve identifies a node on a path from the leaf $\mathcal{S} = \{e\}$ for which either the seeds state or the keys state is stored. (If multiple candidates exist, pick e.g. the one the shortest distance from the leaf.) If it is a seeds state, use DeriveKS to derive the respective keys state. Then the algorithm uses Expand and finally Recover to retrieve the key. For each step, request the necessary ciphertexts from the server. To retrieve the keys for an entire subset of epochs share $\subset \mathbb{N}$, the above steps are generalized by identifying a suitable set of (internal) nodes that cover share with respect to reachability in $\mathcal{D}ag_{\mathfrak{S}}$.

Delegation. Delegation works similarly to the retrieval of keys, except that internal nodes are not further expanded if all or their descendants are part of the set of delegated keys share $\subset \mathbb{N}$. Note that the delegation message can either contain keys states $KS_{\mathcal{S}}$ or $SS_{\mathcal{S}}$. The latter is preferable if it is stored by the delegating user. The accepting user receives those elements. If they already know keys for any epoch $e \in$ share they check consistency by recovering the key k_{e} according to their own state and the retrieved one. Afterward, they add the obtained information to their local state and compact it.

Erasing Keys. Erasure works like self-delegation of the epochs not erased, except that no consistency checks are needed. That is, if a user knows—i.e., can currently recover—keys for epochs $\mathcal{K}$ and wants to erase share, then they self-delegate $\mathcal{K} \setminus$ share.

Functionality and Efficiency. Observe that the efficiency of the above scheme inherently depends on $\mathcal{D}ag_\mathfrak{S}$. As a result, the choice of $\mathcal{D}ag_\mathfrak{S}$ also dictates which sets of epochs can be efficiently retrieved, delegated, and erased as formalized by $\mathcal{R}$, $\mathcal{G}$, and $\mathcal{E}$. We do not make this connection fully formal but only highlight some of the relations.

– *Small covers.* For the user state to be compact, there need to exist nodes that "cover" large sets of epochs, i.e., for which a large set of leaf nodes are descendants. For instance in the all-or-nothing scheme in [7] there exist nodes that cover $[1, n]$, for any n, and in the interval scheme nodes that cover $[2^i, 2^i + 2^j - 1]$ for $i, j \in \{0, 1, \ldots\}$.
  Similarly, delegation and erasure only work efficiently for subsets share $\subset \mathbb{N}$ that have a small cover, sub-linear in share.
– *Limited out degrees.* If a node in $\mathcal{D}ag_\mathfrak{S}$ has too many ancestors on disjoint paths, then U.Append becomes inefficient. In [7], both schemes used a structure where each node has out-degree 1.
– *Short diameter.* If $\mathcal{D}ag_\mathfrak{S}$ contains too long path, then U.Append or U.retrieve can become inefficient. This is, for instance, the reason why the all-or-nothing scheme cannot support efficient (i.e., sub-linear) retrieval of individual keys.

Security and Correctness. The security of the standard-model CKS scheme reduces directly to the respective properties of the iterative CKS scheme. In other words, the integrity of the CKS scheme follows from the integrity of the I-CKS scheme, and analogously for pseudorandomness and correctness. The proof of the following theorem follows by inspection.

Theorem 7 (Informal). *The above sketched CKS scheme is correct and secure if the iterative CKS scheme is correct and secure. The same furthermore applies to the variants considering passive security or security against an honest-but-curious server.*

Legacy Compatibility. Observe that the result from Theorem 3 carries over to the entire CKS scheme.

Corollary 4. *Assume there is an E2E-secure application that provides a secure KDF, that we can evaluate on one additional input, to derive keys from initial seeds (and does not otherwise use the seeds). Then we can build a CKS scheme that is compatible with said application that recovers the keys.*

In particular, this class of legacy applications contains common schemes such as the Double Ratchet or MLS, which use a key schedule based on HKDF.

References

1. Bagherzandi, A., Jarecki, S., Saxena, N., Lu, Y.: Password-protected secret sharing. In: Chen, Y., Danezis, G., Shmatikov, V. (eds.) ACM CCS 2011, pp. 433–444. ACM Press (2011). https://doi.org/10.1145/2046707.2046758

2. Bellare, M.: New proofs for NMAC and HMAC: security without collision resistance. J. Cryptol. **28**(4), 844–878 (2015). https://doi.org/10.1007/s00145-014-9185-x

3. Bellare, M., Keelveedhi, S., Ristenpart, T.: Message-locked encryption and secure deduplication. In: Johansson, T., Nguyen, P.Q. (eds.) EUROCRYPT 2013. LNCS, vol. 7881, pp. 296–312. Springer, Heidelberg (2013). https://doi.org/10.1007/978-3-642-38348-9_18

4. Bellare, M., Lysyanskaya, A.: Symmetric and dual PRFs from standard assumptions: a generic validation of an HMAC assumption. Cryptology ePrint Archive, Report 2015/1198 (2015). https://eprint.iacr.org/2015/1198

5. Brzuska, C., Cornelissen, E., Kohbrok, K.: Security analysis of the MLS key derivation. In: 2022 IEEE Symposium on Security and Privacy, pp. 2535–2553. IEEE Computer Society Press (2022). https://doi.org/10.1109/SP46214.2022.9833678

6. Das, P., Hesse, J., Lehmann, A.: DPaSE: distributed password-authenticated symmetric-key encryption, or how to get many keys from one password. In: Suga, Y., Sakurai, K., Ding, X., Sako, K. (eds.) ASIACCS 2022, pp. 682–696. ACM Press (2022). https://doi.org/10.1145/3488932.3517389

7. Dodis, Y., Jost, D., Marcedone, A.: Compact key storage. In: Reyzin, L., Stebila, D. (eds.) Advances in Cryptology - CRYPTO 2024, pp. 75–109. Springer, Cham (2024). https://doi.org/10.1007/978-3-031-68379-4_3

8. Douceur, J., Adya, A., Bolosky, W., Simon, P., Theimer, M.: Reclaiming space from duplicate files in a serverless distributed file system. In: Proceedings 22nd International Conference on Distributed Computing Systems, pp. 617–624 (2002). https://doi.org/10.1109/ICDCS.2002.1022312

9. Fábrega, A., Pérez, C.O., Namavari, A., Nassi, B., Agarwal, R., Ristenpart, T.: Injection attacks against end-to-end encrypted applications. In: 2024 IEEE Symposium on Security and Privacy (SP), pp. 85–85. IEEE Computer Society, Los Alamitos (2024). https://doi.org/10.1109/SP54263.2024.00082. https://doi.ieeecomputersociety.org/10.1109/SP54263.2024.00082

10. Jafargholi, Z., Kamath, C., Klein, K., Komargodski, I., Pietrzak, K., Wichs, D.: Be adaptive, avoid overcommitting. In: Katz, J., Shacham, H. (eds.) CRYPTO 2017. LNCS, vol. 10401, pp. 133–163. Springer, Cham (2017). https://doi.org/10.1007/978-3-319-63688-7_5

11. Jarecki, S., Kiayias, A., Krawczyk, H., Xu, J.: Highly-efficient and composable password-protected secret sharing (or: How to protect your bitcoin wallet online). In: 2016 IEEE European Symposium on Security and Privacy (EuroS&P), pp. 276–291. IEEE Computer Society, Los Alamitos (2016). https://doi.org/10.1109/EuroSP.2016.30. https://doi.ieeecomputersociety.org/10.1109/EuroSP.2016.30

12. Jarecki, S., Krawczyk, H., Resch, J.K.: Updatable oblivious key management for storage systems. In: Cavallaro, L., Kinder, J., Wang, X., Katz, J. (eds.) ACM CCS 2019, pp. 379–393. ACM Press (2019). https://doi.org/10.1145/3319535.3363196

13. Kamath, C., Klein, K., Pietrzak, K., Walter, M.: The cost of adaptivity in security games on graphs. In: Nissim, K., Waters, B. (eds.) TCC 2021. LNCS, vol. 13043, pp. 550–581. Springer, Cham (2021). https://doi.org/10.1007/978-3-030-90453-1_19
14. Krawczyk, H.: Cryptographic extraction and key derivation: the HKDF scheme. In: Rabin, T. (ed.) CRYPTO 2010. LNCS, vol. 6223, pp. 631–648. Springer, Heidelberg (2010). https://doi.org/10.1007/978-3-642-14623-7_34

Bruisable Onions: Anonymous Communication in the Asynchronous Model

Megumi Ando[1]([⊠]) [iD], Anna Lysyanskaya[2] [iD], and Eli Upfal[2] [iD]

[1] Tufts University, Medford, MA, USA
mando@cs.tufts.edu
[2] Brown University, Providence, RI, USA

Abstract. In onion routing, a message travels through the network via a series of intermediaries, wrapped in layers of encryption to make it difficult to trace. Onion routing is an attractive approach to realizing anonymous channels because it is simple and fault tolerant. Onion routing protocols provably achieving anonymity in realistic adversary models are known for the synchronous model of communication so far. In this paper, we give the first onion routing protocol that achieves anonymity in the asynchronous model of communication. The key tool that our protocol relies on is the novel cryptographic object that we call *bruisable* onion encryption. The idea of bruisable onion encryption is that even though neither the onion's path nor its message content can be altered in transit, an intermediate router on the onion's path that observes that the onion is delayed can nevertheless slightly damage, or bruise it. An onion that is chronically delayed will have been bruised by many intermediaries on its path and become undeliverable. This prevents timing attacks and, as we show, yields a provably secure onion routing protocol in the asynchronous setting.

1 Introduction

The ability to communicate anonymously is an increasingly vital component of digital life and citizenship. From Iranian protesters wishing to safely to inform the world what is happening in the streets of Tehran, to Russian citizens trying to communicate with outside media, anonymity gives people all over the world a chance to exercise their fundamental rights without fear of repercussions. Practical tools such as Tor [DMS04] (i.e., "The onion router," inspired by Chaum's onion routing idea [Cha81] described below) or VPNs have a lot of room for improvement. Both are easily blocked, and neither guarantees privacy even from the network adversary (e.g., a standard model for a resourceful ISP- or AS-level adversary) [MD05, SEV+15, WSJ+18, Rop21].

A communications protocol is anonymous [ALU21] if for any pair of input vectors (σ_0, σ_1) that differ only on the inputs and outputs[1] of honest parties (e.g.,

---

[1] Here, by "output" of a party P we mean a set of messages $\{m\}$ such that some party P' receives (m, P) as part of its input. I.e. P' intends to send m to P.

© International Association for Cryptologic Research 2025
E. Boyle and M. Mahmoody (Eds.): TCC 2024, LNCS 15364, pp. 476–507, 2025.
https://doi.org/10.1007/978-3-031-78011-0_16

Alice sends to Bob in σ_0 and to Charlie in σ_1), the adversary (whose capabilities vary depending on the adversarial model) cannot tell from interacting with the honest nodes in a protocol run whether the input was σ_0 or σ_1.[2]

The goal of research on onion routing [Cha81,Cha88,CL05,vdHLZZ15, ALU18,KBS20,ALU21,AL21,KHRS21,ACLM22] is to achieve this definition in the presence of a malicious adversary corrupting a fraction of the participants, with a communication- and computation- efficient, fault-tolerant and decentralized protocol. In an onion routing protocol, to send a message to Bob, Alice first picks a sequence of intermediary parties $I_1, \ldots, I_{\ell-1}$ and then forms a layered cryptographic object called an onion using the message and the routing path $(I_1, \ldots, I_{\ell-1}, \text{Bob})$. Alice then sends the onion to the first intermediary I_1 on the routing path who peels off just the outermost layer of the onion (i.e., processes the onion) and sends the peeled onion O_2 to the next party I_2 on the routing path, I_2 peels O_2 and sends the peeled onion O_3 to I_3, and so on. This procedure continues until Bob receives the message from Alice.

In an onion routing protocol that uses standard cryptographic onions [CL05], even a powerful adversary who can corrupt (and "look into" or even control) some of the parties cannot link an honest party's incoming onion to its outgoing onion. This lack of transparency allows for shuffling onions when they are batch-processed at an honest party [RS93,BFT04,IKK05,ALU18].

Technical Challenge: Asynchronous Onion Routing. In recent years, several protocols were presented as provably secure yet practical solutions [CBM15, vdHLZZ15,TGL+17,KCDF17,ALU18,ALU21]. However, all these protocols' security analysis requires synchronous communication. In the synchronous communications setting, time progresses in rounds, and message transmissions are lossless and instantaneous. While modeling communications in this way makes designing and analyzing anonymity protocols more tractable, it is somewhat of a cheat. Currently deployed anonymity protocols, such as Tor [DMS04] and Loopix [PHE+17], are known to be vulnerable to traffic analysis attacks [MD05,SEV+15,WSJ+18,AMWB23] that exploit the asynchronous nature of communication in the real world.

Constructing a solution for the asynchronous setting is challenging because the adversary can easily influence the traffic flow, for example, by mounting a BGP interception attack [SEV+15], so that a targeted message arrives with an expected and observable delay. (See Sect. 1.1 for an example of a timing attack on a preciously known solution.) The adversary can do this even if the onions are batch-processed and even if we are willing to pay a cost by increasing the latency and/or volume of dummy traffic. As we explain below, this attack method breaks the anonymity of every known protocol designed and proven secure for the synchronous setting; this is a problem that is not trivially fixable by using sychronizers (which assume no failures) or clock synchronization algorithms (which guarantees that most if not all of the honest parties are synchronized) [Lyn96].

---

[2] Alternative definitions of anonymity exist [BKM+13,KBS+19], but we will be referring to the standard cryptographic definition here.

In this paper, we present the first **provably anonymous** onion routing protocol for the asynchronous communications setting.

1.1 Towards a Solution: A Discussion

Starting Point: Solution for the Synchronous Setting. Let $\mathcal{P} = \{P_1, P_2, \ldots, P_N\}$ be participants in an onion routing protocol. In the synchronous setting, it is possible to achieve anonymity against the passive adversary (who observes all network traffic and passively observes at a constant fraction of the parties) by thoroughly shuffling together the messages. Consider the simple protocol, Π_p. In this protocol, each participant $P \in \mathcal{P}$ receives a message-recipient pair (m, R) as input and forms a single onion using m and the routing path $(I_1, \ldots, I_{\ell-1}, R)$ where each $I_j \in \mathcal{P}$ is chosen independently and uniformly at random from a set of servers (some subset of the participants). Ando, Lysyanskaya, and Upfal showed that Π_p is anonymous so long the expected server load (the number of onions that each server processes in a round) and the round complexity are both at least polylogarithmic in the security parameter [ALU18].

However, Π_p is not anonymous against the active adversary (who controls the corrupted parties and can make them deviate from the protocol). The active adversary can direct corrupted nodes to drop onions and learn who is talking with whom by observing who receives fewer messages than anticipated. For example, if the first intermediary on the routing path from Alice to her recipient (Bob) is adversarial (which happens with constant probability), the adversary can drop Alice's onion in the first round and learn who Alice's recipient is when Bob doesn't receive a message in the end. Additionally, the adversary can direct corrupted parties to replace onions formed by honest senders with ones they generate. In such an attack, the adversary can trick the honest parties into believing that onions (sufficiently) shuffle when they don't since the adversary knows what the onions they generate look like. We can circumvent this attack using checkpoint dummy onions [ALU18, ALU21]. For cryptographic reasons explained in Preliminaries, the adversary cannot forge checkpoint onions; thus, if the adversary drops too many onions, each party independently realizes this when they observe correspondingly far fewer checkpoint onions.

A natural idea for an onion routing protocol is for each party P_i to form a random number (polylogarithmic in the security parameter) of checkpoint onions (each for a randomly chosen recipient), along with an onion bearing the actual payload for the P_i's recipient. In such a scenario, one of two things can happen. If the adversary drops many onions, then the protocol aborts when the parties detect this from the missing checkpoint onions; otherwise, the checkpoint onions provide sufficient cover for the message-bearing onions. That is, as shown by Ando, Lysyanskaya, and Upfal, this protocol (dubbed Π_a – "a" for "active adversary") is differentially private from the active adversary corrupting at most a constant fraction of the parties in the synchronous model [ALU18]. Specifically, the adversarial views corresponding to any two neighboring input vectors that differ only on honest parties' inputs and outputs, are statistically similar as defined by standard differential privacy; see Definition 1.

Defining Local Clocks for Π_a. To adapt Π_a for the asynchronous model, we must contend with the fact that there are no global rounds. Each party may, however, keep a local clock. Our first idea is that a participant P_i advances his clock based on some way of satisfying himself that most of the onions that meant to arrive in the current epoch (according to the local clock) have already arrived; say some τ fraction of them. We can use checkpoint onions to achieve this. Additionally, P_i sends out (processed) onions in batches only when it advances its clock. This way, these onions are guaranteed to shuffle since P_i processes onions only once a sufficient number of them have been received.

Motivation for Bruisable Onions. Unfortunately, this approach does not quite work. As mentioned previously, in the asynchronous setting, the main challenge is preventing the adversary from mounting a timing attack that compromises anonymity. For example, the adversary can delay one of Alice's onions but not delay or drop any other onion. Assuming that the protocol is running continuously, this will ensure that the adversary will observe a late onion delivery at Alice's recipient with (non-negligibly) higher probability than at any other recipient. So, what we want is a mechanism that drops onions that are (chronically) running behind. A first attempt at accomplishing this might be to mark a layer in the middle of each onion. E.g., if the onion O consists of layers $O = (O_1, \ldots, O_\ell)$ for the parties on the routing path $(I_1, \ldots, I_{\ell-1}, R)$, then peeling $O_{\ell/2}$ reveals that it is layer $\ell/2$. The processing party $I_{\ell/2}$ can use this information to determine whether $O_{\ell/2}$ is late relative to its local clock. The problem with this approach is that when $I_{\ell/2}$ is adversarial, $I_{\ell/2}$ may not drop $O_{\ell/2}$.

Our solution is to use cryptographic means to allow a few different intermediaries (polylogarithmic in the security parameter in number and randomly chosen) to each "bruise" an onion if it arrives late. The idea is that an onion that is chronically running behind will be bruised many times and will not reach its final destination (its recipient) because it will have accumulated too many bruises for the innermost onion to be recoverable.

Note that the parties don't immediately drop onions upon late arrivals. If they did, the protocol – even under good network conditions – would not deliver any message. This is because τ fraction of the onions arriving on time "in epoch $j-1$" doesn't translate into each party eventually receiving τ fraction of the expected j^{th} layer checkpoint onions. More likely, some parties will not receive enough checkpoint onions to progress, and the protocol will stall. So, what we want is for onions to be "bruisable;" that is, a party can "bump" an onion so that the damage to it (the "bruise") shows up only later. Within the context of our protocol, a "bruised" onion can travel on, unnoticed by others that it has been modified in any way until it reaches the last intermediary $I_{\ell-1}$ at which point the damage is finally discovered. If the damage is great enough, $I_{\ell-1}$ is unable to extract the identity of the recipient from the bruised onion.

Our Contributions. Our list of contributions in this paper are as follows:

- **A new cryptographic primitive: bruisable onion encryption.** See Sect. 3 for the formal definition including the correctness and security prop-

erties. Other than for the application to onion routing in the asynchronous
model, bruisable encryption is interesting because it is an example of an
encryption scheme that is both malleable in a way that's useful in an application (since an intermediary is explicitly allowed to bruise an onion) and
yet provide security against an adversary who is allowed to adaptively query
participants to process onions of its choice.

- **A construction of a bruisable onion encryption scheme: Tulip Onion
  Encryption Scheme (TOES).** See Sect. 4 for the construction, and Sect. 4.2
  for the proof of security. Specifically, we show that TOES is bruisable-onion
  secure (Definition 2) assuming the existence of CCA2-secure public encryption schemes with tags, block ciphers, and collision-resistant hash functions
  (Theorem 1).
- **The first provably anonymous onion routing protocol in the asynchronous setting: Π_t ("t" for "tulip" or "threshold").** See Sect. 5 for
  the construction and Sect. 6 for the analysis of our protocol. We show that
  for small constant corruption rate (e.g., 10%) and drop rate (e.g., 10%), our
  protocol simultaneously guarantees: a positive constant message delivery rate
  (Theorem 2) and $(\epsilon, \mathsf{negl}(\lambda))$-differential privacy from the active adversary for
  any constant $\epsilon > 0$ (Theorem 3 and Corollary 1). The anonymity guarantee
  holds for any corruption rate strictly less than 50% (and any drop rate). The
  message delivery guarantee holds even in the extreme case where the adversary chooses to bruise every onion layer it receives. In the setting where the
  adversary is maliciously bruising onions only at 5% of the parties and not
  dropping onions, the guaranteed message delivery rate is over 0.85.

2   Preliminaries

For a natural number n, $[n]$ is the set $\{1, \ldots, n\}$. For a set Set, we denote the
cardinality of Set by $|\mathsf{Set}|$, and item $\leftarrow_{\$}$ Set is an item from Set chosen uniformly
at random. If Dist is a probability distribution over Set, item $\leftarrow$ Dist is an item
sampled from Set according to Dist. For an algorithm Algo, output $\leftarrow$ Algo(input)
is the (possibly probabilistic) output from running Algo on input. A function
$f(\lambda)$ of the security parameter λ is said to be negligible if it decays faster than
any inverse polynomial in λ. An event occurs with overwhelming probability
(abbreviated w.o.p.) if its complement occurs with negligible probability in the
security parameter λ. Similar to the convention that $\mathsf{poly}(\lambda)$ means polynomially
bounded in λ, we introduce an analogous notation $\mathsf{polylog}(\lambda)$, by which we mean
polylogarithmically bounded in λ. Throughout the paper, we use the symbol $\perp$
to indicate a dummy object (such as a dummy message or a dummy recipient).

2.1   Modeling the Problem

System Parameters. Let λ be the security parameter. We assume that every
quantity of the system, including the number N of participants, is bounded by
a polynomial in λ.

Parties. Let Parties $= \{P_1, \ldots, P_N\}$ be the static set of participants. We assume a setting with a public-key infrastructure (PKI); more precisely, we assume that every participant knows the set Parties and the public key $\mathsf{pk}(P)$ associated with each party $P \in$ Parties.

Inputs. The input σ_i for each party $P_i \in$ Parties is a set of message-recipient pairs, that is, $\sigma_i = \{(m_{i,1}, R_{i,1}), \ldots, (m_{i,l}, R_{i,l})\}$, where the inclusion of a message-recipient pair $(m_{i,j}, R_{i,j})$ means that P_i is instructed to send the message $m_{i,j}$ to the recipient $R_{i,j}$. By the input vector, we mean the vector $\sigma = (\sigma_1, \ldots, \sigma_N)$ containing everyone's inputs.

   Two input vectors σ_0 and σ_1 are neighboring if they are the same except that the honest destinations for a pair of messages originating at honest parties are swapped. More precisely, there exist $(m, P_u) \in \sigma_{0,i}$ and $(m', P_v) \in \sigma_{0,j}$ such that $\sigma_{1,i} = (\sigma_{0,i} \cup \{(m', P_v)\}) \setminus \{(m, P_u)\}$, $\sigma_{1,j} = (\sigma_{0,j} \cup \{(m, P_u)\}) \setminus \{(m', P_v)\}$, and $\sigma_{1,k} = \sigma_{0,k}$ for all $k \in [N] \setminus \{i, j\}$.

Adversary Model. The adversary is active, meaning that in addition to observing all network traffic, the adversary can also corrupt and control up to a constant χ fraction of the parties. The adversary chooses which parties to corrupt prior to the execution of the protocol. For our result on guaranteed message delivery, we further assume that the adversary may drop (at corrupted parties) up to a constant γ fraction of the honest parties' message packets.

Message Schedule. The N parties form an asynchronous network, connected pairwise by authenticated channels. Every message on the channels is guaranteed eventual delivery after an arbitrarily long delay chosen by the adversary. This setting is in keeping with how the message schedule is modeled in Byzantine consensus literature [Bra84, CR93]; here, the adversary maintains a queue of messages that have yet to be delivered and decides which messages are delivered next. Combined with the adversary's power to control the corrupted parties to behave arbitrarily, this has the net effect that the adversary fixes the message schedule and additionally can add/drop messages at corrupted nodes.

Adversarial View. Given a communications protocol Π, adversary $\mathcal{A}$, and input vector σ, let $\mathsf{View}^{\Pi, \mathcal{A}}(\sigma)$ denote the adversary's view in a run of Π on input σ in the presence of the adversary $\mathcal{A}$; that is, $\mathsf{View}^{\Pi, \mathcal{A}}(\sigma)$ is a random variable representing everything that the adversary can observe including the network traffic and the states and computations of the corrupted parties.

2.2   Definition of Anonymity

The notion of anonymity that we use in this paper is standard (computational) differential privacy:

Definition 1 ((ϵ, δ)-DP [DMNS06]). *A communication protocol Π is (ϵ, δ)-differentially private if for every adversary $\mathcal{A}$ and every pair of neighboring inputs*

σ_0 and σ_1 and every set $\mathcal{V}$ of adversarial views,

$$\Pr\left[\mathsf{View}^{\Pi,\mathcal{A}}(\sigma_0) \in \mathcal{V}\right] \le e^\epsilon \Pr\left[\mathsf{View}^{\Pi,\mathcal{A}}(\sigma_1) \in \mathcal{V}\right] + \delta.$$

We say that Π is computationally (ϵ, δ)-differentially private [MPRV09] if the above bound holds for all polynomially bounded adversaries.

2.3   Checkpoint Onions

A technical challenge in realizing anonymity from the active adversary is preventing the adversary from gleaning information by biasing the number of onions that arrive at the recipients. For example, the adversary who suspects that Alice is sending a message to Bob can try to confirm their suspicion by dropping the onion originating from Alice before it shuffles with other onions.

In prior work, Ando, Lysyanskaya, and Upfal introduced a cryptographic tool called *checkpoint onions* [ALU18] (a.k.a. dummy onions). These onions do not carry a payload; instead, their purpose is to provide cover traffic for "real" payload-carrying onions. They allow intermediary parties to locally determine if the active adversary is disrupting network traffic and causing onions to get dropped. This is accomplished as follows: Each pair of networked parties (the end-users as well as the intermediaries) (P_i, P_j) is associated with a secret key $s_{i,j}$ for a pseudorandom function $F_{s_{i,j}}$. This function mostly evaluates to something other than 0^k, but if $F_{s_{i,j}}(x) = y \ne 0^k$, then party P_i expects to receive an onion containing the string y in round r. I.e. party P_j must form an onion such that, at round r, this onion will reach party P_i and contain the string y. If party P_i is expecting such an onion but does not receive it, it means that the active adversary has disrupted the network.

3   Bruisable Onion Encryption

We introduce a new cryptographic primitive called bruisable onion encryption. Unlike in standard onion encryption, in bruisable onion encryption, each mixer on the routing path has a choice to add an extra bit of information to the onion: to ding (bruise) the onion or not. If the onion sustains too many bruises (i.e., a sufficient number of the mixers on the path bruise the onion), then the identity of the recipient R and the innermost onion O_ℓ for the recipient become unrecoverable.

Another difference between standard onion encryption and bruisable onion encryption is the addition of a new type of intermediaries, called *gatekeepers*. A bruisable onion O travels along its routing path $(M_1, \ldots, M_{\ell_1}, G_1, \ldots, G_{\ell_2}, R)$ consisting of some ℓ_1 mixers, followed by some ℓ_2 gatekeepers and the recipient R. While the role of the mixers is to batch-process the onion (along with other onions) or to bruise it, gatekeepers are responsible for routing the onion all the way to the recipient only if the mixers didn't bruise it too much. Without gatekeepers, an onion that arrives at the last mixer M_{ℓ_1} on its routing path with the threshold number X of bruises (with X bruises the onion can be delivered to the recipient; with $X + 1$, it cannot) can be processed by M_{ℓ_1} with or without further bruising. If M_{ℓ_1} is adversarial, it can try both and learn the number of bruises. So, we need gatekeepers to prevent this line of attack; an honest gatekeeper will detect that this is the same onion except for the number of bruises, and will not process it a second time.

A bruisable onion encryption scheme consists of the following algorithms:

KeyGen takes the security parameter 1^λ and the name of a party P as input, and outputs a public key pair $(\mathsf{pk}(P), \mathsf{sk}(P))$, i.e., $(\mathsf{pk}(P), \mathsf{sk}(P)) \leftarrow \mathsf{KeyGen}(1^\lambda, P)$.

FormOnion takes a (fixed length) message m, a routing path $\boldsymbol{P} = (M_1, \ldots, M_{\ell_1}, G_1, \ldots, G_{\ell_2}, R)$ consisting of ℓ_1 "mixers" and ℓ_2 "gatekeepers," the public keys of the parties in $\boldsymbol{P}$, and a sequence $\boldsymbol{y} = (y_1, \ldots, y_{\ell_1+\ell_2})$ of metadata where the metadata string y_i is intended for the ith processing party on the routing path. (The metadata conveyed to each intermediary is a useful component of an onion routing protocol: it allows the sender to communicate something about the onion to the processing party. For example, in our protocol in Sect. 5, the metadata is the pseudorandom nonces in the checkpoint onions.) FormOnion outputs a list of lists of onions $\boldsymbol{O} = (\boldsymbol{O}_1, \ldots \boldsymbol{O}_\ell)$ where $\ell = \ell_1 + \ell_2 + 1$. That is, letting $\mathsf{pk}(\boldsymbol{P})$ denote the public keys of the parties in $\boldsymbol{P}$, $\boldsymbol{O} = (\boldsymbol{O}_1, \ldots \boldsymbol{O}_\ell) \leftarrow \mathsf{FormOnion}(m, \boldsymbol{P}, \mathsf{pk}(\boldsymbol{P}), \boldsymbol{y})$.

In standard onion encryption as defined by Camenisch and Lysyanskaya [CL05], FormOnion outputs a list of $onions$, $O = (O_1, \ldots, O_\ell)$. This list is called the "evolution of the onion" because it is how the onion should evolve as it travels along the routing path; each O_i is the onion that the ith intermediary should receive and process.

In bruisable onion encryption, the evolution depends on if and when the onion gets bruised. Accordingly, FormOnion outputs a list of lists of onions, $(\boldsymbol{O}_1, \ldots \boldsymbol{O}_\ell)$, where each list $\boldsymbol{O}_i$ contains all possible variations of the ith onion layer. The first list $\boldsymbol{O}_1 = (O_1)$ contains just the onion for the first mixer. For $2 \le i \le \ell_1$, the list $\boldsymbol{O}_i$ contains i options, $\boldsymbol{O}_i = (O_{i,0}, \ldots, O_{i,i-1})$; each $O_{i,j}$ is what the ith onion layer should look like with j prior bruises. For $\ell_1 + 1 \le i \le \ell_1 + \ell_2$, the list $\boldsymbol{O}_i$ contains $\ell_1 + 1$ options, depending on the total bruising from the mixers. The last list $\boldsymbol{O}_\ell = (O_{\ell_1+\ell_2+1})$ contains just the innermost onion for the recipient.

Note that the routing path $\boldsymbol{P}$ may start and/or end with a sub-path consisting of dummy parties, in which case FormOnion outputs onions for only the non-dummy routing parties. For example, if the routing path is $(\perp, \perp, P_3, P_4, P_5, \perp, \ldots, \perp)$, FormOnion outputs $(\boldsymbol{O}_3, \boldsymbol{O}_4, \boldsymbol{O}_5)$.

PeelOnion takes the secret key $\mathsf{sk}(P)$ of the processing party P and an onion O. Its output is (i, y, O', P') where i is the position of the party P on the onion's routing path and y is the metadata, while (O', P') falls into one of four cases: if P is not the recipient, (O', P') is either (1) the peeled onion O' and its next destination P' or (2) $(\perp, \perp)$ if the onion is malformed or too bruised; if P is the recipient, then $P' = \perp$, while O is either (3) a message m or (4) $\perp$. $(i, y, O', P') \leftarrow \mathsf{PeelOnion}(\mathsf{sk}(P), O)$.

BruiseOnion is an algorithm that allows an intermediary to damage the onion, or *bruise* it. This option is only available to the mixers on the routing path, i.e., to the first ℓ_1 intermediaries. BruiseOnion takes as input the secret key $\mathsf{sk}(P)$ of the party P and the onion O to be bruised as input, and outputs a bruised onion O' to send to its next destination, $O' \leftarrow \mathsf{BruiseOnion}(\mathsf{sk}(P), O)$.

3.1 Correctness Definition

If a bruisable onion is processed only either by running the PeelOnion algorithm or the BruiseOnion algorithm at every hop, we require that it should travel along the intended routing path specified by the sender. Further, if the bruising isn't too bad (i.e., it falls under some threshold θ), the gatekeepers should be able to recover the innermost onion and the recipient; otherwise, routing the onion through $(G_1, \ldots, G_{\ell_2})$ should reveal the empty final destination $\perp$. We formalize this intuition below.

Let $\Sigma = (\mathsf{KeyGen}, \mathsf{FormOnion}, \mathsf{PeelOnion}, \mathsf{BruiseOnion})$ be a bruisable encryption scheme. Let Parties be any set of participants. For each $P_i \in$ Parties, let $(\mathsf{pk}(P_i), \mathsf{sk}(P_i))$ be the key pair generated by running KeyGen on P_i. Let m be any message from the message space; let $\boldsymbol{P} = (M_1, \ldots, M_{\ell_1}, G_1, \ldots, G_{\ell_2}, R)$ be any list of parties in Parties; let $\boldsymbol{y} = (y_1, \ldots, y_{\ell_1 + \ell_2})$ be any sequence of metadata. Let $\ell = \ell_1 + \ell_2 + 1$. $(O_1, \ldots, O_\ell)$ is the result of running FormOnion on m, $\boldsymbol{P}$, the public keys $\mathsf{pk}(\boldsymbol{P})$ of the parties in $\boldsymbol{P}$, and $\boldsymbol{y}$, i.e., $\boldsymbol{O} = (O_1, \ldots O_\ell) \leftarrow \mathsf{FormOnion}(m, \boldsymbol{P}, \mathsf{pk}(\boldsymbol{P}), \boldsymbol{y})$.

We say that Σ is correct with respect to the threshold $0 < \theta \leq 1$, the number ℓ_1 of mixers, and the number ℓ_2 of gatekeepers if the following are satisfied:

- **Correct peeling and bruising.** For $1 \leq i < \ell_1 + \ell_2$, $1 \leq j \leq |O_i|$, let (i', y, O, P) be the output of $\mathsf{PeelOnion}(\mathsf{sk}(P_i), O_{i,j})$. Then $i' = i$, $y = y_i$, $O = O_{i+1,j}$, and $P = P_{i+1}$. In other words, when processing an onion, the mixer correctly recovers its position i in the list of processing parties, its metadata y_i, the onion $O_{i+1,j}$ to send forth with the same amount of bruising, and its destination P_{i+1}. Moreover, for $1 \leq i \leq \ell_1$, $1 \leq j \leq |O_i|$, let O' be the output of $\mathsf{BruiseOnion}(\mathsf{sk}(P_i), O_{i,j})$. Then $O' = O_{i+1,j+1}$.
- **Correct gatekeeping.** For $i = \ell_1 + \ell_2$, $1 \leq j \leq \ell_1 + 1$, let (i', y, O, P) be the output of $\mathsf{PeelOnion}(\mathsf{sk}(P_i), O_{i,j})$. If $j \leq \theta\ell_1$, then $i' = i$, $y = y_i$, $O = O_\ell$, and $P = R$. In other words, when processing an onion that is not too bruised, the last gatekeeper correctly recovers its position $i = \ell_1 + \ell_2$ in the list of processing parties, its metadata y_i, the onion O_ℓ to send forth, and the recipient R. However, if $j > \theta\ell_1$, then $i' = i$, $y = y_i$, $O = \perp$, and $P = \perp$. In other words, if the onion is too bruised, the honest gatekeeper still recovers its metadata but not the onion to send forth or the next destination.
- **Correct message.** Peeling the innermost onion layer recovers the intended message, i.e., $\mathsf{PeelOnion}(\mathsf{sk}_R, O_\ell) = (\ell, \perp, m, \perp)$.

3.2 Security Definition

We define security for bruisable onion encryption using the following game, BrOnSHH (which stands for bruisable onion security with an honest mixer and an honest gatekeeper). BrOnSHH is parameterized by the security parameter 1^λ, the adversary $\mathcal{A}$, the bruisable onion encryption scheme $\Sigma = (\mathsf{KeyGen}, \mathsf{FormOnion}, \mathsf{PeelOnion}, \mathsf{BruiseOnion})$, and the system parameters θ (which controls how much bruising can be tolerated) and ℓ_1 and ℓ_2 (which specify the numbers of mixers and gatekeepers for an onion's path).

The challenger controls an honest mixer, an honest gatekeeper, and an honest recipient. The challenge onion might or might not be intended for the honest recipient, but it must be routed through the honest mixer and gatekeeper. The adversary controls all intermediaries other than the honest mixer, the honest gatekeeper, and the honest recipient.

- **Setup:** The adversary $\mathcal{A}$ and the challenger $\mathcal{C}$ set up the parties' keys.
  1. The adversary $\mathcal{A}$ sends the names of the honest mixer P_m, the honest gatekeeper P_g, the honest recipient P_r, and the adversarial parties Bad; and the public keys $\mathsf{pk}(\mathsf{Bad})$ of the adversarial parties to the challenger $\mathcal{C}$.
  2. For each honest party $P \in \{P_m, P_g, P_r\}$, $\mathcal{C}$ generates a key pair $(\mathsf{pk}(P), \mathsf{sk}(P)) \leftarrow \mathsf{KeyGen}(1^\lambda, P)$ and sends $\mathsf{pk}(P_m), \mathsf{pk}(P_g), \mathsf{pk}(P_r)$ to $\mathcal{A}$.
- **First Query Phase:**
  3. $\mathcal{A}$ can direct an honest party to peel or bruise an onion by submitting queries to peel (resp. bruise) an onion O on behalf of an honest party $P \in \{P_m, P_g, P_r\}$, in which case $\mathcal{C}$ responds with the output of $\mathsf{PeelOnion}(\mathsf{sk}(P), O)$ (resp. $\mathsf{BruiseOnion}(\mathsf{sk}(P), O)$).
- **Challenge Phase:** $\mathcal{A}$ picks the parameters of the challenge onion, and $\mathcal{C}$ replies with the challenge onion O_1.
  4. $\mathcal{A}$ sends to $\mathcal{C}$: the message m; the routing path $\boldsymbol{P}$ where $P_m = M_{i_1}$ in position $i_1 \leq \ell_1$ is one of the mixers $(M_1, \ldots, M_{\ell_1})$, $P_g = G_{i_2 - \ell_1}$ in position $\ell_1 < i_2 \leq \ell_1 + \ell_2$ is one of the gatekeepers $(G_1, \ldots, G_{\ell_2})$, and the recipient R may be P_r; and the sequence $\boldsymbol{y} = (y_1, \ldots, y_{\ell_1 + \ell_2})$ of metadata.
  5. $\mathcal{C}$ samples a bit $b \leftarrow\!\!\$ \{0, 1\}$.
     - If $b = 0$, $\boldsymbol{Q} = \boldsymbol{P}$. $\boldsymbol{z} = \boldsymbol{y}$.
     - If $b = 1$, $\boldsymbol{Q} = (M_1, \ldots, M_{i_1-1}, P_m, \overbrace{\bot, \ldots, \bot}^{\ell_1+\ell_2+1-i_1})$. $\boldsymbol{z} = (y_1, \ldots, y_{i_1}, \overbrace{\bot, \ldots, \bot}^{\ell_1+\ell_2+1-i_1})$.

     $\mathcal{C}$ returns the first onion O_1 in the output from running $\mathsf{FormOnion}$ on m, $\boldsymbol{Q}$, the public keys $\mathsf{pk}(\boldsymbol{Q})$, and $\boldsymbol{z}$, i.e., $((O_1), \boldsymbol{O}_2, \ldots, \boldsymbol{O}_{\ell_1+\ell_2+1}) \leftarrow \mathsf{FormOnion}(m, \boldsymbol{Q}, \mathsf{pk}(\boldsymbol{Q}), \boldsymbol{z})$.
- **Second query phase:** $\mathcal{A}$ is again allowed to submit queries to have an onion peeled or bruised by an honest party P.
  6. If $b = 0$; or the request *isn't*
     - to peel or bruise an onion in $\boldsymbol{O}_{i_1}$ as the mixer P_m (query type 1),
     - to peel an onion in $\boldsymbol{O}_{i_2}$ as an honest gatekeeper P_g (type 2), or

- to peel the onion $O_{\ell_1+\ell_2+1}$ as the recipient P_r (type 3);

the challenger processes the request by running the scheme's algorithm (as before).

7. If the query *is* type 1, 2, or 3 (defined above), and *this is not the first request of this type*; the challenger responds with an error message.
8. Else $(b = 1)$:
   i. **Query type 1:** the query is to the mixer P_m to peel or bruise an onion $O_{i_1,j} \in \mathbf{O}_{i_1}$. $\mathcal{C}$ runs FormOnion on the dummy message $\perp$ and the path after P_m to P_g, i.e.,

$$Q_{i_1+1 \to i_2} = (\overbrace{\perp, \ldots, \perp}^{i_1}, M_{i_1+1}, \ldots, M_{\ell_1}, G_1, \ldots, G_{i_2-\ell_1-1}, P_g, \overbrace{\perp, \ldots, \perp}^{\ell_1+\ell_2+1-i_2})$$

$$z_{i_1+1 \to i_2} = (\overbrace{\perp, \ldots, \perp}^{i_1}, y_{i_1+1}, \ldots, y_{i_2}, \overbrace{\perp, \ldots, \perp}^{\ell_1+\ell_2+1-i_2})$$

$$O_{i_1+1 \to i_2} \leftarrow \mathsf{FormOnion}(\perp, Q_{i_1+1 \to i_2}, \mathsf{pk}(Q_{i_1+1 \to i_2}), z_{i_1+1 \to i_2}).$$

Suppose the query was to peel (resp. bruise); $\mathcal{C}$ sets bruisecount $= j$ (resp. bruisecount $= j + 1$) and returns $(i_1, y_{i_1}, O_{i_1+1,0}, M_{i_1+1})$ to $\mathcal{A}$ where $O_{i_1+1,0}$ is the first onion in the output $O_{i_1+1 \to i_2} = ((O_{i_1+1,0}, \ldots, O_{i_1+1,i_1}), O_{i_1+2}, \ldots, O_{i_2})$ of FormOnion. (bruisecount is the number of bruises that the onion acquires before reaching M_{i_1}. The challenger keeps track of this information to ensure that the innermost onion is recoverable only if it should be.)

   ii. **Query Type 2:** the query is to the gatekeeper P_g to peel an onion $O_{i_2,j} \in \mathbf{O}_{i_2}$. Let $m' = m$ if $R = P_r$ or bruisecount $+j \le \theta \ell_1$; otherwise, let $m' = \perp$. Let $R' = R$ if bruisecount $+j \le \theta \ell_1$; otherwise, let $R' = \perp$. $\mathcal{C}$ runs FormOnion on the message m' and the routing path consisting of the gatekeepers after P_g and the recipient R', i.e.,

$$Q_{i_2+1 \to} = (\overbrace{\perp, \ldots, \perp}^{i_2}, G_{i_2-\ell_1+1}, \ldots, G_{\ell_2}, R')$$

$$z_{i_2+1 \to} = (\overbrace{\perp, \ldots, \perp}^{i_2}, y_{i_2+1}, \ldots, y_{\ell_1+\ell_2})$$

$$O_{i_2+1 \to} \leftarrow \mathsf{FormOnion}(m', Q_{i_2+1 \to}, \mathsf{pk}(Q_{i_2+1 \to}), z_{i_2+1 \to})$$

$\mathcal{C}$ returns $(i_2, y_{i_2}, O_{i_2+1,0}, M_{i_2+1})$ to $\mathcal{A}$ where $O_{i_2+1,0}$ is the first onion in the output $O_{i_2+1 \to} = ((O_{i_2+1,0}, \ldots, O_{i_2+1,i_1}), O_{i_2+2}, \ldots O_{\ell_1+\ell_2+1})$ of FormOnion.

   iii. **Query type 3:** the query is to the recipient P_r to peel the onion $O_{\ell_1+\ell_2+1}$. $\mathcal{C}$ returns the message m.
- At the end, $\mathcal{A}$ outputs a guess b' for the bit b and wins if $b' = b$.

We define bruisable-onion security as follows.

Definition 2. *A bruisable onion encryption scheme Σ is bruisable-onion secure for parameters θ, ℓ_1, ℓ_2 if there is a negligible function $\nu : \mathbb{N} \mapsto \mathbb{N}$ such that every p.p.t. adversary $\mathcal{A}$ wins the game $\mathsf{BrOnSHH}(1^\lambda, \mathcal{A}, \Sigma, \theta, \ell_1, \ell_2)$ with advantage at most $\nu(\lambda)$, i.e., $\left| \Pr\left[\mathcal{A} \text{ wins } \mathsf{BrOnSHH}(1^\lambda, \mathcal{A}, \Sigma, \theta, \ell_1, \ell_2) \right] - \frac{1}{2} \right| \le \nu(\lambda)$.*

Intuition for the Security Definition. Our definition captures the idea that if the onion encryption scheme is secure, the adversary cannot determine any meaningful information about an onion that is "hidden behind an honest party:"

- **Layers for parties up to the honest mixer.** The adversary cannot distinguish between the scenario where the challenger forms O_1 as specified by the adversary (case $b = 0$) from the scenario where the challenger forms O_1 without using the message m, the routing path after P_m, or the metadata corresponding to the path after P_m (case $b = 1$). See step 5 of the security game.

- **Layers for Parties after the Honest Mixer up to the Honest Gatekeeper.** The adversary cannot tell whether the peeled (resp. bruised) version O' of the challenge onion $O_{i_1,j}$ for P_m is obtained by peeling (resp. bruising) $O_{i_1,j}$ as specified by the adversary (case $b = 0$), or if O' is a fresh onion formed information-theoretically independently of the message m, the path and metadata up to P_m, the path and metadata after P_g, or the amount of bruising that the onion has incurred so far (case $b = 1$). See step 6 and step 8i of the security game.

- **Layers for the parties after the honest gatekeeper.** If the challenge onion incurs more than (resp. at most) the threshold number ($\theta\ell_1$) of bruises, then the innermost onion and the recipient are unrecoverable (resp. remain recoverable). In this event, the adversary cannot tell whether the onion O'' that the gatekeeper P_g produces as the peeled version of its challenge onion $O_{i_2,j}$ was obtained by peeling $O_{i_2,j}$ (case $b = 0$), or if O' is a fresh onion information-theoretically independent of the bruising so far and, if $R = P_r$, the message m (resp. the message m, the recipient R, and the bruising so far). See step 6 and step 8ii of the security game.

- **Replay attacks.** Note that in both the real world and in our security game, the adversary can send an onion for processing to the same honest party more than once. A feature of bruisable onions is that the adversary can send different versions of the same onion, corresponding to different amounts of bruising. We cannot guarantee security if more than one version is processed according to the protocol since that would reveal how bruised an onion was when it got to the adversary. Thus, in our security game, the challenger will not process the same onion more than once, and this includes differently bruised versions of the same onion. An honest participant in a protocol that uses bruisable onion encryption needs to keep state information and do the same. It is important that a replayed onion be detectable even if it's a different version. In our construction in Sect. 5, different versions of the same layer of the same onion share a symmetric key; storing this key would enable one to identify and reject replayed onions.

Remark. Although we do not provide a UC functionality for bruisable onion encryption in this paper, we note that our definition here should be sufficient to UC-realize any reasonable modeling of such a functionality in the spirit of the ideal functionalities for (regular, non-bruisable) onion encryption of prior work [CL05, AL21]. In this approach, an ideal functionality for bruisable onion encryption would form onions on behalf of honest parties piece-wise. Given a routing path P, the "segments of P" are the subpaths of P that partition P in such a way that each subpath forms a contiguous sequence of adversarial parties followed by a single honest party (or no honest party if the segment is that last subpath containing an adversarial recipient). For example, letting capitalized parties denote honest parties, for the path $P = (P_1, p_2, p_3, P_4, P_5, p_6, P_7)$, the segments are (P_1), (p_2, p_3, P_4), (P_5), and (p_6, P_7). The ideal functionality forms the onion layers for each segment separately, without knowledge of the rest of the path, the message, or the bruise count so far; this ensures that onion layers across different segments are information-theoretically unrelated to each other. For each FormOnion query, the ideal functionality keeps track of which onion layers are part of the onion via an internal table or dictionary, as well as the cumulative bruise count. Our security definition would ensure that, whether the onion layers are formed correctly (as in the real world) or piecemeal by the simulator, no adversary can distinguish; the proof that a bruisable onion encryption scheme satisfying our definition would UC-realize such a functionality would follow the outline of the proof of Ando and Lysyanskaya [AL21], adjusted for the addition of bruises and gatekeepers. Seen in this way, the UC composition theorem allows us to analyze the anonymity of our onion routing protocol separately from the security of the onions.

4   Tulip Onion Encryption Scheme

Our onion encryption scheme produces a type of onion that we call tulip bulbs. A tulip bulb consists of three components: the header H containing the routing information, the content C containing the payload, and the "sepal" S for peeling the penultimate onion layer. (The sepal is the outermost part of a flower that protects the flower while it is still a bud. In our construction, the sepal protects the rest of the content by "absorbing" the bruising.)

Below, we explain on a high level how a tulip bulb is formed and how it will be processed; this will be helpful for understanding our overall construction. Given a party P, let $(\mathsf{pk}(P), \mathsf{sk}(P))$ denote the public key and secret key of P; and let O_i denote the tulip bulb (one of the $|O_i|$ options) for the ith party on the routing path $(M_1, \ldots, M_{\ell_1}, G_1, \ldots, G_{\ell_2}, R)$ of length $\ell = \ell_1 + \ell_2 + 1$.

The Header H_i. In our construction, for each i, all variations in O_i have the same header H_i and content C_i; the only differences are in the sepals. The header $H_i = (E_i, B_i)$ consists of the ciphertext E_i and the rest of the header B_i. E_i is an encryption under $\mathsf{pk}(P_i)$ of the tuple (i, y_i, k_i) where i is the position, y_i is the metadata, and k_i is the layer key. For $1 \leq i < \ell - 1$, B_i is an encryption under k_i of the identity of the next processor P_{i+1} and header H_{i+1} of the tulip bulb O_{i+1} that will be sent to P_{i+1}.

The header $H_{\ell-1}$ for the last gatekeeper G_{ℓ_2} is somewhat different. The ciphertext $E_{\ell-1}$ decrypts to the key $k_{\ell-1}$; using $k_{\ell-1}$, G_{ℓ_2} can process the sepal. If the sepal is not too damaged and processing it yields the bulb master key K, then the rest of the header $B_{\ell-1}$ can be decrypted under K, yielding the identity of the recipient R and the header H_ℓ for R.

The Content C_i. The content C_i is an encryption under the layer key k_i of the content C_{i+1} of O_{i+1}. If P_i is the recipient, then it is an encryption of the message.

The Sepal S_i. The sepal S_i looks different depending on whether the processor P_i is a mixer M_i or a gatekeeper G_j for $j = i - \ell_1$. Specifically:

- For $1 \le i \le \ell_1$, the processor P_i is the mixer M_i. The sepal S_i received by M_i consists of $\ell_1 - i + 2$ blocks, $(S_{i,1}, \ldots, S_{i,\ell_1-i+2})$. For example, if $\ell_1 = 3$, then the first mixer's tulip bulb has four sepal blocks, the second mixer has three, and the last mixer receives a bulb with only two sepal blocks.

  Suppose we want a bulb to be irrevocably lost after d bruises, but $d - 1$ bruises are tolerated.[3] For the first mixer M_1, the first d sepal blocks are encryptions of the bulb master key K, salted and wrapped in layers of symmetric encryption keyed by $k_1, \ldots, k_{\ell-1}$. The rest of the sepal blocks are salted encryptions of 0 (dummies), also salted and wrapped in layers of symmetric encryption keyed by $k_1, \ldots, k_{\ell-1}$. Let $S_{1,1}, \ldots, S_{i,\ell_1+1}$ denote these sepal blocks. I.e., letting "$\langle K \rangle$" denote a sepal block that contains the bulb master key, and "$\langle 0 \rangle$," a dummy block,

$$S_1 = (S_{1,1}, \ldots, S_{1,\ell_1+1}) = (\overbrace{\langle K \rangle, \ldots, \langle K \rangle}^{d \text{ times}}, \overbrace{\langle 0 \rangle, \ldots, \langle 0 \rangle}^{\ell_1-d+1 \text{ times}})$$

To process the tulip bulb without bruising it, M_1 peels a layer of encryption from all the blocks in S_1 and then "drops" the first block from the right. So the sepal S_2 for the next processing party retains the same number of blocks with the bulb master key, i.e.,

$$\text{unbruised } S_2^{(1)} = (S_{2,1}, \ldots, S_{2,\ell_1}) = (\overbrace{\langle K \rangle, \ldots, \langle K \rangle}^{d \text{ times}}, \overbrace{\langle 0 \rangle, \ldots, \langle 0 \rangle}^{\ell_1-d \text{ times}})$$

To bruise the tulip bulb, M_1 forms S_2 by dropping the first block from the *left* instead, i.e.,

$$\text{bruised } S_2^{(2)} = (S_{2,1}, \ldots, S_{2,\ell_1}) = (\overbrace{\langle K \rangle, \ldots, \langle K \rangle}^{d-1 \text{ times}}, \overbrace{\langle 0 \rangle, \ldots, \langle 0 \rangle}^{\ell_1-d+1 \text{ times}})$$

In general, to peel the sepal $S_i = (S_{i,1}, \ldots, S_{i,\ell_1-i+2})$ without bruising it, the ith mixer M_i drops the rightmost sepal block S_{i,ℓ_1-i+2}. To bruise the sepal, M_i drops the leftmost sepal block $S_{i,1}$. Carrying out this procedure ensures that the only remaining sepal block in S_{ℓ_1+1} for the last gatekeeper G_1 contains the bulb master key K if and only if the number of times that the sepal was

---

[3] In our onion routing protocol in Sect. 5, d is set so that the innermost tulip bulb is recoverable when $\le \theta$ fraction of the bruisable layers are bruised, i.e., $d = \theta \ell_1$.

bruised is at most $d - 1$. So, the i options for the sepal S_i correspond to the i distinct $\max(\ell_1 + 2 - i, 1)$ contiguous blocks (with the appropriate number of encryptions peeled off) from $\overbrace{\langle K \rangle, \ldots, \langle K \rangle}^{d \text{ times}}, \overbrace{\langle 0 \rangle, \ldots, \langle 0 \rangle}^{\ell_1 - d + 1 \text{ times}}$.

Note that if the mixer is not honest, they can rearrange the blocks or modify the sepal in an "illegal" way outside the prescribed procedures outlined above. Verification hashes are stored in the header of the tulip bulb to allow honest parties to detect when this happens. Care must be taken that these verification hashes not reveal anything about the possible sepals other than their validity. See the remark below. Moreover, if the last few mixers on the routing path are all adversarial, the adversary can attempt to "open" more than one sepal block, which could potentially leak some information about prior bruisings. The honest gatekeepers prevent this from happening since honest parties will process a tulip bulb only once, and a tulip bulb with a repeating key k_i will be treated as a different variant of the same tulip bulb. See Sect. 4.1 for how the sepal blocks and the verification hashes are formed.

- For $\ell_1 + 1 \leq i < \ell$, the processor P_i is the gatekeeper $G_{i-\ell_1}$. The sepal S_i received by $G_{i-\ell_1}$ is either the encryption of the bulb master key K under symmetric keys $k_i, \ldots, k_\ell$ (if the tulip bulb wasn't bruised too much), or the encryption of 0 (if it was). P_i processes the sepal by peeling a layer of encryption: S_{i+1} is the decryption of S_i under k_i.
- The last gatekeeper G_{ℓ_2} either recovers the master key K from S_ℓ or discovers that it cannot be recovered. If K is recovered, then G_{ℓ_2} can process the rest of the header H_ℓ.

Remark on How to Incorporate Verification Hashes. Mixer M_i receives onion $O_i = (H_i, C_i, S_i)$, where S_i is one of i sepal candidates $S_i^{(1)}, \ldots, S_i^{(i)}$, as described above. In order to ensure that the sepal does not get corrupted in transit but in fact corresponds to the sepal prepared by the sender, our construction includes (in lexicographic order) the values $\{h(S_i^{(j)})\}_{1 \leq j \leq i}$ for a collision-resistant hash function h. Let us go over what can go wrong with if we include only these hashes and how to fix it. First, note that a collision-resistant hash function may still leak information about its pre-image. In a contrived example, $h(S_i^{(j)})$ may leak the position of the first occurrence of the binary string "tulip fever" in its pre-image, if any, and still remain a collision-resistant hash function. Recall that $S_i^{(j+1)}$ is obtained by dropping the first λ bits of $S_i^{(j)}$ and concatenating some additional random bits to the end; in the event that $S_i^{(j)}$ contains the string "tulip fever" in position p, $S_i^{(j+1)}$ will contain "tulip fever" in position $p - \lambda$. Thus, our contrived hash function would leak that $S_i^{(j+1)}$ is the sepal for the onion that has one additional bruising compared to one with sepal $S_i^{(j)}$.

Luckily, we show that this is not a problem if we also include additional dummy hashes of strings that could never be proper sepals. The idea is to create one random, dummy sepal block that is never included in any sepals, but that will be hashed with valid sepal blocks in a circular manner. See Formal description.

4.1   Formal Description

Our onion encryption scheme, Tulip Onion Encryption Scheme (TOES), builds on standard cryptographic primitives: a CCA2-secure public key encryption scheme with tags (KeyGen, Enc, Dec),[4] a block cipher, and a collision-resistant hash function h. In the description below, let "$\{\cdot\}_k$" denote symmetric encryption under the key k, and let "$\} \cdot \{_k$" denote symmetric decryption under k. This notation is consistent with prior work on onion encryption schemes, namely [CL05, AL21, ACLM22].

The onion encryption scheme's key generation algorithm is just KeyGen. We assume a public key infrastructure where the keys (for at least the honest parties) are supplied by running KeyGen. For each party P, let $(\mathsf{pk}(P), \mathsf{sk}(P))$ denote the public-key and secret-key for party P.

Below, we describe how to form a tulip bulb containing the message m for the routing path $(M_1, \ldots, M_{\ell_1}, G_1, \ldots, G_{\ell_2}, R)$, and the metadata $\boldsymbol{y} = (y_1, \ldots, y_{\ell-1})$

Generating the Tulip Keys. To begin with, we pick layer keys $k_1, \ldots, k_\ell$ and master key K independently and uniformly at random from the key space of our symmetric encryption scheme. As explained earlier, each k_i will be used to encrypt the onion layer for the ith processing party on the routing path; the master key is needed to recover the eventual recipient.

Forming the First Sepal. S_1. We describe how to compute the sepal portion of the tulip bulb O_1 for the first mixer M_1 on the routing path. The sepal S_1 consists of d key-blocks (the $\langle K \rangle$-blocks) $S_{1,1}, \ldots, S_{1,d}$, as well as $\ell_1 - d + 1$ null-blocks (the $\langle 0 \rangle$-blocks) $S_{1,d+1}, \ldots, S_{1,\ell_1+1}$.

Each key-block $\langle K \rangle$ is the bulb master key K, salted and encrypted under $k_1, \ldots, k_{\ell-1}$; that is,

$$S_{1,j} = \{\ldots \{K, s_j\}_{k_{\ell-1}} \ldots\}_{k_1} \qquad \forall 1 \le j \le d$$

where $s_j \leftarrow_\$ \mathsf{SaltSpace}$ is a random value from an appropriately large salt space. The procedure for forming a null-block $\langle 0 \rangle$ is essentially the same except that we wrap 0 instead of the value K in layers of encryption, i.e.,

$$S_{1,j} = \{\ldots \{0, s_j\}_{k_{\ell_1+1}} \ldots\}_{k_1} \qquad \forall d + 1 \le j \le \ell_1 + 1.$$

If the sepal S_i was not processed correctly (i.e., not just peeled or bruised), then the processing party P_i should be able to detect this. To that end, we store verification hashes (i.e., hashes of all possible values that a correctly formed and processed S_i can take on, plus a few dummy hash values), denoted by $\boldsymbol{A}_i$, in the header. These hash values are computed as follows: First, let $T_{i,j}$ denote the sepal block $S_{1,j}$ without the $i-1$ outermost encryption layers, and let T_{i,ℓ_1+2} be a dummy sepal block (i.e., a truly random string of length the number of bits in a sepal block, wrapped in layers of encryptions keyed by $k_i, \ldots, k_{\ell-1}$), which we will call the "clasp" for reasons that will become evident in the next sentence.

---

[4] See [CS98] for the original formal description of encryption with tags.

Each hash value $A_{i,j}$ is the hash of one of the $l = \max(1, \ell_1 + 2 - i)$ contiguous blocks on the ring (really a "bracelet") $(T_{i,1}, \ldots, T_{i,\ell_1+2})$ where the block after the clasp T_{i,ℓ_1+2} is $T_{i,1}$. Letting $A'_i = \{A_{i,0}, A_{i,1}, \ldots, A_{i,\ell_1+2}\}$, $\boldsymbol{A}_i$ is the vector, *sorted in lexicographic order*, of the hashes of the elements of A'_i, i.e., letting $T_{\ell-1,\ell_1+2} \leftarrow\$ \{0,1\}^{|S_{1,1}|}$,

$$T_{i,j} = \}\ldots\}S_{1,j}\{k_1\cdots\{k_{i-1} \qquad\qquad \forall j \in [\ell_1 + 1]$$
$$T_{i,\ell+2} = \{\ldots\{T_{i,\ell_1+2}\}k_{\ell-1}\cdots\}k_i$$
$$A_{i,j} = h\left(T_{i,(j \mod \ell_1+2)}, \ldots, T_{i,(j+l-1 \mod \ell_1+2)}\right) \qquad \forall j \in [\ell_1 + 2]$$
$$\boldsymbol{A}_i = \mathsf{Sort}(\{A_{i,0}, A_{i,1}, \ldots, A_{i,\min(i,\ell_1+1)}\})$$

Note that computing the hashes can be accomplished efficiently as the number $|\boldsymbol{A}_i|$ of hashes in each onion layer is $\ell_1 + 2$. See the next section for details on where the hashes are stored. The hash values constitute all possible ranges on the bracelet; this prevents the adversarial intermediary (a mixer or a gatekeeper prior to the last gatekeeper) from learning any information about how bruised the onion is so far. The clasp (and resulting dummy values) are needed to enable detection of any illegal rearrangement of the sepal blocks.

Forming the Header and Content for the Last Onion Layer. After forming the sepal S_1, we obtain the header H_1 and content C_1 via a recursive process. First, we form the last onion layer for the ℓth party (the recipient R). The content C_ℓ is just the encryption of the message m under the key k_ℓ, i.e., $C_\ell = \{m\}_{k_\ell}$. We form the tag t_ℓ by taking the hash of C_ℓ, i.e., $t_\ell = h(C_\ell)$. The tag ensures that R can peel the last layer only if they receive an onion with the correct header and content. The header H_ℓ is completed by taking the encryption under the key $\mathsf{pk}(R)$ of the role "Recipient," the hop-index $\ell + 1$, and the key k_ℓ, i.e.,

$$E_\ell = \mathsf{Enc}(\mathsf{pk}(R), t_\ell, (\mathsf{Recipient}, \ell, k_\ell))$$
$$H_\ell = E_\ell$$

Forming the Header and Content for Penultimate Onion Layer. Next, we form the penultimate layer $H_{\ell-1}, C_{\ell-1}$ for the last gatekeeper G_{ℓ_2}. The content $C_{\ell-1}$ is the encryption of C_ℓ under the master key K, i.e.,

$$C_{\ell-1} = \{C_\ell\}_K = \{\{m\}_{k_\ell}\}_K$$

Block $B_{\ell-1,1}$ is the encryption of E_ℓ and the identity of the recipient R under the master key K, i.e.,

$$B_{\ell-1,1} = \{R, E_\ell\}_K$$

The header $H_{\ell-1}$ consists of blocks $E_{\ell-1}, B_{\ell-1,1}$ where $E_{\ell-1}$ is the encryption under the public key $\mathsf{pk}(G_{\ell_2})$ and the appropriate tag $t_{\ell-1}$ of the role

"LastGatekeeper," the hop-index $\ell - 1$, the nonce $y_{\ell-1}$, the verification hashes $\boldsymbol{A}_{\ell-1}$, and the sepal layer key $k_{\ell-1}$, i.e.,

$$t_{\ell-1} = h(B_{\ell-1,1}, \ldots, B_{\ell-1,\ell-1}, C_{\ell-1})$$
$$E_{\ell-1} = \mathsf{Enc}(\mathsf{pk}(G_{\ell_2}), t_{\ell-1}, (\text{LastGatekeeper}, \ell - 1, y_{\ell-1}, \boldsymbol{A}_{\ell-1}, k_{\ell-1}))$$
$$H_{\ell-1} = (E_{\ell-1}, B_{\ell-1,1}, \ldots, B_{\ell-1,\ell-1})$$

Forming the Outer Layers. For $1 \leq i \leq \ell - 2$, the header and content H_i, C_i builds on the header and content of the previous layer H_{i+1}, C_{i+1}, similar to how the penultimate layer builds on the last layer. Here, E_i is the encryption of the processing party's role (either "Mixer" or "Gatekeeper"), the hop-index i, the nonce y_i, the verification hashes $\boldsymbol{A}_i$, and the key k_i. See below:

$$C_i = \{C_{i+1}\}_{k_i}$$

Letting I_{i+1} be the $i + 1^{th}$ party on the path,

$$B_{i,1} = \{I_{i+1}, E_{i+1}\}_{k_i}$$
$$B_{i,j} = \{B_{i+1,j-1}\}_{k_i} \qquad\qquad \forall 2 \leq j \leq \ell - j + 1$$
$$t_i = h(B_{i,1}, \ldots, B_{i,\ell-1}, C_i)$$
$$E_i = \mathsf{Enc}(\mathsf{pk}(P_i), t_i, (\text{Role}, i, y_i, \boldsymbol{A}_i, k_i))$$
$$H_i = (E_i, B_{i,1}, \ldots, B_{i,\ell-1})$$

See Fig. 1 below for a pictorial description of the tulip bulb O_1.

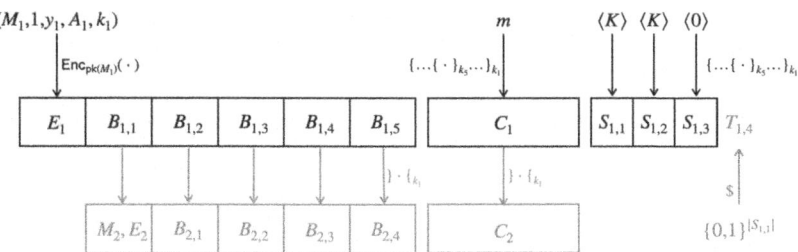

Fig. 1. A pictorial description of how an onion is formed using TOES. The verification hashes A_1 for M_1 are the hashes $h(S_{1,1}, S_{1,2}, S_{1,3})$, $h(S_{1,2}, S_{1,3}, T_{1,4})$, $h(S_{1,3}, T_{1,4}, S_{1,1})$, and $h(T_{1,4}, S_{1,1}, S_{1,2})$ in lexicographical order, where $T_{1,4} \leftarrow\$ \{0,1\}^{|S_{1,1}|}$.

Forming an Onion with an Incomplete Path. We form an onion for a path that begins and/or ends with the empty path, e.g., $(\perp, \perp, P_3, P_4, P_5, \perp, \ldots, \perp)$, by setting the intermediary party for the empty locations (the $\perp$'s) to be the sender; and if the recipient is $\perp$, the sepal blocks are all dummy sepal blocks $\langle 0 \rangle$. In this case, the algorithm outputs only the onion vectors for the parties corresponding to non-empty locations on the path.

Remark on the Onion Size. Recall that ℓ_1 is the number of mixers on a routing path, and ℓ_2 is the number of gatekeepers. Each onion consists of a content block, a number of sepal blocks, and a number of header blocks. The length of each message block is just the length of a message (let us call this ℓ_m). Each onion layer consists of at most $\ell_1 + 1$ sepal blocks and $\ell_1 + \ell_2 + 1$ header blocks, where the length of each sepal block is the length of each layer key (so, roughly λ), and the length of each header block is dominated by the size of the verification hashes in a layer (so, roughly $\mathcal{O}(\lambda\ell_1)$). Thus, the overall size of a tulip bulb is $\mathcal{O}(\lambda(\ell_1^2 + \ell_2)) + \ell_m$.

4.2   Proof of Security

Here, we summarize our proof that our construction satisfies the definition of security provided in Definition 2.

Theorem 1. *Tulip Onion Encryption Scheme is bruisable-onion secure, assuming the existence of CCA2-secure public key encryption schemes with tags, block ciphers, and collision-resistant hash functions.*

Proof (Proof Idea). We first provide a hybrid argument for the case where the challenge onion is too bruised to recover the innermost onion. Proofs for the other cases (when the onion is recoverable and/or when the recipient is honest) are given after the proof of this first case.

Below, we describe a sequence of hybrid experiments $\mathsf{Hybrid}_0, \ldots, \mathsf{Hybrid}_{18}$ and provide a brief explanation (in color) of why each pair of consecutive experiments consists of indistinguishable scenarios. (See full version of the paper for more details.) Recall that in the security game BrOnSHH, the honest mixer is M_{i_1}, sitting in position $1 \le i_1 \le \ell_1$; and the honest gatekeeper is $G_{j=i_2-\ell_1}$, sitting in position $\ell_1 + 1 \le i_2 \le \ell_2$.

Hybrid_0: the challenge onion O_1 is formed correctly. (This is the same as the game when $b = 0$.)
   $\updownarrow$ Indistinguishable from CCA2-secure public key encryption.
Hybrid_1: same as Hybrid_0 except that the ciphertext E_{i_1} is an encryption under $\mathsf{pk}(M_{i_1})$ of the dummy key 0. (The challenger still samples for the layer key k_{i_1} and uses it to form the i_1^{th} onion layers O_{i_1}.)
   $\updownarrow$ Indistinguishable from the collision resistance of the hash function
Hybrid_2: same as Hybrid_1 except that if, in the second query phase, the challenger receives an onion $O = ((E, B), C, S) \notin O_{i_1}$ such that $E = E_{i_1}$, the challenger responds with $\perp$ (rather than processing O).
   $\updownarrow$ Indistinguishable from PRP security.
Hybrid_3: same as Hybrid_2 except that the challenger forms the i_1^{th} onion layers O_{i_1} using a truly random permutation rather than a PRP keyed with k_{i_1}.
   $\updownarrow$ Identically distributed since $O_{i_1-1}, \ldots, O_1$ are wrapped around truly random blocks.
Hybrid_4: same as Hybrid_3 except that the challenger uses the dummy message content $\perp$ and the truncated path $(M_1, \ldots, M_{i_1}, \perp)$ and associated sequence

$(y_1, \ldots, y_{i_1}, \perp)$ of metadata (instead of the real message and full path and sequence of metadata) to form O_1.

$\updownarrow$ Identically distributed since the inner layers $\boldsymbol{O}_\ell, \ldots, \boldsymbol{O}_{i_1+1}$ are independent of the path up to M_{i_1}.

Hybrid$_5$: same as Hybrid$_4$ except that the first query to peel or bruise an onion $O_{i_1} = O_{i_1,k} \in \boldsymbol{O}_{i_1}$ on behalf of M_{i_1} peels to a new onion formed using the message m, the routing path $(\perp, M_{i_1+1}, \ldots, R)$, and the associated sequence of metadata $(\perp, y_{i_1+1}, \ldots, y_{\ell-1})$. (The newly formed onion O_{i_1+1} has the correct number k of bruises.)

$\updownarrow$ Indistinguishable from PRP security.

Hybrid$_6$: same as Hybrid$_5$ except that the challenger forms the i_1^{th} onion layers $\boldsymbol{O}_{i_1}$ using the PRP keyed with k_{i_1} instead of a truly random permutation.

$\updownarrow$ Indistinguishable from CCA2-security.

Hybrid$_7$: same as Hybrid$_6$ except that the ciphertext E_{i_1} is an encryption of the real key k_{i_1} rather than the dummy key 0. (At this stage, the challenge onion O_1 is same as that in the game when $b = 1$, but the onions returned by M_{i_1} and G_j are not quite the same as when $b = 1$. The challenger forms O_1 using the message $\perp$, the routing path $(M_1, \ldots, M_{i_1}, \perp)$, and the metadata $(y_1, \ldots, y_{i_1}, \perp)$. The onion O_{i_1+1} returned by the challenger on behalf of the mixer M_{i_1} is a new onion with the correct number of bruises, formed by running FormOnion on m, $(\perp, M_{i_1+1}, \ldots, R)$, and the metadata $(\perp, y_{i_1+1}, \ldots, y_{\ell-1})$. The challenger obtains the onion O_{i_2+1} returned by the on behalf of the gatekeeper G_j by running PeelOnion on the query onion.)

$\updownarrow$ Indistinguishable from CCA2-secure public key encryption.

Hybrid$_8$: same as Hybrid$_7$ except that the ciphertext E_{i_2} is an encryption under $\mathsf{pk}(G_j)$ of the dummy key 0. (The challenger still samples for the layer key k_{i_2} and uses it to form the i_2^{th} onion layers $\boldsymbol{O}_{i_2}$.)

$\updownarrow$ Indistinguishable from the collision resistance of the hash function

Hybrid$_9$: same as Hybrid$_8$ except that if, in the second query phase, the challenger receives an onion $O = ((E, B), C, S) \notin \boldsymbol{O}_{i_2}$ such that $E = E_{i_2}$, the challenger responds with $\perp$ (rather than processing O).

$\updownarrow$ Indistinguishable from PRP security.

Hybrid$_{10}$: same as Hybrid$_9$ except that the challenger forms the i_2^{th} onion layers $\boldsymbol{O}_{i_2}$ using a truly random permutation rather than a PRP keyed with k_{i_2}.

$\updownarrow$ Identically distributed since $\boldsymbol{O}_{i_2-1}, \ldots, \boldsymbol{O}_{i_1+1}$ are wrapped around truly random blocks.

Hybrid$_{11}$: same as Hybrid$_{10}$ except that the challenger uses the path $(\perp, M_{i_1+1}, \ldots, G_j, \perp)$ and associated sequence of metadata (instead of the real message and full path and sequence of metadata) to form O_{i_1+1}.

$\updownarrow$ Identically distributed since the inner layers $\boldsymbol{O}_\ell, \ldots, \boldsymbol{O}_{i_2+1}$ are independent of the path up to G_j.

Hybrid$_{12}$: same as Hybrid$_{11}$ except that the first query to peel or bruise an onion $O_{i_2} = O_{i_2,k} \in \boldsymbol{O}_{i_2}$ on behalf of G_j peels to a new onion formed using the message m, the routing path $(\perp, G_{j+1}, \ldots, R)$, and the associated sequence of metadata. (The newly formed onion O_{i_2+1} has the correct number k of bruises.)

↕ Indistinguishable from PRP security.

Hybrid_{13}: same as Hybrid_{12} except that the challenger forms the i_2^{th} onion layers $\boldsymbol{O}_{i_2}$ using the PRP keyed with k_{i_2} instead of a truly random permutation.

↕ Indistinguishable from CCA2-security.

Hybrid_{14}: same as Hybrid_{13} except that the ciphertext E_{i_2} is an encryption of the real key k_{i_2} rather than the dummy key 0.

↕ Identically distributed since the sepals are truly random blocks wrapped in layers on encryption, and the verification hashes don't reveal how bruised the sepals are.

Hybrid_{15}: same as Hybrid_{14} except for how bruised the onion O_{i_1+1} is. The onion O_{i_1+1} that M_{i_1} returns will be completely unbruised. The challenger remembers how bruised O_{i_1} was, however, and forms the onion O_{i_2+1} accordingly; thus, O_{i_2+1} is formed identically as in Hybrid_{11}. (At this stage, the challenge onions O_1 and O_{i_1+1} are the same as that in the game when $b = 1$, but the onion returned by G_j is not quite the same as when $b = 1$.)

↕ Indistinguishable from PRP security.

Hybrid_{16}: same as Hybrid_{15} except that the challenger forms the penultimate onion layers $\boldsymbol{O}_{\ell-1}$ using a truly random permutation rather than a PRP keyed with $k_{\ell-1}$.

↕ Identically distributed because since $\boldsymbol{O}_{\ell-2}, \ldots, \boldsymbol{O}_{i_2+1}$ are wrapped truly random blocks.

Hybrid_{17}: same as Hybrid_{16} except that the challenger uses the message ⊥ and the recipient ⊥.

↕ Indistinguishable from PRP security.

Hybrid_{18}: same as Hybrid_{17} except that the challenger forms the penultimate onion layers $\boldsymbol{O}_{\ell-1}$ using the PRP keyed with $k_{\ell-1}$ instead of a truly random permutation. Note that Hybrid_{18} is indistinguishable to the case when $b = 1$.

The hybrid argument for the case where the challenge onion is recoverable, and the recipient is honest is the same as above, except that, in Hybrid_{17}, only the message is ⊥ (the recipient remains R). When the recipient is adversarial, the hybrid argument is just Hybrid_0-Hybrid_{15} above (without Hybrid_{16}-Hybrid_{18}).

5 Our Onion Routing Protocol, $\varPi_t$

5.1 Choosing the Onion Parameters

We describe our anonymous onion routing protocol, $\varPi_t$.

Let TOES = (KeyGen, FormOnion, PeelOnion, PeelOnionHelper, BruiseOnion) be the bruisable onion encryption scheme in Sect. 4. Let ℓ_1 be the number of mixers on the routing path, let ℓ_2 be the number of gatekeepers, and let ℓ_3 be the (expected) number of onions at each intermediary per hop. Let F_1 and F_2 be pseudorandom functions (PRFs) such that F_1 outputs zero with frequency $(\ell_1 + \ell_2)\ell_3/|\mathsf{Parties}| = (\ell_1 + \ell_2)\ell_3/N = \Omega\,(\mathsf{polylog}\,\lambda)\,/N$, and the range of F_2 is superpolynomial in the security parameter λ. We assume a setup with a public key infrastructure (PKI); note that the PKI enables each pair of parties (P_i, P_k) to set up a shared secret key $\mathsf{sk}_{i,k}$,e.g., by using Diffie-Hellman key exchange.

For each sender P_i, let σ_i denote the input for P_i. For each $(m_i, R_i) \in \sigma_i$, party P_i forms an onion bearing the message m_i to the recipient R_i. Additionally, P_i forms a polylog (in the security parameter) number of checkpoint onions.

The algorithms for forming the onions are essentially those of Π_a [ALU18], except we use tulip bulbs instead of standard ones. Specifically, we use tulip bulbs with $\ell_1 = \Omega\,(\text{polylog}\,\lambda)$ mixers per onion, $\ell_2 = \Omega\,(\text{polylog}\,\lambda)$ gatekeepers per onion, and $d = \theta\ell_1$ key-blocks per sepal. For completeness, we describe these algorithms in detail below.

Forming the Message-Bearing Onions. To form the message-bearing onion for the message-recipient pair $(m_i, R_i) \in \sigma_i$, P_i first samples $\ell_1 + \ell_2$ parties $M_1, \ldots, M_{\ell_1}, G_1, \ldots, G_{\ell_2}$ uniformly at random and then runs the onion-forming algorithm FormOnion on the message m_i, the routing path $\boldsymbol{P} = (M_1, \ldots, M_{\ell_1}, G_1, \ldots, G_{\ell_2}, R_i)$, the public keys associated with the parties in $\boldsymbol{P}$ (which we will denote $\text{pk}(\boldsymbol{P})$), and the sequence $\perp = (\overbrace{\perp, \perp, \ldots, \perp}^{\ell_1 + \ell_2 \text{ times}})$ of metadata. Here, "$\perp$" denotes the empty metadata. See Fig. 2 below for the pseudocode.

Fig. 2. Pseudocode for forming the message-bearing onion

Forming the Checkpoint Onions. Next, P_i forms the checkpoint onions. P_i initializes the sets of nonces, $\mathcal{Y}_1, \ldots, \mathcal{Y}_{\ell_1}$, to the empty set.

Then, for every pair (j, P_k) where $j \in [\ell_1]$ is a hop-index and $P_k \in \text{Parties}$ is a party, P_i determines whether or not they should form an onion for party P_k to be verified in the jth hop. This is done by computing the pseudorandom function F_1 on the shared key $\text{sk}_{i,k}$ and the hop-index j. If the output equals zero, P_i sets the checkpoint nonce y to $F_2(\text{sk}_{i,k}, j)$; adds y to the nonce-set $\mathcal{Y}_j$; samples $\ell_1 + \ell_2 + 1$ parties $M_1, \ldots, M_{\ell_1}, G_1, \ldots, G_{\ell_2}, R$ uniformly at random; and forms a checkpoint onion by running FormOnion on the empty message "$\perp$," the routing path $\boldsymbol{P} = (M_1, \ldots, M_{\ell_1}, G_1, \ldots, G_{\ell_2}, R)$, the public keys $\text{pk}(\boldsymbol{P})$ associated with the parties on the path, and the sequence $\boldsymbol{y} = (\overbrace{\perp, \perp, \ldots, \perp}^{j-1 \text{ times}}, y, \overbrace{\perp, \perp, \ldots, \perp}^{\ell_1 + \ell_2 - j \text{ times}})$ of metadata. See Fig. 3 below for the pseudocode.

5.2   Routing Onions

After forming the onions, P_i releases them into the network. From this point on, P_i acts as an intermediary or recipient. That is, P_i first sends each of its onions

```
1 :    𝒴₁, . . . , 𝒴_{ℓ₁} ← ∅
2 :    for (j, P_k) ∈ [ℓ₁] × Parties :
3 :        if F₁(sk_{i,k}, j) = 0 :
4 :            y ← F₂(sk_{i,k}, j)
5 :            𝒴_j ← 𝒴_j.append(y)
                        j−1 times        ℓ₁+ℓ₂−j times
6 :        y = (⊥, ⊥, . . . , ⊥, y, ⊥, ⊥, . . . , ⊥)
7 :        M₁, . . . , M_{ℓ₁}, G₁, . . . , G_{ℓ₂}, R ←$ Parties
8 :        O ← FormOnion(⊥, (M₁, . . . , M_{ℓ₁}, G₁, . . . , G_{ℓ₂}, R), pk(P), y)
```

Fig. 3. Pseudocode for forming checkpoint onions

to the first party on the onion's routing path and then waits to receive onions. In contrast to the setup for Π_a, here, the honest parties must determine when to send out batch-processed onions without relying on a global clock; accordingly, our protocol for processing and routing tulip bulbs (i.e., onions) differs from that of Π_a.

To begin with, P_i sets counters $c_1, \ldots, c_{\ell_1}, j$ to zero.

Upon receiving an onion O, P_i processes it: That is, P_i first peels the onion. P_i drops the onion if this produces a layer key that P_i has seen before; that is, the layer key also serves as a session id for preventing replay attacks. What happens next depends on P_i's role:

– (**Role** = Recipient) If the peeled onion O' is a message for P_i, P_i outputs it.
– (**Role** = Gatekeeper) If P_i is a gatekeeper for O and peeling O produces a peeled onion O' and a destination P' for O', P_i sends O' to P' right away. (Note that if P_i is the last gatekeeper on the routing path, P_i can recover the identity of the recipient R and the onion for R only if a sufficiently small number of mixers bruised the onion en route. See Sect. 4 to recall how the onion encryption construction works and its security properties.)
– (**Role** = Mixer) Otherwise if P_i is a mixer for O, P_i determines whether O was received "on time" or not (relative to P_i's internal clock). If O arrived late, P_i bruises the onion O and immediately sends the bruised onion O'' to its next destination. If P_i is the last mixer on the routing path (i.e., $P_i = M_{\ell_1}$), P_i sends the peeled onion O' to the first gatekeeper G_1.

   Otherwise if O is either early or on time, P_i places the peeled onion O' (along with its next destination P') in its message outbox. If processing O reveals the non-empty nonce $y \neq \bot$, then P_i first checks whether y belongs in a set $\mathcal{Y}_k$. (Recall from Sect. 5.1 that $\mathcal{Y}_k$ is the set of kth layer checkpoint nonces P_i expects to see from the onions it receives.) If it does, then P_i increments c_k by one, and updates $\mathcal{Y}_k$ to exclude y.

   Upon processing sufficiently many j^{th} layer onions (i.e., if $c_j \geq \tau |\mathcal{Y}_j|$ where $0 < \tau \leq 1$ is a system parameter), P_i sends out these onions (but not the onions for future hops) in random order, and advances its local clock (i.e., increments j by one). Note that onions are shuffled at honest intermediaries when they are batch-processed and sent out in random order. See Fig. 4 for the pseudocode.

```
 1 :   c₁, ..., c_{ℓ₁}, j ← 0
 2 :   upon receiving O
 3 :      (Role, k, y, O', P') ← PeelOnion(sk(Pᵢ), O)
 4 :      if Role = Recipient
 5 :         return O'
 6 :      if k < j
 7 :         if Role = Gatekeeper
 8 :            send O' to P'
 9 :         else    // Role = Mixer
10 :            O'' ← BruiseOnion(sk(Pᵢ), O)
11 :            send O'' to P'
12 :      else    // k ≥ j
13 :         place (O', P') in outbox
14 :         if (y ≠ ⊥) ∧ (∃k s.t. y ∈ 𝒴ₖ)
15 :            𝒴ₖ ← 𝒴ₖ \ {y}
16 :            cₖ ← cₖ + 1
17 :   upon cⱼ ≥ τ|𝒴ⱼ|
18 :      j ← j + 1
19 :      send peeled jᵗʰ layer onions out in random order
```

Fig. 4. Pseudocode for processing onions

6   Provable Guarantees

Recall the system parameters set forth in the Preliminaries section: χ is the constant corruption rate. That is, we assume that the adversary can corrupt up to a χ fraction of the parties. γ is the constant drop rate. An onion is *indistinguishable* if it was formed by an honest party and either bears a message or is a checkpoint onion for verification by an honest party; for our result on guaranteed message delivery, we assume that the adversary can drop up to γ fraction of indistinguishable onions. (Note that onions for verification by adversarial parties are distinguishable from other onions when the adversary observes the checkpoint values.)

Recall the onion encryption parameters, ℓ_1, ℓ_2, θ, and the onion routing parameter, ℓ_3, τ, from Sects. 4–5: ℓ_1 is the number of mixers on a routing path. ℓ_2 is the number of gatekeepers on a routing path. θ is the upper bound on the fraction of onion layers that can be bruised before the innermost onion becomes unrecoverable. ℓ_3 is the expected number of onions processed at an intermediary and hop. τ is the fraction of checkpoints needed to progress the local clock to the next hop. See Table 1 for a quick reference to the variables.

Table 1. Table of adversary and system parameters.

	Description
χ	Fraction of nodes that $\mathcal{A}$ can corrupt
γ	Fraction of (indistinguishable) onions that $\mathcal{A}$ can drop
$\ell_1 = \Omega\,(\mathsf{polylog}\,\lambda)$	Number of planned mixers on a routing path
$\ell_2 = \Omega\,(\mathsf{polylog}\,\lambda)$	Number of planned gatekeepers on a routing path
$\theta > \frac{1}{2} + \chi$	Fraction of layers in an onion that cannot be bruised
$\ell_3 = \Omega\,(\mathsf{polylog}\,\lambda)$	Expected number of onions per intermediary per hop
$\tau < (1 - \gamma)(1 - \chi)$	Fraction of checkpoints needed to progress

We present the provable guarantees for our protocol, Π_t. We show that when we set the parameters as in Table 1, Π_t delivers at least (arbitrarily close to) $\left(\frac{1/2 + \tau - 2\theta}{1 - \theta}\right)\left(1 - \mathcal{O}(\frac{1}{\mathsf{polylog}\,\lambda})\right) - \gamma$ fraction of the honest parties' messages differentially privately. For small constants χ, γ (e.g., 10% corruption rate and 10% drop rate), this translates to a constant fraction message delivery rate. In a more reasonable setting where at most 5% of the parties are adversarial and maliciously bruising onions, and with 0% drop rate, Π_t guarantees a much higher message delivery rate of over 0.85; and as the corruption rate goes to 0, the message delivery rate tends to 1. One cannot expect much better solutions since, even in the synchronous setting, the adversary can always bring down the message delivery rate by dropping sufficiently many onions (from known lower bounds [DMMK18], the round complexity of anonymous protocols is at least polylogarithmic in the security parameter, which implies that every randomly chosen routing path includes a corrupted party with overwhelming probability).

In the proofs, we make ample use of the following fact, which is a corollary of the Azuma-Hoeffding inequality [MU05, Theorem 13.7]: Let B be a set of marbles. Let S be a random sample with or without replacement of the marbles, and let X be the number of red marbles in the sample S. If the expected number of red marbles in the sample, $\mathbb{E}[X]$, is at least polylog in the security parameter, then with probability $1 - e^{-\Omega(\mathsf{poly}(\lambda))}$, $X \in \mathbb{E}[X](1 \pm \mathcal{O}((\mathsf{polylog}(\lambda))^{-1}))$. For brevity, we write that a random variable X is w.o.p. arbitrarily close to a value V if $\Pr\left[X \notin V(1 \pm \mathcal{O}((\mathsf{polylog}\,\lambda)^{-1}))\right] = e^{-\Omega(\mathsf{poly}(\lambda))}$.

6.1   Proof of Message Delivery Rate

We first prove that Π_t guarantees a constant fraction message delivery rate in the regime where $(1 + 2\tau - 4\theta)\left(1 - \mathcal{O}(\frac{1}{\mathsf{polylog}\,\lambda})\right) > 2\gamma(1 - \theta)$. Specifically,

Theorem 2. *A run of protocol Π_t with parameters $\ell_1 = \Omega\,(\mathsf{polylog}\,\lambda)$, $\ell_2 = \Omega\,(\mathsf{polylog}\,\lambda)$, $\ell_3 = \Omega\,(\mathsf{polylog}\,\lambda)$, $\theta > \frac{1}{2} + \chi$, $\tau < 1 - \gamma(1 - \chi) - \chi$, and $(1 + 2\tau - 4\theta)\left(1 - \mathcal{O}(\frac{1}{\mathsf{polylog}\,\lambda})\right) > 2\gamma(1 - \theta)$, delivers at least*

$$\left(\frac{1/2 + \tau - 2\theta}{1 - \theta}\right)\left(1 - \mathcal{O}(\frac{1}{\mathsf{polylog}\,\lambda})\right) - \gamma > 0$$

fraction of the honest parties' messages with overwhelming probability.

Proof. Let $j \in [\ell_1]$ be a hop-index, and P_k a party. Let $\mathcal{C}_{j,k}$ be the set of checkpoint values that P_k expects to observe during hop j. Since the number of parties is $\mathcal{O}(\mathsf{poly}\,\lambda)$, $\ell_1, \ell_2 \in \Omega\,(\mathsf{polylog}\,\lambda)$, and intermediate parties on onions' routes are chosen uniformly at random, w.o.p. for all j and k, the actual number of checkpoint values with P_k at hop j is arbitrarily close to its expectation, $\mathbb{E}\,[\|\mathcal{C}_{j,k}\|]$. Thus, in the remainder of the proof, w.l.o.g., we can use the expectations of all these values.

We first need to show that under the conditions of the theorem, the protocol at each party progresses through all the hops of the protocol. Indeed, for every hop-index $j \in [\ell_1]$ and honest party P_k, w.o.p., the adversary can drop up to approximately γ fraction of the indistinguishable checkpoints in $\mathcal{C}_{j,k}$ (Azuma-Hoeffding inequality), plus all of the other checkpoints (the non-indistinguishable ones that the adversarial parties are supposed to send to P_k). Thus, w.o.p., P_k is guaranteed to eventually receive sufficiently many onions in $\mathcal{C}_{j,k}$ to progress to the next hop (i.e., P_k receives at least slightly less than the expected $1 - \gamma(1 - \chi) - \chi = (1 - \gamma)(1 - \chi)$ fraction of the onions in $\mathcal{C}_{j,k}$).

An onion doesn't make it to its final destination for one of two reasons: either the onion was dropped by the adversary (reason 1), or it was too bruised to be reconstructed at the penultimate step (reason 2). The adversary can maximize the total number of onions that don't make it by not overlapping onions that don't make it because of reason 1 and those that don't because of reason 2. That is, the adversary doesn't waste a bruising on an onion that they will ultimately drop.

The fraction of onions dropped by the adversary is bounded by γ. Next we compute the fraction of onion that arrived too bruised at the penultimate step. To bound this number we first bound the total number of bruises of all onions in all iterations of the protocol.

Let us first bound the fraction of the jth layers of indistinguishable onions that P_k bruises. If P_k is honest, they will follow the protocol and only bruise (the jth layers of) onions they receive after observing τ fraction of the values in $\mathcal{C}_{j,k}$. The adversary can fix the schedule so that P_k receives checkpoints in $\mathcal{C}_{j,k}$ from the adversarial parties first. Even so, w.o.p., the number of checkpoint values in onions formed by adversarial parties, $A_{j,k}$, is arbitrarily close to the expected number $\mathbb{E}\left[A_{j,k}\right]$ (Azuma-Hoeffding inequality). Likewise, w.o.p., the number of checkpoint values in indistinguishable onions, $H_{j,k}$, is arbitrarily close to the expected number $\mathbb{E}\left[H_{j,k}\right]$ (Azuma-Hoeffding inequality). It follows that w.o.p., P_k observes at least (arbitrarily close to) $(\tau - \chi)|\mathcal{C}_{j,k}| = (\tau - \chi)(A_{j,k} + H_{j,k})$ checkpoints values embedded in indistinguishable onions. This translates to P_k observing at least (arbitrarily close to) $\frac{\tau - \chi}{1 - \chi}$ of the checkpoints values embedded in indistinguishable onions "on time."

In contrast, an adversarial party can bruise every onion layer it processes.

Thus, the total fraction of *layers* of indistinguishable onions that will be bruised is bounded above by the expression: (fraction bruised when in honest parties) × (fraction of honest parties) + (fraction bruised while in corrupted party) × (fraction corrupted parties) i.e., w.o.p., at most (arbitrarily close to)

$$\left(1 - \frac{\tau - \chi}{1 - \chi}\right)(1 - \chi) + 1 \cdot \chi = \left(\frac{1 - \chi - \tau + \chi}{1 - \chi}\right)(1 - \chi) + \chi$$

$$= 1 - \tau + \chi \qquad (1)$$

An onion is too bruised (i.e., the innermost layer of the onion cannot be recovered) if it is bruised too many times (i.e., for $> \theta$ fraction of the bruisable layers). Thus, from (1), the adversary can sufficiently bruise, w.o.p., at most arbitrarily close to $(1 - \tau + \chi)/(1 - \theta) \le (1/2 - \tau + \theta)/(1 - \theta)$ fraction of the indistinguishable *onions*.

This leaves at least arbitrarily close to $1 - \left(\frac{1/2 - \tau + \theta}{1 - \theta} + \gamma\right) = \left(\frac{1/2 + \tau - 2\theta}{1 - \theta}\right) - \gamma$ fraction of message-bearing onions being both "originating from honest parties" and "ultimately delivered" (Azuma-Hoeffding inequality).

Remark on Censorship. An adversary can censor a party in our protocol by delaying just that party's onions and causing them to be too bruised and eventually undelivered. This is the only way to achieve anonymity: if these delayed onions were ever delivered, they would be de-anonymized. Thus, the lack of censorship resilience is inherent to the asynchronous model. Moreover, note that in the asynchronous model where the adversary controls all the links, censorship is always within the adversary's power (even in a protocol that eventually delivers all messages) since the messages that the adversary aims to censor can be delayed until other parts of the computation are done; so even if they are eventually delivered, the adversary can make sure that by the time they arrive, they are no longer useful for whatever protocol the honest participants need them for. Giving the adversary in our protocol the ability to cause them to be dropped altogether does not provide the adversary extra power.

Here, we prove that Π_t is computationally differentially private.

Theorem 3. *For any constant $\epsilon > 0$, Π_t with parameters $\ell_1 = \Omega\,(\text{polylog}\,\lambda)$, $\ell_2 = \Omega\,(\text{polylog}\,\lambda)$, $\ell_3 = \Omega\,(\text{polylog}\,\lambda)$, and $\theta > \frac{1}{2} + \chi$ is computationally $(\epsilon, \text{negl}(\lambda))$-differentially private from the adversary who corrupts up to $\chi < \frac{1}{2}$ fraction of the parties and drops any fraction $0 \le \gamma \le 1$ of the indistinguishable onions.*

Proof. We prove below that Π_t achieves (statistical) $(\epsilon, \mathsf{negl}(\lambda))$-differential privacy for any constant $\epsilon > 0$ when the PRFs F_1 and F_2 are truly random functions, and the underlying bruisable onion scheme is perfectly secure.[5] From Canetti's UC composition theorem [Can01], this implies that Π_t is computationally differentially private when we use PRFs and our onion encryption scheme from Sect. 4 instead.

Let σ_0, σ_1 be any neighboring input vectors. That is, σ_0 and σ_1 are identical except on the inputs of two honest senders P_i and P_j and the "outputs" of two receivers P_u and P_v. On input vector σ_0, P_i sends a message to P_u, and honest P_j sends a message to P_v; while in σ_1, this is swapped (P_i sends to P_v, while P_j sends to P_v). For $b \in \{0,1\}$, let $(I_{i,1}, \ldots, I_{i,\ell_1+\ell_2}, R_{b,i})$ be the routing path that P_i picks for their message-bearing onion, and let $(I_{j,1}, \ldots, I_{j,\ell_1+\ell_2}, R_{b,j})$ be the routing path that P_j picks for their message-bearing onion.

We prove the theorem by cases.

Case 1: Neither P_i's Message nor P_j's Message is Delivered. The only difference between the scenario when the input vector is σ_0 and the scenario when it is σ_1 is the receivers for P_i and P_j's challenge messages. Everything else is identically distributed. Thus, in this case, the adversarial views for the two settings are perfectly indistinguishable since the adversary never observes the challenge onions' layers for P_u and P_v, i.e., $\mathsf{View}^{\Pi_t, \mathcal{A}}(\sigma_0) = \mathsf{View}^{\Pi_t, \mathcal{A}}(\sigma_1)$.

Case 2: Both P_i's Message and P_j's Message is Delivered. In this case, $\mathsf{View}^{\Pi_t, \mathcal{A}}(\sigma_0)$ and $\mathsf{View}^{\Pi_t, \mathcal{A}}(\sigma_1)$ are statistically indistinguishable, i.e., the total variation distance between $\mathsf{View}^{\Pi_t, \mathcal{A}}(\sigma_0)$ and $\mathsf{View}^{\Pi_t, \mathcal{A}}(\sigma_1)$ is negligible in the security parameter, from Lemma 1 below (proven in the next subsection):

Lemma 1. *Let $O = (O_1, \ldots, O_{\ell_1+\ell_2+1})$ and $O' = (O'_1, \ldots, O'_{\ell_1+\ell_2+1})$ be any two message-bearing onions that were formed by honest parties that make it to their final destinations. Let P be the origin (the honest sender) of O, and let P' be the origin of O'. Let $i_1 < \cdots < i_w \leq \ell_1$ be the hop-indices where O shuffles with other onions (i.e., arrives on time or early at an honest party), and let $i'_1 < \cdots < i'_{w'} \leq \ell_1$ be the moments when O shuffles with other onions. (1) W.o.p., there exists a positive constant $c > 0$ such that $|\mathcal{I}| = |\{i_1, \ldots, i_w\} \cap \{i'_1, \ldots, i'_{w'}\}| \geq c\ell_1$. (2) Let $r = \max \mathcal{I} = \max\{i_1, \ldots, i_w\} \cap \{i'_1, \ldots, i'_{w'}\}$ be the last time that both O and O' shuffle. Given the unordered set $\{O_r, O'_r\}$, the adversary can correctly match P to O_r and P' to O'_r with probability only negligibly greater than $1/2$.*

Case 3: P_i's message or P_j's Message is Delivered. In this case, $\mathsf{View}^{\Pi_t, \mathcal{A}}(\sigma_0)$ and $\mathsf{View}^{\Pi_t, \mathcal{A}}(\sigma_1)$ are differentially private; in other words, $\Pr\left[\mathsf{View}^{\Pi_t, \mathcal{A}}(\sigma_0) \in \mathcal{V}\right] \leq$

---

[5] That is, we assume that the adversary cannot determine any meaningful information "hidden behind an honest party," e.g., the adversary cannot determine the message or the rest of the routing path of an onion that goes into an honest intermediary; see Sect. 3.2 for more details. Further, we assume that the gatekeepers always drop an onion with too many bruises ($> \theta\ell_1$) since w.o.p., at least one of the $\ell_2 = \Theta(\mathsf{polylog}\,\lambda)$ gatekeepers in each onion is honest.

$e^{\epsilon} \Pr \left[\text{View}^{\Pi_t, \mathcal{A}}(\sigma_1) \in \mathcal{V} \right] + \text{negl}(\lambda)$ for every set $\mathcal{V}$ of views. W.l.o.g., we assume that $\tilde{P}_i$'s message makes it to its recipient $R_{b,i}$, but $R_{b,j}$ does not receive P_j's message. Let r be the final hop at which O shuffles with other onions. The indistinguishable onions, including the message-bearing onion O from P_i to $R_{b,i}$, are sufficiently shuffled together by hop r by Lemma 2 below:

Lemma 2. *Let* $O = (O_1, \ldots, O_{\ell_1 + \ell_2 + 1})$ *be any indistinguishable onion. If O shuffles with other onions a polylog (in the security parameter) number of times before some hop r, then given O_r and any r^{th} layer indistinguishable onion O_r' in the adversarial view, the adversary can correctly guess which is the evolved version of O_1 with probability only negligibly greater than one-half.*

Since the adversary cannot determine the origin of any indistinguishable onion at hop r (from the above claim), the only information the adversary has to help determine the input setting is the volumes of onions received by each recipient. W.o.p., the number n of indistinguishable checkpoint onions for either P_u or P_v is arbitrarily close to the expected number $\mathbb{E}[n]$ since $\mathbb{E}[n]$ is poly-logarithmic in the security parameter (Azuma-Hoeffding inequality). Seen this way, the number of indistinguishable checkpoint onions for P_u, which we denote by n_u, and the number of indistinguishable checkpoint onions for P_v, which we denote by n_v, are Binomial random variables with n trials and bias $\frac{1}{2}$, i.e., $n_u, n_v \leftarrow \text{Binomial}(n, \frac{1}{2})$. Thus, the numbers of messages received are obscured by a Binomial Mechanism which, for $n = \Omega(\text{polylog } \lambda)$, was shown [DKM+06] to be $(\epsilon/2, \text{negl}(\lambda))$-differentially private for any positive constant ϵ. It follows from the composition theorem for differential privacy that Π_t achieves (computational) $(\epsilon, \text{negl}(\lambda))$-differential privacy for any positive constant ϵ. $\square$

Recall neighboring input vectors: σ_0 and σ_1 are neighboring if they are the same except for a pair of messages to be sent from honest senders and received by honest recipients. We note that, from the composition theorem for differential privacy, Theorem 3 holds even if we loosen this notion. Specifically,

Corollary 1. *Let the swap-distance $d(\sigma_0, \sigma_1)$ between σ_0 and σ_1 be the length (minus one) of the shortest sequence of input vectors $(\sigma_0, \sigma_{0 \to 1,1}, \ldots, \sigma_{0 \to 1,d} = \sigma_1)$. Consider Π_t with parameters $\ell_1 = \Omega(\text{polylog } \lambda)$, $\ell_2 = \Omega(\text{polylog } \lambda)$, $\ell_3 = \Omega(\text{polylog } \lambda)$, and $\theta > \frac{1}{2} + \chi$. For any constant swap-distance $d \geq 0$, any small constant $\epsilon > 0$, any (computationally-bounded) adversary $\mathcal{A}$ who corrupts up to $\chi < \frac{1}{2}$ fraction of the parties, any pair of inputs σ_0 and σ_1 such that $d(\sigma_0, \sigma_1) \leq d$, and any set $\mathcal{V}$ of adversarial views, $\Pr \left[\text{View}^{\Pi_t, \mathcal{A}}(\sigma_0) \in \mathcal{V} \right] \leq e^{\epsilon} \Pr \left[\text{View}^{\Pi_t, \mathcal{A}}(\sigma_1) \in \mathcal{V} \right] + \text{negl}(\lambda)$.*

7   Conclusion and Open Problems

We present the first provably anonymous communication protocol in an asynchronous environment. Our protocol guarantees differential privacy of the sources and destinations information of the messages under a strong adversity model.

The adversary fully controls the schedule of delivery of all messages, can corrupt a constant fraction of the parties, and drop a constant fraction of all messages.

While our work proves the possibility of anonymity in a fully asynchronous network, many questions were left open for further research. In particular, we are also interested in stronger privacy models than just differential privacy, and in anonymous bidirectional communication in a dynamic network with node churn.

Our work also raised interesting questions regarding the inherent vulnerability of asynchronized communication to adversarial attacks and inherent gaps in security between synchronized and asynchronized models.

Acknowledgments. This work was supported by NSF grants CCF-2312243 and CCF-2312241.

References

ACLM22. Ando, M., Christ, M., Lysyanskaya, A., Malkin, T.: Poly Onions: Achieving Anonymity in the Presence of Churn. In: Kiltz, E., Vaikuntanathan, V. (eds.) Theory of Cryptography. TCC 2022. LNCS, vol. 13748. Springer, Cham (2022). https://doi.org/10.1007/978-3-031-22365-5_25

AL21. Ando, M., Lysyanskaya, A.: Cryptographic shallots: a formal treatment of repliable onion encryption. In: Nissim, K., Waters, B. (eds.) TCC 2021. LNCS, vol. 13044, pp. 188–221. Springer, Cham (2021). https://doi.org/10.1007/978-3-030-90456-2_7

ALU18. Ando, M., Lysyanskaya, A., Upfal, E.: Practical and provably secure onion routing. In: ICALP 2018, LIPIcs, vol. 107. Schloss Dagstuhl (July 2018)

ALU21. Ando, M., Lysyanskaya, A., Upfal, E.: On the complexity of anonymous communication through public networks. In: ITC 2021. Schloss Dagstuhl-Leibniz-Zentrum für Informatik (July 2021)

AMWB23. Attarian, R., Mohammadi, E., Wang, T., Beni, E.H.: MixFlow: assessing mixnets anonymity with contrastive architectures and semantic network information. Cryptology ePrint Archive, Report 2023/199 (2023)

BFT04. Berman, R., Fiat, A., Ta-Shma, A.: Provable unlinkability against traffic analysis. In: Juels, A. (ed.) FC 2004. LNCS, vol. 3110, pp. 266–280. Springer, Heidelberg (2004). https://doi.org/10.1007/978-3-540-27809-2_26

BKM+13. Backes, M., Kate, A., Manoharan, P., Meiser, S., Mohammadi, E.: AnoA: a framework for analyzing anonymous communication protocols. In: CSF 2013 Computer Security Foundations Symposium. IEEE Computer Society Press (2013)

Bra84. Bracha, G.: An asynchronous [(n-1)/3]-resilient consensus protocol. In: PODC (1984)

Can01. Canetti, R.: Universally composable security: a new paradigm for cryptographic protocols. In: 42nd FOCS. IEEE Computer Society Press (October 2001)

CBM15. Corrigan-Gibbs, H., Boneh, D., Mazières, D.: Riposte: an anonymous messaging system handling millions of users. In: 2015 IEEE Symposium on Security and Privacy. IEEE Computer Society Press (May 2015)

Cha81. Chaum, D.L.: Untraceable electronic mail, return addresses, and digital pseudonyms. Commun. ACM **24**(2), 84–90 (1981)

Cha88. Chaum, D.: The dining cryptographers problem: unconditional sender and recipient untraceability. J. Cryptol. **1**(1), 65–75 (1988)

CL05. Camenisch, J., Lysyanskaya, A.: A formal treatment of onion routing. In: Shoup, V. (ed.) CRYPTO 2005. LNCS, vol. 3621, pp. 169–187. Springer, Heidelberg (2005). https://doi.org/10.1007/11535218_11

CR93. Canetti, R., Rabin, T.: Fast asynchronous byzantine agreement with optimal resilience. In: 25th ACM STOC. ACM Press (May 1993)

CS98. Cramer, R., Shoup, V.: A practical public key cryptosystem provably secure against adaptive chosen ciphertext attack. In: Krawczyk, H. (ed.) CRYPTO 1998. LNCS, vol. 1462, pp. 13–25. Springer, Heidelberg (1998). https://doi.org/10.1007/BFb0055717

DKM+06. Dwork, C., Kenthapadi, K., McSherry, F., Mironov, I., Naor, M.: Our data, ourselves: privacy via distributed noise generation. In: Vaudenay, S. (ed.) EUROCRYPT 2006. LNCS, vol. 4004, pp. 486–503. Springer, Heidelberg (2006). https://doi.org/10.1007/11761679_29

DMMK18. Das, D., Meiser, S., Mohammadi, E., Kate, A.: Anonymity trilemma: strong anonymity, low bandwidth overhead, low latency - choose two. In: 2018 IEEE Symposium on Security and Privacy. IEEE Computer Society Press (May 2018)

DMNS06. Dwork, C., McSherry, F., Nissim, K., Smith, A.: Calibrating noise to sensitivity in private data analysis. In: Halevi, S., Rabin, T. (eds.) TCC 2006. LNCS, vol. 3876, pp. 265–284. Springer, Heidelberg (2006). https://doi.org/10.1007/11681878_14

DMS04. Dingledine, R., Mathewson, N., Syverson, P.F.: Tor: the second-generation onion router. In: Proceedings of the 13th USENIX Security Symposium, 9-13 August 2004, San Diego, CA, USA (2004)

IKK05. Iwanik, J., Klonowski, M., Kutyłowski, M.: Duo-onions and hydra-onions-failure and adversary resistant onion protocols. Springer, In Communications and Multimedia Security (2005)

KBS+19. Kuhn, C., Beck, M., Schiffner, S., Jorswieck, E.A., Strufe, T.: On privacy notions in anonymous communication. Proc. Priv. Enhancing Technol. **2019**(2), 105–125 (2019)

KBS20. Kuhn, C., Beck, M., Strufe, T.: Breaking and (partially) fixing provably secure onion routing. In: 2020 IEEE Symposium on Security and Privacy. IEEE Computer Society Press (May 2020)

KCDF17. Kwon, A., Corrigan-Gibbs, H., Devadas, S., Ford, B.: Atom: horizontally scaling strong anonymity. In: Proceedings of the 26th Symposium on Operating Systems Principles, 28-31 October 2017, Shanghai, China. ACM (2017)

KHRS21. Kuhn, C., Hofheinz, D., Rupp, A., Strufe, T.: Onion routing with replies. In: Tibouchi, M., Wang, H. (eds.) ASIACRYPT 2021. LNCS, vol. 13091, pp. 573–604. Springer, Cham (2021). https://doi.org/10.1007/978-3-030-92075-3_20

Lyn96. Lynch, N.A.: Distributed algorithms. Elsevier (1996)

MD05. Murdoch, S.J., Danezis, G.: Low-cost traffic analysis of tor. In: 2005 IEEE Symposium on Security and Privacy. IEEE Computer Society Press (May 2005)

MPRV09. Mironov, I., Pandey, O., Reingold, O., Vadhan, S.: Computational differential privacy. In: Halevi, S. (ed.) CRYPTO 2009. LNCS, vol. 5677, pp. 126–142. Springer, Heidelberg (2009). https://doi.org/10.1007/978-3-642-03356-8_8

MU05.   Mitzenmacher, M., Upfal, E.: Probability and computing: Randomized algorithms and probabilistic analysis. Cambridge University Press (2005)

PHE+17. Piotrowska, A.M., Hayes, J., Elahi, T., Meiser, S., Danezis, G.: The loopix anonymity system. In: USENIX Security 2017. USENIX Association (August 2017)

Rop21.   Ropek, L.: Someone is running hundreds of malicious servers on the Tor network and might be de-anonymizing users (December 2021). https://tinyurl.com/2p999e8e

RS93.   Rackoff, C., Simon, D.R.: Cryptographic defense against traffic analysis. In: 25th ACM STOC. ACM Press (May 1993)

SEV+15. Sun, Y., et al.: RAPTOR: routing attacks on privacy in Tor. In: USENIX Security Symposium (2015)

TGL+17. Tyagi, N., Gilad, Y., Leung, D., Zaharia, M., Zeldovich, N.: Stadium: a distributed metadata-private messaging system. In: SOSP 2017. ACM (Oct 2017)

vdHLZZ15. van den Hooff, J., Lazar, D., Zaharia, M., Zeldovich, N.: Vuvuzela: scalable private messaging resistant to traffic analysis. In: SOSP 2015. ACM (Oct 2015)

WSJ+18. Wails, R., Sun, Y., Johnson, A., Chiang, M., Mittal, P.: Tempest: temporal dynamics in anonymity systems. PoPETs **2018**(3), 22–42 (2018)

Author Index

A

Anastos, Michael   413
Ando, Megumi   476
Arnon, Gal   125
Athamnah, Noor   319
Auerbach, Benedikt   413

B

Baig, Mirza Ahad   413
Ben-David, Shany   125
Bobolz, Jan   90
Boudgoust, Katharina   35
Brandt, Nicholas   191
Brzuska, Chris   287

C

C. Oliveira, Igor   253
Chiesa, Alessandro   67, 158
Couteau, Geoffroy   287

D

Dall'Agnol, Marcel   158
Dodis, Yevgeniy   444

E

Egger, Christoph   287

F

Farshim, Pooya   90
Fenzi, Giacomo   67
Florentz – Konopnicki, Eden   319

G

Guan, Ziyi   158

H

Hirahara, Shuichi   253

J

Jost, Daniel   444

K

Klein, Ohad   383
Kohlweiss, Markulf   90
Komargodski, Ilan   383
Kwan, Matthew   413

L

Liu, Yanyi   222
Loss, Julian   353
Lu, Zhenjian   253
Lysyanskaya, Anna   476

M

Mu, Changrui   3

N

Noval, Miguel Cueto   413

P

Pascual-Perez, Guillermo   413
Pass, Rafael   222
Pietrzak, Krzysztof   413

Q

Quach, Willy   287

R

Rothblum, Ron D.   319

S

Shi, Kecheng   353
Simkin, Mark   35

© International Association for Cryptologic Research 2025
E. Boyle and M. Mahmoody (Eds.): TCC 2024, LNCS 15364, pp. 509–510, 2025.
https://doi.org/10.1007/978-3-031-78011-0

Spooner, Nicholas   158
Stern, Gilad   353

T
Takahashi, Akira   90

U
Upfal, Eli   476

V
Vasudevan, Prashant Nalini   3

Y
Yogev, Eylon   125, 158

Z
Zhu, Chenzhi   383

GPSR Compliance

The European Union's (EU) General Product Safety Regulation (GPSR) is a set of rules that requires consumer products to be safe and our obligations to ensure this.

If you have any concerns about our products, you can contact us on ProductSafety@springernature.com

In case Publisher is established outside the EU, the EU authorized representative is:

Springer Nature Customer Service Center GmbH
Europaplatz 3
69115 Heidelberg, Germany

The manufacturer's authorised representative in the EU is Springer
Nature Customer Service Centre GmbH, Europaplatz 3, 69115 Heidelberg,
Germany. If you have any concerns regarding our products, please
contact ProductSafety@springernature.com

Printed and bound by CPI Group (UK) Ltd, Croydon, CR0 4YY
05/05/2026
02103537-0008